Strategy:
Analysis and
Practice

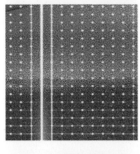
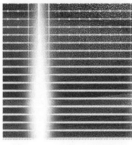
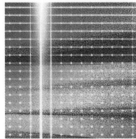

Strategy:
Analysis and
Practice

John McGee
Howard Thomas
David Wilson

Warwick Business School
University of Warwick, UK

The **McGraw·Hill** Companies

London   Boston   Burr Ridge, IL   Dubuque, IA   Madison, WI   New York   San Francisco   St. Louis   Bangkok   Bogotá   Caracas   Kuala Lumpur   Lisbon   Madrid   Mexico City   Milan   Montreal   New Delhi   Santiago   Seoul   Singapore   Sydney   Taipei   Toronto

Strategy: Analysis and Practice
ISBN 0-07-7107063
ISBN 978-0-07-710706-2

 **Education**

Published by McGraw-Hill Education
Shoppenhangers Road
Maidenhead
Berkshire
SL6 2QL
Telephone: 44 (0) 1628 502 500
Fax: 44 (0) 1628 770 224
Website: www.mcgraw-hill.co.uk

British Library Cataloguing in Publication Data
A catalogue record for this book is available from the British Library

Library of Congress Cataloging in Publication Data
The Library of Congress data for this book has been applied for from the Library of Congress

Publishing Director: Catriona King
Acquisitions Editor: Kate Mason
Senior Development Editor: Caroline Howell
Sales and Marketing Director: John Donovan
Marketing Manager: Marca Wosoba

Text Design by Fakenham Photosetting Limited, Fakenham, Norfolk
Cover design by Fielding Design
Printed and bound in the UK by Bell & Bain, Glasgow

ISBN (This edition) 0-07-7107063
ISBN 13 (This edition) 978-0-07-710706-2
ISBN (Text only edition) 0-07-7107055
ISBN 13 (Text only edition) 978-0-07-710705-5

Dedication

To our colleagues, past and present, who have shaped our thinking;
To our students past and present who have contributed more than they know;
And to Jenny, Jo and Lynne who have always inspired us.

Brief Table of Contents

Detailed Table of Contents

Case Study Section *C001*

Preface

The origins of this book grew out of the teaching and the research of the authors recognising that the field of strategy was one of the most central, yet most contested areas of management knowledge. Rather than contribute to the seemingly endless debate about what strategy is (and is not) we chose to write about it in what we hope is a refreshing, analytical, inclusive and accessible way. It is refreshing and analytical, because we are ourselves animated by the topics it embraces and we hope this enthusiasm shows in the text and in our analysis of strategy. It is inclusive and accessible because we have tried to develop a systemic view of strategy which gives breadth and depth to an overall understanding of strategy and its processes.

We hope readers will notice that this text includes some very different approaches to strategy, from viewing strategy as economic analysis to it being embedded in social and broadly contextual processes. Yet we try to blend these approaches in one systemic framework which we present in Chapter 1. As we wrote the various sections of the book we recognized that, far from being incommensurable, different approaches to strategy resonated with each other more than we had realized. It was not so much that paradigms were incommensurable, but rather that approaches could be viewed as being complementary if one highlighted the linkages between them.

We have also tried to be eclectic in the range of topics we have included under the term 'strategy'. Readers may be surprised to find chapters on governance, learning or process improvements in a book about strategy, but we realized as we constructed our framework that we could not talk about strategy in any way holistically without reference to these topics. So, we have tried to seek fit and 'complementarities' (to use the jargon of strategy) between paradigms and approaches and we have tried to be as inclusive as possible in the range of topics we feel contribute toward a more holistic view of strategy. We hope this will enthuse readers more than it may confuse.

It was quite a process and a journey for ourselves in getting to the product you are about to read. The three authors had taught strategy and had researched and written about it in quite different ways. When we came to write together, we discovered commonalities that we had not seen before and which were able to inform the construction of our systemic framework.

Many contemporary authors in strategy have developed a rather dismissive approach to the work that has preceded their own perspectives. Indeed, the field of strategy has been strongly characterised by the almost total substitution of one frame of reference for another as time has progressed. For example, models of rational planning have, over a few decades, been dismissed and ignored by later writers who emphasized a more emergent or politically shaped view of strategy. Whilst we certainly do not want to slow the intellectual progression of this exciting field by ignoring these paradigmatic shifts, we feel that such shift are, in practice, difficult to spot, characterised as much by latest fad and fashion as they are by the substitution of one theoretical lens for another. So marked are these fashions and fads that many authors have published books simply listing the various perspectives that can be taken toward strategy. Rather grandiosely, these have sometimes been called 'schools of thought', but they do not bear scrutiny as such. They are simply ways of looking at strategy, some of which have become fashionable and some of which have not. In this book, therefore, we set out to see if we could weave together in a coherent way what had previously been cited as incommensurable theoretical approaches to the field and we have deliberately avoided the schools of thought approach. Some may feel this is an overly conservative or, even, wrong-headed approach, but our own experience would tell us otherwise. Our students, too, appreciate the linkages and cross-references we make to different epistemologies, as they try and make sense of strategy and develop the field alongside us. What has emerged is a text which we feel has the following defining characteristics:

♦ **Strong emphasis on strategy in practice:** An innovative approach which is informed by academic research but remains highly practical and 'hands on'. Dedicated chapters on Risk Management, Managing Strategic Change, Strategy and the Learning Organization and Corporate Governance.

♦ **An analytical approach to strategy:** A thorough study of competitive advantage provides students with the level of analysis fundamental to understanding business and corporate level strategy.

♦ **An understanding of the link between strategy, knowledge and technological change, and value and performance.** Value and value-based management is shown as central to strategic management. Three themes are treated explicitly because they are particularly close to the core of strategic management thinking. These are (i) performance assessment; (ii) organizational knowledge, learning and value innovation; and (iii) total quality management and customer value.

♦ **A range of contemporary and relevant cases throughout:** Illustrative case examples and end of chapter cases offer insights into a variety of globally recognized companies such as easyJet, Benetton, Deutsche Post, Airbus, Samsung, Disney, Dell and more.

◆ **A section of longer cases in the Text and Cases Edition** places strategy into a variety of contemporary international contexts and offer students the opportunity to analyse strategic decisions across an array of international businesses including BSkyB, Ikea, Honda, Shell, Nike, and Nokia.

◆ **Clear and well-developed pedagogy:** An introduction to each part orients the student to the landscape of the chapters that follow. To aid learning, each chapter introduces its themes and concepts, and leads the student through the topic with key terms highlighted in bold for easy reference. Case Examples contained within the chapters provide illustrations of strategy in practice within real organizations, and at the end of each chapter, a summary and assignments draw together the overarching themes and test understanding. A concluding Chapter-end Case Study encourages the student to analyze how some of the concepts raised in the chapter can be applied within an organization. See the Guided Tour for more information.

◆ **An unparalleled range of supporting resources-** the book is accompanied by an Online Learning Centre website, www.mcgraw-hill.co.uk/textbooks/mcgee, which provides a range of resources for lecturers and students. Lecturers will find PowerPoint presentations, lecture guides, and case study notes to assist them in teaching with the textbook. The student area contains a wealth of extra resources including test questions; help with studying cases, guide answers to the end of chapter assignments questions and more. For more information see our guide to *Technology to enhance teaching and learning* on the following pages.

Like all books, in the writing, it has had its glory moments and its days of drudgery. But we are pleased that the idea with which we began – to try and examine a holistic approach to strategy – was not dismissed as we progressed with the writing. Indeed the reverse was true. We became more committed to the approach as we wrote. And it proved useful, both to ourselves and to our students at all levels from undergraduate to post-experience. As authors, we could be argued to represent something of an eclectic approach. We have tried to synthesize the perspectives and epistemologies of three very different scholars, one who began in mathematics and statistics, a second in economics and a third in organization theory. At least at this level of analysis, we are an example of the inclusive approach to strategy that we present in this book. The final judgement will, of course, be with you, the reader. We hope you enjoy your journey through its pages and, in the process, become as enthusiastic about this area of study as we remain. Happy reading.

John McGee
Howard Thomas
David Wilson   **January 2005**

List of cases

At the end of each chapter from Chapter 3 onwards, you will find a case study that explores the themes and concepts covered on the preceding pages, with study questions. The following cases are featured:

1. The Harder Hard Sell (Ch 3)

There are significant new challenges facing the advertising industry: traditional methods of advertising seem no longer to work – does this mean that the potential to differentiate consumer products and services is diminishing?

2. Made in Japan (Ch 4)

Japan is threatened by competition from low-cost Chinese competitors. What implications does this have for Japanese firms and their competitive advantages? Is it possible for firms to locate in several different countries so as to gain from local comparative advantage without suffering from the disadvantages? In other words can they have their cake and eat it? What can national governments do about this?

3. The Novotel Value Chain (Ch 5)

The strategy of a hotel chain is displayed in its value chain. This shows how the configuration of the value chain relates to competitive advantage and illustrates the importance of the coordination and integration of the different elements in the value chain.

4. Mobile Telephone and the move from 2G to 3G (Ch 6)

The advent of a new technology requires a new business model. This describes how a business model is derived from strategy and the way new technology changes the business model. The example illustrates how the business model is directly derived from the underlying competitive strategy. It also demonstrates how successive technology platforms do require different business models

5. How Dell Keeps from Stumbling (Ch 7)

How supply chain management can be the key to strategy and to sustained competitive advantage. Dell's strategy is well known for its management of suppliers but what is less well known is the direct impact this has on its value proposition to customers.

6. Brand extension with Jacuzzi – Armani (Ch 7)

Should luxury-goods firms go into the hotel business? This case discusses how brands can form the basis for a diversification strategy. It also looks at Armani's businesses in terms of the core competences that underpin a luxury brand. The case allows discussion of the limits to brand strength and also the extent to which luxury brands depend on their founders, such as Giorgio Armani.

7. Stelios Haji-Ioannou (Ch 8)

How important is the entrepreneur? An interview with Stelios shows how his personality and drive is reflected in easyJet's business strategy and operational processes. But is leadership the same as strategy? And how does Stelios compare with other entrepreneurs e.g. Anita Roddick in chapter 21 and Giorgio Armani in chapter 6?

8. Old Dogs, New tricks (Ch 9)

Conventional thinking now holds that conglomerates are undesirable and that industrial restructuring should lead to more highly focused business portfolios. This is examined in the context of major German manufacturing companies. How much notice are industrial giants such as Siemens and Hoechst taking of the antipathy of international investors for industrial diversification?

9. The Battle for the Magic Kingdom: Comcast's bid to acquire Disney (Ch 10)

Comcast, America's biggest cable company, has launched an audacious hostile bid for Disney. The timing is shrewd, for Michael Eisner, Disney's boss, is under attack for poor governance and disappointing results. This illustrates the difficulties faced by hostile bids but also the way in which their targets need to organize their defences.

10. International law firms: getting the right global balance (Ch 11)

London firms want to be more global; New York firms want to be more profitable. Ultimately, more big global law firms will probably emerge to provide services for the international marketplace. But the legal profession does not look as if it will go the way of accounting, with just a few firms dominating the market everywhere.

11. How good is Google: the challenges faced by the search engine (Ch 12)

Will Google become one of the few valuable Internet survivors, joining Amazon and above all eBay? Google the new-age advertising agency makes money, but it is Google the search engine that builds the consumer brand that makes the ad agency powerful. Google's board has decided to bring Google to the stock market next spring in an effort to translate the search engine power into money. But, does Google really have a viable strategy?

12. Browser Wars: Netscape's new Gecko browser challenges Microsoft (Ch 12)

Remember the browser wars, when Netscape and Microsoft fought for dominance of the web? In the end, Microsoft prevailed by bundling its browser with its Windows operating system. Now a new browser war is under way, as software firms compete to provide the browsers for 'information appliances' such as set-top boxes, handheld computers and smart phones. Such devices are still in their infancy, but they are widely expected eventually to outnumber PCs. So the stakes in this new browser war are high. And this time round, the battlefield looks very different.

13. Freud, Finance and Folly: human intuition and risk (Ch 13)

People make barmy decisions about the future. The evidence is all around, from their investments in the stock markets to the way they run their businesses. In fact, people are consistently bad at dealing with uncertainty, underestimating some kinds of risk and overestimating others. Surely there must be a better way than using intuition?

14. Decisions, Risk & Uncertainty and the Use of Game Theoretic Models (Ch 14)

When the environment is predictable and only a few decision variables are involved, all the assumptions for a game theory approach are present. It is possible to identify all the possible moves of each of the players and to identify the consequences of these moves. Therefore, game theoretic thinking allows decision-makers to identify the optimal strategic move(s) for each of the players. This approach is illustrated using examples from Intel Corp., the rivalry between Polaroid and Kodak, and from the ready-to-eat breakfast cereal industry.

15. How to manage a dream factory: the management challenges in the media industry (Ch 15)

One by one, the men of extravagant vision and exaggerated showmanship have been toppled from the upper ranks of the world's media giants. Talk of 'vision', 'synergy' or 'new paradigms' is out; the daily grind of evaluating and improving operating performance is paramount. During the boom, the industry was distracted by gadgets, mergers and convergence theories; now the emphasis is on the relearning of old lessons about fostering creativity and manufacturing entertainment that people are willing to pay for. But, it is really hard to manage the interface between creative thinking and the corporate profit-centre.

16. Future learning: discovering internal conflicts in a strategy (Ch 16)

This describes how to use the framework of a simulation model that allows groups of managers to test out how their mental models of their business operate knowing that the essential real world characteristics of the business are captured in the logic of the simulation model. This allows you to say something with confidence about the future not because it depends on projecting historical data into the future but on understanding the dynamics of an underlying system.

17. Disney: The case against Michael Eisner (Ch 17)

Michael Eisner has been the highly respected leader of Disney for many years. But there has been mounting concern with his leadership style and the governance practices followed by Disney. This case outlines the governance issues at Disney over 20 years and publishes the resignation letter of one of the long-standing directors of the company.

18. Continental Household Mortgage Co. (Ch 18)

This case describes how a major US-based financial services company uses a balanced scorecard approach for assessing progress against its objectives and for assessing the relevance and the sense of its competitive strategy.

19. Proctor and Gamble:

Durk Jager, the new CEO, wants to turn P+G into a innovative company. He blames the consumer-product industry's problems on its failure to innovate. It has 'led to commodity products and pricing pressure.' P&G has done worse than most. It has lost some 10% of its global market share in the past five years and volumes are growing very slowly. The fault, it is said, lies with the culture – it has stifled innovation and prevented new ideas from getting to market quickly.

20. Wasting Disease: crisis in the quality of healthcare (Ch 20)

The health-care industry is a tale of poor quality and inefficiency according to the prestigious U.S. Institute of Medicine. One of the biggest failings of modern health-care systems is that they so seldom provide integrated medical care. Effective co-ordination of care results in better and cheaper treatment, yet too often it does not happen. According to the OECD, 'health-care organisations, hospitals and physicians typically operate separate without the benefit of complete information about the patient's condition, medical history, services provided in other settings, or medications prescribed by other clinicians.' Information technology is said to hold the key to better integration and total quality. Is the way forward with the comprehensive national electronic system, costing £6 billion ($11 billion), that is being adopted by the NHS?

21. 'Oh, the joy of the journey'- Anita Roddick on social responsibility at Body Shop (Ch 21)

Anita Roddick discusses her own conception of a responsible business, and explains how her guiding principles and values allowed the business to grow. The case allows discussion of the role of a founder-entrepreneur in the growth of a successful business.

At the end of the Text and Cases edition of this book, you will find a selection of longer cases to explore.

Guided Tour

Part openers

At the beginning of each part, the authors introduce the topics and themes covered throughout the five Parts of the text.

Chapter introduction

Each introduction section indicates the key ideas that will be discussed within each chapter, linking the chapter to those surrounding it and explaining how the ideas fit together.

Key terms

These are highlighted throughout each chapter and a list of terms at the end of each chapter provides key points for ease of reference.

Case boxes

Each chapter contains a number of brief examples in Case Boxes that serve as illustrations of strategy in action. The examples provide useful insights that highlight the strategy decisions under discussion in the chapter.

Figures and tables

Each chapter provides a number of figures and tables to help students to visualize the various models, and to illustrate and summarize important concepts.

End of chapter summary

This briefly reviews and reinforces the main topics covered in each chapter to ensure students have acquired a solid understanding of the key topics.

Assignments and questions

These questions encourage students to review and apply the knowledge acquired from each chapter and can be undertaken to test understanding.

End of chapter cases

Longer case examples at the end of each chapter provide students with more in-depth discussions of organizations through which to explore the ideas from the chapter and apply their strategic decision making skills.

Case section

The case section at the back of the text and cases book provides a range of case studies from a variety of industries and organizations, offering students real business situations around which to explore, analyse and critique strategy in action.

Technology to enhance learning and teaching

Visit www.mcgraw-hill.co.uk/textbooks/mcgee today

Online Learning Centre (OLC)

After completing each chapter, log on to the supporting Online Learning Centre website. Take advantage of the study tools offered to reinforce the material you have read in the text, and to develop your knowledge of marketing in a fun and effective way.

Resources for students include:

- Student test questions testing your grasp of the concepts in the book
- A guide to how to interpret case studies
- Glossary of key terms from the textbook
- Further reading suggestions for research and assignments
- Chapter by chapter learning objectives
- Suggested answers to the end of chapter assignments
- Web links and more

Also available for lecturers:

- Case study teaching notes to support the cases in the textbook
- Lecture outlines to assist lecturers in teaching with the new book
- PowerPoint slides for presentation
- PowerPoint slides for print
- Figures and tables from the textbook
- A guide to how to teach using case studies
- Tutorial exercises, essay questions and guide answers
- Further mini case study updates, exercises and solutions

For lecturers: Primis Content Centre

If you need to supplement your course with additional cases or content, create a personalized e-Book for your students. Visit www.primiscontentcenter.com or e-mail primis_euro@mcgraw-hill.com for more information.

Study Skills

Open University Press publishes guides to study, research and exam skills, to help undergraduate and postgraduate students through their university studies.

Visit www.openup.co.uk/ss/ to see the full selection.

Computing Skills

If you'd like to brush up on your Computing skills, we have a range of titles covering MS Office applications such as Word, Excel, PowerPoint, Access and more.

Get a £2 discount off these titles by entering the promotional code **app** when ordering online at www.mcgraw-hill.co.uk/app.

Visit **www.mcgraw-hill.co.uk/textbooks/mcgee** today

Acknowledgements

Our thanks go to the following people who have helped us during the writing of this textbook:

Duncan Angwin, Sue Bridgewater, Derek Condon, Ben Knight, Tanya Sammut-Bonnici and Chris Smith for their invaluable assistance in preparing the text, and to Duncan Angwin, Stephen Hodge, Ian Maude, Robert Salter, Tanya Sammut-Bonnici and Bridgette Sullivan-Taylor for creating new case material.

We also thank the McGraw-Hill team who have encouraged and motivated us, channeled our enthusiasms and focused our efforts – Max Elvey, Caroline Howell, Catriona King, Kate Mason and Melissa Rosati.

Our thanks go to the following reviewers for their comments at various stages in the text's development:

Andy Adcroft, University of Surrey
Veronique Ambrosini, University of Cranfield
Lisa Barton, University of Cardiff
Bruce Cronin, University of Greenwich
James Cunningham, NUI Galway, Republic of Ireland
Leanne Cutcher, University of Sydney, Australia
David Jennings, Nottingham Trent
Judith Jordan, University of the West of England
David Lal, Robert Gordon University
Lester Lloyd Reason, Anglia Polytechnic University
Nick Potter, University of Birmingham
John Rudd, Aston University
Shafeek Sha, Rhodes University, South Africa
Gordon Smith, University of Plymouth
Iraj Tavakoli, University of Brighton

We would also like to thank Judith Jordan, of the University of the West of England, for her work in developing the support materials that accompany this textbook, and for her helpful advice as the book developed.

Finally, we thank the following individuals and organizations that granted permission for material to be reproduced within the textbook:

The Economist Newspaper Limited
INSEAD
John Wiley and Sons, Inc.
Palgrave Macmillan
IMD
The Telegraph Group Limited
Ivey Publishing
Institute of Directors
Professor Bernard Taylor, Henley Management College
Elsevier
Kogan Page Publishers
Blackwell Publishing
Westburn Publishers
Simon and Schuster Publishers
Rosalind Beere, Trinity College Dublin
Peter McNamara, University College Dublin
Centre for Asian Business Cases
Harvard Business School Publishing
Professor Ashok Som, ESSEC Business School, Paris

Every effort has been made to obtain permission from copyright holders to reproduce material within this textbook and to acknowledge these sources correctly. We would be pleased to hear from copyright holders whom it has not been possible for us to contact.

Part 1

An introduction to strategy

Part contents

In this part you will find the following chapters:

Introduction

This section forms the key introductory theme music both to the concepts of strategy and to the orientation of this book. In the opening two chapters we try to cover both the basics of strategy – what it is and how we might conceive of it analytically – and how strategy and organization can interact, mutually influencing what happens in practice. This section also presents our own theoretical model (depicted in Figure 1.6 and Figure 2.2) which attempts to show how quite often disparate perspectives on strategy (for example planning, performance, execution and feedback) can be seen as a coherent system. In this respect, these opening chapters form the essential foundation of the book and help inform all the sections and chapters that follow. Each section discusses elements of the overall framework (Figure 1.6). You will see that at the beginning of each section of the book we have depicted which parts of the systemic framework are being emphasized and addressed. The final chapter of the book then attempts to reassemble these component parts into our overall view of strategy and the strategy process.

Chapter 1 points out the contested terrain of strategy, in particular its various definitions and descriptions. Showing how different perspectives on strategy developed, the chapter then provides examples and techniques for assessing strategy. Beginning with planning, the chapter outlines the basics of the planning process and shows the basic analytical tools which can help underpin future plans and trajectories. Taking the perspective that a large proportion of strategy researchers have viewed it largely as a question of alignment (or fit) of the organization with its environment, the chapter covers the various positioning tools and perspectives that can help determine future actions (strategies). Knowing where the organization is positioned in relation to its operating environment allows strategists to plan either for achieving a better (more competitive) position or to try to make it more difficult for others to enter the market and compete. The chapter concludes its analysis of planning by looking at the public face of strategic planning for many organizations. This public face is captured in the notions of goals and mission. A few examples of mission statements shows how such goal-oriented statements can be the overall guide of strategic decisions taken in the organization. Such guiding can take the form of a statement about future economic positioning (we want to be number one in the industry) or can take the form of expressed values (we want to be seen as environmentally friendly and socially responsible).

Nevertheless, we know some curious things can happen when planned strategies are implemented. As the popular expression has it, there can be many a slip between cup and lip. The rest of Chapter 1 and all of Chapter 2 then deal with these questions of what happens when we view strategy as embedded in a particular organizational context. For example, viewing an organization as a constellation of resources (people, knowledge, financial and so on) reveals that some organizations are better endowed with such resources than others. They have more people with more skills and knowledge and are able to resource strategic decisions to a greater extent than other organizations. Taking this perspective leads us to the resource-based view of the organization and we discuss this in some detail.

Similarly, we know that strategy is not always a linear process. By this we mean that strategy is not necessarily a long period of thinking (planning) followed by a long period of acting (implementation). In many cases, strategists implement decisions without much (or, sometimes, any) planning. Decisions emerge from an organization, driven by a wide range of influences such as history (what strategists have done in the past), organizational values (the way we do things around here) and knee-jerk reactions to external threats. Planning, if it exists at all, is then retro-fitted to the process. This debate over whether strategic decisions are planned or emerge is covered in detail in Part 1.

Chapter 2 hinges around what many researchers have termed the more 'process' views of strategy. Taking the view that planning a trajectory is necessary but not sufficient to ensure strategic decisions follow automatically, the chapter shows how animation is as important as orientation for strategists. Animation examines the interplay between strategic intention and how managers interpret the environment, providing a context in which organizational members can become enthused and committed to a particular set of tasks.

The chapter also examines in detail debates over the appropriate levels of analysis we might adopt to understand strategy. In particular, recent work has stressed the importance of relatively micro approaches (what managers think, do and say) over the more macro approaches (level of competition, industry characteristics). Taking the individual as pivotal, the chapter shows how we can conceive of strategy as being essentially a process of individual *interpretation* of events and actions. This view has gathered momentum over recent years and it draws on classic work in the 1950s and 60s about behavioural theories of the firm as well as classic work on strategic decision making in the 1970s and 80s. The point of such debates is that, ultimately, strategists have to make a choice between the extremes of voluntarism and determinism. Determinism implies that all managerial action is shaped and, in the extreme, pre-determined by the context in which they operate. Voluntarism is the opposite view, arguing that strategists can act freely and without environmental constraints. Depending on which perspective you take (or what mixture of each), your view of how strategy processes actually work will be completely different.

Finally, Chapter 2 emphasizes the important role of history. Where an organization and its members have been in the past will have an influence upon its present activities. The longer an organization has been in operation, the longer will be its history of strategic decisions and it is likely to have built up a substantial repertoire of standard responses and actions to particular situations. Organizations can easily become programmed to the degree that they are more accurately described as a collection of ready-made solutions looking for new problems, rather than there being any proactive approach towards taking strategic decisions. Having read both chapters, you should then re-visit Figure 1.6 and 2.2. Here you will recognize both the detail and the bigger pictures of strategy. We have tried to show these as a dynamic and self-reinforcing model that also acts as a frame and as a lens to the rest of the book. The Online Learning Centre (www.mcgraw-hill.co.uk/textbooks/mcgee) shows how we simplify these two figures to create the two maps that we use in the Introductions to Parts 2, 3, 4 and 5. Figure 1.6 becomes the Strategy Resources Concepts map and Figure 2.2 becomes the Strategy Process Concepts map.

Chapter 1

The concept of strategy

Introduction

Why another book on strategy? Given the huge number of books on the subject, an initial conclusion might be that all that needs to be communicated has already been written. There is some truth in this statement if one assumes that the nature and definitions of strategy are pretty well aligned no matter which authors are consulted, or if one assumes that the theoretical and practical aspects of understanding strategy are uncontested. However, congruence in any of these areas is very difficult to find. Strategy remains one of the most contested and ill-defined concepts in management theory. As Magretta (2003) states:

> ... of all the concepts in management, strategy is the one that attracts the most attention and generates the most controversy. Almost everyone agrees that it is important. Almost no-one agrees on what it is.

This book will acknowledge some of the key debates concerning how scholars and practitioners have viewed and practised strategy, but it will not dwell in great detail on either the historical development of the field or on the intense debates which have emerged from five or so decades of theoretical and empirical work. This has indeed been achieved in many textbooks on strategy already (see, for example, Hussey 1998 for a conventional history of strategy, and Cummings and Wilson 2003 for a relatively less conventional mapping of the field). Our intention here is to review briefly some of the key shapers and characteristics of the field and then to see to what extent it is possible both to acknowledge and to combine competing perspectives to create a more holistic approach to understanding strategy. This book analyses the meaning of strategy by breaking it down into its component parts, namely: its *external logic* – how the organization positions itself relative to its external context; its *internal logic* – the levels of the organization at which strategy has different meanings and what distinctive resources and competences it must acquire; its *performance over time* – distinguishing between achievement of long-term objectives, meeting milestones along the way, and preserving short-term stability; and, finally, its *managerial requirements* – the role of general managers and how strategy is planned, managed, monitored and maintained. The next section tries to clarify what we mean by strategy in this book by building upon and trying to synthesize the approaches of key works in the field.

1.1 Key definitions of strategy

In a conference at Harvard Business School in 1963, Cook (reported in Bower 1982) argued that 'the charter of business policy is to focus on the life and death issues of central interest to top management . . . to help top management to deal with these issues effectively, profitably and morally'. Legge (2003), in her chapter on strategy as organizing, points out when discussing Henry Mintzberg's (1994) work that, in general, 'if you ask someone to define strategy, you will likely be told that strategy is a plan or something equivalent – a direction, a guide, a course of action into the future, a path to get from here to there'. Of course, Mintzberg *et al.* (1998) argue that this definition of **intended strategy** fails to recognize strategy as an emergent process, which is best seen as a pattern in a stream of decisions. Strategy, for Mintzberg, is what emerges from actions rather than something planned in advance or in anticipation of future contexts. We explore this planned versus emergent aspect of strategy in later sections of this chapter.

Prahalad and Hamel (1990), have also been very instrumental in influencing how we view strategy. They conceptualized strategy in terms of **strategic intent**, which they define as providing an overarching strategic direction. Strategic intent is, in essence, about winning in a competitive game. This leads to a focus on strategy as a process for reinforcing intent by developing the core competences of a corporation, and leading and managing change.

They also propose the viewpoint of 'strategy as stretch and leverage', in which the strategist sees the advantage of breaking the strategic frame and leveraging the critical core competences in an innovative and distinctive manner. Indeed, the concept of strategy as innovation is dominant in their current thinking and they stress the need for strategists to embrace radical innovation and innovate to stay in front of the competitive game. Their thinking in this respect mirrors that of Christensen (1997) who has discussed the role of the disruptive innovation and the new economy in shaping strategy in the evolving competitive landscape.

Perhaps the definition of strategy that is most common in the field is that attributed to the renowned Harvard business historian Alfred D. Chandler in his landmark book *Strategy and Structure*. The Chandler (1963) definition characterizes strategy as:

> *the determination of the basic long-term goals and objective of an enterprise and the adoption of courses of action and the allocation of resources necessary for carrying out these goals.*

This is the classical view of strategy, very much rational in analysis and following militaristic traditions, including those specified in the Japanese strategy book authored by Sun Tzu entitled *The Art of War* (1990). Quinn (1980), in an equally famous book entitled *Strategies for Change: Logical Incrementalism*, follows Chandler's case study tradition and talks about strategy in a more process-oriented way. Quinn's definition is:

> *the pattern or plan that integrates an organization's major goals, policies and action sequences into a cohesive whole. A well-formulated strategy helps to marshal and allocate an organization's resources into a unique and viable posture based on its relative internal competences and shortcomings, anticipated changes in the environment and contingent moves by intelligent opponents.*

Porter (1987), the Harvard Business School strategy professor, who has also had a tremendous influence on the field of strategic management and competitive strategy, picks up the themes of being different and achieving strategic coherence in organizational strategy. He argues, therefore, that competitive strategy is about being different (i.e. effective strategic positioning). It means deliberately choosing a different set of activities to deliver a unique mix of value. However, a strategic position is not sustainable unless there are trade-offs with other positions. Trade-offs create the need for choice (making strategic decisions) and protect against repositioners and straddlers. Strategy is about combining activities that are complementary and reinforcing. This strategic 'coherence' among many activities is fundamental not only to achieving competitive advantage, but also to the sustainability of that advantage. It is harder for a rival to match an array of interlocked activities than it is merely to match a particular sales force approach, match a process technology or replicate a set of product features. Positions built on a series of coherent activities are far more sustainable than those built on individual activities.

Although the previous definitions might seem at odds with one another (even mutually exclusive in some cases, for example between planned and emergent strategies) there are some common elements which we can identify to help us clarify the analysis a little. Common elements in these viewpoints include the following:

- Strategy as a means of establishing organizational purpose.

- Strategy as a definition of the competitive domains of the firm and the organizational context.

- Strategy as a response to the complexity of external opportunities and threats and internal strengths and weaknesses in order to achieve sustainable competitive advantage.

- Strategy as a way to define managerial tasks and processes with corporate, business and functional perspectives.

- Strategy as a system involving a coherent, unifying and integrative systematic pattern of decisions.

- Strategy as a definition of the economic and non-economic contributions which the firm intends to make to its stakeholders.

- Strategy as an architecture to develop the distinctive competences of an organization.

- Strategy as a vehicle for determining investments in tangible and intangible resources to develop the core capabilities which lead to sustainable advantages.

- Strategy as an expression of strategic intent; stretching the organization to innovate, leverage resources and develop new skills.

These common elements form the backbone of this book. They include the economic analysis of strategy to help plan and inform strategic decisions (Part 2); the analysis of strategy as both a feature of organizational positioning and capabilities, especially in a changing context of globalization and the new economy (Part 3); the analysis of strategy as a series of processes in which decisions have to be implemented and put into practice and which require an understanding of how organizations and individuals change and develop (Part 4); and a view of strategy as monitoring, improving and developing, helping data feedback into the next wave of strategy formulation (Part 5). Complex though all these factors are, the basics of strategy are relatively easily summarized and described. We examine these in the next section.

1.2 The basics of strategy

Figure 1.1 depicts the main basic dynamics and key factors to be taken into consideration when we begin to examine what we mean by strategy. At the most basic level, we mean that actions and decisions need to be analysed and taken in order for the organization to survive and thrive as conditions develop and change around it. These conditions (the external environment in Figure 1.1) comprise a wide range of factors. They include characteristics of the industry (for example the typewriter industry is today completely different from when electronic typewriters were state of the art); characteristics of the market (this may change from being benign to highly competitive and back again); sustainable development is now something all strategists have to consider and political conditions may change the context of business and government markedly (the impact of global terrorism, for example). We take each of the key factors and examine them in more detail in the following sections.

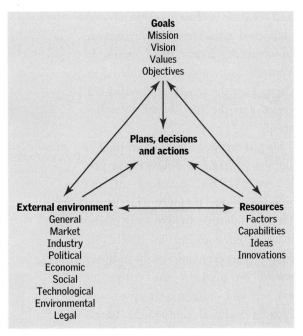

Figure 1.1 The basic dynamics of strategy

1.2.1 Plans, decisions and actions

The notion of planning heralds the beginnings of strategy. Many authors, such as Quinn (1980) and Cummings and Wilson (2003), have traced the military genesis of the term strategy from the Greeks and the Macedonians. The word 'strategos' began as a term describing a commanding role in the army (a general, for example) and by the time of Alexander the Great (330 BC) had become the word which described the successful deployment of troops to overcome the enemy and to the system of governance which facilitated this planning. It is this combined notion of planned deployment and governance which pervades the planning schools of strategy. Authors such as Ansoff (1965; 1972), building on the earlier work of the Stanford Research Institute, epitomize the translation of this planning orientation to the strategic conduct of business and the view of the general manager as a 'strategist' (coining the phrase 'strategic management' in 1972).

Most of today's organizations have some form of corporate plan or strategic plan and some form of planning process. In terms of Figure 1.1, strategic planning is the process by which the firm organizes its resources and actions in relation to an **external environment** in order to achieve its **goals** or **objectives**. This is usually a formal rather than an informal process, the key elements of which are outlined in Figure 1.2.

Planning is conducted in a very hierarchical and formal manner. It is typically top down with the direction and energy being supplied by top management. The process is iterative and the cycle is repeated (typically) on an annual basis. Planning horizons are in practice about three years in Western companies but this does depend on the length of product life cycles and the life of capital equipment.

Formal analysis would go through a number of stages in sequence. The first is typically the statement of the **mission** of the business. This would then be followed by a review of the external environment in which, for example, the economics of the industry would be assessed, the nature of markets and customers analysed, and broader political and social trends identified. In parallel there would be a review of the **internal environment** of the organization. This covers basic strengths and weaknesses, core competences and capability assessments. Based on these, views of the strengths and weaknesses and opportunities and threats (the well-known SWOT analysis which covers the reviews of the internal and external environments) are used as a starting point for formulating the

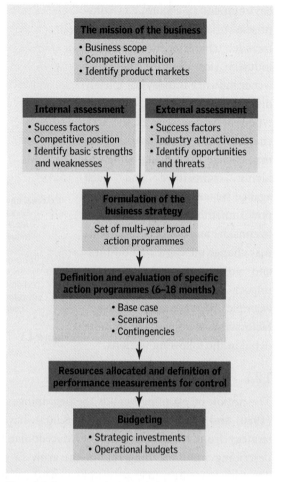

Figure 1.2 A typical planned, formal process of strategy formulation

strategy. From the basic business strategy will come a definition of the specific action programmes required to put the strategy into practice. This is what is usually called the business plan although the way in which this term is used varies widely between firms. This business plan is then submitted to an investment committee (this also goes under a variety of names) for resource allocation along with definition of performance milestones. After the investment expenditures are agreed, budgets are specified and agreed throughout the organization.

However, any person who has had experience of the above process in action in any organization may well have a wry smile on their face as they read the above seemingly rational and militaristic procedure. Great in theory, but never happens in practice might summarize their feelings. According to Mintzberg and Waters (1985) some strategies may be planned, at least in their first stages, but many more just simply *emerge* in an organization without being consciously intended or being deliberate acts. We might make sense of the *pattern* of these actions later and call them a strategy, but we do so with the luxury of hindsight. We construct a logic which was never intended in the first place. **Emergent strategies** can be seen as responses to unexpected opportunities and problems and are usually developed from the locations at which

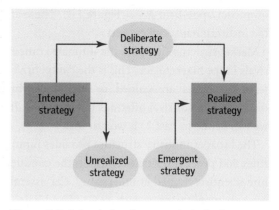

Figure 1.3 Intended and emergent strategies

business-level strategies are usually implemented, i.e. within business units and not at corporate headquarters. The pure definition of emergence requires the absence of any intentions. This is too strong for most occasions but, as Mintzberg and Waters (1985) observe, organizations come close to pure emergent strategies when an environment directly imposes a pattern of actions on them.

Quinn (1980) developed logical incrementalism as a way of explaining the combination of longer-term plans and targets with evolutionary, learning-based patterns of movement on the way (patterns of decisions which emerge). This is an attractive explanation because it seems to combine rational resource allocation thinking with practical learning by doing. Quinn argues that 'properly managed, it is a conscious, purposeful, pro-active, executive practice'.

The twin lenses of intentions and emergence are useful tools with which to analyse strategy since neither as a pure form is likely to be observable. Instead there is a continuum on which different blends can be seen. Figure 1.3 illustrates intentions being formulated as deliberate strategies, some of which come to fruition. But we also see a simultaneous pressure from circumstances producing a stream of emergent (but purposeful) thinking. **Realized strategy** is a blend of intentions and emergence which can be interpreted by reference to the strength of pressure from the external environment – a kind of environmental determinism.

1.2.2 The external environment

The external context of strategic decisions is very broad ranging. In principle, it can include anything and everything that might have an effect on decisions. We could include governments, international trade organizations, buyer and supplier markets, competitors, trade associations, civil servants, and the impersonal progression of science and technology. In order to provide some structure to this variety of influences, we can think of three regions of impact upon firm A (*see* Figure 1.4). These are market structure, industry structure, and the institutional/social context.

Market structure includes the intimate competition for the customers' attention between rivals in the marketplace. This is the competitive battleground within which the firm's long-term objectives are gained or lost and which provides the basis for assessing the distinctiveness of rival offerings to customers. It is here that competitive advantage (which we will define in Part 2) is won or lost.

The broader industry structure provides inputs of traded goods, knowledge and technical rules and procedures that condition the conduct of firms. Thus, pharmaceutical firms will hire scientists trained at universities. Car assemblers such as Ford and GM buy from components manufacturers such as GKN and Valeo. Industry trade associations stipulate rules of conduct and may conduct joint research. Distribution channels act across the board as intermediate customers and sometimes as powerful buyers in their own right. This industry structure has a deep impact on the underlying economic possibilities open to the participants in the market structure.

The broader institutional and social structure sets out the rules of the game in terms of what is morally, legally and ethically possible as well as setting the political terms of reference within which firms are obliged to operate.

These regions represent zones of influence for firms. Most influence is exercised within the market structure and least within the broad institutional context – at least as a general rule. However, firms see it as at least possible that they might shape the rules of the game by seeking to promote changes at various levels. But firms might also see their sphere of

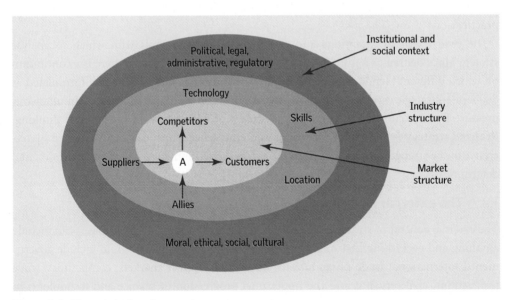

Figure 1.4 The external environment

influence as tightly focused within their market environment and subject, without any recourse, to powerful forces from elsewhere. One way for firms to assess exposure to forces within this broad context is through a PEST analysis. This is an analysis of political, economic, social and technological forces. Occasionally, specific aspects of dealing in particular national legal systems (for example) can be added to this analysis, but for simplicity they are excluded in the following description. Figure 1.5 provides an illustration of the variety of forces that can be identified via a PEST analysis.

In order to make sense of this 'shopping list' some analysis is needed to identify the really significant influences. This involves assigning probabilities and possible outcomes to each event and calculating an 'expected value' (technically the probability multiplied by the outcome). In practice this requires considerable judgement because many of the events can only be described in qualitative terms and because managers may have little, or very partial, information on each factor. We need also to identify ways in which the probabilities of the events and the outcomes of the events might be moderated by management action.

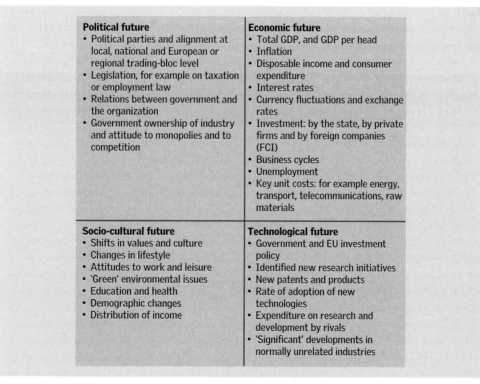

Political future
- Political parties and alignment at local, national and European or regional trading-bloc level
- Legislation, for example on taxation or employment law
- Relations between government and the organization
- Government ownership of industry and attitude to monopolies and to competition

Economic future
- Total GDP, and GDP per head
- Inflation
- Disposable income and consumer expenditure
- Interest rates
- Currency fluctuations and exchange rates
- Investment: by the state, by private firms and by foreign companies (FCI)
- Business cycles
- Unemployment
- Key unit costs: for example energy, transport, telecommunications, raw materials

Socio-cultural future
- Shifts in values and culture
- Changes in lifestyle
- Attitudes to work and leisure
- 'Green' environmental issues
- Education and health
- Demographic changes
- Distribution of income

Technological future
- Government and EU investment policy
- Identified new research initiatives
- New patents and products
- Rate of adoption of new technologies
- Expenditure on research and development by rivals
- 'Significant' developments in normally unrelated industries

Figure 1.5 An example of a PEST Analysis

1.2.3 Goals

As Quinn (1980) observes, goals (or objectives) are statements about 'what is to be achieved and when results are to be accomplished'. Goals do not address the question of *how* these objectives are to be achieved. They are basic statements of desired future objectives.

To communicate goals, organizations typically provide detailed statements of their strategic intent and their major goals in the form of **mission statements**. These are often criticized for their vacuity – indeed, one test of a good mission statement is said to be if employees can recite it without ironic laughter breaking out. It is possible to characterize two approaches to mission statements. One expresses mission in terms of *philosophy* and *ethics*, thereby widening the band of actors that are relevant to the long-term future of the company and capturing the notion of stakeholders. It also captures those forms of corporate behaviour that have implications for the social good and which are not reflected in the pricing mechanisms in marketplaces. The second approach expresses mission as *strategy*, an intellectual discourse that defines the firm's commercial *rationale* and *target markets*. Overall, mission is supposed to answer the question, What is our business and what should it be?

A selection of approaches to mission statements is provided by Collins and Porras (2000). The box below lists a number of well-known mission statements.

Some examples of goals expressed through mission statements

General Electric (rationale)

The first step is for the company to define its destiny in broad but clear terms. You need an overarching message, something big, but simple and understandable. (Jack Welch)

To become No. 1 or No. 2 in every market we serve and revolutionize this company to have the speed and agility of a small enterprise. (Jack Welch)

Sony (business philosophy and ethics)

*The difference between our efforts and those of other Japanese companies lies not in the level of technology, or the quality of the engineers, or even in the amount of money budgeted for development (about 5 per cent of sales). The main difference lies in . . . the establishment of mission-oriented research and proper **targets**. Many other companies give their researchers full freedom. We don't; we find an aim, a very real and clear **target** and then establish the* necessary task forces to get the job done . . . once the commitment to go ahead is made, **never** give up. This pervades all the research and development work at Sony.

Mission as business objectives

To build a car for the great multitude . . . (Ford, Henry Ford 1907)

To change the image around the world of Japanese products as poor in quality. (Sony, Akio Morita 1950)

To make my little Newport store the best, most profitable variety store in Arkansas within five years. (Walmart, Sam Walton 1945)

To become a $1 billion company in four years. (Walmart, Sam Walton 1977)

To double the number of stores and increase the dollar volume per square foot by 60 per cent by year 2000. (Walmart, Sam Walton 1990)

To build the airplane (the 747) even if it takes the entire resources of the company. (Boeing 1969)

Less well-known mission statements also reflect and try to tap into the values of potential customers. Consider the mission statement from Don Hewitson.

Don Hewitson's wine bar: The Cork & Bottle

A MISSION STATEMENT
'LIFE'S TOO SHORT TO DRINK BORING WINE'

Nowadays most wine can be relied upon to be an agreeable tipple. None of the gut-searing acidic whites or over-ripe, jammy oxidised reds which were all I could afford when I arrived in Blighty in 1972. Elton John was on Top Of The Pops with 'Rocket Man' that very day . . . and the charts have gone down the tubes ever since!

BUT . . . and it is a 'big' BUT. In the desire for squeaky clean wines at as cheap as possible prices, have we thrown the baby out with the bathwater? I didn't develop a passion for wine in order to drink virtually the same taste sensation every time . . . I love the bewildering variety of styles and flavours.

STUART WALTON, in his excellent book 'YOU HEARD IT THROUGH THE GRAPEVINE' (Aurum Press £9.99) sums up the desire for conformity brilliantly by blaming the High Street.

'What has happened in the last few years ... is the wholesale mediocratisation of wine in the UK ... As monotony begins to set in, there is the Safebury' wine-buyer at the door, cheque-book in hand and ready to spread this monotony all over the UK high street.'

These wines can be avoided, especially when you are a small operator in a business striving for globalisation. There are thousands of wine producers out there, in all countries, with no interest in producing bland, boring wines. Even if they make wines in sufficient quantities to satisfy the High Street chains, they are not prepared to shave their costs to fit supermarket price points. These days supermarkets invariably require a major financial contribution (a fee to be on their shelves, although they do put it a little less like the Kray twins, it's basically the same approach to business).

My suppliers wouldn't recognise a 'marketing budget' if they fell over one! They are my mates. I trust them implicitly. They are a disparate bunch of individuals dedicated to producing the best wines possible ... I'll drink to that!

Salut Don♀

This is a 'Mission Statement' written on the inside page of an eight-page pamphlet entitled *Wines To Go* – an order form for customers. The Cork & Bottle is a very well-known wine bar in Leicester Square, London, founded by an Australian whose original mission was to bring Australian and New Zealand wines to the British drinking public. It represents an approach to mission statements which is very different from those illustrated earlier. For one thing it is included in a selling/marketing document which is to be read by potential customers. But the main difference lies in the style and content of the narrative. It sets out clear values which are intended to engage with potential customers who share the same values (the charts have gone down the tubes since Elton John's 'Rocket Man') and the statement also acts as both an assessment of the competition (supermarket wines) and as an ethical comment upon them ('like the Kray twins'). Finally, the statement tells the consumer something about the way in which the supply chain is managed (trust – 'they are my mates'). It is also considerably longer than most mission statements, making it suitable for inclusion in a leaflet, but not as useful as a single-sentence strap line to describe the whole organization.

1.2.4 Resources

During the 1980s, the view that organizational resources were important became known as the **resource-based view** (RBV). Its arguments are deceptively simple. An organization has, develops or acquires a range of competences which can then be mobilized by strategists to gain an advantage on the competition. The origins of this way of thinking about strategy can be traced back to Penrose (1959). She adopted what was then something of a unique stance against the conception of the firm by her fellow economists, who had concentrated on conditions external to the firm (such as demand) as drivers of strategy and growth. Penrose took the opposite view, arguing that an organization can be viewed as a collection of resources (in her case she focused particularly on the entrepreneurial resource) which are the drivers of strategy and growth rather than external factors.

In the late 1950s, this was a radical view, but by the time Andrews (1980) had talked about identifying corporate competence and Prahalad and Hamel (1990) had published their article on the core competence of the organization, the RBV had become established. The argument is that strategists can build and mobilize resources which, if unique enough, can bring huge rewards to the organization. One of the most famous examples of this is the 3M Corporation. This organization valued the capacity of its staff to innovate, allowing them up to 25 per cent of company time in which to experiment, regardless of whether the outcome was successful or not. The result of one of these experiments was the Post-It note. Born from an adhesive which did not stick very well (in an organization dedicated to finding better and stronger adhesives) the idea looked initially doomed. But a use for this low-grade adhesive was found by attaching it to small pieces of paper. It could be stuck to paper and other delicate products as a marker, or with a note scribbled on it, and could be removed years later without damaging the paper.

Curiously, no customers were begging 3M or any other organization to produce such sticky notes. In terms of pure economics, there was no *demand* to drive creation of the product. Rather, 3M had produced something that customers did not even know they needed (yet). Here is a core competence according to Prahalad and Hamel (1990). It is the ability to produce something customers need but have never imagined. Conceiving of the firm as a collection of competences allows strategies to be planned 'inside–out'. That is, from the inside of the organization, out to its external environment (markets and industries). In turn, feedback from customers and demand could identify additional competences which might be needed (and may indicate which current core competences might be redundant).

Prahalad and Hamel (1990) define core competences as:

> the collective learning in the organization, especially how to co-ordinate diverse production skills and integrate multiple streams of technologies . . .

For example, Honda's core competence in engine and power trains gives it a clear advantage in car, motorcycle, lawnmower and generator businesses. There are three characteristics of a core competence. Competences should:

- provide potential access to a wide variety of markets;
- make a significant contribution to the perceived customer benefits of the end product;
- be difficult for competitors to imitate.

Prahalad and Hamel (1990) argue that very few organizations are likely to build world leadership in more than five or six competences. Firms may have many capabilities (more than 20 or 30) but they have not aggregated these into the key four or five competences needed for success and growth. Not knowing what are an organization's core competences can create difficulties for strategists. For example, they may outsource a function or operation not realizing that they have saved some costs at the expense of losing a core competence. Prahalad and Hamel (1990) cite the example of Honda, which would never outsource its manufacturing or design to an outside company, versus Chrysler, which has done so. Honda has preserved its core competence in engine and power trains while Chrysler has not. Of course, it is difficult to devise an effective outsourcing strategy if the core competences of the organization have not previously been identified. The crown jewels of the company could easily be outsourced this way in what might seem like a simple (and rational) cost-saving exercise.

So Figure 1.1 provides the basic factors in understanding strategy. Core competences (resources) allow strategists to have strategic intent (goals). These are orientated toward the external environment (market or socio-economic conditions) and these become organizational goals which are often communicated to stakeholders by means of mission statements. However, conceptualizing strategy is a little more complicated than these three factors (important thought they are). The next sections show how we can build upon Figure 1.1 to understand strategy a little more fully.

1.3 Towards a systemic concept of strategy

In this section, we will develop a concept of strategy that builds on Figure 1.1 and which guides the rest of this book. Strategy, as a topic of study, concentrates very much on the situational problems of the general manager (or top management team or CEO). Strategy is different, then, from a more general theory of organizations. It is more specific and more focused than general organizational theories. The general manager's job is to diagnose what is critical in complex business situations and to find realistic solutions to strategic and organizational problems. To solve problems, the general manager must be capable of understanding and using the knowledge from each of the organization's functional areas to provide a holistic 'total business' (systems) perspective on issues pertaining to strategic management. In addition, the general manager must be able to analyse competitive situations within industries in order to understand the sources of the firm's competitive advantage. We see strategy as determined and constrained by the underlying economic and political conditions which prevail in an industry or country, as well as by the resources available to management.

In consequence, we believe that a strategist (or the strategic team) must focus on understanding the specific *context* of the strategic problem. He or she must have an intuitive feel for defining the boundaries of the problem and the issues to include in any analysis. A strategist must also recognize the interrelationships between all the organizational functions, activities and processes, and be able to frame the problem by recognizing the influence not only of history but also of the future on the problem context. The strategist must be willing to act, must have a bias for action and be equally willing to accept the consequences – be they success or failure of the strategies he or she chooses. Therefore, unashamedly, we present in this book a conception of strategy which focuses on the role and the perspective of the general manager.

That said, it is important to develop a discussion about strategy around an appreciation of some of the theories which contribute to current strategic thinking and which help to outline managers' cognitive frames and interpretations of strategy. It is important to understand how these theories develop, how they have evolved and what problems they either seek to solve or begin to explain. What follows, therefore, is a very brief review of the main theories in the strategy field as a basis for showing how they are reflected in the development of the strategic framework and strategic systems model which are the basis for this book.

As noted earlier, the Chandler definition of strategy is the guiding principle underlying the so-called classical or rational view of strategy. A range of other eminent academics, including March and Simon (1958), Cyert and March (1963), Mintzberg (1994), Alchian (1950), Henderson (1973), Williamson (1975), Pascale (1984) and others, personify the main viewpoints in the field of strategy. The so-called **evolutionary view** emphasizes competitive processes of natural selection and environmental determination; survival is everything and nature is the optimiser. In this world, strategy can be a delusion and 'economy is the best strategy'. On the other hand, the so-called **strategy processual** or **organizational process** view of strategy expresses a more agnostic view about a market's ability to produce satisfactory outcomes, which we explain more fully in Chapter 2. In this view, both organizations and markets are sticky and messy, and strategies emerge slowly with much confusion and in small steps. Strategic behaviour is embedded and entrenched in cultures, routines and standard operating procedures. In this view, strategy is programmed by the DNA of organizations. An alternative and more recent viewpoint, focusing on the **strategy-as-systems perspective**, has room for managers and organizations to look forward and make effective plans, in contrast with the agnostic and even nihilistic stance of the evolutionary and strategy process perspectives. The systemic view is drawn principally from the work of organizational sociologists such as Granovetter (1985) and rests on notions of social embeddedness. Embeddedness maintains that people's economic behaviour is embedded in a network of social relations that may involve their families, the state, their professional and educational backgrounds, even their religion and ethnicity. Such influences are absent from the restricted environment of the classical and processual approaches but may find some expression in the evolutionary view.

These viewpoints are largely mutually exclusive but practising strategists in organizations would recognize their presence in strategy as practised. However, there is a new approach which has gained recent significant support. This is the resource-based view attributed to economist Edith Penrose. In this view, the emphasis is on those resources and competences that are distinctive to the organization and are the fundamental underpinning of their marketplace positioning. In this world, competition is a contest for the acquisition of skills and competences and other intangible assets. This represents a theory of core competences (to use the words popularized by gurus Gary Hamel and C.K. Prahalad) that provides linkages between the classical, processual and systemic views. By virtue of its focus on tacit and intangible resources, it links directly with new theories of knowledge management and is the basis for a new knowledge-based view of strategy advanced by Nelson and Winter (1982) and others, in which superior knowledge is likely to be the most valuable resource of all.

Our observation of many of these writers is that they err on the side of conventional rationality, the classical model, and provide the reader with little guidance about how to interpret the changing world of technology and globalization in which we live and the way in which organizations form strategic positions in this world. We observe also that strategizing in the real world is something of a caricature in conventional writing with little attention paid to providing realistic appreciations of the forces at work. It is obvious that the drivers of change have been new structures of scientific knowledge, the internationalization of experience in a time of rapid media access to diverse cultures and the acceleration of technological change in post-industrial society. Thus, we see strategy as marked increasingly by an eclecticism and multicultural nature and a post-industrial, high-tech, internationalistic context. For example, the US and the UK are essentially post-industrial service economies; Asia is entering the industrial stage with specialized industries but markets that are almost entirely international. Structural change is endemic in the world economy and even the largest corporations are caught up in the ebb and flow of outsourcing, refocusing new technologies and intangible, human capital. This is in sharp contrast to the world of the rationalist, where strategy is the preserve of top management and the approach is strategy-as-planning, where organizations are efficient, rational resource-allocation mechanisms designed to achieve competitive advantage and economic rents.

What we propose in our conceptual strategic model is a much more blended, balanced and systemic view of the world. It is a treatment of strategy that builds on the roots provided by the classical model (after all, there is still virtue in rationality) that reflects the modern resource-based and knowledge-based view but uses all the available lenses and viewpoints of strategy and strategic thinking to interpret, make sense and provide a basis for strategic decisions.

As a motivating example to illustrate of the use of multiple viewpoints in framing strategy, we attempt to make sense of Honda's strategic behaviour in the celebrated case of its entry into the US motorcycle marketplace. This has been extensively discussed in the strategy literature but its very familiarity enables us to make the point convincingly. The classical view held that Honda's successful entry was a masterpiece of rational economic calculation, so much so that Boston Consulting Group, in a celebrated report, laid out their view about the importance of market share objectives and economies of scale and experience in the motorcycle industry. They used this argument as a benchmark in providing advice to the British government in its own attempts to revitalize the failing British motorcycle industry in the mid 1970s. The opposing explanation of Honda's success was the processual view advanced powerfully by Richard Pascale. He maintained that Honda's successful entry was, indeed, a masterpiece of strategic thinking but rather of flexible, quick incremental adjustment to the marketplace realities and emergent thinking in framing their ongoing strategy. Honda management did not know what they were taking on but learned very quickly. The broader, all-encompassing systemic view holds that it is not the Japanese management of Honda that determines the strategy, nor is it simply a version of 'muddling through', but it is the local US management of Honda that works out how the game has to be played. Indeed, Honda USA becomes embedded in the network of American social and business relationships, albeit with a very distinctive Japanese flavour. In particular, Honda, like all auto/motorcycle companies, worked out that they face the same industry conditions of scale economies, access, capacity, persistent entry by newly industrializing countries and trends towards commoditization. Although, while Honda may have found short-term distinctiveness in the US market, in the end it will find that this will erode and the only strategy available to it over the long term will be to 'economize', i.e. keep its costs low and its options open.

This commentary on Honda exemplifies the need for contemporary strategic thinking to move away from the purely rational or planned view towards a more eclectic view that embraces the emergent, incremental or processual approaches with a stronger respect for the power or markets and institutions – primarily governments – to shape the behaviour of corporations. Corporate behaviour is neither simply rational nor simply determined by its various environments. Any strategic model has to capture the increasing complexity of modern corporate life by, first, providing alternative lenses (perspectives, theories and rules of thumb) through which to see the world and, second, by articulating a way of telling the strategy story so that the reader can see how organizations frame their strategic positioning in their drive for long-term strategic successes. Thus, the centrepiece – our strategy story – is the juxtaposition of intangible resources at the firm level with imperfectly competitive markets in the context of ever more dynamic and intrusive environments involving globalization and rapid, disruptive technological change. We now move on to a discussion of the strategy systems framework which defines the structure and context of this book.

1.3.1 The strategy systems framework

Figure 1.6 shows the conceptual framework and the logic underlying the approach taken to understanding strategy in this book. It argues that the various models, definitions of strategy and frameworks provided in the book are vehicles for thinking about strategy and policy and carrying out a dialogue about strategic options. In essence, our strategy story is conceptualized in terms of a strategy map, which motivates the strategy team and leads to a discussion of strategy options in a broad, systemic fashion. We believe, following Cummings and Wilson (2003), that:

> strategy frameworks, images or maps help people to do their own mapping, thereby kick-starting an oscillating thinking/acting or strategising process, which instills a momentum that brings other choices and possibilities to the fore. It may not get people 'down the mountain' in a straight line but it gets things moving and, when things move, other things come into view.

In short, the interaction between the general map and the mapping of a particular course of action orientates and animates, and no course is likely to be taken effectively without a measure of each of these things. Cumming and Wilson (2003) go on to propose that strategy is an art in the following terms:

> It is argued that the art of strategy lies both in the combination of frameworks, images or maps and the choice of their focus (e.g. big picture versus certain detail) toward mapping an organization's particular course.

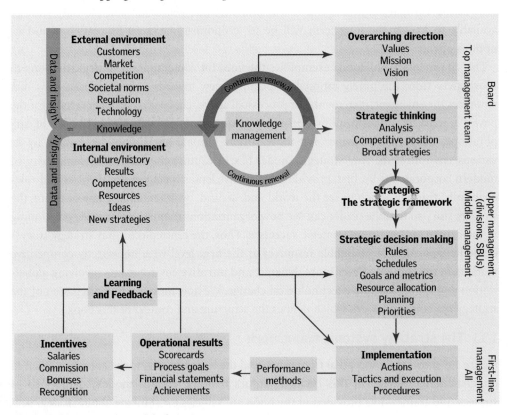

Figure 1.6 A systemic model of strategy

As we shall see, our framework in Figure 1.6 interacts as an organizing framework with strategic processes of animation and orientation (see our introduction in Chapter 2) to produce a preferred strategy for an organization.

What follows now, therefore, is an articulation of the elements of Figure 1.6, recognizing that it is a map and a system model. It 'animates and orientates' the problem of strategy and invites debate and dialogue among those strategists taking part in the strategy process. Note that each of the elements in the diagram (e.g. overarching direction or strategic thinking) encompasses a set of issues and generally poses a specific question. For example, the notion of the overarching direction of an organization begs the question, What do we want to be?

Let us follow through with each of these elements and describe what is going on in each of the boxes.

Overarching direction

Understanding the firm's overarching direction is critical. The general question being asked here is What does the organization want to be? The organization must develop a long-term vision of what it wants to be and take into account the company's culture, reputation, competences and resources in addressing that question. The vision is the core ideology of the organization, which provides the glue that binds the organization together. It encompasses a set of core values that address questions such as why the company exists and what it believes in. The core values may include such things as honesty and integrity, hard work and continuous self-improvement, strong customer service, creativity and imagination. On the other hand, the core purpose is to do with the company's reason for being – in Walt Disney's case, it is simply stated as being to make people happy or, in Hewlett Packard's case, to make a technological contribution to the advancement and welfare of humanity. Purpose, in this sense, is very close to the mission of the organization and, as stated earlier, the vision is the core ideology that binds the organization together. Collins and Porras (2000) argue that what they describe as 'big, hairy, audacious goals' improve long-term vision – for example, Stanford University's statement in the 1940s that they wanted to become 'the Harvard of the West' or Boeing's vision in the 1950s of becoming the 'dominant player in aviation and bringing the world into the jet age'. Thus, a vision breaks down into a more flexible set of aspirations, perhaps sub-goals, which are defined in both qualitative and quantitative terms (e.g. long-term growth or profit), and these aspirations tend to be refreshed more frequently than the overall vision.

Strategic thinking

This element of the strategic concept advances a holistic and integrated view of the business. It asks the question of how, through analysis and strategic positioning, the firm will answer the question, Together, how will we do that?

What we seek to understand here is the relationship between the firm's positioning, resources and capabilities, and organization. We seek to ensure here that the firm's strategy is such that the elements complement and reinforce each other, i.e. the strategies are cohesive. In other words, a co-ordinated framework of high-level enterprise strategies is developed to achieve the vision. This brings together the best strategic thinking and analysis and widely communicates one strategic viewpoint to get everyone pulling in the same direction and to discourage unproductive behaviour.

The agreed enterprise strategy is then broken down into a range of strategies that position the organization in its markets and in its various functional activities (e.g. product strategies, distribution strategies, etc.). They emphasize strategic options and positions, and highlight them in a framework such that they work together. Obviously, strategic thinking requires a whole range of techniques and tools. These include a determination of the broad goals of the organization, thus answering the question, What is most important? Analysts and strategists also have to understand the sources of value creation through revenue drivers, cost drivers and risk drivers.

In other words, strategic thinking begins with a good business model that analyses the economic relationships central to achieving the organization's purpose. These include value creation and analysing industry dynamics – perhaps using the 'five forces' framework developed by Porter (1980). The firm must also recognize the distinctiveness of its own resources and capabilities, because these core capabilities are often long-lasting and provide the linkage with a firm sustaining superior performance over the long run. Porter's (1980) framework is shown in Figure 1.7.

In terms of new entrants, there can be threats from, for example, low barriers to entry, where it is fairly easy for an organization to start trading and enter the market. Equally, if brand identity is weak (say in a commodity product) then the threat of new entrants is likely to be high. Barriers against these threats can be high capital cost of entry (for example, it is very costly to set up a new pharmaceutical manufacturing and R&D organization from scratch) or the development of economies of scale (where bigger and older companies will always benefit from economies of scale and new entrants will not). Substitutes can present a threat if, for example, the cost of a customer switching from one product to that of the substitute is low. Not surprisingly, these are known as switching costs. The lower the switching costs, the greater are the threats from substitution. Substitution can also occur via price. A substitute product at a much lower price (and a

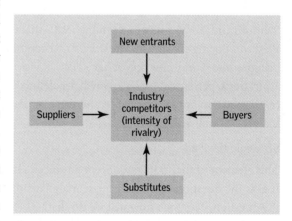

Figure 1.7 Porter's five forces: the elements of industry structure

product which customers will value just as much) will pose a large threat to the company charging higher prices for similar products. Commodity products, such as washing powders, and white consumer goods are examples where customers will switch relatively easily to a lower price product.

Buyers can exert power. If a small number of suppliers serve a large number of firms, then the concentration of supplier power is relatively high. If the reverse situation holds, and there are many suppliers for a few firms, then supplier power is low. In the former case, buyer power is low; in the latter, buyer power is high. An example of the latter case can be found among the large supermarkets worldwide, which exert so much power over their suppliers that they can sometimes charge a premium for stocking and displaying items on their shelves (wine is an example).

Supplier power is really the opposite of buyer power. Where the switching costs of firms in the industry are high, they will not decide lightly to change suppliers. In this case, suppliers have relatively high levels of power over those organizations. However, new suppliers entering the market will have a potential substitution effect and reduce existing levels of supplier power. The relative threat of forward and backward integration will also affect supplier (and buyer) power. For example, if a firm decides it can manufacture its own raw materials (rather than buy from a supplier) then the balance of power between supplier and firm will be changed radically in favour of the firm and to the disadvantage of the supplier.

This kind of framework is useful for picturing the dynamics of an industry but such frameworks do not tell the whole story. They are relatively static frameworks which make a number of assumptions, not least that all players will have perfect knowledge (everyone is aware of the extent of their power or the threat they pose) and will always exercise the power they have. To inject a more dynamic perspective, these frameworks should be seen as one part of a greater process. The strategist has to recognize the source of the power balances or imbalances, but having done that he or she needs to drill deeper into the analysis to analyse not only the sources of such threats and power but also the impact of each on the strategy process. This explains why the five forces model, central to many scholars' strategy frameworks, is only a part of the systemic model presented here. We will be referring to Porter's model again in Chapter 5, where we will use it to explore competitive advantage in more detail.

Strategies: the strategic framework and product goals

In its simplest terms, a strategy consists of a set of goals and a set of policies or actions to achieve those goals. Goals answer the question of what is most important for the organization. The strategy and process also encompass the strategic planning process, which varies from organization to organization in levels of familiarity. However, the most important element in strategic planning is to link the strategic framework and broad goals as guides and allow each of the divisions or sub-units of the organization to develop their own strategies in a co-ordinated fashion. That is, responsibility for strategy formulation should be devolved to the sub-units or entities within the business which have responsibility for products and services. The individual managers running those units are the ones who know the products and services, the product markets and the presence of other competitors in the marketplace. They can then develop a statement of what strategic positioning the organization should reasonably adopt at that level. The role of top management is to co-ordinate those strategies in an enterprise sense, so that it fits the overall strategic framework defined by the vision and the overarching direction of the organization.

Strategic programming

This focuses on the answers to questions such as Who, when and how much? In other words, assuming broad strategies are agreed, an operating plan must be developed to attack such issues as day-to-day priorities, organizational roles and responsibilities, and resource allocation with regard to budgets and systems development. Obviously, this leads to the development of a clearer, tactical plan.

Tactics and execution

This phase of the strategy process answers the tasks of 'Let's get organized and let's do it, and do it right!' In other words, the tactical part of the operating plan fills in the gaps about division plans, unit plans and individual goals, and develops performance metrics at each level, so that monitoring of those plans can be undertaken. The executive focuses not only on the monitoring of performance and targets but the ability to adjust plans quickly and rapidly as new ideas and challenges are developed within the organization.

Performance measurement and purpose

In any organization, there must be a linkage to performance. The feedback that is necessary for any organization in re-framing its strategy in a sensible way is the answer to the question, How do we do a check of performance against targets and cost? Performance metrics are extremely important – they highlight issues such as progress towards goals and, more importantly, how certain tasks and certain strategies can be adjusted better and faster and how change can be incorporated most effectively within the context of the organization.

Information and analysis: the internal and external environment

Obviously, changing the organization through performance monitoring and strategy adjustment is but one process in a series of feedbacks and feedback loops which are absolutely necessary in analysing information about both internal and external environments. In the external environment, we have to question what is happening around us; there must be a process of data gathering and development of insight and knowledge about such issues as new technology and its impact on the business, and the potential impact of regulation and legislation on the activities of the company. The underlying national economic and macroeconomic conditions are also important in setting the global economic context for the organization and, at a more micro level, framing intelligence and analysis about competition, the nature and changing shape of markets and customer needs and opinions. Obviously, key success factors in this external environment enable the firm to focus on appropriate product renewal and generate knowledge and insight about new products and ideas. In the context of the internal environment, the firm needs to analyse and identify its key resources and capabilities and evaluate their impact on competitive advantage. For example, a company's culture and the history of its development can provide a source of competitive strength as in the case of Johnson & Johnson (J&J), which is regarded by many as an extremely ethical and well-run pharmaceutical company. That perception is a result of J&J's strong culture, its history and the strength of its financial resources over a long period of time. Internal analysis also requires a process of continual investigation, discovery and criticism, leading to new ideas, new product concepts, updated financial results and updated metrics. Information about organizational strengths and weaknesses can, in turn, lead to the continual renewal of the strategy process.

Feedback of results and incentives

Kaplan and Norton (1992) have developed processes known as a balanced scorecard for monitoring operational financial results within the organization. Figure 1.8 depicts this scorecard in its simplest form (it is used elsewhere in this book in greater detail; *see*, for example, Chapter 14).

The balanced scorecard attempts to answer questions about progress towards goals and identifies any operational results which can be fed back to continually improve organizational processes. The balanced scorecard also contains an incentive structure which answers the question, What's in it for me? Clearly, if incentives such as salaries, commission and bonuses can be co-aligned with strategic objectives, the employee recognition will lead

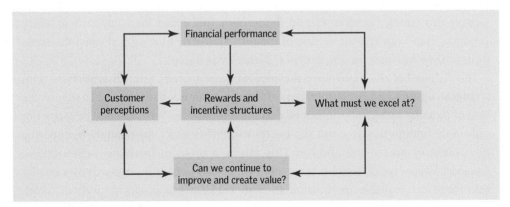

Figure 1.8 The balanced scorecard
Source: adapted from Kaplan and Norton (1992).

to employee loyalty and a strong alignment between individual objectives, organizational objectives and organizational strategy.

In summary, the strategy concept presented here in Figure 1.6 is a map, a framework and a virtuous circle, at the core of which is a process of knowledge management which trades upon analysis of the external and internal environment, analysis of performance, analysis of strategies and competitive updating of values and mission in order to achieve a process whereby the organization is engaged in a continual debate about how it can improve and how it can frame its strategy so that the organization itself fits in a dynamic sense with its current and future strategic position.

1.4 Summary

This chapter has outlined the contested terrain of strategy. The field is full of competing definitions. In order to move beyond a battle of definitions, we have attempted to build a framework which helps show how strategy 'works' rather than debating exactly what it 'is'. Complex though this model might appear at first sight, it provides a framework which the following chapters of this book outline in greater detail.

For example, a solely economics-based perspective would examine the dynamics of *matching the internal environment* of the firm *with its external environment*. As Figure 1.6 makes clear, this is only part of the process – but is an important part. Strategists who do not consider the implications of internal and external do so at their peril. Thus, Part 2 of this book describes in detail the essential elements of this process. In order for strategists to make decisions, they need a detailed appreciation of both the micro- and the macro-economic characteristics of the firm and its environment. But such analysis cannot stand alone. We have already seen in this chapter how values, mission and vision communicate an organization's strategic stance to its wider audience, most importantly its customers. Getting this wrong (as when Gerald Ratner famously called his company's jewellery products 'crap') can seal the demise of the firm no matter how sophisticated the economic analysis has been. In one sentence, Ratner's was doomed.

This chapter has also highlighted the importance of analysis. Strategists are faced with a range of options and rarely are faced with simple go or no-go decisions. Therefore, the skill of *thinking strategically* cannot be overemphasized. Strategists need to be aware not only of the options they face, but also the trade-offs they make, for example, by choosing one course of action over another. This can be a problem for many organizations. Consider Volkswagen's decision to position the Skoda (which it acquired) as a quality mid-range car available in medium to high performance ranges as well as diesel, petrol and dual fuel. What seemed initially like a good decision – to beef up the brand and reputational image of Skoda (Skoda jokes were legendary: what do you call an open-top Skoda? Answer – a skip!) – backfired on Volkswagen since the trade-off this decision produced was to reduce demand for the equivalent Volkswagen products (the Golf and Passat). Skodas were selling at the expense of the firm's existing products. Part 3 of this book examines these sorts of analysis and thinking problems both from the domestic viewpoint (what is our strategic position?) and in the global context (how do we take strategic decisions in an international environment?).

Strategies do not exist independently of organizations, however. The notion of a small number of policy makers sitting in a darkened room formulating key decisions which they then unleash on an unsuspecting organization is a fond and inaccurate characterization. First of all, making strategic decisions involves a wide range of stakeholders and interests which are both internal and external to the organization. Their influences shape and often control what happens. Second, strategies have to be put into practice. They have to be implemented. Moreover, they have to be implemented in often large and complex social environments, which have the convenient label 'organizations' or 'firms' but which contain very high levels of social, individual, elite and irrational behaviours. Organizations are social environments and not solely economic machines. What managers do and how people behave matters. Hence, Part 4 of this book examines in detail the question of strategic acting. It looks at how strategic decisions can be formulated relatively easily but can run into difficulties once managers start to try to implement strategic decisions. The ways in which they organize, oversee and govern decisions matter. Putting decisions into practice means organizations and people are faced with often significant levels of change and new learning. Managers neglect these aspects of strategy (which have often been dismissed as the softer, intangible aspects of strategy) at their peril. Resistance to change and an inability to learn will ensure the death of an organization independently of whether or not it is in a fierce or benign environment. Internal barriers to strategy are just as important as external competitive threats, for example.

Finally, strategies (and organizations) need continuous renewal. Putting decisions into practice is one thing. Knowing and measuring how they have performed and knowing why are completely different skills and processes. Part 5 of this book examines the important questions of performance. How do decision makers know they made the right, or the wrong, decision? This part discusses such topics as performance, quality and process improvements as well as operational results such as financial statements, achievement of stated objectives and process goals. In turn, we view these performance metrics as helping the feedback process into the next set of strategic decisions which managers will take in the future. In this sense, performance metrics also help the learning process and the development of new capabilities as well as the abandonment of old capabilities which might no longer be useful for future strategies.

Before looking at the next parts of the book, it is important to place some of the above arguments in their organizational contexts. The following chapter raises some questions about what happens when 'strategies meet organizations' and provides more detail about the contextual aspects of organization. We would view Chapter 2 as essential pre-reading to Part 4 of this book.

Key terms

Emergent strategy *11*

Evolutionary view *19*

External environment *9*

Goals *9*

Intended strategy *6*

Internal environment *10, 14*

Mission/mission statement *10*

Objectives *see* Goals

Organizational process view *19*

Realized strategy *11*

Resource-based view *16*

Strategic intent *see* Intended strategy

Strategy-as-systems perspective *19*

Strategy processual view *19*

Organizational process view *19*

Online LearningCentre

When you have read this chapter, log on to the Online Learning Centre website at www.mcgraw-hill.co.uk/textbooks/mcgee to explore chapter-by-chapter test questions, further reading and more online study tools for strategy.

Further reading and references

Alchian, AA (1950) 'Uncertainty, evolution and economic theory', *Journal of Political Economy*, **58**, pp. 211–21.

Andrews, KR (1980) *The Concept of Corporate Strategy*, Irwin, Homewood, Il.

Ansoff, HI (1965) *Corporate Strategy*, Penguin, Harmondsworth.

Ansoff, HI (1972) 'The concept of strategic management', *Journal of Business Policy*, **2**, **4**, Summer.

Bower, JL (1982) 'Business policy in the 1980s', *Academy of Management Review*, vol. 7, no. 4, 630–8.

Bower, JL (1986) *Managing the Resource Allocation Process*, Harvard Business School Press, Boston, MA.

Chandler, AD (1963) *Strategy and Structure: Chapters in the History of the Industrial Enterprise*, MIT Press, Cambridge, MA.

Christensen, C (1997) *The Innovator's Dilemma: When New Technologies Cause Great Firms to Fail*, Harvard Business School Press, Cambridge, MA.

Collins, JC and Porras, JI (2000) *Built to Last: Sucessful Habits of Visionary Companies*, Random House, New York.

Cummings S, and Wilson, DC (eds) (2003) *Images of Strategy*, Blackwell, Oxford.

Cyert, RM and March, JG (1963) *A Behavioral Theory of the Firm*, Blackwell, Oxford.

Granovetter, M (1985) 'Economic action and social culture: the problem of embeddedness', *American Journal of Sociology*, **91**, **3**, pp. 481–510.

Henderson, BD (1973) *The Experience Curve Reviewed*, Boston Consulting Group, Boston, MA.

Hussey, D (1998) *Strategic Management: From Theory to Implementation*, 4th edition, Butterworth-Heinemann, Oxford.

Kaplan, RS and Norton, DP (1992) 'The Balanced Scorecard: Measures that Drive Performance', *Harvard Business Review*, Jan–Feb.

Legge, K (2003) 'Strategy as organising', in S Cummings and DC Wilson (eds) *Images of Strategy*, Blackwell, Oxford.

Magretta, J (2003) *What Management is*, Profile Books, London.

March, JG and Simon, HA (1958) *Organizations*, Blackwell, Cambridge, MA.

Mintzberg, H (1994) *The Rise and Fall of Strategic Planning*, Prentice-Hall, Englewood Cliffs, NJ.

Mintzberg, H and Waters, J (1985) 'Of strategies, deliberate and emergent', *Strategic Management Journal*, **6**, pp. 257–72.

Mintzberg, H, Lampel, J and Ahlstrand, P (1998) *The Strategy Safari: A Guided Tour Through the Jungle of Strategic Management*, Prentice-Hall, Englewood Cliffs, NJ.

Nelson, RR and Winter, SG (1982) *An Evolutionary Theory of Economic Change*, Harvard University Press, Cambridge, MA.

Pascale, R (1984) 'Perspectives on strategy: the real story behind Honda's success', *California Management Review*, **14**, **3**, pp. 47–72.

Penrose, E (1959) *The Theory of the Growth of the Firm*, Blackwell, Oxford.

Porter, M (1980) *Competitive Strategy*, Free Press, New York.

Porter, ME (1985) *Competitive Advantage*, Free Press, New York.

Porter, ME (1987) 'From competitive advantage to corporate strategy', *Harvard Business Review*, May–June, pp. 2–21.

Prahalad, CK and Hamel, G (1990) 'The core competence of the organization', *Harvard Business Review*, May–June.

Quinn, JB (1980) *Strategies for Change: Logical Incrementalism*, Irwin, Homewood, Il.

Sun Tzu (1990) *The Art of War*, Sterling Publishing, New York.

Williamson, OE (1975) *Markets and Hierarchies: Analysis and Antitrust Implications*, Free Press, New York.

Chapter 2

Strategy and organization

Introduction

The traditional concepts of strategy outlined in Chapter 1 largely emphasize the dominance of models that highlight the positioning of organizations in relation to their competitive and operating environments. This is certainly an important part of understanding strategic management, but it only tells part of the story. Our eclectic model (see Figure 1.6) emphasizes other key aspects of strategy, locating processes in a wider context, both organizational and societal. This chapter is concerned with the interfaces between strategy and organization. It looks at issues of the *strategy process* – how managers enact and interpret the world around them – and the **organizational *context*** in which such processes take place. Practice focuses on where and how strategic intent has to be formulated, implemented and processed through an organization. Strategy, as a refined and often rarified concept, has to be translated by managers before it can be put into practice. This chapter deals with the key aspects of this translation process and outlines ways of **interpreting strategy** from this perspective.

Translation covers a wide area of topics as well as a wide variety of levels of analysis, ranging, for example, from looking at what managers do when they make strategic decisions to the wider context of organization, such as structure, culture, organizational politics and inter-organizational relations. We shall briefly introduce these concepts in this chapter and expand on each in later chapters (see Part 4).

De Wit and Meyer (1999) provide some useful guidelines for differentiating between strategy content, process and context. They generally define each as:

- *Strategy content:* basically the 'what' of strategy. This means defining what strategic decisions are about (for example, a new product or service) and what their intention is (for example, cost reduction or profit maximization). The content perspective also addresses such questions as where are we going (what are the long term goals?) and what is the scope of the business (what are we going to do?).

- *Strategy context:* the 'where' of strategy. This is the set of factors that comprise the setting for a strategy. This includes the internal context of the organization as well as the characteristics of the external context in the operating environment (such as the nature of inter-organizational relations or the influence of government agencies).

- *Strategy process:* the 'how' of strategy. This details who is involved in the process and when activities take place. It is the story, the drama and the list of players in the strategy as well as the characteristics of the process itself (for example, continuous or discontinuous, short or drawn out over time).

2.1 Linking organization and strategy

The positioning models of strategy introduced in Chapter 1 are deceptively simple. In turn, they can be made sense of by managers in an equally simple way, ignoring the nuances which may lie in the way of thinking and **acting strategically**. As Michaud and Thoenig (2003) point out, a good strategy model is one which is easily readable, can be understood quickly by managers, is transparent to organizational members and outsiders. The philosophy here is that simple is best. The best performances come from adopting and implementing simple models that can be easily understood throughout the organization. Thus, multiple views on strategy and nuances of interpretation are to be avoided as far as possible.

Yet with this view comes a paradox. If all organizations have access to the same models of strategy and to the same external consultants that prescribe best practices, which they distribute in the manner of a cure-all, then what is to differentiate them? Where is the source of competitive advantage, since most organizations will follow similar routes based upon models of best practice and effective strategic positioning?

The answer seems to lie in how managers both interpret such models and how they put strategies into practice in organizations. In short, when strategy meets organization, the actions and processes that ensue have a large impact on the extent to which strategy is effective, competitive and ultimately successful. How managers think and act matters as much as the models that may have informed strategy in the first place.

2.1.1 Thinking and acting strategically

Strategic management, like many other management sub-disciplines, favours dualisms to make conceptual distinctions in the models it uses. These can take many forms, such as competition versus co-operation, or strategy versus structure. While they are useful thinking devices, such dualisms tend to mask the extent to which they are really not polar extremes at all, but are inextricably interrelated. Structure is as much a part of process as process is a part of structure. And certainly, competition and co-operation both inform one another and are part of one another, rather than existing as separate entities. In the same way, the terms thinking and acting strategically are also interrelated and blend together in the strategy process.

The primary reason for focusing on **strategic thinking** and acting is that simply focusing on strategy content (strategic positioning) is insufficient to guarantee desired outcomes (for example, securing a competitive advantage). Consider Porter's five forces model, for example (Porter 1980). This is one of the most well-used and well-described tools for assessing a firm's competitive position. Informed largely by economic models of the firm, the five forces model assesses a firm's position in regard to such factors as the power of suppliers and customers, the ease with which substitution can take place and the barriers to entry for new competitors. The compelling argument from this analysis is that strategic content should be guided by the nature of the interrelationships among the forces and the firm (allowing, for example, a choice of generic versus specialist strategies or quality and customer service strategies). As in many economic models, however, the assumptions that have to be made in order for the analysis to work are fairly heroic and increasingly questionable. For example, the five forces model assumes:

♦ Independence among all the factors.

♦ Organizations can formulate strategies 'at arm's length' in relation to rivals, customers and suppliers.

♦ Structural advantage is the sole key to competitive success (the more a firm has relative power over customers, suppliers etc., the greater is its competitive advantage).

♦ Even where such structural advantages occur, firms can always act to exercise such power without any constraints.

♦ The individual organization is the key unit of analysis.

Even at a common-sense level of analysis, not all of the above assumptions can hold true. Even within the same organization, Chief Executives report severe difficulties in gathering enough information to assess and to mobilize their own operating companies. Looking outside their own organizations to try to implement a forces model is even harder and less realistic.

So what really goes on when managers run with the strategic baton? This chapter begins to unpack this question – the practice of strategy in organizations.

2.1.2 Animation and orientation

At the most basic level, the practice of strategy in organizations is chiefly about defining strategic aims – formulating ambitions and visions (**orientation**). It is also about encouraging and ensuring the various parts of the social system, which is the organization, are mobilised, act in concert with strategic ambitions and contribute to implementation (**animation**). Figure 2.1 illustrates this concept.

Of course, no one believes strategy is as simple as that, but the basic principles of animation and orientation are powerful ideas to begin with (Cummings and Wilson 2003). Everyone knows the story of the group who were lost in the Alps seemingly without a map when one member of the group found a tattered map in a little-used pocket. This find increased morale and animated the group to walk until they were able to orientate themselves by finding familiar bearings. So far so good – but the map was one of the Pyrenees. The value of the map was akin to a strategic framework such as those discussed in Chapter 1. However, what mattered most was this individual's ability to achieve focus and direction, even with the wrong map. The symbolic nature of the framework appears as important as its accuracy in this respect (*see* Weick 1987).

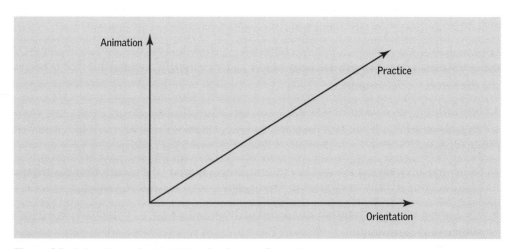

Figure 2.1 Animation and orientation: the drivers of practice

In terms of the strategy model that guides this book (*see* Figure 1.6), animation coincides with the concept of continuous renewal. The interplay between strategic intention and how managers interpret the environment provides a context in which organizational members can become enthused and motivated around a particular set of tasks. Orientation coincides with concepts such as strategic thinking, looking at the broad range of strategies available to decision makers and the processes of analysis undertaken to decide on strategic direction. Orientation embraces values, mission and vision. Orientation is thus inextricably linked with future direction, and all the uncertainty this involves. It is through such statements of future intent (such as we want to achieve 35 per cent market share in two years) that individuals in the organization are motivated to try to achieve. They become animated and oriented towards a particular future or future desirable states of affairs. This is a simple statement to make but a remarkably difficult process to achieve in practice and later sections of this book will explore these social processes of animation and orientation in greater depth (*see* Part 4).

As we argued in Chapter 1, the model of strategy we embrace is eclectic, systematic, attempting to place a resource-based view of the organization in a wider context of cultural, technological and structural changes. How managers interpret and decode the context they inhabit influences the strategies they might choose and colours the desired future states they may articulate. Orientation is thus a combination of interpretation and planning. Equally, the resources at a manager's disposal (either within or outside the organization) will influence the extent to which the manager can successfully animate people and arrange resources around them to achieve desired future states. We examine some of the key interrelationships between context, organization and interpretation in the following sections.

2.2 Context, organization and managerial interpretation

Many authors have called for a view of strategic management that is highly micro, focused on an activity-based view of what managers do (*see*, for example, Johnson *et al.* 2003). The intention is to try to relate what happens in the day-to-day activities of individuals in organizations to strategy processes and outcomes. Some authors go further and argue that the analysis of talk and conversations of all individuals in organizations (not just managers) is relevant for the study of how strategies are formulated, supported and implemented (*see*, for example, Samra-Fredericks, 2003). While we agree that some micro-activities in organizations may reveal a level of analysis previously overlooked by 'traditional' strategic management, such a perspective is nevertheless highly reductionist. As Balogun *et al.* (2003) argue, while micro-perspectives may reveal more about the deeply rooted nature of individual activity (and routines) in organizations, there is a simultaneous need to understand breadth and macro levels of analysis. They argue that if we are to understand any possible relationships between changing forms (structures) of organizations and the characteristics of strategy, we must adopt a broad and more systems-based view of the interactions between context, organization and individual action.

Such a systems perspective is a guiding principle of this chapter. Reductionism allows us to see the detail. It allows us to observe, follow and dissect the activities of individuals as they go about their day-to-day activities and we can learn a great deal about human behaviour in organizations this way, but this prevents us seeing the overall picture. Reductionism, however, can never provide a complete explanation of the strategy process. A more systemic view allows us to move across levels of analysis and across the patterns of organization which any organism adopts in relation to its wider environment (Capra, 1982). In this way we can emphasize the relational aspects of management practice and organizational context.

All organizations are essentially complex systems which interact with their environments. In the case of living systems (such as a species of animal) the relationships between the system and its environment can be characterized by the term structural coupling. That is, a series of interactions between the living system and its environment trigger a set of responses in the living system, resulting in structural and processual changes. These changes can be viewed as the way in which the organism learns, develops and adapts. The same process holds true for complex social organizations. Figure 2.2 shows the main systemic adaptation and strategy processes that help keep the organization aligned with its environment. Managers in organizations *interpret* the environment. They then have to communicate this interpretation among others in the organization. They may have to build

a strategic vision (an ideal goal to aim for) and they may also have to create a new language that can be shared by all organizational members in order to close any gaps between ambition and action. Interpretation and communication allow *strategic options* to be outlined. These are the key choices among a number of possible courses of action which managers might take. Having decided on a course of action, a number of decisions have to be taken in order to *implement* the chosen strategy. In turn, the actions taken by an organization may have an impact on the environment and perhaps modify it slightly. The process then recycles.

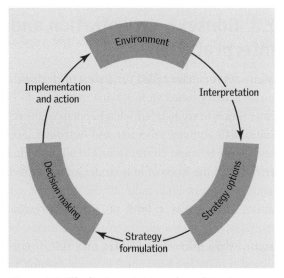

Figure 2.2 The basic systems cycle and strategy

The ways in which managers interpret the environment and instigate changes in their organizations is a fundamental part of the strategy process. Getting this interpretation wrong will increase the risk of demise for the organization and getting it right will increase the chances of growth and success. The following example of Tesco illustrates this point and also shows how the strategic actions of an organization can, in turn, influence and change the operating environment.

Tesco's retail strategies

Tesco (along with other big supermarket chains) has changed the way we shop and the ways we think about shopping. Sensing that 80 per cent of the population have most of the things we want, shopping no longer is a necessity where trolleys are filled to sustain a family for a week, but is a process which happens every two or three days. Many shoppers no longer write lists for the weekly shop, but rely on impulse purchases instead. Recognizing this change in the environment, Tesco moved towards creating the 'shoppable shop' and moved away from competing on volume (stack 'em high) or on price (Sainsbury's is currently the only supermarket competing on low price, perhaps an indication of its poor market position). Tesco now emphasize the shopping experience. Getting the store laid out so customers can get in, shop and get out in the shortest time possible has become a priority. In addition, customers want a one-stop shop. Tesco responds. Almost 50 per cent of the average Tesco store is given over to non-food items such as clothes, homeware and CDs so that the customer does not have to go elsewhere to buy them.

Another change in the 'environment' has been customers' reluctance to drive to large out-of-town stores. Consequently, Tesco are moving back into smaller (less than 2000 square feet) local stores, effectively operating as a corner shop (the average size of an out-of-town store is 50 000 square feet). In another interpretive move, Tesco sensed the organic movement very early – almost before consumers knew what the word meant – and formulated a strategy of providing an uncontaminated, ethically and physically clean food chain. Organic produce now permeates almost all Tesco foodstuffs. In turn, the effects on the consumer (the customer environment) have been marked. Consumers demand more local shops: Tesco sells more DVDs than HMV, more shampoo than Boots and its £4 jeans outsell Levi's, Gap and Wrangler put together. Tesco's strategic actions have modified both the shopping experience of consumers and also their expectations about the quality and type of goods on offer in their stores.

The next environmental challenge for Tesco (and other supermarkets) is the estimate that the average Sunday lunch travels 26 234 miles to the table (e.g. beans from Zambia, chicken from Thailand and carrots from Spain). Cheapest source production is coming under pressure from an increasing number of lobbying groups, including customers, so, according to the simple systems model, Tesco managers will have to interpret these signals correctly and adjust their retail strategies accordingly, perhaps towards a more 'locally produced' initiative.

Source: original data, and the *Observer*, 18 January 2004.

Beer (1981), in his cybernetic view of the firm, crystallizes the systems perspective into five different levels of analysis, showing in each case how the physical analogies of a living organism can be equated with organizational processes. Table 2.1 summarizes this view.

It can be seen from Table 2.1 that 'strategy' can be found in virtually all of Beer's (1981) levels of analysis. The common conception of strategy as being akin to the 'brain' of an organism, telling the rest of the body what to do, is located at levels four and five. Yet, as we have seen from Chapter 1, 'strategy' also comprises controls, monitoring, measurement and procedures and these span levels one to three in Beer's hierarchy. The argument proposed by Beer is that for an organization to be viable (co-exist with and adapt to its environment) all five levels should be present and active. We argue here that the understanding of strategy needs to go beyond a simple understanding of senior management control and direction setting and embrace a broader organizational perspective of tactics, control and execution. The systemic perspective facilitates such a broad perspective.

Nevertheless, the systems view also cannot tell the whole story. While it can show how each level of analysis is important within its own right and that, combined, the levels provide an understanding of complex systems, it makes some rather heroic assumptions about the role of managers, the availability of information and managers' abilities to interpret correctly and communicate effectively under suboptimal conditions of certainty. We explore these issues in the next section.

Table 2.1 The five levels of analysis of the systems view

Level of system	Physical analogy	Function	Organizational analogy
Level one	Muscles, organs	Action and movement	Operational processes
Level two	Spinal cord	Processing and transmission of signals	Information systems and technologies
Level three	Pons/medulla	Autonomic control	Controls embedded in operational processes
Level four	Ganglia, diencephalon (brain connections)	Sensing, arousing and monitoring	Assessing risk and opportunity
Level five	Cortex	Cerebral control and protection	Strategic management processes

Source: adapted from Bell *et al.* (1997).

2.3 **Managerial agency and practice**

The previous parts of this chapter run the risk of making managers seem all-important and pivotal agents of practice and change. In other words, the assumption is that strategy all comes down to managers correctly interpreting an environment 'out there' and taking actions to align their organizations in an optimal interrelationship with that environment. Such a view is equally true of micro-perspectives on the strategy process, since they also give almost absolute primacy to **managerial agency**. The assumption is that understanding micro-practices will reveal more pieces in the strategy jigsaw is equally flawed in this respect.

Many authors, especially in recent years, have suggested that the operating environment of organizations has become increasingly deterministic. However skilfully managers interpret their environments, ultimately strategy is determined by conditions and events external to the organization and outside the direct control of managers or their organizations. Taking this perspective, we could include authors such as Bettis and Hill (1995); Hamel and Prahalad (1996); Hill *et al.* (1998). They argue that the simple feedback loops in systems theory, or the assumptions of perfect knowledge on the part of managers, have been surpassed by changes in what they term the 'competitive landscape' facing organizations. There are two principal drivers of this new landscape – information technology and globalization. Key features are:

- hypercompetition;
- blurring of traditional industry boundaries;
- greater knowledge intensity;
- greater reliance on knowledge as a strategic asset; and
- discontinuous change.

Table 2.2 The new competitive landscape and shifts in strategic emphasis

From	To
General, formal strategies	Local, customized solutions
Strategy content	Strategy process and context
Identifying tangible routines	Managing intangible assets
Certainty seeking	Understanding the dynamics of uncertainties
Competition	Collaboration
Vertical structures	Network and clusters
Learned organizations (distinctive competence)	Learning organizations (open to change and the developments of new competences)

Source: adapted from Cummings and Wilson (2003).

The result is to make traditional models of competitive advantage questionable (such as Porter's five forces) and to render anachronistic traditional efficiency-oriented vertical organizational structures. It also brings into question to what extent managers can act as 'perfect' interpreters of environmental signals and as 'perfect' communicators of strategy within their organizations. Cummings and Wilson (2003) argue that there has been a shift of emphasis from one on strategy content to a focus on contexts and processes. Table 2.2 summarizes some of these changes of emphasis.

From this competitive landscape perspective, strategy is firmly rooted in processes where flexibility, knowledge creation and retention and collaboration within and between organizations are of primary importance (Cummings and Wilson 2003). Performance benefits are likely to be the result of effective combinations of strategy content, process and context and from interlinked systems and practices. Performance benefits are less likely from an organization becoming 'distinctively competent' – in other words, excellent at what it currently does (*see* Table 2.2) since such distinctiveness will soon be eroded in the new competitive landscape.

The majority of the abundant literature on strategy and strategic management tends to emphasize the positioning of organizations in relation to their competitive and

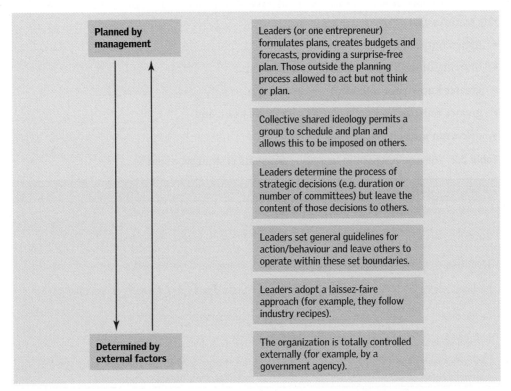

Figure 2.3 Planned versus externally determined strategies: some example characteristics

operating environment. This is certainly an important part of understanding strategic management, but it only tells part of the story. The other parts of the story concern the *strategy process* and the *context* in which such processes take place.

Managerial agency as the sole influence on strategy is certainly questionable in a number of other respects. So far, we have seen that we can make cases for environmental determinism and for managerial choice within a systemic framework. As we saw in Chapter 1, much of the work by Henry Mintzberg and his colleagues sheds light on the middle ground between determinism and choice. As Mintzberg and Waters (1985) argue, strategies do not always come about as a direct result of managerial action. Nor do they come about as a direct result of environmental determinism. Instead, they emerge as a pattern one can detect in a number of strategic decisions made over time in any organization. This emergent pattern in a stream of decisions – taken under conditions of uncertainty – is what we call strategy. It is the interplay between environmental determinism and managerial agency. Mintzberg and Waters (1985) distinguish between planned and emergent strategies:

Planned strategies *are deliberate and are planned as intended in advance.*

Emergent strategies *are patterns which are realized in a stream of decisions, often in the absence of (or in spite of) managerial intentions.*

Obviously, many strategies fall in between these polar extremes of planned versus emergent. Andrews (1987) suggests that, in practice, the only fully planned strategies that can be observed in organizations amount to little more than financial planning statements. Figure 2.3 illustrates a range of planned versus externally determined strategies.

One of the key features of the above debates about managerial agency is that managers have a degree of choice in the strategies they formulate and pursue. As Child (1972) recognized, managers are rarely so constrained by external conditions that they have no discretion to act at all. They simply have varying limits to the autonomy of their actions. Michaud and

	Short term	Long term
External pressure perceived as strong	Mercenary organization	Organic organization
External pressure perceived as weak	Fragmented organization	Self-sufficient organization

Figure 2.4 Strategic orientation
Source: adapted from Michaud and Thoenig (2003).

Thoenig (2003) have characterized how organizational types might emerge over time depending on what degrees of autonomy managers have and to what extent they try to formulate strategies for long-term effectiveness or for short-term gain. Their theoretical arguments owe much to Vincent's (1996) book *La Chair et le Diable* (*Flesh and the Devil*), which has not been translated from the original French. The basic argument is that organizational typologies emerge over time depending on how managers think and act strategically. These typologies can be represented for illustrative purposes in a simple matrix, as in Figure 2.4.

2.3.1 The fragmented organization

Here, managers have been typically exposed to quite benign and calm external contexts. Over time, their strategic thinking and acting has led to the embedding of relatively bureaucratic organizational features. Specialized sub-units have built up, each with its own short-term perspective and each pitched against the other sub-units for resources and senior management attention. Such an organization is fragmented in the sense that there is little incentive to think longer term or to engage in innovation or renewal. In many ways the organization distances itself from the immediacy of the competitive marketplace. Internal co-operation among sub-units is very restricted and formalized and standardized procedures take the place of individual or co-operative initiatives. Referring to Table 2.2, such an organization has become *learned* (very good at what it presently does) but is one which has difficulties in *learning* (changing and developing what the organization does and how it does it). Individuals in the organization have no incentive to change. Examples of such organizations would include many public sector organizations (prior to privatization) and financial services organizations, especially banks, which had a long history of such strategic thinking.

2.3.2 The self-sufficient organization

Here, we have an organization typified by perhaps years of managers facing a benign environment, but is also characterized by managers who think strategically in a particular way – they assume they can find the resources needed for innovation and renewal within their organizational boundaries and can change incrementally towards more longer-term goals. Such an organization may be equally bureaucratic as the fragmented stereotype. However, the key difference is that managers get around specialization and fragmentation by ad hoc and informal processes. Improvisation and informal processes drive strategic thinking. There is strong emotional attachment by individuals to the organization, although strategy may still be imposed from the top rather than be fostered at other levels in the hierarchy. This is an organization characterized by 'in' groups and 'out' groups. Those who are members of the 'in' groups (often informal groups) are those who can influence strategy longer term and can bestow upon themselves privileges which are invisible to the 'out' groups. Examples would include many professional organizations, including universities and further education establishments in the UK.

2.3.3 The mercenary organization

Typified by a threatening and turbulent external context, managers in these organizations permanently seek short-term changes by exploiting the current situation. There are no assumptions that the required skills and knowledge reside within the organization's boundaries, with a readiness to recruit and employ individuals who can bring such needed skills within the organization. In this way, the structure of this organization permanently changes as sections are closed and abandoned in favour of new ones which suit the market more closely. Strategic thinking in these kinds of organization is very much like that of the mercenary soldier. Temporary clusterings of skilled individuals make policy 'on the hoof' as market conditions demand and individual managers (mercenaries) can join or leave the organization at any time. The key to innovation and change is to be found in the engagement of these professionals and the skills they bring with them from outside the organization. Such an organization attracts weak loyalty and, therefore, strategy is inevitably short term in its focus. Nevertheless, such an organization demands strong bonds of co-operation to get the job done. It is also likely to operate in a context where there may be common standards or benchmarks for performance. Examples of such organizations would include many management or professional consulting firms as well as many project-based organizations.

2.3.4 The organic organization

The environment is unstable and perhaps threatening. Competition, regulation and technological changes are all around. Yet, this organization is populated by managers who think and act strategically in very different ways from the mercenaries described above. In this organization socialization and loyalty to the organization are extremely high. Co-operation between people is high and is perhaps seen as something of a normative process (e.g. a moral duty). While there may be differentiated sub-units in the organization, there is mutual loyalty between them. There is also a prevailing assumption that the required skills and knowledge reside inside the organizational boundaries rather than outside them (as in the mercenary organization). As Michaud and Thoenig (2003: 32) note, there is a sense of a shared adventure in such organizations, where cognitive channels spread rapidly across the sub-units to provide a strong and relatively unified organizational culture. Such features allow senior managers to capture ideas and embryonic suggestions made at lower levels in the organization. Internal networks and communities are strongly in evidence and provide a sound platform for longer-term thinking. In more extreme cases, managers may have developed, over time, a community of language and expression unique to the organization in which to express and to short-cut complex ideas and suggestions. In the terminology of organizational cultures, these organizations exhibit strong, cohesive cultures that allow longer-term strategic thinking even in the face of highly turbulent environments

2.4 Summary

In this chapter, we have mapped out the complex terrain where strategies meet organizations. The ways in which managers interpret their environment shapes and influences the ways in which they think and act strategically. They will orientate themselves towards problems and opportunities in different ways, depending on their perspectives and will attempt to animate enthusiasm, support and resources accordingly. Over time, such patterns of strategic thinking and acting become embedded in the infrastructure of the organization and this can lead to the emergence of quite distinct organizational stereotypes.

There are large questions over what are the appropriate levels of analysis to interrogate managerial practice. In this chapter, we have described some of the key levels and the debates each has engendered. These range from a highly focused perspective on the micro-practice of strategy – observing and recording what individual managers do in the strategy process – to a much more macro-level of analysis – showing how the wider context, the organization and managerial interpretation co-exist in a systems model. From this perspective the micro cannot be understood separately from the macro and vice versa.

Finally, the perhaps over-rational and deterministic perspectives of the systems view can be counterbalanced by the consideration of planned versus emergent perspectives. That the majority of strategies seem to err towards emergent processes may come as no surprise to those who participate in strategic decision making. However, even emergent strategies appear to have characteristics which typify them and which, once appreciated, can be of immense help to scholars and practitioners alike.

The sub-themes raised in this chapter (for example, decision making, **strategy and practice**, organizational design and embedded routines) are discussed in greater detail in Part 4 of this book.

Key terms

Acting strategically *34*

Animation *36*

Emergent strategy *43*

Interpreting strategy *34*

Managerial agency *41*

Organizational context *33*

Orientation *36*

Planned strategy *43*

Strategic thinking *35*

Strategy and practice *46*

Online
Learning Centre

When you have read this chapter, log on to the Online Learning Centre website at
www.mcgraw-hill.co.uk/textbooks/mcgee to explore chapter-by-chapter test questions,
further reading and more online study tools for strategy.

Further reading and references

Andrews, KR (1987) *The Concept of Corporate Strategy*, 3rd edition, Irwin, Homewood, Illinois.

Balogun, J, Huff, AS and Johnson, P (2003) 'Three responses to the methodological challenges of studying strategizing', *Journal of Management Studies*, **40**, 1, pp. 197–224.

Bell, TB, Marrs, FO, Solomon, I and Thomas, H (1997) *Auditing Organizations Through a Strategic-Systems Lens*, KPMG Peat Marwick LLP, London.

Beer, S (1981) *Brain of the Firm: The Managerial Cybernetics of Organization*, Wiley, Chichester.

Bettis, R and Hill, M (1995) 'The new competitive landscape', *Strategic Management Journal*, **16**, pp. 7–19.

Capra, F (1982) *The Turning Point: Science, Society and the Rising Culture*, Bantam Books, New York.

Child, J (1972) 'Organizational structure, environment and performance: the role of strategic choice', *Sociology*, **6**, pp. 1–22.

Cummings, S and Wilson, DC (eds) (2003) *Images of Strategy*, Blackwell, Oxford.

De Wit, B and Meyer, R (1999) *Strategy Synthesis: Resolving Strategy Paradoxes to Create Competitive Advantage*, International Thomson Press, London.

Hamel, G and Prahalad, H (1996) 'Competing in the new economy', *Strategic Management Journal*, **17**, pp. 237–42.

Hitt, M, Keats, B and de Marie, S (1998) 'Navigating in the new competitive landscape: building strategic flexibility and competitive advantage in the 21st century', *Academy of Management Executive*, **12**, 4, pp. 22–42.

Johnson, G, Melin, L and Whittington, R (2003) 'Micro strategy and strategizing: towards an activity-based view', *Journal of Management Studies*, **40**, 1, pp. 2–22.

Michaud, C and Thoenig, J-C (2003) *Making Strategy and Organization Compatible*, Palgrave Macmillan, Basingstoke.

Mintzberg, H and Waters, JA (1985) 'Of strategies deliberate and emergent', *Strategic Management Journal*, July/Sept, pp. 257–72.

Porter, M (1980) *Competitive Strategy: Techniques for Analysing Industries and Competitors*, Free Press, New York.

Samra-Fredericks, D (2003) 'Strategizing as lived experience and strategists' everyday efforts to shape strategic direction', *Journal of Management Studies*, **40**, 1, pp. 141–74.

Vincent, JD (1996) *La chair et le Diable*, Odile Jacob, Paris.

Weick, K (1987) 'Substitutes for strategy', in J Teece (ed.) *The Competitive Challenge*, Ballinger, Cambridge, MA.

Part 2

Economic analysis for strategic decisions

Part contents

In this part you will find the following chapters:

Introduction

The logic of Part 2 parallels the logic employed by the strategy analyst. The operation of markets and the nature of supply and demand conditions provides an economics calculus and a toolkit (Chapter 3). There is a context broader and more extensive than markets that we conventionally call the macroeconomy. This (in Chapter 4) shapes and conditions the behaviour of organizations and organizations spend much time and effort in understanding how to cope with or even defy these powerful economic forces. This macroeconomic perspective allied with the microeconomic toolkit gives us the basis for the concept of competitive advantage (Chapter 5). Competitive advantage is the cornerstone of strategy analysis specifically and for strategic thinking generally. It conveys the notion of competitive success in the sense of providing superior (relative to competitors) benefits to customers while earning above average profits (again relative to competitors). Strategy is the pursuit of success and the economic logic expressed in this section gives us an economic language for defining the nature of success. Therefore, this Part should be read as a whole, understanding that competitive advantage is the analytical key to strategy.

Chapters 3 and 4, taken together, present an outline of the basic economic principles that are required in order to understand the detail of strategic management. Economics is a very broad subject, ranging from microeconomics (the organization of markets and the behaviour of firms and individuals), through macroeconomics (the study of whole economies and the determinants of national income, growth etc.), to international trade (the exchange of goods and services by people in different economies). The basic economics in these chapters represent a bare minimum of economics sufficient to gain an understanding of strategic management. For readers who really want to read further in economics we recommend reading McAleese (2004).

Chapter 3 covers the basic economic concepts that are used in strategic management. These include:

- Cost analysis, opportunity cost and economies of scale and scope.
- Market and firm demand and price and income elasticities.
- Competition and rivalry including monopoly, imperfect competition and generic strategies open to firms.

These concepts are fundamental to the way in which economists describe the operations of markets and the operation of the competitive market process. These concepts apply equally to the understanding of the way in which costs arise in the firm and the way in which firms interpret the markets around them. Thus, this chapter presents cost analysis, demand analysis (the analysis of the demand conditions that face individual firms), and analysis of markets and the way in which they operate and the discretion that firms have in their participation in markets. Cost and demand analyses lay the basis for understanding from where cash flows of firms come. Markets are the basis for understanding competition.

The markets perspective in Chapter 3 indicates how strategists need to have an eye to the fit of their organization with its immediate operating environment. Competitors, substitutes and markets can be capricious and their impact immediate. Therefore, a main theme for the strategist is the exploration of the impact of the external economic 'context' on company performance. The strategist is looking to differentiate between those economic forces that are so powerful as to be irresistible and those market conditions that can be conditioned by the choice of appropriate strategy. It is common to observe that economists emphasize the power of markets over organizations whereas organizations adopt strategies for the very purpose of defying environmental pressures and imposing themselves on markets.

The immediate operating environment usually refers to markets for goods and services and to industries – those elements in the supply chain that combine to deliver products and services into final markets. Often overlooked, however, are the apparently more distant influences of an organization's context (such as the impact of government policies or the actions of a regulator). These are present in the deeper context that comprises the infrastructure of government, civil administration, the law, and social custom and practice that shapes the behaviour of businesses and consumers. This deeper context is covered in Chapter 4. The fit of an organization with its environment goes beyond its understanding of the market context of business. All firms and organizations in general are sensitive to events in the wider economy. Even with no change in the strategy of the firm, major changes in its performance and prospects will occur for macroeconomic reasons beyond its control. Whereas the firm might reasonably hope to condition and control its markets, the macroeconomy is typically beyond control but has to be factored into the firm's plans and expectations for the future.

Chapter 4 covers the fundamentals of aggregate demand and supply and the implications for GDP, inflation and unemployment. It also examines the causes and effects of business cycles and what in a global economy causes booms and slumps to come to an end. It goes on to consider issues concerning the sustainability of strong economic growth, especially in emerging markets. The chapter concludes by considering national competitive advantage and the link with company competitive advantage. It also explores issues of uncertainty and risk, and some of the forward-looking strategies business might adopt to limit the effects of exposure to risk. How might uncertain and volatile economic factors (for example, exchange or interest rates) be incorporated into strategic thinking?

Equipped with a microeconomic toolkit and a sense of how to analyse the economic environment, Chapter 5 introduces the key notion of competitive advantage. This is the foundation stone for any strategy analysis. It is a powerful intellectual construct that is used universally. The idea of competitive advantage is gained through the denial of perfect competition, the economist's competitive ideal explained in Chapter 3. Whereas perfect competition leaves no room for individual firms and their strategies, the whole idea of strategy is built on the presence of imperfections in markets. This starting point for strategy is explained in Chapter 5 and further explored in other basic concepts: industry analysis (often referred to as the Porter five forces analysis), the generic competitive strategies and the value chain. Moving from these foundations for strategy analysis, the rest of the chapter introduces a more practical flavour. If we understand the idea of competitive advantage as a key attribute that is specific to the firm, then we have the beginnings of a description of strategy. We describe a template for describing and identifying a strategy – how would you recognize a strategy if you saw one? Whereas competitive advantage is an external positioning concept, strategy also needs to say something about the internal disposition of resources and assets as well. The internal logic of strategy is shown in the strategy cycle and cost analysis is reflected in the value chain. The latter is extremely well known, being another product of Porter's analysis (1985). The strategy cycle illustrates the significance of the balance between internal resources, external market positioning and financial performance. The value chain builds directly on the cost analysis of Chapter 3 and enables us to identify a picture of the internal asset structure and activity structure of the firm. The chapter concludes with a template for a practical overview of strategy – a self-testing of your firm's strategy IQ. This can be turned into a simple questionnaire for assessing the strategy of your own firm or of any firms of which you have some knowledge. By the end of this chapter we will see the significance of competitive advantage for the study of strategy and for strategy making in firms.

Part 2 provides the economic rationale for strategy, a toolkit for analysing strategy, a language for conducting the strategy discourse, and a set of strategy tools. Part 3 goes on to describe how the idea of competitive advantage is translated into practice in a variety of different situations.

You should now refer to the Online Learning Centre where Figures 1.6 and 2.2 are simplified into two maps – the Strategy Resources Concepts map and the Strategy Process Concepts map. As we indicated in the Introduction to Section 1 each Section of the book highlights and uses 'resources' and 'processes' in different ways.

This Part (Economic Analysis for Strategic Decisions) is heavily analytical. Its focus is on the demand and cost conditions that face the firm. On the demand side, this is the typical analysis of the external economic environment in terms of the response the firm can expect from the market given the presence of competitors. It is also in part a contribution to an assessment of the firm's own competitive position. The cost analysis is more focussed on the internal environment in terms of understanding the cost conditions and likewise, is another contribution to understanding its own competitive position. In this chapter the tools from economics are also tools that strategists can deploy in situation assessment.

But the focus on analysis does not mean there are no 'process' implications. In process terms, this Part also contributes to understanding and interpreting the context. The process of analysis here is a strong player in the strategic process that goes on under the heading of 'interpretation'. However, there is little contribution beyond the interpretation activity – interpretation through analysis is largely a discrete activity that once completed becomes an ingredient in later processes.[1]

The shading for each element in the maps indicates the degree of focus on that element. Thus Context and Strategy (content of strategy) are the prime focus in terms of resources. In terms of processes, the rectangles indicate 'orientation' characteristics (see Chapter 2) and the ovals represent 'animation'. Orientation characteristics connect with the resource ideas

---

[1] Although see the events in the British Government in early 2004 to see how analysis and interpretation of intelligence data can become an important and active ingredient in the 'animation' (implementation) stage where other players remain to be convinced about the merits of a proposed strategy.

and animation demonstrates action, implementation and linkage activities. In this Part, the process focus is limited, being confined mainly to the process of understanding the context and interpreting it.

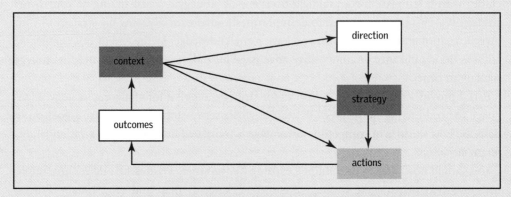

Figure 1.6 Strategy Resources Concepts Map: Outline

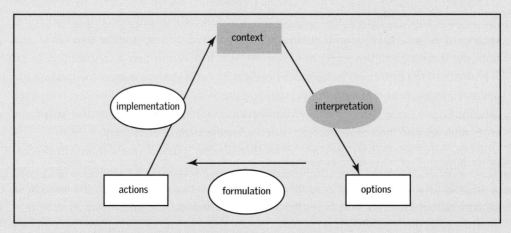

Figure 2.2 Strategy Process Concepts Map: Outline

Chapter 3

The microeconomics of strategy[1]

Introduction

One of the key questions raised in Chapters 1 and 2 is that of the 'fit' of the organization with its environment. For many years, the question of to what extent does an organization need to 'match' the demands of its environment has been debated. Strategists have long argued that there are significant performance pay-offs from an organization which is in tune with its operating environment. For example, the five forces model (see Chapter 1 and later in Chapter 5) identifies key factors in the operating environment of an organization. There may be high levels of competition or the threat of competition may be relatively benign. On the other hand, the threat of substitution may be high and the switching costs of

[1] This chapter is written jointly with K.G (Ben) Knight.

consumers may be relatively low. This means that, in a competitive industry, strategists will have to ensure that the structures and processes of their organizations are flexible enough to undertake rapid changes should the environment become difficult (new organizations enter easily with substitute products, for example).

This seemingly obvious truism – that structures and processes should be increasingly flexible and open to change as environmental conditions become more turbulent – is actually more difficult to analyse and enact in practice. There have been two broad approaches to addressing this key question of organizational fit; one from organization theory and the other from economics. The debate in organizational theory is summarized below and Chapter 3 and the rest of Section 2 then go on to show how a microeconomic analysis can help develop and deepen this organization–environment question.

Organization–environment fit

The key question addressed by organization theorists was: How do organizations adapt successfully to different levels of environment uncertainty? For example, a beer or lager distribution organization operates in a relatively certain environment. Fluctuations in demand for beer are incremental and take place over a long period of time. Beer is also a difficult product to substitute. On the other hand, oil companies and airlines face highly uncertain environments as operating conditions can change rapidly (e.g. terrorist activities, shifting demand patterns) and substitution can be quick and easy (e.g. low-cost airlines).

Building on the work of Burns and Stalker (1961) conducted in England and Scotland, Lawrence and Lorsch's (1967) study of a sample of American organizations facing different levels of uncertainty revealed that two factors were key to sustained performance – differentiation and integration. **Differentiation** refers to the breadth and diversity of individuals' perspectives in departments (broad or narrow; focusing on functional aspects only, for example, versus seeing a broader picture beyond the function). It also refers to the degree of formal structure in a function or department. **Integration** refers to the extent to which functions or departments collaborate. It is also an index of the quality of that collaboration. Lawrence and Lorsch (1967) found that different departments in organizations faced different levels of uncertainty. For example, they found that research and development (R&D) departments faced uncertainties over long time horizons and R&D strategies had to be extremely goal-directed. Sales departments faced uncertainties over short time periods (weeks, not months). In successful firms, R&D departments were structured informally and the sales departments were formally structured but were very socially orientated. The Lawrence and Lorsch study concluded that organizations perform better when the levels of differentiation and integration match the levels of uncertainty in the environment.

Burns and Stalker (1961) had shown earlier that another response to environmental uncertainty lay in the way an organization was structured overall. They depicted two extreme types of structure, **mechanistic** (centralized, formal, with strategic decisions made only by a small number of top managers) and **organic** (decentralized, informal, with strategic decisions made where the relevant expertise lay in the organization). They concluded that organizations which adopt organic structures performed better (were able to innovate, change and thrive) when the environment was highly uncertain. They also found the reverse was true. Mechanistic organizations perform well in very stable and predictable environments.

Both studies provided a firm foundation for a contingency view of strategy and organization which persists today. However, as Rosenfeld and Wilson (1999: 358) point out:

> *there has been a growing body of disquiet over the simplicity of this contingent 'fit' between structure and environment ... environmental characteristics do not wholly fashion organization structures ... managers have choices within certain limits to carve out their own organizational designs and processes ...*

This debate about to what extent managers have autonomy over the strategic decisions they take can be read in detail in Child (1972; 1997), where he introduces the concept of 'strategic choice'. Managers are not wholly constrained by their environments according to Child. But the premise is clear, whether one takes a wholly or a partially contingent view:

> *Environments and organizations are closely interlinked and the nature of those linkages seems to affect organizational performance.*

The perspective of the strategist

For the strategist, therefore, it is essential to analyse such organization–environment relations. They both affect where strategic decisions are taken in the organization (centrally or not) and influence the likely success of their outcomes. Despite this apparent 'Eureka' moment in organization theory, there has been no significant precision and identification of what exactly those environmental variables might be. Which organizational factors are the basis of highly uncertain environments and vice versa? The answers from organization theory remain too broad for the strategist. There is an urgent need for further detail and the identification of key variables. It is here where microeconomics comes to the rescue. It drills deeper than organization theorists attempted to do.

Chapters 3 and 4 present an outline of the basic economic principles that are required in order to understand the subject of strategic management. Economics is a very broad subject, ranging from microeconomics (the organization of markets and the behaviour of firms and individuals), through macroeconomics (the study of whole economies and the determinants of national income, growth etc.), to international trade (the exchange of goods and services by people in different economies). The basic economics in these chapters represent a bare minimum of economics sufficient to gain an understanding of strategic management.

A main theme in both chapters is the exploration of the impact of the external economic 'context' on company performance and the aspects of the business environment over which strategic 'actions' have limited control. Context usually refers to markets for goods and services and to industries – those elements in the supply chain that combine to deliver products and services into final markets. Behind this there is a deeper context that comprises the infrastructure of government, civil administration, the law, and social custom and practice that shapes the behaviour of businesses and consumers. As the book progresses you will see that the theme of strategic management is how the firm can position itself against these economic forces in order to survive and prosper.

This chapter covers the basic economic concepts that are used in strategic management. These include:

- Cost analysis, opportunity cost and economies of scale and scope.
- Market and firm demand and price and income elasticities.
- Competition and rivalry including monopoly, imperfect competition and generic strategies open to firms.

These concepts are fundamental to the way in which economists describe the operations of markets and the operation of the competitive market process. These concepts apply equally to the understanding of the way in which costs arise in the firm and the way in which firms interpret the markets around them. Thus, this chapter presents cost analysis, demand analysis (the analysis of the demand conditions that face individual firms), and analysis of markets and the way in which they operate and the discretion that firms have in their participation in markets. Cost and demand analyses lay the basis for understanding from where cash flows of firms come. Markets are the basis for understanding competition.

3.1 Strategy, markets and macroeconomy

Although there are rival and contrasting views of strategy (set out in Chapter 5), understanding the past and present performance of a company is a key input to strategy making. Skilful analysis of a company and its business environment enables the *separate* effects of factors external and internal to the firm to be carefully identified. Accurate diagnosis of the state of a company is essential for effective competitive strategy, because strategic action is inevitably constrained by a whole host of external events over which managers have no control. For example, the economic crisis that occurred in Asia in 1997/8 derailed the strategies of many companies, not just in the Asian region. The globalization strategy of major Korean companies such as Samsung was thwarted both by the scale of the domestic recession in Korea and the uncontrollable movement of the Korean exchange rate. The impact of these external shocks on the financial position of Samsung and many other companies in the Asian region made it impossible for them to carry out their overseas investment strategy. In late 1997, Samsung were forced to close a new excavator factory and to shelve expansion plans for their electronics factory in the UK.

The effect of this crisis was not confined to Asia. Many non-Asian firms lost large export orders. The Prudential saw its single premium sales drop from £49 million to £9 million in 1997/98. Many EU-based companies with large Asian projects were hit. For example, in the UK the Midlands-based CAD had been commissioned by an Indonesian conglomerate to design and develop a sophisticated multi-purpose vehicle for the Asian market. The crisis in Asia, and in Indonesia in particular, meant that the project could not be completed, with catastrophic consequences for CAD.

Similarly, the 'technology crash' heralded by the collapse in the prices of technology stocks on the NASDAQ in May 2000 signalled the end of the technology boom of the 1990s and led to a significant slowdown of the world economy. In particular, telecommunications companies found themselves to have substantially overinvested in licences for new technology communications, resulting in excessive debt burdens on balance sheets without compensating increases in consumer demand. Most of these companies had still not recovered by late 2003.

The identification of these 'contextual' constraints and an awareness of the severity of their impact on the firm are clearly important. Managers take 'actions' to influence the 'context' in which a firm works, but to do this effectively managers have not only to know what *should* be done, but also to be sensitive to what *can* be done. Recognizing the limitations of strategic 'actions' is fundamental to success. Economic analysis helps us in achieving this understanding of the business environment, so this chapter introduces some key concepts that are used in this stage of the strategy process.

This chapter explores these issues using the example of two real-life manufacturing companies which, for the sake of anonymity, we will call PaperCo (Company A) and MetalCo (Company B). PaperCo and MetalCo operate in different market sectors and

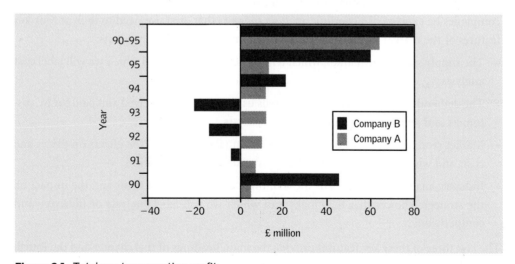

Figure 3.1 Total pre-tax operating profit

produce different goods. MetalCo is a metals manufacturer selling its product to the engineering and vehicle sectors, while PaperCo is a papermaker supplying packaging products to the food industry. The financial performance of these companies over a five-year period in the 1990s is shown in Figure 3.1.

Note that over the five-year period as a whole, the profit performance of MetalCo is significantly better than PaperCo. Both companies are of similar size in terms of capital employed and sales, so that this superior performance is mirrored in the rates of return on both capital and sales. However, it is also clear from Figure 3.1 that there are substantial differences in the pattern of profits over time. PaperCo shows a steady increase in its profits while MetalCo experiences a much more variable performance. Indeed, in three of the five years, MetalCo made a loss, and our view of the comparative performance of these companies in these three years would be completely different from the analysis of the whole five-year period. (The reason the data ends in 1995 is that MetalCo was taken over by a larger company and there is no separate financial data for the years since 1995.)

One explanation for these differences is variation in managerial competence and in particular in strategic capability. Anticipating the discussion in Chapter 5 we set out here the definition of competitive advantage:

> *Delivering superior value to customers and in doing so earning an above average return for the company and its stakeholders.*

One measure of its existence is the ability of a company to outperform its sector rivals. Both PaperCo and MetalCo enjoy substantial competitive advantage in their respective market sectors and this is reflected in their financial performance. Both are in the top 25 per cent of companies operating in their separate market sectors.

How, then, could the differences in the long-run financial performance of these two companies be explained? Economic analysis suggests that, first, we need to look at four key features of the market 'context' in which these two firms sell their products:

- The supply side of the market, which tells us how costs arise and which we will label **cost analysis**.

- The demand side of the market, which tells us how value is perceived and paid for by customers and which we will label **demand analysis**.

- Market rivalry, which tells us how competition takes place and the effects on prices and costs and which we will label **analysis of markets and competition**.

- Industry analysis, which tells us the economic configuration of firms and the impact on the strategic choices that they make and which we will label **analysis of industry and competition**.

The first three of these key features provide the main headings of this chapter and the fourth is discussed in Chapter 5.

Now consider the following simple profits equation:

Profits = total revenue − total costs

The supply side mostly focuses on the cost element of the profits equation, while the demand side and market rivalry mainly deal with revenue issues such as price, sales volume and market share. However, as we shall see, costs are also influenced by sales volume and hence demand and rivalry issues. Analysis of industry and competition assesses the combination of forces that leads to greater or lesser profitability. Note how in our approach to understanding the economic concepts we indicate how the nature of markets affect the way competition works through the interaction of buyers/consumers in the marketplace. But we also show that the economic configuration of the firms in the industry also affects competition by virtue of the cost structures and the nature of their resources and capabilities that condition the competitive offerings that they wish to make.

3.2 **Cost analysis**

The firm needs to examine the implications of its decisions for the costs of the business – the links between decision making and costs is central to an understanding of long-run cost position and competitiveness. The guiding principle is the idea of **opportunity cost.** This is defined as:

> *The sacrifice of alternatives foregone in producing goods or services.* (Seldon and Pennance 1965, p. 253)

For example, the cost of capital for project A is the return foregone by taking project X rather than project Y. It is not simply the cash cost of the funds required for project X. For an individual, the opportunity cost of a new car might be the benefits forgone by not extending the house. For a company, the opportunity cost of expansion into North America might be the return foregone by not investing in China. The notion of opportunity cost rests on the fact of scarcity, that resources are limited in relation to the possibilities that exist. Without scarcity there would be no concept of cost and indeed economics and economic thinking would be irrelevant.

The strength and pervasiveness of the concept of opportunity cost leads us into an understanding of **relevant costs**: the costs associated with a decision are those costs that are directly affected by and are changed by a decision. The significance of this is that costs are decision-specific and therefore are unlikely to be routinely available from those costs reported in the annual accounts for the purposes of reporting to shareholders. Accounting costs are typically backward looking and relate to the firm as a whole whereas relevant costs are decision-specific and relate to future costs. Management accounting strives to bridge this gap by taking a future perspective, although, by its nature, it cannot, in setting budgets, anticipate the characteristics of decisions that are relevant for future costs.

Many costs arise directly from the scale (volume) of operation of a business. The term **cost structure** refers to the technical conditions of production in the markets in which PaperCo and MetalCo operate. The critical issue is the balance of costs between **fixed costs**, which do not vary with output (for example, the cost of machines or buildings or R&D spending), and **variable costs**, which do (for example, labour costs or raw material costs). Table 3.1 sets out the definitions of these different cost concepts together with an example of the impact of different levels of output

Figure 3.2 depicts a cost function that shows the relationship between average total cost and output. It shows how average costs vary with output. Note the shape of the average cost relationship. Average total costs fall and are at the minimum value when output is Q1. The fall in average total costs occurs (arithmetically) because of the fall in average fixed costs (*see* Table 3.1 above).

The shape of cost curves depends critically on the specification of the relevant time period. Economists make a simple but very powerful distinction between the **short run** and the **long run**. The short run is the (short) time within which the fixed factors of production cannot be changed. For example, the nature of a factory and the characteristics of its production lines cannot normally be changed within a period of weeks or even months. However, over a longer period, say five years, the factory can be remodelled and the production lines rebuilt to take advantage of new technology and new working processes.

Short-run cost behaviour has two important characteristics. These are captured in the **law of diminishing returns**. This says that as additional amounts of variable factors of production are added to fixed factors (e.g. factory, production lines), unit costs of output will first decrease up to a point, but will then increase (*see* Table 3.1 above). The first part of this arises

Table 3.1 Cost definitions and cost mechanics

Fixed cost:	Costs which do not vary with output
Variable cost:	Costs which vary with output
Total cost:	Fixed cost + Variable cost
Average total cost:	Total cost ÷ Output
Average fixed cost:	Fixed cost ÷ Output

1 Output	2 Total fixed cost	3 Total variable cost	4 Total cost	5 Average total cost (4 ÷ 1)	6 Average variable cost (3 ÷ 1)	7 Average fixed cost (2 ÷ 1)
100	300	100	400	4.00	1.00	3.00
250	300	200	500	2.00	0.80	1.17
400	300	300	600	1.50	0.75	0.75
500	300	400	700	1.40	0.80	0.60
560	300	500	800	1.43	0.89	0.53

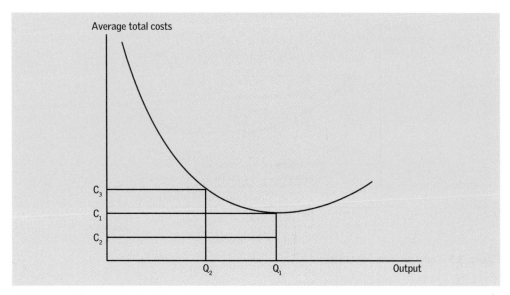

Figure 3.2 Short-run average total costs

because the fixed costs (associated with the fixed factors of production) remain constant as output increases. Therefore unit costs will fall (see Table 3.1 above) and we see the import-ance of attaining the 'right' volumes of output where average costs are minimized. The second part arises because the fixed factors imply capacity constraints on output that might in part be offset by applying more variable factors but at lower efficiencies (such as overtime rates and higher machinery maintenance costs). Thus, output can only be expanded at higher **marginal costs** (marginal cost is the cost of producing one extra unit of output).

In the long run, all factors of production are variable. For the firm this implies investment decisions that pose the question of how much should we invest (in fixed factors such as pro-duction lines) so as to minimize the cost of production in the long term. Figure 3.3 depicts a long-run cost curve that exhibits a range in which increasing returns to scale takes place (to Q_1), a range of constant returns (Q_1 to Q_2), and a range of decreasing returns to scale (beyond Q_2). In this figure the point Q_1 is called the **minimum efficient scale of output (MES)**.

Note that the horizontal axis is the designed scale of the plant whereas in the short-run curve (Figure 3.2) it is the actual volume of output. Figure 3.4 places the short- and long-run curves together. The short-run curve shows the costs that arise given the capital that is actually invested at that scale of plant design. Actual costs will reflect the intensity of use of that invested plant as well as the benefits of having a plant designed for that level of oper-ation. You can, of course, imagine a situation in which the plant has been designed and built to too great a scale (e.g. because of errors in forecasting demand) and the actual short-run cost curve results in very high unit costs because the fixed costs are far too high. In Figure

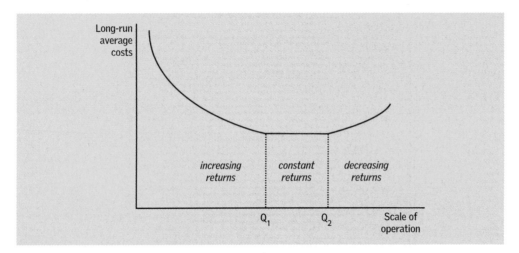

Figure 3.3 Long-run average costs

3.4 you can see that a demand forecast Q_f would require Plant B to be constructed and if the forecast was correct then Q_f would be produced at the minimum point of the short-run cost curve. If, however, demand actually turns out to be Q_a then this has to be produced from Plant B (although Plant A would have been preferable). You can see from inspection that the cost of producing at this level from Plant B is higher than from Plant A. Economies of scale derive specifically from an optimal combination of factors of production and they can be quantified from conventional capital budgeting (net present value) calculations. It is important to recognize that the short-run cost curves (Figure 3.2) represent actual costs identifiable as cash outflows. By contrast the long-run costs should be seen as *planning costs.*

Companies that have cost functions with substantial returns to scale have a strong incentive to sell and produce the large-scale output at Q_1 in Figure 3.3. If they fail to produce Q_1, average total costs will rise and this will damage their financial performance. A common source of scale economies is the opportunity to spread the fixed costs of capital, such as physical equipment, e.g. plant and buildings, or R&D spending. Scale economies usually arise from the efficient use of these fixed *firm-level resources.* There are other sources of *plant* scale economies arising that also have an impact on average variable costs. Large-scale production enables specialization of labour (see the section below on sources of economies of scale) to take place, increasing the productivity of the labour force and reducing average labour costs. It also enables the producer to place large orders with suppliers and negotiate quantity discounts that lower average material and component costs.

PaperCo and MetalCo are both in this category. Their technology is heavily capital-intensive and, as a result, they both benefit from large-scale economies, so Q_1 is their large optimal level of output. In the long term, they are both successful in reaching this optimal scale, so they both appear in the top 25 per cent of their sector's performance, so they enjoy

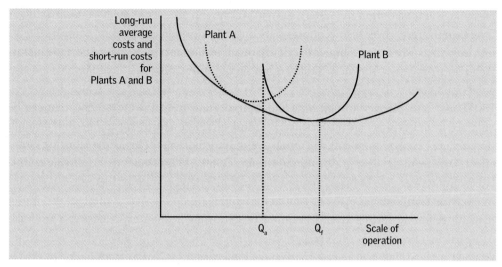

Figure 3.4 Short-run and long-run average costs

a competitive advantage over their competitors as a result of their effective use of *resources*. Although this may be a critical issue in explaining the financial performance of many companies, especially in slow-growing sectors of any economy, it is not crucial to the explanation of the differences between our selected companies PaperCo and MetalCo. This is therefore not the reason for the superior long-run performance of MetalCo. On the other hand, note that in the short-run PaperCo is clearly better able to achieve the optimal scale more consistently. We explore the reasons for this later in this chapter.

Note that economies of scale are much more important in heavy manufacturing industries in which there are substantial capital requirements. Table 3.2 shows the MES (the minimum efficient scale of output – *see* Q_1 on Figure 3.3) for various industries expressed as a

Table 3.2 MES as percentage of EU production

Cellulose fibres	16.00
Aerospace	12.20
Refrigerators	11.00
Steelmaking	10.00
Agricultural machinery	6.60
Cigarettes	6.00
Shoes	0.08
Carpets	0.03

Source: Pratten (1988): Emerson (1988); EU Commission (1997).

percentage of total output in Western Europe. At one end are sectors such as steelmaking or fibre manufacture where scale economies are huge. At the other extreme are companies with low fixed costs where economies of scale are much less important. Carpet and shoe manufacturers are the cases shown in Table 3.2 but service industries such as restaurants are also good examples.

MES may also change through time and an important reason is the benefits that can be obtained from learning from experience. Learning increases a firm's *capabilities* and through time reduces average total cost as cumulative output increases. This is the **learning curve effect**. Data from the Boston Consulting Group (Conley 1975) shows that doubling cumulative output over time reduces average total costs in a range of industries, from 30 per cent in electrical components to 10 per cent in oil refining. A simple way to think of this is as a dynamic economy of scale that arises from a firm learning from its experience as a producer of a particular product over several periods of time. In Figure 3.2 the effect of the economies arising from learning is to reduce the average total cost at Q_1 (MES) from C_1 to C_2. This is another potent cause of differences in cost and profitability, but again is not important to the differences observed in PaperCo and MetalCo.

Another source of superior financial performance is the ability of a firm to exploit **economies of scope**. Economies of scope exist when the cost of joint production of two outputs is less than the cost of producing each output separately (Panzer and Willig 1981). In terms of Figure 3.2 economies of scope arise when the average cost of a single product is lowered by its joint production with other products in a multiproduct firm. When output for each product is at Q_1 (so scale economies for each product are fully exploited), it is possible for average costs at C_2 to be even lower than C_1, if the economies of scope are also fully exploited. In practice, these scope economies can be important. A study (Pratten 1988) of the cost effects of halving the number of products made by each producer in a selection of EU industries shows impacts that range from +3 per cent in carpet manufacture to +8 per cent in motor vehicles. These scope economies may arise from the opportunity to leverage a *core capability* arising from knowledge and learning, organization or management skill, so as to reduce the average total cost of all products produced in a multiproduct firm. A good example is the expertise that arises from technical and scientific knowledge within the firm. Exploiting this distinctive expertise by innovation and product diversification lowers the average total cost of all products. Pharmaceutical manufacture and steel production are both sectors where this kind of cost economy is important. Scope economies can also arise from efficient use of *resources*, for example, where a number of related goods are produced using a common process. Car manufacture of a range of models is an example and part of the reason for the significant scope economies found in Pratten's study. Another source of scope economies arises from spreading the fixed cost of a network over a wider range of products. Commercial banks, for example, incur a large fixed cost from their branch networks. If they spread this cost over a large range of related corporate and retail financial products, the average total cost of each product is reduced. In the area of microelectronics it is possible to realize economies of scope between software and hardware products. Open systems require knowledge of how hardware and software products can be integrated across different vendors' systems. Specifically, software knowledge is essential to design hardware and vice versa (Langowitz 1987). However, there are limits to the economies that scope can offer. Eventually, as the demands for sharing know-how increase, bottlenecks in the form of overextended scientists, engineers and other technical personnel occur.

PaperCo and MetalCo are both able to exploit economies of scope – and do so. Hence, they build competitive advantage and appear in the top 25 per cent of profits performance in their separate industries. However, for reasons outside their strategic control, scope economy opportunities are much larger in Company B, MetalCo. Its core technical competence has more uses and markets, so its product range is much larger than A's, whose core capability is in a tightly demarcated niche. This is the source of the difference in their long-run performance.

A final issue of importance on the supply side in explaining differences in financial performance between industries and firms is supplier power (see the later discussion in this chapter, section 3.4). Powerful suppliers drive up costs and this has an impact on profits. PaperCo and MetalCo are in industries in which suppliers are generally weak, with one major exception: all companies in both industries are heavy users of energy, the suppliers of which have considerable market power.

3.2.1 Sources of economies of scale

The division of labour

Economies of scale figure prominently in modern discussion of the appropriate size of industrial plants. The phenomenon itself has long been recognized and Adam Smith provided the first classic description after witnessing pinmaking processes in the eighteenth century:

> ... one man draws out the wire, another straightens it, a third cuts it,
> a fourth points it, a fifth grinds it at the top for receiving the head;
> to make the head requires two or three different operations:
> to put it on is a peculiar business, to whiten the pins is another;
> it is even a trade by itself to put them into the paper; and the important
> business of making a pin is, in this manner, divided into about
> eighteen distinct operations, which, in some manufactories, are
> all performed by distinct hands ... I have seen a manufactory of this kind
> where ten men ... could, when they exerted themselves, make among them ...
> upwards of forty-eight thousand pins in a day ... But if they had all wrought
> separately and independently, and without any of them having been educated

> *to this peculiar business, they certainly could not each of them have made*
> *twenty, perhaps not one pin in a day …* (Adam Smith, *An Inquiry into the Nature*
> *and Causes of the Wealth of Nations*, 1776)

In this famous passage Adam Smith describes an improvement in labour productivity in excess of 15 000 per cent. He is describing the **division of labour** (also called **specialization**) which came to Britain with the Industrial Revolution of the eighteenth and nineteenth centuries, bringing with it the development and organization of specialized factory trades and an increase in the use of machinery. In Smith's view, these great increases in the productivity of labour were due directly to three consequences of the division of labour: an increase in the dexterity and skill of individual workers due to specialization in one trade; the saving of time lost in moving labour from one type of work to another; and (in his words) '*the invention of a great number of machines which facilitate and abridge labour, and enable one man to do the work of many*.'

The passing of two centuries has not diminished the force of Adam Smith's observations. The assembly line of an automatic plant provides a classic illustration of the impact of labour specialization. The extent of specialization depends technically on the scale of automation and the amount of capital invested in machinery. The greater the automation, the more can a worker specialize in one operation, e.g. 'a left wheel nut tightener' (*see* Scherer 1970). At a rate of output of 500 cars per day, the left wheel nut tightener can be fully employed. But in a smaller plant where output is only 250 cars per day he will be idle for half the time and may be assigned other jobs. However, this inspires losses in his efficiency as he moves to another work location (or as the work flow is re-routed to come to his position) or as he changes his mental gear and finds the correct tool and adopts a different work technique. In general, larger firms can enjoy more specialization than smaller ones but in any event the extent of the division of labour is restricted by the size of the market.

Identical principles apply in the use of specialized machinery. Machines can be designed to perform a range of specific tasks at high speed with great reliability, and considerable savings in time and labour. Such machinery is of little value to the small-scale producer because they cannot be scaled down to his output levels and would be idle for much of the time. Likewise, their preparation for a production run requires much set up time and costs which are only recouped over long production runs. In general, smaller firms must use slower, more labour-intensive machine tools. Nowhere is this more sharply illustrated than in the comparison between the labour productivity of Japanese motorcycle factories (about 200 bikes per man year) and the factories of North America and Western Europe (about 20 bikes per man year) (Boston Consulting Group 1975). Due in part to their privileged access to the large and growing Japanese and Asian markets in the 1950s and 60s, the Japanese industry developed a scale of automation unknown in other countries where the market was more specialized and limited in size.

The benefits of division of labour are fairly obvious and can be summarized thus:

- increase in output at lower unit costs;
- increased use of machinery;
- increased possibility of improvement and quality control;
- the saving of time and tools through the avoidance of moving labour from place to place or the need to own general purpose equipment.

For the individual worker there are also several advantages, for instance hours of work may be shortened and work may be lightened (although productivity gains may have to be shared among the entire workforce). Against this there are problems arising from the loss of traditional skills and pride in workmanship and monotony and strain imposed by the speed of the production line. For the firm there are clear difficulties that arise from the complexity of administration of such large units of production and the risk of failure of production from whatever cause when production is concentrated in one plant.

However, there are consequences to the large-scale adoption of this doctrine of specialization. These are reviewed in Chapter 19. The adoption of the doctrine of specialization and economies of scale has important consequences for the firm in that they develop hierarchical management structures appropriate for the management of specialized tasks but much less so in terms of flexibility and in terms of the costs of adversarial labour relations resulting from specialization.

The cube law

Along with specialization of labour and of capital equipment goes the capital cost savings on large items of machinery due to the operation of the so-called **cube law**. The volume of a vessel (which for process plant determines the volume of output) is roughly proportional to the cube of its radius while its surface area (where the cost is to be found) is proportional to the square. Thus, as the volume capacity of a plant increases, the material requirements and hence its capital cost tend to rise as the two-thirds power of the output capacity. There is considerable empirical support for the existence of this 'two-thirds rule', which is used by engineers in estimating the cost of new process equipment (Moore 1959; Haldi and Whitcomb 1967).

Economies of massed reserves

Another benefit of size comes from the **economy of massed reserves** (*see* Robinson 1958). This rests on the law of large numbers on which the entire insurance industry is based. To preserve continuity of production, the firm must insure itself against the consequences of machine breakdown by maintaining a reserve of excess capacity. The larger the firm and the more identical (or similar) machines it uses, the smaller the proportion required of spare capacity. Such economies exist for stockholding, financial assets, labour, and service department staffing.

Firm-level economies of scale

We should also distinguish between scale economies achievable at the plant level and those achievable at the level of the firm itself. Division of labour and the operation of the cube law each apply at the level of the plant. The economy of massed reserves can apply at both levels. Generally, it is relatively easy to specify and estimate the scale economies at plant level because they rest on technical, engineering considerations. Firm-level economies are more difficult to identify with such clarity and are, surprisingly, more difficult to achieve. But, as we shall see in later chapters, they are, in theory at least, the basis for much merger activity.

The costs incurred by the firm as distinct from the plant can be grouped broadly as: managerial and administrative; research and development; transportation and distribution; and marketing. Where the firm operates many plants, and particularly when there is some degree of horizontal and/or vertical integration, then the firm-level economies can be of great potential significance. Administrative economies can arise through the traditional division of labour and substitution of labour by capital-intensive equipment; for example, word processing equipment replacing typists, automatic document coding and transferral replacing clerks. Financial economies are available by reducing the level of stocks and work in progress relative to the rate of production. Marketing economies are available in advertising to mass markets and using a common sales force to purvey a product line. Risks can be spread in R&D by managing a portfolio of projects rather than a single or few projects. The pooling of risks arises through pooling financial resources across markets with different cyclical characteristics.

Barry Supple (1977) has placed economies of scale in the context of business history and development of large-scale enterprise:

> the specific factors responsible for this trend to large-scale enterprise have varied markedly. The economies of scale in their conventional sense – the unit cost reduction derived from large accumulations of capital equipment, advanced and expensive technology, specialization of functions, bulk purchasing and distribution – played an obvious part ... At the same time, however, the emergence of the giant firm was also a function of financial considerations (stock market buoyancies in particular increased the probability, and profitability, of mergers and flotation) and of market vicissitudes and ambitions. The desire to protect investments and market shares, the ambition to secure market control and stability of sales, the pressure to mitigate competition and to expand sales and profit margins – all illustrate the range, from defensive to offensive, of policies involved, as well as the overall importance of market strategies in the history of large-scale enterprise. And, in the event, many of the most spectacular instances of big business (with Courtaulds, Lever Brothers, Austin Morris) rested as much on product differentiation as on 'pure' cost advantages.

Supple's comments reinforce the earlier statement that the size and the nature of the market place some limits of the extent to which unit costs can continue to fall. Apart from market size, there are other limitations to the extent of economies of scale.

The first relates to the way in which specialized but indivisible units of equipment dovetail in the production process. At some point a stage is reached at which further cost reductions are not possible because all units of equipment are being used at their optimum rates. Any expansion of output in units less than that required for replication of existing equipment will cause unit costs to rise.

A second set of assertions about the management process is probably more significant in bringing potential technical economies to an end. The general hypothesis is that the management of sufficiently large units entails rising unit costs. One variant of this ascribes the problem to the relatively fixed input of senior management time as the scale of operation grows. The cost of communication rises very rapidly, usually evidenced by large numbers of middle managers, staff and so on. The consequence of these managerial and co-ordination problems is upward pressure on costs until diseconomies of large-scale management eventually overpower the technical economies of scale. A concrete analogy is the rise in transport and distribution costs as production is increasingly centralized to obtain production economies. To service a network of distribution points from one central production point entails higher distribution costs than the servicing of smaller numbers of distribution points from a number of decentralized production facilities.

The organization of large-scale management has become highly specialized. Specialized staff functions that supply information for decision making to line executives have been used quite effectively. Communication spurred on by rapid technological developments has been simplified and cheapened beyond our recent expectations. Control techniques based on management accounting, budgetary control and cash flow analysis have been brought to a high state of perfection. Information technology and systems permit the storage, retrieval and analysis of vast amounts of information. These changes in the technology of management, together with more sophisticated views of organizational structure, allow the management of large-scale enterprise to become more and more effective.

Notwithstanding the state of the managerial art, the potential for achieving cost savings through larger plant and from size has often been frustrated by circumstances (for some early examples, *see* HMSO 1978). Examples include the difficulty of phasing out obsolete plant in the steel industry in the face of slow-growing demand and political difficulties. The motor industry in Europe also has a large number of plants in relation to the numbers of cars produced. Similarly the merging of the manufacturing facilities of the aircraft industry and the development of a coherent commercial strategy has taken undue time. However, scale economies are not always frustrated by practical difficulties. More encouraging results have been seen in electricity generation, the restructuring of the bearings industry, and the change of scale in the brewing industry. The limits to the realization of technical economies might be summarized as follows:

- diseconomies of scale in distribution;
- the complexity of large-scale management which requires high investment cost and accumulated experience to reduce it;
- the need to maintain product differentiation and flexibility in the face of changes in tastes;
- the industrial relations problems in managing large plants.

3.3 **Demand analysis**

The demand side of the market is also relevant to an understanding of the 'deep structure of markets', which is so critical to company performance. The first issue is the degree to which market-level product demand is responsive to changes in price.

Figure 3.5 shows a downward sloping relationship of demand with product price. This market 'demand curve' shows that price increases reduce the volume of demand and vice versa. We could measure the degree of responsiveness of demand to a change in price as the:

$$\frac{\text{Change in quantity demanded}}{\text{Change in price}}$$

which is the slope of the demand curve, or by:

$$\frac{\text{\% change in quantity demanded}}{\text{\% change in price}}$$

The latter is the measure preferred by economists who call it the **own price elasticity of demand**. Since demand falls when price is raised and vice versa, real life estimates of the price elasticity are generally negative. Some examples are shown in Figure 3.6.

What factors influence the elasticity? Clearly, as is evident from Figure 3.6, necessities such as basic foodstuffs and fuel are likely to have a low elasticity and demand is therefore relatively insensitive to changes in price. One further important matter is the availability of substitutes for the product. If substitutes are readily available, an increase in price

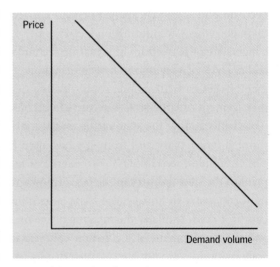

Figure 3.5 Market demand curve

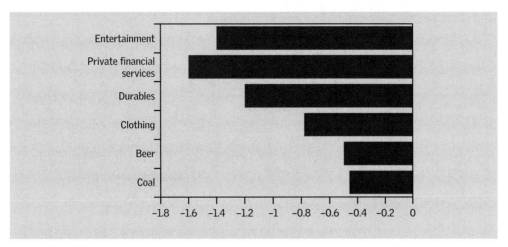

Figure 3.6 Luxuries, necessities and substitutes: market price elasticities of demand (% change in sales ÷ % change in price)
Source: Deaton (1975).
Copyright 1975, with permission from Elsevier.

will have a much larger impact on demand. Petrol, for example, has no close substitutes. If you own a petrol-driven car you have no alternative to petrol and, hence, the elasticity of demand for petrol will be low. This market-level demand relationship gives rise to an aspect of the market environment over which companies have no direct control. It has to be managed. A particular problem arises with products with a very low elasticity. Petrol is one and beer, where firms are concerned, is another. Products like this are an attractive source of revenue for a government. An increase in the rate of tax raises prices, but has little effect on the volume of sales. Because of this, raising the rate of tax has a strong positive effect on tax revenue. The result, from the firm's point of view, is that political forces over which they have no control significantly alter market prices and severely constrain its pricing strategy.

What about the firm-level relationship of price and demand? A crucial issue here is the homogeneity of the product and the ability of the individual firm to differentiate its output from others through branding, thereby reducing the threat of substitute products. If the product is difficult to differentiate, the firm will face a highly elastic **demand curve**, whatever the industry-level relationship looks like.

In the extreme case in which the product is completely homogeneous, the firm will face a horizontal demand curve, as shown in Figure 3.7, so that if an individual firm raises its price above P_1, it will attract no customers. If it lowers its price, it is overwhelmed by demand. The firm in this case is a passive actor with absolutely no power over the market for its products. This is a key feature of perfect competition, in which the individual firm is a price taker with absolutely no impact on prices. In the more normal case, where some differentiation is possible, perhaps by product branding or through service excellence, the firm is able to exercise

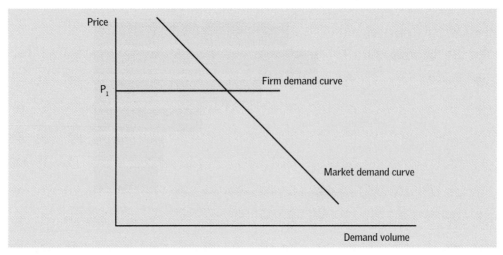

Figure 3.7 Firm and market demand curves

some market power and secure a degree of control, though this will be conditional on the market dominance of its customers. This market power extends not only to price (raising it), but also to the price elasticity, as Figure 3.5 shows. Branding secures the attachment of the buyer to the individual product, so that an increase in its price will have a less adverse effect on demand, because there is less substitution into alternative products available from other firms in the same market.

A good illustration of these concepts is a branded food manufacturer, such as Heinz or Nestlé, operating in the EU or the US. It is possible for these manufacturers to brand the product and hence secure a price premium and improve profitability, and this is what they have done. Since branding also has the helpful effect of reducing the price elasticity, the extra profit margin they get is sustainable over time. However, these benefits are increasingly problematic for the branded food manufacturers, because of the growth in supermarket retailing and hence the growth in the buying power of their customers. Large retailers promote their own brands, weakening the manufacturer's brand and, as a result, demand large quantity discounts from branded food manufacturers which need the supermarket outlet for their products. Clearly, the changing balance of power on the demand side of the market challenges the sustainability of an individual business's competitive advantage, even when they successfully brand their products.

In the case of companies PaperCo and MetalCo, both sell a difficult-to-differentiate product to powerful industrial users. As a result, it is difficult for either to secure premium prices and the profits that go along with them. This is characteristic of all firms in their markets so, in the sector ranking of profitability, both appear in low profitability sectors (PaperCo in paper packaging for the food industry and MetalCo in metal manufacture). Some global data for this is shown in Figure 3.8.

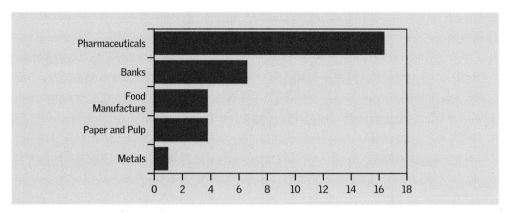

Figure 3.8 Return on revenues (%) in the Fortune Global 500, 2001
Source: Fortune (www.fortune.com).

A further reason for the relatively poor sectoral profits performance of PaperCo and MetalCo is the result of the weak effect of long-run increases in national income on the demand for these products. Both PaperCo and MetalCo have their customer base in the rich industrial economies of North America and the EU. In these markets, the share (or intensity, as it is sometimes called) of the products produced by companies A and B in the total national sales of all products is falling. They produce manufactured products and this sector's share of total sales is declining, while the service sector is expanding. Many manufacturing markets suffer as a consequence of mature and saturated markets. We can measure the response of market-level sales to changes in the long-run income of a country by calculating the long-run income elasticity of demand. This is an analogous concept to 'price elasticity. The long-run income elasticity of demand is:

% change in long-run quantity demanded

% change in long-run national income

Generally, this is a positive number, so increases in national income shift the market demand curve upwards, as shown in Figure 3.9, where the initial curve D_1 is shifted to a new curve D_2 as a result of an increase in income. Since the curve has shifted up, more will be demanded at each price. At a price of P_1, for example, the quantity demanded will increase from Q_1 to Q_2. If national income falls, the opposite happens and the quantity demanded falls.

Where the income elasticity is high, firms will experience large increases in market demand when long-run income increases, and vice versa when it is low. In the mature economies of the EU and the US, the long-run income elasticity of demand is higher in service markets such as tourism or media providers, but low in engineering and food, which are the end users of the output of PaperCo and MetalCo. The result is a progressive decline in the share of GDP produced in the manufacturing sector and a rise in the service

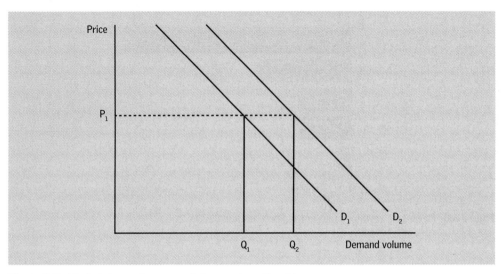

Figure 3.9 Market demand curve and changes in national income

sector's share. Note also the link between the long-run income elasticity and financial performance. Figure 3.8 shows that most of the high-performing sectors are service providers or manufacturers of high-tech products such as pharmaceuticals, while the traditional manufacturing sectors do relatively badly. What makes it worse for the manufacturers A and B is that in an earlier stage of economic development, the long-run elasticity was a good deal higher. In this period, substantial capacity was installed to meet the large long-run growth in demand. Reduction of this capacity in a stagnant manufacturing market is a slow business and this often leaves substantial surplus capacity (refer back to the earlier discussion in this chapter of long-run and short-run costs). This can greatly increase the intensity of market rivalry, driving down prices and contributing to the weak financial performance we see in Figure 3.8.

The long-run income elasticity of market demand is clearly an important feature of markets and a key influence on financial performance. It is also largely out of the strategic control of individual firms.

3.3.1 Demand analysis in practice

Demand analysis is important in two ways: (i) it provides a framework for analysing price and other influences on the sales of the firm's products, and (ii) it provides a baseline for pricing products, and marketing generally, and for forecasting and manipulating demand.

Demand analysis is built around the price–quantity relationship and the many ways in which this relationship is manifested. It is easy to see how important price and volume are to the firm. Price and quantity together determine sales revenue. Sales volume dictates production volume and the scale of production operations together with the capital required

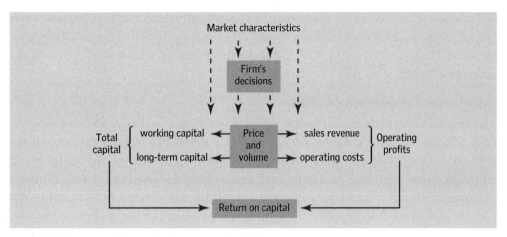

Figure 3.10 Price-volume and return on capital

for production and for working capital. Thus, volume and price fundamentally drive cash flow, profits and return on capital (*see* Figure 3.10). Consequently, the extent to which price can influence volume is of great importance to the firm.

In understanding how return on capital is driven it is helpful to consider those character-istics that shape demand (market characteristics in Figure 3.10) and how the firm's decisions can affect the outcome. We will see below and in later chapters that one of the enduring problems for a firm is how to avoid its activities being totally dictated by market conditions and for its own decisions to provide it with some distinctiveness in markets and therefore some ability to earn profits beyond the minimum rate of return required merely to stay in business. In this section we consider the following:

♦ elasticities and the implications for revenues;

♦ individual versus market demand;

♦ final demand versus derived demand;

♦ producer versus consumer goods;

♦ durable versus perishable (non-durable) goods.

Price elasticity and revenues

Consider a product whose initial price is P_1 and whose initial sales volume is Q_1. If price is reduced to P_2 and volume increases to Q_2 (following the downward sloping demand curve of Figure 3.5) we can see that on the original volume Q_1 a lower price is being earned and there will be a loss in revenue equal to $(P_1 - P_2)Q_1$. But this is to some extent offset by the extra revenue $P_2(Q_2 - Q_1)$. The larger the extra volume from the price cut, the more likely it is that revenue will be greater. Thus, the higher the price elasticity, the larger will be the new revenue. At the other end of the scale, if the elasticity is zero then no extra volume is created, and revenue will fall. When the price elasticity is one, the price effect on the original volume $((P_1-P_2)Q_1)$ – i.e. a fall in revenue – is exactly offset by the extra sales revenue arising from the volume increase $P_2(Q_2-Q_1)$. Table 3.3 shows the general relationship between revenues and price elasticity.

Individual demand versus market demand

The demand curve for a market or any group of consumers is obtained by summing the demand curves of all the individuals concerned. This is done by summing all the quantities demanded at each price level. This submerging of individual differences may matter little if we are concerned solely with predicting total market demand at given price levels. The more stable the individual demand curves are, the easier is the task of forecasting. But, from the point of view of the pricing policy of the firm, matters are not so simple. Price is just one, albeit an important one, of the many instruments with which the product is marketed. Others include distribution channels, advertising and promotion, and support from one's own sales force and also from retailer sales activity. To direct this marketing effort effectively it is helpful to be able to define a target market on which the marketing effort can be focused. So the concept of market segmentation is likely to be useful, i.e. the concept of individual and group differences within the overall market demand curve. A firm may choose to treat its market in a uniform manner, spreading its marketing efforts far and wide in order to bring as much of the market within its orbit as possible. This would normally require uniform pricing and mass advertising campaigns. Alternatively the firm might choose to adopt different price policies for different groups or segments in the market. A high price policy might be indicated for one segment and a low price for another. The success of this approach depends on the two segments being unable to communicate and/or trade with each other and being able to set up a black or grey market (such as happens with UK-sourced cars and European-sourced cars).

Table 3.3 Elasticity and revenue

Elasticity	Effect of price fall	Effect of price rise
Infinite (perfectly elastic)	Sell as much as can be produced	Sell nothing
Greater than 1 (elastic)	Larger sales revenue	Smaller sales revenue
1	Constant sales revenue	Constant sales revenue
Less than 1 (inelastic)	Smaller sales revenue	Larger sales revenue
Zero (perfectly inelastic)	Fall in revenue proportional to fall in price	Increase in revenue proportional to increase in price

In economic terms a market is a group of buyers and sellers who are in sufficiently close contact for the transactions between any pair of them to affect the terms on which the others buy and sell. The existence of individual or group differences cannot be exploited if there is close contact between buyers. Firms can choose to exploit the differences in individual demand curves by pursuing product policies that enable the firm to apply a different 'offer' to different segments. Thus the offer of a standard car to the mass market would result in a price level that would enable those with low price sensitivity (low price elasticity) to buy at prices lower than their reservation price (the highest price that would keep them in the market). To avoid this loss of revenue firms devise product range policies that enable different product characteristics to be directed towards different segments. Thus, higher-income purchasers can be directed towards more expensive cars with more accessories and a higher quality build. Lower-income purchasers would correspondingly be directed to less well equipped and built cars. The bigger the product range, the more the firm can cover the breadth of the market and keep potential customers within its range of offerings. But there is an extra cost of marketing and a potential loss of economies of scale in production as variety of models is increased.

Final demand versus derived demand

When demand for a product is tied to the purchase of another product then this demand is said to be *derived*. The demand for steel is in part derived from the demand for cars and the demand for bricks is derived from the demand for houses. These are instances where the product whose demand is derived is a component part of the final product. Sometimes complementary consumption patterns cause dependence in demand. Thus the demand for film is complementary to the demand for cameras. However, the distinction between final and derived demand should not be pressed too far because in some sense all demand is derived. The demand for golf clubs is derived from a demand for leisure; the demand for washing machines is derived from demand for laundry services. Certainly demand for all producer goods (as distinct from consumer goods) is derived, and so is the demand for labour.

Derived demand is generally supposed to have less price elasticity than final demand. This is attributable to dilution of the cost of the component by other component products whose prices are sticky. It used to be reckoned that a 10 per cent rise in the price of steel would cause only a 1 per cent increase in the cost of a car if all other costs remained unchanged. However, this would be a characteristic primarily of the elasticity in the short run. In the longer term there is the possibility of substitution of one raw material or component part by another. As the possibilities of substitution increase then the price elasticity increases. Thus, glass fibre may rival steel in some applications in ship and boat building: aluminium can displace copper; and synthetic rubber can replace natural rubber.

Some products are so closely tied to the parent products that they have no distinctive demand determinants of their own – television aerials, for example. Here the elasticity will be very low indeed in the short run but such cases of fixed proportions between the parent and component products are rare. More commonly there is considerable leeway for substitution at the margin as well as more than one parent use for the product. In very many instances there is a multitude of parent uses for a product and it becomes impossible to characterize demand in terms of particular final demands. Small electric motors have no final demand of their own but to analyse their demand in terms of their thousands of parent uses would be impossibly tedious. Sulphuric acid and many other chemicals are further examples and integrated circuits provide a contemporary example.

The distinction between derived and final demand is important in understanding the determinants of demand for individual products, and where there is a stable proportional relation between the component and its parent then forecasting of demand can be done by reference to the parent.

Producer goods versus consumer goods

This distinction in some ways is parallel to that between final and derived demand. However, this distinction concentrates attention on who makes the purchase decision rather than the relationship, whether technological or economic, between the component and its parent product. There are two reasons usually cited for expecting purchase decisions made for producer goods to be qualitatively different from those for consumer goods. Buyers are expected to be professional and, hence, more expert. Their motives for buying are expected to be purely economic and not influenced by non-monetary considerations.

It is doubtful whether the distinction between producer and consumer goods can always be maintained. How does one distinguish between cars sold to companies and those sold to private individuals? In addition it is not at all clear that producer goods are evaluated in a cold-eyed professional way. There must be thousands of purchases by any one firm that are incidental in their impact on costs and are purchased with speed and convenience without expensive evaluation. This of course leaves the door open for the human element in purchasing which is supposed to be so characteristic of final consumers.

Durable goods versus perishable (non-durable) goods

By definition durable goods are not completely consumed at the time of their purchase; they yield a stream of services over time (typically measured in years rather than months). They include both consumer and producer durables. The sale of durables can be seen as replacing that part of the existing stock of durables that has worn out (i.e. replacement demand), and as that which is really new (i.e. an expansion of demand). Thus, if the existing stock of cars is 100 of which 10 wear out each year, and the normal growth in demand is 5 each year, then car production (and sales) would be 15, two-thirds of which is to meet replacement demand. If there is now an increase in demand for car stock of 3 units (less than a 3 per cent increase) then production must rise to 18 (a 20 per cent increase) in order to meet this increase. Relatively modest increases in demand for a stock of durables can thus result in large fluctuations in production.

In general, the demand for durable goods fluctuates differently and more violently than the demand for perishable products. The further down the chain of production, the more violent is the cutback in production when final demand falls. If economic activity were to contract by 1 per cent it would not be surprising to see contractions of 10 per cent or even 20 per cent in the output of the steel and metals industries. The volatility of demand for durables is not the only salient feature. Both replacement and expansion have quite distinct sets of demand determinants. When the demand for transportation as a whole goes up, then production tends to take some time to respond and used car values go up relative to scrap values. Then the scrapping rate falls and thus replacement demand also falls. So an increase in demand may initially extend the life of the existing stock and reduce replacement demand. Conversely, if the public desire fewer cars then the scrapping rate accelerates as used car prices fall relative to scrap prices. The most important factor determining replacement demand is the rate of obsolescence that determines prices in second-hand car markets. There are two elements in obsolescence. One is purely financial and requires a comparison of capital costs and running costs of a new car with the scrap value and running costs of the old car. In general, running costs rise with age to a point where the difference in running costs between new and old becomes larger than the required capital outlay. Physical deterioration lies behind these calculations and is an obvious component of obsolescence. However, it is rarely the only factor in replacement decisions. When replacement takes place before the financial criterion is satisfied then in some other way the services of the new car are more highly valued than the services of the (apparently cheaper) old car. For consumer durables, and perhaps also for producer durables as well, style, convenience and youth play an important role in demand.

The determinants of expansion demand for durables are not, in principle, very different from those for perishables but in practice are much more complicated. The key to durables lies in their length of life and the purchase decision is marked by the buyer's difficulty in assessing the future. The buyer has to assess whether they can afford to operate it, whether its services will command a suitable price in the future, whether its price will rise or fall if they postpone their purchase and so on. For durable goods, not only present prices and incomes but also their trends and the buyer's optimism are proper variables to consider. Expectations about technological change are also critical. Should one wait for prices to fall as technology improves (e.g. computers and video games) or might important savings be lost through delay?

Case box: **No End of Luxury**

THE terrorist attacks on September 11th 2001 reverberated even in the world of fashion. Department stores closed their spring-collection orders, the spring 2002 New York Fashion Week was cancelled for the first time ever, and LVMH's net income for the 2001 financial year plummeted from €722m in 2000 to just €10m. After a recovery in late 2002, misfortune struck again in 2003: war in Iraq, the SARS epidemic in Asia and a persistently sluggish economy in Japan. Tourists around the world are responsible for around a quarter of the world's luxury purchases, so anything that lessens international travel hurts the industry.

Yet this apparent vulnerability to world events is actually a sign of strength. The world of luxury is truly global, with all the commercial opportunities that implies: as people get richer, they spend proportionately less on necessities and more on luxuries. This has long been true in Japan, whose fashion-conscious people account for a quarter of the world's luxury-goods sales. That is why corporate analysts anxiously examine the state of the Japanese economy: any change will have an effect on the share prices and sales of luxury-goods houses. And because most Japanese prefer to buy their luxury goods abroad (where prices are up to 40% lower than at home), any change in the value of the yen against the dollar and euro matters too.

But looking a little farther ahead, it is clear that other Asian countries, and particularly China and India, will follow where Japan has led. Between them, those two countries make up more than a third of the world's population, and already the luxury labels of Europe and America are rushing to set up flagship stores in Beijing and Shanghai (though not yet in India). According to the Boston Consulting Group, China already accounts for 5% of the world luxury market – the same share, it is worth remembering, as post-communist Russia.

This suggests that the luxury labels need not fear a shrinking market. They may, however, need to fear a changing market. In the days of Christian Dior, who in 1947 launched his elegant 'New Look' of small waists and full skirts, a fashionable woman would never dream of mixing that look with something designed for the masses. Nor would fans of Coco Chanel, even though in the 1920s, when materials were in short supply, Miss Chanel had more or less invented 'poor chic' by using jersey knit, a fabric previously used for men's underwear.

Yet today it is perfectly acceptable for a smart woman (or man, for that matter, though women outnumber men by four-to-one in their shopping forays) to mix a Chanel or Prada jacket with a pair of blue jeans. The female fashion fad of the moment is the Ugg shoe, an ugly but supremely comfortable sheepskin boot originally made for Australia's surfers, male and female, when they get out of the water. It is perfectly acceptable to wear Uggs with just about everything. Fashion has become democratised, and a market that once belonged entirely to high-fashion brands is being invaded by low-price competitors, from the Gap to Hennes & Mauritz, a Swedish ready-to-wear chain which over the past 57 years has exported its H&M logo to 17 other countries.

The most impressive competitor, however, is Zara, a Spanish company operating in 46 countries, which has shortened the fashion cycle to the point where it no longer exists. By having 200 in-house designers and by controlling the whole process from textile mill to retail shop, Zara can put new items in its 626 stores twice a week. Moreover, it ruthlessly removes its lines – even

Developing nicely

Contribution of China, Russia and India to total sales of luxury-goods companies, %

Source: Merrill Lynch
(Reprinted courtesy of *The Economist*)

the best-selling ones – every three weeks or so. The result is that Zara always has fresh styles, and its customers never feel out of fashion. Perhaps companies such as LVMH, Gucci, Prada and Armani should start to worry.

Yet a Zara sweater or skirt will never be the equal of one by Missoni or Dolce & Gabbana. As long as customers want quality, the high-fashion brands will be safe. Calamities notwithstanding, there still seem to be plenty of people who can afford prices that give the high-fashion brands gross margins of 50–60% on clothes and 80% on leather goods.

Could the internet threaten the luxury brands? There are sites such as bluefly.com that discount their wares heavily, but undiscounted sales by the brands' own sites have been somewhat disappointing. Salvatore Ferragamo used to offer its clothes and accessories on LVMH's eluxury.com site (where Dior's 'latest blonde shoulder bag' sells for a mere $1,280), but the company pulled out. 'Our consumers didn't want internet buying,' says the company's boss, Ferruccio Ferragamo.

What may make a difference is a better way to get clothes to fit. Suran Goonatilake, 'entrepreneur-in-residence' at the London College of Fashion, is the founder of Bodymetrics, a company that uses three-dimensional scanning to get an exact measure of a person's body. At the moment the system is being tested at Selfridges, a store in London's Oxford Street, where customers are being advised which clothes to try according to the print-out. Clothing sizes vary not just from country to country but from manufacturer to manufacturer, so Bodymetrics could be a boon both for the buyer and the manufacturer alike – even for the creative people, who tend to design for clothes horses rather than for normal human beings.

Art, no craft

Yet fashion cannot be reduced to a set of measurements. Some designers insist that fashion is not art. Instead, it is 'design' because, like architecture, it has a function. By contrast, this survey would argue that the best designers, from Balenciaga to Alexander McQueen, are as creative as any painter or sculptor, and even when they borrow from the past they add something new. Indeed, because the designer's medium is the human body, fashion is surely interactive art at its best.

But it is not yet art for the masses, whatever the efforts of Zara and of the talented Isaac Mizrahi, who now works for America's downmarket Target chain. That is not to demean those efforts. After all, when the materials are cheap, it becomes technically more difficult to design good-looking clothes. Nor is it to demean the masses, whose fashion choices are generally limited by price. Instead, this survey would simply praise the self-selected elite who choose to spend their time and money on the kind of clothes and accessories that are plainly luxury rather than necessities. If, for the narrow-minded, that qualifies them as irresponsible wastrels, so what? In an often ugly world, they provide some welcome style.

So forget the threat to luxury brands from the 'democratisation' of fashion and the pressures of mass-market competition. The chances are that as long as human beings apreciate art, and as long as there are enough rich people to pay for it, the world of luxury and high fashion will prosper. Let the designers indulge their fantasies. Today's fantasy becomes tomorrow's fashion, and the-day-after-tomorrow's discard. Hence the paradox that keeps us fascinated: fashion, by definition, is temporary – but it is always with us.

Source: 'No End of Luxury', *The Economist*, 6 March 2004.
© The Economist Newspaper Limited, London (6 March 2004).

Questions for discussion

1　Explain how markets for high fashion products work. In particular, who are the principal customers and what are the driving forces behind their purchases.

2　How are fashion markets affected by external events such as (i) terrorist attacks and (ii) changes in supply markets such as cost inflation?

3　What are the business risks of being in these markets?

3.4 **Analysis of markets and competition**

This section assesses how competition takes place and, in particular, how this is reflected in the different types of competition already mentioned in the previous section. This section looks explicitly at the way in which markets affect the nature of competition and firms' strategic choices. Contrast this with the discussion in Chapter 5 which deals with supply side characteristics usually referred to as industry structure. Market structure (the analysis of markets and competition) and industry structure (the analysis of the economic configuration of firms and their chains of supply) should be seen together as drivers of strategic choice.

The critical market-level influence on firm performance is the form and intensity of rivalry between the existing firms in a market. The economist's approach to market structure and the form and extent of rivalry is to use a taxonomy based on the number of firms in each industry. Figure 3.11 illustrates the economist's approach to market structure.

At one extreme, we have perfect competition, in which products are not differentiable, rivalry is intense and no firm has the power to alter market prices. In such a market the price is determined at the market level by the forces of supply and demand so from the firm's point of view the price of its product is given. The forces of competition limit strategic discretion and drive profits down to the 'normal' level, i.e. a level insufficient to attract new entrants to the market. Markets for agricultural products such as wheat or barley are often viewed as perfectly competitive, because no single producer can alter the market price. Perfect markets are not common. Firms have a huge incentive to adopt strategies which avoid the 'strategic hell' of perfect competition. The exploitation of scale economies is one route through which market power might be obtained and a measure of strategic discretion secured.

Another route by which the 'strategic hell' of perfect competition can be avoided is by product differentiation. Economists often exemplify this by using the example

Market structure	Number of firms	Degree of differentiation	Comments
Perfect competition	many	zero	Fragmented, commodity-like
Monopolistic or imperfect competition	many	some	Multiple niches, localized competition
Oligopoly – undifferentiated	Some to very few	low	Commodity-like with scale economies, e.g. steel
Oligopoly – differentiated	Some to very few	high	Strategic imterdependence, large segments
Dominant firm	One to very few	high	Price leadership, high entry barriers, competitive fringe
Monopoly	single	Not applicable	Natural monopoly due to very high scale economies

Figure 3.11 Market structure: the broad spectrum for competition

of advertising. Advertising is a feature of product differentiation and is characteristic of oligopolistic markets. The producer faces a downward sloping demand curve. The effect of advertising is that it shifts the demand curve out and it probably, and more importantly, steepens the slope of the curve (this means it reduces the price elasticity). This is intuitively sensible; if a product is desired because of its inherent features or quality, price will be less important – you remember the quality long after you have forgotten the price. Consequently the business is taken further away from the perfect competition 'nightmare' of a horizontal demand curve and price taking.

At the other extreme, we have a **monopoly** in which one firm supplies the whole market. Technically a monopoly exists when there is a single seller of a product. As a consequence the monopolist's demand curve is the market demand curve and is thus downward sloping. The monopolist therefore has pricing power, knowing that price reductions expand the market and vice versa. Typically, such markets exhibit low price elasticity and it is therefore in the interest of the monopoly to restrict output, gain higher prices and thereby increase revenues (a straightforward application of Table 3.3). Monopolies (as opposed to dominant firms – see below) exist because of very large economies of scale such that the MES (minimum efficient scale of output/plant size) is greater than the market size. Therefore, there is room for only one efficient firm – as in electricity generation and in water supply. These so called **natural monopolies** are controlled by governments to avoid them exploiting their customers – control is either in the form of public ownership or through regulation (e.g. competition regulators such as Ofcom or Ofwat in the UK – these are offices that regulate the behaviour of the telecommunications and water industries respectively).

Dominant firms may also have de facto monopoly positions. Usually they have risen to dominance over their competitors through superior product differentiation which serves as a highly effect deterrent to entry by new competitors and imitation by existing competitors. The dominant firm enjoys significant market power, is able to fix prices and hence enjoys a high degree of control over its market environment. Patents such as that secured by the UK pharmaceutical company Glaxo in the market for ulcer drugs confer this kind of market power. A high level of market power enables the monopolistic firm to earn higher profits than the competitive firm, as Glaxo did with Zantac in the 1980s and until 1997. There may be a few dominant firms (e.g. three or four), in which case one usually observes very large segments each of which being dominated by a particular player (as in pharmaceuticals where each therapeutic class is dominated by one player).

At a lower level of concentration of competition we have oligopolistic markets, in which a few firms compete against each other, and **monopolistic competition**. Most economists would regard these intermediate cases as the norm. In the monopolistic competition case, there are many firms each with small market shares, but each is able to differentiate its product to some degree and to obtain modest control over its prices and other aspects of its strategy, to build competitive advantage over other players. The restaurant business in a big city such as London or Singapore is a good example of monopolistic competition.

In oligopolistic markets, there are fewer players – perhaps as many as ten, each able to gain competitive advantage by exploiting scale economies, by product differentiation and so on. There are numerous examples of this kind of market including, for example, the global car market and the EU steel market. In both of these cases, a handful of firms compete against each other. This competition could be muted because of collusion between firms aimed at reducing rivalry. Although this collusion is possible and gives market control to all colluding producers, improving both the financial performance of both individual firms and the sector as a whole, it is sometimes difficult to create and to sustain, and is usually illegal.

Some oligopolies are essentially undifferentiated and intense price competition can occur. The large size of the players is determined by large scale economies as in steel or in automobiles and this is the kind of market that confronts both companies PaperCo and MetalCo. Each firm knows that in this case, effective strategic management may create competitive advantage, but also each needs to be aware that its rivals may copy any strategic move. Other oligopolies are much more differentiated, such as the toiletries markets where the degree of product innovation and differentiation is very high and creates sustainable differences between competitors. In both cases the degree of strategic independence is very high, i.e. the strategic moves of one competitor can have an immediate discernible effect on its rivals. This leads to 'gaming' behaviour and a very careful calculation of the risks of precipitating too much competition.

As well as the rivalry from existing players, it is important to take account of the threat of new entrants. This is technically known as '**contestable markets**'. In the case of PaperCo and MetalCo, the threat of new entrants is very low because of the huge entry costs. These arise from the large fixed costs of installing plant, as well as the costs of acquiring the key competencies of these businesses. The existence of static and dynamic scale economies arising from learning curve effects also create market barriers for incumbent firms. In other sectors, this may not be the case.

Case box: **The slumping price of salmon**

'Economics is giving salmon farming more trouble than science is.' This is a common refrain in business. Scientific and engineering problems can usually be solved but business and economic problems are endemic and rarely go away. In this instance the concern is with the salmon farming industry in the Scottish Highlands which has grown and now employs 1500 people but its future looks precarious.

Periodic health scares have claimed the headlines but many believe that the technology is there to reduce health risks to low levels. But the main problem is that supply has been growing faster than demand. Scottish farmed salmon production has grown swiftly from 32 000 tonnes a year in 1990 to 145 000 tonnes in 2002 and output from Norwegian and Chilean fish farms has grown similarly. Wholesale prices have fallen from around £2.70 per kilo in 2000 ($9 a lb) to less than £2.20 a kilo now. Smaller fish farms have been going bust for even large firms have been finding conditions difficult. Graeme Dear, managing director of Dutch-owned Marine Harvest (Scotland) Ltd which produces about 30 per cent of Scottish farmed salmon says, 'Probably no one is making an acceptable return.'

Mr Deare needs price to recover enough to justify the cost of a new ship equipped with seawater tanks whose purpose is to transport live fish to processing factories nearer the markets. This could add 24–48 hours to the salmon's shelf life and this would give Marine Harvest a competitive advantage. But it will cost £1 million a year. Smaller fish farmers cannot afford this so the industry looks likely to consolidate as well as shrink. The industry has a record of mechanization and computerization of feeding but, as cost pressures are prolonged, the larger operators will be looking to gain more efficiencies by grouping their cages together into bigger units.

In addition the industry is under fire from rod fishermen and from conservationists. Rod fishermen blame the falling numbers of wild salmon in Scottish rivers on the parasites that accompany fish farms. Conservationists complain that fish farms kill off sea-bed life beneath them. They both argue that the industry needs more regulation, which would put up costs and reduce profits even more.

Source: adapted from 'Salmon a-slumping', *The Economist*, 17 January 2004, p. 25.

Questions for discussion

1 Explain the mechanisms of supply and demand that are causing these problems for fish farmers.

2 What remedies do farmers have available to them?

3 How would you expect an industry like this to develop over time?

So far in this chapter we have:

♦ Provided a checklist of the key elements of the 'deep structure' of a firm's product market, which we need to consider when explaining differences in the financial performance of firms both within and between markets.

♦ Explored the extent to which these features are outside the strategic control of the firm and, hence, the extent to which effective strategic action is constrained by the business environment.

♦ Illustrated these ideas with respect to two companies. Although there are significant differences in their long-run financial performance, it is clear that they have a very similar 'deep structure'. However, there are differences, of which the most important is the greater opportunity for MetalCo to exploit economies of scope. These arise for reasons largely outside the control of the two businesses and are not the result of effective strategic 'actions'.

As well as the differences in the long run, Figure 3.1 also shows very significant short-run differences between PaperCo and MetalCo. In PaperCo, profits increase steadily and continually, whereas in MetalCo there are large fluctuations with losses made in the middle years. If an appraisal of MetalCo's performance were done in the single year 1993, it would show a very adverse relative position, although it has the superior financial performance in the long run. Why?

The answer is not to be found in the 'deep structure' of the market environment of the two companies but in the wider macroeconomic environment and in its particular impact on each of them. The macroeconomic environment refers to economic forces operating at both the national and the global level, to which all markets are sensitive. Of particular importance is the annual rate of growth of Gross Domestic Product (GDP). GDP is the total amount of all goods and services produced within a national economy or within the global economy (world GDP). It can be measured at the current prices of goods and services to obtain *nominal* GDP or at a single and constant set of prices to obtain a measure of *real* GDP. When GDP increases or decreases, this affects the market demand curve. If GDP growth increases, this shifts the demand curve upwards, increasing the demand at the price P_1 in exactly the same way as shown in Figure 3.9. Similarly, a slowdown in GDP growth shifts it downwards. Why? The answer is that if GDP growth increases (or decreases), there will be an equivalent increase (or decrease) in national income, and this affects the market demand for all products. The impact on market demand is measured by the *short-run (annual)* **income elasticity of demand**, which is defined as:

% change in short-run quantity demanded
_____
% change in short-run national income

Some estimates for the rich industrial economies of the Organization for Economic Co-operation and Development (OECD), which includes both the EU and North America, are shown in Figure 3.12.

Not surprisingly, given the reasoning above, the short-run income elasticity of demand is always a positive number. Note, however, the differences between market sectors. The food sector to which PaperCo in Figure 3.1 supplies its product has a very low short-run income elasticity, while MetalCo in Figure 3.1 is a metals company that supplies 70 per cent of its product to the highly income elastic vehicles sector. The simplest explanation for this difference in volatility is that final consumers are able to postpone their purchases of new vehicles in the short run. They do not and cannot postpone their purchases of food. Food is non-durable and cars are a durable good (recall the earlier discussion of durable and non-durable goods in this chapter). In a nutshell, booms and slumps in GDP have a much greater effect on the quantity demanded in MetalCo's markets.

Why does the greater sensitivity of sales in MetalCo*'s* markets affect its financial performance? Recall from the analysis of Figure 3.2 that if scale economies are important to both of these companies and if they fail to maintain their production at the minimum cost level (Q_1 in Figure 3.2), the average cost of production will rise above C_1 (to, say, C_3 if sales fall to Q_3). This will drive down profits. In years where GDP growth is low or even negative (as in 1993), costs will rise in MetalCo. It is also the case that in recession years (in which GDP growth is negative), prices are driven down in MetalCo's markets so, not surprisingly, its profitability suffers for reasons totally outside its control. What happens in the macroeconomy severely constrains MetalCo's scope for strategic action. In PaperCo's case, its products are used in the low short-run income elasticity food sector, so there are only very small fluctuations

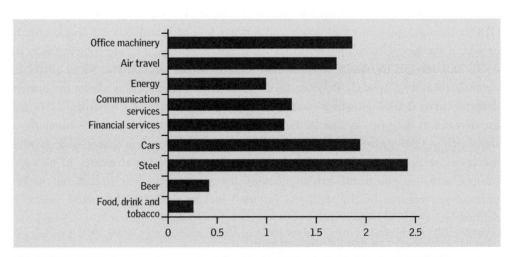

Figure 3.12 OECD short-run income elasticity (% change in 'real' sales/% change in GDP)
Source: KG (Ben) Knight (1999).

in output volumes, costs and also prices. Short-run movements in GDP growth have little effect on its financial performance.

Given the obvious importance of these uncontrollable shocks in the macroeconomic environment to the performance and strategy of individual companies, it is important to understand the workings of the macroeconomy and, in particular, the factors which cause GDP growth to rise and fall. It is also important to scan information sources, to select signals that help to build scenarios of the future. Scenario approaches are discussed in Chapter 14.

3.5 Summary

This chapter has introduced the basic microeconomic concepts that we use in strategic management, namely the basic principles of cost and demand analysis and an understanding of the nature of competition. The discussion in the chapter has given a managerial interpretation of these ideas. By contrast, in a conventional economics textbook you will find the discussion framed in terms of the nature of competitive markets and the government policy implications for fostering efficiency in markets. The concepts in this chapter are used both by economists and by managers. Economists use them to provide a basis for understanding the efficiency of competitive markets whereas managers are more interested in the implications for decision making. This theme is continued in the next chapter where we look at the macroeconomic concepts that condition strategic decisions.

We continue to build on these economic concepts in the chapters that follow. Chapter 4 focuses on the macroeconomy and the way in which this sets out the broad economic backdrop to the operations of firms. Chapter 5 takes the idea of imperfections in markets and the striving for entrepreneurial profits to develop an economic perspective of strategy that sees competitive strategy as a set of firm-specific imperfections around which a long-term business can be developed and defended. Chapter 6 follows directly from the industry analysis and generic strategies of Chapter 5 to create a deeper understanding of the meaning of competitive advantage and the market positioning competitive strategies. Chapter 7 extends this theme into an assessment of the characteristics of resources and capabilities that underpin competitive position in markets. Chapter 8 explicitly introduces time into the analysis and asks how industries change over time, what the implications for strategy are and what kinds of practical problem and opportunity are presented.

Key terms

Analysis of industry and competition *60*

Analysis of markets and competition *60*

Contestable markets *87*

Cost analysis *60*

Cost structure *62*

Cube law *69*

Demand analysis *60*

Demand curve *73*

Differentiation *56*

Division of labour *68*

Durable goods versus perishable goods *80*

Economies of scope *66*

Economy of massed reserves *69*

Final demand versus derived demand *79*

Fixed costs *62*

Income elasticity of demand *89*

Individual demand versus market demand *78*

Integration *56*

Law of diminishing returns *62*

Learning curve effect *66*

Long run *62*

Marginal cost *63*

Mechanistic *56*

Minimum efficient scale (MES) *63*

Monopolistic competition *86*

Monopoly *86*

Natural monopoly *86*

Opportunity cost *61*

Organic *57*

Own price elasticity of demand *72*

Producer goods versus consumer goods *80*

Relevant costs *61*

Short run *62*

Specialization *68*

Variable costs *62*

Recap questions and assignments

To build your strategic awareness, use the framework of this chapter to analyse the financial performance of an organization that you are familiar with. It may be an organization in which you have worked, or a well-known company that you can research online. Alternatively, you might choose an organization featured in one of the case studies in the book.

1 Are economies of scale or scope important?

2 Does your strategic 'action' take full advantage of economies of scale and scope?

3 What is the 'deep structure' of the demand side of the organization's markets and what form of market rivalry does the company have?

4 How exposed is the company to local and global macroeconomic shocks, especially to fluctuations in GDP?

5 Is its financial performance the same if you compared your chosen company to another operating in the same markets?

6 If not, why not?

In particular, try to isolate those factors outside management control which affect the financial performance of your chosen company and which constrain the scope for strategic action to build competitive advantage.

   Guide answers to these questions are given on the Online Learning Centre.

Online
*Learning*Centre

When you have read this chapter, log on to the Online Learning Centre website at www.mcgraw-hill.co.uk/textbooks/mcgee to explore chapter-by-chapter test questions, further reading and more online study tools for strategy.

Case 1 **The harder hard sell**

More people are rejecting traditional sales messages, presenting the ad industry with big challenges

It may have been Lord Leverhulme, the British soap pioneer, Frank Woolworth, America's first discount-retailer, or John Wanamaker, the father of the department store; all are said to have complained that they knew half of their advertising budget was wasted, but didn't know which half. As advertising starts to climb out of its recent slump, the answer to their problem is easier to find as the real effects of advertising become more measurable. But that is exposing another, potentially more horrible truth, for the $1 trillion advertising and marketing industry: in some cases, it can be a lot more than half of the client's budget that is going down the drain.

The advertising industry is passing through one of the most disorienting periods in its history. This is due to a combination of long-term changes, such as the growing diversity of media, and the arrival of new technologies, notably the internet. Consumers have become better informed than ever before, with the result that some of the traditional methods of advertising and marketing simply no longer work.

Ad spending grew rapidly in the late 1990s, but in 2000 – just as the technology bubble was about to burst – it soared by more than 8% in America, which represents about half the world market. The following year it plunged by 8%. Spending is up again, according to ZenithOptimedia, which has long tracked the industry. It forecasts that worldwide expenditure in 2004 on major media (newspapers, magazines, television, radio, cinema, outdoor and the internet) will grow by 4.7% to $343 billion. It will be helped by a collection of big events, including the European football championship, the Olympic Games and an election in America. Historically, when there is an upturn in advertising expenditure, it tends to rise faster than the wider economy. So, provided economic growth can be sustained, ad spending may continue to pick up.

How will the money be spent? There are plenty of alternatives to straightforward advertising, including a myriad of marketing and communications services, some of which are called 'below-the-line' advertising. They range from public relations to direct mail, consumer promotions (such as coupons), in-store displays, business-to-business promotions (like paying a retailer for shelf-space), telemarketing, exhibitions, sponsoring events, product placements and more.

These have become such an inseparable part of the industry that big agencies now provide most of them. Although some are less than glamorous, marketing services have grown more quickly than advertising. Add in the cost of market research, and this part of the industry was worth some $750 billion worldwide last year, estimates WPP, one of the world's biggest advertising and marketing groups.

As ever, the debate in the industry centres on the best way to achieve results. Is it more cost-effective, for instance, to employ a PR agency to invite a journalist out to lunch and persuade him to write about a product than to pay for a display ad in that journalist's newspaper? Should you launch a new car with glossy magazine ads, or – as some carmakers now do – simply park demonstration models in shopping malls and motorway service stations? And is it better to buy a series of ads on a specialist cable-TV channel or splurge $2.2m on a single 30-second commercial during this year's Super Bowl?

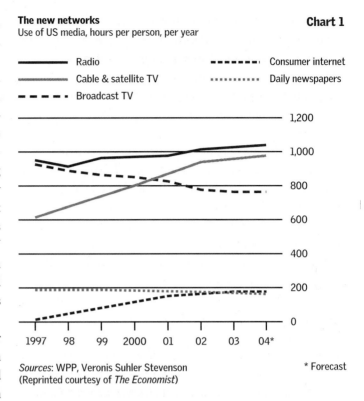

The new networks
Use of US media, hours per person, per year

Chart 1

Radio — Cable & satellite TV — Broadcast TV — Consumer internet — Daily newspapers

Sources: WPP, Veronis Suhler Stevenson
(Reprinted courtesy of *The Economist*)

* Forecast

Such decisions are ever harder to make. Although a Super Bowl ad is still cheaper than in 2000, in general network-TV pricing has risen faster than inflation – even though fewer people tune in. Changes in TV-viewing habits, however, are only part of a much wider shift in the way media is consumed, not least because it has become more fragmented and diverse.

For a start, people are spending less time reading newspapers and magazines, but are going to the cinema more, listening to more radio and turning in ever-increasing numbers to a new medium, the internet (see chart 1).

After the technology bust it was easy to dismiss the internet. But the phenomenal success of many e-commerce firms, such as Amazon and eBay, shows that millions of people are becoming comfortable buying goods and services online. Many more are using the internet to research products, services and prices for purchases made offline. Some 70% of new-car buyers in America, for instance, use websites to determine which vehicle to buy – and often to obtain competing quotes from dealers.

Google that

Such consumers can be targeted by internet advertisers and, in some cases, their responses accurately measured. A surge in online advertising is being led by paid-for text-links dished up by search engines such as Google and Yahoo! The response rate from people clicking on paid links can be as low as 1% – about the same as direct mail, which remains one of the biggest forms of advertising. But there is an important difference: internet advertisers usually pay only if someone clicks on their link. This is the equivalent of paying for the delivery of junk mail only to households that read it.

How are companies and the advertising industry responding to these trends in media consumption? Some people do not believe they amount to a sea-change, while others are simply hoping it will not come to pass on their watch, reckons Sir Martin Sorrell, WPP's chief executive.

Nor is it the only significant force he sees at work. New markets, such as China, are becoming increasingly important for advertisers, especially multinationals. But these markets can have very different characteristics. Clients are also more concerned than ever about getting value for money. What will increasingly matter, says Sir Martin, is not what it costs to put an ad in front of 1,000 people (a traditional industry measure), but 'how effective is that cost-per-thousand?'

At the same time, negotiating advertising deals is becoming tougher because of consolidation, both among clients and among media owners. This could favour the big, integrated agencies. In May, WPP won a contract to handle all the advertising and marketing for HSBC, after the international banking group decided that parent companies and not their individual agencies should bid for the $600m it spends on such services every year. Samsung, a big South Korean electronics firm, is also expected to appoint a single group.

Nevertheless, the smaller agencies believe they can still compete by being more nimble. 'There is definitely a change in the landscape,' says Jane Asscher, chairman of 23red, a London-based agency that describes itself as 'media-neutral' in its choice of outlets for campaigns. Ms Asscher believes that consumers are becoming far more sophisticated in their reaction to all forms of advertising and marketing, so smarter ways have to be used to reach them.

During the slump, some companies tried different forms of advertising and liked the response they got. 'There's lots of ways to skin a cat today,' says Scott Goodson, founder of StrawberryFrog, an agency based in Amsterdam that specialises in international campaigns. While his firm still uses traditional media, such as TV and print, it is often in conjunction with other techniques, such as 'viral'

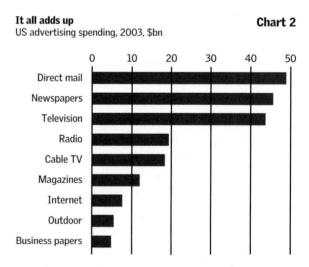

It all adds up   **Chart 2**
US advertising spending, 2003, $bn

Sources: PwC/IAB Internet Ad Revenue Report; McCann Erickson
(Reprinted courtesy of *The Economist*)

marketing. This means trying to spread the message by word of mouth – still considered the most powerful form of advertising. Sometimes that involves using the internet for e-mail messages containing jokes, film clips and games, which recipients are encouraged to pass along to friends.

No one knows just how important the internet will eventually be as an advertising medium. Some advertisers think it will be a highly cost-effective way of reaching certain groups of consumers – especially for small companies operating in niche businesses. But not everyone uses the internet, and nor is it seen as particularly good at brand building. Barry Diller, the head of InterActiveCorp, believes network TV is a great place to promote his company's websites, such as Expedia, his online travel agency, and LendingTree, a consumer lender. Unlike bricks-and-mortar businesses, web-based firms do not worry if their ad is being seen by lots of people in towns where they have no shops. They just want people to remember their website address – or at least enough of their name to be Googled.

So far, the internet accounts for only a tiny slice of the overall advertising pie (see chart 2), although it has been growing rapidly. A joint study by the Interactive Advertising Bureau and PricewaterhouseCoopers found that internet advertising revenue in America grew by 39% to $2.3 billion in the first quarter of 2004, compared with the same period a year earlier. Internet ad revenues are now back above what they were at the height of the tech boom.

And Google and Yahoo! have yet to unleash the full potential of their technology. Google, which already places text ads on other people's websites and splits the revenue with them, recently began testing a system to distribute display ads as well, in effect increasing its role as a sort of online ad agency.

Others are honing new techniques. As part of a recent campaign for American Airlines, the online edition of the *Wall Street Journal* used 'behavioural targeting' to estimate how likely readers were to be frequent-flyers based on how much interest they paid to travel-related stories and columns. The targeted readers were presented with American Airline ads, and not just when they were reading travel stories. According to Revenue Science, a New York company that developed the targeting system, the results were dramatic: the number of business travellers who saw the ads more than doubled.

The potential for advertising on the internet is tempting more firms to join the fray. For instance, Microsoft is working on a search system with the intention of leapfrogging Google. Microsoft and others see that as more types of media, including music and films, start to be distributed over the internet, there will be more opportunities for online operators to put advertising messages in front of consumers.

Indeed, the makers of personal video recorders (PVRs) recently announced that their new machines will be capable of downloading music and films from the internet, as well as from TV. Many advertisers dread PVRs because they can be used to 'time shift' viewing, allowing viewers to record their own schedules with greater ease than existing video recorders. Several studies have shown that users think one of the machine's most-appealing features is the ability to skip past ads. The providers of internet-based content might be able to slip in those ads in other ways than traditional 30-second commercials, perhaps through sponsorship deals or as display ads on the websites which PVR owners will use to select their programming.

Bombarded

People are tiring of ads in all their forms. A recent study by Yankelovich Partners, an American marketing-services consultancy, says that consumer resistance to the growing intrusiveness of marketing and advertising has been pushed to an all-time high. Its study found 65% of people now feel 'constantly bombarded' by ad messages and that 59% feel that ads have very little relevance to them. Almost 70% said they would be interested in products or services that would help them avoid marketing pitches.

It has been calculated that the average American is subjected to some 3,000 advertising messages every day. If you add in everything from the badges on cars to slogans on sweatshirts, the ads in newspapers, on taxis, in subways and even playing on TVs in lifts, then some people could be exposed to more than that number just getting to the office. No wonder many consumers seem to be developing the knack of tuning-out adverts.

'Consumers are getting harder to influence as commercial clutter invades their lives,' says a recent report by Deutsche Bank. It examined the effectiveness of TV advertising on 23 new and mature brands of packaged goods and concluded that in some cases it was a waste of time. Although in the short-term TV advertising would lead to an incremental increase in volume sales in almost every case, there was only a positive cash return on that investment in 18% of cases. Over a longer term the picture improved, with 45% of cases showing a return on investment. Not surprisingly, new products did better than older ones. The study concluded that 'increased levels of marketing spending were less important than having new items on the shelf and increasing distribution'.

The effectiveness of advertising is a hugely controversial area. Conventional wisdom in the industry is that sales may well increase for a certain period even after the advertising of a product ends. But there comes a point when sales start to decline and it then becomes extremely expensive to rebuild the brand.

This supports the idea of continuous advertising. But some people in the industry believe the conventional wisdom is no longer true. When America's big TV networks reached prime-time audiences of 90% of households, they were a powerful way to build a brand. Now that those audiences might be as low as one-third of households, other ways of promoting a brand have become more competitive. Moreover, many clients never really embraced continuous advertising: when times get tough, just as they did after 2000, one of the first things many companies cut is their ad budget.

Robert Shaw, a visiting professor at the Cranfield School of Management in Britain, runs a forum in which a number of big companies try to monitor the 'marketing payback' from advertising. The return from traditional media was, he says, 'never terribly good'. Generally under half of ads provide a return on their investment. And there can be various reasons why ads influence sales, other than their direct effect on consumers. For instance, if a producer announces a multi-million dollar ad-campaign, then retailers are often persuaded to increase deliveries. This can result in a 'distribution effect' that leads to additional sales.

Some companies have profited from re-allocating their spending across different media, adds Mr Shaw. But it is a tricky business to determine what works best. For many companies, and especially the media-buyers who purchase space and slots for ads, greater media diversity and the arrival of the internet has made a difficult job much tougher.

Soap stars

Some big spenders have already made clear choices. With an annual budget of more than $4 billion, America's Procter & Gamble (P&G) is the biggest advertiser in the world. Ten years ago about 90% of its global ad spend was on TV. Now the figure is much smaller. Last year the company launched a non-prescription version of Prilosec, an anti-heartburn medicine. It was one of the most successful brand launches in the company's history, according to Jim Stengel, P&G's global marketing officer. But only about one-quarter of the marketing spend on Prilosec went to TV. The rest was spent on other forms of marketing, such as in-store promotions.

P&G, which helped to launch TV soap operas as a new way to market goods, is now looking once again for novel ways to reach consumers. Three years ago it set up an operation called Tremor to recruit an army of several hundred thousand American teenagers. It uses them to discuss ideas about new products and to help spread marketing messages. In return, the teenagers get to hear about and use new things before many of their peers.

Getting trendsetters to buy (or be given) new products in order to influence a broader market is hardly a new idea. So-called 'early adopters' are a similar group, much sought-after by consumer-electronics companies in order to give their new products a good start. But there is a wider group which marketers sometimes call 'prosumers'; short for proactive consumers. Some people in the industry believe this group is the most powerful of all.

Euro RSCG, a big international agency, is completing a nine-country study of prosumers, which it says can represent 20% or so of any particular group. They can be found everywhere, are at the vanguard of consumerism, and what they say to their friends and colleagues about brands and products tends to become mainstream six to 18 months later. They also vary by category, says Marc Lepere, Euro RSCG's chief marketing officer: a wine prosumer, for instance, will not necessarily be a prosumer of cars.

Such people often reject traditional ads and invariably use the internet to research what they are going to buy and how much they are going to pay for it. Half of prosumers distrust companies and products they cannot find on the internet. If they want to influence prosumers, says Mr Lepere, companies have to be extremely open about providing information.

Despite all of these complications, many in the advertising business remain sanguine. For Rupert Howell, chairman of the London arm of McCann Erickson, which is part of the giant Interpublic group, the industry's latest downturn was the third he has experienced. As it did from the others, he says, the industry is emerging a little wiser. But, he insists, 'the underlying principles haven't changed'. Even the arrival of new media, like the internet, does not spell the demise of the old. Indeed, as he points out, TV never killed radio, which in turn never killed newspapers. They did pose huge creative challenges, but that's OK, he maintains: 'The advertising industry is relentlessly inventive; that's what we do.'

Source: 'The harder hard sell', *The Economist*. 26 June 2004, pp. 83–5.
© The Economist Newspaper Limited, London (26 June 2004).

Case Questions

1   Why is it that traditional methods of advertising 'simply no longer work'? What is it about changes in consumer demand that contribute to this phenomenon?

2   Assess the potential of internet players such as Google and Yahoo! to influence and change the way in which the advertising industry operates.

3   What response do you think advertisers should make to the claim that 'consumer resistance to the growing intrusiveness of marketing and advertising has been pushed to an all-time high'? Does this mean that the potential to differentiate consumer products and services is diminishing?

4   What advice would you offer to an advertising agency such as McCann Erickson and to a major advertiser such as P&G?

Further reading and references

Besanko, D, Dranove, D and Shanley, M (2000) *Economics of Strategy*, 2nd edition, John Wiley & Sons, New York.

Boston Consulting Group (1975) *Strategy alternatives for the British motorcycle industry*, HMSO, London.

Burns, T and Stalker, GM (1961) *The Management of Innovation*, Tavistock, London.

Chandler, AD (1990) 'The Enduring Logic of Industrial Success', *Harvard Business Review*, March/April, pp. 130–40.

Child, J (1972) 'Organizational structures, environments and performance: the role of strategic choice', *Sociology*, **6**, pp. 1–22.

Child, J (1997) 'Strategic choice in the analysis of action, structure, organization and environment: retrospect and prospect', *Organization Studies*, **18**, **1**, pp. 43–76.

Conley, P (1975) *Experience Curves as a Planning Tool*, Boston Consulting Group (pamphlet).

Deaton, A (1975) 'The Measurement of Income and Price Elasticities', *European Economic Review*, Vol. 7, pp. 261–74.

Duncan, R (1972) 'Characteristics of Organisational Environments and Perceived Environmental Uncertainty', *Administrative Science Quarterly*, **17**, **3**.

Economist, The (1999), November, pp. 27–35 and p. 122.

Emerson, M (1988) *The Economics of 1992*, Oxford University Press.

European Commission (1997) 'Economies of Scale', *Single Market Review*, Subseries V, Volume 4, Office for Official Publications of the European Communities, Luxembourg.

Fahey, L and Narayanan, VK (1986) *Macroenvironmental Analyses for Strategic Management*, West, New York.

Haldi, J and Whitcomb, D (1967) 'Economies of Scale in Industrial Plants', *Journal of Political Economy*, **75**, **4**, August, pp. 373–85.

Her Majesty's Stationery Office (1978) *A Review of Monopolies and Mergers Policy*, cmnd 7198, London.

Langowitz, N (1987) 'Sun Microsystems Inc. (A)', Harvard Business School Case 9–686–133, June, revised.

Lawrence, PR and Lorsch, JW (1967) *Organization and Environment: Managing Differentiation and Integration*, Irwin, Homewood, Illinois.

McAleese, D (2004) *Economics for Business*, 3rd edition, Prentice Hall, London.

Moore, FT (1959) 'Economies of Scale: Some Statistical Evidence', *Quarterly Journal of Economics*, May, pp. 232–45.

Panzer, JC and Willig, ND (1981) 'Economies of Scope', *American Economic Review*, **71**, pp. 268–77.

Porter, M (1980) *Competitive Strategy*, Free Press, New York.

Porter, ME (1985) *Competitive Advantage*, Free Press, New York.

Porter, ME (1986) 'What is strategy?' *Harvard Business Review*, Nov/Dec, pp. 61–78.

Pratten, C (1988) 'A Survey of the Economies of Scale', in *Research on the Costs of Europe*, Vol. 2, Office for Official Publications of the European Communities, Luxembourg.

Robinson, EAG (1958) *The Structure of Competitive Industry*, University of Chicago Press.

Rosenfeld, R and Wilson, DC (1999) *Managing Organizations: Text, Readings and Cases*, McGraw-Hill, Maidenhead.

Seldon, A and Pennance, FG (eds) (1965) *Everyman's Dictionary of Economics*, JM Dent & Sons, London.

Scherer, FM (1970) *Industrial Market Structure and Economic Performance*, Rand McNally.

Supple, B (1977) *Essays in British Business History*, OUP.

Teece, DJ (1980) 'Economies of scope and the scope of the enterprise', *Journal of Economic Behaviour and Organisation*, **1**, pp. 223–47.

Chapter 4

The macroeconomics of strategy[1]

Introduction

This chapter focuses on the influence on businesses of changes taking place in the external context of both the market and the macroeconomy. This involves not just the systemic impact of external forces but also, and in particular, the way these forces are augmented and mediated by public policy. The chapter covers the fundamentals of aggregate demand and supply and the implications for GDP, inflation and unemployment. It also examines the causes and effects of business cycles and what in a global economy causes booms and slumps to come to an end. It goes on to consider issues concerning the sustainability of strong economic growth, especially in emerging markets. The chapter concludes

---

[1] This chapter was written jointly with K.G (Ben) Knight.

by considering national competitive advantage and the link with company competitive advantage. It also explores issues of uncertainty and risk, and some of the forward-looking strategies business might adopt to limit the effects of exposure to risk. How might uncertain and volatile economic factors (for example, exchange or interest rates) be incorporated into strategic thinking?

4.1 The context of strategy and the impact of government action

This chapter emphasizes the importance of both the market (inner) context and the macro (outer) context in restricting the strategic discretion of managers. In both of these contexts it is important to take account of the impact of government action and public policy. In the market context there is a particularly important role for competition regulators whose policies and actions impact directly on business strategy.

The activities of the competition regulators (introduced in Chapter 3) are a particularly important source of uncontrollable shock for business because they regulate and maintain rivalry between competing businesses. Most operate on a national basis but the development of the European Union has led to the creation of EU-wide competition regulation. Because of their objective the competition regulators interfere more directly in business strategy, especially when they judge that unacceptable market power and 'unfair' competitive advantage exists. The driving force behind the activities of the regulators is the economic analysis of market power. Much of this is rooted in the social benefits of a high degree of market competition.

The economic analysis of market power identifies the loss suffered by an economy when business is allowed to establish a dominant market position. Consider Figure 4.1, which shows market-level supply and demand curves. The demand curve slopes down, so increases (decreases) in price decrease (increase) market demand. This is discussed fully in Chapter 3. The shape of this market supply curve implies that increases in the market price encourage firms to produce more to take advantage of the higher price. However, the market supply curve is not always upward sloping. In perfect competition, where market entry is free, an increase in price increases the number of firms. As a result there is an increase in long-run supply and price falls to P_c. The long-run supply curve is, therefore, horizontal. The supply curve also shifts in response to a variety of factors including:

- technical changes which reduce costs;
- indirect tax changes;
- changes in supplier cost;
- changes in the cost of labour.

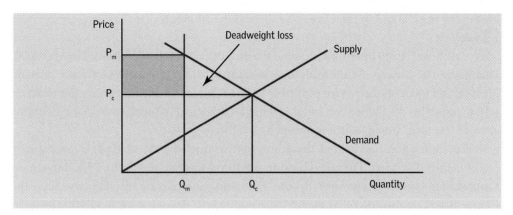

Figure 4.1 Market power and competition

In a competitive market the forces of supply and demand will lead to a price of P_c with Q_c being the volume of product supplied and sold. When firms acquire market power they are able to drive the price above the competitive level (to P_m), and one way to do that is to restrict supply (to Q_m). In this case they are able to earn higher profits, shown by the shaded area. They are clearly better off but consumers are worse off because they are paying a higher price to consume less. In addition, it is evident that this loss is not offset by the producer's gain and this is shown by the white triangle which indicates the 'deadweight' loss, i.e. a loss suffered by one group (consumers) not fully offset by the gain to another group (producers). Society is unambiguously worse off if business is allowed to exploit market power and action must be taken to stop it . This is the mission of the competition regulator.

As an example, Interbrew's strategy has involved acquisition of other brewers in the EU and also in Eastern Europe. This is motivated partly by the desire to reduce dependence on a single national market and also by the need to exploit the cost savings and scale economies from the large-scale production which are inherent in brewing. Achieving these scale economies has been difficult because sales volume has been falling in most EU national economies. In the UK, for instance, beer sales volume has fallen 15 per cent since 1979. The attractiveness of the UK to Interbrew was enhanced by the desire of several well-established UK brewers to divest their beer-making activities. One reason was the decision of the UK Monopolies Commission in 1989 to restrict the number of retail outlets each brewer could own. This was because of concern with the market power arising from the use of 'vertical restraints', which are obtained by the acquisition or control of retail distribution by manufacturers. The traditional British pub tied to a particular brewer is a good example of this practice and hence has been a target for the regulator. The outcome in the 1990s of the 1989 decision was the growth of large independent retail chains, including one owned by the Japanese bank Nomura. These large pub chains have put downward pressure on beer prices, which, with the upward pressure on costs from falling volume, results in lower profits from brewing in the UK and in the EU as a whole and the adoption of an exit strategy by some UK brewers.

As part of its strategy Interbrew acquired the brewing activities of Whitbread in May 2000. Like many UK brewers, Whitbread were anxious to divest themselves of their brewing interests and focus on their more profitable leisure business for the reasons set out above. It was an attractive acquisition for Interbrew not least because Whitbread held the UK franchise for the Stella brand, which is owned by Interbrew.

Similar motivations lay behind the acquisition in August 2000 of Bass, a much larger player in the UK market. The sale of Bass to Interbrew was referred to the UK Competition Commission (www.mmc.gov.uk) by the European Commission. In January 2001 the Competition Commission ruled against the acquisition of Bass on the grounds that it would leave the two top players in the sector (Interbrew and Scottish and Newcastle) with 59 per cent of the UK market which the Commission deemed too large a market share since both would have 'a common interest in raising operating margins' and driving up prices paid by consumers. This decision was a serious blow to Interbrew's strategic ambitions.

As well as national competition regulators, the European Union has its own increasingly active transnational competition regulator. The regulator is a key feature of the EU's programme of economic integration.. The process of EU integration has been driven by a desire to create a larger (US-size) home market for EU business. The first stage was to remove all tariff barriers between member countries in order to encourage the growth of trade within the EU, and this is exactly what has happened, with intra-EU trade as a percentage of total EU trade growing by 20 percentage points between 1974 and 2001. In addition there has been a huge growth in cross-border mergers and acquisitions especially in the run-up to the introduction of the euro in 1999 and also in 2000. Although this process has slowed down since 2000, the European Commission is still keen to ensure that this process of pan-European consolidation does not lead to unwanted accumulation of market power and that the EU maintains a high degree of domestic market rivalry. One area in which the EU competition regulator is actively exerting its influence to limit the market power of producers is in the EU car market, and this has serious implications for the strategy of the EU car-makers.

4.2 The basics of macroeconomics

It is not just a matter of understanding the market context of business. As we saw in Chapter 3, all firms and industries are also sensitive to events in the wider economy. This is true in any economy irrespective of its geographical location or stage of development. The extent of exposure for each industry differs little across countries. As we also saw in Chapter 3, booms and slumps in GDP lead to major changes in the rate of growth of sales and output at both the market sector and firm levels. These feed through to financial performance and, although they have to be managed, are totally outside the control of the individual firm or its managers.

Hence, even with no change in the strategy of the individual firm, major changes in its performance and prospects will occur for reasons outside its direct control. If the threat of adverse developments is to be minimized and the benefit of the opportunity afforded by favourable conditions is to be maximized, these macroeconomic factors need to be taken into account by managers. Chapter 3 suggests that the first critical question to be considered is: what causes the short-run fluctuations in GDP growth which have such a significant impact on firm-level performance?

4.2.1 Short-run fluctuations in GDP

Initially we will focus on national economies. Goods and services in any national macroeconomy as a whole are produced to meet demand, not necessarily immediately, but eventually. Hence, the normal cause of booms and slumps in GDP is fluctuations in the volume of demand for goods and services in the economy as a whole (**aggregate demand**). If aggregate demand goes up, so does GDP, and if it goes down, GDP again follows suit.

This can be seen from Figure 4.2, which shows the close relationship of changes in aggregate demand and output (GDP) for the rich OECD (Organisation for Economic

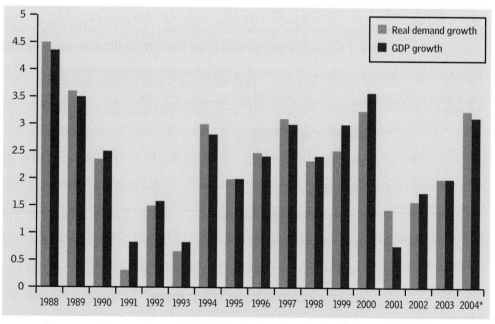

Figure 4.2 Boom and slump in practice: demand and output in industrial economies (annual % growth)
Note: * = estimated.
Source: OECD.

Co-operation and Development) economies of the EU, North America and the Pacific Rim as a whole. This accounts for nearly two-thirds of world GDP. The match between demand growth and GDP growth is not perfect and, where it is not, there will be changes in the stocks of finished goods. If GDP growth exceeds demand growth, for example, stocks rise. When demand growth exceeds GDP growth, stocks fall, as they did in 1994. However, there is clearly a close correspondence between changes in GDP and in aggregate demand and it is this correspondence which we explore next.

What is 'aggregate demand'? It is the total demand for goods and services from all sources in the national economy. Where does the demand originate? Economists identify the following sources of aggregate demand:

1 The demand for consumer goods, both durable (such as cars) and non-durable (such as food), and services by all households resident in the national economy. In most economies this constitutes the biggest source of demand. In the UK, for example, just over 50 per cent of aggregate demand originates from this source and this is very typical of the OECD economies.

2 Demand for investment goods (buildings, plant and machinery) and services by private companies. This varies in importance across economies but is rarely less than 10 per cent of the total aggregate demand for goods and services and in some countries (e.g. the economies of East Asia) can be as high as 25 per cent.

3 Demand for export goods, e.g. pharmaceuticals and services such as tourism, by foreign customers. As Figure 4.3 shows, in some very open (usually small) economies heavily

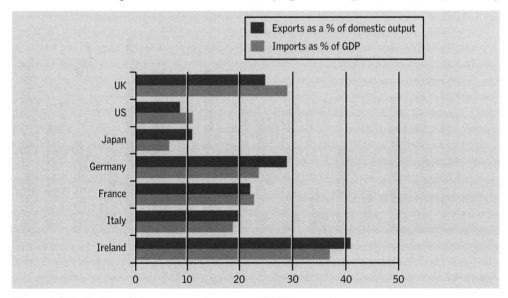

Figure 4.3 Indicators of macroeconomic openness 2003
Source: OECD.

engaged in trade (e.g. Ireland) this can be very high but in the average OECD economy around 25 per cent of the demand for goods in industrial economies comes from this source. In the very large and more self-sufficient economies such as Japan and the US (which together account for over a third of world GDP), the proportion is much lower.

4 Demand for goods and services by the government. This arises from public spending on defence, education, health and so on. It does not include 'transfer payments' (such as state pensions), i.e. payments made to individuals by the government using funds raised from other citizens, because these funds are used by households and hence are included in consumer demand. The share of the government in aggregate demand for goods and services also varies a lot but the 15 per cent level found in the UK is very typical of the industrial economies as a whole.

5 In calculating the aggregate demand for a country's output, account must also be taken of the extent to which demand is met by overseas production, i.e. imports. Increases in imports reduce the level of aggregate demand for home produced goods and vice versa if imports fall. Figure 4.3 also gives an indication of the share of imports in various countries. The most obvious feature here is that the share of imports as a percentage of demand is lowest in the larger more self-sufficient countries such as Japan and the US and highest in a small economy such as Ireland.

Aggregate demand for goods and services in any economy is therefore the sum of each of these sources of demand:

$C + I + G + X - F$ where

$C = $ *consumer demand by households*
$I = $ *investment demand by firms*
$G = $ *public sector demand*
$X = $ *exports to other economies*
$F = $ *imports from other economies*

What determines the level of aggregate demand for goods and services in any national economy? The first and most important answer is the level of aggregate income (wages and salaries *plus* profits) received by all firms and all households in the economy. The government's income is derived from the same source via taxation. In the case of exports, what counts is the income of firms and households in the overseas economies where exports are sold.

Where does this income come from? The most important source is from the proceeds of producing goods and services in the national economy as a whole, i.e. from GDP! We started by wanting to explain GDP and the explanation ends up with GDP!! Not surprisingly, economists refer to this as the **circular flow of income** and this is shown in Figure 4.4.

Figure 4.4 shows the interaction between the three fundamental macroeconomic processes described above, namely:

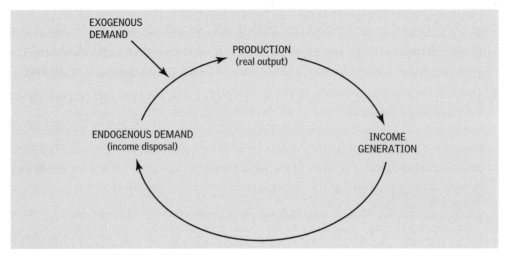

Figure 4.4 The circular flow of income

1   the national production of goods and services;

2   the income generated by this production of goods and services; and

3   the disposal of income to create the aggregate demand for goods and services which completes the circle.

Each of these processes feeds back on the others. Production in an open economy (i.e. one which engages in international trade) would not occur without demand, which in its turn would not happen without income, which depends itself on the production of goods and services. The demand that arises from the circular flow of income is called **endogenous** by economists. It refers to the demand (spending) that arises in the home economy from income earned from the home production of goods and services. Note that some of this income is lost to the home economy because it is spent on imports produced in other economies. Economists call this loss of income a **leakage** from the circular flow of income of any national economy.

Demand, however, can also arise from other sources and this offsets the leakage which arises from imports. This type of demand is called **exogenous** because it does not arise from *within* the circular flow of income but rather from *outside*. It can come from outside the home economy, i.e. from exports of goods and services to the outside world, or from within the domestic economy as a result of spending changes driven by forces other than changes in current income, especially the important spending changes which result from changes in wealth and/or in the level of borrowing.

Changes in any component of aggregate demand can cause fluctuations in GDP. History has taught us that the key drivers of the circular flow of income and the changes observed in GDP are shocks to aggregate exogenous demand. There are many exogenous shocks to aggregate demand which can lead to changes in GDP. In all cases, demand originating in the private sector (consumer demand and investment) and in exports plays a crucial role, not least because in most economies this is at least 80 per cent of the total demand for goods and services. However, there is also a role for government in stimulating exogenous demand. Note this in the examples set out below.

Among the many examples of potent causes of change in the volume of exogenous demand are changes in the following.

The cost and availability of credit

Easy, cheap credit increases consumer spending at any income level. This causes an increase in exogenous demand. The result of this is an increase in output. If, on the other hand, credit becomes more expensive, aggregate demand falls (or increases by less) and this will cause output to fall (or increase by less). In 1999 US interest rates rose to slow down the US economy. The problem is that in 2000 this slowdown happened rather more quickly and dramatically than the monetary authorities thought, so a correction was required. In 2001 onwards US interest rates fell several times to stop the slowdown turning into a severe slump.

Rises in interest rates are sometimes also used to reduce capital outflows and stabilize exchange rates which are under pressure. This is the recent experience of many Asian and Latin American economies and severe recession is the result as demand falls. In November 1998 interest rates in Rio were 49 per cent as the Brazilian government attempted to maintain the real/$ parity! Unsuccessfully as it turned out, so rates fell in 1999 but remain high in 2004. Changes in the interest rate also change the cost of finance as well as the opportunities for gain from financial investment. This has an important effect on both real fixed investment and stockbuilding. When the interest rate rises, firms cut back their fixed investment because borrowing is dearer and financial investment is a more attractive alternative. This response is not, however, immediate. Stockbuilding, in contrast, responds more quickly. Increases in the cost of finance encourage de-stocking, especially of finished goods. When this happens output falls directly.

Changes in wealth

Changes in wealth affect the take-up of credit opportunities by consumers. Increases in wealth encourage consumers to borrow, especially when interest rates are falling. The most important source of wealth for many consumers is equity in houses. When house prices rise, as they did in the UK in the mid 1980s and again in 1999–2004, households experience an increase in wealth, enabling them to increase debt without increasing their debt/wealth ratio. Since additional wealth also encourages greater consumer confidence, increased consumer demand results and output rises. The whole chain of events is reversed when house prices stabilize and then fall as they did in the period 1989–95. This both causes and lengthens a recession because it makes consumers reluctant to increase their spending even when interest rates fall. This was a persistent feature of the UK until 1996/97 when house prices, and hence household wealth, started to rise. Similar effects can occur through changes in the value of non-housing wealth. Rising share prices were profoundly important in explaining the strong growth of private sector demand and GDP in the US from 1992 to 2000. In the opposite direction, falls in the value of shares in Japan, for example, contributed to the slump in consumer demand in 1993 and the subsequent poor and volatile performance of the Nikkei share price index has held back consumer demand and contributed to the difficulty Japan has experienced in getting a strong recovery underway even when base interest rates fall to 0.5 per cent. Falls in world stock markets in 2001 and 2002 also triggered these kinds of 'wealth effects' and contributed to reduced confidence, lower demand and global slowdown despite lower interest rates.

Changes in government spending

Increases in government spending (current or capital) increase aggregate demand, and output increases. This is an important means through which the government can influence the economy. The Japanese government adopted this approach to ending recessions in 1993/4 and 1996 and also in 2000/2001. It is an important reason for the relatively (compared to other G7 economies) strong performance of the UK in the years 2000–2004.

Changes in tax rates

Cuts in income taxes increase consumer spending because they increase net household income and, if government spending is not cut, aggregate demand rises as well. Cuts in the US tax rates in 2001 were intended to boost consumer spending to stop a prolonged recession. Further cuts in both personal and corporate tax rates will have the same effect. In contrast, increases in personal or corporate tax rates have the opposite effect, reducing consumer and investment demand.

Changes in the exchange rate

One critical driver of exogenous aggregate demand is the exchange rate, which sets the price of one currency in terms of another: e.g. if the £/$ rate is 1.50 it tells us the number of US dollars needed to buy £1 – i.e. $1.50. The exchange rates are fixed daily across the world. Changes in the exchange rate have a big effect on cross-border spending, i.e. on exports.

Table 4.1 Exchange rate arithmetic

	$P^x_{£}$	$P^x_{\$}$	$P^f_{\$}$	$P^f_{£}$	
£1 = $2	100	200	300	150	strong £
£1 = $1	100	100	300	300	weak £

Exchange rates also impact on imports, i.e. on leakages from the circular flow of income, so they also impact on the endogenous demand arising from the circular flow of income. The effect is shown in Table 4.1. $Px_£$ is the price of exports in the home currency (£ in this example) and $Px_$$ is the price in export markets. What is the effect of a change in the exchange rate when the home price remains the same (£100 in Table 4.1)? When the exchange rate is £1 = $2, the price in the export market is $200, but when the exchange rate depreciates to £1 = $1, the price in the export market falls to $100. This fall in price increases export sales and leads to faster export volume growth. $Pf_$$ is the price of imports in the overseas currency and $Pf_£$ the price charged in the home market. When the exchange rate falls, the price paid in the home market goes up, benefiting the domestic producer who sells more at the expense of the now dearer imported product, so leakages from the circular flow of income fall. As a result, GDP also goes up.

If the exchange rate goes up (appreciates), exactly the opposite happens. Table 4.1 shows that prices in export markets rise when the pound is stronger. This rise will reduce export volume and hence exogenous demand. Note also the fall in import prices, which increases both import volume and the level of leakages from the circular flow of income.

There are many examples of the effect of exchange rates on exogenous demand and GDP. An increase in the exchange rate, such as that which occurred in the UK between 1996 and 2000, reduces trade competitiveness and exports. It also increases import leakages from the circular flow of income. This reduces the demand for domestically produced goods and output growth falls as a result.

If the exchange rate falls, the opposite happens. The strong growth of the euro-area economies in 2000 was a direct result of the fall in the euro after its introduction in 1999. The depreciation of the Korean won and other Asian currencies in 1997/98 had the same effect on those economies in 1999/2000.

Why does the exchange rate change? The exchange rate is determined in the foreign exchange market and reflects the forces of both supply and demand in that market. The drivers of supply and demand in the foreign exchange (FOREX) market are set out in Table 4.2.

If the demand for home currency rises, the exchange rate also rises (appreciates). What causes this to happen? An increase in the demand for home assets is a common driver.

Table 4.2 Drivers of supply and demand in the FOREX market

Demand for home currency rises (falls) if:
- Exports rise (fall)
- Demand for home assets from overseas investors rises (falls)

Supply of home currency rises (falls) if:
- Imports rise (fall)
- Demand for overseas assets from home investors rises (falls)

This will happen if home interest rates rise, increasing the desire for overseas investors or home-based investors to deposit their money in the home economy. Similarly, if foreign interest rates fall, the impact on investor behaviour will lead to a rise in the exchange rate of the home economy. An increase in exports from the home economy will lead to increased demand for the home currency by foreign buyers, which appreciates the exchange rate. A decrease in imports has the same effect because home residents who want less foreign currency to pay for the imports decrease the supply of home currency in the FOREX market. Test your understanding of these ideas by filling in the blank boxes in Table 4.3. Use arrows to indicate the direction of change.

Knowledge of these relationships helps a business to anticipate government policy, especially with respect to interest rates. Rises in interest rates will take place if a government wants to stabilize exchange rates that are under downward pressure. The idea is to increase the demand from international investors for home assets by increasing the interest rate on them. As noted above, this is the experience of many Asian and Latin American economies.

In summary, booms can only occur if there is an increase in the aggregate demand for goods and services. Similarly, slumps would not happen if the aggregate demand for products did not fall. From a business strategy point of view it is important to keep track of movements both in aggregate demand and in the key determinants of these movements, and to relate this to knowledge of the macroeconomic exposure of the business and its markets.

4.3 Aggregate supply and the end of booms

It is evident from Figure 4.2 that booms end. At the beginning of the 1990s the boom in the OECD economies ended with a bump. Why? The answer to this question is usually found on the supply side of the macroeconomy. At the peak of a boom, shortages of machine capacity begin to appear. Supplies of key skilled labour diminish. As a result, output growth slows down because firms cannot keep up with the growth in demand.

Table 4.3 Exchange rates in the FOREX market

	Demand for £ by overseas residents	Supply of £ by UK residents	£/euro (price of pounds/euros)
Home interest rate down			
Foreign interest rate down			
Current balance of payments worsens			
Home inflation rate up			

In addition to these purely physical constraints there are other effects which bring booms to an end. Emerging supply shortages drive up input (labour and raw materials) prices and this raises costs and hence inflation, i.e. the rate of increase of prices goes up.

This is the idea that underlies the so-called *Phillips curve* which is depicted in Figure 4.5. A boom causes a fall in unemployment from U_1 to U_2. Employers experiencing recruitment difficulties, especially of skilled workers, will bid up their wage offers. To prevent a loss of workers, others will follow suit. Workers will be in a stronger bargaining position to drive up wages. In short, an acceleration of the rate of wage inflation from W_1 to W_2 will occur. Since labour costs are a very significant part of the average costs of production incurred by firms, any increase in the rate of wage inflation will have a positive effect on the rate of price infla-tion. There may also be other more direct routes that lead to higher prices. For example, through, the increase in profit margins that occurs in booms in GDP growth. The evidence from upturns in Europe and North America is that even in historically inflation-prone economies such as the UK, France and Italy, the growth in inflation is much more muted in the 1990s, so there is now much less inflation at all stages of the business cycle.

The result is that inflation no longer takes off as it did in the 1970s and, more spectacu-larly, in the hyperinflations afflicting parts of Eastern and Central Europe in the early 1990s. One reason for this slowdown in inflation is the much lower rate at which imported raw material and energy prices are rising. Other factors may also impinge on the relationship depicted in Figure 4.5, such as prices and incomes policy of the kind still very much in use in Ireland, the strength of trade unions, the rate of growth of labour productivity, and so on. You should try to think through the effects of changes in these factors. The impact of higher inflation on a boom is reinforced by the response of governments and central banks.

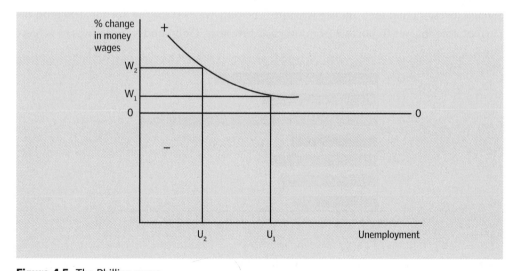

Figure 4.5 The Phillips curve

Banks that target the rate of inflation will tend to drive up interest rates to contain an expected rise in inflation. A rise in the rate increases the costs of borrowing, hence reducing private sector and overall aggregate demand. This slows down GDP growth and brings the boom to an end and brings inflation down to hit the target rate.

A further factor that sometimes brings a boom to an end arises from the effect of a boom on the overseas balance of payments. Rapid growth in output increases income through the circular flow mechanism and this causes an increase in a country's imports to take place. At the same time, the strong pressure of demand can lead to a reduction in exports as home producers seek to meet burgeoning home demand. Hence the balance of trade (exports − imports) worsens.

In fact, this is key to understanding the crisis in the East Asian economies in 1997. This region of the world, almost without exception, grew exceptionally fast throughout the 1990s. So successful were these economies that the World Bank promoted the idea of an 'East Asian Miracle' and urged other emerging economies to look to East Asia to find the ingredients for successful long-run performance.

Figure 4.6 shows GDP growth across the world and it indicates just how successful East Asia was in the period up until 1997 (note that the only OECD country which compares with East Asia is Ireland). However, this rapid growth in GDP led to strong growth in imports and a slowdown in exports, especially in Thailand. The effect on the current account (i.e. where trade flows are recorded) of the balance of payments was substantial deficits. Normally, as you can see from the analysis of exchange rate movements above, this deficit should lead to a fall in the demand for Asian currencies and an increase in their supply in FOREX markets. As a result the exchange rate should have fallen but most of the region's economies had fixed their exchange rates against the US dollar, partly to persuade foreign investors that their money was safe. The only way left to 'pay' for the deficit on the current account was to borrow from overseas investors. Only modest incentives to achieve

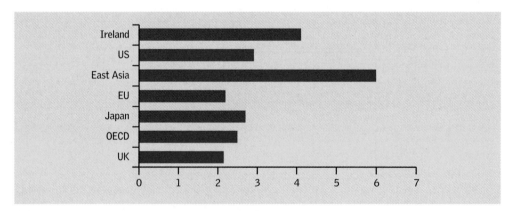

Figure 4.6 Growth of real GDP (% per annum) 1980–97
Source: World Bank.

this were necessary since the international financial community also believed a 'miracle' was happening and lending to East Asian economies was a 'good bet'.

You can see in Figure 4.7 (which also shows the position of Mexico in 1994 when similar events occurred as a result of the same rapid GDP growth) the impact on the overseas debt position of various Asian economies. Much of the debt was short-term lending by East Asian banks from OECD financial institutions which lent it on to local companies to fuel the boom (*see* Figure 4.8).

Problems started (in Thailand) in 1997 when a GDP-boom-driven 'bubble' in the property market burst. Property developers had borrowed heavily and overinvested in projects on which they could not secure a short-run return. Several went out of business with an adverse effect on the poorly regulated banking sector. The ensuing loss of confidence led to a flight of foreign investors and irresistible downward pressure on the exchange rate. This contagion spread to other Asian economies, causing a stock market crash throughout the region. The flight of foreign investors caused exchange rates to fall, as suggested by your answers in Table 3. As a result the US dollar value of East Asian debt soared which, combined with the stock market crash, led to dramatic falls in GDP growth in 1998 (*see* Figure 4.9) as reductions in wealth and increasing debt hit exogenous aggregate demand growth. One exception to these events was Hong Kong, where the monetary authorities were able to resist the downward pressure on the HK dollar by using some of Hong Kong's huge reserves of foreign currencies, including US dollars.

However, the fall in the exchange rate also brought relief to most of the East Asian economies so that by mid 1999 the boost to international competitiveness led to significant increases in GDP being reported in several economies in the region. This emphasizes the important role often played by the exchange rate as a 'shock absorber'.

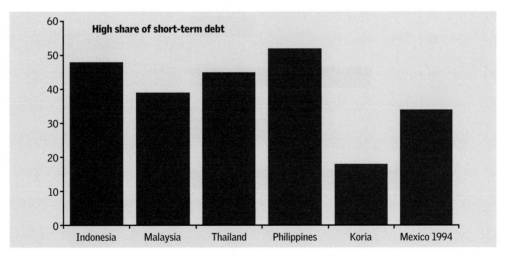

Figure 4.7 Foreign debt as a % of GDP in 1997
Source: World Bank.

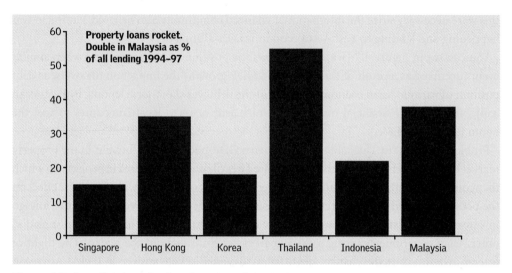

Figure 4.8 Growth in bank lending (% points of GDP) 1991–97
Source: World Bank.

The Asian experience illustrates the importance of **balanced growth** in the emerging economies. Balanced growth implies a growth in the aggregate demand for goods and services that is in line with the growth in aggregate supply, not only of physical assets such as machines and labour (i.e. 'resources'), but also in capabilities such as skill and knowledge, some of which arise from the large learning curve effects evident in emerging economies. More rapid growth in demand is a characteristic of emerging economies where there are few slow-growing mature markets, but if this proceeds at a pace which is faster than aggregate

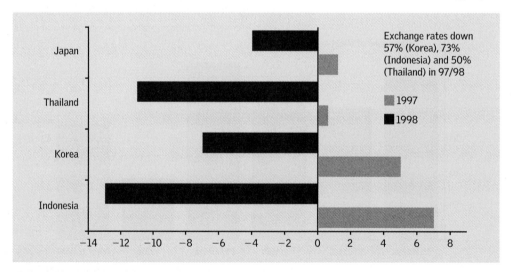

Figure 4.9 GDP growth in Asia 1997/8 (%)
Source: World Bank.

supply, the impact on imports, especially of the capital goods necessary for sustained development, creates financial pressures that are difficult to manage.

The Asian crisis also reflects the development and interdependence of the global economy. Rapid growth in the region would not have been possible without the huge inflows of both long-term (i.e. investment in fixed assets) and short-term (i.e. investment in financial assets) capital from the OECD economies. The growth in global financial markets and the global strategies of large transnational and largely OECD-based businesses are crucial here. Also important is the issue of interdependence. Crisis in Asia carried an important threat for the OECD economies. It had obvious effects on global financial stability but also impacted on global trade and hence global GDP growth. It required the governments of the OECD economies to take an increasingly global view and to take on board the global implications of their domestic policies. This is exactly what happened in 1998 when OECD interest rates were cut at a time when most commentators expected them to rise. The effect was to create OECD markets for goods and services produced not only in the OECD but also in the non-OECD world.

4.4 National competitive advantage and long-run macroeconomic performance

One central feature of the fast-growing economies in Asia is a high degree of **national competitive advantage**, especially in international trade. They have, as a result, achieved strong trade performance and this is reflected in the big increase in their share of world trade, notably in manufacturing goods, which represent 60 per cent of world exports and which is the fastest growing global product market.

Of course, no nation actually engages in international trade itself. This is done by the individual businesses operating in a nation state and competing in the global markets for their products. A competitive economy is, hence, one in which the average business located in the economy enjoys global competitive advantage. Note the emphasis on *average*. Even in the most uncompetitive economies there are still firms with **competitive advantage**. There just are not many of them. Similarly, there are laggards in the most competitive nation states, but not many. What follows from this link is that competitive advantage is not simply to do with a 'natural' endowment of resources, but can be created by policy at *both* company and national level. Company-level global competitive advantage can be facilitated by a favourable political–economic context, but there is still a role for company-level strategic 'actions' in building both *company and national* competitive advantage.

What determines **national competitiveness**? The lessons of the extensive research (including Porter) into this topic emphasize four crucial interdependent factors:

* High levels of investment in 'factors of production' and innovation.
* Effective production and effective business.

- A supportive home market.

- Maintaining domestic competition and maximizing 'external' economies.

Case box: **The Big Mac index**

The world economy looks very different once countries' output is adjusted for differences in prices

HOW fast is the world economy growing? How important is China as an engine of growth? How much richer is the average person in America than in China? The answers to these huge questions depend crucially on how you convert the value of output in different countries into a common currency. Converting national GDPs into dollars at market exchange rates is misleading. Prices tend to be lower in poor economies, so a dollar of spending in China, say, is worth a lot more than a dollar in America. A better method is to use purchasing-power parities (PPP), which take account of price differences.

The theory of purchasing-power parity says that in the long run exchange rates should move towards rates that would equalise the prices of an identical basket of goods and services in any two countries. This is the thinking behind *The Economist's* Big Mac index. Invented in 1986 as a light-hearted guide to whether currencies are at their 'correct' level, our 'basket' is a McDonald's Big Mac, which is produced locally in almost 120 countries.

The Big Mac PPP is the exchange rate that would leave a burger in any country costing the same as in America. The first column of our table converts the local price of a Big Mac into dollars at current exchange rates. The average price of a Big Mac in four American cities is $2.90 (including tax). The cheapest shown in the table is in the Philippines ($1.23), the most expensive in Switzerland ($4.90). In other words, the Philippine peso is the world's most undervalued currency, the Swiss franc its most overvalued.

The second column calculates Big Mac PPPs by dividing the local currency price by the American price. For instance, in Japan a Big Mac costs ¥262. Dividing this by the American price of $2.90 produces a dollar PPP against the yen of ¥90, compared with its current rate of ¥113, suggesting that the yen is 20% undervalued. In contrast, the euro (based on a weighted average of Big Mac prices in the euro area) is 13% overvalued. But perhaps the most interesting finding is that all emerging-market currencies are undervalued against the dollar. The Chinese yuan, on which much ink has been spilled in recent months, looks 57% too cheap.

The Big Mac index was never intended as a precise forecasting tool. Burgers are not traded across borders as the PPP theory demands; prices are distorted by differences in the cost of non-tradable goods and services, such as rents.

Yet these very failings make the Big Mac index useful, since looked at another way it can help to measure countries' differing costs of living. That a Big Mac is cheap in China does not

The hamburger standard

	Big Mac price in dollars*	Implied PPP† of the dollar	Under (−)/ over (+) valuation against the dollar, %		Big Mac price in dollars*	Implied PPP† of the dollar	Under (−)/ over (+) valuation against the dollar, %
United States	2.90	–	–	Aruba	2.29	1.41	−21
Argentina	1.48	1.50	−49	Belarus	1.37	1021	−53
Australia	2.27	1.12	−22	Bulgaria	1.85	1.03	−36
Brazil	1.70	1.86	−41	Colombia	2.35	2241	−19
Britain	3.37	1.54§	+16	Costa Rica	2.61	390	−10
Canada	2.33	1.10	−20	Croatia	2.42	5.14	−17
Chile	2.18	4.83	−25	Dom. Rep.	1.32	20.7	−54
China	1.26	3.59	−57	Estonia	2.27	10.2	−22
Czech Rep.	2.13	19.5	−27	Fiji	2.35	1.47	−19
Denmark	4.46	9.57	+54	Georgia	1.90	1.26	−34
Egypt	1.62	3.45	−44	Guatemala	2.01	5.52	−31
Euro area	3.28**	1.06††	+13	Honduras	1.98	12.4	−32
Hong Kong	1.54	4.14	−47	Iceland	6.01	151	107
Hungary	2.52	1.83	−13	Jamaica	1.88	39.0	−35
Indonesia	1.77	5,552	−39	Jordan	3.65	0.89	26
Japan	2.33	90.3	−20	Kuwait	7.33	0.74	153
Malaysia	1.33	1.74	−54	Latvia	2.00	0.38	−31
Mexico	2.08	8.28	−28	Lebanon	2.84	1483	−2
New Zealand	2.65	1.50	−8	Lithuania	2.26	2.24	−22
Peru	2.57	3.10	−11	Macau	1.40	3.86	−52
Philippines	1.23	23.8	−57	Macedonia	1.84	32.8	−36
Poland	1.63	2.17	−44	Moldova	1.93	7.93	−33
Russia	1.45	14.5	−50	Morocco	0.26	0.82	−91
Singapore	1.92	1.14	−34	Nicaragua	2.19	11.9	−25
South Africa	1.86	4.28	−36	Norway	5.18	12.2	79
South Korea	2.72	1,103	−6	Pakistan	1.90	37.9	−34
Sweden	3.94	10.3	+36	Qatar	0.68	0.85	−77
Switzerland	4.90	2.17	+69	Saudi Arabia	0.64	0.83	−78
Taiwan	2.24	25.9	−23	Slovakia	1.98	22.8	−32
Thailand	1.45	20.3	−50	Slovenia	2.42	166	−17
Turkey	2.58	1,362,069	−11	Sri Lanka	1.41	48.3	−51
Venezuela	1.48	1,517	−49	Ukraine	1.36	2.50	−53
				UAE	0.67	0.84	−77
				Uruguay	1.00	10.3	−65

*At current exchange rates
†Purchasing-power parity
Average of New York, Chicago, San Francisco and Atlanta
§Dollars per pound
**Weighted average of member countries
††Dollars per euro

Sources: McDonald's; The Economist.

in fact prove that the yuan is being held massively below its fair value, as many American politicians claim. It is quite natural for average prices to be lower in poorer countries and therefore for their currencies to appear cheap.

The prices of traded goods will tend to be similar to those in developed economies. But the prices of non-tradable products, such as housing and labour-intensive services, are generally much lower. A haircut is, for instance, much cheaper in Beijing than in New York.

One big implication of lower prices is that converting a poor country's GDP into dollars at market exchange rates will significantly understate the true size of its economy and its living standards. If China's GDP is converted into dollars using the Big Mac PPP, it is almost two-and-a-half-times bigger than if converted at the market exchange rate. Meatier and more sophisticated estimates of PPP, such as those used by the IMF, suggest that the required adjustment is even bigger.

Weight watchers

The global economic picture thus looks hugely different when examined through a PPP lens. Take the pace of global growth. Anyone wanting to calculate this needs to bundle together countries' growth rates, with each one weighted according to its share of world GDP. Using weights based on market exchange rates, the world has grown by an annual average of only 1.9% over the past three years. Using PPP, as the IMF does, global growth jumps to a far more robust 3.1% a year.

The main reason for this difference is that using PPP conversion factors almost doubles the weight of the emerging economies, which have been growing much faster. Measured at market exchange rates, emerging economies account for less than a quarter of global output. But measured using PPP they account for almost half.

Small wonder, then, that global economic rankings are dramatically transformed when they are done on a PPP basis rather than market exchange rates. America remains number one, but China leaps from seventh place to second, accounting for 13% of world output. India jumps into fourth place ahead of Germany, and both Brazil and Russia are bigger than Canada. Similarly, market exchange rates also exaggerate inequality. Using market rates, the average American is 33 times richer than the average Chinese; on a PPP basis, he is 'only' seven times richer.

The way in which economies are measured also has a huge impact on which country has contributed most to global growth in recent years. Using GDP converted at market rates China has accounted for only 7% of the total increase in the dollar value of global GDP over the past three years, compared with America's 25%. But on PPP figures, China has accounted for almost one-third of global real GDP growth and America only 13%.

This helps to explain why commodity prices in general and oil prices in particular have been surging, even though growth has been relatively subdued in the rich world since 2000. Emerging economies are not only growing much faster than rich economies and are more intensive in their use of raw materials and energy, but they also account for a bigger chunk of global output if measured correctly. As Charles Dumas, an economist at Lombard Street Research, neatly puts it, even if a Chinese loaf is a quarter of the cost of a loaf in America, it uses the same amount of flour.

All measures of PPP are admittedly imperfect. But most economists agree that they give a more accurate measure of the relative size of economies than market exchange rates – and a better understanding of some of the dramatic movements in world markets. The humble burger should be part of every economist's diet

Source: 'Food for thought', *The Economist,* 29 May 2004, pp. 75–6.
© The Economist Newspaper Limited, London (29 May 2004).

Questions for discussion

1 Draw up a list of strengths and weaknesses of market exchange rates versus purchasing-power parity for assessing the relative size of different national economies.

2 In assessing a foreign country as a place in which to make investments in plant and machinery, what specific advantages would you get from the use of a PPP approach?

3 The PPP approach suggests that one country (such as Britain) has its currency overvalued against the dollar whereas another country (such as Brazil) has its currency quite heavily undervalued. What does this imply about the relative strength of these two economies and their competitiveness in world markets?

4.4.1 High levels of investment in 'factors of production' and innovation

In competitive economies, the typical firm invests heavily in new products and processes. This enables the firm to produce better and cheaper products and to do so in effective ways. Product innovation is part and parcel of building new markets and the creation of competitive advantage in them. Process innovation is necessary to produce high-quality products in a cost-effective way.

One necessary condition for innovation to take place is a high level of investment in new plant infrastructure and in human capital. Porter calls this the **'factor conditions'** necessary for building national competitive advantage. 'Factors' are factors of production and refer to the resources of capital and labour. Excellence in 'factor creation' is a feature of the fast-growing Asian economies. Consider the facts shown in Figure 4.10. The high level of investment (approximately twice the level of the average OECD economy) in new plant and infrastructure facilitates the rapid diffusion of new up-to-date technologies and speeds up the introduction of new 'state of the art' products. Note that this high level of investment is helped by substantial flows of inward investment from the rich OECD countries and by the very high levels of savings in the region (meaning proportionately less consumption expenditure), which have also grown to a point at which savings as a share of GDP are over twice the level of the OECD countries as a whole.

A high level of investment in fixed capital is necessary for a globally competitive business and for a fast-growing economy, but it is not sufficient. It is also necessary to invest in human capital. A further feature of the East Asia region, emphasized in the research conducted by the World Bank, is a high level of investment in human capital – that is, in the education and training of the workforce. If effective use is to be made of high levels of investment in physical capital, it is important to have a well-educated and trained labour force. This is especially important to securing the innovation benefits of fixed investment. Modern products and processes, even of basic goods such as textiles, require a skilled, flexible and trained labour force.

The World Bank calculates that between 26 and 56 per cent of the growth of GDP experienced in the region (the 56 per cent figure refers to Hong Kong) is the product of high levels of human capital investment. In contrast, the comparative position of the UK within Western Europe, notably in the provision of vocational education, is very weak. Part of this investment, especially on the vocational side, is carried out by business but, clearly, a nation's government has a critical role to play in building both company and national *capabilities*. Ensuring that a nation's workforce is both highly numerate and literate is a basic and essential requirement of any publicly provided or privately sponsored education system.

The reason government's role is so important is because of the presence of the significant market failures in the provision of education. To understand the concept of market failure, refer back to Chapter 3 where the market demand and supply curves are explained. It is shown again in this chapter, in Figure 4.11. The simple idea underpinning the market demand curve is that an increase (or decrease) in price will decrease (or increase) the quantity demanded in the market. In Figure 4.11 recall the market supply curve which implies that an increase in the price of products increases the willingness of producers to increase their supply.

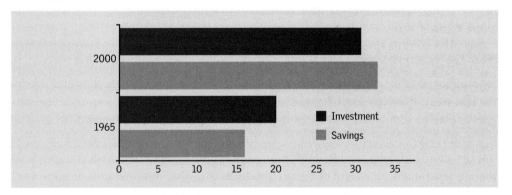

Figure 4.10 Savings and investment in East Asia as % of GDP
Source: World Bank.

In the market the interaction of demand and supply decisions will lead to a price of P_1, with Q_1 being sold and produced. If price were above P_1 at, say, P_2, more would be supplied (Q_3) than could be sold (Q_2), so price would fall to P_1. The opposite would happen if price were below P_1. Competitive market forces rule. If firms succeed in building market power (for example, a monopoly created by merger and/or acquisition), the price can be driven above the market level of P_1, as we saw in Chapter 3.

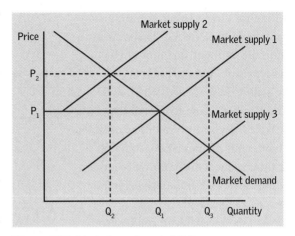

Figure 4.11 Markets and market failure

The market supply curve assumes an underlying relation between costs borne by the firm and the willingness to supply goods. However, the only costs the firm takes into account are the *private* costs of capital, labour, materials, etc. which it bears itself.

However, from society's point of view, there may be important social costs or benefits which the firm does not take into account in its decision making. For example, a firm may pollute a river through its production. In this case, the Market supply curve 1 in Figure 4.11 does not reflect these extra social costs arising from producing the firm's product. On the other hand, Market supply curve 2 does include these pollution costs and it suggests that the price of the polluting product should be P_2, with an amount sold of Q_2. Clearly, the market solution at P_1 and Q_1 leads to significant overproduction. In other words, the market *fails*, because the price charged and the quantity sold in the free market do not reflect all the costs and benefits of production.

Market failure also occurs when there are important social benefits that the private provider does not take into account. A good example is the provision of education and training. Business needs a highly trained and educated labour force and this is also key to long-run macroeconomic success. However, if the provision of education and training is left to the market, there will be substantial underprovision. This is shown in Figure 4.12. DD_1 represents the demand curve associated with the private benefits received from education /training. But there are social benefits that accrue additionally and the real demand curve should be DD_2. Thus, the market fails because it provides less education than it should, viz. $Q_2 - Q_1$. Note that the price effect, $P_2 - P_1$, depends on the slope of the supply curve. If there are economies of scale in education/training, the supply curve could be flat and the price effect could be zero or very small, but the quantity effect (underprovision of education) would be correspondingly larger. One way of dealing with this is for government to provide subsidies for education/training so that the supply curve shifts from SS_1 to SS_2. This would result in the 'optimal' quantity of education provision closer to point Q_2.

The failure is worsened when skills are transferable across firms. All firms want skilled labour to build their own capabilities but the risk of poaching by other firms reduces the incentive to any individual firm to carry out the investment.

The market mechanism could also fail in the provision of education and training because there is a missing market. The missing market is a capital market to finance investment by individuals in their own education and training. As a result of this failure, there is a lower level of investment in human capital than is socially and economically desirable and lower than is needed to build company and national competitive advantage. This problem arises because the providers of capital (for example, banks) have no reliable information to enable them to distinguish individuals who are good risks from those who are bad risks. This phenomenon is called **adverse selection**.

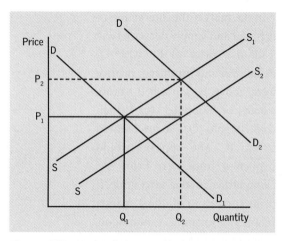

Figure 4.12 Market failure in education and training

The solution to these market failures is some form of government intervention to correct the market failure. Taxes, for example, are often used to correct for the failure to take into account the social costs in private production. Taxes on tobacco are a good example. Smoking damages health and, as a result, causes social costs to be incurred. In the case of social benefits generated by education and training, direct provision by the state, or subsidies to private providers, reflect the social benefit to the economy. To overcome the missing capital market, grants or cheap loans could be given to individuals and businesses to enable them to invest in education and training. However, whatever is done, the key requirement is that the government recognizes its critical role in the provision of human capital and that business understands the motivation for this outside intervention in the operation of the market.

> *Building a highly skilled and well-educated labour force is essential to competitiveness at both the business and national levels, but it is not enough.*

Factor creation in the form of skilled labour facilitates innovation and upgrading, which is fundamental to the creation of company and national competitive advantage. A further necessary condition for rapid innovation to take place is a high level of expenditure on research and development. Examine Figure 4.13, which shows spending on R&D as a percentage of GDP in a number of large OECD economies. In Japan, R&D spending is almost at US levels and has increased between 1981 and 2000 at an impressive rate. Look at the UK for a contrast. The differences in performance shown in Figure 4.13 reflect the different rates of innovation by the business sector, especially in manu-facturing firms. This performance contributed to the competitive advantage of the Japanese nation relative to European nations, and

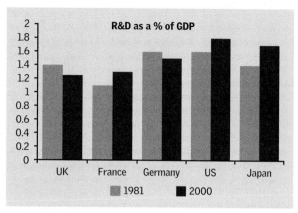

Figure 4.13 R&D as % of GDP
Source: OECD (www.oecd.org).

the strong growth in GDP it achieved in the 1960–90 period. It enabled Japanese industry to increase its share of non-American patents taken out in the US from 1.9 per cent in 1958 to 41.3 per cent in 1988. Over the same period, the UK share fell from 23.4 per cent to 10.8 per cent. It is also important that there is a match between education, training and R&D. Porter (1990) writes, 'To support competitive advantage, a factor (like skilled labour) must be highly specialized to an industry's particular needs'.

> *A high rate of innovation is a key element in business policy and a central ingredient of competitiveness, both in the firm and in an economy.*

Case box: Is outsourcing/offshoring bad for the economy and bad for jobs?

Contrary to what John Kerry and George Bush seem to think, outsourcing actually sustains American jobs

In February 2004 the president's chief economic adviser, Gregory Mankiw, once Harvard's youngest tenured professor, attracted a storm of abuse. He told Congress that if a thing or a service could be produced more cheaply abroad, then Americans were better off importing it than producing it at home. As an example, Mr Mankiw uses the case of radiologists in India analysing the X-rays, sent via the internet, of American patients.

Republicans and Democrats both rebuked Mr Mankiw for approving of jobs going overseas. The White House gave Mr Mankiw only lukewarm support – unsurprisingly, since George Bush recently signed a bill forbidding the outsourcing of federal contracts overseas. And the Democratic presidential contenders? The Wisconsin primary early in 2004 was dominated by the subject of jobs, and the failure of the Bush administration to do enough to protect them from going off to India. Democrat presidential hopefuls such as John Edwards and John Kerry have also seemed very protectionist, using language that criticizes American bosses of betraying American workers by moving jobs overseas, presumably to boost returns for fat-cat investors.

The business lobby seems to be in disarray. 'Tech jobs are fleeing to India faster than ever,' moans the cover of *Wired*. Watch *Lou Dobbs Tonight*, America's main business show, and every factory-closing is hailed as proof of America's relentless 'hollowing-out' at the hands of dark forces in China, India and indeed the White House. Strangely, no mention is made of the fact that a pretty tiny proportion of all jobs lost actually go overseas.

So what is really happening? *The Economist* suggests three themes.

◆ Although America's economy has, overall, lost jobs since the start of the decade, the vast majority of these job losses are cyclical in nature, not structural. Now that the economy is recovering after the recession of 2001, so will the job picture, perhaps dramatically, over the next year.

◆ Outsourcing (or 'offshoring') has been going on for centuries, but still accounts for a tiny proportion of the jobs constantly being created and destroyed within America's economy. Even at the best of times, the American economy has a tremendous rate of 'churn' – over 2 million jobs a month. In all, the process creates many more jobs than it destroys: 24 million more during the 1990s. The process allocates resources – money and people – to where they can be most productive, helped by competition, including from outsourcing, that lowers prices. In the long run, higher productivity is the only way to create higher standards of living across an economy.

◆ Even though service-sector outsourcing is still modest, the growing globalization of information-technology (IT) services should indeed have a big effect on service-sector productivity. During the 1990s, American factories became much more efficient by using IT; now shops, banks, hospitals and so on may learn the same lesson. This will have a beneficial effect that stretches beyond the IT firms. Even though some IT tasks will be done abroad, many more jobs will be created in America, and higher-paying ones to boot.

In the absence of an obvious jobs recovery since the downturn in 2001, it is perhaps not surprising that the myth arose that the American economy was being buffeted by structural, not cyclical, forces. Yet it nevertheless is a myth – as three notable economists, William Baumol, Alan Blinder and Edward Wolff, point out in a recent book (*Downsizing in America: Reality, Causes and Consequences*, Russell Sage Foundation).

Churning, they point out, has being going on in the American jobs market for years, and 'the creation of new jobs always overwhelms the destruction of old jobs by a huge margin.' Between 1980 and 2002, America's population grew by 23.9 per cent. The number of employed Americans, on the other hand, grew by 37.4 per cent. Today, 138.6 million Americans are in work, a near-record, both in absolute terms and as a proportion of the population.

Of course some firms wither – Reynolds Tobacco's workforce shrank by nine-tenths between 1980 and 2002 – but others grow: Wal-Mart's by 4,700 per cent. During the 1990s, about a quarter of all American businesses shed jobs in a typical three-month period, equivalent to 8 million jobs. Yet jobs created greatly outnumbered these, to the tune of 24 million over the decade.

The process leads to incremental shifts that can have profound cumulative consequences for some sectors of the economy. In 1960 only 1 in 25 workers was employed in the business-services and healthcare industries. Today, 1 in 6 is. In terms of output, manufacturing has risen, but, thanks to that productivity spurt, these goods are produced by fewer people – 12 per cent of the workforce, less than half the proportion of three decades ago.

Instead of focusing on jobs lost to the globalization of information technology, Catherine Mann of the Institute for International Economics in Washington looks at globalization's power to reduce prices and so help spread new technology, new practices and job-creating investment through the economy. She uses the example of cheaper IT hardware, one of the main aspects of globalization in the 1990s. Most of the drop in prices for PCs, mainframes and so on was caused by the relentless advance of technology; but she still thinks that trade and globalized production – all those Dell Computer factories in China, for instance – was responsible for 10–30 per cent of the fall in hardware prices. These lower prices led to higher American productivity growth and added $230 billion of extra GDP between 1995 and 2002, equivalent to an extra 0.3 percentage points of growth a year.

Will the trend lead to jobs going overseas? You bet, but that is not a disaster. For a start, America runs a large and growing surplus in services with the rest of the world. The jobs lost will be low-paying ones, such as bank tellers and switchboard operators. Trade protection will not save such jobs: if they do not go overseas, they are still at risk from automation.

By contrast, jobs will be created that demand skills to handle the deeper incorporation of information technology, and the pay for these jobs will be high. The demand for computer-support specialists and software engineers, to take two examples, is expected by the Bureau of Labour Statistics (BLS) to double between 2000 and 2010. Demand for database administrators is expected to rise by three-fifths. Among the top score of occupations that the BLS reckons will see the highest growth, half will need IT skills. As it is, between 1999 and 2003 (that is, including during the recession) jobs were created, not lost, in a whole host of white-collar occupations said to be particularly susceptible to outsourcing.

Yes, individuals will be hurt in the process, and the focus of public policy should be directed towards providing a safety net for them, as well as ensuring that Americans have education to match the new jobs being created. By contrast, regarding globalization as the enemy, as many politicians do, is a much greater threat to America's economic health than any Indian software programmer.

Source: summarized and adapted from 'The great hollowing-out myth', *The Economist*, 19 February 2004.

Questions for discussion

1 Outline the case in favour of outsourcing.
2 Under what conditions would the above reasons not hold good?

4.4.2 **Effective production and effective business**

A second requirement for achieving global competitiveness is achieving effective production. Partly this is about achieving low-cost production through the exploitation of scale and scope economies. That requires the speedy adoption of both production technologies (investment) and production management techniques, which result in high levels and strong growth in input productivity. The World Bank Report on East Asia attributes a third (on average) of the high GDP growth in the region to the effects of rapid improvement in the productivity of all the inputs used in production.

Effective production is not just about low costs. It is also about putting in place the conditions that create competitive advantage at the business level. Porter's 'diamond' analysis identifies the importance to national competitive advantage of firm strategy and structure, and in particular the organizational frameworks which facilitate the development of firm-level competitive advantage. He also emphasizes that no single managerial system is universally appropriate, so that '*competitiveness in a particular industry results from the convergence of the management practices and organisational modes favoured in the country*'. A key issue here is the way management practices encourage commitment and effort from the entire labour force.

National competitiveness requires business to be effective in its use of inputs and to be focused on the development of its own competitive advantage.

4.4.3 **A supportive home market**

This third ingredient is given especial importance in Porter's 'diamond':

> *Nations gain competitive advantage in industries where the home market gives their companies a clearer or earlier picture of emerging buyer needs, and where demanding buyers pressure companies to innovate faster and achieve more sophisticated competitive advantages than their foreign rivals.* (Porter, 1990)

A good example is Denmark's global expertise in windmills for electricity generation. In part, this reflects the 'green' preferences of Danish consumers, but it also reflects local rural community preference for small-scale, local electricity generation. Another example is the competitive advantage of Italian textile and footwear manufacturers. The home market preference for well-designed, innovative and well-crafted clothes and shoes has put pressure on Italian manufacturers to meet the demanding home consumer and this has contributed to their global competitive advantage. Other examples can be found in Porter (1990).

4.4.4 **Maintaining domestic competition and maximizing 'external' economies**

The fourth key ingredient in building a competitive economy noted by Michael Porter (1990) is the responsibility of government for maintaining high levels of domestic competition and, hence, low levels of **horizontal integration**. Horizontal integration is the process of merger in which firms producing the same products come together, thus reducing the degree of competition in the market. As we saw in Chapter 3 market concentration of this kind leads to another form of market failure arising from the growth of market power, which enables firms to charge higher prices than would prevail under competitive conditions. Porter draws attention to the large number of rivals producing the same product in Japan (*see* Figure 4.14) in the period of greatest economic success. Similarly, McAleese (2004) shows that the dominance of large firms in the UK is over three times the rate found in Japan. In Sweden it is nearly seven times the Japanese rate. Domestic rivalry also pressurizes companies to innovate and improve, and hones the skills necessary for successful international competition and this helps explain, in part, the international competitive success of Japanese business.

In apparent contradiction, Porter also emphasizes the need to maximize those business synergies which require a high degree of inter-firm co-operation. These synergies, or **'agglomeration economies'** as economists call them, arise from the location of firms in 'clusters'. These clusters create benefits for all the firms in the cluster which lower their costs and increase their competitive advantage. Porter uses the success of the Italian footwear industry as an example to support his argument. Italian designers and manufacturers of shoes, of leather and leather-working machinery have formed 'clustering' relationships which involve a high degree of co-operative interaction along vertical supply chains. Porter remarks that '*Close and ongoing interchange with suppliers and buyers is integral to the process of creating and sustaining competitive advantage in international competition.*'

A high degree of horizontal competition and of vertical co-operation leads to global competitiveness.

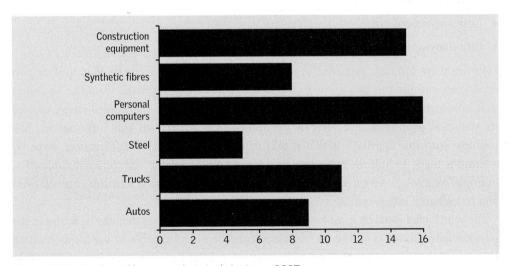

Figure 4.14 Number of home market rivals in Japan 1987
Source: Porter (1990) p. 82. Reprinted with permission of The Free Press, a division of Simon and Schuster Adult Publishing Group. Copyright © 1990 by Michael E. Porter. All rights reserved.

Knowledge of these four requirements for the creation of national competitive advantage is helpful to globalizing businesses, which need to take a long view of the markets in which they plan to locate. When the markets of interest are in the emerging economies, statistical forecasting of the future development of the macroeconomy is difficult, if not impossible. Therefore, in order to make useful judgements about long-run prospects, it makes sense to identify the key determinants of long-run economic success and to benchmark the markets of interest, in terms of their local performance, against these determinants.

Next we explore in more detail the way in which business can use other economic information as part of a strategy to build competitive advantage over its rivals.

4.5 Macroeconometric forecasting and business

Here we examine further the link between business and macroeconomic performance and explore further the implications for business strategy. As we have seen, effective strategy requires an insightful understanding of the macroeconomic environment. In part, this is needed to evaluate and explain past and current performance and this is what we have emphasized so far. However, strategy is about future actions, so a forward-looking view of the macroeconomic environment is also needed. One simple way to do this is to access one of the many published macroeconomic forecasts and to use that. A number of websites are available which contain the kind of forecasts that businesses need. Some of these websites are listed below:

- http://www.imf.org
- http://www.worldbank.org
- http://www.oecd.org
- http://www.niesr.ac.uk

How are these forecasts prepared? A starting point for most forecasters is to look at past experience and use this as a guide to the future. One simple approach would be to collect past information on a particular economic variable (for example, exchange rates), explore its statistical properties and forecast the future time path from this information. The problem with this approach is that it fails to use all the available information, since no attempt is made to link the behaviour of one economic variable with other variables. For example, we know from earlier in this chapter that the link between a nation's interest rates and its exchange rate is critical.

The solution adopted by most forecasters, including the forecasts that can be found in the websites listed above, is to build a macroeconometric model capable of use for forecasting purposes. A macroeconometric model consists of a set of equations that identify the links between macroeconomic variables. It will use all the macroeconomic links discussed before in this chapter and many others as well. One of the basic relationships in a macroeconometric model is that between aggregate demand and GDP. It assumes GDP growth is driven by growth in aggregate demand. It will be accompanied by a set of relationships that set down the variables that cause aggregate demand to change. The interest rate, for example, will feature as a determinant of both consumer demand and investment demand. Share prices and wealth will figure as drivers of consumer demand. Past experience is used to measure the impact of variables on each other. The objective of the model builder is to construct a set of relationships capable of explaining past history.

How do forecasts derived from macroeconometric models of this type perform? The answer is 'not very well'. In an article in the *Financial Times* in 1995, Professor John Kay reviewed the performance of 34 UK forecasts of GDP growth in the years after 1987. He found that the forecasts tended to cluster around an average value, but the average seldom forecasted accurately. He found all the forecasts in 1993 and 1994 were significantly below the actual growth rate, while the opposite was true in 1991 and 1992. A more recent OECD study of forecasts of both GDP growth and inflation for seven countries after 1974 found the same. Detailed results of this exercise can be found in McAleese (2004, Chapter 16).

Why are the published forecasts so notoriously inaccurate? The most important reason is that the models are constructed using past experience. They have to make a number of strong assumptions:

◆ *Links observed in the past continue in the future.* For example, assuming that interest rates will continue to influence investment, as they have done in the past, may not be correct. Cuts in interest rates may not stimulate investment if there is a crisis of business confidence.

◆ *The strength of the relationships embodied in the links in the model stays the same.* This may not be true. Increases in wages tend to follow increases in prices, but the size of the effect is a lot less now than in the 1970s and 1980s, so twenty-first-century inflation of prices will tend to be overestimated in a macroeconometric model which uses 1970s and 1980s data for its estimate of the strength of the link.

◆ *There are no events for which there is no historical experience.* This is clearly not true. When the price of oil quadrupled in the 1990s, forecasts of both inflation and GDP growth across the world were in error, because none incorporated a historical experience of a change of this magnitude.

◆ *Historical data exists and is a good representation of what has happened in the past.* This is especially problematic in emerging markets, where historical data is scarce and where the collection of statistics is at a rudimentary stage. Macroeconometric forecasts are unlikely to be accurate.

What can be done when uncertainty about the macroeconomic future cannot be eliminated by the use of a forecasting model? One solution is simply to accept that the risk is endemic and has to be managed as far as possible by shifting the risk to another party (at a price).

This is what is done when businesses are exposed to exchange rate risk. This may happen because they have a contract to buy a product (for example, raw materials) from an overseas supplier that wants to be paid at some time in the future in an overseas currency. Given the volatility of exchange rates and the notorious difficulty of forecasting movements in the rate, the business cannot predict what the cost of the purchase in the home currency will be at the date of payment. The simplest solution is to 'buy forward' – to enter into a contract with a bank to supply overseas currency at an agreed rate on the date of the payment to the overseas supplier. There will be a cost associated with this forward contract, but it eliminates risk and obviates the need to forecast the exchange rate between the home and the overseas currency. The problem is that forward markets of the kind we see for exchange rate dealings do not exist in many other areas where macroeconomic risk is critical to strategy.

Another solution is to adopt a signalling approach, that is, to use signals that past experience has said are good predictors of the future. This is a good solution to the problem for OECD-based businesses (for example, retailers such as Wal-Mart and Carrefour) seeking to pursue a global strategy. How do they select suitable emerging markets in which to build a presence? There are no reliable long-run forecasts of future macroeconomic performance to guide their decision. What could they do? One solution is to search in the national economies they wish to target for some of the favourable signals set out earlier in this chapter.

The failure of macroeconometric forecasting models to provide a *single* accurate view of the future does not mean these models have no role in strategy. Planning models using this deterministic approach to the future are not the only option for strategic 'actions' that need to be informed by some kind of forward-looking assessment. Another solution is to assess the historical impact of exogenous macroeconomic changes on the individual firm *and* its market(s). This assessment needs to be built upon the same econometric foundations, using the same statistical methodology, as embodied in the macro model.

This extended macroeconometric model enables the creation of a variety of 'what if' scenarios of market prices, volumes and so on. These scenarios set out the impact of a wide variety of uncontrollable shocks from the macroeconomic environment on the business. These shocks need to be managed so this methodology helps to establish some of the limits of strategic action. These scenarios could explore, for example, the impact of different home exchange rates or different rates of growth of world trade over a five-year period. This is no longer difficult. Ten years ago, economists needed up to six weeks to run a full five-year scenario on a mainframe computer. Now relatively inexperienced users can do this in seconds on a PC. It is a simple matter, once the model is built, to use it to think. (This is what you are asked to do in the tasks that accompany this chapter.)

4.6 Summary

A useful proposition with which to end this chapter is:

> *Businesses that do not understand their economic environment make strategic errors, sometimes catastrophic ones, especially if they do not know that booms and slumps are bound to end!*

This chapter is not intended to turn you into an economist. On the other hand, it is critical for managers to be sensible, practical economists because macroeconomics plays such a significant role and has such a direct impact on firms. The argument in Chapters 3 and 4 directs attention to the uncontrollable nature of economic forces and the contextual constraints that it imposes on managerial discretion. This chapter has detailed some of the major forces in the macroeconomy so that managers can, through analysis, understanding and preparation, be able at least to anticipate the pressures on the firm. There are two main themes here. The first considers the nature of the business cycle and the demand and supply characteristics of boom and bust. A well-informed and prepared firm might be able to take strategic decisions contra-cyclically so as to avoid herd behaviour in merely following the economy. The second theme is the nature of national competitiveness and the relation of firms to this. Much of the infrastructure of the economy falls within the range of government spending. Thus, the fortunes of firms in any economy are going to be dependent in part on the ability of governments to foster national competitiveness. But firms also need to respond to these pressures themselves in forming their own strategies so as to mitigate the undesirable effects of economic misfortunes.

All businesses are sensitive to macroeconomic shocks outside their control and have to find ways in which to manage them. Strategic 'actions' need an understanding of the contextual links between an individual company, its markets and GDP growth in both the home and export markets. Exchange rates play a particularly important role for the company that trades outside its own home market but also for those who face competition from imports and whose business is sensitive to GDP fluctuations in its own home economy. It also requires an understanding of how economies in general work and also of the particular economies in which the business's markets are located.

At this point you should read the case box below. This summarizes the dramatic changes that are taking place in Deutsche Post (the German Post Office). This reflects the huge amount of privatization and deregulation that has been taking place across Europe over the last 20 years or so. Privatization has often been associated with diversification (please consult Chapter 9 on corporate strategy for this), with acquisitions (*see* Chapter 10) and with internationalization (*see* Chapter 11). Insights into Deutsche Post can be gained from each of these perspectives but in the context of this chapter the issue of 'fair' competition is raised. Is the growth of Deutsche Post subsidized by a protected home market? From this case, identify the concerns that the EU might have and that its main competitors might have. What would be persuasive grounds on which Deutsche Post might defend itself, or on which its competitors might have a good case? Try also to identify the economic logic on which such a broad expansion of services might be sustained.

Case box: Logistical challenge

Not long ago, Deutsche Post was merely Germany's national post office. Now it wants to be the world's top logistics company

Twice bitten, thrice shy? Not, seemingly, Germany's growing army of shareholders. In the past few weeks, Germans have been inundated with advertisements for 'yellow shares' in the national post office, Deutsche Post. Those who still have shares from offerings by Deutsche Telekom and its internet subsidiary, T-Online, sold amid much hype in the spring, are nursing losses. Yet Germans (as well as a fair number of foreigners) are eager for more. They have been rushing to subscribe to the 25–29 per cent of Deutsche Post that is due to be floated on 20 November 2000, raising somewhere between €5.8 billion ($5 billion) and €7.4 billion.

Whether Deutsche Post will prove a good investment will depend largely on the success of a transformation brought about by its chairman Klaus Zumwinkel. Mr Zumwinkel, who likes to spend his spare time climbing mountains, spent 16 years at McKinsey, a consultancy, before taking over the post office in 1990. He has not only turned a sleepy, loss-making utility into a proper business; he has also tried to turn Deutsche Post from a national post office into an international logistics giant, delivering not just letters, but anything from anywhere to any-where else, at any time.

Over the past two years, the growth of Deutsche Post and the expansion of its activities have been remarkable. In 1998, mail accounted for almost three-quarters of its turnover, with express parcels making up the rest. In the first half of this year, mail, though still the biggest of the company's four divisions, accounted for only 35 per cent of sales. Parcels' share was about one-sixth. The rest (i.e. almost half) was split evenly between new divisions for logis-tics and financial services. Equally striking, the share of sales coming from foreign operations leapt from a mere 2 per cent in 1998 to 28 per cent in the first half of this year. By next year, says Mr Zumwinkel, it will be 40 per cent, thanks to the acquisition earlier this year of a majority stake in DHL, a courier.

To bring about this transformation, Mr Zumwinkel has been buying companies left, right and centre. Since the start of 1999 Deutsche Post has bought, besides DHL, a clutch of other logistics firms: Danzas, a Swiss company; the European operations of Nedlloyd, a Dutch firm; America's Air Express International; and Sweden's ASG. The growth of the financial-services operation began when Deutsche Post took Germany's state-owned Postbank (which already operated in post offices) under its wing. To this deposit-taker has now been added a lender, with the acquisition of DSL, another state-owned bank, which mainly provides finance for new buildings.

There remain three main obstacles for Deutsche Post to overcome if it is to succeed. The first is the long-delayed opening of Europe's national postal monopolies to competition. From 2003 the European Union plans to limit national post offices' monopoly to items weighing less than 50 grams, and to open direct mail and outbound international mail up to full competition.

Some incumbent post offices, especially those in Britain and France, are resisting fiercely. But the Germans are more enthusiastic: in two years' time the monopoly in Germany, already down to 200 grams, is due to drop to 100, well below the limit in other European countries. Analysts reckon that, after TNT Post Groep, a privatized Dutch firm, Deutsche Post is Europe's second-most efficient post office. So it should have less to fear than most from competition. Indeed, it should be well-placed to pinch business from other mail and logistics firms if it gets the chance. And in any case, Mr Zumwinkel points out, a cut in the monopoly from 200 to 100 grams will expose only around 7 per cent of mail sales to competition. 'Maybe we'll lose 1–2 per cent of profits,' he says. 'But on the other hand, we can win market share in other countries.'

The second big challenge is tougher: integrating its huge clutch of recently acquired businesses. Until this is done, the reorientation of Deutsche Post will be incomplete. Although the mail business accounts for only around a third of sales, it still brings in more than 75 per cent of profits. The company's aim is to cut this to 50 per cent by 2004. If this goal is to be met, new acquisitions will have to be woven quickly and successfully into its existing structure.

The third challenge, wrapped as it is in a thick legal mist, is harder to judge, but potentially the most hazardous. Critics of Deutsche Post say that it has, in effect, received illegal state aid in the form of high, government-controlled charges for its domestic mail monopoly, and that it has used these monopoly profits to subsidize its expansion into other markets. The company also stands accused of predatory pricing in its parcels business, which began to turn a profit only last year, after more than a decade of subsidized losses. The European Commission is investigating these and other allegations. The German government and Deutsche Post strenuously deny them.

Should Deutsche Post be required to 'repay' state aid, Mr Zumwinkel insists, the effect on its profits would still be slight. Maybe so. The biggest repayment of state aid ever demanded was €227 million, from Air France in 1995, and in that case the subsidy was explicit. Even something on that scale would scarcely dent Deutsche Post. Nonetheless, an adverse EU ruling would be damaging beyond its one-off blow to the bottom line, because it would show Mr Zumwinkel to be less sure-footed than he has looked so far. With no doubt second and third tranches of yellow shares still to be sold, it could even make investors less eager next time around. For now, though, they seem happy to trudge behind Deutsche Post's determined boss.

Source: 'Logistical Challenge', *The Economist*, 18 November 2000, p. 78.
© The Economist Newspaper Limited, London (18 November 2000).

Key terms

Adverse selection *126*	Exogenous *110*
Agglomeration economies *131*	Factor conditions *123*
Aggregate demand *107*	Horizontal integration *130*
Balanced growth *118*	Leakage *110*
Circular flow of income *109*	National competitive advantage *119*
Competitive advantage *119*	National competitiveness *119*
Endogenous *110*	

Recap questions and assignments

1 Within an economy, what are the main effects of the following on its GDP growth, the rate of price inflation and unemployment?

   (a) A fall in the home rate of interest.

   (b) A decrease in the rate of income tax or social security contribution rates.

   (c) An upturn in World trade.

   (d) A rise in government spending on (i) health and (ii) defence.

2 Access the Virtual Economy Model software available on the website www.bized.ac.uk. Click on 'Virtual Worlds' and then on 'Virtual Economy'. Go to the 4th floor and click on the selected variable model variant. Change the rate of VAT to 20% and record the effects you observe. Reset the model and then explore the effects of a 10% increase in health expenditure and defence spending. Are there any differences and, if so, why? Finally, explore the impact of a fall of 1% in the home interest rates using the model in its full variant.

3 What are the impacts on the exchange rate of the various changes you have made in the Virtual Economy Model? Explain the results you obtain.

Online
*Learning*Centre

When you have read this chapter, log on to the Online Learning Centre website at www.mcgraw-hill.co.uk/textbooks/mcgee to explore chapter-by-chapter test questions, further reading and more online study tools for strategy.

Case 1 **Made in Japan?**

How are Japan's manufacturers faring against low-cost competition from China?

Japan's manufacturing has been steadily moving overseas, most obviously to China. Among the reasons: wages in Japan are much higher, by a factor of between 20 and 30 times. Look more closely, however, and China is far from being the only threat facing Japan's manufacturers. Individual Japanese companies talk as much about competitors in America and Europe as they do about China. Some are most concerned about the technological prowess of South Korean firms such as Samsung and Hyundai.

Many Japanese companies are raising their game, using a range of strategies to fend off low-cost competition from overseas. Some of them are fortunate because they start from positions of relative strength. Leading firms such as Toyota and Canon have developed integrated manufacturing systems that are far more sophisticated and complex than rivals can manage. In other sectors, companies have learned how best to protect trade secrets that have long made them competitive, often bringing back home activities that might otherwise risk exposure to rivals. And most big firms believe that they can keep an edge in future by continuing to invest in new generations of products.

Japan's weak spot is in low-cost, mass production, which has been steadily leaving for lower-wage countries (just as it has also been seeping out of Western Europe and America). There are only rare examples of Japanese companies trying to compete from a domestic base in the low-cost arena. One is Suzuki Motor. Its latest hit is a stripped-down budget scooter that costs one-third as much as regular scooters. Designed for urban short-distance drivers, it has eliminated some parts, such as rear suspension, once thought essential. Clever though this is, low-cost manufacturing in Japan is likely to be limited to niche products; Suzuki admits its efforts could be 'a useless struggle' against an inevitable tide.

Although they interfere less than they once did, Japan's bureaucrats are concerned by the prospect of manufacturing, especially high-tech manufacturing, going abroad. Surely, the thinking goes, if one Japanese company builds a plant in China, and the technology is copied, then all of the firm's Japanese rivals will face cheap competition? Hidetaka Fukuda, who oversees information technology for the Ministry of Economy, Trade and Industry, says that METI stepped in earlier this year to persuade NEC, an electronics giant, to sell its plasma-display business to local rival Pioneer, rather than a foreign investor, as a way to keep its technology in Japan. Mr Fukuda says that he is currently in similar negotiations with roughly ten other companies that might otherwise transfer technology abroad.

Sometimes cheap labour is not the prime motive for moving abroad. For instance, carmakers and construction-machinery makers say they have set up overseas simply in order to follow customer demand. Honda, Japan's second-largest carmaker after Toyota, says that, by building plants close to its markets, it can reduce production times, distribution costs and currency losses. Research facilities are set up overseas in order to tailor cars to meet regional needs, such as sports-utility vehicles in America with extra towing capacity, rarely required in Japan. Manufacturing techniques, such as welding methods, continue to be refined at home.

Indeed, many manufacturers are responding to competition by keeping core technologies secret and at home, while moving low-value-added production and assembly operations abroad. For instance, Toshiba, Japan's biggest chipmaker, is racing to develop high-end chips, and says it is determined not to repeat past mistakes. Initially it co-operated with South Korean chipmakers in basic DRAM memory chips, which have since become commodities, only to find its rivals overtaking it far more swiftly than it had expected.

Others have discovered additional virtues in making things at home. Two years ago Kenwood's new boss, Haruo Kawahara, shifted production of mini-disc players from Malaysia back to Yamagata, Japan. This 'in-sourcing' has raised profits in several ways, which highlight three long-standing advantages of the Japanese approach to manufacturing: specially trained workers, low defect rates and 'lean' processes that hold down inventory costs and boost production flexibility.

Unlike Kenwood's Malaysian workers, who come and go frequently, workers in its Yamagata factory stick around long enough to master several different tasks. A typical Yamagata worker can quickly do four or five steps in the assembly process before handing over to another worker, whereas employees in the Malaysian plant did one step each. These days it takes four employees to put together a mini-disc player in Yamagata, compared with 22 Malaysian workers before the move. The Japanese plant takes up 70 per cent less space, while the defect rate has fallen by 80 per cent.

Mouldy business

An under-appreciated, but critical, sector of Japanese manufacturing is the country's mould-makers. Tiny, secretive firms generally consisting of less than a handful of workers, these craftsmen usually work in what look like dim, grimy, oversize garages, filled with worn machines and piles of scrap metal. Industrial moulds are used to create the shape and form of almost anything that can be picked up, from ballpoint pens and toys to mobile-phone and satellite parts. The work is highly specialized. Many mould-makers, now in their 50s and 60s, started learning their trade when they were children.

The best firms, clustered around Ota, Shinagawa and Sumida wards in south and east Tokyo, make moulds, often prototypes, for the top international names in cars and consumer-electronics – and even for NASA, America's space agency. 'Mould-making technology lies at the base of all manufacturing. If this were to start disappearing, it would be a danger sign for Japanese manufacturing,' warns Mr Kinoshita.

Opinion is split as to whether warning lights are now flashing. Since 1990, almost 40 per cent of mould-makers in Sumida have gone out of business (and only one new one was set up), while more than a third of the remainder had no work at the start of the year, says Yukio Ouchi, an economic commentator who has studied more than 4,000 mould-makers. This reflects a broader trend. One street in Ota, once filled with top-notch mould-makers and other small manufacturers, initially dubbed 'bankruptcy street' was subsequently renamed 'suicide street', reflecting growing pressure from loan sharks.

Kazuo Hori, president of Koyo Seiko, a mould-maker mainly for ballpoint pens, says he has lost almost half his business, mostly to China, over the past year or so. Though some big manufacturers are coming back because quality is higher at home, many mould-makers have gone bust during their absence. More disturbing is a recent trend in which unscrupulous Japanese manufacturers steal mould designs to send to cheaper Chinese makers.

Still, there are bright spots. Business is booming for mould-makers that specialize in car parts and mobile phones. Despite the overall decline, many of the best firms have managed to hang on, says Mr Ouchi. Diversification helps. Tohru Izumi, boss of Izumi Kanagata, counts every Japanese carmaker and, since the late 1990s, an increasing number of foreign carmakers, such as BMW and Jaguar, as recipients of car-audio panels made from his moulds.

Which bits of Japanese manufacturing will survive and flourish will depend on managers' ability to identify, hold on to, and improve, Japan's inherent strengths. In an influential recent article, 'A Twenty-first-century strategy for Japanese manufacturing' (published in Japanese in *Bungei Shunju* in November 2003, translated in *Japan Echo* in February 2004). Takahiro Fujimoto, a professor at Tokyo University, said it is too simple to suggest that Japan should focus on high-value-added production. What Japanese manufacturers really excel at, he argued, are 'products whose functions require many components to be designed in careful detail and mutually adjusted for optimal performance'. This requires close teamwork within a company, as well as co-operation with suppliers.

The Japanese way

This ability to meld different skills and technologies is a common feature among top Japanese manufacturers in several sectors. For instance, successful photocopier companies, such as Canon and Ricoh, combine precision mechanics, advanced chemical processes for toner inks, and servicing skills. Cars, too, are all about mixing different technologies. 'There is no "core" technology in cars,' says Mitsuo Kinoshita, chief production control and logistics officer at Toyota, Japan's top carmaker, which last year overtook America's Ford to become the second-largest seller of cars. For example, he explains, it is not enough to perfect a hybrid system (which combines an engine that runs on petrol with an electric motor) in the laboratory: an equal amount of expertise is needed to make sure it works when actually placed in a car.

It is hard, says Masahiro Sakane, president of Komatsu, Japan's biggest construction-machinery maker, to come up with fresh business models that exploit mixed technologies.

Yet doing this well produces rewards. Komatsu added information technology, such as global-positioning systems (GPS), to hydraulic excavators three years ago to combat theft, and help machinery-rental firms track how much fuel individual excavators had left in their tanks. Yet this has also unexpectedly helped raise sales of Komatsu's excavators in China, where the beginnings of a credit crunch are emerging – banks consider excavators with GPS easier to seize as collateral against soured loans.

One company in an excellent position to see how Japanese manufacturers are faring is Omron, which makes a range of sophisticated sensors and scanning devices that get used on other manufacturers' assembly lines. Omron sells these devices not only to Japan's domestic manufacturers, but also to firms building overseas plants in China (among other countries). Factories in China are upgrading their methods, and are buying more Omron devices to help. Factories in Japan, however, are hardly standing still.

One Omron product that is popular in both China and Japan is a scanner that inspects the substrate of printed-circuit boards for minute imperfections. In China, placing one of these scanners at the end of the line is good enough: defective products can be discarded before the rest are shipped to customers. In super-efficient Japan, however, detecting flawed products so late is seen as shamefully wasteful. So Omron has made a new system for Japanese clients that networks several substrate scanners together. Complex software gives a warning when aberrations start to appear – and then immediately pinpoints which machine needs tweaking.

Canon firing

Canon, which has a high-tech product line ranging from precision photocopiers, to optical components for digital cameras, to expensive equipment for making semiconductors and flat-panel television screens, is a good example of how Japanese firms are regrouping in the face of competition from abroad. Fujio Mitarai, its boss, said earlier this year that over the next three years, 80 per cent of Canon's global capital spending will be in Japan. Among other investments, it is building a high-end digital camera factory in Oita prefecture and a new research centre near Tokyo.

Canon is hardly naive about the benefits of outsourcing: 42 per cent of its worldwide production is overseas. To maintain its technological edge and high profit margins, however, it must balance low-cost manufacturing abroad with the high-tech precision it achieves in Japan. Mr Mitarai told *The Economist* recently that he has a rough cut-off rule for allocating investment: anything for which labour comprises more than 5 per cent of production costs can be done in China or some other low-wage country. Because Canon continues to invest in R&D, Mr Mitarai reckons there should be plenty left to do profitably in Japan. For instance, labour accounts for only 2 per cent of the cost of its lithographic steppers, which are used in making semiconductors and fetch around $22 million each.

Few of Japan's manufacturing bosses, however, are as relaxed as Mr Mitarai is about China. In Japan's vast electronics sector, for example, digitization has forced business leaders to think long and hard about China's changing role. The rapid spread of new digital devices – such as DVD players, mobile phones and digital cameras – has allowed China to do something much simpler than moving from easy technologies to harder ones. Instead, it has actually leap-frogged the harder stuff (i.e. analogue devices) to get to newer and easier digital products.

Manufacturers in China would have a dreadful time producing good conventional film cameras, for example, because of the complex optical, chemical and mechanical processes that must be mastered. But Chinese factories have little trouble assembling digital cameras: all they need to do is to obtain advanced components from Japan that are pre-designed to work in harmony when snapped together.

This combination of digital diffusion and Chinese expansion is driving two profound changes among Japan's electronics firms. First, it has widened an important split between makers of many final consumer products (such as Sony, Sharp and Matsushita's Panasonic brand) and the scores of focused Japanese firms that feed materials, components and equipment into the process. The second, related, change is a rapid erosion of the barriers that have long allowed Japanese manufacturers to protect their trade secrets.

Because China and other low-wage countries need their inputs to make digital products, Japan's focused suppliers and equipment-makers have been doing especially well. They boast large global market shares in specialized niches: ceramics and other fine materials for semiconductors, tiny motors for hard drives and other digital equipment, a range of sophisticated machines for making liquid-crystal display panels, and so forth.

The big consumer electronics companies, by contrast, make a wide range of both components and final products. China's growing production base and the spread of digital products thus presents the big firms with a confusing mix of threats and opportunities. They have lately been enjoying brisk global demand for mobile phones, digital cameras and DVD recorders, along with a rising appetite for flat-panel TVs and other higher-end home electronics. Yet they face tough competition and must rely on cost cutting and a steady stream of new models to maintain profit margins that are already low. They must keep shifting production to China, therefore, to keep up with one another.

Looking Sharp

The rapid movement of manufacturing to South Korea, Taiwan and China is, in turn, forcing Japanese firms to think much harder about which technologies to protect and which activities to leave in Japan. Since much of their edge depends on closely held trade secrets, this is becoming ever more difficult.

Earlier this year, Sharp opened a new 'sixth-generation' plant to make flat panels for televisions in Kameyama, Mie prefecture, which cranks out panels much bigger than those made in fifth-generation plants. Sharp (and rival Samsung) is pushing the frontiers of this technology. Designing a new plant requires the sorting out of dozens of complex steps, each with its own specialized equipment, all of which must work seamlessly to churn out delicate panels with almost no defects. Sharp's reward is good profits at the relatively uncontested high end when it introduces bigger flat-panel TVs from newer and more efficient plants.

Nearly all of the important suppliers to Sharp are Japanese. That has been great news for Mie prefecture, which has been reinvigorated by a cluster of over 50 firms that have built facilities there to be closer to Sharp's Kameyama plant. Unfortunately for Sharp, however, its suppliers also work closely with its rivals, many of them Taiwanese. By the time the paint had dried in Kameyama, imitators in Taiwan were already cobbling together their own sixth-generation plants.

Sharp goes to great lengths to slow its rivals down. When a machine breaks down, engineers now try to fix it in-house rather than telling the supplier – just to keep equipment-makers in the dark about any problems that might occur on the machines they have sold to Sharp's competitors. For the same reason, the company quietly rewrites the software on some equipment once it is installed.

The cumulative effect of many such small steps is to defend Sharp's global market position from erosion, at least for now. Other Japanese manufacturers have absorbed this and other lessons. Having invented lean manufacturing, they are not about to let low-cost rivals have it all their own way.

Source: 'Manufacturing in Japan', *The Economist*, 10 April 2004, pp. 65–7.
© The Economist Newspaper Limited, London (10 April 2004).

Case Questions

1 What actions could and should the Japanese government take to cope with the threat of low-cost competition?

2 Based on this case study, what do you think is Japan's comparative advantage? What implications does this have for Japanese firms and their competitive advantages?

3 Is it possible for firms to locate in several different countries so as to gain from local comparative advantage without suffering from the disadvantages? In other words, can they have their cake and eat it? What can national governments do about this?

Further reading and references

McAleese, D (2004) *Economics for Business*, 3rd edition, Prentice Hall. Once again we recommend this excellent introductory text on economics, Parts 2 and 3 of which provide a much more complete analysis of the macroeconomic environment than could be provided in this chapter.

Porter, ME (1990) *Competitive Advantage of Nations*, Macmillan, London.

World Bank (1993) *East Asian Miracle*, Oxford University Press, New York.

Useful websites

www.bized.ac.uk
Provides excellent supporting material including a glossary of economic terms and the 'Virtual Economy', which is a computer-based model of a real-life macroeconomy. You can carry out a variety of experiments to build your understanding of the concepts developed in this chapter.

The macroeconomic environment changes rapidly so it is important to keep up to date with events. There are many websites which provide up to date information on the macroeconomic context of strategy and which employ many of the concepts developed in this lesson. Examples of the best are:

www.imf.org
www.oecd.org
www.worldbank.org
www.niesr.ac.uk

Chapter 5

Industry analysis and competitive strategy

Introduction

In this chapter we introduce the basic ideas of competitive strategy and indicate some of the issues involved in turning them into practicable propositions. The basic concepts are industry analysis (often referred to as the Porter five forces analysis), the generic competitive strategies, the value chain, and the main sources of competitive advantage. The foundations for these ideas were explained in Chapter 3. Moving from these foundations for strategy analysis the rest of the chapter introduces a more practical flavour. If we understand the idea of competitive advantage as a key attribute that is specific to the firm then we have the beginnings of a description of strategy. We describe a template for describing and identifying a strategy – how would you recognize a strategy if you saw one?

Chapter contents

Whereas competitive advantage is an external positioning concept, strategy also needs to say something about the internal disposition of resources and assets as well. The internal logic of strategy is shown in the strategy cycle and cost analysis is reflected in the value chain. The latter is extremely well known being another product of Porter analysis (1985). The strategy cycle illustrates the significance of the balance between internal resources, external market positioning and financial performance. The value chain builds directly on the cost analysis of Chapter 3 and enables us to identify a picture of the internal asset structure and activity structure of the firm. The chapter concludes with a template for a practical overview of strategy – a self-testing of your firm's strategy IQ. This can be turned into a simple question-naire for assessing the strategy of your own firm or of any firms of which you have some knowledge. By the end of this chapter we will see the significance of **competitive advantage** for the study of strategy and for strategy making in firms.

5.1 Analysis of industries and competition

In Chapter 3 perfect competition is presented as the benchmark by which economists and others such as government departments and regulators judge the efficiency of markets. In general, markets are seen as efficient if they are perfect in their principal characteristics, demonstrating price competition, ease of entry and exit, and wide distribution of relevant knowledge. Conversely, individual firms see it as in their own interest to have specific knowl-edge that enables them to build unique assets and offer distinctive products for which they can charge a price premium. In other words, firms have an interest in constructing imper-fections that favour them in the marketplace. Firms may also have a joint interest in colluding together to create collective imperfections by which they can artificially limit com-petition and charge higher prices than otherwise. This is not the subject of this book but there is a very considerable literature on these monopolistic practices and the ways in which governments pursue pro-competitive policies in order to make industries more efficient and markets more competitive. Firms actually compete on two levels. One level is in the market-place where customers compare rival offerings and make choices and, in doing so, prices emerge from these market processes. Firms also compete through their plans and invest-ments for the future and, in doing so, they construct assets that they hope will be sufficiently distinctive for them to offer distinctive products. Thus, the R&D activities of pharmaceutical firms is intended to create new and unique products that can be protected by patents and which can then be sold as unique high-priced products in the market. Industry analysis is the analysis of assets, resources and capabilities that set out the basic economic conditions under which firms collectively operate (the 'industry context') and which condition their individual abilities to create distinctive individual positions in their industries.

For example, Ford and Toyota operate in the automobile industry. They share some common operating characteristics such as significant economies of scale in assembly operations, a largely common knowledge basis and technology characteristics, and a set of competing products that compete more on price than on product differences. To some extent they share common economic characteristics. However, they each conduct R&D and other development activities in order to gain points of difference versus each other. Toyota might claim a distinctive way of organizing its manufacturing activities with beneficial effects on quality and reliability. Ford might claim a better organization of distribution and servicing activities with beneficial consequences for the way in which consumers experience the service process. This mixture of common economic characteristics coupled with attempts at individual differentiation comprises the content of industry analysis. As we have seen in the section on cost analysis (Chapter 3), the nature of economies of scale in an industry (such as automobile assembly) affects the number of potential competitors in an industry (the greater the minimum efficient scale, the fewer competitors that can survive). Thus, the economic characteristics of the industry shape the nature of competition in the market by affecting the number of players (in this example). More generally, the economic characteristics of an industry are shaped by the investment and planning decisions of firms, and the extent to which firms can sustain uniqueness affects the way in which competition then plays out in the marketplace.

5.1.1 Porter's five forces

Industry analysis is best known as Porter's **five forces** (introduced initially in Chapter 1). This was first popularized by Michael Porter in his path-breaking *Competitive Strategy*, first published in 1980. Figure 5.1 shows the celebrated diagram of the five forces of competition, namely: rivalry, threat of entry, supplier power, buyer power and threat of substitutes. These are the five fundamental forces that determine the 'attractiveness' of the industry, a term which is a surrogate for industry profitability. Thus the weaker/stronger are these forces then the more/less attractive will be the industry taken as a whole and the larger/smaller will be its overall profitability. On the whole, the more attractive the industry, the more likely it is that participants will enjoy 'good' profits.

The supply chain

The heart of the five forces diagram is the horizontal line. Porter draws this as a force diagram with all the arrows pointing towards the central box, which represents the industry in question measured in terms of the competitors present. Alternatively this can be shown as a **supply chain** representing the build-up and flow of goods to the final customer. Thus, for the food industry, goods flow from the farm, to food ingredients companies (such as flour milling), to food manufacturers (such as cake and bread manufacturers), to wholesalers, to supermarkets, and then to final consumers. At each stage of the supply chain there is an industry that invests in assets, that accumulates **fixed** and variable **costs** and then prices its goods to the next stage of the chain. The difference between its revenues and its material

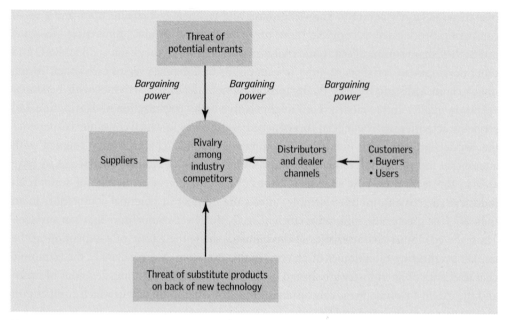

Figure 5.1 The Porter five forces framework
Source: Porter (1980), *Competitive Strategy*. Reprinted with permission of The Free Press, a division of Simon and Schuster Adult Publishing Group, from *Competitive Strategy* by Michael E. Porter. Copyright © 1980, 1998 by The Free Press. All rights reserved.

costs is its added value, i.e. the value it adds to its material input costs.[1] This added value can be partitioned into three parts: labour costs, capital costs and profits. The more attractive the industry, the greater is likely to be the value added, including also the profits, and vice versa. Where perfect competition is the norm, prices will tend to converge downwards and profits will fall to a level that is the minimum rate of return on capital that will enable the capital to be retained in the industry. If profits fall below this there will be pressure to withdraw capital and place it in more profitable employment. If profits are higher then there will be an incentive for more capital to enter the industry. This is the basic mechanism behind the **threat of entry** in Figure 5.1.

The threat of entry

At each stage of the supply chain there is an industry that can be analysed in terms of the five forces. Firms considering investment in an attractive industry will make an entry calculation. This takes the form of a conventional capital investment decision with three components. The revenue stream depends on prices that can be charged (taking account of the price elasticity of demand) and the volumes attainable. The costs depend on the unit costs of production and access to available economies of scale, scope and learning, and on

---

[1] Economists use the difference between revenue and materials costs as the definition of value added (being the value added to materials by the actions of the firm). However, many business analysts use 'value added' in a much more intuitive sense to mean profitability.

the level of marketing and other costs of getting the product to markets. Finally, the capital cost of the investment needs to be reckoned. If any of the cost elements (expressed in cost per unit of output) are higher than those of the incumbents and if the prices relative to incumbents are lower, then the potential entrant faces 'entry barriers', i.e. its profit margins are lower than those of the incumbents and it faces a cost disadvantage or barrier. If the cost disadvantages are high in relation to the profit margins then they serve as an effective barrier to entry. If for other reasons, such as access to technology or to distribution systems, the entrant is effectively barred from entry then we say that entry is *blockaded*.

The power of suppliers and buyers

Suppliers have a natural interest in raising their prices at your expense. To the extent that they succeed, they enhance their margins at your expense. Under what conditions might this happen? Where there are relatively few suppliers you may not have many alternatives to an aggressive supplier. Where the supplier is providing a product that is very important to the eventual performance of your own product, they might be able to charge a 'premium' price. Where you are accustomed to using a particular product there may be costs of *switching* from this product to an alternative. This provides a price umbrella for the supplier in his negotiations with you. If there are no substitution possibilities then price can go up. For example, if as an electricity generator your power stations are configured around coal supplies and conversion to other supplies such as gas or oil are only longer-term possibilities, then coal suppliers have bargaining power. OPEC, in pricing oil, has to be aware that an overaggressive pricing policy provides incentives for its customers to convert to other fuels and/or to invest in energy saving.

The analysis of buyer power is identical. The greater the relative concentration of buyers, the less important is your product to the buyer; the more your product can be substituted by others, the less is your bargaining power and the greater is their bargaining power. In the UK the celebrated example of this is the power of supermarket chains over food manufacturers. The larger and more powerful the chain, the more it can force down its input prices. However, the principal defence of the manufacturer vis-à-vis the supermarket is its ability to differentiate its products. Thus, the more distinctive is Nestlé's Nescafé brand, the less will Tesco be able to force its price down. Nestlé's calculation could be that customers will come into the store having already decided to buy the Nescafé brand regardless of any price differentials between Nescafé and other brands including the supermarket's own brand. However, if Tesco could legitimately conclude that customers respond principally to Tesco's own branding and will therefore buy whatever Tesco put on the shelves (especially its own brand) then Tesco's buying power is strong and it will be more able to treat Nestlé and its other suppliers as providers of commodity products. The threat of vertical integration can be very effective in disciplining suppliers. Some retailers, such as Marks & Spencer, have an own-brand policy that is a form of quasi-vertical integration that leaves strategic power effectively with the retailer. Conversely, the distinctiveness of luxury-brand purveyors such as Louis Vuitton and Gucci has enabled many of these players to invest in their own captive distribution and retailing systems so that they can extract every drop of the product differentiation premium for themselves (see the Louis Vuitton case study).

The balance between supplier power and buyer power is a key issue in business. Very often the biggest threat to your margins comes not simply from your competitors but from the adjacent (and sometimes even the more remote) parts of the supply chain. The biggest threat to food manufacturers probably comes from retailers. In the personal computer business the power in the supply chain lies upstream with the suppliers of components, that is, with Microsoft's operating systems and other software, and with Intel and its microprocessors. Estimates in Harvard Business School's case studies on Apple in the 1980s suggested that more than half of all the profits made in the personal computer industry supply chain were earned by Microsoft and Intel (Yoffie 1992). Thus, the location of power along the supply chain is a key issue in understanding how profits can be earned. The case box on Dell in Chapter 7 shows how a strategic innovation downstream, close to the customer, has been able to create a defensible and profitable position in spite of the power of Microsoft and Intel.

The threat of substitutes

The pressure from substitutes tends to be longer-term pressure. If you conceive of the product from your industry as having a certain benefit–cost ratio to the immediate customer then pressure from substitutes can be calibrated in terms of alternative benefit–cost ratios. A simple but powerful example concerns the substitution of fibre optic cable for coaxial cable in telecommunications in the 1980s. Fibre optic cable offered so many more benefits at relatively low marginal cost that the costs of investing in entirely new cabling systems could very quickly be earned back. Most technological changes can be assessed in the same way, trading off the added benefits, the added costs and the required investments. Complications arise when the products involved are components within larger systems. The increased use of modularity of electronic components and the standardization of electronic interfaces has increased the incentives for substitution. Another problem arises when the scale and scope of substitution is so large as to effectively disrupt the existing supply chains. The advent of photocopying, the laser printer, and the personal computer demonstrate that there can be system-level substitutions that cause industries and supply chains to transform.

Note the similarity and the difference between threat of entry and **threat of substitutes**. Both are about the entry of new capacity into the industry and into the set of competitors. However, entry is essentially about imitation and the entry of new competitors to take advantage of the existing attractiveness of the industry. Substitution, however, is about new dimensions of competition and the ability of new ways of competing to displace existing ways. New entrants reckon to be able to exploit the existing value proposition to customers, whereas substitute products expect to be able to change the value proposition.

Competitive rivalry

The intensity of competition is the fifth force in our list. This is regarded by economists as the first force in that it is the prototype of competitive force present in all economic textbooks (this was summarized in the Chapter 3). The propositions follow from our earlier discussion of perfect competition. Thus, competition will be the stronger (and profits the lower) the more competitors there are and the more commodity-like are the products. In addition, the supply–demand balance directly affects the market price. In declining markets prices fall as excess supply chases deficient demand. The more the cost structure is fixed rather than variable, and marginal costs are therefore low, the more room there is to cut prices before contribution margins become negative. This explains why capital intensive industries with low marginal costs suffer so much in recession. Prices can keep falling as long as cash flows remain positive – remembering that the capital costs are sunk (for example, Eurotunnel) and fixed costs are programmed over a time period – so the only discretionary policy is to place price somewhere above marginal cost. In extreme cases cash flows might remain positive (and sufficient to pay cash costs including interest payments on capital) while accounting losses could be very high.

5.1.2 **Strategy as imperfections**

Many writers have emphasized that strategy is, in the end, a practical matter, as is management studies in general. However, the long-run nature of strategic decisions and their inherent complexity, coupled with the uncertainty attached to futurity, means that there can be a substantial pay-off to strategic thinking. Strategic thinking places a premium on good understanding and use of concepts. Strategy was always recognized to centre on resource allocation decisions that determine the long-term capability of organizations in relation to choices about how and where the organization intends to compete. The foundation for strategic thinking requires an understanding of the nature of markets (see Chapter 3 for a detailed explanation). Perfectly competitive markets are characterized by free entry, perfect information and identical commodity-like products. The consequence of such 'perfect' competition is that price is the only competitive variable, that firms are essentially identical and, therefore, that there are no supernormal profits to be had. Profit is sufficient to provide a normal return on capital and any profits above this will be transitory, either through random shocks or because competition erodes the profit benefits of new initiatives. Thus, the perfectly competitive world is not conducive to super profits ('rents') and does not provide much incentive to entrepreneurial behaviour.

However, imperfections in markets do provide the possibility for **rents** and rent-seeking activities. Imperfections could be differences in information about production possibilities, or consumer ignorance about product benefits. Some imperfections are market-wide, in that monopoly might prevail, perhaps because of government edict, or because of natural economies of scale, or perhaps through cartels. These imperfections are associated with rents, because prices can be held artificially high without (much) fear of competition. The worldwide wave of privatization and deregulation is usually marked by lower prices and greater competition. Figure 5.2 portrays the differences between the conditions under which perfect competition obtains and competitive advantage exists.

Imperfections can be firm-specific. Thus, a pharmaceutical company may, through its R&D activity, develop specific, proprietary knowledge that results in new products that cannot be imitated without a significant time lag. An office equipment company might establish a worldwide service system that allows it to give 24-hour service response to clients. Competitors can only imitate after substantial delay. **Firm-specific imperfections** enable firms to be different from their competitors and to expect this difference to be sustainable over a non-trivial time span. If firms can be different, and if customers value such differences, then these firms can earn supernormal profits, at least for a time. In economic terms, this is the essence of strategy. Firms create advantage by creating assets and positions that are distinctively different from those of their competitors. The essence of these firm-specific imperfections lies, first, in the creation of different assets (either tangible or intangible) and, second, in the creation of distinctive, defensible positions in their chosen product markets. The 'positioning' school (which could be known as the **market-based view**) focuses primarily on the latter, with analysis of the nature and dynamics of competitive advantage. The **resource-based view** is concerned with the former.

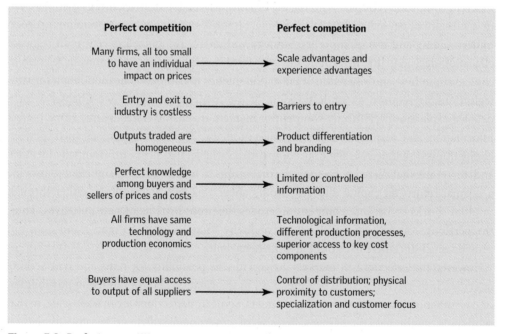

Perfect competition	Perfect competition
Many firms, all too small to have an individual impact on prices	Scale advantages and experience advantages
Entry and exit to industry is costless	Barriers to entry
Outputs traded are homogeneous	Product differentiation and branding
Perfect knowledge among buyers and sellers of prices and costs	Limited or controlled information
All firms have same technology and production economics	Technological information, different production processes, superior access to key cost components
Buyers have equal access to output of all suppliers	Control of distribution; physical proximity to customers; specialization and customer focus

Figure 5.2 Perfect competition versus competitive advantage

What industry analysis does is to create a framework within which all the possible ways in which imperfections arise can be identified, assessed and analysed. The next section looks at how these firm-specific imperfections can be described as generic types of strategy.

Case box: **Profitability of UK retailers**

It is a commonplace to observe that British supermarket groups are much more profitable than their counterparts elsewhere in Europe or North America – isn't it? The companies themselves do not agree, and claims and counter-claims fly around like confetti ... Several factors make comparisons inherently difficult. One factor is that the UK groups are all publicly owned, while many of the continental firms are still private. Definitions of profit, and the motivation to declare a higher or lower figure are different. If you want to please the stock exchange, you tend to declare high profits; if you and your family will be paying income tax on the sum, you may want to minimize it.

Another factor is that accounting conventions vary, in particular in relation to the treatment of goodwill, and amortization of property costs. Sums arising from the purchase of goodwill are amortized against the profit and loss account over 20 years in France; in the UK they will usually be written off immediately to reserves. In France, store assets (land and buildings) are depreciated over a 20-year period, while in the UK this has not until recently been true. The argument in Britain was that because of the high quality of the buildings, they would not decline very quickly in value over time, and the residual asset would have a high resale value. This was clearly not true after the collapse of the property market in the early 1990s, and increasing criticism from analysts eventually led some retailers to acknowledge the validity of the argument. First, Morrison and Asda, then later all the others, agreed from the mid-1990s to depreciate their freehold and long-lease buildings. This reduced profits in the first few years ...

With these preliminaries, we can look at some actual figures. There are (at least) two ways of analyzing profitability: margin on sales, and return on capital employed (ROCE). It turns out that they produce different patterns. With return on sales, which critics most often quote, it is clear that UK supermarkets appear to have an advantage. The profit margins on sales in Britain rose steadily over the decades until the early 1990s, and have consistently been above those for Continental and US operators. Over the period 1988–93, the average operating margin for six French supermarket groups was 2 per cent. For six British groups, the average was over 6 per cent (Burt and Sparks, 1997). Adjustment of the British figures to take account of the differences in accounting treatment mentioned above (and certain other factors), will bring the UK figures down to around 4 to 5 per cent, but the French figures will still be significantly lower at 1–2 per cent. Almost all the US supermarket chains have been nearer the French than the British levels (though in general, US and Continental margins have been rising through the 1990s, while UK rates have been falling).

These comparisons have aroused most attacks from critics. They claim that the UK margins are the result of massive buying power exerted by the supermarkets groups. And the use of oligopoly power to impose on consumers a higher-than-normal price level. It is virtually impossible to compare price levels across countries, and it is also the case that there are large and powerful buying groups in many other countries. The British firms tend to be more centralized than some Continental competitors, and to use a single fascia; this should help in reducing costs. It may also be that British firms are more experienced and more skilful in using their buying power to extract better terms from suppliers.

Other possible explanations for higher British margins flow from lower costs:

♦ British companies have a lead in applying IT to logistics. Their distribution systems are centralized, with deliveries to a small number of company warehouses. Such efficiencies are reflected, for example, in fewer days' stockholding: an average of 20 days in the period 1988–93 for British firms, compared with 35 for French (Burt and Sparks, 1997).

♦ Labour costs are lower in the UK, both because of lower social costs borne by employers, and because in Britain the proportion of part-time labour in supermarkets is higher than elsewhere.

♦ The significantly higher level of own-label penetration in British supermarkets means that the average cost of goods sold is lower than in the rest of Europe, and the gross margin higher.

On the other hand, the costs of buying sites and of building superstores are considerably higher than in other countries; not all cost comparisons favour the British. Another element in the difference between British margins and those of Continental and US operators is the nature of competition in the different markets. Price plays a much more important role in both the USA and in Continental Europe than in Britain, for whatever reason.

When we turn to ROCE, we see a different picture. A study of the years 1988–93 showed an average ROCE for six French companies of 19 per cent, and for six British companies of 21 per cent. A later analysis (Deutsche Morgan Grenfell, 1998) compared store groups in Britain, France, Belgium, and the United States. The results from 1991–7 were consistent, and 1997 showed:

ROCE per cent
Six British companies   16
Nine US companies   21
Eight French companies   20
Three Belgian companies   24

Any comparison of ROCE across countries shows that even the best British supermarket groups are at best similar to their rivals, but certainly not more profitable. The higher capital investment needs servicing by higher margins.

Source: Seth, A and Randall, G (1999), pp. 215–16.
Reproduced with permission of Kogan Page Ltd.

Questions for discussion

1   Are the British supermarkets more profitable than their European and US counterparts?

2   Using the industry analysis framework, why might you expect the profitability of retailers to be different on average in different countries?

When you have read Chapter 6 and the section on the Business Model, you can answer the following questions.

3   Do British supermarkets operate on a different business model than their rivals?

4   On what basis would you judge whether a different business model was sustainable or not?

5.2 Generic strategies

Porter's five forces and the various sources of imperfections are summarized in Figure 5.3. These powerful economic forces on industries, supply chains and markets suggest that firms can have substantial problems in identifying and responding to the competitive pressures that surround them. However, we have seen some examples where firms very deliberately set out to countervail these forces and create space within which they can earn profits at a higher rate than their industry confrères. This is the essence of strategy, the creation of space within which discrete and distinctive actions can secure improved positioning within markets and greater performance. Using the basic economic models popularized by Porter, we can see that competitive position can be improved in two basic ways. A firm might enjoy cost advantages that its rivals will find difficult to imitate. Or a firm might create a differentiated product that its rivals might find difficult to imitate. The essence of perfect competition is that imitation will be easy, not too costly, and speedy. Any differences that emerge will be competed away very quickly. The introduction of an extra feature on a car (such as a rear parking sensor) is generally easy to copy. However, to offer hybrid motors (electric plus gasoline such as in the Toyota Prius) is much more difficult to copy in terms of quality, cost and speed of imitation. Firms with distinctive cost advantages will typically have built up economies of scale and scope over a long period of time and rivals may find it difficult to attain the same low costs. The very well known report on the British motorcycle industry (BCG 1975) identified huge scale economies in Japanese motorcycle factories leading, for example, to labour productivity figures of around 500 bikes per man year compared to the traditional craft-based production processes of European and US producers whose labour productivity was around 18 bikes per man year. This kind of cost advantage is inherently difficult to replicate and would take a very long time even if it were judged sensible to try to emulate.

The other main dimension of strategic choice revolves around the notion of **scope**. We have described **economies of scope** as arising when the average cost of a single product is lowered by its joint production with other products in a multi-product firm. This is based on the indivisibility of certain resources. For example, knowledge is indivisible in the sense that it cannot be divided into pieces, some of which you choose to use or have and some of which you choose not to use or have. Knowing about aluminium means that you will have knowledge relevant to airframe manufacture and to pots and pans. Economies of scope arise when your knowledge or other indivisible resource can be applied in multiple directions without using up that resource. Thus scope becomes interesting strategically. A firm may choose to operate with broad scope (such as Ford in the automobile assembly industry covering a very wide product range and covering also the whole globe). Conversely, a firm may choose to operate

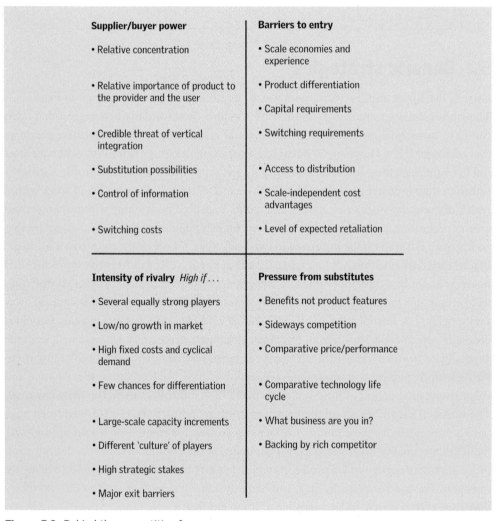

Figure 5.3 Behind the competitive forces

on a very narrow scope (such as Morgan Cars which covers only a particular part of the sports car market). The choice of broad scope suggests a calculation about available economies of scope in such a fashion that once chosen it is a commitment that cannot readily be reversed. The choice of narrow scope suggests an alternative calculation, that the benefits of assets and other resources and capabilities focused and dedicated to specific ways creates differentiation and/or cost advantages of a different sort. Figure 5.4 illustrates these generic strategies.

Generic strategies represent typologies that illustrate the type and range of strategic options that are available in principle. Thus, within the brewing industry, over time it is possible to see some brewing companies as low-cost players relying on size of brewing plants to reduce costs to the lowest possible levels. Other brewers would see themselves as offering a wide range of differentiated products (e.g. cask-conditioned beer). Many well-known breweries are comparatively quite small and offer only a small range of 'real ale' products. Historically, most brewers were small local operations producing cheap and cheerful low-cost products. These typologies are useful in understanding the nature of the strategic options that face firms but they do not in themselves provide prescriptions for strategic choice. Choice depends on the ways in which an individual firm can deploy advantages from cost, differentiation and scope – the key dimensions of the generic strategies box.

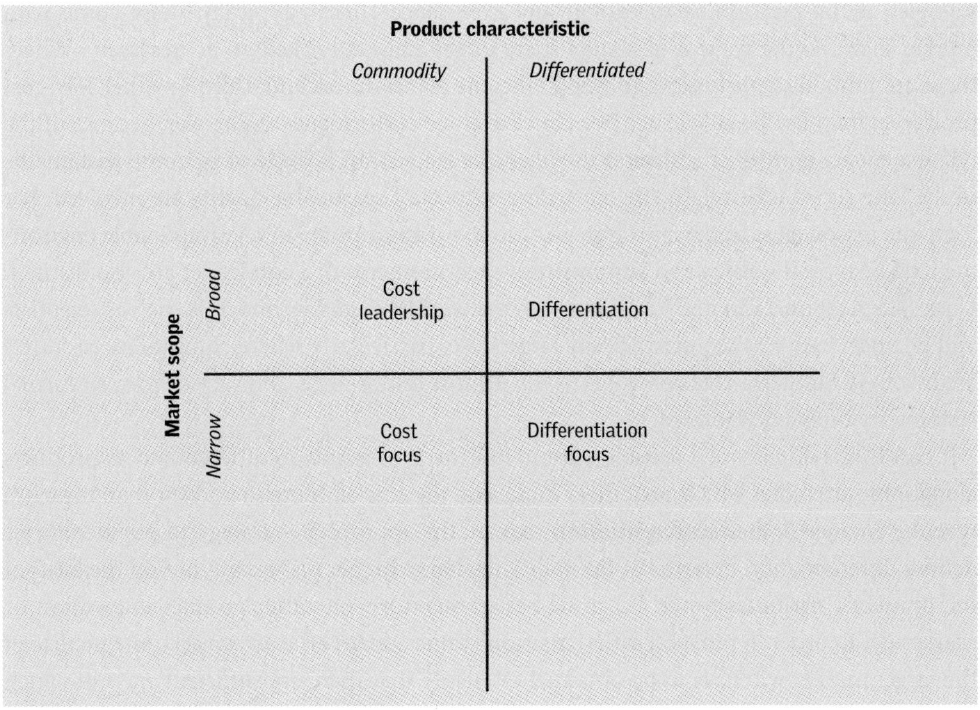

Figure 5.4 Porter's generic strategies

Source: Porter (1980) Chapter 2. Reprinted with permission of The Free Press, a division of Simon and Schuster Adult Publishing Group, from *Competitive Strategy* by Michael Porter. Copyright © 1980, 1998 by The Free Press. All rights reserved.

5.3 **Sources of competitive advantage**

The idea of a generic strategy is a powerful foundation for understanding how competitive strategies are in practice articulated and implemented. A generic strategy is a simple typology that captures the essential economic forces at work in a market (the demand side) and in an industry (the supply side). Porter suggested that there are three generic strategies to choose from, and each business unit can have its own strategy. According to Porter, a business can strive to supply a product or service more cost-effectively than its competitors (cost leadership), it can strive to add value to the product or service through differentiation and command higher prices (differentiation), or it can narrow its focus to a special product market segment which it can monopolize (focus). Not following any of these strategies characterizes a firm as being 'stuck in the middle'. The choice of generic strategy should be based on the firm's business unit's strengths and weaknesses, and a comparison of those with the strengths and weaknesses of competitors.

If a firm can become the lowest-cost producer in the industry then **cost leadership** may be the most appropriate strategy to pursue. Cost reduction should be continuous, so that the cost differential with competitors is maintained, and should involve all stages of the value chain. It can be achieved by methods such as proprietary access to cheaper inputs or technologies, or by positioning to exploit any experience effects. Typically, these come with market share, so the control of a large share of the market is likely to be necessary. Where there are limited opportunities to build efficient plant, the second, third or other low-cost producers may also be able to achieve above average performance. Moreover, because of the reliance on economies of scale and the like, cost leadership is likely to be more sustainable in the long run if relatively stable, no-frills products of reasonable quality are involved. For the same reason, cost leadership strategies are more appropriate in relatively stable environments. The typical staffing and administrative requirements of a cost leader are also distinct. Unskilled personnel can undertake much of the workload, and technocrats such as scientists and engineers are not required on any large scale, particularly where commodity products are involved. Similarly, cost control is of the utmost importance, and very developed formal systems are often encountered.

If cost leadership is not a feasible option, but the firm is able to differentiate its products along some attributes which customers value, and the cost of doing so is lower than the extra revenue envisaged, then **differentiation** may be the appropriate strategy to pursue. Porter defines differentiation in terms of the ability to charge higher prices, and not on the basis of the product's attributes *per se*. It can be based, therefore, on either product innovation or marketing. In order to pursue a differentiation (value added) strategy, an accurate picture of the target market will have to be obtained to ensure that there are sufficient ways in which to differentiate the product, and that the marketplace can be subdivided – and is willing to pay for the differentiation. An effort will then have to be made to avoid imitation, and this typically involves a regular redefinition of the basis of differentiation. For the same reason, it would be desirable for the differentiation to be based on a mix of features and activities rather than a simple product feature or service, and for it to involve many parts of the value chain. Added protection from imitation may also be possible by linking into the value chains of suppliers and buyers. Differentiation, whether innovation or marketing based, is more appropriate in dynamic industry environments, in which it can help to avoid, at least in the short run, potentially more costly forms of competition such as price cuts. However, as it often involves new technologies and unforeseen customer and competitor reactions, it also contributes, in turn, to environmental unpredictability. As far as staffing and administrative requirements are concerned, differentiation typically requires the employment of experts, and the establishment of mechanisms to facilitate the co-ordination of these experts, who may work in different functional departments.

If it is not possible to access the entire market on the basis of either low cost or differentiation, a defensible niche may still be available to provide above average performance. Marketing to such a niche would again involve a choice between low cost or differentiation but, this time, if the niche is well chosen, the scope of the market would enable the firm to advance on more limited cost and differentiation capabilities. In principle, a *focus* strategy exploits the differences in cost behaviour in some segments, or the special needs of the buyers in those segments, so it is only available where such segments are poorly served by the broadly targeted competitors and, of course, only sustainable for as long as the niche can be defended. The difficult point for the focuser is reached when the niche has been exhausted, at which time they may be tempted, out of a false sense of security derived from their success within the narrow scope of the niche, to target the broader market. This can have catastrophic consequences.

From the above discussion it should be evident that each generic strategy makes its own demands on the organization in terms of skills and administrative structure, and is more appropriate in different sets of circumstances. Nevertheless, a firm pursuing one strategy would act foolishly if it did not act to gain from elements of the other strategies too, as long as this did not detract it from its chosen strategy. A differentiator, for example, should pursue all cost reduction which does not sacrifice differentiation, and a cost leader could differentiate until this started to cost too much. However, when a firm confuses its primary goal and source of competitive advantage, and pursues both cost reduction and differentiation indiscriminately (or not at all), then it is said by Porter to be 'stuck in the middle'. This, he said, is an unenviable strategy because, in general, cost leadership and differentiation are inconsistent in principle, and there will typically be a cost leader, differentiator, or focuser that will be able to compete better than the firm stuck in the middle in any one segment of the market. Firms with such a (lack of) strategy, Porter said, typically end up stuck in the middle because they find it difficult to make the necessary choices.

There are a few cases, however, in which cost leadership and differentiation are not mutually inconsistent, at least in the short run. This may occur, for example, when the firm pioneers a proprietary innovation (whether a product, service or process) that enables it to reduce cost and at the same time differentiate successfully. With the appropriate barriers erected, it may be possible to exploit such an innovation for a considerable period of time. Similarly, cost leadership and differentiation may also be pursued together when costs are largely determined by market share, and control of a considerable share enables the firm to use the extra margin to differentiate and still remain the cost leader. The same may be possible if there are interrelationships between industries that a competitor may be able to exploit while others are not. In any case, the profitability of a 'stuck in the middle' company may remain adequate in the medium term in a high-growth environment (as this sustains inefficiencies), in a particularly attractive industry, or if the firm faces similarly stuck in the middle competitors.

Porter's claim that *no* firm should be stuck in the middle has, however, received critical attention and a lot of effort has gone into interpreting and questioning this advice. J.S. Sainsbury, the retailer ('Good food costs less at Sainsbury's'), is often cited as proof that a stuck in the middle strategy can be viable and successful (Cronshaw *et al.* 1990) because Sainsbury exhibits both low cost and differentiation. Gilbert and Strebel (1991) distinguished between one-dimensional and outpacing strategies, and suggested that the latter are designed for being stuck in the middle. The crux of this debate is that there exists no reason to imply that a low-cost base should necessarily be coupled with lower prices, or that a differentiated product should be coupled with premium prices. The low-cost base could simply be used to earn higher margins or, indeed, a differentiated product could be priced low enough to achieve a higher volume of sales (pricing differentiated products low enough to gain entry into a new market is only a temporary strategy which can lead to no competitive advantage, so it is of no relevance here). The underlying cause that leads to the overlap has been identified by Mathur (1988), who observed that whereas differentiation is an output concept, cost leadership is relevant to both inputs and outputs. Finally, some of the most common dangers to sustainability that are inherent in each of the strategies are shown in the tables in Chapter 6.

It is common to hear protests that generic strategies are too simple. But this is to miss the point. Generic strategies are intended to capture and portray the essential underlying economic forces. What firms do is to interpret these in the context of their own circumstances and formulate more or less complex strategies accordingly. Criticism has also focused on the lack of market orientation in the generic strategies matrix (Figure 5.4). Also missing is government and its frequently very significant role in the operation of markets. However, typologies and generics are not intended to be an accurate portrayal of the world – that is the role of the strategist in practice. Thus, the Ansoff diversification matrix is another generic strategies matrix. This sets out to define appropriate types of strategy for the marketing of new or existing products to new or existing markets. This attracted much attention because it drew the distinction between horizontal and vertical integration and conglomerate styles. These are pure types of strategy (like cost, differentiation and focus) that are applied in specific ways according to circumstances. Porter's generic strategy approach enables us to focus on the essence of strategy, which is to seek out and defend competitive advantage, a unique strategic position. This chapter and the one that follows goes behind the three generic strategies to examine the nature of strategic positioning so as to capture a sustainable competitive advantage.

5.4 **Describing strategy**

We are now in a position to set out the key headings under which we can describe an organization's strategy. The basic paradigm is set out in the strategic concepts framework introduced in Chapter 1 and is further developed in Figure 5.5.

Step 1 requires a description of the underlying mission of the organization and the objectives (including financial performance) that it wants to achieve over a defined time horizon. This includes coverage of mission and vision statements, the notion of strategic intent, and an assessment of stakeholders and shareholders (as discussed in Chapter 1).

Step 2 describes the scope of the organization – in which product markets does it choose to compete? Firms obviously cannot compete in any and every market. They must make some choices. However, the logic for making choices is not obvious in itself. Firms might choose to compete in closely related markets where, for example, the technologies and production methods are similar, where distribution channels are common, or where there are common customers for a range of products. But such 'relatedness' or 'synergy' can be difficult to define or achieve and some firms have preferred to adopt more conglomerate-style approaches where the chosen businesses are apparently very diverse (*see*, for example, Hanson plc and Tomkins in the UK). Another facet of scope is geographic markets.

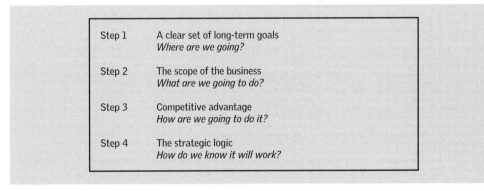

Figure 5.5 Describing strategy

Should one restrict the focus to the home market? Or are there arguments for adopting a more multinational posture? Ansoff's (1965) famous diversification matrix shows the different types of diversification. The grounds for making diversification (that is, scope) decisions are treated more formally in Chapter 9 on corporate strategy, in which business portfolio choices are analysed.

Step 3 articulates the benefits that the firm can bring to its customers and to itself by its positioning within its chosen product markets. Why should the customer buy this product? Why should he or she buy from us? What value can we gain from making this proposition to the customer? These are all ways of describing the nature of the competitive advantage that the firm can achieve.

Our definition of competitive advantage is:

> *Delivering superior value to customers and in doing so earning an above average return for the company and its stakeholders.*

This has implications for positioning choices in product markets. This takes us into Step 4, the strategic logic behind competitive advantage. This has two parts. The first is the positioning logic – the market-based logic which underpins our competitive advantage ambitions (*see* Figure 5.6). The second part is the resource-based logic that states why we think our intentions and actions about resources and capabilities will lead to the products and services that can be positioned in markets in the desired way (*see* Figure 5.7).

Listing the sources of advantage in this way gives us one way of focusing on the resources and capabilities that are needed. In this language we use resources to refer to tangible assets,

---

- Statement of competitive intent.

- The outward evidence of competitive advantage.

- Combination of:

  – superior delivered cost position

  – differentiation advantage

  – protected niches.

- Differences in positional advantage cannot be exploited profitably unless they can be seen to provide *direct benefits* which:

  – are perceived by a sizeable customer group

  – their customers value and are willing to pay for

  – cannot be readily obtained elsewhere both now and in the foreseeable future.

Figure 5.6 Positional advantage

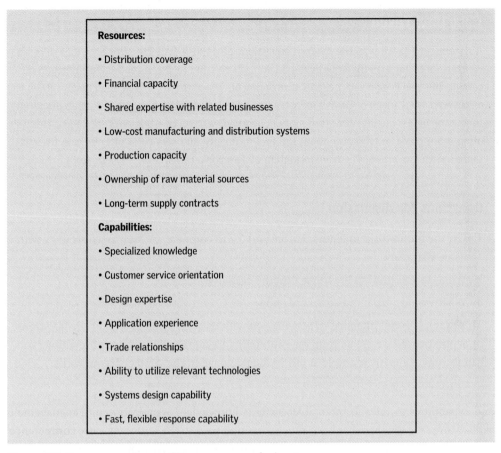

Figure 5.7 Resources and capabilities as sources of advantage

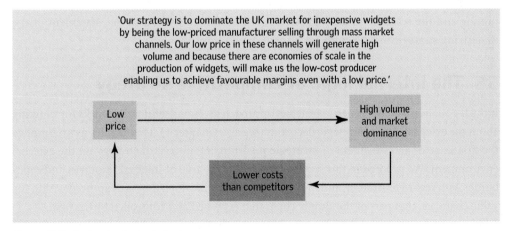

Figure 5.8 A simple strategic logic

Case box: **Tesco**

A decade ago Tesco was the modern equivalent of a music hall joke. But now it is a Tesco which is laughing – all the way to the bank … at the end of the seventies Tesco began discarding the 'pile it high sell it cheap' philosophy on which the chain had been built … then it discovered what much of British industry has been learning; that people are often prepared to pay for better quality, are often more concerned with service than with price and there's often more profit in worrying about the feel of quality and service than in bribing the customers with low prices. The transformation of Tesco is a remarkable success story.

Source: D. Powell (1991) *Counter Revolution: The Tesco Story*, Grafton Books, London.

Questions for discussion

1 Use the frameworks in Figure 5.5, 5.6 and 5.7 to compare the 'old' Tesco strategy with its new strategy.

2 What do you think is the impact on the cash flows?

3 What would a balanced scorecard show?

This example is not intended to provide you with enough detail to answer the questions in depth. Instead we are looking for your ability to capture the essence of retailing (you can use any company example at all) in the language of the strategy frameworks.

and capabilities to refer to intangibles such as knowledge, organization and management skills. More recently there has been much attention paid to the notion of '**core competence**' – an amalgam of the languages of resources and capabilities. We define core competence as the underlying capability that is the distinguishing characteristic of the organization. We explore these ideas further in Chapter 7. Putting together the market-based logic of positioning and the resource-based logic we should be able to make a simple statement of the underlying strategic logic. Figure 5.8 provides an example.

5.5 **The internal logic of competitive strategy**

Industry analysis and the generic strategies approach gives us useful frameworks for thinking about the external logic of strategic decisions (see also Chapter 1). This enables us to complete the first stage of an assessment of **strategic position**, the impact of strategy on the external environment. We proceed in this section to examine the role of internal resources and capabilities with regard to strategy, and in particular the way in which they are captured within the value chain, i.e. that part of the supply chain that is owned and controlled by the firm.

First we look at a map of the interaction between the external world and the internal world of the firm. This is explicit about the nature of strategy over time and asks about the inherent stability or instability of strategy – the strategy cycle.

5.5.1 **The strategy cycle**

Strategy is concerned with fashioning success in the long term, hence there is a performance dimension to the market-based view and the resource-based view. This is demonstrated in Figure 5.9 which shows how the real economy[2] of the firm (the creation of resources and capabilities and the positioning within product markets) interacts with the financial economy of the firm. The top line shows schematically the transformation of 'raw' assets (people, knowledge, and money) into resources and capabilities customized to create goods and services for the chosen product markets. The 'output' of the real economy is cash flow conditioned by the scale of the competitive advantage achieved.

Competitive advantage has two dimensions: the extra value over competitors that customers receive, and the extra value in terms of real profits that are taken back into the firm. These profits, contained within the cash flow, are partitioned between those that are returned to shareholders and debt holders, and those that are retained internally. The returns to shareholders and bondholders as dividends and interest payments serve to maintain the value of the firm in financial markets through two mechanisms. The first is the market value as represented by the share price, which itself is determined through the price/earnings ratio by dividends and by shareholder expectations about future profitability. The second is the credit rating (for example, an AAA rating by Standard & Poors on the New York Stock Exchange) which influences the interest rates a company will have to pay for any new debt issues. Through these mechanisms the value of the firm and its financial capacity are established. Coupled with internal liquidity, this represents the ability of the firm to reinvest in resources and capabilities.

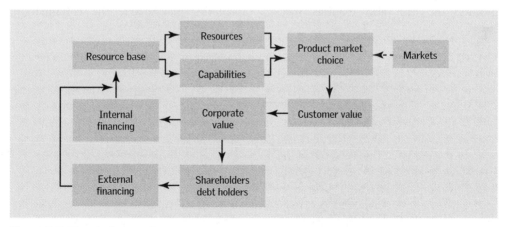

Figure 5.9 The strategy cycle

[2] The 'real' economy is the trade in goods and services as opposed to the 'financial' economy.

We can see the possibility of a virtuous circle whereby the firm enjoys competitive advantage and superior profitability, has the financial capacity to reinvest in its assets, capabilities and competences, from which it can further enhance its competitive advantage and its profitability, and so on. We can see also the possibility of a vicious spiral in which competitive disadvantage and poor profitability could be matched with limited financial capacity and consequent inability to reinvest to restore competitive advantage and so on.

A key role for top management is to manage this balance between the firm's real and financial economy. The dynamics of markets and companies is such that there is rarely a balance; rather, there is continuous adjustment of the key decision variables so as to maintain competitiveness in markets, maintain cash flows, and maintain financial capacity. In this sense we see the firm as taking 'actions' to influence the 'context' in which it works in order to achieve superior 'performance' (*see* Figure 5.10). Context in this language has external dimensions, such as markets and industry membership, and internal dimensions, such as its assets and its organization structure and processes. Strategy, thus, has a focus on actions to affect performance directly and indirectly through context.

The strategy cycle demonstrates (in the top line of Figure 5.9) the conversion of basic *resources* into customized assets which we will call **capabilities**. The ability of a firm to create customer value and corporate value (line 2 of Figure 5.9) depends on the match that can be made between internal resources and capabilities and the opportunities and risks endemic in the external environment. There is an important distinction to be made between resources and capabilities. Resources are typically inputs into the real economy of the firm. They include finance, skills of individual employees, purchased components and items of capital equipment, and anything else purchased on open markets. Resources on their own do not provide a distinctive characteristic to the firm. To obtain a distinctive strategic position the firm also requires specific capabilities that enable the combination,

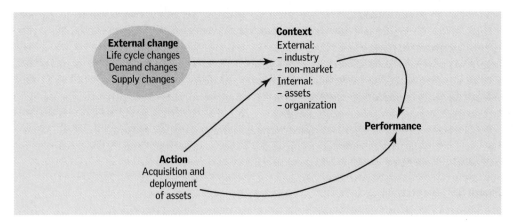

Figure 5.10 The dynamics of strategy

development and co-ordination of basic resources. Capability (often called competence) is the capacity to perform tasks or activities and distinctive capabilities (or core competences) are the capacities to perform these tasks in a sufficiently distinctive way so as to create unique strategic positions (see Figure 5.7), as explored further in Chapter 7.

5.5.2 The value chain

We have seen that the supply chain forms the basic spine of the five forces analysis. It contains all the activities required to bring the final product or service to the customer. Along the way many different firms or businesses have their own activities along the supply chain. Each firm has its own **value chain**, a subset of the supply chain. Figure 5.11 is Porter's classic picture of the value chain. It has two parts. The lower part contains those activities (labelled primary activities) that are organized in sequence, just like a production line. Thus, inbound logistics is the first step, leading to manufacturing operations, then outbound logistics, marketing and sales, and eventually service. This is a caricature and each firm's value chain will contain different headings according to the nature of the operations. These categories can be described as follows:

- *Inbound logistics.* Activities associated with receiving, storing, and disseminating rights to the product, such as material handling, warehousing, stock management and the like.

- *Operations.* All of the activities required to transform inputs into outputs and the critical functions which add value, such as machining, packaging, assembly, service, testing and so on.

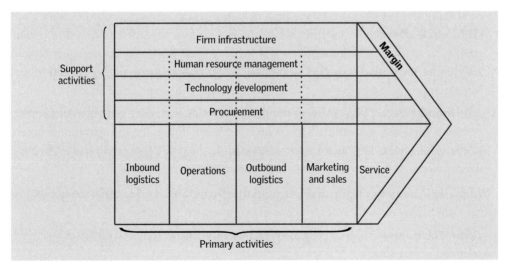

Figure 5.11 The generic value chain
Source: adapted from Porter (1985).

- *Outbound logistics.* All of the activities required to collect, store and physically distribute the output. This activity can prove to be extremely important both in generating value and in improving differentiation, as in many industries control over distribution strategies is proving to be a major source of competitive advantage – especially as it is realized that up to 50 per cent of the value created in many industry chains occurs close to the ultimate buyer.

- *Marketing and sales.* Activities associated with informing potential buyers about the firm's products and services, and inducing them to purchase by personal selling, advertising and promotion, and so on.

- *Service.* The means of enhancing the physical product features through after-sales service, installation, repair and so on.

The second part of the value chain is the upper section which contains all the overhead service elements (labelled support activities) required by the firm. In Porter's picture he named four elements: firm infrastructure, human resource management, technology development and procurement.

1 *Procurement.* This concerns the acquisition of inputs or resources. Although technically the responsibility of the purchasing department, almost everyone in the firm is responsible for purchasing something. While the cost of procurement itself is relatively low, the impact can be very high.

2 *Human resource management.* This consists of all activities involved in recruiting, hiring, training, developing, rewarding and sanctioning the people in the organization.

3 *Technology development.* This is concerned with the equipment, hardware, software, technical skills and the like used by the firm in transforming inputs to outputs. Some such skills can be classified as scientific, while others – such as food preparation in a restaurant – are 'artistic'. Such skills are not always recognized. They may also support limited activities of the business, such as accounting, order procurement and so on, and in this sense may be likened to the value added component of the experience effect.

4 *Firm infrastructure.* This consists of the many activities, including general management, planning, finance, legal, external affairs and so on, which support the operational aspect of the value chain. This may be self-contained in the case of an undiversified firm or divided between the parent and the firm's constituent business units.

Within each category of primary and support activities, Porter identifies three types of activity which play different roles in achieving competitive advantage:

- *Direct.* These are activities directly involved in creating value for buyers, such as assembly, sales and advertising.

- *Indirect.* These are activities that facilitate the performance of the direct activities on a continuing basis, such as maintenance, scheduling and administration.

◆ *Quality assurance.* These are activities that insure the quality of other activities, such as monitoring, inspecting, testing and checking.

The value chain is another generic framework that permits a range of applications and analyses. It permits the analyst to decompose the firm's activities into broad categories (as above) and increasingly into finer categories. Thus, operations might be refined into sub-components and assembly; marketing and sales into market research, product development, sales force and so on. The usefulness of this is to be able to identify those activities that are the source of the competitive advantage and to be able to locate them within the value chain. For example, if Intel's competitive advantage is product performance and this is derived (at least in large part) from R&D activities, then this can be isolated within the value chain and measured, compared to competitors, and provided with support.

Competitive advantage is often quite subtle in its manifestation and in its sources. Cost advantage might arise from the way in which every single activity in the value chain is linked to the others and managed for efficiency. The story of the low-cost airlines such as easyJet, RyanAir and SouthWest Airlines is about system management of the costs as well as focus on driving down each cost component. Differentiation may be delivered as a service quality perception driven by the way in which each element of service delivery is managed systematically, along with all other elements, in order to differentiate the product. The case exercise at the end of the chapter illustrates this for the hotel chain Novotel.

The Novotel example shows how the value chain can be a powerful tool in diagnosing and explaining how the management of competitive advantage takes place within the firm. The interrelationships between the elements of the value chain provide an important explanation of the nature of competitive advantage in large, complex organizations. Such organizations typically are rich in tacit knowledge. This is the kind of knowledge that you call upon to ride a bicycle. We all know how to do this – but it is impossible to explain it. Similarly, large corporations are used to making links between complex and far-flung activities, and between related and unrelated technologies. This is a glue that binds these companies together and makes it impossible for others to imitate quickly. The 'hidden' part of the value chain is these linkages that contain the tacit knowledge. In the Novotel example we can see how the authors use Novotel's own management processes to describe how the elements of the chain are linked together. The way this glue works determines the level of vertical integration, i.e. those elements of the supply chain that can be brought within the value chain and within the firm, and those that should remain outside the firm. The guiding principle is that when the costs of internal transactions (making the glue work properly) exceed the costs of buying outside, then the firm should source outside its boundaries. This glue is part of the core competence that we will be discussing in Chapter 7. We turn now to the issues of cost analysis and outsourcing.

The value chain and cost analysis

The value chain provides a good basis on which to conduct a cost analysis. Its principal advantage is that the elements of the value chain are already organized around those issues that are important in driving competitive advantage and profitability. Porter was therefore able in his 1985 book to make very strong links with the array of literature and practice on cost cutting that was already available. A criticism of the cost analysis literature was the difficulty of defining the correct units of analysis, an issue which the value chain solved brilliantly at a stroke!

Therefore a normal cost analysis procedure can take place with the following stages:[3]

1 Define the value chain in terms of those elements that relate to the sources of competitive advantage. Key considerations are:
    - The separateness and independence of one activity from another.
    - The importance of an activity in relation to competitive advantage and to the margin.
    - The dissimilarity of activities in terms of requiring different cost drivers.
    - The extent to which there are differences in the way competitors perform activities (i.e. where there are differences there are potential advantages to be gained).

2 Establish the relative importance of different activities in the total cost of the product. This means assigning costs to each activity based on management accounts or other customized analysis procedures. The distinctions made in Chapter 3 about fixed and variable costs sunk costs, and cost allocations are really significant issues at this stage. Errors in cost analysis can lead to significant misunderstanding of the what contributes to profits and how valuable a competitive advantage is.

3 Compare costs by activity and benchmark against competitors. The comparison is not in terms of how big are the costs but how different are they from efficiency benchmarks and from competitor standards.

4 Identify cost drivers. These are the forces that move costs up or down. Planned scale of activities is a driver of overall plant cost and so also is degree of capacity utilization. A driver of sales force costs might be product range – if the range is too small, costs will be high. Another driver will be geographical concentration of customers and another might be sales communication methods (face to face or remote teleconferencing). For labour intensive activities critical drivers might be wage rates, speed of production line and defect rates. It is the understanding of cost drivers that signifies how well you understand the nature of your business. One needs to look behind the obvious in order to identify the fundamentals.

5 Identify linkages between activities. As we see from the Novotel example, interrelationships may be very many in number – the critical cost drivers may seemingly relate to

---

[3] This section draws on Grant (2002), Ch. 7.

another activity entirely. We will see in later chapters a comparison between Xerox and Canon in the photocopying industry. Xerox found that its service costs were driven by design complexity and manufacturing inefficiencies. Grants observes that:

> *the optimisation of activities through the value chain has become a major source of cost reduction, and speed enhancement has become a key challenge for computer integrated manufacturing.* Grant (2002, p. 271)

6 Identify opportunities for reducing costs. By identifying areas of obvious inefficiency (i.e. deviations from designed machine performance standards) and of deficiencies against competitive benchmarks, opportunities for cost reduction become evident. Very often the option is posed of contracting outside the firm for components or services. Some firms have subcontracted entire IT departments. Currently European firms are outsourcing their call centres to India. The automobile companies are going through an extensive process of outsourcing. The Ford Fiesta plants in Cologne outsource fully made-up doors (as a subsystem) to plants adjacent to the Ford plant.

Value chain in summary[4]

The value chain concept thus helps to identify cost behaviour in detail. From this analysis, different strategic courses of action should be identifiable in order to develop differentiation and less price sensitive strategies. Competitive advantage is then achieved by performing strategic activities better or cheaper than competitors.

To diagnose competitive advantage, it is necessary to define the firm's value chain for operating in a particular industry and compare this with those of key competitors. A comparison of the value chains of different competitors often identifies ways of achieving strategic advantage by reconfiguring the value chain of the individual firm. In assigning costs and assets it is important that the analysis be done strategically rather than seeking accounting precision. This should be accomplished using the following principles:

- operating costs should be assigned to activities where incurred;
- assets should be assigned to activities where employed, controlled, or influencing usage;
- accounting systems should be adjusted to fit value analysis;
- asset valuation may be difficult, but should recognize industry norms – particular care should be taken in evaluating property assets.

The reconfiguration of the value chain has often been used by successful competitors in achieving competitive advantage. When seeking to reconfigure the value chain in an industry, the following questions need to be asked:

- How can an activity be done differently or even eliminated?

---

[4] See Channon (2005).

- How can linked value activities be reordered or regrouped?
- How could coalitions with other firms reduce or eliminate costs?

5.6 Strategy making in practice

5.6.1 Intended versus emergent strategies

As we saw in Chapter 1, strategic management deals essentially with four questions:

1 How do we develop and formulate strategy?
2 How do we make choices between strategic options?
3 How do we put the strategy into operation and sustain it over time?
4 How do we manage the processes of strategic change and strategy renewal?

The first question raises issues of intended and planned strategies (typically top-down) versus emergent strategies, which arise from experience and learning and where the emphasis is on knowledge that is distributed throughout the organization, versus accidents, serendipity and 'muddling through', within which strategy is very much the junior partner to flexibility, operations expertise, tactical acumen and speed of response.

The second question focuses on the nature of data and information required, the analytical processes used and how trade-offs are made. It confronts the logic approach of economic and quantitative models with the uncertainty and risk endemic in long-term decisions and raises questions about criteria for decision making and the nature and role of organizational influences.

The third question is widely regarded as the key to superior performance. This view is based on the nostrum that ideas are cheap but action is difficult. However, we argue throughout this book that these questions are linked and, for example, difficulties in implementation are partly (if not largely) to do with over-ambition and error in the first two parts. Nevertheless, implementation is distinctively difficult. It is complex in the range and the depth of detail making operational planning and control highly complex. It often requires the adoption of path-breaking new knowledge beyond the known best practice. Thus it is clear that matters may not proceed as expected and contingencies have to be anticipated. If operational matters were clear-cut and lacked complexity then it would almost always follow that the strategy would lack distinctiveness and competitive advantage would not be attained. The points at which competitive advantage are delivered are generally through specific operations and activities. Where these are unique, or at least new to the firm, successful implementation is clearly not assured. The issue of sustainability is to be seen in similar fashion. Keeping ahead of competitors involves continuous reinvestment and reappraisal of key operations. Thus, the firm is continually having to prospect into new territory in order to keep ahead, with all the risks and uncertainties that this implies. These issues are all taken up in detail in Part 4 of this book.

The fourth question has provided significant employment and fee income for consultants. Referring back to the strategy cycle diagram (Figure 5.9), we observed that strategies get out of date and performance suffers when markets change faster than organizations can respond. This gives rise to the need for strategic change and renewal. The management of strategic change has been one of the central practical and theoretical issues of the last 25 years. The era since 1979 has been one of radical external change resulting in radical changes to the business portfolios and activities of firms and to their traditional ways of doing business. The most common management responses have been to divest businesses and product lines in order to refocus on sustainable core businesses in which competitive advantage can be pursued. The pressures for internationalization have been very strong and companies have used acquisitions, alliances and organic growth in order to enter new markets. This combination of retrenchment plus expansion has obliged firms to undertake major programmes of change in which these changes in strategy have had to be matched by internal changes in organization structure and habitual ways of doing business (culture), and management processes have also had to be adapted and re-engineered.

5.6.2 Assessing progress

Bearing in mind the complexities arising from the proposition that at least part of your strategy may in practice be emergent or accidental (see Chapter 1), there is nevertheless a need to assess progress against your intentions. This section suggests a number of questions that you can use to judge the underlying logic of a strategy and the validity of the fundamental planning process.

Judging a competitive strategy

1 What does the customer really want and is willing to pay for?

2 What is the economic logic of the industry and how is it changing?

3 What are the key forces for change and how are we planning to take advantage of them?

4 What is the company's competitive advantage (business idea) that makes it unique?

5 How can it gain this competitive advantage?

6 How are the competitors likely to react?

You can see that these questions are closely related to our description of strategy in the strategy cycle.

How good is the strategic thinking?

1 Is strategy clearly articulated:

◆ in product-market terms?

◆ with measurable objectives?

◆ with clear milestones?

◆ specific on source of competitive advantage?

2 Is it evident that strategy has been created with reference to the external environment?

3 Does strategy provide a clear guide to resource allocation?

4 Are business unit strategies clearly stated and linked to corporate strategy?

5 Is strategic planning linked to operational decision making?

6 Is the budgeting process subservient to the strategic planning process?

Points 1 to 6 relate directly to the content of the strategy and the way it is linked up and down the organization to its main systems and processes.

7 Is strategy consciously set by senior management?

8 Is the company's culture and value system conducive to strategic thinking?

9 Is strategy widely understood by division and middle level managers?

10 Is the concept of strategy understood by those providing 'strategy inputs'?

Points 7 to 10 bring in managers and management and provide a basis for asking how strategy processes and the values in the company actually support the production of 'good' strategy content.

Ten questions for judging a strategic plan

1 Will a high-quality business position result?
   ◆ At the end of the planning period we should feel good about the character and quality of our achievement, that is, a strong foundation and competitive position, and attractive financial results.

2 Is it clear what we want to have in our value chain?
   ◆ What will we invest in and what will we discard? Resource priorities should be focused in order to develop a healthy portfolio and a value chain of activities that can be managed with economies of scale and scope.

3 How are we anticipating and managing change to our advantage?
   ◆ The environment is changing rapidly: how will competitors respond and what are we planning to do?

4 Are the assumptions sound?
   ◆ Major changes in volume, share or margins should be firmly based on plans that support such changes, taking into account market realities and competitor reactions.

5 Are there specific concrete ideas driving the plan?

- Avoid 'hollow' plans that are superficially attractive but lack a solid idea capable of good execution.

6 Is there a sustainable competitive advantage?

- What is it that is going to result in superior performance over time and will warrant investment?

7 Is the implementation clear and specific?

- The organization must be able to understand, accept and carry out the key actions involved.

8 Are the financial results achievable?

- Is cash generation evident within an appropriate time frame with clear milestones identified?

9 Are the necessary resources identified?

- The plan must be within the existing capabilities of the company or have identified how these will be obtained.

10 Will the organization be able to adapt to the plan and its implementation?

- How much change in current operations and motivation of key managers will be required for successful achievement?

5.6.3 Assessing progress: the balanced scorecard

A critical element in successful strategy implementation is an appropriate performance measurement system (we develop this theme at greater length in Chapter 18). Conventional accounting systems often do not provide the critical information required by management to assess the company's progress to achieving its strategic vision and objectives because of their focus on reporting the past rather than assessing the future consequences of decisions made now. The **balanced scorecard** is a performance measurement system developed by Kaplan and Norton (1992) which, although including financial measures of performance, also contains operational measures of customer satisfaction, internal processes, and the company's innovation and improvement activities. These are seen collectively as the key drivers of future financial performance and individually as key success factors.

The balanced scorecard examines a business from the four important perspectives of:

- How do customers see the firm?
  (*customer perspective*)

- What does the firm excel at?
  (*internal perspective*)

- Can the firm continue to improve and create value?
  (*innovation and learning perspective*)

◆ How does the firm look to shareholders?
  (*financial perspective*)

This approach avoids information overload by restricting the number of measures used so as to focus only on those seen to be essential – the key success factors.[5] The balanced scorecard presents this information in a single management report and therefore brings together often disparately reported elements of the firm's strategic position such as short-term customer response times, product quality, teamwork capability, new product launch times and the like. As a result, the approach guards against suboptimization by forcing management to examine individual operational measures systematically and comprehensively.

A typical scoreboard is illustrated in Figure 5.12. From this you can see how management can translate its general mission statements into the four perspectives, each of which contains a series of specific measures. The precise scorecard design should reflect the vision and strategic objectives of the individual company. The key point is that the scorecard approach

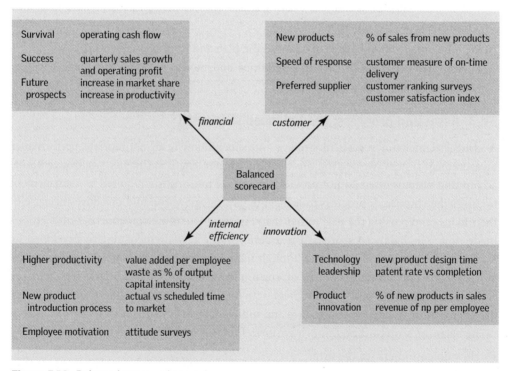

Figure 5.12 Balanced scorecard example

---

[5] The term '**key success factors**' is widely used but rarely defined. In the next two chapters we will provide a useable definition, but for this chapter just think of it as referring to the range of competitive advantages evident in an industry from which firms make profits.

puts strategy and corporate vision, rather than financial reporting, as the key driver of performance management design (see Chapter 1). This is consistent with the development of corporate transformation techniques, cross-functional organizations, customer–supplier interrelationships and other major corporate programmes that are designed to have major effects on business performance.

> Question: Using Figure 5.12 and the previous case box examples on Tesco and the profitability of UK retailers, try to create a balanced scorecard for Tesco (or any other major retailer).

The case box below is included here for you to look at a specific characteristic of retailing, namely capital intensity, and ask, how does this affect the way we look at a business and how, therefore, does it affect the way in which we judge progress over time?

Case box: **Capital intensity in retailing**

A distinctive feature of the UK supermarket industry has been that it is far more capital intensive than in other countries. This stems, first, from certain aspects of the property market in the UK. Britain is a small country, and land for development is scarce and therefore expensive. During a long period of rising prosperity and therefore of increased demand it has become more scarce (as Mark Twain noted, 'They've stopped making it'). In these circumstances leases always contain regular, upward-only rent reviews. Ownership of commercial sites is concentrated among institutional investors, who are interested only in their capital gains and revenue streams. British leasehold law allows the lessor to recover all rent due from the head lessee, even though the lease may have been assigned, often many times. The original lessee may thus find that – when the latest tenant has defaulted, and even if the premises are shuttered – the owner will pursue him for all rent owing. British supermarket companies have therefore concentrated almost entirely on freehold properties.

Further, the planning authorities have insisted on high building standards, so the cheap, large sheds of Continental or US hypermarkets are not an option for UK grocers. One estimate suggests that a US supermarket can be built for half the cost of its UK equivalent.

High investment is also needed for the IT systems on which a modern retail chain depends. It would be impossible to run a group of several hundred stores, each with 20 000 or more SKUs (stocking units) without a formidably effective IT system. All the UK chains have invested hundreds of millions of pounds over the years on IT.

Finally, compared with France at least, UK retailers have to fund more of their own working capital. In France, the large food retailers take at least 90 days credit from their suppliers; in Britain, the figure is nearer 30 days. UK food manufacturers may feel that they are supplying their retail customers with much of their working capital along with their products, but the situation is much worse in Continental Europe.

High capital investment has been forced on the UK chains, and has dictated much of their strategy; they *have* to achieve higher margins. Their drive for efficiency has led them inexorably to the superstore format (seemingly unique to Britain, because of the market size and population density), and to take over much of the distribution chain themselves. Return on capital, the ultimate measure of profitability, shows that they achieve results similar to their rivals elsewhere but the route is different – higher margins and higher capital intensity.

Source: adapted from Seth and Randall (1999), pp. 226–7.
Reproduced with permission of Kogan Page Ltd.

Questions for discussion

1   How does capital intensity affect the way in which profits are earned?
2   What does this imply for strategic decisions such as store expansion and pricing?

5.7 Summary

This chapter, along with Chapters 3 and 4, provides a foundation for the strategy analysis that comes in Part 3. In this chapter we have introduced the idea of competitive advantage as a firm-specific imperfection that is the foundation and cornerstone of all strategy analysis. Strategy cannot be understood without this concept and it cannot exist without it existing in practice. Without competitive advantage we are consigned to the 'strategic hell' of perfect competition in which profits are elusive, products are commodities and firms are creatures of their environments. With competitive advantage, firms can be different, managers and managements can exercise choice and discretion, and entrepreneurial profits are possible. With competitive advantage we can have strategic choice. We can observe industries in which the participants can pursue similar or different strategies. Above all, with diverse and changing consumers firms can be entrepreneurial in constructing new value propositions. The ways in which competitive advantage can be deployed in different strategic clothes is the subject of the next section of seven chapters. The way the practice of strategy is carried on in the pursuit of competitive advantage is the subject of the six chapters of Part 4.

Alongside the idea of competitive advantage we have introduced some other well-known ideas. Generic strategies provide a typology of strategies based on competitive advantage. The value chain gives us a framework for identifying and analysing the internal disposition of assets, resources and activities. The balanced scorecard enables us to relate performance outcomes to these strategy ideas. We have also looked at some practical ways of categorizing strategy and assessing a firm's progress in setting out its own strategic thinking.

Key terms

Balanced scorecard *177*

Capabilities *168*

Competitive advantage *148*

Competitive rivalry *153*

Core competence *166*

Cost leadership *160*

Differentiation *160*

Economies of scope *157*

Firm-specific imperfections *154*

Five forces *149*

Fixed costs *149*

Generic strategies *159*

Key success factors *178*

Market-based view (MBV) *154*

Positioning *154*

Power of suppliers and buyers *151*

Rents *153*

Resource-based view (RBV) *154*

Scope *157*

Strategic position *166*

Supply chain *149*

Threat of entry *150*

Threat of substitutes *152*

Value chain *169*

Recap questions and assignments

1   Undertake a strategy audit of a business with which you are familiar. How attractive is the industry in which it competes? What strategies seem to be available in this industry? How would you describe the strategy of your selected business (Cheat: use Figure 5.5)?

2   Choose two companies in the same industry – preferably direct competitors – and compare the configuration of their value chains. Explain how these relate to their competitive positioning.

3   Do a SWOT analysis for your chosen business. Explain why you have chosen each of the key items.

Online LearningCentre

When you have read this chapter, log on to the Online Learning Centre website at www.mcgraw-hill.co.uk/textbooks/mcgee to explore chapter-by-chapter test questions, further reading and more online study tools for strategy.

Case 1 **The Novotel value chain**

Figure 5.13 captures some of the key elements in the Novotel value chain. Each of the elements of the chain is important in itself for service delivery. But also most of them interact with other elements.

To expand further on the *hospitality concept*, one would need to describe intangibles such as 'greeting', 'welcome for the traveller' and personal warmth. It lends a relevant insight into the nature of the management task in services to reflect on the robustness of internal systems and processes to deliver these service elements to the customer on a routine basis. Indeed, Novotel use the layout of their hotel (part of *Service Design*, the first lower half (primary) activity in column 1) to lead the customer immediately to the 'hospitable' public spaces of bar and restaurant, which are always on the entry floor adjacent to reception.

Marketing (lower half, column 2) is extensive, sophisticated and linked closely to *distribution systems*. Novotel operates within both the individual and corporate business and leisure markets. Its special promotions and advertising themes (column 2, lower half) address these different segments. For example, Dolphi, a baby dolphin, is the marketing and promotional symbol for children's events worldwide. However, although all *locations* worldwide (column 1, lower half) will use the co-ordinated symbol and marketing materials for this (or any other) segment, general managers at different locations and in different countries will tailor promotions to local holidays and lifestyles.

Partnership programmes (column 2, lower half) are common nowadays. Novotel links them with deepening *relationship marketing* (column 2, top half). Particularly noteworthy are the supplier partnership programmes, linked with purchasing and learning efficiencies (see *firm infrastructure* and *procurement* in top half of value chain), delivering both scale and scope economies. An example of this would be an agreement to purchase televisions from a sole *preferred supplier worldwide* (column 1, top half) – a recent innovation at Novotel where local purchasing had been common. The television (or any other) supplier would be expected to develop a reciprocal relationship through utilizing their customer's hotels for corporate travel purposes (column 3). *Purchasing efficiencies* are thus linked to *internal and external relationship marketing* (see linkages between columns 1, 2 and 3 in top half).

The *hospitality concept* is further implemented by other key elements in *Service Delivery* (column 4). *Staff exchanges* (column 4, lower half) (between countries, locations and type of customer mix) contributing to *multi-culture* (column 1, top half) are essential to the philosophy of 'welcome'. They provide a means of motivating staff in an industry where labour turnover is typically high (column 4, top half – *staff retention*) and service delivery is dependent on the quality of the service encounter, to which staff motivation is crucial (column 4, lower half – *responsiveness* etc.). It also ensures an international mix of hotel staff to interact sympathetically with an international client mix.

HIGH EXPERIENCE EFFECTS (eg. site selection, hotel construction)
EFFECTIVE MANAGEMENT OF LINKAGES

	SERVICE DESIGN	MARKETING	DISTRIBUTION	SERVICE DELIVERY	SERVICE MONITORING & ENHANCEMENT
FIRM INFRA-STRUCTURE	– Central design unit – NPD	– Global branding & positioning – Image management	– Central systems – Accor HQ	– Académie Accor – G M autonomy	– Flat reporting structure – WAR ROOM – Transfer of best practice
HRM	– HOSPITALITY CONCEPT – Core values – Multi-culture	– Relationship marketing (internal & external) – Incentive programmes	– Relationship-building:	– Superior recruitment & selection – TRAINING – Superior staff retention	– Extensive training – Skills grading
TECHNOL DEVELPT	– Customer interface – Service needs – Rapid roll-out of new specifications	– Software & systems development	– Global reservation systems – Network linkages – Dedicated suppliers (global)	– Unique service features	– Process development
PROCUREMENT	– Standardization – Worldwide global best suppliers – High quality components & features	– Media selection placement & negotiation – Market research	– Dedicated software/systems	– Best available inputs – EOS	– Continuous enhancement & upgrading

PURCHASING SCALE EFFICIENCIES

SERVICE DESIGN	MARKETING	DISTRIBUTION	SERVICE DELIVERY	SERVICE MONITORING & ENHANCEMENT

– Tight design specifications
– Global coverage
– 3-star
– Features:
  – hotels
  – rooms
  – restaurants
– Layout
– Locations
– Image
	– Corporate travel management
	– Partnership programmes
	– Special promotions
	  – segmentation
	– Advertising themes
	  – for segments
	– Materials
	  – brochures
	  – give-aways
	– Campaign mgt.
	– Pricing
	– Supplier partnerships
	– Personal relationships with suppliers
		– Geographic network
		– Best locations
		– Centralized systems
		– Corporate agency network
		– Travel agency network
		– Availability
		– Rapid response/ timelines
		– Capacity utilization
		– Vertical & horizontal integration
			– Staff multi-skilling
			– Staff exchanges
			– Transferability of staff & skills
			– Languages
			– Responsiveness to customer requirements
			– Interface mgt.
			– High service recovery
			– Attractive styles/ appearance (people & hotels)
				– High quality controls
				– High conformance
				– Standard setting/quality measures
				– Skills – testing & banding/ grading
				– Extensive supplier training
				– Directors Clubs
				– Progress Groups (all staff levels)
				– 'Progress Novotel'
				– Customer surveys/feedback
				– Staff surveys/feedback
				– Staff empowerment
				– 'Pilot Case'
				– 'Quick' meetings
				– Refurbishment

Figure 5.13 Value chain for Novotel
Source: McGee and Segal-Horn (1997).

However, the more interesting elements of the Novotel offering for the purposes of this discussion are the management processes which enable the standardized service levels to be delivered at all locations worldwide.

Since hotel design and guest bedrooms are standardized, basic housekeeping and maintenance functions can in turn be standardized (see all *Service Design* and *Firm Infrastructure* elements in Figure 5.13). That means that training of staff in all basic functions may be simplified and the procedures for training can be themselves standardized (see all *HRM* and *Service Delivery* elements). Indeed, one of the features of the Accor Group (Novotel's parent) is the 'Academie Accor' set up in 1985, as the centre for all staff training within the Group. It's 'campus' is located on the site of Group corporate headquarters just outside Paris. From there, all training is designed and delivered. This standardized approach to the core service concept places special requirements on the staff as the key medium for delivery of consistent service standards wherever the customer is staying. Standardized procedures and centrally designed training programmes are one of the core mechanisms for securing such consistency (columns 4 and 5).

Taking the notion of consistency one stage further, the Novotel senior management developed a new approach to staffing in the hotel sector which is described as 'multi-skilling'. The idea behind multi-skilling is to develop staff as a team able to perform tasks and work as needed in a flexible manner. Obviously, this would have many advantages for hotel management, not least in smoothing the need for certain types of staff at peak bottleneck periods of the day or evening. Pressures on checking-in or checking-out at reception and getting rooms cleaned while guests are at breakfast are common bottlenecks dramatically affecting patterns of staffing. With the Novotel approach to flexible skilling and team working, a new pattern is emerging. Flexible working patterns have broken down some of the staff demarcation normal within the hotel industry. Reception and front-of-house activities (e.g. showing guests to rooms) may be carried out by the same staff as serve in the restaurant at peak mealtimes or perform housekeeping or room-cleaning tasks at other times of the day. The benefits of this to the firm have been enormous in a reduction of core staff levels and a more resourceful workforce. However, maintaining universal quality standards as the chain grew rapidly over a 25-year period became more and more problematic, especially when many new staff were recruited from other hotel groups with different working practices.

A system to monitor standard procedures was introduced in 1987 which became known as the '95 Bolts'. This system was intended to be, and duly became, a template for learning. It was a hierarchical system, centrally-designed and centrally-driven. It emphasized structural elements of service and was authoritarian in both concept and style. It was about managerial direction and control. The 'Bolts' were 95 points or regulated systems applied to the 13 main points of staff/customer interaction. These key service encounters or 'moments of truth' included: reservation, arrival/access, parking, check-in, hall, bedroom, bathroom/WC, evening meal, breakfast, shops, bar, outdoor games/swimming-pool and check-out. Each of these key interaction points were divided into a series of compulsory directives for staff, e.g. how to set out a bedroom, lay a place setting in the restaurant or welcome a guest. A booklet containing the 95 Bolts was issued to all staff and was a mainstay in induction for new staff. Monitoring of standards was carried out by an internal team of inspectors who visited each hotel approximately twice each year. They functioned in the same way as 'mystery shoppers' in that they made reservations, arrived, stayed and departed incognito. On completion of their stay they would make themselves known to the General Manager (GM) for review and discussion. Percentage grades were awarded and recommendations made. The 95 Bolts, while helpful to control and consolidate after a period of rapid growth, gradually became over-rigid and procedural in orientation and was replaced by a more adaptive system in 1992.

Source: McGee and Segal-Horn (1997).

Case Questions

1 Describe Novotel's strategy using the 'Describing strategy' framework (above).

2 What are its competitive advantages?

3 How does the value chain configuration help us to understand how the competitive advantages are managed and delivered?

Further reading and references

Andrews, KR (1980) *The Concept of Corporate Strategy*, Irwin.

Ansoff, H (1965) *Corporate Strategy*, Penguin.

Boston Consulting Group (1975) *Strategy alternatives for the British motorcycle industry*, HMSO, London.

Buchelle, RB (1962) 'How to Evaluate a Firm', *California Management Review*, Fall.

Chandler, AD (1962) *Strategy and Structure: Chapters in the History of the Industrial Enterprise*, Cambridge, MA, MIT Press.

Chandler, AD (1977) *The Visible Hand: The Managerial Revolution in American Bussiness*, Harvard University Press, Cambridge.

Channon, DF (2005) 'Value chain analysis', in J McGee and DF Channon (eds) *Encyclopedic Dictionary of Management*, 2nd edition, Blackwell Business, Oxford.

Cronstraw, MJ, Davis, E and Kay, J (1990) 'On being stuck in the middle – good food costs less at Sainsbury's', *Proceedings of the British Academy of Management Annual Conference*, Glasgow.

De Geuss, A (1988) 'Planning as Learning', *Harvard Business Review*, **66**, **2**, pp. 70–4.

Eccles, RG and Nohria, N (1992) 'Strategy as a language game', from *Beyond the Hype: Rediscovering the essence of management*, Harvard Business School Press.

Gilbert, X and Strebel, P (1991) 'Developing competitive advantage', in H Mintzberg and JB (1991) *The strategy process: Concepts, contexts, cases*, Prentice-Hall, Englewood Cliffs, NJ, pp. 82–93.

Grant, RM (2002) *Contemporary Strategic Analysis: Concepts, Techniques and Applications*, 4th edition, Blackwell Business, Oxford.

Hamel, G and Prahalad, CK (1993) 'Strategy as stretch and leverage', *Harvard Business Review*, March/April.

Hamel, G and Prahalad, CK (1994) 'Competing for the Future', *Harvard Business Review*, July/Aug, pp. 122–8.

Kaplan, RS and Norton, DP (1992) 'The balanced scorecard: measures that drive performance', *Harvard Business Review*, **1**, Jan/Feb.

Mathur, S (1988) 'How Firms Compete: A New Classification of Generic Strategies', *Journal of General Management*, **14**, **1**, pp. 30–57.

McGee, J and Segal-Horn, S (1997) 'Global competences in service multinationals', in H Thomas, D O'Neal and R Alvarado (eds) *Strategic Discovery: Competing in New Arenas*, J Wiley & Sons, pp. 49–77.

Mintzberg, H (1987) 'Crafting Strategy', *Harvard Business Review*, **65**, **4**, pp. 66–75.

Mintzberg, H (1994) *The Rise and Fall of Strategic Planning*, Prentice Hall.

Mintzberg, H (1993) 'The Fall and Rise of Strategic Planning', *Harvard Business Review*, Jan/Feb, pp. 107–14.

Mintzberg, H and Waters, J (1985) 'Of strategies, deliberate and emergent', *Strategic Managment Journal*, **6**, pp. 257–72.

Porter, M (1980) *Competitive Strategy*, New York, Free Press.

Porter, ME (1985) *Competitive Advantage*, New York, Free Press.

Porter, ME (1986) 'What is strategy?' *Harvard Business Review*, Nov/Dec, pp. 61–78.

Porras, JI and Collins, JC (1996) *Built to Last*, Century Books, New York.

Quinn, JB (1980) *Strategies for Change: Logical Incrementalism*, Irwin.

Rumelt, R, Schendel, D and Teece, D (eds) (1994) *Fundamental Issues in Strategy*, Boston, MA, Harvard Business School Press.

Seth, A and Randall, G (1999) *The Grocers: the rise and fall of the supermarket chains*, Kogan Page.

Sloan, AP (1983) *My Years at General Motors*, Doubleday.

Whittington, R (1993) *What is strategy and does it matter?* Routledge.

Yoffie, DB (1992) 'Apple Computer 1992', Harvard Business School Case Study, revised August 1994, 9–792–081.

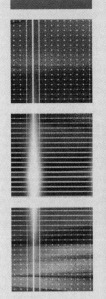

Part 3

Strategy analysis

Part contents

In this part you will find the following chapters:

Introduction

Part 2 set up the economic logic that gives us the tools for analysing and formulating strategy. The key concept introduced here is essentially the logic of competitive advantage supported by specific frameworks such as industry analysis, generic strategies and the value chain. The strength of these concepts lies in the way of thinking about strategy. These are intellectual constructs – they are not cookbooks into which one uncritically feeds data. They apply in different ways to different contexts. By themselves they have limited interest. Their value lies in the way in which they can be applied in different circumstances. Part 3 contains a variety of different contexts for which specific strategies have to be formulated.

Chapter 6 articulates the nature of strategic positioning. We call this the market-based view and others have called it the activity-based view. What strategic positioning is about is what activities have to be pursued in chosen markets so as to gain competitive advantage. Positioning is about the deployment of cost and differentiation-based advantages. It is about the identification of distinctive cost strategies and distinctive differentiation strategies. In practice we see the need for detailed analysis of markets and industries, first, to see what the 'rules' are and how to play them but, second (hopefully) to see how we might innovate with our strategies so as to break the rules and get ahead. In industry terms this means understanding how we can be better than our competitors. In market terms it means understanding what the customer wants. Strategy is about value creation and value analysis is an important element of this chapter.

Chapter 7 steps back into the firm and asks what capabilities are needed for the desired positioning to be achieved. This has become known as the resource-based view often captured in the term 'core competence'. This approach to strategy has become very widespread but suffers from a high degree of subjectivity and lack of agreement about terminology and definitions. This chapter sets out to review some of the main contributions and to indicate a basic language to which we might all subscribe. Core competence, like competitive advantage, is an intellectual construct that is useful because it can be deployed in a wide range of situations. The chapter goes on to examine how competence-based competition can be conducted in practice and suggests some practical ways of relating these ideas to value creation.

Following Chapters 6 and 7 we should now have the ability to develop our own strategic theory of the firm comprising both a view of competitive advantage and core competence *and* the way in which they support and complement each other.

Chapter 8 adds a number of important practical dimensions to the strategic theory that has come from Chapters 6 and 7. Basically it introduces the timeline in the form of life cycle analysis – a notable deficiency of Porter-style work is its static character with only a nodding acknowledgement of the importance of dynamics. In exploring different parts of the time line, going from embryonic stages to decline, the chapter picks out some salient issues. First, we discuss entrepreneurs and start-ups – individualism and idiosyncrasy of both people and events but subject to some overarching strategy context. Second, we examine entry strategies, where we look at the extraordinary difficulty of gaining a foothold in attractive industries in the teeth of organized opposition. Third, we look at turnarounds. These come about typically (but not exclusively) when differentiation advantages have been competed away, the strategy is worn out, and performance is not acceptable. This chapter sets out to put strategic thinking into practical contexts, suggesting as we go along how elements such as personal leadership may be crucial.

Chapter 9 shifts the focus from the single business to the multibusiness portfolio. This is the arena of corporate strategy where the task of the corporate centre is to choose what portfolio it wants and to design and manage the organization structure and its management processes. There are other key tasks: the mission statement and the choice of strategic objectives are discussed in Chapter 1. Managing performance is mentioned in many places but Chapter 18 is devoted to the analysis and measurement of performance. In Chapter 9 the key issue is the way in which the portfolio creates value. This revolves around the economies of scope that we introduced and discussed in Part 2, often called synergy by practitioners and relatedness by analysts and academics. Depending on how synergies arise, there are implications for the fit of strategy and structure and for the styles by which the organization is managed. These are discussed in Chapter 9 and also recur throughout Part 4.

Chapter 10 continues the corporate-level theme with mergers and acquisitions (M&A). These are the biggest and riskiest decisions that most companies make. Mistakes can destroy a company but companies can also grow and prosper very quickly. This chapter lays out the context for M&A decisions and explores in some detail the planning of an acquisition and then its implementation. M&A is a highly controversial area: the risks are very high, the rewards are enticing, but the track record of companies is very varied with perhaps more glaring failures than conspicuous successes. But remember that we said strategy is about risk – a theme we return to in Chapter 14.

Chapter 11 introduces the international domain. This again is controversial and risky (you should be getting used to the idea that these are defining characteristics of strategy) because of the difficulties inherent in moving out of one's home base to international markets and to international suppliers. Globalization is presented in its specialized meaning as global standardization (e.g. the 'world car'). This forms the basis for discussion of the two contrasting strategies of global standardization versus local differentiation. These are a replay of our old friends cost and efficiency on one hand, and differentiation on the other. Not surprisingly, therefore, there is the possibility of combining globalization and localization into a joint approach characterized as 'transnational'. Some think this is just a theoretical possibility but it has led to widespread discussion about the nature of the multinational firm. The chapter concludes with a profile of the 'flagship firm', a concept originated by Alan Rugman in which he portrays how some international firms can sit at the nexus of opposing forces – international versus local forces, global customers versus global suppliers, and different host governments. Overall the theme for the international company is how to blend and balance host-country-specific advantages (CSAs) with firm-specific advantages (FSAs).

Chapter 12 uses the 'new economy' as a rallying cry. This rests on the observation that information technology and knowledge intensity, driven by highly successful R&D programmes over the last forty years, have transformed the cost conditions and demand conditions to which we became accustomed on the old manufacturing-based economy. Cost structures have become predominantly fixed cost in nature with vanishingly small variable costs. Markets have been transformed by the flood of new products that have redefined the elements of consumer leisure time and the patterns of consumer expenditure. Also significant (but quite how much is not yet known) is the emergence of a consumer phenomenon based on standardization and complementarity.[1] Customers increasingly and consciously buy products that conform to known standards and that technically complement their existing products and the products that other people have (one buys a new 'Wintel' computer because your Windows-based software and that of your friends will run on it). This means that we are increasingly buying products because other people have them.[2] It also results in very large, quasi-monopolistic market positions for some companies (e.g. Microsoft), dependency positions for others so that, for example, one is obliged to buy Microsoft's operating systems, and expensive market failures for others (On-Digital versus BSkyB). Business risk has risen markedly in these conditions. Strategies have to be adapted to these specific conditions. Maybe, also, these industries are becoming a bigger proportion of the whole economy. Chapter 12 and some of the case studies at the end of the book discuss the reasons why these new economy characteristics have taken hold and indicates how new economy strategies represent significant adaptations to the strategies common in the traditional manufacturing economy.

The chapters cover the areas depicted below in the strategy resources concepts map and the strategy process concepts map (introduced in Chapters 1 and 2 of this book). The shaded boxes represent the primary focuses of this part of the book. The non-shaded boxes are covered in other parts of this book. The degree of shading in the boxes reflects the degree to which these topics are covered here and also indicates the interconnections explored in each chapter.

The maps show that this section concentrates heavily on resource concepts but only lightly on process concepts. Notably this section says little about 'direction', taking it largely for granted and leaving it mainly to the introduction in Part 1 and to the discussions in Part 5. Throughout this part there are references and allusions to process issues. Sometimes the organization structure issues are covered in some depth. Overall, however, process issues are covered in detail in Part 4 but the allusions herein are important in setting the stage.

---

[1] Strictly speaking it is a re-emergence: it was well known back in the nineteenth century as a characteristic of utilities (e.g. railways and the telegraph) but in a sense was forgotten as manufacturing-style cost conditions became pervasive in the twentieth century.

[2] This is characteristic of fashion products as well, where the benefit is psychological rather than practical.

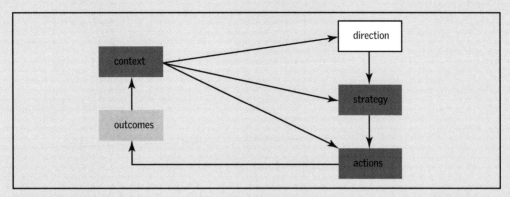

Figure 1.6 Strategy resources concepts map

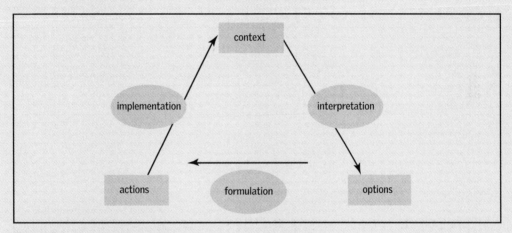

Figure 2.2 Strategy process concepts map

Chapter 6

Competitive strategy: the analysis of strategic position

Introduction

This chapter sets out the essence of strategy as the denial of perfect competition and the search for firm-specific advantages that we call competitive advantage. Chapter 3 developed the economic concepts that underpin the operation of markets. These concepts give us the frameworks and the language for analysing markets and costs. Chapter 4 set out the large-scale macro forces that can shape the fortunes of firms. In Chapter 5 we saw the fundamental importance of the idea of competitive advantage. In this chapter we set out the basic framework of competitive strategy and how it enables us to analyse the **market-based view** that is, as its name suggests, the **positioning** of the firm in its markets versus competitors. The central pillar of this is *competitive advantage*. Chapter 8 presents the *resource-based view*.

Chapter contents

This focuses on the distinctive nature of the resources and capabilities that are required to produce competitive advantage. The central pillar of this is *core competence*. Chapter 8 concludes by relating the ideas of competitive advantage and core competence to managerial tools such as SWOT analysis, PEST analysis, and critical success factor analysis.

Much of this chapter is built upon Porter's original description (1980) of generic competitive strategies, where strategies are characterized as being cost or differentiation based on the one hand or narrow versus broad focus on the other hand (see Figure 6.1). This derives directly from the economist's view of strategy as explained in Chapter 5, where competition can be seen as cost based at one extreme and pure differentiation based at the other extreme. It also includes fundamental ideas of **economies of scope** (from Chapter 3) that are reflected in the vertical axis of Figure 6.1. This idea of a generic strategy is a powerful foundation for understanding the nature and variety of competitive strategies. A generic strategy is a simple typology that captures the essential economic forces at work in a market (the demand side) and in an industry (the supply side). Porter suggested that there are three generic strategies to choose from, and each business unit can have its own strategy. According to Porter, a business can strive to supply a product or service more cost-effectively than its competitors (cost leadership), it can strive to add value to the product or service through differentiation and command higher prices (differentiation), or it can narrow its focus to a special product-market segment which it can monopolize (focus). Not following any of these strategies characterizes a firm as being 'stuck in the middle'. The choice of generic strategy should be based on the firm's business unit's strengths and weaknesses, and a comparison of those with the strengths and weaknesses of competitors.

Generic strategy ideas are pervasive in strategy analysis but not for their operational value. They provide a sound conceptual framework from which more operational ideas can be developed. This chapter develops the ideas of cost advantage and differentiation advantage beyond the introduction given in the previous chapter. It then goes on to look at two powerful grouping concepts – markets segments and strategic groups. The former is well developed in marketing and is explored here for its basis for differentiation strategies and for pricing and value capture. Strategic groups is the idea of industries within industries. It is useful in trying to understand complex industry structures. But it is also valuable in looking ahead to ways in which industries might evolve.

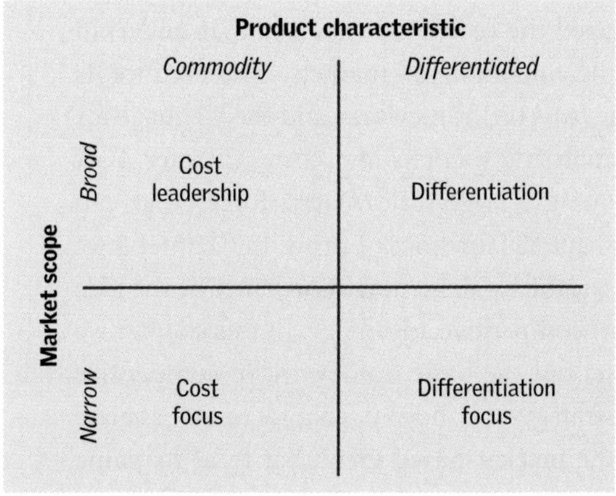

Figure 6.1 Porter's generic strategies
Source: Porter, 1980 Chapter 2. Reprinted with the permission of The Free Press, a Division of Simon and Schuster Adult Publishing Group, from *Competitive Strategy* by Micheal E Porter. Copyright © 1980, 1998 by the Free Press. All rights reserved.

Industry transformation looks at bigger, more revolutionary changes in structure. Finally, we look at business models. This phrase has become current in the new world of e-business, being used to show how the internet creates new rules and new ways of making profits – hence the ideas of new business models.

All of the ideas in this chapter contribute to the way in which the firm positions itself in markets to gain competitive advantage. The concepts and frameworks can be deceptively simple, even generic. But the applications require care with data and with interpretation. Above all, application requires a strong grasp of what the competitive strategy concepts are and how to think through their implications. This chapter should be powerful in helping you turn concepts and frameworks into tools for strategic thinking.

6.1 Industry analysis and competitive strategy: the market-based view

In this section we develop the market-based view in some more detail. Building on Chapter 4, we look at cost analysis, especially at the nature of economies of scale and learning effects, as the basis for cost leadership strategies. We consider further the nature of advantage and the different forms in which it can be seen. Finally, we look at some practical advice when formulating competitive strategy.

6.1.1 Cost advantage

The microeconomics of strategy is built initially on an understanding of the nature of costs. Cost for economists is essentially opportunity cost, the sacrifice of the alternatives forgone in producing a product or service. Thus, the cost of a factory building is the set of houses or shops that might have been built instead. The cost of capital is the interest that could have been earned on the capital invested, had it been invested elsewhere. In practice, money prices may not reflect opportunity costs because of uncertainty, imperfect knowledge, natural and contrived barriers to movements of resources, taxes and subsidies, and the existence of externalities (spillover effects of private activities on to other parties; for example, pollution imposes costs on more than just the producer of pollution). Opportunity cost provides the basis for assessing costs of managerial actions, such as in 'make or buy' decisions, and in all those situations where alternative courses of action are being considered.

Costs are also collected and reported routinely both for purposes of stewardship and for control. The behaviour of these costs in relation to the scale of output is of much importance. We see, for example, that break-even analysis is based on the extent to which costs vary in relation to output (in the short term) or are fixed in relation to output. The distinction between fixed and variable costs has implications for the flexibility a firm has in pricing to meet competitive conditions. Thus, one would always wish to price above variable cost per unit in order to maintain positive cash flow. Fixed costs in this example are **sunk costs**;

they are paid and inescapable, and the only relevant costs are those that are affected by the decision under consideration. It is the behaviour of costs in the long term that has strategic implications for firms and for the structure of industries. The long term is the time horizon under consideration and affects what is considered to be 'fixed'. In the very long term, all economic factors are variable, whereas in the very short term, nearly all economic conditions are fixed and immutable. An economy of scale refers to the extent to which unit costs (costs per unit of output) fall as the scale of the operation (for example, a factory) increases (in other words, as more capital-intensive methods of operation can be employed).

In Figure 6.2 we can see that Plant 1 exhibits increasing returns to scale or, simply, economies of scale. By contrast, Plant 2 shows decreasing returns to scale, diseconomies of scale. The strategic significance of economies of scale depends on the minimum efficient plant size (MES). This is important in relation to market size. The higher the ratio of MES to market size, the larger the share of the market taken by one plant, and the more market power that can be exercised by the firm owning the plant.

Table 6.1 contains estimates of the ratio of MES to market size for various industries in the US and the UK. It is evident, for example, that the refrigerator industry will be much more *concentrated* than the shoe industry (it will have many fewer players) because economies of scale are so much bigger in relation to the market size.

The major sources of economies of scale are usually described as:

◆ Indivisibilities and the spreading of fixed costs.

◆ The engineering characteristics of production.

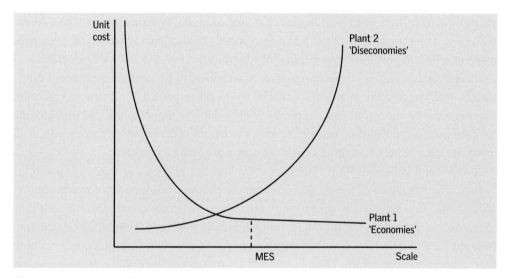

Figure 6.2 Minimum efficient plant size

Indivisibility means that an input cannot be scaled down from a certain minimum size and can only be scaled up in further minimum size units. Thus, costs per unit diminish after the initial investment until a further new block of investment is required. The original examples of 'specialization' (the term coined by Adam Smith) were often engineering in nature. As volumes go up, it is usually cheaper to make work tasks more specialized – as exemplified dramatically in Henry Ford's mass production assembly line operations in the first decade of the last century. Economies of scale also arise because of the physical properties of processing units. This is exemplified by the well-known cube-square rule. Production capacity is usually determined by the volume of the processing unit (the cube of its linear dimensions), whereas cost more often arises from the surface area (the cost of the materials involved). As capacity increases, the average cost decreases, because the ratio of surface area to cube diminishes. (For a full discussion of economies of scale, *see* Besanko, Dranove and Shanley (2000) Chapter 5.)

These general principles apply to functional areas other than production. In marketing, there are important **indivisibilities** that arise out of branding and the creation of reputation effects. There are important scale effects in advertising, as the costs of campaign preparation can be spread over larger (for example, global) markets. Research and development requires substantial minimum investments – another indivisibility – in advance of production, and the costs of R&D therefore fall as sales volumes increase. Purchasing in bulk exhibits economies of scale, in that the price per unit falls as the number of purchased items goes up. Sometimes this is because of monopolistic buying power (for example, supermarkets in

Table 6.1 Minimum efficient scale for selected industries in the UK and the USA

Industry	% Increase in average costs at ½ MES[1]	MES as % of market	
		UK	USA
Cement	26.0	6.1	1.7
Steel	11.0	15.4	2.6
Glass bottles	11.0	9.0	1.5
Bearings	8.0	4.4	1.4
Fabrics	7.6	1.8	0.2
Refrigerators	6.5	83.3	14.1
Petroleum refining	4.8	11.6	1.9
Paints	4.4	10.2	1.4
Cigarettes	2.2	30.3	6.5
Shoes	1.5	0.6	0.2

[1] This gives a measure of the sensitivity of costs across the range of plant sizes.

Source: Scherer and Ross (1990) *The Economics of Mutiplant Operations*, Tables 3.11 and 3.15.

the UK). But each purchase does have a certain element of fixed costs attached to it (writing contracts, negotiation time, setting up production runs) and these may be significant.

The **experience curve**, sometimes called the **learning curve**, has similar strategic implications. The experience curve is an empirical estimate of the proportion by which unit costs fall as experience of production increases. An 80 per cent experience curve arises when costs fall to 80 per cent of their previous level after production has doubled (see Figure 6.3). Strategically, this means that a firm which establishes itself first in the market and manages to build a cost advantage by being twice the size of its nearest competitor would have a 20 per cent production cost advantage over this competitor if an 80 per cent experience curve existed. Experience and learning effects arise where there are complex, labour-intensive tasks. The firm can facilitate learning through management and supervisory activities and coaching. It can also use incentives to reward learning.

In general, economies of scale and experience effects provide the basis in terms of cost advantage for those strategies that depend on cost leadership. The objective of cost leadership strategies is to realize a price discount to the customer and/or a margin premium that reflects the size of the cost advantage. Cost advantages are also available through vertical integration and the exercise of buying power.

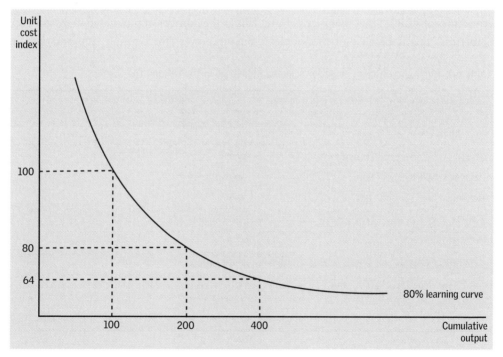

Figure 6.3 The learning curve
Source: Besanko *et al.*, 2000, p. 197. Reprinted with permission of John Wiley and Sons Ltd.

The example in Figure 6.4 is taken from a case study on Du Pont's attempt in the 1970s to dominate the market for titanium dioxide in the USA by virtue of its superior cost position. The cost advantage is based on economies of scale, on experience effects, on vertical integration, and on lower raw material prices. In total, the cost advantage over typical competitors is around 40 per cent. As a result, the competitors were unable to stop Du Pont building scale-efficient new plant to take advantage of market growth – a classic example of a pre-emptive strategy. Similar arguments lay behind the analysis of the rapid growth of Japanese companies in the 1970s. Significant economies of scale gave the opportunity for lower prices, the building of market share, even lower costs, and the gradual dominance of markets. In general, the analysis of **first mover advantage** relies on the existence of significant scale and experience effects, a price-sensitive market, and the willingness to commit capital ahead of competition.

6.1.2 Differentiation advantage

We first encountered product differentiation in Chapter 3, where we saw that it was a characteristic of imperfect markets where 'non-price' strategies are important. Product differentiation is the act of making products different from one another. This might involve tangible differences such as quality, reliability, performance or design. Alternatively (or in addition) it might be based on intangible elements such as reputation and branding.

	Ilmenite Chloride	Rutile Chloride *1972 cents/lb*	Difference
From exhibit 3	18.80	21.50	−2.70
Less depreciation	−3.00	−2.50	−0.50
Capital charge	6.80	5.60	1.20
	22.60	24.60	−2.00
Learning effect	−4.75	0.00	−4.75
Scale effect	−3.75	0.00	−3.75
Integration effect	−1.30	0.00	−1.30
Capacity effect	1.30	1.00	0.30
Cost per lb	14.10	25.60	−11.50

capital charge = investment requirements per lb multiplied by hurdle rate (say 15%)
learning effect = 79% learning curve and double the experience
scale effect = 85% doubling effect and twice the scale
capacity effect = differences in capacity utilisation

Figure 6.4 Du Pont's calculation of its cost advantage
Source: Du Pont in Titanium Dioxide (A), Harvard Business School case 9-385-40 (1984) exhibits 2 and 3.

Thus, Subaru's cars might be differentiated on the basis of their performance characteristics as attested by their success in motor sport. But Mercedes would rely heavily on accumulated reputation in addition to other tangible differentiators such as build quality.

Differentiation[1] requires the investment of resources – typically time, capital cost and higher variable costs – in a risky bet that the customer will respond to the differentiated product by buying it at a premium price and/or more frequently. The bet is risky because the attempt to differentiate might fail:

1   product quality might fail to improve as a result of the product development activity;

2   a competitor does it better (for example Jaguar is involved in an attempt to catch up with the differentiation power of the German brands BMW and Mercedes);

3   customers fail to respond to the new proposition (see, for example, the failure of laser disks in the consumer electronics market);

4   the costs of differentiation might be in excess of the gains from differentiation – the capital costs and any higher variable costs might not be offset by the new price–volume combination. The classic case of this is IBM's attempts to differentiate its personal computers from the stream of IBM-compatible new entrants in the 1980s. IBM offered a new operating system, OS2, but the benefits of this were not apparent to customers who preferred to stay with the Microsoft DOS system that had become the industry standard.

Successful differentiation makes the market less perfect (see the discussion in Chapter 3) because the firm that has created the differentiation has in fact created a firm-specific imperfection. Product differentiation is therefore the process of creating a competitive advantage by making the product (or service) different from those of rivals to the extent that superior performance results.

In Table 6.2 we can see that there are different bases for cost advantage and differentiation advantage. Cost leadership typically requires large (mass) markets in which minimum efficient plant sizes can be reached. Differentiation, by contrast, prospers in market segments in which different customer needs can be identified and products designed for those needs. The approaches to the market are distinctive. Cost leadership is accompanied by price (low price) strategies, whereas differentiation is based in non-price strategies. Different competences are also indicated. Cost leadership is usually manufacturing and procurement based, whereas differentiation activity is marketing based and R&D intensive. Michael Porter argued, controversially, that firms could not do both and if they tried they would get '**stuck in**

---

[1] It is important to distinguish product differentiation from differentiation as applied to organization structure. The building blocks of organization structure are differentiation and integration. In this context differentiation is the way in which a company allocates people and resources to different organization tasks – the greater the number of functions and activities, the higher is the level of differentiation (*see* p. 56).

	Cost leadership	Differentiation
Cost advantage	Scale and scope	None required
Differentiation advantage	Low (price strategies)	High (non-price strategies)
Market segmentation	Low (mass market)	High (many markets)
Distinctive competences	Manufacturing and buying	Marketing, R&D

Table 6.2 Comparison of cost and differentiation strategies

the middle'. However, his position clearly depends on a particular view of the competences that support cost and differentiation positions. The case box (below) describes the emergence of the scale economy brander in the food processing industry.

Case box: The scale economy brander

The consumer packaged goods industries (including the food processing industry) enjoyed halcyon days in the 1960s when manufacturers were dominant. This was a period when mass markets in processed foods were growing quickly, retail distribution was highly fragmented, economies of scale were available, and processing technologies were proprietary. These substantial economic advantages were buttressed by the creation of mass marketing systems comprising national media advertising, national sales forces and increasingly sophisticated marketing support services. The visible output of this business system was the brand, the repository of guarantees to the customer of product qualities arising from proprietary technology. The creation of the brand was subject to many economies of marketing scale, and fostered scale economies available elsewhere in the system. The brand was the visible symbol of the manufacturer's strength, and was the visible barrier to entry behind which grew a series of oligopolies earning monopoly rents. There were seven entry barriers around these brand positions:

1 National sales force and distribution: 'filling up the backroom and stealing shelf space'.
2 Listing muscle: fragmented retailers felt they had to stock the leading brands on manufacturers' terms.
3 Intensive media advertising bought at preferential rates and defrayed across large volumes.
4 Superior product quality arising from proprietary processing technology and/or from consumer perceptions.
5 Low-cost processing either from superior technology or from scale economies.
6 Sophisticated support services, e.g. market research, product management support structure, advertising skills.
7 Discounts on raw material purchases based on volume.

Branding economics was all about premium prices, consumer pull and economies of scale. The association of market share and profitability was well attested in this regime of the scale economy brander. Behind the brand lay a technology edge and a new management structure and style – the style of the marketing company.

These marketing companies came in two forms. The first was the multinational major branders (e.g. Unilever, BSN, Heinz). These were multinational companies operating multiple, related consumer goods businesses across the world, with strong perceived product differentiation accompanied by strong branding. These companies have been traditionally multi-domestic in character as opposed to global (Porter 1986) or transnational (Bartlett and Ghoshal 1989) (see the discussion in Chapter 11 on the nature of international advantage).

The second was the national major branders (e.g. St Ivel). These were nationally based and focused companies with very high levels of marketing support for a product range which, by the standards of the multinationals, were more limited.

Source: McGee and Segal-Horn, 1992.

Questions for discussion

1   Why was it possible for scale and differentiation effects to be simultaneously present?

2   What effect do you think this could have on the pattern of competition?

Sources of differentiation advantage

Product differentiation opportunities arise from the physical characteristics of the product, from the technological foundations of the product, and from the nature of customers and markets. As a shorthand we can observe that 'quality' reflects the physical characteristics of the product; 'innovation' captures the technological dimension; and 'customer responsiveness' reflects market and customer factors. If we correlate these with the tangibility/intangibility dimension we can see Table 6.3 describing the arena in which product differentiation works.

Table 6.3 is a simple representation of the complexity of differentiation. However, you can see the elements that can make up differentiation. Performance and reliability of products (such as durable goods, computers, cars, washing machines) are obvious characteristics but

Dimensions of differentiation	Tangible	Intangible
Quality	Performance and Reliability	Reputation
Innovation	New functional attributes New usage patterns	Modernity
Customer responsiveness	New distribution system	Brand Relationship management

Table 6.3 Dimensions of differentiation

ones which can be imitated. However, reputation is less easily gained and less easily lost. So a Rolls-Royce reputation for automobile quality may linger for a long time even if the objective data on tangible characteristics might suggest that others have long since caught up.[2] Innovation allows for a reshaping of the way in which the product works and the way in which customers use the product. Thus laptop computers are an innovation sitting alongside the desktop alternatives but operating in different ways and places and requiring different technical solutions. Sometimes innovation captures a style (which we have called modernity) that reflects lifestyle choices. Thus, architectural innovation may have tangible effects on the nature of buildings but much of the benefit may be felt in the feel, style and texture of the space. The (high) fashion industry is one where intangibles are predominant and functionality unimportant. Customer responsiveness captures the extent to which products have value because of the degree and style of interaction between buyer and seller. Dell Computers offer the lesson that product features are not all-important. Michael Dell's innovation was to identify that customers valued close interaction between buyer and seller through the distribution system. Dell's competitive advantage rests on the closeness of links to the customer and the entire business is about creating the logistics that give the customer maximum choice and timeliness of choice.

Dell Computers is a good example of how differentiation advantages can be built in self-reinforcing pyramids. Dell innovated, created a new tangible marketing and distribution process, and has also created an enviable reputation and brand name. The more diverse the bases and dimensions of differentiation, the more powerful will be the differentiation effect. As a result companies that are successful at this (see the scale economy branders above) become infused with the differentiation culture. Witness, or example, how the scale economy branders such as Procter & Gamble, General Foods, Unilever and others are known as marketing companies despite their very considerable talents in manufacturing and other non-marketing functions. The prime source of advantage is differentiation secured through core competences (see Chapter 7) in marketing.

Differentiation covers many approaches to the customer. It might rest on a broad market appeal or it might rely on narrow market niches in which it offers highly specific solutions for customers. Figure 6.5 suggests a methodology by which you can begin an assessment of the market and the potential for differentiation. In looking at the product and customer dimensions in this figure you are trying to work out whether this is a market in which common needs prevail or where there is a diversity of needs. Where you might identify commonality and make your differentiation investments accordingly, you are open to the niche player who might target a niche in your market to which a more specific and valuable customer proposition can be made. In mature markets this process of continuous segmentation

---

[2] This is *not* true of the Rolls-Royce reputation for aero engines which continues to be high on both tangible and intangible dimensions.

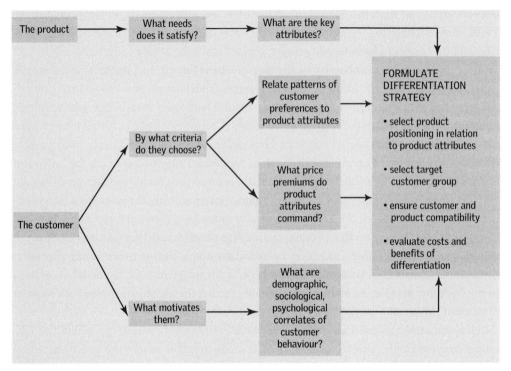

Figure 6.5 Identifying differentiation potential
Source: Adapted from Grant, 2002, p. 287.

allows smaller firms to chip away at the bigger but broader positions of the market leaders. Conversely a niche play is susceptible to innovation by large players such that the niche offer is swept up in a bigger and better offer that covers many segments. The decline of small and medium-size retailers is testament to the ability of large retailers to provide an unmatchable price proposition together with different differentiation propositions.

6.1.3 **Competitive advantage**

In the case examples on retailing in Chapter 5 we drew the connection between strategy choices and profitability. We argued that strategy choices are resource allocation decisions that enable the firm to create distinctive assets and capabilities (this is the language of core competences, as we shall see below). These enable the firm to create imperfections in markets that are specific to itself and therefore the firm can capture the benefits of this positioning in terms of higher prices or lower costs or both. Figure 6.6 illustrates the point. A successful strategy can earn superior financial returns because it has an **unfair advantage**, that is, it creates, exploits and defends firm-specific imperfections in the market vis-à-vis competitors. We deliberately use the term unfair advantage as a colloquial simile for competitive advantage in order to underline that such advantages are achieved in the face of organized opposition, both from competitors that wish to emulate your success and from customers that will exercise bargaining power to achieve lower prices.

In theory, competitive advantage is the *delivering of superior value to customers and, in doing so, earning an above average return for the company and its stakeholders.* These twin criteria impose a difficult hurdle for companies because competitive advantage cannot be bought by simply cutting prices or by simply adding quality without reflecting the cost premium in higher price. Competitive advantage requires the firm to be sustainably different from its competitors in such a way that customers are prepared to purchase at a suitably high price. Classic perfect competition works on the basis that all products are so alike as to be commodities and that competition takes place solely on the basis of price. The

Figure 6.6 Firm-specific imperfections as the source of profits

search for competitive advantage is the search for differences from competitors, and for purchase on the basis of value (that is, the offer of an attractive performance-to-price ratio). Competitive advantage is a statement of positioning in the market and consists of the following elements:

♦ A statement of competitive *intent*

♦ Outward evidence of *advantage* to the customer

♦ Some combination of:
  ♦ superior delivered cost position
  ♦ a differentiated product
  ♦ protected niches

♦ Evidence of *direct benefits,* which:
  ♦ are perceived by a sizeable customer group
  ♦ these customers value and are willing to pay for
  ♦ cannot be readily obtained elsewhere, both now and in the foreseeable relevant future

The sustainability of competitive advantage depends on the following:

♦ *Power* – maintaining the levels of commitments in resource terms relative to competitors

♦ *Catching-up* – ease of copying and nullifying the advantages

♦ *Keeping ahead* – productivity of one's own continuous search for enhanced or new advantages

♦ *The changing game* – rate of change of customer requirements

♦ *The virtuous circle* – the self-sustainability and mutual reinforcing of existing advantages

Economists argue that competitive advantages are by their nature temporary in character and therefore decay quickly. This is to argue that product markets and the market for underlying resources is reasonably competitive. Indeed, much of the analysis of competitive advantage is concerned with assessing just how defensible, durable and large the advantages can be. The Porter five forces framework (Porter 1980) (*see* Figure 5.1) provides a useful basis for categorizing and understanding the industry economics that lie behind competitive advantage and Figure 5.3 summarizes the competitive forces. Notice that the barriers to entry shown in Figure 5.3 are, in essence, the competitive advantages that are available in the industry. They represent the cost premiums that entrants would have to pay in order to enter the industry and compete on equal terms. In other words, these are the imperfections that the incumbents have created (or are the beneficiaries of). It is important to note that the barriers to entry may be generic, meaning that the incumbents do not have advantages over each other, but have a shared advantage with a shared rent. Or the barriers may be firm-specific, implying that different

Supplier/buyer power	Barriers to entry
• Relative concentration	• Scale economies and experience
• Relative importance of product to the provider and the user	• Product differentiation
• Credible threat of vertical integration	• Capital requirements
• Substitution possibilities	• Switching requirements
• Control of information	• Access to distribution
• Switching costs	• Scale-independant cost advantages
	• Level of expected retaliation
Intensity of rivalry *High if . . .*	**Pressure from substitutes**
• Several equally strong players	• Benefits not product features
• Low/no growth in market	• Sideways competition
• High fixed costs and cyclical demand	• Comparative price/performance
• Few chances for differentiation	• Comparative technology life cycle
• Large-scale capacity increments	• What business are you in?
• Different 'culture' or players	• Backing by rich competitor
• High strategic stakes	
• Major exit barriers	

Figure 6.7 Behind the competitive forces

incumbents are protected by different advantages and are themselves different from one another. Barriers are also entrant-specific in that different potential entrants have different assets and therefore different ways in which they might compete.

Figures 6.8 and 6.9 show a reworking of Porter's generic strategy table (Figure 6.1) to emphasize that the three routes to advantage are potentially reinforcing. Figure 6.9 outlines

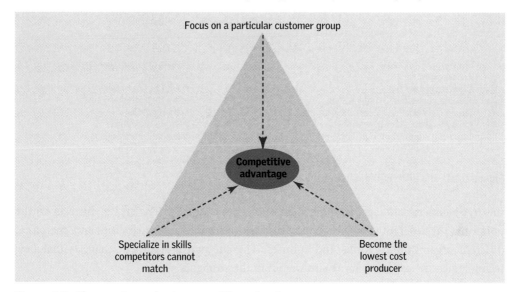

Figure 6.8 Three major routes to competitive advantage

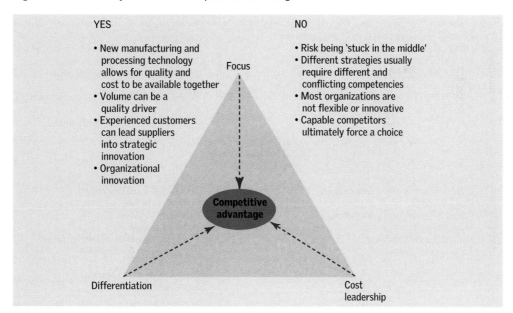

Figure 6.9 Is more than one generic strategy possible?

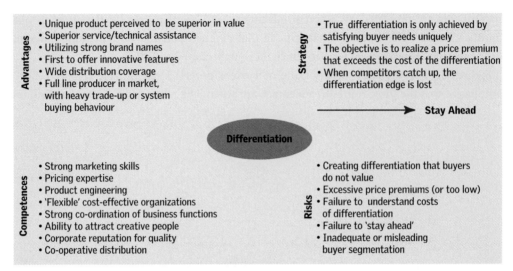

Figure 6.10 The differentiation strategy

the arguments for and against more than one generic strategy. The argument rests on the point that the different strategies require different resources and capabilities and, therefore, different organizational forms and cultures. The alternative argument suggests that new technologies are leading to more similarities in the strategies.

Figures 6.10, 6.11 and 6.12 summarize the generic strategies in terms of the essence of the strategy, the nature of its advantages, the competences required and the risks that it has

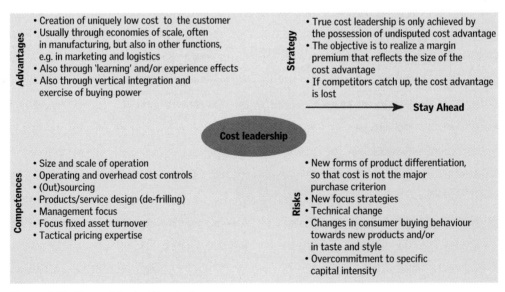

Figure 6.11 The cost leadership strategy

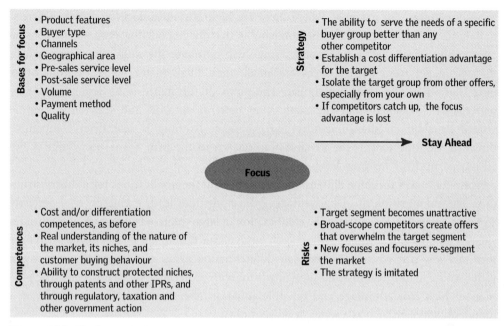

Figure 6.12 The focus strategy

to face. This should reinforce the idea that strategy is about making a commitment and about the deliberate calculation and taking of risk.

Figure 6.13 shows the implications of composite differentiation and cost strategies. The figure arrays cost advantage against a composite differentiation and

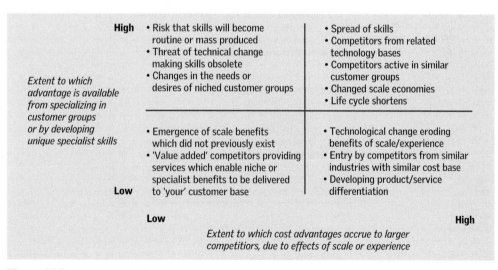

Figure 6.13 How industry dynamics shape competitive threats

focus dimension. For example, where there are high cost advantages and high differentiation advantages, the risk for the company is that the supporting skills might become mass produced or that technological change will outmode the skills. Conversely, where the advantages from both sources are small, then there might be entry from other industries where the skills are similar. The point of the figure is to demonstrate how patterns of advantage (and the supporting patterns of skill and capability) can be eroded by shifts in the competitive environment. Nothing is safe from competitive threat in the long term – the variables of concern to the firm are (i) how large is my advantage, and (ii) for how long can I retain it?

Figure 6.14 takes the same dimensions and draws out the implications for industry structure. The combination of low advantages from both sides leads eventually to a perfectly competitive market. By contrast, the combination of large (high) advantages from both sides yields a kind of specialization, where each large player dominates a large segment. Where there are low-cost advantages but high differentiation/focus advantages, we often see a variety of small or medium-sized speciality firms with protectable niche positions. The position of high-cost advantage and no differentiation effects is typically the profile of a monopoly supplier, such as a water or power utility.

Industries and firms differ markedly in the size and shape of the advantages that are available. In Figure 6.15 we array the number of advantages against the size of the advantages. The point of origin is the perfectly competitive solution, where there are very few

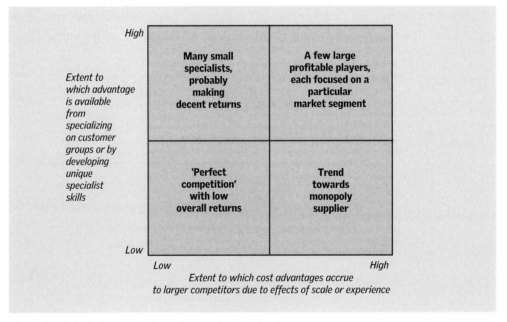

Figure 6.14 Industry dynamics and competitive advantage

advantages and/or the advantages are extremely small. The typical comparison is between the 'blockbusters' and the 'inch by inch' polar alternatives. The blockbuster situation arises where there are very few, usually one or two, sources of advantage, but these are very large in size. The prescription pharmaceuticals industry is like this. Its sources of advantage are research and development (including product registration) and sales force. But products are protected by patent and are typically price insensitive in the markets, so the advantages are huge. Perhaps more typical in most situations is the pattern of multiple sources, but each being of small consequence – the inch by inch situation. This would be typical of much of retailing, where there are a great many ways to compete through choice of product ranges, locations, sourcing policy, staff training and skills, and so on. A more dramatic example is Formula One racing, where the racing teams are very close to each other in terms of performance, but performance does depend on myriad different dimensions. What Formula One does demonstrate is that it is possible for the compounding of many different sources of small advantage to result in predictable and sustainable differences between teams. The source of performance differences here lies in the way in which the resources and capabilities are systematically managed – another resource-based argument.

Read the case box on the video gaming industry and interpret the rules of the game in terms of Porter's five forces analysis. Do this for the original rules of the game and for the new rules that Sony is trying to establish. What benefits is Sony expecting to gain? How would you expect its competitors to react?

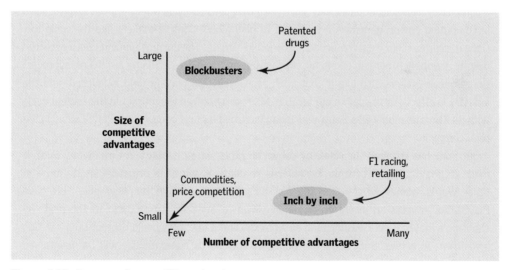

Figure 6.15 Degrees of competitive advantage

Case box: **Changing the game in video gaming industry**

Something funny is going on in the video gaming business. Sony, the market leader, is changing the technological and business rules that have defined this cut-throat industry for two decades. By doing so, it hopes both to improve its fortunes – earlier this year the company admitted that its revenues and profits had unexpectedly plunged – and to fend off a challenge from Microsoft, which launched its first games console, the Xbox, in 2001. Though motivated by Sony's self-interest, these new rules are also good news for consumers, whether they are seasoned gamers or occasional players, since they impose some stability on a volatile and cyclical industry.

The existing rules are simple: every five years or so, console-makers release new consoles that are far more powerful than the previous generation. The current crop consists of Sony's PlayStation 2, Microsoft's Xbox and Nintendo's GameCube. The PlayStation 2, launched in March 2000, is the most successful by far, with over 60 million units sold, compared with around 15 million units each for the Xbox and GameCube. Just as shaving companies make money on blades rather than razors, the industry works by selling consoles at knock-down prices and making a profit on the games. A game typically costs $50, around $10 of which is passed from publisher to console-maker as a licence fee.

The result is a regular 'console cycle', as one generation succeeds the next. At the end of each cycle, gamers abandon their old consoles and buy new ones, and the whole process starts again. Games written for one console do not work on another, so they also have to buy a completely new set of games. But since each new console cycle offers a great leap forward in computing power, gamers are prepared to play along. Console-makers like the cycle too, since it isolates them from the broader economic climate. The current gaming boom occurred despite a wobbly American economy; the last but one, in 1991–93, came amid a global recession. Console-makers also like it that with each cycle, the playing field is levelled, and the industry in effect starts again from scratch. Microsoft entered the market in the current cycle with its Xbox; its model was Sony, which had launched its first console, the PlayStation, in the previous cycle.

But Sony has changed the rules, by subverting this state of affairs in three ways. First, it made its PlayStation 2 console 'backwards compatible' with the original PlayStation – in other words, games written for the old console also work on the new one. This gave PlayStation owners an incentive to remain loyal to Sony from one cycle to the next. By choosing a PlayStation 2, rather than an Xbox or GameCube, they could protect their existing investment in games. Sony says this policy of backwards compatibility will be maintained when the PlayStation 3 appears in 2005 or 2006: it will be able to run games designed for previous consoles. Since each generation is so much more powerful than the last, this trick is relatively easy to pull off by getting a console to impersonate, or emulate, its less powerful predecessors.

Next, Sony did not kill off the PlayStation when it launched the PlayStation 2, but instead cut its price and aimed it at new, more price-sensitive markets. In 2002, Sony sold 20 million PlayStation 2s and 4 million PlayStations – compared with sales of about 6 million each for the Xbox and GameCube. In other words, successive console cycles are starting to overlap.

Sony's third move is intended to extend this trend still further. It has just launched the PSX, a home-entertainment device that combines a PlayStation 2 with a DVD recorder, a hard-disk based video recorder, satellite and analogue TV tuners, and photo-album and music playback features. As well as cutting down on spaghetti-like wiring behind the TV, this jack-of-all-trades is the first example of Sony's new strategy to combine its games consoles with other consumer-electronics devices. By throwing in PlayStation 2 functionality with other devices at a small premium – made easier by Sony's recent cramming of a PlayStation 2 on to a single chip – it hopes to broaden the market and appeal to people who would not normally dream of buying a stand-alone games console. 'Once they get it down to a single chip, then economies of scale come in, and the potential for integrated devices becomes very real,' says Nick Gibson of Games Investor Consulting.

Playing to win

Together, these three moves have the effect of damping the industry's cyclicality, maintaining loyalty and widening ownership. They also make life more difficult for Microsoft, which is expected to be Sony's chief rival in the next cycle. The Xbox, which was launched more than a year after the PlayStation 2, could never have caught it up in sales. Instead, it was widely seen as Microsoft's trial run for the next round, in which the Xbox 2 will battle the PlayStation 3 on more equal terms. Sony's strategy changes that calculation. As the winner of the previous cycle, it has the most to gain by trying to reduce the industry's cyclicality, in order to maintain its dominance. By overlapping console cycles and spreading the PlayStation 2 into a range of other devices, it hopes to make the coming fight between the Xbox 2 and the PlayStation 3 just one front in a larger battle on a wider landscape. Indeed, says Toby Scott of *Games Analyst*, an industry publication, it now makes sense to consider the PlayStation's collective market share across multiple console cycles. Since Microsoft is now under pressure to make the Xbox 2 backwards compatible too, the next cycle will arguably not start from scratch after all.

That does not mean the console cycle is dead. But it will matter less, which is good news for consumers. In the old days when consoles were killed off and there was no backwards compatibility, says Mr Scott, 'gamers were the playthings of manufacturers'. The changing dynamics of the industry now mean that buying a console, particularly late in the cycle, is much less dangerous than it used to be. If you buy a console this Christmas, in short, you are much less likely to end up getting stuck with a turkey.

Source: 'Changing the Game', *The Economist*, 4 December 2003.
© The Economist Newspaper Limited, London (4 December 2003).

6.2 **Strategic market segments**

In Chapter 3 we saw that the basis for market segmentation lies in the existence of different responses to price (and other marketing variables) by individuals or groups of individuals. Earlier in this chapter we saw how differentiation activities are intimately related to the existence of market segments. One of the most creative endeavours in strategy making has been the seeking out of new markets or market niches to which customized products can be directed. In general we can see that a market can be divided into **strategic segments** based on product range and on associated price differentials. Figure 6.16 illustrates the general case.

Customers are faced by an **offer curve** that summarizes the range of options open to them. This shows what groups of customers exist for each combination of product performance and price. Thus, group A is content with a low product specification and a correspondingly low price. Group B is the larger segment, where both the product specification and price are higher. Group C is higher still on both counts, the premium market. Given this offer curve, firms would be unwilling, in general, to offer a product at point X for two reasons. First, it does not fall into any of the established segments A, B or C. Second it falls above the offer curve, meaning that it is overpriced for that level of product performance. Another way of putting it is to say that at that price the product is under-specified. The shape of the offer curve depends on customer price sensitivities – how much are they prepared to pay for extra product performance? It also depends on the cost characteristics of the product. Thus, the premium product may require different product development routines, and specialized attention in production and marketing. The existence of only a small market for the premium product is likely, due to the high costs

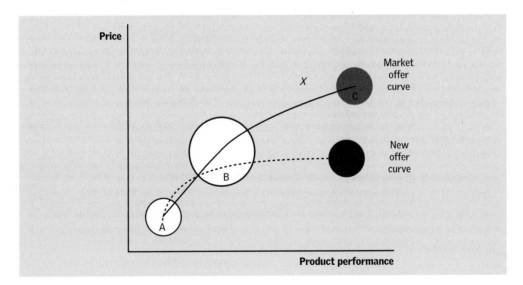

Figure 6.16 The offer curve

involved and the level of the minimum price that has to be charged in order to make a profit. Innovation in the market can transform the offer curve, as shown in Figure 6.16. The innovation, for example, could be due to cost reductions in product development and manufacturing so that lower prices can be charged. A good example is the way the Lexus intruded on the premium car market in Europe and the USA by creating its own version of a premium offer at lower prices than Mercedes. The unfair advantage was the application of the Toyota production system to the Lexus (which is Toyota's premium brand), giving Toyota considerable cost advantage over Mercedes.

Another way of looking at strategic segmentation is to compare price and differentiation patterns across a market. Figure 6.17 suggests a pattern of locations along which the price differentiation trade-off takes place. Starting from point A you can charge relatively higher prices for modest increases in differentiation. This, however, flattens out so that a plateau is achieved around point B, where the price is relatively stable whatever the level of differentiation. This implies a stable price point at which product changes make little difference. Eventually the plateau is broken because differentiation differences are so large as to be able to command higher prices. In this example point C represents a journey through progressively steep trade-offs where customers are prepared to pay disproportionately high prices for modest changes in differentiation. This locus of trade-offs enables us to locate different market positioning strategies. Around point A but below the curve we could see low-cost strategies being deployed. Around point C but above the curve we could see premium-quality strategies. Below the curve and to the right of the mass market located at B we could see a combination of low-cost and high-quality strategies in region D. Although strategies

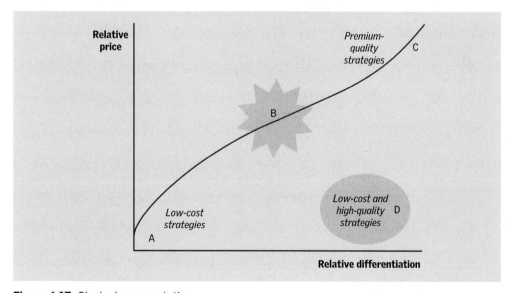

Figure 6.17 Strategic segmentation

around A, B and C are stable and consistent in relation to each other, the offerings in D have the potential to destabilize the market.

6.2.1 Identifying segmentation variables

The bases for segmentation have always been major issue for companies. The conventional approach is to look at the characteristics of buyers and the characteristics of products, as in Figure 6.18. This is a very well known approach and is probably more useful for identifying existing patterns of segmentation than for discovering new and untested segments. Figure 6.18 should remind you of the earlier section on differentiation because the drivers are very much the same in each case. This is to be expected, but what is difficult to do is to develop new bases for segmentation and differentiation. However, the more that all competitors follow the same logic, the more likely they are to end up with the same kinds of strategies. By definition these will cancel out and competitive advantage will be elusive.

The end-of-chapter case study describes the move from 2G standards in mobile telephony to 3G standards. This describes the value proposition of the 3G service, the differentiation required and the segmentation on which it is based. 3G allows for internet connection to mobile telephones, whereas the 2G standard has become almost a commodity-style offer.

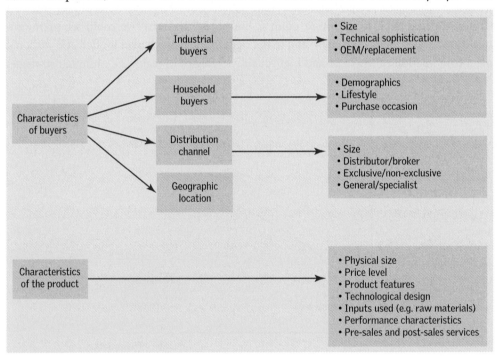

Figure 6.18 Bases for segmentation
Source: Grant, 2002, p. 121.

You should use this example to think about how new technology and development of standards require effective segmentation and differentiation for success.

The analysis of strategic segments leads towards the firm's choice of pricing strategy. In assessing pricing options the firm is essentially concentrating on issues of *value*; that is. how to price in order to gain value to the firm while still delivering value to the customer. The next section addresses this.

6.2.2 Value creation and value analysis

The concept of value is central to economics and to the understanding of competitive advantage. The **theory of value** in economics deals with the determination of final market prices (as opposed to factor prices, which are determined by the theory of distribution).

Perceived benefit and consumer surplus

If you buy a car for $15 000 but it is worth $20 000 to you in terms of the services it renders, then you are better off by $5000. This is known as the **consumer surplus**. Given a choice of cars with identical service values, you would (rationally) buy the cheaper car – this would save you money and increase your consumer surplus. The idea of consumer surplus is a profit idea – it is the 'profit' that the consumer makes from a purchase. If the 'consumer' was a firm buying a machine for $15 000 but as a result lowering its costs by $20 000, the value created by the purchase (i.e. the profit) is $5000.

In tabular form:

> Perceived gross benefit
> less   user costs
> less   transactions costs
> = Perceived net benefit
> less   price paid
> = Consumer surplus

Value maps

A firm must deliver consumer surplus to compete successfully. **Value maps** illustrate the competitive implications of consumer surplus analysis. The vertical axis shows the price of the product and the horizontal axis shows quality or performance characteristics of the product. Each point corresponds to a particular price–quality combination. At any time, the series of price–quality combinations available to consumers is shown by an upward-sloping schedule, an indifference curve. The slope shows the trade-off between price and quality; the steeper the slope, the higher the extra price to be paid for increased quality. This is an 'indifference' curve because at each point on the curve the consumer surplus is the same. Above the curve is lower consumer surplus, because prices are higher. Below the curve is higher consumer surplus because prices are lower. Without any innovations in product or process, any firm wishing to price below the indifference curve to gain volume will do so at the expense of profit. Genuine innovation might enable a competitor to make a different 'offer' in the form of a new indifference curve below the original one. This will offer higher consumer surplus, will divert volume towards the new competitor and take volume and profit away from the non-innovating competitor.

This is illustrated in Figure 6.19 by the luxury car market in the USA (the example is taken from Besanko *et al.* 2000). When the Japanese luxury automobiles Lexus, Infiniti and Acura were introduced in the late 1980s they offered comparable quality to Mercedes but at lower prices. Not surprisingly they gained market share. Eventually the Japanese firms increased prices and Mercedes lowered price, converging on a new and lower indifference curve. Overall the consumer gained – consumer surplus increased. The suppliers would have benefited if their costs had fallen by at least an equivalent amount.

Value creation and pricing

As goods move along the supply chain and into and along the firm's value chain, economic value is created. Firm A in Figure 6.20 illustrates the different value creation packages:

- Consumer surplus is benefit less price paid: B – P
- Firm profit (or producer surplus) is price paid by the consumer less costs: P – C
- Total value created is consumer surplus and firm profit: B – C
- Value added (as measured in the national accounts and used as a measure of output of the economy) is technically firm profit less costs of raw materials: P – RM

The firm's pricing decision can be seen as critical in partitioning total value between consumers and firms. A high price claims more for the firm, giving less to the consumer and running the risk that Firm B, for example, might opt for lower prices and attract volume

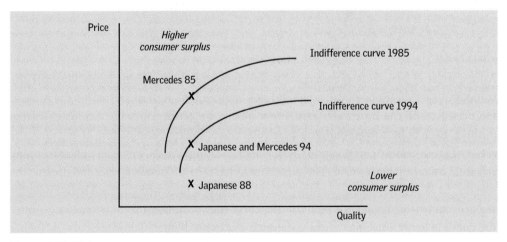

Figure 6.19 Value maps

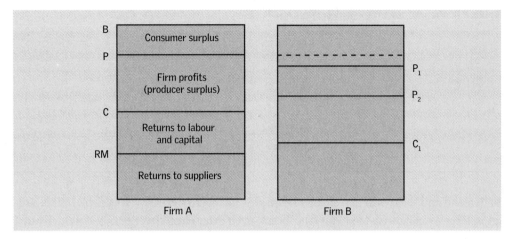

Figure 6.20 Pricing, consumer surplus and profit

away from Firm A. With similar costs competitive forces will move the market towards a common price level P. However, if Firm B is innovative and reduces costs to C_1, then it has the option of various prices below P, such as P_1 or P_2. The choice of price depends on the price elasticity of demand.

Pricing, price elasticity, costs and profits

Table 6.4 illustrates the interactions between **price elasticity** for the firm (not the market) and type of advantage – differentiation (benefit) or cost. The four boxes tell different stories:

- With a cost advantage and high price elasticity, it pays to underprice competitors to gain share.

- With a differentiation (benefit) advantage and high price elasticity, it pays to maintain price parity and let the differentiation advantage increase volume and thereby pull profits through.

- With cost advantage and low price elasticity the best option is a margin strategy whereby prices are maintained and profits are increased through the margin benefit.

- With a differentiation (benefit) advantage and low price elasticity, a margin strategy is again indicated where prices can be substantially raised because of the low elasticity and high benefits – profits accrue through increased margins with only small volume offsets.

In setting prices the task is to create a competitive advantage by (i) creating unique value to consumers (best possible consumer surplus) and (ii) creating above average profits for the firm. If every firm were like Firm A in Figure 6.20, there would be no competitive advantage. If one firm can innovate and create lower costs (like Firm B) or higher benefits, then a competitive advantage is possible for a range of possible prices depending on the price elasticities

Table 6.4 Pricing, advantage and profits

	Cost advantage	Differentiation (benefit) advantage
High price elasticity	SHARE STRATEGY Underprice competitors to gain share	SHARE STRATEGY Maintain price parity and let differentiation gain share
Low price elasticity	MARGIN STRATEGY Maintain price parity and gain profits through high margins	MARGIN STRATEGY Charge price premium relative to competitors

of demand and the type and scale of advantage available to the innovating firm. In this situation Firm B would wish to identify the '**break-even price elasticity**', that is the elasticity that would enable it to identify the borderline between a share strategy and a margin strategy.

6.3 Strategic groups

In the same way that there are segments on the demand side, there are groups on the supply side. We call these **strategic groups**. From Figure 6.14 you can see that we have arrayed differentiation characteristics against cost characteristics to obtain a map of different locations for firms within an industry. In this case we looked in terms of the consequences for profits for firms in different locations. The dimensions of this matrix are strategic choices and thus difficult to change and difficult to imitate. Strategic groups are configurations of this kind. They represent substructures within an industry that enable us to identify groups of firms with similar strategies.

A strategic group is formed when:

> *A firm within a group makes strategic decisions that cannot readily be imitated by firms outside the group without substantial costs, significant elapsed time, or uncertainty about the outcome of those decisions.* (McGee and Thomas, 1986, p. 150)

Strategic groups are based on the notion of **mobility barriers**, the sources of which are illustrated in Table 6.5:

> *Mobility barriers are a corollary to the existence of strategic groups. They are factors which deter or inhibit the movement of a firm from one strategic position to another and, more generally, the expansion of firms in one group to a position held by another group. Therefore a mobility barrier is essentially a limitation on replicability or imitation. It acts like an entry barrier, but it acts for the group within the industry rather than for the industry as a whole.*
>
> *A group structuring carries no meaning without costs attached to the imitation of strategy by other firms. Mobility barriers thus reflect the decisions of firms and*

Table 6.5 Sources of mobility barriers

Market-related strategies	Supply and cost characteristics	Characteristics of firms

Product line
User technologies
Market segmentation
Distribution channels
Brand names
Geographic coverage
Selling systems
	Economies of scale:
	    production
	    marketing
	    administration
	Manufacturing processes
	R&D capability
	Marketing and distribution systems
		Ownership
		Organisation structure
		Control systems
		Management skills
		Boundaries of firms:
		    diversification
		    vertical integration
		Firm size
		Relationships with influence groups

Source: McGee and Thomas (1986) *Strategic Management Journal*, p. 151.

are a way of defining the set of key strategies available to a firm. The essential characteristic is relative cost advantage over all other competitors. The remedy for cost disadvantage of this kind probably involves investment expenditure on tangible or intangible assets with significant elapsed time before the investment comes to fruition. Moreover, the investment expenditures are irreversible ... and there will typically be considerable uncertainty attached to the outcome of the investment expenditures. (McGee and Thomas, 1986, p. 153)

6.3.1 The implications of strategic groups

Groups may exist for many different reasons. Investments in distinctive assets and therefore in competitive advantage are risky investments and firms may have quite different risk aversion postures. Thus, strategic positions, which are the outcome of patterns of decisions over time, can be seen in terms of return–risk trade-offs calculated ex ante. Corporate structure may also affect the nature of strategic groupings. Business units can vary considerably in their relationship with their corporate parents and may pursue different goal structures in ways that lead to strategy differences (see Sjostrom 1995). More generally, the historical development of an industry bestows differential advantages on firms depending on their timing of entry (first mover advantages versus follower advantages), geographical location (country-specific advantages), and sheer luck. Whatever the historical genesis of strategic groups, the essential characteristic is similarity along key strategic dimensions. The patterns of similarity and the extent of variety in an industry will have consequences along three dimensions:

1 the structure of the industry and its evolution over time;

2 the nature of competition; and

3 implications for relative performance of firms.

Industry structure analysis is intended to identify the nature and range of profit-earning possibilities for the participants. There are benchmark but simple models of perfect competition and monopoly (see Chapter 3), but the real interest lies in oligopolistic market structures within which different groups of firms may behave in systematically different ways protected (at least for a time) by their mobility barriers. Figure 6.14 illustrates the variety of structural types. Where there are significant opportunities available for both cost and differentiation there will be firms or groups of firms with different strategies and differing expansion paths. This becomes more important as the concept of industry becomes more fluid as entry conditions change, as boundaries become flexible and as 'new' industry groupings are formed (e.g. new media industries, new electronic commerce industries). Industry definition is in itself a form of classification process. Strategic group analysis provides a more fundamental basis for assessing future strategic possibilities and the emergence of new industry boundaries.

Strategic groups affect the nature of competition. Because of their structural similarities, firms in the same group are likely to respond in the same way to disturbances from outside the group and to competitive activities within the group. Here we can see oligopolistic interdependence at work on the basis of ability to imitate the moves of rivals. The interdependence here does not arise from targeting the same customers (although this may be a consequence of similar strategies) but stems solely from the possession of structural similarities.

The ability to explain the relative performance of firms is a central theme in strategic management research. Wide variation in profitability is characteristic of many industries and means that industry structural characteristics are not likely to be a good or stable predictor of profitability. However, mobility barriers (i.e. strategy differences) can explain persistent differences in profit rates between groups in an industry. Porter (1979) argued that the pattern and intensity of inter-group competition and the consequences for profitability in the industry depends on three factors:

1 *The number and size distribution of groups.* Other things held constant, the more numerous and more equal in size are the strategic groups, the higher is the rivalry. On the other hand, if one strategic group constitutes a small portion of an industry while another is a very large portion, then strategic asymmetry is likely to have little impact on rivalry since the power of the small group to influence the large group is probably low.

2 *The strategic distance between groups.* This is the degree to which strategies in different groups differ in terms of the key strategic decision variables. The greater this distance, the more difficult tacit co-ordination becomes and the more vigorous rivalry will be in the industry.

3 *The market interdependence between groups.* Diversity of strategies increases rivalry between groups the most, where market interdependence is high. However, those

strategic groups that possess high mobility barriers are relatively more insulated from rivalry. On the other hand, when strategic groups are targeting very different segments, their effect on each other is much less severe.

Profits may be differentially affected across strategic groups for other reasons:

◆ There may be differences in **bargaining power** that some strategic groups may have towards customers and/or suppliers. These differences may be due to differences in scale, threat of vertical integration or product differentiation following from differing strategies.

◆ There may be differences in the degree of exposure of strategic groups to *substitute products* produced by other industries.

◆ There may be great differences in the degree to which firms *within* the group compete with each other. While mutual dependence should be fully recognized within groups that contain few firms, it may be difficult to sustain if there are numerous firms in the strategic group or if the risk profiles of the firms differ.

There are also firm-specific factors that influence profitability within a group:

◆ *Differences in firms' scale within the strategic group.* Although firms within the same strategic groups are likely to be similar in the scales of their operations, differences in scale *may* exist and may work to the disadvantage of smaller firms in the group where there are aspects of the strategy subject to economies of scale.

◆ *Differences in the cost of mobility into a strategic group.* If there are absolute cost advantages of being early in establishing brand names, locating raw materials, etc., a later entrant in a specific strategic group may face some disadvantages with respect to established firms. Timing is in this case a factor that may impact profit differences. This may also be the case if an established firm also possesses assets from its operations in other industries that could be jointly utilized.

◆ *Ability of the firm to execute or implement its strategy* in an operational sense. Some firms may be superior in their ability to organize and manage operations, develop creative advertising themes, make technological breakthroughs with given inputs of resources and the like. While these are not structural advantages of the sort created by mobility barriers, they may be relatively stable advantages if the market for managers, scientists and creative personnel is imperfect. Those firms in a group with superior abilities to execute strategies will be more profitable than others firms in the same group.

6.3.2 Strategic mapping

It is convenient and conventional to turn the multidimensional concept of strategic groups into a practical tool by drawing **strategic maps**. These are two-dimensional replications of the larger group structure within which the important strategic dimensions can be seen and through which key opportunities and threats can be depicted. The key steps in this process are (following Fiegenbaum *et al.*, 1990, and Fiegenbaum and Thomas, 1990):

1   choice of the strategy space (industry);

2   choice of organizational levels to be incorporated (corporate, business or functional);

3   identification of the variables which best capture firms' strategies;

4   identification of stable time periods;

5   clustering of firms into strategic groups.

The main issue concerning choice of strategic space relates to the identification of the boundaries of the 'industry'. The concept of industry is fuzzy but in practice we often over-rely on Standard Industrial Classification (SIC) codes. However, these mirror product variation and are typically bounded by nationality. The term strategic space is used as an alternative to industry to indicate that the relevant criterion for choice is competitive interaction.

When choosing the organizational level at which to analyse firms' strategies one must not simply focus on business level characteristics such as product and geographical scope, and relative emphasis on cost versus differentiation. Corporate parenting can provide a significant element of the eventual competitive advantage and it would be an oversimplification to exclude corporate effects. Similarly, functional strategies such as advertising intensity and sales force characteristics can be critical investments in support of the business strategy.

On the identification of the variables representing firms' strategies it is common to argue that there are a small number of dimensions that capture the essence of strategy differences between firms and between groups. This suggests that it is entirely possible to adopt a pragmatic approach. Typically an in-depth case study can reflect the views of industry participants, can give peer group judgements on competitors' strategies, and can also give the analyst a database for independent judgement. The alternative is to use clustering and other statistical techniques to determine, de facto, what groups exist and then to interpret the groupings using independent data on strategy dimensions. This is typically the route taken by academic researchers.[3]

---

[3]   A number of different methods exist for clustering firms into groups. Analysis of empirical research indicates that most researchers use cluster analysis. Once strategic variables have been identified, researchers generally use clustering techniques to form groups so that homogeneity is at its maximum internally and at its minimum externally. There is considerable debate about the nature of cluster analysis; see Ketchen and Shook (1996) for a review of the way it has been used in strategy research. The advantage of cluster analysis is that it indicates the distance that exists between strategic groups and between companies within the same strategic group. The distance between groups can be considered as approximating the height of mobility barriers while the distance between firms can be used as a basis to analyse the differences between them. The main difficulty with cluster analysis is that it identifies clusters regardless of the presence or absence of any underlying structure (Ketchen and Shook, 1996). Then there remains the question of how to describe and empirically validate the dimensions that the analysis reveals.

Much research in strategic management has studied industry change over long periods of time. This contrasts with research in economics where the emphasis has been much more on cross-section, relatively short-period studies. When studying strategic groups longitudinally there is a problem about identifying the nature of change and the way it affects the groupings. The typical approach is to think in terms of '**punctuated equilibria**'. Periods of stability are punctuated by periods of change within which strategies are changed, new positions taken up, and rivalry adjusts in response. Firms' strategies and industry structure are seen in equilibrium during each strategic time period. When the equilibrium ends (maybe because of exogenous shocks in the environment or alternatively triggered by autonomous firm actions), some firms change their strategies, new strategic groups are formed and others disappear. Statistical techniques can be used to identify the relatively stable sub-periods within which strategic groups are identifiable (see Bogner, Thomas and McGee 1996) and the transition points or periods from one equilibrium to the next.

6.3.3 **Strategic groups in practice**

We illustrate these points by looking at a study of the food processing industry in Europe at the time of the enactment of the European Single Market Act 1987–1992 (McGee and Segal-Horn 1990 and 1992). This looked across conventional market (national) boundaries and asked how the industry might evolve given the exogenous legislation shocks to the industry.

The practical question concerned the possible emergence of a pan-European food industry from the existing mosaic of separate nationally focused industries, i.e. transnational companies emerging from multidomestic structures. This possibility was mooted in the context of the Single European Act, conceived in 1987 for implementation by 1992. This was expected to reduce the costs of access to separate European markets and, along with expectations about increasing homogeneity of consumers across Europe, constituted external triggers for structural change.

The approach to this was to develop a model of '**strategic space**' on to which the prospective movements of firms could be mapped. A historical overview enabled the identification of periods of stability and the conditions causing breaks between periods. On the basis of this history, key variables were identified as the basis for strategic group identification. These were market scope (territories covered), marketing intensity and brand strength, manufacturing focus, and R&D intensity (the latter two were not statistically validated). These were used to identify the strategic group configuration in 1990, enabling the identification of at least four distinct groupings. However, the real interpretive power of the configuration lay in the specification of the mobility barriers between the groups. The strategic space idea is the converse of the strategic group, i.e. why is there no group present in a particular location on an n-dimensional map. The first possible answer is that some spaces are currently infeasible and the asset structures implied by that space are competitively dominated by other asset structures. The second possible answer is that some spaces have never been entered because the construction of the implied assets was not thought to be competitively viable. This second insight allowed the analysis of certain empty spaces to suggest that certain assets could technically be constructed (e.g. European marketing systems and brands) and that changing market conditions might yield a pay-off for those new asset structures.

Thus the strategic group/space analysis allowed the juxtaposition of a changing market situation in Europe with a lowering of mobility barriers between existing groups and the empty spaces. The conclusion drawn is that certain kinds of new asset structures of firms are very likely to be constructed and that these will fall into two or three key new groups. The processes by which this might happen can be identified, including a wave of mergers and acquisitions. The consequences for competition both in the transition period and for a period of subsequent stability can be analysed, although the time period over which the transition will take place could not be identified. The analysis is distinctive in that it is almost entirely prospective in character, laying out a framework for analysing future change in the industry.

Figures 6.21, 6.22, 6.23 and 6.24 summarize the analysis. Figure 6.21 shows the existing strategic group structure in the late 1980s. Figure 6.22 summarizes the mobility barriers that protect each group. Figure 6.23 contains the strategic space analysis and Figure 6.24 shows the authors' conjectures about the group configuration in 2000. The dimensions of the matrix are key strategic decisions faced by firms in this industry, namely geographical coverage of the EC (representing internationalization strategy) and marketing intensity (representing brand focus). The map distinguishes different kinds of brand players, national versus European in scope, and cost-based own-label suppliers.

The authors conclude:

> First, two major new strategies are likely to emerge, the pan-European own label supplier and the pan-European brander. Second, the strategic space analysis tells us something about the pathways to achieving these positions. Third, it also tells us something about the nature of competition both en route and in the new structure. This approach does not tell us how long the process of change will take, nor does it say

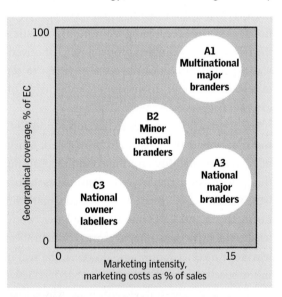

Figure 6.21 European food processing industry strategic groups, late 1980s
Source: McGee and Segal-Horn (1990) *Journal of Marketing Management*. Reproduced with permission of Westburn Publishers Ltd.

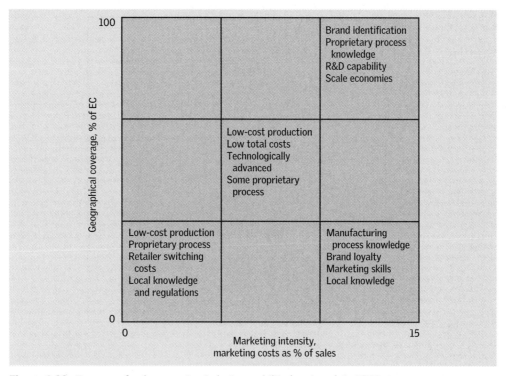

Figure 6.22 European food processing industry mobility barriers, late 1980s
Source: McGee and Segal-Horn (1990) *Journal of Marketing Management*. Reproduced with permission of Westburn Publishers Ltd.

who will be the winners and losers. It does, however, say a great deal about the characteristics of the winners and losers. (McGee and Segal-Horn, 1990, p. 190)

After the passage of time since this paper was written, it is interesting to reflect on the extent to which the pan-European brander space has been occupied. At that time it seemed like an attractive space since it offered economies of scale across a European market that was showing signs of converging consumer tastes, developing its logistics networks and creating fewer larger factories. In the 1990s it becomes clear that Unilever, Nestlé and Mars were beginning to focus on just such a strategy (Johnson and Scholes 1999, p. 129).[4]

Strategic group maps do not have to be historical and therefore 'backward-looking'. History is important in developing an understanding of the nature of mobility barriers and the time and cost involved in investing to overcome them. However, one can assess the present and make forward-looking conjectures. For example, Figure 6.25 is a speculative map constructed in 1996 of retail banking in 2000 in order to assess the implications of new

---

[4] Note that the Pan-European group emerges with lower marketing/sales ratios because transnationals (and trans-regionals) save costs by eliminating duplication of marketing costs across country markets.

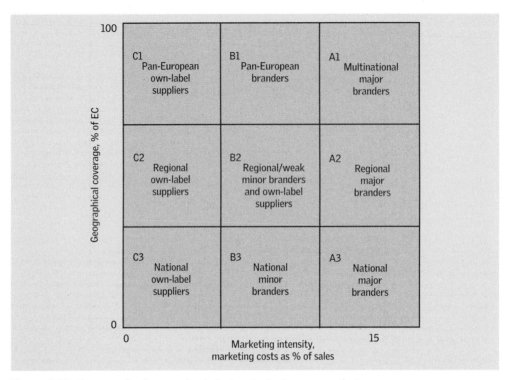

Figure 6.23 European food processing industry strategic space analysis
Source: McGee and Segal-Horn (1990) *Journal of Marketing Management*. Reproduced with permission of Westburn Publishers Ltd.

possibilities such as banking through the internet. The two strategy dimensions are degree of vertical integration and brand novelty. Traditional banks have a 'complete' value chain and do everything in-house whereas the new e-banks focus for the most part on electronic distribution and sub-contract everything else such as cheque processing. The new e-banks have enormous brand novelty indicated by the plethora of 'cute' names such as Egg, Goldfish and Smile. Thus, we have two utterly distinct groups. The first question to ask is, are these groups highly rivalrous, or is the emergence of the new group merely indicative of a new market segment? This poses a degree of threat to traditional banks which need to ask whether they can remain where they are with some strategic adaptation such as opening of new electronic channels of distribution in parallel to their existing channels (viz. the High Street). Or should they seek to develop some brand novelty? Or perhaps deconstruct their integrated value chains into separate upstream and downstream businesses? Or is there a different dimension on which they can play, for instance TV banking? For the new e-banks the question is, to what extent is this strategic group defensible? Should a highly deconstructed value chain be supported by a series of alliances to secure access to best-in-class highly complementary activities?

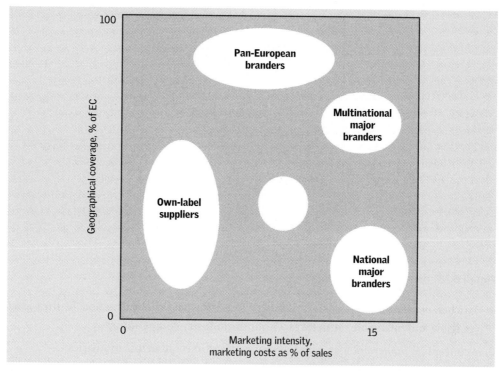

Figure 6.24 European food processing industry strategic groups, 2000
Source: McGee and Segal-Horn (1990) *Journal of Marketing Management*. Reproduced with permission of Westburn Publishers Ltd.

These two examples demonstrate some key themes:

1 Strategic group analysis enriches our discussion of the nature of strategic choice.

2 The formation of groups reflects strategy innovations and risky decisions.

3 The stability of group structures over time tells us, through mobility barriers, about sustainability.

4 The nature of mobility barriers forces us to think about the investments that underpin market position and competitive advantage. It points us towards the nature of resources and the idea of core competences.

Any analysis of group structures leads very quickly from history to predictive ability. The essence of strategic decision is investment in distinctive assets against an uncertain future and therefore strategy innovations and industry evolution are closely linked. Innovation disturbs the industry equilibrium and foreshadows the emergence of new ways of competing and new group structures. Ex ante analysis of possible strategy innovations gives an indication of new strategy dimensions and therefore the nature, pattern and intensity of future rivalry. The pay-offs from this approach can be summarized in terms of interpretation, framework and language, viz.:

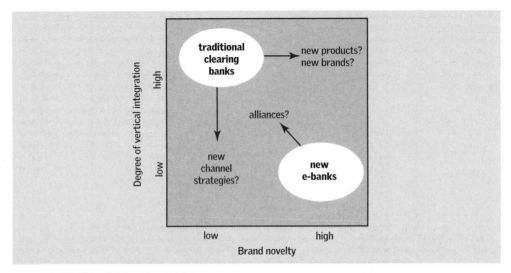

Figure 6.25 UK retail banking, 2000

1 a richer *interpretation* of current industry structures and the interaction of firm asset (tangible and intangible) structures with intra-industry competition;

2 a conceptual *framework* for analysing change over time and across industries;

3 a *language* for interpreting change in terms of asset structures of firms and the ensuing effects on competition in the long run.

6.4 **Industry transformation**

It is common to observe that change is endemic and many consulting firms have been very successful in promoting programmes of strategic change. However, many also note that strategies by their nature are not things that one changes readily or frequently. Strategies involve investment in lumpy and sticky assets without the comfort of knowing that mistakes can be easily undone. Nevertheless, markets and industries do evolve and grow. Growth very often is continuous and cumulative, especially when research and development follows cumulative trajectories. The experience of the last quarter of a century shows that new knowledge has very often moved sideways into adjacent industries and done an excellent job of unsettling long-held beliefs and strategies. Thus, new materials such as plastics have undermined the steel industry and the coming of the internet has caused major changes in distribution industries. So are there any patterns in the way in which industries are transformed? In what ways does Porter's famous picture of the five forces change systematically? Figure 6.26 suggests the major possibilities.

The principal **industry transformation** routes, as a result of which the five forces are reconfigured, are:

1 redefining the market

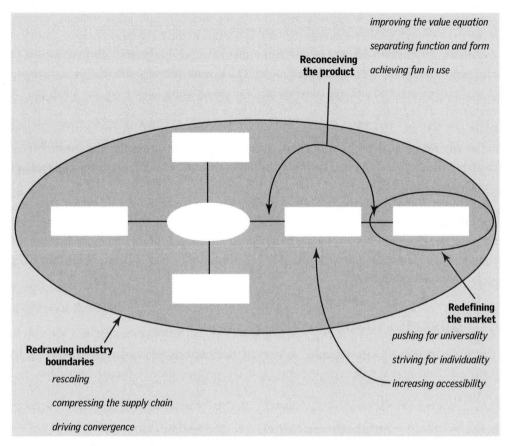

Figure 6.26 Industry transformation routes

2   reconceiving the product

3   redrawing the industry boundaries

Market redefinitions involve changing the relationship with the customer. At one level firms may seek universality, that is, striving to get a wider take-up of their products across hith-erto distinct market segments. This is the approach typically taken in internationalization and we could say that Coca-Cola has succeeded in achieving a universal market. The oppo-site approach is individualization with segments of one person – an approach typical in modern electronic and internet-based industries. Most redefinition strategies have some element of higher accessibility involving major changes in logistics and distribution.

Rethinking the role of the product is also an attempt to capture changes that are taking place in the psychology of consumers. There have been fundamental and controversial changes in the nature of drinks on offer to young people (alco-pops, for example), where the producers have been trying to tap into the rapid changes that are taking place.

Similarly, sports cars are being redefined as toys for the retired. Product changes typically involve changing the value equation (benefit–cost ratio to the customer).

Redrawing industry boundaries stems from major changes in the underling economics of production and of the supply chain in general. The drivers of change are usually rescaling to obtain economies, and driving convergence and eliminating variety to the same end. A simple way of reducing costs has been to outsource more and more but this in itself is not strategic – it is more a rebalancing of the location of costs along the chain. More significant is the compressing of the supply chain, where new technology raises the possibility of changing the nature of the operations in the chain with the effect of changing the product and its cost characteristics.

In Chapter 5 and in this chapter we have often referred to the 'economic model' that captures the essential economic characteristics and cash flows of the firm. In assessing strategic position we wish to be able to relate the intended strategic position and the nature of the competitive advantage to the performance of the firm. In the next section we introduce the idea of the **business model**.

6.5 **Business model**

This is a widely used term intended to provide the link between an intended strategy, its functional and operational requirements, and the performance (typically cash flows and profits) that is expected. It usually applies to single businesses where a specific competitive strategy can be identified but it can also apply to those multi-business portfolios that are linked by strong synergies and therefore have common or similar strategies.

Chesbrough and Rosenbloom (2002) cite their experience in turning up 107,000 references to 'business model' on the World Wide Web while only finding three citations in the academic literature. In the usual practitioner sense, a business model is the method of doing business by which a company can sustain itself – that is, generate revenue. The business model spells out how a company makes money by specifying where it is positioned in the value chain. A more precise definition has been offered by the consultants KM Lab (2000): 'business model is a description of how your company intends to create value in the marketplace. It includes that unique combination of products, services, image and distribution that your company carries forward. It also includes the underlying organization of people and operational infrastructure that they use to accomplish their work.'

Chesbrough and Rosenbloom (2002) describe the functions of a business model as:

- to articulate the value proposition
- to identify a market segment
- to define the structure of the value chain
- to estimate the cost structure and profit potential

- to describe the position of the firm within the supply chain
- to formulate the strategic logic by which the firm will gain and hold advantage

The simple Du Pont accounting identities are a good starting point for identifying a business model. Thus:

$$\pi = (p - c)Q - F$$

and

$$NA = WC + FA$$

where

π is profits
p is price
c is variable costs
Q is quantity sold
F is fixed costs
NA is net assets
WC is working capital
FA is fixed assets

An intended strategy should have specific effects on the variables in these equations. For example, a cost leadership strategy would be expected to reduce variable costs, to increase fixed costs, and to increase fixed assets – according to the economies of scale available. Accordingly, profits and return on investment (π/NA) will be expected to increase because the rise in fixed costs and fixed assets due to the investment will be more than offset by the increase in contribution margin ($p - c$). A more ambitious business model might also specify a price reduction that will result in a volume increase through the medium of a high price elasticity and no imitation by competitors. The validity of such an assumption about lack of competitor response depends on judgements about competitor cost levels and their willingness to sacrifice margin for volume.

Similarly, a differentiation strategy would be expected to raise both costs and prices. Costs would go up because of the variable costs (such as quality and service levels) and fixed costs (such as advertising and R&D) of differentiation. Prices would be expected to increase disproportionately if the value to customers was sufficiently high to make the product price inelastic. This business model then calls for a higher margin game, offset to some degree by higher fixed costs. A more ambitious model might also aim for a volume increase on the basis of higher product 'value' stimulating demand (a rising demand curve rather than a negatively sloped one).

What the business model does is to articulate the logic of the intended strategy in terms of the specific operations that have to take place. With this detailed plan the consequences for cash flows can be determined and the link between (intended) strategy and (expected) performance can be established. Beyond the obvious benefit of quantifying the strategic logic of the firm, the business model also enables sensitivity testing and risk analysis. In the case of the cost leadership example the intention might be to reduce variable costs by a target percentage. The implications of a shortfall in cost reduction can easily be calculated and expressed in terms of the percentage change in profits in relation to a given percentage shortfall from the target cost reduction. Where the business model calls for price changes, the implications of competitor imitation or non-imitation can also be calculated.

In practice a business model can be articulated in terms of detailed plans and budgets that provide guidance to managers relating to their operational responsibilities. The logic that drives plans and budgets lies within the business model. The business model itself is the mechanism through which a business intends to generate revenue and profits. Figure 6.27 shows a schematic (Yip, 2004) that describes the process from inputs to customers – in many ways this is simply a restyled value chain. This should not be surprising – the value chain is an activity map on to which can be placed assets and costs. Figure 6.28 shows an application to the existing mobile telephony business (*see* end of chapter case study). The merit of this is the explicit nature of the choices made and from this the implications for cash flows will follow. A different example is shown in Figure 6.29. This describes the leasing operations of a London bank. This shows clearly the performance dimensions at the top of the figure. Shareholder value is decomposed into components such as market share, price and costs. The bottom of the figure shows the drivers of the cash flows, starting with characteristics such as flexibility and moving upwards to a higher level of aggregation to customer satisfaction and brand strength from which the cash flows stem directly. This is an unusual picture of a business

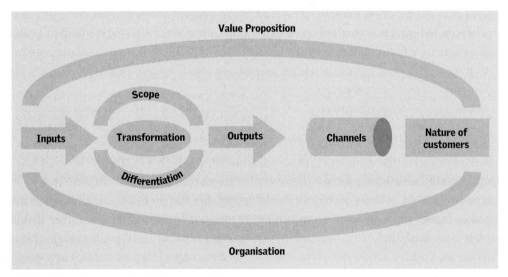

Figure 6.27 Elements of a business model
Source: Yip, 2004.

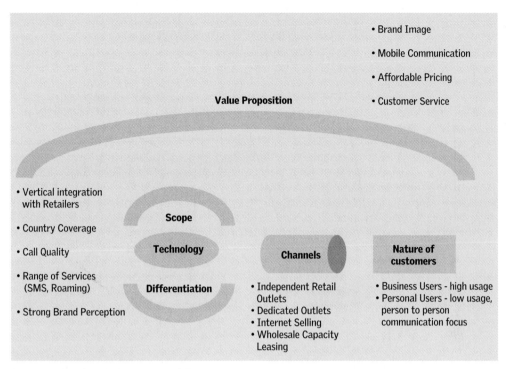

Figure 6.28 The 2G business model
Source: Puri, 2004.

model because it is not faithful to the value chain idea – only selected activities are shown. You should look at this and ask yourself (i) is this likely to be an accurate model if some variables are excluded? (ii) not all the variables are observable and quantifiable – does this matter? and (iii) what extra information would you require (hint: consider sensitivity analysis)?

6.5.1 Commitment and sustainability

The business model has become a standard part of the business lexicon to indicate the way cash flows are underpinned by a strategic logic. For the business model to be genuinely useful it needs to reflect the sustainability and defensibility of its strategic position and the nature of the commitment that is required in the strategic assets of the firm. Recall the strategy cycle (Figure 5.9) and note that the top line requires a balancing of resources and assets with the market position. The resource and asset component of this is discussed in the next chapter. Sustainability of the strategic position is to do with the imitability (or otherwise) of the competitive advantage. The five forces model gives an indication of the overall attractiveness of the industry – attractiveness means the degree to which the profits of the industry players are protected from erosion by the five competitive forces. More specifically, sustainability is to do with the insulation of the net cash flows (and the net present value of

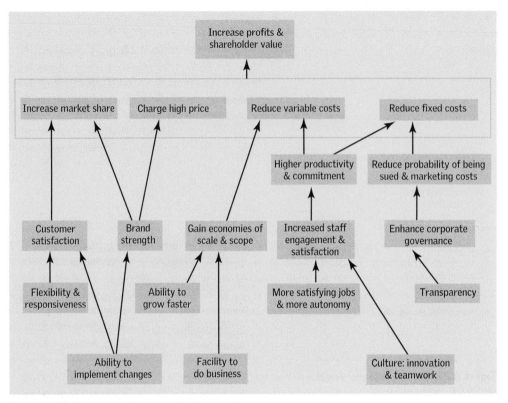

Figure 6.29 London bank: leasing business model
Source: Tello, 2004.

the firm) from attack by any individual competitor. A failing of the generic five forces model is its inability to move beyond the industry on average or in general. Sustainability analysis involves analysing potential responses by competitors and potential entrants and the impact of those actions on the degree of competition and on the cash flows that are generated by the competitive advantage of the incumbent firm. Richard Rumelt invented the term **isolating mechanisms** to refer to the economic forces that limit the extent to which a competitive advantage can be neutralized or duplicated. Isolating mechanisms are to the firm what entry barriers are to an industry – they are the forces that inhibit other firms from competing away profits from incumbent firms. There are different approaches to identifying and classifying isolating mechanisms (*see* Rumelt 1984; Ghemawat 1991, 1994a, 1994b; Yao 1988). Besanko *et al.* (2000) put them in two distinct groups.

Impediments to imitation

These isolating mechanisms prevent firms from imitating and/or surpassing the resources, competences and strategic assets that underpin the incumbent's advantage. Thus, many firms compete in the executive car markets but few, if any, can match the approach of BMW and Mercedes. Note, however, the concerted efforts of Audi, Jaguar and Lexus to do so. In the soft drinks industry Coca-Cola has been unrivalled in fostering its brand name as a symbol of uniqueness. These impediments include legal restrictions, superior access to inputs or to customers, and intangible barriers (resource-based) to imitating the incumbent's core competences.

Early mover advantages

Once a firm establishes a competitive advantage then certain economic forces can protect its position. We saw earlier in this chapter the example of Du Pont in titanium dioxide. Its first move pre-empted the market by establishing a requirement for sufficiently large size to attain competitive costs that there was insufficient room in the market for followers. Similarly, Microsoft's position as the effective standard in the personal computer industry (see Chapter 13 for an analysis of network effects) has meant that no follower has been able to create a value proposition for consumers such that they would be willing to incur the costs of switching to a new (and presumably much improved) standard. These impediments are all related to market size and scale economies, and also to technological change and the creation of legally recognized or de facto standards.

Firms usually analyse isolating mechanisms through a process of competitor analysis (*see* Channon, 1988). This can take a variety of forms but usually contains a number of common headings:

- Identifying which competitors to track
  - existing direct competitors
  - new and potential entrants
- Establishing a competitor database
  - surveying sources of competitor intelligence
  - collecting data regularly and systematically
  - building and using the database
- Analysing competitor strategies
  - functional strategies
    - marketing
    - production/operations
    - R&D
    - financing strategy
  - business unit strategies
  - corporate/group objectives
  - long-term financial capability

Competitor analysis is capable of giving insight into ways in which the incumbent's core competences might be imitated or outflanked. Sometimes this can be done by direct observation of the activities of competitors and making appropriate inferences. A longer-range warning might come from studying the stated and sometimes covert intentions of significant competitors. Thus, Citibank and Chase Manhattan might have credited the possible appearance of HSBC[5] as a global competitor as it began its move out of its Hong Kong base in the early 1980s. It is now bigger than Chase.

These ideas are captured in the case box below, which discusses changes in the business model for large pharmaceutical companies.

Case box: **Big trouble for Big Pharma**

Why Big Pharma urgently needs a new business model

When GlaxoWellcome and SmithKlineBeecham announced their merger in 2000 to form GlaxoSmithKline (GSK), the world's second-largest drug firm, its new boss, Jean-Pierre Garnier, said that the merged firms would be 'the kings of science.' This week GSK unveiled its crown jewels: a full pipeline of compounds in research and development, the result of a £2.6 billion ($4.5 billion), 16,000-researcher-strong effort. 82 new drugs and 20 vaccines are in development, 44 of them moving into later-stage trials. Yet if Mr Garnier hoped that these numbers would impress his shareholders, he had to think again: GSK's share price actually fell on the news. Like investors in many other big drug firms, GSK's shareholders have little confidence that many of its new compounds will earn them a cent anytime soon. Of the 20 drugs that GSK plans to put into final-phase human testing in the next three years, the chances are, on current industry averages, that less than half of them will make it to market.

Next, consider Merck. On November 20th, news that the firm was stopping development of a diabetes drug after finding tumours in lab mice was met with dismay – and a wave of selling that knocked 11% off the firm's already-battered share price. With another vaunted project – an experimental anti-depressant – also failing last month, Merck's near-term pipeline now looks horribly empty. Even an upbeat profit forecast for next year, on December 3rd, did not cheer investors much.

Merck and GSK are not alone. In 1998–2002, according to Lehman Brothers, Big Pharma firms launched on average 59 drugs per year. In 2002–06, reckons Lehman, they will launch just 50 per year. Moreover, as many patents for the industry's existing products expire in the next five years, competition from generic-drug makers will threaten $30 billion (one-fifth) of annual sales in America alone, says AT Kearney, a consultancy.

When the drugs don't work

Big Pharma now faces two big challenges. First, control costs better. Stuart Walker, head of the Centre for Medicines Research International, reckons that total industry spending on R&D

---

will reach $50 billion this year, over 25% up on 1998. Sales and marketing overheads have soared, too. In the past four years, says Dean Hart, head of North American sales at Takeda, a Japanese drug firm, the number of sales representatives employed by drug firms in America has risen by 54%, to 90,000. Each rep costs on average $200,000 a year. Sales, general and administrative expenses account for 17% of a typical big American firm's revenues, says Christopher White of AT Kearney. In the drug industry, such overheads (even excluding the big American sales forces) account for 33% of revenues. Standard management practices such as consolidating procurement, outsourcing personnel and finance functions and automating transaction processing all compare poorly with other industries, says Mr White. Many firms still make pills in-house, a job perhaps better done by a contract manufacturer.

But the tougher challenge is to improve the productivity of R&D. As Mr Walker points out, it is not just the number of new products that has fallen in recent years, but also their originality. Less than 30% of drugs launched last year were first or second in their class. The proportion was far higher in the late 1990s. Roughly 40% of R&D spending by Big Pharma is now on 'line extensions' – improving existing drugs, not creating entirely new ones.

Many big drug firms have begun to license more of their technology and products from outside companies, especially biotechnology start-ups: having slumped in recent years, the value of biotech firms is now rising again. Novartis has set up a big R&D centre in Cambridge, Massachusetts, in part to better position itself to collaborate with outside academics. Eli Lilly's InnoCentive subsidiary runs a website where problems confronting drugmakers, such as how to generate a particular compound in chemical synthesis, are posted to be tackled by more than 25,000 registered problem-solvers as far afield as Russia and China. For a reward of $10,000–100,000, the firm gets a solution that would have cost more time and money to solve itself.

Others hope to improve the way they manage in-house R&D. Wyeth is encouraging its researchers to perform their tasks better by changing how it pays them. Unusually for the industry, its scientists get to share a bonus pool which depends, in part, on how many new drugs they launch each year. There used to be a temptation for Wyeth's early-stage researchers to throw their work 'over the wall' before it was ready to the scientists who run clinical trials, says Robert Ruffolo, the firm's head of research. Because early-stage researchers now share incentives with later-stage scientists, the later-stage researchers have begun to 'pull' the development of the most promising compounds forward. A corresponding 'push' from early-stage workers hastens the process. GSK fundamentally reorganised its R&D in 2001, splitting its more creative arm into smaller 'centres of excellence', and enlarging the arm that enjoys economies of scale. Mr Garnier claims that his 'best of both worlds' strategy is now paying off.

The industry's bloated overheads appear to be driving its decisions on the sort of drugs it seeks to develop. Like a supermodel who will not get out of bed for less than $10,000 a day, Big Pharma has decided that it is simply not worth investing in anything but a blockbuster.

This means that lesser, albeit interesting, compounds fall by the wayside. An oft-quoted figure from the Tufts Centre for the Study of Drug Development puts the average cost of bringing a new drug to market at $897m. But as F.M. Scherer, an economist, points out, this is an average cost for big firms producing drugs for chronic diseases. Other firms can bring drugs for other complaints – infectious diseases or rare conditions, say – to the market for around $100m–200m.

Big Pharma also needs to do something about its poorly trained, generalised sales force, which is simply not equipped to chase smaller, more specialised markets. Most sales calls end, at best, with just a few seconds of a doctor's time, laments Mr Hart of Takeda. Some reps do not even make it past the reception desk before dropping off their free samples. Drug firms lag behind other industries in the way they use information technology to discriminate between profitable and unprofitable customers. Only one in five drug companies invests in any sales force training beyond initial courses offered to recruits. Who, after all, needed to bother with trifles such as training and IT when, without much effort, a drug such as Lipitor, Pfizer's cholesterol-lowering medicine, was making sales of $8.6 billion last year alone?

Can Big Pharma achieve transformation without changes at the top? The bosses of big drugs firms have been horribly slow to grasp the enormity of their problems. Until recently, Merck's boss, Raymond Gilmartin, has been reluctant to license much technology from outside, instead putting his faith in the firm's own scientists. With Merck's in-house R&D now struggling, it will be no surprise if Mr Gilmartin's head is the first to roll.

Source: 'Big Trouble for Big Pharma', *The Economist*, 4 December 2003.
© The Economist Newspaper Limited, London (4 December 2003).

6.6 Summary

This chapter has examined the notion of competitive advantage from the viewpoint of establishing and defending strategic position in the marketplace. This requires a deep understanding of the economic drivers of the firm, its essential cost position, its approach to differentiating itself in the market from its competitors, and its chosen position in the market in terms of ability to exploit natural economies of scale and scope. We have also looked at what competitive advantage means to customers and to firms and the ways firms have of understanding their positions in terms of strategic market segments (on the demand side) and of strategic groups (on the supply side). This leads to an understanding pricing and value and the sustainability of value over time. Any competitive strategy has to be turned into action – the notion of the business model is the way in which the firm's individual theory of its business (its competitive strategy) is turned into cash flows. A proper understanding of the business model leads to an appreciation of how the strategy might be sustained into the future (sustainability).

In the next chapter we turn our attention to the assessment of strategic capability, those core competences that underpin competitive advantage and are the target of the firm's strategic investment programmes.

Key terms

Bargaining power *225*
Break-even price elasticity *222*
Business model *234*
Consumer surplus *219*
Early mover advantages *239*
Economies of scope *196*
Experience curve *200*
First mover advantage *201*
Indivisibilities *199*
Industry transformation *232*
Isolating mechanisms *238*
Learning curve *200*
Market-based view *195*
Mobility barriers *222*

Offer curve *216*
Positioning *195*
Price elasticity *221*
Punctuated equilibria *227*
Strategic groups *222*
Strategic maps *225*
Strategic market segments *216*
Strategic space *227*
Stuck in the middle *202*
Sunk costs *197*
Theory of value *219*
Unfair advantage *206*
Value maps *219*

Recap questions and assignments

1   Read the case box on the video gaming industry and interpret the rules of the game in terms of Porter's five forces analysis. Do this for the original rules of the game and for the new rules that Sony is trying to establish. What benefits does Sony expect to gain? How would you expect its competitors to react?

2   Read the case box that discusses changes in the business model for large pharmaceutical companies. Identify the original business model by which these companies have traditionally earned high profits. Why has this model become unsustainable? Is this because industry forces have gradually eroded the traditional imperfections upon which firms could build their profits? Or, alternatively, have there been significant shifts in the business environment that have outdated their strategies. Define the new business model. What are its risks?

Online
*Learning*Centre

When you have read this chapter, log on to the Online Learning Centre website at www.mcgraw-hill.co.uk/textbooks/mcgee to explore chapter-by-chapter test questions, further reading and more online study tools for strategy.

Case 1 **Mobile telephony and the move from 2G to 3G standards**

The 3G business model

The transition from 2G to 3G business model is not a radical step change. With the introduction of WAP and GPRS services, the 2G business model is continually evolving. The proposed 3G business model is the culmination of this evolution. Of course business models are dynamic, like strategy, and will continually alter with rapid technology introduction (Yip 2004).

The 3G business model is muddied by the number of services that an operator can offer. The 3G platform allows enhanced data services and therefore the complexity of the service offering is increased. Obviously, since 3G is essentially offering 2G services, part of the business model stays the same; however, many new business models need to be amalgamated with this existing voice telephony model.

The 3G business model identifies two distinct uses a mobile operator may offer its customer base: a provider of communication and a mobile exchange. The network operator must try to provide the characteristics that will make each of these offerings successful in the marketplace and build a business model that will be sustainable.

3G as communication provider

The role of the communications provider is to allow customers to send and receive communications over the mobile network to which they are connected.

- **The value proposition** – in this case, is similar to that in the 2G case. Mobility and convenience of communication is clearly an advantage to the customer. The value proposition is enhanced by a strong brand image that confers the psychological risk reduction of branding on the customer. The newest entrant to the market, 3 UK, may suffer from this as they have no particular brand image at present. Negative publicity over network problems will further disadvantage the company, which has obviously spent millions in trying to build a brand. Although Vodafone and Orange may hold premium place in the branding stakes, it is important to realize that a branding strategy needs to be aligned with the customers you intend to target. Vodafone's premium position may be a disadvantage if pressure on call charges increases. Customers are looking to pay the least they can for what is now viewed as a commodity market and Vodafone's perceived higher prices may put customers off.

- **Differentiation** – is the step that operators must take if indeed they are to price calls higher than competitors. In the 2G world, Vodafone (and to a certain extent O_2) was able to create the impression that its network was of higher quality and dropped less calls than T-Mobile and Orange. These factors lead business customers and other high-value users to subscribe to the Vodafone connection as being the premium network. In the world of 3G, voice will be the main driver and to protect revenues operators must establish a differentiation between themselves and competitors. Handset range is a potential differentiator. 3 UK has suffered badly from being unable to provide customers with a handset range that meets the standards of the newest 2G phones. 3G phones need significant improvement in aesthetics and battery power if they are to be considered a viable alternative to the current crop of 2G phones. The average customer is looking for a phone that can be considered a fashion accessory and it could take some time before 3G phones reach this stage (Morrison 2003). Another strong avenue of differentiation must be customer service. T-Mobile ploughed millions of pounds into the renovation of the customer service department before and after rebranding from One2One. One2One was always associated with poor levels of customer service and high levels of churn. Rebranding meant that T-Mobile was focusing on new market segments and customer services had to be of industry standard before marketing to these customers could occur.

◆ **The channels of distribution** – are also not greatly changed for this particular 3G offering. Independent retailers offer an excellent way of getting phones to market and do not require the expense of building expensive prime-located stores. Carphone Warehouse dominate this market and more than 27 per cent of customers say that it would be the first place they would go if they wanted to find out more about their phone (ICM Research 2003). Interestingly, dedicated retailers Orange and Vodafone, which have invested large sums in building up the branding of their stores, come second and third in the poll. O_2 and T-Mobile stores lag further behind after a string of independents such as The Link and Phones 4 U. The findings show that the companies that lead the branding stakes are also foremost in the minds of customers when they are thinking about their phones. Vodafone and Orange consistently score higher on brand awareness surveys than other networks and customers automatically think of these brands when they want to make changes to the way they use their phones (Wolff Olins 2004).

Preferred mobile phone retailers

Retailer	Percentage of customers
Carphone Warehouse	27%
Orange shops	18%
Vodafone shops	16%
The Link	16%
Phones 4 U	9%
O_2 shops	5%
T-Mobile shops	5%

Source: ICM Research, 2003.

◆ **Segmentation of customers** – is an extremely important stage that requires operators to begin thinking in different ways. Operators must think of the consumer base as different sub-groups, which can be characterized by different needs, some of which will overlap. Remembering that voice is very much the main driver, tariff plans must be altered to accommodate the needs of a majority of these groups. In August 2003, 51 per cent of customers on 3 UK admitted to voice and SMS being the primary reason they purchased a new phone and connection (Deutsche Bank 2003). An analysis of the market shows that there are many types of users, each with different usage patterns of voice and SMS products. By mapping these on to axes we can see which particular services operators will have to target when putting together tariffs to appeal to these different segments. The business community can be seen as a large range of users that primarily use voice services but may be high users of text messages as well. Users in an older demographic can be considered low users of either service, with mobility and convenience being their main concern. The main group of users relates to customers in a middle-age demographic, but even this must be segmented. Traditional users continue to use their handset as a voice-calling instrument and do not use other services heavily. Prepay customers look to receive more calls and send more SMS messages, while the upwardly mobile users are high-worth customers that use their phone for all occasions. Between these groups are students, who look to minimize payments by sending SMS messages, and children under 15, who may have parental limits on the amount they spend. It must be remembered that there are many other variables to be considered when deciding tariff and this analysis is simply a guide.

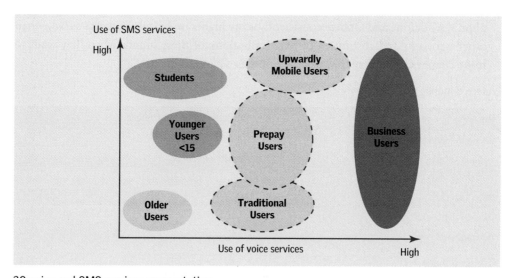

3G voice and SMS services segmentation

Other segmentation factors

Factor	High-end user	Low-end user
Handset style	Upwardly mobile user	Older user
Price sensitivity	Prepay user	Business user
Interconnect allowances	Upwardly mobile user	Older user
International options	Upwardly mobile user; students	Younger users

Source: Puri, 2004.

Case Questions

1 Describe the strategy being followed to move to the 3G standard.

2 What are the bases for differentiation and segmentation? Try to describe these in terms of Table 6.3 and Figures 6.5 and 6.18.

3 Is there anything novel about the approach described here?

4 Can you suggest alternative, new ways for differentiating innovative products?

Further reading and references

Bartlett, C and Ghoshal, S (1989) *Managing Across Borders*, Hutchinson, London.

Besanko, D, Dranove, D and Shanley, M (2000) *The Economics of Strategy*, (2nd edition), John Wiley & Sons, New York.

Bogner, WC, Thomas, H and McGee, J (1996) 'A Longitudinal Study of the Competitive Positions and Entry Paths of European Firms in the US Pharmaceutical Market', *Strategic Managment Journal*, **17**, **2**, pp. 85–107.

Chesbrough, H and Rosenbloom, RS (2002) 'The role of the business model in capturing value from innovation: evidence from Xerox Corporation's technology spin-off companies', *Industrial and Corporate Change*, **11**, **3**, pp. 529–55.

Deutsche Bank (2003) 'European Wireless Review', May, Deutsche Bank Equity Research, London.

Economist, The, 'Big Trouble for Big Pharma', 4 December 2003.

Fiegenbaum, A and Thomas, H (1990) 'Strategic Groups and Performance: The US Insurance Industry 1980–84', *Strategic Management Journal*, **11**, pp. 197–215.

Fiegenbaum, A, Tang, MJ and Thomas, H (1990) 'Strategic Time Periods and Strategic Group Research: Concepts and an Empirical Example', *Journal of Management Studies*, **27**, pp. 133–48.

Ghemawhat, P (1989) 'Du Pont's Titanium Business (A)', Harvard Business School Case Study 9–390–112.

Ghemawat, P (1991) 'Commitment: the Dynamic of Strategy', Free Press, New York.

Ghemawat, P (1994a) 'Du Pont in Titanium Dioxide (A)', Harvard Business School Case Study 9–385–140.

Ghemawat, P (1994b) 'Capacity Expansion in the Titanium Dixoide Industry', *Journal of Industrial Economics*, XXXIII, December, pp. 145–63.

Grant, RM (2002) *Contemporary Strategy Analysis*, 4th edition, Basil Blackwell, Oxford.

HMSO (1978) *A Review of Monopolies and Mergers Policy*, cmnd 7198, London.

ICM Research (2003) 'Do People Want More from their Mobiles?', ICM Research Review, July, pp. 3–4, ICM Research, London.

Johnson, G and Scholes, K (1999) *Exploring Corporate Strategy*, Prentice Hall, Hemel Hempstead.

Ketchen, DJ and Shook, CL (1996) 'The Application of Cluster Analysis in Strategic Management Research: An Analysis and Critique', *Strategic Management Journal* **17**, pp. 441–58.

Kitchen, S (2000) 'Connections in the Wireless World', Warwick Business School, September.

KM Lab (2000) www.Kmlab.com/4Gwarfare.html, 20 June.

MacMillan, I and McGrath, RG (1997) 'Discovering New Points of Differentiation', *Harvard Business Review*, July/August, pp. 3–11.

McGee, J and Thomas, H (1986) 'Strategic Groups: Theory, Research and Taxonomy', *Strategic Management Journal*, **7**, **2**, pp. 141–60.

McGee, J and Segal-Horn, S (1990) 'Strategic Space and Industry Dynamics', *Journal of Marketing Management*, **6**, **3**, pp. 175–93.

McGee, J and Segal-Horn, S (1992) 'Will There Be a European Food Processing Industry?' in S Young and J Hamill (eds) *Europe and the Multinationals: Issues and Responses for the 1990s*, Edward Elgar.

McGee, J and Channon, DF (eds) (2005) *The Encyclopaedic Dictionary of Strategic Management*, 2nd edition, Blackwell Publishing, Oxford.

Miller, D (1992) 'The Generic Strategy Trap', *Journal of Business Strategy*, **13**, **1**, pp. 37–42.

Morrison, D (2003) 'Calling up a New Strategy', *New Media Age*, October, pp. 24–7.

Porter, ME (1979) 'The Structure within Industries and Company Performance', *Review of Economics and Statistics*, **61**, May, pp. 214–27.

Porter, ME (1980) *Competitive Strategy: Techniques for Analysing Industries and Competitors*, Free Press, New York.

Porter, ME (1985) *Competitive Advantage*, Free Press, New York.

Porter, ME (1986) *Competition in Global Industries*, Harvard Business School Press, Boston.

Puri, R (2004) 'Mobile Telephony: The Move from 2G to 3G Standards', Warwick Business School, September.

Rumelt, RP (1984) 'Towards a Strategic Theory of the Firm', in RB Lamb (ed.) *Competitive Strategic Management*, Prentice-Hall, pp. 566–70.

Rumelt, RP (1991) 'How much does industry matter?' *Strategic Management Journal*, **12**, pp. 167–85.

Scherer, FM and Ross, D (1990) *The Economics of Multiplant Operations*, Harvard University Press, Boston.

Sjostrom, C (1995) 'Corporate Effects on Industry Competition: a Strategic Groups Analysis', unpublished doctoral dissertation, University of Oxford.

Tello, M (2004) 'Opportunities in the Leasing Market for London-based Banks', Warwick Business School, September.

Wolff Olins (2004) 'Significance of Mobile Branding', Wolff Olins Orange Case Study, April, Wolff Olins Brand Consultancy, London.

Yao, D (1988) 'Beyond the reach of the invisible hand: impediments to economic activity, market failures, and profitability', *Strategic Management Journal*, Special Issue, **9**, pp. 59–70.

Yip, G. (2004) 'Using Strategy to Change your Business Model', *Business Strategy Review*, **15**, **2** (Summer), pp. 17–24.

Chapter 7

Competitive strategy: the analysis of strategic capability

Introduction

In setting out to understand strategic management we are in effect building our own strategic theory of the firm. The usual starting point of this endeavour is provided in Chapters 5 and 6, which describe the behaviour of firms in markets, the nature of competition, and the search for unique and sustainable market positions. To attain competitive advantage is to open the door to higher profits, other things being equal. This chapter sets out the internal agenda for the firm seeking to create competitive advantage. What resources and capabilities should the firm create and protect that will be the critical underpinning of its desired competitive advantage? In common parlance this is the concern with 'core competences'. In the academic discourse this is the **resource-based view** (RBV) of the

Chapter contents

firm in which it is recognized that firms are internally heterogeneous and in effect possess unique clusters of resources. Thus firms in the same industries and markets will very likely have different strategies and different performance levels. Critics of the **market-based view** (MBV) have argued that it is nonsensical to place the MBV at the centre of strategy making, leaving the inside of the firm to operate as a black box. Some, therefore, use the RBV to place the firm, rather than the industry or the market, at the centre of strategy making. However, the emphasis of this chapter is that the RBV and the MBV provide complementary perspectives on how to compete and jointly provide the basis for a strategic theory of the firm.[1]

7.1 The resource-based view in theory

Economists see the firm as a bundle of productive resources, where resources are defined as inputs into the firm's operations so as to produce goods and services. In this view resources are generic and specific categories are not suggested, but typical examples include patents, capital equipment, and skilled and unskilled human resources. Strategists go further and distinguish **capabilities** from **resources**. A capability is the ability to perform a task or activity that involves complex patterns of co-ordination and co-operation between people and other resources. Capabilities would include research and development expertise, customer service and high-quality manufacturing. Skills, by contrast, are more specific, relating to narrowly defined activities such as typing, machine maintenance and book-keeping.

Strategists are interested in those resources and capabilities that can earn **rents** (a surplus of revenue over cost). These collectively are known as **strategic assets** or **core competences**[2] and are a subset of but distinct from those other resources and capabilities that do not distinctively support the competitive advantage. The strategic task for the firm is to sustain these rent streams over time by creating and protecting the competitive advantage and the strategic assets that together underpin them. The inherent value of the strategic assets for the firm depends on the ways in which the firm combines, co-ordinates and deploys these assets in concert with the other firm-specific and more generic resources and capabilities.

The internal economy of the firm can be seen as sets of discrete activities (e.g. a product line), each of which leads to market positions and each of which is supported by assets of resources and capabilities. *Similar* activities (for example the Ford Mondeo and Ford Focus product lines) share some common strategic assets and some common generic assets. This sharing can lead to economies of scale (if different components share the same production line), to economies of scope (where products might go through common distribution

---

[1] However, this is to ignore important contributions such as the theory of the growth of the firm by Edith Penrose (1954) and the evolutionary theory of Nelson and Winter (1982).

[2] But note that there are many other labels, such as distinctive capabilities from Selznick (1957), that are and have been current.

channels), and experience effects. *Complementary* activities require dissimilar sets of strategic assets which would then require degrees of co-ordination (for example marketing activities and production activities). The skills of co-ordination and internal co-operation are in fact high-level capabilities with considerable strategic significance.

In the real world of uncertainty and imperfect information the firm may have (and usually does have) considerable problems in knowing which particular configurations of its strategic assets will maximize profits. Managers do not have perfect knowledge of future states of the world, of alternative actions that could be taken, or of the pay-offs from adopting various alternatives. Moreover, the way a manager chooses to allocate resources will be a function of past personal experience, the firm's experience, values, biases and personality. Accordingly, even if two managers were given identical bundles of resources they would use them in different ways. The result is that a firm's set of resources and capabilities will diverge from those of its competitors over time. Managers in competing firms in the same markets do not face the same sets of choices – rather, they have different menus with different choices. The future, as firms sees it, is to a greater or lesser degree uncertain and unknowable and their capacities for addressing the unknowable are diverse. Further, no amount of information gathering can resolve this fundamental uncertainty of what the future will hold.

Case box: **The game of chess**

If the theory of chess were really fully known there would be nothing left to play. The theory would show which of the three possibilities (white wins, tie or black wins) actually holds and, accordingly, the play would be decided before it starts ... human difficulty necessitates the use of incomplete, heuristic methods of playing, which constitute 'good' chess; and without it there would be no element of 'struggle' and 'surprise' in the game.

Rationality and full information would give us the ability to solve well-specified problems like chess. The initial resources (i.e. whether you start with white or black) would fully determine the outcome. Furthermore, no one would read or write books on how to play chess well, because all the optimal moves would already be known. In practice, people differ widely in their ability to play chess and many find that studying books on chess ('rules' for winning) improves their play. People rely on heuristics, on search, on experience and on training to aid their decisions. Such individuals can learn better heuristics and search patterns from books and can improve their performance.

If we assume in both chess and in strategy that no one knows all the 'rules' then there can exist rules for riches that can benefit many participants. Indeed, half the firms in any industry could improve their status by becoming average. Neither in chess nor in strategy is there a fully fledged theory with optimization procedures in place. Participants have therefore to make progress by adopting heuristics (or intellectual constructs) that help them make sense of the possible varieties of moves and counter-moves. There cannot exist simple nostrums or simple rules for riches that apply universally.

Thus, strategy making is a long way from the simplistic assumptions of the economic model. Strategies tend to be unique and idiosyncratic and simplistic theories for success are usually 'magic theories', i.e. theories which explain everything but predict nothing.[3] Nor are there simple rules for riches, i.e. there are no automatic rules that provide benefits in the long run. The case box above uses the game of chess as an analogy.

This means that strategic management is not captured in the form of a strategic theory of the firm in a way that enables equations to be identified, data collected and analysed and simple rules be inferred. Strategic management is much more eclectic and diverse. Contexts external to the firm and internal to the firm are highly idiosyncratic. This places a premium on the ability to diagnose situations and formulate options. The specific routes to high performance are many and varied and not readily susceptible to simple generalizations. This goes some way to explaining why the RBV is widely seen as lacking specificity and definable concepts, and having no traceable connection to real performance improvements.

7.2 The language of the resource-based view: what is core competence?

In Chapter 5, we introduced the resource-based view with a figure similar to Figure 7.1. The top line of this diagram shows how the firm's investment programmes are directed towards the creation and development of resources and capabilities, and that these underpin the positional advantage from which superior value can be delivered to customers. The bottom line shows the value and financial consequences, in terms of the capacity of the firm to finance its investment programmes. The resource-based view focuses on the resources and capabilities of the firm, asserting that it is the distinctiveness of these that enables **sustainable positional**

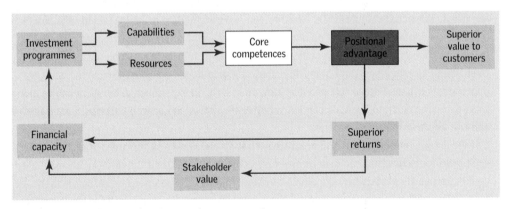

Figure 7.1 Competitive advantage and core competence

[3] Lave C and J March (1993) *An Introduction to Models in the Social Sciences*, University Press of America, NY.

advantages to be constructed. The added element in this diagram is the presence of core competences as representing those resources and capabilities that are distinctive to the firm. As a result, competitive advantage is seen as the joint product of core competences and positional advantage. What many writers observe is that imperfections in the resource and capability markets are more in number and larger in size than those in product markets. This places the burden on firms to pay attention to the underpinnings of competitive advantage in resource and capability terms. What many writers have also observed is that markets are changeable and even volatile, but it is quite difficult to get firms to change their internal cultures and processes quickly enough to keep pace with market changes.

Here we follow Grant's (1991 and 1998) lead in using 'resources' to describe inputs that can in general be purchased on open markets and customized for use by the purchasers. Thus, production capacity might be generally available, but will be configured for specific use by each purchaser. The activities of individual purchasers may lead to imperfections in supply markets. For example, a company may seek to monopolize certain raw materials through acquisition, or maybe through offering long-term supply contracts. But, on their own, few resources are immediately productive. By contrast, the 'capabilities' described here are firm-specific. They are developed internally against the specific needs and ambitions of each company. They often depend on tacit knowledge, are path-dependent in that they emerge and develop over time, and are not in the form of assets that can be traded. These resources and capabilities have individual characteristics, but a large part of their value-in-use to a firm is related to their configuration and their co-ordination. Figure 7.2 compares typical resources and typical capabilities (we introduced their distribution in Figure 5.7 on p. 165). The distinctiveness of the firm's specific set of resources and capabilities is a function of which resources to acquire and what capabilities to develop (the *configuration* issue), the way in which each of these is developed (the *firm-specificity* issue), and the way in which they are internally managed to create positional advantage (the *co-ordination* issue).

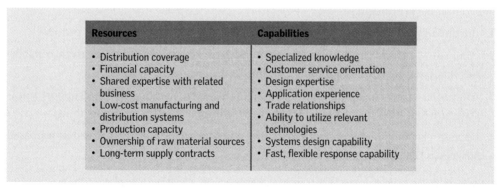

Resources	Capabilities
• Distribution coverage • Financial capacity • Shared expertise with related business • Low-cost manufacturing and distribution systems • Production capacity • Ownership of raw material sources • Long-term supply contracts	• Specialized knowledge • Customer service orientation • Design expertise • Application experience • Trade relationships • Ability to utilize relevant technologies • Systems design capability • Fast, flexible response capability

Figure 7.2 Resources and capabilities

7.2.1 Prahalad and Hamel on core competence

The language of assets, resources and capabilities can be confusing. The Grant (1998) distinction between resources and capabilities is as easy a distinction as any to maintain. However, it is laborious to keep referring to strategic resources and capabilities as those that systematically and uniquely underpin the competitive advantage relative to those other resources and capabilities that do not. Thus it is attractive to refer to these as core competences, the language popularized by Prahalad and Hamel in the *Harvard Business Review* (1990). They provided an unusual metaphor:

> *The diversified corporation is a large tree. The trunk and the major limbs are core products, the smaller branches are business units; the leaves, flowers, and fruit are end products. The root system that provides nourishment, sustenance, and stability is the core competence. You can miss the strength of competitors by looking only at their end products, in the same way you miss the strength of a tree if you look only at its leaves . . .*
>
> *Core competences are the collective learning in the organization, especially how to coordinate diverse production skills and integrate multiple streams of technologies.*

7.2.2 BCG and capabilities-based competition

Prahalad and Hamel's approach is to define core competence as the combination of individual technologies and production skills that underlie a company's product lines. Sony's core competence in miniaturization allows it to make everything from the Sony Walkman to video cameras and digital cameras. Honda's core competence in engines and powertrains allows it compete from lawnmowers to racing cars. But this latter example shows a difficulty in their approach in that Honda's dealer network would be invisible – because of the focus on competences that lead directly to products. A development of their idea is contained in a Boston Consulting Group paper in 1992[4] on 'capabilities-based' competition. This contained four basic principles:

1 the building blocks of strategy are not products and markets but business processes;

2 competitive success depends on transforming these key processes into strategic capabilities that consistently provide superior value to the customer;

3 companies create these capabilities by making strategic investments in a support infrastructure that links together and transcends traditional strategic business units;

4 because capabilities necessarily cross functions, the champion of a capabilities-based strategy is the chief executive officer.

---

[4] Stalk, G, P Evans and L Shulman (1992) 'Competing on Capabilities', *Harvard Business Review*, March/April.

This approach has the real merit of focusing on business processes as the integrative glue that binds together the various lower-level ingredients and on the investments that are required to make this effective. Unfortunately, the continued use of capabilities makes for some confusion. The essence of the idea here is that these business processes should connect to real customer needs. Things are only strategic when they begin and end with the customer because that is where value is sensed and created. The box below is an extract from the same paper and summarizes the five dimensions on which a company's strategic resources and capabilities should aim to outperform the competition.

◆ **Speed:**	the ability to respond quickly to customer or market demands and to incorporate new ideas and technologies quickly into products
◆ **Consistency:**	the ability to produce a product that unfailingly satisfies customers' expectations
◆ **Acuity:**	the ability to see the competitive environment clearly and thus to anticipate and respond to customers' evolving needs and wants
◆ **Agility:**	the ability to adapt simultaneously to many different business environments
◆ **Innovativeness:**	the ability to generate new ideas and to combine existing elements to create new sources of value

Source: Stalk, Evans and Shulman, 1992.

Boston Consulting Group present this discussion in the language of strategic capabilities in an attempt to avoid an overuse of competences, which is a feature of the Prahalad and Hamel approach.

7.2.3 Amit and Schoemaker on strategic assets

A similar approach can be seen in another classic paper from the same era. Amit and Schoemaker (1993) build on the resource and capability language to create 'strategic assets'. By resources they mean stocks of available factors of production that are owned and controlled by the firm. Capabilites refer to the firm's capacity to deploy resources, usually in combination, using organizational processes to effect a desired end. They are information-based, tangible and intangible processes that are firm-specific and are developed over time through complex interactions with each other and with the firm's resources. Unlike resources, capabilities are based on developing, sharing and exchanging information through the firm's human capital – as information-based assets they are often called 'invisible assets'. The authors describe 'strategic assets' as:

> the set of difficult to trade and imitate, scarce, appropriable and specialised resources and capabilities that (underpin) the firm's competitive advantage.

In practice it is difficult to draw clear distinctions between the core competences of Prahalad and Hamel, the capabilities-based competition of Boston Consulting Group, and the strategic assets of Amit and Schoemaker. They all convey the sense of firm-specific assets that are typically process and information based and intangible in character.

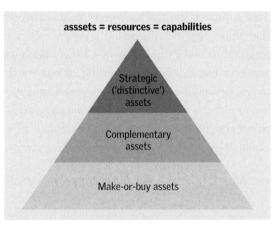

Figure 7.3 The asset triangle

There are other assets and activities in the value chain, notable complementary assets that, when linked to strategic assets (core competences), are necessary for the existence of the competitive advantage. Thus, a research-based pharmaceuticals company such as Merck or SmithKlineGlaxo would identify research expertise as a core competence but would regard management of government regulations as a complementary asset, essential but not unique. Many other assets and activities in the firm can be classified as 'make-or-buy', that is, the firm makes a financial calculation as to make or buy. Figure 7.3 distinguishes 'strategic assets' from 'complementary' assets and 'make-or-buy' assets. Strategic assets are those that are truly distinctive and unique to the firm and provide the underpinning of positional advantage in product markets. Complementary assets are those assets that are jointly required with the strategic assets in order to produce and deliver the product or service. Thus, product development might be a strategic asset, but production capacity is required for product trials and for product adaptations, even though that capacity is not unique to the firm. These assets are sometimes called **co-specialized assets**, in that they are complementary to the specialized assets and (lightly) customized to interface with them. Make-or-buy assets are those that you choose to include in the assets portfolio solely on the basis of financial calculations. For example, the decision to own or lease company cars might be made solely on financial criteria, because there are no strategic implications. In principle, if there are no strategic implications (which means that there is no need to customize the assets for specific purposes), then there will, in general, be a free outside market. This in turn generally means that the market is able to supply cheaper than is possible internally. You can see from this that the pressure to outsource can be very high and depends critically on the characteristics of supply markets.

7.2.4 **Core competence = distinctive capability = strategic asset**

In this chapter we propose to follow the terminology shown in Figure 7.1. This means that we follow the definition of resources and capabilities as discussed by Grant (1998) and that we use the term 'core competences' to cover the capabilities language of Boston Consulting

Group and the strategic assets approach of Amit and Schoemaker. This language of core competences is nevertheless abstract and hard to put into practice. This reflects the idiosyncratic and unique nature of the strategic problems faced by individual firms. But it also reflects the need to have a clear concept upon which to base strategic thinking. The two building blocks of strategy (identified so far in this book) are competitive advantage and core competence. They are both intellectual constructs. Each relies on situational characteristics for their application in practice. Each provides a way of thinking so that strategists can develop a 'theory in use' that applies to their own situation. Gary Hamel (1994) has attempted to codify the idea of core competence further. He offers the following essential characteristics of a core competence:

1 A competence is a bundle of constituent skills and technologies rather than a discrete skill or technology and a core competence is the integration of a variety of individual skills.

2 A core competence is not an asset in the accounting sense of the word. A factory, a distribution channel or brand cannot be a core competence but an aptitude to manage that factory, that channel or that brand may constitute a core competence.

3 A core competence must make a disproportionate contribution to customer-perceived value. The distinction between core and non-core competence thus rests on a distinction between the relative impacts on customer value.

4 A core competence must also be competitively unique. This means either that (i) a competence is held uniquely by one firm in the competitive set or that (ii) a competence that is ubiquitous across an industry must be held at a superior level in the firm (for example, powertrains are ubiquitous in the automobile industry but one could argue that Honda has unique strength in this area and thus it is a core competence for Honda).

5 From the corporate (multi-business) perspective[5] a core competence should provide an entrée into new markets. A particular competence may be core from the perspective of an individual business, but from a corporate perspective it will not be core if there is no way of imagining an array of new product-markets issuing from it.[6]

The language of core competence has become widespread. Core competence and competitive advantage together have become the central conceptual terms in the analysis of competitive strategy. We define core competence quite simply as:

> the underlying capability that is the distinguishing characteristic of the organization.

◆ It is the way we do things.

◆ It is how we organize the way we do things.

---

[5] See Chapter 9 for an explanation of the way in which competitive advantage should be deployed across multiple businesses within one company.

[6] For an excellent example, see the case study Canon: Competing on Capabilities, HBS in the text and cases version of this book.

- ◆ It is how we *communicate* systematically this knowledge and build upon it.
- ◆ It is understanding the difference, and building bridges, between tangible and intangible assets, tacit and explicit knowledge, and individual and team knowledge and skill.

More formally, we define core competences as:

> *the set of firm-specific skills and cognitive processes directed towards the attainment of competitive advantage.* (McGee and Segal-Horn, 1997)

Core competence is a fundamental concept in our understanding of what strategy making is. It is *only* through core competence that the firm attains competitive advantage and is therefore the mainspring of sustainable distinctiveness. But it is also the lens through which the world is seen and interpreted. Different firms (and people) see different things in their environments and this is a function of their inheritance and their experience. In the same way, firms (and people) differ in the way in which they see themselves and therefore in their understanding of what they might achieve. In this way we can see core competences as the link between managerial cognition and the economics of the firm (*see* Figure 7.4). The key tasks of a strategy analyst are interpreting the external environment, understanding the dynamics of markets and of competition, and understanding the internal dynamics of one's own organization. Core competences provide the links to these economic assessments through a clarity of perception about the shared values and beliefs in the firm (often explicit in the mission statement), through tacit knowledge and understandings (that are possibly unique to the firm), and through flexible routines and recipes that enable non-standard challenges to be comprehended.

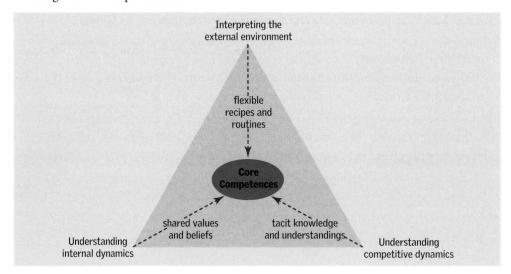

Figure 7.4 Core competences as the link between managerial cognition and the economics of the firm
Source: McGee and Segal-Horn, 1997.

7.3 Related issues and the management of core competences

There are some mistakes that managers make very frequently. The first is to assume that acquiring and leveraging generic resources will be a major source of advantage in a new market. Advantage requires some degree of difference between firms and this requires the construction of assets that are unique to the firm. Another common mistake is to overestimate the transferability of specific assets and capabilities to a new product market. Assets are unique to the firm in relation to the use for which they have been designed. New uses require some degree of further customization or re-adaptation. Even where the firm has constructed unique assets, it is easy to overestimate their capability to compete in highly profitable markets. This is merely to say that strategic choices are highly risky. Even if one can create a distinctive asset base it does not necessarily follow that customers will like the product offering that follows. Through this observation, you can see that competitive advantage is a composite of a resource-based view and a market-based view. Both are necessary: neither is necessary and sufficient on its own.

7.3.1 Resource leverage

Managers often neglect ways of creating advantage from a resource-based perspective. It is common to see firms paying much attention to the detail of product positioning in attempts to create those pieces of unique advantage that can make a difference. However, attention to the resource side can have significant pay-offs. For example, the approach of the Japanese automobile assemblers, especially Toyota,[7] show the benefits from rearranging the supply chain in such a way that essential customer values such as reliability can be fundamentally changed. There are five ways in which management can **leverage** its resources so as to create the conditions under which a core competence can emerge.[8] The idea of leverage (a much-used word of strategists) is to focus attention and effort an a specific object to the exclusion of rival objects so as to create a desired outcome. The exercise of leverage requires clear strategic intent and the possession of the relevant assets and competences.

Concentrating resources: convergence and focus

Convergence is the idea of focusing resources on few rather than many objectives and focus itself prevents the dilution of resources being applied to a specific target. The basic principle is the concentration of resources and the avoidance of dissipation of effort.

---

[7] See 'Competitive Advantage the Toyota Way' by Gary Fane, Reza Vagheti, Cheryl Van Deusen and Louis Woods, *Business Strategy Review*, 14, 4, 51–60, Winter 2003.

[8] This is taken from Gary Hamel and CK Prahalad (1993) 'Strategy as Stretch and Leverage', *Harvard Business Review*, March/April.

Accumulating resources: extracting and borrowing

Extraction is the ability to surface resources and capabilities that exist within the firm but might be lying concealed or dormant. The capacity to draw from the stockpile of resources is a facet of the ability to learn. Borrowing resources is the ability to tap into the resources of other companies. A simple example is the use of one company's basic research as an input to another company's commercialization. Thus Sony commercialized the transistor that was pioneered by Bell Laboratories. As Hamel and Prahalad (1993) point out:

> *Increasingly, technology is stateless. It crosses borders in the form of scientific papers, foreign sponsorship of university research, international licensing, cross border equity stakes in high-tech start-ups and international academic conferences. Tapping into the market for technology is a potentially important source of resource leverage.*

Complementing resources: blending and balancing

Blending resources is similar to what we called co-specialization (above). How resources fit together in planned and unplanned ways gives the possibility to transform the value of resources while using them. Blending requires integrative skills such as technological integration, functional integration and new product development. The blending of functional skills is a new way of restating the nature of general management. This traditionally has involved the integration of functions such as production, marketing and R&D. Balancing requires the firm's resources and capabilities to be able to support a business model. Unbalanced firms would have gaps such that resources and capabilities would be required from others for a sustainable revenue stream to be achieved. A balanced firm may benefit from tapping into the resources of others but has a defensible position on its own.

Conserving resources: co-opting and shielding

Conserving resources simply means retaining resources so that they are reusable – the basis for economies of scope. The issue is how to retain knowledge in the memory banks so that it is addressable and recyclable to other activities. Co-option has the same theme as recycling but involves collaborative efforts to work collectively towards new standards or new products. Shielding resources is about not wasting non-renewable resources (such as cash) on difficult targets. Attacking competitors directly in their home markets is an example of a difficult target where the probabilities are more of failure than of success. The example of Canon taking on Xerox in plain paper copying is a classic example. Xerox's R&D budgets were very much higher than those of Canon, but Canon chose to compete in areas where the Xerox business model was weak, e.g. small machines, third-party distribution systems and machine reliability.[9]

---

[9] See the case study Canon: Competing on Capabilities, HBS in the text and cases version of this book.

Recovering resources: expediting success

Pace is a significant dimension of performance. The faster the cycle time from investment through to sales, the quicker that resources can be renewed and redeveloped (see Figure 7.1, where the strategy cycle indicates the process). The speed at which Japanese automakers and motorcycle manufacturers operated gave these companies higher cash flows than their Western counterparts but also more up-to-date products and a greater ability to respond to changing markets.

7.3.2 Identifying intangibles

The expression 'intangible' is being applied more and more frequently to resources and to capabilities. For our purposes it refers to the following:

- Intellectual property rights of patents, trademarks, copyright and registered designs
- Trade secrets
- Contracts and licences
- Databases
- Information in the public domain
- Personal and organizational networks
- The know-how of employees, advisers, suppliers and distributors
- The reputation of products and of the company
- The culture of the organization

Richard Hall conducted a study of the relative contribution of intangible resources and capabilities to business success.[10] Some of the results are summarized in Tables 7.1, 7.2 and 7.3. Table 7.1 summarizes the average weightings for each intangible drawn from the above list. Hall found that the results were common and systematic across a wide sample of companies. Four factors stood out as most important namely, company reputation, product reputation, employee know-how and organization culture. By contrast, intellectual property rights and trade secrets were by far the least significant. Table 7.2 unpacks the employee know-how factor seen in Table 7.1. Here CEOs were asked which business function was the most important contributor to employee know-how. Operations scores highly because of the high tacit content of know-how (learning by experience). In contrast, in finance, know-how has a large external knowledge content, which means that skills can be formalized and transferred. The importance attached to sales and marketing by both manufacturers and retailers is to be expected, whereas the contribution of technology is quite modest.

---

[10] Richard Hall (1992) 'The Strategic Analysis of Intangible Resources', *Strategic Management Journal*, 13, 135–44.

Table 7.1 Relative importance of intangible resources in overall business success

Ranking (1 = highest, 2 = lowest)	Average weight (crucial = 10, insignificant = 1)
1 Company reputation	8.6
2 Product reputation	8.4
3 Employee know-how	8.1
4 Organization culture	7.9
5 Networks	7.1
6 Specialist physical resources	6.1
7 Databases	6.0
8 Supplier know-how	5.8
9 Distributor know-how	5.3
10 Public knowledge	5.2
11 Contracts	4.7
12 Intellectual property rights	3.2
13 Trade secrets	2.9

Sample size = 95
Source: Hall, 1992. © Copyright 1992, John Wiley and Sons Ltd. Reproduced with permission.

Table 7.2 Percentage of CEOs quoting the function as the most important area of employee know-how

	Total sample	Manufacturing	Retailing
Operations	43	27	8
Sales and marketing	29	46	46
Technology	17	18	31
Finance	6	0	15
Other	5	9	0
Total	100	100	100

Source: Hall, 1992. © Copyright 1992, John Wiley and Sons Ltd. Reproduced with permission.

Table 7.3 Replacement periods

	Average replacement period (years)
Company reputation	10.8
Product reputation	6.0
Employee know-how	4.6
Networks	3.4
Supplier know-how	3.1
Databases	2.1
Distributor know-how	1.6

Source: Hall, 1992. © Copyright 1992, John Wiley and Sons Ltd. Reproduced with permission.

Table 7.3 looks at the time it takes to replace an intangible asset. The question posed was, How many years would it take to replace the *particular resource* if you had to start from scratch? This gives an indication of protection from new entrants depending on the transferability of existing reputation. Reputational resources dominate this list. Company reputation, in particular, gives strong incumbents a significant advantage. By contrast, much know-how can be replaced or rebuilt over quite a short period (around three years), suggesting that speedy imitation is quite probable in most situations.

The importance of reputation suggests that it should receive constant management attention. The distinction between company and product is interesting, implying, first, that attention to both is probably necessary and, second, that in multi-business companies the corporate name could have a significant halo effect across businesses and product lines. The experience of companies such as Sony, Hewlett-Packard and IBM provide good examples of this. The high scores for employee know-how support the idea of invisible assets that are information and experience rich. This is clearly fertile ground for the development of core competences. In Table 7.1 the term culture has a specific meaning: it refers to ability to manage change, ability to innovate, teamworking ability, participative management style, perception of high quality standards, and perception of high standards of customer service. These are also ingredients that are information and experience rich.

7.3.3 What determines the value of a core competence?

Figure 7.5 summarizes the conditions that determine the value of a core competence (strategic asset). The basic foundations of value are *imitability*, *durability*, *substitutability*

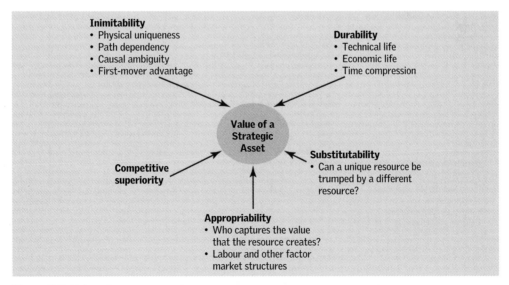

Figure 7.5 Value of a core competence
Source: Peteraf, 1993.

and *appropriability*. The ability of competitors to imitate your assets is in part to do with *physical uniqueness*. More subtle issues around inimitability are:

♦ **Path dependency** – cumulative learning and experience over time, which is difficult to replicate over short periods.

♦ **Causal ambiguity** – not really knowing what it is that is the important element in a complex asset.

♦ **First-mover advantage** – the pre-emption of a market by being the first to create scale efficient assets.

Substitutability is often an unknown, in that new technologies can emerge which very quickly outdate older solutions. For example, the battle between satellite and cable television systems is still raging – substitutability is high, but it is not clear which standard will prevail. Appropriability is an important but subtle issue. A central question about a strategic asset is: Who can capture the value that is created? Is it the firm? Could it be the skilled technicians? Might it be patent owners? Perhaps there are long-term supply contracts?

7.4 Linking core competence to competitive advantage

The resource-based view (RBV) is not a theory in its own right. But coupled with the market-based view (MBV) it enables the strategist to link the firm's internal behavioural

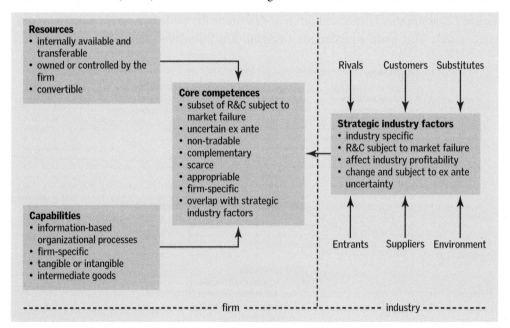

Figure 7.6 Strategic industry factors and core competences
Source: Amit and Schoemaker, 1993.

decisions and organizational choices with the need to secure a defensible positional advantage in the market. RBV and MBV together provide a theory-in-use for the strategist. Figure 7.1 shows the link between RBV and MBV as a juxtaposition of core competence and competitive advantage. Amit and Schoemaker (1993) went a stage further. Their full model is shown in Figure 7.6, adapted only to use the phrase core competence for strategic asset. The extra dimension (compared to Figure 7.1) provided here is contained in the phrase 'strategic industry factors'. These are the sources of market imperfections that firms can capture as elements in their competitive advantage.[11]

From our earlier discussion of industry analysis and Porter's five forces we obtained a general description of the characteristics of an industry. Porter's model provides five generic characteristics and others have suggested more, such as government and deeper environmental variables. Other ad hoc analyses have developed over the years, particularly the idea of key success factors (KSFs). Later in this chapter we suggest a way of using KSFs in practice, but in general KSFs can be seen as those elements in the industry that are deemed as *important* for customers. Strategic industry factors are a way of articulating KSFs as those elements in the industry and in the market that are subject to market failure and therefore where firms can provide them they will have an advantage. Using our language of advantage, these factors are those firm-specific imperfections that represent competitive advantage. Amit and Schoemaker synthesize contributions from many writers in producing this list of characteristics that apply to strategic industry factors.

1 They are determined through a complex interaction among industry rivals, new entrants, customers, regulators, innovators, suppliers and other stakeholders.

2 They are strategic in that they are subject to market failures and may be the basis for competition among rivals.

3 They are known ex post but not ex ante; in particular, not all aspects of their development and interactions with other factors in the market will be known or controllable.

4 Their development takes time, skill and capital: they may be specialized to particular uses.

5 Investments in them are largely irreversible (i.e. sunk costs).

6 Their pace of accumulation is affected by own prior knowledge and experience and that of rivals (i.e. path dependent) and cannot be readily increased (doubling the investment will not usually halve the time).

7 Their value to any particular firm will depend on its control of other factors – the complementarity property.

---

[11] Economists often refer to these imperfections as market failures, that is, inabilities to trade in these factors in perfect markets. Our view of competitive advantage as firm-specific imperfections in the market rests on this notion of market failure.

You will observe that this list is similar to, and is a development of, the discussion in section 5.1, where we discussed the essential ingredients of strategy. In examining Figure 7.6 you will see that the list of core competences has similarities to the list of strategic industry factors. This is not an accident, nor is it an error. The difference is that firms seek to design their core competences in anticipation of their usefulness in creating and sustaining an intended competitive advantage. The strategic industry factors are those imperfections in the market that have succeeded. The core competences are ex ante in nature; they are intentions. The strategic industry factors are ex post, those characteristics that have actually worked in the market to produce competitive advantage.

7.4.1 Competence-based competition in practice

In 1977 Dan Bricklin, an MBA student at the Harvard Business School, developed on his Apple computer a type of 'electronic blackboard' that allowed him to display a grid of numbers linked together by formulae. His professor told him (allegedly) that it had no future as a product. Why? Because software was (and is) easily imitated. There was virtually no entry barrier. There were established firms selling mainframe languages to do pro-forma calculations. Moreover, the Apple was a mere toy! What was wrong with the professor's reasoning?

In 1973 one of the authors wrote a case on the Japanese motorcycle industry. The final discussion question asked, Should Honda enter the emerging global automobile business? It was a 'giveaway' question – anyone who said 'yes' flunked, because markets were saturated, efficient competitors existed in Japan, the USA and in Europe. Honda had little or no experience in automobiles and it had no automobile distribution system or access to one. In 1985 his wife drove a Honda! What was wrong with this answer?

This was a common fault in the strategy analyses of that period. Why was it that Canon could beat Xerox? How did Komatsu manage to beat Caterpillar? The fault lay in the lack of a proper resource-based perspective. There are three parts in an answer to this question: strategic intent, strategic innovation and core competences.

Strategic intent

Strategic intent has a particular meaning in encouraging people to go beyond 'business as usual'. It appeals to the resource language that we reported above, particularly the sense of concentration, convergence and focus, and to the idea of resource leverage.

It has been argued that US firms seeking strategic fit have often found themselves overtaken by firms, especially the Asian conglomerates, driven by long-term visions of the future, which are then relentlessly and ruthlessly pursued with *strategic intent*. Companies such as CNN, Honda, NEC and Sony have succeeded (according to this argument) because of their sustained obsession with achieving global dominance in their industries. This obsession has been labelled strategic intent (Hamel and Prahalad 1989). The significance of this is that the intent of these companies was out of proportion to their existing resources and capabilities.

Table 7.4 The Xerox position in 1980

	Xerox
Technology	Leading edge product technology: 7000 patents
Distribution	Worldwide direct sales: 7000 in USA, 5000 in Europe, 3000 in Japan
Financing	Leasing
R&D investment	$600 million p.a.
Manufacturing	Worldwide network of plants
Scale	Market share = 90%
Image	Photocopy = Xerox

Source: Ackenhusen (1992) 'Canon: Competing on Capabilities', case study.

This gap between ambition and resources is known as **strategic stretch**. These companies had to expand and adapt their current stock of resources and create new ones. They were more concerned with 'leveraging' resources than with achieving **strategic fit** between their current resources and their industry environments.

Strategic intent can thus be used as a psychological target which provides a focus that all members of the organization seek to adopt. Becoming the industry leader or dominating a specific segment are frequent missionary goals. The fundamental focus of the firm's strategy commits well beyond its current resource profile. The prophecies can therefore become self-fulfilling provided that employees have faith in their leadership and that, in many cases, the existing industry leaders fail to recognize that the challenge is on. The logic of expansion coupled with economies of scope provides an economic basis for justifying strategic intent. However, there are limits to economies of scope which arise when industries and markets require more variety than the fixed factors that sustain scope effects can support.

Strategic intent implies a stretch beyond current resources, capabilities and means. But for those companies that have adopted this style it became a necessity and was not a luxury.

Table 7.5 How Canon rewrote the rules of the game

	Xerox existing business	**Canon's new rules**
Customer definition	Medium/large companies	Small companies/individuals
Use pattern	Centralised copying	Decentralised
Product	High copy volume features	Utility, value for money
Distribution	Own sales force	Office products dealers
Service	Own network	By dealers
Financing	Lease	Sale
Technology	Leading edge dry toner	Low cost liquid toner

Source: Ackenhusen (1992) 'Canon: Competing on Capabilities', case study.

Strategic innovation

Strategic investments are bets against an unknowable future. These bets often require technical progress and substantial investment in R&D and in new products. In 1980 Xerox had a stranglehold on the copier industry. IBM were poised to enter, attracted by Xerox's huge profits. Canon also had an interest in fine optics and precision mechanics on the basis of their existing camera business. On whom would you have bet? Table 7.4 shows the Xerox hand.

The barriers to entry were formidable. In IBM's favour was their own large scale that meant it could probably afford to spend as much money as Xerox (but note that Kodak had had the same thoughts earlier without too much success). Canon had no obvious points of superiority given the nature of the market and the strategic industry factors that were present at that time. The idea of strategic innovation is to rewrite the rules of the game. Table 7.5 catches the essence of what Canon did to outflank Xerox and one can do similar analyses to show how Komatsu outflanked Caterpillar by changing the point of competition from quality to cost and reliability, and how Honda managed to enter the global automobile industry by emphasizing quality.

Strategic innovation leads to a new form of competitive advantage, a different conception of the required core competences and a different business model through which the cash could be seen to flow. In the case of the Apple computer and Dan Bricklin's spreadsheet invention, the spreadsheet became the killer application that placed the new Apple personal computer on millions of desks by appealing to a similar sense that Canon identified – the customers' wish to have desktop capability.

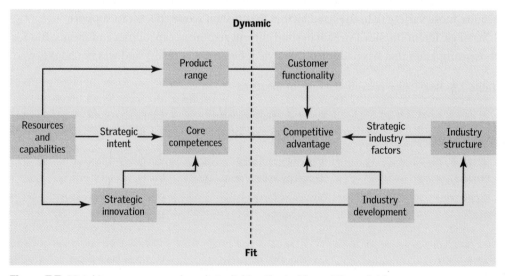

Figure 7.7 Matching resources and markets: linking the inside and the outside

Core competence

The core competences in each of these examples were created by investments in the operational and organizational infrastructure of the strategic innovators. The new capabilities spawned through these investments were linked across business units and the learning and experience of diverse business units was captured and leveraged across the company. Canon's distinctive management processes (compared to Xerox) were high levels of decentralization, strong internal co-ordination processes and external co-operation. Canon exemplified the value of external co-operation through importing knowledge from strategic alliance partners and joint ventures The complex core competences that arose could be described as (i) a high pace of learning and innovation, (ii) a long-term approach to developing capabilities, and (iii) the systematic transfer of competences across businesses and into new businesses.

The risks associated with the Japanese approach – most of the examples have been Japanese companies – is that an overdependence on a resource-based perspective can lock you into your own view of the world, away from changing markets and customer preferences. In an earlier discussion of the strategy cycle in Chapter 5 we commented on how Marks & Spencer became trapped in their own conception of the world just as the textile market became more fashion conscious, new entrants were appearing and product offers were changing rapidly (the strategic industry factors were obviously in a process of change).

How do we balance the inside view with the outside view? Figure 7.7 summarizes inside and outside perspectives and the links between them. The firm is driven by the link of resources and capabilities through strategic intent to core competences. This is the crux of the firm's intended strategy culminating in the match between core competences and competitive advantage. A failed strategy would have empty boxes in the middle of the diagram. The core competences are captured in products which have to match customer functionality. The dynamics of the process are shown by strategic innovation which through 'newgame' strategies match with and/or drive industry development.

The demand side, the outside, is captured by the link between industry structure through strategic industry factors to competitive advantage. Industry structure has multiple industry factors and competitive advantages associated with it. The firm's task is to identify one of the set and match with it – this implies a set of customer functionalities to be satisfied. The dynamics are captured through industry development and other exogenous factors.

The design of the firm's theory-in-use is shown by the strategic fit between core competences and competitive advantage. The practical present-day fit is shown by the fit between product range and customer functionality. The dynamic fit is between strategic innovation and industry development. Lack of fit in the short term can be a result of (i) the requirements of the outside moving too quickly for the inside to keep pace, or (ii) by the strategic drive from the inside missing its targets. There may be a short-term fit that erodes because the dynamic linkages through innovation and industry development do not work properly.

7.4.2 The role of learning

When we compare product markets and resource markets, we can see that fundamentally competition is a contest for the acquisition of skills. Moreover, competition in product markets is a superficial expression of the more fundamental competition over competences. Looked at in this way, the dynamics of markets, of industries and of firms is about 'learning' rather than technical theories of product market evolution; hence, all the current concern with the 'learning organization' and with 'knowledge management'. Core competences arise through the collective learning of the firm, through accumulated experience with the coordination of diverse production skills and the integration of multiple streams of technology. Prahalad and Hamel (1990) take the proposition further. They argue that core competences span across businesses and products within a corporation – they can support several products or businesses. Thus, they argue that the narrow focus of strategic business units is dysfunctional. It is also clear that core competences have temporal dominance over products. They evolve slower than the products that they make possible, or core competences support several generations of essentially the same product classes. Figure 7.8 suggests a framework within which all these strands can be seen. The focus of the diagram is on the way in which the resource-based view is becoming accepted as the genesis of advantage in the firm, but also reflects the modern debate about the contribution of learning and knowledge to our understanding of how firms compete. Chapters 16 and 19 take this discussion further.

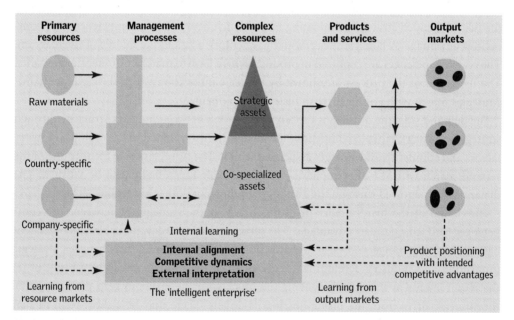

Figure 7.8 A synthesis of positioning, the resource-based view and learning
Source: McGee and Segal-Horn, 1997.

7.5 Competitive strategy in practice

We start from the premise that there can be great differences between the abilities of firms to succeed – there are fundamental inequalities between most competitors. This contrasts with the conventional economics textbook view of perfect competition that holds that firms are essentially similar, if not the same, and that over time their performances will converge on a minimum rate of return on capital. Less efficient firms will be obliged to exit and the more efficient firms will be subject to imitation. But the competitive strategy view of the firm is that understanding and manipulating the factors that cause these inequalities, so as to give the firm a sustainable competitive advantage, largely govern long-term business success. These factors vary widely; so different businesses, even within the same industry, often need to be doing different things. Thus, there are many strategies open to firms. The usual starting point is to recognize that strategy is the outcome of the resolution of several different, conflicting forces. These are summarized in Figure 7.9. Society has expectations of its business organizations. Owners, managers and other implementers of strategy have their own personal values and ambitions. The company has strengths and weaknesses, and the industry context offers opportunities and threats. The traditional top-down view of strategy is encapsulated in the *strategic planning view*. This involves deciding on long-term objectives and strategic direction, eliminating or minimizing weaknesses, avoiding threats, building on and defending strengths, and taking advantage

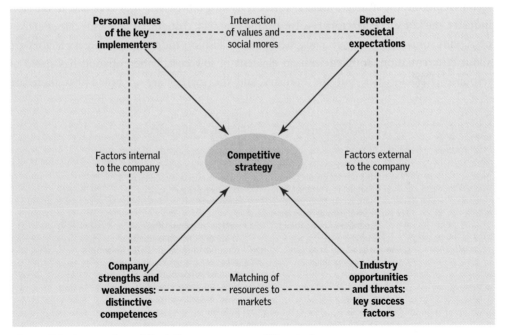

Figure 7.9 An overview of the influences on competitive strategy

of opportunities. But, from reading this chapter, it should be clear that given the strategic direction, the key strategic decision is product market selection. This should be based on the existence of long-term viable business opportunities (not merely the existence of growing markets), together with the prospect of creating the relevant core competences. Viable business opportunities depend on:

◆ The existence of valuable market segments.

◆ The existence of a sustainable positional advantage.

◆ The creation of the appropriate strategic assets.

In conducting the assessment of viable business opportunity, the term *key success factors* is often used. Intuitively, this means 'What do we have to do to succeed?' We can put some analytical flesh on these bones. Figures 7.10 and 7.11 illustrate the process (see Grant 1991). There is a set of key questions to ask:

◆ Is there a market?

◆ Do we have some advantage?

◆ Can we survive the competition?

These lead us into two pieces of analysis: the analysis of customers and demand, and the analysis of competition (summarized in Figure 7.10). Figure 7.11 shows how these can be put together to identify key success factors in three different industries. The key success factors represent the strategic logic(s) (there is usually more than one) available. In the steel industry, the key success factors revolve around low cost, cost efficiencies and scale effectiveness, with some scope for speciality steels. In the fashion industry, key success factors are about differentiation, coupled with an element of low cost. Differentiation has speed of response characteristics, but the industry and the market are so broad that there are

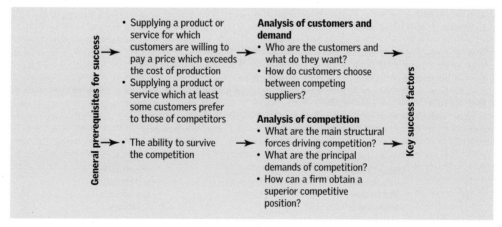

Figure 7.10 Identifying key success factors

Industry	What do customers want? (analysis of demand)	How do firms survive competition? (analysis of competition)	Key success factors
Steel	Customers include automobiles, engineering, and container industries. Customers acutely price sensitive. Also require product consistency and reliability of supply. Specific technical specifications required for special steels.	Competition primarily on price. Competition intense due to declining demand, high fixed costs and low-cost imports. Strong trade union bargaining power. Transport costs high. Scale economies important.	Cost efficiency through scale-efficient plants, low-cost location, rapid adjustment of capacity to output, low labour costs. In special steels, scope for differentiation through quality.
Fashion clothing	Demand fragmented by garment, style, quality, colour. Customers willing to pay price premium for fashion, exclusivity, and quality. Retailers seek reliability and speed of supply.	Low barriers to entry and exit. Low seller concentration. Few scale economies. Strong retail buying power. Price and non-price competition both strong.	Combine effective differentiation with low-cost operation. Key differentiation variables are speed of response to changing fashions, style, reputation with retailers/consumers. Low wages and overheads important.
Grocery supermarkets	Customers want low prices, convenient location and wide range of products.	Markets localized, concentration normally high. But customer price sensitivity encourages vigorous price competition. Exercise of bargaining power a key determinant of purchase price. Scale economies in operations and advertising.	Low-cost operation requires operational efficiency, scale efficient stores, large aggregate purchases to maximize buying power, low wage costs. Differentiation requires large stores to provide wide product and customer convenience facilities.

Figure 7.11 Identifying key success factors in three industries

distinctive segments, some of which are cost driven, while others are differentiation driven. This industry provides a good example of the multiplicity of available strategies.

In formulating competitive strategy, there are some important things to remember:

- *Resources are limited*, opportunities are infinite. The essence of strategy lies in saying 'Yes' to only some of the options and, therefore, 'No' to many others. *Trade-offs* are essential to strategy – they reflect the need for choice and they purposefully limit what a company offers.

- Always factor in *opportunity costs*. A dollar invested 'here' is a dollar not invested 'there', or not given back to shareholders.

- The essence of strategy is choosing to perform activities *differently* than rivals.

- In the long run, what matters is not how fast you are running, but whether you are *running faster than your competitors*.

- A company can only outperform rivals if it can establish a difference that it can sustain. So always test for the *sustainability* of your competitive advantage. Competitors are likely to view relieving you of your competitive advantage as their cardinal duty. Further, not all of them are likely to be stupid.

- The competitive value of individual activities cannot be separated from the whole. So, *fit* locks out imitators by creating a value chain that is stronger than its weakest link.

- The long-run test of any strategy lies not in what it contributes to market share or profit margins but in what it contributes to long-term *return on investment*.

- Strategic positions should have a *time horizon* of a decade or more, not just of a single planning cycle and/or product cycle.

7.5.1 Managing the business for value

Firms are often poor at devising practical procedures for carrying out the strategy analyses of the kind suggested in this chapter. The ideas are frequently expressed only as concepts. Data is often not collected nor organized as evidence to test out alternative possibilities. This section outlines one way of capturing the analysis of competitive advantage.

Competitive advantage is about creating value both for the customer and for the firm. The first task is to define what this means in practice. Thus, value to the customer can be defined as:

1 firm's ability to position a product better/different than competitors;

2 firm's ability to persuade customers to recognize, purchase and value the difference.

Value to the firm can be defined as

1 firm's ability to create and sustain core competences that underpin the positioning at manageable cost premiums;

2 firm's ability to run (the rest of) the business efficiently and at best practice levels.

These definitions can be operationalized according the schema shown in Figure 7.12. The four elements of value are coded as positioning, customer persuasion, capability and efficiency. Note that efficiency is not enough! Each of these requires strategic indicators by which performance can be measured. The figure suggests some starting points.

Strategic indicators		Company 1	Benchmark
Price: performance segment maps	Positioning		
Repeats; price premium; share	Customer		
Peer ratings; tech benchmarking	Capability		
Engineering studies cost analysis	Efficiency		
Financial indicators	Sales margins asset T/O RoI		

Figure 7.12 Managing the business for value

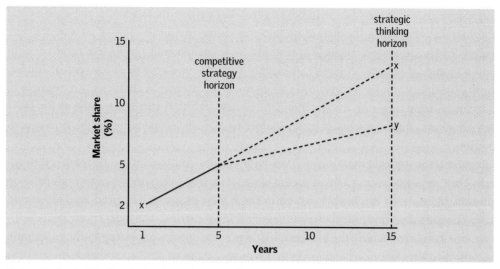

Figure 7.13 Positioning the business for growth

Then data should be collected to identify the firm's own performance on these measures and then some benchmark comparisons. To complement this strategic performance analysis financial indicators can also be shown remembering that these reflect the outcomes of previous strategies whereas the strategic indicators will presage future financial performance.

7.5.2 Positioning the business for growth

Competitive strategy will usually have a limited time scale over which assessments can be made reliably. This is usually related to the tangibility of assets and to the speed with which the product life cycle operates. As a rule of thumb firms can see to the end of the current product life cycle and are actively engaged in the planning and the next cycle. The cycle beyond that is much less clearly seen. Thus, in practice, we can expect firms to see one and a half life cycles ahead (subject to the life expectancy of their capital assets). Thus, if a car manufacturer has a product life cycle of four years, we would expect it to be able to see and forecast about six or seven years ahead. So how do we plan beyond this if the numbers are missing? Figure 7.13 shows the break in our planning horizons.

The shorter period of competitive strategy horizon (shown for example as five years) should not and does not mean that we do not do any strategic thinking beyond that. One way of dealing with this is to compare

Growth target =	%		
	Technical	**Internal**	**External**
Enables			
Blockers			

Figure 7.14 Enables and blockers

alternative growth targets (shown in the figure). For each of these, identify the enables and the blockers and assess the nature of these as either technical, internal or external (*see* Figure 7.14). An enabler might, for example, be a creative and productive research team and it would be internal in nature. A blocker might be the growth of low-cost manufacturing capability among competitors and it would be external in character. An example of a technical issue might be the development of new technical standards (such as for DVD rewriting) and this might either be an enabler or a blocker depending on the firm's capabilities.

Longer-term strategic thinking requires both enables and blockers to be managed properly. Thus we would expect a focus on the key enables to develop measures and information sources, to create an intelligence system to track their progress. The need is to assess and keep assessing the prior probability of these enables occurring. The blockers are more difficult. The task is to identify the blockers, sort them into groups according to their common factors, discover the underlying forces and dynamics, and to develop strategies to shift the blocks or to get round them (note how in the reprographics industry in the 1970s Canon developed an R&D strategy to get around Xerox's network of blocking patents). For blockers we need (as for enables) to assess and track over time the prior probability of controlling the blockers and moderating their influence. This analysis should then be repeated for different growth targets. The outcomes will of course be quite qualitative and multidimensional, but Figure 7.15 suggests a way of summarizing the outputs.

The vertical axis is the prior probabilities of facilitating the enables and controlling the blockers (a joint probability of achieving a target would be one way of operationalizing this). The horizontal axis is time. The first part of this is a commitment period during which the foundations are being established (typically the first part of a J-curve), shown here for example as four years. Beyond this period we are looking for a confidence that growth can be managed – *the ring of confidence* in the figure, or not, i.e. *the undesirable region*. More generally you would expect to see a curve showing the prior probabilities rising over time. The key question is whether the probabilities are sufficiently high early enough. The bad position is when the probabilities remain low well beyond the commitment period. Conversely, happiness occurs when they rise quickly.

Approaches such as this one require considerable judgement and they often will defy the objective tests implied by quantification. However, the advantage here is of applying a systematic procedure that is rooted in the economics of the firm, in the nature of customer behaviour and that seeks to balance opportunity against risk.

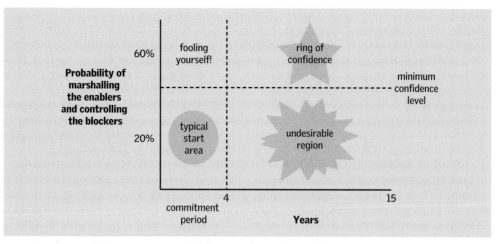

Figure 7.15 Positioning the business for growth: assessing feasibility

7.6 **Summary**

This chapter asserts that competitive advantage and core competence are two key intellectual constructs that together provide the foundation for understanding strategy. Competitive advantage is the basis for the market-based view, providing us with a way of assessing the positioning of the firm relative to its competitors. Core competence is one of many phrases that capture the resource-based view. The idea of *the underlying capability that is the distinguishing characteristic of the organization* and that underpins competitive advantage.

We have reviewed the various languages of the resource-based view, mentioning resources, capabilities, competences and strategic assets. However, rather than pursue semantic differences between such an array of titles, we have chosen to follow the definition of resources and capabilities as discussed by Grant (1998) and to use the term 'core competences' to cover the capabilities language of Boston Consulting Group and the strategic assets approach of Amit and Schoemaker. Further, we suggest Hamel's clarification as both practical and theoretically sound, namely:

1 A competence is a bundle of constituent skills and technologies rather than a discrete skill or technology and a core competence is the integration of a variety of individual skills.

2 A core competence is not an asset in the accounting sense of the word. A factory, a distribution channel or brand cannot be a core competence but an aptitude to manage that factory, that channel or that brand may constitute a core competence.

3 A core competence must make a disproportionate contribution to customer-perceived value. The distinction between core and non-core competence thus rests on a distinction between the relative impacts on customer value.

4 A core competence must also be competitively unique. This means either that (i) a competence is held uniquely by one firm in the competitive set or that (ii) a competence that is ubiquitous across an industry must be held at a superior level in the firm.

5 From the corporate (multi-business) perspective a core competence should provide an entrée into new markets. A particular competence may be core from the perspective of an individual business, but from a corporate perspective it will not be core if there is no way of imagining an array of new product-markets issuing from it.

The language of the resource-based view can be confusing and it is no surprise that the concept of core competence has been difficult to apply. However, it is an intellectual construct in just the same way that competitive advantage is, and it should be used to clarify thinking. It is not intended as a simple framework or tool (such as SWOT or PEST) that contains within it simple practical guidelines. The second half of the chapter is devoted to practical applications of the core competence concept. Core competence leads directly into issues of resource leverage (for value and profit). We discuss the importance of identifying intangibles. We have discussed the link to competitive advantage using the language of strategic industry factors and fey success factors. We have looked at strategic intent, strategic innovation and the role of learning. What core competence does is to focus attention on the managerial processes, information content and communications that are the intangible heart of the resource-based view. Core competences are hardly ever tangible assets – they reflect intangible, sometimes designed but sometimes informal managerial process. As intangibles it is then not surprising that firms are essentially different from one another (as opposed to the traditional view of economists who hold that firms are essentially similar in the long term). Bringing competitive advantage and core competence together as competitive strategy in practice we see how managing the business for value and managing the business for growth depends on both concepts.

In the following chapters we explore how strategy (i.e. competitive advantage plus core competence) is manifested in a number of different situations. In Chapter 8 we look at competitive strategy in a variety of different situations. Chapter 9 introduces multi-business or corporate strategy and Chapter 10 develops this into mergers and acquisitions. Chapter 11 focuses on international strategy and Chapter 12 asks how these ideas translate into the world of the 'new economy'.

Key terms

Capabilities *252*

Causal ambiguity *266*

Core competences *252*

Co-specialized assets *258*

First mover advantage *266*

Intangibles *263*

Leverage *261*

Market-based view (MBV) *252*

Path dependency *266*

Resource-based view (RBV) *251*

Rents *252*

Resources *252*

Strategic assets *252*

Strategic fit *269*

Strategic intent *268*

Strategic stretch *269*

Sustainable positional advantage *254*

Recap questions and assignments

Guide answers to these questions are given on the Online Learning Centre website.

1   Undertake a resource audit of an organization with which you are familiar, then identify which resources, if any, are unique in the sense that they are difficult to imitate. Has the organization gained competitive advantage as a result of this uniqueness?

2   Refer to Question 2 (Chapter 5). For these same two companies identify the core competences and show where they are located within their value choices.

3   Refer to Question 3 (Chapter 5). For the same organization show how its core competences are contained within the SWOT analysis. Convert your SWOT analysis into a diagram based on Figure 7.7.

Online LearningCentre

When you have read this chapter, log on to the Online Learning Centre website at www.mcgraw-hill.co.uk/textbooks/mcgee to explore chapter-by-chapter test questions, further reading and more online study tools for strategy.

Case 1 How Dell keeps from stumbling: It's the supply chain, says its boss, Dick Hunter

In the high-tech universe, Dell Computer Corp. is a force of nature. In less than 20 years, company founder Michael S. Dell has amassed a personal fortune of $16 billion and built a $25 billion company, besting the likes of IBM, Hewlett-Packard, and Compaq Computer in the process. Along the way, his build-to-order model has blossomed into a new manufacturing paradigm. Impressively, the Austin (Tex.) company also has weathered the technology meltdown—at least so far. Rival Gateway Inc. just posted its second consecutive quarterly loss, and Hewlett-Packard Co. is planning to eliminate 3,000 management jobs. Outside the PC sector, things are far worse: Cisco Systems Inc. is slashing up to 8,500 jobs after writing off $2.5 billion in unsold inventory.

What insulates Dell from these troubles? Says Dick L. Hunter, the vice-president overseeing supply-chain management, the difference comes from Dell's super-efficient supply chain. 'Michael [Dell] focuses relentlessly on driving low-cost material from the supplier through the supply chain to our customers,' he says. The low-cost producer, he adds, will be the ultimate winner, and that's reflected in Dell's steadily rising market share. According to IDC in Framingham, Mass, Dell nabbed top spot in global PC sales in the first quarter, with a 13.1% share. Hunter brought 25 years of manufacturing experience to Dell. Before joining the company in 1998, he worked in operations and supply-chain management for General Electric, Texas Instruments, and Ericsson. Today, in addition to his supply-chain responsibilities, he manages Dell's largest manufacturing site, a cluster of four factories in Austin that produces most of the systems sold in the Americas. Hunter recently spoke with *Business Week* Industries Editor Adam Aston about the nuts and bolts—and chips and monitors—of Dell's supply-chain operations.

Q: How central to Dell's success is the efficiency of its supply chain?
A: It's absolutely critical. Materials costs account for about 74% of our revenues. We spent around $21 billion on materials last year. Shaving 0.1% off [that] can have a bigger impact than, say, improving manufacturing productivity by 10%.

Q: Dell is famously lean. How does that affect your performance?
A: We carry about five days' worth of inventory. Our competitors carry 30, 45, or even 90 days' worth. This is critical because in our industry, materials costs fall by about 1% per week. So if a competitor has four weeks' worth of inventory and we have one week's, right there we have 3% worth of materials cost advantage. That can mean a 2% or 3% advantage on the bottom line.

Q: Dell has been growing at double-digit rates for its entire life span. Does software play a big role in that?
A: A couple of years ago, realizing we couldn't grow to $75 billion with the tools we had in

place, we selected i2 Technologies' software. Now, 10 months later, all our global manufacturing sites are operating on the same i2 resource-planning and execution systems.

Q: And the result?

A: We now schedule every line in every factory around the world every two hours—we only bring into the factory two hours' worth of materials. With i2, we typically run a factory with about five or six hours' worth of inventory on hand, including work in progress. This increased the cycle time at our factories and reduced warehouse space. We replaced this space with more manufacturing lines.

Q: It takes a tightly knit supplier base to deliver on a schedule like that. How many suppliers do you rely on?

A: Our top 30 suppliers represent about 75% of our total costs. Throw in the next 20, and that comes to about 95%. We deal with all of those top 50 daily, many of them many times a day.

Q: How do the new systems help you manage supply crises?

A: The software tells us where we are. We monitor practically every part, every day. If we're running out of a part, it might be because demand is outstripping supply. We'd try to solve the supply problem first. We'd call the supplier to see if he can increase the next shipment. If it's a generic part—like a hard drive—we might check alternate suppliers. Once we've exhausted our supply options, we go to the sales and marketing guys to help shift the demand to something else. This happens within a few hours.

Q: But isn't demand beyond your control?

A: One of coolest things about Dell is that we talk to 10,000-plus customers every day. That gives us 10,000 opportunities to balance supply and demand. If I'm running out of a part, then I know ahead of time. I'd communicate with our sales department and we'd move demand to material that we have. For example, we can alter lead times. We might extend the lead time on a high-demand item from the standard 4 to 5 days to 10. In this case, we know statistically how much demand will move. Or we may do a promotion. If we're short on Sony 17-inch monitors, we could offer a 19-inch model at a lower price, or even at the 17-inch price. We know if we do this an awful lot of demand will move. We can alter pricing and product mixes in real time via Dell.com. Our competitors that are building to sell through retail channels can't do that.

Q: What effect does this have on excess inventory?

A: Perpetual balance of supply and demand is my main goal in life. If I'm in perpetual balance, I can always meet my customers' delivery expectations. It also helps to minimize excess and obsolete inventory. Dell writes off between 0.05% and 0.1% of total material costs in excess and obsolete inventory—that's about $21 million across our global business in a year. In other industries that figure is probably 4% to 5%. Our competitors probably have to write off 2% to 3% worth of excess and obsolete inventory. There's no way we'd end up with months of inventory someplace. If we see two or three days of softening demand for a particular product, alarm bells go off. On an end-of-life product, we'll name a number—say 50,000 more of this computer model will be built. Then that's it — we will not build a 50,001st.

Q: At this volume of transactions, and at this speed, how do you coordinate your suppliers?
A: All of the data goes back and forth on the Internet. From the long-term planning data—volume expectations over the next 4 to 12 weeks—to the two-hourly execution systems, which are making automatic requests for replenishment, every supplier can view our order information via the Web.

Q: How far has automation gone—are even your smallest suppliers wired up?
A: The issue isn't how to get the last 5% online—that's easy, everyone can see our information via the Web. The real question is: How do I get true machine-to-machine connection between me and my supplier, because today there is still manual intervention by the supplier to get the data off the Web. We're fairly automated internally at Dell. Now we want to get the suppliers connected machine-to-machine.

Q: Are you advising the suppliers on particular technologies?
A: Yes. We have a lot of leverage with our suppliers. And all of them understand our model and supply-chain management systems. We constantly ask them, 'How can you become more like Dell?' We're very loyal to these guys. I'd say just two or three of our top suppliers have changed in the past three years.

Q: So what's the next step?
A: Folks ask if five days of inventory is the best Dell can do. Heck no, we can get to two.

Q: How have Dell's operations been affected by the PC downturn?
A: We had 1,700 layoffs a couple of months ago. And our use of contract workers fluctuates depending on the cycle. As we have a downturn, we will have a smaller percentage of contract workers. As we increase production, we have a higher percent. But this recession could be a very good thing for Dell. We're able to pass on lower costs to our customers more quickly, which allows us to gain market share and put a hurt on our competitors.

Q: Some big names, such as Cisco, have been burned by excess inventory. Your thoughts?
A: Our goal is to replace inventory with information. The more information we get to our suppliers quickly, the faster we build product, the faster we receive materials from suppliers, the faster [we] alleviate a problem like Cisco is having. Cisco might have communication problems in the supply chain about what's real demand and what's real supply. It could be that they had bad high forecasting, and the suppliers never knew better.

Case Questions

1 What resources and capabilities does Hunter identify in his answer?

2 Which of these do you think are core competences? Why?

3 How does Dell keep the inside (the firm) and the outside (the industry and the market) in balance?

Case 2 Brand extension, with jacuzzi

Should luxury-goods firms go into the hotel business?

Giorgio Armani is already one of the most diversified brands in fashion. As well as haute couture and everyday clothes, Mr Armani and his eponymous firm create scent, cosmetics, spectacles, watches and accessories. Dedicated followers of Mr Armani's minimalist aesthetics can buy furniture at Casa Armani, chocolate, other sweets, jam and even marmalade at Armani dolce and flowers at Armani fiore. There are Armani cafes and restaurants in Paris, New York, London and other cities. An Armani nightclub recently opened in Milan. Now the great Giorgio is branching out further still. On 22 February his firm announced a $1 billion hotel venture with Dubai's Emaar Properties, the Middle East's largest property developer. Mr Armani will be in charge of the design for ten new luxury hotels and four resorts, to be built in the next six-to-eight years.

Armani's is the boldest move so far by a luxury-goods company into the hotel business. But it is by no means the first. In September 2000, a hotel designed by Donatella Versace opened on Australia's Gold Coast. In February 2001, Bulgari, an Italian jeweller, announced a joint-venture with Ritz-Carlton, the luxury-hotel division of Marriott, to build six or seven hotels and one or two resorts. Bulgari and Marriott are each investing some $70m. The first Bulgari hotel, located immediately behind Milan's La Scala opera house, will (belatedly) open in May. Salvatore Ferragamo, an Italian shoemaker, has designed four hotels in Florence, his hometown. The latest Ferragamo hotel, the Continentale, opened in January last year.

Does it make sense for designers of luxury goods to go into a tricky service business? Hotels are not even a good hedge against the fickleness of the fashion world. Travel and luxury follow the same economic cycle. In the first half of last year both industries were in bad shape because of the war in Iraq, SARS and the rise of the euro. (Many luxury-goods firms are from euro-zone countries, but their revenues are mostly in dollars or yen.) In the second half of the year the two industries both started to recover, albeit timidly. Armani and Bulgari say that their hotels are managed by outside professional managers, and that they are only in charge of making the hotels beautiful. Mr Armani considers hotels a logical extension of his aim of promoting his brand in all walks of life (can Armani toilet paper be far behind?). Rita Clifton, chairman of Interbrand, a consultancy, says that this strategy can work. A strong product, strong images and a strong experience, such as staying at a fashion designer's hotel, can combine to make a super-strong brand, claims Ms Clifton.

To fit the firm's luxurious image, Bulgari says that its hotels must be as upmarket as it is possible to be. Because small is considered more exclusive, Armani and Bulgari plan to launch mostly smallish five-star hotels. Armani's Dubai hotel, due to open in 2007, will be an exception, however, with 250 rooms. Bulgari's Milan hotel will have no more than 60 rooms.

Losing control of their brand is the biggest risk for luxury firms expanding abroad or venturing into a new line of business. Over the years, Pierre Cardin, Yves St Laurent and Christian Dior have each lost their good names by doling out licences all over the world to firms that did not deliver the appropriate quality. Calvin Klein's current troubles are related to the company's loss of control of the distribution of its wares in many countries. Designers' hotels can create good publicity, as they have done for Ferragamo with its easily controllable properties in Florence. Even if Bulgari's hotels turn out not to make any money, the venture could be considered an expensive, yet effective, advertising campaign, says Antoine Colonna of Merrill Lynch in Paris. Mr Armani's hotel plans are altogether more ambitious, and the danger of brand dilution much greater. Armani says that the management company for its hotel venture will be headquartered in Milan rather than Dubai, and that Mr Armani will be fully in charge of design. So far Mr Armani has managed to control his brand tightly despite dabbling in many different businesses. Hotels, however, are a bigger challenge than flowers and marmalade.

Source: 'Brand extension, with jacuzzi', *The Economist*, 26 February 2004.
© The Economist Newspaper Limited, London (26 February 2004).

Case Questions

1 What are the core competences of the typical luxury-goods business and Armani in particular?

2 Explain why these core competences are to be transferred to other businesses such as hotels.

3 What would be the limits to this?

4 To what extent is the core competence of Armani dependent on Giorgio Armani himself? How might his family plan for life after Giorgio?

Further reading and references

Ackenhusen, M (1992) 'Canon: competing on capabilities', INSEAD case study, reprinted in B de Wit and R Meyer (1998) *Strategy: Process, Context, and Content*, 2nd edition, International Thomson Business Press, London.

Amit, R and Schoemaker, PJ (1993) 'Strategic assets and organisational rent', *The Strategy Management Journal*, **14**, pp. 33–46, reprinted in Segal-Horn, S (ed) (1998) *The Strategy Reader*, Blackwell Business.

Barnet, JB (1991) 'Firm Resources and Sustained Competitive Advantage', *Journal of Management*, **17**, pp. 99–120.

Besanko, D, Dranove, D and Shandley, M (2000) *The Economics of Strategy*, 2nd edition, John Wiley & Sons, New York.

Collis, D and Montgomery, C (1995) 'Competing on Capabilities', *Harvard Business Review*, **73**, **4**, pp. 118–28.

Fane, G, Vagheti, R, Van Deusen, C and Woods, L (2003) 'Competitive Advantage the Toyota Way', *Business Strategy Review*, **14**, **4**, Winter, pp. 51–60.

Grant, RM (1991) 'The Resource-Based Theory of Competitive Advantage: Implications for Strategy Formulation', *California Management Review*, Spring, pp. 114–35.

Grant, RM (1998) *Contemporary Strategy Analysis*, 3rd edition, Basil Blackwell, Oxford.

Hall, Richard (1992) 'The Strategic Analysis of Intangible Resources', *Strategic Management Journal*, **13**, pp. 135–44.

Hamel, G (1994) 'The Concept of Core Competence', Chapter 1 in G Hamel and A Heene (eds) *Competence Based Competition*, in the Strategic Management Series, John Wiley & Sons.

Hamel, G and Heene, A (eds) (1994) *Competence Based Competition*, the Strategic Management Series, John Wiley & Sons, Chichester.

Hamel, G and Prahalad, CK (1989) 'Strategic Intent', *Harvard Business Review*, **67**, **3**, pp. 63–76.

Hamel, G and Prahalad, CK (1993) 'Strategy as Stretch and Leverage', *Harvard Business Review*, **71**, **2**, pp. 75–84.

Lave, C and March, J (1993) *An Introduction to Models in the Social Sciences*, University Press of America, NY.

McGee, J and Segal-Horn, S (1997) 'Global Competences in Service Multinationals', in Thomas, H and O'Neal, D (eds) *Strategic Discovery: Competing in New Arenas*, the Strategic Management Series, J Wiley & Sons, Chichester, pp. 49–77.

Nelson, RR and Winter, SG (1982) *An Evolutionary Theory of Economic Change*, Harvard University Press, Boston.

Penrose, E (1995) *The Theory of the Growth of the Firm*, 3rd edition (original edition 1954), Oxford University Press.

Peteraf, MA (1993) 'The Cornerstones of Competitive Advantage; a Resource-based View', *Strategic Management Journal*, **14**, **2**, pp. 179–91.

Porter, ME (1980) *Competitive Strategy: Techniques for Analysing Industries and Competitors*, Free Press, New York.

Porter, ME (1985) *Competitive Advantage*, Free Press, New York.

Prahalad, CK and Hamel, G (1990) 'The Core Competence of the Corporation', *Harvard Business Review*, May/June, pp. 79–91, reprinted in S Segal-Horn (1998) (ed.) *The Strategy Reader*, Blackwell Business.

Schoemaker, P (1992) 'How to Link Strategic Vision to Core Capabilities', *Sloan Management Review*, Fall, pp. 67–81.

Segal-Horn, S (ed.) (1998) *The Strategy Reader*, Blackwell Business, Oxford.

Selznick, P (1957) *Leadership and Administration*, University of California Press.

Stalk, G, Evans, P and Shulman, LE (1992) 'Competing on Capabilities: the new Rules of Corporate Strategy', *Harvard Business Review*, **70**, **2**, pp. 57–69.

Chapter 8

Competitive strategy: moving from theory to practice[1]

Introduction

Alfred P. Sloan once said that no company ever stops changing. Our discussion in earlier chapters has indicated that competition is a dynamic process within which firms never stop trying to pursue changing market demands. Nor do they stop trying to imitate and emulate each other. Some of this dynamism is the natural consequence of rivalry and of ambition. But some of it is due to persistent changes that take place in markets as knowledge grows and experience accumulates – the forces of technological change and economic growth. This chapter starts to move us from the basic model of competitive strategy with its notions of positioning and strategic capability to arenas where practical complexities

Chapter contents

---

[1] This chapter is written jointly with Duncan Angwin.

are important. Later chapters explore these in terms of multi-business companies, multi-territory (international) companies, and the new economy in which knowledge and information economics prevail.

This chapter uses the **industry life cycle** model as a backdrop against which we can observe different kinds of strategies at different stages of evolution of an industry or of a firm. A general life cycle model is presented to create another generic strategy model – this one being a time-based model. But the bulk of the chapter is concerned with three practical themes. The first is the theme of start-ups and the role of entrepreneurs. The second reviews how entry strategies are conceived and deployed to overcome organized resistance and substantial entry barriers. The third theme is concerned with issues of corporate failure and turnarounds, problems that occur typically in maturity and beyond. Each of these themes enables us to reflect on the balance of forces between the need for powerful analysis of the strategic context and the personality, capability and leadership of individuals. Entrepreneurs and start-ups reflect strongly on the last point – entrepreneurs are quintessentially individualistic. Entry strategies into the complex economics of embedded firms and industries requires powerful strategizing. Turnarounds and the remedy of corporate failure require a blending of powerful leadership and operational capabilities with the need to bring the firm's economics in line with the dictates of the markets. In practice (and looking ahead to Part 4 on practice), strategies always require a blending of strategic thinking and analysis (strategizing) and personal leadership skills and capabilities. This chapter introduces these issues.

8.1 The life cycle model

Porter's famous five forces model is a static view of competition in which industry structure is seen as a stable determinant of performance of firms. In practice we know that industries evolve over time. They have a genesis and a start-up period; they have periods of rapid growth and then maturity sets in. Maturity might last a long time or the industry may pass quite quickly into decline and eventual decay. The question is whether competitive strategies have distinctive characteristics over this life cycle. Are there distinctive success factors at each stage of the cycle?

The industry life cycle model is the supply side analogue of the better-known **product life cycle**. Products are born, their sales grow, they reach maturity, and they eventually decline and maybe die. If products have life cycles then so do industries, albeit on a longer time scale. For example, the products in the computer games industry may have lives of just a few years (e.g. Sega, Sony, Nintendo) but the life of the industry continues beyond these and into successive generations of products. The life cycle is conventionally divided into four phases, as shown in Figure 8.1.

The life cycle curve has over its whole a distinctive, somewhat asymmetric bell shape. In practice we can usually observe only portions of the life cycle even though we might be

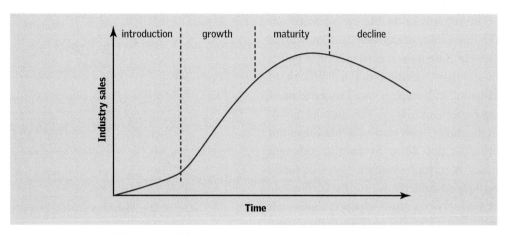

Figure 8.1 Industry life cycle model

conscious of issues of industry evolution. Robert Grant (2002) emphasizes two key factors behind industry evolution: demand growth, and patterns of knowledge creation and diffusion. Demand growth is also important for the product life cycle and can be characterized by S-shaped patterns (see Figure 8.2). In the introduction stage, the pace of growth can be slow as the new product gains acceptance and overcomes customer inertia. The growth stage is marked, if successful, by rapidly increasing sales as product formulations become more standardized and as customers become accustomed to the benefit–cost offer of the new product class. Maturity is a reflection of market saturation and sales are predominantly due to replacement demand. Finally, new technology and new knowledge cause obsolescence of the product-class and sales fall away.

The knowledge driver is more complex in its operation and much more varied in its manifestations. New knowledge is captured in the form of product innovation and rival forms of this new knowledge can result in a range of new propositions before the customer – for example, the range of videotape options, VHS, Betamax and Philips 2000, and also the different technologies behind the original automobiles: expert opinion 100 years ago favoured the steam car! In economic terms there is no dominant technology and rival designs compete for attention. The industry evolution normally evokes processes of standardization and the number of competing designs often falls to a single dominant design. This standardization reassures customers and firms are encouraged to cut costs by increasing scale and standardization. At this point the emphasis shifts to process innovations from product innovation. The most dramatic example is the automobile industry. The essential nature of the technology has barely changed for 80 years but the extent, scale and significance of process innovation has been dramatic. As Grant points out (pp. 244–5), product innovation has been incremental and not systemic, e.g. disc brakes and engine management systems whereas electric power innovation has barely made any mark at all.

The patterns of the life cycle result from the interaction of demand and knowledge (supply). Often the crucial inflection points in industry evolution can be difficult to pinpoint and much is owed to patterns of consumer psychology. The 'tipping point' in the choice between rival technologies can often be put down to fashion although many observers maintain that economic realities do underlie seemingly fashionable choices. For a contemporary view on this, read Leibowitz and Margolis (1999, pp. 119–134) on the tipping point between VHS and Betamax and see also Chapter 12.

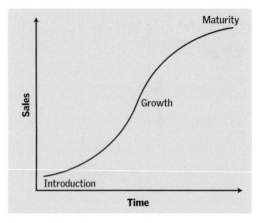

Figure 8.2 S-shaped growth patterns

The industry life cycle is a highly generic concept. It does not imply any standardization in terms of time taken at various stages. Some industries are very long-lived (e.g. railroads and automobiles). As the twentieth century progressed and as the pace and scope of technological development increased, product life cycles became progressively compressed. Many industries introduced in the last 25 years have grown very quickly (e.g. the PC industry). Some have grown and vanished (e.g. the vinyl LP record). Some started and never grew beyond the early stages (e.g. laser discs).

However, there is a standard approach to analysing life cycle effects. First, the stages of the cycle are identified, typically embryonic, growth, maturity and decline (or ageing). Second, the generic characteristics of the industry are identified. Different authors emphasize somewhat different elements but Arthur D. Little Inc. (ADL) (which pioneered and marketed much of this analysis as a consulting product in the 1970s)[2] suggest growth rate, market potential, products, number of competitors, market share stability, purchasing patterns, ease of entry, and technology. Figures 8.3a and 8.3b show how patterns of evolution can be seen in the data. From this there is arguably a general pattern over the life cycle as volumes increase, standardization increases, consumer knowledge grows and entry barriers eventually fall. Strategically the incentive to innovate and grow rests on the chances of being able to generate volumes, to protect knowledge, develop brands and have a good run at making profits before entry erodes margins and profitability. For example, a dominant position is ideal but rarely achieved. It comes about because a competitor has managed to establish a quasi-monopoly or has achieved technological dominance. Such positions have been claimed by IBM in mainframe computers, Kodak in colour film, Xerox in copying,

---

[2] The academic pioneers of the concept of the product life cycle were Everett R Rogers, 1962 and Theodore Levitt, 1965.

Description	Stages of the industry life cycle			
	Embryonic	Growth	Mature	Ageing
Growth rate				
Market potential				
Product line				
Number of competitors				
Market share stability				
Purchasing patterns				
Ease of entry				
Technology				
Overall				

Figure 8.3a Factors affecting the stages of the industry life cycle
Source: Arthur D Little Inc., 1974, 1980.

and much more recently by Microsoft and Intel in the PC industry. In the case of the first three we can see that the dominant position was eventually competed away. Mainframes were outmoded by smaller computers. Conventional colour film slowly became more competitive but digital technology has provided the real push towards obsolescence. Xerox was eventually caught by new technologies from Canon and other Japanese copier manufacturers. In each of these three cases the anti-trust authorities were sufficiently concerned about the existence and potential exploitation of dominant position to the extent of prolonged legal proceedings against all three. It is interesting to observe similar processes at work with Microsoft.

ADL was among the first to collect data on financial flows over the life cycle and Figure 8.4 shows sales following the familiar bell-shaped curve. But profits and cash flow are negative in the first two stages, significantly profitable in maturity, and appropriately declining in the ageing stage. This represents the desirable pattern in which the returns on investment have to be garnered in maturity with real profitability occurring the longer decline can be delayed. Conversely, profitability would be significantly challenged (i) if the industry fails to

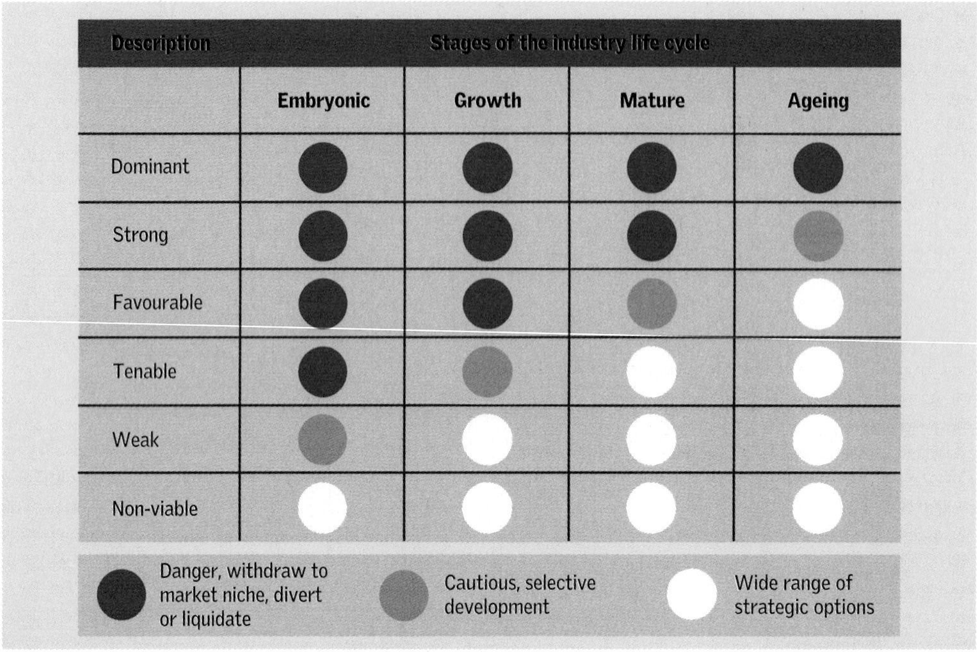

Description	Stages of the industry life cycle			
	Embryonic	Growth	Mature	Ageing
Dominant	●	●	●	●
Strong	●	●	●	◐
Favourable	●	●	◐	○
Tenable	●	◐	○	○
Weak	◐	○	○	○
Non-viable	○	○	○	○

● Danger, withdraw to market niche, divert or liquidate   ◐ Cautious, selective development   ○ Wide range of strategic options

Figure 8.3b The life cycle portfolio matrix
Source: Arthur D Little Inc., 1974, 1980.

grow to large enough size, (ii) if it declines early, and (iii) if it attracts too many competitors too soon.

If Figure 8.4 indicates desirable patterns of cash flow then there are likely to be strategies that are particularly helpful at each stage. ADL calls these **natural strategic thrusts**. These are:

♦ *Start-up strategies* are applied in the embryonic phase to achieve high and/or defensible market position while market growth is high.

♦ *Growth with industry strategies* applies when the firm is content with its industry position and seeks to maintain market share: this is indicated when enjoying dominant or strong competitive position, especially in maturity.

♦ *Gain position gradually* is applicable when a modest share increase is necessary in order to consolidate position and defend cash flows.

♦ *Gain position aggressively* is an aggressive share-building strategy in an attractive industry while the growth rate is still high: it often comes in the form of pre-emptive strategies where entry-deterring capacity is built aggressively ahead of demand – this is a high-risk double-or-quits bet.

♦ *Defend position* applies when enjoying a dominant or strong position: the cost of defending position should be lower for industry leaders than for attackers and cash flows should be protectable,

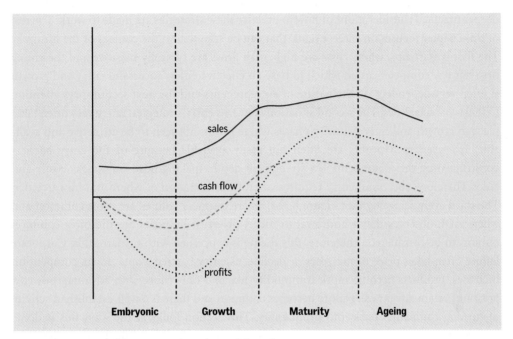

Figure 8.4 Financial flows over the industry life cycle
Source: Arthur D Little Inc., 1974, 1980.

- *Harvest* is possible at any stage. The important factor is the speed of harvest. From a strong position harvesting may be slow because the erosion of competitive position might be slow. Issues here include how strongly to defend versus harvest, given the other strategic demands for cash. Rapid harvesting may have to take place from weaker positions and may imply early closure.

The industry life cycle model needs to be used with care. Criticisms of the approach include:

1 its underlying validity and usefulness;

2 the stages vary widely in terms of time;

3 industry activity does not necessarily evolve into a well-behaved S-curve;

4 markets can be rejuvenated and maturity can turn back into growth through changes in fundamental industry conditions;

5 firms can themselves fundamentally transform life cycle positions through innovation and repositioning (see comments on industry transformation in Chapter 6);

6 the nature of competition varies greatly from industry to industry.

The life cycle is a generic model (like Porter's generic strategies) in which the general characteristics of the strategic environment can be seen in broad strategic relief unfettered by deeper practical considerations of how in practice these strategies are made to work. The rest of this chapter focuses on three 'events' that can be seen within the context of the life cycle. The first is start-ups, where costs are high, cash flows are typically negative and the young firm has few competences on which to base an effective entry; successful entry and growth is often very dependent on the nature of entrepreneurs and the next section pays attention to their characteristics. The second situation concerns entry strategies. Entry very often takes place in growth and early maturity phases where profits are seen to be attractive and available. However, such profits are often not easily available because of the entry barriers constructed by the incumbents – a strength in depth, making head-on attacks costly and risky. Therefore, successful entry requires careful consideration of where and how to enter. The third event is ageing (see Figure 8.3b), where business failures are most common and where ADL observes that withdrawal to niche, divert or liquidate are the most common options to be considered. Therefore, this theme is concerned with turnarounds. Corporate failure often takes place in the years of decline, as entry barriers come down, competition increases, products become more commodity-like and only those with advantageous cost positions retain advantage. Failure becomes common and there is a well-established activity of turning companies back into profitability. This section looks at the ways this is done. Clearly it is not correct that start-ups only occur in the early stages of the industry life cycle, nor are turnarounds only required in the maturity and decline of industries. However, both are most common in these periods and the distinctive characteristics of entrepreneurs and turnaround specialists are seen in sharp relief when placed against these portions of the industry life cycle.

8.2 **Strategy and the entrepreneur: start-ups and sustainability**

Take a moment to think of the names of a few highly successful business executives. The chances are that you have tended to pick the names of entrepreneurs such as Richard Branson, Anita Roddick, Sir Clive Sinclair, Alan Sugar and Sir James Goldsmith of the UK; Bill Gates, Steve Jobs, Donald Trump and T-Boone Pickens of the US; and Rupert Murdoch, Alan Bond and Holmes á Court of Australia.

However, such entrepreneurs are but a minority among the business leaders of the world's largest and most successful companies – and many entrepreneurs do not remain successful for reasons we shall discuss later. Why, then, do we, and the business press, give such prominence to entrepreneurs? What is it about entrepreneurs that we find compelling and what are the implications for the way our businesses, and indeed we ourselves, interpret the business world?

8.2.1 **Entrepreneurs: an overview**

Entrepreneurs are a global phenomenon. However, in Anglo-American cultures, where individualism is encouraged, they are glorified, whereas in 'collectivist' cultures they result in significant tensions. While it has been shown that entrepreneurialism declines as 'collectivism' increases, it is important to note that a balance of individualism and collectivism is important for entrepreneurship to flourish. For example, the Asian entrepreneurs in North America have sufficient autonomy to exhibit creativity and entrepreneurial behaviour, and yet their cultural background, emphasizing collectivism, helps them promote co-operation and group ownership of innovation (Li 1993). In addition, then, to perceiving entrepreneurs in purely psychological terms, focusing upon their potential as individuals, we must also recognize their positions in society at large, where social backgrounds can help to inspire and enable.

In the UK, entrepreneurs were the potent symbol of the 'Thatcher decade' and today they are once again being encouraged. They are the source of contemporary myths and legends; they are romantic, larger than life, modern buccaneers, who hold enormous wealth. They are rebels, trail-blazers and risk takers. We focus on them, for they are our 'proof' that the individual counts; that one can make a difference.

Entrepreneurs are being encouraged, with the UK Government giving substantial tax incentives and advice for the starting up and developing of businesses. There is also a more positive attitude towards entrepreneurs in society at large, as we move ever more towards an individualistic society and a 'can do' attitude. Implicit in governmental encouragement is that entrepreneurialism is good for the economy in terms of stimulating growth and encouraging innovation. Indeed, recent speeches by the UK Government aim at fostering the use of the internet, nationwide, as a major facilitator of entrepreneurial growth and, so it is hoped, economic prosperity.

This raises the questions of what entrepreneurialism is and how we would recognize it. To answer these questions, we examine:

♦ What an entrepreneur is

♦ What it takes to be an entrepreneur

♦ Where we find entrepreneurs

♦ Whether entrepreneurs have a shelf life

8.2.2 **What is an entrepreneur?**

The **entrepreneur** is often a single leader with personal charge in a highly dynamic situation, such as in a new firm, or a small one in a growing market, or sometimes within a large organization facing a crisis. This individual has a clear and distinct vision of purpose and directs an organization that is structured to be as responsive as is possible to his or her personal wishes. Such entrepreneurial vision tends to have a high potential pay-off, such as the commercial success of an idea or the turnaround of a firm in crisis.

Through 'memories of the future' (Ingvar, 1985), entrepreneurs mentally rehearse 'pathways' into the future and 'envision' a new world for their business. They seek to create the future and, to do so, they must take risks, be aggressive, proactive and innovative. Fondly, then, we think of entrepreneurs as visionary leaders. They have a profound ability with language and – often in symbolic form, as metaphor – cause others to see things from a new perspective. A good example is Edwin Land, who invented the Polaroid camera. In speaking of photography, he said, 'It's not merely the camera you are focusing: you are focusing yourself. Part of you is now permanent' (Mintzberg *et al.* 1998, p. 610).

Entrepreneurs, then, have a number of characteristics, the most widely cited of which is being visionary. However, there are many other 'traits' that are commonly associated with them. They are said to have self-confidence, the ability to bounce back, are innovative, results-oriented, professional risk takers and have total commitment (Barrow 1991). In addition, they have the ability to conceptualize and plan, manage others, manage their own time and to learn as well as adapt to change (Gaedeke and Tootelian 1985). They require technical competence, mental ability, human relations skills, high achievement drive and creativity (Hodgetts 1982).

Furthermore, a visionary leader requires integrity – a genuine feeling behind what the leader says and does. This is what makes leadership truly visionary, and what makes impossible the transition of such leadership into any formula (Mintzberg *et al.* 1998, p. 610). To take an example, when employees of Richard Branson's company Virgin are interviewed, we find this level of belief in Branson's integrity. From his idiosyncratic style and beliefs, high-profile dramatic activities (such as ballooning around the world) and high commitment, we find employees buying into and motivated by his vision. We find entrepreneurship as the 'art of turning work into play: entrepreneurial leadership creating drama' (Mintzberg *et al.* 1998).

8.2.3 What does it take to be an entrepreneur?

The interest in researching entrepreneurial traits has been driven by the question of whether entrepreneurs are born or made, as this may mean that executives can be trained to be entrepreneurial and revitalize their businesses.

It has been shown that while the 'need for achievement' is essential for the entrepreneur, it is not genetically bound. Indeed, lifetime experiences are just as important as hereditary variables. Such experiences are often externally determined by social and economic pressures, which force entrepreneurial activity as a legitimating channel or means of expression. Such groups have tended to be those groups outside or debarred from the predominant managerial or social class, such as immigrants, ethnic minorities, socially or educationally deprived groups. 'Outsiders', then, the victims of social marginalization, often have the incentive to exhibit entrepreneurial behaviour and also tend to have the support of their disadvantaged group.

At the individual level, there are three groups of factors influencing the entrepreneurial decision. The first group comprises antecedent influences, such as generic factors, family influences, educational choices and previous career experiences. The second is the incubator organization, where the geographic location may provide impetus (for example, if the entrepreneur would rather live in the country than the town), where the nature of knowledge and skills may allow transferability, where other 'co-conspirators' may be met, and where the organization may pressurize or facilitate departure. The third group consists of environmental factors, such as general economic conditions, availability of funding, other examples of entrepreneurial activity, opportunities for interim consulting and availability of supporting services (Cooper 1981).

Therefore, the choice to become an entrepreneur will be affected by the above factors and the balance between the strengths of specific competencies and self-confidence, and the restraints in terms of career, life-stage and income needs. Critical will be the presence of a trigger to prompt the entrepreneur into 'life'.

A *Wall Street Journal*/Gallup survey shows that entrepreneurs are significantly different from the senior executives of Fortune 500 firms. They take fewer holidays, are more likely to have suffered stress, have a greater need to be recognized as leaders, have made an earlier start in business, have worked for several companies, have lower socialization needs and are more likely to have been expelled or suspended from school. The 'needs' of entrepreneurs are illustrated in Figure 8.5, which shows the high level of importance of having the power and freedom to act, as well as receiving recognition, and the much lower importance of personal comfort and relationships.

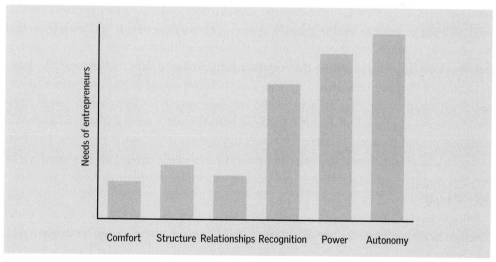

Figure 8.5 Personal profiles: the 'needs' of entrepreneurs
Source: Hunt, 1981.

8.2.4 **Where do we find entrepreneurs?**

Entrepreneurs, new and small businesses

To get started, new firms, regardless of sector, seem to need personalized leadership to establish their basic direction or strategic vision. Such situations also attract strong leaders, as they can put their own stamp on things. It is not surprising, then, to find that most entrepreneurs are at the head of new and small businesses, where they have control.

By definition, entrepreneurs need to innovate, but this capacity is threatened by constraints in terms of resources and controls. It is an essential characteristic of entrepreneurs that they use more resources than they control, for they are motivated primarily by the *pursuit of opportunity,* rather than working within resource constraints.

> The entrepreneur always searches for change and responds to it, and exploits it as an opportunity. (Drucker 1985, p. 42)

Entrepreneurial firms are often young and aggressive, continually searching for new opportunities that may be perceived as too risky by large firms or, indeed, not perceived at all. There is a tendency to concentrate not on complex markets, but on niche markets, which the leader can understand. The small size of these firms, with their focused strategies, allows the organizational structure to remain simple, so that the leader can retain tight control and the firms move quickly, their flexibility out-manoeuvring the big bureaucracies. Indeed, such an intimate knowledge in one mind provides an unexcelled focus. Nothing else permits so clear and complete a vision and also allows flexibility to elaborate and rework the vision.

Firms that exhibit entrepreneurial actions are those with internal or external resource disadvantages in relation to a competitor. Such firms need to avoid competition to prevent losing in head-on battles. Their best option is to discover and seize new opportunities that rivals will not perceive or be able to easily counter. The key issue here is 'uncertainty', in that the resource-rich firm might easily duplicate the action of the firm with inferior resources, but the uncertainty surrounding the entrepreneurial action delays the response. A classic example is in the early 1980s, when Bill Gates of Microsoft played on the competitive uncertainty surrounding the development of the software industry. Clearly many larger firms could have out-competed Microsoft at the time, but Microsoft's small size and the uncertain nature of the industry meant that competitors did not pay it too much attention. The sorts of action that might be taken by entrepreneurial firms include developing new products or services, improving products or services, making geographic transfers and satisfying shortages of supply.

Entrepreneurial strategy, then, is deliberate rather than emergent. It is critically about '*seizing new opportunities early*' (Oster 1990) rather than being resource-based. Entrepreneurial strategy is characterized by creativity and first-mover advantages, which can provide industry leadership and influence the structure of competitive domains in a way that may create potentially sustainable competitive advantage.

Intrapreneurship

In the face of large declining firms in the 1980s, both the US and the UK saw entrepreneurial characteristics as a way of reinvigorating stagnating corporate behemoths. The promotion of entrepreneurial characteristics in large companies was to be a form of 'corporate renaissance', where the spirit of enterprise would be reawakened and organizational alchemy performed, to transmute smokestack industries into high-technology firms (Kanter 1983). This form of entrepreneurship gave rise to the term '**intrapreneurship**', where employees other than 'the boss' could champion some technology or strategic issue by means of an entrepreneurial role – a role in which there are not only the ideas, but also the innovation – the doing of new things. Ideas generally abound in organizations; the scarce people are the ones who have the know-how, energy, daring and staying power to implement ideas.

> *The champion is not a blue-sky dreamer, or an intellectual giant. The champion might even be an idea thief. But above all, he's the pragmatic one who grabs onto someone else's theoretical construct if necessary and bull-headedly pushes it to fruition.* (Peters and Waterman 1982, p. 207)

So, if many agree that 'champions' are pivotal to the innovation process, why not just go out and hire them? Part of the reason is that champions' working styles are at odds with the ways that most businesses are managed. In the words of Tait Elder, at 3M:

> *We expect our champions to be irrational.* (Peters and Waterman 1982, p. 202)

> *Most corporations fail to tolerate the creative fanatic who has been the driving force behind most major innovations. Innovations, being far removed from the*

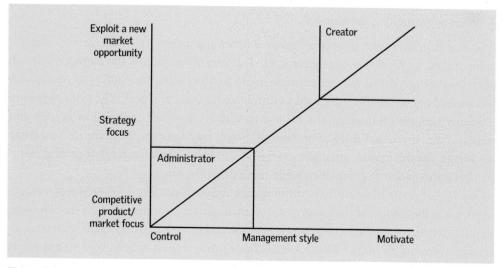

Figure 8.6 Entrepreneurial type versus administrator type
Source: Stevenson and Gumpert, 1985.

mainstream of business, show little promise in the early stages of development. Moreover, the champion is obnoxious, impatient, egotistical and perhaps a bit irrational in organizational terms. As a consequence, he is not hired. If hired, he is not promoted or rewarded. He is regarded as 'not a serious person', 'embarrassing', or 'disruptive'. (Quinn, in Peters and Waterman 1982, p. 206)

This difficulty is at the core of the debate over the place of the entrepreneur in the large firm: the debate over 'innovation versus administration'. As firms grow and become more complex, there becomes an increasing need for greater administrative control. However, such controls generally constrain innovation and so result in the loss of entrepreneurial spirit. This is illustrated by the changing importance of administrative and entrepreneurial executives (*see* Figure 8.6).

The entrepreneur asks:

- Where is the opportunity?
- How do I capitalize on it?
- What resources do I need?
- How do I gain control over them?
- What structure is best?

Whereas the administrator is characterized by asking:

- What resources do I control?
- What structure determines our organization's relationship to its market?
- How can I minimize the impact of others on my ability to perform?
- What opportunity is appropriate?

It is clear that, over time, the entrepreneur will find the increasingly bureaucratic organization stifling, as his or her autonomy is eroded. As a consequence, the entrepreneur will often leave or be pushed out. An example might be Steve Jobs, the founder of Apple, who was pushed out as the company tried to instill 'big business practices'. The price of greater efficiency and control through systems and procedures, however, may well be rigidity and staidness that drives out innovation and ultimately may threaten the company's strategic advantage. For this reason, attention has been focused heavily upon ways of getting entrepreneurialism back into companies, while minimizing tension.

One way of revitalizing business without such dramatic conflict is by viewing intrapreneurs not as the authors of the grand gesture, but of quiet innovation. They are the ones who translate strategy set at the top into actual practice, and in so doing, they shape what strategy actually turns out to mean (Kanter 1983). These intrapreneurs are the ones to test limits and create new possibilities. They generally do not start businesses, but improve them by pushing the creation of new products, leading the development of new production technology or experimenting with new humanly responsive work practices. Occasionally they may become heroes, but often by the time the achievements have found their way into company announcements, it is hard to attribute. So these 'quiet' intrapreneurs may not in themselves bring about big changes; they are, however, cumulatively, a major force for change – their micro-changes are often the first steps in major reorientations (Kanter 1983).

Internal innovation may contribute to the development of sustainable competitive advantage, but with the pace of knowledge accelerating, many, regardless of their size, cannot keep pace. Knowledge is also becoming far more specialized and often embedded within different contexts. To harness this proliferation of entrepreneurial activity, and to avoid the risks of forcing one's own organization to learn new tricks, firms are embarking more than ever before upon strategic alliances. For example, the large pharmaceutical firms are eagerly searching for opportunities to team up with biotechnology companies that can perform early-stage research, so that they can reduce their fixed costs, reduce risks and not impair their chances of discovering and marketing new blockbuster drugs.

Other methods of harnessing entrepreneurs include outright corporate acquisition, although this often leads to the types of tension mentioned above, and forms of investment whereby the large firm supplies venture capital into funds for start-ups. This allows ground-floor entry, the ability to observe and the possibility of future benefits, without the domination and stifling of the entrepreneur. However, as part of a syndicate group, returns to the large firm may be diminished.

8.2.5 Do entrepreneurs have a shelf life?

New organizations may grow rapidly and require specialized forms of expertise. As Greiner's (1972) five-stage model of evolutionary and revolutionary growth suggests, to cope with greater size and complexity over time, there will be an impetus towards new ways of organizing, which have important implications for the way in which the business is managed. However, these pressures can be, and very often are, in direct contradiction to the entrepreneur's instinctive need to retain power and avoid any formalization of activities that may erode his or her right 'to rule'.

In large organizations, where strong entrepreneurial leaders are used in times of crisis, such as managing a turnaround, the normal powers of existing groups are suspended, so that the leader can impose a new integrated vision. With the aversion of the crisis, the organization may revert to its traditional level of complexity and the entrepreneurial leader may then become perceived as an obstacle to the smooth running of the business.

It would seem that entrepreneurs as corporate leaders are excellent at providing vision and leadership for start-ups and in times of crisis. However, their powerful appeal is often to a specific audience at a specific time. As the business environment changes, perhaps with increasing organizational complexity as a direct consequence of their own achievements, entrepreneurs face the danger of 'the Icarus paradox':

The fabled Icarus of Greek mythology is said to have flown so high, so close to the sun, that his artificial wax wings melted and he plunged to his death in the Aegean Sea. (Miller 1992)

In other words, like Icarus, whose greatest asset led to his demise, entrepreneurs are captured by the causes of their very own successes. Success leads to specialization and exaggeration, to confidence and complacency, to dogma and ritual. We can have too much of a good thing.

Successful entrepreneurs, then, need to build an enterprise that will function without them. While they may rarely ever come to play the purely visionary role, as they will remain deeply engaged in their organizations, their roles must change for the organization to continue to flourish. They need to move from doing the work to teaching others how to do it. They will always strive for increasing impact and will aim to achieve this by focusing more on the strategy – the common purpose and organizational norms, rather than moving the product out of the door. Sir Michael Edwards – well-known for turning around high-profile businesses in the UK – always left after the firm had pulled through its crisis, rather than staying on to manage for sustained growth. He felt his management style suited a crisis situation rather than steady build. The different ways in which the role of the entrepreneur may change, as a small business evolves, is well illustrated by Churchill and Lewis's (1983) five stages of small business growth, namely, existence, survival, success, take-off and resource creativity.

In some cases, entrepreneurial CEOs cannot adjust their styles or bring themselves to leave. Especially when they were the founders of the business, it can be impossible for them to proactively manage their departure or countenance changes. They then find themselves in a dilemma: with each success they fly ever closer to the sun, blinding them to the increasing complexity and changing needs of their organizations. The heat of these tensions will melt the wings of even the most determined entrepreneur. 'Heroic' figures of the past, like those listed below, are now just names with which we struggle for association:

Alan Bond	Asil Nadir	Clive Sinclair	Holmes á Court
Cyril Lord	David Bloom	Eddie Shah	Freddie Laker
George Walker	Ivan Boesky	Jim Slater	John Ashcroft
John De Lorean	John Gunn	John Milken	Tony Berry

8.2.6 Reflections upon entrepreneurs and strategy

The topic of entrepreneurs opens many avenues in the strategy field. In terms of our view on strategy, **entrepreneurial strategy** is deliberate rather than emergent. It is top-down and directive, binding behind the entrepreneur's vision. Linked with the vision is the ability to innovate 'with 'controlled boldness' – the ideas are bold, the execution careful. Thus, there is an interesting interplay between problems and opportunities, as the entrepreneur will tend to treat problems as a crisis, which he will then turn into an opportunity. *By overselling* *the problem, he creates energy and the need for coherence.* By this means, an entrepreneur is able to achieve frame-breaking change within both the business and the industry itself. Such innovation is under-represented in traditional strategy models, where the emphasis is upon deliberate outcomes to plans to exploit unique resources, as in emphasizing lower cost or differentiation. Entrepreneurial actions are more spontaneous, based on opportunities created from market disequilibrium. Unlike the traditional approaches, which are based upon present-day or known resources, where future results should be predictable, these models understate the outcomes from entrepreneurial action, which are far more uncertain.

The powerful combination of vision and innovation in one person can give tremendous strategic punch to an organization sufficiently receptive and flexible to such autocratic power. However, increasing organizational complexity raises the issue of managerial sustainability. Traditionally, the entrepreneur would be associated with start-ups and crises, and would then be edged out, as organizational complexity increased. However, in a rapidly globalizing world experiencing a technological revolution and increasing competition, innovation is of critical importance. Those firms competing globally that invest more in innovation achieve the highest returns (Price 1996; Franko 1987). More than ever before, entrepreneurship is driving economic growth in general, and the harnessing of entrepreneurship is increasingly the secret of corporate renewal. This presents companies with significant new challenges in terms of how they should be organized, as innovators need to be woven into their very fabric and yet dysfunctional tensions must also be avoided. Within the firm, successful entrepreneurial activity and innovation require flexibility and a move away from the M-form. This is currently driving research into an N-form, which has optimistically been described as 'a new form', but in reality is a *set* of new forms of organizing. We might argue that the proliferation of strategic alliances and their many variants, the wide range of acquisition types, networks and the 'corporatization' of venture capital, are companies' attempts to organize more flexibly in order to harness innovation and yet give entrepreneurs the autonomy they need to flourish.

8.3 **New entry strategies**

Entrepreneurs give a very vivid picture of the strategic and operational challenges that face managers. We have used them as a device to illustrate some of the problems that typically arise at the beginning of the industry life cycle. It is worth remembering that entrepreneurs (like the turnaround specialists that we discuss later) are very real people operating in very challenging circumstances. However, the industry life cycle is simply an intellectual construct that is useful in helping us to structure and analyse problems. In this section we look a little more broadly at some of the strategic implications of the life cycle but noting as we go along that the life cycle idea is not a strategic law – there are in practice many irregularities and paradoxes as is evident in the very real world of start-ups, entry and turnarounds.

Figure 8.3a is map that displays the factors that help us define the stages of the life cycle. This leads to a view that there are four generic styles of strategy over the life cycle corresponding to the embryonic, growth, maturity and ageing phases shown in Figure 8.3a. Figures 8.3b and 8.4 show the implications in terms of strategic objectives (e.g. selective development) and financial outcomes. We need also to look at the implications for industry structure, competition and sources of competitive advantage. Figure 8.7 (taken from Grant 2002) shows demand/growth conditions and technology as drivers and other variables such as products, manufacturing and distribution, competition and key success factors as outcomes. Thus, competition changes predictably going from few firms, through multiple entries, to stabilization, then shakeout and eventual exits of many firms. The forms of

	Introduction	Growth	Maturity	Decline
Demand	Limited to early adapters: high income, avant-garde	Rapidly increasing market penetration	Mass market, replacement/repeat buying. Customers knowledgeable and price sensitive	Obsolescence
Technology	Competing technologies. Rapid product innovation	Standardization around dominant technology. Rapid process innovation	Well-diffused technical know-how: quest for technological improvements	Little or no product or process innovation
Products	Poor quality. Wide variety of features and technologies. Frequent design changes	Design and quality improve. Emergence of dominant design	Trend to commoditization. Attempts to differentiate by branding, quality and bundling	Commodities the norm: differentiation difficult and unprofitable
Manufacturing and distribution	Short production runs. High-skilled labour content. Specialized distribution channels	Capacity shortages. Mass production. Competition for access to distribution	Emergence of overcapacity. Deskilling of production. Long production runs. Distributors carry fewer lines	Chronic overcapacity. Re-emergence of specialist channels
International trade	Producers and consumers in advanced countries.	Exports from advanced countries to rest of world	Production shifts to newly industrializing countries then to developing countries	Exports from countries with lowest labour costs
Competition	Few companies.	Entry, mergers and exits	Shakeout. Price competition increases	Price wars, exits
Key success factors	Product innovation. Establishing credible image of firm and product	Design for manufacture. Access to distribution. Building strong brand. Fast product development. Process innovation	Cost efficiency through capital intensity, scale efficiency, and low input costs. High quality	Low overheads. Buyer selection. Signalling commitment. Rationalizing capacity

Figure 8.7 The evolution of industry structure and competition over the life cycle
Source: Grant, 2002, p. 311.

competitive advantage go from simple product novelty, through innovation, to differentiation alternatives, moves towards commoditization, and eventual commodity status. The implications for functional strategies such as marketing and manufacturing follow directly from this. Cost advantage plays a minor, even negligible role in start-up and growth, grows more important in maturity as a major contributor to profit, and eventually becomes central as the power to differentiate wanes.

The growth (and early maturity) phase attracts entry. In particular a successful pioneering of a new industry is often buttressed by significant barriers to entry, such as by patents (see the examples of Kodak in film, Xerox in photocopying, Microsoft in PC operating systems, and Intel in microprocessors). The role of the pioneers in establishing such new industries is well known. Less well known are the successful strategies of competitors striving to enter across the barriers. Table 7.4 outlines the strength of the Xerox position in 1980 behind its wall of patents and the other entry barriers that it had had time to construct. What is less well known (perhaps forgotten) is how waves of entry head on against the Xerox barriers were dashed and broken. These include many firms well known in their day but now forgotten (such as Gestetner and Agfa) but also major players such as IBM and Kodak. However, Xerox's position was eventually undermined and broken by patterns of entry that stepped around the formidable Xerox defences and offered alternative value propositions to customers. Table 7.5 outlines how Canon rewrote the 'rules of the game'. What this means is that the old rules, the Xerox competitive advantages, were replaced by new rules, the new competitive advantages. These new rules came about through a 'sequential entry strategy' pursued by Japanese competitors, notably Ricoh and Canon. The way these new rules are put in place can be codified as **sequential entry strategy**.

A sequential entry strategy takes place gradually over time and has four main elements (McGee and Thomas 1994).

1 Gateway to entry

The process of gradual entry will lead firms to choose as gateways to entry (Yip 1982) either:

(a) a unique entry point in strategic space reflecting unmet demand-side characteristics; or

(b) a competitive positioning in the new industry based on the asset configurations of the current dominant strategic group in the industry; or

(c) a competitive positioning based on a new asset configuration representing the creation of a new strategic group.

The first represents an entry based on a new segmentation of the market where demand is currently unmet and probably unrecognized. The second is an emulation of the industry leaders and a head-on challenge to them. The third is a 'new-game' strategy where the entrant, often through new technology, intends to play the game a different way with a new and unusual mix of assets (see Steffens, 1986, for a discussion of how the PC industry was characterized by new games in its early, formative stages). Firm choice will be a function of its current strategic assets, the speed of technological change, and the costs and risks of entry which will be asymmetric between individual firms. In particular, costs will be related to differences in the height of entry barriers between market segments and risk will be related to the firm's existing asset configuration and financial resources. Typically positions (a) and (b) are not desirable or feasible. Unmet demand based on standard assets in the industry is highly unlikely and already easily captured by incumbents. Position (b) is risky given the defensive strengths of the incumbents.

2 Initial entry point

Successful entry occurs first into segments where barriers are lowest. This means that in the short run firms prefer risk minimizing as opposed to profit maximization. According to Caves and Porter (1977):

> It may be optimal to enter groups characterized by tangible asset outlays (e.g. producing for private label with no advertising outlay) first and groups requiring more risky intangible asset outlays only after a viable base in the industry is attained; the lower risk barriers are vaulted earlier.

Thus, short-term risk minimization might be a necessary prerequisite for long-term wealth creation. Therefore, on the above analysis, position (c) would be the preferred **entry point**. However, The costs of entry with a **new-game strategy** are very high and the uncertainties also high. So the temptation to go for entry points with lower costs is high even though the chances of making a successful entry might in fact be low.

3 Mode of entry

The **mode of entry** concerns the nature of the investments undertaken in order to use the particular gateway. Thus:

(a) gateways to entry are distinguished by differences in entry costs between them;

(b) within each gateway a range of different investments are possible given the nature of the assets required;

(c) the nature of the entry is conditioned by the risk proclivities of firms and ways available to them for managing risks.

Different gateways require different classes and types of assets, but at each gateway there will be a variety of possible entry moves. The larger the number of strategic groups, the wider the range of possible entry strategies. The more complex an individual strategic group, the wider the range of possible strategies for entering that group. Following the example of Canon vs Xerox in Chapter 7, Canon had to construct an entirely new value chain (or business system) in order to make use of its preferred gateway. As we now know, this worked very well, but the entry cost was high and the perceived risks very high.

Dell represents a similar example. In order to get into the PC industry how do you get around the power wielded upstream by Microsoft and Intel? The answer is by appealing to buyer needs that are not addressed directly by these two orchestrators of the industry. This meant getting close to the customer and building a direct link to the customer through the telephone and through the internet. This was a different gateway and new entry point, requiring a distinct mode of entry. The rest is history and Dell is now a major force in the industry.

4 Expansion path

The **expansion path** (following Penrose's (1959) ideas about the nature of growth of the firm) concerns the subsequent strategic decisions about the path that growth should take. The subsequent entry pathway (the route for expansion) is dependent on the initial mode of entry and the firm's ability to develop firm-specific assets.

The initial entry point contains an immediate market opportunity which is assessed in the context of the systematic risk relating to the chosen gateway and the specific risks assumed by the entrant. The development of longer-term competitive advantage will require further investment in **co-specialized assets** (e.g. technology) and appropriate access to complementary assets (e.g. marketing and distribution) (Teece 1987). For example, for short-term success new entrants (innovators) may need to forge alliances with incumbents to gain access to complementary assets such as marketing and distribution. But in the longer term a different view is likely to be taken of the appropriate mix of co-specialized and complementary assets. The process of moving towards the desired mix can be thought of as the expansion path.

The idea of sequential entry can be distilled into four elements: the gateway to entry, the initial entry point, the mode of entry and the expansion path. The central concern is how to get around the existing entry barriers. Entry barriers are simply competitive advantages – the bigger the advantage, the higher the barriers. To get into an existing industry against established incumbents means being able to beat them at their own game. Where this is unlikely, a circuitous route to find a different entry point is required.[3] Entry is about the cost of imitation. This involves assessing the advantage of the incumbent and one's own capabilities.

The case box below places these themes of technology, entry and competition into a Schumpeterian '**creative destruction** context'. The example makes the claim that these processes of sequential entry are widespread in industries marked by technology discontinuities. List as many industries as you can that fit this pattern. The result may surprise you.

---

[3] This may remind some readers of Winston Churchill's strategy in the First World War to make landings in the Dardanelles against the Turks rather than waste resources taking on the Germans who were well embedded on the Western Front. This was a good strategic thought that foundered on two practical, operational points: the Allies botched the invasion and the Turks were much better prepared than had been anticipated.

Case box: **Creative destruction**

Certain themes recur throughout the history of industries such as reprographics. First, step changes in technology that are 'competence-destroying' can fundamentally change an industry's knowledge base, can lead directly to new dominant designs, and can spawn new, powerful competitors in new strategic groups. The nature of competitive rivalry changes with serious implications for the survival of incumbent firms.

Second, incumbents are affected in a number of ways. Incumbent monopolists (because of the potential erosion of profits of existing products and processes) have a smaller incentive to innovate than potential entrants (the Arrow effect, Arrow, 1962).

Third, technological change enables firms from outside the industry to capture a series of sub-markets. Entry is a complex, sequential process taking many years and involves systematic moves from a circumscribed initial entry point through a series of expansionary investments.

Fourth, sequential entry processes are important in determining the eventual competitive conditions that prevailed. Thus, the industry structure observed at any given time is the result, to a great extent, not only of exogenous technological change but also of the strategic decisions of firms.

Finally, with every step-change in technology, the market is enlarged. New product 'spaces' emerge and are filled up. Market boundaries are redefined. New ways of product differentiation and new possibilities for segmentation become available to suppliers. This creates new dimensions of competition.

These recurring patterns constitute the Schumpeterian process of creative destruction (Schumpeter, 1942). There are two steps to the argument here. The first simply states that technology can change industry structure. It can do so by changing conditions on the demand side and/or by causing adjustments on the supply side. Thus, the nature of competition changes and the nature and level of entry barriers can alter, sometimes dramatically. The second step is more fundamental to an understanding of the process and concerns the role of the firm in the way it takes advantage of technological change. The centre-piece is the idea that technology changes the asset base of the firm. The key issue for the firm concerns its ability to invest in the creation of assets that are, relative to competitors, sufficiently distinct so that it can compete in the market in ways that cannot be imitated. The distinctiveness of the assets relates to the 'uncertain imitability' of those assets by competitors and thus constitutes the basis for economic profits. The ability of the firm to create distinctiveness for itself by investing in R&D is a prime source of competitive power and taken far enough (as in the case of Xerox and plain-paper copying) is sufficient to change industry structure.

This second point underlines the possibility for firms to act so as to make technological change endogenous to the system. It is evident from this that firms will be concerned to protect their distinctive assets (which, ex post, are sunk costs) with other kinds of differentiation strategy to lock in their customers in the face of similar or newer forms of competition.

> Initially the asset base is a potential entry barrier but in the course of time it might also become a prison wall inhibiting investment by the firm in new directions. In contrast, the successful firms are the ones that re-defined the industry boundaries and the relevant assets for the firm, and engaged in a continuous series of innovations.
>
> *Source*: McGee and Thomas, 1994.

This section is arguing two points, one general, the other more specific. The first point is exemplified by the life cycle idea that says, as a general rule, that changes in demand growth and technology over the life cycle have implications for industry structure, competition and sources of competitive advantage. At each phase of the life cycle there are general conditions suggesting that specific competitive strategies need to evolve over the cycle and that firms should therefore plan for these changes. However, as Grant points out (2002, p. 313) generalization can be dangerous and the particulars of strategy may go beyond the simplicity of the life cycle model.

Therefore, our second point becomes relevant. Whereas the life cycle depends on a simple time line and equally simple growth extrapolation, we are concerned with more powerful theories that build on the ability of technology to create new assets, new competitive spaces, which in turn are destroyed by new rounds of technical change. The idea of sequential entry is a theory built on the interplay between these factors. All strategy development has a time line but behind the time line are powerful forces of discovery and change which Schumpeter called 'creative destruction'. The life cycle model is a useful starting point for recognizing how strategy must change over time. But we always need a more powerful model that can capture the interplay between technology, markets, costs and investment. Strategy is the taking of considered risks against the odds and against an unknown future but there are recognizable patterns for us to use.

8.4 **Corporate failure and turnaround strategies**

What happens when things go wrong? What are the competitive forces and managerial mindsets that lead to **corporate failure**? This chapter looks at the anatomy of failure and at the analytical and management procedures that constitute a 'turnaround' of a failing company. It covers the links between financial analysis, strategy analysis and strategic choice.

Why should we look at corporate turnarounds? They are part of the life and death of all businesses and, while the Western business culture is firmly focused on success, we should not ignore lessons that can be gleaned from when things start to go wrong. Indeed, it is worth noting that several large companies specifically ask their best managers to manage the turnaround of 'dogs' before appointing them to the main board – a trial by fire if ever there was one.

Substantial numbers of turnarounds arose after the massive wave of corporate diversifications during the 1960s–1980s. The bureaucratic inefficiencies of **diversification** resulted in poor management of subsidiaries, and stock markets began to downgrade **conglomerates**, realizing that the sum of the parts exceeded the whole. A trend-setting bid of this nature was Hoylake's £15 billion bid for the tobacco giant BAT industries, where the aggressors promised to 'unbundle' the assets to realize greater value for shareholders. New sophisticated financing methods helped corporate raiders to launch bids for even the largest corporate, so that size was no longer a guarantee of independence. In response to such threats, conglomerates began to recognize that continuous expansion had given rise to the twin problems of managing the extremities as well as expansion taking its toll on the core of business. It was the time of Tom Peter's famous homily: '*stick to the knitting*'[4]. Turnarounds of divested businesses, as well as the core, are an important feature of organizational life.

8.4.1 **Issues**

The Boston Box, while designed as a corporate portfolio technique for reducing financial risk, has been widely used as a prescriptive strategic planning tool, with some disastrous consequences. This is well illustrated by 'dogs', which are characterized by business units with low relative market share in low-growth markets. According to the Boston Box, and other directional policy matrices of this ilk, such businesses are in decline, generate low profits, and should be divested: they will not attract equity finance and there is greater financial risk in this context with debt finance. However, in times of recession, some 80 per cent of UK businesses can be described as 'dogs', and so it is dangerous to conclude that they should all be divested. For instance, there are alternative strategies, which may lead to successful outcomes, such as recovery/rejuvenation, maturity, the end game and internationalization. All of these strategic options offer significant potential for shaking off the negative image of 'dogs'.

We shall be concentrating in this chapter on 'turnarounds', or corporate recovery. Hofer's (1976) classic article on turnarounds draws the distinction between operating and strategic forms. Operating turnarounds are about 'doing things differently', so that the firm's efficiency can be improved. This may be achieved by a fundamental change in a firm's operations, by using advanced manufacturing technology, for instance. Strategic turnarounds are about 'doing different things'. In this instance, companies attempt to change their fortunes by fundamental adjustments to their strategy, in terms of acquisition and divestment, for instance.

Hofer's distinction between strategic and operating turnarounds has been challenged by Hambrick and Schecter (1983). They argue that the difference becomes blurred as we move

---

[4] In other words, concentrate on the core business, and do not be distracted by non-core activities.

from the corporate to the business unit level. They suggest three categories: traditional asset cost surgery, product-market pruning and, their largest category, piecemeal strategies. This suggests that there is such difference between individual companies that it is difficult to establish a single turnaround framework.

Grinyer, Mayes and McKiernan (1988) have extended this discussion by carrying out a detailed examination of types of recovery employed by UK manufacturing companies, and relating these to contextual variables. In their rigorous study, they do find sufficient commonalities to suggest that turnarounds have distinct stages, even though there are different types of turnaround in existence. Their work is reviewed here, to give insight on types of turnaround and the anatomy of a turnaround.

8.4.2 **Types of turnaround**

In their study of 1200 of the UK's largest companies, Grinyer, Mayes and McKiernan (1988) examined the different types of corporate turnaround that had been experienced, as well as analysing the anatomy of such events. To enable them to determine between different types of turnaround they broadened their frame of reference to embrace all firms that had experienced a decline, followed by a sharp upturn in performance. It is important to note that this means that the study is also examining firms that are not facing extinction, as in the classic turnaround definition, but includes firms which, while suffering declining performance, may still be healthy. Figure 8.8 shows the different types of '**sharpbender**' identified.

- ◆ **Case A** is the firm showing *early recovery*. The firm is aware of its decline in performance and *anticipates* that on such a trend it is likely to breech its managerial-determined minimum acceptable level of performance. Although the firm is far from extinction, actions are taken in advance, the crisis averted, and a path of sustained improvement achieved.

- ◆ **Case B** is the firm taking *intermediate* action to break through its line of minimum acceptable standards. Alarm bells are ringing and actions taken to recover. However, such actions are insufficient – perhaps superficial, addressing symptoms rather than causes – and the firm returns to its decline trajectory. At this point, the firm may countenance

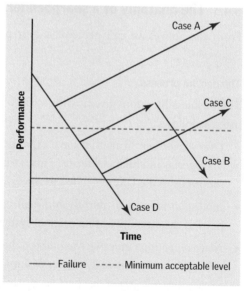

Figure 8.8 Types of sharpbender
Source: adapted from Grinyer, Mayes and McKiernan, 1988, p. 14.

more sweeping changes to restore the firm to a trajectory of sustained improvement. However, should this step not be taken, it is likely that the firm will continue to oscillate around the line of minimum acceptable standards, with successive uplifts being more difficult to achieve than previously, before ultimately failing.

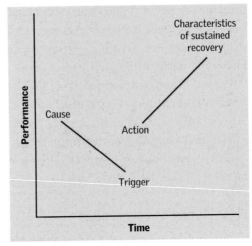

Figure 8.9 The four phases of a sharpbender
Source: Grinyer, Mayes and McKiernan, 1988.

- **Case C** is a firm which is late in reacting to the crisis. The firm has breached its managerial-determined minimum level of performance and has begun to approach the line of failure. It is the classic turnaround, as described by Slatter (1984). In this instance, the firm needed the spur of breaking its internal standards, as well as the threat of extinction, to begin to take substantial action. By so doing, sustained recovery is achieved.

- **Case D** is the firm that does not perceive the threat of extinction, despite breaking its own minimum acceptable standards, or is unable to make any changes before termination.

8.4.3 **The anatomy of a sharpbender**

From the above, we can perceive a four-phase model for a 'sharpbend', as depicted in Figure 8.9.

The decline process

The business literature gives a wide variety of reasons for corporate decline. These can be listed as follows:

- *Over-expansion*: firms that have expanded too far find that they are stretched in both managerial and financial terms. This is the classic criticism of the diversification boom of the 1960s in the UK, which led to massive under-performing conglomerates.

- *Inadequate financial controls and high costs*: these often occur when a business grows beyond the capability of its original systems, so that costs spiral out of control.

- *New competition entering the market*: the arrival of a new competitor can substantially distort the competitive dynamics of a market and damage a firm's health.

- *Unforeseen demand shifts*: the nature of the market may change dramatically. Where a firm has substantial and rigid asset configurations, this can spell disaster – the classic example being the impact on IBM of the widespread switch from mainframe to desk-top computers. The area most on people's minds at the moment is the potential impact of the internet.

- *Poor management*: managers may have a false sense of confidence in their own abilities. This can arise from experiencing a period of success, causing an atmosphere of infallibility, and the screening of information. Of course, poor management may also just mean poor management.

From their interviews, the sharpbender researchers concluded that primary causes of decline were in changes in total market demand, falling revenues from more intense competition and a high cost structure. In Table 8.1 we show that such variables impact differently, depending on whether the firms are staging early, intermediate or late recoveries.

How do managers react to a crisis?

Most systems within businesses, such as control systems, reporting and accounting systems, are backward-looking or historic in nature and designed for steady state environments. As a result, managers may find themselves in a situation of false security. As signals emerge, there is at first the issue of whether the managers know or accept that there is a crisis. The natural tendency is to deny that there is a crisis, on the grounds that any negative signal may well be a temporary 'blip' or extraordinary factor. The tendency is also to rationalize the signal away in terms of thinking that 'Everyone is in the same boat' and to suggest that 'We've all seen it before'. With this urge to preserve the status quo, top management will see the situation as temporary and be inclined to 'sit it out' – wait and see what happens next. This inactivity will be reinforced by a general view that knee-jerk reactions are dangerous and panic should be avoided. To maintain this stance, there may be a degree of self-delusion in terms of massaging, delaying and even hiding figures. An example of this situation might be Midland Bank's exposure to Latin American debt in the secondary banking crisis in the late 1980s. All the major banks were heavily exposed and the City waited nervously for Midland's results, as the bank had one of the largest exposures. However, instead of reporting a massive loss as

Table 8.1 Causes of decline

	Early %	Intermediate %	Late %
Market decline	25	55	75
Financial	25	55	67
Project failure	25	36	75
Strategic Problems	0	9	25
Poor marketing	75	9	8

Source: McKiernan, 1992, p. 64.

everyone anticipated, they announced a substantial profit. To achieve this, they had used an accounting sleight of hand, which was subsequently contested in court. The outcome was that the accounts had to be restated and the new results showed an even greater loss than anticipated. This extraordinary course of events shows a management team trying to preserve confidence in the bank among its stakeholders, by suggesting that the debt situation was a one-off, temporary blip, which did not impact in any substantial way upon the bank's prospects.

Stages of reactive behaviour

When the crisis is too obvious to ignore, managers tend to react in a sequential way, which may be perceived as taking the least risky actions at first, and then becoming progressively more daring if the crisis worsens and they have time to act.

Initially, managers will tighten up on existing control systems. They will go for the easy targets, which are almost invariably costs. Many investment expenditures and current experimental programmes will also be abandoned. If the crisis continues, the tendency is to tighten costs even further. To those executives who have lived through such turnarounds, it will come as no surprise the extent to which costs can be tightened. One such symbol of straitened times is the pencil trolley. Suddenly people will appear and raid everyone's desks for all writing implements. These will be carted away and a brand new pencil left behind. For the executive to qualify for a new pencil at a later stage, the stub will need to be taken to the stores to ensure that it is less than one inch in length!

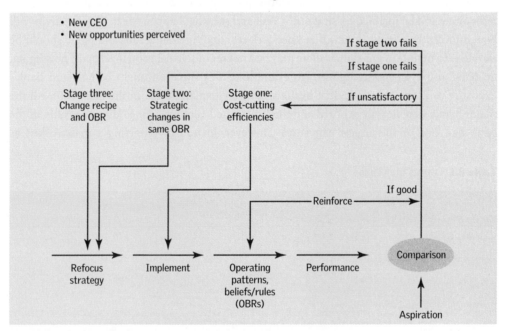

Figure 8.10 A conceptual model of the stages of reactive behaviour
Source: extended Cyert and March model (McKiernan 1992) p. 58.

If the crisis persists, then the smart executives will be preparing their own alibis and the organization will be looking for victims. Strategy may be reviewed incrementally and there may be some product market changes. If there is no improvement, the organization may descend into a state whereby no one will act unless receiving direct instructions from the top, or the prevailing modus operandi, or recipe, of the business may be challenged. This will entail a fundamental review of the organization – its purpose and logic.

These stages of reactive behaviour are well captured in Figure 8.10. Comparisons are continually drawn between reference points such as competitor performance, share performance and ambitions and aspirations for profit performance. Should this comparison be favourable then the innermost loop will be followed, with the current behaviour being reinforced. Should the comparisons prove unfavourable then the first stage will be followed.

If desirable results are not forthcoming, executives may move progressively outwards in Figure 8.10 until the third stage of a fundamental review of strategy is undertaken.

Living in crumbling palaces

Organizations build up excessive rigidity to change – as the sub-heading suggests. The difficulty with needing to change is that it is perceived to have unforeseen and frightening consequences. In addition, there are barriers to change from those executives who owe their positions to the status quo. Organizational members have to unlearn their current ways of doing things, unpackage their assumptions about how the business works and engage with a new set of parameters. This in itself can lead to a downturn in performance, and so cause despondency and sap energies. It is important to note, therefore, that change will not just happen, but requires considerable power to enforce. If left to its own devices, the likelihood is that the result will just be a series of 'cosmetic changes', rather like rearranging the chairs on the *Titanic.*

> When an organization is in this serious a state, it is rare that a turnaround can be accomplished by the incumbent senior management – the ritual sacrifice of the old leader is almost obligatory. (Grinyer, Mayes and McKiernan, 1988)

Triggers for action

While it may be clear that an organization is on a decline trajectory, it is vital that triggers are identified to bring about action. If triggers cannot be identified then it is likely that nothing will change, despite the abundance of warning signs.

The *Sharpbenders* study identifies a number of important triggers for bringing about change (see Table 8.2). It is important to note that acquisitions were specifically excluded from the study, and so we do not know how prevalent this important trigger might be. A well-known example of an acquisition as a trigger prompting a strategic change is the Hanson bid for ICI. In fighting off the bid, ICI announced the de-merger of Zeneca.

Table 8.2 Triggers

		Sharpbenders citing this factor
1	Intervention from external bodies	30%
2	Change of ownership or the threat of such a change	25%
3	New chief executive	55%
4	Recognition by management of problems	35%
5	Perception by management of new opportunities	10%

Source: Grinyer, Mayes and McKiernan, 1988, *Sharpbenders*, p. 47.

The main trigger identified is a new CEO. His or her importance is in terms of supplying a new vision and symbolizing that things need to change. Indeed, such a person has undoubtedly been appointed with a mandate for change.

In terms of early, intermediate and late stage recoveries, the broad pattern, as one might expect, is for the early stagers to have internal triggers and have a management able to perceive problems and opportunities. As we move to the late stagers, all triggers are important with an increased external emphasis.

Table 8.3 Actions taken

	% of firms citing factor		
	Sharp-benders	Control companies	% diff
Major changes in management	85	30	55
Stronger financial controls	80	70	10
New product market focus	80	80	0
Diversified	30	70	(40)
Entered export market vigorously	50	30	20
Improved quality and service	55	50	5
Improved marketing	75	30	45
Intensive efforts to reduce production costs	80	30	50
Acquisitions	50	80	(30)
Reduced debt	50	80	(30)
Windfalls	85	70	15
Other	25	20	5

Source: Grinyer, Mayes and McKiernan, 1988, *Sharpbenders*, p. 64.

Actions taken

If there are triggers in place then the sorts of action that might be taken to bring about a recovery are contained in Table 8.3. We are interested to know the actions that sharpbenders took and in particular those actions that are specific to them. For this reason we show the percentage of sharpbenders citing an action in column one, the percentage of other randomly selected companies citing an action in column two and the difference between the two scores in column three.

The major difference between sharpbenders and control companies in terms of action taken is management changes: 85 per cent of sharpbenders cited management changes, some 55 per cent more than the control companies. They also devoted considerable efforts to improving marketing and reducing production costs. Unlike the control companies they were very reluctant to diversify and there were markedly reduced levels of acquisition. Interestingly, they were also reluctant to reduce debt, and here there is a distinction with pure turnarounds in that the latter make considerable efforts to reduce debts. Sharpbenders are more likely to invest to improve performance.

Characteristics of sustained performance

Following the turnaround, sharpbenders needed to adopt characteristics that would enable sustained levels of performance – to refer back to Figure 8.8 organizations want cases A and C, rather than B (where the recovery achieved is only short term). The characteristics identified in the *Sharpbenders* (1988) study are contained in Table 8.4.

♦ Good management is seen to be critical to sustained recovery.

♦ Appropriate organizational structure often meant a much leaner one, with fewer layers in the hierarchy.

♦ Tightly controlled costs meant better controls, rather than cutting costs.

Table 8.4 Key features of sustained improved performance

	Number of characteristics cited	% of firms cited
1 Good management	4+	90
2 Appropriate organizational structure	4+	75
3 Effective financial and other controls	4+	50
4 Sound product market posture	5+	45
5 Good marketing management	2+	55
6 High quality maintained	2+	35
7 Tightly controlled costs	3+	40

Source: Grinyer, Mayes and McKiernan, 1988, *Sharpbenders*, p. 110.

Case box: The destruction of Marconi

Major shifts in strategic directions can work for some companies. But more often they can lead into areas that the management does not understand – with disastrous results.

General Electric Company (GEC), the UK company with no relation to America's GE, grew rapidly in the 1960s under Arnold Weinstock's domineering but effective leadership.

Like its American counterpart, GEC grew into a conglomerate with interests in such diverse businesses as white goods, defence electronics, telecoms and power systems. While there was no real logic underlying this array of businesses, Weinstock held the company together through a combination of his imposing personality and a strict system of financial controls. At its peak, GEC had sales of £11bn and a cash pile of £2bn.

Simpson's masterplan

Lord Weinstock retired in 1996 and was replaced by George Simpson, a former executive at Rover. Over the course of the next five years, Simpson and his finance director John Mayo masterminded a complete rethinking of GEC's corporate strategy.

They decided to focus the company on the fast-growing telecoms equipment industry. They bought two mid-sized US competitors (Reltec for $2.1bn and Fore for $4.5bn) for large sums of money and invested in developing a range of new products to compete with industry leaders Cisco and Nortel. To pay for this growth, most other businesses, including defence electronics, white goods and power systems, were sold off. To reflect this change in strategy, GEC was renamed Marconi.

The dénouement

Marconi's share price peaked in August 2000 at £12. Then things started to go badly wrong. The dot-com bubble burst and demand for new telecoms equipment dried up. Lucent, Cisco and Nortel all announced profit warnings. Marconi's share price dropped even though it denied that its sales had been hit. Then, when the profit warning finally came, angry investors dumped the stock.

The downturn was far more severe than anyone anticipated and with large and mounting debts Marconi was facing bankruptcy, its shares worth less than one per cent of their peak value. Simpson and Mayo were forced out. A new executive team was brought in; £37bn of market value had been destroyed in just a year and a half. In November 2003, Marconi announced half-year losses of £149m in the period to September, down from £485m a year previously.

The lesson

Marconi's story is a classic tale of an over-ambitious growth strategy and subsequent collapse. But the lesson to take away is that despite their ultimate failure, Simpson and Mayo did some important things right.

First, they correctly reasoned that if Marconi were going to become a major player in telecoms it would have to grow aggressively and it would need a strong US position. Hence its acquisitions of Fore and Reltec. This approach worked for Cisco.

Where Marconi went wrong was that it paid cash – partly because it had plenty of it, and partly because it did not have a full listing in the US (so its paper was not attractive currency).

So rule one: if you are going to overpay for an acquisition, better to overpay with your own overpaid shares. The cash drain from these acquisitions is what ultimately killed Marconi. Second, Marconi's decision to major on one business – and sell the rest – is exactly what the markets were asking for. Conglomerates were OK in the 1970s and 1980s but the trend during the 1990s was towards highly focused corporations. And, indeed, Simpson was lauded for his courage in breaking up and focusing the company he took over from Lord Weinstock.

But Marconi's failure underlines how risky this sort of refocusing can be. Simpson put all his eggs in one basket but it was a relatively untested and new basket at that. Such dramatic changes in corporate strategy can work. For example, Spirent made a successful transition from industrial conglomerate to fast-growing telecoms company during the late 1990s.

But more often than not major changes in strategy take a company into new areas that it does not really understand and the results end up being disastrous – as the shareholders of Vivendi and Enron will confirm.

Source: Julian Birkinshaw, *Business Strategy Review*, Spring 2004, Volume 15, Issue 1, pp. 74–5.
Reproduced with permission of Blackwell Publishing.

Case box: **A Rose-tinted vision**

Has Stuart Rose seen the future for M&S?

'A bit boring,' is how Stuart Rose describes some of the products sold by Marks & Spencer (M&S). Mr Rose says that he can transform M&S by going back to retailing basics – not easy in the era of Wal-Mart. M&S's relationship with its customers and suppliers was once admired worldwide. But that was when its St Michael brand of underwear could be found in the top drawer of almost every house in Britain. Retailing has since changed dramatically and traditional stores in almost every country face similar challenges. Speciality retailers, such as America's Gap in casual clothes, Victoria's Secret in underwear and Sweden's H&M in low-cost fashion, are taking business away from department stores and established chains. At the same time, supermarkets have moved aggressively into selling clothes, household goods and prepared meals (pioneered by M&S). The British firm has struggled, sacrificing its legendary high quality and employee-friendly culture to make the cost savings needed to keep profits growing through the 1990s and so meet the short-term expectations of many shareholders.

By 3 June, when Mr Green, a Monaco-based billionaire who owns the Bhs and Arcadia store chains, launched his latest attempt to buy M&S, the firm was deteriorating fast. Its efforts to transform itself had begun to stall. Its management was floundering. Rumours of Mr Green's pending bid led to a boardroom rout. Mr Rose was quickly made chief executive only days before Mr Green made his bid. That bid was rebuffed, as was his now-withdrawn later offer, which was potentially worth up to £4 a share.

The appointment of Mr Rose, aged 55 – a retail professional with an impressive reputation – was a masterstroke. Early in his career, he spent 17 years working for M&S. Selling M&S to Mr Green never seemed to be on Mr Rose's agenda. Even at £4 a share, he maintained that Mr Green's final offer undervalued the company significantly. That bid, however, has set the hurdle over which Mr Rose must climb. He believes he can deliver a company worth more than £4 a share. To sweeten shareholders he is selling M&S's financial-services business to HSBC, a big bank, in order to fund a share tender offer worth £2.3 billion, the equivalent of returning £1 per share to investors. Costs will be cut, leading to savings of some £320m in the 2006 financial year. The group's extensive property holdings have also been revalued, upwards.

Yet the really crucial thing for M&S's future is what Mr Rose describes as a return to its core. 'It doesn't need revolution,' he says, but, rather, the application of basic retailing skills in lots of areas. For a start, the business has to be made simpler. Compared with when he worked at M&S before, Mr Rose now finds each division operating like a separate company. The supply chain has become slow and overcommitted, and stores are cluttered with too many product lines. 'Do we need 23 varieties of tomato?' he asks. Mr Rose's new management team has already started to edit the products on offer, adding some new ones to plug the gaps but eliminating many more. Some 10,000 lines of clothing will be reduced to around 9,000. Its roughly 8,500 lines of home goods will be cut to 4,500. A new venture, Lifestore, specializing in homewares, has been cancelled and the unit's first giant store will be closed. Some of the company's smaller food-only stores will also be closed.

Too many sub-brands have left shoppers confused, adds Mr Rose. Some will be kept, such as Per Una, which has been a successful range of women's clothing for M&S. As part of the new strategy, he has bought this business for £125m from George Davies, the designer who developed it, in order to have control over it. Mr Rose reckons M&S's customer relationship is defined by womenswear. So, if his new team can produce appealing styles at good prices, he believes he can regain the trust of the company's most important group of shoppers.

But the transformation cannot be completed overnight; this autumn's fashion lines, for instance, are already fixed, so the new team will not have a chance to make their mark on womenswear until spring 2005. Mr Rose is adamant that he can succeed, and perhaps he can – if his shareholders have patience. Despite its troubles, M&S has much going for it: with 25m customers – around half of the adult British population – it retains a large market share, even in women's underwear (26%).

Source: 'A Rose-tinted vision', *The Economist*, 15 July 2004.
© The Economist Newspaper Limited, London (15 July 2004).

Questions for discussion

1   Apply the four-phase sharpbender model to Stuart Rose's M&S recovery plan.

2   What is different about the M&S situation? Is it a conventional turnaround?

3   In what ways does the turnaround plan take sufficient account of the causes of decline? In what ways do you suspect that M&S might be a 'crumbling palace'?

8.4.4 Generic turnaround strategies

Grinyer, Mayes and McKiernan's (1988) rigorous work has suggested a time ordering of actions to achieve a turnaround. This supports a review of practitioners' work by Hoffman (1989), which suggests a three-stage process for recovery, although not all organizations need to go through all three stages. This is shown in Figure 8.11.

8.4.5 Lessons for managers

The practical lessons for managers are that:

♦   Financial and behavioural criteria need to be monitored for declining trends in operational or strategic performance. Strategic health requires proactive management, rather than reactive financial reporting.

♦   During decline, ensure that there is sufficient management talent.

♦   The new CEO needs to establish a reliable top team.

♦   Management will need a two-stage plan – an operational plan to stop the decline and generate positive cash flow and a strategic plan to reposition the organization to sustain recovery.

♦   It is critical to get to the root causes – there will be a temptation to address symptoms rather than causes. If one is really tackling fundamental issues then it is likely to be painful, as it will challenge the very way that executives see their roles.

♦   Both strategy and success are communicated effectively by and through the workforce.

We began this section with the BCG portfolio view of strategy, which perceived turnaround situations as best divested. However, turnarounds can be very successful, if well managed. By taking an anatomical view of turnarounds, we have exposed some core issues for effective management, in particular, showing the necessity for confronting basic premises upon which the organization has operated.

Turnarounds are just one example of crisis situations in corporate strategy, and readers should be aware that this has particular implications for how strategy is viewed in such circumstances. In the case of turnarounds:

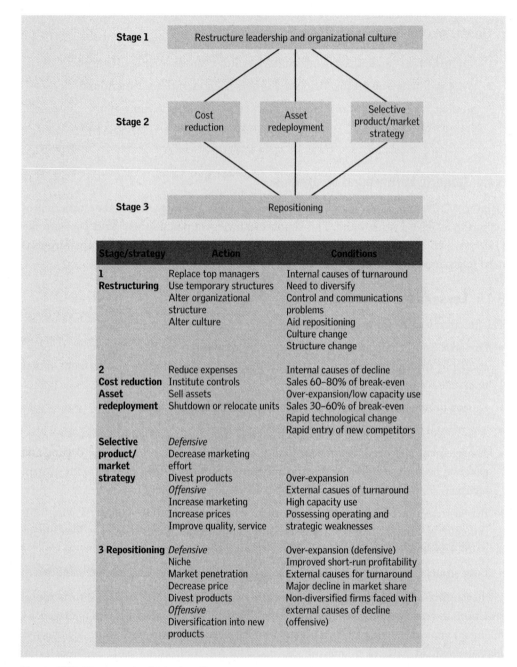

Stage/strategy	Action	Conditions
1 **Restructuring**	Replace top managers Use temporary structures Alter organizational structure Alter culture	Internal causes of turnaround Need to diversify Control and communications problems Aid repositioning Culture change Structure change
2 **Cost reduction** **Asset** **redeployment**	Reduce expenses Institute controls Sell assets Shutdown or relocate units	Internal causes of decline Sales 60–80% of break-even Over-expansion/low capacity use Sales 30–60% of break-even Rapid technological change Rapid entry of new competitors
Selective **product/** **market** **strategy**	*Defensive* Decrease marketing effort Divest products *Offensive* Increase marketing Increase prices Improve quality, service	 Over-expansion External casues of turnaround High capacity use Possessing operating and strategic weaknesses
3 Repositioning	*Defensive* Niche Market penetration Decrease price Divest products *Offensive* Diversification into new products	Over-expansion (defensive) Improved short-run profitability External causes for turnaround Major decline in market share Non-diversified firms faced with external causes of decline (offensive)

Figure 8.11 Five generic strategies of recovery
Source: adapted from Hoffman (1989) Vol. 14, No 3.

- A *proactive top-down* style of management has been advocated as necessary and effective. In other areas of strategy, you will encounter a Mintzbergian bottom-up view, or indeed a middle-up-down perspective.

- *Rapid change* is critical to survival in a turnaround, although currently dominant in strategic management is the processual (Whittington 1993) view, which emphasizes the complexity and difficulty of change, so that it is perceived as a long and involved process (cf. Pettigrew 1973).

- *Structure comes before strategy* in so far as changes are made for the company's very survival before the luxury of a strategy can be considered. This is contrary to the strongly held Chandlerian view that structure follows strategy.

In an increasingly turbulent environment, businesses have to concern themselves with adjusting far more rapidly than ever before. Turnarounds and the crisis literature then, while positioned at one extreme in the strategic management literature, are a useful counterpoint to the 'incremental' 'emergent' schools of thought.

8.5 Summary

This chapter began with the industry life cycle model as a means for displaying the need for strategies to change over time. This is an unexceptional proposition but the model does have a systematic thread running through it that shows a natural progression from innovation and differentiation through to eventual commoditization. With this progression goes a series of propositions about he way in which the firm should arrange its functional strategies and how it should expect to earn profits.

This is useful for setting out a framework within which change can be seen to be taking place. But we have chosen to place against this generic model three essentially practical and difficult circumstances. One concerns entrepreneurs and how they start businesses. The second is how firms gain entry to heavily defended marketplaces. Each of these practical examples brings out its own lesson. An the third is how businesses are turned round. The entrepreneurial lesson is that the magic of start-up success is almost certainly more to do with the characteristics of entrepreneurs themselves rather than with the merits of the economic case for the start-up (otherwise we would leave everything to venture capitalists and bankers). The essence of the turnaround is the ability to reconcile the cash flows of the company with competitive exigencies. This takes operational and practical skills but it also takes a sense beyond survivability to sustainability. Entry requires much more careful consideration of the longer term, how one strategy can displace an incumbent's strategy. This requires a mix of calculation and risk taking that is different in style from either the entrepreneur or the turnaround specialist. The personal characteristics of the decision makers are less obviously important and the time scales are usually more extended.

Thus strategy over time has many faces. The underlying discipline of aceing and defeating competition is always there but the mix of personal characteristics and capabilities can vary substantially. The strategic frameworks and models that we build give us a baseline and a context against which to work. In some situations the strategic calculus (as in entry) is prominent and must be constructed with some degree of precision. In other cases the strategic context shapes the situation but is not necessarily decisive. Our concern is to recognize these different situations both as managers and as strategists so that we can operate in the right manner.

Key terms

Conglomerates *314*

Co-specialized assets *311*

Corporate failure *313*

Creative destruction *311*

Diversification *314*

Entrepreneur *299*

Entrepreneurial strategy *306*

Entry point *310*

Expansion path *311*

Industry life cycle *292*

Intrapreneurship *303*

Mode of entry *310*

Natural strategic thrusts *296*

New entry strategies *307*

New-game strategy *310*

Product life cycle *292*

Sequential entry strategy *309*

Sharpbender *315*

Sustainability *298*

Turnaround strategies *313*

Recap questions and assignments

1 Choose an entrepreneur with whom you are familiar and comment on:
   ◆ What elements are responsible for his or her success so far.
   ◆ What characterizes his or her strategic style.
   ◆ Whether he or she will continue to lead his or her business to further successes.

   You might wish to consider two issues: (i) Does your entrepreneur have a capability that is transferable to another entrepreneurial situation? (ii) Can your entrepreneur's capability apply equally as well to his or her organization as it becomes significantly larger?

2 What are the corporate arguments for and against carrying out a turnaround?

3 What are the difficulties for management in recognizing that its firm is in a turnaround situation?

4 Referring to a turnaround situation with which you are familiar, comment on the critical ingredients that contributed to its success or failure.

Online
*Learning*Centre

When you have read this chapter, log on to the Online Learning Centre website at www.mcgraw-hill.co.uk/textbooks/mcgee to explore chapter-by-chapter test questions, further reading and more online study tools for strategy.

Case 1 **Stelios Haji-Ioannou**

Known simply as Stelios, easyGroup's founder has become the embodiment of the business. And like one of his heroes, Richard Branson, he's already created a thriving airline business and is now parlaying that brand into ventures as diverse as buses, pizzas and hotels. But can he replicate easyJet's success, asks Richard Cree.

Stelios Haji-Ioannou hands me a bright orange business card. Under his name it says 'serial entrepreneur'. There's little doubt that this is how he views himself. Whether others agree with him is less clear. To some he is a genial buffoon who stumbled onto a good idea for a budget airline and was lucky to be in the right place, at the right time, to exploit it. His lack of entrepreneurial flair, claim his detractors, has been exposed by a series of disastrous attempts to extend the easy brand into everything from cinemas to car rental to internet cafes (with pizzas, buses, cruises and hotels all on the way). To others he is a pioneering entrepreneur and role model, with a flair for launching businesses and the courage to know when to get others to manage them.

In reality he is a little bit of both. Behind a funny man facade lurks a serious intellect with a predilection for talking about risk management and asset utilisation. It is also worth remembering that for all his recent setbacks, he is founder and majority shareholder in two highly successful businesses (easyJet and Stelmar Tankers).

For his part, Stelios admits to still finding his feet: 'I'm learning an awful lot about the job of being a serial entrepreneur,' he says, as we settle into a bland side office at easyGroup's nondescript HQ. 'I have decided to be a serial entrepreneur – I don't want to be a Plc chairman and I don't want to be a beach bum yet. I'm unemployable, I don't want a salary, and I don't want to work for anyone else. I either have to pick one business and run it, which doesn't excite me, or I have to get into the habit of creating a lot of companies and as soon as I feel confident about them, hand them over to managers.'

Never scared to contradict himself, Stelios claims this learning includes both doing more himself and getting the right people to help him with each project. 'I've discovered that what I'm best at is doing the research and deciding on the business model,' he explains. 'As soon as I've found the business model, I hire a manager to run it. But when I start a company, rather than hiring an army of people to do research, the best way is to do it all myself. If there is someone who ought to learn everything there is to know about an industry, it's me. When I decided to get into the airline industry, I didn't hire consultants. I started plane spotting at airports and talking to people. The pre start-up expense of easyJet was half a million pounds.'

The latest ventures to benefit from this hands-on approach are his planned hotel and cruise ventures, easyDorm and easyCruise, which will both use a new type of modular room. 'By accident I came across some sophisticated techniques used on cruise ships for prefabricated cabins. That is the benefit of doing the research myself. I spent a day in Finland and as a result, I've latched on to something which will allow me to develop an interior that is cheap to manufacture, easy to clean and easy to maintain.'

And with that he is off again, outlining detailed plans for a central London hotel (from £5 a night) and cruises on a 'floating hotel on the Med' (from £29 a day). Both ventures are based on the concepts of yield management and demand-based pricing, internet distribution and unbundled services that he developed at easyJet.

It's an approach Stelios says leads to better returns on invested capital. 'The Four Seasons will get an average room rate higher than my hotel, but if you calculate return on capital employed, my ratios come out ahead. With little investment and a lower price than the competition, you can still make a profit. The brand allows you to offer very little and lower expectations but people still like it.'

Which leads naturally to a discussion of easyJet the budget airline that made his name in the UK. 'My claim to fame in the airline industry is that I am the first person to sell coffee on an aircraft,' he jokes. 'Coffee had never been sold before. In 1995 this orange plane appeared and when the first passengers got on board we said "here's a coffee, that's a pound". Ryanair wasn't doing that in 1995. Some people forget that O'Leary copied more things from easyJet than the other way round. It's Ryanair that learnt from easyJet and transformed itself into a successful company, rather than them being the pioneers.'

It's the sort of comment that you expect between rivals in the airline business, an industry which attracts more than its share of characters. Mark Pilling, managing editor of *Airline Business,* says part of the attraction of the industry is the opportunity for would-be Davids to take on industry Goliaths and win, especially in the era of budget airlines. 'To want to take on the big guys you need to be the sort of character who's reaching out for a dream, someone prepared to take risks,' he says. Pilling also points out that O'Leary and Stelios both copied the ideas of Herb Kelleher at Southwest Airlines.

According to Stelios, the attraction of airlines is all to do with gravity: 'The airline industry has always attracted loonies, starting from the Wright brothers. As an industry it attracts far more attention than it deserves in terms of its size and importance. The only way to explain it is this feeling of defying gravity. There have been other monumental inventions that are not as celebrated as flight. Look what happened on the retirement of Concorde last year. This magic of flight creates media and public attention and as a result it attracts very high-profile characters, because they are the ones who survive. It's an industry where you need to outshine your competitors and those who shout the loudest get the customers.'

And so publicity stunts have become part of the marketing mix for the industry. If such stunts appear a dangerous way of raising consumer awareness, it's a risk Stelios is happy to take, and one that he hasn't left behind. Last year he made a cheeky offer to Matt Barrett, chief executive of Barclays, to give him £100,000 on an easyMoney credit card if Barrett cut up his Barclaycard, after the Barclays man admitted to a government select committee that he didn't use his Barclaycard because it was too expensive. Having been voted by *Campaign* magazine as one of the best tactical ads of last year, Stelios shows no sign of stopping. But are there risks in tying the business so closely with his personality? Laura Haynes, director of brand consultancy Appetite, thinks so. 'Heroes have feet of clay and one mistake can have a disproportionate impact across all parts of the business. Having said that, building a business around a personality rather than a product or service makes it easier to stretch into new areas. Stelios is also doing something more subtle. His personality is part of the brand, but there are other aspects to it, such as the idea of taking on the big bad guys.'

For his part Stelios is unconcerned: 'It's the only way to start a business,' he states boldly. 'By lending my name to a start-up I improve its chances of success. How do easyJet share-holders feel about that risk? I spend my own money promoting the easy brand and that creates more customers for easyJet. The rewards outweigh the risks. If *my* reputation suf-fered irreversibly, easyJet would survive. It has a good product at a good price and is a hell of a company to dislodge.'

Although he says he started his business in the UK because of its favourable climate for business, he admits that the start-up climate is better still in the US. He says he is happy with the way the UK media have treated him, but gives the impression that the sniping gets to him. 'Given the size of our company, small mistakes get exaggerated. By any other standards easyCinema is a respectable cinema in Milton Keynes. OK it hasn't set the world alight, but then nobody in Milton Keynes has ever set the world alight.

'The attitude to failure in the US is much better for entrepreneurship than in the UK. Whether that has to do with bankruptcy laws or whether it has to do with the attitude and education of the media, I don't know. Most American entrepreneurs take pride in having had a couple of failures in their past. In the UK people are ashamed. If you expect people to take risks, you have to allow them to fail, otherwise they become too risk-averse. I take more risks than most people, but I temper my risk-taking to levels I can afford rather than risk bankruptcy.'

But the criticism most often levelled at Stelios and easyGroup is that his failures are racking up across a wide front. Is he worried about spreading himself too thinly, stretching across too many start-ups at once? 'The danger of spreading yourself too thin is always there,' he admits. 'But learning to control things and acting as a bottleneck is a skill I have to develop. I've created this brand, been through several start-ups already and it's unlikely I will focus for the rest of my life on one company. I like the idea of a portfolio. In some ways I'm spreading risk because I'm not going to place a life threatening bet on any of those indus-tries. I'll keep them small enough so I can manage them.'

Despite his positive outlook, he has begun to learn from recent mistakes, and change his approach to new ventures. Wherever possible, he is now getting others to share what he calls the execution risk.

'There was a shift in approach last year. I've started to think about how to manage the downside risk as well as managing the upside. I could hire people and learn to operate buses (for the soon-to-launch easyBus) but why? There are so many people who know how to do it. The best way to do it is to hire people from the industry, either licensing a company or hiring individuals, which is how easyJet started. We didn't have an airline certificate until 1998. It was flying for three years under other people's licences. It was a glorified travel agent. And that was how we wanted it.' He adds that having believed in this approach, he began to underestimate the risks involved in industries he knew nothing about. 'I'm going back to thinking that industry expertise has merit,' he says.

The two biggest companies created since easyJet – easyCar and easyInternet – have, according to Stelios, 'turned the corner'. Both have been reinvented, with new business models, new management teams ('by implication, perhaps the first management teams were not the best,' he says). In both cases he has hired an industry expert from the car rental business and from American Express's ATM business for the internet cafes. The objective means the same – getting the businesses strong enough to look after themselves. But where that used to mean flotation, Stelios is now happy to use licensing or franchise agreements. Last year he struck deals with Lloyds TSB to run the easyMoney credit card, and with Kellkoo to run the internet cost-price comparison engine easyValue. Not too familiar with the concept of modesty, Stelios explains that these moves are evidence he is following in the footsteps of his hero Richard Branson. 'It's the shape of things to come. I've built a brand and one of the ways you exploit a brand is by licensing deals.'

He has also become a big fan of franchising. 'I think franchising is an amazing tool. It's capitalism at its best. I'm using it for the internet cafes. I've made enough mistakes in that industry and I now have technology that works, I have a brand that people recognise. It's all about branding and then allowing local entrepreneurs to use the business method and name and reputation to make money. If your asset is your brand, the best thing you can do is sell it to entrepreneurs. I have a great rapport with these people. They are small versions of me and aspire to be me.'

With a delightful mix of metaphors he describes his style as 'leadership by the chin'. He repeats that he only wants to work in start-ups and will never be a manager of large groups of people or a big company. 'I wouldn't take the job of running General Electric and motivating 300,000 people I've never met,' he says. 'I think I can just about carry with me a small group of people into the unknown. I lead by example. If I expect people to work hard, I work hard. I can just about manage the 100 people I have in this room. As soon as a business is profitable and successful we kick it out.'

The problem is that he hasn't managed to 'kick out' a business since easyJet. So will the pressure to produce another success mean he loses his appetite for being a serial entrepreneur?

'I still have fun. I refuse to do anything else except have fun. As soon as chairing the board of a Plc became too claustrophobic for me or tedious I said, I'm out of here, let's hire someone else to do this job. You can never pretend to be anything other than what you really are. I like fun and humour. I'm the guy who tells the jokes at dinner parties. Having fun while doing business, poking fun at competitors through advertising, will always be my way.

Source: taken from *The Director*, February 2004.
© Reproduced with permission of *The Director* magazine.

Further reading and references

Arthur, D Little Inc. (1974) *A system for managing diversity*, Arthur D Little, Cambridge MA.

Arthur, D Little Inc. (1980) *A management system for the 1980s*, Arthur D Little, San Francisco.

Barrow, C (1991) *The New Small Business Guide*, 3rd edition, BBC Books, London.

Bhide, A (1996) 'The Questions Every Entrepreneur Must Ask', *Harvard Business Review*, **74**, **6**, pp. 120–30.

Bull, I, Thomas, H and Willard, G (1995) *Entrepreneurship: Perspectives on Theory Building*, Pergamon Press, Oxford.

Cascio, W (1993) 'Downsizing: What do we know? What have we learnt?' *Academy of Management Executive*, **7**, **1**, pp. 95–104.

Caves, RE and Porter, ME (1977) 'From Entry Barriers to Mobility Barriers: Conjectural Decisions and Contrived Deterrence to New Competition', *Quarterly Journal of Economics*, **75**, **4**, pp. 515–43.

Churchill, NC and Lewis, VL (1983) 'The Five Stages of Small Business Growth', *Harvard Business Review*, May/June, pp. 30–50.

Cooper, AC (1981) 'Strategic Management: New Ventures and Small Businesses', *Long Range Planning*, **14**, **5**, pp. 39–45.

Drucker, PF (1985) *Innovation and entrepreneurship*, Harper & Row, London.

Franko, LG (1987) 'Global Corporate Competition: Who's winning, Who's Losing and the R&D Factor as One Reason Why', *Strategic Management Journal*, **10**, **5**, pp. 449–74.

Gaedeke, RM and Tootelian, DH (1985) *Small Business Management*, 2nd edition, Glenview, London.

Gopinath, C (1991) 'Turnaround: Recognising decline and initiating intervention', *Long Range Planning*, **24**, **6**, pp. 96–101.

Grant, RM (2002) *Contemporary Strategy Analysis*, 4th edition, Blackwell Publishing, Oxford.

Greiner, LE (1972) 'Evolution and Revolution as Organizations Grow', *Harvard Business Review*, **50**, **4**, pp. 37–46.

Grimm, CM and Smith, KG (1997) *Strategy as Action: Industry Rivalry and Co-ordination*, South-Western College Publishing, An International Thompson Publishing Company.

Grinyer, P, Mayes, D and McKiernan, P (1988) *Sharpbenders*, Basil Blackwell, Oxford.

Hambrick, DC and Schecter, SM (1983) 'Turnaround Strategies for Mature Industrial Product Business Units', *Academy of Management Journal*, **26**, **2**, pp. 231–48.

Hodgetts, RM (1982) *Effective Small Business Management*, Academic Press, London.

Hofer, CW (1976) 'Turnaround Strategies', in WF Glueck (ed.) (1980) *Business Policy and Strategic Management*, 3rd edition, McGraw-Hill, Maidenhead, pp. 427–33.

Hoffman, RC (1989) 'Strategies for Corporate Turnarounds: What Do We Know About Them', *Journal of General Management*, **14**, **3**, Spring, pp. 46–66.

Hunt, J (1981) Managing People at Work: A Manager's Guide to Behaviour in Organizations, Pan, London.

Ingvar, D (1985) 'Memories of the future, an essay on the temporal organization of conscious awareness', *Human Neurobiology*, No 4.

Jarillo, JC (1988) 'On strategic networks', *Strategic Management Journal*, **19**, **1**, pp. 31–42.

Kanter, RM (1983) *The Change Masters: Corporate Entrepreneurs at Work*, Routledge, London.

Leibowitz, SJ and Margolis, SE (1999) Winners, Losers and Microsoft: Competition and Antitrust in High Technology, Oakland: The Independent Institute.

Li, PS (1993) 'Chinese investment and business in Canada: Ethnic entrepreneurship reconsidered', *Pacific Affairs*, 66.

McGee, J and Thomas, H (1994) 'Sequential Entry Paths and Industry Evolution', in H Daems and H Thomas (eds) *Strategic Groups, Strategic Moves and Performance*, Pergamon Press, Oxford, pp. 143–54.

McKiernan, P (1992) *Strategies of Growth*, Routledge, London.

Miller, D (1992) 'The Icarus Paradox', *Business Horizons*, **35**, **1**, pp. 454–67.

Mintzberg, H, Quinn, JB and Ghoshal, S (1998) *The Strategy Process*, Revised European Edition, Prentice Hall, Englewood Cliffs, NJ.

Oster, S (1990) *Modern competitive analysis*, Oxford University Press.

Penrose, ET (1959) *The Theory of the Growth of the Firm*, Basil Blackwell, Oxford.

Peters, TJ and Waterman, RH (1982) *In Search of Excellence*, New York, Harper and Row.

Pettigrew, A (1973) *The Awakening Giant: Continuity and Change at ICI*, Blackwell, Oxford.

Price, R (1996) 'Technology and strategic advantage', *Californian Management Review*, **38**.

Segal-Horn, S (ed.) (1998) *The Strategy Reader*, Blackwell Business, Oxford.

Schumpeter, JA (1942) *Capitalism, Socialism, and Democracy*, Harper & Row, New York.

Slatter, S (1984) *Corporate Recovery*, Penguin.

Steffens, J (1986) Entry Behaviour and Competition in the Evolution of the United States' Personal Computer Industry 1975–83', PhD thesis, University of London.

Stevenson, HH and Gumpert, DE (1985) 'The heart of entrepreneurship', *Harvard Business Review*, **63**, **2**, March/April, p. 85.

Teece, DJ (1987) 'Profiting From Technological Innovation: Implications for Integration, Collaboration, Licensing and Public Policy', in DJ Teece (ed.) (1987) *The Competitive Challenge*, Ballinger, Cambridge, MA.

Whittington, R (1993) *What is Strategy and Does it Matter?* Routledge, London.

Yip, GS (1982) 'Gateways to entry', *Harvard Business Review*, Sept–Oct, pp. 85–92.

Chapter 9

Corporate strategy: adding value in multi-business firms[1]

Introduction

This chapter concerns the portfolio of businesses held within a common, 'corporate' ownership, and the organization structure and management processes required to manage such portfolios. It covers the economic analysis of portfolios using, for example, BCG and McKinsey models, the concept and practice of parenting advantage, and the role of the corporate headquarters. It also covers the elements of the organization design and structure, and methods of resource allocation and control.

The importance of the study of corporate strategy stems from the fact that large businesses are increasingly *multi-businesses* and networks between businesses (for example, strategic alliances) are becoming more

Chapter contents

---

[1] This chapter is written jointly with Chris Smith.

common. This is true across the globe, from the *chaebols* of Korea and the *keiretsus* of Japan to the corporate sweep of America's GE and Europe's ABB. As such, it is not just ongoing competitive strategy – the long-term dynamics of serving customers better than the competition – that occupies the minds of the top managers and investors. It is also ongoing *corporate* strategy – the value gained from the mixture of businesses and how to manage those businesses to optimize that value. Corporate strategy for

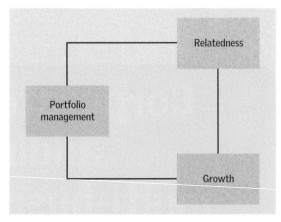

Figure 9.1 The three essential insights of corporate strategy

multi-business firms goes far beyond the traditional ideas of the choices of which industry/markets/products to be in. Figure 9.1 captures the three main ideas or insights that are fundamental to corporate strategy:

1   **Portfolio management** – the businesses that should make up the portfolio.

2   The growth idea – the way in which profitable growth is to be achieved through internal investment and/or external acquisitions.

3   **Relatedness** – the way in which the synergies between businesses are to be managed and exploited.

9.1 **The changing organizational structure**

The modern, hierarchical business enterprise arose in the 1850s in the United States and Europe, to administer the new railroad and telegraph companies. An organizational structure based on a split into functional responsibilities (the **U-form** – unitary form) was the norm at this time (*see* Figure 9.2).

Expanding size, however – particularly where expansion included diversification – compromised the effectiveness of the U-form.

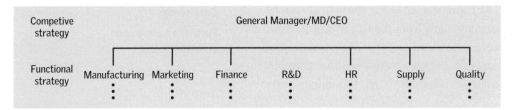

Figure 9.2 The U-form organization

The inherent weakness in the centralised, functionally departmentalised operating company ... became critical only when the administrative load on the senior executives increased to such an extent that they were unable to handle their entrepreneurial responsibilities efficiently. This situation arose when the operations of the enterprise became too complex and the problems of co-ordination, appraisal and policy formulation too intricate for a small number of top officers to handle both long-run, entrepreneurial, and short-run, operational administrative activities. (Chandler, 1962, p. 299)

To overcome such problems, the large American companies Du Pont, General Motors, Jersey Standard and Sears Roebuck pioneered a movement to an innovative organizational form in the early 1920s. This innovation, which became known as the 'multidivisional' or **M-form**, divided tasks and responsibilities into semi-autonomous operating units (profit centres) organized on brand, product or regional lines (see Figure 9.3).

After slow early growth, the spread of the M-form increased dramatically following the Second World War. In 1949 less than a quarter of the Fortune 500 were divisionalized. This had risen to just over a half in 1959. By 1969 only one-fifth of companies in the top 500 were not divisionalized (Hill 1994). Similar trends have been evident in Europe and the UK and today the multidivisional form is the most prevalent organizational structure in large companies in Western economies.

The basic reason for its success was simply that it clearly removed the executives' responsible for the destiny of the entire enterprise from the more routine operational activities, and so gave them time, information, and even more psychological commitment for long-term planning and appraisal ... Thus the new structure left the broad strategic decisions as to the allocation of existing resources and the acquisitions of new ones in the hands of a top team of generalists. Relieved of operating duties and tactical decisions, a general executive was less likely to reflect the position of just one part of the whole. (Chandler, 1962, pp. 309–310)

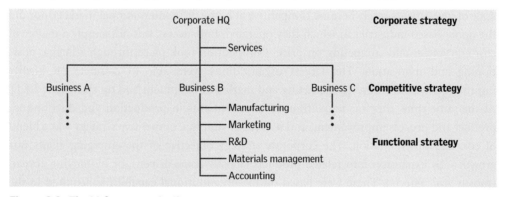

Figure 9.3 The M-form organization

The M-form has several positive attributes. It enables business managers to maximize economies of specialization, by allowing them to focus on their products and markets, while freeing corporate managers from the distractions of day-to-day operations. It makes it easy for corporate management to measure and compare the performance of business units through financial statements, and facilitates the addition (acquisition) or deletion (divestment) of businesses. On top of this, the stand-alone business ethos fits well with Western values of individualism and accountability, and encourages the development of autonomous general managers.

Alfred Chandler, the eminent business historian, chronicled the rise of the M-form organizations in the USA in his celebrated book *Strategy and Structure* (1962). He also provided a telling and powerful argument for the benefits of size in papers such as 'The Enduring Logic of Industrial Success' (1990a, 1990b). He argued that economics of scale and scope were the motive power behind large organizations. These enable large plants to produce at much lower costs than small ones (*scale*). Large plants use many of the same raw and semi-finished materials and intermediate production processes to make a variety of different products (*scope*). To capitalize on the new, larger scale of manufacturing, investment firms needed to make two further, related sets of investment. The first was to create national, then international, marketing and distribution organizations (both scale and scope effects). The second was to develop new management teams. The lower/middle levels were to co-ordinate flow of products through production and distribution. The top level was to co-ordinate and monitor current operations and to plan and allocate resources for future activities. The new levels of investment thus require an integrated and balanced economic and managerial infrastructure to ensure constant flow of product and high-capacity utilization. In simple economic terms the scale and scope driven savings in operations have to be balanced in part by higher administrative and managerial costs. But these too offer scale and scope benefits as long as volumes are maintained.

Chandler took the argument further. He observed that first movers quickly dominated their industries and continued to do so (for decades). Those who failed to make the right scale of investments rarely became competitive at home or in international markets, nor did the home-based industries in which they operated. But success was not simply a matter of cost efficiencies and competing on price. Competition took place through strategic positioning and innovation. The largest organizations were able to compete on quality improvement, innovations in marketing and market development and on systematic R&D. At the same time, they made continuous improvements in production and distribution, product and process improvement, and sources of supply. Competitive strategy was a blend of cost and differentiation. The corporate strategy objective of the emerging giants was growth – by expansion into related products (mostly *scope*-driven), or by moving abroad (mostly *scale* effects). These were based on the organizational capabilities acquired in the process of domestic oligopolistic competition. There were also some horizontal movements

Diversification strategy	
Single:	core business > 95% of turnover
Dominant:	core business 70–95% of turnover
Related:	diversified > 30% but market/tech linkages
Unrelated:	diversified > 30% but weak linkages

Organizational structure	
Functional:	centralized around key functions
Functional holding:	core centralized around key functions; remainder decentralized
Holding:	highly decentralized: little central control
Multidivisional:	centralized strategically: decentralized operations

Figure 9.4 Strategy and structure

(acquisitions) and some vertical integration to control material supplies or distribution outlets.

This is the history of the emergence of international oligopolies, founded initially on scale and scope advantages in production and distribution but enhanced and secured by scale and scope effects in marketing, R&D, supply management and organization. However, large is not always logical. The giants can and do stagnate, with Ford Motor Co. providing the leading example in the 1920s. In its case the direct competition between two giants, Ford and GM, was to leave at least one of them injured. In post-war years, particularly the 1960s, the compulsion for growth led companies to much broader based diversification. This became known as conglomerate style diversification and was, and is, highly controversial.

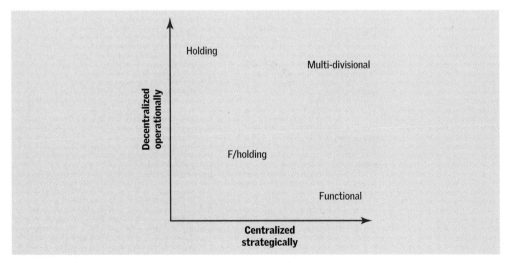

Figure 9.5 Structural types

The economic argument for large size required an organization structure that was capable of managing both scale effects (which require specialization and depth) and scope effects (which need variety and breadth). The divisionalized corporation, M-form in style, was clearly appropriate for the task in comparison to the earlier U-form. Figures 9.4 and 9.5 illustrate the strategy–structure choices. The term *U-form* has given way to *functional*, emphasizing the focus on functional specialization as the source of managerial economies. Figure 9.5 indicates the value of the divisionalized (M-form) in that it allows for both operational decentralization as well as strategic direction.

The relationship between strategy and structure has been established for a long time. The concept has been broadened to include other variables, with a further extension that a successful 'fit' between these elements and corporate strategy is essential for success. McKinsey and Company introduced the 7S Model (see Waterman (1982) and Waterman *et al.* (1980)) with seven broad areas that need to be integrated together. The seven variables are structure, systems, style, staff, skills, shared values, and strategy. Figure 9.6 shows how the McKinsey 7S model can be applied to the M-form organization, demonstrating the nature of the fit between its different components. In Chapter 10 we will show how the new network form of organization can be described by the 7S model.

However, there are also manifest drawbacks. Because corporate managers are free from operational distractions, they also tend to get out of touch with business and divisional issues and hence, are reliant on the input of their politically aware general managers. The clear structural split does not necessarily mean there is a clear split of responsibilities, and confusion often reigns as to which level is accountable for various outcomes or processes. Further complications arise due to the (rational) tendency of business units to compete

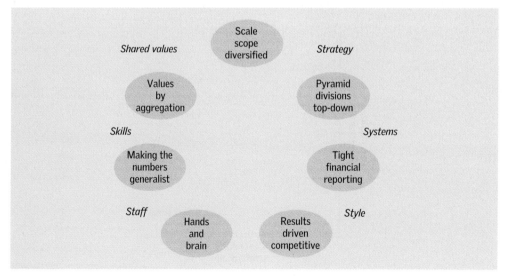

Figure 9.6 The classic M-form

rather than co-operate with each other for the limited resources available. This leads to general managers 'selling' their business needs to the corporate level, with the resultant blurring of reality that selling frequently entails. As will be discussed in more detail below, perhaps the most significant problem with the M-form is its tendency to impede the development of trans-firm competencies.

9.1.1 Issues

Given these opposing dynamics and their prevalence, the multidivisional firm has attracted the interest of academics and management authors. Two major questions have been the focus of research and writing:

1 *What is the additional value generated by such firms?*

This is an economic question which addresses what value is inherent in having a group of potentially stand-alone businesses under one management. Writings on this question are found mainly in academic journals and focus particularly on the value of groupings of *related* businesses and the associated issue of *synergy*.

2 *How are they best managed?*

This is an organizational/strategic question which addresses how value is optimized and, in particular, what is the role of the corporate head office in all this. This question addresses what is known as 'corporate strategy' in the strategic management literature. While 'corporate strategy' is still used by some in an all-encompassing sense, most authors now identify 'corporate strategy' with multi-business firms. Porter's (1987) view is typical:

> *Corporate strategy,* **the overall plan for a diversified company** ... *concerns two different questions: what businesses the corporation should be in and how the corporate office should manage the array of business units.* (Porter, 1987, p. 43, emphasis added)

Thus, corporate strategy is concerned with the choice of industries to compete in, the setting of an organizational context for the operations of the component business units, and managing the relationships between those businesses.

9.2 Theory and concepts

9.2.1 The inherent value

The M-form originated as a response to the complexity of large U-form organizations. Its continued existence as the dominant structure of large companies, however, suggests that it possesses ongoing 'ecological' advantages over other organizational forms. It has been proposed that its ubiquity is driven by the status, power and material hunger of managers –

a bigger company means more benefits for the top people. The ecological argument still suggests that, even if managerial greed were a significant driver, competitive forces in free markets would select out these forms if they were sufficiently inefficient relative to other structures. (*Note*: 'Ecologists' might suggest that we should 'watch this space', as the time frame in which the M-form has existed is very short in population ecology terms.)

Writers in economics and strategic management are agreed that the *economic* logic of multi-business corporations, and hence a potential reason for their proliferation, is that the whole is worth more than the sum of its parts:

$$V_c = A_s + B_s + C_s + M_c$$

where:

V_c	=	the value of the corporation
A_s, B_s, C_s	=	the respective values of the stand-alone businesses A, B and C
M_c	=	the total net[2] value of corporate membership, that is, *membership benefits*

so: $V_c > A_s + B_s + C_s$ by the value of M_c

In many cases M_c has proven to be negative. When this situation prevails, the break-up of the corporation is a financially attractive strategy, as proved by the corporate raiders – asset strippers of the 1980s.

M_c has different sources. Organizational gain, derived from the splitting of strategy and operations, has a value-logic grounded in managerial efficiency and focus. This traditional rationale, allied to the benefits of size and scale, seems an adequate explanation of the *reorganization* of growing companies from (inefficient) U-form to (efficient) M-form. However, this argument does not explain why the total value of the component businesses can be higher under a corporate umbrella than if they were stand-alone. (*Note*: This is a very important issue for investors, who are free to invest directly in the stand-alone businesses without the necessity of a corporate layer.)

Theorists in the general area of what is known as **transaction cost economics** (TCE)[3] offer some of the most persuasive ideas about the potential added value of the M-form. They propose two major categories of benefit: *governance* and *scope* advantages.

---

[2] The idea of 'net' value acknowledges that there are a variety of 'costs' of membership. These are more than the financial overheads of corporate staff etc. Examples of other costs include business time and resource invested in corporate or inter-business activities; the potential loss of entrepreneurial drive, as market incentives are replaced by more focused, internal rewards that encourage 'satisficing' behaviour; the containment of business activities to a more narrow product, process or geographic range than might be attainable in stand-alone mode; the sustained cross-subsidizations of businesses that, in a stand-alone capacity, would be bankrupt etc.

[3] TCE breaks with neo-classical economics by dropping several of the latter's (unreal) assumptions. In particular, it concerns itself with the effects of the costs of interactions (transactions) between businesses, between businesses and customers, etc.

Governance

Under this category, the corporate office takes the role of a more informed and involved investor. Unlike arm's-length investors, it is fully knowledgeable about the businesses via direct reporting and auditing mechanisms and can pressure business managers for improved performance, while paying market-rate salaries. In a stand-alone business, a manager can take advantage of the fact that he or she controls the information flow to the investment community and can hide the true nature of any problems. In a multi-business firm, the corporate office has all the necessary information and can sanction or replace managers of underperforming units. The corporate office also has an overview that the business manager lacks, and can thus add further information and insight to his or her decisions. In stand-alone units, business managers can maximize what has been called 'on-the-job consumption', for example, making (unnecessary) spouse-accompanied weeklong, visits to desirable locations, flying first class and staying in five-star hotels. The additional corporate layer can police and prevent such dissipation of shareholders' funds. (*Note*: This 'advantage' begs the obvious question of who guards the guards. In the light of increasingly spectacular returns to directors of public companies, this is a question worth asking.)

Scope

As well as potentially dealing with the tensions between owners and managers through governance mechanisms, the multi-business organization is argued to have value-enhancing properties in that it can facilitate economies of scope. *Related* businesses (those with similar markets/technologies/processes) can share specialized physical capital, knowledge and managerial expertise. The sharing process is overseen and controlled and disputes are resolved by corporate management. With stand-alone businesses, such sharing is problematic. Potential problems include ongoing haggling, the risk of one partner exploiting the trust of the other, the risk of being let down, and the tendency for partners to try to benefit more than their input would warrant.[4] Under normal circumstances, stand-alone businesses attempt to control these problems through formal contracts and a 'trading relationship'. However, such sharing is not amenable to formal contract, particularly in the case of specialized organizational knowledge embodied in people. Tacit components, team embeddedness and the uncertainty of its value make such learning particularly difficult to trade.

It is through scope economies between related businesses that corporate *synergies* (the total being more than the sum of the parts) are hypothesized to be most attainable. A relatively recent expression of scope economies has been the popularization of the concept of *core competences* that are 'the collective learning in the organization, especially how to coordinate diverse production skills and integrate multiple streams of technology' (Prahalad and

---

[4] This is an example of the 'free-rider' problem and is familiar to students undertaking group work, when one member seems to get out of most of the duties, but shares in the overall assessment.

Hamel, 1990, p. 82). The importance of core competences for multi-business firms is that they can '*span businesses* and products within a corporation. Put differently, powerful core competencies *support several* products or *businesses.*'

Prahalad and Hamel (1990), emphasizing the importance of trans-business capabilities, assert that core competencies are the 'central subject of corporate strategy' (p. 220) and that multi-business companies should see themselves as a 'portfolio of competences' (p. 221) – as well as a portfolio of products and services, that is. Economies of scope are the nub of corporate strategy and the fundamental rationale for the M-form company.

9.3 Managing the multi-business firm

9.3.1 The strategy–structure balance

We have seen from earlier chapters that, at the level of the business, strategy has three key dimensions: competitive advantage (how to compete), the key resource allocation decisions at the business level, and the organization of the business. At the corporate level there is a parallel concern with resource allocation decisions, and with organization structure and process. But the distinguishing characteristic of the multi-business firm is that at the centre it is concerned with what businesses to be in – the portfolio question. The answer is, of course, contingent on the nature of competitive advantages, but decisions about the portfolio are taken at corporate level whereas the responsibility for securing competitive advantage is at the business level.

The economics of corporate strategy revolve around three issues (see Figure 9.1):

1 The characteristics of the portfolio expressed as its overall return and its overall risk. This allows for gains from the statistical nature of pooled variances, which means that imperfectly correlated risks of the individual businesses result in lower overall risk. This is on the basis of avoiding having all one's eggs in the same basket.[5]

2 How synergies between businesses are captured – the idea of relatedness.

3 The growth ambitions of the firm and how these are to be achieved by internal investment and/or expansion.

There are insights and traps attached to each of these. Portfolio analysis arrays the strengths and weaknesses of each business. In particular, the sources of cash and profit can be established and investment needs specified. Thus it is possible to assess for the portfolio what are its cash flow and profit characteristics in relation to its overall risk. However, if taken too literally portfolio analysis can focus excessively on eliminating unprofitable,

---

[5] We should note that the gains from diversification may mitigate against disaster but by themselves don't promote competitive advantage.

low-potential businesses and expanding high-potential businesses without attention to any underlying synergies and complementarities.

Relatedness determines whether interdependencies between businesses can create value and competitive advantage or whether each business should be treated on its own merits. The trap is that poor-performing businesses should not be maintained from 'overall strength' without strong evidence of value potential from relatedness.

Sensible growth objectives and analysis identifies how resources can be deployed to maintain a balance between investment, cash flow and profits over time. Proper analysis prevents misdirected growth that focuses on growth for its own sake, leading to inappropriate timing and falling into cash traps.

Corporate organization has to be consistent with the economics of the strategy. This too can be described in three parts:

1   Definition of division and business unit boundaries.

2   The intended lateral integration and co-ordination between business units.

3   The vertical relationships between corporate tasks and roles and line operations – the corporate–business interface.

Business unit boundaries and groupings of businesses (divisions or sectors) can be the natural and powerful way to exploit relatedness opportunities. Superior performance frequently requires that businesses be properly focused on relevant markets – that the boundaries should be drawn correctly. New boundaries should be drawn[6] when the value of increasing the focus (narrowing the scope) exceeds the cost of lost relatedness benefits, and vice versa.

The corporate–business interface sets out authority and accountability in the firm. Three particular styles are commonly observed (see the discussion below). **Strategic planning** involves corporate executives in defining and monitoring corporate and business strategies. It is most appropriate for capital-intensive operations and highly interrelated businesses. **Strategic control** involves corporate executives in influencing business-level strategies and monitoring financial results. It is a 'loose-tight' approach. **Financial control** decentralizes control of business strategy to the business and relies solely on financial control at the corporate level. It is deemed to be most appropriate for conglomerate-like strategies.

Integration mechanisms are used to balance choices made on boundaries and on the corporate–business interface. The formality of the latter two can be supplemented by less formal arrangements that can pick up on related possibilities not captured within business boundaries and neglected by the corporate level need to have strong vertical controls. Therefore, self-interested lateral co-operation has a natural place in complementing the formal organizational arrangements. More formal lateral mechanisms include centres of

---

[6]   This is often called 'reorganization'.

excellence, people transfers, transfer pricing systems, special study teams, lead business arrangements and internal consulting. Vertical mechanisms are also possible such as intermediate levels of organization and arrangements of cross-functional authority. Strategic control styles of management typically require more explicit processes for lateral integration than other forms of control.

9.3.2 Corporate strategies

Adding value through buying and selling businesses has been one form of corporate strategy. The corporate centre acts as a funds investor and seeks opportunities to buy companies that are undervalued by the market and then waits until the inherent value is recognized and sells them on at a profit. A more active role than this entails buying companies that are underperforming, and hence are available at a relatively low price, and acting to improve performance and selling price. A variant of this was undertaken by the so-called 'raiders' and 'asset strippers' of the 1980s, who bought conglomerates and then sold off the component parts for a total price far in excess of the overall purchase price. Opportunities to profit from this mode of corporate strategy are now rare, as the general market is more attuned to such opportunities, as are potential targets.[7]

Porter (1987) terms this corporate buy-and-sell approach *portfolio management*. The Ashridge researchers Goold, Campbell and Alexander (1994) call it *corporate development*, and include the reshaping of existing businesses by amalgamation or division and the creation of new businesses by internal venturing. Both sets of authors agree that this is no longer a viable value-generating corporate strategy, as the market now anticipates the potential undervaluation and reflects this in the (speculative) premium in the price paid. Such premiums ensure that profitable acquisitions must now be based on better management of the acquired business, or other forms of synergistic benefits of belonging to the new corporation.

In discussing the aspect of corporate strategy that is to do with the management of the multi-business organization, Porter (1987) identifies three organizational/process concepts of corporate strategy: *restructuring*, *sharing activities* and *transferring skills*:

◆ **Restructuring** occurs when businesses are acquired with the specific intent of achieving value by active intervention and improvement. The centre needs the capability to effect such transformation and thus it exerts strong direct influence on business performance and processes. In Porter's view, once restructuring has been successful, the business should then be sold to capture the new value, unless it benefits in some way from ongoing membership of the corporation.

---

[7] The trend for conglomerates to become focused on fewer 'core' businesses was a consequence of such threats.

- **Sharing activities** is a value activity that is based on the component businesses using the same facilities, services, processes or systems and thereby reaping utilization, learning curve (scope) scale or differentiation benefits. Management is based on interrelationships, but not necessarily interdependencies between the business units, that is, the shared facility can be a corporate-level activity.

- **Transferring skills** is managing ongoing interrelationships between the businesses. In this case, the corporate centre actively fosters the sharing of expertise or skills among the businesses, even though they might have different value chains. As with 'sharing activities', the centre is actively involved, but this time it develops and promotes linkages and interdependencies between business units.

Goold *et al.* (1994) have spent a considerable time focusing on the multi-business company and how its corporate strategy adds (or subtracts)[8] value. Consistent with the well-known 'competitive advantage', they coined the intuitively attractive term *parenting advantage* to denote the additional value that an insightful parent company can add to its component businesses through appropriate orientation and management. They suggest three requisites for parenting advantage:

1 the corporate advantage must translate into more competitive advantage in at least one business, or membership of each business in the portfolio must create extra value somewhere in the portfolio;

2 must create more value than the cost of the corporate overhead;

3 must add more value than any other possible parent otherwise the market for corporate control might eventually challenge your ownership and parenting credentials.

Goold *et al.* (1994) also identify three classes of value-adding corporate strategy: *stand-alone influence, functional and services influence* and *linkage influence,* which parallel Porter's categories. They emphasize that these are not either/or choices but can all be in operation at the same time. Figure 9.7 illustrates the range of sources of value creation.

- *Stand-alone influence* is the value created by the influence on the individual business strategy and performance. The major focus is on vertical linkages, mainly between the CEO and the MDs of the businesses. In this category, successful corporate parents have to overcome the '10% versus 100% paradox' – the idea that part-time, organizationally removed managers can enhance the performance of the business's dedicated management.

- *Functional and services influence* is again a vertical process, with the focus on adding value through the influence of a range of centrally controlled staff functions. These may replace

---

[8] This is more than a technical parenthesis, as the general thrust of their findings is that value destruction is the norm in multi-business companies.

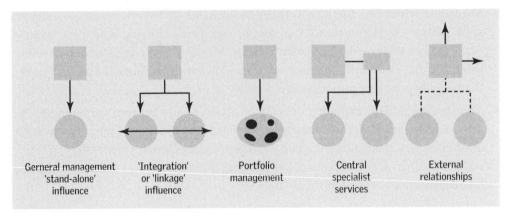

Figure 9.7 Sources of value creation

or augment those already in place in the businesses. The problem the corporate centre faces here is offering a higher value-added service than specialist outsiders – the 'beating the specialist' paradox.

◆ *Linkage influence* aims to increase value through the relationships between the businesses. The focus is on horizontal processes and incorporates both the 'shared activities' and 'transfer of skills' categories of Porter. It is difficult to explain, however, why the managers of the businesses would not do this themselves if extra value would accrue as a result, that is, the 'enlightened self-interest' paradox.

The general management influence is generally reckoned to be the key (only) justification for long-term survival of conglomerates. Linkages, portfolio effects and specialist capabilities are all part of the synergy and relatedness themes. The external relationship management theme harks back to much earlier thinking about the role of the top team and the board. This maintains that the specialist skills at the top are about understanding the external environment and finding ways to cope with it and to position against it. Modern thinking has focused very much on the internal management and dynamics of the organization, perhaps to a fault.

Case box: **Benetton: the other colours**

Diversifying from fashion into motorways and restaurants has paid off for the Benetton family

Almost 50 years ago Luciano Benetton came up with an idea that took the world of fashion by storm. His bright, casual sweaters would be dyed after they had been knitted so that stores could restock faster with the most popular colours. From artisanal origins in Ponzano Veneto, a small town about 30 kilometres (19 miles) north of Venice, the shops of the United Colors of Benetton spread across Europe and America, promoted by provocative and controversial advertising.

Benetton on the road
Edizione Holding's main businesses

	2003 sales €bn	2003 profit before tax, €m	Edizione's share*, %	Edizione's share of market cap*, €bn
Autogrill	3.143	98	56.7	1.71
Autostrade	2.570	532	31.2	2.94
Benetton Group	1.859	165	67.1	1.09

Source: Company reports: Thomson Datastream   *On August 31st 2004

But times change and colours fade. Early this year, there were whispers that the Benetton family might be in financial trouble. The figures, though, show something rather different: Edizione Holding, the Benettons' holding company, owns investments with a market value, after deducting debts, of around €6 billion ($7.3 billion). Diversifying out of the business that the Benettons knew well, the fashion industry, has worked surprisingly well for one of Italy's best-known family concerns.

The Benettons' success in clothing relied on a supply chain of outsourced production tied together with a computerised logistics system, which was well ahead of its time. But by the late 1980s, imitators and competitors were catching up. Firms such as Sweden's H&M and Spain's Zara have recently given the Italian company a tough time in high streets and shopping malls.

Rumours about financial worries, however, seem to have been prompted by the Benettons' big spending on other businesses. Not content to stick to its knitting, the family has invested heavily over the past ten years in Italian privatisations, usually as part of a consortium.

In 1994, Edizione Holding was the leading partner in a consortium that acquired Autogrill, an Italian motorway-catering business. Then came Autostrade, the largest operator of toll motorways in Italy. Stakes in municipal energy utilities, the refurbishment of railway stations, Turin's airport and Telecom Italia followed. Over two-thirds of the Benettons' wealth—they are the third-richest family in Italy—is now in Autogrill and Autostrade (see table).

Idyllic Ponzano Veneto seems a long way from the centres of power. 'We never needed to get close to politicians. I personally feel distant from politics. We like the idea of being in the countryside,' explains Mr Benetton. Yet this aversion to politicians did not hamper the family's diversification efforts much.

Edizione Holding now has a 56.7% stake in Autogrill, which became a global concern in 1999 with the acquisition of Host Marriott Services, an American catering firm. It is, says Gianni Mion, Edizione Holding's managing director, 'a nice business, well-managed and self-standing'. North America is now Autogrill's most important market; it accounted for over half of revenues in 2003. And the group's tills at airports were nearly as busy as those on the motorways.

The privatisation of Autostrade in 2000 presented another opportunity. Edizione Holding owns 60% of the consortium that obtained control of Autostrade by buying 30%. Last year, the consortium raised its stake in Autostrade to 62% with a public tender offer at €10 per share; in July it sold 10% of this at almost €16 per share, leaving it with virtually no debt.

Why have investors been so impressed? Autostrade's revenues are regulated, so tight management of costs is essential. Mr Mion says that Autostrade's spending on items such as road surfacing, guard rails and maintenance is now much lower per kilometre than was envisaged at the time of privatisation. Yet pleasing investors has proved easier than managing complaints about conflicts of interest. Autostrade grants concessions to restaurants and petrol stations on its motorways and, inevitably, Autogrill pitches for some of them. Although a firm of independent consultants handles the tendering process, there have been complaints that the process favours Autogrill. Magistrates are investigating these complaints, but Mr Mion appears unflustered, insisting that both firms have behaved correctly.

While Autogrill and Autostrade have been excellent investments, that cannot be said about all of the Benetton family's diversifications. Moves into sports equipment (Nordica ski-boots and Rollerblade skates) were a disappointment. These businesses were finally ditched in 2003. 'I like to keep the mistakes in mind,' says Mr Mion. The group did not understand the sports equipment business, he admits. More significant than the losses was the distraction for management.

There is another mistake that Mr Mion should keep in mind. In 2001, the Benettons joined forces with Marco Tronchetti Provera, the boss of Pirelli, to take over Telecom Italia through Olimpia, a highly leveraged company. That has not paid off either: Edizione Holding's 16.8% stake in Olimpia is now worth only half its cost of €1.16 billion. 'It is an investment that gives less satisfaction,' Mr Benetton remarks dryly. But at least the success of Autostrade and Autogrill means he can afford this blooper. Operating toll motorways and selling pizzas may be rather dull compared with the glitz of the fashion world, but at least they promise a steady cashflow for the next generation of Benettons.

Source: 'The other colours', *The Economist*, 9 September 2004.
© The Economist Newspaper Limited, London (9 September 2004).

Questions for discussion

1 Assess the extent to which Benetton has diversified its activities; for example, what proportion of its total revenue is taken by the core (original) business?

2 What synergies are there between these lines of business?

3 How would you judge whether these investments have been worthwhile?

9.3.3 **Corporate styles**

In an earlier study, Goold and Campbell (1987) examined high-performing corporations and concluded that the *style* of the parent is an important factor in the level of performance achieved. They examined the extent to which management styles varied along the dimensions of *planning influence* (that is, the extent to which the corporate level became involved in the strategic and operating planning of the business) and *control influence* (that is, the extent to which the businesses were held to budgetary and operational targets) (*see* Figure 9.8).

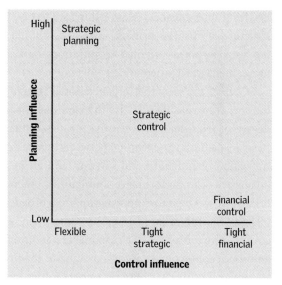

Figure 9.8 Parenting styles
Source: Goold and Campbell, 1987.

Three styles seemed to stand out. In *financial control* companies (for example, BTR), the centre allowed a high degree of strategic and operational autonomy to the businesses (low planning influence). The budget, however, was sacrosanct and any slippage from planned performance needed swift correction, if it were not to mean the curtailment of the career of the responsible GM (high control influence). At the other end of the continuum, *strategic planning* companies (for example, ICI) involved themselves on an ongoing basis in the strategic planning and management of the businesses (high planning control). They were more flexible if strategic contingencies caused operational performance to slip against budgeted targets, that is, the budget was a reflection of the strategy (low control influence). In between these two extremes were the *strategic control* companies.[9]

This work on styles is consistent with the view that optimizing corporate strategy is contingent on the appropriate organizational structures, systems, processes, etc.

> *Corporate strategies which predominantly use one or other of these three roles to realise the value inherent in their resources should, according to contingency theory, align their structure, systems and procedures according to those roles.* (Collis, 1991c, p. 7)

In accordance with this view, corporations do not need large corporate staffs if they are relying on a stand-alone influence role, whereas a co-ordinated and integrated staff is

---

[9]   In a summary of this work in their 1994 text, the authors conclude that there is a continuing movement away from the *financial control* to the strategic *planning/control styles.*

needed if inter-business relationships are to be a major source of value. In a similar way the structure of business manager incentives should vary, with group-based incentives needed for 'inter-business'-oriented corporations and stand-alone incentives appropriate for the more 'managerial' orientations.

As well as the view that organizational structure, processes etc. should be contingent on the corporate role, there is also the view that the optimal corporate role is contingent on the degree of *relatedness* between the business units. To realize economies of scope (synergy) from relatedness, *co-operation* between businesses is required. This leads to increased centralization of functions and systems, and an increase in integrating mechanisms between businesses. The performance ambiguities inherent in sharing facilities and functions are tackled by seeking more information on a broader, less financial, range of indicators, and by business incentives based on group rather than individual performance. A value-enhancing, co-operative form may be a sustainable parenting advantage for a firm, as its unique history and social context make it idiosyncratic to the firm and, thus, more difficult to imitate.

Unrelated businesses have no opportunities for increased value from economies of scope and are argued to benefit from M-form membership due to governance benefits (Williamson 1975). Within such a framework, the corporate office of the M-form takes on the role of informed investor and runs the businesses on a *competitive* basis, as stand-alone entities that are rivals for capital which is allocated on a 'best-use' basis, consistent with external capital markets. Performance incentives are based on unambiguous, financial outputs. A summary of the proposed relationships between inherent value, basic corporate strategy and organizational factors is shown in Table 9.1.

Table 9.1 Comparing co-operative and competitive strategic orientations

| | Source of inherent (economic) value | |
	Economies of scope (related businesses)	Governance (unrelated businesses)
Basic corporate strategy:	Co-operative multidivisional	Competitive multidivisional
Operating and business-level strategic decisions:	Some centralization of critical functions	Complete decentralization
Inter-business integrating mechanisms:	Moderate to extensive	Non-existent
Business performance appraisal:	Mix of subjective and objective criteria	Primary reliance on objective financial criteria
Business incentive schemes:	Linked to corporate performance	Based on business performance only

Source: adapted from Hoskisson *et al.*, 1993, pp. 269–98.

In contrast to the optimism of multiple, coexistent corporate roles expressed by Porter (1987) and Goold *et al.* (1994), Hill (1994) points out that the 'radical differences' between these two types of M-form are such that:

> *it may be difficult for diversified firms to simultaneously realise economic benefits from economies of scope and efficient governance ... Competitive and co-operative organizations have different internal configurations with regard to centralisation, integration, control practices and incentive schemes. As a result **the internal management philosophies of co-operative and competitive organizations are incompatible.** (Hill, 1994, pp. 312–13, emphasis added)*

This means that co-operative and competitive philosophies are different strategies with different organizational and managerial arrangements. Thus, if an M-form firm comprises a set of businesses, some of which are related and others which are not, it is faced with an economic and organizational dilemma. One resolution of this dilemma is to divest units and focus on a *core* business grouping.

Another resolution is through the creation of another organizational level – the *division*, into which all the businesses related in a particular way (for example, all those in the automotive components industry) are placed. In this sense, the division becomes an internal (quasi) corporation and the divisional-level managers can focus on optimizing the relatedness of their component businesses.

9.4 **Practical frameworks and applications**

The M-form seemed a boon to managers as an apparent answer to the complexities of size, growth and diversity. The intuitive value of divisionalization was further boosted during the 1960s, as diversification became a strategic imperative in its own right and acquisition and merger became a major mechanism for growth. Emboldened by shareholder approval, and armed with increasingly all-encompassing definitions of synergy[10] and faith in the transferability of general management skills, companies embarked on a diversifying buying spree.

In many cases, senior managers had no previous occupational experience of the operations and/or markets of the businesses that they bought and subsequently 'controlled'. Seemingly, however, the corporate office had no need to fully understand operational details, as this was the domain of the general managers of the business units. While demand exceeded supply, industries experienced stable growth and, hence, even relatively inefficient firms were able to prosper. By the early 1970s, a more complex and turbulent economic environment highlighted the unwieldy nature of many conglomerates. Senior managers sought different rationales and tools to manage their set of businesses. The new portfolio planning techniques and most notably, the growth-share matrix (Figure 9.9) developed by the Boston Consulting Group (BCG) seemingly met their needs. (*See* Day, 1977 for a critical review.)

---

[10] For example, Goold *et al.* (1994) cite the example of the British Oxygen Company (now BOC) buying a manufacturer of frozen pizza on the synergistic basis that gases were used in the freezing process.

Based on the cost-reducing effects of experience curve dynamics,[11] the **growth-share matrix** gave a cash flow rationale for business linkage, acquisition and divestment. Companies needed a balanced portfolio of investments. The 'mid-point' for relative market share was 1.0 and for market growth the mid-point was commonly the growth of the economy/GDP as a whole. The route to success implied by 'the boxes' approach was deceptively simple. (Relatively) large businesses in mature markets ('cash cows') generated free cash flow above their reinvestment needs. This cash could then be invested in the high growth (and, hence, cash-consuming) businesses, so that the 'question marks' became 'stars', and the 'stars' maintained their strong positions, until eventually they became 'cash cows'. Relatively small businesses in low-growth industries ('dogs') were targets for divestment, or the basis for acquisition of similar businesses, to achieve the critical mass necessary to have the highest relative market share (a 'kennel of dogs'). The disaster route was equally simple to understand (*see* Figure 9.9).

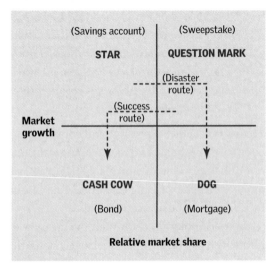

Figure 9.9 The growth-share matrix
Source: adapted from research by the Boston Consulting Group.

When it was first used as an analytic aid with the Mead Corporation in the early 1970s, the boxes were described in neutral, investment-oriented terms – that is, 'bond', 'savings account', 'sweepstake' (lottery ticket) and 'mortgage'. The commonly known descriptors that came later are more colourful, but also more implicitly prescriptive, particularly in the case of 'dogs'. (On the way to being 'dogs', they were also known as 'pets', which, in the American context, is markedly less negative.) (*Note*: by definition, most businesses are 'dogs' and the wholesale divestment of such units by all corporations is not logically feasible. See McKiernan (1992) for a good discussion of the 'boxes' in general and the 'dog' box in particular.)

A variety of other portfolio techniques followed, with differences centred on the dimensions along the axes, such as industry attractiveness/competitive position (GE) and stage of product-market evolution/competitive position. The helicopter view offered by such techniques encouraged managers to correct past mistakes by divesting weak businesses and

---

[11] The critical *assumption* being that having a *larger market share* than competitors meant higher volumes of production, leading to swifter progress down the experience curve (each doubling of cumulative volume bringing a known percentage reduction in costs) and, hence, the advantage of lower costs.

establishing a seemingly more solid rationale for the corporate mix than some tenuous definition of synergy. By the end of the 1970s, nearly half the Fortune 500 companies were using portfolio planning in some way to deal with a collection of businesses that were often beyond the scope of senior executives to manage and control other than at arm's length. What started off as an *aid to analysis* became a strategic paradigm in its own right and one that was accepted relatively uncritically by managers.

The oversimplistic assumptions underlying such techniques became apparent with the wholesale value destruction manifest in acquisition-driven conglomerates in the 1980s and the associated success of corporate raiders, who bought (using very high debt levels) and immediately broke up and sold their acquired conglomerates at vast profits. The era of the boxes was at an end:

> In most countries the days when portfolio management was a valid concept of corporate strategy are past. (Porter, 1987, p. 51)

(*Note*: although no longer the core of corporate strategy, some of the analytic language and assumptions of portfolio management are still reflected in annual reports today; for example, the almost universally accepted idea of the need for a 'balanced' portfolio – 'balance' often being discussed in terms of three-legged stools.)

9.5 Evidence and experience

The concept of the M-form, and its associated corporate strategy, as a value-adding entity receives little support from *academic* or practical (*market*) evidence.

9.5.1 Academic

It has always been difficult to mount a successful academic defence of the pure conglomerate as a value-adding grouping. *Governance* as a justification per se assumes sufficiently endemic and material opportunism, incompetence, goal displacement and so on among managers of stand-alone businesses that the reduction of these creates corporate value, despite the added corporate overhead and lack of market incentive. It is feasible that in the relatively early days of large businesses, the development of professional management skills in formerly stand-alone units may have added value, but this offers no rationale for ongoing membership.

Academic research has tended to focus on the presumed benefits of groupings of *related* businesses. Related businesses are those where a 'common skill, market or resource applies to each' (Rumelt, 1974, p. 29) and, hence, where scope benefits are appealing as a source of potential value. Rumelt produced a landmark study of 246 US firms over the period 1949–69, which supported the performance superiority of the multidivisional form, but questioned the relative value of different forms of diversification. He confirmed the intuitive logic of academics and managers that companies that had undertaken related

Case box: **Abbey's losing portfolio**

If we don't deliver we will be hung from the lampposts. (Luqman Arnold)

A decade ago, Abbey National was a pioneer that was streets ahead of its rivals. As a leading mortgage and savings bank, it was the first building society to demutu-alise, the first to snap up a life insurer and the first to diversify into supposedly lucra-tive wholesale lending.

Now it is in crisis. The diversification strategy has gone badly wrong and Abbey has acquired the unfortunate title of Britain's most troubled bank. Few can doubt the scale of its problems after a bank statement last week revealed that Abbey will be the first British bank in a decade to slash its dividend.

The bank is facing crippling losses at its wholesale arm, a huge bill to cover write-downs on four overambitious acquisitions – such as Scottish Provident, the life insurer – and a £500m one-off accounting charge to revalue Scottish Mutual, its ailing life insurer. Overall, the cost is expected to be well over £1bn and could push Abbey to a thumping loss for 2002. The most bearish analysts believe the loss could be a massive £1.5bn, against a £1.9bn profit in 2001.

So late in 2002 Luqman Arnold, the new chief executive, and Stephen Hester, the finance director, face a daunting challenge. Arnold's plan is to reconstruct Abbey to focus on its core retail banking and personal financial businesses. Operations which are deemed to be non-core, including much of the wholesale bank, will be placed in a new Portfolio Business Unit and sold off or wound down.

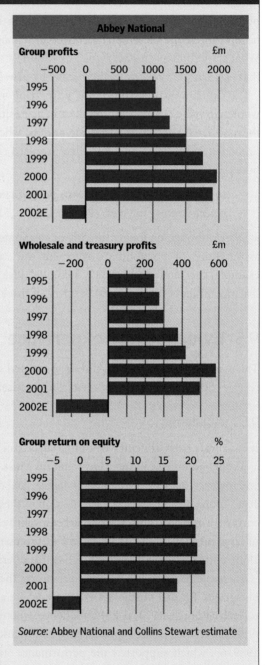

Source: Abbey National and Collins Stewart estimate

> What is very evident is just how badly Abbey has lost its way. Critics argue that as the bank devoted more capital to the once booming wholesale bank, which in 2000 made a huge £575m profit, the core retail bank has suffered from years of under-investment. 'What started as a small division became a core strategy to reduce the proportion of earnings from the core retail banking business,' says Arnold. 'The result was not just a loss of focus but there was an imbalance in terms of risk. We are concentrating now on rebalancing that risk.'
>
> Hester is more blunt: 'If I had a criticism of the direction of Abbey's strategy in the past it was that in a number of cases there was not enough assessment of competitive advantage. There was too much "gosh, that is a big market that is growing fast and we should have a slice of that" but not enough asking whether we would be any good in that business.'
>
> *Source*: adapted from the *Sunday Telegraph*, 1 December 2002.
> © Telegraph Group Limited (2002).

diversification outperformed those that had undertaken unrelated (that is, conglomerate) diversification.

Following Rumelt's work, the relationship between the make-up of business groupings and their economic performance became a major research focus. While some authors were supportive of Rumelt's main contentions, a significant body of research was in disagreement. Factors such as industry structure and specific firm characteristics played important roles and, once these were controlled, 'relatedness' seemed to have little explanatory power. Using market-based measures of relatedness has produced equivocal evidence on the link between firm performance and the composition of the corporate business portfolio, with few *strong* findings on either side.

The problem with the demonstrated lack of relationship between relatedness and performance is argued to lie primarily with the validity of the traditional market or industry-based relatedness measures, which, while they incorporate surface characteristics of *similarity*, do not capture relatedness of *strategic importance*. The relatedness that is really valuable is that between 'strategic assets', which are important to competitive advantage and cannot be quickly or cheaply gained by non-diversified competitors. The second drawback is that traditional researchers have tended to have a narrow, static view of relatedness, which does not take into account the *dynamic* creation and accumulation of trans-business competences, so managers must specifically manage for the benefits of relatedness across the businesses, to achieve added (corporate) value.

Hamel and Prahalad (1994) are particularly scathing about the inherent structural bias of the M-form *against* the exploitation of scope economies (core competences) inherent in relatedness. They decry what they see as a dominant focus on strategic business units (SBUs) in multidivisional firms being defined in *external* terms of markets, products and competitors. The 'tyranny of the SBU', as it promotes its own autonomous functioning, does not facilitate the complex interactions and sharing that are necessary for corporate-wide development and exploitation of core competences. This ultimately results in the demise of capabilities linking the businesses and thus impairs the exploitation of potentially valuable relatedness.

9.5.2 **Market**

As mentioned above, value destruction became the norm for multidivisional companies throughout the late 1970s and the 1980s. So much was this the case that the value of the M-form and, in particular, the value-adding capability of its head office, became a significant focus of research and discussion. While diversified conglomerates have been seen as the main cause of value loss it has yet to be proven (see above) that corporations of *related* businesses are much better. Perhaps it is true, as some authors contend, that the future of value creation lies in huge one-business companies, although these entities will still have to deal with the complexities of size, growth, and local–global dilemmas that gave rise to the M-form in the first place. Certainly, the mid to late 1990s saw the rise of the mega-merger between businesses in the same industry, as globalization became a driver for senior executives.

(*Note*: market valuation is not a good guide to the value-creation of businesses. As Collis (1991a) points out, a *significant* loss of value is necessary before takeover-break-up-and-sell becomes a viable option. With typical transaction costs of 2% and an acquisition premium of 20%, a corporation 'can be creating only 78% of the value that could be generated . . . and yet still be immune to the threat of a change in corporate control', p. 6.)

9.5.3 **Issues for the future**

The past problems of optimizing the management of multi-business corporations continue to challenge managers in the modern world. However, superimposed on the 'traditional' dilemmas of centralization versus **decentralization**, business (vertical) versus pan-corporate (horizontal) focuses, and (internal) co-operation versus competition, are the local versus global issues inherent in globalization. The increasing pace of change, turbulence and complexity of the business environment continue to test the structures, systems, processes and underlying rationale reflecting and underpinning corporate strategy, as managers strive to achieve a material parenting advantage which exceeds the value-generating capability of the stand-alone units. Perhaps the biggest issue facing these managers is to be able to demonstrate to increasingly sceptical stakeholders that there are tangible benefits of corporate membership. If the whole is not demonstrably more valuable than the sum of the parts, then corporate managers will continue to battle against the inexorable economic and market forces for disintegration.

9.6 The role of headquarters: the case of ABB and Percy Barnevik

9.6.1 *The Economist* on Barnevik and ABB

By trusting in multiculturalism and decentralization, Percy Barnevik has created a world beater. Could the firm hang together without him?

If Europe has a management superstar it is Percy Barnevik, boss of ABB Asea Brown Boveri, an electrical engineering giant. A tall, bearded and fast-talking Swede who has the restless manner of a man over-endowed with energy, Mr Barnevik has won almost every honour bestowed upon his profession, from 'emerging markets CEO of the year' to (twice) boss of Europe's most respected company. His name is dropped by management theorists and by the Harvard Business Review almost as frequently as that of Jack Welch of America's General Electric. And the gap is closing fast. 'Our greatest rival is no longer GE,' confesses one Japanese competitor. 'The one we have to be most on guard against is ABB.'

For once, the hyperbole is largely warranted. There are several reasons to praise Mr Barnevik. One is that he has shown how a company can be big and small at the same time: ABB consists of 1,300 separate companies divided into 5,000 profit centres. He has also pioneered such fashionable practices as internal benchmarking, centres of excellence and corporate parenting. But perhaps his most striking idea is the 'multicultural multinational'.

Not long ago, pundits held that globalization would erase national differences and homogenize consumer tastes. Mr Barnevik's view is more nuanced. He argues that purely national companies have little chance of thriving as governments deregulate and as the cost of travel and information plummets. But he stresses that companies need to keep deep roots in local markets, because markets will continue to differ. His answer is a cosmopolitan conglomerate diverse enough to respond to local tastes but united enough to amount to more than the sum of its parts.

ABB was born with such diversity, In 1988 Mr. Barnevik fashioned the organization from two century-old companies: ASEA, the Swedish engineering group which he ran from 1980, and Brown Boveri, an equally proud Swiss competitor. Since then, the company has been involved in more than 100 acquisitions and joint ventures, expanding into Eastern Europe and Asia, and adding (after many layoffs) 18,000 workers in 40 different countries.

This makes for an impressive array of dots on the map. But how do you join them up? Remember, for instance, the recent national rivalry between different parts of Royal Dutch Shell, another multicultural multinational, over its oilrig fiasco. That is where Mr Barnevik has been particularly successful. He forces all employees to read his 'bible', a short booklet on the company's aims and values. He made English his firm's official language, although only a third of the employees speak it as their mother tongue (Mr Barnevik himself has a strong Swedish accent). He moved ABB's headquarters to Zurich so that the merger would not look like a Swedish takeover. But he keeps the headquarters staff small (currently 171 people from 19 different countries) in order to avoid the impression that ABB is now a Swiss company. In making cuts, he has made sure that the burden is spread fairly evenly. Indeed, the most common criticism is that he treats his native Sweden rather too harshly; he once needed a bodyguard there to protect him from angry former employees.

Mr Barnevik's leadership style is not risk-free. He has always relied on speed to pre-empt nationalistic passions, either within the company or in national parliaments. Merging ASEA and Brown Boveri took a mere six weeks, and Mr Barnevik has been adding companies ever since.

Some critics say that this relentless expansion has prevented ABB from putting down any deep common roots, and that it runs on nothing more substantial than the adrenalin of permanent revolution. This, remember, is a company with a small core and only a thin layer of managers to supervise myriad subsidiaries and profit centres. ABB's retort is that its identity is buttressed not only by its possession of a coordinating executive committee (with members from eight countries) but also by an elite cadre of 500 global managers, a Praetorian Guard that Mr Barnevik selects carefully, paying particular attention to the cultural sensitivity of its members, and to their spouses' willingness to move. He shifts them through a series of foreign assignments, and takes a close interest in their careers. Worth more than their weight in gold, according to Mr Barnevik, their job is to knit the organization together, to transfer expertise around the world, and to expose the company's leadership to differing perspectives.

In the end, however, a lot of ABB's corporate glue comes down to Mr Barnevik's own relentlessness. ABBers around the world speak reverently about his ability to get by on four hours' sleep a night and his familiarity with every nook and cranny of the organization. He reckons he speaks personally to 5,500 of his employees every year. He spends only a couple of days a week at headquarters (often Saturday and Sunday); much of the rest of the time he is in an airborne office in a corporate jet.

'So what?' one of ABB's many happy shareholders might ask, adding that it is difficult to imagine Mr Barnevik sitting still anywhere. But ABB's current structure – and indeed the modern management fashion which Mr Barnevik has done so much to influence – has thrust an awesome amount of responsibility to the very top of the organization. The more global it has grown, the more it has relied on a strong leader to hold it together. The bigger test of Mr Barnevik's skills may be not how

well the company performs while he is still in charge, but what happens to it after his departure.[12]

9.6.2 *Time* magazine on Barnevik

Barnevik [is] analytical, quick, blunt and, above all, global. As chairman of ABB Asea Brown Boveri, the world's largest electrical engineering group, Barnevik, 57, presides over a $36 billion federation of more than 1,000 companies with 217,000 employees in 140 countries. Zurich-based ABB is the biggest single investor in Eastern Europe and the former Soviet Union, a Western pioneer in India and a aggressive player in East Asia and Latin America. For three years running it was voted 'Europe's most respected company' in a poll of executives by the Financial Times *newspaper. The structure Barnevik devised to run this globe-girdling behemoth 'has become the new prototype for the post-industrial-age corporation,' says Manfred Kets de Vries of the INSEAD business school outside Paris.*

The champion of globalisation started life in a provincial setting: the isolated west coast of Sweden. Educated as an economist, Barnevik left a management-consulting job to help a troubled Swedish steel company. Success there led to the CEO spot at Asea, a large electrical-engineering firm then in decline. Barnevik carried out a radical and initially painful shake-up, dubbed 'Percy's reign of terror'. He completed the ABB merger, Europe's biggest cross-border deal, in six weeks, following a key Barnevik rule: act fast, even at the risk of making mistakes. Or as the ABB 'bible' he inspired puts it, 'Not to take action is the only non-acceptable behavior.'[13]

9.6.3 Barnevik on Barnevik's management style

On his organizing principles

The only way to structure a complex, global organization is to make it as simple and local as possible. ABB is complicated from where I sit. But on the ground, where the real work gets done, all of our operations must function as closely as possible to stand-alone operations. Our managers need well-defined sets of responsibilities, clear accountability, and maximum degrees of freedom to execute.

We are fervent believers in decentralization. When we structure local operations, we always push to create separate legal entities. Separate companies allow you to create real balance sheets with real responsibility for cash flow and dividends. With real balance sheets, managers inherit results from year to year through changes in equity.

[12] *The Economist*, 6 January 1996.
[13] Jay Branegan, *Time*, 24 February 1997, p. 34.

ABB is a huge enterprise. But the work of most of our people is organized in small units with P&L responsibility and meaningful autonomy. Our operations are divided into nearly 1,200 companies with an average of 200 employees. These companies are divided into 4,500 profit centres with an average of 50 employees.[14]

On the organization structure

ABB is an organization with three internal contradictions. We want to be global and local, big and small, radically decentralized with centralized reporting and control. If we resolve those contradictions, we create real organizational advantage.

That's where the matrix comes in. The matrix is the framework through which we organize our activities. It allows us to optimize our business globally and maximize performance in every country in which we operate. Some people resist it. They say the matrix is too rigid, too simplistic. But what choice do you have? To say you don't like a matrix is like saying you don't like factories or you don't like breathing. It's a fact of life. If you deny the formal matrix, you wind up with an informal one – and that's much harder to reckon with. As we learn to master the matrix, we get a truly multidomestic organization.[15]

On the difficulty of managing the transition into ABB

It does require a huge mental change, especially for country managers. Remember, we've built ABB through acquisitions and restructurings. Thirty of the companies we've bought had been around for more than 100 years. Many of them were industry leaders in their countries, national monuments. Now they've got BA managers playing a big role in the direction of their operations. We have to convince country managers that they benefit by being part of this federation, that they gain more than they lose when they give up some autonomy.[16]

On creating a culture: why the 13 members of the group executive management team meet every three weeks for one day

Sitting in one room are the senior managers collectively responsible for ABB's global strategy and performance. These same managers individually monitor business segments, countries, and staff functions. So when we make a decision-snap, it's covered. The members of the executive committee communicate to their direct reports, the BA managers and the country managers, and the implementation process is under way.[17]

---

[14] William Taylor (1991) 'The logic of global business: An interview with ABB's Percy Barnevik', *Harvard Business Review*, March/April, reprint no. 91201, p. 99.

[15] ibid. pp. 95–6.

[16] ibid. p. 98.

[17] ibid. p. 100.

On diversity

We can't have managers who are 'un-French' managing in France because 95% of them are dealing every day with French customers, French colleagues, French suppliers. That's why global managers need humility. A global manager respects a formal German manager – Herr Doktor and all that – because that manager may be an outstanding performer in the German context.[18]

On building a culture of trust and exchange

Sharing expertise does not happen automatically. It takes a trust, it takes familiarity. People need to spend time together, to get to know and understand each other. People must also see a payoff for themselves. I never expect our operations to coordinate unless all sides get real benefits. We have to demonstrate that sharing pays – that contributing one idea gets you 24 in return.[19]

On selecting top managers for ABB

We sought people capable of becoming superstars – tough-skinned individuals who were fast on their feet, had good technical and commercial backgrounds, and had demonstrated the ability to lead others . . . For the merger to work it is essential that we have managers who are open, generous, and capable of thinking in group terms.[20]

On decision making

Nothing is worse than procrastination . . . When I look at ten decisions I regret, there will be nine of them where I delayed . . . Better roughly and quickly than carefully and slowly.

Take the initiative and decide – even if it turns out to be the wrong thing. The only thing we cannot accept is people who do nothing.

To emphasize the point Barnevik banned the phrase 'I think' at meetings: 'either you know or you don't.'[21]

On managers

Global managers are made, not born . . . you rotate people around the world. There is no substitute for line experience in three or four countries . . . you encourage

[18] ibid. p. 95.

[19] ibid. p. 97.

[20] Jules Arbose (1988) 'ABB: The new energy powerhouse', *International Management*, June.

[21] Jonathan Kapstein and Stanley Reed (1990) 'Preaching the Euro-gospel: ABB redefines multinationalism', *Business Week*, 23 July, p. 36.

people to work in mixed-nationality teams. You force *them to create personal alliances across borders … You have to force people into these situations.*[22]

On information used by the executive committee

We look for early signs that businesses are becoming more or less healthy … I stop to study trends that catch my eye … [I don't] start giving orders. But I want to have informed dialogues with the appropriate executives.[23]

On communications

You don't inform, you over-inform.[24]

On the role of headquarters

We operate as lean as humanly possible. It's no accident that there are only 100 people at ABB headquarters in Zurich. The closer we get to top management, the tougher we have to be with head count. I believe you can go into any traditionally centralized corporation and cut its headquarters staff by 90% in one year. You spin off 30% of the staff into free-standing service centres that perform real work – treasury functions, legal services – and charge for it. You decentralize 30% of the staff – human resources, for example – by pushing them into the line organization. Then 30% disappears through head count reductions.[25]

Questions for discussion

1 How does ABB's organization work? What are the key roles of managers at the country level? At the Business Area (BA) level? At the front line and the business unit level?

2 What role does headquarters play in getting this organization to work? Which of the four archetypes of headquarters is most like ABB? Does ABB have its own blend of these archetypes?

....

[22] William Taylor (1991) 'The logic of global business: An interview with ABB's Percy Barnevik, *Harvard Business Review*, March/April, reprint no. 91201, p. 95.

[23] ibid. p. 100.

[24] ibid. p. 104.

[25] ibid. p. 99.

Case box: **Conglomerates on trial**

Conglomerates have taken a battering from management theorists. But is there something to be said for them after all?

The case against conglomerates can be summed up in two words: size and complexity. Size is said to slow down decision making; complexity to create confusion. These things make it hard even for good managers to cope with the demands of specialized markets and rapid change. Breaking companies into their constituent parts, in contrast, allows managers to focus on businesses they know something about. And investors who want to spread their risk by diversifying – once thought a good reason to invest in a conglomerate – can nowadays do so by buying shares in many different companies.

Making the case for conglomerates BCG argues[26] that the 'conglomerate discount' is little more than prejudice, and that what really determines a company's success is not the narrowness of its focus but the quality of its management. A 'premium conglomerate', as BCG likes to call the well-managed ones, manages its portfolio aggressively, setting its subsidiaries clear targets and ditching underperforming companies (Mr Welch operates on a 'fix, sell, or close' principle). But it also invests heavily in creating and transferring company-wide skills. Samsung, for instance, spends about $400m a year on training.

In addition, say the men from BCG, conglomeration can be a strength at a time when disparate businesses are tending to converge. By remaining omnivorous, Britain's Virgin Group has transferred its marketing skills from music to airlines and financial services. By contrast, British Petroleum (BP) made a conscious decision to stick to energy businesses. It has lately found, as petrol stations have become more like grocery stores, that it has had to learn more 'normal' retailing skills. Focus, argue the men from BCG, can be a straitjacket.

VEBA is a highly diversified German company. In 1991 it considered breaking up but chose instead to manage its companies more aggressively; it has since produced above-average returns. Samsung, a South Korean firm with 166 different businesses, has grown tenfold every six years since the 1960s. And how do conglomerate bashers explain away America's General Electric? This unfocused giant has given shareholders an average annual return of 20.8% (six percentage points better than the stockmarket average) since Jack Welch took over in 1979. Mr Welch wants the firm to grow bigger still: he dismisses the infatuation with focus as 'trendy'.

These are not isolated examples. Dieter Heuskel, of the Boston Consulting Group, and Timothy Plaut, of Goldman Sachs, an investment bank, reckon that between 1985 and 1995 the 40 largest American, European and Australian conglomerates generated returns for their shareholders which were virtually identical to the market average, and that the top quartile of conglomerates turned in annual returns which were almost five points above the market average.

---

[26] 'Premium Conglomerates', The Boston Consulting Group.

A verdict?

To say that a well-run conglomerate can sometimes succeed is hardly proof that conglomeration is a sound principle. BCG is frustratingly unclear about how diversified it thinks a conglomerate can be before the costs outweigh the benefits. Look behind many apparently diversified successes and you will find either or both of the following: first, some degree of focus (for instance Virgin usually concentrates on the marketing side of its admittedly varied businesses); and, second, a rare business mind, such as GE's Mr Welch or Virgin's Richard Branson, capable of holding the group together. When these rare traits are absent, as they normally are, conglomerates often lose their way.

As academics and others continue to document the failings of conglomerates, the case for them – except when they are blessed with unusually talented and disciplined bosses – remains unproven.

Adapted from *The Economist*, 3 April 1997.

You should consider the ABB experience in the light of the debate on conglomerates (see case box above). Does ABB have the management experience and talent to manage such a wide spread of businesses? Alternatively can you argue that there is a focus and a thread running through the business so that synergies can be achieved? To what extent does a management team depend on its leader? Consider again the role of Percy Barnevik. What is the nature of the management talent that can make conglomerates succeed beyond the expectations of the stock market?

9.7 Summary

This chapter has introduced a new dimension to our strategy discussion – the multibusiness portfolio. The job of designing, managing and adapting the portfolio of businesses lies generally with the corporate centre. It is concerned with the issues of competitive advantage just like individual strategic business units but it is particularly concerned to (i) make sure that SBUs do what they are supposed to do (the 'control' question) and (ii) ensure that the patterns of competitive advantage within the portfolio are mutually reinforcing (the 'synergy' question). In order to fulfil these tasks the corporate centre has to pay close attention to the structure of the organization so that patterns of specialization are created and that management responsibilities can be properly defined. Issues of organization structure and process are discussed in more detail in Part 4 and in this chapter we have gone so far as to argue that the strategy–structure fit and balance is a key task for the corporate centre.

Although the corporate centre has a distinct role to play compared with the SBUs, it still deals with the same economic issues. In particular the centre is concerned with synergy, introduced in Chapter 3 as economies of scope. This is reflected in the many practical frameworks and strategy tools that have been marketed over time. The BCG growth-share matrix is the grandfather of all these and has been succeeded by many other portfolio management frameworks. In noting these it is sensible to remember that all strategy tools and frameworks are highly contextual. They depend critically on the situation of the particular organization. Frameworks in and of themselves do not convey truth or 'good' theory: they are merely ways of presenting data and alternatives. The trick with tools is to note the exclusions or, rather, to be clever with choosing a focus on just a few elements of the strategic context.

The role of the centre is to find a way of managing the whole organization that fits its overall context. This is reflected in the range of strategies available. We discussed restructuring, activity sharing and skills transfer. These capture different ways of creating value. We also discussed how companies have different styles that also reflect the same point – how to actually create extra value.

We have also noted the academic debate. This has focused on the defensibility of the conglomerate where, in general, academics are unconvinced that this is a sustainable approach. Also, we have noted that this is an area where many big mistakes can be made. Experience suggests that these mistakes are all too common. The next chapter goes on to look at the area in which there is a high degree of controversy – mergers and acquisitions.

This chapter concludes with an extended discussion of Percy Barnevik's creation of ABB. This has been both highly celebrated and controversial. It ranks as one of the most radical and significant corporate experiments ever undertaken in Europe. It put together a wide range of businesses under a distinctive management style with a wholly new concept of a matrix structure. This exemplifies the significant role of corporate-level decisions and the high risks attached to them.

Key terms

Decentralization *360*

Financial control *347*

Growth-share matrix *356*

M-form *339*

Portfolio management *338*

Relatedness *338*

Restructuring *348*

Sharing activities *349*

Strategic control *347*

Strategic planning *347*

Transaction cost economics (TCE) *344*

Transferring skills *349*

U-form *338*

Recap questions and assignments

1 Make a critical appraisal of the importance of the centre-division relationship in the strategic direction and development of large multi-business companies. Illustrate your answer by describing the relationships that you feel would be most important to a chosen company. You may wish to choose one from the text and cases version of this book:

Diageo (in case section)

HSBC (in case section)

Rank Xerox (in case section)

2 Evaluate the nature of the additional value that is being suggested as a rationale for an ongoing merger or acquisition being reported in the current financial press. What actions need to be undertaken to realize this value? How would you classify this value in the terms used in the above chapter and how would you describe the parenting role best suited to the merged corporation?

Online
Learning **Centre**

When you have read this chapter, log on to the Online Learning Centre website at www.mcgraw-hill.co.uk/textbooks/mcgee to explore chapter-by-chapter test questions, further reading and more online study tools for strategy.

Case 1 **Old dogs, new tricks**

Focus is no longer a minority pursuit

Shortly after Jürgen Dormann took over at Hoechst in 1994, he made a big decision. With 16 different businesses to its name, ranging from photocopiers and cosmetics to dyes and drugs, the German chemicals group was far too diversified. Its future, he figured, lay in pharmaceuticals, which at that time accounted for only a fifth of its turnover. In 1997, a restructuring plan involving the spin-off of several divisions was put before analysts, who lapped it up. But then things started going wrong. Egged on by politicians, Hoechst's unions went on the offensive. As the overhaul was taking shape, but before anyone had been fired, a group of 8,000 angry demonstrators marched on the company's headquarters to protest against the dismantling of a great industrial name. Mr Dormann held firm, but the share price wobbled, reflecting investors' belief that he would have trouble implementing his plan.

Re-engineering old-established companies in Europe is bound to be tough. As the Hoechst example illustrates, managers often find themselves caught between two powerful forces: unions backed by job-protection laws on one side, the financial markets on the other. Long-standing links between business and politics have made it hard to resist the pressure to form conglomerates. And without a strong steer from the stockmarket, as in America, managers have been able to indulge their empire-building urges. With a few notable exceptions, Europe's companies have tended to lose focus as they grow.

International investors doubt the wisdom of industrial diversification, and most studies suggest that they are right. Champions of conglomerates always point to America's highly diverse and highly successful General Electric, which hawks everything from aircraft engines to financial services. But GE is the exception that proves the rule. No European company has come close to pulling off the same trick for any length of time.

At long last, the message is sinking in. Industrial focus, until recently the mantra of a few pioneers, has become a common chant. It is notable that this chant has grown loudest in Germany, Europe's most conglomerate-stuffed economy. Since the beginning of last year, around half of Germany's top 30 companies have announced plans to sell or hive off big subsidiaries that they no longer consider part of their core business.

Fresenius, whose main activity is making medical equipment, says it plans to float all its subsidiaries on the stockmarket – so long as doing so will add value. Thyssen Krupp, a smokestack business if ever there was one, is cutting down its 23 divisions to eight, and mulling the sale of businesses worth €5 billion ($4.8 billion), including a chunk of its once-untouchable steel operations. Its cool new phrase for this is 'portfolio optimisation', which makes trade unionists' blood boil. Germany's big utilities, RWE and Veba/Viag, are undoing past, untidy diversification (into logistics, telecoms and electronics) in favour of concentrating on an area they know well: Europe's fast-deregulating electricity markets.

Why the mass conversion? For some companies, selling peripheral activities means killing two birds with one stone: it raises money for acquisitions in their main businesses, but also boosts another takeover currency, their shares, by making their operations more transparent. For others, it is simply the only option left when their excuses for doing nothing have run out. No company exemplifies this better than Siemens.

For many years Siemens was a lightning rod for criticism of the European way, and deservedly so. Its vast spread, from heavy engineering, electronics and white goods to light bulbs, mobile phones and computers, grew ever more difficult to manage from one boardroom. One problem was that its labs came before its customers. Technicians were allowed to over-engineer, and managers struggled to turn good ideas into products that sold. Moreover, the board was usually stuffed with specialists rather than general managers with a feel for strategy. Profits were often woefully thin: the old joke that Siemens would do better by selling itself and sticking the cash on deposit contained more than a grain of truth. The group was stifled by its own sense of history.

By the early 1990s, a combination of high wages, tough competition and weak management began to take its toll. Something had to be done, but the reorganizations that followed were half-hearted. Nudged by politicians, the company invested heavily in eastern Germany, but saw scant profit for its trouble. Management was spending most of its time trying to patch up holes. Some were worse than others: Heinrich von Pierer, the chairman, once described the troubled nuclear-energy division as '2% of our business and 90% of our headaches'.

Last-chance saloon

In 1998, with Siemens's share price in the doldrums, Mr von Pierer announced a grand 'ten-point plan', quickly dubbed 'von Pierer's last chance'. This time, against expectations, it has come off. The number of basic operating divisions has been slimmed from 15 to five, and businesses employing a third of the workforce have been put up for sale. Some of the assets have attracted enormous attention: the recent flotation of the recovering semiconductor business, Infineon, was 30 times oversubscribed. At long last, Siemens's share price has started to reflect its underlying technological strengths.

That is partly because the latest restructuring is about more than just sales and spin-offs. Mr von Pierer has taken a knife to the company's culture of complacency and concentrated on financial performance, installing a former investment banker as finance chief. Some 60% of top managers' pay has been linked to targets for return on capital, a radical move in a country used to predictable pay packets. Now the company's accounts are being overhauled in preparation for an American stockmarket listing next year.

None of this has been easy for Mr von Pierer, who harbours a natural distrust of financial analysts, and prefers consensus to conflict. Still, he seems a genuine convert. 'Siemens is a living organism,' he says. 'I can't promise my people that any overhaul will be the last.'

Coming from a veteran with 31 years' service in a German industrial behemoth, that is radical talk. There are still taboos, however. Mr von Pierer is clearly uncomfortable with the suggestion that the group might be worth more broken up than in one piece. That, he insists, would destroy all sorts of synergies.

Whatever it does, Siemens still has some turning around to do. After restructuring comes repositioning. Does it want to be a manufacturer or a service-provider, an engineering company or a technology specialist? It is investing heavily in its pure-technology businesses, and wants to generate a quarter of its revenue from the Internet within a year. But turning a supertanker into a flotilla of nippy motor boats will be a far greater challenge than merely throwing the unwanted lifeboats overboard. As Europe's start-up culture spreads, keeping talented employees and encouraging them to innovate in-house is becoming increasingly hard.

Several of Europe's industrial champions may be forced down the same route as Siemens, including Philips, a Dutch electronics giant that makes everything from food blenders to digital-disc players. Cor Boonstra, the first outsider to be brought in as boss, has rejigged the group's mix of businesses and cut staff numbers several times, but analysts have yet to be convinced that even after the latest overhaul, announced earlier this year, it is sufficiently nimble on its feet.

As with Siemens, the solution for Philips may be to pare its range of businesses to a more manageable number, and to do more to foster entrepreneurship in its own ranks. Were it not protected by a web of trusted shareholders, it would probably have been taken over years ago. 'Focus is especially important during times of fast technological change like this, because bigger ships take so much longer to turn,' says Mr Nilsson of Ericsson, which has just sold its century-old energy-systems business to concentrate on its mobile-phone operation.

But what happens if not just a few, but all of a company's businesses turn out to be dispensable? Europe already has several examples of companies that have thrived on getting out of everything they were in and starting afresh. In the early 1990s, Germany's Preussag was a company nobody wanted to invest in. It had mediocre managers in unexciting industries such as shipbuilding. Today, it is one of Europe's most profitable travel and tourism groups.

Preussag's transformation owed more to stealth and serendipity than to any grand restructuring plan: a well-timed asset sale here, a shrewd acquisition there, all supported by its largest shareholder, WestLB. At times like this, patient owners can be a help. When Finland's Nokia switched from rubber products to mobile telephones in the mid-1990s, its largest shareholders balked as revenues dipped and the share price halved. But they decided to stick by the chief executive, Jorma Ollila, and have since been handsomely rewarded. Had Nokia been American, he might easily have been ousted.

Not every company has the far-sightedness or the market opportunities of Preussag or Nokia, but excuses to waste money on ill-judged diversification are running out everywhere.

For one thing, political patronage is on the wane. For another, companies have acquired tools with which to manage their capital more sensibly. Buy-backs, which involve a company purchasing its own shares to reduce its capital base, became legal in France and Germany in 1998, and are starting to take off. Last year, European companies bought $25 billion-worth of their own shares, up from a mere $4 billion-worth in 1995. As buy-backs become more widely accepted, European companies should become less prone to acquire for acquisition's sake when they have more capital than they need.

Halfway there

Managers are beginning to learn that bigger is better only when supported by industrial logic. And yet much restructuring remains held up by misguided patriotism and ideology. Last autumn, Michelin, a French tyre maker, unveiled a sharp increase in profits but at the same time announced a 10% cut in its workforce. It was duly lambasted for putting profits ahead of people, even though it tried to explain that without reorganization its profitability would wane. Outraged members of parliament are still trying to introduce legislation that would give employees more say over changes in company strategy.

Nor do all the remaining barriers to change come from the outside. There are still plenty of chief executives in Europe who pay lip service to shareholders, yet pursue their own agenda. The boss of one German company explains with a chuckle that he bundles its various engineering units into a single grouping for analysts' roadshows, 'so we don't look as messy as we really are.' And not all large companies are really convinced of the importance of their share price. 'It's not our first priority', says Stefano Giussani, the investor-relations chief of Montedison, an Italian chemicals concern, to explain why he cannot recollect how his company's share price has moved over the past year.

For those managers who do embrace restructuring, the hardest part is yet to come. If laying off workers and setting financial targets were all it took, Siemens would have been a glittering stockmarket star long ago. But once a company has cut away its flab, it has to find new ways to grow profitably, which involves more fundamental change. American firms, having streamlined a decade ago, are now free to expand revenues and bring together converging industries, as in last year's merger of America Online and Time Warner. Catching them will take quite some doing.

Source: 'Old dogs, new tricks', *The Economist*, 27 April 2000.
© The Economist Newspaper Limited, London (27 April 2000).

Case Questions

1 Outline the case against conglomerates and for more closely inter-related business portfolios.

2 How would you counter the arguments often advanced by workforces and politicians that restructuring merely results in transferring jobs overseas?

3 It is often claimed that conglomerates are not able to grow profitably. Explain this argument? Is it correct?

Further reading and references

Bartlett, CA (1990) 'Matrix Management not a Structure, a Frame of Mind', *Harvard Business Review*, **68**, **4**, pp. 138–45.

Bartlett, CA and Ghoshal, S (1993) 'Beyond the M-form: Toward a New Managerial Theory of the Firm', *Strategic Management Journal*, **14**, pp. 23–46, reprinted in Segal-Horn (ed.) (1998).

Campbell, A and Goold, M (1994) 'Adding Value from Corporate Headquarters', in B De Wit and R Meyer (eds) *Strategy: Process, Content, Context*, West Publishing Company, New York.

Campbell, A, Goold, M and Alexander, M (1995) 'Corporate Strategy: The Quest for Parenting Advantage', *Harvard Business Review*, March/April, pp. 120–32.

Campbell, A and Luchs, K (1992) *Strategic Synergy*, Butterworth-Heinemann.

Chandler, AD, Jr (1962) *Strategy and Structure: Chapters in the History of the Industrial Enterprise*, MIT Press, Cambridge MA.

Chandler, AD, Jr (1994) 'The Functions of the HQ Unit in the Multibusiness Firm', in R Rumelt, D Schendel and D Teece (eds) *Fundamental Issues in Strategy*, Harvard Business School Press, Boston, MA.

Chandler, AD, Jr (1990a) 'Scale and Scope: The Dynamics of Industrial Capitalism', Cambridge, MA: Belknap.

Chandler, AD, Jr (1990b) 'The Enduring Logic of Industrial Success', *Harvard Business Review*, March/April, pp. 130–40.

Collis, D (1991a) 'Corporate Strategy: A Conceptual Framework', *Harvard Business School Case Study*, 9–391–284.

Collis, D (1991b) 'Corporate Strategy: Identifying and Exploiting Resources', *Harvard Business School Case Study*, 9–391–285.

Collis, D (1991c) 'Managing the Multibusiness Corporation' *Harvard Business School Case Study*, 9–391–286.

Collis, DJ (1996) 'Corporate Strategy in Multibusiness Firms' *Long Range Planning*, **29**, pp. 416–18.

Day, GS (1977) 'Diagnosing the Product Portfolio', *Journal of Marketing*, April, pp. 264–80.

Ghoshal, S (1987) 'Global strategy: an Organising Framework', *Strategic Management Journal*, **8**, pp. 425–40, reprinted in Segal-Horn (ed.) (1998).

Goold, M and Campbell, A (1987) *Strategies and Styles*, Blackwell, Oxford.

Goold, M, Campbell, A and Alexander, M (1994) *Corporate Level Strategy: Creating Value in the Multibusiness Company*, John Wiley & Sons Inc., New York.

Hamel, G and Prahalad, CK (1994) *Competing for the Future*, Harvard Business School Press, Boston MA.

Hill, CWL (1994) 'Diversification and Economic Performance: Bringing Structure and Corporate Management Back into the Picture', in R Rumelt, D Schendel and D Teece (eds) *Fundamental Issues in Strategy*, Harvard Business School Press, Boston MA.

Hoskisson, RE, Hill, CWL and Kim, H (1993) 'The Multidivisional Structure: Organizational Fossil or Source of Value?' *Journal of Management*, **19**, 2, pp. 269–98.

McKiernan, P (1992) *Strategies of Growth*, Routledge, London.

Porter, ME (1987) 'From Competitive Advantage to Corporate Strategy', *Harvard Business Review*, May/June, pp. 2–21.

Prahalad, CK and Hamel, G (1990) 'The Core Competence of the Corporation', *Harvard Business Review*, May/June, pp. 79–91.

Rumelt, R (1974) 'How Much Does Industry Matter?' *Strategic Management Journal*, **12**, pp. 167–85.

Segal-Horn, S (ed.) (1998) *The Strategy Reader*, Blackwell Business, Oxford.

Teece, DJ (1982) 'Towards an Economic Theory of the Multiproduct Firm', *Journal of Economic Behavior and Organization*, **3**, pp. 39–63.

Waterman, R (1982) 'The seven elements of strategic fit', *Journal of Business Strategy*, **3**, pp. 68–72.

Waterman, R, Peters, T and Phillips J (1980) 'Structure is not organization', *The McKinsey Quarterly*, Summer, pp. 2–20.

Williamson, OE (1975) Markets and Hierarchies: Analysis and Antitrust Implications, Free Press, New York.

Chapter 10

Corporate strategy: mergers, acquisitions and strategic alliances[1]

Introduction

Corporate portfolios can change quickly through mergers and acquisitions. During the 1990s dissatisfaction with acquisition performance drove the search for an alternative form of expansion. Strategic alliances became a popular alternative. Subsequently firms learned that these forms of expansion, and partial control and ownership, also suffer from high failure rates. Attention again focused on **mergers** and **acquisitions**. This chapter covers the elements of pre-acquisition planning and the issues involved in post-acquisition integration. We also present a framework for assessing co-operative strategies (alliances), setting out the ways in which alliance planning and alliance management ought to proceed.

---

[1] This chapter is written jointly with Duncan Angwin.

Mergers,[2] acquisitions and strategic alliances are a major force for restructuring industries and companies. Barriers to such activity have been eroding rapidly during the 1990s with the opening up of new markets, deregulation of industries, increased sophistication of financing techniques and more active stakeholders.

As a consequence, one major feature of the last M&A boom has been the large increase in volume of cross-border acquisitions. Even if companies prefer organic growth to acquiring or making alliances, all must guard against the way in which these phenomena can radically redraw the competitive arena.

10.1 Acquisitions: an overview

General reading of the business press and of academic writings suggests that acquisitions, although common, are not so tractable and it is worth pausing to consider why this is so (see Tables 10.1 and 10.2). Acquisitions touch all aspects of corporate life and so can be viewed from a multiplicity of angles. From a strategic perspective, much attention has been devoted to understanding the drivers for acquisition and identifying suitable targets. The underlying assumption with this approach is that if one can correctly identify such targets then the acquisition will be successful. This exposes us to Mintzberg's criticism of

Table 10.1 Consultancy and business press evidence on acquisition failure

Consultancy	Date	Method	Failure Rate
Business International	1975	400 postal questionnaires	49%
	1978	150 postal questionnaires	48%–56%
Coopers and Lybrand	1992	Qualitative in-depth interviews with senior executives in the UK's top 100 companies	54%
Coopers and Lybrand	1996	125 companies. Low revenues, cash flow, profitability	66%
Mercer MC	1995	150 companies. Poor returns to shareholdes after three years	50%
McKinsey & Co	1995	Examined 58 acquisitions. Success was measured as financial return exceeding the cost of capital	58.6%

Source: KPMG.

---

[2] The terms 'merger' and 'acquisition' are often used interchangeably in the literature. There are differences in so far as mergers are generally the bringing together of businesses of equal size, paid for by the exchange of shares and with no premium. Acquisitions imply a dominant party controlling another, and often there is a premium paid. Where the distinction becomes problematic is in the post-deal phase, where 'mergers' often become 'zero premium acquisitions', and some acquisitions become rather like mergers in having a 'level playing field'.

Table 10.2 Academic evidence on failure rates

Types of academics	Conclusions	Authors	Date
Financial economists	Target shareholders benefit by c.20% whereas acquirer shareholders do not, benefiting by c.0–2%	Jensen and Ruback	1983
		Jarrell and Poulsen	1989
		Sudarsanam *et al.*	1993
Industrial economists			
◆ Using accounting data	◆ Bidders suffer an immediate decline in relative profitability	Hughes	1993
◆ Subsequent market share	◆ Subsequent market share showed dramatic decline	Mueller	1985
		Caves	1988
◆ Divestment	◆ 58.5% of 2,021 acquisitions (1950–1986) subsequently divested	Porter	1987

the planning school: Mintzberg questions whether successful results will inevitably follow from a good plan. Indeed, this author has often heard CEOs remark that if the acquisition failed then it was due to a poor plan! This circular argument is not helpful and, indeed, obscures the point that the causal link between plan and performance is weak at best – the relationship being substantially mediated by *implementation strategies*. As a consequence, strategy research efforts have turned to the post-acquisition phase, where 'implementation is the bridge between the islands of plan and performance'.

In focusing on implementation, a new set of strategic agenda has arisen. Implementation has opened up the black box of the 'messy' detail of organizations, which pre-acquisition planning frameworks largely overlook. This has implications for our view of strategy and the role of the HQ. Pre-acquisition frameworks tend to assume a top-down approach to strategy, whereas the latter is embedded within the organization, and is multilevel and complex. Focusing internally on the resources and capabilities of the business echoes a shift in emphasis, as noted in Chapter 5, in the field of strategy itself, from the positioning school to the resource-based school. However, rather than being an 'either/or' choice, this is really a question of emphasis, with the recognition that success in the latter is crucial to achieving the former.

10.1.1 **The context**

While 2002 has seen a slump in activity from the record wave experienced in the previous five years, totalling $10.84 trillion, 2003 has seen an upturn. Interestingly, mega-deals, which characterized the boom of the late 1990s, continue, as do the large-scale cross-border transactions.

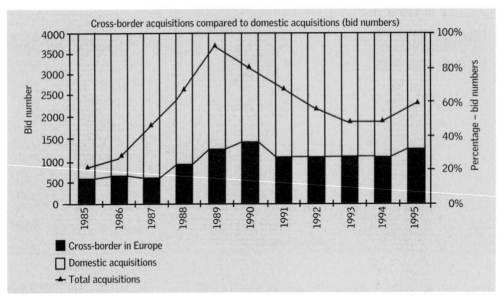

Figure 10.1 The growing relative importance of European cross-border acquisition activity
Source: Angwin and Saville, 1997.

Acquisitions come in waves. The 1960s were characterized by a wave of diversification activity designed to spread financial risk across a portfolio of businesses. Companies such as the tobacco giant BAT industries spent vast sums trying to establish sound footings in other industries, but with very poor results. The 1980s exposed the fallacy of diversification, as its supposed advantages were more than offset by the difficulties of managing such large diverse groups. It was realized that shareholders could diversify more effectively themselves, and, with the rise of more aggressive financial techniques, such giants were no longer bid-proof. Break-ups became the new order, as businesses streamlined, downsized and generally 'stuck to the knitting'. The 1990s saw a massive resurgence in acquisition activity, spurred by deregulation, globalization and technological change. Differences from previous waves of activity are the number of mega-mergers to create global giants, such as Travelers/Citicorp forming the world's biggest financial services group, Exxon and Mobil creating an oil behemoth, and the intention of Deutsche Telekom and Telecom Italia, in a $162 billion deal, to create Europe's first supranational.

In Europe, the drive towards a single market has encouraged internal, cross-border acquisitions. Free of the political barriers that have fragmented their markets, many European companies have sought to consolidate their efforts as a means of matching the advantages in economic scale of their US and Far East counterparts (Calori and Lubatkin 1995).[3] At the same time, the initial fears of Fortress Europe, as well as its size and sophistication, have

---

[3]   Refer back to the scale economy brander, pp. 203–4 and the discussion of the European food processing industry, pp. 227–31.

made it an attractive hunting ground for non-European multinationals. This has not only resulted in a sharp increase in acquisitions on the Continent, but also resulted in the rise of the almost unheard-of hostile takeover. While almost a thing of the past in the US and UK, where they attract little attention, Continental Europe is in the grip of such acrimonious deals which regularly feature in its business press.

Another feature of this recent wave of acquisition activity is the rise in cross-border acquisitions. In the ten years 1985–1995, the value[4] of cross-border acquisitions rose tenfold from £2 billion to some £20 billion and the numbers of deals fivefold, to 655. Cross-border deals gained steadily in significance over that period from 15 per cent to 30 per cent of total deals.

Recent data (see Figure 10.1) suggests that this trend in cross-border activity continues to surge forward, totalling $229.6 billion in 1998 (KPMG 1998), an increase of 60 per cent on the previous year, and already in the first quarter of 1999, European-wide deals[5] have amounted to $345 billion.[6]

In the case box below, *The Economist* reports on an awakening of acquisition fever among chief executives in the early months of 2004. Given what we know about the historic record of successes and failures of acquisitions, identify the principal reasons for and against undertaking major acquisitions.

Case box: Some notes for company bosses out on the prowl

After a long hibernation, company bosses are beginning to rediscover their animal spirits. The $145 billion-worth of global mergers and acquisitions announced in January was the highest for any month since October 2000, and the figure for February seems likely to beat that. Two deals alone (the bids for Walt Disney and AT&T Wireless) account for over $100 billion, and there is a week of the month still to run. There is now no shortage of chief executives tossing in their beds at night as they contemplate what target they might attack in order to add growth and value to their companies and glory to themselves. They might have been chastened briefly by the excesses of the dotcom boom, but they are once again on the prowl. Hostile bids, the corporate kingdom's way of culling feeble stock, are in favour again. Disney, target of a hostile bid from Comcast, has looked like a three-legged wildebeest for some time now.

What should CEOs do to improve their chances of success in the coming rush to buy? First of all, they should not worry too much about widely quoted statistics suggesting that as many as three out of every four deals fail to create value for the acquiring company's shareholders. The figures are heavily influenced by the time period chosen, and they can never be compared with what would have happened had the deal not taken place. In any case, one out of four is

---

[4] These figures undoubtedly understate the case, as the values of many cross-border deals are not publicly known. The numbers of deals, however, are a more reliable measure of activity.

[5] This figure may include domestic deals.

[6] Although this figure has been inflated by the Telecom Italia deal, there were also a record number of deals.

not bad odds when compared with the chances of getting a new business off the ground. So they should keep looking for good targets ...

If CEOs wish to avoid some of the errors of the 1990s, they should not forget that they are subject to all the failings that flesh is heir to – and in particular the eternal tendency of business planners to be over-confident. It is a near certainty that, if asked, little short of 99% of them would describe themselves as 'above average' at making mergers and acquisitions work. Sad as it may be, that can never be true. They should also be aware that they will be powerfully influenced by the herd instinct, the feeling that it is better to be wrong in large numbers than to be right alone. In the coming months they will have to watch carefully to be sure that the competitive space into which the predator in front of them is so joyfully leaping does not lie at the edge of a cliff.

Source: Adapted from 'Spring in their steps', *The Economist*, 21 February 2004, p. 14.

10.2 Pre-acquisition planning

10.2.1 Motives for acquisition

Most texts on acquisitions will cite the following main strategic motives for making acquisitions:

- *Industry restructuring* – removing competitors in an over-saturated industry.
- *Increased market power* – the enlarged company may be able to achieve monopolistic or oligopolistic power over its customers and better control its competitors. This might also be achieved by acquiring suppliers that can allow the firm to be more competitive in the market, as well as influence the competitive balance if supplying competitors.
- *Access to new markets* – this can be an effective way of entering new countries without the difficulties of establishing new distribution systems.
- *Economies of scale and scope* – for instance, closing acquired factories and transferring production to your own factory can create economies of scale. Overhead costs can also be spread, such as with common advertising or a single head office.
- *Acquisition of new skills* – particularly in fast-developing industries, this will help the firm develop more rapidly than may be possible internally.
- *Diversification* – this may allow the firm to find opportunities for generating superior returns to those available within the sector.

All of these strategic motives are designed to achieve improved financial performance. In addition, there are also motives we might classify as purely financial:

- *Buying a bargain* – a company that is perceived to be cheap and will be sold on for a quick profit. This would also include asset stripping.

- *Tax advantages* – where companies have a significant tax liability in one country and earnings elsewhere.
- *Financing advantages* – more attractive financing means easier access to finance and/or lower cost of capital. For example:
  - a company may acquire a business in another country to gain advantages from different tax laws;
  - a private company may acquire a listed company to obtain a lower cost of capital; or
  - a company may acquire a business with a strong cash flow.

Strategists have endeavoured to identify the characteristics of a target that link with acquisition performance. These are:

- *Avoid sprat-catching* – acquisitions of less than 5 per cent of parent turnover will tend to underperform, as they are often neglected.
- *Market share* – the risk of failure increases substantially as market share decreases.
- *Avoid financially weak companies* – poor financial health will damage your wealth (unless you are a turnaround specialist).
- *Pre-acquisition experience* – only useful in so far as knowing what not to do based upon small errors in the past.

A hotly debated topic is the issue of 'relatedness', as managers believe intuitively that acquisitions should be more successful where the acquirer knows the business. However, the evidence remains contradictory on this issue and, rather like experience, the acquirer may suffer from a false sense of security.

Perhaps it is not surprising with this small list of recommendations that so many acquisitions fail – the overwhelming weight of evidence is that only some 50 per cent succeed. It is a rather sobering thought that a multi-billion-dollar merger has only a one in two chance of success!

So far, we have reviewed the 'managerial' reasons for making acquisitions that would be found in any acquisition offer document. This is not the whole picture, however, and we should not overlook:

- *Chief executive characteristics* – ego, the need for a challenge, addiction to doing deals, prestige and empire building – these will be downplayed.
- *Process issues* – the decision in a large company may be the result of many disconnected impulses, rather than a single rational decision. A top management team is likely to rationalize the process post-hoc.
- *Environmental pressures* – external pressures may force the company into action, rather than the company being proactive – for instance, the City may threaten to down-rate a company if an acquisition is not made. A top management team is unlikely to admit to not being in charge.

All of these 'drivers' for mergers and acquisitions also interact, as discussed in Angwin (2000).

10.2.2 Selecting a target

To select a target, we should consider the following:

- Resist perceiving acquisitions as one-off events, but remember that they are part of a larger strategy – how will the acquisition build on core competences and enhance competitive advantage?

- Careful analysis of industry structures to judge long-term profitability – Porter's 1980 techniques are ideally suited to this approach.

- Detailed examination of possible targets in that industry to clarify potential synergies – the value chain may be useful in identifying such synergies.

- Detailed examination to expose possible incompatibilities – the use of a cultural web (Johnson and Scholes, p. 230) will expose differences in management style and culture.

- Assessment of the target's worth and the price the company can afford – there are many ways to value a business, such as using price/earnings ratios, discounted cash flow, asset valuation (Weston *et al.* 2003). However, the final price will be the result of negotiation, rather than precise calculation.

- The acquirer must also be mindful of regulatory restrictions to prevent mergers that are against the public interest. In the US there are severe 'anti-trust' provisions. In the UK, the Monopolies and Mergers Commission is empowered to investigate any merger (combined assets greater than £30 million or combined market share of 25 per cent or more), and can recommend to the Secretary of State for Industry that the deal be prohibited. There is also a City code on takeovers and mergers, which is designed to protect shareholder interests and is administered by the City's takeover panel.

10.2.3 Doing the deal

Bidding tactics

Launching a bid is a very expensive exercise in terms of fees to professional advisers. Experts can include investment banks, commercial banks, equity houses, lawyers, accountants and PR advisers. How these experts are used depends on the nature of the bid, the expertise of the protagonists, and the national/international context (Angwin 2001). The success or failure of the bid can have very widespread ramifications for all stakeholders and directly affects adviser and management credibility (Angwin 2003).

Essentially, the bidder needs to persuade the target's shareholders that they are able to produce better performance from the target company than the current management. This gives rise to *puffing* and *knocking copy*. The bidder will embark on a vigorous campaign of propaganda designed to puff up its own management abilities and knock those of the target management team. This will involve formal presentations, circulars, and 'wining and dining' key institutional shareholders, influential analysts and financial journalists. A good example of the importance of managing the media was the acrimonious bid by Granada for Trusthouse Forte. The bid was launched on the day that the Granada group knew that Rocco Forte was on holiday, shooting game. With immediate media attention, and no one to put the Forte case, newspapers polarized the two CEOs in terms of Granada's Jerry Robinson as an industrious working-class hero, versus Forte's Rocco Forte as an aristocratic hobbyist. This unjust image of Rocco Forte did considerable damage to his defence campaign.

During the 1980s, the importance of aggressive campaigning led to a string of sensational newspaper advertisements proclaiming the virtues of each position, to the extent that there are now regulations in place to tone down such campaigns.

Defender tactics

Defence may be about trying to preserve the independence of the company or just ensuring that the best price is paid (Angwin 1996, 2004). There are numerous tactics that can be used, but countries have different restrictions upon their usage.

- **Revaluation of assets**
  Assets, especially property, can quickly become undervalued in companies' accounts; revaluing to a realistic level can force the bidder to raise its offer. Other types of asset, particularly intangibles, have been a particular focus of attention.

- **Improving profit forecasts**
  Incumbent managements will almost certainly proclaim that they are able to produce higher levels of profit than before and will issue forecasts to this effect. There are strict rules about such forecasts, and financial advisers have to be very careful in agreeing to these new estimates. Clearly, some managements may have credibility problems in this respect, although it is worth noting the unusual case of Sketchley, the dry cleaning company, which, when approached by an unwelcome bidder, decided to show that the company was a great deal worse than the bidder anticipated – the bidder withdrew.

- **Crown jewels**
  Where the bid is made for one particular asset within a business, then the sale of this asset removes the threat upon the whole business. As an example, in 1982, the American Whittaker Corporation (AWC) made a bid for the Brunswick Corporation. The latter sold its crown jewel, Sherwood Medical Industries, and AWC then withdrew.

- **Pac-man**
  Although common in the US, this is rare in the UK. Nevertheless, this strategy (named after the video game) was recently employed by two breweries in the Midlands. The idea is that the target firm launches a counter bid for the acquirer.

◆ **White knight**

As a last resort, the target may seek an alternative bidder which may offer a higher price, or retain the existing management.

Other tactics that may be considered, depending on the country, are: restrictive voting rights; dual-class stocks; employee share ownership; leveraged recapitalization; poison pill; greenmail.

10.3 Issues in post-acquisition integration

It is in the post-acquisition phase that value from the acquisition is created or destroyed. Many attempts have been made to produce diagrams that show clearly how the strategic intention behind an acquisition translates into **post-acquisition integration** actions. One such diagram is shown in Figure 10.2.

While diagrams such as Figure 10.2 indicate how the level of complexity may increase with different types of deals, it is clear that the class of acquisitions labelled 'horizontal', for instance, can give rise to almost all of the types of functional change suggested.

We are now shifting from issues of strategic fit to issues of organizational fit, from viewing companies holistically to looking at the complexities within. As Figure 10.3 shows, strategic fit offers the potential upon which organizational fit acts as a series of constraints.

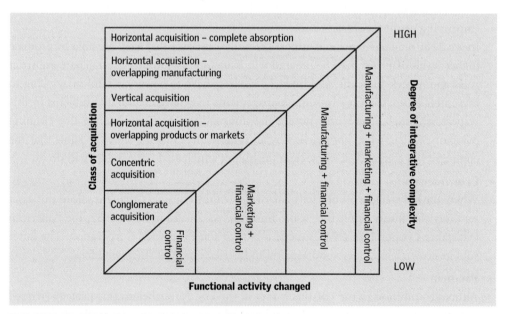

Figure 10. 2 Complexity of post-take-over integration
Source: Jones, 1982.

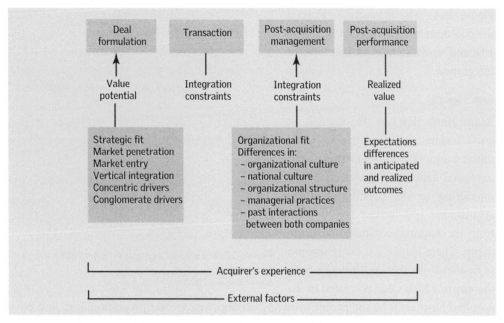

Figure 10.3 The tension between strategic and organisational fit
Source: adapted from Angwin, 2000, p. 4.

10.3.1 **Organizational fit**

Acquisitions are often associated with substantial redundancies. For this reason, there are numerous articles on the psychological impact of being acquired (Buono and Bowditch 1989; Mirvis and Marks 1992; Cartwright and Cooper 1996). There are many layers to culture and the number affected by acquisition will depend on the differences between the companies in terms of nationality, regionality, industry, corporate structure, history and managerial style. A further important dimension is the relative importance of employees to the organization's offering. Where employees are an integral part of the offering, for instance consultants are not separable from their advice, then cultural differences can have serious outcomes. In the words of one chief executive of a service firm, if the key employees walk out, what have you got?

10.3.2 **Post-acquisition integration styles**

The impact of organizational constraints, such as a culture clash, is largely a function of two factors. First, the inherent difficulties between the companies and the strategic independence of the acquired company (the need for strategic direction from the centre in Figure 10.4). Second, the extent to which value can be created from the acquisition through resource transfer or resource sharing between the two businesses (the need for resource transfer in

Figure 10.4). The interaction between the two dimensions is shown in Figure 10.4 and results in four distinct types of integration.

Arm's length

Acquisitions that are maintained at arm's length are most often in unfamiliar business areas – perhaps classic unrelated takeovers. Acquirers avoid interfering in the running of these acquisitions and instead try to learn from the acquired company's achievements. There may be a modest amount of financial/risk sharing, but essentially the way in which value is created in the

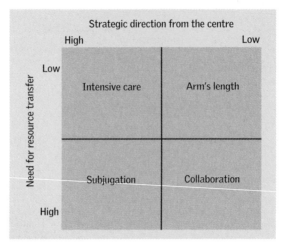

Figure 10.4 Types of acquisition integration approach
Source: Angwin, 2000.

acquired business is by the parent company encouraging greater professionalism and positively influencing the ambition of the management group. The post-acquisition phase tends to be rather gentle and it can take years for real benefits to show.

Intensive care

These acquisitions are often in poor financial shape at the time of acquisition and they are usually held in isolation to avoid infecting the group. In most cases, a turnaround strategy will be employed to restore them to a healthy condition. Owing to the poor state of the acquired company, post-acquisition actions tend to occur very rapidly, with the post-acquisition phase being relatively short. As an acquisition technique, isolation acquisitions are quite risky, but, as with all turnarounds, success can be very marked.

Subjugation

Acquisitions that are subjugated rapidly lose their identity and structure and are subsumed within the parent group. Such acquisitions are often based on clear similarities between both companies, so that amalgamation will bring economies of scale and scope. The integration process is complex, potentially occurring throughout all aspects of the business. The post-acquisition phase of subjugation acquisitions tends to occur quickly and brings rapid results.

Collaboration

Acquisitions of a collaborative nature show the acquired company having considerable independence from the new parent. The acquired company has its own head, but future projects and arrangements show joint efforts for the benefit of the group. Over time, there is substantial interchange of capabilities, but this is a gradual process. Collaborative acquisitions are difficult to manage, have substantial risks, and the benefits are long term.

In theory, collaborative acquisitions offer the greatest potential for gain. However, the gains require the acquired company to retain a high degree of strategic independence, to retain the configuration of its core capabilities, while at the same time experiencing interaction of resources with the parent. This is something of a paradox, as the acquired company, in order to receive resources from the acquirer, loses some of its precious independence and has its capabilities threatened.

The Hewlett-Packard/Compaq casebox is an adaptation of a report in the *New York Times* on the way in which Hewlett-Packard is approaching the integration of Compaq into the HP business. Using the frameworks in this section, try to identify the approach that HP is taking.

Case box: **Integrating Hewlett-Packard and Compaq**

Three days before the deal between Hewlett-Packard and Compaq was announced in September 2001 Carleton S Fiorina, the chief executive of HP, tasked Webb McKinney to lead the team that would plan how the two companies would fit together, with what products and how the proposed company would achieve its cost savings and its revenue targets. Industry analysts were sceptical. Big mergers are always tricky. In the computer industry putting two companies together has been a recipe for trouble (for example the merger of Compaq with Digital Equipment Corporation). Typically, as the new combined company grapples with the internal turmoil created in the wake of the merger, the fast-moving technology markets move on and customers defect to competitors.

The integration team had grown to more than 1,000 employees from bit companies by March 2002. By that date they had worked an estimated 1.3 million hours on the integration planning and had studied and talked to veterans of a dozen successful large mergers.

Yet, for all the detail work, one thing was clear – the need for speed. 'We make quick decisions and get on with it,' McKinney said. 'Out of the blocks, we have to move as fast as we can,' said Barbara Braun, a senior manager on the team. To do this the team has taken as one of its operating principles the need to make tough decisions instead of 'trying to make everybody happy'. The key decisions include the product line – what products will be promoted and supported most aggressively. The top 100 customers were planned to be visited by HP representatives with bound 'play books' detailing HP's product plans and who the customers' account teams will be. A crucial element will be how convincing the corporate customers find the 'migration path' from discontinued product lines to other offerings the company will feature.

The cost of not making the difficult product decisions can be far greater in terms of wasted time and investment. A big mistake after Compaq acquired Digital Equipment in 1998 was not moving early to focus the Digital Unix business on its niche strength in technical computing rather than trying to compete broadly in the Unix market against bigger rivals such as Sun Microsystems, Hewlett-Packard and IBM.

McKinney is said to be analytic and unflappable and has the temperament suited for arbitrating the tough decisions that the team must make. He and the other senior members of the integration team will stay in place to push the merger along for 12 months after the deal is closed.

Source: adapted from the *New York Times*, 25 March 2002.

The framework in Figure 10.4 is important for making sense of different post-acquisition styles and attempting to integrate this backwards into the pre-acquisition process. There is now a growing literature on the mechanics of creating value through resource sharing and transfer. This resource-based view is based on an enhanced utilization of core competences and resources. Resource redeployment is the dominant value-creating mechanism of acquisition, primarily through capability enhancement, but also to a lesser extent through cost savings. Interesting recent research suggests the acquirer is better skilled at rationalizing its own assets and redeploying its own resources than those of the target (Capron 1999).

The case box on the DaimlerChrysler merger tells the story of the difficulties of making the new entity work. Identify the problems that have occurred in the post-merger integration. Contrast these with the benefits that were expected to flow from the merger. Then assess the probabilities and time scales associated with a successful resolution of all these problems. What does this tell you about the inherent difficulties and rewards of such large-scale mergers?

Case box: **DaimlerChrysler stalled?**

Chrysler Group Chief Executive Dieter Zetsche says, 'We have to deal with the hand we have, and turn it into a winning hand.' There's no masking the stark reality behind the biggest industrial merger in history. Five years after Daimler-Benz CEO Jürgen E. Schrempp carried out a $36 billion fusion with Chrysler Corp., his promise of creating the world's most profitable carmaker is a financial blow-out. After an unexpected $1 billion loss in the second quarter, Chrysler may end 2003 in the red, despite Schrempp's boast a year ago that the unit would earn $2 billion this year. That wipes out the gains of 2002 and follows on the heels of the $5.8 billion loss in 2001.

Chrysler is not the only thing Schrempp, 59, is worrying about these days. In July, a J.D. Power & Associates Inc. survey revealed embarrassing quality deficiencies at Mercedes itself, raising questions about whether the drain on management from Chrysler is affecting the classiest of German marques. Mitsubishi Motor Corp., another troubled imperial possession, has warned of a $683 million first-half loss and has slashed its full-year earnings forecast by

75%, as U.S. sales plunge. In July, Daimler's $30 billion truck business embarked on a sweeping reorganization to reap savings from sharing parts and pooling purchasing for its various units after losing $960 million in two years. And in August, Daimler agreed to pay $300 million to settle a lawsuit by institutional investors and still faces a $2 billion claim by shareholder Kirk Kerkorian.

Was the merger a colossal mistake? A growing chorus of voices says it was. Many experts think Chrysler, whose competitiveness Schrempp badly misjudged in 1998, might have gone bankrupt by now without its German parent. Schrempp promised a swift integration and a world-spanning company that would dominate the industry. But five years later, new products have failed to pull Chrysler out of a rut. And DaimlerChrysler dominates only where it did before – in luxury cars. It now owns or controls struggling players in both the U.S. and Asia. Analysts even speculate that DaimlerChrysler might jettison Chrysler altogether. The CEO refuses to admit defeat. 'There are one or two things we didn't do right [at Chrysler] in the beginning. But we will get it right,' a subdued Schrempp told journalists at the Frankfurt motor show. Many institutional investors and small shareholders are fed up. They want to see Schrempp replaced and the deal unwound. The market capitalization of DaimlerChrysler, at $38 billion, is well below the German auto maker's $47 billion market cap before its marriage to Chrysler. BMW, the company closest in size and market segment to Mercedes, has seen its market value rise by 27%, to $26 billion, since the end of 1998. But the most stinging criticism comes from those within the vaunted 119-year-old auto maker, who point to top management error, not market woes, for the company's dismal performance. 'The entire management board is too removed from the business. Things have being going in the wrong direction for a long period of time,' says one senior DaimlerChrysler manager.

Poor execution isn't the only problem. The logic behind Schrempp's vision of Welt AG, a world auto company with integrated parts, looks increasingly flawed. Sure, Chrysler and Mitsubishi may be able to cut their costs by sharing parts and engineering. But many auto-industry experts and top executives agree that Schrempp erred fundamentally in merging a luxury auto maker with a mass-market brand – an unnatural combination that offers limited benefits and requires twice the expertise and effort to manage. Moreover, luxury has proved a better source of growth and profits than mass-market cars.

True, when Mercedes management sets its mind to change, it can be very successful. In the early '90s when Mercedes was losing ground to the Japanese, it revamped models and invested in new market niches and factories. But the global auto market today is brutally competitive. Car sales in Asia, Europe, and the U.S. are all in a long slump, and the Japanese continue to seize market share from Chrysler. The toughest challenge may be the relentless downward pressure on prices in the U.S. Big Three rebates now average nearly $4,000 per vehicle, more than double 1998 levels. That makes it hard to earn a premium on even the newest, snazziest models. Witness Chrysler's $38,000 2004 Pacifica minivan-SUV crossover.

Consumers considered the price tag steep for a Chrysler, and it now comes with a $1,000 rebate. In August, Chrysler lost to Toyota its 53-year position as America's No. 3 carmaker. 'Chrysler could prove impossible to fix,' says Garel Rhys, professor of automotive economics at Cardiff Business School in Wales.

The Germans who are doing the driving at Mercedes and Chrysler still counsel patience. They insist that the integration of process know-how and parts sharing is just starting to kick in and that, over time, productivity gains will reduce costs while quality improvements and new models boost Chrysler. But Chrysler's problems are overwhelming the gains. The new products vital to a Chrysler rebound have been slow in coming. The first joint Chrysler-Mercedes engineering product – the sleek Chrysler Crossfire roadster – only recently hit the market. While the $35,000 car offers German engineering finesse and quality at a bargain, thanks to borrowing 40% of its components from Mercedes, the experiment is a one-of-a-kind. Future Chrysler cars will share most with Mitsubishi, not Mercedes, in order to avoid diluting the luxury German brand image.

In Stuttgart, the fear and loathing of Chrysler is palpable. 'Chrysler is the downfall of Mercedes-Benz. It is a hole for billions of euros,' says one Mercedes dealer. For the first half, DaimlerChrysler's revenues fell by 11%, to $75 billion, and net profit declined by 81%, to $773 million. For now, Jürgen Hubbert, the respected boss of Mercedes Car Group, has kept Mercedes pumping out steady profits. But there are signs that could portend an erosion of competitiveness. The C-Class compact sedan is straining under competition from BMW's older 3 Series model, while less expensive cars that were developed to spur growth, including the A-Class, are unprofitable. Worse, Mercedes recently suffered a spate of quality problems, including faulty transmissions. J.D. Power's July report on customer satisfaction flagged a number of quality problems on three Mercedes models from the year 2000: the E-Class sedan, the M-Class SUV, and the CLK coupe.

How much more bad news can Schrempp survive? His fate – and that of DaimlerChrysler – depend on Deutsche Bank, DaimlerChrysler's largest shareholder, which has seen the value of its 12% stake plunge by more than $15 billion since the merger. 'The key question is: What does Deutsche Bank think? Do you throw good money after bad, or cut your losses,' says David E. Cole, president of the Center for Automotive Studies in Ann Arbor, Mich. Deutsche Chairman Josef Ackermann says he wants to sell the bank's stake, but not at today's price. The bank is still backing Schrempp, but if Chrysler posts huge losses in the quarters ahead that push the mother company into the red, Ackermann could oust Schrempp. Dissatisfaction with the merger is growing within Daimler Benz, especially among Mercedes executives. Says one insider: 'The race is on to be [Schrempp's] successor.' The front-runners: Zetsche and Eckhard Cordes, head of commercial vehicles who edged the struggling division into the black in the second quarter, even though its margins are still way below target. Getting rid of Chrysler could be tougher than firing Schrempp. A parent company can put a subsidiary into Chapter 11 bankruptcy and shrug off its pension and health-care obligations. But that works in this case only if Chrysler's obligations aren't guaranteed by parent DaimlerChrysler. Otherwise, creditors and unions would simply take their demands to the parent.

A more likely outcome: Daimler could spin off Chrysler to its shareholders. The question is whether Chrysler's research and development, engineering, and leadership could be disentangled from Daimler's. Daimler might also sell Chrysler in pieces, as BMW did with its money-losing Rover unit. Daimler, the theory goes, could sell off Chrysler's profitable Jeep SUV and Dodge truck units for a profit and hand off the money-losing passenger-car business to diehard Chrysler loyalists for $1. That, however, would surely trigger massive political and labour reactions as thousands of car-unit jobs were destroyed, and benefits jeopardized. Short of that, DaimlerChrysler could merge Chrysler and Mitsubishi car operations into a single unit.

Deutsche Bank will probably keep Schrempp at the helm for now, barring another dramatic setback at Chrysler. But DaimlerChrysler executives concede that a real turnaround will take three to five years and billions in investment. In short: a new generation of cars built in updated plants. Zetsche and Schrempp are confident they can pull that off. But many argue that Schrempp, who quadrupled his salary after the merger and ranks in compensation reviews as Germany's top-paid CEO, with an estimated $12.1 million pay package in 2002, does not deserve a third chance. If he fails again, Chrysler's problems will overwhelm its German parent in less than five years, warns an insider. 'It will be the biggest industrial cleanup job Germany has ever seen.' Given Schrempp's chequered track record, that's a high-stakes gamble.

Source: extracted from Gail Edmondson and Kathleen Kerwin, *Business Week*, 29 September 2003, Issue 3851, p. 54.

10.4 **Managing strategic alliances**

The poor performance record of mergers and acquisitions led to corporate disenchantment with this method of expansion. Corporate indigestion meant that acquirers found the immediate advantages of acquisition to be frequently undermined by the trauma of integration. Acquirers often had difficulty in assimilating the expertise of the target company and, where the target company had considerable flexibility and innovative capacity, these characteristics were often lost in the subsequent bureaucracy. Added to this disenchantment there has also been a shortage of appropriate targets to purchase. These twin constraints led companies to search for alternative means of rapid, safer expansion, so as to improve their control over the competitive environment.

Strategic alliances appeared to overcome many of the limitations of mergers and acquisitions. They seemed to avoid culture and organizational shock and yet achieve rapid presence in specific areas for the companies concerned. However, it is worth recording that there now appears to be something of a backlash with companies recognizing problems of sustainability with strategic alliances and some feeling strongly that acquisitions would have been preferable.

10.4.1 Types of co-operative strategies

Strategic alliances are just one of two broad sub-sets of **co-operative strategies**; the other is collusive strategies. They may be defined as follows:

♦ **Collusive strategies**: where several firms in an industry co-operate to reduce industry output below the competitive level and raise prices above the competitive level (Scherer 1980). Such strategies are normally between firms in the same industry and may be perceived as a defensive strategy to ward off a threat by competition. Collusion may be deliberate in which case it constitutes illegal price-fixing (in most countries). It may, however, be tacit. In that case firms recognize a common interest in raising prices without explicit agreement being reached. This is not currently regarded as illegal.

♦ **Strategic alliances**: where several firms co-operate but industry output is not reduced (Kogut 1988). Such alliances can exist between firms in different industries and can be perceived as aimed at creating and enhancing the competitive positions of the firms involved in a very competitive environment.

The term *strategic alliance* itself covers a multitude of different arrangements and there is no agreed typology in the literature. However, it is critical to understand the different forms in existence, as they have profound implications for the way in which the alliance is to be managed. In particular, there is an important distinction on the grounds of whether or not the partner is a competitor – note that even if the partner is a competitor, this may not mean collusion.

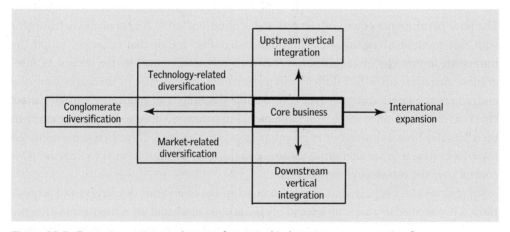

Figure 10.5 Expansion options and types of partnership between non-competing firms
Source: Adapted from Dussauge and Garrette, 1999, p. 51.

Strategic alliances between non-competitors

The following provides a useful way of linking alliance types among competitors to options for strategic expansion. These growth options may be grouped into three categories:

- *International expansion*: where a company extends its activities into a new geographic market, often after having established a dominant position in their domestic market.

- *Vertical integration*: where a company extends its activities upstream or downstream to become its own supplier or customer.

- *Diversification*: where a company expands outside its industry of origin.

In Figure 10.5 the implications for these expansion options for types of strategic alliance among non-competing firms are shown. We can see there are three main types of strategic alliance among non-competing firms:

- **International expansion joint ventures**: these are formed by companies that originate in different countries. One company often has a product that it seeks to market in another country in which the other firm has privileged access. The mutual benefits are that the local firm gains a product to distribute, while the manufacturer gains a foothold in a new country. Often these alliances are between partners with unequal skills and resources, one coming from the developed world with technical skills and considerable resources and the other from the developing world without the ability to develop such a product on its own but having a profound understanding of the local market.

- **Vertical partnerships**: these bring together two companies that operate at two successive stages in the same production process. For instance, fast food chains are critical customers of soft drinks suppliers, so Coca-Cola has set up an alliance with McDonald's and Domino's Pizza.

- **Cross-industry agreements**: these are co-operations formed by companies from totally different industries to leverage their complementary capabilities. For instance, BMW forged an alliance with Rolls-Royce in aircraft engines in order to enter that market. Although for Rolls-Royce this meant the emergence of a new competitor, it also provided the opportunity to control their long-term development. This raises the issue of competing agendas, with the newcomer trying to close the expertise gap as rapidly as possible, while the established company attempts the reverse. Such alliances may also occur where there is technical convergence between two industries. For instance, Philips has teamed up with Du Pont de Nemours for the production of surface coatings for data storage applications.

Strategic alliances between competitors

Alliances among competitors seem rather paradoxical, but according to Morris and Hergert (1987) they account for approximately 70 per cent of all co-operation agreements. Maybe it is in recognition of this that Hamel and Prahalad's (1989) article is entitled 'Collaborate with your competitors – and win'. While some put these alliances in the collusive category, it is a question of degree, with some being more collusive than others. Through the use of cluster analysis techniques on 200 alliances, Dussauge and Garrette (1999) identified three main alliance types between competitors (*see* Figure 10.6) in terms of balance of power between the partners (degree of symmetry) and impact on competition.

The three types of alliance identified may be characterized in the following way:

+ *Pre-competitive* or **shared supply alliance:** this may only cover one stage in the production process, so that while the final product contains inputs from both companies, these are specific to the parents and the alliance is not apparent to the market. These alliances occur when the minimum efficient size at a particular stage in the production process is much greater than for the entire product and when neither firm produces enough volume to achieve this critical size. These sorts of alliances are mainly between firms of similar size, often intra-zonal, and in areas of R&D and manufacturing. Industries with such alliances are automotive, electronics and data processing.

+ **Quasi-concentration alliance:** this covers the entire production process and results in a common product marketed by all allies. The assets and skills brought by each partner are similar in nature and the goal is to benefit from economies of scale. Such an alliance is clearly visible to the customer, such as in the Airbus consortium or the production of the Tornado fighter aircraft. Clearly, such alliances eliminate competition between competitors, although there can be internal rivalry within the alliance. These sorts of alliances are found mostly in the aerospace and defence industries.

+ **Complementary alliance:** when the assets contributed by the partner firms are different in nature. Most commonly, one may be a manufacturer and the other a distributor. For instance, Matra manufactures the Espace, a mini van, which is marketed in Europe

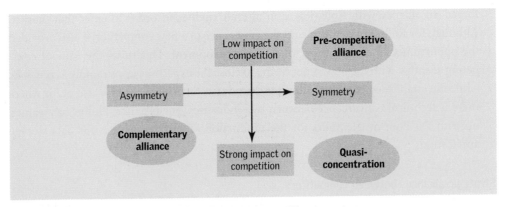

Figure 10.6 Mapping strategic alliances between competitors
Source: Dussauge and Garrette, 1999, p. 61.

by Renault. For such alliances to work, the product brought in by an ally must not compete directly with the products of the other firm. Complementary alliances are usually between two firms (unlike the other two styles) and the companies may be very different sizes. These alliances are often found in the automotive and telecommunications industries.

10.4.2 **How to manage alliances**

International expansion joint ventures

The aim of the multinational is to develop its business in the targeted country, while the local partner wishes to derive adequate profits. Both need the **joint venture** to be successful, but there are clear grounds for conflict:

◆ Profitability of the joint venture is strongly affected by the multinational partner, which controls the transfer pricing of inputs such as technology, expertise, products etc. The local partner cannot readily assess this aspect, but is totally dependent upon the profits of the joint venture.

◆ For the multinational, the joint venture is only one part of a much larger system and will manage its joint ventures to optimize the system as a whole. If profits and sales are reduced in a joint venture, the local partner suffers, as there is no other benefit.

To avoid such conflicts a management structure needs to be set up to manage day-to-day operations while respecting the views of each party.

◆ *Balance of power.* Unlike traditional shareholders, these partners[7] get involved in the day-to-day operations of the joint venture. For this reason, some partners push for a dominant equity stake. However, the link between equity distribution and performance is far from conclusive and research in developing countries suggests that there is greater chance of success as the balance of ownership moves towards the local partner (Schaan and Beamish 1988).

Equity ownership, though, is not necessarily reflected in degree of influence, which appears to have a greater impact upon performance. In Table 10.3 we can see that independent joint ventures where the general manager enjoys considerable autonomy from either parent would appear to be more successful. However, with the parents merely acting as investors and shareholders, it is difficult to see how the complementary capabilities of the partners can be leveraged.

The lower success rate of joint ventures with shared management results from problems in the balance of power, as all major decisions require consensus and, because key

---

7 The partners (typically the multinational partner and local partner) act as both shareholders and managers, and therefore are mutually involved in the day-to-day operations of the joint venture.

Table 10.3 Balance of power and performance of international joint ventures

	JV performance*			Number of JVs terminated/restructured
	Bad	Average	Good	
Dominant parent	23	23	54	15
Shared management	55	20	25	50
Independent JV	25	0	75	0

*Assessed by managers
Source: Killing, 1983.

areas are allocated to each partner, must be tightly controlled. While the other forms remove this endless negotiation and the problems of co-ordination, they also lose the opportunity to take advantage of the parents' complementarities.

♦ *Quality of joint venture manager.* It is vital for the manager to capture and preserve substantial autonomy compared to the parent firms (Killing 1983), establishing from the outset that leaving the manager to manage guarantees success and avoids untimely interventions from the parents. The manager must also manage each parent separately and work towards consensus without the parents confronting each other.

Vertical partnerships

It is not enough to just examine operational effectiveness for vertical partnerships. Other factors must be considered:

♦ The degree of mutual trust between partners.

♦ The commitment to invest jointly for the long term.

♦ The fit between the partners' strategies.

Commitment, then, is at least as important as technical capabilities.

Moving from subcontractor to full partner requires radical organizational change. In particular, each organization needs to be organized around projects rather than functions. This allows a greater account of people's opinions throughout the process, and so enhances overall unity, consistency and quality of product. Ways of facilitating these changes are to move people between firms for extended periods and indeed set them up in separate sites for the purpose of better understanding the partner's perspective and improving communication.

Cross-industry agreements

These can be in the form of combining complementary technologies to create a new business, or to exploit converging technologies, or to diversify into a partner's industry.

Where it is intended to combine complementary technologies, while the intention may be to blur the boundaries of existing industries, few such alliances have really achieved this, remaining a particular and limited segment of the previously existing businesses.

However, alliances between biotechnology companies and the pharmaceutical sector, for the testing, marketing and manufacture of products on a large scale, are at the very core of the biotech firm's development and the pharmaceutical firm's innovation process.

In terms of diversifying into another's industry, there may be financial benefit to the 'host'. The speed with which the entrant is capable of operating on its own in the targeted industry depends on how quickly it can acquire necessary skills and capabilities. This depends on three factors (Hamel 1991):

◆ *Appropriability of the incumbent's expertise* – such skills are not equally accessible, with more formalized areas being replicable upon observation, whereas more tacit knowledge is more embedded in context and far more difficult to abstract (Nonaka 1991).

◆ *Openness and transparency of the incumbent firm* – there may be procedures, systems and language that act as barriers to learning.

◆ *The ability of the entering partner to internalize new skills* – this will be affected by the similarities between the firms, the style of management and the mobility of the personnel.

Shared supply alliances

The two main areas of shared supply are in R&D and manufacturing:

◆ *Managing R&D alliances.* This occurs through dividing up the work between the firms' respective R&D facilities, rather than setting up a joint site that would result in technology leakage. To manage this, R&D alliances are implemented through informal structures, such as steering committees, to agree the division of work. The difficulty with this approach is that there are few incentives to make the joint work a priority over researchers' own projects, so that joint projects often drag and have disappointing outcomes. In addition, there is suspicion that when it comes to jointly applying, developed concepts to prototypes, entrusting one partner with the task becomes tantamount to subsidizing a competitor's new product development.

  The leakage of know-how is virtually unavoidable as even in scoping out projects a firm defines its areas of technical interest. A firm therefore must not rely too heavily on an alliance for developing its technological base and must maintain independent expertise alongside the project.

◆ *Manufacturing alliances.* Manufacturing shared supply alliances are often long-lived, but this may not be an indicator of success, as there are often barriers to dissolution. These alliances can often lack flexibility. The partner firms become captive customers of the alliance that is the 'in-house' supplier, isolated from the competitive marketplace. Contractual obligations to purchase make it difficult for the partners to carry out corrective action, which in itself is difficult, due to physical and human resource commitments. The partners also have to agree as to the way in which the alliance would be altered, which may be increasingly difficult, as their requirements of the alliance change over time.

For this reason, it is critical at formation to assess the similarity of needs between the parties, in terms of volume and technical specifications of the product, and the durability of the strategic fit, in terms of the stability of the industry and the way in which respective product lines will evolve.

Quasi-concentration alliances

These alliances aim to achieve economies of scale without merging. To achieve this, it is important that investment be minimized and economies of scale maximized. Duplications should be avoided, so that a single operator handles a specific task. Occasionally it may be necessary to pool tasks, where a separate structure is set up on behalf of the partners. If this is for the long term, such a pooling may become a business-based joint venture and is an efficient way of maximizing economies of scale.

While duplication will tend to undermine the advantages of these alliances, in many cases partners may choose to allow a certain amount of duplication, for one of the effects of the alliance may be to cause each partner to specialize to an unacceptable degree and consequently lose important skills. Although through specialization the extent and degree of rivalry will lessen, the loss of a partner can pose a serious threat to remaining partners. For this reason, in industries such as aerospace, partners allow the duplication of final assembly, as it involves a range of strategic competences; in particular, systems integration. An alternative is to rotate tasks and responsibilities.

Managing complementary alliances

In such alliances each partner contributes different and complementary assets and capabilities to the joint endeavour. However, it can be a classic case of the Trojan Horse, with each partner trying to capture the other partner's most valuable skills, to enhance its own position in the industry in general and tilt the balance of power in the alliance in particular. There is also the wish to make the other partner more dependent, so that the alliance can be influenced favourably.

Whether the alliance will remain as a win-win or degenerate into a Trojan Horse is determined by:

- The appropriability of the capabilities of the other partner.
- The value and attractiveness of those capabilities.
- The organization of the alliance – the amount of interaction will affect the amount of learning
- The '**absorptive capacity**' of the firm (Cohen and Levinthal 1990) – the extent to which the firms have appropriate organizations and cultures to facilitate learning.
- The impact of a change in environment – this may affect the balance of power, as a partner's contribution may lose value.

For the alliance to prosper it is critical for the firms to continuously improve their specific capabilities and enhance the value of their contributions to the alliance, while also preparing for possible termination. Learning from the alliance is an important aspect of complementary alliances, and often leads to early termination by the partner who has captured the desired capabilities first, with the winner operating on its own and the loser having to either form a new alliance or pull out altogether. When the race to learn is over, in many cases the winner acquires the partner.

10.4.3 Evaluations and outcomes

Assessing the outcomes of alliances is no easy matter. As we have shown, there are many different types and the partners have very different reasons for pursuing them. Tables 10.4 and 10.5 show the variety of outcomes for both non-competing and competing firm alliances.

For alliances between competitors, the most frequent outcomes overall are either an extension of the alliance or premature termination – it seems it is unusual to have a natural end or be acquired. In most cases, alliances between competitors had significant strategic consequences for the partner firms, with one-way skills appropriation in particular, and such alliances tend to affect the levels of competition in the industry. However, there is considerable variation between the different types of alliance between competitors, as Table 10.5 shows.

Table 10.4 Outcomes of alliances between non-rival firms

Alliance type	Evolution of the alliance	Strategic consequences for each firm	Impact on competition
International expansion joint ventures	High mortality rate in their first years in existence, followed by stability	Stability in the partners' relative positions	Globalization
Vertical partnerships	Long-term relationship between the partners	New division of the value added within the industry	Concentration of the upstream industry and changes in the relative bargaining power of suppliers and buyers
Cross-industry agreements	Results are frequently disappointing when compared to initial expectations	Joint venture becomes independent or intensification of competition between partners	Creation of new activities and arrival of new competitors

Source: Dussauge and Garrette, 1999, p. 209.

Table 10.5 The evolutions and outcomes of strategic alliances between competitors

Alliance type	Evolution of the alliance	Strategic consequences for each firm	Impact on competition
Shared-supply	Natural end or premature termination	No consequence	No impact on the intensity of competition
Quasi-concentration	Extension	Mutual specialization	Reduced intensity of competition
Complementary	Extension or continuation by one partner	One-way skill appropriation	Increased intensity of competition

Source: Dussauge and Garrette, 1999, p. 220.

10.5 Summary

We began the chapter with a discussion of the advantages and disadvantages of mergers and acquisitions as a method of corporate renewal. Disenchantment with the method has spurred businesses to seek alternative avenues to improve their competitive advantage. A whole new set of options has arisen in the form of strategic alliances, although the chapter has pointed out that the term embodies a substantial range of different forms. However, we are now beginning to perceive something of a backlash, as managers become disenchanted with the instability of alliances, the difficulties of realizing anticipated benefits and the risks of knowledge leakage. The irony, then, is that strategic alliances, like mergers and acquisitions, also have considerable implementation difficulties that need to be fully considered before the deal is signed.

On a broader canvas, both mergers and acquisitions and strategic alliances are good examples of the difficulties strategic management as a subject has had with the planning–implementation dichotomy. Doing the deal still obscures managing the aftermath. One can only hope that the lessons that may have been learnt with managing strategic alliances may now feed back into making better acquisitions.

Key terms

Absorptive capacity *400*

Acquisition *377*

Collusive strategy *394*

Complementary alliances *396*

Co-operative strategies *394*

Cross-industry agreements *395*

International expansion joint ventures *395*

Joint ventures *397*

Merger *377*

Post-acquisition integration *386*

Quasi-concentration alliances *396*

Shared supply alliances *396*

Strategic alliances *394*

Vertical partnerships *395*

Recap questions and assignments

Choose an acquisition/merger or an alliance which has featured prominently in the business press or with which you have been involved.

1 Critically assess the motives behind the making of the deal. In answering this question, you should consider different levels of analysis and specifically address the question of how the deal contributed to the creating and/or sustaining of competitive advantage.

2 *Either* assess the outcome in terms of subsequent events, *or* comment critically upon what you perceive to be the main difficulties ahead in realizing the intentions of the deal.

3 Why do you feel that acquisitions and alliances continue to be made, when so many fail?

Online
*Learning*Centre

When you have read this chapter, log on to the Online Learning Centre website at www.mcgraw-hill.co.uk/textbooks/mcgee to explore chapter-by-chapter test questions, further reading and more online study tools for strategy.

Case 1 Disney: The battle for the Magic Kingdom

Comcast, America's biggest cable company, has launched an audacious bid for Disney. The timing is shrewd, for Michael Eisner, Disney's boss, is under attack for poor governance and disappointing results

With viciously perfect timing, Comcast, a cable-TV company, last week launched a hostile takeover bid for The Walt Disney Company, arguably America's best-known entertainment company. Comcast is taking advantage of a particularly weak point in Disney's history. Last month Disney's most important business partner, Pixar, an animation studio, abandoned it. At the end of last year, two board members, Roy Disney and Stanley Gold, resigned and started a campaign to oust Michael Eisner, Disney's boss. On the day that Comcast announced its bid, Disney's executives started an investor conference in Florida, an occasion they had counted on to boost the company and its share price. The share price did indeed jump, but this was thanks to Comcast's bid, initially worth $66 billion, rather than to any of Disney's business plans.

At its get-together with investors, the Disney high command behaved as if the Comcast bid had never happened. Indeed, the bidder's name was barely mentioned, until Mr Eisner joked that 'we're buying Comcast' when asked about possible acquisitions. The Disney boss also argued against the sort of consolidation that media distributors like Comcast have pursued. Perhaps foreshadowing the arguments that Disney's lobbyists will make in Washington, Mr Eisner said: 'Concentration of distribution usually hurts the small guy [not] the large player.'

Mr Eisner's dismissal of Comcast's approach was backed up by Disney's board, which formally rejected the hostile bid on Monday February 16th and expressed confidence in Mr Eisner's leadership. However, the board also said it would 'consider any legitimate proposal'. The problem was that Comcast's all-share bid, which by then had fallen in value to $60 billion, did not 'reflect fully Disney's intrinsic value and earnings prospects'.

Mr Eisner's rejection of merger talks was 'unfortunate', Comcast argued in a letter to him, because strategically the deal makes sense. Putting Comcast, which has 21m cable subscribers, together with Disney, wrote Brian Roberts, president and chief executive of Comcast, would unite its distribution power and technology know-how with Disney's peerless content businesses. Although the jury remains out on whether vertical integration really delivers value, other companies have already pursued such a strategy. Rupert Murdoch's News Corp, for instance, has satellite distribution plus its Fox content businesses. Time Warner unites cable with a film studio and television programming – as well as, thanks to its horribly bubbly merger with AOL in January 2000, the internet. But a merger between Comcast and Disney would create by far the biggest vertically-integrated entertainment giant of them all, with a market capitalization of over $120 billion, says Comcast, compared with Time Warner's current $78 billion. There are no obvious competition grounds for blocking the proposed deal, since Comcast and Disney mostly operate in different businesses. However, the sheer size of the proposed company has prompted regulators and politicians to insist that they will scrutinize it aggressively.

Weapons of mouse destruction

Beyond grand strategic dreams – which some observers reckon that the hard-nosed sorts who run Comcast cannot really take seriously – Disney's appeal may be that its assets are undervalued, while those of Comcast are arguably overvalued. Disney's crown jewel, for instance, is ESPN, America's most-watched sports network. Comcast is particularly keen to own ESPN, as it currently has to pay high and rapidly rising fees to carry it on its cable channels.

Under Disney's current management, the group's profits are now a third lower than they were in 1998, and its share price is at the level it was in 1997. Part of the reason for the poor performance is sheer bad luck: Disney's theme parks, which make up nearly a quarter of its revenue, suffered badly in the wake of the terrorist attacks of September 11th 2001 and because of subsequent economic weakness – they are recovering now, if slowly. A more intractable problem is the broadcast network, ABC, which Disney bought in 1995 and is still losing money. With some exceptions, Disney's movie-making has struggled for ages. It has had big hits, such as 'Finding Nemo' last year, which have propelled a significant improvement in financial performance, but these triumphs have mostly been the work of Pixar, the studio which is now divorcing Disney.

Would Comcast, a family-controlled firm with few creative credentials, be any better at managing Disney's assets? Possibly. In a sort of government-in-exile conference which ran in tandem with Disney's own efforts this week to talk to its shareholders, Comcast's management described its plans to improve profits at its target, with special focus on ABC and on the cable networks. Steve Burke, a former Disney executive who used to run ABC, and who is now Comcast Cable's president, also stressed the need to revitalize Disney's animation business, which has languished of late. In addition to improved profitability, Comcast said, cost savings could be $300m–500m a year, bringing a total cash-flow boost from the merger of as much as $1 billion annually. Wall Street, to be sure, loves the deal, with one analyst, Jessica Reif Cohen, hailing it as a 'perfect, brilliant combination'.

Comcast, which has a well-deserved reputation as a tough negotiator of deals, also has a fine record in arguably an even harder part of the merger process – execution. It bought AT&T Broadband, a company twice its size, 15 months ago, and so far the acquisition is working well – Comcast has managed to slow dramatically the number of cable subscribers being lost by AT&T Broadband. Indeed, Comcast is considered to be America's best-run cable operator. It has managed – thanks, again, to those negotiating skills – to get cheap programming without ruining relations with its content providers. In 2000, for instance, a war broke out between Time Warner and Disney over the cost of Disney's cable channels and ended up with Time Warner blocking ABC from transmission. Comcast, meanwhile, had the same fight with Disney, but carried it out in secret, winning what are believed to have been favourable terms.

Above all, Messrs Roberts and Burke appear to believe that most of Disney's long-term problems have one (easily removed) root cause: Mr Eisner, chairman and chief executive of Disney since 1984. In his first 13 years in charge he impressively raised revenues from $1.65 billion to $22 billion, and market value from $2 billion to $67 billion. But he lost his way some years ago, and the swelling crowd of influential critics of Mr Eisner has surely emboldened Comcast to make its bid hostile.

Mr Eisner seems to have difficulty getting on with people and thereby retaining senior talent. A long list of executives, such as Paul Pressler and Steven Bornstein, have left Disney. Mr Eisner seems to have made insufficient effort to keep up good relations with Steve Jobs, chief executive of Pixar, which has been responsible for over half of Disney's studio profits in recent years. That Mr Eisner infuriated Mr Jobs, himself a fiery and short-tempered man, was confirmed recently when Mr Jobs unexpectedly ended talks to re-negotiate Pixar's co-production deal with Disney.

Mr Jobs noted that Mr Eisner told Disney's board that, after seeing an early cut of 'Finding Nemo', he didn't think the film was as good as its others – an embarrassing incident since it went on to become the highest-grossing animated feature film of all time. Mr Eisner told the board that, once the film hit movie-theatres, the Pixar people would get a reality check and become easier to negotiate with. On another occasion, Mr Eisner called Mr Jobs a 'Shiite' in a Disney board meeting, according to a board member who participated in it.

Losing Pixar should not immediately hurt Disney's results because the contract between the two firms obliges Pixar to deliver two more films, in 2004 and 2005. Wall Street analysts have thus been fairly upbeat about Disney's shares, even before the bid – the success of 'Finding Nemo' and a cyclical recovery in advertising and visitors to theme parks should boost profits sharply in 2004. Also, Disney has the rights to make sequels to all the films it co-financed with Pixar, a thought that Mr Jobs said makes his executives 'sick' since they will have no control over creative quality.

In the longer term, however, Disney faces a huge problem if it cannot improve the quality of its animated films: characters such as Snow White and Mickey Mouse have historically been the creative heart of the firm. Mr Jobs cruelly pointed out last week that not even Disney's marketing and brand could turn Disney's latest two home-grown animated films – 'Treasure Planet' and 'Brother Bear' – into successes: they both 'bombed at the box office'. With Comcast in charge, would Mr Jobs reconsider the divorce?

Unhappy family

The Comcast bid provides both succour and a conundrum for two of Disney's noisiest critics, who would presumably prefer the firm to stay independent: Roy Disney and

Stanley Gold, two former board members who resigned their positions in December in order to mount a public campaign against Mr Eisner. Mr Disney, the nephew of Walt, is derided by some Disney allies as a 'nut'. But the support of Mr Gold – a shrewd, tough lawyer who put Mr Eisner in his job in the first place—has been helping to create a following among some institutional investors for his 'Save Disney' internet campaign.

Whilst Messrs Disney and Gold clearly regard Comcast's bid as vindication for their campaign, they are as yet uncertain about whether to support the takeover. Perhaps they would prefer Mr Eisner simply to go, so that the firm can remain independent, or (less attractive) a 'white knight' to acquire Disney. Indeed, Comcast's offer may yet trigger either of those outcomes.

Meantime, Messrs Disney and Gold will try to persuade shareholders to oppose the election of Mr Eisner, and three other Disney directors, at Disney's annual general meeting in Philadelphia on March 3rd. So far, before Comcast bid, Mr Gold was believed to have mustered as much as 15% of Disney's shareholder vote. Messrs Disney and Gold have also attacked Disney's corporate governance and choice of directors. Investors should vote against George Mitchell, a former senator, they say, because he has been a paid consultant to Disney and because his other directorships leave him too little time for Disney. Institutional Shareholder Services, a firm which advises institutions on how to vote, has added its support to Messrs Disney and Gold by advising investors not to vote for Mr Eisner's re-election.

Whether any plausible white knight would be a more attractive partner than Comcast is debatable; indeed, it is easy to imagine blacker knights now joining the tournament to win Disney. True, Mr Murdoch has ruled out bidding for Disney. But Viacom, Liberty Media and even Microsoft may fancy the firm. Even likelier bidders are two internet firms, Yahoo and InterActiveCorp, whose respective bosses, Terry Semel and Barry Diller, hail from the entertainment world.

In theory, regulators might ride to Mr Eisner's rescue and block a merger of Disney and Comcast, but it seems unlikely. After the bid was announced, Michael Powell, chairman of the Federal Communications Commission, said that it would go through the 'finest filter'. Mike DeWine, a Republican from Ohio and the chairman of the Senate Judiciary antitrust subcommittee, said that his panel would hold hearings on the transaction. Yet Comcast says that it would make the same undertakings not to discriminate against other content firms and distribution networks that News Corp did last year when it acquired DirecTV. With luck, that should do the trick.

Mr Eisner, one of the entertainment world's great survivors, will no doubt try to fight to the death. He may offer yet more corporate governance reforms – though the easy ones are mostly done. He will point out that Comcast's opening offer, originally worth $27 a share and falling, is too low – though Comcast has surely known all along that it will have to raise its offer closer to the $35 that Lawrence Haverty of State Street Research says would tempt institutional investors. The fact is, if Disney's board really wants to keep one of the world's iconic companies independent, its best strategy may be to replace Mr Eisner forthwith. Otherwise, Comcast will soon be doing it instead.

Source: 'The battle for the Magic Kingdom', *The Economist*, 17 February 2004.
© The Economist Newspaper Limited, London (17 February 2004).

Case Questions

1 Why has Disney become an acquisition target?

2 What strategies would an acquirer pursue in order to restore profitability?

3 Do you think Comstat have the capabilities to pursue these strategies?

4 If you were a Disney shareholder, what would you wish should happen and why?

5 What conclusions do you draw from Roy Disney's (public) letter of resignation and public criticism of Eisner?

Further reading and references

Angwin, DN (1996) 'After the fall', *Management Today*, April, pp. 56–8.

Angwin, DN (2000) *Implementing Successful Post-Acquisition Management*, Pearson Education Ltd, London.

Angwin, DN (2001) 'Mergers and acquisitions across European borders: national perspectives on pre-acquisition due diligence and the use of professional advisers', *Journal of World Business*, Spring.

Angwin, DN (2003) 'Strategy as exploration and interconnection', Chapter 8 in S Cummings and D Wilson (eds) *Images of Strategy*, Blackwell Publishers, Oxford.

Angwin, DN, Stern, P and Bradley, S (2004) 'Condemned or redeemed: the target CEO in a hostile takeover', *Long Range Planning*, Vol 37, 3 June.

Angwin, DN and Saville, B (1997) 'Strategic Perspectives on European Cross-Border Acquisitions: A View from Top European Executives', *European Management Journal*, **15**, **4**, pp. 423–35.

Buono, AF and Bowditch, JL (1989) *The Human Side of Mergers and Acquisitions: Managing Collisions Between People and Organizations*, Jossey-Bass, San Francisco.

Calori, R and Lubatkin, M (1995) 'Euro-mergers 1993: Viewpoints and Predictions', in G Von Krogh, A Sinatra and H Singh (eds) *Perspectives on the Management of Acquisitions*, Macmillan.

Capron, L (1999) 'The long term performance of horizontal acquisitions', *Strategic Management Journal*, **20**, **11**, pp. 987–1018.

Cartwright, S and Cooper, C (1996) *Acquisitions – the Human Factor*, Butterworth-Heinemann

Child, J and Faulkner, D (1998) *Strategies of Co-operation: Managing Alliances, Networks, and Joint Ventures*, Oxford University Press, Oxford.

Cohen, WM and Levinthal, DA (1990) 'Absorptive Capacity: A New Perspective on Learning and Innovation', *Administrative Science Quarterly*, **3**, pp. 128–52.

Contractor, FJ and Lorange, P (eds) (1988) *Cooperative Strategies in International Business*, Lexington Books, Lexington MA.

Dussauge, P and Garrette, B (1999) *Co-operative Strategy: Competing Successfully through Strategic Alliances*, John Wiley & Sons, Chichester.

Hamel, G (1991) 'Competition for Competence and Inter-Partner Learning within International Strategic Alliances', *Strategic Management Journal*, **23**, special issue, pp. 83–103.

Hamel, G and Prahalad, CK (1989) 'Collaborate with your competitors – and win', *Harvard Business Review*, **67**, **1**, pp. 133–9.

Haspeslagh, P and Jemison, D (1991) *Managing Acquisitions*, Free Press, New York.

Johnson, G and Scholes, K (2002) *Exploring Corporate Strategy*, 6th edition, Pearson Education, Harlow.

Jones, CS (1982) *Successful Management of Acquisitions*, Derek Beattie, London.

Killing, JP (1983) *Strategies for Joint Venture Success*, London, Croom Helm, London.

Kogut, B (1988) 'Joint Ventures: Theoretical and Empirical Perspectives', *Strategic Management Journal*, **19**, **4**, pp. 319–32.

KPMG (1998) *KPMG Deal Watch*.

Mirvis, PH and Marks, ML (1992) *Managing the Merger: Making it Work*, Prentice Hall, Englewood Cliffs, NJ.

Mockler, RJ (1999) *Multinational Strategic Alliances*, Wiley, Chichester.

Morris, D and Hergert, M (1987) 'Trends in International Collaborative Agreements', *Columbia Journal of World Business*, **19**, **4**, pp. 319–32.

Nonaka, I (1991) 'The Knowledge Creating Company', *Harvard Business Review*, November/December, pp. 96–104.

Porter, ME (1987) 'From Competitive Advantage to Corporate Strategy', *Harvard Business Review*, May/June, pp. 2–21.

Porter, M (1980) *Competitive Strategy*, Free Press, New York.

Schaan, JL and Beamish, PW (1988) 'Joint Venture General Managers in LDCs', in FJ Contractor and P Lorange (eds) *Cooperative Strategies in International Business*, Lexington Books, Lexington MA.

Scherer, FM (1980) *Industrial Market Structure and Economic Performance*, Houghton Mifflin, Boston.

Sudarsanam, S (1994) *The essence of mergers and acquisitions*, Financial Times Prentice Hall

Weston, F, Chung, KS and Siu, JA (2003) *Take-overs, Restructuring and Corporate Governance*, 2nd edition, Prentice Hall, Englewood Cliffs, NJ.

Chapter 11

Global strategies and international advantage

Introduction

This chapter reviews the forces that are shaping the global economy and the responses that are being made by firms. We look at the characteristics of 'global' and 'multidomestic' strategies. We review the evolution of the multinational enterprise (MNE) and examine the contrasts between MNEs that are multidomestic, global and transnational.

Over the past few years the concept of global strategy has taken the world of multinational enterprises (MNEs) by storm. Scores of articles in the Harvard Business Review, Fortune, The Economist, *and other popular journals have urged multinationals to 'go global' in their strategies. The topic has clearly*

Chapter contents

captured the attention of MNE managers. Conferences on global strategy, whether organized by the Conference Board in New York, The Financial Times in London, or Nomura Securities in Tokyo have attracted enthusiastic corporate support and sizeable audiences. Even in the relatively slow-moving world of academe the issue of globalization of industries and companies has emerged as a new bandwagon, as manifest in the large number of papers on the topic presented at recent meetings of the Academy of Management, the Academy of International Business, and the Strategic Management Society. 'Manage globally' appears to be the latest battle cry in the world of international business. (Ghoshal, 1987.)

11.1 International business: the context for international strategy

11.1.1 Definition of terms

This interaction of world, country, industry and company is inherently complex. In this section we introduce some of the terminology used in international business so that we can distinguish the concepts that we use from the words and phrases that are used in practice. The approach used here follows that of Rugman and Hodgetts' (2003) excellent introduction to **international business**.

International business is the study of transactions taking place across national borders for the purposes of satisfying the needs of individuals and organizations. These transactions consist of trade (called **world trade**), which is exporting and importing, and capital transfers – foreign direct investment. Over half of all world trade and about 80 per cent of all foreign direct investment is carried out by the 500 largest firms in the world. These companies are called **multinational enterprises** (**MNEs**). Typically they are headquartered in one country but have operations in one or more other countries. In 2000 the MNEs that earned over $100 billion annual revenue were:

Exxon (USA)

Wal-Mart (USA)

General Motors (USA)

Ford Motor (USA)

DaimlerChrysler (Germany)

Royal Dutch/Shell Group (UK/Netherlands)

British Petroleum (UK)

General Electric (USA)

Mitsubishi (Japan)

Toyota (Japan)

Mitsui (Japan)

Citigroup (USA)

Itochu (Japan)

TotalFinaElf (France)

Nippon Telegraph & Telephone (Japan)

Enron (USA)

Each of these comes from one of three geographic locales: the USA, Japan or the EU. This group is called the *triad*. Of these sixteen companies, seven are from the USA, five from Japan and four from the EU. The North American Free Trade Association (NAFTA) is a regional free trade agreement between Canada, the USA and Mexico. NAFTA is often used in place of the USA as the North American element of the triad. Also Asia can be used in place of Japan to reflect the size and growth of markets such as China, India and Indonesia etc. Table 11.1 shows the breakdown of world trade by region. World trade is the sum of all export and imports. The EU is the biggest 'trader', accounting for 35 per cent of world trade, with Asia at 25 per cent and North America at 22 per cent.

Foreign direct investment (FDI) is capital invested in other nations by MNEs through their control of their foreign subsidiaries and affiliates. Most of the world's FDI is invested both by and within the triad. This has implications for the pattern of trade and industrial activity and is a highly controversial issue (see, for example, the discussions at the Cancun meeting of the World Trade Organization about access by underdeveloped regions and countries to the rich markets of the OECD countries). The USA is an excellent example of a country that is a major target of investment as well as a major investor in other countries. In 1999 nearly $990 billion was invested in the USA and the USA itself (through its MNEs) invested over $1132 billion in all other countries. Table 11.2 shows a breakdown of US inward and outward FDI by region. This demonstrates the concentration of Europe and Asia.

Table 11.1 World trade 2000

	Imports $bn		Exports $bn		World trade $bn	
North America	1692.8	25.6%	1213.6	19.2%	2906.4	22.4%
EU	2284.9	34.6%	2283.0	35.8%	4567.9	35.2%
Asia	1563.5	23.7%	1742.6	27.4%	3306.1	25.5%
Othres	1067.5	16.2%	1129.5	17.7%	2197.0	16.9%
Total	66087.7		6368.7		12977.6	

Source: adapted from Rugman and Hodgetts, 2003, p. 6.

Table 11.2 USA: inward and outward FDI 1999

	Into USA $bn	From USA $bn
Total	987	1133
Europe	686	582
Latin America	45	223
Africa	2	15
Middle East	7	11
Asia and Pacific	168	186

Source: adapted from Rugman and Hodgetts, 2003, p. 8.

Trade and investment is subject to various rules and procedures. There are many international or supra-national bodies that help to set trading rules and resolve trade disputes. For example:

◆ *The Organization for Economic Co-operation and Development* (OECD) is a group of the 30 wealthiest countries that provides a forum for the discussion of economic, social and governance issues across the world.

◆ *The World Trade Organization* (WTO) is an international body that deals with the rules of trade among member countries. One of its most important functions is to act as a dispute-settlement mechanism.

◆ *The General Agreement on Tariffs and Trade* (GATT) is major trade organization that has been established to negotiate trade concessions among member countries.

The patterns of trade and investment are highly significant and are reflected in the nature of MNEs. The United Nations has identified over 60 000 MNEs but the largest 500 account for 80 per cent of all FDI. Of these 500, 430 are from triad countries (interpreted narrowly to mean USA, EU and Japan); 185 come from the USA, 141 from the EU and 104 from Japan. This means that the triad is a basic unit of analysis for international strategy. It also means that for MNEs the actions and policies of a few key countries are highly important for their corporate strategies. Countries are concerned to maintain and foster their own economic competitiveness. As we have seen from Chapter 12, countries have strong incentives to invest in physical infrastructure and in human capital. In doing so they hope to provide conditions under which business and trade can prosper and macroeconomic goals such as low employment, low inflation and high growth can be sustained.

11.1.2 'National' competitive advantage

Why are some firms able to innovate consistently while others are not? Michael Porter (1990) provided an intriguing answer to this question. He undertook a comprehensive study of 100 industries in 10 countries. It is not simply due to the strength of individual corporate strategies. He found that the success of nations and their individual firms is determined by four broad attributes – factor (supply) conditions, demand conditions, related and supporting industries, and market (industry) structure. He called this the **diamond of national advantage** (*see* Figure 11.1).

First, it is not just factor endowments and factor conditions that are an index of competitiveness – these are the typical concerns of government policy. Also on the supply side is the supporting, related industry infrastructure, through which various externalities come into play. Thus, an automobile assembly industry is advantaged by a domestic infrastructure of auto component suppliers, which themselves have sustainable competitive advantages. Similarly, domestic rivalry and intensity of competition are seen to have a direct effect on competitiveness.

Finally, Porter points to demand conditions as a determinant of competitiveness. The size, growth and character of demand shape the supplying industries. The sophistication of local demand will be reflected in the developing characteristics of domestic suppliers. The point to take away from Porter's diamond is that the companies are embedded in and influenced by their industries, and these industries are in turn embedded in a wider economic and social structure. However, it is not clear from this analysis, nor is it asserted in this analysis, that competitive advantage is necessarily determined by the broader economic context. It is possible to see that clusters of firms and clusters of industries might have shared benefits from a common location, at the expense of (in terms of competitive advantage) firms located elsewhere. Thus, it has been advantageous to be an auto assembler in Japan and a chemical manufacturer in Germany. It may also be the case that in these circumstances it might not pay any one local player to attempt to be different[1] from other local players.

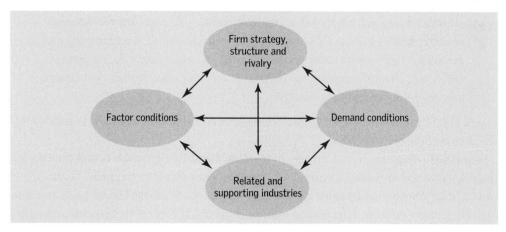

Figure 11.1 The determinants of national advantage (Porter's diamond)

[1] 'Different' in this context meaning in the strategic sense of different generic strategies or different strategic groups.

Strategically, any one firm can choose between shared local benefits ('nationality is destiny') and striving to create a unique and distinctive position.

11.1.3 The internationalization process

From this discussion we can see that the MNE has two areas of concern: its home country and its host country/countries. The linkages across these areas are in the end manifested by the cash flows across country boundaries. These are influenced by home and host government policies and by the actions of supra-national bodies in setting trade rules and regulations. Rugman and Hodgetts (2003, pp. 39–40) identify three main characteristics of MNEs:

1 MNEs have to be responsive to a number of forces across and within countries, some of which are competition related (as per the five forces) and some of which are government related (as per the diamond).

2 MNEs draw on a common pool of resources that are typically founded in the home country and which are made available throughout the MNE's affiliates.

3 MNEs link their operations through a common strategic vision and a unified international strategy.

What is **international strategy?** According to Hill and Jones (1995, p. 233):

> *Companies that pursue an international strategy try to create value by transferring valuable skills and products to foreign markets where indigenous competitors lack those skills and products. Most international companies have created value by transferring differentiated product offerings developed at home to new markets overseas. Accordingly they tend to centralise product development functions (for instance, R&D) at home. However, they also tend to establish manufacturing and marketing functions in each major country in which they do business … Ultimately, in most international companies the head office retains tight control over marketing and product strategy.*

Figure 11.2 illustrates the stages by which companies enter into foreign markets and eventually become fully blown MNEs.

Domestic firms go through a process of learning about foreign markets and minimizing the risks attached to them. Licensing, for example, gives access to the firm's standardized products for distribution by third parties in new markets. Similarly, export gains access to markets initially through independent local sales agents. If exports to particular countries become sufficiently large then there is the possibility to set up one's own sales force. This is an important stage. It marks the arrival of sales in sufficient quantities to gain efficiencies from the fixed costs of own sales activities. It also represents a stage at which direct contact with customers becomes possible with potential for customization and differentiation.

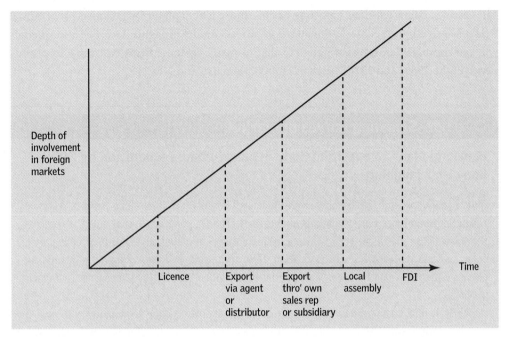

Figure 11.2 The internationalization process

It also results in familiarity at first hand with local conditions and could lead to direct investment in production and marketing and possible other value chain activities. This stage of FDI is what marks out an MNE from domestically rooted companies. At this stage there is a risk investment in a new territory and the MNE has to manifest the three characteristics shown above, namely local responsiveness, distinctive central resources and an overarching strategy.

There are many reasons why companies decide to take the plunge and take on the new, often unfamiliar, risks facing a multinational company. The usual reasons are:

1   to diversify against the risks and uncertainties of the domestic (home country) business cycle;

2   to tap into new and growing markets;

3   to 'follow' competitors;

4   to reduce costs by (i) building larger volumes and gaining scale effects, (ii) gaining access to lower factor costs, and (iii) 'internalizing' control by eliminating middlemen and other transactions costs;

5   to overcome barriers to trade; and

6   to protect intellectual property rights by undertaking value chain activities in-house rather than giving third parties access through licensing and sales agreements.

The case box below tells how Samsung has become a global player in a relatively short time. Relate its growth to the internationalization process model in Figure 11.2. See also whether you can compare Samsung's progress to that of many Japanese firms that came to prominence in the 1960s and 1970s (such as Honda, Komatsu and NEC).

Case box: **Samsung moves upmarket**

Samsung plans to overtake Sony in brand-name recognition by 2005 – Sony isn't laughing

Only a few years ago, cell phones were built just for talking. Then along came a company called Samsung Electronics selling us phones that are voice activated, that surf the Internet, that play MP3 tunes. Last year Samsung rolled out stylish models that keep our calendars in color and can pinpoint our exact location. Now the South Korean company is introducing phones with always-on text messaging and wireless video that lets us play games and watch movie clips.

Like a lot of Samsung's new devices, these combine cutting-edge technology with award-winning design—at premium prices. That's something new for a company that only a few years ago was known as a mass marketer of cheap TVs and VCRs. Since 1997, however, Samsung has begun rubbing shoulders with the market leaders in high-end cell phones, DVD players, elegant flat plasma TVs and a wide range of other consumer products. These gadgets are sometimes less expensive than those of Japanese or Finnish competitors—but by no means inferior.

Eric Kim, 47, Samsung's savvy Korean-American marketing chief, boldly suggests that he hopes to surpass Sony in brand recognition by 2005. Don't laugh; Sony CEO Nobuyuki Idei certainly isn't laughing. Samsung has the second most recognizable consumer-electronics brand in the world, according to Interbrand, the New York City-based consultancy. Idei has said privately that Samsung is on the verge of overtaking Sony in the consumer-products race. Graeme Bateman, head of research in Seoul for Japanese investment bank Nomura Securities, says Samsung is 'no longer making poor equivalents of Sony products. It is making things people want.'

What's more, at a time when most of the world's tech companies are still shuttering plants and trimming R & D to weather the global economic slump, Samsung is extending its reach. Bolstered by the resurgent Korean economy—which is expected to grow 3% to 6% this year after nearly collapsing during the 1997 Asian financial crisis—Samsung Electronics' worldwide revenue reached $25 billion last year.

That's not even half the revenue stream of giant Sony, but Samsung Electronics is growing fast. It is the best performer in the family-controlled conglomerate that spawned it, the Samsung Group. Investors are pouring money into the stock. Korea's consumers are spending more than ever, and they just happen to be among the most wired people on the planet, with easy access to broadband connections and new wireless local-area networks. So Samsung has an unparalleled testing platform for new gadgets right in its backyard.

Since the early 1990s, Samsung has led the global market in dram semiconductors, the memory chips that are vital to almost every digital product we use. During the current slump, as competitors like Hitachi and NEC have been backing away from the chip business, Samsung has been diving in, introducing two new lines. The company has leveraged its digital know-how to dominate the manufacturing of computer monitors and state-of-the-art flat-panel displays. In 2002 Samsung, in conjunction with Texas Instruments, introduced the world's first 50-in. TV with digital light-processing technology, now used mostly in movie theaters. Analysts who have seen the picture say it is sharper than anything on the market. And Samsung revolutionized the world of microwave ovens with a technology that senses when your food is properly cooked.

Samsung got into the U.S. phone business only in 1997, through a $600 million deal with Sprint and pledged that it would become a Top 5 phone maker within five years. It made it in two, with the clamshell-shaped 3500, which became America's top-selling cell phone in 2000. Last year, among a rush of other introductions, Samsung started selling the I300, a Palm-based PDA with a built-in wireless phone. Although there are plenty of combo PDA phones on the market, none have sold as well or enjoyed as much acclaim. 'People pull these out at meetings to show off, which makes them a walking brand advertisement,' says Peter Skarzynski, a Samsung Telecommunications America vice president. 'That's what Sony's Walkman did for them.' And that's what Samsung's products and a big advertising investment are doing for it. In 2001 its global brand recognition grew a stunning 22%.

Throughout the global slump of 2000–2, Samsung has continued to invest in new processes and research. The company refined its semiconductor and liquid-crystal-display operations so effectively that traditional competition from Tokyo was upended. 'Samsung is more cost effective, and its manufacturing technology is better than at companies like Sharp and Hitachi,' says Shiro Mikoshiba, a Nomura Securities analyst in Tokyo. 'The Japanese stopped competing two years ago.'

The next stop in Samsung's digital march is the living room. To that end, the company has worked with Microsoft to develop Home Media Center, designed to control everything from your DVD player to the PC. Last June, Texas Instruments and Samsung signed an agreement to develop ultra thin, large-screen televisions based on TI's digital light-processing technology. In 1999 TI turned down a Samsung partnership offer, thinking it would be better to work with 'established' brands. By last year it was clear that TI's initial partners were moving too slowly to get anything to market in good time. With Samsung, it took only a matter of months. The new 50-in. television made its debut in January 2002 at the Consumer Electronics Show in Las Vegas, and videophiles like Evan Powell of ProjectorCentral declared it an instant hit.

For all its technical prowess, Samsung faces big-league competition in its quest to dominate the digital home. Microsoft, AOL Time Warner, Apple and Sony are among the heavy hitters that are also betting that someday everything from our alarm clocks to our refrigerators will be linked to a constant stream of information and entertainment from the Internet. (AOL Time Warner has formed partnerships to develop digital hardware with both Samsung and Sony.) Samsung is gambling that it can move faster than its bigger rivals.

Samsung has demonstrated a century's worth of catch-up in a very short time. Now the question is whether they can fulfill the new expectations for Samsung's future.

Flat-panel monitors	DRAM chips	DVD players	Mobile handsets
1. Samsung 13.1%	1. Samsung 27.9%	1. Sony 23.3%	1. Nokia 35.6%
2. Philips 11.3%	2. Philips 20.3%	2. Samsung 11.7%	2. Motorola 15.0%
			3. Samsung 7.2%

Sources: Frank Gibney Jr, iSuppli Stanford Resources, Semico Research Corp., NPD Intellect
Source: extracted from *Time.com* March 25, 2002. © 2002 by Time, Inc. Reprinted by permission.

11.2 Globalization

There is no doubt that **globalization** and internationalization have, as ideas, fired the imagination, even though the words themselves are cumbersome and awkward. In this section we intend to give an economic meaning to the term globalization.

11.2.1 Global markets and industries

International trade incorporates many different types of competition, and across industries we can observe marked differences in the patterns of international competition. On the supply side of industries, the dimension of competition and of strategic choice in which we are interested is geographic scope, the extents to which firms' activities extend across national borders. But it is the demand side that is more important. We use the term *multidomestic* (or *multilocal*) to describe industries where the competition in any one country is independent of competition elsewhere. We use the term *global* when competition in one country is influenced by competition elsewhere. Multidomestic is the situation where markets are different in their consumer behaviour patterns. Thus, the market for foods can be seen to be very different across the countries of the European Union and even wider across the countries of the world. By contrast, the market for Coca-Cola is broadly similar across the world, with consumers exhibiting similar if not the same utility functions and buying behaviour. **Global** markets lead to standard products, whereas **multidomestic** markets lead to product differences and diversity. Multidomestic industries are, as the name implies, a collection of domestic industries. A global industry leads directly to international rivalry. In a multidomestic industry a firm can and should manage its worldwide activities as a portfolio of independent subsidiaries in each country – this is a country-centred strategy and relatively little co-ordination is necessary or valuable. In a global industry, to have a global strategy a firm must develop and implement a strategy that integrates its activities in various countries, even though some portion of the firm's activities must take place in each individual country.

Figure 11.3 puts this approach to globalization in a broader context. 'Global' refers, broadly speaking, to an entwined web of economic forces. The world dimension indicates the extent to which there is economic interdependence between countries, as indicated by the cross-border flows of goods, services, capital and knowledge. At the country level, countries will differ in their degree of linkage between their economy and the rest of the world, using the same indicators. Our definition of global industry has thus to be seen in the context of the worldwide pattern and the role of individual countries. At the firm level, we are looking at the extent to which its revenue and asset bases are spread across borders.

11.2.2 Global companies

Table 11.3 indicates the degree of internationalization of Fortune 100 companies. Although we have a reasonably clear concept of what constitutes global at the industry level, it is much harder to distinguish a 'global' firm from any other. From Table 11.3 we can see that many firms have a high proportion of sales and production abroad. But there are deeper levels of internationalization. Table 11.3 picks out research and development, management style and membership of boards of directors as indicators of the extent to which firms can transcend national boundaries.

The nature of globalization is complex and multidimensional, even without bringing in broader issues of culture, behaviour, national tastes and so on. Accordingly, there have been

Figure 11.3 Determinants of 'globalization'

Table 11.3 Degree of internationalization of Fortune 100 companies (early 1990s)

- *c.*40 companies generate >50% of sales abroad
- <20 companies maintain >50% of production capacity abroad
- 13 companies have >10% of shareholdings abroad
- R&D remains firmly domestic
- Executive boards and management styles remain solidly national
- Almost all highly internationalized companies originate from 'small' economies:
  - Netherlands: Philips, Royal Dutch/Shell (60% Dutch), Unilever (40% Dutch)
  - Sweden: Volvo, Electrolux, ABB (50% Swedish)
  - Switzerland: Nestlé, Ciba-Geigy, ABB (50% Swiss)

many attempts to capture the term in a single definition. The original proponent of globalization was Theodore Levitt (1983), whose concept was that of *global standardization* – a single global market with standard products and a corporate focus on gaining efficiencies through standardization. Kenichi Ohmae (1985) introduced the idea of the 'triad' – to compete effectively, firms should be present in each of the three major regions of the world. This has become known as *global localization.* Wisse Dekker, an erstwhile chairman of Philips, saw globalization as *assembly abroad* to *circumvent competition.* More recent commentators see *global niches* sitting alongside domestic redoubts. Toyota in its Annual Report in 1995 said:

> *Our global strategy used to centre on 'world cars' which we would modify slightly to accommodate demand in different markets. To-day our focus is shifting to models that we develop and manufacture for selected regional markets.*

We seem to be moving from a market-based focus on standardization (standard products and centralized production facilities) to a resource-based view of standardization. This would argue for a common approach to knowledge and learning, and resources and capabilities across the world, but with products adapted to local or regional needs from a common core competence.

Table 11.4 suggests what might be the deeper drivers. There are five forces at work. The first is a *cultural homogenization* – a 'global village' argument that we leave for you to reflect

Table 11.4 Why globalization?

- Cultural homogenization ('global village')
- Convergence of markets
- Globalization of customers
- Cost drivers
  - economies of scale and scope
  - increase in levels of fixed cost
- Fundamental changes in industry structure
  - deregulation, privatization
  - technological change

upon using your own experience. Two of the forces are from the demand side, *convergence of markets* and *growing similarity of customers*. Markets in this context are about the infrastructure and the processes by which markets work. This covers legislation, application of competition law, organization of selling and distribution systems, consumer protection laws, local tariffs and so on. The markets for agricultural products are vastly different between Russia and the United States. The markets for packaged groceries are different between European countries, to the extent that the laws governing price promotions and use of television advertising are different and the extent to which superstores are allowed to develop as between France and Italy, for example. One of the aims of the Single Market Acts in the EC in 1992 was to create broadly similar market conditions across Western Europe – the 'level playing field'.

The customer argument is more plainly about the degree of similarity between the utility functions of customers in different locations and the impact this has on buying behaviour. This can be exemplified by considering two buyers of auto components, one for Ford Motor Company's plants in Europe the other for General Motors. Their buying criteria are likely to be very similar and component companies are very likely to be designing and selling very similar components across Europe. It is less clear that Italian and English shoppers in supermarkets will have the same attitudes and ideas about buying food products. To the extent that these buyers are fundamentally different in their behaviour, the suppliers will be adapting their products to reflect different requirements in Italy and in England.

On the supply side of industries, the cost drivers are very important. We learned in Chapter 3 of the significance of economies of scale and experience. The costs of investment can be so high that single national markets, even those of the USA, might be too small to support them. It is difficult to see how the design and development costs of large aeroplanes can be economically supported from even the USA. The development costs of automobiles, prescription drugs, many high-technology new products, and much military hardware require a large international market. It is in the interests of companies, then, to make the offer of a standardized product across the world in competition with the more locally differentiated, but more expensive, options offered by local companies. From a cost point of view, the presence of significant scale and experience effects drives customers towards the cheaper, more standardized options. This is the basis of Levitt's approach to global standardization.

Finally, fundamental changes in industry structure can result in major changes to the underlying economics of industries (for example, through technological change). Coupled with new management teams (for example, through privatization and deregulation) this can change the terms on which companies approach their marketplaces and their opportunities to move across borders. For example, the worldwide trend to the privatization of telecommunications and utility companies has challenged the presumption that the natural market for utilities is domestic only.

Scale is commonly considered to be a major characteristic of being global. But there are other benefits:

+ exposure to the world's 'best' practice;
+ learning and transfer opportunities of best practice;
+ access to technology;
+ ability to serve new customer groups;
+ ability to anticipate moves of global competitors;
+ ability to defend national profit sanctuaries through counter-attack.

In looking at global industries and the firms that compete in them, you should be able to examine and test the proposition that industries do not go global by accident. They are global because of innovations in strategy. **Global strategies** can create advantage only if they:

+ change the economics of the industry;
+ serve local markets better than the local incumbents;
+ are hard to emulate;
+ are sustainable;
+ are capable of further development.

As a firm gains experience in operating within a global industry, some of the original strategic innovations become embedded into the industry structure and thus, the industry economics will have characteristics such as large-scale economies – high and rising R&D costs, extensive interaction with governments, and links with changes in country infrastructures. But there are still many strategy choices open to each firm: for example, how to increase local content without sacrificing global scale, how to increase product homogeneity through design, how to shape demand, how to develop systems to make co-ordination easier. Some firms will be striving to develop local/domestic niches, others will be focusing on global segments, and others might be attempting global standardization.

11.2.3 Globalization and the value chain

The key strategic choices in globalization revolve around local differentiation versus global standardization. These might be seen as polar opposites, but more usually the question is how to secure the right blend between the two. What would this mean for how we conduct our business?

Figure 11.4 enables us to think of the implications of global choices in terms of how we manage the activities in the value chain, where we locate them, and how we co-ordinate the whole chain. The opportunity for global standardization occurs when:

+ upstream value chain activities can be decoupled from downstream activities and, in particular, from buyer locations;

- these activities are a large part of total costs;
- scale effects are important in these activities.

We see that these conditions hold with automobiles. Production does not need to be close to the customer, nor even to the sales channel. Assembly is a very large part of the cost and there are very big scale economies. Conversely, multidomestic industries exist where:

- downstream activities are tied to buyer locations and market-specific entry barriers can be created;
- these activities are a large part of total costs.

These are situations where the competitive advantages reside primarily with the downstream, and the focus of strategic attention lies with managing its capacity to differentiate the product offering. This is typical of retailing, many service operations, such as investment banking, and consumer packaged goods.

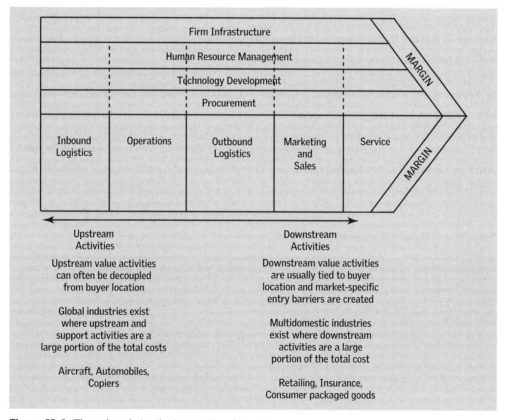

Figure 11.4 The value chain: the international strategy
Source: Adapted from Porter, 1985, p. 46. Reprinted with permission of The Free Press, a division of Simon and Schuster Adult Publishing Group. Copyright by the Free Press. All rights reserved.

The possibility for globalization usually means that the value chain has to be partitioned in some way. The key strategic dimensions of choice are:

◆ Where to perform each activity in the value chain – the *configuration* question.

◆ How to link similar activities wherever they are located.

◆ How to co-ordinate all the activities in the value chain – the *co-ordination* question.

The degree of co-ordination is in general dependent on how globally standardized the product is or, conversely, how varied the local market conditions are. Table 11.5 summarizes the kinds of high and low co-ordination patterns that might be observed. The contrast between high and low degrees of co-ordination stem from the balance between the two types of competitive pressure that are evident in global markets: pressures for cost reductions and efficiency, and pressures for local responsiveness. Typically, local differentiation requires low co-ordination, as each country operation contains much of the value chain that it needs, and those inputs it does need, such as components, will be relatively standardized. Pressures for global efficiency usually mean that there is product standardization and close integration of production and service delivery across all the value chain activities, which themselves will have been located in the lowest-cost regions/countries.

The tension between the pressures for efficiency and for local responsiveness is a constant concern for multinational companies. The efficiency dimension can be seen as pressures for global co-ordination and integration. This is a subtle restatement of cost and efficiency pressures, coupled with product standardization, taking account of the variety and diversity that takes place at the margin around simple standardization. The pressures for national or local responsiveness represent a complex aggregate of differentiating forces, namely differences in consumer tastes and preferences, differences in local infrastructures and traditional practices, differences in distribution channels and other forms of access to markets, and host government demands.

Table 11.5 Co-ordination across international markets

Reasons for high co-ordination	Reasons for low co-ordination
Share know-how and learning Reinforce brand reputation Supply identical differentiation worldwide Differentiate to local buyers by meeting their needs anywhere Seek bargaining counters with governments Respond to competitors' flexibility	Respond to diverse local conditions - product needs - marketing systems - business practices - raw material sources - infrastructure Circumvent government restrictions on flow of goods or information Avoid high co-ordination costs Acknowledge organizational difficulties of achieving co-ordination across subsidiaries

11.2.4 **Sources of competitive advantage**

As we have seen in Chapter 8, corporate strategy is about exploiting economies of scope across the business units of the corporation. Global strategy requires the exploitation of economies of scale, scope, knowledge and learning across national boundaries. Ghoshal (1987) provides an excellent framework (*see* Table 11.6) for understanding the sources of advantage that can spring from 'globalization' and the strategic objectives that can be pursued. As Segal-Horn puts it:

> *Ghoshal creates a roadmap to guide managers of multinational companies through their choices for global strategic management.* (Segal-Horn, 1998, p. 325)

Ghoshal refers to this framework as a mapping of means and ends. The means are the sources of advantage and the ends are the strategic objectives. The goals are an elegant articulation of three contrasting but complementary themes:

- *Achieving efficiency* is the dominant perspective in strategic management, where the objective is to maximize the value of the ratio between outputs and inputs. The basic strategies of cost leadership and differentiation are both maximizers in this sense, cost strategies reducing the value of inputs and differentiation strategies increasing the exchange value of the outputs.

- The notion of *managing risks* gets far too little attention in the academic and in the business literatures. Ghoshal identifies several different categories of risk:
  - macroeconomic risks
  - political or policy risks
  - competitive risks, and
  - resource risks.

- *Innovation, learning and adaptation* are an outcome of resource-based thinking. Here Ghoshal makes an interesting argument that increasing geographic scope ('globalization') is in effect an exposure to diversity and variety. The twin pressures of managing for efficiency and for local variety impose a greater need to innovate, to learn and to adapt than is faced by a purely domestic firm.

Ghoshal maintains there are three fundamental tools for building global competitive advantage:

- The first is to exploit the differences in input and output markets in different countries. This is to exploit **comparative advantage** – the economic characteristics that make national economies different.

- The second is to achieve *economies of scale.*

- The third is to exploit *economies of scope.*

Table 11.6 Global strategy: sources of competitive advantage

Strategic objectives	National differences	Scale economies	Scope economies
Achieving efficiency in current operations	Benefiting differences in factor costs – wages and cost of capital	Expanding and exploiting potential scale economies in each activity	Sharing of investments and costs across products and businesses
Managing risks	Managing different kinds of risk arising from market policy-induced changes in comparative advantages of different countries	Balancing scale with strategic and operational flexibility	Portfolio diversification and risks of options and side bets
Innovation, learning and adaptation	Learning from societal differences in organizational and managerial processes and systems	Benefiting from experience-based cost reduction and innovation	Shared across organizational components in different markets or businesses

Source: Ghoshal, 1987.

The term **national differences** refers to what economists call **factor conditions** or differences in factor costs between different countries. According to international trade theory a country will export those goods that make use of the factor conditions with which it is relatively well endowed. Thus, a country such as China is concentrating on modern assembly plants in which the low cost of Chinese labour plays a significant role in reducing costs. MNEs seek to locate their activities in regions with specific factor advantages. For example, BT along with many UK-based banks are relocating their call centres to India to take advantage of low costs but a skilful labour force. Rugman and Hodgetts (2003, p. 17) cite the example of the Netherlands as the world's leading exporter of flowers. It has maintained its position by creating research institutes in the cultivation, packaging and shipping of flowers. Therefore, any company wishing to compete in this industry has to have an operation in the Netherlands. Similarly, in Formula 1 racing the central cluster of activity is to be found in Motor Sport Valley in the South of England. Here are to be found skilled labour and craftsmen in engineering, advanced materials, software and project management. For Ferrari to become successful again in F1 racing it had to gain access to these skills by first establishing an operation in England and then finding ways to transfer this knowledge throughout their Italian home base.

From Ghoshal's framework we are able to articulate the nature of the trade-offs between alternative strategy choices. In other words, the framework is not deterministic, but it does enable discussion of the consistencies and contradictions among different moves.

In the next section we will re-visit some of the basic concepts that lie behind globalization and will return to Ghoshal's organizing framework at the end of the chapter. But before we move on, it is helpful to examine the internationalization of service industries (Segal-Horn, 1993). Service industries have traditionally been seen as domestic or local, but there have been many celebrated attempts to go global, some of which have been seen to fail (for example, Saatchi & Saatchi) and some of which are clearly successes (for example, American Express). Segal-Horn's contribution is to take Chandler's logic of internationalization (and also Ghoshal's later framework) as developed for manufacturing firms and show how the basic assumptions are now relevant for service organizations. Thus, we see that scale and scope economies – the roots of strategy analysis – are as relevant for service firms as for any others. With service firms, it is clear that the source of scope economies is rooted for the most part in the way in which knowledge and information can create scope benefits. It is worth noting also that the service element of hitherto traditional manufacturing has increased dramatically and that the role of services in the advanced economies now outweighs that of manufacturing (Quinn 1992). Thus, the consequences of Segal-Horn's approach are significant both in terms of the economy as a whole and for the nature of internationalization as a knowledge-based phenomenon.

Read the case box on US multinationals, which argues that the conventional assumption of globalization is misplaced. You should also look again at Table 11.3, which uses the same data sources. What is the criterion you would use to assess whether a company is 'global'? Also, what difference would this make to the strategies that companies should follow and the relationships that they should cultivate with their home governments and with their many host governments?

Case box: US multinationals are regional not global

Karl Moore and Alan Rugman argue that globalization is not what it seems

'Go global'. That's what CEOs have been hearing from gurus and academics for a while now. But how global are the US' biggest MNEs? We argue not very global at all. Each year *Fortune* magazine ranks the world's largest MNEs in its annual *Fortune 500*. The US accounts for 185 of the companies: the ERU has 141 and Japan 104. Together this 'triad' has 430 of the top 500 companies.

But, if you examine the data on the US' 25 largest multinationals it becomes clear that they are what we would call home-region based. Of the US' 25 largest MNEs 22 have more than 50% of their sales in their home region of North America. None of these US MNEs are 'global'. For example, Wal-Mart has 94.1% of its sales in the North American Free Trade Area (NAFTA); GM has 81% – and so on. Indeed, the average intra-regional sales figures for all the 185 US MNEs is 77.3%. With well over two-thirds of their sales in North America, these are home-based triad MNEs. So much for the globe-girdling US MNE.

Only IBM, ranked at number seven, is a truly 'global' firm, with over 20% of its sales in each region of the triad. Other US global firms (not in the top 25) are Intel and Coca-Cola. Indeed, only eight of the *Fortune 500* firms in the world are global – the others are Sony, Philips, Canon, Flextronics, and LVMH.

'So what?' the hard-nosed CEO may ask. Good question: what this data tells us is that US companies should focus corporate energies and push government policies to secure access to the vital regional NAFTA market. At the same time US companies should continue to increase their involvement in the two other regions of the triad economies, the EYU and the small number of critical Asian economies. That is the reality of today's global economy.

Source: extract from Karl Moore and Alan Rugman, *Business Strategy Review*, vol 14, no. 4, p. 2. Reproduced with permission of Blackwell Publishing.

11.3 **Strategic choices**

11.3.1 **Strategic positioning**

There are four basic strategies that companies use to enter and compete in the international environment: multidomestic, international, global and transnational. These are covered in detail in Bartlett and Ghoshal (1989) and are depicted in Figure 11.5.

Multidomestic strategies are, as we described above, country centred with extensive customization for local markets and with an almost full set of value chain activities in each major market. They do transfer skills and products developed at the home base, but high degrees of local discretion are given to meet local conditions. Typically, these strategies cannot realize value from centralized, scale-effective, experience-rich production facilities. Bartlett and Ghoshal describe multidomestic companies as decentralized federations (Figure 11.5) and regard them as typically European, being conceived in days of higher transport and communication costs and higher tariffs.

International strategies create value by transferring key skills, capabilities and products to local markets. The degree of differentiation developed in the home base is advanced and the intent is that the differentiation delivered in each local market reflects this. Thus, local differentiation is complementary to that from the centre. However, the organization is usually country centred and local managers have important degrees of discretion in deciding what product portfolio to offer and how it should be presented locally. Product development and R&D tends to be centralized in the home base, but other value chain activities are usually closer to market. Head office retains close control over marketing strategy and product strategy, and also exercises close financial control. Bartlett and Ghoshal regard this as typically North American – born in the 1950s and 1960s, as US companies began to realize the benefits of the scale and technological achievement of 50 years of distinctively large, progressive markets. They see this form

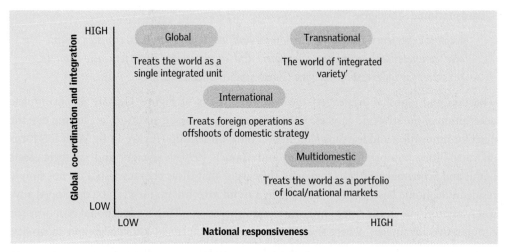

Figure 11.5 International strategic environments: late 1990s
Source: Adapted from Prahalad and Doz, 1986.

as a co-ordinated federation, the degrees of co-ordination (especially in marketing and finance) being distinctive American contributions to management practice in the post-war years. Many writers are tempted to place international strategies into the bottom-left corner of Figure 11.5. This would be to deny the distinctive co-ordinating power of these companies (for example, Procter & Gamble, IBM, Kellogg, McDonald's, Merck). Moreover, with low co-ordination and low responsiveness, there would not appear to be a sustainable strategy.

Global strategies focus on increasing profitability through product standardization, and capturing the cost reductions that come from location economies (exploiting comparative advantage in Ghoshal's framework in Table 11.6), economies of scale and experience effects, and the organizational focus on procedures and processes that support low costs. Bartlett and Ghoshal see these strategies as quintessentially Japanese, having emerged in the growth years and tariff reduction years of the 1970s and 1980s. These companies are typically highly centralized, with little attempt to build local differentiation (marketing) activity. They do, however, often pursue global branding and 'quality' positioning, along with or after their initial focus on low cost (for example, Sony). Toyota was a good example of a global strategy in the 1980s – its productivity (cars per employee) was about 37 com-pared to 20 at Ford, which would be regarded as having an international strategy. Many industries can be seen to be global in character. Thus, the semiconductor industry has global standards with enormous worldwide demands for standardized products. Not sur-prisingly, the players such as Intel, Texas Instruments and Motorola pursue global strategies. Bartlett and Ghoshal describe global companies as centralized hubs, reflecting the high degree of centralization.

Transnational strategies:

> *Exploit experience-based cost economies and location economies, transfer distinctive competences within the company, and at the same time pay attention to pressures for local responsiveness.* (Bartlett and Ghoshal, 1989)

Bartlett and Ghoshal argue that the two dimensions of Figure 11.5 are an incomplete description of the strategic choices. They offer a resource-based addition, suggesting that the need for innovation and learning should be a third dimension (Figure 11.6). With this focus on capabilities, competences (Prahalad and Hamel, 1990, language) and strategic assets (Amit and Schoemaker, 1993, language), they argue that these characteristics do not simply reside in the home base. On the contrary, by careful investment, they can be developed anywhere appropriate in the company's worldwide operations. This is a locational economy (or comparative advantage), where the advantage is in the form of knowledge and capability, rather than low cost. So the flows of skills and products can be in any direction within the worldwide configuration of activities.

The role of the centre is to provide an organizational and strategic context within which the complex flows and interactions can take place. Toyota is a good example, as are other Japanese auto manufacturers such as Nissan and Honda. We saw earlier that Toyota has moved from a focus on the 'world car' to something more regional. This initially involved the development of manufacturing capabilities and sites in North America, Europe and

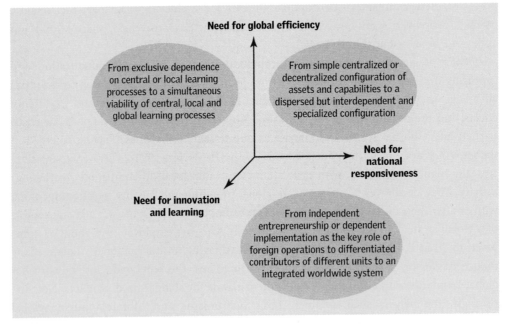

Figure 11.6 The strategic tasks
Source: based on and freely adapted from Bartlett and Ghoshal, 1989.

elsewhere in the world. Along with this goes a spreading of product development beyond Japan.

Unilever is another example. Once it was a classic multidomestic company in the European tradition. It has moved from 17 different and largely self-contained detergents operations in Europe toward a single European entity with detergents being manufactured in a handful of cost-efficient plants, and with standard packaging and advertising across Europe. Unilever's estimate of the cost savings is over $200 million per year. However, Unilever recognizes that there are major differences in distribution channels and that brand values and brand awareness vary a lot across Europe, and therefore, that local responsiveness must not be sacrificed for simple standardization benefits. In other words, Unilever have taken some steps to move from multidomestic to transnational. By contrast, Procter & Gamble have seemingly moved more in the direction of a global strategy from an international position. The transnational company is likely to need a matrix structure (see below) and is increasingly likely to move towards a network organization (Figure 11.7).

Strategic choice involves making trade-offs. It is not always clear what strategies should be followed because it is rare that one choice will dominate all other possibilities. The advantage of a pure global strategy is the ability to become a low-cost player, but the disadvantage is the lack of local responsiveness (*see* the Matsushita example in Bartlett and Ghoshal 1989).

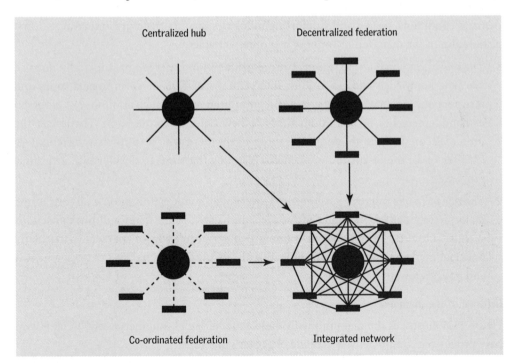

Figure 11.7 Alternative organizational solutions
Source: adapted from Bartlett and Ghoshal, 1989, Chapters 3 and 4, pp. 50–2 and 89.

The multidomestic has the opposite trade-off. It is able to differentiate to local markets and respond to local conditions, but it cannot manage itself into a distinctive low-cost position. The international company is able to transfer distinctive competences to new markets, but it can be caught between the inability to differentiate enough locally or to be sufficiently low cost. It could be a case of 'stuck in the middle' – this seems to be Procter & Gamble's own diagnosis. The transnational appears to solve all of these conventional trade-offs, but it clearly has major difficulties of implementation, because the network organization is so fundamentally different from more traditional 'command and control' organizations.

11.3.2 Country issues

The double diamond

The balancing of efficiency, responsiveness and innovation is in a sense an elaboration of Porter's classic generic strategies (cost, differentiation and focus), bringing in the dynamics of innovation to his essentially static model. Porter's later model (1990) on the diamond of national advantage and its implications for companies can also be elaborated in this context. According to the diamond model the MNE takes sustenance from its home markets and these provide the strategic asset base from which advantage can be gained.

First, here is a reminder of the four key variables in the diamond: factor conditions, demand conditions, related and supporting industries, market structure and rivalry. A first elaboration of the diamond introduces two other variables:

1 *The role of chance and uncertainty.* Unforeseen developments are paradoxically normal, viz. new knowledge and inventions, interventions of foreign governments, wars and insurrections, financial market crises, discontinuities in costs such as oil shocks, surges in demand, emergence of new competitors or new types of competition. The longer the time scale of strategic thinking, the more likely there will be unforeseen events (see Chapter 14 for the discussion on scenario planning that aims to deal directly with these problems).

2 *The role of (home country) government.* Government's task is to influence all four of the major determinants of national advantage summarized in the diamond through actions such as subsidies, education and training policies, regulation of markets (particularly financial markets), establishment of standards, its purchasing policy, tax laws, antitrust and policies towards competition.

Critique of the diamond

Figure 11.8 illustrates the diamond with these extra variables. Rugman and D'Cruz (1993) have provided a comprehensive critique of Porter's diamond.

First, they observe that the data on which the diamond is founded contains only triad-based countries and therefore refers only to firms with strong home bases. MNEs in non-triad countries would not expect such a supportive home base and these must therefore look elsewhere for strategic assets.

Second, government is a crucial player but not all governments, even in triad regions, follow identical policies. Mistakes are possible that might, for example, result in the creation of sheltered domestic industries that cannot compete in international markets. Policy fashions might also result in misdirected investments intended to create national flagships.

Third, the diamond is uncomfortably positioned between the determinism of governments and the discretion of companies. In the end it is companies that make the strategic investments and these may often be at odds with the prevailing national orthodoxy. See, for example, the rise of Honda in spite of Japan's MITI officially disapproving of its international ambitions.

Fourth, behind Porter's model is an assumption of a life cycle of evolution of national development. This proceeds in linear fashion through factor driven (e.g. China currently), to investment driven (such as Korea's support of its chaebol), to innovation driven (such as Japan), and eventually wealth driven (such as the UK – this is Porter's rather unlikely example). Over a short period of, say, a decade this may have some merit. But over a longer period it is plainly unsatisfactory by leaving no prospect for fundamental reappraisals of national policy. Since the stage of development greatly influences the way in which a company responds, the placement of a country in the cycle is clearly critical.

Fifth, the model is peculiar in crediting only outbound FDI as a source of change and profits. But surely inbound FDI also has the same effects and thus the home country's position in the cycle can be changed. The McKinsey study (1993) of the world automobile industry is explicit in its recognition of the way in which Japanese FDI into the USA had a significant impact on Detroit.

Sixth, Porter implicitly states that factor-driven strategies will not promote international competitive advantage for MNEs from such countries. However, Canadian researchers have been quick to criticize this (Safarian, Rugman, Crookell) observing many Canadian counter-examples. In addition, the growth of Asian MNEs suggests (although the evidence is not yet conclusive) that Korean and Chinese and maybe Indian MNEs will soon be as large and as strategically well founded as their triad counterparts.

Finally, the model does not adequately address the role of the multinational in creating a distinctive position for itself. Dunning has observed:

> there is ample evidence to suggest that MNEs are influenced in their competitiveness by the configuration of the diamond in other than their home countries, and that this in turn may impinge upon the competitiveness of home countries. (Dunning, 1983, p. 11)

Thus, Nestlé earns the vast bulk of its revenues outside its home base (Switzerland), as also do virtually all Canada's multinationals. Nearly every country outside the main triad regions and the big industrial countries within these regions has a small home diamond whereupon its MNEs overcome this problem by gaining access elsewhere. Rugman and Hodgetts conclude (2003, p. 423):

different diamonds need to be constructed and analysed for different countries.

These criticisms of the original diamond model can be captured under two broad headings. First, there is the neglect of government as a major driving force. Essentially government actions create externalities that can give MNEs (or local firms) firm-specific advantages (FSAs) in terms of location decisions and the emergence and sustenance of regional clusters of economic activity. Second, the diamond has quite different implications for the big as opposed to the small MNEs. The larger the MNE, the more capability it has to take advantage of market imperfections, especially government-induced externalities. The MNEs from small home bases gain less advantage from their home locations and are impelled to seek advantages elsewhere. It is the combination of these effects that has led to the formulation of the *double diamond*. The value of this is that it gives a more realistic basis for analysing the international competitiveness of smaller MNEs. But it also captures the complex interactions (and rivalry) between the policies of governments. Figure 11.8 shows the basic figure.

In the double diamond the MNE is at the centre of the diamond but is focused on (at least) two 'home' bases. From each it gains resources and factor characteristics. From each it benefits from the nature of demand conditions. And from each it is sustained by the supporting infrastructure. However, it gains by taking a highest common factor approach, that is,

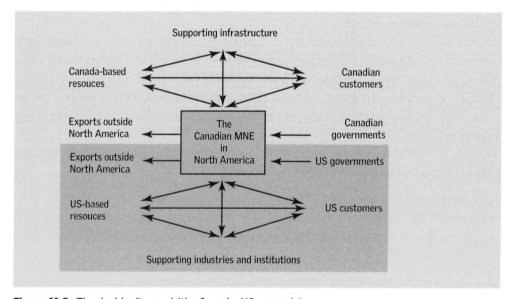

Figure 11.8 The double diamond (the Canada–US example)

it takes advantage of the best infrastructure, it locates in the lowest-cost region, it learns from the most advanced customers and so on. Rugman and D'Cruz (1993, p. 32) use the example of Canadian businesses within the North American Free Trade Area (NAFTA). Thus, Canadian plants gained economies of scale by producing for the North American market as a whole. They argue that the result of North American economic integration has been the development of a Canadian–US double diamond, which shows that, for strategy purposes in the Canadian companies, the two countries have become integrated. This suggests that the double diamond results from government policies, in this case the creation of NAFTA. However, companies themselves can take the initiative. We saw earlier that the emergence of the transnational is a deliberate attempt to be both centralized and localized and the double diamond is a facet of this. Figure 11.9 illustrates a double diamond for McDonald's, taking the USA and Europe as the two 'home' countries. We can see that any moves from the security and sanctuary of a single home base will involve the MNE with a multiple set of close interactions with its markets. For the MNE from smaller homes this enables an entry into a larger game (see, for, example, the power of Nestlé from its small Swiss base, the restored power of Philips from its Dutch home, and the growth of ABB from its Swedish-Swiss base). But multiple homes are not just the prerogative of the 'small' MNE.

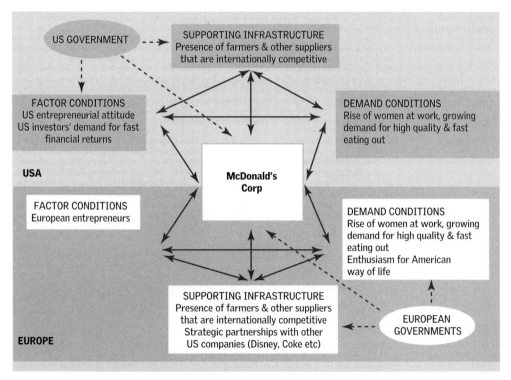

Figure 11.9 The double diamond and McDonald's Corporation
Source: case material: ENPC, Paris.

We see that companies such as Toyota and McDonald's deliberately took the transnational line and effectively work in the context of double/multiple diamonds.

The competitive advantage matrix: CSAs and FSAs

Firm-specific advantage (FSA) is a term used in the international business literature to describe the unique capabilities of an organization and is identical to the concept of *core competence* that we discussed in Chapter 7. **Country-specific advantage** (CSA) arises from the above discussion of the diamond, the double diamond, and the impact of the home base(s) on the MNE. These can be interrelated to produce a competitive advantage matrix (Figure 11.10) that provides a useful framework for discussion. Quadrant 1 firms rely on strong CSAs and are usually in mature markets that are globally oriented, commodity in style and marked by price competition. Typical CSAs would be low factor costs and low energy costs. Cost leadership would be the desired strategy. Firms in quadrant 2 display no advantages, would typically be inefficient in scale and would be candidates for exit, restructuring and/or absorption. Firms in quadrant 4 are generally differentiated firms with strengths in marketing, product development and customization. Their home base is largely irrelevant and these firms are very self-sufficient. Firms in quadrant 3 can benefit from both low cost and differentiation with major contributions from the factor costs and supporting infrastructure of the home base.

From quadrant 4 a firm can have ambitions to develop FSAs that will take into quadrant 3 with an even stronger position. However, firms in quadrant 4 are faced with exogenous CSAs and cannot in general expect to develop new CSAs unless they deliberately undertake to shift location or adopt a double diamond approach. Note, however, that firms may not be homogeneous if their portfolios are not: individual businesses may be in different quadrants and require different strategic approaches. This raises the questions posed in Chapter 8 about the nature of the portfolio and the dangers of excessive diversification. It is also worth noting that changes in the trading environment can and do affect the CSAs. The foundation of trading areas such as NAFTA have affected the positioning of Canadian companies (some companies moving from 2 to 1, and better still some moving from 4 to 3). Similarly the thinking behind European integration and the creation of the single market in 1992 was to create the conditions under which European-based MNEs might compete more effectively by enjoying stronger CSAs.

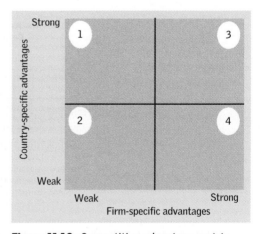

Figure 11.10 Competitive advantage matrix
Source: Rugman and Hodgetts, 2003, p. 583.

The flagship model

Much of the above discussion and indeed discussions within governments has been about the way government policy can affect the success of companies. But the theme of this discourse is more on the ability of companies to construct their own destiny and not have to be mere respondents to market and institutional change. In international business this has been evident in the ways by which successful MNEs have business networks and relationships that have the effect of creating a favourable context without being dependent on the policy whims of others. The main theme in this is the replacement of the traditional adversarial supply chain structure with co-operative supply networks. This stems from the success of Japanese companies in the 60s and 70s and in particular the Toyota production system. The Japanese recognized that creating additional value by creating close relationship with buyers/suppliers can add more to profitability than simple value extraction strategies (exemplified in the traditional explanation of the five forces). These strong co-operative relationships typically require sharing information on costs and manufacturing processes and the co-ordination of logistics to minimize inventories and waiting times. These characteristics are evident in the successful working of alliances (recall Chapter 10). The implication of this is there must be a de facto recognition of how such co-ordination takes place. In the world of value extraction this is a simple exercise in economic power. But in the world of value creation there must still be an orchestration of events by the most powerful or influential firms. This is described by Rugman and D'Cruz (2000) as the **flagship model** and is depicted in Figure 11.11.

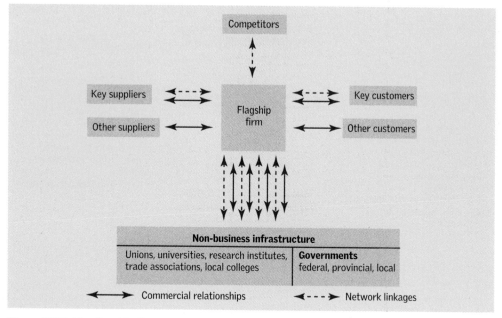

Figure 11.11 The flagship firm
Source: Rugman and D'Cruz, 2000.

This is derived from a diamond framework but is distinctive in the way it parallels commercial relationships with network (co-operative) relationships. This extends not just to suppliers and buyers but also to competitors and the non-business infrastructure. The point about the conventional supply chain relationships is the observation that co-operation along the chain can result in better outcomes for customers. This is not always easy to prove and can easily be confounded with convenience to the players. More challenging are the emerging sets of relationships with competitors in the form of joint ventures, technology transfers and market-sharing agreements. Again there is tension between co-operation and competition and economists would argue that such co-operation is only productively possible if markets are not too concentrated with the result that co-operation would shade into monopolization. The international automobile industry provides a dramatic example of multiple linkages in a highly competitive arena. Other elements of the business infrastructure are also being pulled into co-operation. MNEs are now sharing their strategies with the unions (*see*, for example, the Detroit discussions in the summer of 2003 with the UAW in the face of intense competition). Partnerships are being effected with universities (e.g. by pharmaceutical companies). Above all, governments and MNEs are increasingly co-operating not only around issues of FDI but also about local content and other forms of local reinvestment in infrastructure. Figure 11.12 shows a picture of L'Oréal as a flagship company.

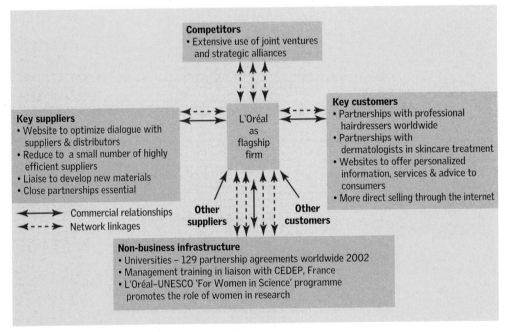

Figure 11.12 L'Oréal as a flagship firm
Source: case material: ENPC, Paris.

Case box: **The first multinationals: Assyria circa 2000 BC**

In an effort to fill an important gap in the history of MNEs, Karl Moore and David Lewis presented evidence suggesting that the first MNEs appeared in the old Assyrian kingdom shortly after 2000 BC. Using the eclectic paradigm as a model to analyse ancient international trade it demonstrates that the major characteristics of MNEs were a part of the Assyrian business organizations of the time. The definition of MNE accepted by the OECD and the UNCTC (the United Nations Centre for Transnational Corporations), 'an enterprise that engages in foreign direct investment (FDI) and owns or controls value-adding activities in more than one country' leads us to conclude that there were MNEs in ancient Assyria around 2000 BC. Characteristics found in modern MNEs, such as hierarchical organization, foreign employees, value-adding activities in multiple regions, common stock ownership, resource and market seeking behaviour, were present in these ancient firms. These early MNEs successfully operated considerable business empires in multiple foreign locations from their corporate headquarters in the capital of Ashur. Undoubtedly more will be learned about the commerce of the old Assyrian kingdom as records from archaeological finds continue to be translated and new finds uncovered.

Were there early MNEs or proto-MNEs earlier than the Assyrian Empire? There may well have been. The records have yet to be uncovered.

Source: extracted from Moore, K and Lewis, D (1998) 'The first multinationals: Assyria circa 2000 BC', *Management International Review*, 38, 2, pp. 95–107.

Note: The eclectic paradigm can be readily summarized by the acronym OLI which indicates ownership, location and internalization advantages. Ownership advantages are firm-specific advantages (FSAs) owned or controlled by the firm. Location advantages are country-specific advantages (CSAs) that arise from the location(s) of the MNE. Internalization advantages are those that accrue to a firm when it internalizes or brings inside the hierarchy of the firm activities which could be performed by the market (remember the discussions on make versus buy and the boundaries of the firm).

11.4 **Managing international organizations**

The international company has always had a tendency towards complex organization structure and difficulties of management control. Stopford and Wells (1972) demonstrated how multinationals tend towards matrix structures (Figure 11.13).

Multinationals historically have moved along the route of increasing product diversity, followed by geographic expansion, or geographic expansion followed by product diversity. A multiproduct firm with limited overseas commitment will naturally organize around product divisions. A multicountry, single-product firm will naturally organize around area or country divisions. The difficulty comes with multiproduct, multicountry operations –

should it be organized around geography or around products? The pure strategies offer clear advice. A global company should operate product divisions, because of the imperative to standardize and achieve cost efficiencies. The multidomestic company should organize around countries, because the foundation of competitive advantage lies within the countries. Trade-offs have to be made in international firms and in transnational organizations.

Where there is a fine balance to be struck, there has been much experimenting with matrix structures. The **matrix** attempts to substitute formal, vertically oriented control and planning processes with more direct contact between individuals. It does this by placing line managers in situations where they have two bosses and are required to meet the needs of both. Figure 11.14 illustrates this with reference to a global chocolate company. This example is inspired by the acquisition of Rowntree by Nestlé, when the new parent argued for the continuation of its country-centred structure, and Rowntree managers argued that because the chocolate industry was global (at least it was European), there should be a product division structure. However, many managers have been very uncomfortable with matrix structures for numerous reasons, including:

- The time taken to make decisions may be too long.

- Priorities may be confused, because equal priorities are implied in the matrix.

- Responsibilities may not be clear because of dual reporting lines.

- A matrix may engender conflict because of the lack of vertical control processes.

Many MNEs use matrix structures and some seem to work quite well but, in general, they provoke much controversy. The dual line of reporting is the source of many problems and

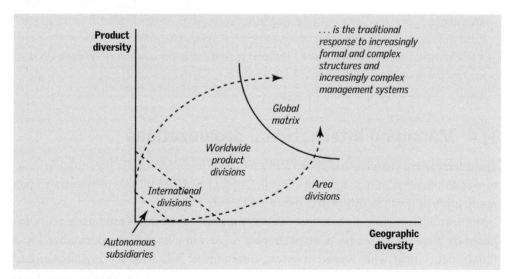

Figure 11.13 The global matrix
Source: Stopford and Wells, 1972.

requires explicit procedures that can resolve the inherent tensions. Bartlett and Ghoshal (1990) suggest three important criteria for making a matrix structure work well. These are clarity, continuity and consistency. *Clarity* refers to how well people understand what they are doing and how well they are doing it. It is built on clear corporate objectives within which relationships in the structure have to be spelt out in simple, direct terms. *Continuity* means that the company remains committed to the same values, objectives and principles of operation. This means that people know what is required and what the company stands for and how it operates. *Consistency* relates to how well all parts of the company work in relation to each other. This means that different parts of the operation should work in the same way without (too many) unnecessary variations and adaptations.

One of the difficulties with organizational design and the management processes that support each design is that they have a 'one size fits all' character. The multi-business company has more complexity than any single organization structure can accommodate. Sometimes a central policy is needed; sometimes local discretion is required; often there needs to be a debate about how something should be done. The need for innovation, learning and adaptation usually requires local discretion within a clear strategic intent (*see* ABB and Percy Barnevik for an attempt to achieve this: Taylor 1991). A useful approach is to seek to build our diagnosis of a company from the bottom up and not from the top down. Figure 11.14 implies that an overall judgement can be made about which type a company belongs to. Solid lines indicate the regulating line whereas dotted lines show information and consultation lines.

Alternatively, consider Figure 11.15. This breaks down the unit of analysis into its constituent parts (rather like a parts explosion diagram). An international-type industry

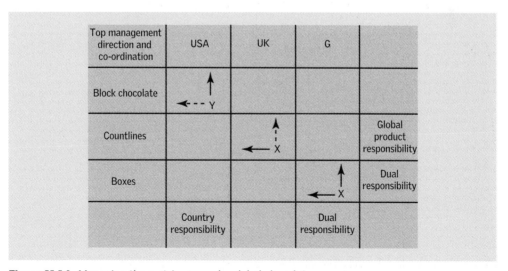

Figure 11.14 Managing the matrix, example: global chocolate company

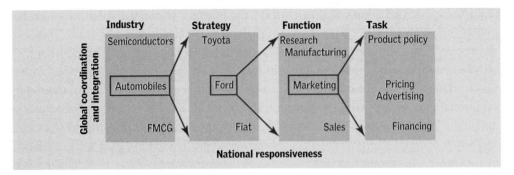

Figure 11.15 Integration and differentiation
Source: Adapted from Bartlett and Ghoshal, 1989, Ch 6.

(automobiles) is broken down into its member companies, some of which are global, some international etc. The Ford Motor Company, international in type, is broken down into its major functions. Research is seen to be global and centralized, sales are multido-mestic and decentralized, and marketing is international (and it is probably difficult to decide how it should be organized).

Breaking marketing into its constituents, we see that some parts, such as product policy, should be centralized, whereas others, such as advertising, still have a complex mixture of local and central contributions. In practice, the diagnosis can be built from the bottom as well as from the top. Thus, the bottom-up approach identifies how things are done. The top-down approach can challenge this and ask how things should be done. The result might look like Figure 11.16. In this we show the integration–responsiveness trade-off diagram for KFC (Kentucky Fried Chicken, now part of Tricon Global Restaurants Inc). The company is

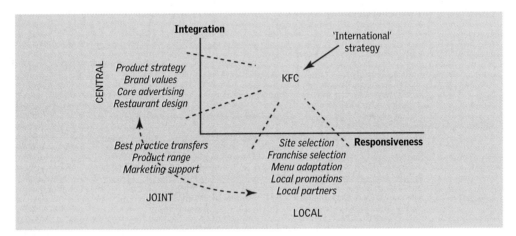

Figure 11.16 Integration and differentiation at KFC
Source: adapted from Bartlett and Ghoshal, 1989, Ch 6.

diagnosed in general as International in type. The vertical axis displays the tasks and functions that are to be done centrally, to gain the integration benefits. The horizontal axis displays those tasks and functions that ought to be carried out locally. Grouped around the origin of the diagram are those activities that require both central and local contributions. It is in these areas that a matrix-style structure would be relevant. Rather than adopting a one-size-fits-all structure, it would be appealing to be able to differentiate the structure according to needs.

11.5 Summary

In this chapter we have positioned international strategy as a significant extension of the logic of competitive advantage. We do not go into a full discussion of how the economics of trade interrelates with the genesis and nature of multinational firms – this is the province of international business as a subject. However, the subjects do overlap and what we do is reflect on how the eternal verities of competitive strategy (cost and differentiation) are played out on the international stage.

The chapter opened with a review of international trade and its institutional context and the significance of 'national' competitive advantage. This should be read as an extension of the discussion on macroeconomics in Chapter 4. The core of the chapter revolves around the nature of globalization and the sources of competitive advantage that flow from this. Whereas internationalization of companies (exemplified in the internationalization process) is seen as the general consequence of international trade, globalization is presented here as a particular form of this – the (debatable and controversial) trends towards international standardization.

The second key element of the chapter concerns the application of standardization strategies (crudely speaking, cost-based) versus differentiation strategies (differentiation-based). Following from this is the tantalizing debate as to whether both are possible (the transnational solution). You will recall from earlier chapters that exactly the same debate has taken place within competitive strategy about the possible simultaneity of cost- and differentiation-based strategies.

The importance of these discussions is profound because they effect the balance between country-specific advantages (CSAs) and firm-specific advantages (FSAs). These issues are discussed against the broad backdrop of Porter's diamond and the double diamond extensions popularized by Rugman. They are also discussed specifically in terms of the advent of the 'flagship firm' with its ability to manage its context and secure its position.

Just as in corporate strategy (Chapter 9) the nature of the (international) strategy has to be complemented by appropriate organization structures and processes. The logic of strategy and structure implies that complex strategies seem to require complex organizations such as the matrix form. Note that ABB, as discussed in Chapter 9, is not simply a complex corporate structure; it is also essentially an international portfolio for which Barnevik prescribed a matrix structure.

Key terms

Comparative advantage *427*

Country-specific advantage *438*

Diamond of national advantage *415*

Double diamond *434*

Factor conditions *428*

Firm-specific advantage *438*

Flagship model *439*

Foreign direct investment (FDI) *413*

Global *420*

Globalization *420*

Global markets *420*

Global matrix *442*

Global strategy *424*

International business *412*

International strategy *416*

Internationalization process *416*

Multidomestic *420*

Multinational enterprise (MNE) *412*

National differences *428*

Transnational *432*

World Trade *412*

Recap questions and assignments

1 Compare the structures of ABB, Diageo, Canon and DaimlerChrysler. To what extent do you think they are in line with current thinking on organizational structures for multinational corporations? What suggestions can you make for any changes in approach?

2 Consider the argument for global standardization as advanced originally by Ted Levitt in the *Harvard Business Review* and as popularized in the business press and in popular journalism, then:

(a) Outline the main arguments against this view.

(b) Identify an alternative to global standardization and explore its implications for multinational corporations.

When you have read this chapter, log on to the Online Learning Centre website at www.mcgraw-hill.co.uk/textbooks/mcgee to explore chapter-by-chapter test questions, further reading and more online study tools for strategy.

Case 1 International law firms: trying to get the right balance

London firms want to be more global; New York firms want to be more profitable. So far, the two are irreconcilable

'We're leading the way. Others will have to follow,' said the senior partner of Clifford Chance four years ago when the London lawyers merged with New York's Rogers & Wells and Germany's Pünder, Volhard, Weber & Axster. At the time, the three formed the world's biggest and most international law firm. But nobody did, in fact, follow their pioneering route, at least not on anything like the same scale.

The only proximate followers were the big accounting firms which had ambitions to build legal practices as global as their accounting businesses. 'We are aiming to be one of the top global players in legal services in the next five to ten years,' said a managing partner of Arthur Andersen, a year or so before the firm ceased to be a global player in anything.

In the late 1990s, over-confident accounting giants thought they could take the legal field by storm thanks to their extensive global networks. But they did not snap up multinational companies' big deals, nor did they lure top lawyers to their firms. Today, sobered by their experience in the intervening years, all the remaining 'Big Four' accountants are retreating from the legal arena, with KPMG the first to throw in the towel altogether.

Is it time then to abandon the idea of assembling a truly international law firm? Is commercial law such a different service to accounting, say, or advertising that it merits a very different industry structure, one characterised by small local specialists rather than big global generalists?

Non-intersecting circles

Not all firms have abandoned the attempt to become big and global. Multinational clients, they say, are clamouring for firms with a global reach. Cross-border deals are increasing, in Europe in particular where ten new countries are about to join the European Union. What's more, after the recent spate of corporate scandals, a slew of new rules on corporate governance calls for greater transnational legal expertise.

The drive for globalization of the profession has been stymied by the different nature of the business in its two biggest markets—London and New York. These two cities dominate the world of commercial law. The ten biggest firms and the ten most international are all based in one or the other (see chart 1).

Each city has a small group of highly reputable firms whose list of blue-chip clients marks them out as special. In New York, this group is seven strong and known as the 'Charmed Circle'. In London, it is known as the 'Magic Circle' and consists of five leading firms, including Clifford Chance. These two circles, however, find it peculiarly hard to intersect.

For a start, the New York firms are markedly more profitable than their London counterparts. Nine of the world's ten most profitable firms (in terms of profit per partner) are based in New York (see chart 2). While internationalisation has led to an increase in size and revenue, it has not produced an equivalent increase in profits. Of the two British firms in the 20 most profitable, one of them—Slaughter and May—has deliberately chosen not to internationalise its operations. The other, Herbert Smith, has only a quarter of its lawyers outside Britain. By contrast, Clifford Chance, Britain's leading international law firm with nearly two-thirds of its lawyers overseas, comes a poor 31st in the profit per partner league table.

At the time of its mergers it was Clifford Chance's ambition to rank among the top three firms wherever it practised. Yet its American strategy quickly ran into trouble.

Taking a chance?   Chart 1
World's most international law firms
by % of lawyers outside their home country, 2002

Rank by total number of lawyers

Firm	% chart	Rank
Baker & McKenzie, US		2
Clifford Chance, UK		1
Freshfields Bruckhaus Deringer, UK		3
White & Case, US		10
Lovells, UK		9
Allen & Overy, UK		4
Linklaters, UK		5
Simmons & Simmons, UK		39
Shearman & Sterling, US		17
Denton Wilde Sapte, UK		28

Source: Legal Business

Briefcase money   Chart 2
World's most profitable law firms by profit per equity partner

Firm	2002-03 $m
Wachtell, Lipton, Rosen & Katz (New York)	2.92
Cravath, Swaine & Moore (New York)	1.96
Simpson Thatcher & Bartlett (New York)	1.85
Kirkland & Ellis (Chicago)	1.80
Milbank, Tweed, Hadley & McCloy (New York)	1.79
Davis Polk & Wardwell (New York)	1.78
Paul, Weiss, Riflkind, Wharton & Garrison (New York)	1.74
Sullivan & Cromwell (New York)	1.72
Skadden, Arps, Slate, Meagher & Flom (New York)	1.61
Cleary, Gottlieb, Steen & Hamilton (New York)	1.45

Source: Legal Business

Several of the firm's big-name New York partners defected, and morale among its junior lawyers fell. After stagnating in the 2002–03 financial year, the firm's revenue is believed to have dropped sharply in the first half of 2003–04, with profits per partner down by as much as 15% according to the *Lawyer*, a trade magazine.

Peter Cornell, Clifford Chance's global managing partner, admits that the firm's American venture has proved more difficult than anyone imagined. 'We reckoned we'd need three years to do it. Now we see it's going to take a bit more time,' he says.

The law of the asphalt jungle

The firm's biggest difficulty was its 'lock-step' system of remuneration, espoused by most English firms. Under this system, profits are shared among partners according to a sliding scale of seniority. Clifford Chance's New York arm, Rogers & Wells, however, like most American firms, used an 'eat-what-you-kill' system under which profits are shared among partners according to how much business each of them brings in.

To keep its American partners happy, Clifford Chance introduced a modified lock-step system in New York with fat bonuses for the most productive partners. But it did not do the trick. Since the merger, the firm has lost 19 of its top New York partners, including two stars. During that time, the firm points out, it has recruited twice as many new American partners. But the damage to its reputation and ability to retain top talent remains.

British firms will never succeed in America without adopting at least a modified system of 'eat-what-you-kill', says John Lynch of Latham & Watkins, a Californian firm that is expanding rapidly in Europe. A merit-based system of pay has always existed in America, but rewarding by results has become much more prevalent in the past few years. It is now beginning to undermine the traditional career path of gradual progress to the top.

Marc Bartel at Lovells, a British firm that used to harbour American ambitions, agrees that compensation is the core of the problem for British firms wanting to gain a foothold in the highly competitive American market. In the most profitable British firms, a senior partner may earn £1m ($1.87m) a year, but a top American partner can expect to earn almost twice as much. While some British firms are beginning to consider the introduction of a modified lock-step system, most are reluctant to go all the way down the American road. 'Pure eat-what-you-kill can be very ugly,' says Hugh Crisp, who takes over in April as chief executive of Freshfields Bruckhaus Deringer, another of London's Magic Circle firms.

Freshfields is the third-biggest law firm in the world (with more than 2,400 lawyers) and the third most international. It has offices in 18 countries and some two-thirds of its lawyers are based overseas. However, its presence in America is still small. 'We'd love an American merger,' admits Mr Crisp, 'but not at a risk to our culture or quality.' Linklaters and Allen & Overy, two other Magic Circle firms once in search of American brides, fared no better than Freshfields in finding a suitable transatlantic partner.

One big problem is that none of the top New York firms is interested in a merger. Relatively small and hugely profitable, they are happy to go on exploiting the biggest and richest legal market in the world on their own. Why should they bother with the risk and expense of a merger with a less-profitable foreign entity?

With the exception of Baker & McKenzie (83% of whose lawyers are abroad), White & Case (60% of whom are abroad) and Shearman & Sterling (37%), few American firms have more than a quarter of their legal staff based outside America. All London's Magic Circle firms, by contrast, have more than a quarter of their lawyers abroad. Significantly, the seven Charmed Circle firms have shown a particular resistance to moving their operations away from their own back yard.

Some British firms, such as Linklaters, seem to have abandoned the idea of a transatlantic merger in favour of organic growth in America. But with American firms offering much higher salaries, it is difficult for newcomers to attract America's brightest. Apart from Clifford Chance, no British firm has so far managed to establish a significant New York practice.

Yanks abroad

A few New York firms outside the circle have, however, been pursuing an international strategy, spurred on both by the needs of their increasingly globalised clients and by growing competition from the British. Some are convinced they would miss out on lucrative deals were it not for their presence in several different markets. Weil, Gotshal & Manges (WGM), an American firm with about 1,000 lawyers in offices in America, Europe and Asia, committed itself to an international strategy 13 years ago. In 1991 the firm did not have a single lawyer in Europe; today one quarter of its staff is there.

WGM says its international expansion was well worth the effort. 'Without our international platform, we could not have been involved in the Vivendi or the Yell deals,' says Stephen Dannhauser, chairman of the firm. In 2002, WGM advised Vivendi, a French media and utilities group, on the $1.7 billion sale of Houghton Mifflin, a publisher, to a consortium of private-equity firms. That same year, it also handled the flotation of Yell, an international-directories business, on the London Stock Exchange. In Vivendi's case the firm's Paris and New York lawyers worked together. In the Yell transaction, British and American teams co-operated.

Baker & McKenzie, one of the first American firms to pursue an international strategy actively, also believes strongly in the advantages of diversification. Baker has 12 separate practices—including antitrust, employment, tax and corporate law—each of which it runs on a global basis. This broad range of business, it says, helped it to ride out the bear market and the economic slowdown at the beginning of the decade. The firm 'could limit the pain, because it is not a big player in capital markets,' says Christine Lagarde, Baker & McKenzie's chairman.

Others also benefited from being diversified. WGM kept busy with work related to distressed deals, troubled loans and corporate restructuring, while Cravath, Swaine & Moore and Sullivan & Cromwell, members of New York's Charmed Circle (and also financial-market specialists), continued to lead charmed lives thanks to their expertise in litigation, an especially lucrative area in times of trouble.

On the other hand, several firms did not make it through the bear market, either because they decided to grow at the wrong moment or because they were over-dependent on financial deals. Altheimer & Gray, a Chicago firm, for example, and Brobeck, Phleger & Harrison, a Californian firm, both went into liquidation last year. Some of London's Magic Circle firms that specialise in financial markets were also badly hurt by the stockmarket slump.

Horses and courses

Instead of buying up other firms around the world, Slaughter and May, Britain's most prestigious and profitable firm, has built up an informal network of what it describes as non-exclusive referral relationships with the 'best of the best' firms around the world. All of them have agreed not to compete in each other's home jurisdictions, and to share documents, exchange lawyers, invest in joint developments, run joint training programmes and pool bills. All but two of America's Charmed Circle have signed up to the network. The aim, says Slaughter and May's David Frank, is to provide 'horses for courses'—the very best lawyer for any particular client in any particular jurisdiction. Mr Frank maintains that no single firm acting alone can provide this.

There is evidence to suggest that this is what multinationals really want: the best legal horse for whatever litigious course they find they have to run. For example, when Gesparal, the French holding company through which Nestlé, a big Swiss food group, and the French Bettancourt family controlled L'Oréal, a leading cosmetics firm, was dissolved earlier this month, Nestlé was advised by a French firm, an expert in its local market, despite the fact that the transaction involved both Swiss and French jurisdictions.

At the same time, there are occasions when Nestlé will seek out cross-border expertise. If it were involved in a cross-border deal within the EU, for example, it would, it says, choose an international firm as an adviser. 'In some cases we prefer international law firms, in others we go for local players,' says François Perroud, a spokesman for the company.

A growing number of legal areas are demanding cross-border expertise—the environment, shipping, aviation, antitrust, employment law, pensions, international arbitration, property rights, and so on. Small specialist firms exploiting a particular niche can benefit from this. Schulte Roth & Zabel, a small New York firm, for instance, specialises in advice for hedge funds and opened a London office when a growing number of its hedge-fund clients set up shop there. But Brad Hildebrandt, chairman of Hildebrandt International, a consultancy specialising in legal services, says that large companies and financial institutions 'are moving away from the "best firm in each location" approach to using a firm with an international capability for specific needs'.

It is becoming essential, particularly in Europe where there are EU directives as well as national laws, that one firm, or a network of close alliances, is able to pull all the threads together. 'This is increasingly difficult to do,' says Mr Hildebrandt, 'when no one firm has responsibility for the overall co-ordination and integration of the advice.' Baker & McKenzie, for instance, acts as intellectual-property enforcement counsel for Calvin Klein, a fashion designer, in countries in Europe and elsewhere. The firm fights counterfeiting and grey-market sales of jeans, underwear and sunglasses by prosecuting offenders in a number of jurisdictions.

If it ain't broke, don't mix it

British firms remain the strongest advocates of a global strategy. French law firms have stayed largely independent. Siméon et Associés, which has joined forces with Britain's Lovells, is an exception. Other top French law firms are big, diversified and predominantly French.

German law firms, on the other hand, have tended to follow the British path. In recent years they have started to merge among themselves and with British firms. Linklaters joined forces with Oppenhoff & Rädler, for instance, while Freshfields Bruckhaus Deringer is the result of a union between London's Freshfields and two top German practices.

As Americans are still giving them the cold shoulder, some British firms have started to become American, but in Britain. With 75 lawyers who have qualified in America on its payroll, Allen & Overy, a Magic Circle firm, employs more Americans in London than any American firm. Its ambition is to be 'the best non-US American law firm'. This leads to a somewhat odd segregation at the firm's offices, where Americans work almost exclusively on American business and earn considerably higher salaries than their British colleagues. Despite the resentment this can create among staff, it is the way that Allen & Overy hopes to attract and keep top American lawyers.

Michael Goldhaber, a journalist with *American Lawyer*, a trade magazine, does not think a transatlantic merger wave is imminent. At the moment, he says, mid-sized, second-tier American firms, usually not based in New York, are buying medium-size European firms. For example, in January 2002, Chicago's Mayer, Brown & Platt bought London's Rowe & Maw and created the world's 14th-largest law firm. And in the same year New York's Fried Frank, a firm with about 540 lawyers, very nearly merged with Britain's Ashurst Morris, a company with some 700 lawyers.

Rumours of a merger of Freshfields and New York's Cleary, Gottlieb, Steen & Hamilton have been denied several times by both firms in recent years. As Cleary already has a presence in Europe, the firm has little interest in joining forces with Freshfields. A merger with Freshfields might make more sense for two other Charmed Circle firms, Davis Polk & Wardwell or Sullivan & Cromwell. But they are both hugely profitable. So, since there is no urgency for top New York firms to merge, any transatlantic union is likely to be among second-tier players.

Ultimately, more big global law firms will probably emerge to provide services for the international marketplace. But the legal profession does not look as if it will go the way of accounting, with just a few firms dominating the market everywhere. Alongside any global legal giants, first-rate firms that decide to remain at home—such as Cravath, Swaine & Moore in New York and Slaughter and May in London—will probably continue to thrive as long as they can remain pre-eminent in their niches.

Despite efforts at cross-border harmonisation of certain areas of law, such as taxation, there remain big differences between legal systems. For instance, in countries with systems based on English common law the protection of investors is much stronger than in those based on French civil law. On the other hand, the recent victory in a French court of LVMH, a luxury-goods group, in a lawsuit against Morgan Stanley, an American investment bank, over allegedly tainted reports by an equity analyst probably would not have happened in an English jurisdiction.

That is why the legal profession has remained relatively parochial while its best clients have become increasingly global. Lawyers are currently catching up. But a small number of huge firms is unlikely ever to dominate the industry.

Source: 'Trying to get the right balance', *The Economist*, 26 February 2004.
© The Economist Newspaper Limited, London (26 February 2004).

Case Questions

1 Why should law firms in London and New York wish to globalize?

2 Why are these law firms reluctant to expand by acquisition – whereas other professional service firms in advertising and in property surveying have done so?

3 In what ways are the strategies of London-based and New York-based law firms different?

Further reading and references

Amit, R and Schoemaker, PJH (1993) 'Strategic Assets and Organizational Rent', *Strategic Management Journal*, **14**, pp. 33–46, reprinted in Segal-Horn, S (ed.) (1998) *The Strategy Reader*, Blackwell Business.

Bartlett, C and Ghoshal, S (1989) *Managing Across Borders: the Transnational Solution*, Harvard Business School Press, Boston MA.

Bartlett, C and Ghoshal, S (1990) 'Matrix Management: Not a Structure, a Frame of Mind', *Harvard Business Review*, July/August, pp. 138–45.

Bartlett, C and Ghoshal, S (1992) 'What is a Global Manager?' *Harvard Business Review*, **70**, 5, pp. 124–32.

Bartlett, CA and Ghoshal, S (1993) 'Beyond the M-form: Toward a New Managerial Theory of the Firm', *Strategic Management Journal*, **14**, pp. 23–46, reprinted in S Segal-Horn (ed.) (1998) *The Strategy Reader*, Blackwell Business.

Douglas, SP and Wind, Y (1987) 'The Myth of Globalization', *Columbia Journal of World Business*, Winter, pp. 19–29.

Dunning, JH (1983) 'Internationalising Porter's Diamond', *Management International Review*, **33**, Special Issue 2, pp. 7–16.

Economist, The, 19 November 1999, pp. 27–35 and 122.

Ghoshal, S (1987) 'Global strategy: an Organizing Framework', *Strategic Management Journal*, **8**, pp. 425–40, reprinted in S Segal-Horn (ed) (1998) *The Strategy Reader*, Blackwell Business.

Ghoshal, S and Nohria, N (1993) 'Horses for Courses: Organizational Forms for Multinational Corporations', *Sloan Management Review*, Winter, pp. 23–35.

Harvard Business School (1986) *Kentucky Fried Chicken (Japan) Ltd*, Case Study 9–987–043, Harvard College, Boston, MA.

Hill, CW and Jones, GR (1995) *Strategic Management Theory: An Integrated Approach*, 3rd edition, Houghton Mifflin, Boston MA.

Jarillo, JC (1993) *Creating the Borderless Organization*, Butterworth-Heinemann.

Levitt, T (1983) 'The Globalization of Markets', *Harvard Business Review*, May/June, pp. 92–102.

McKinsey & Co. (1993) 'Manufacturing Productivity Units', *McKinsey Global Institute Report*, October 1993.

Ohmae, K (1985) *Triad Power: the Coming Shape of Global Competition*, Free Press, New York.

Porter, ME (1985) *Competitive Advantage*, Free Press, New York.

Porter, ME (1990) 'The Competitive Advantage of Nations', *Harvard Business Review*, March/April, pp. 73–93.

Prahalad, CK and Doz, YL (1986) 'The Dynamics of Global Competition', in CK Prahalad and YL Doz (eds) *The Multinational Mission: Balancing Local Demands and Global Vision*, Free Press, New York.

Prahalad, CK and Hamel, G (1990) 'The Core Competence of the Corporation', *Harvard Business Review*, May/June, pp. 79–91, reprinted in S Segal-Horn (ed) (1998) *The Strategy Reader*, Blackwell Business.

Quinn, JB (1992) *Intelligent Enterprise*, Free Press, New York.

Rugman, AM and D'Cruz, JR (1993) 'The "Double Diamond" Model of International Competitiveness: the Canadian Experience', *Management International Review*, **33**, Special Issue 2, p. 32.

Rugman, AM and D'Cruz, JR (2000) *Multinationals as Flagship Firms: Regional Business Networks*, Oxford University Press.

Rugman, AM and Hodgetts, RM (2003) *International Business*, FT Prentice Hall, London.

Segal-Horn, S (1993) 'The internationalisation of service firms', *Advances in Strategic Management*, **9**, pp. 31–55, reprinted in Segal-Horn (ed.) (1998) *The Strategy Reader*, Blackwell Business.

Segal-Horn, S (ed.) (1998) *The Strategy Reader*, Blackwell Business.

Segal-Horn, S and McGee, J (1997) 'Global Competences in Service Multinationals', in H Thomas and D O'Neal (eds) *Strategic Discovery: Competing in New Arenas*, the Strategic Management Series, J Wiley & Sons, Chichester, pp. 49–77.

Stopford, J and Wells, LT (1972) *Managing the Multinational Enterprise*, Basic Books, New York.

Taylor, W (1991) 'The Logic of Global Business: an Interview with ABB's Percy Barnevik', *Harvard Business Review*, March/April, pp. 91–104.

Yip, G (1995) *Total Global Strategy*, Prentice-Hall.

Chapter 12

Strategy in the new economy[1]

Introduction

This chapter is concerned with the 'new' world of information technology and knowledge intensity. This is a world marked by big investments in R&D, different cost structures and significantly changed demand conditions. You should read this chapter in conjunction with Chapter 19, which deals with knowledge, information and innovation. In this chapter we are concerned with how the logic of competitive advantage applies to the new conditions in which we find ourselves. To anticipate the conclusions, we will see that the strategic context has shifted a great deal. This means that fundamental demand and cost conditions have changed, resulting in different strategies

---

[1] This chapter is written jointly with Tanya Sammut-Bonnici.

being pursued. The new world and the new economy does mean that the old strategic logic is outmoded. Instead we see a significant change in the strategic context that results in the logic of competitive advantage being applied in different ways.

The chapter presents and contrasts the differences between the old world of scale and scope economies and the new world of **network externalities**. There is an extensive discussion of what network externalities are and how they arise but the reader should read this in the context of addition, not replacement – scale and scope have not been replaced; there is, however, another important practical phenomenon to consider. Networks are supported by many layers of infrastructure and we go into some detail to show how the technological infrastructure can be identified and analysed. There are many implications for competition which we review. Finally, we summarize the implications for strategy – although it is a new world, the logic of competitive advantage still applies.

12.1 **The need for a new strategic perspective**

The new information and communication technologies of the last decade are fundamentally transforming the operating methods of most manufacturing and service companies and are provoking wholesale reappraisal of the nature of support functions. These technologies have become institutionalized in the new ICT (information and communications technology) industry across the world and are now having a revolutionary effect on corporate strategy. Executives are rethinking the strategic fundamentals of business practices not just in technology and communications industries but also across the entire spectrum of industries.

Many of the component parts of this new ICT industry, such as telecommunications, the internet, computing and software, are shaping significant parts of the corporate environment into a new 'network economy'. The essence of networks is the existence of multiple nodes, the interconnectivity between them, and the co-operative (as opposed to competitive) behaviour of the nodes. As we will see, networks have increasing returns to scale characteristics. The dynamics of corporations and the new information economy will increasingly reflect these increasing returns to scale and, therefore, understanding how such networks work is the key to developing a new set of strategies in this new information-based corporate landscape (Kelly 1998).

The 'old world' was driven by economies of scale and scope, where the benefits of size are moderated by eventual diminishing returns. The 'new world', spawned by information and communications technology, is not moderated by the normally powerful influence of diminishing returns. Network effects, also known as network externalities, can result in 'winner-takes-all' phenomena (for example, the Wintel standard for PCs) and therefore result in new industry dynamics and new sets of corporate responses (for a discussion of network effects, *see* McGee and Sammut-Bonnici 2002).

The burgeoning growth and influence of the new ICT industry is making it possible for more individuals, corporations and companies to reap the benefits of the information economy. The internet has provided a free infrastructure for the rapid exchange of information and is creating new distribution opportunities in regional and global economies. The development of the 'self-organizing' web of new economy industries is affecting all elements of trade and brings commercial gains to regional and global economies. The Digital Planet 2002 report indicates the scale of this effect. At the regional level, Eastern Europe's spending grew faster in 2001 than the North America, Latin America, Middle East and Africa regions combined. Mature economies such as the US will become less dominant, as China, Poland and a host of other developing countries play an increasing role. At a more micro level, information industries are giving rise to geographic hot-spots of commercial activity, created from economic webs, corporate clusters and commercial ecosystems. California's Silicon Valley, Taiwan and Tokyo are such examples. Local concentration of ICT activity may develop spontaneously or can be created by governments and regional planners. Malaysia is developing two of the world's first Smart Cities: Putrajaya, the new seat of government providing e-government facilities, and Cyberjaya, a city for multimedia industries, R&D centres, a multimedia university and operational headquarters of multinationals wishing to direct their trading activities using information technology. The underlying feature of smart cities is the high level of ICT infrastructure, on which the whole city is developed. Another example of regional growth due to the information economy is Northern Virginia. Its economy has boomed with the explosion of internet and telecommunication companies. America Online, which set up in Northern Virginia in 1985, employs over 13 000 people, and generates over $1.5 billion in online revenues. The presence of a number of multinational companies such as AOL, UUNet and Worldcom MCI in the area attracts competitors as well as vendors through the normal multiplier effects. ICT Industries have well-documented, substantial effects on the local, regional and global economies through the **multiplier effect**.

The extent to which the ICT industry and associated network industries have proliferated in the economy is a recent phenomenon. However, network effects have been recognized for some time, since the onset of industrialization, but particularly with the advent of the first infrastructure industries (especially railroads) in Victorian times. Literature on network externalities dates back by almost a century to the works of Young (1913), Knight (1924), and Ellis and Fellner (1943). Contemporary research on networks tends to be econometric in nature (Shy 2001) and charts industry evolution over time in a series of snapshots. We adopt Shapiro and Varian's (1999) strategic perspective on network industries and develop a strategic framework that transcends ICT and non-ICT companies. We start this journey by analysing the structure of network industries and go on to look at the dynamics endemic in each level within that structure.

12.2 **The emergence of a new economy**

In this section we look at how the old industrial economy was characterized by economies of scale and scope, while the new information economy is driven by the economics of positive feedback in network industries. We will discuss the nature of network industries, such as railroads, telecommunications, software and hardware networks. We will see how network companies benefit from positive feedback on both the demand side and supply side. On the demand side, the more customers join a network, such as a telecommunications service, the higher the incentive for other customers to join. On the supply side, the larger a network becomes in terms of users and also in size of assets deployed, the easier it is for a company to lower costs and prices. The lower the price introduced by a network company, the more subscribers will join the network and positive feedback kicks in. The result is a self-reinforcing spiral. The importance of critical mass, competition and standards is discussed in the light of the dynamics of positive feedback.

12.2.1 **The old world: economies of scale and scope**

The theory of strategic management was given impetus by the realization that industrial organization as a subject could be turned around to give a perspective on the entrepreneurial profit-seeking activity of firms. This led to the notion of firms seeking market power in which rents could be protected, at least for a time, by barriers to entry. These barriers were derived from the cost functions of firms, the dominant theme being the ability of firms to sustain differential cost positions through economies of scale.[2] In the world of scale economies, where minimum efficient plant sizes are a significant fraction of the market, oligopolistic market structures prevail and are overturned principally by the growth of markets or by the advance of technology enabling the creation of new assets with more advantageous cost positions. The notion of economies of scale is therefore fundamental to strategic management because it provides a rationale for firms to be different in terms of asset configuration and in terms of performance. However, this is an insufficient argument on its own for the existence of diversified firms. Diversification requires the notion of economies of scope. These are defined as 'the cost savings realized when two different products are produced within the same organization rather than at separate organizations' (Saloner *et al.* p. 364). They arise because the products share a common input such as plant or equipment, obtaining volume discounts on purchases (exercising monopsony power), or applying

---

[2] Saloner, Shepard and Podolny (2001) identify three types of entry barriers: barriers from production or distribution technology, barriers from brand name or reputation, and legal barriers (p. 138). The first two are essentially cost barriers in that replication of the incumbent's assets is inhibited by the costs of so doing. The third type is an absolute barrier that arises from institutional characteristics that are idiosyncratic from a market point of view.

common expertise or reputation. The advantages conferred by economies of scope are not, however, inherent in the jointness of production but in the barrier to entry which protects the 'original' asset. There is nothing to prevent two firms enjoying identical economies of scope if there is free competition for the underlying asset. Thus, economies of scale convey the fundamental advantage that underpins superior profitability in single-product and multiple-product firms.

The discussions in strategic management textbooks about competitive advantage are all variations upon this same theme. The simplest articulation of the theme is the cost differential that arises in production. The more complex argument concerns knowledge assets, where the essence of the argument is about the cost to reproduce knowledge and not the possession of knowledge per se. The subtlety in strategy making resides in the variety of ways in which knowledge and expertise is acquired (which is where the cost function of knowledge acquisition is important) and then captured in products and services (the generic differentiation theme). In this almost bucolic world the supply side and the market side are linked through some form of arm's-length market exchange process. Customer desires are conveyed through the pattern of their purchasing decisions and producers respond by adjusting the nature of their offerings. Where competition is monopolistic (or imperfect) producers may attempt to shape customer preferences, and to the extent they succeed, demand functions become downward sloping in the conventional manner and producers can then price according to the nature of their marginal cost curves and the price elasticities in the market. But demand and supply are mediated through a market mechanism in which product demand is independent of other products[3] and demand is not time dependent. This latter point is crucial.

12.2.2 **The new world of network industries**

However, there is a class of markets and industries that do not conform to these assumptions. These are known as **network industries**.[4] According to Economides and Flyer (1997):

> *The value of nearly every good is influenced by aggregate consumption levels in its market and in the markets for related goods. In many cases, high aggregate consumption in its own market, and in the markets for complementary goods affects positively the value of a good. Traditionally such effects have been called network externalities, since they were first identified in network industries. While such effects are salient in some markets, such as for telephones, fax machines and computer operating systems, for most goods these influences are more subtle and tend to be smaller.*

[3] This exaggerates the point, as we will see later when we discuss product complementarity.

[4] In this discussion the terms 'industry' and 'market' are used as if interchangeable.

Network industries are not uncommon. Many physical networks have been around for a long time, e.g. railroads, telephone, electricity. So-called virtual networks have arisen largely through information technology and include facsimile machines and computer operating systems. These are 'virtual' because the key knowledge and information assets are intangible. We can distinguish intuitively between pure networks and indirect or weak networks. Pure networks exist where it is an essential characteristic of the product that it is organized through complementary nodes and links, such as a railway network or the telephone system. A key element is the notion of complementarity, thus the value of a railway station is derived from the existence of other railway stations on the network. A weaker definition relies also on complementarity between products (or nodes, in network language) but allows the links to be created *by* the customer rather than *for* the customer. Economides and Flyer (1997) have some powerful examples:

> *the value of a washing machine is affected by the aggregate consumption of washing machines and the consumption level of the particular brand, since this determines the availability of parts, repairmen, detergents, fabric softeners and various other related goods and services. The value of a sporting event is influenced by the aggregate size of the audience, as this enhances the excitement level, analysis, discussion and remembrance of the event. Even a grapefruit is influenced by network externalities, since the variety of accessible complements, such as peeler, slicers, juicers, recipes, nutritional information and specialized spoons, are affected by the aggregate consumption of the fruit.*

The essence of this idea is that the demand for a product is influenced by total demand for the product class or by total demand in a complementary product class. Thus, demand is conditioned by a consumer externality. Where these **consumer externalities** are powerful, the feedback effect on demand is such that there is a tendency towards a single network, or platform, or standard. The value for consumers of being on a common standard outweighs any specific differences between alternative standards. We see that the VHS standard was preferred to a 'technically better' Betamax rival to the extent that the rival standard disappeared. The Wintel standard is greatly preferred to the Apple standard although the rival does still exist as a small niche in the market. Where the externality is smaller and the intrinsic difference between standards is relatively larger then we might observe multiple competing and co-existing 'platforms'.[5] An example of a platform can be seen in the automobile industry, where a company might develop a core of components and sub-assemblies that can be used to support alternative body styling to create a product range. Such a platform can co-exist with other platforms because the scale efficiencies associated with platforms is modest in relation to market size.

---

[5] To observe multiple standards defies common sense, hence the term 'platform' which denotes an array of linked complementary products that together are compatible with other products.

12.3 **Networks**

What is the significance of networks and network externalities? To answer this we need to look first at what we mean by networks. Then we look at the implications for the demand function and the consequences for the market and the industry structure.

A network is a set of connections (links) between nodes. A two-way network allows the links to be operated in both directions, whereas a one-way network has distinct direction-ality. Two-way networks include railroads and telephone systems. Figure 12.1 shows a simple star network where A can communicate with B through a switch S. B can also communicate with A by reversing the direction of the link (viz. a telephone call). In Figure 12.1 we have eight nodes (A through H) linked through a switch, S. If this were a two-way network, AB and BA would be distinct products (different telephone calls, different rail journeys). The total number of products in the network is 56, i.e. $n(n-1)$ where n = the number of nodes. If there were to be a ninth member this would increase the total number of products to 72 (n is now 9), a total increase of 16 products available from the expanded network. If the value to each user of being in the network is proportional to the number of users then the value of this network has just increased by 28.5 per cent (16 as a percentage of 56) even though the size of the network has increased by only 12.5 per cent (one added to eight).[6] This is an algebraic characteristic of network economies of scale: that the value rises dispro-portionately higher than the increase in network size as long as prices are constant and products are independent. Intuitively we might expect that an increase in network size beyond a certain point has little value.[7] If this network were a one-way network there would be half the number of products but the value of the network would nevertheless increase at the same rate but achieving only half the value.

The analysis of complementarity is equivalent to the analysis of a one-way network. Figure 12.1 can be extended, as in Figure 12.2, to show a typical one-way network. Here we can interpret the A_i as ATMs[8] and the B_j as banks. The network runs only from A to B. The sig-nificance of the two switches S_A and S_B is that they have only one link. This means that there is compatibility between all ATMs and all banks. This maximizes the value of the network but increases the competition between banks for customers through ATMs.[9] It is this com-patibility that makes the complementarity actual and the network operational. For complex

---

[6] Assuming for convenience in this example that prices are constant.

[7] Using calculus we would expect the first derivative to be positive but the second derivative to be nega-tive. Therefore, total value increases but at a decreasing rate.

[8] Automatic teller machines

[9] Two complementary components, A and B, are compatible when they can be combined to produce a composite good. A VHS player is compatible with VHS tapes. Two substitute components A_1 and A_2 are compatible when each of them can be combined with a complementary good B to produce a composite good. Thus two VHS tapes are compatible, and two VHS players are compatible.

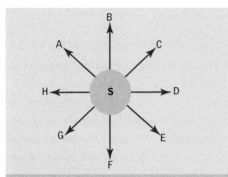

A star network has a collection of nodes clustered around some central resource. Movement of resources/products must pass through this central node, e.g. a local telephone exchange.

Figure 12.1 A simple star network

products actual complementarity has to be achieved through adherence to specific technical standards. Other complementary products can be visualized in terms of

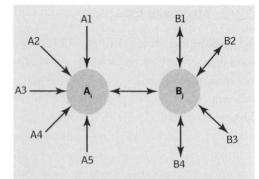

Occurs when the central resouces are distributed among connected star networks. In a normal star network, movement can occur from any point on the network to any other point. Movement from one star to another will involve both central connections (hubs). Movement within one star will require only one – e.g. long-distance telephone network

Figure 12.2 A crystal 'one-way' network

Figure 12.2. VHS tapes could be the A_i and VHS players could be the B_j. Think also of copier paper and copiers, or printer paper and printers, or car accessories and cars, or local and long-distance telephone networks.

Case box: **Real and virtual networks**

The concept of network can be segmented into real and virtual networks (Shapiro and Varian 1999). Real networks are found in industries such as telephony and railways where a physical network is present. Virtual networks are typified by computer and software platforms where the interconnection between users is intangible. The two types of networks are discussed below.

In real networks the interconnection between users is tangible. Examples are cable networks for telephone users and radio transmissions in mobile phones. Electricity grids, telecommunications networks encompassing telephones, fax machines, online services and the internet are typical examples of products or services within real networks. There are one-way networks, such as broadcast television, where information flows in one direction only. In two-way networks, such as railroads and telephone systems, links are operated in both directions. Any network may be viewed as a set of connections (links) between nodes. A two-way network allows the links to be operated in both directions whereas a one-way network has specific direction. Two-way networks include railroads and telephone systems.

In virtual networks the interconnections between users are intangible, but users remain interdependent. Computer systems are typical of virtual networks. For example, Mac users are part of the Mac network, with Apple as the sponsor of the network. Mac users are locked into a network determined by the technology standard of this platform. They can only use software that is compatible to the system and will exchange files with users within the system. Operating systems such as Windows and Unix are other examples of virtual networks. Virtual network dynamics also operate in the entertainment industry for Sony PlayStation, Microsoft Xbox and Nintendo's Gamecube networks.

Network size is still important in virtual networks in that a large consumer base makes production viable and usage possible. In addition, the value of a product increases as the number of, or the variety of, the complementary goods or services increases. Indirect network effects in the computer industry are referred to as the hardware–software paradigm. The success of an operating system for personal computers depends on the variety of software applications available in the market. Value may depend more critically on software applications.

12.3.1 Network externalities: the new economic force

Earlier in this chapter we looked at the traditional economic model for the 'old world', which was driven by economies of scale and scope. The 'new world', characterized by information and communications technology, is governed by a different dynamic. Network externalities are the new drivers of the network economy. It is important to recognize that economies of scale/scope and network externalities represent the extreme ends of a spectrum of effects, and that the presence of one does not imply the exclusion of the other. Companies may experience the effects of both to varying degrees, with a tendency for network externalities to have more strategic relevance in the new network economy.

The concept of network externalities has attracted the attention of academics and practitioners alike. The extent to which network industries have proliferated in the economy is a recent phenomenon. The effects of network externalities, however, have been recognized for some time with the development of the older network companies such as the railroads and the electricity systems. In 1804 Trevithick constructed the first practical locomotive in England. In 1882 the Edison Electric Lighting Company completed the first commercial generating station at Holborn Viaduct in London. The first commercial telephone line was installed in Boston, Massachusetts, in 1877.

Network externalities are defined as the increasing utility that a user derives from consumption of a product as the number of other users who consume the same product increases (Katz and Shapiro 1985). For example, the more people there are in a telephone network, the more users can be reached on the network, thereby increasing its usability. Fax machines, broadcast industry services, credit card networks, and computer hardware and software are examples of products exhibiting network externalities.

Networks were originally analysed on the assumption that each network was owned by a single firm and research concentrated on the efficient use of the network structure and on the appropriate allocation of costs (Economides 1996; Sharkey 1993). With the anti-trust cases against AT&T and its later break-up, attention shifted towards economies of scope, the efficiency gains from joint operation of complementary components of networks (Baumol et al. 1982). This led to issues of interconnection and compatibility in parallel with the reduced role of IBM in the 1980s and 1990s in the setting of technical standards in computer hardware and software. As technology has advanced, there have been significant reductions in telecommunications costs and a shift towards fragmented ownership of telecommunications networks. Market structure has shifted from natural monopoly to oligopoly. Similar trends are evident in other IT-intensive industries. Thus, the focus of interest in network economics has shifted from the analysis of natural monopoly towards issues of interconnection, compatibility, interoperability and co-ordination of quality.

12.3.2 **Network externalities and the battle for critical mass**

For normal goods, the demand curve slopes downwards. As price decreases, more of the product is demanded. Other elements in the demand function, such as income or advertising, serve as 'demand shifters' that elevate demand to a higher level. Figure 12.3 illustrates the traditional role of a demand shifter. Higher levels of consumption are derived from higher incomes (positive income elasticities) or from lower prices (negative price elasticities).

This fundamental relationship is greatly distorted in the presence of network externalities. In the presence of network externalities, we specify that sales rise as accumulated sales (the

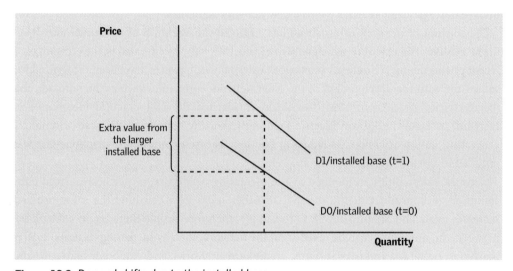

Figure 12.3 Demand shifts due to the installed base

installed base) rise and there arises a chicken and egg problem. Customers may not be interested in purchasing because the installed base is small and/or not expected to grow. For example, imagine the purchase of complex software without internet support, help lines and user groups. Alternatively, there may be confident expectations that the installed base will grow substantially and therefore consumers will confidently make purchases. The paradox is that consumers will not buy if the installed base is too low. However, the installed base is too low because customers will not buy. The crux of the paradox lies in the management of expectations. In markets for normal goods, equilibrium is explained in terms of a balance between costs and demand, between marginal costs and marginal utility. In network markets, there is also equilibrium to be struck between actual demand and expectations of total demand.

This gives rise to an economic paradox. Almost the first law of economics is that value comes from scarcity. However, in the new economy value comes from plenty: the more something is demanded and the more it is expected to be demanded then the more valuable it becomes. Expectations are so important in driving demand that a point exists where the momentum is so overwhelming that success becomes a runaway event and we observe a 'winner takes all' phenomenon (see Figure 12.4).

The '**tipping point**' is when the installed base (or size of network) tips expectations sharply towards one player (or one network) and away from its rival. We have experienced this effect when the market moved towards Windows as the prevailing computer operating system, rather than OS2. Another example of tipping would be IBM-compatibles versus Apple, as shown in Figure 12.5. The tipping point comes somewhere in 1984–5 when IBM-system sales overtake those of Apple.

The exception to the winner takes all phenomenon would be a regulated network market with strong interconnections between competing platforms. The mobile telephone

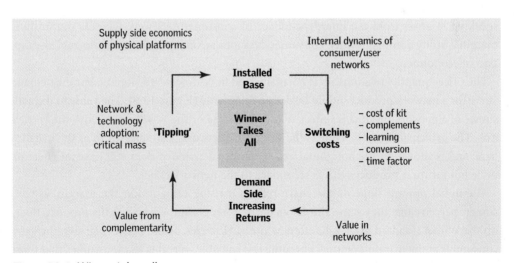

Figure 12.4 Winner takes all

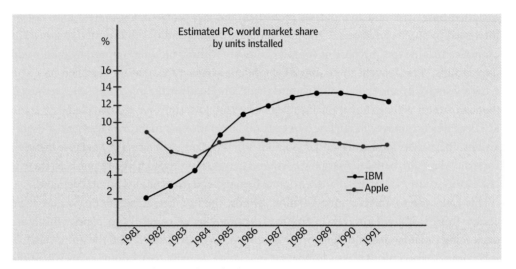

Figure 12.5 Market share of IBM and Apple

industry is a classic example. The standards are harmonized across the network providers, at least by continental region. The platforms are interlinked and the sales curves of the regulated network providers follow the pattern of the overall subscription curve for the industry.

Traditional economic thinking is based on **negative feedback systems** in which the strong get weaker at the margin and the weak get stronger, thus providing a drive towards a competitive equilibrium. This is captured in economics by the concept of diminishing marginal utility as consumption grows. In the new world of networks, feedback rules. In this world the valuation of a product increases the more that others consume the product. Strictly speaking, it arises from the interdependence of consumer decisions, whereas diminishing marginal utility dominates when consumer decisions are independent – the normal assumption in economics.

The price–quantity relationship is normally held to be downward sloping, but the demand curve for a network product should be drawn differently (Figure 12.6). The value to the consumer of a network product is reflected in the price he or she is willing to pay – the vertical axis. The principal driver of value is the size of the network, also referred to as the installed base, and is shown on the horizontal axis. Quantity demanded does still have an effect on price but for these products, this is secondary to the network effect.

The initial upward slope of the curve reflects a rising valuation at the margin, as consumers perceive that they gain value by virtue of other consumers having the product. Being on the Wintel standard gives value to new users. However, as the network grows, the extra consumers at the margin eventually become less valuable – i.e. this shape assumes that those users with higher potential valuation of the network will join first. As the network gets very

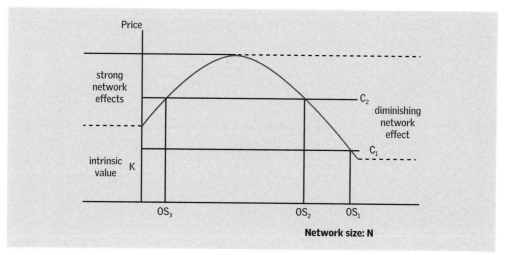

Figure 12.6 The network demand curve: the idea of optimal size

large, further growth has less value for future customers.[10] The intercept on the vertical axis represents the value the network product has as a stand-alone product. Thus a Wintel computer has some stand-alone value, but a telephone has no value on its own and is a **pure network good**.

There is a notion of an optimal size of a network. This can be seen from the interaction of demand and cost so that as less and less valuable customers join the network there may come a time when the costs of acquiring and servicing new customers begins to exceed the price those customers are willing to pay. This determines the optimal size and has significant implications for competition.

The three configurations shown in Figure 12.7 indicate the range of possibilities. The first is a pure network good, such as a telephone system, in which the optimal size of network is a very high proportion of the available market. This implies there is little or no room for rival networks. The second is a product with a significant intrinsic value that attracts a modest size group of users. For example, this could be a corporate software package (e.g. enterprise solutions) that attracts dedicated user support from the supplier through the web. Alternative networks could co-exist. The third case is one of very high intrinsic demand but extensive consumer interactions (small in size but very many in number) provide a substantial total network value. The obvious example is word processing software where the value from standardizing on MS Word is very high, with the result that alternative standards (such as WordPerfect) are being frozen out of the market even though the intrinsic value of any word processing package is high.

---

[10] In the language of demand curves, this is an average revenue curve.

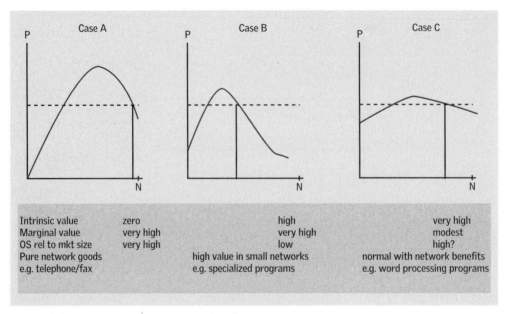

Intrinsic value	zero	high	very high
Marginal value	very high	very high	modest
OS rel to mkt size	very high	low	high?
Pure network goods		high value in small networks	normal with network benefits
	e.g. telephone/fax	e.g. specialized programs	e.g. word processing programs

Figure 12.7 Alternative network demand configurations

12.4 **The technological infrastructure of network industries**

Much of the popular discussion of technology and its effects makes powerful but general claims for the effect of technology but is less than clear about the underlying mechanisms. We observe four nested levels of infrastructure within network industries. Each of these levels has its own economic dynamics and each makes a contribution to the overall network (increasing returns characteristic). These levels are (i) technology standards, (ii) the supply chain driven by such standards, (iii) the physical platforms that are the output of the supply chains and are the basis from which the company delivers its product (e.g. the digital TV, the decoder, the satellite system, and the telephone lines that are the platform from which Sky TV delivers its programmes), and (iv) the consumer network (Figure 12.8). The economic characteristics of the first three levels are the prevalence of fixed costs and joint products coupled with economies of scale. Networks of interacting and interdependent customers provide the increasing returns characteristic of networks. Then the whole can have such powerful positive feedback characteristics that the winner might be able to take all.

Each level displays distinctive economic characteristics of significance. Technology standards can be achieved either by rule or by emergence and in the latter case early mover advantages are important. The economics of modularity and the specialization of knowledge shape the structure of supply chains. Physical platforms are a melding of standards and components in which modularity and the economics of substitution also play a

	Language of networks	Wintel	WWW	Mobile phones	Satellite TV
Network externalities, consumer lock-in, market equilibrium and tipping	Consumer network	PC producers, retailers, offices and homes	PC producers, retailers, offices and homes	Individual corporations	Households
Economies of scale, critical mass, positive feedback, externalities, path dependence	Physical platform	PC producers, retailers, offices and homes	Global net of millions of computers, ISPs, online services, software	Mobile phones, transmitters, land lines, BT phones	Satellite transponder, decoder, TV shopping signal via phone
Supply-side economics, economics of substitution, versioning, switching costs	Technology standards	Win95 runs on x86 only. WinNT runs on non-x86 chips. Linux runs on x86	HTML IP, TCP/IP, VoIP	3G, 2.5G, GSM, GPRS, UMTS	Proprietary decoder vs CPSI
Technical capabilities ahead of markets: R&D races, JVs and alliances	R&D supply chain	New 'itanium' chip is being held back to preserve current version	Integration of internet with cable TV: Microsoft Mobile Internet	I-mode technology by DoCoMo	IoS – Internet over Satellite Currently for ISPs

Figure 12.8 Strategic levels of network industries

significant role. Consumer networks, of course, require positive feedback effects for their full power to be gained. We use the mobile telecommunications business as a running example to show how these technological dimensions and strategy interact.

12.4.1 Technology and standards

The significance of the economics of information is attributed to two key factors: the continuing reduction in cost of information technology hardware products and the scale effect of global standards. Gordon Moore, founder of Intel Corporation, created a corporate empire on his eponymous Moore's Law, which states that every year and a half processing power doubles while costs hold constant. Moore's foresight proved prophetic and 'Moore's Law' is expected to remain valid for the foreseeable future (but *see* Leyden 1997). Computer memory, storage capacity and telecommunications bandwidth are all going through a similar pattern of cost reduction. This makes it very affordable for individuals and small businesses to be equipped with the electronic means to conduct commerce and transfer information as fast and freely as large corporations can. Hence, the demand for the products of the ICT industries continues to grow.[11]

[11] In spite of the feast and famine evident in the telecommunications industry reminiscent of the fragility of corporate structures during the railway boom of the 1840s.

However, the rapid growth of products from the ICT economy depends on operating technology standards as well as on production costs. For example, automated teller machines across the world must work on an agreed standard to ensure customers can use one card in different countries. A technology standard is the important enabler to create wide reach and to capture a wide network of subscribers. With the globalization of commerce, national and regional boundaries blur and the need for international standards is more urgent and critical.

A new **standard** can be registered with organizations such as the British Standards Institute, the American National Standards Institute or the International Standards Organization. But the process to determine the prevailing standard does not stop there. The path to achieving a de facto standard stems from three modes of selection process: market-based selection, negotiated selection and a hybrid selection process where both market competition and negotiation operate jointly.

Market-based selection is reflected in standards wars such as that between VHS and Betamax, where consumers decided on the dominance of the VHS standard. The marketing strategies of firms are key to which firm and standard is most likely to win. VHS gained a decisive advantage from a strategy of wider distribution channels and a range of complementary products (Hollywood films) as well as longer recording time than Betamax, in spite of other more advanced features available only on Betamax.

Negotiated standardization is becoming more widespread. Organizations that determine prevailing standards are emerging to reduce the cost and the uncertainty associated with adopting new standards. Negotiated standard setting guarantees the smooth interchange of information, technical components and services along different networks. The telecommunications industry was able to keep up with the speed of technological development by opening up the negotiation process to market players (David and Steinmueller 1994; David and Shurmer 1996). Groupe Speciale Mobile (GSM), the current mobile technology in Europe, is an association of 600 network operators and suppliers of the mobile phone industry. The UMTS Forum is a similar association, developed to speed convergence between telecommunications, IT, media and content suppliers for the 3G industry. As with GSM the name of the UMTS association is synonymous with the name for the industry technology standard.

The internet has a different history of standardization to telecommunications. Standards were completely open and established within the research communities of universities. As the internet has become a commodity for the domestic and the commercial communities, other players are increasingly influencing its evolution.

Hybrid standard setting emerges as private firms adopt strategies to undercut collaborative decisions taken in negotiated standardization. They introduce new products, which initiate unprecedented developments but also create incompatibilities, lock-in effects, and pockets of market power. Internet telephony is a typical example, where companies, standards organizations and governments create a hybrid standard setting environment (Vercoulen and Wegberg 1998).

Case box: **Standards versioning**

Standards organizations are playing an increasingly important role in the process of upgrading standards (called 'versioning'). The GSM Association is guiding the evolution of the mobile industry through a family of wireless technology standards from today's standard through to GPRS, EDGE and 3GSM. Each subsequent standard offers a higher level of service. GPRS provides open internet. EDGE facilitates faster data streaming, and 3GSM will provide video streaming. The network of companies supporting the technologies will go through grades of service levels in order to phase out older standards and introduce new ones (Figure 12.9). At the end of the life span of a standard the technology platform is decommissioned, with the exception of equipment and software that is forward compatible with the next generation of standards.

Software standards follow a similar versioning strategy. Microsoft publishes the *Windows Desktop Product Lifecycle Guidelines* to provide advanced notice of changes in product availability and support. Microsoft makes Windows licenses available for purchase for a minimum of five years and provides assisted support for a further four years. The guidelines are important so that companies can plan their investment through software upgrades of Windows 98, NT, 2000, ME, and the latest version of Windows XP.

Switching costs are minimized when standards are designed to evolve from one another. The introduction of revolutionary standards, however, is costly. The pay-off is superior performance against the high cost of switching standards. The telling example is the price paid by mobile telephone operators to switch to third-generation technology. Mobile spectrum auctions earned European Governments £200 billion with Britain and Germany raising £22.5 and £60 billion respectively. The mobile operators had to bid – to renounce third-generation spectrum was to opt out of the future (but did they have to pay so much?). The outcome of these auctions left mobile operators with increased debt, depleted cash flow, and delay in third-generation launches, all of which became the more significant as the stock market faltered and then stopped dead.

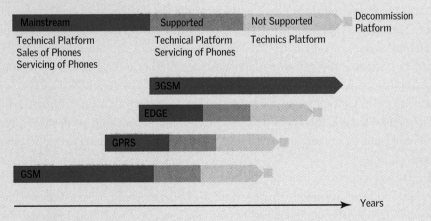

Figure 12.9 Standards versioning in the mobile telecommunications industry

12.4.2 **Supply chain**

In the last twenty years, the structure of the information economy has evolved through the interaction of three factors: the increase in computational capacity for data mining; the growth of telecommunication networks both fixed and mobile; and the explosion of information sharing via the internet.

These new, powerful characteristics of information have created opportunities for all industries, including network industries, to take advantage of new ways of managing supply chains. How to integrate company functions became the key concern and enterprise resource planning (ERP) systems provided the solution. Integration of the elements of the supply chain was seen as a move to dilute the boundaries of the rigid corporate departmental structures that were restricting business growth. The ERP era was the first wave of change in supply chain management. Deconstruction policies soon followed. Based on the example set by the automotive industry, many companies split their business processes and pushed some of them out to suppliers. Companies would retain the processes they liked and outsource the remainder. The elements of the supply chain would then be controlled through proprietary resources, which are difficult to replicate, such as a strong brand identity. MMO2, the UK mobile network provider that has recently faced upheaval is deconstructing its value chain as a means of strengthening its position (Pesola 2002). The company will move all its IT systems, including such functions as customer care, e-payments and billing to IBM. The outsourcing agreement covers ten years and is worth £50m in its first year. MMO2's tactics are an interesting pointer of how the European mobile industry is changing its operating model in order to emulate the US model.

With the outsourcing of functions and the need for specialist knowledge in handling electronic transactions, the number of organizations involved in the supply chain is increasing. As a result of integration and deconstruction, suppliers are developing modular structures with Lego-like snap-together interconnectivity. The complexity of the new supply chain structure is becoming akin to a business ecosystem of networked co-operation, rather than the traditional chain of competing suppliers, manufacturers and distributors (*see* Mathews 2002).

Figure 12.10 depicts the modular structure of the ICT industries, which constitute the new information economy. The structure is built on layers of communication network companies, hardware and software manufacturers, internet service providers, e-commerce transaction companies, media and content companies, and myriad service companies.

The network infrastructure suppliers are companies such as Alcatel, Nortel Networks, Motorola and Ericsson that provide communications networking equipment. Intel and 3Com form a sub-set of companies in this category, which supply interfacing hardware and software.

The network operators provide the basis of the exchange of information between companies and their customers. The medium they operate could be based on satellite, telephone, mobile, television or area networks. British Telecom, AT&T, Vodafone and T-Mobile

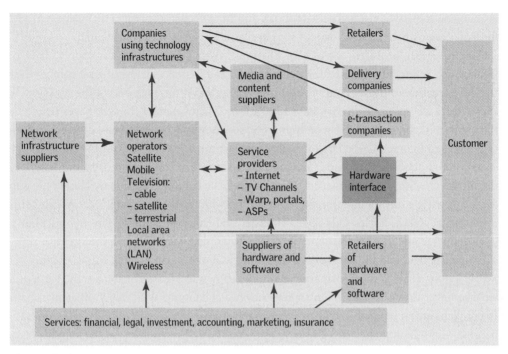

Figure 12.10 The modular infrastructure of the ICT economy

offer landline and mobile telecommunications networks. The operation of these companies is interconnected with other companies. For example, Vodafone uses BT's network. Credit card companies use Vodafone's mobile network for off-site credit verification. Vodafone has sold fixed-line telephone services from Energis and Racal Telecom networks. The interoperability of different telecom networks has become a complex business operation. British Telecom set up BT to develop and manage such relationships. BT Wholesale sells its fixed network product to independent service providers: businesses that wish to provide telecom services to end consumers without owning their own networks. The independent SP purchases the network facility from BT and other network operators, adding their own value and service brand.

Satellite networks provide the infrastructure for long-distance television, telephony and data interchange transmission. SES GLOBAL, Gilat Satellite Networks and Alcatel Space/SkyBridge have formed a €200 million joint venture to provide two-way satellite broadband services in corporate and home office markets across Europe. The new company plans to cater for the growing demand for broadband communications services in Europe via advanced VSAT satellite technology.

Digital television networks operate on a host of platforms such as satellite, copper or optic fibre cable. Interactive television has opened a host of business opportunities for retailing. The use of two-way cable networks, or a return medium via a normal telephone line, is changing the way consumers use and respond to television content. The business model for this service implies a new form of supply chain, for a new form of retailing.

Internet service providers are part of a complex web that provides the supply chain of information to the internet user. ISPs such as AOL and Fastnet convey internet content over the infrastructure of the telecommunication companies. At the back-end of the supply web, ISPs receive web pages from various organizations. The owners of the web pages would be the media and content suppliers, or, in many cases, they may have purchased the services of the media and content suppliers to create their web presence. At the front-end, where the supply web touches the customer, ISPs have to collaborate or conform to consumer interface manufacturers, which in the internet scenario would be computer suppliers. The supply web for the internet is due for another major revolution with third-generation (3G) mobile communication, which carries high-speed internet and video streaming. The 3G telephone, which will become the new customer interface, could dictate a change in internet transmission management and the nature of media content all the way down the supply chain.

The supply chain in the information economy shown in Figure 12.10 takes the form of a weblike network where each member may have to collaborate with many other members. Intercollaboration is possible because of software and hardware compatibility, and necessary because of the high degree of knowledge specialization at each point on the supply chain. An example of this weblike structure is the relationship between e-transaction companies, ISPs and media content providers and the companies that own the web pages. The four types of organization have to ensure the compatibility of their services across the supply network.

The infrastructure of the information economy does not look like a normal, traditional and competitive supply chain in the 'old' industrial economy. Telephony and the internet have made it possible for corporations to have commercial partnerships with many more companies. The notion of 'information is power' is turned on its head. As more companies have access to more information through communication, power is dissipated to more members in the supply chain. This increase in information exchange has become the overriding equalizer of power throughout the supply networks.

The basis of this new economy is the increase in connectivity among the various players in the chain. The connectivity level itself is rapidly evolving as communication and computational technologies become faster. The whole supply network is in a state of flux. Flexibility and adaptability have become essential strategic stances. Faster connectivity within the supply chain not only implies more interconnections between companies, but it also creates more volatile and replaceable interrelationships.

The concept of replaceable interrelationships has come about because companies are becoming '**isomorphic**' or similar in nature. DiMaggio and Powell (1983, p. 149), drawing from Hawley (1968), define isomorphism as 'a constraining process that forces one unit in a population to resemble other units that face the same set of environmental conditions'. With the standardization of technology, products are becoming more similar in design and quality. With the standardization of internal operations, through materials resource planning (MRP), enterprise resource planning (ERP) and electronic customer relationship management (eCRM), the service levels of competing companies are becoming similar in content and in construction. The implication is that suppliers are easily replaced with similar companies that have similar products and similar delivery attributes.

The information economy is creating a web of companies that have lower barriers of entry but fewer safety nets for retaining business. The older, hierarchical value chains of the industrial economy reinforced exclusivity, while the information economy is more inclusive.

Case box: **The rise of co-evolution and co-operation**

The new weblike value chain gives rise to a 'self-organizing' system. In nature, flocking is a form of self-organization. The formation of flocking birds is a self-organizing form of collaboration, with simple goals of direction and velocity. Similarly, companies organize and adapt their relationships with vendors and distributors. They select and substitute their partners in the value chain according to changes in the consumer market. Vendors and distributors in turn adapt to new market scenarios. For example, a wave of collaborative buying (when competitors join forces for purchasing) is counteracted by a wave of collaborative vending from vendors. The system eventually normalizes the balance of power.

The 'self-organizing' aspect in the information economy leads to the concept of 'co-evolution' (*see* Kelly, 1994, for an overview of the implications of adaptive behaviour). Evolving to meet the needs of other members in the value chain is becoming a more effective strategy than satisfying the company's own needs. Adapting to meet other companies' need leads to more business. Riding the new wave of co-evolution, companies are avoiding costly races against each other in favour of a strategy to join forces to gain more customers. We are observing this effect in NEC and Siemens, which have joined forces to supply the networks for Hutchison 3G, a key network provider of third-generation telecommunications in Europe.

Co-evolution and collaboration are even more relevant in industries where network externalities are a vital part of corporate success. The more customers join a network, such as a telecommunications service, the higher is the incentive for other customers to join. This effect is causing companies to collaborate on issues of compatibility. With 3G mobile phones on the horizon for Europe and the US, the standards war for a mobile internet operating system has begun. Microsoft, Linux, Symbian and Openwave are in the race to establish a widely accepted standard. This is an example of old-style competition, but it has caused a wave of co-evolution in another layer of competitors. The issue of standards has motivated Nokia and Siemens, Europe's largest manufacturers of mobile phones, to collaborate. They have teamed up to accelerate the introduction of third-generation mobile services. The collaboration of two companies will guarantee that Nokia and Siemens handsets can communicate with each other seamlessly. In this way the two companies, which have a combined global market share of 45 per cent, will benefit from network externalities and the positive feedback generated from providing a larger compatible technology network. Nokia and Siemens anticipate that other equipment vendors will link up with them to minimize industry fragmentation.

12.4.3 Physical platforms

A **physical platform** is the tangible infrastructure (such as computers, telephones, satellites, digital TV and local area networks) that delivers a service to consumers. A simple example of a platform is the PC on your desk. This comprises a set of hardware and software items joined together to provide a computing service. The component items are built according to to explicit technology standards and are delivered through separate but parallel supply chains to the PC assembler. Similarly, to obtain Sky's pay-TV service one needs a physical platform consisting of digital TV receiver, set-top decoder, telephone landlines, satellites and ground stations. The physical platform is an assembly of items, each constructed to specific standards and integrated to deliver service to the customer.

Case box: **Globalstar**

Globalstar is another example of a physical platform. Globalstar provides mobile telecommunications using Low Earth Orbiting (LEO) satellites. Its telephones look like mobile or fixed phones but the difference is that they can operate in areas outside normal reach. The satellite platform picks up signals from the Earth's surface, and relays them to the terrestrial gateway. Gateways distribute the calls to existing fixed and mobile networks. Terrestrial gateways are vital to integrate the company's services with existing local telephony networks.

The size of a physical network does not guarantee success. Iridium had a larger physical platform of satellites than Globalstar, but faced marketing-related difficulties at start-up. When it launched in 1998 it targeted the consumer users, who rejected the service because of its cost and bulky first-generation phones. Iridium filed for bankruptcy in 2001 and planned to decommission its satellite platform. It was purchased by a consortium, which paid $25 million for the inactive satellite system, which cost $5 billion when it was built in 1998. Iridium has recuperated most of its losses by changing its marketing segmentation strategy. Its current major user is the US Department of Defence, which is in line with its sales strategy to service large industrial users in remote locations (Weiss 2001).

Physical platforms have evolved from the simple structures, such as the older regional railway system, to a complex structure of interconnected sub-platforms. For this reason, the joints between the sub-networks become the strength of the whole structure, or, conversely, it could be its Achilles heel. It is therefore vital to define standards for joints. The standards that govern how a system and its modules interact is called the network's architecture (Morris and Ferguson 1993).

Henderson and Clark (1990) review two kinds of dynamic processes in modular systems: **modular innovation** and **architectural innovation**. The former type retains the architecture of the network, including its joints, but modifies the modules. By preserving the basic architecture of a system, network providers offer users enough compatibility to shift from one product generation to the next. The changes occur in the innovations and improvements of the modular components. They are be fitted into the system when required, and will be removed when obsolete. The result is a hybrid dynamic of change that preserved the platform's architecture while creating innovations within the module structure. A series of minor incremental modular changes can lead to an overall network platform that is radically new (Vercoulen and Wegberg 1998).

In architectural innovation, the modules are largely unchanged, but the architecture that connects them (the jointing system) is changed (Henderson and Clark 1990). The speed of innovation can be fast, as a key part of the system, the modular structure, is retained. New joints between these modules are installed. In some cases, adopting new standards and installing some new modules that embody these standards create an architectural innovation. The development of the internet in the late 1990s is an example of an architectural innovation in a network platform. The main proponents of the internet evolution are standard-setting bodies such as the World Wide Web Consortium and the Internet Engineering Task Force (Vercoulen and Wegberg 1998).

Case box: **Managing interoperability**

Physical platforms in the telecommunications industry are typically open platforms (like Wintel is for PCs) that provide interconnectivity with other telecom networks to add value and create network externalities. Open platforms have stipulated protocols, which are implemented by a large user base, as in the case of IBM clones. Closed platforms or proprietary platforms make it difficult for others to interact properly with those systems. Microsoft software and Apple computers are examples of closed platforms.

Open networks require interconnections and compatibility with surrounding networks. Telecommunications platforms have had to cope with the complexity of interoperability among different systems, as well as the agility required to shift rapidly to newer standards. The dynamics of complexity and agility used to be opposing forces (Vercoulen and Wegberg 1998). A complex interconnected physical platform tends to develop slowly. Railway systems and the telecom networks in many countries show this inertia. Communications and technology firms progressively created a solution to these opposing dynamics of development. As in the supply chain case discussed earlier, companies divided their platform structure into separate modules, each with some degree of autonomy (Langlois and Robertson 1992; Garud, Kumaraswamy and Prabhu 1995). Each module is designed with the flexibility for rapid change, such as the shift from ETACS to GSM. The complexity feature is retained because each module is interoperable with other modules to form a weblike complex system. The modules are therefore interdependent through the nodes, or joints between the modules. Interoperability between modules creates value for the user, as we observe in the ability to call overseas on a mobile telephone. Roaming of mobile telephones from country to country is another example. Interoperability exists between platforms of different network providers in the same country, or different platforms in different countries.

Building alliances

The reach of a technical platform determines the size of the consumer base. For this reason, companies are building alliances to gain the rewards of positive feedback. Apple and Microsoft have collaborated to create a version of Office that operates on an Apple computer. The effect is to allow the Apple computer platform to overlap with the Microsoft Office platform. In the mobile industry, competing telephone manufacturers are clamouring to create a communications platform with a common operating system. Ericsson and Nokia use the Symbian operating system on their third-generation mobile phones. Panasonic and Motorola are planning to introduce telephones with the software platform. Symbian will receive a total of $17.95 million in funding from Nokia Corp., Motorola Inc., Panasonic, Sony Ericsson and Psion to support its development (Evers 2002).

The Ethernet is an earlier example of alliance formation intended to increase the size of a physical platform. In 1973 Metcalfe and Boggs invented the Ethernet, the local area networking (LAN) technology that acts as a means to send vast amounts of data at high speed to the laser printers that Xerox was designing. Interestingly, the Ethernet came before the PC, yet it was to create a breakthrough in computer networking that would eventually tie together over 50 million PCs worldwide. The Ethernet quickly attracted Digital and Intel's interest to adopt the communication platform. Metcalfe had moved on to form 3Com but remained the key player in the discussions between Xerox, Digital and Intel. The DI3X group was formed, named after the first letter of the company names. The alliance lobbied for Ethernet to become a standard approved by the IEEE. Xerox agreed to license Ethernet to all users at a nominal fee of $1000. It realized that it would have to provide an open standard to get computer manufacturers to take on Ethernet as an interface to their printers. The strength of Ethernet was that it allowed PCs and workstations from different manufacturers to communicate by using an agreed standard, hence increasing the size of its physical platform and therefore its reach.

12.4.4 **Consumer networks**

A **consumer network** requires interdependencies between consumers. In a consumer market there are two levels of value attached to a product. 'Autarky' value (Liebowitz and Margolis 1999) refers to the value associated with a product irrespective of the number of other users. In marketing terms, this would be the 'core' value of a product. In economics this is the normal assumption and the theory of the firm is based on assumptions about the independence of individual consumer preferences. 'Synchronization' value is the augmented value derived from being able to interact with other consumers. The latter fuels the dynamics of the network effect discussed earlier in this chapter and in McGee and Sammut-Bonnici (2002). For example, the relative abilities of Microsoft, Symbian or other companies to capture synchronization value will determine who will gain critical mass first and win the race to establish the new operating system for third-generation mobile telephones. Customers will buy the 3G phones with the operating system they expect to be the most popular in the future. In this way they will be able to communicate and exchange video clips and photos with the widest possible set of users. The success of the winning operating system might depend on the psychology of consumer choice, or it could depend on technology characteristics from supply chain strategies and technology standards. For example, Microsoft and Intel co-operated to make Windows 95 exclusively compatible with Intel x86 microprocessor architectures and vice versa. The media coined the effect the 'Wintel Advantage'. In the case of mobile operating systems, Symbian and Microsoft are rallying their respective set of supporters to establish separate supply networks.

Lock-in and switching costs

The Wintel case led to a situation of **lock-in** for Windows users. The Wintel operating system quickly gained critical mass through rapid adoption and it became the most popular system throughout the world. On top of this, Windows users then invested in complementary software such as the Microsoft Office suite. Lock-in arises whenever users invest in the multiple complementary and durable assets of a physical platform and then find the costs of switching to an alternative to be prohibitive. Lock-in can occur on an individual level, company level and even a societal level. Thus, individuals may face switching costs in adopting a rival to Microsoft software, but so also do companies in having to provide systematic retraining costs, and so might whole communities in having to move from one software product to another. The key is that it would usually be necessary to switch from one dominant product to retain the interdependencies and complementarities between consumers. Private users were locked into the long-playing record technology because records could not be used on CD players (but were persuaded to switch when the benefit–cost ratio of the new products became sufficiently large). Note that the benefits of tape recording were never large enough to persuade customers to make a wholesale switch from LPs but the extra benefits of tapes (ability to record) were sufficient to persuade customers to invest in parallel systems. Companies became locked into Lotus 1-2-3 spreadsheets because their employees were trained in using the program command structure but later were persuaded to switch to Excel within Microsoft Office because of the extra complementarities. On a societal level, millions of users throughout the world are locked into using Microsoft's Windows desktop operating environment, as it has become the standard software in offices around the world.

Case box: **Lock-in and switching costs in mobile communications**

Telecommunication systems providers have chosen to offer new, superior technologies despite high switching costs. The industry has undergone three generations of technologies – TACS, ETACS, and GSM – and is now in the early days of introduction of 3G, incurring significant investment costs. Their calculation is made on the basis that the new systems will provide backward compatibility plus the expected benefits of new services.

Switching costs and lock-in at the consumer level can be deliberately used to inhibit or prevent consumers from adopting newer technologies or moving to alternative networks. In mobile communications, users may switch to another network provider with the same technology but with a different price structure. They may choose to switch to another technology when they replace their handsets with higher-level models. The strategies of the mobile telecommunication companies have focused on manipulating the tangible and intangible consumer costs when switching networks. In the introductory phase customers were contractually bound to a network for a year. They had to pay a release fee to end the contract and a connection charge to go to the next network. In the later 1990s switching networks became easier with the introduction of pay-as-you-go cards. But the hidden, intangible costs of switching remains, irrespective of payment structures and Oftel's recent pressure to minimize switching cost in the industry. Customers are deterred from switching by the investment in the time required to get used to a new product and are further inhibited by the uncertainty about the quality of untested products. The influence of brand loyalty is also significant. To the consumer, another very relevant switching cost is the loss of the mobile number when moving to another network (this was also a very big issue in the development of the telephone system in the USA over a century ago). Subscribers' reluctance to give up their familiar numbers resulted in the introduction of subsidized phones and more competitive tariffs. The power of switching costs can be observed in the entry strategies against powerful incumbents. Vodafone and Cellnet started to operate in 1984 and had a captive customer base by the time Orange and One2One entered the market in 1993 and 1994 respectively. The new entrants had to generate new customer-winning strategies with stronger branding and lower costs.

On a societal level economists observe that the practice of using lock-in strategies can have negative welfare effects as new superior technologies are suppressed. Liebowitz and Margolis (1990) discuss the fascinating example of typewriter keyboard layouts. In the 1870s the QWERTY configuration was selected by the creators of the TypeWriter brand in order to slow down typists in order to reduce jamming of the keys. The Dvorak layout patented in the 1932 is a more efficient layout and allows faster typing. This would suggest that QWERTY should then give way to the more efficient keyboard layout. The phenomenon of sticking to the slower QWERTY system is explained in terms of switching costs.

The collective switching costs are far higher than the individual switching costs because the co-ordination for mass switching to Dvorak is so difficult. With the advent of electric type-writers if the 1950s and then computer keyboards the expectation is even stronger but QWERTY still remains.

12.5 **Networks, standards and competition**

According to Economides and Flyer (1997):

> *Firms that compete in markets where network externalities are present face unique trade-offs regarding the choice of a technical standard. Adhering to a leading compatibility standard allows a firm's product to capture the value added by a large network. However, simultaneously the firm loses direct control over the market supply of the good and faces (direct) intra-platform competition. Alternatively, adhering to a unique standard allows the firm to face less or no intra-platform competition, but it sacrifices the added value associated with a large network.*

This trade-off is a key strategic decision that depends in part on the control that firms have in making their output compatible with competitors' outputs and complementary products. The ability to conform to a common standard opens the opportunity to make this trade-off. Where standards are proprietary, the decision rests with the owner of the standard. The owner's trade-off is the pay-off associated with developing the existing network and its spillovers versus the introduction of more intra-platform competition. Essentially the trade-off is the same: to adhere to a common standard or to seek uniqueness. This can be expressed as a sequential game: at the outset, one chooses the appropriate technical standard (and, therefore, the network to join), and later one chooses how to compete. Normal markets do not have this choice of network and there are consequences for market structure and competition in the presence of network externalities. The mathematical model in Economides and Flyer (1997) defines networks as coalition structures and analyses the stability of coalitions under different standards regimes and varying levels of network externalities. There are a number of implications for market structure in the presence of network externalities.

First, it is intuitively clear that industry output will be higher when there are network externalities and when standards are open. Firms are free to choose which standard to adopt and are deterred only by the costs of adoption. Second, when standards are incompatible and the owners of standards can exercise proprietary control, incumbents are more strongly protected against the consequences of new entrants. Moreover, there will usually be considerable asymmetries between firms in terms of outputs, prices and profits. (Under incompatibility regimes, firms are equivalent to platforms and constitute one-firm networks.) For pure network goods the asymmetries are particularly marked.

In general, with total incompatibility of standards market concentration, output inequality and price and profit inequality increase with the extent of the network externality. This is an important result because it explains why one or two firms so often dominate network industries. The mechanism is straightforward. The leading network establishes its critical mass, leaving the second network to establish a critical mass across the remaining untapped market coverage. The third network follows in the same fashion and so on. It follows that there will be a tendency to provide large incentives to organize customers into few platforms so as to maximize the added value from the available networks. Firms will be keen to abandon their own weak standards in favour of the higher value obtainable from a leading network.

There is a third implication. Where there are proprietary standards and strong network effects, there is no natural equilibrium in terms of network offerings. There are always incentives for at least one firm to move to a stronger network and the consequence of any one move is to shift the incentives for all other firms. However, equilibrium can be reinforced by the refusal of firms to make their proprietary standards available. Again, the mechanism is straightforward. Under strong externalities, the owner of a standard has a considerable incentive to exploit the standard by itself and to exclude other firms with weaker standards. Conversely, where the externality is weak, the owner will find a stronger incentive to admit other firms to its proprietary standard in order to grow the network through collective effort and thus generate more added value.

In summary, strong network externalities suggest the following conclusions:

1 Larger industry output.

2 Very large asymmetries between firms/platforms.

3 Likelihood of market dominance.

4 Enhancement and protection of proprietary standards.

5 Equilibrium market structures that are the reverse of the world without network externalities.

12.6 Implications for strategy

This chapter argues that there are major differences between the economic and strategic characteristics of the **new economy** compared to the old industrial order. These major differences can be summarized as follows:

1 The information economy depends on connectivity. Without connectivity, consumer interdependence is indirect. Positive feedback gives an economic law of plenty – more gives more.

2 Upfront costs are very large and revenues can be substantially delayed and are

significantly at risk. As a result, the nature of business models is different, with higher degrees of risk embedded in them.

3 It is also a world of immense uncertainty where even the range of potential outcomes is not known, but also where there is a significant probability that future technological change might undermine an apparently winning position.

4 The competition between rival networks/standards can be hard to call in advance.

5 'Tippy markets' substantially raise the level of risk.

In this new world there is much more uncertainty and companies need to take bigger risks in order just to survive. The prospect of entrepreneurial profits is enticingly large but there are probably greater probabilities of failure. The list of failures and near failures in the last decade by large companies is very long. There are some new strategic 'rules' for competing in the new economy. While these are quite generic in nature they illustrate that companies need to come to these markets with a different mindset about how to compete:

1 **Expectations management** is central to the way in which marketing strategy is conceived (see the case box below).

2 **Open standards** are the key to volume. Protected standards are only viable as small high-priced niche markets. The old preoccupation with protection of intellectual property is giving way to a sharing and co-operating approach.

3 There is a law of inverse pricing. The best (i.e. the most valuable in the future) products are given away, such as web browsers, in order to create a consumer standard, and sheer volume causes both marginal costs and prices to fall over time as the product becomes more valuable. The cash flow machine consists of modest (even small) margins multiplied by gigantic volumes to defray massive investments. The machine is volume driven and protected by very large switching costs.

4 The first strategic choice is which network to join (which standard to adopt). The second, and a long way behind, is how to compete within the network of choice.

5 Networked complementarities and co-operative strategies are replacing the old order of hierarchical business organization and competition.

6 In a world of uncertainty, customers are also uncertain about which standards, technologies and products will prevail. This will increase the power of brands and place upon marketing the need to manage customer expectations so as to speed adoption rates towards tipping points in the market.

The economic characteristics of network industries are dependent in large part on the interconnectivity that is characteristic of the technologies of information goods. Interconnectivity allows customers to view, use and link products, giving rise to virtual networks of customers. In these networks, powerful demand-side increasing returns can operate. Where consumer-based externalities are powerful there are strong pressures towards 'winner takes all' phenomena (e.g. Wintel globally, and Sky TV in the UK). In these circumstances conventional economic laws are challenged. De facto monopoly can emerge: but uncertainty is high and markets may be intrinsically unstable. Successive waves of technology may outmode old monopolies and serve as the basis for new monopolies.

The rate of growth and now the sheer size of the ICT industry has been the progenitor of major changes in the economy. We have seen major effects on other industries through the new value possibilities that information technology offers and through the substantial fixed costs and minimum scales required for effective deployment of these technologies. When linked to networks of interdependent customers we see the potential emergence of 'winner takes all' strategies and the emergence of new monopolies.

We have decomposed the ICT industry into its component parts in order to see who the players are and how they interact with one another. In doing this we argue that we are beginning to see a new type of industrial order – one marked by networked complementarities and co-operation in place of the traditional model of hierarchy and competition. We have also decomposed the industry into four horizontal levels – technology, supply chain, platform, and network – to show that these have different economic characteristics and therefore that corporate strategies have different dynamics. The examples quoted indicate the range and extent of the possibilities inherent in the new technologies and for the nature of rivalry in the form of pre-emptive strikes and technology races. We note particularly the pervasive changes that are taking place in supply chains generally. The increasing importance of connectivity and modularity is forcing a shift from competitive mode towards co-operative mode. This raises thoughts of self-organizing systems and the notion of co-evolution, rather a long way from the search for and exercise of crude bargaining power. The sheer size and cost of physical platforms also create new dynamics. The pervasive use of alliances is an obvious example. Less obvious is how the need for interoperability requires new attitudes towards complexity and requirements for agility.

A new set of strategies is emerging to offset the risks and pressures exerted by these rules. This is visible in the setting up of global standards and their ensuing platforms. For example, Group Speciale Mobile, commonly known as GSM, is an association of 600 network operators and suppliers of the mobile phone industry. Their primary objective is to set a common standard for mobile communications in order to create a homogeneous industry where equipment, software and networks can seamlessly talk to each other. Strategies of standardization are stabilizing the markets and charting the course for research and development policies.

Finally, we remark on the significance of interdependence between consumers. This effect at its strongest completely shifts our thinking from the prevalence of oligopolistic competition (size matters but so do diminishing returns) to the possibility of winner takes all and the monopoly (size matters – full stop). Clearly such network effects are not always going to be so extreme but there is a real possibility that the combination of high fixed costs, significant economies of scale, and high degrees of knowledge specialization will, when taken together with consumer bandwagons, create massive new corporate structures to which the major (and perhaps only) discipline will be further developments in technology. However, the analysis of consumer lock-in suggests the real possibility that switching costs might inhibit the adoption of valuable new technologies.

Case box: **Expectations management**

When consumers choose products in network markets, their expectations play a crucial role on sales of the products or their network components, since consumer utility depends on the number of other consumers purchasing the same products. Rival firms in the network industry influence consumers' expectations in order to maximize their profits. The process is facilitated by consumers' imperfect information about the size of the installed base in the market. Sales figures are often exaggerated to impress consumers about leadership in the installed base over rivals. The competition between OS/2 and Microsoft Windows in 1992 is an example of firms' intentions of influencing consumer expectation. IBM and Microsoft both announced wider adoption of their operating systems than actual. Later on, each company disputed the estimated numbers of sales of the other (Bensen and Farrell 1994).

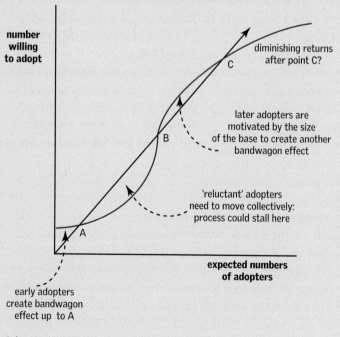

Figure 12.11 Adoption processes: networks and technologies

Expectation manage-ment is a strategic device that goes beyond the inflation of penetration figures and moves into the realms of brand and corporate image building. In competing to become market leaders in the mobile communications industry, or at least to achieve critical mass, consumer expectations

Market to create momentum:
    create the belief that this technology will be the standard
Leverage reputation:
    brands and reputation matter
Commit to 'open' standards:
    open standards can give access to volume
    proprietary standards can result in small niches
Win over an influential buyer
    e.g. supermarkets and UPCs (barcodes)
Advance sign ups:
    prior commitments create confidence
Wink at piracy:
    adoption at zero price is better than no adoption
Pricing:
    leasing, long-term contracts, give-aways, penetration pricing

Figure 12.12 Managing the adoption process

were significant. The mobile company that was expected to grow the fastest would gain most market share. Self-fulfilling expectations are one manifestation of positive feedback econ-omics and bandwagon effects. The mobile industry has made consistent use of semiotics in expectations management through its media campaigns. Images, music themes and slogans are used to imply magnitude and leadership.

The model in Figure 12.11 illustrates the adoption process. Adoption typically follows an S-shaped pattern around the long-term trend growth rate. The early adopters ('anoraks') rush in. There is then a pause while the prospective early adopters make up their minds – marketing is focused on persuading them to move quickly and decisively so as to create a rapid growth that will become self-sustaining (through point B in the diagram). Following this, the push to sustain the market through attracting late adopters is the next marketing focus. This suggests some rules for marketing – these are summarized in Figure 12.12. Marketing is about creating momentum so as to minimize the risks that are endemic in this new world. Brands and reputation are, if anything, even more important. The emphasis is on volume, so open standards are attractive and low, penetration-style pricing will be common.

Vodafone's corporate image campaign in its early days included images of the Thames Barrier and the cliffs of Dover. Symbols of national interest were used to give the subliminal message that Vodafone will succeed throughout the UK. The musical theme in the Thames Barrier campaign was from *Close Encounters*, implying universal reach. The cliffs of Dover campaign involved the draping of a large section of the cliffs with material, by a contem-porary artist. The message could have been directed at conquering 'coverage' issues of radio transmission. Orange has had one of the most famous slogans in UK media history: 'The future is bright, the future is Orange'. One2One has had equally expansionist media campaigns, par-ticularly with its award-winning 'Welcome to Our World'. All these campaigns imply market leadership and a sense of network growth.

The effects in Figure 12.11 can be seen in research by Huberman (1988), which shows how consumers' expectations are being linked to the critical mass. The stronger the consumers' expectation that a new network will be widely adopted in the future, the faster the market reaches critical mass. Once a critical number of users is achieved, the rate of increase of new users increases exponentially, up to the limit of the user population (or to some other natural limit; *see* Figure 12.11). The implication for strategists it that the time required to achieve critical mass can be reduced in proportion to the degree of optimism of people's expectations.

Hence, strategic action aimed at increasing consumers' expectations of the success of a new product would have a double effect of inducing more new users, who in turn influence even more users. This effect can be powerful – Huberman's simulations demonstrate that even if there is only a small group of individuals with double the propensity for innovation in relation to the group average, the critical mass can be reached very rapidly. This has been evident in the mobile telecommunications industry. Once the phones were affordable and accessible to the youth market (the early adopters), sales boomed for this particular segment. As a result even more users from other segments were attracted to the market.

12.7 Summary

Thus, the brave new world has a sting in the tail. The pervasive development of the ICT industries has promoted, and continues to promote, very substantial consequential changes throughout the economy. In doing so, industry economics and dynamics do change and significant adaptations have to take place in order to avoid getting run down by the juggernaut. Changes are needed in the nature of the corporate strategies and in the mindsets required. Where the conjunction of certain technological and consumer circumstances takes place, the strategy game becomes a very direct race to establish dominant position. Even where such games fail to achieve their objectives, the cost of unproductive investment could be enormous. Where they in fact succeed, many will nevertheless have failed, and we would also face the difficulties in managing the consequences of de facto monopoly. The data available does not suggest that winner takes all is likely to be a frequent phenomenon. However, all the other indications suggest that various forms of scale-intensive, pre-emptive strategies will become much more common (see, for example, the telecommunications boom and bust). But as a counterpoint we can also see that there are very considerable forces promoting more co-operation and stronger incentives towards a much more subtle blending of co-operative and competitive modes of practice within industries.

Key terms

Architectural innovation *478*

Consumer externalities *462*

Consumer network *480*

Critical mass *466*

Expectations management *485*

Installed base *467*

Interoperability *479*

Isomorphism *476*

Lock-in *481*

Modular innovation *478*

Multiplier effect *459*

Negative feedback systems *468*

Network externalities *458*

Network industries *461*

New economy *484*

Open standards *485*

Physical platforms *478*

Pure network good *469*

Real and virtual networks *464*

Standards *472*

Standards versioning *473*

Switching costs *473*

Technical platform *473*

Tipping point *467*

Recap questions and assignments

1   Explain how network externalities might (or might not) occur in the following situations, paying particular attention to the way in which critical mass is reached:

(a)   The Apple–IBM PC battle in the PC industry;

(b)   The mobile telecommunications industry;

(c)   BSkyB and the satellite TV market.

2   For the situations in question 1, give examples of co-evolution and/or cooperation. In which case is co-operative behaviour most marked? Why?

3   For any internet-based business with which you are familiar, explain its business model and compare it to any one of the business models discussed in Chapter 6.

Online
*Learning*Centre

When you have read this chapter, log on to the Online Learning Centre website at www.mcgraw-hill.co.uk/textbooks/mcgee to explore chapter-by-chapter test questions, further reading and more online study tools for strategy.

Case 1 **How good is Google?**

If the ultimate measure of impact is to have one's name become a new verb in the world's main languages, Google has reason to be proud. When they founded the company five years ago, Sergey Brin and Larry Page, friends at Stanford University, chose a word play on 'googol' – the number 1 followed by 100 zeros – because their ambition was to organize the information overload of the internet in a transparent and superior way. These days, singles 'google' suitors before agreeing to a date, housewives 'google' recipes before cooking, and patients 'google' their ailments before visiting doctors. Dave Gorman, a comedian, even has a popular show, the 'Googlewhack Adventure' – a Googlewhack being what happens when two words are entered into Google and it comes back with exactly one match.

As search engines go, in other words, Google has clearly been a runaway success. Not only is its own site the most popular for search on the web, but it also powers the search engines of major portals, such as Yahoo! and AOL. All told, 75% of referrals to websites now originate from Google's algorithms. That is power. For some time now, Google's board (which includes two of Silicon Valley's best-known venture capitalists, John Doerr of Kleiner Perkins Caufield & Byers and Michael Moritz of Sequoia Capital) has been deliberating how to translate that power into money. They appear to have decided to bring Google to the stockmarket next spring. Bankers have been overheard estimating Google's value at $15 billion or more. That could make Google Silicon Valley's first hot IPO since the dotcom bust, and perhaps its biggest ever. That alone is enough to have some sceptics whispering 'Netscape'. Now that the worst of the dotcom hangover is clearing, they wonder, will Google become one of the few valuable internet survivors, joining Amazon and above all eBay? Or will it simply be the next over-hyped share sale to make its founders rich only to wither away miserably, either for lack of a sustainably profitable business model, or, like Netscape, because it finds itself in the path of that mighty wrecker, Microsoft?

The search for profits

Google, naturally, is determined to avoid Netscape's fate at all costs. This was why it made Eric Schmidt its chief executive in 2001. Mr Schmidt was 46 at the time – Messrs Brin and Page were in their twenties – and was the boss of Novell, a software firm decimated by Microsoft but given another lease of life under his leadership. He seemed suitably 'adult' to turn Google into a money-making machine.

Mr Schmidt understood that the key to monetising all those customer searches (now 200m a day) was to place small, unobtrusive and highly relevant text advertisements alongside Google's search results. Advertisers like this system because they pay only if web surfers actually click on their links. And consumers either do not mind, or even learn to love these commercial links for their relevance, just as they appreciate the Yellow Pages.

Google did not pioneer this 'paid search' advertising. That honour falls to Overture, a Californian firm bought this year by Yahoo! which still has about half of the $2 billion-or-so market. Nor did Google's founders readily embrace the concept. Mr Page was once heard to say at a trade show that commercial exploitation was 'bastardising' the search industry. Mr Schmidt made the concept uncontroversial at Google, thereby helping paid search to become the fastest growing part of the advertising industry today.

The next step is to take this approach to advertising from the results pages of search engines and on to other web pages. Increasingly, web publishers – from hobby bloggers to small businesses – allow firms such as Google to crawl through the content of their pages and place relevant text advertisements in the right margin. Once page visitors click on the links, the webmasters share the revenues with Google. At a stroke, this so-called 'contextual advertising' makes much of web publishing self-financing. This may result in better web content by making hitherto unprofitable online activities economically viable.

Meta Group, a consultancy, reckons that the market for paid search and other contextual advertising will grow to $5 billion by 2006. This is Google's main market opportunity (although it also gets some revenues from licensing its search technology). Currently, Google is thought to make annual profits of about $150m. To be worth the rumoured $15 billion for longer than it takes a bubble to burst, it will need to raise its profitability substantially. That means matching such internet stars as eBay (market capitalisation $37 billion), but without the natural-monopoly advantages that have made eBay so dominant – the classic network effect of buyers and sellers knowing they do best by all trading in one place. For Google to stay permanently ahead of other search-engine technologies is almost impossible, since it takes so little – only a bright idea by another set of geeks – to lose the lead. In contrast to a portal such as Yahoo!, which also offers customers free e-mail and other services, a pure search engine is always but a click away from losing users.

The arrival of competitors

Yahoo!, in fact, will probably be the first to attack. It now owns rival search technologies including AltaVista, AlltheWeb and Inktomi. With the contextual-advertising technology of Overture, Yahoo! now has under its own roof all the elements of the business model that made Google such a success. It cannot be long before Yahoo! turns from a lucrative customer of Google's into a powerful rival.

Even more frightening (especially to those who remember Netscape's fate in the browser wars), Microsoft smells blood. It is currently working on its own search algorithm, which it hopes to make public early next year, around the probable time of Google's share listing. Historically, Microsoft has been good at letting others (Apple, Netscape, Real) pioneer a technology before taking over, exploiting its dominance in desktop operating systems.

Google the new-age advertising agency makes money, but it is Google the search engine that builds the consumer brand which makes the ad agency powerful. Whenever users click on advertisements on Google's own site, Google gets all the revenues. Whenever users stray to other search engines, even ones where Google has placed sponsored links, Google has to share the revenues with the site owner. As the competition between Google, Overture and others heats up, Google's profit margins will fall.

This may already be happening. Craig Pisaris-Henderson, the chief executive of FindWhat.com, a smaller rival to Overture and Google in contextual advertising, reckons that Google's operating margins on sites other than its own must be much worse than FindWhat.com's (23%) or Overture's (12%) because it has been wooing advertisers away from Overture by being more generous to webmasters.

One thing that might help against Microsoft, says Danny Sullivan, the editor of SearchEngineWatch.com, an online consumer guide to the industry, is Google's image of 'niceness' – at least by implicit comparison with the forces of darkness in Redmond. Scott Banister, a pioneer of paid-search technology (and now a founder of IronPort, an e-mail infrastructure firm), thinks that Google has already built sufficiently deep networks with advertisers to mount an effective resistance to Microsoft's impending assault.

Even so, Google is no sure thing – as those who hope to sell its shares are no doubt aware. John Doerr and Michael Moritz, for instance, between them also brought Netscape and Yahoo! to market, and may remember their lessons. With luck, Google's owners will remember to work out a viable strategy for Google beyond the point at which they cash out.

Source: The Economist, 11 January 2003, Vol. 369, Issue 8348, p. 57.

Case Questions

1 Describe Google's strategy and explain how its business model works.

2 What are the risks facing Google and how can it defend itself against them?

3 What characteristics of the 'new economy' are present in this case? To what extent do these characteristics make the analysis of Google's competitive position and its future strategic choices unique or unusual?

Case 2   Browser wars, part two

Remember the browser wars, when Netscape and Microsoft fought for dominance of the web? For a while, each rushed out ever more complex browsers in the software equivalent of an arms race. In the end, Microsoft prevailed by bundling its browser with its Windows operating system.

That fight may, however, prove to have been just a warm-up. Now a new browser war is under way, as software firms compete to provide the browsers for 'information appliances' such as set-top boxes, handheld computers and smart phones. Such devices are still in their infancy, but they are widely expected eventually to outnumber PCs. So the stakes in this new browser war are high. And this time round, the battlefield looks very different.

For a start, Microsoft is almost nowhere to be seen. Its strongest weapon in the desktop browser wars – the ability to include new software as part of Windows, and thus ensure its installation on millions of PCs – no longer works. Microsoft's cut-down version of Windows for appliances has been a flop, and the firm's strategy of tying its browser to its operating system is no help if that system is not dominant. But Netscape, which is now part of AOL, is still very much in the running, alongside dozens of rivals including Opera, OpenTV, Lineo, QNX and Pixo.

Another difference is that the appliance makers and service providers (such as cable-TV and mobile-phone companies) will decide which browser comes installed on a particular device. On a PC, a new browser can be downloaded and installed with a few clicks. Not so with appliances, whose users will have no choice in the matter. Rival browser makers are thus courting appliance makers and service providers, rather than trying to woo users. To maximise its chances in this beauty contest, a browser must be fast and work with many different kinds of hardware.

With so many firms in the race, it seems unlikely that any browser will win a dominant share. The resulting diversity will mean that, for everything to work properly, it will be vital that web pages and the browsers that display them conform to the technical standards laid down by the World Wide Web Consortium (W3C). So browser makers are rushing to show how well-behaved their software is. Contrast this with the old Microsoft-Netscape battle, when both firms added proprietary extensions to existing web standards in an attempt to lock in users.

Netscape claims that its software, called Gecko, is the most standards-compliant browser around. Jon Stephenson von Tetzchner, Opera's boss, makes a similar claim about his firm. The problem, he says, is that only 5% of web pages comply with W3C standards. Most are designed to look good on Netscape's or Microsoft's old browsers, rather than playing by the rules. On December 6th, Opera said it will offer the Windows version of its browser free. The idea, says Mr von Tetzchner, is to increase Opera's market share and to encourage web designers to look beyond the 'big two' browsers to a more diverse future.

This is just one of the many subtle links between the old and new browser wars. Netscape's new strategy is similarly informed by its bruising previous encounter with Microsoft. By making Gecko freely available, and encouraging its use with the free Linux operating system, it hopes to allow appliance makers to avoid 'vendor lock-in'. Netscape does not benefit directly from this strategy, but the result is to make it hard for any single firm (i.e., Microsoft) to establish a stranglehold on the market. Although the new browser wars are very different from the old, in some respects little has changed.

Source: 'Browser wars, part two', *The Economist* 14 December 2000.
© The Economist Newspaper Limited, London (14 December 2000).

Case Questions

1 What was Microsoft's strategy in the first browser wars? How important were network externalities in its thinking?

2 Why is the new generation of browser wars different? Does Microsoft now have a competitive disadvantage?

Further reading and references

Arthur, B (1996) 'Increasing Returns and the New World of Business', *Harvard Business Review*, July/Aug.

Arthur, WB (1989) 'Competing technologies, increasing returns, and lock-in by historical events', *Economic Journal*, **99**, pp. 116–31.

Arthur, WB (1990) 'Positive feedback in the economy', *Scientific American*, **262**, pp. 92–9.

Baumol, W, Panzar, J and Willig, R (1982) 'Contestable markets and the theory of industry', *American Economic Review*, 72.

Bensen, SM and Farrell, J (1994) 'Choosing How to Compete: Strategies and Tactics Standardization', *Journal of Economic Perspectives*, Spring.

David, PA and Shurmer, M (1996) 'Formal standards-setting for global telecommunications and information services: towards an institutional regime transformation', *Telecommunications Policy*, 20, 10.

David, PA and Steinmueller, WE (1994) 'Economics of Compatibility Standards and Competition in Telecommunication Networks', *Information Economics and Policy*, 6.

Digital Planet (2002) *The Global Information Economy*, Data by International Data Corporation, World Information Technology and Services Alliance, USA.

DiMaggio, PJ and Powell, WW (1983) 'The iron cage revisited: institutional isomorphism and collective rationality in organizational fields', *American Sociological Review*, **48**, April, pp. 147–60.

Dumont, B (2000) Book Review of Carl Shapiro and Hal R. Varian, Information Rules: A Strategic Guide to the Network Economy, *Journal of Network Industries*, **1**, **1**, pp. 101–7.

Economides, N (1996) 'The economics of networks', *International Journal of Industrial Organization*, **14**, **2**, pp. 675–99.

Economides, N and Flyer, F (1997) 'Compatibility and Market Structure for Network Goods', Discussion Paper EC–98–02.

Ellis, HS and Fellner, W (1943) 'External economies and diseconomies', *American Economic Review*, 33.

Evans, P and Wurster, TS (2000) *Blown to Bits*, Harvard Business School Press, Boston, MA.

Evers, J (2002) 'Siemens joins Symbian Consortium', IDG News Service, Amsterdam Bureau, ITworld.com 4/23.

Garud, R, Kumaraswamy, A and Prabhu, A (1995) 'Networking for Success in Cyberspace', *IEEE Proceedings of the International Conference on Multimedia Computing and Systems*, pp. 335–40.

Henderson, RM and Clark, KB (1990) 'Architectural Innovation: The Reconfiguration of Existing Product Technologies and the Failure of Established Firms', *Administrative Science Quarterly*, 35.

Huberman, BA (1988) *The Ecology of Computation*, Elsevier Science Publishers, Amsterdam.

Katz, M and Shapiro, C (1985) 'Network externalities, competition and compatibility', *American Economic Review*, **75**, **3**, pp. 424–40.

Kelly, K (1994) *Out of Control – The New Biology of Machines*, Addison Wesley.

Kelly, K (1998) 'New Rules for the New Economy: 10 ways the network economy is changing everything', Fourth Estate.

Knight, FH (1924) 'Some fallacies in the interpretation of social cost', *Quarterly Journal of Economics*, 38.

Langlois, RN and Robertson, PL (1992) 'Networks and Innovation in a Modular System: Lessons from the Microcomputer and Stereo Component Industries', *Research Policy*, **21**, **4**, pp. 297–313.

Leyden, P (1997) 'Moore's Law Repealed, Sort of', *Wired*, Issue 5.05, May.

Liebowitz, SJ and Margolis, SE (1990) 'The Fable of the Keys', *Journal of Law and Economics*, Vol. XXXIII, April.

Liebowitz, SJ and Margolis, SE (1999) *Winners, Losers & Microsoft*, The Independent Institute, Oakland.

Mathews, JA (2002) 'Strategizing vs Economizing: Theorizing dynamic competitive behaviour in disequilibrium', unpublished paper, November.

McGee, J and Sammut-Bonnici, T (2002) 'Network Industries in the New Economy: the Effect of Knowledge and the Power of Positive Feedback', *European Business Journal*, September, **14**, **3**, pp. 116–32.

Morris, CR and Ferguson, CH (1993) 'How Architecture Wins Technology Wars', *Harvard Business Review*, **71**, **2**, pp. 86–96.

Pesola, M (2002) *Financial Times*, 11th April.

Saloner, G, Shepard, A and Podolny, J (2001) *Strategic Management*, Wiley, New York.

Sammut-Bonnici, T and McGee, J (2002) 'Network Strategies for the New Economy: Emerging Strategies for New Industry Structures', *European Business Journal*, December, **14**, **4**, pp. 174–85.

Shapiro, C and Varian, H (1999) *Information Rules: A Strategic Guide to the Network Economy*, Harvard Business School Press, Boston, MA.

Sharkey, NE and Sharkey, AJC (1993) 'Adaptive generalisation and the transfer of knowledge', *Artificial Intelligence Review*, Special Issue on Connectionism, **7**, pp. 313–28.

Shy, O (2001) *The Economics of Network Industries*, Cambridge University Press, Cambridge, UK.

Vercoulen, F and Wegberg, M (1998) 'Standard Selection Modes in Dynamic, Complex Industries: Creating Hybrids between Market Selection and Negotiated Selection of Standards', NIBOR Working Paper, nib98006, Maastricht.

Weiss, T (2001) *Computer World*, April 2.

Young, AA (1913) 'Pigou's Wealth and Welfare', *Quarterly Journal of Economics*, 27.

Part 4

Strategy and practice

Part contents

Introduction

This section moves on from the micro and macroeconomic analyses of strategy and focuses on more *process-based* analyses to help our understanding of what happens in the strategy formulation and implementation phases. A briefer description of the section would be that it investigates 'what happens when strategy meets organization'.

The objectives of this section are to introduce the reader to the more process-orientated perspectives on strategy. Part 2 began with the economic analysis of strategic decision making, while this part opens with a *process* analysis for strategic decision making. This sets the scene for the following chapters. The logic for this section is that we neglect the influence of organizations, interest groups (stakeholders) and individuals on strategy at our peril.

The interactions of external context, organizational context, behaviours and strategy are complex, yet they colour what happens in practice. There can be 'many a slip between cup and lip' in the strategy process. It is only by taking the perspectives outlined in this part that we can fully appreciate how these factors may interact to shape, block, change or radically modify strategy.

Chapter 13 characterizes the strategic decision making process. First, it deals with the concept of choice. How do strategists make choices between competing avenues for action? Three important techniques are introduced: game theory, sensitivity analysis and options theory. Each of these helps decision makers choose between alternative courses of actions. However, the chapter shows that choice is only one aspects of understanding decision processes. The chapter goes on to show how we can identify different processes that are more associated with the characteristics of the decision (how complex and how politically contested between stakeholders) than with the topic itself (e.g. a new product or a reorganization) or the choice process between alternatives. All decisions have to be put into practice, so the chapter also shows how characteristics of implementation can relate to performance. In particular, two factors stand out as being important, the *knowledge base* of the organization and the *receptivity* of the organizational infrastructure to the strategic decision.

Chapter 14 builds naturally on the decision making perspective by introducing the concepts and practicalities of risk and uncertainty. The chapter first of all distinguishes between risk and uncertainty and provides some working definitions of each. The chapter then identifies the sources and types of risks typically faced by decision makers. It depicts ways risk may be both assessed and handled as a natural part of the decision making process. The chapter outlines models for risk analysis. These include models based on expected utilities and introduces techniques such as net present value, internal rate of return and the use of decision trees to reduce both uncertainty and risk. The chapter concludes by looking at scenario building, a way of reducing risk and uncertainty by looking forwards to plausible futures. The chapter outlines a method for conducting scenario analysis and reflecting this back on the firm so that scenario building can help inform the strategy process.

Chapter 15 takes on board the fact that the implementation of any strategic decision will involve both individuals and organizations in often substantial degrees of change. This chapter examines the organizational and individual aspects of managing these changes. The chapter outlines the many different approaches that have been taken to understanding change in relation to strategies and it covers a number of levels of analysis ranging from the contextual to the individual. This chapter argues that looking at strategy without also looking at questions of organizational change exposes strategies to increased risks and, in the worst case, problems with organizational and individual change can prevent strategic decisions from being implemented altogether.

Chapter 16 deals with how organizations ensure survival and continuity by not simply adapting to their operating environment, but also by learning. Organizational learning is a much debated and contested concept and the chapter takes the reader through the main debates, showing how foresight, insight and learning are key to long-term development and growth for the organization and its individuals. The chapter emphasizes the dynamics between learning and strategy, showing how the process can be viewed as recursive. The one informs the other. Without strategy, there can be little learning. Learning from doing is necessary, but not sufficient. Organizations and individuals must also create, sustain and feed learning back into the strategy process so that new decisions can be made, based on the new knowledge created by learning. The chapter examines the benefits and the pitfalls in this theoretically virtuous circle between learning and strategy.

Chapter 17 looks at the most senior echelons of organization, the board or the top policy making team. In particular, the chapter examines the processes of governance and assesses what we know about more effective and less effective boards. Drawing on a wide range of literature and research the chapter outlines the role of the board as the top strategic team of the organization and emphasizes its pivotal role in shaping both the strategy process and the fortunes of the organization overall. The chapter provides details of recent changes in regulations and recommended guidelines for effective governance. The bulk of these guidelines have been formulated in the UK and apply directly to UK companies. However, as the chapter emphasizes, other countries are struggling with very similar problems of trying to ensure effective governance. So the chapter should not be read as solely a UK-specific chapter, but as one which shows how different governance characteristics can impede or enhance the strategy process.

The chapters cover the areas depicted in the strategy resources concepts map and the strategy process concepts map (introduced in Chapters 1 and 2 of this book). The shaded boxes represent the primary focuses of this part of the book. The non-shaded boxes are covered in other parts of this book. The degree of shading in the boxes represents the degree to which these topics are covered here and also indicates the interconnections explored in each chapter. These maps also appear overleaf.

Clearly this part deals in far more detail with the process concepts but there are also key references to the resource concepts, in particular the interrelationships between internal and external environments (context), actions and outcomes.

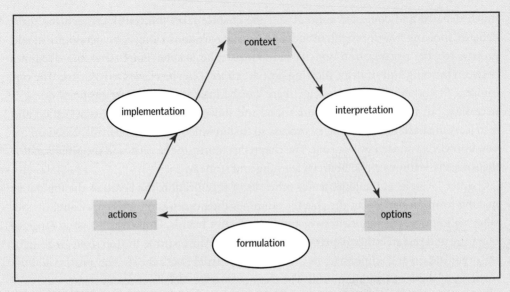

Based on Figure 2.2
Strategy process concepts map

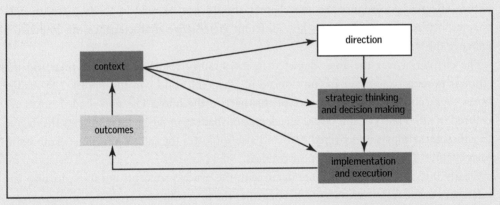

Based on Figure 1.6.
Strategy resources concepts map

Chapter 13

Process analyses for strategic decision making

Introduction

At the heart of strategy lies decision making. Having analysed the environment, assessed organizational capabilities and investigated technological shifts, managers have to take preferred courses of action. They have to examine possible alternatives and choose among them. As Coyne and Subramaniam (1996) observe, strategic decisions are the handful of decisions that drive or shape most of an organization's actions, are not easily changed once made and have the greatest impact on organizational performance. Strategy may be a grand concept, but it is the individual strategic decisions that matter.

At its simplest, decision making may be considered an instantaneous action, a choice between two or more known alternatives, made by individuals or groups.

However, this 'point of decision' approach is unable to capture the richness and complexity of the processes that lead up to the point of decision, the influences on putting the decision into action and the ultimate performance of that decision. It also assumes that managers have full agency and control over decisions. Sometimes they may have very limited discretion to make decisions or choose among alternatives. This could be the case, for example, where strategic decisions in organizations are heavily constrained by interventionist government policies (such as privatization or deregulation) where all strategic decisions are framed and shaped by this wider **context**. Nevertheless, managers still have some degree of **strategic choice** (Child 1972) even if the wider context (e.g. privatization) is firmly set in place. Managers can still make strategic decisions, concerning for example, such key topics as organizational design, choice of suppliers, choice and sophistication of information systems and general product or service portfolios.

Of course, most people are aware that much of decision making is not a simple process that happens in a linear sequence a period of thinking followed by a period of acting. Decision making and the development of alternative courses of action are fashioned in their doing. Therefore, factors such as previous experience or whether things 'feel' right are likely to have as much influence over strategic choices (and what follows) as analysis and planning. Yet, these decisions are what will influence the fortunes or otherwise of any organization (from a sports club to a multinational enterprise) and understanding strategic decision making processes therefore represents a key aspect of examining how strategies are put into practice. A great deal of what has been discussed in Part 3 of this book has enabled us to see how strategy, as an overall direction an organization might take, can be achieved by analytical and rational thinking. Strategy is a positioning process by which organizations chart their ways through the seas of competition, internationalization and changing markets and technologies. Positioning alone, however, leaves open the question of how particular choices are made among a set of alternatives however incomplete those alternatives might be. In short, to understand strategy fully we need to understand the processes of strategic decision making.

13.1 Different perspectives on the nature of decision making

Like many theories of how we organize, plan and act, decision making has multiple lenses through which we might try to understand its complexity. We examine some of these perspectives in this section. For example, Mintzberg, Quinn and Ghoshal (1998) identify five different (and sometimes mutually exclusive) perspectives on strategic decision making:

- Decision making as a *plan*: the decision is a consciously intended course of action. In the same way that you might intend to catch an aeroplane to a specific destination at a particular time, decision making is a process that is carried out in advance of the action that follows and is developed with a clear purpose.

◆ Decision making as a *ploy*: a decision from this perspective is a set of actions designed to outwit the competition and may not necessarily be the 'obvious' content of the decision. For example, a decision to construct a new building in order to expand may not be the overt strategy, but is more concerned with increasing barriers to entry for potential competitors. There are obvious connections here with game theory (Van Neumann and Morgenstern 1944), which examines the choices players make in every possible situation. Forcing one's opponent to move (to achieve a short-term win), so that this puts them at a longer-term disadvantage, is an example of such a ploy. Equally, there are connections with strategy as conceived in its military roots, where the plans of campaigns may have similar intentions to the game analogy (Von Clausewitz 1976).

◆ Decision making as a *pattern*: decisions are not necessarily taken with a planned purpose and decision makers do not always have access to the range of knowledge required to plan wholly in advance. What happens is that multiple decisions taken over time form a pattern. It is this pattern of resulting (emergent) behaviour that we call the strategy of the firm. Strategy is therefore characterized as a pattern that emerges from a stream of decisions.

◆ Decision making as a *position*: decisions are less about the dynamics of planning or gamesmanship and more about trying to achieve a match between the organization and its environment (Hofer and Schendel 1978). This position can be one of alignment, so that the organization matches its environment (for example, highly decentralized structures to match a turbulent and unpredictable environment) or one of trying to secure competitive advantage (where the organization achieves a unique position in the market for some time). Positions, of course, can be planned, emerge or be a combination of both emergent and planned processes.

◆ Decision making as a *perspective*: decisions here are characterized as a reflection of how strategists in an organization see and perceive the world and their organization. For example, the strategic perspective of Nokia is one of continuous and sometimes radical change (Nokia began as a paper and pulp company); IBM favours a dominant marketing perspective, while Hewlett-Packard favours an engineering excellence perspective. This perspective, if pervasive enough, can influence the kinds of decision taken, in respect of their content and their processes. We can see the effects of this embedded view of decision making by observing that organizations in similar industries often choose similar strategic decisions. They become institutionalized. Universities tend to follow broadly similar strategies as do large retailers or service organizations.

Whittington (1996) reminds us that not only can we identify different perspectives on decision making, but the past forty or fifty years has also seen radical changes in the ways in which links between strategic decisions and corporate strategy have been established. For example, the 1950s/1960s saw an emphasis on the planning approach to decision making.

The focus was on tools and techniques to help managers make informed decisions about future business directions. Such tools included industry structure analyses and portfolio matrices (for example, the Ansoff matrix or the Boston Box, see Part 3 of this book). Decision making was mostly about planning. The 1970s onwards saw a changed emphasis. Decisions were now supposed to emphasize the pay-offs to organizations that may accrue if they pursued different strategic directions. Typical **options** were diversification decisions, but this was also the era of innovation (R&D), acquisition, joint venture and internationalization decisions.

The 1980s saw a move away from examining the content of strategic decisions (that is, what they were about) to examining them more as processes. The question now became whether we could map the progress of a strategic decision and make any inferences about why such processes might occur. Hickson *et al.* (1986) characterized such processes as sporadic (discontinuous), fluid (continuous and smooth) or constricted (restricted to a small group of stakeholders). Mintzberg *et al.* (1976) had also identified a number of specific process types in a similar vein. Pettigrew (1986) underscored the importance of such processes since they underpinned the recognition among managers for strategic change. Here Pettigrew established a clear link between strategic decision making and change (a theme which will be described in greater detail in Chapter 15). The 1990s onwards have seen a continuing interest in unfolding the characteristics of decision processes, but the emphasis has changed to focus on whether or not there are any links between decision making activity and performance (did the decision succeed or fail?). We examine this aspect of decision performance later in this chapter.

13.2 Choice selection and strategic decision making

The question of how individuals make decisions is deceptively simple. Deeper analysis reveals that trying to explain the *how* of decision making, even if limited to trying to explain how managers make decisions in organizations (rather than, say, the cognitive processes of individuals generally), is still very complex indeed. One of the enduring features of complex organizations is that they operationalize and codify the knowledge and experience of individuals. As managers take decisions, the rules of thumb they may use become standardized as procedures and activities for *planning* and *evaluating*. This allows a degree of *strategic programming* to take place (*see* Figure 1.1). Resource allocation, schedules and priorities can be planned, evaluated and assessed by such metrics and they become embodied in the formal planning system of the organization.

The links between planning and forecasting metrics and strategy vary, depending on how strategy is viewed. If the classic Chandler (1962: 13) perspective is taken – strategy is 'the determination of the long-term goals of an enterprise' then tools such as **scenario planning** and **macroeconomic forecasting** are appropriate metrics. These help assess complex environments often over long time horizons (25 years is not unusual in scenario analysis, for example) from the perspective of the organization–environment interaction. We describe these techniques in more detail in Chapter 14. Alternatively, if we define strategy as the sum of its parts – a pattern among a handful of decisions – then we need metrics that are finer grained. Once the level of analysis becomes the decision itself, managers need more specific tools and techniques to help them in option selection from a range of alternatives. Table 13.1 summarizes some typical planning and forecasting techniques.

13.2.1 Game theories

Game theories help decision makers to make sense of (and react to) the actions of others. By posing choice among alternatives in the form of different games, decision makers can judge to what extent their assumptions about others' rationality are valid. Typically portrayed as a matrix between two 'players', **game theory** examines what is likely to happen when two players make choices and what are the best outcomes or pay-offs. Powell (2003: 392) gives an example, using two firms facing investment opportunities in an existing market. Each firm can invest in process, quality or can make no investment. Investment in process should reduce price, and investment in quality should improve differentiation. Table 13.2 shows the pay-offs.

Table 13.1 Planning and forecasting techniques and strategy

Strategy is viewed as ...	The remit of strategists	Typical techniques
The long-term alignment of an organization with its economic, social and political environment	Long-term, wide span control of organizational affairs	• Scenario building • Macroeconomic analysis and forecasting
The handful of strategic decisions that drive and shape the fortunes of an organization and which characterize its strategy	The management of shorter-term decisions that involve the disposition of limited resources	• Game theory • Sensitivity analysis • Options

Table 13.2 A simple example of game theory

Company B	Company A		
	Invest in process	Invest in quality	Make no investment
Invest in process	50 : 50	30 : 70	85 : 15
Invest in quality	60 : 40	45 : 55	80 : 20
Make no investment	25 : 75	20 : 80	30 : 30

Source: adapted from Powell, 2003.

The rules of the simple game depicted in Table 13.2 are that Company A chooses first which column to play. In the cells of the table are the pay-offs in percentages to Company B and Company A (in that order). The pay-offs are not symmetrical since each company has different capabilities. If both companies choose not to invest then it will be easier for new entrants to come into the market, hence both Company A and B will only receive 60 per cent.

Company A logically chooses the least worse case. This is a decision to invest in quality where, whatever the choice of Company B, Company A will receive at least 55 per cent pay-off. Company B would also reason similarly. The least worse choice is to invest in quality where Company B would receive at least 45 per cent. The game assumes that these decisions are made at the same time, although even if they were made in sequence, the inbuilt time lags in the market would reduce immediate effects of the investment.

If the game is played deliberately in sequence, making the assumption that Company B moves first and immediately sees the choices of Company A, then Company B has the following decision choices. Investing in process would be likely to make A choose quality (this would yield a pay-off of 70 per cent). Investing in quality would persuade A to choose quality as well since the pay-off will be larger for them (55 per cent) than B. If B were to choose not to invest then A would invest in quality to gain an 80 per cent return. The best case is, therefore, for B to invest in quality and gain 45 per cent, with A gaining 55 per cent.

There are many variants of this simple game. The most well known is perhaps the prisoner's dilemma where two criminals are in separate cells and have to decide whether or not to betray each other (having agreed not to betray in advance of the game). The greatest pay-offs come from both prisoners sticking to their agreement, but most betray each other and the pay-offs are significantly reduced.

From a decision making perspective, these type of game may vary depending on whether the game is played more than once with the same 'players'. If both parties know that they will be playing the same game again, under the same rules, then the evidence suggests that they will be more predisposed to co-operate and trust each other than if the game were only played once.

Of course, these simple heuristics make some heroic assumptions. For example, players are assumed to be perfectly rational in their behaviours and choices. They are also assumed to have perfect knowledge of the rules (shared equally between them) and will always want to maximize their returns. Nevertheless, they do show clearly some of the choices and returns which may happen, should managers make best use of the resources and knowledge at their disposal.

13.2.2 Sensitivity analysis

In many respects, this heuristic is akin to scenario planning but **sensitivity analysis** operates at a much more operational level. It is a technique for investigating what happens if the assumptions underlying a strategic decision are questioned and changed. For example, a strategic decision may be taken to launch a new product with a five-year horizon over product price (no increase for two years and a small increase after that). However, even small changes in price might yield large changes in volumes sold; therefore, managers need to know what will happen if they make even slight changes to product price. This technique requires that a portfolio of variables are entered on to a spreadsheet and can then be subjected to simulation on the computer.

Again, this technique makes an array of assumptions which decision makers need to take into account, but the exercise of 'mapping' the decision trajectory under different pricing structures (for example) can be very useful in revealing the multi-variate interaction of key variables in the process, such as demand, cost and levels of competition.

13.2.3 **Options**

This technique helps managers make key decisions about future activities when current strategic decisions seem to be failing or not working as well as they might. This is often called **strategic decay** (Williamson 1999). Decay indicates the urgent need to take strategic decisions in order to try to reverse the process of decline. There are a number of measures of decline, but the most evident are:

◆ Reaching limits to profit generation: diminishing returns.

◆ Revenue grows faster than profits year after year (efforts are to run a growing organization harder, but with a diminishing contribution to profit).

◆ The firm records high profits but share prices fall (confidence in the sustainability of returns is low).

◆ **Core competences** (strategic assets) begin to depreciate in the amount of profit they generate. These include, for example, patents, long-term contracts which are nearing their end and intellectual capital which other firms can now recruit or train.

◆ Industry convergence: over time major competitors begin to adopt similar strategies. Products and service are hard to differentiate; the only firms which survive over the long term are low cost and highly competitive. Profits of all survivors are squeezed.

All of the above can contribute individually or together to create decline. Perhaps the least self-evident cause of decline is where the organization is earning good profits but the share price collapses since confidence in maintaining profits over the long term erodes. For example, in the retail industry Tesco managed to increase its return on capital employed by some 35 per cent (1995–2002). British Airways was not far behind with a return of 23 per cent. Yet the share prices of each organization differ markedly. British Airways has seen an almost static price/earnings ratio for the last ten years while Tesco has seen its p/e ratio rise by over 40 per cent (*The Economist* 2003). Confidence in British Airways is significantly less.

In order to maintain profits they have had to make savage cuts in the organization, laying off large numbers of staff as well as cutting back on the range and type of routes offered to customers. Other airlines are creating stiff competition, especially low-cost providers. Tesco, on the other hand, has engendered confidence and has managed to stay well ahead of the competition without having to savage the fixed costs of its organization. On this basis, British Airways is in urgent need of strategic decisions that will help stem the decline and that will help create value in the near future. Once identified, these decision choices are known as options.

The formal analysis of options can help inform an organization and its decision makers about likely ways forward. From a decision making perspective, the word options can be misleading in that it can be taken to refer to the micro-detail of operations (costs, sales volumes and so on) so that forecasts can be 'exact'. In fact, options techniques are relatively macro in their focus. They rely on two related dimensions: the identification of additional or alternative organizational capabilities that might be needed to meet product or service needs in the future; and the identification of potential future markets and/or new customer behaviours. In order to assemble an accurate set of options, decision makers need to assess both of these dimensions. For example, in the mobile telephony industry, customer needs might be predicted to change towards using the mobile telephone as the major way of accessing internet and telephony needs. Thus the mobile telephone becomes the key focus in terms of an organization's capabilities to deliver such technologies. Bandwidth and voiceover internet protocols will all be capabilities that will have to be developed and honed in order to meet market demands. Figure 13.1 illustrates how the need both to address capabilities and to develop a knowledge of new potential markets is important for decision makers.

Figure 13.1 simply outlines the options available to organizations which fall into the various cells of the matrix. While this is a useful analysis, it tells decision makers little about actions or the types of action they may take. For example, decision makers may have

Knowledge of new markets

	Low	High
Capabilities Low	**No options** Decision making limited to being reative and becoming part of others' strategies	**Trading options** Aware, but unable to do anything, so best option is to trade the information
Capabilities High	**Bounded options** Capable but little awareness of new markets	**Full set of options** Ability to identify and follow strategy options is high

Figure 13.1 Strategic options in decision making

identified two or three options but then chosen to retain these as ideas which might be explored sometime in the future. Just holding these options as ideas is fairly cost free, but is obviously low on action. Decisions between options and **implementation** require often significant analysis and investment. Choosing between options is necessary since pursuing all identified options would be prohibitively expensive. Then decisions have to be made over how to implement the chosen option or options. We explore these processes of strategic decision making in the following sections.

13.3 **The processes of strategic decision making**

The processes of making decisions can appear deceptively simple. Actions are formulated towards the solution of a particular problem. The problem with this approach is that there may be discernible actions and there may be observable outcomes, but they need not necessarily be wholly related to one another. Problems may be solved by factors other than strategic decisions and, sometimes, taking a strategic decision can create a whole new set of problems (without solving the initial problem the decision was supposed to address).

These polar views can be represented by the *planning* versus the *chaotic* processes of strategic decision making. They are extremes and, although most decisions lie somewhere between the planned and the chaotic, both perspectives are useful for understanding the processes of strategic decision making. Viewing processes as basically a set of planning tools allows *actions, procedures* and *measurement* to be explicitly addressed (*see* Figure 1.6) Planning facilitates decision makers in analysing and codifying what appear initially as complex problems. Planning simplifies complexity and helps reduce uncertainty. Because of this, planning can also help decision makers examine current planning practices in their organization and assess their utility in the light of current problems. From a behavioural perspective, planning can ensure that others in the organization are involved and are communicated with as fully as possible. Note that although involvement and communication can be explicit parts of the plan, this may not endow those participants with any influence over the process or its eventual outcome. Finally, planning processes help decision makers identify key performance indicators by which progress of the decision can be monitored and judged.

Chaotic processes (Cohen *et al.* 1972; Stacey 1993) argue that organizations can be viewed as an 'anarchy' or as a system with chaotic tendencies. Hence decision makers can neither understand fully nor control decision processes. Means and ends are unlikely to be coupled (Weick 1976), which implies that actions do not lead to expected outcomes and are swayed one way or another by other decisions, other actions and unforeseen circumstances. The main components of a strategic decision making process (problems, solutions, participants and choice situations) interact in an apparently haphazard way, a stream of demands for the fluid attention and energies of managers. Participants move in and out of the decision making process (every entrance is an exit elsewhere) and this can create discontinuity. At other times, participants fight for the right to become involved and then never exercise any influence they may have.

Viewing decision making processes as chaotic also has some advantages for decision makers. Unlike the planning approach, the chaos perspective does not seek to simplify and to reduce uncertainty. It avoids any oversimplification of the process and allows decision makers to appreciate and expect the role of politics and influence to be a natural part of the decision making process. In theory, the chaos perspective should encourage decision makers to think creatively around complex problems and help them to avoid thinking solely in linear sequences. Creativity and innovation may be enhanced by decision makers being encouraged to take actions which seem unrelated to the decision under consideration. On the other hand, we should bear in mind that the distinction between creativity and madness is a rather fine line (March 1999)! From a decision making perspective, this means that no one will know whether the tangential explorations were useful or folly until a long way down the track of the decision process. Figure 13.2 summarizes four polar types of **decision process characteristics** which can arise from counterposing planned versus chaotic and political versus planned perspectives.

13.4 **The architecture of strategic decision making**

Trying to put together the above perspectives is a complicated task but is one that decision makers are required to understand. This is because strategic decision makers need to understand how such perspectives may predominate and hence characterize their organization and how decisions might flow through its structures. If you know how decisions might be configured in your organization, you stand a greater chance of being able to predict and perhaps influence what is going on.

	Problem solving	**Political process**
Chaos/ anarchy	**Uncoupled** strategic decision making (means unrelated to ends)	**Uncontrolled,** random strategic decision making
Planning/ coherence	**Intended** strategic decision making (means related to ends)	**Incremental** strategic decision making (step by step, mutual adjustment to stakeholders)

Figure 13.2 A typology of decision processes
Source: adapted from Cummings and Wilson, 2003.

Any attempt to configure the architecture of strategic decision making will necessitate some degree of integration of at least three aspects. These are:

◆ Decision-specific characteristics.

◆ The organizational context.

◆ The influence of the wider environment.

This chapter will look at decision-specific characteristics and the organizational context. The wider environment is covered in detail in Part 3 and Chapter 14.

13.4.1 **Decision-specific characteristics**

We can categorize decision-specific characteristics into two broad areas:

◆ The interpretation of a problem or problems by decision makers.

◆ The characteristics of the decision or problem to be solved.

Research into decision making cognition and labelling suggests that the same internal or external stimulus may be interpreted differently by managers across different organizations, or sometimes even within the same organization. Therefore, relying on the stimulus itself is unlikely to tell us much about what follows in terms of strategic decision making.

It has also been shown that the ways in which managers categorize decisions strongly influences the ways in which subsequent processes happen. For example, decisions may be perceived as an opportunity or as a crisis. Where managers perceive decisions to be more of a crisis than an opportunity, the process is characterized by the overarching threat of the crisis. The search for alternatives becomes wider and the collection of information and intelligence relevant to the decision becomes greater. Overall, the decision making activity becomes more comprehensive in scale and scope (since it tends to involve more participants).

The characteristics of the problem to be solved have been shown to have links with the strategic decision making process and to influence its trajectory through an organization. For example, problems have been characterized as 'wicked' or 'tame' (de Wit and Meyer 1999). Wicked problems are not evil, but are complex. They are permeated with uncertainty caused by either the technical nature of the decision or by the politics and intrigue it engenders among decision participants. Hickson *et al.* (1986) characterized these 'wicked' decisions as complex, political or both. Complex decisions are those that are unprecedented, carry high levels of uncertainty and may have fundamental precedent-setting consequences for subsequent decisions. They may also require information of a different type and from a different source to be gathered and interpreted. Political decisions are those that draw in a specific set of stakeholders (inside and outside the organization). The more interests that are represented in the decision (multiple and conflicting voices), the more political is the strategic decision.

Complex and/or political decisions share some or all of the following characteristics:

◆ They are difficult to define precisely (the nature of the problem is elusive).

◆ Understanding the problem is also part of understanding the solution.

◆ There is rarely one best solution, but a series of possible solutions.

◆ Each solution is associated with different trade-offs and priorities.

◆ They are difficult to assess in terms of performance since they tend to continue through the organization without a clear, final end point against which performance can be judged.

◆ They are highly inter-connected with other problems in the organization.

◆ They have high levels of uncertainty associated with them.

◆ They require strategists to accept fairly high degrees of risk in making decisions.

◆ Once made, they are difficult to reverse.

◆ They are likely to be discontinuous and political, with different competing interests trying to influence the outcome in line with their preferences.

Simple (or tame) decisions reflect the opposite characteristics to those listed.

13.4.2 **The organizational context**

There are many ways of defining the organizational context, but the major descriptors are:

◆ Systems

◆ Structure

◆ Ownership and control

◆ Organizational culture

Internal *systems*, such as information or formal planning processes, both influence the flow of information across the organization and, to some extent, determine the nature and context of human interaction. It is not surprising, then, that they have a strong influence over strategic decision making and its practice. Control systems and measurement and reward systems also prescribe what is given priority and therefore what decision makers focus most of their attention upon. In decision making, such systems will set parameters around trade-offs and what levels of risk are tolerable, for example:

◆ The more regulated the formal systems, the more strategic decision making tends to be routine and predictable and the more it will have to accommodate a large number of specialist functions.

◆ The more complex the systems, the more decision making becomes reliant on knowledge experts, and information gathering and synthesis.

- The more automated systems become, the more flexibility and space there is for strategic decision making that relies on expertise (or the intellectual capital of the organization). The obsession with control tends to be reduced, since controlled systems do not require watching over. (When they go wrong, however, they can cause havoc!)

- The greater the scope of the system, the greater the reliance on expertise and intellectual capital. This is true of e-commerce and e-business, for example, where the scope of information goes beyond the single organizational unit.

The *structure* of an organization also has an impact on strategic decision making. The most obvious example of the interrelationship between strategy and structure is the debate (which still rages) about whether structure follows strategy or vice versa. In this book we take the view that strategy and structure are like two legs. You need both to walk, but whether you lead with the left or the right leg is fairly arbitrary. One may be said to follow or to lead the other. No matter, you are still walking. Decisions both *create* structures and are also *influenced* by them.

That there are a set of relationships between strategic decision making and structure can be identified in a number of aspects of management. In relation to strategic decision making, some of the key influences are listed below:

- Formalized structures are associated mainly with older organizations. Decision making becomes formalized and has a tendency to become more predictable. This is especially so in the 'seen it all before' attitudes that may prevail, and repeating what was done in the past as solutions to today's problems.

- Larger organizations formalize processes more, even if they are structured into smaller business units. Strategic decision making becomes more about rule-following than rule-bending (or breaking) practice.

- Decentralized structures may appear to avoid the above, but decision making can become dominated by trying to ensure co-ordination and communication across the decentralized organization (rather than producing new products and service for example). Decentralized structures often require more, rather than less, hands-on management before they can become effective and efficient.

Organizational structures reflect the age of the industry from its founding date. Industries which pre-date the Industrial Revolution (for example, the Church or the military) are characterized by centralized and formal structures (whatever the age of the organization in the industry). It seems that industry age is a better predictor of the organizational structure, even of a new entrant into the industry.

In terms of organizational size, the main effect on strategic decision making appears to be formalization rather than size itself. Hickson *et al.* (1986) found no differences in strategic decision making processes which could be attributed to organizational size. So large organizations that manage to retain less formal structures may not necessarily exhibit the rule following strategic decision making processes of their more formalized counterparts.

Ownership and control exert separate influences over strategic decision making. In family-owned firms, for example, the overlap between the two social systems of the family and the firm create decision processes in which personal stakes are high and delegation may be rare, since decision making authority and the strategic direction of the firm are controlled by the owners. Interestingly, there is strong evidence to show that public versus private ownership seems to make little difference to the ways in which strategic decision making occurs (at least in the UK).

According to Hickson *et al.* (1986), public sector organizations:

◆ Take no longer than privately owned organizations to make strategic decision.

◆ Do not have more committees involved in the decision making process.

◆ Do not have more stakeholders than private sector organizations (but the type of stakeholder may differ, with government agencies such as the Treasury prevailing).

It is still debatable whether national ownership exerts much influence on strategic decision making. There is some evidence to show that patterns of national cultural stereotypes permeate the practice of decision making. For example, North American organizations decide quicker than UK firms and both are significantly faster than Swedish organizations. But the results are far from conclusive.

The *culture* of an organization can be described as:

> *the underlying assumptions, beliefs and values in an organization which inform,*
> *influence and shape strategic decision making.*

The influence of organizational culture on decision making reveals what is often taken for granted in decision making processes. The impact of organizational culture often goes unnoticed by members of an organization. Culture is continually reinforced by symbols, stories and routines, as well as by organizational structures and the power plays of

Basic assumptions	Value-led decision making	Artefacts
e.g. Taken-for-granted beliefs	e.g. Goals and strategies	e.g. Organization structures
Perceptual habits (ways of thinking)	Answers to the question 'why?'	Technologies
Basic attitudes	Vision and mission	Jargon and dress code

Figure 13.3 Artefacts and assumptions in strategic decision making
Source: adapted from Schein, 1992.

various interests. Culture tends to be self-reinforcing. In addition, culture provides a set of values which are reflected in choice behaviours and processes. Schein (1992) shows how decision making is influenced both by artefacts and basic assumptions held by individuals in organizations, as illustrated in Figure 13.3.

Organizational culture, therefore, colours decision making from a palette that can include such things as ritual and language alongside the influence of technology and organizational structure. These factors all intermingle to colour decisions that we would be tempted otherwise to view as rational choices. The cultural perspective shows how values are added to the decision process. Sometimes such values are overt. They can be seen in mission statements such as Yamaha's 'Kill Honda', Federal Express's 'Absolutely on Time', or 3M's 'To solve unsolved problems innovatively'. At other times, values can be shaped by taken-for-granted behaviours, jargon or dress codes (for example, we all wear business suits in sober colours). These are more covert influences.

Simpler versions of how strategic decisions are influenced by the context or culture of organizations can be found in the work of Collins and Porras (1996). They argued that successful companies were those where the core decisions were influenced by timeless guiding principles which require no external justification. This cherished core ideology represents the key values of the organization and is the cultural glue that holds it together in the face of other changes. So long as key decisions were taken in line with these cherished principles, outstanding performance over a sustained period was the result.

However, organizations can also become trapped by their coherent cultures into routines which impair the development of new and different strategies. The practice of strategic decision making, therefore, becomes constrained rather than enhanced by the organizational culture. Decision makers can only think along the rigid lines demarcated by the strong culture. Innovation and creative thinking are precluded and invoking learning into the organization becomes very difficult, since the culture resists new ideas.

Decision makers, therefore, have to be very clear whether the culture of the organization is working for its success, or is actually constraining choice activities. Spotting the difference can be very difficult since the choice-enhancing factors identified by Collins and Porras (1996) very closely resemble the 'mindguards' that can detract from innovative thinking.

13.5 **Strategic decision making and performance**

What are the relationships between decision processes and their outcomes? Does it matter what managers do in the strategic decision making process? What difference, if any, do managerial actions make to both processes and outcomes?

For nearly thirty years, practitioners and scholars alike have argued about what brings success. So complex have some of these arguments become that there is virtually a whole industry of analysts devoted to arguing whether planned or emergent strategies (for example) capture the essence of strategy, and whether the effective positioning of the organization in its industry and value chain leads to greater or lesser performance. Sub-industries also sprung up, including, for example, focusing on whether organizations could learn from failures and successes and whether key technological advancements (for example, killer applications) rendered any form of strategic planning redundant. Other analysts focused on the levels of uncertainty facing decision makers, arguing that when faced with extreme uncertainties, success was more probable if managers took action (leaps of faith in the dark) than if they took no action at all. Of course, this rich analysis has not only provided a large number of industry overviews and industry shake-outs (for example, in the telecommunications industry) but has also provided many case studies and war stories for others to pick over and make sense of.

Focusing on strategic decisions rather than sectors (for example) allows us to examine the many slips that can occur 'between cup and lip' (that is, between decisions processes and outcomes). Spotting decision 'failures' is easy after the event. They can take the organization into decline or, in extreme cases, can seal the demise of the organization. Typical decision failure characteristics include such features as:

- Failure to address the original (or the real) problem.
- The decision made the problem worse rather than better.
- The decision becomes irreversible when things begin to go wrong and decision makers get deeper and deeper into crisis.

So where do things go wrong in this process view of decision making? If we knew in advance that decision pathways were going to result in failure then we would not waste our time on them and would choose other alternatives. However, such is the level of uncertainty surrounding strategic decisions that this predictive dimension is almost impossible to identify, especially at the early stages of decision making. For example, it can be in the implementation stages of decision making that things can go wrong, despite what may have seemed like good ideas during formulation. Of course, there is a critical temporal element here. Before implementation, it is extremely difficult to differentiate what will be an effective strategy from one which ultimately fails. Despite all the attempts to assess the degree of future risk (through techniques such as risk analysis), strategic decisions seemingly succeed or fail independently of such criteria.

Research is beginning to identify patterns of implementation which indicate key factors associated with higher-achieving decisions (Hickson *et al.* 2003; Miller *et al.* 2004). These factors are a combination of organizational features, such as structures and the receptiveness of organizational culture to the decision; features of what actions managers take during the process, such as how far they can specify what must be done in advance or whether the required expertise can be accessed inside the organization; and features of the decision process itself, such as its **duration**. We look at duration in the next section.

13.5.1 **Duration and decision success**

Hickson *et al.* (1986) produced an empirical classification of strategic decision processes up to the point of authorization. One aspect of process was duration. They found that from first mention to the point of authorization, the bulk of decisions take between 4 and 24 months to process. The mean for 150 cases was 12.4 months. Implementation, however, covers a far greater range of time, with some decisions only taking a few months to put into practice and others taking many years.

Implementation is defined here as the time taken from the point of authorization to when the decision is put into practice (for example, the new building is constructed or the reorganization is put in place). Duration of implementation is not associated directly with success. It seems that the time taken to implement strategic decisions matters little in terms of decision performance. Long-drawn-out implementation processes can be associated with very successful decisions, while faster implementation times are no guarantee of success. The following two vignettes show examples of these temporal extremes, one decision taking four years, the other nine months.

Case box: Long implementation time (successful)

Organization:	Glass manufacturer
Strategic decision:	Build a new manufacturing plant
Implementation time:	4 years
Achievement:	Highly successful

This organization has always enjoyed a worldwide reputation for technical excellence in process and product innovation, especially in the revolutionary float glass process it pioneered. However, first mover advantage in float glass was soon eroded, and market share reduced considerably, as competitors moved to float glass technology. Benchmarking revealed that the glass division in general was becoming increasingly inefficient compared to competitors producing similar products with similar technology. Competition was hotting up, especially after the expiry of its manufacturing process licences.

The senior planning team assessed the situation and set up a lengthy process of working parties and committees to consider whether to increase dramatically the production of float glass by building a new plant. The decision was made even more dramatic since it would signal this organization's possibly complete move into float glass technology. Parallel production processes of other types of glass might have to be abandoned.

Fortunately, the necessary technical expertise was in-house. A very strong R&D team provided up-to-the minute technical information to the planning team, assisted by very strong design information from the engineering department. The decision was by no means clear to the planning team and a further two years were spent deliberating the costs and benefits associated with the investment. During this time, the business environment was becoming increasingly competitive, but the planning team chose to consult widely across the organization, so that managers and workers could absorb the need for change and could become its supporters once the decision had been put into practice.

The new site was built following this two-year deliberation and consultation period. It subsequently became the most successful plant of its type worldwide and became a role model for change within the organization, spreading out to other divisions such as insulation and opthalmics.

Case box: **Short implementation time (unsuccessful)**

Organization:	Paint and model manufacturer
Strategic decision:	Expand capacity
Implementation time:	9 months
Achievement:	Unsuccessful

This highly successful international organization had developed a very profitable business, manufacturing and supplying plastic model kits of planes, cars, ships and so forth. They also had a successful business manufacturing and selling the specialized paints model builders needed to decorate their plastic models. All was going well in the market and a possible joint venture with a French company was being considered. Such a move would make this the largest plastic model manufacturer in the world.

The operations manager, who was associated with a number of successes in the plastic kit business, had been looking at alternative materials for model kit-building. In this case he was assessing the potential for balsa wood kits as an alternative to plastic construction. Margin on balsa wood kits was, however, not attractive, since the supply of balsa wood around the world was virtually a price monopoly. However, the managing director located another supplier in Chile who was prepared to undercut the balsa monopoly. A hastily convened meeting between the managing director and the operations director ended with the realization that if they were to enter the balsa kit market on any scale, they would have to invest in a new production line in a new factory to accommodate it.

Coincidentally, a new site for the new factory became available. A government grant was available with the only proviso that an extra 20 people were employed. Neither manager thought this to be a problem and the investment was made. Almost immediately, the first shipment of balsa wood became a problem. It was full of dead insects and other debris, which made it unsuitable for building model kits. While trying to negotiate with the balsa wood suppliers, the joint venture with the French plastic kit manufacturer was abandoned (the French company pulled out of negotiations). It now became even more crucial to get good-quality supplies of balsa wood.

The French company introduced a range of innovative plastic kits which were an immediate success. Demand for balsa wood kits plummeted worldwide. The organization was left with a supply contract for material they did not now need, a factory with rent to pay and a workforce to lay off. It took five years to recover financially from this strategic decision.

From the boxed examples it can be seen that success and the speed at which implementation occurs seem to be unrelated. So which factors seem to be associated with success? We explore these in the next section.

13.5.2 **Factors of success**

Curiously, there have been relatively few studies at the level of strategic decisions that focus on the performance of the decision. Recent research (Hickson *et al.* 2003; Miller *et al.* 2004) has summarized this work, relating characteristics of how a strategic decision was made to how successful the decision was in practice.

Using achievement as a surrogate measure of performance (to what extent did the decision achieve stated objectives?), two key factors emerge:

- The knowledge base of managers.

- The receptivity of the organizational context to the strategic decision being implemented.

The knowledge base of managers

The key factors which emerge as related to performance are how *familiar* managers are with the problem to be addressed. Where managers are clear about the parameters of the problems and what information is needed to address it, they can begin to take action toward implementation. Two other processes are associated with this knowledge base. They are the *ability to plan* and *to resource* strategic decisions. Knowledge facilitates planning and argues a good case for resourcing. Strategic decisions do not succeed on knowledge alone; they need resources to back them up.

The receptivity of the organizational context

The key factor here is how ready the organization is to adopt the changes incurred by the strategic decision. The greater the readiness in the organization's culture to undertake the change, the easier it is for managers to take action and to begin to prioritize their various strategic decisions.

However, even a high state of cultural readiness can be blocked by organizational structures that are overly formal or bureaucratic. Hence, both organizational culture and structure have to be co-aligned if higher levels of performance are to be expected from the strategic decision making process.

13.6 Summary

To look at strategy through the lens of decision making is a complex activity. Decisions can focus on choices made or on how managers make decisions. The focus can also concentrate on the characteristics of the decision process itself and recent work has begun to establish some relationships between these process characteristics and decision performance.

Key features of these decision making processes are knowledge, planning, resourcing and specifying. Stakeholders must also be broadly aligned to be supportive of the decision. Organizational culture should be open to the changes the decision will bring about, and organizational structure should not impede the process of implementation by being too formal or cumbersome.

Key terms

Chaotic processes *511*

Context (and decision making) *504*

Core competences *509*

Decision process characteristics *512*

Duration (of strategic decisions) *518*

Game theory *507*

Implementation (of strategies) *511*

Macroeconomic forecasting *506*

Options *506*

Scenario planning *506*

Sensitivity analysis *508*

Strategic choice *504*

Strategic decay *509*

Recap questions and assignments

1   Pick a strategic decision with which you are familiar, or in which you were a participant. How would you describe its key process features?

2   Using the same example (or you can choose another strategic decision), describe what was done and by whom during the process.

3   What, in your view, were the major influences on the decision and its final outcome?

When you have read this chapter, log on to the Online Learning Centre website at www.mcgraw-hill.co.uk/textbooks/mcgee to explore chapter-by-chapter test questions, further reading and more online study tools for strategy.

Case 1 **Freud, finance and folly**

Human intuition is a bad guide to handling risk

People make barmy decisions about the future. The evidence is all around, from their investments in the stockmarkets to the way their run their businesses. In fact, people are consistently bad at dealing with uncertainty, underestimating some kinds of risk and overestimating others. Surely there must be a better way than using intuition?

In the 1950s and 60s, a group of researchers at American universities set out to find a more scientific method. They created a discipline called 'decision science' which aimed to take the human element out of risk analysis. It would offer a way of making soundly based decisions for a future fraught with uncertainties. This would involve using computer models for forecasting, estimating the probabilities of possible outcomes and determining the best course of action, thus avoiding the various biases that humans brought to decision-making. Such models, the researchers thought, would provide rational answers to questions such as whether to build a factory, how to combat disease and how to manage investments.

Business schools soon adopted their teachings, and even some policymakers were persuaded. Decision science's heyday may have been the Vietnam war when Robert McNamara, then America's defence secretary, used such techniques to forecast the outcome of the conflict (though, as it turned out, without much success). But mostly the approach did not quite catch on. Decision-makers, whether in business or politics, were loath to hand over their power to a computer. They preferred to go with their gut instincts.

Think like a machine

Daniel Kahneman, now a professor at Princeton, noticed as a young research psychologist in the 1960s that the logic of decision science was hard for people to accept. That launched him on a career to show just how irrationally people behave in practice. When Mr Kahneman and his colleagues first started work, the idea of applying psychological insights to economics and business decisions was considered quirky. But in the past decade the fields of behavioural finance and behavioural economics have blossomed, and in 2002 Mr Kahneman shared a Nobel prize in economics for his work.

Today he is in demand by organisations such as McKinsey and PartnerRe, and by Wall Street traders. But, he says, there are plenty of others that still show little interest in understanding the roots of their poor decisions. The lesson from the analyst's couch is that, far from being random, these mistakes are systematic and predictable:

- **Over-optimism**. Ask most people about the future, and they will see too much blue sky ahead, even if past experience suggests otherwise. Surveys have shown that people's forecasts of future stockmarket movements are far more optimistic than past long-term returns would justify. The same goes for their hopes of ever-rising prices for their homes or doing well in games of chance. In a recent study of Dutch game-show contestants, people's estimates of their odds on winning were around 25% too high. Americans are perhaps the most optimistic: according to one poll, around 40% of them think they will end up among the top 1% of earners.

Such optimism can be useful for managers or football players, and sometimes turns into a self-fulfilling prophecy. But most of the time it results in wasted effort and dashed hopes. Mr Kahneman's work points to three types of over-confidence. First, people tend to exaggerate their own skill and prowess; in polls, far fewer than half the respondents admit to having below-average skills in, say, love-making or driving. Second, they over-estimate the amount of control they have over the future, forgetting about luck and chalking up success solely to skill. And third, in competitive pursuits such as betting on shares, they forget that they have to judge their skills against those of the competition.

- **The anchor effect**. First encounters tend to be decisive not only in judging the character of a new acquaintance but also in negotiations over money. Once a figure has been mentioned, it takes a strange hold over the human mind. The asking price quoted in a house sale, for example, tends to become accepted by all parties as the 'anchor' around which negotiations take place, according to one study of property brokers. Much the same goes for salary negotiations or mergers and acquisitions. If nobody has much information to go on, a figure can provide comfort—even though it may lead to a terrible mistake.

- **Stubbornness**. No one likes to abandon a cherished belief, and the earlier a decision has been taken, the harder it is to give up. In one classic experiment, two groups of students were shown slides of an object, say a fire hydrant or a pair of spectacles. The slides started out of focus and were gradually made clearer until the students could identify the object. Those who started with a very blurry image tried to decide early and then found it difficult to identify it correctly until quite late in the process, whereas those who started less out of focus kept a more open mind and cottoned on more quickly.

  The same sort of thing happens in boardrooms or in politics. Drug companies must decide early to cancel a failing research project to avoid wasting money, but find it difficult to admit they have made a mistake. Bosses who have hired unproductive employees are reluctant to fire them. Mr Kahneman cites the example of Israel's failure to spot growing threats in the lead-up to its 1973 war with its Arab neighbours. Part of the explanation was that the same people who had been watching the change in political climate had to decide on Israel's response. Similar problems have arisen in recent counter-terrorism work in America. In both cases, analysts may have become wedded early to a single explanation that coloured their perception. A fresh eye always helps.

- **Getting too close**. People put a lot of emphasis on things they have seen and experienced themselves, which may not be the best guide to decision-making. For example, many companies took action to guard against the risk of terrorist attack only after September 11th, even though it was present long before then. Or somebody may buy an overvalued share because a relative has made thousands on it, only to get his fingers burned.

  In finance, too much emphasis on information close at hand helps to explain the so-called 'home bias', a tendency by most investors to invest only within the country they live in. Even though they know that diversification is good for their portfolio, a large majority of both Americans and Europeans invest far too heavily in the shares of their home countries. They would be much better off spreading their risks more widely.

◆ **Winning and losing**. Fear of failure is a strong human characteristic, which may be why people are much more concerned about losses than about gains. Consider the following bet: with the flip of a coin, you could win $1,500 if the coin turns up heads, or lose $1,000 on the tails. Now describe it in another way: with heads, you keep all the money you had before the bet, plus $1,500; with tails, you also keep everything, except $1,000. The two bets are identical, and each one, on average, will make you richer by $250 (although that average will be little consolation to the punter who has just lost $1,000). Even so, people will usually prefer the second bet.

Behavioural economists say that is because the prospect of losses seems far more daunting in isolation, rather than in the context of looking at your entire wealth, even if the average outcome is the same. This sort of myopia in the face of losses explains much of the irrationality people display in the stockmarket.

◆ **Misplaced priorities**. More information is helpful in making any decision but, says Mr Kahneman, people spend proportionally too much time on small decisions and not enough on big ones. They need to adjust the balance. During the boom years, some companies put as much effort into planning their Christmas party as into considering strategic mergers.

◆ **Counterproductive regret**. Crying over spilled milk is not just a waste of time; it also often colours people's perceptions of the future. Some stockmarket investors trade far too frequently because they are chasing the returns on shares they wish they had bought earlier.

Mr Kahneman reckons that some types of businesses are much better than others at dealing with risk. Pharmaceutical companies, which are accustomed to many failures and a few big successes in their drug-discovery programmes, are fairly rational about their risk-taking. But banks, he says, have a long way to go. They may take big risks on a few huge loans, but are extremely cautious about their much more numerous loans to small businesses, many of which may be less risky than the big ones.

But at least when businesses try to assess their risks, they have to worry only about making money. Governments, on the other hand, face a whole range of sometimes conflicting political pressures. This makes them even more likely to take irrational decisions.

Source: 'Freud, finance and folly', *The Economist*, 22 January 2004.
© The Economist Newspaper Limited, London (22 January 2004).

Case Questions

1 Why do you think individuals find it difficult to accept and utilize the tools and techniques of decision science?

2 Taking each of Kahneman's roots of poor decisions (over-optimism to counterproductive regret) suggest ways in which organizations and decision might be designed to alleviate some or all of them.

3 To what extent do you think Kahneman's roots of poor decisions are generalizable across different nations and different types of organizations (e.g. public, private, non-profit). What differences (if any) would you expect to encounter? Why or why not?

Further reading and references

Chandler, AE Jr (1962) *Strategy and Structure: Chapters in the History of the American Industrial Enterprise*, MIT Press, Cambridge, MA.

Child, J (1972) 'Organizational Structure, Environment and Performance: The Role of Strategic Choice', *Sociology*, **6**, pp. 1–22.

Cohen, M, March, J and Olsen, J (1972) 'A Garbage Can Model of Organizational Choice', *Administrative Science Quarterly*, **17**, pp. 1–25.

Collins, JC and Porras, JL (1996) *Built to Last*, Century Books, New York.

Coyne, K and Subramaniam, S (1996) 'Bringing Discipline to Strategy', *The McKinsey Quarterly*, pp. 14–25.

Cummings, S and Wilson, DC (eds) (2003) *Images of Strategy*, Blackwell, Oxford.

De Wit, B and Meyer, R (1999) *A Strategy Synthesis*, International Thomson Press, London.

Hickson, D, Butler, R, Cray, D, Mallory, G and Wilson, D (1986) *Top Decisions: Strategic Decision Making in Organizations*, Jossey-Bass and Blackwell, California and Oxford.

Hickson, D, Miller, S and Wilson, D (2003) 'Planned or Prioritized? Two options in managing the implementation of strategic decisions', *Journal of Management Studies*, **40**, **7**, pp. 1803–36.

Hofer, CW and Schendel, D (1978) *Strategy Formulation: Analytical Concepts*, West, New York.

March, JG (1999) *The Pursuit of Organizational Intelligence*, Blackwell, Oxford.

Miller, S, Wilson, D and Hickson, D (2004) 'Beyond planning: strategies for successfully implementing strategic decisions', *Long Range Planning*, **37**, **3**, pp. 201–18.

Mintzberg, H, Raisinghani, D and Theoret, A (1976) 'The structure of "unstructured" decision processes', *Administrative Science Quarterly*, **21**, pp. 246–75.

Mintzberg, H, Quinn, JB and Ghoshal, S (1998) *The Strategy Process*, Prentice Hall, New York.

Pettigrew, A (1986) *The Awakening Giant: Continuity and change in ICI*, Blackwell, Oxford.

Powell, JH (2003) 'Game theory in strategy', in D Faulkner and A Campbell (eds) *The Oxford Handbook of Strategy*, Oxford University Press, Oxford.

Schein, E (1992) *Organizational Culture and Leadership*, Jossey-Bass, San Francisco.

Stacey, R (1993) *Strategic Management and Organizational Dynamics*, Pitman, London.

Van Neumann, J and Morgenstern, O (1944) *Theory of Games and Economic Behaviour*, Princeton University Press, Princeton.

Von Clausewitz, C (1976) *On War* (translated by M Howard and P Paret), Princeton University Press, Princeton.

Weick, K (1976) *The Social Psychology of Organizing*, Wiley, New York.

Whittington, R (1996) 'Strategy as practice', *Long Range Planning*, **29**, 5, pp. 731–5.

Williamson, PJ (1999) 'Strategy as options on the future', *Sloan Management Review*, **40**, 3, pp. 117–26.

Chapter 14

Risk, uncertainty and strategy

Introduction

All strategic decisions are taken in the context of both uncertainty and risk. Decisions are about future states of affairs and are based on incomplete information. They also commit resources which could otherwise be used elsewhere in organizations, hence there is a large degree of opportunity cost. Putting resources into one project therefore carries with it varying degrees of risk. It might be a poor choice and jeopardize the chances of taking an alternative course of action which may have yielded better results. On the other hand, the decision itself may turn out to be poor, yielding poor results or, in the extreme, financial disaster for the organization, for example.

The concepts of risk and uncertainty are, however, difficult to define precisely. This is made even more difficult because many authors define one aspect (risk) in terms of the other (uncertainty). For example, Hertz and Thomas (1983: 9) note that many authors define risk as 'degrees of variability or uncertainty'. This does not help distinguish the key elements of risk and uncertainty. To do this, we need to add more precision to the definitions of each concept. Uncertainty is relatively easier to define. In this chapter, we take **uncertainty** to mean:

> the limits to the precision and the extent of knowledge about a subject or an event.

For decision makers, phrases they associate with uncertainty include 'it is likely' or 'the chances are' or, in the case of little uncertainty, decision makers may say 'it is quite certain that'. All of these phrases, while in themselves imprecise, cluster around the notion of probabilities. Another way of defining uncertainty, therefore, is to describe uncertainty as:

> the subjective interpretations of probability by decision makers and analysts of problems in organizations.

Risk is harder to define. Dictionaries typically describe risk in terms of the possibility of destruction, loss or damage. In business organizations, however, risk also takes on other characteristics. For example, insurance companies categorize risk into at least two distinct types 'pure' risk and 'speculative' risk. An example of a pure risk is the likelihood of damage to assets and liabilities through fraud or criminal acts. It either will happen or it will not. However, speculative risks are characterized by the likelihood of gains *and* losses from which decision makers hope profit will eventually accrue (Hertz and Thomas 1983). Risk and reward are the essence of business. Investment in marketing, production and financial underpinning for a project are all risks undertaken by decision makers – and are risks from which they eventually hope to make some profit. Knight (1921) argues:

> The only 'risk' which leads to a profit is a unique uncertainty . . . profits arise out of the inherent, absolute unpredictability of things.

This takes us nearer to defining risk. It is about the *degree and type of unpredictability* (rather than the notion that unpredictability exists, which is closer to describing uncertainty). We may say, then, that risk can be defined generically as:

> The assessment, severity, amount and nature of losses which an action may incur, whether such actions are generated within an organization (such as a decision,) or are imposed upon it (such as a natural disaster). Risk is the measurable consequence of uncertainty for an organization.

Taking risks appears endemic to human behaviour in social groups. In the 1960s social psychologists such as Stoner (1968) showed that individuals will accept higher levels of risk when taking decisions in groups. He found that there was tendency for groups to go for risky and high pay-off decisions, while individuals favour relatively safe decisions with moderate pay-offs. Groups do not represent the 'average' risk of their members. Stoner referred to this tendency for higher risk taking in groups as 'risky shift' decision making.

Since organizations comprise many groups, the likelihood of many examples of risky shift decision making increases. In addition, degrees of uncertainty will vary from sector to sector and from decision to decision. We explore these aspects of uncertainty and risk in the next sections. First, we need to explore the many different images and origins of risk.

14.1 Different images of risk

From one perspective, risks faced by organizations can be viewed (and defined) as a set of wholly exogenous influences or shocks which they have to face. These could include changes in the natural environment or macroeconomic stability. Natural disasters such as hurricanes, earthquakes or tornados would fall into this category, as would disruptive technological changes which force decision makers to make choices not of their own making (technologies may be invented outside the organization, forcing decision makers in the organization to respond reactively). However, few analysts of risk maintain that uncertainties due to these exogenous shocks are wholly key to understanding how organizations both create and deal with risk. A noticeable movement has taken place over the last twenty or so years toward viewing risk as 'man-made' (Turner, 1978) or manufactured (Beck 1992). Both these authors argue that these organizationally created risks influence the social and natural environments. Furthermore, they may also influence national and global economic systems. The number of completely exogenous shocks to organizations is very small indeed, according to these theorists.

Events which seem to be 'natural' are argued to have an organizational origin. For example, the risks posed by earthquakes have been argued to have an organizational component, namely poor or disregarded building regulations. However, the possible occurrence of the earthquake itself is undeniably an exogenous risk. Technological failures, such as the Bhopal disaster, or the *Challenger* space shuttle, are argued to be rooted deeply in organizational processes. Perrow (1984) argued that one common factor in disasters that places people at risk is the mismatch between organizational structure and its technology in use. The explosion in the Union Carbide plant in Bhopal, India, was argued to be a result of the firm growing in size but not adapting to new technologies. When a fault occurred in the plant, it was not immediately noticed since the specialization of roles together with the remoteness of the manufacturing process (relying on arm's-length safety checks) did not accommodate inter-role communication, which would have been needed to avert disaster. When a switch was thrown (accidentally), giving a false 'all systems OK' message, role specialization meant there was no possibility of checking this, despite it being obvious that something was wrong. By the time the problem was recognized it was too late. No individual had the capacity to stop the inevitable explosion which caused long-term damage to human and plant life.

Alexander (1996) accounts for the bursting of a gas pipeline in New Jersey in March 1994 as being attributable to the structure of the Texas Eastern Transmission Company, which was traditional, centralized and inflexible, unable to cope with the demands of gas transmission. Greening and Johnson (1996) argue that highly interactive, tightly coupled and high-risk technologies can spell high risk in an organizational structure which is bureaucratic and inflexible. They argued that one of the problems of such organizations is the inability of top-level managers to cope with (or to prevent) disasters. This was seemingly prophetic, given the economic disasters which were to follow as a result of top-level failures (such as Enron; *see* Chapter 17). The events of 11 September 2001 and the subsequent invasion of Iraq have also been blamed on organizational failures, in this case the paucity of information exchange between security agencies worldwide. Therefore, we can view risk as being something organizations create, as well as have to manage when external events (such as natural disasters) are imposed directly upon them.

Table 14.1 Categories of risks facing organizations

Risk category	Examples	Endogenous/exogenous to the organization
STRATEGY	Changing patterns of demand	Mostly exogenous
	Competitor actions	Mostly exogenous
	Changing markets	Mostly exogenous
	Business/government relationships	Endogenous and exogenous
	New disruptive technologies introduced	Exogenous
OPERATIONS	Manufacturing/process systems	Endogenous
	Financial/accounting controls	Endogenous
	Regulators	Exogenous
ECONOMIC	Poor cash flow	Mostly exogenous
	Changes in interest rates	Exogenous
	Currency exchange	Exogenous
	Poor credit	Exogenous and endogenous
HAZARDS	Natural disasters such as earthquakes or volcanoes	Exogenous
	Terrorist attacks	Exogenous
	Criminal activity	Exogenous and endogenous
	IT failure	Exogenous

To try to bring some order to understanding risk in an organizational context, it is useful to break down risk into subcategories that correspond to organizational activities. This allows decision makers to assess risks which are internal to the organization and those which are external to it. Table 14.1 gives some examples of how this might be done.

Table 14.1 is not intended to be exhaustive. There are many more risks than those illustrated here, but breaking down risks into these (or similar) categories allows decision makers to assess what would happen in the worst case if one or more of these were to occur. In that way, decision makers can rate each risk for severity and potential loss. In total, such a rating can produce an overall risk assessment score for an organization.

It is difficult for many of these risks to label them either as endogenous or as exogenous. In the majority of cases, they are a combination of both. For example, new technologies and scientific developments (such as genetic engineering or gene therapy) have been described as the 'new' risks by a number of commentators (Jorian 2000). Mostly these are seen as exogenous risks to organizations (and to individuals in society). Nuclear power and biotechnology are developed 'out there' and provide sources of cheap energy or improved crop production for organizations. But they are considered risky since the 'downsides' of each are well known. Yet, decision makers inside organizations can actually increase (or multiply) these risks. For example, decision makers in Monsanto ignored public anxieties about the testing of gene technologies and it incurred heavy financial losses as a result. What began as an external risk was badly managed internally and resulted in Monsanto facing even greater levels of risk.

However, even narrowing down risk to categories and origin (endogenous or exogenous) is not without its problems. Several strands of research have emphasized different attributes of and meanings to risk. The main difficulties stem from the difficulties in disentangling *organizational* risk from *managerial* risk. We explore this difficulty in the next section.

14.1.1 Organizational risk and managerial risk

Many authors have grappled with the many different definitions and descriptions of risk. Baird and Thomas (1990) argue that risk is multidimensional and that it is important to distinguish between *managerial* and *organizational* risk. **Managerial risk** taking is where managers make choices associated with uncertain outcomes. **Organizational risk** is where organizations face volatile income streams which are associated with turbulent and unpredictable environments. It is important not to confuse the two. If, for example, we use organizational risk as a substitute term for managerial risk, we make the unwarranted assumption that managerial risk taking leads to variations in organizational performance. This may not be the case. There is little empirical evidence on the relationships (if any) between organizational and managerial risk. Miller and Bromiley (1990) found that risk loaded on three separate factors (managerial, firm performance, market performance) but their study concluded little about the possible interrelationship of these factors.

Table 14.2 Organizational and managerial risks

Organizational risk factors	Characteristics
COMPLEX–SIMPLE ENVIRONMENTS	The more complex the environment, the greater the degree of organizational risk. Complexity corresponds to industry size as well as the number and heterogeneity of competitors. Simple environments, such as oligopolies, have institutional rules of behaviour. Complexity is likely to lead to blind spots, making it difficult for organizations to calculate risk or prepare for the responses of rivals since not all are understood or even known.
SCARCITY–MUNIFICENCE	Munificence refers to the abundance of resources, which include human, financial and capital. Abundance provides a context in which greater risk can be tolerated more easily. For example, mergers are tolerated to a greater extent in periods of growth rather than periods of economic closure. The reverse is true of scarcity, when firms face less risk as they all look inward to tighten controls and to reduce costs.
DYNAMISM	Dynamism refers to the stochastic characteristics of the environment. These include, for example, discontinuities caused by the introduction of new technologies or novel products from competitor organizations.
Managerial risk	**Characteristics**
ASPIRATIONS AND EXPECTATIONS	Aspirations are used to judge the quality of actual performance. Expectations indicate the level of anticipated future performance. Higher aspirations induce higher risks. Higher expectations mean better performance is more likely and this will induce lower levels of risk taking. The framing of a situation as either a gain or a loss may also influence propensity to take risk. For example, when managers/decision makers are faced with the likelihood of failing to meet their objectives, they are likely to accept greater levels of risk in order to try to reach their objectives and to avoid losses. When managers/decision makers are faced with the likelihood that they will achieve objectives, they are likely to favour safer options and avoid risk.
TOP-TEAM CHARACTER-ISTICS	High levels of heterogeneity in top teams are likely to promote greater risk taking. Managers with varied backgrounds (educational, international, other companies) will bring different perspectives and interpretive schema to bear upon decisions. Such groups are more likely to consider and take action on more risky, uncertain and non-routine decisions. High levels of homogeneity will induce a greater tendency to preserve the status quo and only take action on less risky decisions.
OWNERSHIP	Managers/decision makers who do not hold an equity stake in their organizations are less likely to take risky decisions than managers/decision makers who do hold a stake. Equity ownership prompts owner-managers to make decisions which are in line with shareholder goals through carefully calculated risk taking. Other things being equal, equity ownership mitigates the risk aversion of managers who hold risk-neutral preferences held by diversified shareholders. Non-owner-managers may feel that taking risks puts their employment at risk, because gambles which do not succeed can result in them being fired or, in the extreme, firm bankruptcy. They also have a less strong interest in the outcomes of successful risky decisions.

Table 14.2 continued

Managerial risk	Characteristics
SLACK	Slack means an organization has spare resources which can buffer it against fluctuations in environmental conditions. It acts to absorb shocks which could otherwise harm performance. Slack allows managers/decision makers to avoid risky decisions and major strategic changes. Low levels of slack induce more risky decisions. This 'hunger-driven' view of risk taking is shared by some authors and not by others. For example, Wiseman and Bromiley (1996) provide evidence that supports the argument. On the other hand, Singh (1986) found a positive relationship between slack and risk taking by managers. Firms do not necessarily have to be hungry for managers to take risks in this perspective. Palmer and Wiseman (1999), however, found evidence in favour of the hunger-driven view of risk taking, showing that organizations which have greater levels of slack take fewer risks.

Source: adapted from Palmer and Wiseman, 1999.

Despite the relative lack of empirical evidence and the theoretical confusion, Palmer and Wiseman (1999) provide some clear and concise definitions of risk at the managerial and organizational levels. These are summarized in Table 14.2.

Differentiating between these two levels of analysis (organizational and managerial) allows decision makers a clearer evaluation of both the location and source of risks. Hazards that are clearly identified as being at the organizational level help decision makers focus on (say) environmental characteristics and help avoid needless and perhaps pointless examination of managerial processes (such as the composition of top teams). Clarity, not only over the source of risk (Table 14.1,) but also its levels of analysis (Table 14.2), helps decision makers begin the process of **assessing risk**.

However, the interrelationships (if any) between organizational risk and managerial risk are much more in dispute. Some authors (for example, Fiegenbaum and Thomas 1988) assume managerial risk taking to be congruent with organizational risk. The one and the other are essentially the same. Others (for example, Palmer and Wiseman 1999) argue that decisions which have high levels of uncertainty (such as R&D investments) provide only a partial explanation of organizational risk. There is presently too little empirical evidence to support one view or the other. It is clear that there are some interrelationships between managerial and organizational risk, but the extent of that relationship is, as yet, unknown.

14.1.2 **Prospect theory and risk**

Fiegenbaum and Thomas (1988) utilize 'prospect theory' to reach their conclusions. Prospect theory is a modification of expected utility theory. It helps explain choice behaviours which do not fit with expected **utility theory**. For example, decision makers can be observed to persist in committing resources to risky and uncertain projects in an attempt to try to recover prior sunk costs which were invested earlier in the decision process. This behaviour considers *sunk costs to be relevant* to future decision trajectories, but it is in violation of the assumptions of expected utility theory which argue that *sunk costs should be ignored* in risky decision making. **Prospect theory** holds that decision makers make choices between risky alternatives influenced by both the magnitude and the probabilities of outcomes. Outcomes are evaluated as gains or losses (positive or negative deviations) from a neutral reference point. Gains and losses are evaluated using an S-shaped value function which illustrates that (say) the disappointment at losing a lot of money is greater than the pleasure associated with winning the same amount. It also implies that decision makers will tend to prefer a sure gain over a probable gain of expected equal value. This means that a sure chance of winning 20 000 euros is preferred to a 50 per cent chance of winning 40 000 euros, but a 50 per cent chance of losing 40 000 euros is preferred to a sure chance of losing 20 000 euros.

One critical aspect of prospect theory is that gains and losses are assessed relative to a neutral (or reference) point. However, this point is not really neutral. Options can be framed or presented in a highly positive way, thus affecting the placement of the supposedly neutral point (Kahneman and Tversky, 1973). A set of prospects presented as likely losses will induce risk taking, whereas a set of prospects presented in terms of gains will induce less risky decision making.

However, prospect theory appears to explain many decisions one can observe in organizations. Organizations with returns which are above target level are characterized by having managers who are risk-averse. Organizations which have returns below target levels are characterized by managers who are risk-seeking in their decision making. Prospect theory also helps explain what may seem, at first sight, to be odd behaviour. This is because individual managers are likely to set different levels of aspiration. For example, one manager may have set his or her aspirations very high (say for a new product). These may be aspirations about brand strength for example. The new product may indeed reach the aspirations of one manager in terms of brand strength, but may actually perform less well in the market. Few people buy the new product. A second manager whose aspirations centred around sales would likely argue against further investment and take the sunk costs as something to write off. The first manager, however, is much more likely to commit more money to advertising and promotion of this product which (by another's criteria) is failing. So prospect theory helps us untangle the relativism which pervades individual choice processes. Gains or losses are subjectively constructed and a so-called neutral point from which potential gains and losses are calculated is rarely neutral. Finally, this begs the question of whether the reference point is individually or organizationally constructed. Organizations, as well as individuals, have goals and objectives. Organizational goals can mask what appear to be behaviours at solely managerial levels and vice versa.

14.2 **Uncertainty**

Uncertainty is the principle that there is a limit to the precision and the extent of knowledge about a subject or an event. Uncertainty creates risk for strategic decision makers. Uncertainty arises because we cannot know everything:

> We do not perceive the present as it is, and in its totality, nor do we infer the future from the present with any high degree of dependability, nor yet do we accurately know the consequences of our actions. In addition ... we do not execute our actions in the precise form in which they are imagined and willed. (Knight 1921: 203)

Such uncertainties vary in themselves, with some strategies being taking in response to a relatively predictable future, while others are taken in the face of highly unpredictable and sometimes unknowable futures. This may be seen as a scale of uncertainty, ranging from *predictable uncertainty* at one end to *uncertain uncertainty* at the other (Luhmann 1993). An example of a relatively predicable uncertainty would be world demographics. An uncertain uncertainty might be trying to predict technologies which have not yet been invented or developed.

As far as demographics are concerned, we already know, for example, that the worldwide population is estimated to grow by 29 per cent by 2021 (a rise of 1.79 billion people). In the UK, estimates are for a 4 per cent population increase in the same period (2.5 million people). The number of 16–34-year-olds will decline by 15 per cent (1995–2021) and the number of 55–64-year-olds will have increased 40 per cent in the same time period (source: Office of National Statistics). The question for the strategic decision maker is what effects will such knowable futures have on business and what strategic decisions might be taken now in anticipation of these changes? Table 14.3 lists some of the factors a clothes retailer might take into consideration to inform future strategies in relation to the relatively predictable uncertainties of demographics.

Uncertainties also stem from not being able to anticipate changes in the macro or competitive context or not being able to predict the consequences these might have for the firm. Uncertainties also stem from the nature of the business you are in. An example of this can be seen in the film industry (*see* case box).

Table 14.3 Some typical effects of demographic changes on clothing retailers

◆ Larger market for clothers in the late-middle-aged group of the population
◆ More opportunities for design and style in this market (feeding the 'Jeans Generation' which comprises this segment of the population).
◆ A declining number of high-spending fashion-conscious 15–24-year-olds (and 25–34-year-olds)
◆ A greater number of more affluent 'grannies' (who may spend more money on clothes for the fewer babies that will be around)

Case box: **The film business and uncertainty**

The film business is one of the most unpredictable (and costly) in the world. It occupies a space which is at the nexus of art and commerce and is one where directors, actors and producers want to make a lot of money and get noticed for doing it. Yet it is notoriously difficult to tell what is going to be a successful film at the outset of the decision process. Many seemingly good ideas crash badly at the box office. Some films become the disaster stories they seek to portray. For example, *Cutthroat Island*, a pirate-thriller, made a splash for all the wrong reasons on its release in 1995. The film cost $100 million to produce, promote and distribute, but made only $11 million at the box office. As well as walking the plank commercially, the film was heavily criticized. The *Washington Post* remarked, '*Cutthroat's* lame cliff-hangers are enough to make you a cliff jumper.' This film destroyed Carolco, a studio known for big-budget sci-fi films such as *Terminator 2, Judgement Day* and *Total Recall*. At the time of its making, *Cutthroat* was judged by the studio likely to be a sure-fire success.

Yet, a film argued at its inception to be a stupid idea (everyone knows the ending before they see the film) became the biggest-grossing film to date. *Titanic* (Paramount) became the first film to ever take US$1 billion at the international box office. The film set included a replica of the ill-fated luxury liner, a model only 10 per cent smaller than the actual vessel and an enormous 7-acre tank that could hold 77 million litres (17 million gallons of water). Computer-generated effects helped to recreate the world's worst single peacetime maritime disaster, as well as sink the biggest film budget. It cost over US$200 million to make, when the industry average was around US$30 million (today it is US$ 60 million – still significantly under Titanic's budget). Director James Cameron persuaded Fox and Paramount executives to accept budget overruns, arguing that there was an urgent need for a film which could blow the market away. He gained commitment from executives for reasons which, at the outset, were little different from those used to support *Cutthroat Island. Titanic*, however, was the success, with the most number of Oscars awarded to a single film: 11 accolades including Best Picture, Best Director, Best Actress and Best Visual Effects.

Source: interviews by the author with *Entertainment Data International* (EDI) and *Prescience Film Finances*, July 2004.

Uncertainties in the film industry lie in the intractable problems of prediction of success. They also lie in making decisions to continue, even though the film is going over-budget and over-time. Such decisions are, of course, key, since the question becomes: if we continue, what might happen? Or do we just stop and take as losses expenditure to date? Since there are no data which can reliably inform these decisions, gut feel, persuasion and ego can be the factors which drive continuation in this uncertain industry.

Yet decision makers are always surrounded by uncertainties. What techniques have they developed over time to cope with and to reduce uncertainty and risk?

Table 14.4 Macro and micro-level influences

Environmental uncertainties	Industry uncertainties	Firm uncertainties
Political War Revolution Coup d'état Other political turmoil Raw materials shortages	**Input market** Quality uncertainty Shifts in market supply Changes in quantity used	**Operating** Labour uncertainties Labour unrest Employee safety Input supply
Governmental policy Fiscal and monetary Price controls Trade restrictions Nationalization Trade restrictions Government regulation Barriers to earnings Inadequate provision of public services Repatriation	**Product/market** Quality changes Changes in consumer tastes Spare parts restrictions Availability of substitutes Production uncertainties Scarcity of complementary goods Machine failure	
Macroeconomic Inflation Changes in relative price Exchange rates Foreign exchange rates Interest rates	**Competitive** Rivalry among competition New entrants Technological uncertainty Innovation	**Liability** Product liability Emission of pollutants
R&D Terms of trade Uncertain results of R&D	**Credit** Problems with collectibles	
Social Social unrest Riots Changing social concerns Demonstrations Small-scale terrorist movements		
Natural uncertainties Variations in rainfall Hurricanes Earthquakes Other natural disasters		

Source: adapted from Miller, 1992.

One well-known tool for this assessment is the PEST analysis. This will be familiar to many readers (it was also introduced in Chapter 1 of this book) and includes:

- **Political/Legal**: legislation (e.g. monopolies), environmental protection, taxation and foreign trade regulations, employment law, government stability.

- **Economic**: business cycles, interest rates, inflation, income and GNP trends, market share and price/volume relationships.

- **Socio-cultural**: demographics, income distribution, lifestyle changes, levels of education, attitudes to work and leisure and social mobility.

- **Technological**: levels of research spend (government and industry), rates of obsolescence and innovation, speed of technology transfer, e-commerce and the impact of digital technologies more broadly.

However, such macro-changes also need to be assessed alongside the more micro-changes which organizations face (such as industry structure, the influence of suppliers, competitors and customers). Although complex, Miller (1992) provides an example of combining macro and micro influences. These are shown in Table 14.4.

Some factors (such as product/market) in Table 14.4 span both industry- and firm-level uncertainties. Hence they can appear 'between columns'. Complicated though Miller's list is, it nevertheless allows the strategist to consider simultaneously both macro- and micro-level factors. It also presents the strategist with the problem of both measuring and analysing these factors. Many of them are difficult to measure with any level of precision or probability. We examine techniques to assess probabilities in the next sections of this chapter.

14.3 **Risk analysis and assessment techniques**

A variety of methods have been proposed to assess the level of risk associated with pursuing a particular strategy in the face of uncertainty. These range in complexity from observation (taking action and seeing what happens) through to quantification via Delphi techniques and multivariate analyses such as econometric and computer models.

Risk analysis provides a set of techniques for assessing the effects of uncertainty on decision making, especially capital investment decisions (Hertz and Thomas 1983). There are a number of variations in a set of different techniques, but they tend to be variations on a theme. The theme is that:

> *the assessment of whether or not the decision is 'worth' making is achieved by taking into account the varying degrees of uncertainty surrounding the input variables to a decision.*

There are a number of commonly used measures of worth, such as **net present value** (NPV) and **internal rate of return** (IRR). The decision maker first has to define the input variables to a decision and then has to make subjective assessments of the probabilities of each. Typically, the uncertain variables are costs, prices and economic factors, and these can be identified and quantified.

For example, decision makers may be considering an investment decision in a research and development (R&D) project. In a totally certain world, decision makers would know the cash flow pattern that would occur over the life cycle of the project and a definite value could be calculated for NPV. Uncertainty, however, means that there will be unpredictability in the various factors which comprise the cash flow pattern for the project. Risk analysis provides a technique whereby the decision maker can assess and characterize the impact of these uncertainties on NPV. The probability of the NPV distribution is derived from the input variables and the expected value of NPV can be mapped out and evaluated. The basic steps in such a risk analysis comprise:

◆ Identify the main factors of the decision which are uncertain (e.g. raw material costs, selling price of final product, likely level of sales).

◆ Estimate the range of values within which each variable is expected to fall and assess the likelihood of occurrence. For example, raw material costs may be expected to lie within a range of 20–45 euros per tonne. Decision makers, however, might assign a probability of 0.5 that the cost will be 40 euros and 0.1 that it will be 20 euros. Each variable in the decision can thus be assessed. However, some variables may be interdependent (raw material costs will influence selling price) and the decision maker must estimate the strength of the correlations between them. This can be done by a series of probability distributions in a specified range of values.

◆ Select at random from the distribution of values for each factor one particular value. Then, combine the values for all the factors and compute the rate of return (NPV) from that combination. For example, the lowest in the range of prices might be combined with the highest in the range of growth rate.

◆ Conduct the previous stage many times to define and evaluate the odds of occurrence of each possible rate of return (NPV). There are, of course, potentially many thousands of possible combinations of values. Therefore, we need to work out the likelihood that various specific returns on the investment will occur. This whole procedure has been referred to as the simulation method or the Monte Carlo method. The distribution of NPVs thus obtained can be used to calculate its mean and variability, ranging from a loss (if the factors go against the decision) to whatever maximum gain is possible (if all factors support the decision).

Obtaining this distribution has been likened by Hertz and Thomas (1983) to tossing two die and assessing how many times we may expect the total of seven to be thrown. A total of seven can be achieved by more than one combination of die values (e.g. by throwing a three and a four; a six and a one; a five and a two). The greater the number of combinations for a given value, the higher are the chances of achieving it. The average expectation is the average of the values of all outcomes weighted by the chances of each occurring. The variability of outcome values from the average also needs to be calculated since it is preferable to have a lower variability for the same NPV if given the choice.

Figure 14.1 shows some possible shapes for NPV distributions derived from the risk analysis. Faced with these data, decision makers would want to know:

- What is the probability of making a loss? (NPV < neutral)
- What is the average NPV?
- What is the probability of making a gain greater than some pre-specified level?
- How risky is the project? Is the variability or spread of the NPV distribution large in relation to the mean?

With reference to Figure 14.1, we can see that project C has about a 50:50 chance of an NPV exceeding zero. Project B has about a 75 per cent chance of an NPV below zero. Project C is highly risky (it has a large spread in relation to the mean) and project B is unlikely to yield a positive NPV. Project A always yields a positive NPV and this is low risk. Based on this analysis, decision makers would choose project A.

Knowing the shapes of possible NPV distributions helps decision makers assess the expected NPV. Of course, the shape of the distribution depends for its validity on the degree of accuracy with which subjective probabilities of the key variables in the decision or project are assessed. In addition, the decision eventually arrived at by using this technique does not take into account later decisions which may be dependent on the original decision. Risk analysis only considers the levels of risk of one decision at a time. Decision makers, however,

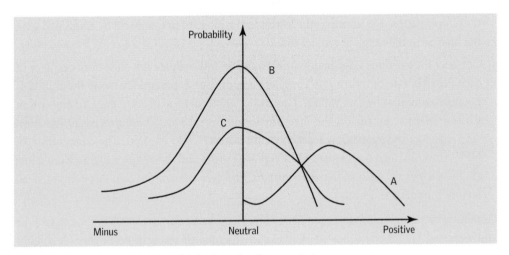

Figure 14.1 Three possible NPV distributions for three projects
Source: adapted from Moore and Thomas, 1976.

want more than just knowing the level of risk as assessed by probabilities; they also want to make choices. In making choices, decision makers build up multiple and interrelated patterns of decisions. They rarely just make one stand-alone decision (*see* Chapter 13). To consider risk in multiple related decisions, we need to combine risk analysis with techniques such as **decision trees**.

14.3.1 Decision trees and risk analysis

Hespos and Strassmann (1965) developed the stochastic decision tree method as a way of representing and analysing a series of decisions over time. It puts together classic decision tree analysis (where individual decisions are built up over time) with risk analysis techniques such as those described in the previous section. This technique is designed to handle situations of sequential investment decision making (e.g. new product launches, downsizing or internationalization) and assess risk across a series of related decisions.

According to Hespos and Strassman (1965), such stochastic decision trees assume that:

- All quantities and factors, including chance events, can be represented by continuous, empirical probability distributions.

- The information about the results from any, or all, possible combinations of decisions made at sequential points in time can be obtained in a probabilistic form.

- The probability distribution of possible results from any particular combination of decisions can be analysed using the concepts of utility and risk.

Hertz and Thomas (1983) give an example of structuring an investment decision using this technique. First the decision team identifies the range of alternative options and assesses the chance events which might occur along the way. They also examine potential ways of measuring performance and outcomes. Then they can begin to structure the decision tree, as in Figure 14.2.

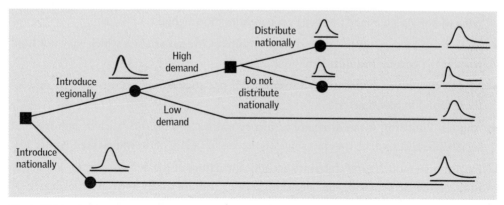

Figure 14.2 Stochastic decision tree for the launch of a new product
Source: adapted from Hertz and Thomas, 1983.

Figure 14.2 shows that the initial decision is whether or not to market the product nationally or regionally. If the decision is to market regionally, the firm can later expand nationally or can remain regional. Once the decision to launch the new product has been made, uncertain cash flows can be associated with each branch and represented by individual probability distributions by employing a Monte Carlo simulation. The process is repeated and the net cash flows resulting are accumulated to give separate frequency distributions for each of the four possible final net cash flows in the tree.

It should be noted that Figure 14.2 represents an unusually simple set of strategic decisions. In practice, decision makers are faced with more complex situations (each with associated risks) and the decision tree becomes more complicated with a large number of branches. A variety of option-reduction techniques can be employed to 'prune' the branches of the decision tree. These can involve working backwards through the tree, using expected monetary value (EMV) as an outcome. Where a branch has a lower EMV and higher variance than another branch it would be eliminated. This process would be reiterated until the decision tree was in a more simplified form and decision makers could begin working forwards again through the probabilities in the branches. Computer simulations can also have a similar effect. Setting up decision rules before any simulation will reduce the number of branches. For example, one rule could be to abandon branches where chance events exceed some previously specified value; then that option would not be considered and the branch of the decision tree would be removed.

14.3.2 **Limitations of risk analysis techniques**

- They can easily be interpreted as falsely precise (since they are numerically complex). Complex numbers give the impression of more certainty than perhaps is the case.
- When carrying out decision analysis, it is crucial that the decision structuring phase has been carried out with sufficient thought and attention to detail. This includes the specifying of key variables and assessing probabilities thoroughly.
- Models can be over-reliant on past relationships between variables which may not hold true for the current or future situations.
- Models may have important (and overlooked) parameters built into equations such as those found in econometrics.
- Another limitation is the difficulty of incorporating 'soft' factors, such as cultural and social differences, which may be critical to success or failure of decisions (see Chapter 12).
- Finally, such models rarely take into account the nature of the decision, or the characteristics of the firm making the decision. Models cannot easily measure the degree of 'perceived' risk which individuals may feel. Such perceptions may vary widely (such as people's perceived risk in eating genetically modified foods for example).

14.4 **Risk indices**

There are a range of published risk indicators, such as those from Business Environment Risk Indicators (BERI) or the Economic Intelligence Unit (EIU), which allow firms to use data based on expert opinions. These indices tend to select a range of variables covering a range of political, economic and financial or operational aspects of the country. The variables will be weighted. Not all may be of equal importance, so some may be given a higher weighting than others. In the BERI system, weights range between 0.5 and 3.0. The weighting makes some variables count more strongly in measuring overall attractiveness than others.

For example, in foreign market entry decisions, an expert panel gives each country a score for each variable. Scoring systems vary. In the BERI index, scores range between 0 (unacceptable risk) and 4 (superior conditions). The score and its weight are multiplied for each variable to reach a total 'risk' score for each country. The maximum country score is 100.

Broadly speaking, a score of over 80 is very attractive and less than 50 unattractive. Other systems may use letters, A = very attractive ... E = unattractive, or a range from 'hot' or attractive countries, through to 'cold' or unattractive (Goodnow and Hansz 1972; Litvak and Banting 1968).

14.4.1 **Limitations of risk indices**

- **Risk indices** may give initial insights but are macro-level and cannot be easily tailored to inform specific decisions.

- It is possible that a country rating as unattractive may be the best choice for a particular firm depending on its circumstances. If, for example, a multinational corporation already operates in a large number of countries, it may be choosing between remaining investment targets that are all high risk.

- Similarly, markets which appear attractive may be subject to intense international competition, whereas in a market with difficult conditions, a firm that masters these may achieve high levels of success.

- Indices assume we can say something about the future based on what has happened in the past. This assumption may not be true in rapidly changing market conditions – known as discontinuous change (high uncertainty). If the future is uncertain, can history help us predict what might happen?

14.5 **Using scenarios to help reduce risk and uncertainty**

Alternative techniques for understanding and trying to reduce both risks and uncertainty use more qualitative approaches. One dominant approach of this type is the use of scenarios.

According to Bain & Co. (website):

> *Scenario planning is not about predicting the future. Rather it attempts to describe what is possible. The result of a scenario analysis is a group of distinct futures, all of which are plausible. The challenge then is how to deal with each of the possible scenarios.*

In Shell's words (website)

> *Scenarios are carefully crafted stories about the future embodying a wide range of ideas and integrating them in a way that is communicable and useful. They help us link the uncertainties we hold about the future to the decisions we make today. When we reflect on situations, we see the world through our own frames of reference. The purpose of scenario work is to uncover what these frames are, respecting differences rather than aiming for a consensus that puts them to one side.*

These definitions remains broadly unchallenged. More recent approaches use language such as 'visualizing alternative futures' so that we can design 'flexible options for strategy' to cope with the 'diversity within these futures'.

In practice, scenarios are:

- Attempts to look into the future by bundling together plausible and logically consistent factors.

- Together, these factors help tell a story about the future influences in an organization and give it key characteristics (no matter how apparently wild these seem today).

- Such characteristics are key to helping strategists plan and effect changes to meet the anticipated futures.

14.5.1 **Which organizations should use scenarios?**

- In theory, all organizations can use scenarios, but it is clearly important for large, capital intensive firms (such as oil companies) to get the future context as right as possible. Sunk costs and opportunity costs are very high in these industries and getting it wrong can have disastrous consequences. Equally pharmaceutical firms have very high R&D levels and manufacturing costs. Getting the future wrong can be a disastrous problem in such industries.

- Scenarios can be projections of up to (and beyond) ten years into the future. The advantage of this that strategies for change can be formulated which are relatively independent of business and economic cycles.

- Organizations which need to use scenarios are especially those which are unable to react quickly and effectively to changing events as they occur.

- Organizations which can react quickly and maintain high levels of flexibility have the option of pursuing a 'trading' strategy involving rapid changes and quick fixes. So long as this capability lasts, such organizations need not necessarily concern themselves with longer-term scenarios.

14.5.2 Scenarios and scenario thinking

In Chapter 6 we considered the difficulties of planning over time scales that fall beyond the limits of competitive strategy. In particular we noted that most companies have difficulty in quantifying any factors beyond two product life cycles. Yet strategic thinking cannot be neglected. It was Alvin Toffler who said;

> There is a slightly odd notion in business today that things are moving so fast that strategy becomes an obsolete idea. That all you need is to be flexible or adaptable or, as the current vocabulary puts it, 'agile'. This is a mistake. You cannot substitute agility for strategy. If you do not develop a strategy of your own you become a part of someone else's strategy. You, in fact, become reactive to external circumstances. The absence of strategy is fine, if you don't care where you're going. (Source: Bain & Co. website)

We suggested in Chapter 6 an adaptation of competitive advantage thinking that would in a qualitative way enable strategic thinking to be taken beyond two product life cycles. In this section we look at scenario planning, a method of longer-run thinking that has become very well known and adopted in a great many diverse situations. A search on the internet through Google reveals over 50 pages of sites whose prime descriptor is scenario planning. It is said to have its roots in military strategy studies and notably through Herman Kahn, who was famous for his work related to the possible scenarios associated with thermonuclear war ('thinking the unthinkable'). It was transformed into a business tool in the late 1960s and early 1970s at Royal Dutch Shell, firstly through Pierre Wack, Kees van der Haydn and Peter Schwartz. At a time of very low oil prices Shell's use of scenario planning enabled it to be better prepared for the oil shocks of the 1970s, the oil crisis followed by the oil glut. Indeed the subsequent success of the method owes much to Shell's success in predicting the first oil price shock in 1973. High-profile users in the USA include the White House, the Pentagon and the Economic Planning Agency.

14.5.3 How useful are scenarios?

A scenario is useful in assessing the long-term ramifications of a firm's overall strategy. Analysis of multiple scenarios enables the assessment of the implications of different futures for alternative strategies and the uncertainties and risks associated with them. According to Shell (again, from their website):

> Scenarios are particularly useful in situations where there is a desire to put challenges on the agenda proactively (for example when there are leadership changes

and major impending decisions) and where changes in the global business environment are recognised but not well understood (such as major political changes and emerging technologies).

A well-constructed scenario enables the ordering of one's perceptions about alternative future environments in one of which it is likely that one's decisions might be played out.

Therefore, there are two key characteristics of a good 'story'. The first is that it results from the subjective assessments of a wide range of informed individuals or groups. A valid story has to be built on facts and assumptions that can be validated and supported in a reasonably objective way. This requires that the process of scenario development should be objective and replicable and not rest simply on guesswork, however inspired. Second, it recognizes that decision makers have some influence on future development. The simple assumption is that decision makers are in position to react to the dimensions of the story as it unfolds. The stronger view is that the unfolding story allows for the dynamic interaction of the decision makers with the environment.

14.5.4 **Writing a scenario**

A scenario starts with the focal issue or decision. A generic worry about, for example, the implications of new technologies will lead in myriad directions. The issue for the firm must revolve around key dilemmas or challenges that are on the horizon (or just over) but for which there is little early guidance. The purpose of the scenario is to provide a frame within which some guidance for major commitments can be developed. Nevertheless, the focal issue can be described in quite broad terms (e.g. what will be the future for technology in banking?). Or they could be quite specific (what are the implications of new technologies for traditional banking organizations?). The longer the time frame, the broader will be the focal issue. The shorter the time frame, the easier it is to collapse scenario thinking into detailed forecasting and planning.

The second stage is to identify the primary driving forces of the future. This is usually based on the PEST analysis that we introduced in this chapter and Chapter 6. Because the scope of PEST includes politics, economics, technology and social dynamics, this encompasses most of the forces that are likely to be relevant.

You are now ready to construct your story of the future (Schoemaker 2002).

A structured view of the **scenario planning** process might look as follows:

1 Identify the focal issue(s).

2 Specify the scope of the planning and its time frame.

3 Establish the broad background that includes the organization within its 'deep' structure (PEST characteristics).

4 Identify the driving forces that link the focal issues with the long-term future: these are events that are predetermined and virtually certain to occur.

5   Identify the critical uncertainties in the environment. At this point macroeconometric forecasting will be useful.

6   Combine the driving forces with the uncertainties to create alternative futures (the scenarios).

7   Validate the alternative futures (e.g. by Delphi-style processes or by qualitatively assessing their likelihood of occurrence). The latter can easily be assessed on a probability scale ranging from 0 (little likelihood of occurrence) to 1 (high likelihood of occurrence).

8   Analyse the scenarios for similarities, differences and sources of difference, mutual dependence.

9   Quantify the effect of each scenario on the firm and formulate appropriate strategies. Again the impact on the firm can be assessed on a 0 to 1 scale where 0 equals little impact and 1 equals high impact.

10   Develop strategy options and criteria for future choices and paths.

Although some of the above may seem similar to the probabilities and assessments made in risk analyses described earlier in this chapter, there are two main differences with respect to scenarios. First, the time horizon considered is significantly longer. Scenarios typically look ten or fifteen years into the future. Second, the specificity of the analysis is far broader and, of necessity, less precise.

The processes around points 3, 4, 5, 6, 7 and 8 may take place typically in workshop settings where executives, technical experts and policy analysts bring together a wide range of experience and expertise in order both to identify and to validate the key assumptions about the driving forces and the uncertainties, and how they interact to create the basic scenarios. Figure 14.3 shows the basic drivers of two scenarios distilled into three sets of variables, some common to both scenarios and some exclusive to one or the other.

The analysis methods at points 8 and 9 involve testing each scenario in two ways. The first is a cross-impact analysis to establish the extent to which scenarios have common drivers and different drivers. And the second is to relate each scenario to a short list of the key variables to test for sensitivity/robustness.

Figure 14.4 shows the early stages of the analysis in which the PEST environment is determined and the competitive strategy horizon for the firm (see Chapter 6) is established,

	Common variables	Variable one	Variable two
Scenario one	Yes	Yes	No
Scenario two	Yes	No	Yes

Figure 14.3 Distinguishing the drivers of scenarios

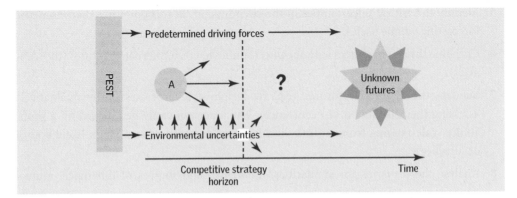

Figure 14.4 Setting out the assumptions

leading to a specification of the focal issues. The futures are unknown and even the points of arrival on the competitive strategy horizon are uncertain.

Figure 14.5 shows the establishment of the basic stories, here characterized as 'optimistic' and 'pessimistic'. They depend on the specification of the assumptions from the first figure and the way in which the drivers and the uncertainties interact. A difficult part of this is initially to keep the stories distinct it is all too easy to end up with minor variants on a common theme. The second problem is to restrict the number of stories to a manageable number, typically two or three. Here the need is to sacrifice complexity for the tractability of analysis. This is why at this stage it is important to restrict the key drivers and uncertainties to only the most important. Hence you can appreciate the need to consult opinion from far and wide so as to avoid our normal perceptual filters.

Figure 14.6 articulates the strategies, the options, and the paths. The paths illustrate the potential complexities. First, the starting point at the competitive strategy horizon may not be clear, points a, b and c are possible, but are broadly similar. However, point d is

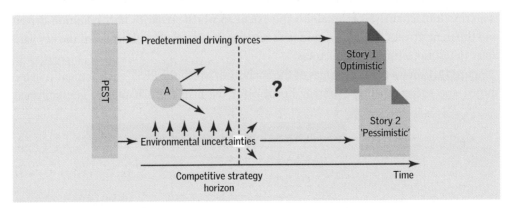

Figure 14.5 Establishing the stories

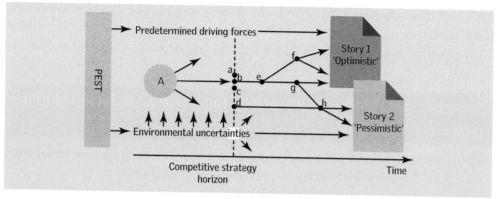

Figure 14.6 Figuring out the strategy options and paths

quite different (i.e. the current competitive strategy has failed to deliver). Second, common paths are possible and choices might be deferred until the situation becomes clearer. Thus, points e, f and g represent choices to be made along the top path. Point f leads unambiguously (as far as we can see now) towards the 'optimistic' story with the possibility of two paths onward, one being more optimistic than the other. Point g represents a more difficult choice where either story is possible but a commitment must be made. Point h is a point along the low path to the 'pessimistic' story, the main question being how pessimistic?

The process of scenario planning seeks to achieve a set of options with assessments of potential pay-offs and risks that can be unfolded over time, taking account of events as they emerge, correcting errors and acknowledging expert opinion as it changes (which it will do). Scenarios are not intended or expected to be 'right' in the sense that forecasts are intended to anticipate the correct outcome. They are intended to:

1 explore the long term beyond conventional planning horizons;

2 build on a wide set of assumptions;

3 explore a wide range of outcomes;

4 meld assumption-outcome sets to derive ranges of possible futures;

5 explore paths required to move from the present to these futures.

In doing this we need to keep our mindset very strategic. Look for common paths. Watch out for forks in the road divergences. Identify the key risks. Find common paths where possible. Do not commit too early avoid the avoidable commitments. But, in the end, the commitments have to be made against the risk. If scenario planning achieves anything (and it is not a panacea) it helps to *assess risk* over the longer term and identify strategic options for the organization. It should be emphasized that organizations are unlikely to survive by scenarios alone. In the short and medium terms, decision and risk analysis alongside the risk/return trade-offs introduced earlier in this chapter, are more useful and immediate ways of formulating strategies.

The following short case example, from a real situation, shows how scenario analysis can be used.

Case box: **Strategic considerations for a European business in a global economy**

This case is taken from a study conducted on the implications for European-based firms of a more global economy and greater economic integration within Europe. It demonstrates three levels of analysis, the world economy, Europe, and (European) companies (see Figure 14.7). It also shows the distinctive variables established at each level of analysis. These then were taken to be distinctive factors that shaped each level, although recognizing that there were other actors common across the levels.

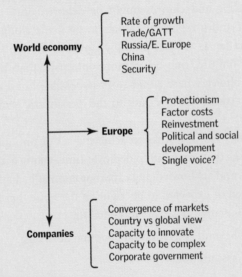

World economy
- Rate of growth
- Trade/GATT
- Russia/E. Europe
- China
- Security

Europe
- Protectionism
- Factor costs
- Reinvestment
- Political and social development
- Single voice?

Companies
- Convergence of markets
- Country vs global view
- Capacity to innovate
- Capacity to be complex
- Corporate government

Figure 14.7 Establishing the assumptions

Two scenarios were established – 'pessimistic' and 'optimistic'. For the world economy this elicited the following comparison:

Pessimistic	Optimistic
Low growth	Sustained growth
Inability of LDCs to grow	LDC and ex-communist growth
Protracted difficulties in China and Russia	Islam and Christian rapprochement
Inability to balance budgets: welfare costs and macro policy problems	Welfare reforms
The 1990s bubble remains burst	Radical Right makes a breakthrough?
	New surge of innovation

For Europe, there is a similar dichotomy:

Pessimistic	Optimistic
Regulation and protection increases	Political voice
Divergence from rest of world	Major trading bloc
Politically inchoate	Thrives on variety and innovation
High cost	Good home base for global companies
Low innovation	Transformation of labour markets

In staying with a dichotomy the distinction is probably too sharp and a third possibility should be explored but a simple middle of the road. The dichotomy for companies is also sharp:

Pessimistic	Optimistic
Country managers remain	Strong global market growth
Global view restrained	New federal organizations
MNEs do not evolve into more complex federal forms	Innovation becomes central to profitability
Efficiency concerns outweigh innovation challenges	Service and financial companies have v. high growth
Country–company difficulties	Emergence of new breed of MNEs from China, Russia and East Asia

The simple interaction between the pessimistic columns produces the overall 'pessimistic' scenario, and likewise for the 'optimistic' columns.

Pessimistic scenario

1 Failure to resolve the current set of dilemmas against background of stagnation, insecurity (anarchy?) and weakening of political control and influence. There is continued failure of macroeconomic policy to resolve excessive government spending. Consumer pessimism continues to hold back aggregate demand.

2 Growth will be around 'polar' points rather than uniformly spread. World increasingly has different speeds.

3 Companies seek national or regional patronage from host countries. Trade becomes politicized politico-economic trade-offs become the norm; trade fortresses re-emerge.

4 Power of existing MNEs is likely to be reinforced because of lack of effective competition.

Optimistic scenario

1 Marked by prosperity and high growth across the world. Multiplier effect of major investments enhanced by rapid learning in newer economies. Emergence of major new markets plus increased innovation and opportunity for development of large, new corporations.

> **2** Corporate environment is competitive but highly dynamic. Political influence focused primarily on investing and opening up rather than on protection.
>
> **3** Companies are able to change through growth. They are able to develop transnational and federal character but against a background of increasing segmentation, thus not dominated by the largest players. Look for emergence of Chinese and Russian MNEs.

The scenarios in the case box lead to the development of two possible strategies for an organization. Companies either seek to become expert at politico-economic trade-offs, or they seek to grow transnationally and become expert on innovation and segmentation and seek to establish new organizational structures to support the federal approach. So far, so good. But as Schoemaker (2002) points out, strategy formulation is only one (important) part of the story. Should the firm pursue such strategies, there will need to be a careful assessment of the extent to which the organization is capable and able to implement these chosen strategies

14.6 Back to the organization: identifying gaps

The above examples (and the use of scenarios in general) show that it can be easy to treat scenarios as ends in themselves. That is, the question of whether or not the organization *is capable* of implementing the future strategies informed by the scenario is either not addressed or is overlooked. Scenarios are simply tools which help reduce uncertainty and risk. They also help identify one or two future strategic directions which the organization might take, but they cannot help determine to what extent such strategies are capable of being implemented, or what changes would need to occur to make such strategies a realistic proposition for the organization concerned. The same holds true for strategies identified by risk and decision analyses. Our mythical firm in Figure 14.2 may decide to market the new product nationally rather than regionally. But the key question is, to what extent it can do this effectively?

Fahey and Randall (1998) suggest that, following the identification of future strategies, decision makers should:

- Reflect the formulated strategy back against the organization. What gaps are there (if any) in key factors such as capabilities, capacities, competences and structures?

- Identify what changes may need to be made to the organization in the light of the above 'gap' analysis.

- Identify and select key indicators and signposts which will help monitor and assess the implementation and the performance of the chosen strategies. This will involve careful selection and imaginative choice as well. Using current performance indicators may not be appropriate.

There are a number of ways of doing the above, but most revolve around some form of **gap analysis**. This is where core competences of the organization are assessed against future strategies that have been crafted following the scenario analysis.

Table 14.7 shows a typical gap analysis. This is based on defining an organization's core competences and then assessing to what extent each competence contributes towards (supports) the chosen strategy. This can be done simply by using plus, minus or neutral signs. Plus signs indicate where a **core competence** supports the strategy. Neutral is where the core competence provides little or no support and minus signs indicate where a current competence actually detracts from a future strategy. Core competences are difficult to define as we have seen earlier in this book, but they can be thought of as distinctive capabilities of the organization which:

- create value in terms of economic rent;
- are difficult to imitate (why can't competitors do that?);
- are 'implicit' as part of an organization's history, routines and social capital.

In our mythical example organization in Table 14.7, we can see that two future strategies had been crafted, each based on a particular scenario. One strategy (based on an optimistic scenario that there will still be demand for these types of products) is to retain the existing technology base, but to compete on the strength of expanding the existing product range. A second strategy (based on a pessimistic scenario that new products will be needed as well as new technologies to produce them) is to develop an entirely new product range and to invest in new or emerging technologies. The table also records the firm's current strategy.

Table 14.5 Gap analysis: future strategies and core competences: an example

Core competences (examples)	Current strategy	Future strategy one (e.g. expand product range incrementally; retain existing technologies)	Future strategy two (e.g. adopt new technologies and develop new product ranges to meet anticipated future)
Product advantages (lighter, smaller, cheaper)	+	+	0
Time to market (faster)	+	+	0
Ability to innovate (high)	0	0	+
Proprietary knowledge	+	0	+
Flexible structures	0	0	+

The existing core competences of the organization had been identified as ranging from product advantages (lighter, smaller and cheaper) to flexible organizational structures. For each competence, its utility in each strategy has been assessed on a scale ranging from minus, through zero to plus. In the example there are no core competences which actually detract (or work against) any strategies, but there are core competences which vary from neutral to positive.

For example, having a flexible organizational structure does not positively support either the current or future strategy one. It is needed and will be a positive support under strategy two, when R&D and innovation will need to be communicated and processed effectively and swiftly around the organization. Having proprietary knowledge is a core competence now, but under strategy one its potency will become eroded as other organizations compete using the same or similar products. Under strategy two, where R&D will be crucial, proprietary knowledge again becomes key. Other competences, such as time to market and product advantages are eroded under strategy two (presuming new advantages will be needed and that time to market may not be a key aspect of competition).

The utility of doing this gap analysis (which can be carried out by a small focus group) is that it identifies the transient nature of core competences. It also shows how the constellation of competences shifts depending on the strategy adopted. The gap analysis may also reveal much longer lasting capabilities in the organization, its distinctive long-lived assets. Finally, it may show where new competences are needed in the future and where existing competences may be abandoned. For example, under strategy two in Table 14.5, the organization may be advised to switch resources into additional competences such as high investment in R&D and a greater emphasis on environmental scanning and benchmarking as well as ensuring the selection and recruitment of the 'best and the brightest' staff to grow the firm's intellectual capital, or what March (1999) terms 'organizational intelligence' (*see* Chapter 16).

14.7 Summary

All organizations and all managers face uncertainties. The effects are to increase the degree of risk faced by strategic decision makers. Most techniques of strategic decision making under uncertainty (e.g. risk analyses) assume that the returns from a decision are arranged on a probability distribution conditional on the choices made. In general, decision makers are assumed to have a preference for alternatives which have higher expected values, but at the same time, they consider the riskiness of other alternatives.

Risk itself is a variable concept. In the consideration of alternatives, risk taking is co-related to the risk takers' changing fortunes (March and Shapira 1999). For example, if risk is perceived to be life-threatening, then individuals, it seems, will either take highly risky decisions or will be traumatized to take very risk averse decisions and play safe.

We currently know these are the polarized choices decision makers may take, but we do not yet know enough to predict when and under what circumstances they will opt for high risk or will play safe.

Higher levels of organizational slack seem to encourage experimentation and innovation and encourage risk taking (probably because of a relaxation of controls). Lower levels of organizational slack (or when slack becomes negative) means tighter controls, and efforts to improve efficiencies and procedures encourage lower levels of risk taking. Decision makers' aspiration levels are also not fixed. Over time they will vary, often considerably, and therefore the degree of perceived risk will vary depending on where the aspiration level is fixed. This is because risk averse behaviour will be defined as being below the aspiration threshold and risky behaviour will be defined as being above it. Equally, individuals' self-confidence changes over time. Past successes can breed confidence (and sometimes overconfidence) in taking risky decisions. Overconfidence can occur when decision makers wrongly assume they were wholly responsible for past successes (and do not attribute success to exogenous factors, such as errors by competitors or a munificent macroeconomy where resources are easily available).

Risk itself is subject to varying interpretations and definitions. Risk can be viewed as something totally exogenous to organizations and therefore out of managers' control. Equally, risk can be seen as wholly endogenous. Even seemingly external events and threats (such as terrorist attacks) can be attributed ultimately to the actions, or inactions, of individuals and groups. From this perspective, all risk is argued to be ultimately man-made. Typically, decision makers will face some level of uncertainty between these polarized views. There will always be earthquakes, flooding and volcanoes and there will always be man-made disasters.

A key question for strategists is how to manage risk and how to craft strategic decisions in the face of risk. Many empirical models of risk have been developed and some of the main ones have been mentioned in this chapter. The limitation of all these approaches is that they are essentially short term in their time horizons. In order to build in a time dynamic, scenario analysis can be beneficial to strategists, enabling them to plan future decisions based on a contingent view of what a plausible future (or set of futures) may be. This chapter has described in some detail one way of dealing with scenarios, both to develop strategies and to help make decisions in the face of uncertainties. Finally, the chapter returns to the level of analysis of the organization, since the ability to implement such strategies depends very much on the capacities and capabilities built into the organization's infrastructure. In particular, we have highlighted the role of core competences, effective governance and ensuring the organization can undertake strategic change and continue to learn. Each of these topics is developed in the following chapters.

Key terms

Assessing risk *535*	Organizational risk *533*
Core competence *555*	Prospect theory *536*
Decision trees *543*	Risk *530*
Gap analysis *555*	Risk indices *545*
Internal rate of return *540*	Scenario planning *548*
Managerial risk *533*	Uncertainty *530*
Net present value *540*	Utility theory *535*

Recap questions and assignments

1 Build three scenarios for an organization with which you are familiar. Name them and provide a thumbnail sketch of their key characteristics.

2 Choose the scenario you consider to be most likely and assess the impact of this on organizational factors such as customer demand, costs, levels of competition, changes in technology etc.

3 From the story told in (2) above, suggest one or two strategies the organization might adopt now to prepare for the future you have outlined.

4 Assess the organization's capabilities in implementing your identified strategies. What additional core competencies will be needed (if any) and which current competences may become redundant?

Online
*Learning***Centre**

When you have read this chapter, log on to the Online Learning Centre website at www.mcgraw-hill.co.uk/textbooks/mcgee to explore chapter-by-chapter test questions, further reading and more online study tools for strategy.

Case 1 **Decisions, risk and uncertainty and the use of game theoretic models**

The examples of Intel Polaroid vs Kodak and the breakfast cereals industry

When the environment is predictable and only a few decision variables are involved, all the assumptions for a game theory approach are present. In particular, it is possible to identify all the possible moves of each of the players and the financial consequences of these moves. This allows decision-makers to identify the optimal strategic move(s) for each of the players. We illustrate this approach using three examples.

Intel's dilemma: a prisoner's dilemma game

The rivalry between Intel and Advanced Micro Devices Inc. (AMD) (Business Week, 1999b) has some similarities with the classic game of prisoner's dilemma (Luce and Raiffa, 1957; Rappaport and Chammah, 1965). In this game, two players are suspected of a hypothetical major crime, such as murder. They are imprisoned and held incommunicado, so each must decide whether to cooperate or to defect, without knowing what the other will do. The authorities possess evidence to secure conviction on only a minor charge, such as illegal possession of weapons. If neither prisoner squeals, both will draw a light sentence on the minor charge – this state is called a mutual cooperation (MC) pay-off. If one prisoner squeals and the other stonewalls, the squealer will go free (unilateral defection, UD), and the stonewaller, or 'sucker,' will draw a very heavy sentence (unilateral cooperation, UC). If both squeal, both will draw a moderate sentence (mutual defection, MD).

Each prisoner's preference ordering is UD > MC > MD > UC. Each prisoner will be better off squealing than stonewalling, no matter what his partner chooses to do, because UD > MC (the temptation of cheating) and MD > UC (the fear of being cheated upon). But if both defect, both do worse than if both had cooperated (MC > MD). Hence the dilemma (Parkhe, 1993, pp. 796–7).

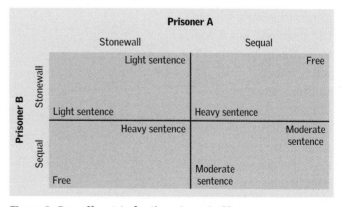

Figure 1 Pay-off matrix for the prisoner's dilemma

Figure 1 shows the pay-off matrix of the prisoner's dilemma.

Intel's situation in 1999 was as follows:

> Intel's aggressive marketing and price cuts have delivered big share gains, but the impact on its rivals has been so severe that some are now struggling to survive. For anti-trust enforcers who continue to watch over Intel's practices since it settled a Federal Trade Commission (FTC) suit in March 1999, the failure of one of its competitors would set off alarm bells. At the end of 1998, Intel had 75 per cent of the PC processor market, down from 86 per cent the year before, as a result of gains by rivals Advanced Micro Devices Inc. (AMD) and National Semiconductor Corp. (National), whose low-cost knockoffs of Intel's Pentium chip were getting a huge chunk of the hot sub-$1000 PC business. Although Intel still dominated the chip market and had a lock on the upper-end of the business, that wasn't enough. Intel responded by cutting the price of its low-end Celeron chips in half and courting PC makers with discounted packages of PC parts. Since February 1999, US retail sales of sub-$1000 Celeron PCs have surged 50 per cent. Rivals, meanwhile, are reeling. On May 5, National dropped out of the PC processor business, saying it couldn't make a profit in it. AMD has lost 10 points of market share in cheap PCs. Intel can be super aggressive on price in Celerons because it generates big profits on other lines. Nearly all of Intel's expected $7.7 billion profit this year will come from processors used in computers costing $1200 or more. What Intel is doing is perfectly legal. But antitrust experts say Intel could run foul of regulators if they found that its actions were meant to protect a monopoly through predatory pricing. If for no other reason than to keep the FTC at bay, Intel needs AMD and other rivals to stick around. If AMD collapsed, the FTC would surely react. (Business Week, 1996b).

For Intel, the dilemma is the following: it can pursue its aggressive marketing and price cuts to gain market share (that is a UD situation), but if AMD leaves the market, the FTC will punish Intel for antitrust practices (a MD situation). Therefore, Intel would be better to try to keep AMD in the market even if its market share would suffer (an MC situation). Figure 2 shows the pay-off matrix for Intel and AMD.

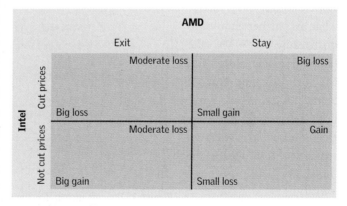

Figure 2 Pay-off matrix for the Intel and AMD

Polaroid–Kodak

Another example of the prisoner's dilemma is the competition between Polaroid and Eastman Kodak in instant photography in 1976 and 1977. Prior to 1976 Polaroid had faced no serious competition in instant photography. In 1974 Kodak for the first time revealed that it was working on its own system of instant film and cameras. On April 20, 1976, Kodak announced that it would challenge Polaroid's 28-year monopoly of the instant photographic field (HBS Case 376–266, 1984; Bettis and Weeks, 1987). At that time, the competitive environment was characterized by a limited number of competitors and innovation was incremental and regular in nature thus making the environment quite predictable. The number of decision variables was also limited: Kodak could either enter the instant camera market (fight) or not (détente). Then, Polaroid could either cut its prices (fight) or not (détente) and Kodak could either choose to follow Polaroid (fight) or not (détente). This is clearly a situation where game theoretic models apply. The decision tree presented in Figure 3 shows the different alternatives for Kodak and Polaroid.

In this situation, a sequential model with repeated moves could have helped Kodak to anticipate what Polaroid would do and then, based on this information, determine an optimal decision path. The main rule of competitive strategy in a situation of sequential moves has been described by Dixit and Nalebuff (1991) and can be summarized as follows: *look ahead and reason back*. Kodak had to think about the possible reactions of Polaroid to its entry into the instant camera market and how to react. Kodak could have predicted the fact that Polaroid would cut its prices to maintain its market share and highlight the necessity of Kodak's own subsequent price cuts. It was another example of a prisoner's

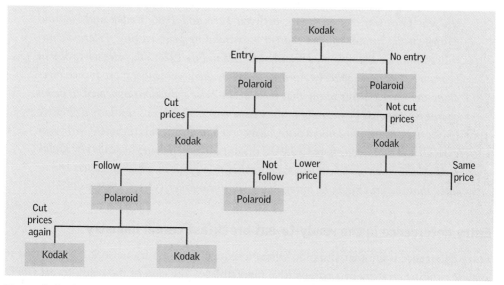

Figure 3 Decision tree for Kodak's entry into the instant camera market

dilemma is presented in Figure 4. All the elements of a price war existed. At that time, Kodak clearly dominated the US conventional photographic market with market shares of 90 per cent for film and 85 per cent for cameras. Protected by its patents, Polaroid earned monopoly profits in the instant camera market. By April 1976, its Colorpack

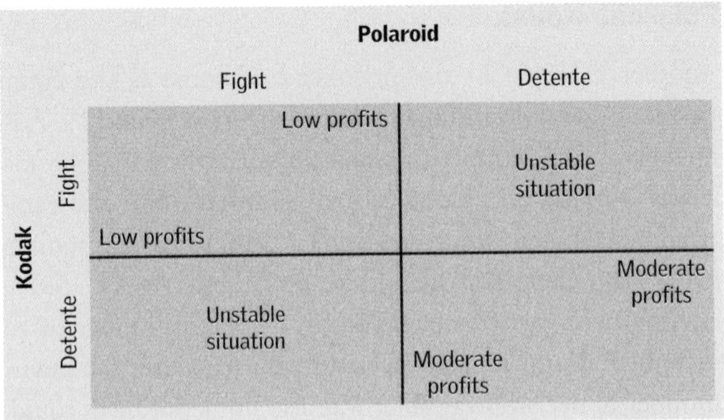

Figure 4 Pay-off matrix for Polaroid and Kodak

system contributed at least 95 per cent to Polaroid's earnings; therefore, Kodak's entry into the instant camera market was clearly a threat for Polaroid's market share and profitability. Therefore, it was predictable that Polaroid would react aggressively to protect its market share.

If Kodak had used a game theoretic model to analyze the situation, it is likely that it would not have entered the instant camera market and the subsequent price war would have been avoided. The following quote presents Polaroid and Kodak's moves after Kodak's entry.

> 'On April 20, 1976, Eastman Kodak Company announced that it would challenge Polaroid Corporation's 28-year monopoly of the instant photographic field' (HBS Case 376–266, 1984). The entry of Kodak into the instant camera market starts a ten-year price war. For ten years, between 1976 and 1986, Kodak and Polaroid battled in the instant camera market essentially by price-cutting. Polaroid's no-frills Pronto, for example, was priced at $79.95 in July 1976. The price fell to $59 in February 1977 and $39.95 by April 1977. While there were modest product changes along the way, it is fair to say that most of the price reductions appeared to be an aggressive response by Polaroid to the Kodak entry. Kodak was similarly aggressive in its prices. Its instant camera price fell by over $20 during this turbulent early year of rivalry, so that it too offered a $39.95 instant camera. Rebates to dealers by Kodak reduced the price of the camera even further to a point at which outsiders speculated that the firm might be losing money in this market. (Oster, 1999, p. 282)

Entry deterrence in the ready-to-eat breakfast cereal industry

Entry deterrence is another situation where a sequential-game framework may be used to analyze product strategy in a competitive marketplace. The case of the ready-to-eat (RTE) breakfast cereal industry (Schmalensee, 1978; HBS Case 9–795–191, 1997; HBS Case

9–796–122, 1997) is a good example of such a game, because the environment is quite predictable and the number of decision variables is limited.

In this situation, entry into a market normally occurs one or two firms at a time. As a new firm enters, it will position itself by looking at its costs, at consumer preferences, and at the position of other firms already in the market. It may also be important for firms to take into account the likely future product behaviour of current and potential rivals in market. Firms will wish to pursue product positions that are least destabilizing to the existing industry and most defensible against entry threats in the future by filling the gaps in the product space (Schmalensee, 1978; Gruca and Sudharshan, 1995). In sum, a firm will take into consideration what it believes will be the final shape of the market in making its own product-line choices.

In the RTE breakfast cereal industry in the USA, between 1950 and 1972, the six leading producers introduced over 80 brands (Schmalensee, 1978). During the same period of time, there was no significant firm entry into the market. The product strategy of the leading producers in the RTE breakfast cereal industry may be described by a competitive game in which each firm positions its brands in market space so that new launches by insiders cannot erode its profits, and therefore, entry by price-matching outsiders is deterred. More formally, the game may be described as follows: RTE cereals provide different attributes relevant to consumers (sweetness, protein content, shape, grain base, vitamin content, fibre content, and crunchiness, for instance). These different attributes define a multi-dimensional space in which cereal brands are positioned. The strategy of the existing firms in the RTE cereal industry is to continually launch new brands to occupy all the cells of the space. There are only two rules for the choice of the position of a new brand: (i) The new brand should be positioned as far away as possible from the position of any other existing brands to avoid price competition and cannibalization of the existing brands of the firm; (ii) The new brand should also be positioned to maximize the space occupied by the brands of the same firm. The brand launches stop when all the cells are occupied by one and only one brand. For simplification, the product map of Figure 5 uses only two dimensions: Sweetness and Fibre content and shows an example of the possible first few launches for two competitive firms A and B.

Moreover, a pattern of rivalry focusing solely on advertising, launching new brands and avoiding price competition seems likely to be self-reinforcing once established. The logic of the pattern follows. The more effectively the established brands are differentiated, the less incentive any seller would have to engage in price competition. The less the price competition among established sellers, the greater the typical price-cost margin, and the greater the

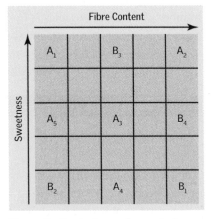

Figure 5 Product map for ready-to-eat-cereals

incentive to advertise. To the extent that advertising outlays resemble fixed costs, increased advertising intensity increases the asymmetry between the positions of potential entrants and established sellers. The latter's brands will be kept on the market as long as variable costs are covered, while an entrant will only launch if it can expect to cover total costs. The greater the difference between variable and total cost, the less attractive aggressive price-cutting entry appears to the new firm (Schmalensee, 1978).

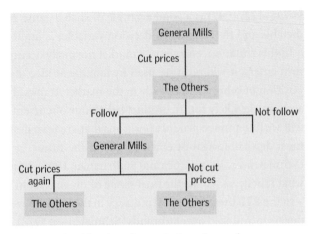

Figure 6 Decision tree for ready-to-eat cereals

This game was profitable for the players, as long as all followed the same rules. However, in April 1994 after a drop in its stock price, General Mills decided to change the rules of the game and announced that it planned to cut $175 million out of its trade promotions and couponing budget, and simultaneously to reduce price. This created a new game similar to the one between Polaroid and Kodak in which players either had to follow the General Mills strategy and reduce prices to maintain market share or continue with the old strategy of brand proliferation. If they decided to cut prices, a destructive price competition may develop like that described earlier (cf. Figure 6) and 'private-label' producers may be forced to exit the industry.

These examples show that game theoretic modelling may be applied to various competitive situations, such as market entry, product positioning and pricing strategy. However, such models are limited to situations where the environment is predictable and where the number of decision variables is limited. When the environment becomes less predictable, other models such as simulation, scenarios or systems are more appropriate.

Source: abstracted from Furrer, O and Thomas, H (2000) 'The rivalry matrix: Understanding rivalry and competitive dynamics', *European Management Journal*, 18, 6, pp. 619–37.

Case Questions

1   Given the analysis of Intel in the prisoner's dilemma matrix, what would you advise Intel to do next? Why?

2   Using Polaroid and Kodak as examples, what are the limitations of using game theoretic models in assessing risk and deciding future strategies? What would you suggest could reduce such limitations?

3   Are scenarios of any more utility than game theoretic models? Assess with reference to Intel, Kodak and the cereal industry.

Further reading and references

Scenarios and scenario-based planning

Peter Schwartz (1991) *The Art of the Long View – Planning for the Future in an Uncertain World* Doubleday 258pp; ISBN 0-385-26731-2, paperback 1996; ISBN 0-385-26732-0)
This is one of the best starting books describing the fundamentals of scenario planning. Peter Schwartz is a futurist and a founder of the *Global Business Network* (GBN) but has also worked at Stanford Research Institute (SRI) and Shell.

Kees van der Heijden (1996) *Scenarios – The Art of Strategic Conversation,* Wiley, 305pp; ISBN 0-471-96639-8)
An excellent book about scenario planning in a business context because it connects to strategy and its practice in a strategic context. The author Kees van der Heijden is one of the founders of GBN and has also a history as head of the Scenario Planning group at Shell.

Gill Ringland (1998) *Scenario Planning – Managing for the Future,* Wiley; 401pp, ISBN 0-471-97790-X
This is mainly focused on providing experiences from a number of scenario planning projects in different companies. Gill Ringland works for ICL and the book reflects scenario projects within ICL, but there are also examples from a number of other projects in other contexts.

Liam Fahey and Robert M. Randall (1998) *Learning from the Future,* Wiley 1998; 446pp; ISBN 0-471-30352-6
This contains a number of articles focusing on different application areas or aspects of scenario planning.

Art Kleiner (1996) *The Age of Heretics,* Doubleday, 414pp; ISBN 0-385-41576-1
This book relates stories about the heretics who challenged the prevailing views at companies like Royal Dutch/Shell. By using scenario planning they saw possible future events which management didn't see at all. Art Kleiner, among other interests, teaches a scenario class focusing on the future for telecommunication infrastructure at New York University.

Wilkinson, Lawrence (1996) 'How to Build Scenarios', *Scenarios: Special Wired Edition,* January, pp. 74–81.

Useful websites

www.library.nijenrode.nl/library/publications/nijrep/1997-01/1997-01.html
Scenarios, strategy and the strategy process
Interesting paper by Kees van der Heijden, a strategic planning veteran from Shell who is also a member of GBN. Scenario planning is treated as a strategic tool that can be used to develop business idea by testing it in several futures and getting a more powerful and more robust strategy.

www2.shell.com
Current Royal Dutch/Shell scenarios and introductory texts
Shell provides both introductory information about scenario planning as well as several downloadable scenarios.

www.innovation.gov.uk/projects/converging_techn/summary/html
Converging Technologies – consequences for the new knowledge-driven economy
A UK government initiative on innovation has produced a number of scenarios on the effects of technology on an economy.

References

Alexander, CB (1996) 'Planning for disaster', *American Gas*, **78**, **2**, 24–7.

Baird, IS and Thomas, H (1990) 'What is risk anyway? Using and measuring risk in strategic management' in Bettis, RA and Thomas, H (eds) *Risk, Strategy and Management*, JAI Press, Greenwich CT, pp. 21–52.

Beck, U (1992) *Risk Society: Towards a New Modernity*, Sage, London.

Fahey, L and Randall, R (1998) *Learning from the Future: Competitive Foresight Scenarios*, West.

Fiegenbaum, A and Thomas, H (1988) 'Attitudes toward risk and the risk-return paradox: prospect theory explanations', *Academy of Management Journal*, **31**, pp. 85–106.

Goodnow, JD and Hansz, JE (1972) 'Environmental Determinants of Overseas Entry Strategies', *Journal of International Business Studies*, **3**, pp. 33–50.

Greening, DW and Johnson, RA (1996) 'Do Managers and strategies matter? A study in crisis', *Journal of Management Studies*, **33**, **1**, pp. 25–51.

Hertz, D and Thomas, H (1983) *Risk Analysis and its Applications*, Wiley, New York.

Hespos, RF and Strassmann, PA (1965) 'Stochastic decision trees for the analysis of investment decisions', *Management Science*, **11**, **10**, pp. 244–59.

Jorian, P (2000) 'Value, risk and control: the call for integration', *The Financial Times*, 16 May.

Kahneman, D and Tversky, A (1973) 'Judgement Under Uncertainty', in Kaufman, GM and Thomas, H (eds) *Modern Decision Analysis*, Penguin: Harmondsworth.

Knight, FH (1921) *Risk, Uncertainty and Profit*, University of Chicago Press, Chicago.

Litvak, IA and Banting, PM (1968) 'A Conceptual Framework for International Business Arrangements', in RL King (ed.) *Marketing and the New Science of Planning*, AMA Fall Conference Proceedings.

Luhmann, N (1993) *Risk: a Sociological Theory*, Aldine de Gruyter, Berlin.

March, JG (1999) *The Pursuit of Organizational Intelligence*, Blackwell, Oxford.

March, JG and Shapira, Z (1999) 'Variable risk preferences and the focus of attention', in JG March (ed.) *The Pursuit of Organizational Intelligence*, Blackwell, Oxford.

Miller, KD (1992) 'Framework for Integrated Risk Management', *Journal of International Business*, Summer, pp. 311–31.

Miller, KD and Bromiley, P (1990) 'Strategic risk and corporate performance: an analysis of alternative risk measures', *Academy of Management Journal*, **39**, pp. 91–122.

Moore, PG and Thomas, H (1976) *The Anatomy of Decisions*, Penguin, Harmondsworth.

Palmer, TB and Wiseman, RM (1999) 'Decoupling risk from income stream uncertainty: a holistic model of risk', *Strategic Management Journal*, **20**, pp. 1037–62.

Perrow, C (1984) *Normal Accidents: Living with High Risk Technologies*, Basic Books, New York.

Schmalansee, R. 1978. '*Entry Deterrence in the Ready to Eat Breakfast Cereal Industry*', *The Rand Journal of Economics*, **9**, pp. 305–327.

Schoemaker, PJH (2002) *Profiting From Uncertainty: Strategies for Succeeding no Matter What the Future Brings*, Free Press, New York.

Singh, JV (1986) 'Performance risk and slack taking in organizational decision making', *Academy of Management Journal*, **29**, pp. 562–85.

Stoner, J (1968) 'Risky and cautious shifts in group decision: the influence of widely held values', *Journal of Experimental Social Psychology*, **4**, pp. 442–59.

Turner, B (1978) *Man-Made Disasters*, Wykeham, London.

Wiseman, RM and Bromiley, P (1996) 'Toward a model of risk in declining organizations: an empirical examination of risk, performance and decline', *Organizational Science*, **7**, pp. 524–43.

Chapter 15

Managing strategic change

Introduction

As de Wit and Meyer (1999) point out, thinking and acting strategically will, of necessity, involve an organization in some degree of strategic change. Such changes can be to structures, processes, technologies, markets, products and services, ownership and so forth. Change processes themselves can also be characterized, for example, as relatively continuous (that is, piecemeal and evolutionary) or discontinuous (that is, dramatic and revolutionary). The story of strategy implementation is also the story of strategic change.

It is obviously important to understand the change process, since no matter how sophisticated strategic thinking is, a poorly managed implementation is likely to result in a more difficult or complex set of strategic changes, or no change at all. This chapter examines change in organizations from the perspectives of strategic management.

Chapter contents

Many management disciplines cover the topic of change, most notably organizational behaviour (OB) and human resource management (HRM), and they do so from very specific perspectives. This chapter will not cover such topics as individuals' reactions to change, stress and coping mechanisms, and best practice in HRM in change management. These areas are the central subject matter of OB and HRM. Here, we will be concerned with:

◆ Analysing and understanding the characteristics and dimensions of change processes.

◆ Their relationship to organizational strategies.

◆ What we know about relatively more and less successful change strategies.

15.1 Levels of change

Change is called strategic (rather than operational) when it involves relatively high-level and pervasive changes to the structures, processes and core businesses of the organization. Such changes are usually novel to the organization in question (although not necessarily novel in themselves). They are changes which set precedents for subsequent strategic decisions made in the organization, and they are difficult to reverse once in motion and tend to be capital hungry (in terms of both human and financial capital). Table 15.1 summarizes one way of viewing change along a scale which moves from status quo to revolutionary change, at the same time distinguishing between strategic and operational changes.

Table 15.1 Levels and degrees of operational and strategic change

Degree of change	Level of change	Characteristics
Status quo	Can be both operational and strategic	No change in current practices. A decision *not* to do something can be strategic as well as operational
Expanded reproduction	Mainly operational	Change involves producing 'more of the same' (for example, goods and services)
Evolutionary transition	Mainly strategic	Sometimes radical changes occur but they do so within the existing parameters of the organization (for example, existing structures or technologies are retained)
Revolutionary transition	Predominantly strategic	Change involves shifting or redefining existing parameters. Structures, processes and/or technologies likely to change

Source: Wilson, 1999: 20.

15.2 **Analysing and understanding strategic change**

Researchers and practitioners in strategic management have all proposed various ways in which we might understand strategic change and, more importantly, which perspectives will yield the most useful results in making changes work successfully. Nutt *et al.* (2000) provide a useful summary of the main approaches taken. They argue that there are five predominant ways to craft a strategy in the face of strategic change issues. These are:

- Analytical approaches
- Stakeholder approaches
- Adaptive approaches
- Gap analyses
- Systems-based analysis of strategic 'tensions'

In brief, *analytical approaches* examine the strategic portfolio of the organization (services and products) to see how well its portfolio of activities fits with its commitment to find resources to change the mix to improve performance. Strategic change, therefore, is a constant process of aligning and shifting the mix of products and services, clients, funding sources, skills and image (for example, brand strength).

Stakeholder approaches argue that strategies are crafted in line with those stakeholders who are in a position to be influential over strategic decision making or who can place heavy demands on the organization. Thus, strategic changes are designed to satisfy stakeholder interests.

Adaptive approaches take the view that strategic change is more a process of alignment of an organization's activities, structures and cultures with the characteristics of the external operating environment it faces. Classic contingency studies of organizations fit into this category (for example, the nostrum that decentralized structures out-perform centralized structures in turbulent environments).

Gap analyses focus on assessing the current core competences of the organization and seeing where there are 'gaps' in competences to provide a changed future portfolio of products and services. This current versus future thinking, and the requirements in terms of organizational resources (human and financial), is the essence of gap analysis.

The **strategic tensions** approach attempts to move beyond position-based bargaining (as may characterize the stakeholder perspective, for example) and attempts to see their wider interests in the context of the organization. Such a perspective also accords with that taken by Pettigrew and Whipp (1991) who argue that change can only be understood in terms of its content (what the change is about); its processes (how organizations craft strategies to get from state *a* to state *b*; and its context (the wider environment of infrastructure, culture, sector, nation etc.). This approach relies on managers being able to identify as accurately as possible the various tensions in the wider system. Easy to say, but difficult to do!

However, the approach argues that even a partial identification of wider tensions is better than a fuller analysis of more focused and local issues (but which ignore context).

Examples of some common strategic tensions are illustrated in Table 15.2.

Nutt *et al.* (2000) argue that the systemic tensions perspective gives a better chance of success in crafting change strategies than any of the other approaches. They cite examples from the public and private sectors, showing that context (in the organization or the wider system) is crucial for facilitating win–win situations among competing interests. Like Pettigrew and Whipp (1991), Nutt and his colleagues argue that a co-operative organizational culture (context) will create commitment and support for actions to be taken, since competing interests will always see something of value to them in the change.

Practical steps for managers crafting such change strategies would be to 'widen the arena' of the issues discussed (and hence of the change process). One way of achieving this is to communicate both the *how* and the *why* of change. Various techniques can be used for this,

Table 15.2 Examples of strategic tensions and their main characteristics

Examples of strategic tensions	Characterized by
Equity–Equity	Clashes between different interests (e.g. between clients, suppliers) all of whom call for a different set of actions to be taken. The key question is whose interests will be served?
Transition–Transition	Where several competing plans for what should change are in conflict. The usual characteristic of these tensions is where there are disputes over diagnostics (that is, 'my data is better than yours' arguments). The result is having to choose between several plans for change.
Preservation–Preservation	Difficulties in maintaining the status quo when it is unclear what are the organization's core values and strategic direction. Characterized by debates about what this organization *should* be doing and what is *appropriate*.
Preservation–Innovation	Where there are disputes over anticipated pay-offs from strategic changes. The tensions are about who gets what out of the change, once implemented. The key danger here is that of inertia (that is nothing happens other than conflict).
Expansion–Contraction	Where departments (for example) are expected to produce more with fewer resources. This can happen to organizations, to sectors and to national economies.
Innovation–Tradition	The tension here is between values. There are those who argue that current practices are to be preserved and that what is being proposed violates central norms and values in the organization.
Change–Ethics	Similar to the above, but the urgency is to try to reconcile changes with ethical considerations such as commitment to environmental principles or to humanizing the workplace.

Source: adapted from Nutt *et al.* (2000) and Wilson (1999).

the most popular being a simple laddering exercise. At the bottom of the ladder are placed the *how* factors of strategies and then in logical ascending order the *why* factors are listed. A simple example of such a ladder is given in Figure 15.1.

In Figure 15.1, the objective of the change is to improve the standard and provision of healthcare over all the regions of a country. The ladder then begins at the bottom with three sets of actions (the how factors) and then ascends through a series of why factors to complete the loop, since the last why factor very closely resembles the first objective.

The reason for using the laddering technique is to create a context in which the likelihood of 'buy-in' to the change is increased. Buy-in is a much misunderstood idea. Many senior managers ask how they can achieve 'buy-in' as if there were some kind of magic formula which they could apply to the organization after the fact, to win the hearts

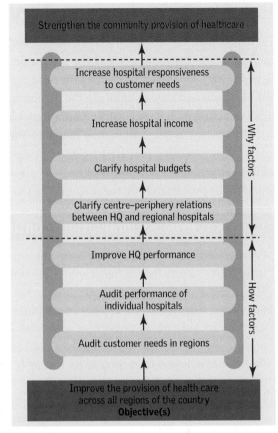

Figure 15.1 An example of a strategic outcome ladder

and minds of all individuals. The problem is that strategic changes are about meanings and interpretations, not simply process maps; and meaning grows from the opportunity to engage at early stages in the formulation and discussion processes. Newsletters, corporate social events, prizes and vision statements communicate facts and can provide a route map of the change, but they can never communicate behaviours or help individuals make sense of what is happening in the change process. Therefore, even a broad understanding of the wider context is only part of the answer to implementing change. We also have to understand the role of individuals in the process, both change initiators and those who are recipients of the process and the outcome. A contextual assessment of what happens when strategy meets organization has been depicted in Chapter 2 of this book. In the current chapter, we examine some specific issues of what happens when strategic changes happen in an organization. We will consider both the role and influence of organization as well as the impact and influence of individuals. First, we examine the change–organization interrelationships

15.3 **Strategic change and organization**

The basic question which surrounds **change and organization** is in the tension between continuity and discontinuity and the size, scale and scope of the change (Greiner 1972; Gersick 1991). **Continuous change** assumes a gradual evolution of changes which emanate out of the current state of affairs in the organization. Change is thus incremental, taken in small steps and each change effort continuously builds upon the previous phase of change activity. Strategy implementation is therefore concerned with ensuring that current strategies 'fit' with existing practice by either not deviating too far from the existing script, or adding incrementally to what is already in place. Key examples of this approach can be found in the process improvement approaches in manufacturing industries.

Case box: **Process innovation: continuous change in Airbus UK**

Process innovation is a way of stealing a march on rivals by firms getting better at what they do and the way they do things – their practices and processes. Beginning in Japan in the 1950s, these process improvements have a lot of empirical evidence to back them up. Continuous improvements in the ways organisations manufacture products (or provide services) pay off in terms of competitive advantage. For example, in 2004, Airbus UK boosted productivity in wing assembly by 25% and increased product quality by 40% in six months. All this was achieved by looking at the assembly process and continually refining it over a period of months. It became obvious that there had to be a shift from a mass production mindset (and technologies) to a lean production mindset and technologies. Employees take a much bigger role in production and assembly – for which they need different mental as well as physical equipment. Managers are required to stop managing at one remove and engage with the shop floor or the design team, wherever the issues appear. The series of changes which have led to this shift of emphasis from machinery to people has been smooth and continuous, including revision of pay and administrative systems. Continuous change seems to have paid off at least in the case of Airbus UK.

Source: S. Caulkin, 'Lean times for innovation', *The Observer*, 23 May 2004.

We deal in more depth with process and quality issues later in this book (Part 5) but the Airbus example is a typical one of continuous and incremental change to production methods which, in turn, have led to quite significant changes in organizational design and practices. This model of continuous change embraces a business model which goes far beyond manufacturing improvements. Its philosophy is that only by ensuring continuity in strategic changes will organizations be able to realize their strategies. As de Wit and Meyer (1999: 144) point out, the tortoise of Aesop's fable keeps moving slowly, but surely and continuously. It wins the race. The hare, on the other hand, shows off its ability to sprint and take great leaps forward, but eventually loses the race. Diligent tortoises, it seems, win the day. Endurance, persistence and small, but significant, improvements to the ways in which we organize help ensure survival and growth for firms.

Advocates of continuous change cluster around three basic principles:

- Continuous improvement
- Continuous learning
- Constant adaptation to changing conditions

Continuous improvement means that all individuals in an organization should always be driven to change, which is rooted in their dissatisfaction with the status quo. This attitude needs to be constructive so that changes can be suggested, designed and put in place. The overall philosophy is that things can always be done better (Stacey 1993).

Continuous learning means that all individuals in an organization should continually update or increase their knowledge base. This means acquiring new knowledge and techniques as well as acquiring knowledge sufficient for decision makers to say 'no' to what might seem reasonable proposals at first sight and to be able to challenge taken-for-granted behaviours and attitudes in the organization. Crises need to be avoided as far as possible since they inhibit longer-term thinking and promote short-term reactions and decisions (Senge 1990).

Constant adaptation to changing conditions means that organizational design must be such that it avoids becoming inflexible and hence a barrier to further change. Flexible structures and systems, coupled with open and change-receptive cultures, provide sufficient motivation, security and curiosity for individuals to tolerate the inevitable uncertainty and insecurity associated with change (Kagono *et al.* 1985).

On the other hand, many scholars and practitioners argue that continuous change is a false friend in terms of trying to plan change (intention) and in terms of accurately describing what happens in practice. This is the argument for understanding change as a *discontinuous* process. The basic principles of discontinuity derive from the maxim that both organizations and individuals resist change. This is not resistance for its own sake but is a function of the organizing process whereby most organizations develop routines over time (accepted and settled ways of working) and individuals feel comfortable in such rather predictable structures. Indeed, this is one of the ways that can bring about the demise of many organizations (Miller 1990). Success can breed the seeds of its own destruction since it further embeds and reinforces routines and practices in organizations which run deep and are resistant to change.

Organizations are very effective at creating stabilities which act as strong barriers to change. These stabilities can be found in formal and informal systems, standard operating procedures, the distribution of power and the strong ties of organizational culture. They can also be found in factors such as long-term contracts and commitments, fixed investments and inflexible financial and accounting procedures (Arthur 1996; Ghemawat 1991).

So, long terms of stability occur in organizations, held together by these multi-ingredients of the corporate glue. If significant change is to happen then crises (real or constructed) need to be created. The organization becomes jolted into action. This kick-start effect is known as the punctuated equilibrium view of change (Gersick 1991). Change happens in bursts of activity (followed by further periods of consolidation). These discontinuities can be analysed at different levels of analysis. At the individual level, reluctance to change and settled ways of doing things makes individuals predisposed to maintain the status quo and only embark upon change when things become too tough to remain as they are. Groups (social or work) will also exhibit the same behaviours. Organizations will have structural and cultural – institutional – arrangements which act as barriers to change unless significant and threatening events spur action. Industries, too, will exhibit inertia until a crisis point means the equilibrium is punctured and radical change occurs. The airline industry is a good example of **discontinuous change** at this level of analysis.

Case box: Airlines in crisis: forcing the pace of change

Of the top eight US airlines, only two are making profits and the remaining six are making sizeable losses (at least two are under bankruptcy protection from their creditors). Things are going to have to change radically in the industry. The two profitable airlines (JetBlue and Southwest) are low-cost carriers just like many of the internet-based airlines which service European destinations (e.g. easyJet, Ryanair and Thompson). The challenge of low-cost carriers and greater price transparency via the internet has created a crisis among full-cost airlines.

Frederick Reid, President of Delta Airlines, suggests that this environmental shock to the

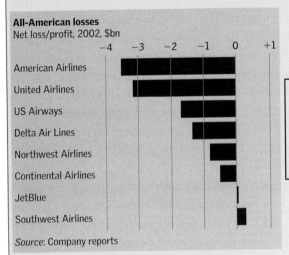

All-American losses
Net loss/profit, 2002, $bn

American Airlines	
United Airlines	
US Airways	
Delta Air Lines	
Northwest Airlines	
Continental Airlines	
JetBlue	
Southwest Airlines	

Source: Company reports

These huge losses act as 'crisis' trigger, points for strategic change in the mainstream carrier industry. These organizations will have to change both their business model the ways in which they organize their systems, structure, processes and people.

Source of data: OECD.

industry is like the meteor which struck Earth and created a winter which the planet's then rulers (the dinosaurs) could not survive. He paints a picture of full-cost airlines getting fat on the high returns they could extract from business travellers, especially those who were looking for last-minute and flexible tickets. Those days have gone forever. The metaphorical meteor has struck this industry in the form of travellers being able to surf the net for cheap unsold seats. The only ways for mainstream airlines to survive are to cut costs and to raise productivity to a level where they can compete with the profitable low-cost carriers.

This is true discontinuous change. For the first time, mainstream airlines have been forced into making major changes (the 1980s shakeout in the industry which saw the demise of PanAm, TWA and Eastern Airlines was just that a shakeout which did not significantly see a change in the structure of the industry or the firms in it). Some of the changes now required may prove to be a little too difficult to achieve. For example, most need to reduce costs by over 50 per cent per seat. And they need to cut their workforce, but a strongly unionized organization (especially in the USA) could make this very difficult. For example, American Airlines is losing around $5 million per day which is covered by borrowing. At the same time, it needs to cut costs by $4 billion. It has already introduced leaner flight operations and ticketing has been streamlined. Simplifying the fleet (from 12 types of aircraft to 5 types) and using fewer gates has brought some benefits but these are a drop in the ocean in comparison to what is needed for this airline (and the other mainstream carriers) to survive.

Now the airlines need to cut labour costs. This means renegotiating labour contracts to try to save at least $1.8 billion off the wage bill in the short term. Unions will resist if past form is anything to go by. If many mainstream airlines fail to persuade staff to take a pay cut in order to keep their jobs, bankruptcy looks the only option.

Discontinuous change can also occur as a result of perhaps risky, rash or ill-informed decisions which can trigger a series of unplanned and unanticipated events (see also Chapter 13). These strategic decisions can lead the organization into a series of bad moves which, in the worst case, can seal the demise of the firm. Another example from the airline industry (European) illustrates this process clearly (*see* the Sabena case box).

Case box: **Bankruptcy at Sabena**

This Belgian airline Sabena became bankrupt in 2001. There were many explanations for the bankruptcy, but a report to the Belgian government in 2003 has revealed that the organization undertook a series of key strategic decisions which together led to Sabena's demise. The final of these 'fateful' decisions was made when McKinsey were called in to advise Sabena on future strategy. Just as they had with Swissair (which controlled Sabena), McKinsey recommended the airline embark upon a high-risk growth strategy. Swissair went bankrupt trying to follow the same strategy in 2001.

McKinsey's strategy for growth, however, was based on some flimsy foundations in the airline. In 1996, Sabena's then Swiss boss, Paul Reutlinger, took a series of strategic decisions which embarked Sabena upon a era of deal making with Virgin Express (part of the Branson airlines). The first of these was a one-year deal on Sabena's London–Brussels route. Virgin's planes and crew flew the route using Sabena's Heathrow slots. Sabena payed Virgin Express for 85 seats whether or not they were filled. This decision was quite normal in the airline industry and was a way of reducing competition. However, Reutlinger followed up this decision with another two similar deals signed later the same day (29 October 1996). These were eight-year deals with Virgin for flights to Rome and Barcelona. During these decisions, the London–Brussels deal was also extended from one to eight years. These deals became a huge cash drain in Sabena, costing over 30 million euros a year. Virgin were kept well afloat financially by these deals while Sabena haemorrhaged. Moreover, over 80 per cent of passenger complaints to Sabena originated in these Virgin flights. In March 1997, Reutlinger sold Sabena's slots at Heathrow for $8 million to Virgin Atlantic Airways. The report to the Belgian government alleges that these decisions were taken without full consultation and ratification by the Sabena board. When McKinsey was called in and recommended a strategy of growth, the strategy was in effect built upon a financial house of cards. It failed and the airline went bankrupt.

The Sabena example vividly illustrates discontinuous changes which were prompted by the strategic decisions of one individual (or a small groups of individuals) and the perhaps misplaced external advice from McKinsey to embark upon a high-risk growth strategy, which proved fatal to both Swissair and Sabena.

In addition to examining the continuity or discontinuity of change processes, the size, scale and scope of change relates both to organization and to the likelihood of success in implementing the change. There is relatively little empirical work in these areas, but work by Hannan, Polos and Carroll (2003) uncovered some revealing (if mathematically complex) relationships. Using the collapse of Barings Brothers (a British Bank) in 1995 as an example, these authors argue that reorganization in the bank had created an infrastructure (organizational architecture) which allowed Nicholas Leeson (the so-called 'rogue trader') to operate in a way which sealed the demise of the bank. Without letting Leeson off the hook for rogue trading activities, these authors explain that the organizational conditions under which these activities took place allowed his actions to go undetected. In a different firm with a different architecture, Leeson would have been identified early on in the process and prevented from trading.

In brief, the context of Barings allowed a number of activities to take place which amounted to significant changes in its size, scale, scope and eventual disaster for the organization. According to Hannan, Polos and Carroll (2003: 428):

- The structure of the organization was porous with no clear lines of responsibility and accountability. This allowed Leeson to operate undetected for at least two years.

- Confusion of the reporting lines in the organization could be traced to the recent reorganization of the bank.

- The matrix structure which resulted from the reorganization failed to work in practice. It was never clear who Leeson's product managers were (a common problem of ambiguous responsibility in matrix structures) and they had little knowledge of his trading activities.

- Leeson was in charge of both the front and back office functions of the bank and was therefore in a position to override any internal controls.

- The organizational sub-units (departments) which dealt with Leeson's activities were very poor at communicating with one another and this allowed Leeson to trade in the now infamous account 88888, of which senior managers of the Baring Group claimed they had no knowledge.

The conclusion drawn from the above example is that changes can go badly wrong when organizations change their architectures. The new design of the organization can allow large changes to sweep through the organization, with often few or no controls to keep them in check. These authors derive two concepts from their mathematical model. These are:

- **Opacity:** low opacity occurs when there is limited foresight about how different units in the organization are interconnected and work together. The lower the opacity, the higher the likelihood of changes becoming out of control and beyond the capacity of the organization to deal with them when things go wrong.

- **Asperity:** high asperity indicates an organizational culture (see Chapter 2) which will not readily accept changes and which will cling to the 'old' ways of working. The higher the asperity, the greater the likelihood that changes will fail.

Key explanations for failure lie in the scale and scope aspects of change processes. For example, high opacity leads to individuals underestimating the time a reorganization will take as well as the associated costs of change, thereby prompting them to undertake changes with adverse consequences. Put simply, complex, opaque organizations which have a high level of cultural asperity will tend to get themselves into trouble by implementing changes that cost far more than was foreseen. In the worst cases, these can be costs that cannot be covered by whatever new organizational form or circumstances the change has brought about. Like Barings, the organization may well go bankrupt.

The Barings and the Sabena examples also illustrate the impact one person, or a small group, can have on the fortunes of an organization and the speed with which change (mostly discontinuous) can occur. We examine these aspects of change in the next section.

15.4 Change, individuals and strategic leadership

Popular literature (both management and non-management) is replete with the contribution that individuals can make to the success (or otherwise) of the processes and outcomes of change. Much of the literature focuses on the contribution of individuals through the process of leadership, although a sizeable proportion of work also examines the contribution of, for example, creative or innovative individuals to drive change in organizations. To cover the field of leadership is beyond the scope of this chapter. Instead, we focus on what has become termed 'strategic leadership' (Senge 1990). This term describes how individuals may lead changes in ways which are non-individualistic and are not necessarily related to the charisma or power of the individual concerned. Strategic leadership is concerned with teaching, learning, stewardship and the ability to challenge prevailing modes of thought in the organization.

Whatever their position in the organizational hierarchy, strategic leaders are strongly associated with the strategic changes which occur in their organizations. In some cases this may mean that other individuals (who may be more senior in the hierarchy) defer to these strategic leaders since their abilities or their reputation ensures they have credibility and support. In other cases, strategic leadership may be more systemically rooted. For example, the founders of a family firm or the owners of a small business will almost certainly assume a strategic leadership role since they are the 'owners' of the business idea as well as the business philosophy. Another way in which strategic leadership may be systemically rooted is through organizational history. For example, an individual chief executive may have implemented very successful strategies in the past, or may have saved the company from decline. Such a history endows this individual with a position of strategic leadership since they embody, or personify, the organization, its development and its success.

Some organizations which rely on individual leaders to drive strategic changes have difficulty in sustaining this process through time. In particular, family firms seem to suffer from this lack of continuity. The Motorola example below gives an illustration of this problem (*see* case box).

Case box: **Strategic change and leadership at Motorola**

In September 2003, Christopher Galvin, the grandson of Robert Galvin, founder of Motorola, resigned as Chair of Motorola, Christopher Galvin had been Chair since 1997. Investors and the City were relieved at his resignation. He had failed to implement much needed changes in the organization, which had been making losses in its mobile phone business.

The problems started with Robert Galvin, who invested very heavily in the ill-fated Iridium satellite mobile phone. Motorola also missed the technology shift from analogue to digital with Nokia leading the competitive charge. A radical change was needed, but Christopher Galvin did not provide it. Instead, he continued with business as usual. Motorola's share of the mobile phone market (40 per cent of its revenue) continued to fall. Galvin laid off 56,000 employees. He also closed a number of plants. Revenue continued to fall.

For almost four years the firm continued to fail, with a share price fall to match (a high of $60 in 2000 and an all-time low of $8 in 2003). In 2000, things began to change. The board, previously filled with Galvin family acolytes, was restocked with outsiders. These were influential individuals from successful companies. They included Indra Nooyi (from Pepsico), Douglas Warner (JP Morgan Chase) and John Pepper (Procter & Gamble). These directors had none of the family affiliation which Galvin embodied. They are able to seek a new successor for Christopher Galvin as well as make decisions which a family member would have found difficult if not impossible to make. For example, a likely strategy is to sell off some of Motorola's businesses (such as wireless infrastructure and semiconductors). One of the first suggestions of the new directors was to talk to Siemens about the possibility of exchanging the wireless business for Siemens' mobile phone business, but Galvin still at the helm prevented this deal progressing. Now he has gone, the board can explore new and perhaps radical directions for Motorola.

As the Motorola example illustrates, some powerful individuals can both drive change and act as effective barriers to further change. The offspring of founding fathers are prime examples of individual leadership that can prevent an organization thinking and acting strategically and effecting change.

Just as there are polarized views on whether or not strategy is planned or emerges as a pattern in a stream of decisions, strategic leadership can be viewed from the same, mutually exclusive perspectives. Assuming that strategic leadership is planned means that we view leaders as:

- Predominantly people who plan a path forward by thinking analytically.

- Predominantly people who bring past experience to bear on the present situation (the change worked successfully last time, so it should work again in the new situation).

- Appointable chiefly through their demonstrable analytical ability and foresight and their ability to think systematically through a problem and come up with an implementation plan.

On the other hand, we may take the position that strategic leadership emerges in organizations rather than it being planned. This perspective means we would view strategic leadership as:

♦ Less associated with individuals in key positions, but something which emerges from new and sometimes competing ideas from all parts of the organization. Capturing such ideas is a key activity and it may be that this is the key role of individual leaders.

♦ A role in which highly intuitive individuals who have demonstrable vision should be favoured in any appointment process. These individuals can see what others cannot and are happy to embrace new ways of seeing the organization or undertake new ways of working.

The small amount of empirical evidence so far produced on this topic suggests that both approaches can bring performance benefits and can enhance change processes. Peters and Waterman (1982) argued that strategic leadership was about an individual being able to take a highly abstract and perhaps intuitive view as well as being able to handle the operational detail involved in change implementation. Leavy and Wilson (1994) demonstrated how these abilities may be time dependent. In some circumstances, change requires hands-on detail; in others, change requires abstract and perhaps lateral thinking, leaving the processes of implementation to others in the organization. Debates as to whether any of the above approaches are connected to the personality of individual leaders are many, but inconclusive. We just do not know whether or not personality makes a key difference to a leader's ability to handle or manage change (*see* Farkas and Wetlaufer 1996).

15.4.1 Creative individuals and change

Once we shift our focus from key 'leadership' positions in an organization, we may see that individuals who can see beyond the self-evident, and often in quite creative ways, can be the drivers of organizational change wherever they are in the organizational hierarchy. For example, writers and artists (such as Baudelaire or Picasso) challenged established beliefs with new ideas, which in turn transformed our understanding and appreciation of art and literature. Political leaders (such as Gandhi or Luther) were individuals who were also able to effect such transformations. In business organizations, people such as Sloan, Carnegie, Packard and Barnevik (ABB) are commonly cited as those who questioned received wisdom about organizational designs and manufacturing procedures. They said the unsayable and thought the unthinkable.

In change strategies, the temptation is to seek individuals who have this special insight and foresight. However, they are remarkably rare. As March (1999: 226) reminds us:

most current leaders seem to be competent and analytical rather than imaginative and visionary … they seek to refine the establishment rather than challenge or transform it.

This may be a product of modern times and organization, or it may simply be that we have learned to distrust creativity alone as a guide for strategic change.

The difference between visionary genius and delusional madness is much clearer in history books than in experience.

The problem lies in identifying which novel ideas will turn out to be successful and which will turn out to be little more than crackpot visions. The ratio of successful creative ideas (in practice) to ones which turn out unsuccessful is not good. Most new ideas will not pay-off, so we usually retreat into what is knowable, familiar and do-able. The paradox here is that without a heavy reliance on conventional thinking, highly creative leadership is in more danger of failing than it is in succeeding.

At the same time, organizations need to have stimuli which prevent ossification and encourage new ideas and new ways of thinking and acting strategically. Such leadership (which can come from any part of the organization, not just senior executives) is commonly termed 'transformational' in the management literature. Such leadership seems to centre upon:

♦ Successfully coping with and developing the intellectual challenge of new ideas (for example, a new or unique competitive position in an evolving environment). Many 'dot.com' companies are founded on such expertise and yet many fail because individuals cannot successfully continue to differentiate their companies from other dot.coms.

♦ Meeting the social and political challenges of keeping dialogue and communication going when different stakeholders view the same world through very different lenses.

♦ Having a design in mind which will align the activities, structures and processes in organizations with the strategic intentions. This involves being able to synthesize a great many ideas which may come from all parts of the organization.

♦ Being able to live with the results of the change in terms of both ethics and performance.

Such a list of factors is a tall order. Individuals are notoriously poor at achieving even one of the above factors, never mind all of them. In relation to strategic management, we can identify a number of reasons why this is so.

Managing change by individual foresight is only possible if environmental signals are seen clearly and in time to act. This is a conundrum which has beset organizations from the very beginning. As Arie de Geus, strategy analyst with Shell, pointed out:

You cannot see what your mind has not experienced before.

> ## Case box: **Mind traps: locked in our own worlds of experience**
>
> We are all familiar with the example of explorers who stumble upon a tribe of natives isolated from the outside world. Their chief is highly intelligent and has a rich and deep understanding of the world from the tribe's perspective. The explorers begin to explain the modern world. They take the chief to a large city and show him what is going on. He is exposed to thousands of signals from a new environment. However, when the explorers ask him what he has learned, he mentions only one thing. He has seen a market trader pushing a cart full of vegetables, more vegetables than he has ever seen before. This is what he wants to bring back to the tribe from his experiences, more vegetables. All other signals had been discarded as irrelevant to the chief's needs!

Individuals with different backgrounds pick up different signals. Yet even long-standing and highly experienced companies miss important and relevant signals. Why?

One explanation lies in the ways in which individuals relate to knowledge and the future independently of their prior experience. We are all familiar with the adage that experienced managers utilize more knowledge from the past than the present and future. The path, looking backward, is relatively clear. Looking forward, the path is full of uncertainty and ambiguity. However, even in looking forward, strategists can become locked into what de Geus terms the 'memory of the future'.

He argues that managers are constantly looking at potential futures and making plans and programmes for these futures. These plans become organized in an almost sequential way so that they create time paths into the future. The variable nature of this activity lies only in how many alternative paths are created (de Geus argues that this is dependent upon how healthy is the brain, with more healthy brains seeing more alternative time paths). However, all brains store and code these alternative future paths and commit them to memory. Paradoxically, therefore, strategists can create a memory of the future! The implication of this way of thinking is that individuals will tend to pick up only those signals which are relevant to a future they have already worked out. The rest are likely to be missed.

15.4.2 Subjectivity: emotion and organizational change

An emerging perspective on individuals, organizations and change is that strategic change is a complicated and highly emotional psycho-social drama (O'Donnell 2000). The ability to trust your own and others' emotions is argued to be at least as important as viewing intelligence or creativity as a set of cognitive attributes which a person 'has'. The ability to be aware of one's own mental processes lies at the heart of understanding change as an emotional activity. It is key to understanding change as a *subjective* phenomenon (Sparrow 2000). This ability has become known as **emotional intelligence**. It is argued that managers who display emotional intelligence are able to use meta-abilities or meta-cognitions to understand both how they act and how their actions are interpreted by others, and they are able to develop better information networks, generate higher levels of trust and have greater levels influence in implementing change. Although much work on emotional intelligence has been conducted outside formal work organizations, its attributes can easily be seen. According to Sparrow (2000: 26), emotional intelligence:

◆ Emphasizes pre-conscious thought and shares many common neurological processes with creativity and intuition.

◆ Is a strong source of energy (feelings and personal drive) which can sustain individuals through a change process and can guide individuals to see unexpected or previously unseen possibilities.

◆ Helps individuals cope with change since it emphasizes self-awareness, empathy, personal style and communications.

A key difficulty is one of assessing or measuring emotional intelligence. Many of its reflections (such as high levels of trust or effective communication and empathy with opposing viewpoints) are best assessed through the eyes of others (Steiner 1997). Dulewicz and Herbert (1998) assessed emotional intelligence as:

◆ Sensitivity

◆ Resilience

◆ Influence and adaptability

◆ Decisiveness and adaptability

◆ Energy and leadership

They found that managerial advancement was positively related to the 'possession' of emotional intelligence (36 per cent of managerial advancements could be traced to emotional intelligence). This finding should be put in the context of other findings from the same study: 27 per cent of promotions could be traced to rational and intellectual analysis (such as judgement, planning and organizing) and only 16 per cent to management process effectiveness (such as business sense, initiative and independence). Although we are not yet at a stage where we can clearly demarcate emotional intelligence as a valid construct with a set of valid measures, it nevertheless seems to have a beneficial influence both on smoothing change processes and on advancing the careers of managers who display higher levels of it.

Emotional intelligence would also seem to be vital to underpinning Beer and Eisenstat's (1996) principles of the relatively more successful implementation of strategic change:

◆ Change should be systemic: the focus of the change should accommodate and recognize the complex system that is the organization. Such factors include strategy, structure, behaviours, analysis and emotions.

◆ Change should allow the discussion of barriers: people cannot develop realistic and implementable plans for change unless all impediments are taken into account.

◆ Change should involve a partnership between all stakeholders in the process.

Argyris (1992) suggests that individuals mostly operate on the basis of what he terms 'defensive routines' and hence never engage with the emotional desiderata listed above. He suggests individuals:

1 Bypass embarrassment or threat wherever possible.

2 Act as if they were not bypassing them.

3 Refuse to discuss bypassing behaviour or actions as above.

4 Don't discuss the undiscussability of the undiscussable.

It remains to be seen whether or not emotional intelligence develops into a valid construct and stops being potentially perceived of as a yet another management fad and fashion. Nevertheless, Argyris's four principles, above, apply to virtually all change processes and can act as significant barriers to the implementation of strategic change.

15.4.3 Using outsiders to implement change

The 'external' aspects of change are rather less well covered in the literature than the 'internal' features of structures, cultures and individuals. Outsiders can take a number of forms. They can include, for example, bringing in a new chief executive from a related industry where he or she has had demonstrable success. Or, a significant influx of new managers to an organization (especially over a short time period) can also help break down high asperity cultures (strong cultures which are change resistant). The old guard can be swept away effectively by these newcomers. Taking a stakeholder perspective, there are likely to be a large number of strong influences from outside the organization which have an impact on the change process. These can include suppliers, customers, investors and government agencies.

By far the most obvious of external **change agents**, however, are management consultants. The role of the vast majority of consultants (both individual consultants and consultancy firms) is that of providing expert advice. It is hardly surprising, therefore, that the majority of large consulting firms (e.g. McKinsey, PricewaterhouseCoopers) become involved with the execution of strategic changes in organizations. These processes are complex, take time and (perhaps cynically) can create the opportunity for new or continuing relationships between consultant and organization.

Different consulting firms become involved in different phases of the change process. For example, McKinsey have a reputation as being excellent at the analytical and planning phases of strategic change, but are rather less well involved in the implementation phases (putting idea into practice). KPMG are the reverse. These consultancies, offshoots of audit practice, are centrally involved in the performance aspects of implementation (such as standardized solutions for cost reduction, or the application of programmatic 'solutions' to change such as business process re-engineering). Technical and functional expertise (for example, human resource management) can be found in consulting firms such as Hay or PA Consulting. Given the longevity of change as an organizational problem, some consulting firms (such as Cap Gemini) have specialized in producing customized change models (such as the 'transformation' model of Gemini) and these have become major products in their own right. The Gemini model is described briefly in the case box below.

Case box: The Gemini model of corporate transformation

The high failure rate of business process re-engineering (BPR) projects has led to the development of a more subtle approach which has been called a biological model of corporate transformation, identifying the corporation as essentially an organic evolving entity. The model consists of four broad categories of activity leading to transformation and, as developed by Gemini Consulting, corporate transformation is defined as 'the orchestrated redesign of the genetic architecture of the corporation, achieved by working simultaneously – although at different speeds – along the four dimensions of Reframing, Restructuring, Revitalisation and Renewal'. These four dimensions are seen as a biological process as follows:

♦ *Reframing* is seen as shifting the company's perception of what it is and what it can achieve and is designed to open the corporation's mindset and allow it to refocus.

♦ *Restructuring* deals with the body of the corporation and addresses competitive fitness. This activity is most akin to the BPR approach and involves similar techniques.

♦ *Revitalization* endeavours to link the revised corporate body to its environment, and is considered to be the factor which most clearly differentiates transformation from the harshness perceived of re-engineering. The intention is not to obliterate activities but, rather, to change them positively to encourage revitalized performance.

♦ *Renewal* is concerned with the 'people' side of transformation and with the spirit of the company. It is concerned with investment in skills and purpose to allow the company to self-regenerate with new confidence and enthusiasm rather than the often morale-sapping impact of re-engineering projects, which are a major cause of failure. This activity is perhaps the most difficult to achieve, and is seen by many critics of re-engineering change to be the point at which many consultants, brought in as change agents, leave their clients.

Gemini believes that 12 corporate 'chromosomes' comprise the biocorporate genome, three for each of the four Rs. While each chromosome can be considered independently they are all integrated into a total system. The chief executive officer and the executive leadership are seen as the genetic architects of the corporation and are thus not expected to be involved in operational detail.

The reframing chromosomes

1 *Achieve mobilization.* This activity is the process of bringing together the mental energy required to initiate the transformation process, and involves moving motivation and commitment from the individual to the team and ultimately to the total corporation.

2 *Create the vision.* The development of a corporate vision is essential to provide a shared mental framework which stretches the future dimensions of the corporation and in human terms provides a common sense of purpose which people can identify with. The role of the CEO in establishing such a vision is crucial.

3 *Building a measurement system.* Once the corporation is mobilized and provided with a vision, new measurement systems which allow management to monitor progress towards the future will usually be required. While often quantified, such measures will usually emphasize the strategic progress rather than the financial history. In human terms, the system should also create an identifiable sense of commitment; *see* balanced scorecard.

The restructuring chromosomes

4 *Construct an economic model.* This involves the systematic top-down disaggregation of a corporation in financial terms from shareholder value-based planning to activity-based costing and service level assessment. It provides a detailed view of how and where value is created or cost allowed in the bio-analogy of the cardiovascular system for resources to be deployed where they are needed, and redistributed from where they are not needed.

5 *Align the physical infrastructure.* This element is analogous to the corporate skeletal system and consists of the appropriate alignment of the resources of the corporation's assets, such as plants, warehouses, transportation, equipment and the like. While these are relatively fixed, there is also a need for continuous monitoring and, on occasion, change as when a bone is fractured, to allow for strategic healing.

6 *Redesign the work architecture.* The work of the corporation is achieved via a complex network of processes which is identified as the work architecture. These need to be correctly configured and aligned and this process can be linked to re-engineering.

The revitalization systems

7 *Achieve a market focus.* To Gemini, revitalization implies growth. To achieve this, customer focus provides the starting point, as developing new and perhaps undiscovered benefits that the corporation can offer to its customers leads to business growth. For the corporation, market focus provides the senses in the biological analogy.

8 *Invent new business.* Growth can also occur as the result of the development of new businesses. These can emerge from the cross-fertilization of capabilities from within the corporation or by the introduction of activities from outside via mergers and acquisitions,

strategic alliances, joint ventures and the like. The biological analogy of this concept can be seen as the reproductive system.

9 *Change the rules through information technology.* The strategic use of information technology can produce new ways to compete by redefining the rules of the game in many traditional industries. Biologically, the use of such technology is analogous to the nervous system.

The renewal systems

10 *Create a reward structure.* An appropriate reward structure is seen as a major motivating force on human behaviour. When the motivation system is wrongly aligned with desired behaviour it can also act as a serious demotivator and encourage undesired behaviour.

11 *Build individual learning.* Corporate transformation can only successfully take place when the skills and learning of many individuals are also transformed. Individual learning promotes self-actualization of the people who constitute the corporation.

12 *Develop the Organization.* Corporations are seen as needing to organize for continuous learning, enabling them to constantly adapt to an ever-changing environment in which the pace of change is often accelerating. Organizational development thus allows the corporation to evolve and fosters a sense of community among individuals.

Conclusion

The corporate transformation process has been applied in many corporations around the world. Such transformations often involve modifying the behaviour of many thousands of people, often on a global basis. Such transformations take time, often involving a number of years, but the end result is expected to produce transformed corporations capable of continuous adaptation to permit successful evolution.

Source: McGee, J and Channon, D (eds) (forthcoming 2005) *Encyclopedic Dictionary of Strategic Management*, 2nd edition, Blackwell, Oxford.

Whether or not consulting firms help or hinder organizational change processes (or are relatively neutral in their influence) is an open question for which there is insufficient evidence to present any firm conclusions. On the positive side, there are arguments that consultants learn from academics and from their client organizations. In these ways, consultants both codify often abstruse and complex academic thinking (mostly form business schools) and also develop their own knowledge base from clients so that effective knowledge can progress from one client to another ideally from leaders to laggards (Abrahamson 1991).

On the more negative side, some authors argue that consultants 'borrow your watch to tell you the time' (they are simply symbolic agents, often engaged to fulfil a political motive of driving a change through an organization which would have been more difficult if solely an internal process) or they overgeneralize their solutions so that one size fits all (Alvesson 1993).

15.5 **Creative organizational contexts**

If creative foresight and heretical, off-the-wall ideas are so elusive (and likely to be just as dangerous as they are useful), then how can organizations be designed and arranged to encourage strategic thinking to enable the strategic change process? This is an approach to strategic change which relies less on the creativity of individuals and more upon designing the creative organizational contexts in which strategies for change can be crafted.

Kanter (1999) argues that such creative contexts are formed and sustained by three major elements:

♦ *Concepts*: These are ideas and technologies which are driven by innovative thinking and the innovations produced by other organizations.

♦ *Competences*: These are the repertoires of skills and abilities of individuals in the organization. They also involve the ability to use such skills in the organization. Many individuals who work in organizations have useful skills which they only use in hobbies (for example) away from the workplace. The trick is to engage these competences in the workplace.

♦ *Connections*: These are the important strategic relationships which individuals, teams and organizations create (such as networks). They are nurtured by collaboration rather than competition and can be extended and reconfigured as new ideas emerge.

Chapter 16 picks up some of these organizational themes in more detail in the context of assessing how organizations might remain innovative and how they might continue to learn.

15.6 **Summary**

This chapter has examined the issues of, and widely differing approaches to, strategic change. Since the implementation of virtually any strategy will involve an organization and its members in a degree of change, understanding its processes and its problems can be an advantage.

The chapter has highlighted variation in both the degree of change (radical to incremental) and the extent to which change is discontinuous or is smoother and more continuous. It has also shown how we can examine change from a multitude of levels of analysis.

There are important links in this chapter to the themes and debates of other chapters in this book. In particular, readers should work through this chapter in conjunction with the material in Chapters 2, 13 and 16.

Key terms

Asperity *579*

Change agents *586*

Change and organization *574*

Continuous change *574*

Discontinuous change *576*

Emotional intelligence *584*

Mind traps *584*

Opacity *579*

Process innovation *574*

Strategic tensions *571*

Recap questions and assignments

1 Identify an *unsuccessful* strategic change with which you are familiar. You may wish to choose an example from the business press, a case example you have studied, or you may draw on experience of a strategic change in which you were involved in an organization. What were the key characteristics which contributed to this being an unsuccessful change process?

2 Identify a *successful* strategic change and identify its key characteristics as above.

3 What aspects would you introduce in your organization to improve the implementation of strategic change and why?

Online
Learning Centre

When you have read this chapter, log on to the Online Learning Centre website at www.mcgraw-hill.co.uk/textbooks/mcgee to explore chapter-by-chapter test questions, further reading and more online study tools for strategy.

Case 1 How to manage a dream factory

Harder times are reminding the industry of the critical importance of creating good content. But that means managing the tensions between artists and suits

One by one, the men of extravagant vision and exaggerated showmanship have been toppled from the upper ranks of the world's media giants. The departure of Steve Case from AOL Time Warner and of Tommy Mottola from Sony Music are only the latest in a lengthening line-up that includes Bertelsmann's Thomas Middelhoff, AOL Time Warner's Jerry Levin and Bob Pittman, Vivendi's Jean-Marie Messier, Canal Plus's Pierre Lescure and EMI's Ken Berry. Into their places has stepped a parade of dull men in suits, such as Andrew Lack, new head of Sony Music, who has never worked in the record industry, Jean-René Fourtou, an ex-pharmaceuticals boss, at Vivendi or, at Bertelsmann, Gunter Thielen, ex-head of the group's printing and industrial operations.

This trooping of grey faces into the unruly media world marks a distinct change of mood. Talk of 'vision', 'synergy' or 'new paradigms' is out; the daily grind of evaluating and improving operating performance is paramount. Gone are the days when moguls such as Mr Messier posed jauntily for *Paris Match*, a French celebrity magazine, while skating in Central Park. Except for the two wise old birds of media – News Corporation's Rupert Murdoch and Viacom's Sumner Redstone – today's rising media stars, such as Tony Ball at BSkyB, Britain's leading pay-TV operator, or Jeff Bewkes, co-deputy head of AOL Time Warner, go largely unrecognised on the streets and unquoted in the press.

The need to return to the basics of the business was summed up recently by Peter Chernin, Mr Murdoch's right-hand man at News Corp. 'What the hell were we thinking?' he asked. 'Where did [the industry] get our grandiose ideas the media business was on the way to complete and utter re-invention?' His point was that during the boom, the industry was distracted by gadgets, mergers and convergence theories; now it is time to relearn old lessons about fostering creativity and manufacturing entertainment that people are willing to pay for.

The rediscovered importance of content is encapsulated at perhaps the most troubled media giant, AOL Time Warner. Recent news of the departure of Steve Case as chairman, under heavy pressure, marks the end of an era when new media held any sway at all. Mr Case, the founder of AOL, masterminded the merger with Time Warner three years ago (and pocketed a handsome profit). None of the architects of that deal remains in charge. Yet another battered division, CNN, saw its head, Walter Isaacson, quit in 2003. Today, it is the success of such traditional old-media assets as 'The Lord of the Rings' and 'Harry Potter' films that keeps the group afloat.

But how to get content right? Why is it that Walt Disney, once a finely tuned Hollywood dream factory, has lost its touch in animation? Its latest offering, 'Treasure Planet', which cost $140m to make, flopped at the pre-Christmas box office and forced the company to revise its 2002 results to reflect a $74m write-down. How can Home Box Office (HBO), by contrast, consistently turn out genre-busting television dramas, from its hit comedy 'Sex and the City' to such dark series as 'The Sopranos' and 'Six Feet Under', which are at once critical and commercial successes?

Oiling the dream machine

The answer is not simply the burden of scale, as some observers suggest. HBO is, after all, yet another part of the AOL Time Warner empire. It comes down to a less tangible factor. As Viacom's Mr Redstone puts it: 'Size is not the barrier to creativity, it's bad management.'

Pinning down the elusive quality of good management is particularly hard in entertainment because it is such an odd industry, in two ways. First, it is hugely hit-driven. Most films flop, most records lose money, most TV series fail. A single hit – 'American Idol', say, for the FOX network – can transform profits. The fizzling out of a hit – as Disney's ABC found when viewers tired of the over-exposed 'Who Wants to be a Millionaire?' – can drag down an entire division.

Entertainment bosses therefore need certain qualities: a readiness to take big risks, laser-quick reactions to fickle changes of taste, and a supreme confidence in their own gut instincts – all virtues, as Michael Wolf puts it in his book 'The Entertainment Economy', that reinforce the mogul model of leadership. But the best moguls trust their managers to take decisions too. 'Show business doesn't attract leaders who know how to listen properly or leave people alone,' comments Roger Fransecky, head of the Apogee Group, which advises many media bosses. 'But when you manage creative people, you must intrude carefully.'

Resisting the temptation to interfere, but at the same time enforcing operational control, makes for a delicate balance. With their unpredictable, autocratic management styles, Messrs Murdoch and Redstone might look like ruthless meddlers. Yet in fact each gives his trusted division heads and right-hand men – respectively, Mr Chernin at News Corp and Mel Karmazin at Viacom – the freedom to get on with their jobs.

The second oddity of entertainment is that managers have to be able to handle talent, or at least to handle the handlers of talent. Manufacturing content is not like manufacturing furniture. Armchairs do not get in a strop, go into rehab or become hospitalised for 'exhaustion' – as Mariah Carey, a singer who had just signed an $80m contract with EMI's Virgin Records, did shortly before releasing a new album in 2001. Six months later, EMI sacked her, at a cost of $28m.

Because of the allure of fame, the entertainment industry attracts an unusual mix of aspirant managers, from the star-struck to the ice-cool. 'Most people in the creative world think that they are artists themselves,' comments Alain Levy, head of EMI Recorded Music. Up to a point, this is necessary. Simply navigating the star system, with its shifting alliances of publicists, agents, record labels and studios, requires unnatural quantities of ego. But managing creative types, and imposing some order on their whims, is tricky.

'What is really hard is managing the interface between the creative thinking and the corporate profit-centre,' says Peter Kreisky, a media consultant who is writing a book about the management of creatively driven industries. The two cultures – of the ponytail and the suit – are a world apart, and combustible together. Few managers combine both creative credibility and commercial discipline. But the best entertainment companies manage to impose operational control without squashing artistic freedom.

Three companies illustrate how, or how not, to go about this. In each case, success – or failure – hinges on getting the balance between creative and operational leadership right. The first, HBO, shows that it is possible even for a vast corporation to retain an edgy creative outfit that achieves both critical and commercial success. HBO's series were nominated for twice as many Golden Globe awards this year as those of any of the broadcast networks. Insiders suggest that profits at HBO for 2002 could be up by 17% from the previous year, to $850m, on revenues of about $2.8 billion, or 8% ahead of 2001.

The second company is EMI, the world's biggest independent record company. It is busy trying to bring an end to an era of creative extravagance and financial excess, and to refashion itself as a tightly controlled music company that invests for long-term creative return. The improvement is beginning to show. In the six months to September 2002, EMI made a post-tax profit of £138.4m ($208m), after a loss of £54.4m in the same period of 2001.

The third company, Disney, a media conglomerate built from an animated-film studio, offers a lesson in how creative supremacy can be lost – even during the reign of a single boss. Michael Eisner, in charge since 1984, was once widely admired for transforming a faltering film studio into a slick entertainment empire. Today, the company's creative touch has faded, and Mr Eisner is battling to keep his job.

It's not TV

To the untrained eye, HBO might look like just another bit of the sprawling AOL Time Warner empire. But it is fiercely independent, and has carved out a distinct identity. Employing only 1,770 people, less than 2% of the group total, HBO is physically and operationally removed from even the group's other TV activities, notably Warner Brothers in Los Angeles. That nobody ever suggests merging New York-based HBO into the other TV studios points to its strength as an autonomous operation. The secret has been twofold: the creation of a small boutique-like identity within a huge corporate institution; and the granting of creative independence within a tightly controlled operation.

On the first count, people working at HBO have a clear sense of what they are trying to achieve. As the company's slogan puts it: 'It's not TV. It's HBO'. HBO prides itself on making difficult original drama that would not ordinarily find a place on the ratings-driven broadcast schedules. 'We all know what we're looking for, we know how to smell it,' explains one HBO executive. This sense of purpose has been entrenched by stable management in an industry notorious for high turnover. Mr Bewkes, its former boss, was at HBO for 23 years until last year; Chris Albrecht, today's head, has been there for 17 years.

By itself, a boutique-like identity is no guarantor of creative strength. What drives HBO's success in original drama is its determination to grant writers artistic freedom – always to a commercial end. Talk to screenwriters in Hollywood and they enthuse about HBO. 'It's an amazing place to work,' gushes one. 'Once they have hired the right people, they give you the liberty to do what you want.'

Part of this luxury stems from the business model. HBO's revenues come from subscriptions, not advertising, so it does not need to chase ratings and can afford to be daring. But there has also been a deliberate effort by Messrs Bewkes and Albrecht to liberate creative people in order to keep pushing at the edges of television drama.

Unlike such media bosses as Harvey Weinstein at Miramax, who notoriously meddles with scripts and edits, HBO bosses let the creatives off the leash. When Alan Ball, who won an Oscar for his screenplay for 'American Beauty', began to discuss 'Six Feet Under,' he was hardly pushing what looked like a commercial hit: a dark series set in a family-run funeral parlour and starring a repressed gay funeral director. The reaction from Carolyn Strauss, the commissioning executive at HBO? Make it weirder. Today, it is often the directors and writers who come knocking at HBO's door, not the other way round.

Escapology

Across the Atlantic, in its oddly cramped headquarters – by record-industry standards – in London's West End, EMI has been grappling with a similar effort to invest in artistic freedom while mopping up after an era of excess. When Eric Nicoli, EMI's chairman, hired Alain Levy, a music-industry veteran and former head of Polygram, as his head of recorded music in 2001, the Frenchman inherited a company that had turned profligacy into an art form – notably at Virgin Records in America. In an industry already troubled by piracy and illegal online file-sharing, the company did itself no favours by letting spending on marketing, salaries, parties and first-class travel spin out of control.

Mr Levy purged the place. He changed more than 30 heads of record labels; he trimmed the headcount by about 20%; he pruned the roster of artists by nearly 400, or about a quarter (all 49 artists in Finland got the chop). Out went Ken Berry, along with his wife, Nancy, vice-chairman of Virgin Music Group, whose reputation for partying and jetting about with stars was legendary. In came a two-headed structure that Mr Levy refers to as 'my creative head and his Mr No'. At Virgin Records, he installed a new duo: Matt Serletic, a young creative type in charge of sniffing out new talent, and Roy Lott, whose job is to keep him from financial excess.

Mr Levy, who mixes a business-school background (MBA from Wharton) with a creative's uniform (shock of curly salt-and-pepper hair, charcoal polo sweaters), does not pretend to second-guess musical taste. 'My people just laugh at my French accent and remind me of my age [56].' But he does keep a tight watch on the profitability of his operations. He meets monthly with the financial head of each of the American record labels to go through the numbers; and every three months with the creative heads, to discuss artist development.

This is not meant to squash creative freedom. On the contrary, it is an attempt to put the right people in charge of signing and managing artists, but under tighter financial control. Mr Levy argues that the industry has lost sight of the need to invest in artists for the long term, and become mesmerised by overnight, overpackaged success. 'Nobody is going to be successful if they don't have number ones,' he concedes. 'But it all depends on how you get them.' TV talent shows may create instant hits and help grab market share, but will not develop lasting acts that build up a back catalogue for the future. This is the reasoning behind EMI's apparently extravagant new contract with Robbie Williams, which gives the music company a greater share in all his future revenues, not just those from record sales.

Nobody pretends that the record industry is an easy business to be in right now. But there are signs that EMI's new approach might help, not only from the company's financial improvement. Upcoming or new EMI acts, from Coldplay to Norah Jones, are doing well in America, EMI's traditional weak spot. *Billboard*, the American record-industry bible, named Coldplay's new album the best of 2002. Norah Jones's debut album hit number one in the American charts this week.

Over on the west coast, meanwhile, Disney's troubles throw light on how easily such creative feel can be lost. In his early years, Mr Eisner transformed a faltering company whose film studio had only a 4% share of the American box office into a global entertainment empire. By the early 1990s, Disney was a polished creative machine, turning out a stream of well-crafted animated films, such as 'Beauty and the Beast' (1991) and 'The Lion King' (1994). It was a commercial success too, pioneering the concept of generating branded characters that could be pumped out profitably as TV series, theme parks, fluffy toys, lunch-boxes and so on. Between 1984 and 1993, net profits at Disney shot up nearly sevenfold; by 1993, its box-office share was 16%.

In recent years, however, the Disney machine has sputtered. The most cutting-edge animated output it has distributed – 'Toy Story', 'Monsters Inc' – has not been made in-house, but by Pixar, Steve Job's computer-animation studio. There are now only two more films left in its partnership deal with Pixar. And Disney's home-grown animated output tends to be charmless. In the year to September 2002, Disney's operating profits dropped by 33% from 2001, to $2.8 billion. The group has just replaced its head of animation.

What went wrong? There are various competing theories, including Mr Eisner's decision in 1995 to buy the ABC TV network, now the group's biggest single headache. But the two most persuasive explanations turn on the problem of balancing creative freedom with operational restraint. The first is that Disney has never recaptured the fine balance that existed when Mr Eisner's creative strengths were tempered by the operational sense of Frank Wells, his chief operating officer, who was killed in an accident in 1994. Since then, Mr Eisner's instinct for meddling, along with his increasingly centralised and controlling management style, has gone largely unchecked. Managers feel second-guessed; artists fear surrendering creative freedom. 'Disney's problem isn't management,' says one Disney executive, 'it's over-management.'

The second reason is Mr Eisner's inability to retain his top talent. The loss in 1994 of Jeffrey Katzenberg, whom he recruited to revamp the film studios, was searing. Frustrated at Disney, Mr Katzenberg went on to found, with Steven Spielberg and David Geffen, DreamWorks SKG, which has since released such superb animated films as 'Shrek'. More recent defectors range from Joe Roth, who quit as the studio head in 2000 to found Revolution Studios, to Paul Pressler, who threw in his job last year running theme-parks to join Gap, the clothing chain. That there is now no credible successor to Mr Eisner within Disney's own ranks, in contrast to the smooth transition at HBO after Mr Bewkes's departure, only emphasises this failing.

Dedicated followers of fashion

On paper, the recipe for successfully managing an entertainment company appears simple: carve out small creative units within big companies to give them their own identity; grant them creative freedom from meddling bureaucracies; but do not do either recklessly. Yet striking the right balance between the artists and the suits remains remarkably hard.

Over the years, entertainment companies have often failed, and have instead swung, alternately, from being too strongly in favour of letting creative types rule, towards being too much in hock to the bean-counters. EMI has lurched from periods when the suits were in charge, notably under Jim Fifield's stewardship from 1988 until his sacking in 1998, to times of financial excess, when the creatives went untamed, as happened with the rise of Mr Berry in the late 1990s until his eviction in 2001. The firing of Mr Mottola from the loss-making Sony Music represents yet another attempt to bring an end to an era of creative and financial extravagance: Mr Mottola was so close to the talent that he ended up marrying – and later divorcing – one of the artists he had once signed in her pre-EMI days, Ms Carey.

If the pendulum theory of managing the creative industries is right, today's gallery of grey faces may last only as long as the downturn. Boom times tend, after all, to unleash profligacy – and not just in the entertainment business. The best companies are likely to be those that avoid swinging too wildly in favour of either ponytails or suits: both have their place.

Source: 'How to manage a dream factory', *The Economist*, 16 January 2003.
© The Economist Newspaper Limited, London (16 January 2003).

Case Questions

1 What are the key issues in managing 'creatives' as opposed to managing 'suits' in strategic change? What lessons can be learned from HBO?

2 Taking Disney as your example, what would you advise them to do next? What difficulties are they likely to encounter as they embark upon your suggested change route? Can you suggest ways in which such difficulties might be minimized or alleviated?

3 To what extent do you think strategic change is more or less difficult to achieve and manage in different organizations (e.g. creative organizations, media firms).

Further reading and references

Abrahamson, E (1991) 'Managerial fads and fashions: the diffusion and rejection of innovations', *Academy of Management Review*, **16**, pp. 586–612.

Alvesson, M. (1993) 'Organizations as rhetoric: knowledge intensive firms and the struggle with ambiguity', *Journal of Management Studies*, **30**, **6**, pp. 997–1015.

Argyris, C (1992) *Organizational Learning*, Blackwell, Oxford.

Arthur, WB (1996) 'Increasing returns and the new world of business', *Harvard Business Review*, July/August pp. 100–9.

Beer, M and Eisenstat, RA (1996) 'Developing an organization capable of implementing strategy and learing', *Human Relations*, **48**, **2**, pp. 97–126.

De Wit, B and Meyer, R (1999) *Strategy Synthesis: Resolving Strategy Paradoxes to Create Competitive Advantage*, International Thomson Press, London.

Dulewicz, V and Herbert, PJ (1998) 'Predicting advancement to senior management from competencies and personality data: a seven year follow-up study', *British Journal of Management*, **10**, **1**, pp. 13–23.

Farkas, CM, and Wetlaufer, S (1996) 'The ways chief executive officers lead', *Harvard Business Review*, May–June, pp. 110–12.

Gersick, CJG (1991) 'Revolutionary Change Theories: A Multi level Exploration of the Punctuated Equilibrium Paradigm', *Academy of Management Review*, **6**, pp. 10–36.

Ghemawat, P (1991) *Commitment: the Dynamics of Strategy*, Free Press, New York.

Greiner, LE (1972) 'Evolution and Revolution as Organizations Grow', *Harvard Business Review*, July/August, pp. 37–46.

Hannan, M, Polos, L and Carroll, GR (2003) 'Fog of Change' *Administrative Science Quarterly*, **48**, **3**, pp. 399–432.

Kagono, T, Nonaka, I, Sakakibara, K and Okumara, A (1985) *Strategic versus Evolutionary Management: A US-Japan Comparison of Strategy and Organization*, North Holland Press, Amsterdam.

Kanter, RM (1999) 'Change in Everyone's Job: Managing the Extended Enterprise in a Globally Extended World', *Organizational Dynamics*, Vol 28, No 1, pp. 7–23.

Leavy, B and Wilson, DC (1994) *Strategy and Leadership*, Routledge, London.

March, JG (1999) *The Pursuit of Organizational Intelligence*, Blackwell, Oxford.

Miller, D (1990) *The Icarus Paradox: How Excellent Companies Bring about Their Own Downfall*, Harper Business, New York.

Nutt P, Backoff, R and Hogan, M (2000) 'Managing the Paradoxes of Strategic Change', *Journal of Applied Management Studies*, **9**, No 1, pp. 5–31.

O'Donnell, D (2000) 'The Emotional World of Strategy Implementation', in P. Flood, T. Dromgoole, S Carroll and L Gorman (eds) *Managing Strategy Implementation*, Blackwell, Oxford.

Peters, T and Waterman, R (1982) *In Search of Excellence: Lessons from America's Best Run Companies*, Harper & Row: New York.

Pettigrew, A and Whipp, R (1991) *Managing Change for Competitive Success*, Blackwell, Oxford.

Senge, P (1990) 'The Leader's New Work: Building Learning Organizations', *Sloan Management Review*, Fall, pp. 7–23.

Sparrow, P (2000) 'A World Turned Upside Down', in P. Flood, T. Dromgoole, S. Carroll and L. Gorman (eds) *Managing Strategy Implementation*, Blackwell, Oxford.

Stacey, R (1993) 'Strategy as Order Emerging from Chaos', *Long Range Planning*, **26**, **1**, pp. 10–17.

Steiner, C (1997) *Achieving Emotional Illiteracy*, Bloomsbury Publishing: London.

Wenger, E and Snyder, W (2000) 'Communities of Practice: The Organizational Frontier', *Harvard Business Review*, January–February, pp. 139–45.

Wilson, D (1999) *A Strategy of Change: Concepts and Controversies in the Management of Change*, International Thomson Press, London.

Chapter 16

Strategy and the learning organization

Introduction

As the competitive environment has become more dynamic, strategic management as a discipline has widened its scope to include the internal resources of firms and how these might create competitive advantage. De Geus (1988) argues that learning is the key internal resource of the firm. He argues that learning is a fundamental strategic process and the primary way in which sustainable advantage can be secured in the future. The 1990s has seen an increasing interest in the dynamics of 'the learning organization' as a means of configuring value. Senior managers in many organizations have come to believe that the way an organization learns is key to its effectiveness and potential to innovate and grow (Garavan 1997). However, the concept of organizational learning is by no means clear

Chapter contents

or consistent (Vera and Crossan 2003) and finding work which builds cumulatively is very difficult indeed. Different authors use different concepts or different terminologies to describe learning. The following section attempts to outline the key authors and approaches in the field and concludes by presenting an overall framework by which we might interpret and understand organizational learning.

16.1 What is learning?

Garvin (1993) defines a learning organization as one able to create, acquire and transfer knowledge and to change its behaviour to reflect new knowledge. Organizational learning involves experimentation, creative moments, learning from experience as well as best practice and transferring knowledge quickly and efficiently throughout the organization.

However, as Senge (1990: 285) argues:

> Human beings are designed for learning ... children come fully equipped with an insatiable drive to explore and experiment. Unfortunately, the primary institutions of our society are oriented predominantly toward controlling rather than learning, rewarding individuals for performing for others rather than for cultivating their natural curiosity and impulse to learn.

Here, Senge is pointing out two important aspects of learning:

- Learning can be viewed from different levels of analysis, ranging from individual learning to organizational learning.

- Organizations appear rather less adept at learning than individuals.

We will examine these different levels of analysis later in this chapter. For the moment, it is necessary first of all to examine the generic features of the processes of learning. Only then can we sensibly examine learning across different levels of analysis.

Senge (1990) suggests that learning is both an *adaptive* process and a *generative* process. **Adaptive learning** describes the processes whereby an organization can adapt to its environment and to accelerating or decelerating rates of change. Adaptive learning can thus best be described as the processes organizations engage in to cope with changing external conditions. But the learning process is much deeper than a desire to respond and adapt to external changes. Such responses may render an organization more efficient or effective in the short term, but cannot generate increased or new capabilities – the bedrock of innovation and creativity. Only **generative learning** can provide this. Generative learning requires new ways of looking at the world, whether this involves making sense of the external environment or in understanding how to manage internal business processes better. Such learning is important for the visionary aspects of strategy formulation. To achieve new ideas, an organization needs to develop its capacity for strategic thinking, which is the generative (or creative) learning to which Senge refers. However, in order to understand an organization's capacity to implement strategy as well as to formulate it (thinking and acting strategically), it is necessary to engage and develop both adaptive and generative learning.

These two types of learning originate from what Argyris and Schon (1987) termed single and double-loop learning. This has been variously referred to in the literature as first and second order learning, exploitation and exploration, or convergence and reorientation (see Table 16.1). When learning enables the organization to carry out its present activities and goals without disturbing existing cultural values and norms, it is termed **single-loop learning**. Single-loop learning is important for increasing effectiveness in implementing strategy because it ensures that the organization is becoming better at undertaking its existing strategies. In the terminology of Peters and Waterman (1982) this form of learning helps an organization to 'stick to the knitting'. Single-loop learning is embodied in the experience curve of an organization. The more experience a firm has of an activity, the greater its efficiency and effectiveness become *in that activity*.

However, single-loop learning does not expose an organization to new activities or new ways of conceptualizing old activities. When learning involves modification of an organization's underlying cultural values, assumptions and norms, it is termed **double-loop learning**. In terms of complexity, single-loop learning is relatively simple to achieve while double-loop learning is far more complex. This is because individuals are constrained by their mental models to identify familiar patterns for solving problems. As existing patterns are within the managerial 'comfort zone' of tacit knowledge and experience, this occurs even when the problem is significantly different and requires new solutions. The longer an organization has been using an existing set of practices, the harder it is to conceptualize new ways of doing things. Thus, paradoxically, single-loop learning, which involves existing mental models, is necessary for improving efficiency and effectiveness in existing strategic practices, but poses a barrier to developing new ways of learning.

Double-loop learning may occur when a change in strategy is so difficult to implement that it exposes the problems in existing practices, causing fundamental changes in the way the organization approaches strategic problems. Senge (1990) provides a classic example of this at Shell. Realizing 'that they had failed to change behaviour in much of the Shell organization', Group Planning set about altering the mental models of managers. They developed tools, such as scenario planning, to encourage managers to envision alternative futures. In this way, managers learned flexibility in their current practices. Using scenarios, they could work backwards from a series of anticipated futures to change the practices in the current organization. The capacity to learn enabled Shell to be more responsive than its competitors to changes in the political environment, such as the development of OPEC.

However, for many organizations, the gap between efficient current practices, which involve single-loop learning, and the capacity to double-loop learn, that is to create viable futures, is only exposed during a performance downturn. An organization needs to engage

Table 16.1 Theories and approaches to organizational learning

Learning type (key authors)	Definitions/key words	Advantages	Disadvantages
Adaptive (Senge, 1990) Single loop (Argyris & Schon, 1987) First order (Lant & Mezias, 1992) Exploitation (March, 1991) Convergence (Tushman & Romanelli, 1985)	Increases effectiveness Incremental adaptation Refinement Efficiency Implementation Execution Stability Routine Conservative	Increases familiarity with existing strategy and routines Improves short-run effectiveness Improves capacity to make decisions and act Enhances strategy implementation	Provides a barrier to conceptualizing new ways of evaluating strategies Becomes rigid and resistant to change May result in performance downturn in the long term
Generative (Senge, 1990) Double loop (Argyris & Schon, 1987) Second order (Lant & Mezias, 1992) Exploration (March, 1991) Reorientation (Tushman & Romanelli, 1985)	Expanding capabilities New paradigms Reflexivity Exploring alternatives Discontinuity Risk taking Experimentation Flexibility Discovery Innovation	Encourages creative thinking Improves flexibility and speed in changed environments Associated with innovation and redefining products/markets Prevents long-run myopia	Risky, new ventures have potential to fail Difficult to 'manage' In excess, can lead to dilution of distinctive competences

Source: adapted from Jarzabowski (2004).

in both types of learning; single-loop learning to improve familiarity with existing practices, aiding strategy implementation, and double-loop learning to encourage exploration of new opportunities. A firm that can manage to encompass both has the capacity for continuous learning, thus potentially improving performance and avoiding crisis. Table 16.1 summarizes some of the major authors and their conceptual orientation to the field of organizational learning.

16.2 Levels of analysis: individual, group and organizational learning

It is obvious that learning occurs at the levels of the individual, group and organization, but it is less obvious what processes underpin this learning. It is equally less obvious how (or if) these various levels of analysis are interrelated. For example, an organization may be full of individuals who are constantly learning new capabilities and developing new skills, but the organization neither harnesses these nor benefits from them. The organization does not learn in this example only individuals, who presumably find outlets for their new-found skills outside the formal confines of the organization.

One of the problems with the theories of learning described in the previous section is that they present learning as a static phenomenon. While they indicate the importance of both single- and double-loop learning, they are characterized by being difficult to understand how dynamism or interaction between the two types of learning occurs. In order to understand how organizations can manage single- and double-learning as part of their strategic capabilities, it is necessary to identify where learning is located. That is, who learns and at what level? Figure 16.1 shows how learning may be considered across different levels of analysis. At the primary or basics level, learning is located within individuals. At more complex levels, learning occurs in one-to-one interactions, in groups and in the organization as a whole.

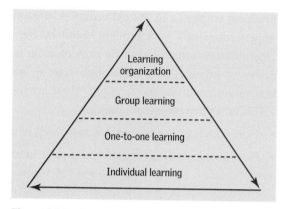

Figure 16.1 The learning pyramid: four levels of analysis
Source: adapted from Garavan (1997) and Mumford (1995).

Learning will occur at all these levels, regardless of whether the organization may be considered a 'learning organization', meaning the innovative, value-creating aspects of learning that can contribute to strategy formulation and implementation. This perspective on learning as continuous moves beyond more static views of learning to show how the potential for interaction between the two types of learning may occur. As Nicolini and Meznar (1995) suggest, learning is continuous at a tacit level, since individuals are continually learning from their own experiences and their interactions with others. However, for that learning to be utilized as part of organizational strategy, it must be made explicit. This involves a reflexive process by which individuals, groups and organizations pause to reflect on the learning that has taken place. By interjecting a phase of reflection, the ongoing learning and creativity in an organization, which may be largely unconscious and unrecognized, is surfaced and made objective. In this way, an organization can become aware of where learning occurs at *all* levels of the company, and how best to make use of that knowledge.

16.2.1 Learning across levels of analysis: interaction effects and the knowledge-based organization

Once we begin to analyse how learning might be a product of interaction across levels of analysis, we have explicitly adopted a **knowledge-based view** of organization. This means that knowledge can be viewed as an organizational asset (created and enhanced by learning) and can thus be deployed as part of strategic management. The importance of this asset needs no emphasis. In the old economy, organizations sought advantage through market imperfections that were brought about by the unequal distribution of economic assets. Organizations sought to out-do each other in terms of a competitive strategy. In the new economy, organizations increasingly have to out-know each other, putting emphasis on innovation, creativity and foresight. These are the new tools of competition.

This raises two important questions:

♦ How does learning take place across levels of analysis?

♦ How does **knowledge transfer** take place in organizations?

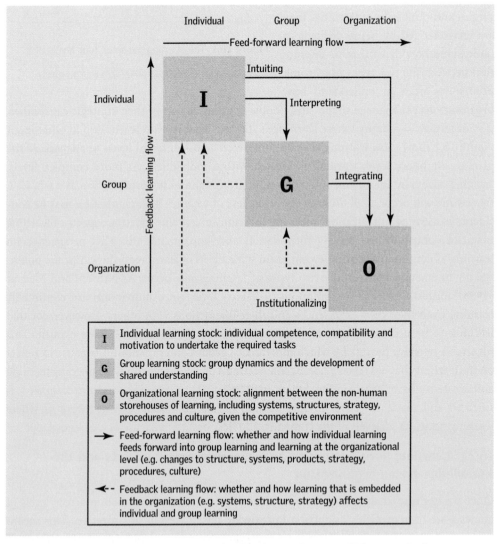

Figure 16.2 Interrelationships between levels of analysis in learning: 4I framework of organizational learning
Source: adapted from Crossan *et al.* (1999: 532).

In addressing the first question, the 4I framework captures the key processes that need to be enacted before learning can take place across levels of analysis. This framework is shown in Figure 16.2.

The three levels (individual, group and organizational) are linked together in a learning process that rests on four social and psychological processes. These processes are described by Crossan *et al.* (1999) as *intuiting, interpreting, integrating* and *institutionalizing*. Within these processes, behaviours (what people do) influence cognition (what people think). We do not know to what extent this is a linear process since cognition also influences behaviours, but these are the key processes that underpin the 4I model and facilitate learning across levels of analysis. Note that Crossan *et al.* have subsumed one-to-one learning (see Figure 16.1) as part of group learning; hence they deal with three (and not four) levels of analysis.

As Vera and Crossan (2004) explain, *intuiting* represents two important elements in learning. First, it is the start of learning. It occurs at the level of the individual. Second, intuiting can only occur in an individual's mind since this is largely a subconscious process. Nevertheless, this represents a stock of knowledge that resides at the individual level in organizations. In order to extract the conscious elements of this intuition, *interpretation* allows this knowledge to be articulated and shared at group level. Individuals thus inform groups and help increase the stock of knowledge at group level. *Integration* is the process by which group learning and the group stock of knowledge is collectively identified (from many groups for example) and is translated into understanding at the organizational level. Finally, *institutionalizing* is the process by which learning is incorporated in the organization by embedding this stock of knowledge in organizational structures, systems, practices and routines.

Vera and Crossan (2004) emphasize the importance of recognizing stocks and flows of knowledge within an organization. Stocks of knowledge can be found at each level of analysis. They underpin the inputs and the outputs of the learning process. Flows of learning are where knowledge passes from one level to another, feeding forward from individual to group and organization and feeding backward from the organization to the individual and group. As Vera and Crossan (2004: 226) explain:

> *The tension between the feed-forward and the feedback flows of learning represents the tension between exploration and exploitation (March 1991). The feed-forward process allows the firm to innovate and renew. The feedback process reinforces what the firm has already learned and ensures that organizational level repositories of knowledge (such as culture, structures, systems, procedures and strategy) guide individual and group learning.*

Vera and Crossan's work demonstrates graphically how information flows and resides in organizations at various levels. These knowledge assets become part of the organization's infrastructure. However, while the 4I framework explains that knowledge flows (or transfers) take place, there is little evidence on how this might take place. To address this issue (the second question raised earlier in this section), we refer to the work of Nonaka's (1994) model of **knowledge creation**.

16.2.2 Knowledge transfer

Nonaka's (1994) model of knowledge creation (*see* Figure 16.3) shows how knowledge transfer may occur through processes of *socialization, internalization, externalization,* and *combination*. In order for the knowledge that is located across the levels of the organization to be realized as learning, a knowledge-creating dynamic is necessary. In this type of organization, there will be opportunities for individuals to share their tacit knowledge through socialization. Such sharing will largely involve shared experiences, participating in tasks together in order to learn from each other within a specific context. Learning of this type occurs through participation in small group interactions.

While socialization deals with sharing, combination is more concerned with exchange. Learning occurs through the exchange of explicit forms of knowledge that may be articulated in conversation, or in written form. Such knowledge may be shared through databases, memos and other forms of information transfer that may be accessed by the wider organization. Clearly email, intranet and other types of information systems play a large part in this type of knowledge transfer. Externalization involves the conversion of tacit knowledge to explicit knowledge, which may then be available for others in the organization to access. This type of learning is accessible through stories and metaphors. Tacit knowledge of a specific situation may be made available to others in different situations, not through a prescription

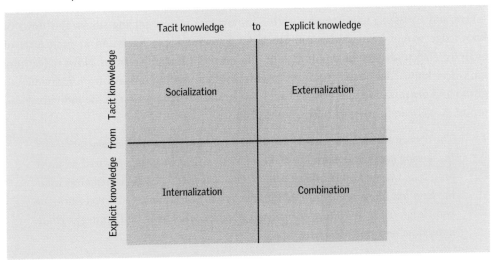

Figure 16.3 Models of knowledge creation
Source: adapted from Nonaka (1994: 19).

of how to do something but through a metaphor. A metaphor is a process of thinking that enables concepts from one situation to be used in another different situation by constructing similarities and differences. It utilizes the creative or intuitive aspects of strategic thinking, allowing an individual to build a connection between familiar and unfamiliar situations.

For this type of learning to be realized, an organization needs to be rich in stories from which metaphors may be constructed. Finally, learning occurs through internalization, the process by which individuals adopt external information and build it into their existing values and assumptions. In a learning organization, these four types of knowledge creation are inter-active, enlarging and amplifying individual knowledge across the whole organization.

Many organizations have implemented Nonaka's and Crossan *et al.*'s frameworks. For example, Unilever's current head of knowledge development emphasized the importance of knowledge assimilation and transfer to underpin marketing and new product strategies. Knowing more about consumers' preferences and demographics, spending patterns and shopping habits all feed through the organization and help inform new product strategies. Rover has also been tapping into the internal competences of the organization in order to enhance product design. Previously, Rover would take a design to its suppliers to see which one could make it the cheapest. Now, Rover feeds these questions internally into the group's experience of different designs and their performance on various models and then the team collaborates with suppliers to design simultaneously one standard (and better performing) design.

However, knowledge is not a standardized commodity, however, across all firms. Organizations will have very different stocks of knowledge that are vital to their competitive success. A pharmaceutical company has very different knowledge requirements from (say) a telecommunications firm or an airline. It is also vital that knowledge flows, rather than knowledge stocks, are continually revitalized. Sometimes this flow can be planned. At other times, serendipity plays a huge role. The short example of Pfizer, below, illustrates the importance of not overlooking serendipity.

Case box: The potency of knowledge and serendipity at Pfizer: Viagra

Drug companies are leaders in the knowledge management field for the obvious reason that the majority of their competitive advantage depends on how they accrue and use R&D knowledge and turn this into drugs and related products. When Pfizer began testing a new drug to control angina in 1992, tests and trials revealed the drug had limited effects and failed most of the performance criteria the organization used in assessing whether or not to proceed with the mass production of a product. However, a small group of Pfizer researchers in the UK recognized that the drug was very effective in correcting male impotence. They communicated these data to the US parent. This knowledge was taken very seriously in the US and immediately trials began on the drug which was to become Viagra and the product which turned Pfizer's financial prospects around.

Of course, these stories continue and the news that Viagra has been cited as a major cause in marital breakdowns is something that Pfizer may want to consider! But serendipities such as the discovery of Viagra are not uncommon. Most of us will know the story of the development of the Post-it note (a 3M product), which was born out of the company producing an adhesive which failed all the tests for effective glues. It would not stick anything together, but the knowledge that it would adhere to paper and could be removed on many occasions without damaging the paper to which it had been attached was soon communicated around the organization and the Post-it note was born.

British Telecom is another organization which takes knowledge stocks and flows seriously. To facilitate this the knowledge management division have concentrated on trying to transform a company whose sole strategic ambition was to become a cost-effective utility, to an entrepreneurial culture which values and acts upon originality and creativity.

Case box: Utilizing knowledge to increase organizational learning at BT

Only a short time ago, executives at BT were expected to communicate only with one layer up or one layer down the extensive hierarchy which characterized BT's organizational structure. Today, BT UK is structured into nearly 40 business units and is organized into a network structure where communication across many levels is via email and the group's intranet. The top executives have their own websites which detail their priorities and their strategies. Anyone can ask a question of anyone else via email or online discussions. The result is that anyone is approachable with an idea and responses are usually fairly rapid. The company has an organization-wide directory which lists the contact details of everyone in the organization, together with their whereabouts and a hot link to their personal and their departmental websites. Around 80 000 staff use the intranet every day. BT is careful to ensure that knowledge flows and that learning occurs as a result. To do this, BT assesses how well knowledge flows and how well people collaborate. The focus is on four areas: the economic case for sharing knowledge more effectively; the level of sophistication of the unit's knowledge management technology; the cultural environment and a leadership commitment to a new way of working. The results of the assessment are fed back to the management team so that they can identify knowledge problems, barriers to learning or opportunities in each unit. Then the unit can begin to formulate an action plan, reduce the unnecessary or the irrelevant and emphasize what are identified as key competences for the development of future plans. Learning to value what people know is the hardest task of all, but the BT approach seems to be successful in revealing this hidden (tacit) aspect of knowledge and learning.

16.2.3 **An alternative perspective on organizational learning models: neo-institutionalism**

One of the key questions which surrounds both Nonaka's and Vera and Crossan's models of learning is that they, perhaps, naively assume the dominant flow of learning to be from the individual to the organization and that, in turn, the organization codifies and reinforces such learning back to groups and individuals. The alternative view is that organizations are effective systems for ensuring that all learning at both the group and individual levels of analysis is institutionally bounded. That is, organizational systems, procedures and dominant coalitions predominantly decide who is recruited, how they behave, which ideas are taken forward and which are discarded. In terms of Crossan *et al.*'s model (Figure 16.2) the bold arrows and the dotted arrows should change places. The *organization* is where the dominant logic of operations and learning resides. Everything else (individuals and groups) have to fit into place and their behaviour as well as their learning is bounded by the organization. Groups and individuals are recipients of organizational constraints and the dominant flow of knowledge is from the organization to groups and individuals.

This institutional view of organizational learning has strong support among a number of scholars. Organizations are, as Morgan (1986) argued, self-producing systems of learning. The institutionalised system of interactions, systems and forms in the organization drive both strategy and learning (or, arguably the lack of learning at the organizational levels of analysis). The Arthur Andersen example illustrates this process.

Case box: **Arthur Andersen**

Prior to the collapse of Enron, Arthur Andersen was a highly successful professional service organization. In such firms, differentiation is via the collective ability of its professionals the intellectual capital of the organization – and this becomes embodied in the brand. Andersen was one of the top five employers of choice of graduates; it selected its graduates from top universities and provided glittering salary packages. In return, entrants were socialized into a workaholic lifestyle in which responsiveness to the client was the priority at all times. To further their stock of intellectual capital Andersen invested heavily in an MBA for their staff. This was designed to serve three major objectives central to what, at first sight, appeared to be a model of a learning organization. First, the MBA was designed to retain middle rank professionals (retention being a key aspects of keeping the knowledge within the firm). Second, it represented an investment in their intellectual capital, developing the idea of a one-stop shop for their clients, cross-selling high-value consultancy to a client base that had been developed on the basis of a now maturing auditing service. The MBA was considered useful in broadening and developing the perspectives and knowledge base of specialist processionals. Third, the MBA signalled to the client the significant levels of investment the firm was making in learning and developing individual and organizational competences.

However, on closer inspection, Andersen turned out to be a firm which had a structure and a culture that precluded organizational learning. Although, formally, Andersen declared itself to aspire to becoming a learning organization, there was little evidence of this happening. The partnership structure and the culture of individualism (you became a senior partner on the basis of your client base) prevented intuitive knowledge ever being shared with peers and thus developing into interpretive knowledge. Individuals did not network. They rarely, if ever, shared their MBA assignments with others (even with peers taking the same MBA). Knowledge was seen as private and an asset from which the individual, rather than the organization, could benefit. Knowledge was shared, but outside the organization – with clients. It could be used to impress clients through better (or better packaged) advice. Client acquisition and retention were key to securing a senior partnership.

Source: adapted from Legge, Sullivan-Taylor and Wilson, 2004.

In the Andersen case, the explanation of why individual learning took place, but organizational learning did not, can be found in institutional theories of organization (*see* for example, Greenwood and Hinings 1996). Although the stocks of knowledge are significant at the level of the individual, these stocks are rarely transferred, shared or embedded in the organization. More precisely, this barrier to learning can be seen as a facet of **neo-institutionalism** (Powell and DiMaggio 1991). Old institutionalism argued that the influence of key managers, dominant coalitions of interests groups and the general exercise of power were the barriers to organizational development, change and learning. In other words, organizations were precluded from learning because powerful people within the firm prevented the process from happening. It was in their interest to block learning and this helped sustain and maintain their power base.

Neo-institutionalism, on the other hand, is the effect we see in the Andersen example. Here, it is much less the power of elites which is the barrier to learning and much more the embeddedness of routines, legitimacy and taken-for-granted behaviours in the organization which preclude learning. Neo-institutionalism explains stability and similarity of organizational arrangements within and between organizations (it is likely that Andersen is very similar to other professional service firms in these respects). This phenomenon is called 'isomorphism', which is a powerful force against organizational learning.

The links between isomorphism and strategy are obvious. If organizations do not learn, they are unable to adapt to (or to anticipate) change. Stability on learning translates into stability and ossification in strategy. Isomorphism is a powerful force against both innovation and learning (*see* Chapter 15 on organizational change).

Bringing the concept of isomorphism into the world of practice reveals that one of its key effects is to produce what is known as 'dominant logic' among managers who formulate and participate in strategy.

16.3 Learning traps: dominant logic

Dominant logic is 'the way in which managers conceptualize the business and make critical resource allocation decisions' (Prahalad and Bettis 1986). Based on their experience, managers evolve mental models that influence their selection and retention of relevant information about the business and the business environment. These mental models or cognitive maps, arising from top management's existing knowledge banks, affect the selection of strategic choices for the firm. Thus, the breadth and depth of the experience base of the top management team influences firm strategy. A team with a lower degree of diversity in its experience base will have less capacity to envision diversity in its strategic portfolio.

Furthermore, when a team has had long experience in a particular type of business environment, it will build up a strong managerial logic that constrains any capacity to select new environments. The degree of cohesion in the dominant logic has varying influences on the strategic portfolio depending on the different phases of strategic decision-making. High diversity is important in the early phases for conceptualizing a broad business domain and conducting a wide search and evaluation of potential businesses. Lower diversity and high top team consensus are necessary, however, in order for strategic actions to be implemented.

Therefore, while wide diversity, associated with a broadly defined but also potentially diluted dominant logic, is important in the early phases of strategic decision-making, a narrower, more cohesive dominant logic is instrumental in implementing strategic decisions (Ginsberg 1990). As dominant logic aids strategy implementation, the managerial challenge is to create a unitary dominant logic by achieving a similar strategic understanding across all levels of the organization (Von Krogh and Roos 1996). From this perspective, dominant logic is a form of corporate glue, providing a cohesive set of core beliefs that guide consistency in strategic action across divisions (Lampel and Shamsie 2000).

When dominant logic is cohesive across the organization, it becomes embedded within the routine tasks and processes by which strategy is put into practice. The relationship between the way that managers think and how organizations act strategically may be understood through the notion of procedural memory. Procedural memory is the skill-base associated with thinking. This is the familiar routinized actions, developed from experience, which managers undertake without conscious thought (Cohen and Bacdayan 1994). They simply 'know' how to approach certain strategic tasks, such as strategy formulation, resource allocation and performance monitoring.

Managerial mental models for conducting strategic action readily transmit to the organization through the formal administrative processes and the informal, tacit, locally understood methods of acting. These routines and processes make up the knowledge infrastructure of the firm. This knowledge base provides learning about, response to, and understanding of problems in the organization. Over time, such knowledge becomes a key component of the firm's dominant logic, reinforcing existing patterns and procedures for acting strategically. The dominant logic forms the basis of decision-making and action whenever a problem is perceived. However, a strongly cohesive dominant logic results in a tendency to interpret and solve all problems in essentially familiar ways, even where the business environment may have changed, requiring new ways of thinking and solving problems.

Thus, managerial thinking and the administrative processes and organizational knowledge arising from it tend to become static over time, predisposing an organization to single-loop learning. Organizations with a very cohesive dominant logic will not be receptive to creative ideas that may be arising at the peripheries. They will lack the methods for surfacing learning (as discussed above). Rather, employees will rapidly socialize to the unitary dominant logic and understand that rewards and incentives are tied into the existing practices and procedures. As dominant logic is such a self-reinforcing process, adapted to the existing procedures, interpretations and strategies, it is likely to remain largely unchanged until declining performance reaches a level of crisis where new learning is imperative for survival (Bettis and Prahalad 1995; Cote *et al.* 1999).

16.3.1 **The counter argument: groups help organizations learn and combat dominant logic**

The role of communities of practice

In spite of pressures for isomorphism, learning in organizations is argued to occur continuously in individuals and in the groups in which those individuals interact. Such groups are called **communities of practice** because they involve people participating in the actual practices of work (Brown and Duguid 1991). The practice of work may not mirror the formally documented rules and regulations by which work is supposed to occur. In practice, people innovate and experiment with ways of getting the job done more easily or more efficiently, or may improvise because the existing rules (organizationally codified procedures) fail to provide them with sufficient information to get the task done. The immediate work community provides a learning context because people tell each other stories about work and they share information and concepts through the social processes of the group.

Such learning is occurring at the peripheries of the organization all the time and may be extremely valuable to the firm. However, its value and its occurrence can easily be overlooked in the wider organizational context (and by neo-institutionalists) for two reasons. First, it occurs at the margins or peripheries where the specific task is located, therefore, it is not within the 'mainstream' of organizational activities. Second, since such practices do not always mirror the formal descriptions of how to act, they may be suppressed in discussion with supervisors or senior managers. Indeed, the community may not see itself as a valuable learning resource, simply regarding itself as a group of people who help each other.

However, as senior management and organizations generally have begun to understand the value-creating properties of knowledge, they have become more interested in ways of tapping into the existing knowledge and learning potential of their companies. Wenger and Snyder (2000) suggest that communities of practice are a means of doing this. Communities of practice help to drive the emergent properties of strategy and help to surface organizational innovation. Furthermore, they provide an important learning forum for the various forms of knowledge creation proposed by Nonaka (1994).

Members of a community learn through participation in tasks together, transferring practices, ideas and concepts about the work process. As they do so, the individuals in the group increase their own knowledge and skill base, creating a virtuous circle of enlarging knowledge at the individual and group level. Such communities provide particular benefit where they bring together individuals with different skills and backgrounds. As communities are spontaneous, informal and free forming, they are difficult to manage, particularly since much of the work such communities do does not look like work in any traditional sense.

However, as Wenger and Snyder (2000) note, while communities of practice cannot be organized, they can be cultivated by providing a fertile environment. They suggest that managers can:

- Identify potential communities of practice that will enhance the company's strategic capabilities.
- Provide the infrastructure that will support such communities and enable them to apply their expertise effectively.
- Use non-traditional methods to assess the value of a community of practice.

In most organizations informal networks of people already exist and may be considered part of the core competences. The manager's task is to identify such groups and encourage them to come together. Shell has a structured method of encouraging communities of practice. If a person wants to develop a community, he or she teams up with a consultant to determine the problems and challenges that different units have in common, which might serve as the basis for a community. People are then interviewed for their views on how a community might support them and their capacity to advance the company's strategic agenda. This flags up the idea of a community of practice, provides information on what the community would value, and generates enthusiasm and interest in joining such a community. This is one of the ways in which Shell has built upon its early success with scenario planning in order to develop itself as a learning organization.

In order to bring the work of communities from the periphery into the mainstream of organizational information flows, they need to be given legitimacy. Communities need to be given resources, such as IT support and reward structures that create incentives for collaboration, if they are to be recognized as important to the strategic development of the company. American Management Systems (AMS) has managed this through a formalized system of sponsoring communities. Recognizing that they were losing their capacity to leverage knowledge due to their rapid growth during a period of global development, AMS encouraged business units to nominate 'thought leaders'. The company paid for up to three weeks of the leaders' time each year to be devoted to developing communities of practice in strategic areas. Community membership is seen as a privilege for people recognized as experts by their business units. The communities are actively involved in developing knowledge-creating projects for which they are funded. An annual conference brings together all the communities of practice once a year to share knowledge across the organization. In this way, communities of practice are recognized, given resources and perceived as prestigious because their work is important to the company. Many companies do not have such formal processes for developing and recognizing communities, but they may, nonetheless, provide senior management support for informal groups that arise.

While it is generally accepted that developing the capabilities of individuals should help to develop firm capabilities, the process of transfer from individual to firm capabilities is poorly understood (see Figure 16.2). As such, it is difficult to assess the value of a community of practice in terms of wider value of the organization. First, the outcome of a community of practice may not occur in a measurable way within the community itself, but in the work of the business units that surround the community. Second, since communities have informal processes, it is difficult to know whether innovative ideas are a result of the community or whether they may have occurred anyway. It is complex to evaluate the motivational, knowledge-sharing opportunities and outcomes that communities provide. Wenger and Snyder (2000) suggest that senior managers need to listen to the *stories* arising from communities of practice to understand how such communities provide value. They note that AMS, which has formal processes for developing and recognizing communities, conducts an annual 'audit' of such stories. An analysis of a sample of stories revealed that the communities had saved the company between $2 million and $5 million and increased revenue by more than $13 million in one year. Other companies, such as Shell, recognize the value of communities' stories as learning resources for the wider organization, publishing them in internal newsletters and reports. We explore the value of stories in developing organizational learning through stories in the next section.

16.4 Using storytelling to develop organizational learning

Shaw *et al.* (1998) note that **storytelling** plays an important role in strategic learning. In a discussion of strategic planning as storytelling, they show how stories have, for example, helped 3M to become a learning organization, as illustrated in the case box.

> ## Case box: Organizational learning in the 3M Corporation through storytelling
>
> Through stories, managers and scientists at 3M are able to discuss organizational failures as well as strokes of genius and intuition. Such stories allow employees at 3M to explore reasons for failures in a non-threatening way, enabling learning from mistakes. Equally importantly, successes arising from creative thinking can be disseminated, serving as examples of what is important and valued at 3M. They allow ideas to be shared throughout the company. Storytelling has become so important to the culture at 3M that it has replaced traditional forms of strategic planning. Gordon Shaw, the executive director of planning at 3M, realized that traditional strategic plans were too 'thin' to inspire commitment or generate learning. Traditional plans could articulate goals and provide extensive lists of what the organization should do in each of its divisions. However, they could not build links between divisions to illustrate the complex relationships involved in putting the strategic plans into practice. Neither could they encourage participants to internalize company goals. Stories, on the other hand, were able to provide these links and enable individuals to understand the complexity of strategy implementation.

The 3M example is a good illustration of what happens when traditional strategic planning methods and approaches are converted into stories. There were several advantages:

- Strategic stories enable learning by increasing the capacity to think through issues. When strategic plans are told as stories, it is necessary to envision the steps involved in a particular action, building a rich picture of what such an action may involve.

- During this process ideas emerge as part of the construction of the story. Thus, stories increase the creativity involved in planning.

- Because stories are visual, involving characters and situations, they capture the imagination. A strategic story can inspire commitment to the firm's goals and the processes for achieving them.

- Stories build identity and image. Identity is the internal representation of the company; what members believe the firm is. Image is how people would like their organization to be perceived in the outside world. Stories can be used to build a strong picture of what the company's identity currently is and how it relates to what the company would like to become. Stories then show how current realities can be translated into future images. Thus, storytelling can be used to build commitment to the strategic goals of the company.

- As stories are rich in detail, they explain complex relationships between divisions and actions. They can be used to paint a picture of how a strategy will happen and the role that each part of the organization will play in bringing that strategy to fruition. Such richness is inclusive, creating a sense of ownership over organizational goals.

♦ Storytelling also allows assumptions that underlie the organizational strategy to be brought to the surface. Thus, implicit or tacit beliefs about the future of the market, organizational capabilities, products, probable areas of growth and the relationships between them can be made explicit and better evaluated.

Stories are a means of creating a strategic dialogue within an organization. Shaw *et al.* (1998) propose some general guidelines for developing strategic stories that can replace traditional strategic plans. Good stories:

♦ use analysis to set the stage and paint in the background to the current situation;

♦ introduce dramatic conflict by showing what has to be done and why it is important; in this way, a sense of urgency and excitement is developed; and

♦ reach a resolution by explaining what can be done and how it should be put into action.

Essentially, storytelling increases communication and allows strategic planning to assume a reality for the organizational participants. They can envision the strategy being enacted and see how their role contributes to the whole. This builds a sense of inclusion, excitement and confidence about achieving strategic goals. Clearly, such commitment and participation is an important feature of organizational learning. Storytelling creates a sense of community in the wider organization. It is a method of putting Nonaka's (1994) models of knowledge creation into practice.

16.5 Enhancing organizational learning

16.5.1 Risk taking

In order to counteract the tendency for dominant logic to become overly unitary, managers need to encourage diversity, creative conflict and dissonance in organizations. Such conflict, well managed, provides an opportunity for debate and discussion, enabling new ideas to be surfaced. This is difficult since organizational cultures frequently suppress innovation because of an underlying fear of risk taking. In a learning organization it is necessary for managers to avoid a culture of blame, to be open to risks where these are well considered, and to accept the occasional failure. As the chief executive at 3M notes:

> *The freedom to persist implies the freedom to do things wrong and to fail. We accept that . . . but at the same time, we expect mistakes to have originality. We can afford almost any mistake once.* (Easterby-Smith, 1991: 26)

In this way, risk-taking can occur within a supportive culture with the expectation that, where ideas fail, this experience is used to generate further learning.

16.5.2 Devil's advocacy and dialectic inquiry

Some techniques can help to generate and surface ideas and manage the creative tension arising from multiple points of view. Devil's advocacy (DA) and dialectic inquiry (DI) are decision making techniques designed to improve the quality of decision-making (Schwenk 1984). DA involves appointing a member of the group to act as devil's advocate for a particular decision. This member's role is to pose all the reasons why a decision should not be implemented. The group must then work through the countervailing views, encouraging them to debate the decision and surface underlying assumptions. DI is another technique designed to improve the levels of debate and creative tension surrounding decision-making. In DI, multiple options are put forward for major strategic decisions. These possible choices, even where they appear inappropriate, must be debated, creating a wider pool of thought and discussion surrounding the decision. Such techniques deliberately impose tension and conflict into the decision-making arena in order to enhance decision quality.

16.5.3 Leadership

While learning is not a top-down initiative, the behaviour of senior management is very important in developing an appropriate context for organizational learning. Senge (1990) suggests that leaders are responsible for building shared vision, surfacing and challenging mental models, and engaging in systems thinking, meaning helping employees to see the big picture and their role in it. He outlines three leadership roles. First, the leader is a designer, building a foundation of purpose and core values within the organization. Second, the leader is a teacher who facilitates the surfacing of tacit knowledge and underlying assumptions within the organization. Finally, the leader is the steward responsible for the sense of ownership and commitment of employees, as well as having a personal commitment to furthering the mission and goals of the organization. Such participative and supportive leadership is consistent with Nonaka's (1994) advocacy of middle-up-down management to stimulate knowledge creation in organizations. Nonaka is critical of top-down management as it presumes that knowledge creation and learning are the province of senior management. However, he notes that bottom-up management is unlikely to be feasible in large corporations because it is time consuming and difficult to co-ordinate:

> The middle-up-down model takes all members as important actors who work together horizontally and vertically. A major characteristic of the model regarding knowledge creation is the wide scope of cooperative relationships between top, middle and lower managers. No one major department or group of experts has the exclusive responsibility for creating new knowledge. (Nonaka, 1994: 30)

In middle-up-down management, senior management are seen as the sponsors and catalysts for creating knowledge. They build the goals, set the deadlines and develop a supportive and receptive context in which learning can occur. Middle managers provide the bridge between lower-level experience in the daily operations of the company and top-level visions. They translate both viewpoints into reality, allowing visions and experience to be combined in the actual practices and strategic actions of the organization. Organizations that embrace middle-up-down management are characterized by self-organising teams, intrapreneurship, diversity, and shared tacit and explicit knowledge. The benefits for both strategy formulation and implementation the practice of strategy would seem to be substantial.

16.6 Summary

This chapter has explored the relationships between organizational learning and organizational strategy. In particular, it has focused on the practice of strategy and how this relates to the ways in which knowledge and learning are arranged and designed in organizations.

It should be clear from reading this chapter that there is no single standardized agreement about what constitutes organizational learning. There are many conflicting theories and many of them have been covered in the chapter. However, the prevailing message seems to be clear. The practice of strategy depends on both knowledge and learning. The ability of an organization and individuals to learn and to communicate and share that knowledge is vital for innovation and strategic renewal.

Even authors who subscribe to the dominant logic or isomorphism schools of thought subscribe to the above view that learning, knowledge and knowledge flows are a vital trio of competences that can help inform and shape strategy.

Key terms

Adaptive learning *602*

Communities of practice *614*

Double-loop learning *603*

Dominant logic *613*

Generative learning *602*

Isomorphism *612*

Knowledge-based view *605*

Knowledge creation *608*

Knowledge transfer *606*

Neo-institutionalism *612*

Single-loop learning *603*

Storytelling *616*

Recap questions and assignments

1 What would you describe as being the key features of a learning organization?

2 Pick an organization with which you are familiar (or is in the public domain) and assess to what extent it is a learning organization, or to what extent it is an organization trapped by routines, stories and dominant logic.

3 If you were asked by an senior manager to help improve learning in his or her organization, which features would you analyse first?

4 Lex Donaldson has criticized much of the 'learning and knowledge' aspects of strategy, saying that the links between knowledge, learning and organizational performance have not been demonstrated at all. What is your view on this statement? Do you agree or disagree? Why?

Online
*Learning*Centre

When you have read this chapter, log on to the Online Learning Centre website at www.mcgraw-hill.co.uk/textbooks/mcgee to explore chapter-by-chapter test questions, further reading and more online study tools for strategy.

Case 1 Future learning: Discovering internal contradictions in a strategy

In his well-known book on the art and practice of the learning organisation, *The Fifth Discipline*, Peter Senge introduced the idea of the *Microworld*.[1] It is a common observation that human beings learn through firsthand experience – 'learning by doing'. The repertoires of children's play (dolls, building blocks, swings and other playground equipment) create learning by doing through experimentation with transitional objects (the dolls etc.) in small self-contained worlds (microworlds). Adults create microworlds in which complex phenomena can be examined. Senge mentions wind tunnels (aeronautical engineers) and wave tanks (naval designers). Managers use role playing exercises for supervisory training and outdoor exercises for team building. But Senge observes that there are few microworlds available to managers for creating and testing new ideas and new insights. In particular:

> *few existing microworlds develop individual or team capacities to deal productively with complexity. Few capture the dynamic complexity that confronts the management team when it seeks to craft new strategies, design new structures and operating policies, or plan significant organisational change.* (Senge 1993, p. 315)

Senge's new world of microworlds is built on the use of computer simulation models that enable complex team interactions to be integrated with complex business interactions. The framework of the simulation model (the new microworld) allows groups to test out their mental models of how their business operates, knowing that the essential real world characteristics of the business are captured in the logic of the simulation model. This is, then, a microworld that is essentially a 'practice field'[2] where teams can learn how to learn together while engaging their most important business issues. This is captured in the old adage 'practice makes perfect'. This is readily achieved in performance activities such as sports and theatre where the polished performance seen by the customer is the result of many, many hours on the practice field. But the manager has fewer mechanisms for practice and microworlds are one attempt to remedy this situation.

The case that follows constructs one microworld in which a management team discovers internal contradictions in a strategy that is being put into place.

Lying behind all strategies are assumptions, which often remain implicit and untested. Frequently, these assumptions have internal contradictions. When they do, the strategy also has internal contradictions, which will prove to make it difficult or impossible to implement. One benefit of microworlds is bringing these assumptions into the open and discovering these inconsistencies.

---

[1] Senge (1993) pp. 313–16.

[2] Senge's term.

One such case occurred at a highly successful manufacturer of microcomputers (here called the 'Index Computer Company').[3] The top management team had introduced a microworld as a part of a two-day planning retreat. They had taken on a strategic goal four months earlier: to reach $2 billion in sales in four years. They were all committed to the goal, from Index's President Tom Jamison on down. And everyone seemed happy with the progress so far.

That's why the vice-president of sales, James Sawyer, felt so uneasy. It was difficult enough to keep and train his present sales force – how did they expect him to double it? He had shared his qualms with other top managers, but they had only responded with platitudes: 'You'll work it out. After all, you'll have the budget for it.' Now he was in a bind. He didn't want his fellow executives to think he lacked their commitment to that magic $2 billion figure. He didn't want to get the reputation of a 'nay sayer'. And he certainly didn't want to let on that he thought he might not rise to the occasion, especially since he had a reputation as a 'fixer' who could solve any problem. But every time he thought about the future, an 'involuntary shudder of pain' ran through his stomach.

Soon the executives split into three-person microworld teams to explore the consequences of the sales plan. Their first task was to construct an explicit model on the computer of the assumptions behind the plan.[4] The plan called for a 20 per cent annual sales growth, a continuation of the growth rate of the past ten years. And it also called for 20 per cent more salespeople each year. As they looked at sales figures for the next four years, it didn't take them long to recognize that the official plan implicitly assumed that the productivity of salespeople would hold steady as the sales force expanded. Hire 20 per cent more salespeople, you make 20 per cent more sales.

Making the assumption explicit prompted Sawyer to say, 'Well, wait a minute. Not all salespeople are equal. There is so much they have to learn – about office automation, software, training, accounting, engineering, consulting, and manufacturing – before they can place a single system. Much of our historic growth,' he continued, 'came from hiring experienced salespeople whom we lured away from our competitors. We could do that as long as we were small. But now the numbers of new hires we need to sustain our 20 per cent are getting much larger. We will not be able to get this many people by hiring away from our competitors. We'll be hiring many more inexperienced salespeople in the future.'

Sawyer's comment sparked a lively debate about the differences between experienced and inexperienced salespeople. All agreed that it was necessary to distinguish new,

---

[3] The name and the company are changed, but the insights are based on a real case involving Barry Richmond, of Dartmouth College and High Performance Systems.

[4] The teams were using a software package called STELLA with which simulation models can be built at a screen of a personal computer with advanced graphics capabilities. STELLA is available from High Performance Systems, Inc., Lyme, N.H.

inexperienced salespeople from veterans. When they split back into teams, each team modified their models to make more realistic assumptions. Sawyer's team, for instance, assumed that veterans would be four times as productive as rookies. Some groups assumed less, some groups assumed more, but everyone assumed that training and developing an experienced salesperson required two to four years.

Now, however, none of the models reached that $2 billion sales goal. Sawyer's model projected sales under $1.5 billion.

The problem came from the average productivity of the growing sales force. As the computer simulated the consequences of the projected hiring, it showed more and more rookies, because the rate of new hires exceeded the rate at which rookies became veterans. Although they hired enough total salespeople to meet their plan, the mix of inexperienced and veteran salespeople shifted progressively toward the inexperienced, pulling down average productivity.

The different work teams tried furiously to find a set of assumptions they could believe which would produce $2 billion in sales in four years. No one could do it. To see just how extreme the situation might become, one group asked the question, 'How many salespeople would we have to hire if we simply kept hiring until our sales targets were met?' They found that 'We'd end up almost doubling the sales force in the fourth year alone, if we doggedly kept adding bodies until our sales target was reached.' All knew that this magnitude of personnel growth would wreak havoc on the sales organization, not to mention the overall personnel budget.

After an hour, the president stood up and asked, 'Is there anyone here who still believes that our strategic plan is internally consistent?' No one responded.

The managers had known both halves of the contradiction: that novices are less productive salespeople, and that the new sales goals would require them to hire more novices. But the assumptions came together only when they were put into a microworld that simulated their interaction over time. Now that everyone could see the internal inconsistency, Sawyer found himself able to articulate, for the first time, his general reservations.

'I've felt for some time that executing the new strategic plan will cause problems,' he told the group. 'And the problems might be even worse than even these simulations suggest. We have a tradition of not revising our business goals once we've announced them publicly. So, not only would we be likely to hire a lot more new salespeople than our official plan projects, but there will be a lot more pressure on our veterans. Couple that with the distractions and frustrations for our veterans who have to help all these new people get up to speed and I wouldn't be surprised if we end up with more veterans leaving and lower productivity from those who stay. We could get into a really vicious cycle. Many of our veterans came to us in the first place to escape this kind of situation somewhere else.'

The other managers sensed that Sawyer's fears might well materialize. 'Perhaps,' said the president, 'it's time to step back and consider some of the challenges we face.' He had hardly finished his sentence before Susan Willis, the vice-president of human resources, had motioned for the floor.

'This is crucial,' said Willis. 'Our people have some problems with the sales managers that I'd like to get on to the table.' Willis talked about the strained relationship between human resources and sales. The sales managers, she said, especially resisted any call to invest their time in training and developing new salespeople. Why, she asked Sawyer, were they so reluctant?

'Well we grew our sales organization by attracting the most aggressive people, the kind of people who spend all their time out in the field,' said Sawyer. 'They don't want to mentor any new hires. They thrive on closing a sale. That's not just where they get their kicks, it's where they make their money. Thanks to our strong incentives, the sales managers with high quotas are among the best-paid people at Index. There are no comparable incentives for helping newcomers; our organization is a lot stronger at rewarding individual accomplishment.'

Sawyer added that the new strategic plan would simply reinforce this problem. 'You must keep in mind that our whole sales organization is geared to meet aggressive targets,' he said. 'Give them a tougher target, and they'll respond by selling harder. I'll have a tough time getting them to think about taking time in developing new hires. I understand Susan's problems. I have the same problems.'

The microworld had brought to the surface a set of frustrations which had been brewing for some time. Moreover, it focused those frustrations on critical changes which needed to occur if the organization hoped to sustain past success. Most important, the declining sales productivity had failed to galvanize action to date, because *it had not yet taken place in the real world*. The microworld gave them a unique window on the future.

As their strategy retreat continued, the management team saw the core issue as either lowering their growth targets or transforming their sales organization. They concluded that the growth target was realizable *if* new salespeople could be trained much more quickly. This presented a significant challenge, because it meant that veteran salespeople would need to be more committed to mentoring inexperienced colleagues. There would need to be new rewards for sales managers to develop their staffs. More support to help senior salespeople in mentoring and training would be needed. And they'd need to look more carefully for new hires who wanted to work in a collaborative team environment, where people helped one another become more effective. The changes were significant but achievable.

One tool for change would be another microworld – this one designed for sales managers, in which they could learn to balance, week by week, their time allocation between direct sales efforts, recruitment, training and management. The salespeople could then discover the long-term benefits of allocating time to personnel development rather than to direct sales efforts.

Predictions such as those achieved at Index are different from normal business forecasts. As former Shell planner Pierre Wack observed: 'Suppose heavy monsoon rains hit the upper part of the Ganges River basin. With little doubt you know that something extraordinary will happen within two days at Rishikesh at the foothills of the Himalayas; in Allahabad, three or four days later; Benares, two days after that.'[5] This is a prediction, not a forecast. It is something you can say with confidence about the future because it depends not on projecting historical data into the future but on understanding the dynamics of an underlying system. By analogy, some of the most interesting learnings that come out of microworlds come from discovering implications for the future, when decisions play out in what had been unrecognized organizational systems.

Source: adapted from Peter Senge (1993) *The Fifth Discipline: the art and practice of the learning organisation*, Doubleday, London, pp. 316–20.

Case Questions

1 What are the key lessons you can learn from the Index Computer Company's use of microworld methodology?

2 What do you consider to be the major weaknesses of microworld thinking in strategy formulation?

3 Can microworld thinking (and similar techniques) enhance both individual and organizational learning? How?

---

5 Pierre Wack, 'Scenarios: Uncharted Waters Ahead,' *Harvard Business Review*, September/October 1985.

Further reading and references

Argyris, C and Schon, DA (1987) *Organizational Learning: A Theory of Action Perspective*, Addison-Wesley Publishing Company, Reading MA.

Bettis, RA and Prahalad, CK (1995) 'The Dominant Logic: Retrospective and Extension', *Strategic Management Journal*, Vol 16, pp. 5–14.

Brown, JS and Duguid, P (1991)'Organizational Learning and Communities of Practice: Toward a Unified View of Working Learning and Innovation', *Organization Science*, **2**, **1**, pp. 40–57.

Cohen, MD and Bacdayan, P (1994) 'Organizational Routines are Stored as Procedural Memory: Evidence from a Laboratory Study', *Organization Science*, **5**, **4**, pp. 554–68.

Cote, L, Langley, A and Pasquero, J (1999) 'Acquisition Strategy and Dominant Logic in an Engineering Firm', *Journal of Management Studies*, **36**, **7**, pp. 919–52.

Crossan, M, Lane, H and White, R (1999) 'An organizational learning framework: from intuition to institution', *Academy of Management Review*, **24**, pp. 522–38.

De Geus, A (1988) 'Planning as learning', *Harvard Business Review*, **66**, **2**, pp. 70–4.

Easterby-Smith, M (1991) 'Creating a Learning Organization', *Personnel Review*, **19**, **5**, pp 24–8.

Garavan, T (1997) 'The Learning Organization: A Review and Evaluation', *The Learning Organization*, **4**, **1**, pp. 18–29.

Garvin, DA (1993) 'Building a learning organization', *Harvard Business Review*, (July–August) pp. 78–91.

Ginsberg, A (1990) 'Connecting Diversification to Performance: A Socio-cognitive Approach', *Academy of Management Review*, **17**, **3**, pp. 514–35.

Greenwood, R and Hinings, CR (1996) Understanding Radical Organizational Change: bringing together the old and the new institutionalism', *Academy of Management Review*, **21**, **4**, pp. 1022–54.

Huber, GP (1991) 'Organizational Learning: The Contributing Processes and the Literatures', *Organization Science*, **2**, **1**, pp. 88–117.

Jarzabowski, P (2004) 'Recursiveness and adaptive strategic practices in use', *Organization Studies*, **25**, **5**, pp. 412–25.

Lampel, J and Shamsie, J (2000) 'Probing the Unobtrusive Link: Dominant Logic and the Design of Joint Ventures at General Electric', *Strategic Management Journal*, **21**, **5**, pp. 593–602.

Lant, TK and Mezias, SJ (1992) 'An Organizational Learning Model of Convergence and Reorientation', *Organization Science*, **3**, **1**, pp. 47–71.

Legge, K, Sullivan-Taylor, B and Wilson, DC (2004) Organizational Learning and Corporate MBAs, paper presented at the EGOS Colloquium, Ljubljana, Slovenia, July.

March, JG (1991) 'Exploration and Exploitation in Organizational Learning', *Organization Science*, **2**, **1**, pp. 71–87.

Mason, B (1998) 'Switchboard: Exchange Culture', *People Management*, **4**, **21**, pp. 46–9.

Morgan, G (1986) *Images of Organization*, Sage, London.

Mumford, A (1995) 'The Learning Organization in Review', *Industrial and Commercial Training*, **27**, **1**, pp. 9–16.

Nicolini, D and Meznar, MB (1995) 'The Social Construction of Organizational Learning: Conceptual and Practical Issues in the Field', *Human Relations*, **48**, pp. 727–46.

Nonaka, I (1994) 'A Dynamic Theory of Organizational Knowledge Creation', *Organization Science*, **5**, pp. 14–37.

Peters, T and Waterman, R (1982) *In Search of Excellence*, Harper Row, London.

Powell, W and DiMaggio, P (1991) (eds) *The New Institutionalism in Organizational Analysis*, University of Chicago Press, Chicago.

Prahalad, CK and Bettis, RA (1986) 'The Dominant Logic: A New Linkage between Diversity and Performance', *Strategic Management Journal*, **7**, pp. 485–501.

Schwenk, CR (1984) 'Devil's Advocacy in Managerial Decision-Making', *Journal of Management Studies*, **21**, pp. 173–88.

Senge, P (1990) 'The Leader's New Work: Building Learning Organizations', *Sloan Management Review*, Fall.

Shaw, G, Brown, R and Bromiley, P (1998) 'Strategic Stories: How 3M is Rewriting Business Planning', *Harvard Business Review*, May–June pp. 41–50.

Tushman, ML and Romanelli, E (1985) 'Organizational Evolution: A Metamorphosis Model of Convergence and Reorientation', in *Research in Organizational Behaviour*, LL Cummings, and BM Staw (eds) (7th edition), Greenwich, CT, JAI Press, pp. 171–222.

Vera, D and Crossan, M (2003) 'Organizational Learning and Knowledge Management: Towards an Integrative Framework', in M. Easterby-Smith and M. Lyles (eds) *Handbook of Organizational Learning*, Blackwell, Oxford.

Vera, D and Crossan, M (2004) 'Strategic leadership and organizational learning', *Academy of Management Review*, **29**, **2**, pp. 222–40.

Von Krogh, G and Roos, J (1996) 'A Tale of the Unfinished' *Strategic Management Journal*, **17**, pp. 729–37.

Wenger, EC and Snyder, WM (2000) 'Communities of Practice: The Organizational Frontier', *Harvard Business Review*, Jan/Feb, pp. 139–45.

Chapter 17

Strategy and corporate governance[1]

Introduction

In recent years the importance of **governance** has become of prime concern in the strategic management of organizations of all kinds. Effective, honest, accountable and transparent modes of governance are now sought of organizations by stakeholders of all varieties.

There is no single model of good governance. However the OECD (2004) has identified corporate governance as one of the key elements in improving economics efficiency and growth as well as enhancing investor confidence. The OECD (2004) describes corporate governance as:

> ... *involving a set of relationships between a company's management, its board, its*

---

[1] Contributions to this chapter were made by Derek Condon, Warwick Business School.

> *shareholders and other stakeholders. Corporate governance also provides the structure through which the objectives of the company are set, and the means of attaining those objectives and monitoring performance are determined. Good corporate governance should provide proper incentives for the board and management to pursue objectives that are in the interests of the company and its shareholders and should facilitate effective monitoring.*

The OECD's *Principles of Corporate Governance* go on to say that:

> *Corporate governance is only part of the larger economic context in which firms operate that includes, for example, macroeconomic policies and the degree of competition in product and factor markets. The corporate governance framework also depends on the legal, regulatory and institutional environment. In addition, factors such as business ethics and corporate awareness of the environment and societal interests of the communities in which a company operates can also have an impact on its reputation and its long-term success.*

There have been a number of recent scandals and exposés of alleged poor governance ranging from Enron, through Parmalat to Shell. These failures expose some of the key principles and the importance of governance structures, processes and accountabilities. We outline the case of Enron below.

Case box: **The Enron collapse**

On 2 December 2001, Enron filed for bankruptcy. On the same day, Irwin Steltzer writing in the Business News of the *Sunday Times* praised Kenneth Lay (Enron's Chairman) for 'converting this American Industry into a lean, mean and internationally competitive machine'. Houston-based Enron went bankrupt amid revelations of hidden debt, inflated profits, questionable accounting and governance. Thousands of workers lost their jobs and millions of investors who hadn't already bolted watched their shares become worthless. Dozens of people, including Enron founder and former Chairman Kenneth Lay, former Chief Executive Jeffrey Skilling and former finance chief Andrew Fastow, have been charged with crimes in the Justice Department's continuing investigation of what caused the collapse. Mr Fastow is among 10 former executives who have pleaded guilty, while Messrs Lay and Skilling are among the 20 who have pleaded innocent and are facing trial. The ventures that once defined Enron as a leader in energy and other markets, such as trading and broadband, are long gone. Unsecured debts in the UK alone reached over £600 million involving Barclays, the Royal Bank of Scotland and Abbey.

Since the collapse of Enron, a key focus has been on how organizations are governed and how boards of directors in particular can let such events happen – and how they might prevent them happening again. The Enron story reveals a board which effectively turned a blind eye to events which should have sounded alarm bells. In brief, the story goes: Enron forged a close relationship with the then Secretary of State for Energy (John Wakeham) in 1990. Wakeham gave Enron permission to build a large gas-fired power station on Teesside. John Wakeham was an accountant by training and was trusted and largely left alone by his two Prime Ministers (Margaret Thatcher and John Major) to secure the deal. In 1994, John Wakeham left the government and joined the main board of Enron. The Tories' policy of energy privatization was vigorously opposed by Labour (especially by its spokesman on industrial affairs, Tony Blair). Once appointed Prime Minister in 1997, Blair began to change policy and secured close relationships with private energy companies and with John Wakeham (now Lord Wakeham, a Tory peer). Enron made small donations to both US political parties, including $10,000 to support the Florida recount in the Presidential elections. Kenneth Lay subsequently secured a seat on a key advisory committee on energy policy (a post previously unavailable to anyone outside government). Enron also lobbied New Labour in the UK.

In 1998, Peter Mandelson (then Trade and Industry Secretary) gave permission for Enron to purchase Wessex Water without referring this decision to anywhere else in the Government. Wessex Water became the core of Enron's new water unit, Azurix. In 1999, Azurix went public and Enron began commercial operation of its nationwide fibre network for high bandwidth uses. Also in 1999, Helen Liddell (Industry Minister) gave Enron permission to build a gas-fired power station on the Isle of Grain, Kent, also without referring the decision elsewhere. By 1999 the Labour government had reversed their energy policies and were strongly backing gas-fired power stations. Labour ministers insisted that the regulation of privatized industries would ensure fair play and healthy business practices.

The response of the Enron board was to recruit the regulators. In October 2000, Claire Spottiswoode, the Gas regulator joined the board of Asturix (the new title of Wessex Water) and in August 2001, Stephen Littlechild, the electricity regulator, was appointed to the board of Teeside Water (a subsidiary of Enron). Following this, the Enron board turned a blind eye to several deals carried out by executives and sanctioned their actions.

These deals put large dents in Enron's funds but were not recorded on the balance sheets. Billions of pounds were used to support these initiatives. In February 2001, a group of Andersen partners met to discuss Enron's accounting and disclosures, but decided to retain the company as a client. Kenneth Lay discussed energy policy with Dick Cheney, US Vice-President, and Cheney's energy task force included some recommendations favourable to Enron. During a public appearance in June 2001, Skilling was hit by a cream pie thrown in protest for Enron allegedly profiteering from California's energy crisis which had begun in May 2000. In August 2001, Skilling resigned as President and CO and Kenneth Lay returned to the position of CEO. In October 2001, the *Wall Street Journal* revealed that Fastow made at least $7 million from running LJM partnerships in order to hedge investment in an internet company. In October 2001, Andersen began shredding Enron-related documents despite knowing of an SEC inquiry.

Enron replaced Fastow as CEO with Jeffrey McMahon from the industrial markets division and the SEC elevated its inquiry into Enron's financial dealings to a formal status. Enron restated its earnings for 1997 to 2001, reducing net income over that time by $586 million and boosting debts by $2.6 billion. By November 2001, major credit rating agencies had downgraded Enron's bonds to junk status at 61 cents per share. The bankruptcy file (for Chapter 11 protection) in December was the biggest in the US at the time ($62 billion in assets).

In 2002 Enron's trading operations were sold to UBS Warburg. Enron received no money but did secure the promise of one-third profits. Enron's board fired Andersen as auditors. Andersen claimed the relationship ended when Enron went into bankruptcy. On 23 January 2002, Kenneth Lay resigned as Chairman and CEO, replaced by Stephen Cooper as acting CEO. The Powers Report, commissioned to investigate blame, spreads the reason for Enron's collapse among Lay, Skilling, Fastow and Andersen, among many others.

Stephen Cooper revealed reorganization plans in May 2002 and one month later a jury found Andersen guilty of obstruction of justice in the investigation of Enron, sealing the demise of the accounting firm in the process. Between October 1998 and November 2001, Lay sold shares with gross proceeds of $184 million; Skilling $71 million; Fastow $34 million and Rebecca Mark $83 million.

By July 2004, the US Government had launched 31 Enron-related prosecutions including the criminal case which brought down Andersen in 2002. It has also set up criminal investigations into around 20 former Enron employees including Lay, Skilling and Fastow. So far, 11 have resulted in convictions or guilty pleas.

Source: authors' own data.

In New York in July 2004, US bankruptcy judge Arthur Gonzalez signed off Enron's plan to exit Chapter 11 bankruptcy protection with no notable adjustments. The reorganization plan aims to pay most of the more than 20,000 creditors about $12 billion of the approximate $63 billion they are owed in cash and stock in one of three new companies created from Enron's remains. Sales are pending for two of those companies – CrossCountry Energy Corp., which comprises Enron's whole or part interest in three domestic natural-gas pipelines, and Portland General Electric, its Pacific Northwest utility. The third is Prisma Energy International Inc., a smattering of pipeline and power assets in 14 countries, mostly in Latin America.

If the sales of CrossCountry and Portland General close later this year as expected, the $11 billion will be distributed to creditors with 92 per cent in cash and 8 per cent in Prisma stock. If one or both of the sales crumble, creditors will receive less cash and more stock in the multiple companies. The Enron name will disappear.

CrossCountry has so far attracted two buyers. In May the first bidder, Texas billionaire and Coastal Corp. founder Oscar Wyatt Jr, offered $2.2 billion. Then, a joint venture of Southern

Union Co. and GE Commercial Finance a unit of General Electric, offered $2.3 billion. Both offers include $430 million in assumed debt. Judge Gonzalez is to consider those and any other bids at a 1 September auction, and he is to approve the winning bid by 9 September.

CrossCountry's holdings include the 2600-mile Transwestern pipeline, which transports natural gas from west Texas, Oklahoma, eastern New Mexico, the San Juan Basin in north-western New Mexico and southern Colorado to California, Arizona and Texas markets; half-ownership with El Paso Corp. of Citrus Corp., a holding company that owns the 5000-mile Florida Gas Transmission pipeline from southeast Texas to Florida; and a less than 2 per cent interest in Northern Border Partners, which transports natural gas from Canada to the Midwest.

Last year Enron announced plans to sell Portland General to an investment group backed by Texas Pacific Group for $1.25 billion in cash and $1.1 billion in assumed debt.

Stephen F. Cooper, Enron's acting CEO and chief restructuring officer, said in a news release:

> *Undoubtedly, this was an extremely complex bankruptcy. Today's court approval acknowledges not only the tremendous amount of work that has been accomplished during the last two and a half years, but also the overwhelming support of our economic constituents.*

The Enron debacle was seen as a serious failure of strategists at board level. It heralded a new era of reviews and prescriptions for board behaviours and regulation, which will be discussed later in this chapter. A new era, since the first code of good governance originated in the USA in 1978. There were, of course, other high-profile failures in the US WorldCom, Global Crossing and Tyco. In Asia the economic crisis of 1997 was laid firmly at the door of poor governance by the Asian Development Bank. And, in Europe, Parmalat and Shell Oil have also been blamed for poor governance. Clearly not just a problem in US companies; nevertheless, the US Business Roundtable issued a report concerning the roles and composition of boards of directors of large publicly owned companies. Monks and Minnow (1992) argued that the origin of this code was in response to increasingly criminal corporate behaviour and included guidelines to quell the occurrence of hostile takeovers. This focus on board behaviours and processes was essentially about the structure, composition and conduct of boards. The main points identified the chairman's main duties as:

- Overseeing board members' selection and succession.
- Reviewing the organization's performance and allocating its funds.
- Overseeing **corporate social responsibility**.
- Adherence to the law.

It was not until 1989 that the next **code of governance** was issued, this time in Hong Kong by the Hong Kong Stock Exchange and this was rapidly followed in 1991 by a best practice set of guidelines issued by the Irish Association of Investment Managers (Aguilera and Cuervo-Cazurra 2004). After this date, the Cadbury Committee Report in the UK (1992) heralded the authorship of many codes of good conduct with Aguilera and Cuervo-Cazurra (2004: 419) concluding that there were 72 codes of good governance by the end of 1999 spread across 24 industrialized and developing countries. Table 17.1 summarizes the position.

The codes produced under different **legal systems** have often been customized to particular national settings and this has reinforced the governance differences identified by Charkham (1999). However, institutions such as the World Bank and OECD are calling for

Table 17.1 Numbers of codes of governance worldwide (to end 1999)

Country	Total number of codes
English-origin legal system:	
Australia	4
Canada	4
Hong Kong	4
India	2
Ireland	2
Malaysia	1
Singapore	1
South Africa	1
Thailand	1
UK	11
USA	17
French-origin legal system:	
Belgium	4
Brazil	1
France	4
Greece	1
Italy	2
Mexico	1
Netherlands	2
Portugal	1
Spain	2
German-origin legal system:	
Germany	1
Japan	2
Korea	1
Scandinavian-origin legal system:	
Sweden	2
Total countries 24	Total codes 72

Source: adapted from Aguilera and Cuervo-Cazurra, 2004, p. 423.

common principles and common governance structures and processes, at least to a minimum level. *Exogenous* forces are influencing the adoption of reasonably common codes. As organizations become more a part of the global economy for example, the transmission of common practices becomes easier and, some would say, necessary. Government liberalization and the increasing influence of foreign institutional investors also force the pace for common codes and standards. In this way, exogenous pressures force countries to show that their codes of corporate governance are 'legitimate' in the global economy.

17.1 The context of corporate governance

As early as the 1930s, Berle and Means (1932) drew attention to the growing separation of power between the executive management of major public companies and their increasingly diverse and remote shareholders. This view focused on the problem of control. The central question was to what extent could boards control executive management and thereby maintain the rights and influence of the shareholders as owners of the organization? This question has been addressed in terms of **agency theory**, in particular in economics. In this theory, the *agents* are corporate management, and the *principals* are the shareholders. In agency theory, the board is viewed as an alternative monitoring device which helps to control the agents to further the interests of the principals. It is assumed in agency theory that effective boards will identify with shareholder interests and use their experience in decision making and control to exert leverage over any self-interested tendencies of corporate management – the agents. For boards to exercise their vigilant role over the chief executive officer (CEO), the board needs power (Keasey, Thompson and Wright 1997). For the CEO to engage in self-interested activities there must presumably be a power imbalance between the CEO and the board.

Cadbury (2000) and Cassidy (2000) offer accounts of the rise and rise of corporate governance as an issue in the USA and Europe since the 1980s. Central to their argument about why this issue has risen so far up the policy agenda have been:

- a succession of corporate scandals;
- performance weaknesses of many firms which could be attributed at least in part to poor governance and leadership;
- disjunctures between the compensation of CEOs and executive directors and the financial performance of the companies they are managing (Conyon and Murphy 2000).

Despite these varying accounts, it is clear that there are a common set of *endogenous* pressures and questions which revolve around the purposes, responsibilities, control, leadership and power of boards. These questions include:

- How is oversight to be exercised over those delegated to the executive management of the firm?

+ How are owners' interests to be protected?

+ How are the interests of the other stakeholders such as consumers, employees and local communities to be protected?

+ Who sets the purpose and direction of the organization and ensures its accountability?

+ How is power over the organization legitimized and to whom is an organization accountable and responsible?

17.2 **Corporate governance in the UK**

Modern UK corporate governance regulations began with the Cadbury Report (1992), which reviewed the financial aspects of corporate governance and led to the publication of the Code of Best Practice. This was followed by the Greenbury Committee (1995), which reviewed directors' remuneration, while the Hampel Committee on corporate governance (established in 1995 and reporting in 1998) had a broader remit that built on Cadbury and Greenbury, essentially picking up new issues that had arisen from both reports. Following the report of the Hampel Committee, the first edition of the **Combined Code** was published by the London Stock Exchange (LSE) Committee on Corporate Governance and was added as an appendix to the LSE Listing Rules. The code superseded all previous codes for UK-listed companies and was derived from Cadbury, Greenbury, Hampel and the LSE's Listing Rules. The principles behind the code were those of market and self-regulation. The code was not legally enforceable, but a company was required to explain how the principles of the code had been followed and to disclose when and why they did not follow the code. If these reasons were not deemed acceptable by the stock market, it would be reflected in the company's stock price.

Since the publication of the first edition of the Combined Code, three other important reports have been published to date. These are the Turnbull Report, which provides guidelines for directors on how to meet the code's provisions on internal control; the Smith Report, which relates to the provisions on audit committees and auditors; and the Higgs Report, which was a review of the role and effectiveness of **non-executive directors**. The findings of these reports have been incorporated into the latest edition of the Combined Code (Higgs 2003). It represents something of a 'capstone' on the previous reports and it has had a significant impact on the structures and processes of boards in the UK. Like all previous codes, the Combined Code seeks to influence board structure and conduct by means of codes of practice and not through legislation. Boards are expected to *comply or explain* why they have not complied in their reporting mechanisms. The key requirements of the Combined Code are summarized in Table 17.2.

The reasons for not choosing a legal requirement for disclosure and relying on codes of practice lie, on the one hand, in the less than adequate provision of the legal structure in the

Table 17.2 Key elements of the Combined Code

> ***The main disclosures required are***:
> ♦ A statement of how the board operates and which types of decision are taken by the board and which are delegated to management.
> ♦ Number of meetings of the board and its committees including a list of annual attendance by directors.
> ♦ A description of how performance evaluation of the board, its committees and its directors is conducted.
> ♦ What steps have been taken to ensure that members of the board, especially non-executive directors, understand the views of major shareholders about their organization.
> ♦ A description of how the nomination committee works and why open advertising or an external search agency have not been used in either the appointments of a chairman or a non-executive director.
> ♦ A description of the processes and activities of the remuneration and audit committees.
>
> ***The main principles of the code are***:
> ♦ Every company should be headed by an effective board which is collectively responsible for the success of the organization.
> ♦ A clear division of responsibilities. The roles of chairman and chief executive should not be exercised by the same individual and no one individual should have unfettered powers of decision. It is worth noting here that almost 10 per cent of UK-listed companies have a joint chairman/chief executive (Hemscott 2003).
> ♦ The board should include a balance of executive and independent non-executive directors.
> ♦ Transparency of all procedures.
> ♦ The board should undertake a formal and rigorous evaluation of its own performance and that of its committees and individual directors.
> ♦ All directors should be submitted for re-election at regular intervals subject to continued satisfactory performance. Refreshing the board with new members should be planned and implemented.
> ♦ Levels of remuneration should be sufficient to attract, retain and motivate directors but this should not include paying more than is necessary for this purpose. There should be a transparent policy on remuneration.
> ♦ Financial reporting should be understandable and transparent and subject to strict internal controls.

UK to ensure good practice and, on the other, to encourage the spirit of self-regulation. For example, UK law rests on the principle that the owners (shareholders) appoint agents (directors) to run the business, and the directors report annually on their stewardship. In practice, in public limited companies (of which there are around 2,000 in the UK), there is a two-link chain of accountability. Management is accountable to directors, and directors are accountable to shareholders. PLCs registered after 1 November 1929 are legally required to have at least two directors. There is no distinction between classes of directors; for instance, between executive (inside or full-time) directors and non-executive (outside and part-time) directors. The law refers only obscurely to chairmen and barely mentions boards. This legal minimalism leads Charkham (1999) to conclude that *the superstructure as we know it: boards, board committees, chairmen, non-executive directors are pragmatic adaptations. In law none is essential; to this day ICI could legally be run by two directors, like the consulate of the Roman Republic.*

Many UK boards divide the chairman and chief executive officer (CEO) roles, and the position of chairman is often part time. Chairmen have major responsibilities in determining the size, balance, composition and agenda of the board. They can also play a significant part in handling external relationships with key stakeholders such as government, institutional investors, regulators and banks. Chairmen are normally appointed by non-executive directors. Non-executive directors play an increasingly important role in influencing board processes, heading up important committees of the board such as the audit or remuneration committees. Audit and remuneration committees comprise only non-executive directors and nomination committees are headed by a non-executive director or the chairman, who must meet the independence criteria laid out in the Combined Code.

17.2.1 Compliance with codes of governance in the UK

Conyon (1995) reveals a clear pattern of company adherence to the Cadbury recommendations. There is no statutory requirement for a company to reveal its board committee structure, so the failure of a company to reveal the existence of a committee does not necessarily mean it does not exist. (Since Cadbury, however, it is in companies' interests to be as transparent as possible in reporting non-controversial matters about board structures.) Tables 17.3, 17.4 and 17.5 summarize the main patterns in the data from the Conyon study and is reported in Pettigrew (2004).

Table 17.3 Board composition and size in the UK

	Average size of board	Average number of non-executive directors	Average number of executive directors
FT-SE top 100 Companies	12.30	6.15	6.16
FT-SE mid 250 Companies	8.89	4.57	4.32
FT-SE top 350 companies	9.87	5.02	4.85

Source: Conyon, 1995.

By 2003, these data had hardly changed. On average, a UK-listed board has around 7 directors. FTSE 100 boards are still larger, with an average of 11.5 directors (Hemscott 2003).

Table 17.4 Remuneration committee structures in UK companies, 1994

	Number of companies with remuneration committee	Average size of remuneration committee	Average number of non-executive directors on remuneration committee	Number of non-executive-only remuneration committees
FT-SE top 100 companies	100	4.61	4.28	73
FT-SE mid 250 companies	233	4.07	3.63	161
FT-SE top 350 companies	333	4.23	3.82	234

Source: Conyon, 1995.

Table 17.5 Audit committee structures in UK companies, 1994

	Number of companies with audit committee	Average size of audit committee	Average number of non-executive directors on audit committee	Number of non-executive-only audit committees
FT-SE top 100 companies	100	4.24	4.05	92
FT-SE mid 250 companies	246	3.94	3.59	208
FT-SE top 350 companies	346	4.03	3.73	300

Source: Conyon, 1995.

Again, the Hemscott (2003) survey of boards reveals very few changes in the above data from the Conyon study.

Key points from the Conyon study are:

• The overall average board size for the FTSE 350 companies is 9.87. The ratio of non-executive directors to executive directors for large UK companies is approximately equal. The average of 5.02 non-executive directors per company considerably exceeds the Cadbury minimum recommendation of three.

  In a 1993 postal survey of 400 of the *Times* 1000 top UK companies between 1988 and 1993, Conyon (1994) found the average proportion of non-executives on the main board in 1993 to be 44 per cent, up from 38 per cent in 1988. There is possibly a rising trend in the use of non-executive directors in large UK plcs.

• Table 17.4 indicates close adherence to the Cadbury and institutional shareholders' committee recommendations on the creation and composition of remuneration committees. Almost all the FTSE 350 companies have remuneration committees that set top pay. Table 17.4 also shows the minimal presence of executive directors on such committees. Even so, among the 1994 FTSE 100 companies, there were still 33 executive directors who sat on their company's remuneration committee. According to Conyon's 1993 study, in contrast, only 54 per cent of companies sampled had had remuneration committees in 1988.

♦ The Cadbury Report states that 'all listed companies should establish an audit committee' (1992, 4.35, p. 28) in order to help safeguard shareholder interests. Table 17.5 shows that by 1994, 98.9 per cent of the FTSE 350 companies had audit committees and that non-executive directors were a dominant feature of the audit committee. This high disclosure of the existence of audit committees again shows considerable change from the disclosure rate in 1988, when a Bank of England (1988) company survey found that only 56 per cent of the *Times* 1000 top 250 companies reported the existence of audit committees.

The picture that emerges from the Conyon studies (1994 and 1995) is one of substantial change in the prevalence of remuneration and audit committees between 1988 and 1994. Bostock (1995), however, has shown a lesser rate of adoption of board-nominating committees. Nominating committees, when available, may be able to bring a more objective approach to the selection of executive and non-executive board members. Using publicly available data disclosed in company annual reports, Bostock (1995) showed that 53 per cent of the top 100 UK companies by market capitalization did not have a nominating committee. The incidence of nominating committees trebled between 1998 and 1993, yet Conyon (1994) found that only approximately 40 per cent of UK quoted companies had them in 1993, despite the Cadbury code of practice.

The Cadbury code of practice does not recommend companies to split the roles of chairman and chief executive. It does, however, recommend that where the roles are not

Table 17.6 Number of companies with women on the board for 1995

	Number with at least one woman non-executive director	Number with at least one woman executive director	Number with at least one woman board member (exec or non-exec)
FT-SE top 100 companies	34	7	40
FT-SE mid 250 companies	29	7	33
FT-SE top 350 companies	63	14	73

Source: Conyon and Mallin, 1997.

Table 17.7 Percentage of females on the board in 1995

	Percentage of female non-executive directors on main board	Percentage of female executive directors on main board	Percentage of all female directors on main board
FT-SE top 100 companies	3.08	0.56	3.65
FT-SE mid 250 companies	1.44	0.40	1.84
FT-SE top 350 companies	2.02	0.46	2.49

Source: Conyon and Mallin, 1997.

split, there should be a strong independent element, with a recognized senior member, on the board. The Cadbury Committee's own research on compliance (CADS, 1995) shows that by 1994 the roles of chairman and chief executive were split in 82 per cent of UK firms in the top 500 by market capitalization. Conyon's (1994) postal survey of 400 firms in the *Times* 1000 found that, in 1993, 77 per cent of quoted companies had split the two roles, compared with 57 per cent in 1988.

In a slightly later study, Conyon and Mallin (1997) report on women's participation rates in the UK boardrooms. Tables 17.6 and 17.7 report respectively on the number of companies with women on the board, and the percentage of females on the board of UK plcs in 1995.

These data reveal the very limited participation of women in the main boardrooms of the UKs top plcs. IN 1995, there were just 73 companies with at least one female director on the main board and very few of those were executive directors. In 1995 there was only one company in the FTSE 100 with a female CEO. In 2000, this figure had doubled to two. Only 2.49 per cent of the directors were female and females are more likely to be non-executive than executive directors. By 2003, just over one in ten FTSE non-executive posts were held by females and one in forty FTSE executive posts were held by women (Hemscott 2003). Things do not seem to be changing in terms of the gender imbalances in the boardroom. Most strategists are male.

Although the above data show the extent which UK organizations comply with the various codes, the data should not be taken to imply anything about the effectiveness of these boards. Ticking the boxes of compliance and working effectively are two very different processes. In the next sections, we look at **board effectiveness** generally (i.e. in companies worldwide) and in the UK, referring to a recent empirical study of UK boards by McNulty and Pettigrew (1999).

17.3 **Board effectiveness**

Conger *et al.* (2001), Ward (2000) and the OECD (2004) all offer principles against which board effectiveness might be judged. In particular, these authors emphasize that the board should be able to exercise judgement in decision making and corporate affairs generally, independently of other influences, particularly the voices of management. Since boards should appoint non-executive directors to exercise independent judgements over key areas such as financial reporting, nomination and remuneration, the board ought to be able to exercise independent and informed judgements away from the day-to-day managerial concerns of the organization. In addition, these authors emphasize the importance of boards being able to access and be supplied with accurate, timely and relevant information in order to carry out their strategic decision making roles effectively. Finally, the role of accountability is emphasized, not only compliance with the law and acting on good faith, but also in the interests of all shareholders and the social responsibilities of the organization. These issues are summarized in the next sections.

17.3.1 **The board as a team**

Surprisingly, the board as an organizational team has been relatively neglected in empirical study. While there are plenty of studies on teams (and top teams) in organizations (see Katzenbach and Smith 1992; Hambrick *et al.* 1998), there are very few studies of boards using the key variables identified from these team studies. Applying the empirical knowledge of team processes and performance to boards would emphasize a number of key aspects.

First, boards should ensure they focus on the correct issues during their meetings and avoid much of the side-tracking which can take place in groups. For example, this would mean being able to focus on and distinguish between long- and short-term factors with full discussions at board meetings before any strategic decisions are taken. As with all organizational groups, size is important. Extrapolating from the team-based literatures, boards should restrict their size as far as possible to around six or eight members for a small organization to ten or twelve members for a larger organization. All members should feel that they can contribute freely and effectively to meetings and be well prepared in advance of the meeting. Regular meetings with high levels of attendance would also be beneficial in terms of effective decision making.

Second, the board needs to build in maintenance and learning functions to its operations and processes. The board's role as the key strategic decision making body calls for a high level of commitment of all members as well as the ability of those members to learn from experience and apply that learning to decisions and judgements they are required to take. Training and development (e.g. perhaps an induction programme for newly appointed directors) should also be beneficial as should specific training in the key areas of decision making (see Chapter 13) such as strategy, risk and evaluating performance. Like all groups in organizations, some assessment of their own performance as a team and as individuals in that team should ensure greater effectiveness.

17.4 **The board and strategic decision making**

As the key group in strategic decision making processes, the board needs both to understand how decisions are made (on what basis and with what stated objectives for example) and how they go about decision making as a team. This is another aspect of the interface between organization and strategy (see Chapter 2). In making strategic decisions, the board stamps its mark on the organization and, in turn, the organization becomes a distinctive entity with

Table 17.8 Levels of non-executive board member involvement in strategy

	Taking strategic decisions	Shaping strategic decisions	Shaping the content, context and conduct of strategy
Definition	Influence is exerted inside the boardroom at the end of the capital investment decision process	Influence occurs early in the decision process as part-time board members shape the preparation of capital investment proposals by executives	Influence is continuous and not confined to decision episodes
Board behaviour	Inside the boardroom, boards take decisions to accept, reject or refer capital investment proposals	Consultation with part-time board members by the executive, either formally or informally, while a capital investment proposal is being prepared enables board members to test ideas, raise issues, question assumptions, advise caution, and offer encouragement. *Executives 'sieve' capital investment proposals in anticipation of the need for board approval*	The board develops the context for strategic debate, establishes a methodology for strategy development, monitors strategy content and alters the conduct of the executive in relation to strategy
Board involvement	All boards take strategic decisions	Some boards shape strategic decisions	A minority of boards shape the context, content and conduct of strategy

Source: adapted from McNulty and Pettigrew, 1999.

its own structure, culture and philosophy. A resource-based view of the organization would imply that a key role of the board is to ensure precisely what is the core business or purpose of the organization and to ensure that organizational competences and resources are in place to support that core purpose. This is akin to creating and preserving that 'cherished core ideology' that Collins and Porras (2000) argue is the vital constant of successful organizations when all else around them is subject to change. In essence, the board represents and needs to preserve the glue which holds the organization together and which symbolizes the guiding principles by which key decisions are made.

The board also has the responsibility of overseeing not only its own internal processes in this respect, but also of ensuring that this 'strategy with values' is disseminated effectively throughout the organization and that processes, rewards and organizational structures are aligned with the strategy. Opinions differ about the level of involvement that is both possible and desirable for boards in the strategy process. Some argue that boards should have a proactive or initiating role of shaping strategy. Others contend the board should challenge, question and eventually approve strategic ideas and decisions formulated below the board in the executive team. McNulty and Pettigrew (1999) have examined the contribution to strategy by chairmen and non-executive directors of large UK companies. The collective label of part-time board member was used to refer to individuals performing these two roles (although a limited number of chairmen in the UK have executive and virtually full-time positions). Table 17.8 summarizes the forms of strategic involvement of boards in strategic decision making.

Most non-executives claimed they were much more influential in stopping initiatives than in starting them (McNulty and Pettigrew 1999). The executives interviewed claimed that around 80 per cent of the strategic decisions they took to the boardroom were approved or confirmed by the whole board.

Shaping strategic decisions entails a higher degree of non-executive board member influence. Here the non-executives are consulted and involved earlier in the strategy process and thereby can shape the assumptions, alternatives and actual choices in the process. Shaping also occurs when executives restrict the range of their own proposals (knowing that certain alternatives will not be accepted at board level).

The ultimate way for a board to shape strategy is to fire the CEO and other executive directors. This is happening with increasing frequency in UK boardrooms. The new generation of CEOs entering UK boardrooms are likely to be younger, to have had experience in more than one company and industry, and to have a shorter tenure in post than their predecessors of the 1980s and early 1990s.

17.4.1 **The board and performance**

Like any process, it is vital that boards have some way of agreeing what the key drivers of performance are. These can include a variety of measures such as financial results, corporate reputation or customer satisfaction, or can be a holistic grouping of such measures. An example of such a broad-based performance measurement system is Kaplan and Norton's (1992) balanced scorecard approach to using multiple measures for assessing performance. These include financial and non-financial measures of performance with a view to assessing future potential as well as assessing current performance.

A broad-based performance measure means boards must be clear about:

- How do our customers see us.
- What we must excel at.
- How we can continue to improve and create value.
- How good our financial performance is.

Each of these measures can be sub-divided into two component parts. These are outcomes, which *measure* the results of actions in the past, and performance drivers (*goals*), which predict future success. This allows future strategies to be reflected in today's goals and targets. Figure 17.1 shows the multi-dimensional nature of the balanced scorecard.

Measures can be metrics such as return on capital employed or return on net assets. They can also include factors such as employee attitudes, extent of customer satisfaction or core competences. *Goals* are future desired states which predict future success.

Of course, such a broad-based performance tool requires boards to be effective at both *prioritizing* strategic decisions (see Chapter 13) and assessing *risk*. The task of the board is to manage risk effectively rather than try to eliminate risk altogether. Bernstein (1996) reminds us that risk is a choice rather than a fate. The degree of risk taken by boards is really an expression of the amount of action (in an uncertain world) they dare to take. In this sense, risk is also an integral part of strategic decision making alongside prioritization. It is also

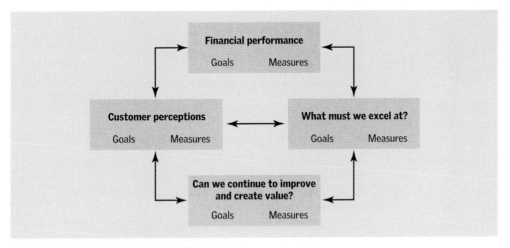

Figure 17.1 The balanced scorecard
Source: adapted from Kaplan and Norton, 1992.

management's responsibility (as well as that of the board) to monitor and assess risk as well as to keep the board informed of future risk-related projects or developments.

Handling risks (and setting the appetite for risk in an organization) are the responsibility both of the board and management. Effective risk management means there must also be good patterns of communication and understanding between the board and the management of an organization. Risks can arise from virtually all organizational activities. Some boards establish risk committees to look explicitly at some of the risk factors outlined in Table 17.9.

The main challenge to boards is to incorporate risk assessments into their own processes and to be able to prioritize significant or key risks (which may range from ethical issues to health and safety). Many practitioners advise that the board should make a detailed risk analysis every time they make (or ratify) a strategic decision. The Turnbull Report recommended a risk-based approach to designing, operating and maintaining a sound system of internal governance. Kirkbride and Letza (2003) note that Turnbull is the first official UK corporate governance document where the role of risk in corporate governance practice has been explicitly included and articulated.

Table 17.9 Some risks facing boards

Source of risk	Examples
Corporate strategy	♦ Strategy and organizational capabilities not aligned ♦ Unsuccessful acquisition ♦ Major change programme goes wrong
Financial	♦ Major accounting irregularities ♦ Fraud ♦ Cash flow problems
Legal	♦ Health and safety risks ♦ Breach of regulatory laws ♦ Failure to protect intellectual property
Supply chain and alliances	♦ Strategic alliances and joint ventures do not work ♦ Supply chain problems (e.g. suppliers) ♦ Overdependence on outsourced services
The operating environment	♦ Not responding to market trends ♦ Failure to innovate ♦ Overdependence on a few customers/suppliers
Human resources	♦ Loss of key people ♦ Poor motivation and communication among staff ♦ Leadership unable to take the organization forward (unable to formulate/implement strategies)
Social responsibility	♦ Stakeholder concerns about ethics of organization ♦ Dealing with unethical suppliers or contractors ♦ Human rights violations

The board is responsible for the company's system of internal control and it is the role of management to implement board policies on risk and control. Reports to the board should provide a balanced assessment of the significant risks and the effectiveness of the internal control mechanisms to handle those risks.

Other risks identified in the Turnbull Report include the following.

Strategic risk

- Changing conditions in the regional, national or world economy having an effect on the company's business
- Becoming a takeover target
- The risk of obsolescent technology
- Being in an industry in decline

Financial risk

- Shortage of cash (liquidity risk)
- Trying to expand the business too quickly
- Having unrecorded liabilities (e.g. guarantees about which senior management is unaware)
- Taking decisions with incomplete or inaccurate financial information.

Compliance risk

- Breaching financial regulations
- Litigation risks
- Breaching the requirements of the Companies Act (or its legal equivalent)
- Incurring tax penalties

Operational risk

- Vulnerability of IT systems to unauthorized access (e.g. hackers)
- Loss of key people
- Succession problems
- Reputation damage or loss

17.5 Boards and corporate social responsibility

A question of increasing importance to all organizations is to what extent the board has ensured that strategic decisions incorporate ethical, socially responsible and sustainable factors. It is the duty of a diligent board to assess and to take into consideration issues of a sustainable environment. In many respects, corporate social responsibility (CSR) is not a separate issue but is one which permeates all board activities (in particular decision making and risk assessment).

An organization which operates in a manner contrary to CSR faces the risk of poor market ratings and adverse publicity. Those which face large ethical concerns also face the results of poor and adverse publicity. A well-known example of this is the case of BP-Amoco which suffered greatly as a result of its exploration activities in Colombia. Eventually accused of working for a corrupt government, BP Amoco suffered bad publicity, a drop in market value and a drastic drop in reputation. Few boards would want to ignore CSR. They would do so at their peril.

Two aspects of formalizing CSR have now become the remit of boards worldwide. The first is known as the 'triple bottom line'. This means that, alongside financial and other hard measures of performance, a measure of CSR (the third measure) should be included as an equal arbiter of performance. The second is known as the 'global compact', resulting from a meeting of the World Economic Forum in 1999. The then UN Secretary General, Kofi Annan, set out nine principles on human rights, labour and the environment that organizations need to address (and be judged against). Table 17.10 summarizes the nine core principles of the global compact.

A study by Contardo and Wilson (2001) revealed a patchy take up of these nine principles by the boards of twenty organizations. These twenty organizations were drawn from ten different nations in order to see if country of origin had any significant impact on the implementation of the nine principles. The results revealed that country of origin had no

Table 17.10 The nine principles of the global compact

Human rights	Businesses should:
	• Support and respect the protection of international human rights within their sphere of influence • Ensure their own corporations are not involved in human rights abuses (implicitly or explicitly)
Labour	• Recognize the right of labour to collective bargaining and freedom of association • Eliminate forced and compulsory labour • Abolish child labour • Eliminate discrimination in terms of employment and occupation
Environment	• Take a precautionary approach to environmental challenges • Promote greater environmental responsibility • Encourage the development and diffusion of environmentally friendly technologies

impact at all. The data from this study revealed that boards were experiencing some difficulties in implementing the nine principles, especially in older organizations. Boards in older organizations experienced difficulties in assessing the relative priority of these principles in relation to other externally determined standards (such as International Standards or Health and Safety). In general, the boards of older organizations were making progress in networking with stakeholders in order to try to establish partnerships and had often set up new functions in the organization to deal with CSR issues. For example, Unilever had created a special department addressing CSR issues and had engaged with many stakeholders (including strong critics of the organization) in order to weave environmental consciousness throughout their business. Shell Brazil has introduced a clause in its contracts with distillers forbidding the use of child labour. Shell Brazil was awarded the title 'Child Friendly Company' for its work in discouraging the use of child labour in the production of sugar cane alcohol, which it is legally obliged to sell on its forecourts and include in its gasoline. BASF has established a sustainability council at board level to try to make sustainability a part of everyday processes in the company. Overall, however, the data from Contardo and Wilson (2001) point to a very patchy worldwide take up of the nine principles by a wide range of organizations, with boards in particular finding it difficult to add these responsibilities to their existing portfolio of activities.

17.6 **What is an effective board?**

There are many autobiographical accounts by practitioners of board effectiveness but few independently conducted analyses of board conduct and performance. Recently a study conducted by Pettigrew and McNulty has generated first-hand data on board conduct, power relationships and strategy processes (Pettigrew and McNulty 1995 and 1998; McNulty and Pettigrew 1999). This study used a multi-method approach combining a survey of the chairmen, CEOs and non-executive directors of the top 500 plcs, with personal interviews with 65 part-time and 43 full-time board members and the analysis of publicly available documentary material.

Most of the board members we interviewed acknowledged that it was somewhat easier to identify the characteristics of an ineffective board than to catalogue the features of an effective one. Indicators of ineffectiveness included:

- Poor chairing of the board
- Over-dominance by the chair
- Marginalization of the non-executives
- Cliques and politicking between and inside board meetings
- Failure to reveal critical information to board members
- Failure to encourage open discussions and allow issue spotting

- ◆ A board focused on a narrow set of issues and fixated by historical reporting and operational matters
- ◆ A closed process of recruitment to the board

Looking more broadly at board effectiveness, there are some important conceptual distinctions. These include considering effectiveness both against a set of agreed board purposes and against a trinity of design choices (inputs, processes and outputs); recognizing that effectiveness has to be customized to local circumstances; and being clear that performance in the boardroom is a dynamic issue and may require continuous performance assessment, learning and change. McNulty and Pettigrew (1999) characterized effective boards as 'maximalist' and less effective boards as 'minimalist'. Table 17.11 summarizes their characteristics.

The maximalist board does not have the extreme power asymmetrics to be found in the minimalist board. With greater sharing of power and information, and more clearly defined purposes and roles, better relationships and communication flows are apparent in the maximalist board. In time, with greater trust and better shared understandings between the chair and CEO, the board culture changes. With greater trust, more challenge and dissent becomes

Table 17.11 Characteristics of maximalist (successful) and minimalist (less successful) boards

Characteristics of minimalist boards	Characteristics of maximalist boards
Run by individuals and small factions	Trigger for change often a performance crisis
Big power asymmetries between chair or chair/CEO and rest of board and executive	Top-level change: new personalities and purpose and processes
Non-execs have low legitimacy; selected to maintain power asymmetries; starved of information; confined to the boardroom; isolated from the strategic process	Attempts to distinguish roles more clearly
	Recruitment of new non-executive directors: given greater legitimacy
Board agenda is stylized and predictable in its historical reporting	Board agenda and process opened up
	Space for issue spotting and resolutions
No space to spot issues, even less for dealing with them	Non-execs allowed into strategic process
	Non-execs allowed to roam outside boardroom
Little or no conflict, challenge or dissent	Roaming enhances perspective, judgement, confidence and trust
	Greater trust and openness allows greater challenge and dissent and more informal working and better relationships
	Often tensions about power. Non-execs are prepared to use it, and executives have felt it
	Checks and balances and fluidity of information and relationships allow control and leadership purposes to be realized

possible and more fundamental strategic issues are opened up for discussion and possible resolution. Although there is a more comfortable dynamic balance of power on maximalist boards, there may still be an appropriate tension about power. This tension may be a left-over from the company performance crisis, when the non-executives were prepared to use power and when the executives felt the use of power. Without this tension about power there would be no checks and balances, and without these the apparently contradictory board purposes of control and strategic leadership would be less likely to be realized.

17.7 Summary

This chapter has examined some key aspects of boards and their role in strategic decision making. Board have a strategic and public responsibility to provide direct returns for shareholders and employees, suppliers and have a responsibility towards the communities in which they operate. In the wake of recent corporate scandals and collapses, governments worldwide have been reviewing the role and the processes of governance.

Because the board is in place to lead and control the organization, it should have a clearly defined set of responsibilities and codes of operation. This chapter has outlined the main features of those responsibilities and it has outlined some of the major features of the emerging guidelines.

Although board structures differ from country to country, most countries have a common set of principles of governance, namely that no individual director has unrestrained power to control and direct the organization and that there should be a countervailing influence (on insiders on the board) from outside directors who act as the guardians of board conduct and decision making processes

Key terms

Agency theory *635*

Board effectiveness *641*

Code of governance *633*

Combined Code *636*

Corporate social responsibility *633*

Governance *629*

Legal systems *634*

Non-executive directors *636*

When you have read this chapter, log on to the Online Learning Centre website at www.mcgraw-hill.co.uk/textbooks/mcgee to explore chapter-by-chapter test questions, further reading and more online study tools for strategy.

Recap questions and assignments

1 Why are governance processes and structures important to our understanding of strategy?

2 With regard to an organization you know well (or is in the pubic domain) what would you assess as its good and less good features in terms of governance structures and processes?

3 What do you see as the key changes and challenges for the future for corporate governance

Case 1 **Walt Disney Company: 'The case against Michael Eisner'**

Timeline

1984   Following a long period of relative decline, reflected in both its stock price and profits, corporate raider Saul Steinberg launches a takeover bid for Disney. Although unsuccessful it leads to a power struggle that is eventually won by a group of shareholders led by directors Roy E. Disney (nephew of Walt Disney and son of Roy O. Disney the co-founders of Walt Disney Productions) and Stanley Gold (Disney's close friend, attorney and financial advisor). The existing management – Raymond Watson (Chairman) and Ron Miller (CEO), Walt Disney's son-in-law – is replaced by Michael Eisner (Chairman and CEO), the President of Paramount Pictures (a division of Gulf & Western), and Frank Wells (President), a former CEO of Warner Bros (a division of Warner Communications). Both were equals in the sense that they reported directly to the board, with Eisner seen as the 'creative talent' and Wells the 'businessman', an arrangement similar to that found in the original Walt Disney Productions where Walt Disney (creative) was Chairman and CEO and Roy O. Disney (businessman) was President.

Roy E. Disney (who had previously resigned his executive position at the company while remaining on the board of directors) returns as Head of Animation.

Jeffery Katzenberg joins as Head of the Film Division.

1984–94   Over the next 10 years as the stock price rises 6000%, the company opens EuroDisney, makes numerous successful films and TV shows targeting all types of audiences, expands Disney World, buys TV stations and the Anaheim Mighty Ducks ice hockey team. Eisner is lauded as one of the great CEOs of the 1980s and 1990s.

1994 (April)   Frank Wells is killed in a helicopter crash.

1994 (July)   Katzenberg (seen by many commentator's as Eisner's eventual successor) leaves after a clash with Eisner. Only one month after *The Lion King*, overseen by Katzenberg, becomes the most successful animated film ever.

1994 (July)   Eisner undergoes quadruple bypass surgery.

1994   Prince Alwaleed invests in the failing EuroDisney preventing the collapse of the project which is renamed Disneyland Paris.

1995 (Oct) 'Super-agent' Michael Ovitz, frequently described as the 'most powerful man in Hollywood', leaves Creative Artists Agency (CAA) to become Disney President. He is seen as a potential successor to Eisner by many industry insiders and institutional investors.

1995 George Mitchell joins the board.

1996 (Feb) Disney purchases Capital Cities/ABC for $19 billion. It is the largest media takeover to date and the second largest acquisition of a US firm.

1996 Disney purchases the Anaheim Angels baseball franchise.

1997 (Jan) Ovitz leaves the company after a public clash with Eisner with a $140 million severance package.

1997 *Business Week* names the Disney board the worst board in America (for the first time).

1999 Disney's lawsuit with Katzenberg, regarding future profit participation, is settled when he accepts a $275 million payout.

2000 Roy E. Disney and Stanley Gold begin their campaign to force the board to develop a programme to identify Eisner's eventual successor and become more independent. The board of directors includes Eisner's friends such as actor Sidney Poitier, architect Robert A.M. Stern, who has designed many Disney properties, and former Sen. George Mitchell, who consults for Disney. The board's judgement is particularly questionable with regard to the compensation packages awarded to Eisner. In the spring of 2001, *Forbes* concluded that in the previous five years, Eisner made $737 million. This was in a period when the company's profits fell and in which the company's stock performed poorly.

2001 (Oct) Disney acquires the Fox Family Channel for $5.3 billion, a price that is seen by many as far too high.

2002 (Aug) During the previous five years, Disney performed worse than all but three of the 30 Dow stocks. Eisner's failures are becoming increasingly common-place, they include the poor performance of the ABC network, the leading network, possessing an envied news organization and cutting-edge original programming such as *NYPD Blue* when it was purchased seven years earlier; a botched plan to build an American history theme park; the loss of millions of dollars on an expensive new California Adventure attraction at Disneyland, which failed to draw significant crowds; and a loss of more than $1 billion in an attempt to replicate Yahoo!'s portal with the go.com network.

2003	The Securities and Exchange Commission began investigating whether Disney failed adequately to disclose payments made by the company to directors and their family members in 2001.
2003 (April)	Disney sells Anaheim Angels baseball franchise.
2003 (May)	Disney announces plans to sell its badly performing Disney Stores.
2003 (Nov)	Roy E. Disney learns he will not be entered on the slate of directors for the next election (March 2004).
2003 (Nov)	Roy E. Disney resigns from the board and publishes his letter of resignation in which he claims that some of his associates have been required to report his conversations and activities back to Eisner, the company has lost its creative direction, Eisner is guilty of micro-management and has refused to establish a clear succession plan. He concludes by saying '... it is my sincere belief that it is you who should be leaving not me. Accordingly, I once again call for your resignation or retirement.'
2003 (Dec)	Stanley Gold resigns from the board and publishes his letter of resignation in which he criticizes the board for 'not actively engaging in serious discussions regarding the Company's flawed plans and management's unmet projections and unfilled promises'. He also questions the board's adoption of its Corporate Governance Guidelines which he describes as 'another example of this Board's commitment to image over substance'.
2004 (Jan)	Pixar, the company behind blockbusters such as *Finding Nemo* and *Monsters Inc*, ends its distribution deal with Disney following the failure of the two parties to negotiate a new distribution deal. The five movies created by Pixar for Disney have grossed more than $2.5 billion at the box office.
2004 (Feb)	Comcast announces a hostile bid for Disney ($54 billion in stock). The bid is rejected.
2004 (Feb)	Institutional Shareholder Services (Proxy Advisor) recommends shareholders to withhold their vote on the re-election of Michael Eisner.
2004 (Feb)	Glass Lewis & Co. (Proxy Advisor) recommends shareholders to withhold their vote on the re-election of Michael Eisner and George Mitchell.
2004 (March)	A five and half hour annual shareholder meeting sees 43% of shareholders withhold their vote for Eisner and 24% for Mitchell (final results including proxy voting show 45.37% and 25.69% respectively). Later in the day it is announced that Eisner will be replaced as Chairman of the Board by Mitchell.

2004 (April)	*Forbes* magazine names Eisner as one of the five worst CEOs in America (based on annualized total return of minus 5% and average compensation over the six year period of $121 170 940).
2004 (April)	Comcast drops bid for Disney (now worth $48 billion).
2004 (Sept)	Eisner announces that he will retire when his contract expires in September 2006. The two-year period of transition to a new CEO is heavily criticized for being too long, increasing uncertainty, handicapping the development of corporate strategy and creating a 'lame duck' CEO. The search for Eisner's successor will be led by Chairman George Mitchell, who will also be leaving the board in September 2006, who announced the company's intention to name the new CEO in June 2005, leading to uncertainty as to whether Eisner would leave the company earlier than planned. Mitchell also announced Robert Iger (a long-time executive at Capital Cities/ABC before its sale to Disney, who became Disney's President in 2000). This was Eisner's personal choice as his successor and the only internal candidate for the post.

Following initial suggestions that he would not rule out continuing to serve on the board and reclaiming the Chairmanship if asked to by the board after his 'retirement', Eisner said in a *Fortune* magazine interview that his assumption is that he would not continue on the board or as Chairman. Mitchell added that 'as far as the Board is concerned that is the end of it.'

The California Public Employees' Retirement System (one of the US's largest investors and a leading advocate for improved corporate governance) called for Eisner's resignation, saying in a press release that Eisner's 'continued presence on the board would prevent the company from the clean break that is needed to restore investor confidence.'

Upcoming	A lawsuit filed by shareholders against Disney is expected to be tried in Delaware's Court of Chancery in October 2004. The suit is challenging Ovitz's $140 million severance package. Eisner, and the directors of the company will defend against allegations that their mishandling of Mr Ovitz's hiring and termination cost shareholders millions.

The defendants will have to face claims they breached their duty to Disney in 1995 when Mr Ovitz negotiated the terms of his employment deal, and in 1996, when he was allowed to leave the company under a 'no-fault' clause.

Attorneys for shareholders argue that Mr Ovitz's performance was so poor in the president's slot that the company should have fired him for cause, a move that would have meant a much smaller severance package. Mr Ovitz's attorneys say the evidence will prove otherwise.

In a pre-trial hearing, the judge ruled that instead of resigning or being fired, Disney's president may have colluded with Mr Eisner to engineer a no-fault departure. In court papers, Mr Ovitz's attorneys have said the $140 million no-fault payment was justified and a bargain, compared with the $320 million in damages that Ovitz could have won had Disney fired him unfairly for cause. If shareholder allegations that Mr Ovitz lied and alienated Disney executives prove to be true, the judge may find that the no-fault termination was unjustified and that Disney's board is to blame for not firing him.

The Disney directors are already in a difficult position as the board never met to approve Ovitz's departure or the payment of his severance package and it is unclear whether the payment ever was properly authorized.

Upcoming   Disney and Gold have promised to run an alternate slate of potential Disney directors if the board does not remove Eisner by the March 2005 annual meeting.

The above case covers many of the key issues in the present debate on corporate governance:

1 CEO rewards

2 Chairman/CEO split

3 Succession planning

4 Board independence

5 Effectiveness of the board

6 Communication among and to board members

7 Responsibilities of directors

8 Payments to directors' companies and family members

9 Ceremonial adoption of corporate governance guidelines

10 The role of financial institutions

The letter from Stanley Gold is below:

[Letterhead of Stanley P. Gold]

December 1, 2003

To the Board of Directors of the Walt Disney Company:

It is with regret that I resign effective immediately from the Board of Directors of the Walt Disney Company and second Roy Disney's call for the removal of Michael Eisner as Chairman and C.E.O. I am proud of my more than 15 years of service and my role in reshaping the Company in 1984 by bringing Frank Wells and Michael Eisner to the Company. I do, however, lament that my efforts over the past three years to implement needed changes has only succeeded in creating an insular Board of Directors serving as a bulwark to shield management from criticism and accountability. At this time, I believe there is little that I can achieve by working from within to refocus the Company. I hope that my resignation will serve as a catalyst for change at Disney.

The most recent evidence of the drive for insularity is reflected in the Governance Committee's determination that Roy Disney should no longer serve on the Board, ostensibly because Roy had surpassed the expected retirement age established by the Board's Corporate Governance Guidelines. In fact, these very rules regarding age, by their terms, only apply to non-management directors, not to Roy, who, as the Committee knows, has been deemed a management director. The Committee's decision and George Mitchell's defense of it yesterday are clearly disingenuous. The real reason for the Committee's action is that Roy has become more pointed and vocal in his criticism of Michael Eisner and this Board. This is yet another attempt by this Board to squelch dissent by hiding behind the veil of 'good governance.' What a curious result.

Roy has devoted a lifetime to Disney as both an employee and Director. He has served with renewed vigor during these times of malaise, disappointment and instability at the Company, trying to maintain the morale of employees, focusing on the magic that makes Disney special and attacking bonuses to the CEO and increased compensation for Board members while the Company falters and shareholder value erodes. He and his family have a very large financial stake in the Company. Unlike Messrs. Watson and Murphy who have asked to be replaced, Roy has sought even more involvement only to be told that his input in animation will continue to be minimized and that his role as a Director is no longer welcome. This Board has become an enabler to entrenched management and, in so doing, is not effectively discharging its duties to the shareholders. This conduct has resulted in yet another valuable human asset of the Company slipping away. Within the last year this Board will have managed to cull from its ranks Andrea Van de Kamp and now Roy, two of the staunchest critics of Michael Eisner and the Company's poor performance. I cannot sit idly by as this Board continues to ignore and disenfranchise those who raise questions about the performance of management.

As this Board knows, during my tenure I have tried to be an active, engaged Director. I believe a board should not merely rubber stamp decisions of senior management. I decided in August of 2002 that it was not enough just to express my views in the limited time set aside for our infrequent Board meetings. I therefore began a series of written communications to the Board regarding the Company, its management and the Board. I wrote to express my disagreement and growing concern with management, its policies and the effectiveness of the Board. I focused on the failed initiatives of the Company over the past five or six years and admonished the Board for not actively engaging in serious discussions regarding the Company's flawed plans and management's unmet projections and unfulfilled promises. In particular, I have urged the Board to concentrate on the Company's 'poor performance, lack of credibility and accountability and poor capital allocation.' In an effort to get Directors to seriously assess management's 5-year strategic plan (a plan that is only discussed with this Board, but not submitted for Board approval), I wrote to the Board to detail the Company's unsatisfactory financial performance for the past several years and to suggest a process, a so-called Diagnostic Review, designed to give the non-management directors the tools necessary to evaluate performance and establish a comprehensive framework and baseline from which the Board could be active partners in developing plans to maximize the value of Disney's existing assets and businesses. That approach was opposed by management and then, not surprisingly, rejected by the Board. The Board and its Chairman even criticized me for putting on paper these serious questions about fundamental matters.

I believe the Board's adoption of its Corporate Governance Guidelines was yet another example of this Board's commitment to image over substance. Among other things, those Guidelines were carefully crafted to stifle dissent while allowing those supportive of senior management to continue business as usual. This was apparent when the Board applied its Guidelines to conclude that I was not 'independent' despite the fact that I frequently challenged management at Board meetings and criticized both the Board's and the Company's performance. That decision was initially based on my daughter's employment in a non-executive position at Disney and, then, after that reason became insufficient under the new NYSE Governance Guidelines, because of my association with Roy. This resulted in my further isolation as I was no longer permitted to serve on the Governance and Nominating Committee or the Compensation Committee. On the other hand, John Bryson was deemed 'independent' and appointed Chairman of the Nominating and Governance Committee despite the fact that his wife is an executive officer at Lifetime Entertainment Television, a 50% owned subsidiary of Disney, where she earned in excess of $1 million in total compensation in fiscal 2001. In addition, Senator Mitchell was appointed Presiding Director, despite having been recently employed as a Company consultant and notwithstanding that the law firm of which he was chairman received in excess of $1 million for legal services on behalf of the Company in fiscal 2001.

At the time the Company's new Corporate Governance Guidelines were being considered, I also urged the Board to separate the positions of Chairman of the Board and CEO. This separation would empower the Board and help establish its independence and oversight role. Not only did the Board reject that initiative, the Board failed to give the newly established Presiding Director any real substantive powers.

Continuing through March of this year I wrote to express my concerns regarding the financial performance of the Company and the repeated failures of management to achieve its forecasts. I urged this Board to feel a sense of urgency in dealing with the issues of leadership, performance, operations and accountability. Those efforts failed. Instead, Mr. Eisner was awarded a bonus of $5 million in Disney shares by the Compensation Committee despite objections by Roy and me. I believe that bonuses for senior management must be tied to performance; by that measure, no bonus was warranted.

In a similar vein, I recently wrote to express my objection to the Compensation and Governance Committee's joint recommendations that fees paid to Disney Directors be increased dramatically, that stock grants to Directors be substituted for options (and thereby render meaningless the requirement that Directors own $100,000 in Disney shares) and that greater compensation be paid to the Presiding Director. Raises for the Disney Directors at this time are inappropriate based on my assessment of the Company's performance. I objected to the increase for the Presiding Director on the grounds that it did not reflect a reasonable payment for the only slightly increased duties. Finally, I could not make sense of a share ownership requirement for Directors that would be satisfied by a direct issuance from the Company at the same time Directors' cash compensation was being increased.

It is clear to me that this Board is unwilling to tackle the difficult issues I believe this Company continues to face – management failures and accountability for those failures, operational deficiencies, imprudent capital allocations, the cannibalization of certain Company icons for short-term gain, the enormous loss of creative talent over the last years, the absence of succession planning and the lack of strategic focus. Instead, the Board seems determined to devote its time and energies to adopting policies that focus not on substance, but on process and, in reality, only serve to muzzle and isolate those Directors who recognize that their role is to be active participants in shaping the Company and planning for executive succession. Further, this Board isolates those Directors who believe that Michael Eisner (when measured by the dismal results over the last 7 years) is not up to the challenge. Perhaps acting independently, from outside the Boardroom, not hamstrung by a recently enacted Board policy barring Board members from communicating with shareholders and the media, I can have greater success in shaping the policies, practices and operations of Disney than I had as a member of the Board.

In accordance with Item 6 of Form 8-K and Item 7 of Schedule 14A, I request that you disclose this letter and that you file a copy of this letter as an exhibit to a Company Form 8-K.

Very truly yours,

(Signed) Stanley P. Gold

The letter from Roy Edward Disney is as follows:

Letterhead of Roy Edward Disney

November 30, 2003

Dear Michael,

It is with deep sadness and regret that I send you this letter of resignation from the Walt Disney Company, both as Chairman of the Feature Animation Division and as Vice Chairman of the Board of Directors.

You well know that you and I have had serious differences of opinion about the direction and style of management in the Company in recent years, for whatever reason, you have driven a wedge between me and those I work with even to the extent of requiring some of your associates to report my conversations and activities back to you. I find this intolerable.

Finally, you discussed with the Nominating Committee of the Board of Directors its decision to leave my name off the slate of directors to be elected in the coming years, effectively muzzling my voice on the Board – much as you did with Andrea Van de Kamp last year.

Michael, I believe your conduct has resulted from my clear and unambiguous statements to you and to the Board of Directors that after 19 years at the helm you are no longer the best person to run the Walt Disney Company. You have a very successful first 10 plus years at the Company in partnership with Frank Wells, for which I salute you. But, since Frank's untimely death in 1994, the Company has lost its focus, its creative energy, and its heritage.

As I have said, and as Stanley Gold has documented in letters to you and other members of the Board, this Company, under your leadership, has failed during the last seven years in many ways:

1 The failure to bring back ABC Prime Time from the ratings abyss it has been in for years and your inability to program successfully the ABC Family Channel. Both of these failures have had, and I believe will continue to have, significant adverse impact on shareholder value.

2 Your considered micro-management of everyone around you with the resulting loss of morale throughout this Company.

3 The timidity of your investments in our theme park business. At Disney's California Adventure, Paris, and now in Hong Kong, you have tried to build parks 'on the cheap' and they show it and the attendance figures reflect it.

4 The perception by all our stakeholders – consumers, investors, employees, distributors and suppliers – that the Company is rapacious, soul-less, and always looking for the 'quick buck' rather than long-term value which is leading to a loss of public trust.

5 The creative brain drain of the last several years, which is real and continuing, and damages our Company with the loss of every talented employee.

6 Your failure to establish and build constructive relationships with creative partners, especially Pixar, Miramax, and cable companies distributing our products.

7 Your consistent refusal to establish a clear succession plan.

In conclusion, Michael, it is my sincere belief that it is you who should be leaving and not me. Accordingly, I once again call for your resignation or retirement. The Walt Disney Company deserve fresh, energetic leadership at this challenging time in its history just as it did in 1984 when I headed a restructuring that resulted in your recruitment to the company.

I have and will always have an enormous allegiance and respect for this Company, founded by my uncle Walt, and father, Roy, and to our faithful employees and loyal stockholders.

I don't know if you and other directors can comprehend how painful it is for me and the extended Disney family to arrive at this decision.

In accordance with Item 6 of Form 8-K and Item 7 of Schedule 14A, I request that you disclose this letter and that you file a copy of this letter as an exhibit to a Company Form 8-K.

With sincere regret,

(Signed) Roy Edward Disney

cc. Board of Directors

Case Questions

1 What went wrong on the Disney Board? Suggest ways you might avoid or alleviate these factors.

2 To what extent do you think any of the regulatory and advisory codes of conduct for Boards would have been useful in addressing Disney's problems of governance? Why would they have been useful (or why not)?

3 Examine the letters from Stanley Gold and Roy Disney. What do they reveal about board structures, processes and ethos?

4 What are the implications of poor governance (such as in the Disney case) for strategic thinking and acting in organizations?

Further reading and references

Aguilera, RV and Cuervo-Cazurra, A (2004) Codes of good governance worldwide: what is the trigger? *Organization Studies*, **25**, **3**, pp. 415–43.

Bank of England (1998) 'Composition of Company Boards', *Bank of England Quarterly Bulletin*, May, pp. 242–5.

Berle, AA and Means, GC (1932) *The Modern Corporation and Private Property*, Macmillan, New York.

Bernstein, PL (1996) *Against the Gods: The Remarkable Story of Risk*, Wiley, New York.

Bostock, R (1995) 'Company Responses to Cadbury', *Corporate Governance: An International Review*, **3**, **2**, April, pp. 72–7.

Cadbury Report (1992) *Committee on the Financial Aspects of Corporate Governance*, Moorgate, London.

Cadbury, A (2000) 'The Corporate Governance Agenda', *Corporate Governance: An International Review*, **8**, **1**, pp. 7–15.

CADS (1995) *The Financial Aspects of Corporate Governance: Compliance with the Code of Best Practice*, May, Stock Exchange, London.

Cassidy, DP (2000) 'Wither Corporate Governance in the 21st Century', *Corporate Governance: An International Review*, **8**, **4**, pp. 297–302.

Charkham, JP (1999) *Keeping Good Company: A Study of Corporate Governance in Five Countries* (2nd edition), Oxford University Press, Oxford.

Collins, JC and Porras, JI (2000) *Built to Last: Successful Habits of Visionary Companies*, Random House, New York.

Condon, D (2003) 'The Role of the Turnbull Guidelines and the Management and Identification of Risk in UK Multi-National Companies', PhD in progress Warwick Business School, UK.

Conger, JA, Lawler, EE and Finegold, DL (2001) *Corporate Boards: Strategy for Adding Value at the Top*, Jossey-Bass Pfeiffer, San Francisco and Wiley, Chichester.

Contardo, I and Wilson, DC (2001) 'The United Nations' Global Compact: A Report on Case Study Evidence', Research Paper, Warwick Business School, UK.

Conyon, MJ (1994) 'Corporate Governance Changes in UK Companies between 1988 and 1993', *Corporate Governance: An International Review*, **2**, **2**, pp. 97–109.

Conyon, MJ (1995) *Cadbury in the Boardroom*, in Arthur Anderson Corporate Register, Hemmington Scott, London.

Conyon, MJ and Mallin, C (1997) 'Women in the Boardroom: Evidence from Large UK Companies', *Corporate Governance: An International Review*, **5**, **3**, pp. 112–17.

Conyon, MJ and Murphy, KJ (2000) 'The Prince and the Pauper? CEO Pay in the US and UK', *The Economic Journal*, **110**, F640–F671.

Greenbury, R (1995) *Directors' Remuneration: Report of a Study Group Chaired by Sir Richard Greenbury*, Gee Publishing, London.

Hambrick, DC, Nadler, DA and Tushman, ML (1998) (eds) *Navigating Change: How CEOs, Top Teams and Boards Steer Transformation*, Harvard University Press, Boston, MA.

Hampel, R (1998) *Committee on Corporate Governance: Final Report*, Gee Publishing, London.

Hemscott (2003) 'The current population of non-executive directors', Hemscott Group Limited, London

Higgs, D (2003) Review of the Role and Effectiveness of Non-Executive Directors, Department of Trade and Industry, London. Printed in the United Kingdom by The Stationery Office 19585 809438 01/03.

Hutton, W (1996) *The State We're In*, Vintage Press, London.

Institute of Chartered Accountants (1999) 'Internal Control: Guidance for Directors on the Combined Code', ICA, London.

Institute of Chartered Accountants (1999) 'Implementing Turnbull: A Boardroom Brief', ICA Centre for Business Performance, London.

Kaplan, RS and Norton, DP (1992) The Balanced Scorecard: Measures that Drive Performance, *Harvard Business Review*, Jan/Feb.

Katzenbach, JR and Smith, DK (1992) *The Wisdom of Teams: Creating the High Performance Organization*, Harvard Business School Press, Boston, MA.

Keasey, K, Thompson, S and Wright, M (eds) (1997) *Corporate Governance: Economic Management and Financial Issues*, Oxford University Press, Oxford.

Kirkbride, J and Letza, S (2003) 'Establishing the boundaries of regulation in coporate governance: Is the UK moving toward a process of collibration?', *Business and Society Review*, **108**, **4**, pp. 463–85.

McNulty, T and Pettigrew, AM (1999) 'Strategists on the Board', *Organization Studies*, **20**, **1**, pp. 47–74.

Monks, RAG and Minnow, N (1992) *Power and Accountability: Restoring Balance of Power Between Corporations, Owners and Societies*, Harper Business, New York.

OECD (2004) *Principles of Corporate Governance* (available at www.OECD.org).

Pettigrew, AM (2004) 'Corporate Governance', *Distance Learning MBA Notes for Strategy and Practice*, Warwick Business School.

Pettigrew, AM and McNulty, T (1995) 'Power and Influence in and Around the Boardroom', *Human Relations*, **48**, **8**, pp. 845–73.

Pettigrew, AM and McNulty, T (1998) 'Sources and Uses of Power in the Boardroom', *European Journal of Work and Organizational Psychology*, **7**, **2**, pp. 197–214.

Ward, RD (2000) *The Boardroom Insider Guidebook*, New York, Wiley.

Part 5

Strategy and the future

Part contents

In this part you will find the following chapters:

Introduction

In Parts 2 and 3 we introduced the language of competitive advantage. Coupled with industry analysis (five forces analysis) and the value chain concept, this provided the kickstart for the modern theory of strategy and was the genesis of an entire academic and consulting industry devoted to the production of analysis-based concepts, frameworks and tools. The idea of strategy as the design of firm-specific market imperfections in the pursuit of profit gave rise to the language of *value*, for example value creation, value capture, value-based management, shareholder value, economic value added and so on. The term value encompasses multiple stakeholders: distinctive value for customers (remember we used the idea on consumer surplus in Chapter 6), superior profits for firms (we used the term rents in Chapter 5), and returns to the labour force in terms of higher rewards for higher productivity. If value is created by skilful strategic management then that value filters through to all the stakeholders and beyond (e.g. through taxes and through larger business volumes).

In Part 4 the focus shifted from the strategic positioning of the firm in relation to its competitors and its customers to those internal arrangements from which an external value-creating position derives. From this perspective we see the roots of value lie within the organization, through its structure, through its management processes and decision rules, through its governance arrangements, and by virtue of its ability to adapt, to change itself, and sometimes to transform itself. All these internal foundation stones rest on the ability of its people to manage strategically so as to achieve long-term objectives. In this part we also created an important counterbalance to the simple idea of value in the earlier sections. Here we looked at risk and uncertainty leading us to the idea of risk-return trade-offs – a concept central to strategy and especially the evaluation of alternative strategies. Along with this we used the idea of scenario planning as a way of creating and understanding strategic options that can then be evaluated in a risk-return way.

From the building blocks in these earlier parts we can see the idea of value and value-based management taking a central role in strategic thinking. In Part 5 we extend our strategy discourse into a more holistic view of how value creation and capture takes place. There is an entire literature on the topic of value-based management and its many variants. The purpose of this discussion is to give this literature a foundation in strategic management thinking. One variant is the idea of *value disciplines* (Treacy and Wiersema 1994).[1] These disciplines are operational excellence, product leadership and customer intimacy. Some prestigious public awards for management excellence focus more on internal management processes. The Baldridge Award, which is highly respected in the USA, is a good example. This identifies seven arenas of management activity that are used to assess the management system and its capability for excellence. These arenas are leadership; strategic planning; customer and market focus; measurement, analysis and knowledge management; human resource focus; process management; and business results. These approaches underline the point that excellence and value creation are a joint product of external positioning and internal management processes. Management is the process, and positioning is the external manifestation of it.

In this part we take up three of these arenas as themes because they are particularly close to the core of strategic management thinking. These are (i) performance assessment; (ii) organizational knowledge, learning and value innovation; and (iii) total quality management and customer value. The assessment of *strategic* performance is central to any strategy discussion. Innovation and learning has been the dynamic behind economic growth and the

---

[1]   Treacy, M. and Wiersema, F. (1994) *Discipline of Market Leaders*, Addison Wesley.

stock market value of companies. Total quality management has been the major innovation that has transformed the thinking of companies since the traumas of the 1970s.

Chapter 18 is concerned with analysing and measuring strategic performance. This is not a replay of the financial calculus of shareholder value of the accounting detail of return on investment. Nor is it a wider review of the social responsibility of companies, their corporate citizenship or their ethical standards. Both of these are dealt with in other textbooks. This chapter is about how to distinguish *strategic* performance from conventionally measured financial performance. To do this we use the balanced scorecard approach and we build on the business model approach that was introduced in Chapter 6.

Chapter 19 is about the nature of innovation and technological change. We introduced the idea of creative destruction back in Chapter 8. This chapter builds on that and discusses the effects of disruptive technologies and the dilemmas that face innovators (should we or should we not cannibalize our existing business?). The chapter develops a knowledge-based view of strategy that enables us to discuss ways of fostering organizational commitment to innovation and how to structure organizations so as achieve growth through innovation.

Chapter 20 builds on the writings on operational excellence, much of which is in the operations management area. Much of this literature is about the pursuit of excellence in every corner of the firm's operations. But a strong element of it is concerned with the nature of *quality* and *quality management*. We focus here on the implications of quality for the process of strategic management and the way this is driven by customer perceptions of value. We see from the examples how the rethinking of supply chain and value chain concepts from a total quality perspective actually enables firms to compete differently and often to out-compete those with conventional approaches.

In this Part you will see how a 'systemic' view of strategy begins to emerge. Parts 2 & 3 gave most emphasis to context and strategy. Part 4 opened up the process view of strategy showing how organisations, stakeholders and individuals bring important influence to bear on strategy in practice. In this Part the many elements in our Resource and Process maps appear simultaneously, requiring careful coordination – i.e. requiring a 'systems' view.

Chapter 18's focus on the measurement of performance, Chapter 19's introduction of the knowledge-based view and Chapter 20's attention to the elusive concept of quality all emphasise the elements of direction, actions and outcomes. Chapter 21 integrates all the key elements of the Resources map, showing how these elements need to be robustly linked together.

The Process map shows how strong linkages between the elements of this map result in the ability to 'think and act strategically'. The orientation elements – context, options and actions – are fulfilled as shown in the Resources map. However, the elements of animation – interpretation, formulation and implementation – are essential for strategy in action to be attained. In process terms, Chapter 18 asks how the balanced score card integrates in practice with the human resource system. In Chapter 19 the knowledge-based view is shown to be embedded in organisational routines and in learning processes. The quality concept in Chapter 20 shows how the apparently simple idea of quality requires complex links between strategy, organisation and operations.

This Part, taken as a whole, shows how the strength of the linkages within and between the maps gives strategy that integrated, systems-like characteristic that is essential for the sustained ability to create value.

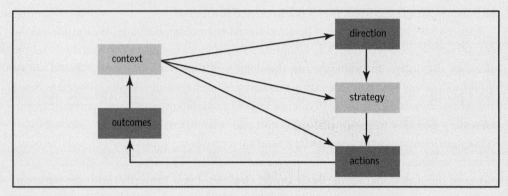

Figure 1.6 Strategy Resources Concepts Map: Outline

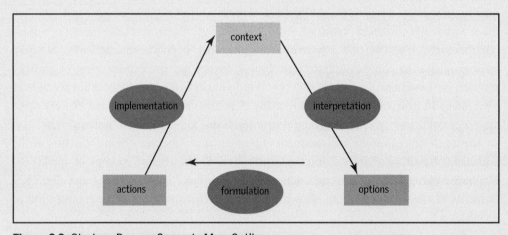

Figure 2.2 Strategy Process Concepts Map: Outline

Chapter 18

Analysing and measuring strategic performance

While the principle that the fundamental objective of the business corporation is to increase the value of its shareholders' investment is widely accepted, there is substantially less agreement about how this is accomplished.
(Rappaport, 1986, p.1)

Introduction

The concept of strategic performance and its measurement is a central issue in the field of strategic management. In earlier sections of this book, performance constructs such as a 'business model' (Chapter 6), managing a business for value (Chapter 7) and the **balanced scorecard** (Chapters 5 and 17) illustrate the fundamental importance of analysing the performance and health of

Chapter contents

the firm. And, our organizing framework – the systemic model (*see* Figure 1.6) – shows that performance feedback provides the framework within which organizational renewal and strategic reorientation take place.

In this chapter, we note that firms have a range of targets or goals with profit maximization or shareholder value maximization often stated as one of the key strategic objectives. We will also discuss the following issues about performance metrics:

- The idea of multiple measures of performances, e.g. accounting-based, market-based, etc.
- The concepts of economic value and, in particular, 'shareholder value' and 'economic value added'.
- An examination of the 'value-based' management approach.
- An analysis of the 'balanced scorecard' approach to performance measurement, with its focus on key performance indicators to address the multiple goals and foci of the business (e.g. financial, marketing, internal process and learning goals).

In summary, organizations and managers must link their choice of performance measures and key performance indicators with the overall strategy and any likely re-evaluation of strategic priorities. Appropriate and robust performance metrics allow managers to evaluate strategic success and 'fine tune' the **business model** to achieve corporate goals and targets.

18.1 **The domain of business performance**

Venkatraman and Ramanujam (1986) present a very useful conceptualization to explain the domain of business performance. This is shown in Figure 18.1. We shall use this as an organizing structure for this chapter.

In this diagram, three perspectives of performance are offered, namely, financial performance, operations performance and organizational effectiveness. We will discuss each briefly in turn.

Financial measures of performance

The narrowest view of performance (represented by the inner circle) focuses on *financial performance* and argues that well-crafted strategy pursues primarily profitability goals, well examined in the accounting literature, such as return on investment, return on equity or earnings per share. This approach assumes the dominance of financial goals and associated measures, whether they are accounting based or financial-market based.

Operational measures of performance

Operational performance indicators (the middle ring of the diagram) examine a range of internal performance factors which might lead to success for the company and its set of

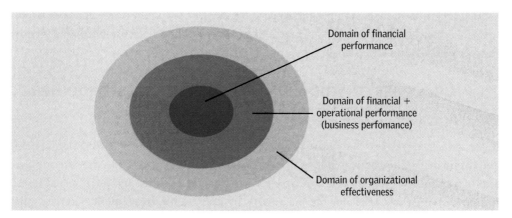

Figure 18.1 Domain of business performance
Source: Venkatraman and Ramanujam, 1986, p. 803.

businesses. These include market position indicators such as the absolute level or growth rate of sales, market share (as a percentage of sales) and the rate of new product introductions. Other measures might involve a focus on efficiency and include value added in manufacturing, product quality and other indicators of technological efficiency (e.g. potential economies of scale and scope).

Measures of organizational effectiveness

Beyond economic and operational performance fundamentals, the selection of performance factors that should be monitored and benchmarked must respond to the strategic goals of the entire firm (the outer ring of the figure), and their often multiple and conflicting nature (Cameron and Whetten 1983). Management's challenge, therefore, is to build systemic relationships with all stakeholders and constituents of the firm from shareholders, suppliers and employees through to consumers, in order to build value throughout the organization. For example, they might measure such human-resource indicators as employee job satisfaction and labour turnover and examine supply-chain relationships in order to build and create long-term strategic knowledge and value for the organization.

In summary, value creation in performance terms is clearly the central task and purpose of senior management. It means that managing performance outputs rather than resource inputs is an imperative and requires a perspective that encompasses a systemic and dynamic understanding of performance. In other words, if performance is sound then it can be assumed that there is a clear 'fit' between the elements of strategy (e.g. competition, capabilities, etc.) and organizational success. If, on the other hand, there is evidence of performance weaknesses, these may indicate that there are problems in the strategic framework, involving perhaps a weak competitive strategy or a shortfall in organizational core competences and capabilities.

What is critical in managing performance is the existence of appropriate and robust performance metrics, which enable managers to predict economic performance and identify necessary changes in strategic and operational positioning.

18.2 **Concepts of value and performance management**

18.2.1 **Accounting-based performance metrics**

In the industrial era's search for efficiency, managerial thinkers such as Alfred P. Sloan (1963) and his financial director, Donaldson Brown, put forward the proposition that the strategic aim of a business is to earn a satisfactory return on capital (or the money invested in the business). Financial efficiency as measured by **return on investment** (ROI = net income/capital investment) became perhaps the most commonly used of the measures of financial position alongside **return on equity** (ROE = net income/shareholders' equity), **return on sales** (ROS = net income/sales revenue) and **return on assets** (ROA = net income/assets employed in business). The financial press and corporate analysts' reports also placed great emphasis on measures of **earnings per share** (EPS = net income/number of shares outstanding) and **price/earnings ratios** (P/E = ratio of stock price/net income) as a scorecard of corporate performances.

Managers and analysts use accounting earnings and accounting profits as a benchmark because financial accounts are readily available and the measures themselves are easy to calculate. Yet, according to Doyle (2000, pp. 26–7), the measurement of accounting earnings can be arbitrary and subjective and easily manipulated by management (*see* also Smith 1992). Accounting profits also exclude investments, ignore the time value of money (*see* Rappaport 1986) and produce a focus on short-term results. Indeed, many of these criticisms stress the fact that managers may uncritically focus on accounting numbers without recognizing the judgements, conventions and realities involved in the construction of those numbers.

Writers, such as Rappaport (1986) in particular, demonstrate the detailed shortcomings of accounting numbers and advance the concept of shareholder value creation as the new standard for business performance. Indeed, Rappaport points out that research confirms that satisfactory earnings growth (for example, growth in EPS) does not necessarily lead to a concomitant increase in the market value of the company's shares.

Hayes and Abernathy (1980) also point out the shortcomings of management who wrongly assume that by improving ROI, ROE, etc., consequent improvements in share price must necessarily follow. Indeed, they criticize ROI for helping to hasten the process of 'managing our way to economic decline'. They point out that ROE, with its short-term emphasis, can lead to a decline in investments of a long-term character such as those in innovations, which provide the growth paths and long-term strategic direction for many organizations.

Quite apart from the accounting judgements necessary to measure accounting earnings, there are a similar set of problems in measuring assets. Typically, financial accounts recognize and measure physical assets but ignore the intangible assets increasingly developed by knowledge-based companies, e.g. patents, R&D, new technologies, brands and customer loyalty. With the wide growth of knowledge-based companies in IT, biotechnology, pharmaceuticals etc., measures of ROA will be over-recorded with such companies, since knowledge assets will be under-recorded. There will also probably be similar over-recording for mature manufacturing companies that have gradually depreciated their assets over time, making the book value of the assets quite small in the denominator of the ROA measure. Such anomalies in the measurement of ROA, therefore, suggest that comparing the financial performance of companies in the FTSE (*Financial Times* Share Exchange), for example, using ROA would provide a very questionable measure of comparative performance. Indeed, there may be an inverse relationship between ROA performance and improvements in share price performance.

In summary, writers such as Rappaport and others hastened the value creation trend in measures of financial performance.

18.2.2 Economic value added (EVA) and financial performance

Consultants such as Stern Stewart (1996) promoted the movement from a focus on accounting profit to economic profit, or economic rent as exemplified in our earlier discussion of the resource-based view (RBV), (*see* Chapter 7). Indeed, Kay (1993) defines added value as the difference between the value of a firm's output and the cost of the firm's inputs. Stern Stewart define an essentially similar concept, which they call **economic value added** (EVA). They define EVA as net operating profit after tax minus the weighted average cost of capital. The resulting value of EVA can then be interpreted as a measure of the strategic value of the business and a useful metric for judging ongoing performance. In consequence, the EVA approach argues that a firm and its set of businesses are creating value when they earn returns in excess of the firm's weighted average cost of capital – a position which is consistent with an objective of maximizing shareholder value. However, EVA links value creation to current operating performance, i.e. it is a single-period measure of value creation, developed from balance sheet measures, and provides a tight financial discipline for a company to address whether it is adding value for shareholders.

It is important to recognize that measures such as 'economic profit' or EVA help firms identify the value for the business. However, the main problem with the 'economic profit' metrics is that they do not help to address the issues associated with future investments such as new product development, whose time period, future earnings and capital requirements are somewhat uncertain and unpredictable. In this situation, the **shareholder value approach** (SVA), with the emphasis on discounted cash flow, and the shareholder value principle popularized by Rappaport (1986) is the more appropriate methodology. This is discussed in more detail in the next section.

Case box: **Freeserve's business model**

Freeserve described their mission in their flotation prospectus as being: 'to become the UK's preferred internet portal by delivering both free internet access and an integrated offering of UK focussed content, e-commerce and community'.[1]

Freeserve believed when they launched that they could improve on the fundamental Internet business model with their 'free access' approach. In their presentation to investors at the time of flotation they describe the traditional business model with the diagram below:

The Traditional Internet Business Model[2]

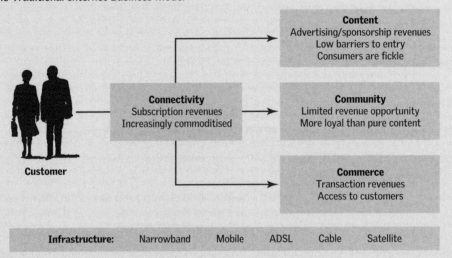

| Infrastructure: | Narrowband | Mobile | ADSL | Cable | Satellite |

They recognized income as being gained either as an ISP through subscriptions or as a portal through advertising, sponsorship and commission from commerce.

They positioned themselves to provide their customers with both of these services:

- a dial-up mechanism to access the internet, in which they compete with other ISPs such as AOL and BT; and
- an internet portal which offers content,

Freeserve's 'improved' Business Model

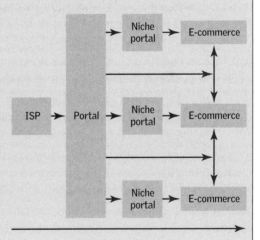

---

[1] Freeserve. The Freeserve Solution. Freeserve Mini Prospectus (12/7/99), p. 4.

[2] Freeserve. Freeserve Investor Presentation (1999) URL: http://www.aboutfreeserve.com/investor/presentations/index.html

tailored web services and a virtual marketplace for consumers to buy and sell products or services, in which they compete with the likes of AOL, Yahoo!, Microsoft, Lycos, etc.

They proposed to change the business model described above profoundly by not charging users for connect time to their ISP. They went on, in the same presentation to investors, to describe their improved business model with the diagram on p. 676.

Their belief was that by offering free access to the internet they would corner the market in people dialing-up to get online. Some income would be generated by agreements with the telephone companies to split the revenue from the telephone call charges, but more importantly, those people would, by default, come to the Freeserve portal first. If the Freeserve portal was good enough, offering sufficient flexibility and a wide range of niche areas, the user would stay with Freeserve, access the internet through its pages and its search engine, read its adverts and buy goods through its sponsors. In that way, the free ISP would be a loss leader to get people into the portal, which would generate the income.

Questions for discussion

1 Examine the Freeserve business model using the Yip framework in Figure 18.2. What, if anything, is missing from Freeserve's model?

2 Can you describe how Freeserve proposes to generate cash flows and profits?

3 What risks does its business model identify?

18.2.3 The shareholder value approach (SVA)

The clear operating principle underlying the SVA is that the company's dominant strategic goal is to maximize its shareholder wealth. In essence, this means that corporate and business strategies should focus on the economic gains they produce for shareholders, i.e. in terms of maximizing the value of their shares through dividend policies and share price rises.

Rappaport (1986) then addresses the issues of how to value the company's shares and advances the view that share prices should be calculated by evaluating expectations of the cash flows that will arise from the company's corporate and business strategies over time. SVA, then, measures the total value of the corporate strategy by discounting these cash flow predictions to allow for the time value of money and risk. Any introductory textbook (e.g. Brealey and Myers (2002)) explains clearly the discounted cash flow (DCF) approach and it has been widely used for many years in practice, for example, to evaluate the worth of alternative capital projects or capital investments (*see* also Chapter 14 in this book). However, it is only over the last fifteen years or so, through Rappaport's influence, that the focus of DCF has switched to shareholder value and the evaluation of strategic planning and management strategies. Ultimately, the SVA calculates an NPV (**net present value**) for each alternative strategy option available to the company, using the company's weighted average cost of capital as the discount rate. That strategy that has the highest NPV of all the options is generally selected as the preferred alternative.

It is important to stress that SVA is not simply a financial approach or a financial technique. It requires all of the corporate knowledge, core capabilities and strategy development processes that have been discussed in this book for the senior managers to outline a viable series of strategic options before putting them under the 'financial' microscope of the SVA.

Case box: Punch Taverns

Punch Taverns is a public limited company which owns about 7400 pubs across the UK. The company has agreements with retailers, who are self-employed and operate a retail business within our pub. The company does not directly manage the retail business in the pubs.

The agreements are generally leases (10 to 25-year agreements assignable after two years and with full repairing liability), or tenancies (non-assignable non-repairing agreements of up to 6 years). Lease agreements generally apply in bigger outlets. The primary lease offer currently is the Punch Growth Lease (PGL). Other short-term agreements exist for temporary situations (notably the tenancy at will – TAW). We also have a legacy of older agreements.

Under all agreements the retailer pays a rent based on a share of the estimated fair maintainable profitability of the pub. The rent is usually index-linked and subject to upward-only rent reviews (after 5 years in leased pubs).

The retailer is also required to buy certain products from the company ('the tie'). In general the tie covers all beer and lager products (sometimes with the exception of one guest ale). Depending on the agreement it may also cover cider, soft drinks, and flavoured alcoholic beverages.

The gross price charged for products is the brewer's or manufacturer's national wholesale price. Discounts are offered off invoice in the Growth Lease. In certain other agreements we offer a retrospective volume target based discount incentive scheme.

In some agreements the company agrees to manage the machine income opportunity in the pub and shares the net income, usually 50:50, with the retailer. The company also receives a rebate from machine suppliers where their machines are sited in our pubs.

The agreements provide a low cost entry into running a business with professional support. We expect adherence to the terms of the agreement, but we are prepared to consider special situations.

The key operational output is business planning, with the objective of helping the retailer to build a better business. The main activities that drive success are:

◆ Recruiting and training the right retailer.

- Agreeing the right business lease, and ensuring adherence to this lease.
- Developing the pub to give the right consumer offer, often using shared investment with the retailer.

Fundamentally, the two key company objectives are to maximize the profitability of each pub, and to optimize the company's share of that profit.

The company has organized support functions to assist the retailer to build his business. Support activities range from essential processes (order taking, debt collection), through care and maintenance (business manager support, customer administration) to development (estate management and investment). In addition the company maintains an infrastructure covering finance, systems, purchasing, HR etc.

A third key company objective is to expand the estate by acquiring more pubs. This can be successful as the company is able to add value to a pub through its purchasing power and support services, thereby earning a good return on investment.

The profitability of the company is driven by two main income streams of beer margin and rent. Machine income and non-beer margin are important growth areas, but of smaller scale. Overhead costs are relatively low and with fairly stable income streams the company has very low operational gearing risk, and is very cash generative.

The company is financed by debt and equity, having floated on the London Stock Exchange in May 2002, and ranked within the UK FTSE 250. Debt comprises some 70% of enterprise value, relatively high but secure due to the nature of the income model. The main debt is securitized in two pub groupings, known as security nets, with further debt capacity for new acquisitions. The business is asset rich, with pub values being comparable to the enterprise value of the company.

Questions for discussion

1 Rewrite the Punch Tavern's business model using the Yip framework in Figure 18.2. What, if anything, is missing from the Punch model?

2 Can you describe how Punch Taverns proposes to generate cash flows? Profits?

3 What risks does its business model identify?

4 Compare the Freeserve and Punch Tavern's approaches to describing and presenting their business models. Which do you prefer? Why?

First and foremost, therefore, the senior managers must develop their own *business model* (*see* the discussion in Chapter 6 and particularly Yip 2004), which is essentially a 'theory' about how their particular business system (i.e. the total corporate set of businesses) operates. Such a model is a set of assumptions about the processes and structures necessary for the business to achieve competitive success. It involves a clear outline of how the whole business system will work and provides full details about the economic and business relationships that must be in place for the corporate strategy to work in the competitive marketplace. As such, it will include many of the strategic system features (*see* Figure 1.6) already discussed in this book: an environmental and competitive model; a capability (core competence) framework; a marketing/consumer model; an operations model and an overall organizational structure and systems model which links people, incentive systems, vision, leadership etc. with the economic relationships necessary for effective strategy implementation. In practice[1] a business model can be articulated in terms of detailed plans and budgets that provide guidance to managers relating to their operational responsibilities. The logic that drives plans and budgets lies within the business model. The business model itself is the mechanism through which a business intends to generate revenue and profits.

Yip (2004, p. 20) identifies the following elements in his conceptualization of a 'business model', as shown in Figure 18.2:

◆ Value proposition (i.e. the strategic concept)

◆ Nature of inputs

◆ How to transform inputs (including technology)

◆ Nature of outputs

◆ Vertical scope

◆ Horizontal scope

◆ Geographic scope

◆ Nature of customers

◆ How to organize

What Yip's business model does is to articulate the logic of the intended strategy in terms of the key strategic choices and the specific operations that have to take place. With this detailed plan the consequences for cash flows can be determined and the link between (intended) strategy and (expected) performance can be established. In many ways this is simply a restyled value chain – an activity map on to which can be placed assets, and revenues and costs. The value chain reflects the firm's strategic choices – the business model goes one step further in making the link to cash flows.

Yip demonstrates the application of his business model using a range of examples including easyGroup's core value proposition of bringing cheap and efficient services (airlines, rent-a-car, etc.) to the mass market. Chapter 6 shows two examples, the 2G (mobile telephony) model (Figure 6.27), and a model of a leasing business at a London-based bank (Figure 6.28).

---

[1] See Chapters 2 and 6 for further discussion.

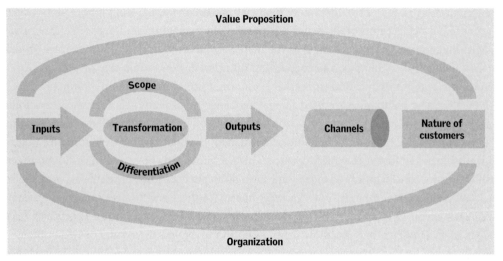

Figure 18.2 Elements of a business model
Source: Yip, 2004.

Assuming, then, that a sound 'business model' is developed, the elements and steps involved in the SVA for valuing strategies are:

1 Clear identification of the 'business model', including the organization value drivers (e.g. capabilities), operational drivers (including supply chain management), marketing drivers (including brands, image, loyalty, etc.) and financial drivers (including cash flows, financial strength, risk profile, etc.).

2 Derivation from the 'business model' of the set of viable strategic options for the company in the competitive marketplace.

3 Evaluation and estimation of the cash flow profiles associated with each strategic option.

4 Estimation of the company's cost of capital (weighted average cost of capital) in view of the company's current and future projected investments (e.g. debt and loan structure implications).

5 Discounting the cash flow profiles for each strategic option (using the weighted average cost of capital) and calculating a net present value for each option.

6 Choosing the strategic option/alternative with the highest net present value.

In summary, therefore, the highest NPV strategy ensures that the option chosen maximizes firm value from the perspective of shareholders and provides the positive net cash flow to satisfy the claims of other stakeholders/constituents in the business system.

However, as with all such 'financially oriented' approaches, there are limitations and issues involved in its application. First, an objective of shareholder value maximization is not always understood by employees and senior managers who feel that the objective of share maximization is too short-term and financial-market oriented, may ignore options for growth and neglect important issues associated with managing the long-term future strategic direction and competitiveness of the firm. Second, as indicated in our chapter on risk (*see* Chapter 14), estimating and forecasting future cash flows must rely on the quality of judgements about such factors as market evolution, technological change, competition, etc. Typically, most companies are used to making range or probabilistic forecasts (and scenarios) over a five-year planning horizon and, as a consequence, knowledge and learning about forecasting capabilities is being accumulated in organizations over time, leading to improvements in forecasting performance. Third, as indicated above, SVA techniques do not allow for the consideration of more long-term strategic decisions, particularly with regard to 'option-type' investments. For example, pharmaceutical and biotechnology companies regularly invest in new research programmes which, at the outset, do not necessarily have clear goals. However, they do allow firms an option to exploit the results of R&D obtained at a later date for the future development of new products. Option-pricing models in finance such as the Black-Scholes model (see Brealey and Myers, 2002) provide a basis for attacking this problem and writers in the strategy field such as Bowman and Hurry (1993) have suggested adaptations to strategy valuation processes using option-type models.

Overall, therefore, the evolution of performance measurement techniques based on 'economic profit' such as EVA and more systemic 'value-based' management techniques as SVA have usefully linked strategy to the finance literature and have provided vehicles for companies to both understand the 'business models' and drivers underlying shareholder value and develop the capability to identify further strategic options and alternatives to create value for the business.

The 'balanced scorecard' approach is a logical development of EVA and SVA techniques, and provides a broader perspective and framework for managers to use in determining which key performance indicators should be used to monitor and, subsequently, drive organizational strategy.

18.2.4 **The balanced scorecard concept: managing for value**

We introduced the idea of the balanced scorecard in Chapter 5 and showed an example in Figure 5.12. The context for this in Chapter 5 was to show how progress against objectives might be assessed and how the scorecard approach enables managers to relate progress to the concepts of competitive strategy and to the content of a strategic plan.

The balanced scorecard concept developed by Kaplan and Norton (1992) is a clear example of how **value-based management** approaches have become much more than a toolkit of financial techniques to apply to critical business issues. The scorecard concept provides insight into the linkages between the *strategic value drivers* (e.g. operational efficiency at Toyota, high-quality production engineering and engine design at Honda) and *strategic outcomes*, and forces senior managers to question both the soundness of the overall corporate strategy and the potential need to reorient the strategy towards an alternative set of strategic priorities.

Case box: **The National Model Agency**

Sales Memorandum

Confidentially offered for sale

The National Model Agency
Profits available to the owners
Exceed £176,000 per annum
Asking Price
£800,000
Business profile

This model and promotional agency provides more services for clients and models than either the high profile London based agencies, which act for a limited number of big name professional models or the provincial agents who serve small local communities. The difference being that none of these traditional agencies have the number of models or geographical coverage that this successful national agency has to offer, by way of choice and a full United Kingdom wide promotion campaign.

The National agency represents professional and amateur models regardless of race, gender, ethnic or national origins, marital status, sexuality, education, age, physical impairment, religion or belief, language, appearance or class. The agency offers access to the world of fashion, film, television and photography.

Several thousand prospective models approach the agency each month.

Online use of the unique bespoke software enables their national database of more than eighteen thousand contracted models to be searched precisely and accurately for clients' requirements producing for them comprehensive data including instant photographic images.

Clients who employ the agency can call for a choice of models at very short notice, for various work fields including advertising, promotions, television, film, fashion, photographic, catalogue, and media and see a national selection immediately downloaded from their PC.

Commercial photographic shoots, television commercials, and magazine layouts that are being shot every day used to expect expensive, time-consuming postal portfolios to be sent by small inefficient agencies. Now these same clients, casting directors, and magazine editors can look at the models portfolio on the web from the computer on their desk and find the model they require in minutes, versus several days or weeks!

The agency avoids so-called glamour work.

The length of management contract between each model and this agency is one to three years.

Ancillary services to models include photographic shoots, training courses, videos, books and merchandise together with access to over 400 professional United Kingdom Master photographers.

As a 'Client focused' agency the agency has achieved excellence in understanding and responding to the demands of new and existing clients, thus generating maximum satisfaction and profitability.

This agency has a strong ability to identify trends and establish itself in new markets thereby exploiting the most profitable opportunities. This has led to heavy investment in a sophisticated computer structure and an increasing focus in establishing a significant Internet presence.

The ten thousand quarterly newsletter and merchandising range provide a potentially strong marketing platform.

The agency is now poised for global development with a licensed franchised system ability to encompass European and Intercontinental business.

Types of Clients

Clients represent a wide variety of organizations:

- Retailers
- Restaurants
- Hospitals
- Religious organizations
- Universities
- Manufacturing firms
- Film & Video producers
- Television Companies
- Racecourses
- Motor Racing Groups
- Luxury Hotel Groups
- Hairdressers
- Drinks Companies
- Dairy Companies
- Newspapers
- Car Rental
- Theatres
- Publishing Houses
- Car Manufacturers
- Building Societies
- Hospital
- Brewers
- City Councils
- . . . and others.

Financial information

The business and property are being offered for sale on a going concern basis.

All financial discussions will take place directly between the vendors and interested party.

Market and competitors

There is no known direct national competitor.

Management and staff

The operation is fully managed with guidance provided by the principals.

Future prospects

The media requirement for the human image for advertising and promotion remains almost insatiable.

The business model could grow to a worldwide operation should the new owners have the drive and ability to manage an operation of this size.

Reason for sale

The owners feel the business is reaching the optimum size for their management ability.

Questions for discussion

The above is a notice advertising the sale of the National Model Agency.

1 From the content of this notice for sale, identify the business model that is in place.

2 Also how would you assess the performance of the National Model Agency from this data?

3 If you were selling a company of this kind, how much information would you give about the underlying business model and the historic performance of the company?

The balanced scorecard allows managers to examine each business and the overall corporate vision and strategy through four perspectives or lenses: financial, customer, internal, and innovation and learning. Figure 18.3 shows the logic of the approach.

What the basic concept of a balanced scorecard provides is a disciplined framework through which to impose a series of questions (Kaplan and Norton, 1992, p. 22) that should be addressed by the company and its senior managers:

- *How do we look to shareholders?* (The financial lens): Metrics in this area encompass the SVA and the EVA approach, as well as accounting-based measures of performance.

- *How do customers see us?* (The customer lens): Metrics in this area include market share, brand image and customer satisfaction.

- *What must we excel at?* (The internal lens): The issues in this area involve the internal business processes necessary to develop a successful strategy. Metrics would include supply-chain processes, quality etc.

- *How can we continue to improve and create value?* (The innovation and learning lens): Metrics in this area address the firm's ability to innovate and develop new capabilities through new product growth and development and improved R&D processes.

Doyle (2000, pp. 152–4) provides a basic and more extended checklist of potential measures or **key performance indicators** (KPIs) for each of these lenses. Broadly, these comprise:

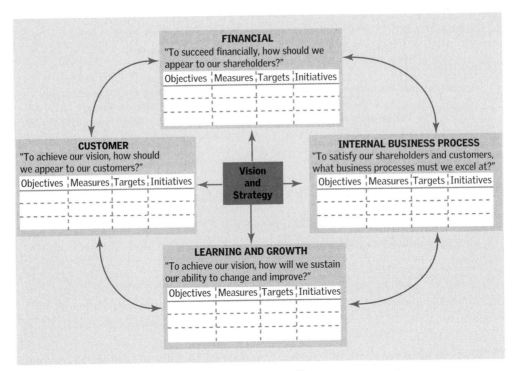

Figure 18.3 Translating vision and strategy: four perspectives
Source: Kaplan, RS and Norton, DP (1996) 'Linking the balanced scorecard to strategy', *California Management Review*, Fall, 39, 1, p. 54.

- ◆ **Financial lens measures**
  - ◆ Return on capital employed
  - ◆ Operating margins
  - ◆ Economic value added
  - ◆ Cash flow
  - ◆ Sales growth

- ◆ **Consumer lens measures**
  - ◆ Market share
  - ◆ Brand image and awareness
  - ◆ Customer satisfaction
  - ◆ Customer relations
  - ◆ Customer acquisition

- ◆ **Internal lens measures**
  - ◆ Percentage of sales from new products
  - ◆ Manufacturing cost
  - ◆ Manufacturing cycle time

- ◆ Inventory management
- ◆ Quality indices
- ◆ Supply chain management processes
- ◆ **Innovation and learning lens measures**
  - ◆ New product development capabilities
  - ◆ R&D core competences
  - ◆ Technological capabilities
  - ◆ Human resource development and capabilities
  - ◆ Improved manufacturing and business processes
  - ◆ Improved sales methods and techniques

Checklists of measures, however, beg the question of what the best set of measures or key performance indicators (KPIs) are for any company. Fundamentally, we argue that important KPIs must link to the company's strategy and vision and track/monitor the key elements of that strategy. They must also take account of any changes in the broader economic and technological environment the company faces. In essence, the KPIs chosen should be regarded as a future-oriented set of metrics that will allow the company to benchmark and monitor the economic and competitive outcomes and examine the stability of the firm's strategy (the long-term perspective) and operations (the short-term perspective).

These KPIs relate back to the discussions in earlier chapters. Whereas KPIs are a manifestation of performance that we seek to measure, the drivers of KPIs are deep within the firm and within the logic of the strategy analysis in Part 3 and within the process analysis of Part 4. Performance analysis and the analysis of progress against strategic milestones was introduced in Chapter 5. The idea of rents and 'superprofits' as goals for strategy making stems for the economic analysis of markets that was introduced in Chapter 3. These discussions provide essential background for the very financially oriented KPIs in the financial lens measures. The trade-off between long- and short-term profits (the time horizon problem) is unresolved by any of these measures. The correct way to account for long-lived assets is captured to some degree by EVA measures.

The customer lens relates to the ideas that were germinated in Chapters 5 and 6 and discussed explicitly in Chapter 7. **Key success factors** (KSFs) and KPIs can be confused. KSFs are often portrayed as intuitive in their conception but Chapter 7 shows how they derive from what customers want (analysis of demand; see Chapter 3 for a close discussion of this) and from how to beat competitors (analysis of competition). Thus, KSFs are manifestations of strategic choice and should reflect the intended competitive advantages. They should therefore be drivers of KPIs and high scores on KPIs would be an indication that the KSFs are in place as intended. Furthermore, Chapter 7 shows a framework for analysing value (*see* Figure 7.12). This captures elements of customer value and shows some examples of KPIs of customer value. It also captures elements of costs and efficiency inherent in the strategy (the internal lens measures). Chapter 20 goes further into the internal process characteristics of the firm in terms of total quality management and supply chain management and these also contribute to the internal lens.

The innovation and learning lens presents many complexities, largely because the issues involved are process-sensitive and are both subtle and complex. The usual KPIs are relatively crude and often do not do justice to the underlying strategic choices. Chapter 16 introduced learning as an organizational phenomenon. Here the idea of the learning pyramid and its four levels of activity (from individual, to one-to-one, to group, to organization) in Figure 16.1 and the framework for organizational learning in Figure 16.2 provide important perspectives that allow general managers and strategists to 'unpack' the KPIs shown in this lens. Chapter 19 takes further the discussion on knowledge and learning. This is driven from the resource-based view (Chapter 7) and provides a strong, albeit subjective, framework for generating useful KPIs for the innovation and learning lens.

The strength of the balanced scorecard approach is its inclusivity of the range of strategy concepts and the way of linking them together in a single map (Figure 18.4). There is strength also in the way in which measurable KPIs are used to ground the map in reality and to make it an operational tool for managers. But this is also its weakness. Not all elements of competitive strategy are easy to measure, although many firms have strategic planning

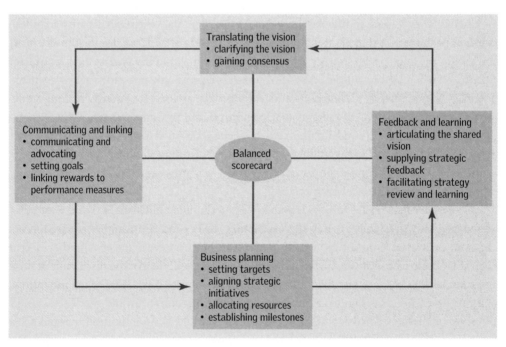

Figure 18.4 The balanced scorecard as a strategic management system
Source: Kaplan, RS and Norton, DP (1996) 'Using the balanced scorecard as a strategic management system', *Harvard Business Review*, Jan/Feb.

processes that make a heroic attempt to do this. More difficult is the area of management process which, as we have seen in Part 4, provides an essential grounding for strategy analysis decisions. Without good or appropriate process, good decisions cannot be made – decisions do not make themselves. The balanced scorecard is relatively silent on matters of process. The balanced scorecard should really be seen as a designed set of KPIs that provide early warning indicators rather than as a diagnostic system that indicates the nature of problems and the sources of them. This is a controversial area that will benefit from progress on two fronts: (i) better conception and measurement of KPIs, and (ii) better linkage of strategy process elements to strategic decisions. The management process issues have been the subject of much attention and are discussed below.

As Kaplan and Norton note (1996, p. 75), the earlier version of the balanced scorecard as a balanced multi-perspective performance measurement system has evolved to a new strategic management system, linking long-term strategic objectives with short-term actions (*see* Figure 18.4), following the usage and experience gained from applying the original scorecard concept in a wide range of 100 or so organizations. Each of those organizations found that the balanced scorecard approach supplied a structure and a framework for such critical management processes as goal setting, business planning, capital allocations, strategic initiatives, and feedback and learning that facilitated strategic thinking and stimulated the analysis of alternative policy options for the organization.

The new strategic management system involves a set of four management processes that interact to enable the management of the strategic balance between short-term productivity objectives and long-term growth perspectives. The first of these processes is that involved in the *translation of the vision and strategy statements* using the model shown in Figure 18.3, so that they form a clear and well-understood set of objectives and measures that are agreed and endorsed by all senior managers.

This vision/strategy facilitates the framing of the strategy map and identification of the long-term drivers, whether marketing, organizational or financial, that will determine the long-term success of the company. Ultimately, a well-structured vision and strategy statement builds organizational commitment.

The second of these processes – *communicating and linking* – requires managers to discuss and communicate their strategy as the corporate vision throughout the company and link that strategy to departmental and individual objectives. Thus, the scorecard provides a vehicle for debate and undertakes a strategic role in ensuring that the organizational strategy is understood by all organizational levels and, more importantly, that both departmental and individual objectives are linked and closely aligned to the strategy.

The third of these processes – *business planning* – provides a basis for the integration of business and financial plans. Since the balanced scorecard links strategy to performance measures (KPIs), managers can use the scorecard measures and associated goals to allocate resources and set priorities to achieve long-term strategic objectives at the business unit level. In other words, business unit scorecards are designed to link with the corporate scorecards.

The fourth of these processes – *feedback and learning* – allows the company to use feedback from the balanced scorecard and benchmarking processes to provide an insight into, and evaluation of, existing strategy at business unit and corporate levels. Thus, strategies can be changed, or reoriented, to take account of the real-time learning and feedback achieved by the company and its employees. Thus, corporate and business unit scorecards can be reviewed and updated. As Kaplan and Norton point out (1996, p. 77), the balanced scorecard in this context can be viewed as a systems dynamics model that provides a comprehensive, quantified model of a business's value creation process and enables the corporate strategy and vision to be continually refined and reviewed.

Kaplan and Norton also argue that the strategic plan should ultimately describe how the company intends to maximize shareholder value and continually create and sustain that shareholder value over time. By focusing on value, the strategic scorecard approach breaks the organizational effectiveness value equation into at least three main elements, namely, operational effectiveness (improving the efficiency of core business processes), customer management (understanding and leveraging customer relationships better) and product innovation (developing new products, markets and relationships to sustain future growth). Operational effectiveness strategies have a relatively short-term focus; customer management strategies have a more medium-term focus; and product innovation strategies are much longer-term in orientation. In each case, management must set 'stretch' objectives/targets for each of the KPIs and benchmark them on a regular basis. It is important to note that corporate strategy may be modified as economic and other conditions change (for example, in recessionary environments) with, in some cases, shorter-term productivity and operational strategies taking precedence over more innovative, longer-term product strategies.

18.3 How does the strategic management system work in practice?

The vision and strategy element of the balanced scorecard process in Figure 18.3 is the core process owned by the senior management team. It leads to a strategy map such as that shown in Figure 18.5.

This strategy map unfolds the four lenses of the balanced scorecard (the core process) and builds them systematically from workforce and operational issues to a customer value proposition that leads to improved shareholder value. The important KPIs are outlined in the diagram.

Once the vision and strategy has been identified through the strategy map, different senior managers must take responsibility for managing the four strategy processes shown in Figure 18.4, with the balanced scorecard activity as the 'hub' and organizing framework of the

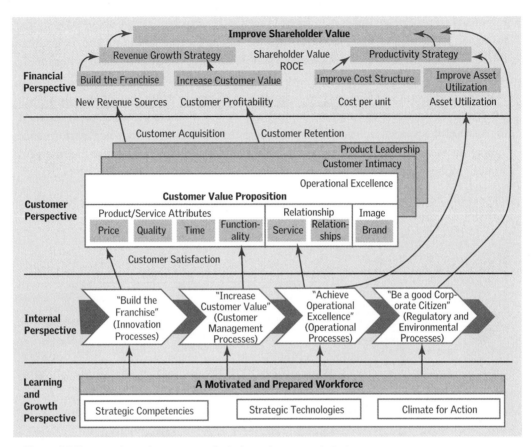

Figure 18.5 Describing the strategy: the balanced scorecard strategy map.
Source: Kaplan, RS and Norton, DP (2001) *The Strategy-focused Organisation*, HBS Press, Boston, MA, p. 96.

process. It is likely that the director of strategic planning or a very senior executive officer will manage the strategic planning process to clarify and translate the vision and strategy exemplified in the strategy map. Normally, the CFO (chief financial officer) has responsibility for annual planning and budgeting and can be assigned the management of the business planning process, including target setting and resource allocation. The process of strategic feedback and learning may be given to a chief information officer, or a strategic planning director. He or she would have clear responsibility for competitive intelligence benchmarking and the management of strategic databases/management information systems. The important role of communicating and linking should probably be the function of the director of human resources, who would manage the goal-setting, incentive and reward systems in the organization.

A number of points are of critical importance in implementing the scorecard as a strategic management system. First, it is critical that the CEO and the senior management team responsible for the scorecard system should meet and exchange dialogue about system performance on a regular basis. Second, the role of managerial intuition and judgement throughout the organization will be important in drawing conclusions from system feedback and the wide range of KPIs offered by the scorecard (often 25 or so in Kaplan and Norton's framework). The underlying logic of how to interpret this data relies critically on the creativity, openness and rapport among members of the senior management team. At the heart of the process is the capability to translate KPIs into a 'bottom-line' performance view of the business and the willingness to continually amend, craft and evolve the emergent strategy of the business.

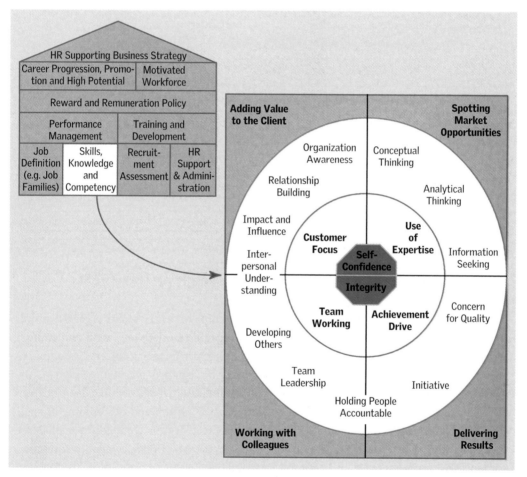

Figure 18.6 Winterthur International's human resource management process
Source: Kaplan, RS and Norton, DP (2001) *The Strategy-focused Organisation*, HBS Press, Boston, MA, p. 243.

18.3.1 An example of the scorecard in practice: integration with the human resource process

Kaplan and Norton (1996, p. 81) ask the following question: 'Should compensation systems be linked to the balanced scorecard measures?' Clearly, the attractiveness of linking financial compensation rewards to performance is a powerful motivator discussed at length in the literature of strategic human resource management (e.g. Tichy, Fombrun and Devanna 1982).

The main potential pitfalls are whether the performance reward process involves too many risks in implementation. For example, are the right measures on the scorecard? Are valid and reliable data available for each of the selected measures? Other questions could clearly be posed here. To illustrate the dilemma, we offer an example from Kaplan and Norton (2001, pp. 242–3) based on the experience of Winterthur International, a major insurance company, which tried to link the balanced scorecard to a performance management model for the HR function. The diagram shown in Figure 18.6 presents a new HR management structure that Winterthur executives designed and which specifies job families and defines KPIs, skills and knowledge/competences associated with each job family.

The company's experience was that many of the skills and competences were difficult to measure, e.g. conceptual thinking, relationship building, etc. However, the exercise of proposing the measures and identifying the organization's strategic themes made clear to many employees how they could contribute to achieving the strategic objectives of the organization. This alone made them more motivated employees. It should be noted from this evidence that the eventual goal may be to spend more time on the HR processes of translating organizational and business scorecards and associated KPIs into personal development scorecards, which employees can use with HR personnel to review and monitor performance. This may, in turn, lead to subsequent design of rewards/incentive systems as a longer-term goal.

18.4 Summary

The underlying theme of this chapter has been that the performance feedback loop is critical in terms of both assessing and making strategic choices. Taking purely a planning approach to strategy (for example) is rather a one-eyed perspective, since it ignores the value of the feedback from actual (or expected) performance. Curiously, much of the field of strategic management has paid relatively scant attention to analysing and measuring performance as it relates to the strategy process. This chapter has attempted to fill that gap. The importance of the performance feedback loop cannot be overstressed. It enables strategists to assess strategic decisions, of course, but, more importantly, it facilitates the generation of new ideas, allows human resource managers to assess appropriate rewards, and underpins organizational as well as individual learning.

In this chapter we have discussed the evolution of concepts of performance measurement and their linkage to the strategy process. Given a goal of shareholder value maximization, we have presented a range of performance measures, including accounting-based measures of performance, economic value added (EVA) metrics, based on concepts of 'economic profit', and shareholder value approaches (SVAs), based on discounted cash flow concepts from finance. We concluded with a discussion of a set of more holistic value-based management techniques known as the balanced scorecard approach. We believe that this approach has considerable value as a strategic management tool, particularly in its linkage to strategy and a range of KPIs. We continue to develop this theme in the next chapter, when we focus on managing innovation/knowledge and the development of the future strategic path for the organization.

Key terms

Balanced scorecard *671*

Business model *672*

Earnings per share (EPS) *674*

Economic value added (EVA) *675*

Key performance indicators (KPIs) *685*

Key success factors (KSFs) *687*

Net present value *677*

Price/earnings ratio (P/E) *674*

Return on assets (ROA) *674*

Return on equity (ROE) *674*

Return on investment (ROI) *674*

Return on sales (ROS) *674*

Shareholder value approach (SVA) *675*

Value-based management *682*

Recap questions and assignments

1 Based on your analyses of the business models used by Freeserve, Punch Taverns and the National Model Agency, identify (i) the principal use and value of business models, and (ii) the practical difficulties in using business models.

2 What is the difference between a business model and a balanced scorecard process?

3 Does the existence of a performance feedback loop invalidate the idea of top-down planning? How much of a deviation from planned performance can an organization tolerate before abandoning a planning approach?

Online
*Learning*Centre

When you have read this chapter, log on to the Online Learning Centre website at www.mcgraw-hill.co.uk/textbooks/mcgee to explore chapter-by-chapter test questions, further reading and more online study tools for strategy.

Case 1 **The Continental Household Mortgage Company**

The Continental Household Mortgage Company (known internally simply as 'the Company') is a US-based financial services company specializing traditionally in household mortgages and latterly in personal savings products. Tom Howlett is a newly appointed strategic planner with a remit to review the planning and performance assessment processes.

The Company's strategic planning process uses a balanced scorecard approach for assessing progress against its objectives and for assessing the relevance and the sense of its competitive strategy.

It describes its strategy as follows:

1 Scale is central to all products and services.

2 All business units are required to make accounting profits.

3 Customer relationships are central to business retention and development of new products.

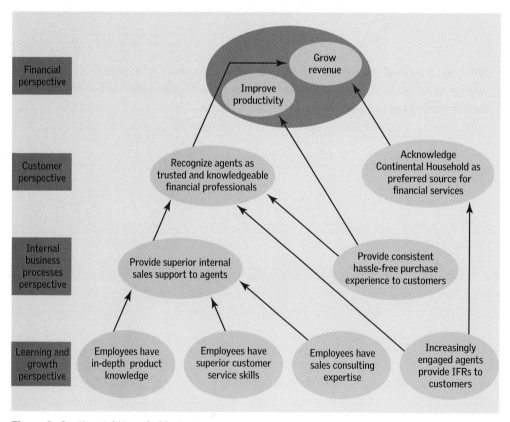

Figure 1 Continental Household: strategy map

4 Product development relies on the core product (mortgage services) being able to attract customers and then to generate interest in other products.

Its approach to assessing its strategy is captured in the strategy map (Figure 1). In this the four lenses of the balanced scorecard are used to identify the key management processes that will 'deliver' the strategy. For example, the learning and growth lens identifies the need for in-depth product knowledge and customer service skills (and other elements as well). From a customer perspective there is a need for the company's agents to be 'trusted'. The strategy map provides a linkage between key processes and financial measures relating to sales growth and productivity.

Behind the strategy map is another document that provides a strategy perspective (Figure 2). This shows how the four lenses of the balanced scorecard are reflected in 'vision' statements. The financial vision is about profitability. The customer vision is about access to professional advice. The internal perspective concerns the nature of the customer contact experience. Finally, the learning and growth vision is about how these customer relationships will evolve and be developed in the future.

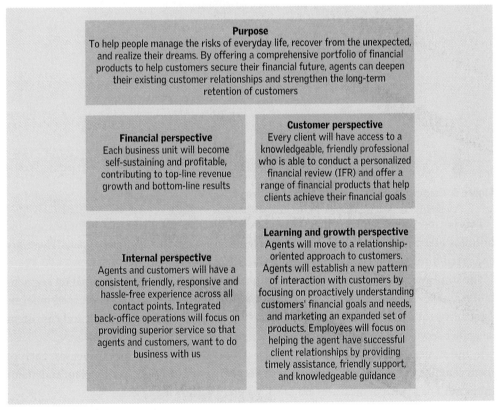

Figure 2 Continental Household strategy perspective

Strategic position
To become the provider of choice for customers who want help securing their financial future, we must offer financial products that are perceived by customers as better value than those offered by our competitors. At the same time, our offering has to be matched by a cost structure that is capable of delivering an acceptable rate of return on investment

Customer perspective
The Company's reputation and brand will extend to all financial services so that our existing customer base readily acknowledges the Company as a preferred source for quality financial products. In addition, more customers than ever will recognize their agent as a knowledgeable and trusted financial professional capable of delivering personalized, high-quality service and meeting their needs with a full line of financial products

Financial perspective
At least three of our four business units will be profitable. Regardless of profitability, all business units will contribute significantly to top-line revenue growth and meet expense management targets

Learning and growth perspective
More than half of our agents will be increasingly engaged in marketing and selling products that meet the broad financial goals of our customers by providing a personalized financial review (IFR) to interested customers. These engaged agents, with the support of their staff, will be achieving sales success that meets or exceeds scorecard levels of production. While employees in every business unit will be providing superior customer service to agents and customers, those employees in support roles will also possess in-depth product knowledge and sales consulting skills so that they can help agents build deeper relationships with clients

Internal perspective
The application process for core, high-volume financial services will be integrated and simplified so that our customers' purchase experience is consistent and hassle-free. Agents will be receiving superior internal sales support for core financial products from an integrated contact and support system

Figure 3 Continental Household strategy objectives

This perspective is supplemented by a strategy objective statement that identifies specific business objectives so as to make measurable progress towards company goals. These are expressed through each lens of the balanced scorecard (*see* Figure 3).

The strategy is then elaborated in terms of products scope, market scope, market segmentation and key target markets, capped by a clear value proposition. This is phrased in terms of quality products, simple transactions, skilled and friendly staff, convenient and consistent customer service, and a professional approach to sales.

In the strategic plan there are entries for each of the balanced scorecard lenses. Each of them contains the following headings: business goal and its measure, action plan, and major initiative. The principal measures are as shown in the following table.

Balanced scorecard lens	Business goal	Measures (KPIs)
Financial	1 Increase sales revenue 2 Improve productivity	1 Percentage revenue growth (12% pa 2004–6) 2 Expense ratio (21% falling to 16% 2004–6)
Customer	1 Wide recognition by customers of Company products 2 Customer recognition of sales agent as financial professional	1 Percentage households with a company product (20% to 25% 2004–6) and number of Company products per Company customer (1.8 to 2.25 2004–6) 2 Percentage Company agents fully participating in the product line
Internal	1 Customer-facing business processes integrated and simplified 2 Company agents receive superior sales support from integrated contact and support system	1 Percentage agents satisfied with the application process (increase over 2003 of 0% in 04, and 10% by 06) 2 Percentage agents satisfied with internal support (increase over 2003 baseline of 5% in 04, 10% in 05 and 15% in 06)
Learning and growth	1 More agents providing a personal financial review to actual and potential customers 2 Employees in internal sales support possess in-depth product knowledge, sales consulting expertise, and superior customer service skills	1 Percentage agents fully participating in marketing Company product-line 2a Percentage agents very satisfied with employee product knowledge (increase over 2003 of 5% in each yr to 06) 2b ditto with customer service 2c ditto with sales consulting skills

Note that sales agents are self-employed and typically marketing financial services products from a range of providers.

Tom Howlett is worried about a number of things.

Case Questions

1 Is the strategy described properly?

2 What are the key success factors?

3 Do these relate to the key performance indicators?

4 What initial steps should the company take to improve the process?

Further reading and references

Bowman, EH and Hurry, D (1993) 'Strategy through the option lens: An integrated view of resource investments and the incremental choice process', *Academy of Management Review*, **15**, **4**, pp. 760–82.

Brealey, RA and Myers, SC (2002) *Principles of Corporate Finance*, 7th edition, McGraw-Hill, London and New York.

Cameron, KS and Whetten, DA (eds) (1983) *Organisational Effectiveness: A Comparison of Multiple Methods*, Academic Press, New York.

Doyle, P (2000) *Value-based Marketing*, John Wiley & Sons, Chichester and New York.

Hayes, RH and Abernathy, WH (1980) 'Managing our way to economic decline', *Harvard Business Review*, July/August, pp. 67–77.

Kaplan, RS and Norton, DP (1992) 'The balanced scorecard: Measures that drive performance', *Harvard Business Review*, Jan/Feb, pp. 71–9.

Kaplan, RS and Norton, DP (1996) 'Linking the balanced scorecard to strategy', *California Management Review*, Fall, **39**, **1**, pp. 53–79.

Kaplan, RS and Norton, DP (1996) 'Using the balanced scorecard as a strategic management system', *Harvard Business Review*, Jan/Feb, pp. 75–85.

Kaplan, RS and Norton, DP (2001) *The Strategy-focused Organisation*, Harvard Business School Press, Boston MA.

Kay, J (1993) *Foundations of Corporate Success: How Corporate Strategies Add Value*, Oxford University Press, Oxford.

Rappaport, A (1986) *Creating Shareholder Value: The New Standard for Business Performance*, Free Press, New York.

Sloan, AP (1983) *My Years with General Motors*, MIT Press, Cambridge MA.

Smith, T (1992) *Accounting for Growth*, Century Business Books, London.

Stern Stewart (1996) *The Stern Stewart Performance 1000: A Ranking of America's Most Value-adding Companies*, Stern Stewart, New York.

Tichy, NM, Fombrun, CJ and Devanna, MA (1982) 'Strategic Human Resource Management', *Sloan Management Review*, Winter, pp. 47–60.

Venkatraman, N and Ramanujam, V (1986) 'Measurement of business performance in strategy research: A comparison of approaches', *Academy of Management Review*, **4**, pp. 801–14.

Yip, G (2004) 'Using strategy to change your business model', *Business Strategy Review*, **15**, **2**, pp. 17–24.

Chapter 19

Knowledge, information and innovation strategy

Introduction

A theme evident in Chapter 18 discussion of the balanced scorecard approach was the strategist's need to balance short-term and long-term performance. In order to create value in the long term, managers must commit current resources in an uncertain environment in order to create a sustainable future for the organization. They must gather the appropriate information and use judgement feedback and intuition from the accumulated knowledge and experience base in order to innovate, i.e. to develop new ideas, products, markets and business relationships that will facilitate expansion of existing markets or create entirely new markets.

In the strategy field there is increasing interest in the nature of 'knowledge', for example, how it is generated and fed back to

Chapter contents

individuals to improve strategies and to organizational members to facilitate organizational learning. New areas of strategy and organizational science such as knowledge management (Nonaka 1994), organizational learning (de Geus 1997) and the knowledge-based view of strategy (Grant 1996; Spender 1996) have mushroomed and have, in turn, posed critical questions about processes of **innovation** and the meaning of knowledge.

In this chapter we discuss the literature on innovation and technological change and introduce a number of competing concepts including 'disruptive innovations and the innovator's dilemma' (Christensen 1997), 'innovation as revolution' (Hamel 2000), and 'value innovation' (Kim and Mauborgne 1999). We try to define key terms such as knowledge, technology, innovation and core competences as a basis for examining four different perspectives on knowledge: knowledge as assets, knowledge through innovation, knowledge embedded in routines, and knowledge through learning. We then try to present the elements of the knowledge-based view of strategy and provide insights about how to foster organizational commitment to innovation and to structure the organization to achieve growth through innovation.

19.1 Concepts of knowledge and innovation

In their path-breaking book *The Knowledge-creating Company* (1995), Professors Nonaka and Takeuchi have stressed clearly the proposition that the *systemic knowledge* ingrained in the firm, its processes and its people is the single most important resource for the firm. This systemic knowledge is slowly developed, is distinctive and unique to the firm, is not easily transferable to others and may be protected by intellectual property regulations or other competitive barriers. The ease with which the knowledge is capitalized by the firm depends in part on how the knowledge is managed internally in the firm and transferred and replicated easily throughout the organization. Wal-Mart's inventory management and replenishment systems and McDonald's knowledge transfer of restaurant technology throughout its restaurant system are prime examples of good knowledge management and transfer in successful organizations. We define knowledge management as follows:

> *The process of identifying, extracting and managing the information, intellectual property and accumulated knowledge that exists within a company and the minds of its employees.*

Strategists such as Cooper and Schendel (1976) point out the nature of strategic responses to technological threats and indicate that incremental technological changes (competence-enhancing changes) reinforce the competitive positions of established firms in the industry, whereas more radical technological innovations (competence-destroying changes) may pressure existing incumbent firms to develop new competences, skills and capabilities. Dussauge, Hart and Ramanantsoa (1996, p. 14) emphasize the distinction

Table 19.1 Product innovators and winners

Product	Innovator	Product winner (follower)
Jet plane	British Aerospace: Comet	Boeing (707)
CT scanner	EMI	GE
Video-cassette recorder	Ampex	Sony/Matsushita
Video games	Atari	Nintendo/Sega
Photocopier	Xerox	Canon
Office P/C	Xerox	IBM

Source: D.J. Teece, 1987; P Anderson and M. Tushman, 1990.

between 'incremental' innovations (refining and improving existing products or processes) and 'radical' innovations (introducing totally new concepts). Innovation may involve the development of new technologies, such as bio-engineering and genetic engineering which define new industries, or the application of existing technologies to create new products, such as PCs, or to enhance existing products, such as digital cameras versus 35mm cameras. Generally, new products such as the CT scanner or the PC are new product configurations which link existing technologies and components in a new way. In these cases of new innovations (arising from *inventions* that create new products from new knowledge or distinctive combinations of existing knowledge) the product innovator is often not the eventual product winner. For example, Table 19.1 shows a range of innovative products for which the innovator is not the product winner. From a British viewpoint Sir Geoffrey Household of EMI won the Nobel Prize for the CT scanner yet the innovation was capitalized by GE. As a counter-example, however, Pilkington Glass of the UK was the innovator for float glass and also the winner in the marketplace despite US competition from Corning.

19.1.1 Disruptive technologies

Christensen (1997) focuses very closely on what he calls the innovators' dilemma in confronting different innovation types. He distinguishes between **sustaining technologies**, which foster improved product performance among existing firms and **disruptive technologies**, which result in worse near-term product performance and which precipitate the leading firm's failure. The dilemma for incumbent leading firms is that any adoption of disruptive breakthrough technologies requires cannibalization of purchases of existing products by current mainstream customers. This loss of revenue can lead these firms to go slow on implementing breakthrough technologies. Their mainstream customer focus, and associated market research, can then prevent leading firms from new product development, new markets and new customers in the future. This strategic weakness can allow entrepreneurial firms to exploit the new product pathway left open by the incumbent, leading firms.

Table 19.2 shows a list of the impacts of such disruptive innovations on the economic performance of leading incumbent firms.

19.1.2 Value innovation

Writers such as Kim and Mauborgne (1999) extend the concept of technological innovation to **value innovation**. They point out that while an innovator such as Ampex failed to capture the rents from inventing the VCR, their inventions nevertheless benefited the economy because later value innovators such as Sony and Matsushita made a success of the Ampex innovation. Value innovation places emphasis on the buyer as the centre of strategic thinking. To *value innovate*, companies must ask two questions:

1 Are we offering customers radically superior value?

Table 19.2 Examples of disruptive technologies (innovations)

Company	Disruptive innovation	Firms disrupted	Prior industry leader
DEC (Digital Equipment Corporation)	Mini computer	Mainframe computer manufacturers	IBM
HMOs e.g. Kaiser Permanente	Health maintenance organizations	Conventional health insurance	Blue Cross/Blue Shield
Compaq	Personal computer CPC	Mini-computer manufacturers	IBM, DEC
Dell	Direct order, customized PCs	Retail stores	Compaq
Charles Schwab	Discount trading/ broking	Investment banks	Merrill Lynch
Ford	Model T	Specialized car makers	Many
Toyota	Small cars and lean manufacturing	Large-volume car manufacturers	GM, Ford
Canon	Desk top photocopiers	High-speed photo-copying manufactuers (IBM, Kodak, Xerox)	Xerox
Wal-Mart	Discount retailing	Department stores	Macy's
Sony	Portable radios, TVs	Vacuum tube-based electronic products	RCA, Zenith

Source: Christensen, 1997.

2   Is our price level accessible to the mass of buyers in our target market?

As a consequence, the major inputs for value innovation are knowledge and ideas, new product concepts etc., which reject competitive strategies based on imitation but do not necessarily require new technology in order to succeed.

Table 19.3 shows a range of examples of value innovation given by Kim and Mauborgne (1999). It is instructive to note that in virtually all the cases given, the innovation shown is generally not a new 'technology' of a technical kind, but really a new product concept or a new way of framing a business opportunity using existing technologies and knowledge.

19.1.3 Revolutionary innovators

In his book *Leading the Revolution* (2000), Gary Hamel also stresses the importance of innovation as the engine to sustain corporate growth. Like Kim and Mauborgne, he believes that imitative strategies based on competitive strategy analysis have no basis in today's marketplace. He believes that the time has passed for strategies based on efficiency models (e.g. productive efficiency or benchmarking 'best practices' in competitors or the

Table 19.3 Example of value innovation

Company	Innovation
Callaway Golf – 'Big Bertha'	– made playing golf less difficult and more fun
SWATCH	– a price-competitive watch as a fashion accessory
Starbucks	– good coffee in a 'coffee bar'
Wal-Mart	– discount retailing
Charles Schwab	– investment and brokerage account management
CNN	– innovation in news broadcasting (24-hour news)
IKEA	– fashion home products and furniture retailing
SAP	– business applications software
Barnes & Noble	– book retailing
Southwest Airlines	– short-haul
Body Shop	– organic cosmetic retailing
Home Depot (B&Q)	– home improvement retail
Virgin Atlantic	– 'Upper class' – first-class service at a business-class price

Note: In virtually all these cases, with perhaps the exception of SAP, the concept is not a patentable innovation i.e. a scientifically excludable innovation.
Source: Kim and Mauborgne, 1999.

best-run companies). Senior managers must recognize the clear differences between innovation and imitation. Imitative approaches to the market mean that companies act reactively and try to emulate existing competitive strategies. In so doing, they misunderstand the customer demands and buyer needs in emerging mass markets.

Table 19.4 gives a few examples of companies seen as revolutionary innovators by Hamel.

Again, many of the ideas here rely on creative ideas and product concepts, and creative reconfigurations of existing technologies. New economy strategies are different and are discussed in Chapter 12.

The chapter now takes us systematically through four perspectives on knowledge which encompass economic concepts discussed earlier (for example, the resource-based view of the firm), alternative definitions of innovation (for example, radical, incremental, disruptive or value-based) and organizational approaches based on organizational evolution, routines and organization learning.

The traditional economic approach treats knowledge as an entity which affects the nature of the economic equilibrium, like so many other variables, but does not feature as a central player with regularity of effects on the competitive outcome. As we move towards placing knowledge at the centre of strategy theory we argue that there are four distinct approaches of how knowledge works. The first is the resource-based view (RBV) that provides us with the 'knowledge as asset' metaphor. A second view is Schumpeterian (Schumpeter 1934) in origin, picturing knowledge as innovation and as an essential element in the general theme of creative destruction of existing technological/knowledge bases. Third, evolutionary economics[1] moves away from a decision orientation towards a focus on the internal organization

Table 19.4 Hamel's revolutionary innovators (Hamel, 2000)

Company	Innovatory idea
SWATCH	Small objects of desire – combines Swiss watch making with Lego plastics
easyJet/Ryanair	Reinvented basic economics of airline business – real value to customers
Dell	Reinvented product cycle and cost structure of PCs
Nokia	Understood youth culture and its linkage to mobile phones

Source: Hamel, 2000.

---

[1] Nelson and Winter (1982) are most commonly identified with evolutionary economics. But the roots run deeper: *see* Veblen, 1898, on cumulative change; Marshall, 1920, on 'economic biology' and his well-known appreciation of dynamic analysis, and Alchian, 1950, 1953, on the implications of selection for the economic system.

of the firm and the role of organizational routines. The use of a Darwinian natural selection process coupled with adaptive feedback mechanisms explains the nature of organizational routines in large organizations. Such routines and their adaptation over time require embedded knowledge, acquisition of knowledge and transfer and integration of knowledge within organizations. Finally, the Teece, Pisano and Shuen (1997) approach to dynamic capabilities adds the elements of learning and other dynamics to the RBV and suggest paths by which both RBV and evolutionary approaches can take place in practice. The writers of these approaches did not place knowledge per se at the centre of their writing so, to a large degree, what follows is a reinterpretation of existing theory in terms of our view of knowledge and the role of knowledge in the processes of competitive strategy formulation and strategy development.

Case box: **What do we know about the knowledge economy?**

Pundits and politicians are forever proclaiming that we live in a knowledge economy, where success depends increasingly on brains not brawn. Yet little is actually known about the knowledge economy. An OECD study in 1999 made a start at filling in the picture – and debunks some myths.

For starters, Germany, not America, tops the OECD's knowledge-economy table. Knowledge-based industries accounted for 58.6% of German business output in 1996, compared with 55.3% in second-placed America (see chart). Japan is third, with Britain and France close behind, and Italy a notable laggard. In the OECD as a whole, knowledge-based industries accounted for over half of rich-country business output in the mid-1990s, up from around 45% in 1985.

The OECD's definition of the knowledge economy is pretty broad. As well as high-technology industries, such as computing and telecoms, the Paris-based think-tank counts sectors with a highly skilled workforce, such as finance and education. One reason that Germany is ahead of America is because of its big car, chemicals and machinery industries. Yet even in high-tech industries, where America is widely thought to be streets ahead, the United States comes behind Japan and Britain. High-tech industries produce 3.7% of Japan's business output and 3.3% of Britain's, but only 3% of America's. The United States is level-pegging with France, and only a bit ahead of Germany.

Growth in knowledge-based industries requires investment in knowledge as well as in physical capital. Such intangible investment is pretty hard to measure. By adding together spending on research and development (R&D), investment in software and public spending on education, the OECD puts it at 8% of rich-country GDP. Throwing in incomplete data on private education spending brings the total up to 10% of GDP, compared with physical investment in plant and machinery of 20% of GDP.

Sweden is the keenest investor in knowledge. Its investment in intangibles came to 10.6% of GDP in 1995; it spends far more of its national output on R&D than other countries.

France ranks second, thanks to its generously financed public-education system. America lags behind, because its government spends so little on schools. Japan, which spends a whopping 28.5% of GDP on physical investment, invests a puny 6.6% in intangibles.

Another myth that the new study pokes holes in is that the service sector, unlike manufacturing, does not innovate. Admittedly, R&D spending in services has traditionally been low. But in most countries it is now rising faster in services than in manufacturing. In 1980 services accounted

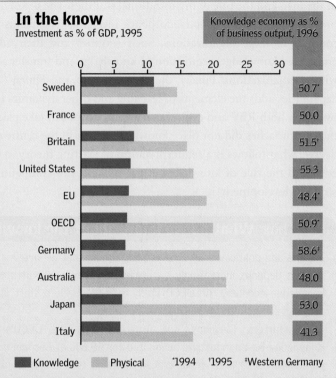

In the know
Investment as % of GDP, 1995

Knowledge economy as % of business output, 1996

Country	Knowledge economy %
Sweden	50.7*
France	50.0
Britain	51.5†
United States	55.3
EU	48.4*
OECD	50.9*
Germany	58.6‡
Australia	48.0
Japan	53.0
Italy	41.3

■ Knowledge   ■ Physical   *1994   †1995   ‡Western Germany

for only 4.1% of business R&D in America; by 1996 its share had risen to 19.5%.

Moreover, spending on R&D is only a fraction of total business spending on innovation. According to new evidence from business surveys compiled by the OECD, service industries spend far more on innovation than previously thought. Indeed, in Britain, spending on innovation in services is higher, at 4.02% of business sales in 1996, than in manufacturing, at 3.16%.

There are inevitably many gaps and flaws in the OECD's study. Its definition of the knowledge economy is far from perfect. It lumps together investment banking, a high-tech and pretty high-skill business, with estate agents, where knaves with badly written brochures still prosper. Another problem is that it includes many unskilled workers who work in knowledge industries. So, for example, hospital cleaners are counted as knowledge workers. But despite these shortcomings, the new report sheds new light on the knowledge economy.

Source: 'Knowledge gap', *The Economist*, 14 October 1999.
© The Economist Newspaper Limited, London (14 October 1999).

Questions for discussion

1 How would you define the 'knowledge economy'?

2 What are 'knowledge workers' and how are they different from other workers?

3 How do you expect the knowledge economy to develop over the next 10 years? 20 years? What implications does your answer have?

19.2 **Knowledge as assets**

Figure 19.1 portrays the market-based view commonly found in economic models in resource-based terms. The internals of the firm are here fleshed out in terms of resources and capabilities, the conventional description that permits discrimination between assets based on knowing and skills based on experience and actions. We do not summarize the key elements of the resource-based view here. They are familiar enough (see Wernerfelt 1984, Barney 1991; Grant (1991) and presented in depth in Chapter 7. Instead we suggest some conclusions in the language of *core competences*.

First, core competences can have a very significant impact by their effect on firm scope (boundaries), and by the (long) time scales over which they exist and change. They arise typically through collective learning – very much in the economics tradition of **objectified knowledge** (Spender 1996). Also, their impact is to create a framework through which we can view competition. This view is about contests for the acquisition of distinctive skills, in which competition in product markets is a 'superficial expression' of the more fundamental competition over competences. Therefore, the dynamics of the strategic theory of the firm focus on the process of core competence acquisition and collective learning because it occurs logically prior to product market evolution.

Figure 19.2 is a simple expansion of the range and nature of asset positions that are implied in Figure 19.1.[2] The broad categories give some idea of the differing demands on internal processes and on the challenge for integration of these different positions through some form of *corporate glue*, which integrates and binds these diverse asset positions for corporate value maximization. Many authors have provided classifications and explanations of the language of resources, assets, capabilities and competences. Grant (1991), for example, distinguishes between resources and capabilities, viewing resources as inputs and capabilities as those intermediate processes derived within the production function that are

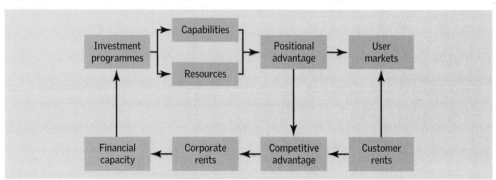

Figure 19.1 Resource-based view

---

[2] See the teaching notes in De Wit and Meyer (1994) for a practical illustration. Also see Barney (1991) and Grant (1991) for similar deconstructions of resources.

the main source of competitive advantage (refer back to the discussion in Chapter 7). Both are hard to define objectively and indeed Grant goes as far as to say that capabilities are organizational routines. Amit and Schoemaker (1993) (first discussed in Chapter 7) also deploy the language of resources and capabilities but seek to draw links with the industry analysis framework. Resources for them are intermediate goods (in contrast to Grant), and capabilities are '*based on developing, caring and exchanging information through the firm's human capital*'. They are built by combining physical, human and technological resources at the corporate level. The link with industry (or product market) arises when certain resources and capabilities become the prime determinant of economic rents and value. This can only occur if these resources and capabilities are subject to market failure and their possessions can therefore be firm-specific. Amit and Schoemaker refer to these as 'strategic assets'. This enables a distinction to be drawn between those resources and capabilities that are generally attainable and those that are asymmetrically distributed between firms, and difficult to trade and imitate.

Prahalad and Hamel (1990) (also first introduced in Chapter 7) have made famous the language of core competence and avoid using the language of resources and capabilities. For them, '*core competences are the collective learning in the organization, especially how to co-ordinate diverse production skills and integrate multiple streams of technologies*'.

Just as Amit and Schoemaker extend their notion of strategic assets towards product markets with a concept of strategic industry factors, so also do Prahalad and Hamel in making core competences the foundation for core products. For them the insight is not what is a core competence and how to build one, but a view of the strategic architecture

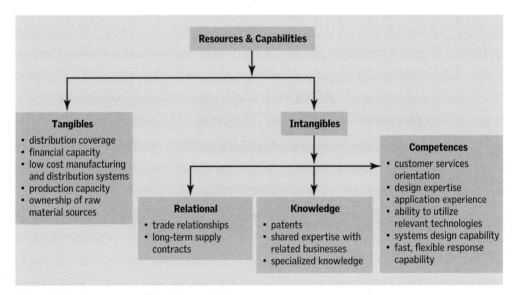

Figure 19.2 Resource positions (expanded)

of the firm, by which they mean '*a road map of the future that identifies which core competences to build and their constituent technologies*'. For these and other authors writing in the same vein, the common characteristic is the appeal to economic reasoning in the form of asymmetric distribution of assets to support economic rents and value. But the mainspring of firm-specific resources can lie anywhere between inputs and outputs with alternative scenarios about the contributory roles of organization structure and process, and managerial culture.

Our own approach in Figure 19.2 is more modest in intent. We seek only to distinguish between some categories or resources and capabilities so that we can see more clearly the different roles that knowledge can play. The distinction between tangible and intangible assets occurs prior to any distinction between resources and capabilities. We divide intangibles into three parts. The first companies those assets that are relational in character and involve the relationship of the organization with the outside world. The second is more explicitly concerned with knowledge and know-how. Although some entries under this heading suggest explicit knowledge (such as patents) they are surrounded by or produced by know-how that is essentially tacit. In the third part, our term competences can be used interchangeably with capabilities without any loss of meaning. There are, following Grant, intermediate processes, some of which are explicit in their design but many are likely to display characteristics of organizational routines.

19.3 **Knowledge as innovation**

The resource-based view provides a theory of protection and sustainability of competitive advantage. For an understanding of the genesis of advantage we have to turn elsewhere. The Schumpeterian approach (Schumpeter 1937) offers innovation as the medium through which creative destruction of existing technologies and knowledge bases takes place (see Box 1, Chapter 8). The element of destruction depicts intuitively and vividly but also convincingly how the old is replaced by the new. But it also sets these mechanisms in waves and floods of change, suggesting that a calculation of the benefits of change and innovation is overwhelmed by the magnitude of the opportunities on offer. Thus, Schumpeter suggested there were patterns of change and ferment (radical innovation) interspersed with stability (incremental innovation). In this way Schumpeter emphasized dynamic efficiency above static efficiency. Some recent writings clearly have their origins in Schumpeter. See, for example, d'Aveni's (1994) approach to hypercompetition, where he argues that the sources of competitive advantage are being created and destroyed at an increasingly rapid rate. Hamel and Prahalad (1993) use the language of dominance to assert a doctrine of strategic intent and define the gap between ambition and resources as strategic stretch. But the Schumpeterian world of enormous opportunity is not the only context for innovation. Firms may wish to create their own shocks or, more modestly, may seek to calculate finer pieces of sustainable advantage.

19.3.1 **Innovation competition**

But who innovates? Economists such as Kenneth Arrow have formulated models to explain whether new entrants have advantages over incumbents, whether monopoly can innovate more readily than competitive markets, and whether potential entrants can outwit monopolists. Of course, the answers depend on the situation but there is good reason for thinking that incomers often provide the wellspring of innovation – eventually. The behaviour to be explained is not that of the innovator who rationally examines the balance between costs and revenues in the light of prevailing competition and makes innovations when the return–risk ratio looks promising. The more difficult behaviour to explain is the reluctance of incumbents to refrain from innovating in the light of expected innovation from new entrants (*see* also Christensen 1997). The two rational economic reasons for this are the **sunk cost effect** and the **replacement effect**. The former arises when the incumbent assesses his existing technology by comparing its contribution margin to no new costs of investment beyond that of simple replacement. By contrast a new technology has a stiffer hurdle because the contribution margin (assuming for simplicity the same revenue stream from both technologies) has to cover new investment as well (*see* Besanko *et al.* 2000, pp. 488–9). The replacement effect was first formulated by Arrow (1962) in considering who has the greater propensity to invest, the monopolist or the new entrant. The incentive for the monopolist to invest in a radical new technology requires a comparison of the new stream of monopoly profits with the existing stream. However, for the new entrant who, if successful, will become the new monopolist, the incentive is simply the new stream of monopoly profits.

Through innovation an entrant can replace a monopolist but a monopolist can only replace itself, hence this is called the replacement effect. Thus, established firms under this thinking are less willing to stretch themselves to innovate. However, where the monopolist anticipates that new entry is likely then the incentives reverse to favour the monopolist. The incentive for the monopolist to innovate in the teeth of potential competitive intrusion is that of retaining monopoly profits from successful innovation versus sharing the market with a new entrant as a duopoly within which prices will be lower due to competition. This is greater than that of the new entrant who, expecting the monopolist to defend by innovation, can only anticipate the profit streams from sharing a competitive duopoly. Arrow called this the **efficiency effect.** The balance between these three effects depends on the probability of successful innovation by potential entrants. Where this is low, the sunk cost and replacement cost effects will dominate and the monopolists will prefer to maintain their existing cash flows. Where the probability is high then the efficiency motives will dominate and monopolists will seek to maintain their market position even if it is less favourable in absolute terms.

Case box: **Outsource your innovations**

When Frito-Lay added a little curl to its snacks, the company's sales improved. Of such seemingly modest innovations are great fortunes made. Next month Gillette will launch the successor to its sensationally successful Mach3 razor. Much as the company would like it to be as revolutionary as the Mach3 was in its day, the battery-operated vibrating beard-remover is unlikely to be more than evolutionary. That may not, however, prevent it from making a sizeable contribution to Gillette's profits.

Big firms still aspire to make truly great breakthrough inventions – products that will underwrite their profits for at least a decade. They are, however, coming up with such inventions less and less often, even though many industries, notably pharmaceuticals, continue to spend vast sums trying. Indeed, for most of industrial history, small firms have been responsible for the bulk of breakthrough products. America's Small Business Administration claims that the pacemaker, the personal computer, the Polaroid camera and pre-stressed concrete all emerged from small entrepreneurial outfits, and those are taken only from the list of items beginning with the letter P.

Big firms are better at less eye-catching forms of innovation – for example, Frito-Lay adding a little curl to its snacks, the clever twist allowing consumers to scoop up their guacamole or salsa dip and place relatively more of it in their mouths and less on their rugs, and generally improving the ways in which products invented elsewhere are manufactured, marketed and continually enhanced. Henry Ford did not invent the automobile. He 'merely' invented a far superior way to manufacture it – namely, the mass-production assembly line. And on that was built an industrial empire that has thrived for almost a century. Likewise, in the past few decades most of the companies that have created truly extraordinary amounts of wealth have done so by inventing great processes, not great products. Dell, Toyota and Wal-Mart, for example, have risen to the top of their respective industries by coming up with amazingly efficient ways of getting quite ordinary products into the hands of consumers more cheaply than their rivals.

Does this mean that big firms should sack all their scientists and leave inventing to others? In practice, more and more are doing just that. For some time, the computer industry has, in effect, relied for much of its research and development on small firms backed by venture capital, and the telecoms industry is outsourcing more and more research to smaller firms in India and elsewhere. Without their own in-house labs, however, big firms fear that they will be taken by surprise by what a Harvard professor, Clayton Christensen, famously described as a 'disruptive technology', an innovation so revolutionary that it will enable an upstart outsider to crush them, much as the PC did to the mainframe-computer business.

But, as history has shown time and time again, a bevy of in-house scientists gives no guarantee that their output will protect their employer from technological change. Xerox, AT&T and IBM spent billions on research but all failed to exploit much of what came out of their labs, and all ended up being caught out by new technologies. It is far better if big firms' managers keep their binoculars well trained on the outside world and their minds open to any new ideas they spot there. They can then buy them and do what they do best: find innovative ways to bring them to market.

Source: 'Less glamour, more profit', *The Economist*, 22 April 2004.
© The Economist Newspaper Limited, London (22 April 2004).

Questions for discussion

1 If in-house R&D is so risky, what are the arguments for doing it?

2 What are the arguments for outsourcing R&D?

19.3.2 Technology races

This analysis of innovation competition focuses on the pay-offs to innovation. There is also a literature on choosing the right levels of R&D under market uncertainty and under uncertainty about the response of rivals. The analysis of first mover advantage is well known. It asserts that the first mover gains advantage by establishing explicit knowledge protected by patents and trademarks and goes on to build advantages of scale, experience and scope so that later movers can never erode the early advantage (*see* the discussion in Chapter 6 of Ghemawat's 1997 analysis of Du Pont in titanium dioxide). There is also an interesting empirical literature on technology races and patent races (Gottinger 2003). These races describe the battles between firms to complete a successful R&D programme and to be the first to market with an innovation with all the benefits of first mover advantage. A race is an interactive pattern of competition characterized by firms constantly trying to get ahead of their rivals, or trying not to fall too far behind. Like the **dominant design** literature,[3] racing behaviour is also a dynamic story of how technology unfolds in an industry recognizing the fundamental importance of strategic interactions between competing firms. A simple race between two firms might involve the following. The leader may consider further investment to outdistance its rival and get to the winning post first. But it is aware of the diminishing marginal productivity of research for itself and the uncertainty of innovation for its rival. It therefore has to balance the risks and expenditures associated with pressing on with the benefits of delay in terms of consolidating its own knowledge and the difficulty for its rival of catching up. By contrast the follower is faced with the need to catch up, but has the same concerns about the productivity of research offset to some degree by at least some knowledge about the successful path followed by its rival. The leader has considerable incentives

---

[3] Dominant design can be defined as 'after a technological innovation and a subsequent era of ferment in an industry, a basic architecture of product or process that becomes the accepted market standard', from Abernathy and Utterback 1978, cited by Anderson and Tushman 1990. Dominant designs may not be better than alternatives, nor innovative. They have the benchmark features to which subsequent designs are compared. Examples include the IBM 360 computer series and Ford's Model T automobile, and the IBM PC.

to be cautious, whereas the follower might be more inclined to plunge ahead. Clearly the variables are many and imponderable given the uncertainty of success in R&D and the difficulty of predicting the responses of rivals. Gottinger summarizes the implications:

> At one level, racing behaviour has implications for understanding technology strategy at the level of the individual firm and for understanding the impact of policies that aim to spur technological innovation. At another level, racing behaviour embodies both traditions that previous writings have attempted to synthesize: the 'demand-pull' side emphasized by economic theorists and the 'technology-push' emphasized by the autonomous technological innovation school. (Gottinger 2003, pp. 37–8)

Gottinger observes from his research on telecommunications and computer industries the apparent inability of technology-oriented companies to maintain leadership in fields that they pioneered (op. cit. p. 51). These failures might be due to agency problems or other suboptimal managerial behaviour. But of more interest to our thesis here is the existence of market asymmetries that affect racing behaviour: (i) risk-driven and (ii) resource-driven asymmetries. The latter are clearly linked to the replacement effect (above). All this literature (Abramowitz 1986; Gottinger 1998 and 2001; Lerner 1997; and Scherer 1991) carries implications for knowledge in terms of its creation, how it is accessed, transferred and integrated, and who has the incentives for these activities.

Case box: **Does IT matter?**

Nicholas Carr has foisted an existentialist debate on the mighty information-technology industry

His argument is simple, powerful and yet also subtle. He is not, in fact, denying that IT has the potential to transform entire societies and economies. On the contrary, his argument is based on the assumption that IT resembles the steam engine, the railway, the electricity grid, the telegraph, the telephone, the highway system and other technologies that proved revolutionary in the past. For commerce as a whole, Mr Carr is insistent, IT matters very much indeed.

But this often has highly ironic implications for individual companies, thinks Mr Carr. Electricity, for instance, became revolutionary for society only when it ceased to be a proprietary technology, owned or used by one or two factories here and there, and instead became an infrastructure – ubiquitous, and shared by all. Only in the early days, and only for the few firms that found proprietary uses for it, was electricity a source of strategic – i.e., more or less lasting – advantage. Once it became available to all firms, however, it became a commodity, a factor of production just like office supplies or raw materials, a cost to be managed rather than an edge over rivals, a risk (during black-outs) rather than an opportunity.

Computer hardware and software, Mr Carr argues, have been following the same progression from proprietary technology to infrastructure. In the past, American Airlines, for example, gained a strategic advantage for a decade or two after it rolled out a proprietary computerised reservation system in 1962, called Sabre. In time, however, its rivals replicated the system, or even leap-frogged to better ones. Today, the edge that a computer system can give a firm is fleeting at best. IT, in other words, has now joined history's other revolutionary technologies by becoming an infrastructure, not a differentiator. In that sense, and from the point of view of individual firms, 'IT no longer matters.'

And what's IT all about?

Surely though, Mr Carr's critics counter, IT is different from electricity or steam engines. Even if hardware tends to become a commodity over time, software seems, like music or poetry, to have infinite potential for innovation and malleability. True, it may have, answers Mr Carr, but what matters is not whether a nifty programmer can still come up with new and cool code, but how quickly any such program can be replicated by rival companies. Besides, today's reality in the software industry has nothing to do with poetry or music. Many companies are furious about the bug-ridden, pricey and over-engineered systems that they bought during the bubble era and are doing their best to switch to simple, off-the-shelf software, offered in 'enterprise-resource planning' packages and the like. If there is any customisation at all, it tends to be done by outside consultants, who are likely to share their favours with other clients.

But surely Mr Carr does not appreciate the impressive pipeline of new technologies that is about to hit the market – the wireless gadgets, the billions of tiny radio-frequency identity tags that will turn Aspirin bottles, shirt collars, refrigerator doors and almost everything else into smart machines, and so on? Those are impressive indeed, says Mr Carr. But again, the issue is whether they will be proprietary technologies or open infrastructures. And everything points to the latter.

This is not a debate for the ivory tower. Since IT can no longer be a source of strategic advantage, Mr Carr urges CIOs to spend less on their data-centres, to opt for cheaper commodity equipment wherever possible, to follow their rivals rather than trying to outdo them with fancy new systems, and to focus more on IT's vulnerabilities, from viruses to data theft, than on its opportunities. As it happens, CIOs have been taking exactly this approach for the past three years, and their bosses like it that way.

Source: 'Does IT matter?', *The Economist*, 1 April 2004.
© The Economist Newspaper limited, London (1 April 2004).

Questions for discussion

1 If all innovations are destined to become commodities, what is the incentive to innovate?

2 What is it about knowledge that makes it 'strategic' for the economy and for society but a mere commodity for firms?

3 How might a firm resist the move towards commoditization of its intellectual property?

19.4 **Knowledge embedded in routines**[4]

Recently the strategy literature has paid attention to the organizational processes that form the basis for the development of the firm's strategy (Teece *et al.* 1997; Eisenhardt and Martin 2000). These scholars, along with others, focus on the routines, competences and capabilities of the firm that shape its development in the long run. This approach shifts the focus of attention from the market-positioning view (described earlier) to a more micro-analytic approach that aims to go even deeper than the resource-based view, aiming to understand the way in which competitive advantage is actually developed (Johnson and Bowman 1999). Our interest here is in the routinized elements of strategy making. This is well grounded in the literature (March and Simon 1958; Nelson and Winter 1982; Cyert and March 1963; and Teece *et al.* 1997).

Less well known and certainly less commonly cited alongside the above scholars is the long-standing preoccupation of economists with evolution.[5] Veblen (1898, p. 397) talks about *the process of cumulative change.* Marshall used the term *economic biology* and argued that the '*the key-note is that of dynamics rather than statics*' (Marshall 1920, p. xiv). These represent early arguments about economic evolution. Although economists have spent considerable time developing the neoclassical theory of the firm (a misnomer for a theory of markets), the notion of *evolutionary economics* has gained considerable momentum. Some of the impetus for this derived from the long controversies about *marginalism.*[6] This led to the breaking open of the black box that was the firm in traditional microeconomics and the onset of the new theory of the firm. The essence of this is to throw light on the internal organization of the firm. Whereas the traditional theory is concerned with prices and output, the new theory is interested in how transactions are organized. The intellectual progress of this strand of economics is marked by Coase's (1937, 1988) path-breaking paper on the nature of the firm, new approaches to understanding the nature of ownership bringing in property rights (Alchian and Demsetz 1972) and agency costs (Jensen and Meckling 1976), and Williamson's transaction cost economics (1985, 1987). Coase anticipated all of this in pointing out that the essential differentiating feature of intrafirm transactions, as opposed to interfirm transactions, is authority and hierarchy. This stream of thinking does reinforce the idea of 'efficiency management' – Williamson expressed it as the strategy of *economizing* (1981), and this has strong resonance with the idea of cost minimization from neoclassical theory. But, more important than this, it opens the door to ideas about the evolution of efficient organizational forms. Vronen (1995, p. 2) maintains that evolutionary economics is inspired by the new institutional economics. This examines

---

[4] The approach adopted in this section owes much to Menuhin (2001) and Menuhin and McGee (2003).

[5] This is described and analysed in great detail by Vronen (1995).

[6] See, for example, the anti-marginalist critique exemplified by the Oxford Research Group in the 1930s, especially Hall and Hitch (1939) and the American economist Lester (1946).

processes through which institutions evolve (Langlois 1986). Similarly, the sociologist Granovetter (1985, p. 488) argues that:

> *social institutions and arrangements previously thought to be the adventitious result of legal, historical, social or political forces are better viewed as the efficient solution to certain economic problems.*

The central part of evolutionary theory is the selection proposition that argues that competitive markets select for the most efficient organizational forms. Although there are considerable debates about the precise forms and implications of this process, the selection argument is the hard core of evolutionary theory. Evolution is a form of organizational ecology where firms engage in behaviour that is routine rather than purposive. Adaptation takes place by mimicking the survivors which are accidentally well adapted. Managers get little credit in this view. Scholars such as James Brian Quinn have argued for processes that are typically fragmented, evolutionary and intuitive. He describes this as *logical incrementalism* (Quinn, 1978) in which minor changes in strategy take place as a response to changes in the external environment in an evolutionary and adaptive manner.

Nelson and Winter's (1982) approach (drawing heavily on Winter, 1964) is a sustained argument that selection is not an ad hoc or involuntary response, but is systematic and purposeful firm behaviour. They – famously – argued for collections of routines based on **tacit knowledge** supplemented by organized search behaviour for modifications or substitutes. This allowed, in our view, for the evolution of economic thinking (over many decades) to map on to the newer thinking from management theorists attempting to understand and map organizational processes. The essential link is the purposive behaviour of managers and we shall argue that this is characterized by asset and knowledge accumulation and by learning processes that allow knowledge to be transformed from a tacit to an explicit form (a distinction also offered by Nonaka and Takeuchi 1995). Thus we see Burgelman (1983) arguing that the intellectual basis for activist and explicit roles for top managers is based on complex organizations that are subject to both evolutionary and planned processes.

Nelson and Winter introduced us to evolutionary economics but much is owed to Simon (1955, 1959) with his seminal concepts of *satisficing* and *bounded rationality* and Penrose's (1959) theory of the growth of the firm. Although Nelson and Winter's tone is somewhat hostile to traditional economics, their approach can be seen as a rehabilitation of the theory of the firm by providing (far more) realistic assumptions. They shift attention away from an overarching organizational decision calculus (how can one continually make these complex trade-offs about everything?) to internal organization where organizational routines regularly and automatically make 'decisions' based on the knowledge and best practice embedded in those routines. The argument for routines that make 'good decisions' is based on two points: one, a Darwinian natural selection process at an organizational level that ensures that only the 'best' routines are kept in operation and, two, on an adaptive feedback mechanism at the individual level that permits new knowledge to be accessed and then diffused through the organization to be eventually embedded in routines. Routines are thus embodiments of organizational memory – better called organizational genetics.

The evolutionary approach is saved from ecological sterility by the learning process (based on Simon). Through this we can see the essential elements and characteristics of a **knowledge-based view (KBV)** starting to take shape: tacit versus explicit knowledge; relative roles of individuals, groups and organizations; sourcing and accessing of knowledge, transfer and integration of knowledge (note the classic formulation by Nonaka and Takeuchi 1995).

19.5 **Knowledge as learning**

Nelson and Winter's second set of routines are those that determine the long-run changes in the firm's stock of capital – hence they are called *strategizing routines*. Attention has been paid to the contribution of planning and budgeting processes to the accumulation of fixed assets over time. But more central to our argument are the product and technology development processes. For example, Henderson and Clark (1990) developed the concept of *architectural knowledge* explaining how the dominant organizational design '*incorporates a range of choices about the design that are not revisited in every subsequent design*' (1990, p. 15). They go on to link this architectural knowledge to the development of innovation processes.

Strategizing routines contribute to strategy and strategy making as they store the firm's experience in such a way that it can be used in a new context (for example, consultants such as McKinsey and Bain discuss how they develop experience libraries of problems and problem solutions through their ongoing consulting activities). They channel the structure of decision-making processes into the type of behaviour that has brought success in the past. But such routines have a negative side. Over time, as the environment changes, new forms of organization become appropriate and gaps emerge between environmental requirements and existing capabilities. These gaps cause routines to become dysfunctional (Teece *et al.* 1997; Leonard-Barton 1992) and inhibit future development of the firm (Levitt and March 1988; Henderson and Clark 1990; Leonard-Barton 1992; Teece *et al.* 1997). This leads to the processes of organizational learning by which routines are modified over time.

The literature makes many references to types of organizational learning. Cyert and March's (1963) view of organizations as complex adaptive systems suggest *modes of learning*. Levitt and March (1988) refer to change processes at several *nested levels*. Cohen and Baclayan (1994) illustrate the role of *experimental learning*. Bettis and Prahalad (1995) suggest that firms *unlearn* ineffective routines. Hedberg (1981, p. 18) suggests that unlearning is 'a process through which *learners discard knowledge*'. All of these notions build on the idea that routines flow from history and serve as the organizational memory in which knowledge about best practice is stored. The propositions about learning fall into two camps. The cognitivists (e.g. Porac, Thomas, and Baden Fuller 1989; Porac and

Thomas 2002) focus on learning at the individual level and on individual mental maps. Structuralists suggest that learning is an organizational phenomenon based on the firm's routines and that these routines are subject to formal change processes. Nonaka and Takeuchi (1995) combine these two views into their knowledge-creation spiral. This begins with a distinction between tacit and explicit knowledge and maps how tacit knowledge starts with the individual and proceeds through socialization and integration processes so that knowledge becomes a key ingredient in the organization's capital stock (see Figure 19.5 which is shown later in this chapter). More generally, such learning can be described as a *sense-making process* (Weick 1979, 1995) through which the members of an organization construct a *common reality* that influences the way they seek to achieve an *objective economic reality*.

Teece, Pisano and Shuen (1997) in their well-known paper on dynamic capabilities may have intended to add primarily to the RBV but they also provide a sense of the internal mechanisms by which learning and adaptation may actually take place. Their definition of dynamic capabilities is '*the sub-set of the competences and capabilities which allow the firm to create new products and processes and respond to changing market circumstances*' (1997, p. 270). In some ways this is a restatement of Nelson and Winter's strategizing routines but inherent in their discussion is recognition of learning. They identify three characteristics that permit learning. The first is the nature of the internal processes: co-ordination/integration (a static notion), learning (dynamic), and reconfiguration (a renewal or transformational concept). Second, they are specific about the variety of resource positions that might need to be addressed. Finally, they pay attention to the paths by which developments can take place. It has to be said that these concepts can be very slippery. Path dependency, for example, is celebrated only as an idea. However, they are on more firm

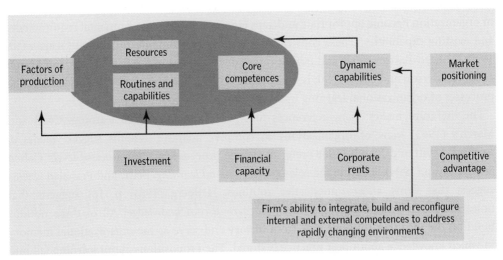

Figure 19.3 Dynamic capabilities view

ground in outlining the ways in which technological opportunity can shape the future. The hints they provide on the nature of increasing returns are suggested here.

We revisit our schematic again in the form of Figure 19.3. This time the resource side is further elaborated by the inclusion of learning and dynamics (feedback loops). Note, however, that the resource (knowledge) element defies construction in linear form – we begin here to see it as an interconnected whole (via the multiple arrows). Learning, moreover, creates multiple feedback effects.

19.6 **Towards a knowledge-based view**

We have reviewed four different perspectives on knowledge in strategy and in strategy making: knowledge as assets for protection, knowledge through innovation, knowledge embedded in routines, and knowledge through learning. In doing this we have touched on a wide variety of themes in strategic management, competitive advantage, the resource-based view, strategy making, and strategizing routines. We have also commented on developments in economic thinking ranging from neoclassical theory, through Schumpeter to evolutionary economics, with a hint also of institutional economics. Thus we have progressed from market positioning and the firm as a black box to serious consideration of internal organization and those processes that underpin competitive advantage. Knowledge makes its entry as an asset, albeit largely invisible, that protects competitive position. But we have moved to a more subtle position where knowledge is embedded in individuals and by complex processes is socialized and reintegrated into the organization at large. Do these various perspectives on knowledge enable us to articulate a *knowledge-based view of strategy* whose implications allow us to draw inferences about strategy and strategy making that are either absent from other theories or in contradiction to them? What are the essential ingredients of the knowledge-based view?

19.6.1 **Organizational knowledge**

Grant and Spender in a Special issue of the *Strategic Management Journal* in 1996 have two much quoted papers that step outside conventional economic approaches. Grant sees the firm as an institution for integrating knowledge, where knowledge is individually held and is typically tacit. The organization's role is to access, transfer and integrate that tacit knowledge within and throughout the organization. His approach is very similar to that of Nonaka and Takeuchi (see below). In Grant's view, the firm is a co-ordinating mechanism with implications for organizational design and for the nature of organizational process. Spender sees knowledge as too contentious a concept to easily bear the weight of a theory. The biggest problem, he sees, is the multitude of types and definitions. He therefore argues (as Grant does implicitly) for a pluralistic viewpoint and advances the idea of interplay between explicit and tacit knowledge, and between different units within the organization (from individuals through to collectives). This leads to a set of ideal types (see Figure 19.4). He moves from this to knowledge as activity and argues eventually for a Penrosian view – a historical, path-dependent process in which the individual rather than organizational machine bureaucracies are the important strategists. It is useful to start with Spender's view that our concepts of knowledge are highly varied and in many ways inconsistent or incapable of being interrelated:

> *Knowledge is a highly contentious concept, far too problematic to bear the weight of a useful theory of the firm without a clear statement of the epistemology which gives it meaning* (Spender 1996, p. 48).

He then proceeds by making three points.

1 Knowledge is interplay between the *tacit/implicit* and the *explicit*, the vertical dimension in Figure 19.4.

2 This distinction allows for several different *adaptation mechanisms* – for example, Nelson and Winter's own use of adaptive feedback mechanisms where the interplay between tacit and explicit takes place through individual choices that are eventually embedded in organizational routines ('organizational genetics').

3 Many theorists, starting with Polanyi (1966) and famously in Nonaka and Takeuchi (1995), see the origin of all knowledge in individual intuition. So the third element is the transformation and communication of what is known tacitly by individuals into collective or social knowledge. Hence the second, horizontal dimension in Figure 19.4.

Therefore, Spender advances four ideal types connected by an adaptation mechanism. He observes that the organizational intent is to transform tacit, individual knowledge into collectively owned, objectifiable knowledge – this is the world of standards, procedures, practices, patents, science, training, but still recognizably a world that remains dependent on the knowledge held by individuals although, in this diagram, the adaptation mechanisms of transformation and conversion process operate in silence. Given different types of knowledge, are there different types of knowledge-based theory, Spender asks. A theory of *conscious* knowledge would have to solve agency problems – how can inventors be persuaded to pass on their codified knowledge to an organization? A theory based on *automatic* knowledge also has agency problems where the brilliant man must be persuaded to stay with the firm (cf work-out clauses for entrepreneurs when they sell their businesses).

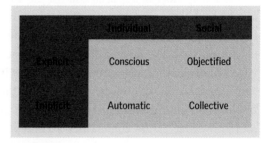

Figure 19.4 Different types of organizational knowledge
Source: Spender, 1996.

A theory of *objectified* knowledge raises problems of imitability in a world where knowledge is explicit. A theory based on inherently immobile *collective* knowledge (this is where Nonaka and Takeuchi would wish to take us and where Nelson and Winter go with their extra-rational learning processes) leads to a conclusion that this is the most secure and strategically significant kind of organizational knowledge.

Nonaka and Takeuchi's knowledge spiral (Figure 19.5) predates Spender by some three years. Their arena (matrix) has become a standard framework of its kind. Their focus is on a *knowledge spiral*, an adaptation mechanism through which knowledge is converted and then transferred between the tacit and the explicit (it can go either way) and among individuals, groups and the whole organization. *Socialization* is the sharing of experiences so that tacit knowledge is shared between individuals, from individuals to the organization through the development of culture and shared mental models, and from the organization to individuals. *Externalization* is the conversion of tacit into explicit knowledge through its articulation and systematization within the organization. *Combination* involves the conversion of explicit knowledge held by individuals and groups into explicit knowledge at the organizational level, and subsequent conversion of organizational knowledge back to the individual in different form. This is the key role of information systems within the firm. *Internalization* is conversion of explicit knowledge back into tacit knowledge in the form of individual know-how and organizational routines. The *knowledge spiral* is the dynamic process by which knowledge is translated through separate but related stages, through socialization to combination and externalization, and back to internalization.

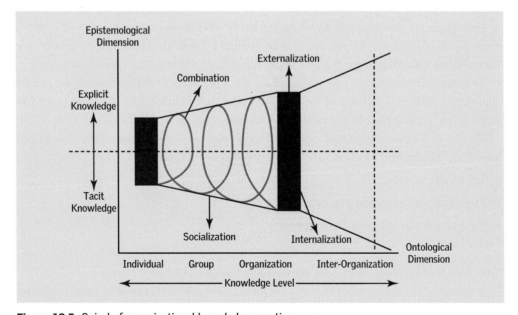

Figure 19.5 Spiral of organizational knowledge creation
Source: I Nonaka 'On a knowledge creating organization', Paper presented at AIF National Congress, Posma, October 1993.

Thus, individual creativity can be linked to the growth of collective knowledge.[7] Spender's contribution relates to the different types of organizational knowledge whereas Takeuchi and Nonaka use the same intellectual space to portray the adaptation mechanisms that organizations can use to convert and transfer various kinds of knowledge to inimitable and therefore rent-earning organizational knowledge.

19.6.2 **From value chain to value web**

The value chain, popular for its simple and robust character, can be restated firstly in the language of core competences and the RBV but more fundamentally in this language of knowledge. This characterization restates the linear chain of activities as a similar chain of core competences. The activities of the value chain might be dispersed across different owners but in any event they are controlled in economic terms through the operation of core competences. Thus economic power is operated through the conjunction and interaction of core competences. However, the linearity of the chain metaphor is uncomfortable where the empirical record suggests knowledge is multifaceted and capable of being attached to other pieces of knowledge in a variety of expected and unexpected ways, particularly as interface standards are developed and 'knowledge as Lego' becomes more and more possible.

The notion of a web is intuitively appealing (Figure 19.6). At the centre is the *corporate glue* (McGee 2003), that is, the organizationally held tacit knowledge that cannot readily be imitated – the *collective knowledge* according to Spender, and the *knowledge architecture* according to Henderson and Clark. This is characteristically a collective concept but also a tacit and sticky concept, meaning that the organization can be readily and sustainably differentiated by it. This corporate glue supports and is supported by a set of core competences within which elements of objectifiable knowledge may be evident.[8] These are buttressed by closely held partnerships with other organizations where the ability to control the agency costs becomes really important. More remotely managed are the subcontract relationships where market contracting suffices. The value of the web is a framework within which the *activity sets* formerly given pride of place in the value chain are now replaced by *knowledge concepts.*

Inherent in a knowledge-based view of strategy (and also in an economist's concept of a knowledge production function) are three key linkages between:

1 knowledge as assets;

2 knowledge embedded in processes; and

3 the pathways to competitive advantage.

---

[7] We are indebted to Rob Grant for this articulation of Nonaka and Takeuchi's model.

[8] An alternative description would be to describe the corporate glue as supported by elements of objectifiable knowledge and the conjunction of the two being core competence. This has the merit of defining core competence explicitly in terms of knowledge concepts.

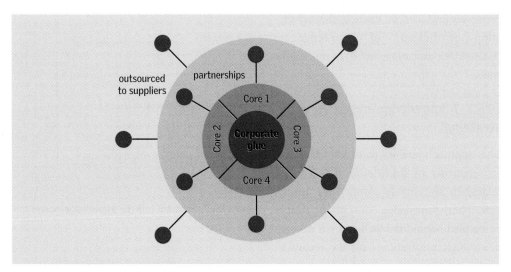

Figure 19.6 The knowledge web
Source: McGee, 2003.

According to the Teece *et al.* (1997) discussion of dynamic capabilities, there are four knowledge processes:

1   entrepreneurial (creative);

2   coordinative and integrative (static);

3   learning (dynamic); and

4   reconfigurational (transformational).

In asset or resource terms we see knowledge as embedded in many different classes of assets such as technology, complementary, financial, reputational, structural, institutional, and market structure. For example, Amit and Schoemaker (1993) provide an excellent description (see Chapter 7) of strategic assets and their linkage to organizational rent (competitive advantage). Following but not replicating Teece *et al.* (1997), we express the linkages to competitive advantage in terms of *dynamic pathways*. Whereas Amit and Schoemaker (1993) and Peteraf (1993) only assert that assets create profit possibilities, in this approach the dynamic pathways are defined in terms of path dependency (which allows us to call on an evolutionary perspective) and technological opportunities (which allows for returns to scale,[9] first/early mover advantage, and oligopolistic gaming). The strength of this approach lies in its organizational inclusivity, ranging from internal process to asset positions, linked over time through management of the pathways. Empirical evidence here is patchy but attracting research interest as we speak. In summary, this approach includes entrepreneurial (creative)

---

[9]   Especially network externalities where 'winner takes all' strategies are possible; McGee and Sammut-Bonnici (2002, 2003), summarized in Chapter 12.

processes and a more explicit characterization of linkages of knowledge to competitive advantage as dynamic pathways.

19.6.3 A knowledge-based view of strategy?

This approach enables us to see that there are elements of knowledge that can be related to sustainable competitive advantage. These knowledge concepts lie deeply embedded behind the well-known notions of strategic positioning and the resource-based view and are powerful in that they, in a fundamental sense, are the drivers behind core competences and competitive advantage. So, is it possible to draw this thinking together into a perspective that we might call the knowledge-based view of strategy? Our approach is to suggest three categories (Figure 19.7) called specific knowledge, organizational knowledge, and the **knowledge web**.[10]

Specific knowledge (Figure 19.8) relates to the knowledge production function and draws links between knowledge, production, access to knowledge, knowledge diffusion, connections between elements of knowledge, and knowledge renewal (including the discarding of knowledge). The foundations of this are highly dispersed throughout the academic literature. There is a considerable economic literature on innovation competition and on R&D. There is a considerable scientific and social science literature on innovation processes. There is also some considerable mystery about creativity, usually captured under the heading of serendipity.

Organizational knowledge (Figure 19.9) is the process by which various elements of specific knowledge are taken into the organization, transformed into social/collective knowledge and, through dynamic pathways, linked into other organizational activities. The key elements are characterized as types of organization knowledge, the knowledge creation

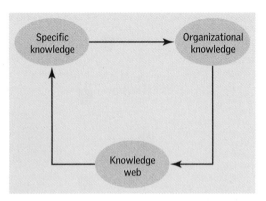

Figure 19.7 Elements of the knowledge-based view

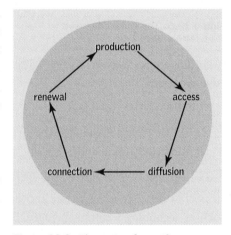

Figure 19.8 Elements of specific knowledge

---

[10] Alternatively knowledge in action.

process, and dynamic pathways. The inheritance from such writers as Spender, Takeuchi and Nonaka, and Teece *et al.* is self-evident.

The knowledge web (*see* Figure 19.6) represents the way in which specific knowledge and organizational knowledge is captured into value-creating activities within the firm (discussed above) (*see* also Winter 1987 for an earlier exposition of this point). Both specific and organizational knowledge feed into the knowledge web. The notion of corporate glue or knowledge architecture stems

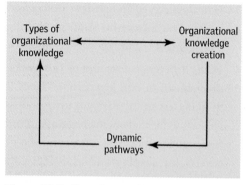

Figure 19.9 Organizational knowledge

directly from the conjunction of tacit and social knowledge. But specific knowledge is also evident from its role within core competences and within the core competences of strategic partners. The knowledge web is also dynamic in that incentives to innovate and to create new linkages between knowledge components are created here and therefore provide the link back to the knowledge production function that is captured within the category of specific knowledge.

This approach allows us to connect three strands. The first concerns the ways in which knowledge is produced, accessed, diffused, renewed and discarded. The second concerns the notion of organizational knowledge as an essentially invisible asset fostered and conditioned by visible and defined organizational routines and ad hoc processes. The third is a strategic theory of the firm in which positioning and resource-based approaches are recast in the form of knowledge.[11] Again, knowledge is the invisible asset but captured here in the form of specific activities on which management focuses attention. This does not answer all the questions but perhaps does allow us to define the arena of interesting questions and permit the formation of some conjectures. We suggest the following list.

1 *How is knowledge produced and accessed?* This includes the imponderable of 'knowledge creation' as well as 'knowledge conversion' (a word used by Grant (1996) and by Nonaka (1994) and has a parallel to the economists' idea of a production function). We know more about the processes of innovation and we also know quite a lot about the economic analysis of new technology decisions.

2 *How does knowledge fit into supply chain and value chain thinking* – in other words, how does it link and co-ordinate with the other activities of the firm to produce competitive advantage? The knowledge web is a useful framework but much needs to be done to identify the specifics in actual cases and applications.

---

[11] A link here could be made with Rumelt (1984) by developing the argument that our use of knowledge as corporate glue is directly analogous to his use of isolating mechanisms.

3 *How do pieces of knowledge connect up?* How do they change the nature of the corporate 'glue' – the integrative strategic architecture? The burgeoning function of knowledge management within knowledge-intensive organizations reflects these considerations.

4 *What difference does any of this make for the analysis of strategic decisions such as diversification and acquisition?* Does this have anything to contribute to economists' thinking about increasing returns industries – another arena where the 'new economy' appears to be challenging basic assumptions behind traditional thinking (*see* McGee and Sammut-Bonnici 2002, 2003, and the discussion in Chapter 12)? These are not simply criteria for shaping and assessing a theory but they are also conjectures. They are conjectures about the nature of knowledge itself, whether such a multi-faceted concept can be marshalled into the constraints inherent in a normative, organizationally focused theory.

Case box: **Patient money at Corning Glass**

Some companies prosper by making continuous improvements to their business practices. Others grow by using their market clout to acquire rivals for the skills and markets they covet. A few thrive by making patient investments in far-sighted ideas of their own that can take decades to pay off. Rarely does any company attempt to do all three things at once.

Corning, a glass maker that was founded 150 years ago, is one of those rare manufacturing enterprises that has managed to cling to its innovative roots. Apart from the upheaval of the 1970s and 1980s, which affected many American companies that had grown fat in the decades after the second world war, Corning has been remarkably consistent in giving full rein to the ingenuity of its researchers while pursuing total mastery over its process technologies.

Its reputation for continuous innovation over a century and a half is unrivalled anywhere. Without Corning's ribbon machine, electric light bulbs, vacuum flasks and cathode ray tubes would have been far costlier and more fragile affairs. Without its patented borosilicate glasses, there would have been no Pyrex ovenware. The glass ceramics called Pyroceram, which the company developed originally for missile nose cones, has not quite made Corning a household name. By contrast, its Corelle line became one of the world's most popular brands of tableware.

The firm's successful casting of the 200-inch (five-metre) mirror for the Hale telescope on Mount Palomar in 1934, a feat that even the mighty General Electric had attempted but failed to achieve, reinforced the company's reputation in the scientific world. Its patented vacuum-deposition processes, secretly used for years in the optics aboard American spy satellites, have made Corning the mirror maker of choice for optical astronomers everywhere since the end of the cold war. Corning's invention of ceramic substrates for catalytic converters made the firm the darling of Detroit. And then there was the optical waveguide – the invention, better known as optical fibre, that has transformed telecommunications the world over.

'Patient money' was the principle that guided the Houghton family when it first invested in a small glass company in Somerville, Massachusetts, in 1851. (The firm moved to the city of Corning, New York in 1868.) And the Houghton dynasty has influenced the company according to that principle ever since. Lacking access to the cheap immigrant labour, raw materials and exploding markets that rival glass makers enjoyed across the Alleghenies in the Ohio valley, to the west, the Houghtons also insisted that their fledgling corporation should focus exclusively on the specialist end of the business and use inventiveness as its principal competitive weapon. Producing me-too products was out of the question, so Corning's only choice was to be endlessly unorthodox – and so, for the most part, it has remained.

Central to Corning's success in turning unorthodoxy into a winning way has been the management's profound understanding of the value of the company's intellectual property, and its willingness to protect that at any cost. This has meant investing in research and development at a rate almost double that of the rest of the industry. It has also meant refusing to blink when bigger companies with deeper pockets infringed Corning's patents and sought to outspend it in the law courts, as when, one by one, wealthy corporations tried to muscle their way into Corning's optical fibre business. Even giants such as ITT in America and Sumitomo in Japan found to their cost that the feisty little glass maker from upstate New York refused to roll over and play dead. Today, Corning has 40% of the market for optical fibre – nearly three times more than its nearest rival. But it took Corning 15 years of patient investment in optical-fibre technology to make a profit.

Only once has Corning stumbled badly. The 20-odd acquisitions the company made building its MetPath business into the largest medical-testing organization in the world smacked of impatient money. Yet in the end, this helped the company rediscover its innovative roots. Once again, the Houghtons, still around and still influential, were there to help nudge Corning back to its 150-year-old formula for patient innovation.

Source: 'Patient money', *The Economist*, 5 July 2001.
© The Economist Newspaper Limited, London (5 July 2001).

Questions for discussion

1 Why should Corning Glass have succeeded in its close control of intellectual property when so many others (see the case box on the knowledge economy) have outsourced their R&D?

2 What risks did Corning take and how did it manage them?

3 Use the 'knowledge spiral' (Nonaka and Takeuchi) to describe and classify Corning's approach to intellectual property.

19.7 Summary

Having taken a reasonably broad view of the writings in and around knowledge and strategy we have made a number of observations about current thinking:

1 Whereas knowledge is only implicit in the market-based view it is a central element of the resource-based view.

2 Dynamic theories of the firm cannot operate without some clear and operational concepts of knowledge. For example: (i) tacit and explicit and (ii) a knowledge production function incorporating innovating, accessing, transferring, integrating, and codifying.

3 However, we sympathize with assertions that knowledge is a highly contentious concept. For example: know-how vs know-what; explicit vs. implicit; individual vs collective; knowledge as knowing, as learning, as activity etc.

4 Nevertheless, our conjectures about the applicability of knowledge as a significant explanatory variable may be supported empirically; for example, see the wide range of citations in Eisenhardt and Santos (2001).

5 The writing on organizational knowledge has shown it as the lynchpin between internal organizational structures and processes and the capture of economic rents.

6 More controversially, there is a case for an evolutionary theory incorporating dynamic pathways as the external manifestation of organizational knowledge.

Our own approach to this has not been to attempt to provide 'a unified theory of absolutely everything'.[12] Rather, we have attempted to find a way of incorporating knowledge variables into the explanation of the long-run performance of firms, their long-run sustainable competitive advantages. To do this we offer a simple categorization that links three types of literature: on specific knowledge (a very dispersed literature), on organizational knowledge (which made considerable progress in the 1990s), and on the strategic theory of the firm. These strands we suggest are mutually reinforcing and interconnected. In particular, from a managerial perspective we can see how knowledge issues have a very direct economic content via the knowledge production/diffusion function, and a very organizational and individual element through analysis of organizational knowledge. These do not stand, however, as separable issues although elements of the problem can be treated in isolation. Rather, the system-wide characteristics of knowledge are evident particularly in the knowledge web through which value creation activities are composed.

We would also offer the final organizational observation that the knowledge web is a framework that allows firms to monitor threats. It should allow managers to question

---

[12] See the debates that have taken place in theoretical physics on just this issue.

the adequacy of existing business models and to analyse the unconventional responses that new entrants and innovators may be 'cooking up' to attack the entrenched positions of leading firms. In fact we believe that many leading firms fail to innovate because they act like hierarchies, not markets. They allocate resources for bureaucratic, political but not economic reasons. Too few of them make their organizational processes and routines receptive to idea and value innovation. Unfortunately they do not see innovation, learning and knowledge acquisition as key elements of the corporate DNA.

Key terms

Disruptive technologies *703*

Dominant design *714*

Efficiency effect *712*

Innovation *702*

Knowledge-based view *719*

Knowledge web *726*

Objectified knowledge *709*

Replacement effect *712*

Sunk cost effect *712*

Sustaining technologies *703*

Tacit knowledge *718*

Value innovation *704*

Recap questions and assignments

1 Compare the discussion of the knowledge economy in this chapter with the discussion of the new economy in Chapter 12. Identify the common elements and their effect on strategic discussions.

2 Consider also the discussion of risk in Chapter 14. What does a knowledge-based view of strategy imply for strategic risk and strategic decision-making?

3 Compare the action of disruptive technologies in this chapter with Schumpeter's 'Creative destruction' explained in Chapter 8. What role does tacit knowledge play in these ideas?

When you have read this chapter, log on to the Online Learning Centre website at
www.mcgraw-hill.co.uk/textbooks/mcgee to explore chapter-by-chapter test questions,
further reading and more online study tools for strategy.

Case 1 **Procter & Gamble: Jager's gamble**

Durk Jager, Procter & Gamble's new chief executive, wants to turn it into an innovative company. Easier said than done

A few years back, scientists at Procter & Gamble hit upon a big idea. Combining know-how in absorbent paper with a new 'dry-weave' polyethylene mesh, they came up with a thin, highly absorbent sanitary towel, the first breakthrough in feminine hygiene in 50 years. Today, P&G's 'Always' pads, now jazzed up with wings and even thinner, are sold in 80 countries, and are the mainstay of a product family that generates around $1.6 billion in annual sales.

This is just the kind of innovation that Durk Jager, who took over at P&G in January, sees as essential to rekindling growth at the world's largest consumer-products group. As its latest move, P&G announced on October 26th that it is prepared to give away or license any of its 25,000 patents, including those used in established brands. Chuck Hong, the firm's director of R&D for corporate innovations, thinks this will 'force us to continually invent'.

But why must P&G be forced to invent? Surely a firm with $38 billion in sales, more than 300 brands and 110,000 employees in 70 countries, with patents spanning fats and oils, plant fibres, surfactants and calcium, with vast marketing and financial resources, ought to be churning out exciting new products all the time? The trouble is, the new sanitary towel, which Mr Jager himself admits was the company's last big innovation, was launched away back in 1983. The story at P&G is not so much 'Always' as 'almost never'.

Mr Jager blames the consumer-product industry's problems on its failure to innovate. It has, he told this month's annual meeting in Cincinnati, 'led to commodity products and pricing pressure'. P&G has done worse than most. It has lost some 10% of its global market share in the past five years. Volumes this year will grow by 2% at best.

Turning a marketer into an innovator requires money, ideas and a nimble culture. P&G's problem has never been a lack of money or even ideas. Last year it was America's 21st-largest investor in research and development, spending $1.7 billion. Its R&D budget has grown from 2.9% to 4.5% of net sales over the past decade – still well below the 15% typical in the pharmaceuticals industry, but double that of Gillette. That spending has, however, yielded little. Less than 10% of P&G's thousands of patents are used in its hundreds of brands.

The fault lies with the culture. The firm has stifled innovation and prevented new ideas from getting to market quickly. Years after P&G developed its tissue-towel products, they have only just started to be rolled out globally. 'We're slower than my great-grandma,' says one executive.

Mr Jager is trying to change all that. In June he announced a big internal shake-up, sacking 13% of the workforce to streamline management and speed up decision-making. He is tying strategy and global profit targets to the performance of brands, rather than countries, and handing responsibility for new ideas to new business managers, not ones steeped in existing businesses. He has set up innovation teams to shoot promising ideas rapidly around the company and rush the best to market. And P&G plans to take more risks, cutting pre-market laboratory testing and putting products on sale earlier.

Spiffy Swiffer

P&G has had some success with the recent launch of products, including Swiffer, a dry mop that traps dust, Febreze spray to eliminate smells in fabric and Dryel, a home dry-cleaning kit, all of which he says are 'new-to-the-world' products, not just variants of old ones. Febreze, which was introduced in June last year, is already America's fifth-most successful new packaged product, with sales of $230m in its first year. And whereas Febreze took forever to be launched, Mr Jager boasts that Swiffer went from test marketing to global roll-out in a record 18 months.

P&G has even started looking outside for new ideas. To develop 'NutriDelight', a fortified orange powdered drink unveiled at the annual meeting, P&G worked with Unicef and licensed in the technology that lets iron exist with iodine and vitamin A in a stable form, helping undernourished children put on weight. And the group recently bought Iams Petfoods, admired for a scientific approach to pet health that includes low-calcium nosh for big dogs prone to overgrown bones, and oil and mineral formulas for 'senior' pets with bad joints.

Mr Jager is getting on the Internet, too. In November P&G will launch its majority-owned venture, reflect.com, an Internet-only range of 50,000 beauty products sold direct to consumers. Nathan Estruth, who helps run reflect.com, calls the venture 'heresy' for a mass-market company that has always sold through retailers.

Yet turning a marketing giant into a nippy innovator will be hard. P&G's line managers and country chiefs are trained to squeeze the last drop of sales out of existing products, not back risky new ones. Sam Stern, a professor at Oregon State University who has written a book on creativity in consumer-goods companies, points out that new ideas threaten the status quo.

However esoteric they sound, most consumer-goods technologies are unlikely to fend off imitators for long. A drug's effect is tied closely to its complex technology. Having gone through rigorous approval and lengthy clinical trials, patent challenges on drugs are rare. By contrast, Gillette's patent on a new toothbrush may specify with utmost precision how bristles are laid out; but there are lots of different 'technologies' that can clean teeth just as well. Lynn Dornblaser, director of the Global New Products Database, estimates that only 10% of the 55,000 brand new products that were launched globally last year are really innovative.

Even when consumer-products companies do come up with something novel, competitors catch up fast. 'Always' went unchallenged for ten years. Now, only one year after the launch of Febreze, Johnson & Johnson, Clorox and others have launched their own improved versions – mainly because Febreze was in pre-market testing for two years.

Similarly, Gillette took ten years and spent $1 billion developing its Mach3 triple-blade razor, launched last year. Within a few months, Asda, a British supermarket, rushed in with its own product, Tri-Flex, claiming that it was just as good and 40% cheaper.

What is more, packaged-goods companies not only have to develop the product, but also try to get jaded consumers to think they need it. That sometimes works. Upbeat marketing turned a very ordinary orange drink, Sunny Delight, into one of P&G's best brands.

But few new products are so successful. Information Resources, which researches packaged goods in America, finds that less than 1% of products launched in 1998 achieved $100m of sales in their first year. More than two-thirds flop in their first year. Hence, many managers in consumer-goods firms associate innovation with failure. Mr Jager has to persuade them that it is a condition for success.

Source: 'Jager's gamble', *The Economist*, 28 October 1999.
© The Economist Newspaper Limited, London (28 October 1999).

Case Questions

1 Why must P&G 'be forced to invent'? (p. 733)

2 Describe the incentives to innovate and the rewards and risks of innovation in terms of this P&G experience.

Further reading and references

Abramowitz, M (1986) 'Catching up, forging ahead, and falling behind', *Journal of Economic History,* **66**, pp. 385–406.

Alchian, AA (1950) 'Uncertainty, Evolution and Economic Theory', *Journal of Political Economy*, **58**, pp. 211–21.

Alchian, AA (1953) 'Biological Analogues in the Theory of the Firm: Comment', *American Economic Review*, **43**, pp. 600–3.

Alchian, AA and Demsetz, H (1972) 'Production, information costs, and economic organisation', *American Economic Review*, **62**, pp. 777–95.

Amit, R and Schoemaker, PJ (1993) 'Strategic assets and organisational rent', *Strategic Management Journal*, **14**, pp. 33–46.

Anderson, P and Tushman, ML (1990) 'Technological Discontinuities and Dominant Designs', *Administrative Science Quarterly*, **35**, pp. 604–33.

Argyris, C and Schon, D (1978) *Organisational Learning: A Theory in Action Perspective,* Addison-Wesley, Reading, MA.

Arrow, K (1962) 'Economic Welfare and the Allocation of Resources for Inventions,' in RR Nelson (ed.) *The Rate and Direction of Economic Activity,* Princeton University Press, Princeton, NJ.

Barney, J (1991) 'Firm resources and sustained competitive advantage', *Journal of Management,* **17**, pp. 99–120.

Besanko, D, Dranove, D and Shanley, M (2000) *Economics of Strategy,* 2nd edition, John Wiley & Sons, New York.

Bettis, RA and Prahalad, CK (1995) 'The dominant logic: retrospective and extension', *Strategic Management Journal*, **16, 1**, pp. 5–15.

Brandenburger, AM and Nalebuff, BJ (1995) *Co-opetition,* Doubleday, New York.

Brown, JS and Duguid, P (1991) 'Organisational learning and communities of practice: Toward a unified view of working, learning and innovation', *Organization Science*, **2**, pp. 40–57.

Burgelman, RA (1983) 'A model of the interaction of strategic behaviour, corporate context, and the concept of strategy', *The Academy of Management Review*, **8, 1**, pp. 61–70.

Chandler, AD Jr (1990) *Scale and Scope: The Economics of Industrial Competition,* Harvard University Press, Cambridge, MA.

Christensen, CM (1997) *The Innovator's Dilemma,* HBS Press, Boston, MA.

Coase, R (1937) 'The nature of the firm', *Economica*, **4**, pp. 386–405.

Coase, R (1988) 'Lecture on the nature of the firm, III', *Journal of Law, Economics and Organisation*, **4**, pp. 33–47.

Cohen, MD and Baclayan, P (1994) 'Organisational routines are stored as procedural memory: evidence from a laboratory study', *Organisation Science*, **5**, **4**, pp. 554–68.

Cooper, AC and Schendel, DE (1976) 'Strategic Response to Technological Threats', *Business Horizons*, **19**.

Cyert, RM and March, JG (1963) *A Behavioral Theory of the Firm*, Prentice-Hall, Englewood Cliffs, NJ.

D'Aveni, RA (1994) *Hypercompetition: Managing the Dynamics of Strategic Manoeuvring*, Free Press, New York.

De Geus, A (1976) *The Living Company*, HBS Press, Boston, MA.

De Wit, R and Meyer, R (1994) *Strategy: Process, Context, and Content*, West, St Paul, MN.

Dussage, P, Hart, S and Ramanantsoa (1996) *Strategic Technology Management*, Wiley, New York.

Eisenhardt, KM and Martin, JA (2000) 'Dynamic capabilities: what are they?' *Strategic Management Journal*, Special issue, pp. 1105–21.

Eisenhardt, KM and Santos, FM (2002) 'Knowledge-based view: a new theory of strategy?' in AM Pettigrew, H Thomas, and R Whittington (eds) *The Handbook of Strategy and Management*, Sage Publications, London.

Evans, P and Wurster, T (1997) 'Strategy and the New Economics of Information', *Harvard Business Review*, Sept/Oct, **75**, **5**, pp. 70–82.

Evans, P and Wurster, T (1999) *Blown to Bits: How the New Economics of Information Transforms Strategy*, Harvard Business School Press.

Ghemawat, P (1984) 'Capacity expansion in the titanium dioxide industry', *Journal of Industrial Economics*, **32**, pp. 145–63.

Ghemawat, P (1991) *Commitment: The Dynamics of Strategy*, Free Press, New York.

Ghemawat, P (1997) *Strategy and the Business Landscape*, Addison-Wesley, Reading MA.

Gottinger, H-W (1998) 'Technological races', *Annual Review of Economics* (Japan), **38**, 1–9.

Gottinger, H-W (2001) 'Stochastic innovation races', *Technological Forecasting and Social Change*, **68**, pp. 1–18.

Gottinger, H-W (2003) *Economics of Network Industries*, Routledge, London.

Granovetter, M (1985) 'Economic action and social structures', *American Journal of Sociology*, **91**, pp. 481–510.

Grant, RM (1991) 'The resource based theory of competitive advantage: implications for strategy formulation', *California Management Review*, Spring, pp. 119–45.

Grant, RM (1996) 'Toward a knowledge-based theory of the firm', *Strategic Management Journal*, 17 (Winter Special Issue), pp. 109–22.

Hall, RL and Hitch, CJ (1939) 'Price theory and business behaviour', *Oxford Economic*

Papers, 2, reprinted in T Wilson and PWS Andrews (eds) (1951) *Oxford Studies in the Price Mechanism*, Clarendon Press, Oxford.

Hamel, G (2000) *Leading the Revolution*, HBS Press, Boston, MA.

Hamel, G and Prahalad, CK (1993) 'Strategy as stretch and leverage', *Harvard Business Review*, March/April.

Hedberg, BLT (1981) 'How organisations learn and unlearn', in PC Nystrom and WH Starbuck (eds) *Handbook of Organisational Design*, Volume 1, pp. 2–27, Oxford University Press, New York.

Henderson, RM and Clark, KB (1990) 'Architectural innovation: the reconfiguration of existing technologies and the failure of established firms', *Administrative Science Quarterly*, **35, 1**, pp. 9–30.

Huff, AS (1994) 'Mapping strategic thought', in AS Huff (ed.) *Mapping Strategic Thought*, 2nd edition, pp. 11–52, John Wiley & Sons, Chichester.

Jensen, MC and Meckling, W (1976) 'Theory of the firm: managerial behaviour, agency costs, and ownership structure', *Journal of Financial Economics*, **3**, pp. 305–60.

Johnson, G and Huff, AS (1998) 'Everyday innovation/everyday strategy', in G Hamel, CK Prahalad and H Thomas (eds) *Strategic Flexibility: Managing in a Turbulent Economy*, John Wiley & Sons, Chichester.

Johnson, G and Bowman, C (1999) 'Strategy and everyday reality: the case for study of micro-strategy', working paper, 15th EGOS Colloquium.

Kim, W Chan and Mauborgne, R (1999) 'Strategy, Value Innovation and the Knowledge Economy', *Sloan Management Review*, **40, 3**, Spring, pp. 41–54.

Kogut, B and Zander, U (1992) 'Knowledge of the firm, combinative capabilities, and the replication of technology', *Organisation Science*, **3**, pp. 383–97.

Langlois, RN (1986) 'Rationality, institutions, and explanation', in RN Langlois (ed.) *Economics as a Process: Essays in the New Institutional Economics*: Cambridge University Press Cambridge, pp. 225–55.

Leonard-Barton, D (1992) 'Core capabilities and core rigidities: a paradox in managing new product development', *Strategic Management Journal*, **13** (Special Issue), pp. 111–26.

Lerner, J (1997) 'An empirical exploration of a technology race', *The Rand Journal of Economics*, **28, 2**, pp. 228–34.

Lester, RA (1946) 'Shortcomings of marginal analysis for wage-employment problems', *American Economic Review*, **36**, pp. 63–82.

Levitt, B and March, JG (1988) 'Organisational learning', *Annual Review of Sociology*, **14**, pp. 319–40

March, JG and Simon, HA (1958) *Organisations*, John Wiley, New York.

Marshall, A (1920) *Principles of Economics*, 8th edition, Macmillan Press, London.

McGee, J (2003) 'Strategy as Orchestrating Knowledge', in D Wilson and S Cummings (eds) *Images of Strategy*, Basil Blackwell, Oxford.

McGee, J and Sammut-Bonnici, T (2002) 'Network Industries in the New Economy', *European Business Journal*, **14**, **3**, September, pp. 116–32.

McGee, J and Sammut-Bonnici, T (2002) 'Network Strategies for the New Economy: Emerging Strategies for New Industry Structures', *European Business Journal*, **14**, **4**, December, pp. 174–85.

Menuhin, J (2001) *Strategising Routines: The Emergence of Strategic Initiatives*, unpublished PhD thesis, University of Warwick.

Menuhin, J and McGee, J (2003) 'Strategising routines in HSBC (UK), unpublished working paper, University of Warwick, Warwick Business School.

Nelson, RR and Winter, SG (1982) *An Evolutionary Theory of Economic Change*, Belknap Press, Cambridge, MA.

Nonaka, I and Takeuchi, H (1995) *The Knowledge-creating Company: How Japanese Companies Create the Dynamics of Innovation*, Oxford University Press, New York.

Nonaka, I (1994) 'A dynamic theory of knowledge creation', *Organization Science*, **5**, pp. 14–37.

Penrose, KT (1959) *The Theory of the Growth of the Firm*, Basil Blackwell, Oxford.

Peteraf, MA (1993) 'The cornerstones of competitive advantage: a resource-based view', *Strategic Management Journal*, **14**, **3**, pp. 179–91.

Porac, JF, Thomas, H and Baden Fuller, C (1989) 'Competitive groups as cognitive communities: the case of the Scottish knitwear manufacturers', *Journal of Management Studies*, **26**, pp. 397–416.

Porac, JF and Thomas, H (2002) 'Managing Cognition and Strategy: Issues, Trends and Future Directions', in AM Pettigrew, H Thomas and R Whittington (eds) *Handbook of Strategy and Management*, Sage Publications, London.

Polanyi, M (1966) *The Tacit Dimension*, Anchor Day Books, New York.

Porter, ME (1980) *Competitive Strategy*, Free Press, New York.

Porter, ME (1982) *Competitive Advantage*, Free Press, New York.

Prahalad, CK and Hamel, G (1990) 'The core competence of the corporation', *Harvard Business Review*, May/June, pp. 79–81.

Quinn, JB (1978) 'Strategic Change: Logical Incrementalism', *Sloan Management Review*, (Fall).

Rumelt, RP (1984) 'Towards a Strategic Theory of the Firm', in Robert Boyden Lamb (ed.) *Competitive Strategic Management*, Prentice-Hall, Englewood Cliffs, NJ.

Scherer, F (1991) 'International R&D races: theory and evidence', in L-G Mattsson and B Stymme (eds) *Corporate and Industry Strategies for Europe*, Elsevier Science Publishers, New York.

Schumpeter, J (1934) *The Theory of Economic Development*, Harvard University Press, Cambridge, MA (first published in 1911, republished 1968).

Simon, HA (1955) 'A behavioural model of rational choice', *Quarterly Journal of Economics*, **69**, pp. 99–118.

Simon, HA (1959) 'Theories of decision-making in economics and behavioural science', *American Economic Review*, **49**, pp. 253–83.

Spender, J-C (1996) 'Making knowledge the basis of a dynamic theory of the firm', *Strategic Management Journal*, 17 (Winter Special Issue), pp. 45–62.

Teece, DJ (1980) 'Economics of scope and the scope of the enterprise', *Journal of Economic Behaviour and Organisation*, **1**, pp. 223–47.

Teece, DJ (ed.) (1987) *The Competitive Challenge: Strategies for Industrial Innovation and Renewal*, Ballinger, Cambridge, MA.

Teece, DJ, Pisano, G and Shuen, A (1997) 'Dynamic capabilities and strategic management', *Strategic Management Journal*, **18**, **7**, pp. 509–33.

Tsoukas, H (1996) 'The firm as a distributed knowledge system: a constructionist approach', *Strategic Management Journal*, **17**, Winter Special Issue, pp. 11–25.

Veblen, T (1898) 'Why economics is evolutionary science', *Quarterly Journal of Economics*, **12**, pp. 373–97.

Vronen, J (1995) *Economic Evolution*, Routledge, London.

Weick, KE (1979) *The Social Psychology of Organising*, McGraw-Hill, New York.

Weick, KE (1995) *Sense making in Organisations*, Sage, Thousand Oaks, CA.

Wernerfelt, B (1984) 'A resource-based view of the firm', *Strategic Management Journal*, **5**, **2**, pp. 171–80.

Williamson, OE (1981) 'Strategizing, economizing, and economic organization', *Strategic Management Journal*, **12**, Winter Special Issue, pp. 75–94.

Williamson, OE (1985) *The Economic Institutions of Capitalism*, Free Press, New York.

Williamson, OE (1987) 'Transactions costs economics', *Journal of Economic Behaviour and Organisation* **8**, pp. 617–25.

Winter, SG (1964) 'Economic "natural selection" and the theory of the firm', *Yale Economic Essays*, **4**, pp. 225–72.

Winter, SG (1987) 'Knowledge and competence as strategic assets', in DJ Teece (ed.) *Competitive Challenge – Strategies for Industrial Innovation and Renewal*, Ballinger, Cambridge, MA.

Chapter 20

Total quality, customer value and process impacts

Introduction

Almost any business studies student now has a compulsory course (or courses) in the areas of operations management and strategy as part of their degree. The subject is considered an essential element of a manager's toolkit. Indeed, Slack and Lewis (2002, p. 3) in their recent text, on operations strategy, pose the question, 'How can "operations", which is generally concerned with the day-to-day creation and delivery of goods and services be considered strategic?' They argue that operations is a key part of a firm's strategic system and define operations strategy as the strategic reconciliation between the requirements of the markets in which the firm operates with the capabilities of its operational resources – i.e. what they can and cannot do. In other words, a continual and critical element of strategic process design, feedback and renewal is the analysis of how to achieve 'fit' between the company's resources and processes (i.e. capacity, supply network, process technology and organization) on the one hand and the requirements of its market positioning (i.e. customer segmentation, product differentiation, branding etc.) on the other hand.

From a strategic systems perspective two elements of this 'fit' process are particularly important and are considered thoroughly in this chapter. The first is the concept of quality (and the associated phrase **total quality management**) as a value driver for customer satisfaction and coherence across internal **business operations processes**. The second is the feedback impact of understanding **customer value** on the strategic redesign of the company's processes and market positioning.

Therefore, we examine in this chapter:

- Concepts of quality and their linkage to strategy.
- Examples of quality processes in practice explaining the Kaizen process (i.e. step-by-step improvements) and continuous improvement processes.
- Linkages between quality concepts and customer perceptions of value.
- The close linkage between operations management and strategy.
- The relationship between value and operations in creating value and achieving value innovation.

20.1 **Quality concepts**

> *When everything would seem to be matter of price, there lies still at the root of great business success the very much more important factor of quality ... After that, and a long way after, comes cost.* (Carnegie 1920)

The principles, practices and tools that comprise quality management have become a major focus of managerial attention in the West recently, in part because Japanese firms have used them with great commercial success in areas such as product quality, sales growth and profitability. Nonetheless, it seems to us that there is still a lack of clarity about the implications of quality for the process of strategic management in particular. Too many managers still think of quality as essentially an operations' problem: a functional issue of importance only to marketing or to production. On the other hand, many managers have been subjected over the last decade to innumerable siren calls urging them to view quality as the centrepiece of business activity. However, despite the significant attention paid to quality in recent years, strategic management practice and research remain a key area for extension of the quality concept (Godfrey 1993). In this discussion, we briefly review some perspectives on quality, offer an integrative strategic-level definition, and raise a series of issues that we believe are central to understanding the relationship between quality concepts and strategy.

20.1.1 **What is quality anyway?**

Goodness

Often, people will describe quality as meaning that something is outstanding in an indefinable way: 'even though Quality cannot be defined, you know what it is' (Pirsig 1974, p. 213). This common perspective can be found even in organizations which already seem quality-orientated. For example, one of the authors recently conducted a series of workshops at a large public-sector pension system well-known for productivity, innovation, and excellent client service and relations. However, despite the organization's reputation for high quality, not a single employee, form senior manager to clerk, could provide a specific operational definition of quality that the organization used to guide its work. Indeed, Pegels (1995 p. 4) notes that quality definitions have broadened to include quality processes and quality products, e.g. a definition of total quality management (TQM) is *providing the customer with quality products at the right time and the right place*.

A valuable product

Economists tend to view quality in a way familiar to many managers and consumers – as something valuable contained in a product, and hence a basis for price differences. Leffler (1982) suggests that quality is not the entire good but the amounts of an unpriced desired attribute contained in each unit of a priced attribute. For example, the cost of down comforters (duvets) depends mostly on the quantity of down, but most buyers are probably seeking a warm comforter, not a heavy one per se. In other words, what people want when they buy a good or a service is not necessarily the product itself but what it does for them. Marketing experts address this problem by disaggregating product quality into generic dimensions or attributes from the user's point of view. Figure 20.1 summarizes some of these marketing views of quality.

Physical Goods		Services	
Garvin (1987)	**Moen, Nolan and Provost (1991)**	**Parasuraman, Zeithaml, and Berry (1985)**	**Zeithaml, Parasuraman and Berry (1990)**
Performance	Time	Tangibles	Tangibles
Features	Consistency	Reliabilty	Reliabilty
Reliability	Uniformity	Responsiveness	Responsiveness
Conformance	Harmlessness	Access	Assurance
Durability	**Personal interface** ⟶	Courtesy	Empathy
Serviceability		Communication	
Aesthetics		Credibility	
Perceived quality ⟶		Security	
		Knowing customer	

Figure 20.1 Customer-based dimensions of quality

The marketing perspective has two elements of particular importance. First, customer perceptions of the quality of *tangible* goods have much in common with the quality of *services*. Service quality may be more difficult to evaluate (Parasuraman, *et al.*, 1985), but this only highlights the importance of service perceptions. Second, it emphasizes customer satisfaction as the core of organizational purpose. Figure 20.1 is from the market's point of view, not the firm's.

Doyle (2000, p. 79), a marketing expert, stresses that customers require strong value and unique benefits relative to competing products. And he adds that customer loyalty is an asset: loyal customers repurchase and buy more of the firm's products. Obviously, a firm needs more than the customer's point of view to gauge its activities. Internal standards, ranging from process quality to financial performance, are equally necessary. However, while many of a firm's internal measures may not be of direct concern to customers, they still must be *linked* to market preferences.

The change to a marketing focus by the earth-moving equipment maker Caterpillar provides a useful example here. In conversations with the authors, Caterpillar managers noted that the company used to focus on internally developed standards of product quality. Marketing served to communicate product superiority as defined by engineers rather than customers. The result was a marked tendency toward 'over-engineered' (and overly expensive) products.

In another instance, one manager at a large European telecommunications manufacturer noted that his firm's quality standards still remain internally focused and relatively unlinked to market preferences. The function of marketing is essentially limited to pushing product on to customers.

A question of process

Frederick Taylor, the father of scientific management, wrote that our 'larger wastes of human effort, which go on every day through such of our acts as our blundering, ill-directed, or inefficient … are less visible, less tangible, and are but vaguely appreciated' (Taylor 1911). His point was that most if not all productive systems are profoundly wasteful in subtle ways. This reality underlies much of the current thinking about managing for quality. Work approaches such as total quality management (TQM), certification programmes such as the ISO 9000 series, and conceptual frameworks such as W. Edwards Deming's fourteen points for management all emphasize processes.

TQM began as an approach to continuously improve product and service quality. Over time, however, through the efforts of Juran (1951), Deming and others, TQM now covers a range of performance and process improvement factors including productivity, flexibility, timeliness, customer responsiveness, benchmarking, improving supplier relationships, improving internal communications and re-engineering. TQM is seen as a management philosophy (Aguayo 1990). For example, Figure 20.2 shows Deming's philosophy

Standard Company	Deming Company
Quality is expensive	Quality leads to lower costs
Quality control experts can assure quality	Quality is made in the boardroom
Buy at lowest costs	Buy from vendors committed to quality
Play off one supplier against another	Work with suppliers
People can be treated like commodities – buying more when needed, laying off when needed less	People should be made to feel secure in their jobs
Profits are made by keeping revenue high and costs down	Profits are generated by loyal customers

Figure 20.2 Differences in belief between a Deming company and a standard company
Source: adapted from Aguayo, 1990.

more clearly, following his famous quote 'Where is quality made? Quality is made in the boardroom.'

In fact, it is common for managers to recognize problems in their firms' organizational processes; however, many apparently find it easier or cheaper (in the short run) to simply live with the problems. A plant manager of a major truck equipment maker, we will call it Truckco, commented:

> *I know our production and coordination are a mess, but demand is booming. When times are good, my top management is busy getting all the orders they can, and they just pressure us to work harder and faster. There's no time for investment. When times are bad, they continue to defer investment because there's no money coming in. Either way, our systems don't get any better.*

Clearly, there are costs of accepting problems or defects in organizational systems. Cycle time and work-in-process may rise for *all* activities, not just the production department. Departmental or functional parochialism and frustration also rise. Investments in non-value-added activities increase. Although management seems like firefighting (Mintzberg 1973), it is clear that these fires often are of managers' own making, caused by flawed management processes and assumptions.

For example, at Truckco, weak links between the sales team and the factory have led each to blame the other for missed delivery schedules. The sales force promises highly customized products without much concern for production constraints. In turn, the factory has devoted an ever-increasing percentage of floor space to storing unused specialized components that were ordered in excess, or that remain from cancelled orders. Afraid of the financial impact of writing off this inventory, the factory's management has resorted to routing its production lines around stores of materials. The factory functions only with the aid of myriad materials handlers and forklifts shuttling a large volume of work-in-process back and forth through the building. Top management is concerned about high costs and marketing problems, but has not addressed the key issue of functional integration.

Analytical tools	Practices
Pareto charts (frequency of occurrence	Quality circles
Ishikawa (fishbone) diagrams	Team-based organization with specialized roles
Run charts	Benchmarking
Histograms	Design for manufacturability
Control charts	Vendor certification
Scatter diagrams	Customer certification
Flowcharts	Mistake-proofing (poka-yoke)
Forcefield analysis	Predictive maintenance
Process capability analysis	Design of experiments
Taguchi loss function	
Quality function deployment (house of quality)	
Failure and effects analyses	

Figure 20.3 Some quality management tools and practices

The process improvement view of quality is grounded in work on process control. Anchored in Shewhart's (1930) theory of variation and process improvement, it emphasizes the use of data analysis (Ishikawa 1982; 1985) and other managerial tools and practices to support a focus on data-driven, process-centred decision making (Crosby 1979; Deming 1986; Juran 1978; Juran and Gyrna 1988). This view has, however, moved far beyond considering just the production process. Quality is as much about design as it is about process (e.g. Susman 1992; Taguchi 1986). Organizational links to suppliers and customers, and the use of integrative planning techniques, are efforts to build quality into product design, production, delivery and service. A key in this perspective is the development and use of tools to guide decision making (Figure 20.3)

Case box: Deming's 14 points of management

The fourteen points of management of Dr W. Edward Deming represent for many people the essence of total quality management (TQM). Deming's fourteen points are:

1 Create constancy of purpose for improvement of product and service (organizations must allocate resources for long-term planning, research and education, and for the constant improvement of the design of their products and services)

2 Adopt the new philosophy (government regulations representing obstacles must be removed, transformation of companies is needed)

3 Cease dependence on mass inspections (quality must be designed and built into the processes, preventing defects rather than attempting to detect and fix them after they have occurred)

4 End the practice of awarding business on the basis of price tags alone (organizations should establish long-term relationships with [single] suppliers)

> 5 Improve constantly and forever the system of production and service (management and employees must search continuously for ways to improve quality and productivity)
>
> 6 Institute training (training at all levels is a necessity, not optional)
>
> 7 Adopt and institute leadership (managers should lead, not supervise)
>
> 8 Drive out fear (make employees feel secure enough to express ideas and ask questions)
>
> 9 Break down barriers between staff areas (working in teams will solve many problems and will improve quality and productivity)
>
> 10 Eliminate slogans, exhortations, and targets for the workforce (problems with quality and productivity are caused by the system, not by individuals. Posters and slogans generate frustration and resentment)
>
> 11 Eliminate numerical quotas for the workforce and numerical goals for people in management (in order to meet quotas, people will produce defective products and reports)
>
> 12 Remove barriers that rob people of pride of workmanship (individual performance reviews are a great barrier to pride of achievement)
>
> 13 Encourage education and self-improvement for everyone (continuous learning for everyone)
>
> 14 Take action to accomplish the transformation (commitment on the part of both [top] management and employees is required)

Strategy-based definition

Strategic management raises several issues central to any integrative definition of quality. First, the very notion of strategic management suggests the significance of the firm's environment. Some of the significant external forces that affect a firm include the actions of other firms. Technological change, customer needs and preferences and governmental and social influences; each of these may be relevant to quality. Other firms provide both areas and competitive standards for quality. Change drives and is driven by quality. The evolution of customers' expectations presents a moving target for firms, but what customers expect is partly a function of how firms choose to manage quality. Further, government and society look to business for guidance, yet they also mold firms' approaches. For example, the proliferation of government-sponsored quality awards has substantially raised firms' awareness of the significance and complexity of quality issues.

Second, strategy means little without a clearly-defined purpose (mission). Leadership and the importance of defining purpose are common themes in quality literature.

Third, if strategy is about finding better ways to pursue the mission, the methods of managing seem relevant to strategy. Since much of quality management research and practice is indeed centred on the basic structure and approach to work, there clearly is potential for substantial bonds between quality management and strategic management.

Perspective	Core message	Element of systems perspective
Quality as goodness	Quality permeates the whole of a thing	Quality is greater than the sum of the parts
Production	The processes to accomplish purposes can be improved	Quality can be pursued through broad methodical improvement
Marketing	Quality is in the eye of the beholder and can be defined	Quality is the purpose of serving others well
Strategy	Purposeful actions are needed in an uncertain world	Organizations 'do' and 'change' subject to a system of supplier-organization-user links, an environment, and guiding purpose

Figure 20.4 Summary of themes

Last, although strategy places a primary focus on the firm, it implicitly recognizes that the firm is but one element in the value-chain system leading from raw physical and human inputs to the delivery of goods and services to final customers. Since any one firm is only part of a larger process, the micro-level concepts and techniques used to manage for quality within a firm's operations also may be useful at the corporate and industry levels. These four elements – the environment, leadership, method, and a systems view – are the contributions that a strategic management view can make to an integrative concept of quality management.

The themes discussed thus far can be integrated. Clearly, quality includes notions of the goodness and value of a product or service as experienced by the user, as well as some notion of the relative merits of the process which produced it. The process view suggests that superior, less-costly quality is possible through improvement mechanisms. Both the process and marketing perspectives provide specific tools and practices to pursue quality. Finally, the strategy perspective suggests that the firm must seek beneficial change including the effects of technological change in order to cope with changing environments, that planning matters, and that a firm is only part of a larger system. Figure 20.4 summarizes these themes.

20.2 Quality and strategy

Quality is a strategic firm-level concept which has become a competitive necessity. However, it also highlights the significance of the larger system of which the firm is a part, including suppliers and customers. Suppliers and customers have much in common in a systems perspective. Each provides needs, capabilities, and resources to the rest of the system. Finally, each can benefit from, and contribute to, the strengthening and integration of the overall system's efforts, purposes and understanding. The quality-focused firm adopts the role of partial 'co-ordinator' for the system. The firm's involvement and influence may decrease further up or down the demand–supply chain of which it is a part, but it can nonetheless foster self-aware-ness and co-operation into the system. This concept of systemic improvement is potentially a strategic issue of central relevance to a firm's senior management: the firm is not simply a narrow independent unit competing with suppliers, customers, and 'direct competitors'.

Thus, a strategic construct of quality which incorporates the perspectives we have raised is as follows: the strategic management of quality means that the firm using quality, co-operation and long-term viability as interrelated guiding themes works to inform, educate and motivate itself, and those with which it interacts, in order to continually improve and strengthen the human and processual inputs, interactions, dependencies, relations and outputs which constitute the firm and the system to which it belongs. In other words, quality is the continuing pursuit of system optimization (Deming 1986, 1993).

Quality-driven changes can be characterized on a least two dimensions, *locus* and *type*, as shown in Figure 20.5. In terms of *locus*, firms initiate changes internal to the firm or in interactions with its environment. For clarity Figure 20.5 considers only environmental interactions with upstream suppliers and downstream customers (key elements of the **value chain**).

In terms of *type*, since the techniques that managers employ depend in part on assumptions underlying their approach to management, the philosophical changes required by the quality approach must at least partly precede the technical ones. Quality 'problems' can be traced to either lack of information/knowledge or lack of motivation, both of which are problems of management, not of quality (Crosby 1979). A predominant theme in quality management literature is that the only members of a system who can intentionally and fundamentally change its philosophical underpinnings are those who manage it (Deming 1986; Hayes and Abernathy 1980; Ishikawa 1985; Taylor 1911). Of course, the dynamics between and within type and locus are more interactive than Figure 20.5 suggests.

Figure 20.6 provides another way of understanding this systemic impact on productivity. On the upstream or input side, the firm which pursues system improvement may enjoy lower negotiating costs for inputs, less cumbersome relations, better inputs and, in some cases, lower direct input costs. Inside the firm, outputs may improve and direct costs decline due to reductions in system waste and reworked or discarded output. Note that the

Type	Locus		
	Upstream interactions (suppliers)	**Internal to 'firm'**	**Downstream interactions (customers)**
Philosophical	Less cost-bidding Move toward sole-sourcing. Focus on improving supplier fit, quality, capability Acknowledge shared destiny	Systems, not people, as source of problems. Acceptance of human variation Systems optimisation Primacy of purpose	Commitment to customer delight Customer retention based on value, not price Acknowledge shared destiny
Technical	Shared planning and strategic information Suppliers linked with internal demand and development Training	Institutionalised mechanisms for systems analysis and change Management by fact Functional integration Training	Mechanisms to know customer Education of customer

Figure 20.5 Representative changes suggested by the quality paradigm

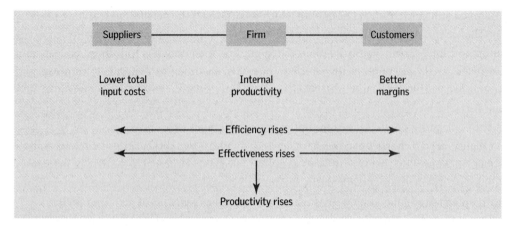

Figure 20.6 Effects of the quality paradigm

concept of productivity improvement includes elements that, although hard to assess, are known to have substantial impact on a firm's productivity – morale, absenteeism and turnover, decision processes, planning and so on. On the downstream or output side, stronger ties with buyers improve the firm's ability to satisfy them, may allow higher prices, and reduce total selling costs (including costs of poor quality such as reputation cost, lost customers and warranty support).

Further, as quality performance improves, the types of problems change (Garvin 1986). By identifying increasingly subtle problems and opportunities, technological changes, and systemic and environmental changes (which in turn lead to new problems and opportunities) the firm shifts its productivity horizon, as illustrated in Figure 20.7.

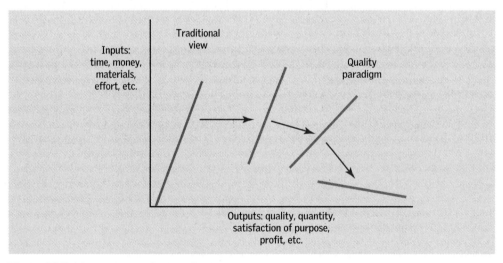

Figure 20.7 Alternative productivity horizons

Adding value is the salient feature of Figure 20.7. Widening the gap between quality (expressed as a broad set of desirable outputs) and cost (expressed as a broad set of inputs) means adding value. Although higher quality may mean lower cost, investments in quality are not entirely free. There may be significant direct and indirect expenses associated with change, and the most important ones may be the ones that cannot be quantified (Deming 1986).

Case box: Illustrative examples of the impact of TQM and value principles on competitive advantage

The automobile industry: Toyota v Ford v GM

The battle for dominance in the automobile industry is an important demonstration of the break between the old industrial order (an efficiency focus) and the new order (a focus on TQM and knowledge specialization).

In the first instance, Henry Ford's dream of the Model T Ford ('you can have it in any colour as long as it is black') in the early 1900s led to the principles of economies of scale and highly specialized mass production. His 'value innovation' was the assembly line focused on a single model (Model T) whose necessary components were carefully analysed and standardized to achieve cost efficiency and economies of scale. Ford's mass production strategy was, in turn, matched by an organizational structure which was highly functional and centralized – it was essentially a pyramid-shaped organization with Henry Ford at the apex, issuing orders and maintaining quality through efficiency management and application of the Taylorist principles of scientific management. In fact, by the 1920s Ford had a very significant cost advantage over the competition.

Competitors realized that they couldn't compete with Ford simply on a focused 'low cost' leader strategy. General Motors, formed in the early 1900s by William Durant through acquisition of a number of car assemblers and suppliers, realized that it needed to differentiate itself from Ford. Alfred P. Sloan (see *My Years with General Motors*) suggested that GM, with its range of brands, could offer 'a car for every purse and purpose'. Sloan's strategy for GM was, therefore, to understand the customer, offer the customer added value in each segment and cater for customer needs through product variety. However, the problem in implementing this differentiation strategy is how to offer such product variety at an affordable cost of production for GM. This problem was solved by Sloan by his invention of the multidivisional corporate structure. In essence, as noted by Alfred D. Chandler, the eminent Harvard business historian, this organization structure exploited economies of scale in production and design and economies of scope and focus in marketing and sales across the product range. Over time, in order to reduce costs further, GM decided to become vertically integrated and, for example, bought Fisher car body works to guarantee a supply of car bodies for its production schedules. Extending the organization structure in this fashion along the value chain offered two main advantages, namely, the guarantee of raw material sources and lower costs through better co-ordination across the value chain.

The preoccupation with scale and scope economies, vertical integration and hierarchical multidivisional structures lasted until the early 1970s and the oil crisis. Toyota had been a minion in the car industry since the 1950s, unable to exploit the principles of economies of scale and vertical integration. Indeed, Toyota relied on outside suppliers for parts and components such as gear transmissions and braking systems. In addition, because of the physical space limitations imposed by the geography of Japan and its lack of working capital, it could not afford to hold inventory and 'buffer' stocks to create slack in the production process.

As a consequence Toyota developed the now well documented system of lean production (Womack, Jones and Roos, 1990) and *just-in-time* inventory. Toyota demonstrated clearly that a supply chain (involving a range of suppliers) could be managed effectively without tying up capital in ownership of elements of the supply chain. It also pointed out that flexible, lean production meant that the production process allowed workers to stop production when problems occur, thus addressing the basic causes of poor quality. Toyota's system of continuous improvement, in essence, meant that through the mechanism of quality circles, problem solving in the production process was the preserve of the assembly line workers. They all participated in decision making and, as a result, Toyota developed a wide range of tools and techniques known as TQM (total quality management) to improve the quality of manufacturing and organizational processes. Not surprisingly, product quality also improved at a very rapid rate. Clearly Toyota has generated a sustainable competitive advantage based on cost and quality arising from its organizational practice, its 'value innovation' in supply-chain management and its continuous improvement (Kaizen) philosophy.

Lessons learned from the Toyota experience

In summary, the Toyota experience has a number of key characteristics:

- Auto firms were originally assemblers of components sourced from a supply network. **Vertical integration** (VI) plus scale gives high profits due to standardization, mass production and mass marketing. The market thus becomes concentrated where the key success factors are uncontroversially seen as VI with in-house assembly supported by hierarchical management structures.

- The Japanese came to this industry with a different set of initial conditions (and therefore assumptions). Japan was resource-poor, leading to high import content and the need to trade. They had technical capability but underdeveloped financial markets and a hostile labour force (post-war conditions). The Japanese observation of the US business model was high waste and low flexibility in production. Thus, initial assumptions were that (i) the work environment needed to be changed (hence life-time employment), and (ii) less waste was essential.

- At this point we see a gradual transition from the industrial age to the information age. With a reliance on a different intellectual capital model they created (i) a continuous improvement model of manufacturing processes, and (ii) new ways of working. The new intellectual capital was more intangible in nature – intellectual property (patents, copyright, trademark, trade secrets), concepts, information, etc.

- The Toyota production system has two key features: (i) outsourcing and just-in-time inventory to give reduced investment in working capital and space, and (ii) a human dimension in which labour is seen as an asset requiring constant on-the-job training, job rotation, skills and techniques programmes for production line workers and operations training for middle managers.

- The industrial age requires specialized capital, high task specialization, and separation of planning and management functions from actual production efforts (mental from physical). The information age requires team production with consensus and co-operation, flexible production with multi-purpose equipment and cross-trained workers running their own environments. This results in a new demarcation of responsibilities between managers and front-line workers (see Table 20.1).

  Note that the Toyota model is an example of 'value innovation' through creative destruction – a Schumpeterian approach – i.e. the upgrade and move to more sophisticated types of production assets. The industrial age focuses on refining capital assets and on the tangibility of knowledge and its incorporation into assets. The information age maintains the shift towards capital-intensity but has a parallel deployment of capital – intensive tangible assets with capital-intensive intangibles.

- The horizontal structures typical of the information age have a number of interesting characteristics: (i) team production (flexible work teams, quality circles, job rotation); (ii) cross-training labour for multi-task performance; (iii) empowering workers to participate in continuous process improvement and to control their immediate work environment. These are the **Kaizen**. Also the **Keiretsu** – the creation of close networks of supply linkage – and the **Kanban** – co-ordination among related units. The management of this depends on a particular form of intellectual capital (which can be contrasted with the industrial age's need for intellectual capital to manage vertically controlled organizations). This capital-induced expansion increases the marginal product of labour

Table 20.1 Staff responsibilities in the information age

	Technical and functional activities	Administrative and operations planning	Strategy, conceptual and entrepreneurial
Senior	10%	20%	7%
Middle	30%	50%	20%
Front line	75%	20%	5%

automatically and the benefits are shared between firms, shareholders, labour, and consumers (lower prices thus fuelling further growth …).

The innovation is in new methods of production, new forms of organization, new sources and organization of supply, and new trade routes to markets (a completely different *business model*). Overall, the Toyota production system is a combination of lean production and new organization, more specifically:

+ Flexible batch production (complete with cross-trained workers etc.)
+ JIT (just-in-time inventory) invented
+ Waste elimination
+ Minimum use of capital equipment
+ Higher labour productivity
+ Continuous product and process improvement
+ Line workers identifying and controlling problems
+ Supplier organization

Case box: General Electric

General Electric, as can be seen from the extensive range of Harvard Business School cases and Jack Welch's exploits as CEO for 20 years from the 1980s, has been a leader in strategic management and one of the most closely examined of modern corporations. Since the Second World War, it has had relatively few CEOs and its structure has mirrored the changes outlined by Alfred D. Chandler in his seminal work on the structure and scope of US corporations – Borch, the CEO in the 50s, stressed functional, Vertical Integration (VI)-type structures; Cordiner, the CEO in the 60s, stressed departmental, divisionalized structures; Jones, the CEO in the 70s, advanced the concept of GE as a portfolio of strategic business units (SBUs) whereas Jack Welch in the 1980s and the 1990s moved the company through several phases marked by simple messages and themes. Indeed, Gordon Walker (2003, p. 225) summarizes the various corporate mandates and leadership themes (in chronological order) which Welch devised to create a flexible, quick and adaptable organization:

+ Reduce bureaucratic behaviour
+ Define markets globally
+ Develop managers as leaders
+ Promote sharing across business units
+ Set very aggressive goals
+ Build service businesses
+ Implement six-sigma quality programmes

◆ Identify and remove managers who are underperforming compared to their peers
◆ Force all business units to implement e-commerce strategies

It can be seen that these range from Welch's earlier mandates to be 'number 1 or number 2 in any market or else get out' to an increasing focus on organizational learning, sharing promising practices and moving planning to the business unit level (with short five-year plans). In the middle 1990s for example, Jack Welch began his TQM approach based on the six-sigma principles advocated by quality theorists such as Deming and Juan. However, Welch took a very strong systems approach to the quality process and focused very closely on the customer and the customer value proposition (*see* also Doyle 2000). GE asked customers to state exactly what they value about a specific product or service and, in essence, define the value he or she wants. These are the customer value drivers, the value innovations/proposition, that are the critical quality elements for the specific GE product or service. GE then manages its organizational and strategic processes from a systemic, customer value viewpoint so that every process element along the value chain, from product design through manufacturing operations to the selling and distribution chain, is geared to provide the maximum value and delight to the eventual customer. When quality levels are below the six-sigma requirements managers must analyse and address the fundamental causes of poor quality and provide quick, workable solutions. For example, in one exercise GE found that customers had a very low tolerance for late deliveries of electrical appliances, leading GE to examine the service offered regularly by its dealers.

Table 20.2 Quality matrix

	Goals (organizationally determined)			
	A	B	C	D
KEY FACTORS				
Quality leadership				
Supplier management				
Process control and improvement				
Quality management and processes				
People commitment				
Customer value programme				
New product innovations				
Change capabilities				

Note: Rating scale to table (within matrix): 1 = No Activity; 2 = Ongoing efforts; 3 = Competent; 4 = Best practice; 5 = Leader
Source: adapted from Walker, 2003.

It is clear that Jack Welch, in developing each of his strategic themes, was adamant that employers must be encouraged to follow common goals. In the six-sigma (TQM) quality situation, GE developed tools such as the **quality matrix** (Walker 2003, p. 227) shown in Table 20.2 (p. 755) to ensure that each business unit and product category continually assessed and monitored its progress towards the production of the highest quality products.

In summary, GE's experience of TQM shows that when a company has a 'value innovation' focus, and a value proposition espousing customer value, it looks at its products closely from the outside-in perspective (as Robert Burns, the Scottish poet, said, 'try to see ourselves as others see us'). This allows the firm to focus on providing innovative products of high quality which address customer needs and wants – not simply producing products from the inside perspective without recourse to the customer. For example, when GE realized that locomotive customers did not want bigger and more powerful trains but more reliable, productive and easily scheduled vehicles, it addressed those needs and this, in turn, opened a whole new lucrative market in providing service, back-up and other services for operators of railroads and railroad operators.

Case box: Processes of improvement: how to survive in difficult times

One thing that helps companies survive in recession and in the teeth of fierce competition is having good business processes, and improving them all the time. The best Japanese companies, for example, are extremely good at logistics, both in their global operations and at home. Honda has a network of factories around the world, all hooked into the same supply chain. Each operates in the same way, so each is able to make any vehicle in the product range according to demand. This gives the company tremendous flexibility, thanks as much to slick logistics as to excellence in manufacturing.

Honda pays meticulous attention to detail to help ensure that its products are made on time. It has special data systems installed in each of its factories to monitor weather forecasts. These allow factory managers to talk in advance to parts suppliers about bad weather and how it might affect deliveries. They can decide what and when to stock up.

One of the best Japanese companies at logistics is Seven-Eleven, the largest convenience-store chain in the country. It is a rare example of a company whose business is largely domestic that is doing well despite Japan's deflationary environment. Its biggest strength is its custom-built information system that compiles extensive sales data (collected three times a day and analysed in 20 minutes). The system helps improve **quality control** and assists the company in pricing, product development and inventory management.

In the Japanese economy, any excess inventory can quickly translate into losses for firms that become too anxious to shift stock. For this reason, Kao has been working hard to improve its supply-chain management. Just as Toyota and other carmakers gained competitive advantage from honing their 'just-in-time' delivery systems in the 1980s, so Kao has been steadily improving its inventory management – to the extent that it has saved around ¥10 billion ($85m) a year for the past 15 years. Companies such as Canon, Takeda Chemicals and Yamato Transport, the biggest parcel-delivery company in the country, are also strong in logistics and supply-chain management.

In many cases, these process improvements have gone against the grain. Japan is remarkably backward in its use of information technology. Its spending on IT jumped to 4.4% of GDP in 2001, from 3.9%. But the comparable figure for Europe was 5.2%, and for America, 5.3%. There is no shortage of computers on Japanese workers' desks, but many are still connected to old mainframes and run outdated software. Access to the internet is often available only via the one or two PCs around the office that are wired to the web.

Many of the firms that seem to have made the biggest productivity gains from IT are big exporters – car manufacturers and electronics firms. They are the ones with the global strategies that enable them to see what the rest of the world is up to.

Source: 'Rising above the sludge', *The Economist*, 3 April 2003.
© The Economist Newspaper Limited, London (3 April 2003).

Questions for discussion

1 How can process improvement lead to a sustainable competitive advantage?

2 Explain how process improvement is more than just engineering management.

3 Is process improvement objectified, explicit knowledge (in terms of Figure 19.4) or is it collective, implicit knowledge? What is the significance of your answer?

20.3 Implications for strategic management

European and American attempts, beginning in the early 1970s to explore the ill-understood quality paradigm emerging from Japan had a fairly narrow emphasis on tools and techniques. Although understanding in many firms has moved beyond this narrow view, as is clear from the GM, Ford, Toyota and GE examples, we believe that there still are strategic issues which merit increased attention, from both senior management and strategy researchers.

20.3.1 How strong is self-interest?

A variety of traditional management practices and concepts rest on the subtle assumption that human behaviour is dominated by self-interest and that people (and firms) will often cheat if conditions permit.

Transaction costs and agency theories are often seen in strategy research and are used to provide insight into basic strategic issues faced by firms. **Transaction cost theory** is concerned with the efficiency of organizational forms – given alternative ways to structure economic activity, what is the most efficient way to do so? It is applied most often to the traditional 'make-or-buy' question (Williamson 1985). **Agency theory** asks how non-owners (agents) charged with managing resources will treat those resources and their outputs, and how owners (principals) can select, motivate and control agents to get the most productive, equitable resource employment (Eisenhardt 1985, 1989). Both of these perspectives emphasize that a firm risks being cheated by people and other firms.

The quality paradigm does not argue against self-interest. It does, however, argue that opportunistic (unfair) behaviour may be largely an outcome, the *result* of a system of beliefs and practices, not a dominant genetic element in human behaviour. In other words, many people and firms cheat when taught to cheat and when they do not perceive themselves as part of an interdependent system. The potential problem with efforts to control cheating is that the systems devised to prevent problems may also have a substantial, adverse impact on non-cheaters. Just as surveillance cameras breed mistrust, so too can adversarial, control-oriented management practices. The American retailer Wal-Mart had a reputation of subjecting suppliers to a particularly difficult bargaining process. However, in order to fully exploit the potential of the tightly integrated distribution system it was building, Wal-Mart discovered that its semi-adversarial, 'arm's-length' relations with suppliers could not provide the co-operation and commitment it needed.

On the other hand, consider the popularity of vendor certification programmes. In the certification process, a firm's probing and participation may extend deep into suppliers' fundamental planning and management practices. Even relying on third-party certification such as ISO 9000 means that a firm cares how its suppliers conduct their operations. On the downstream side, if a firm's marketing efforts include managing inventory for its customers, then the firm must become tightly linked with the customer's production system. Such activities internalize upstream and downstream elements beyond the formal boundaries of the firm, and help to overcome the failure for co-operative learning which can be found in a more competitive supplier–buyer market relationship. In other words, 'arm's-length' business relationships make it more difficult for firms to learn together.

Open co-operation is a matter of degree, of course, but firms are becoming increasingly focused on the benefit of building knowledge ties with suppliers and customers and with other firms, rather than focusing on the possibility that 'outsiders' will exploit their openness. For example, although winners of the American Baldridge Award for quality are *required* to share their experiences, many well-known firms have pursued the award. Further, the increasingly popular practice of benchmarking cannot take place without an attitude of openness regarding information and knowledge. (Interestingly, some of these knowledge-sharing ties, in the United States at least, could be interpreted as anti-trust violations.

The inability of anti-trust law to cope with co-operative learning systems may pose a growing problem as more firms move towards the quality paradigm.)

Motorola, for example, is famous for its efforts to educate not only employees but also suppliers, customers, and interested firms and parties. Motorola actively seeks to improve the generation, processing and dissemination of knowledge both within and beyond the firm's formal boundaries. The sharing of ideas and data is seen as the key to creativity and prosperity, as opposed to the presumption that knowledge is to be hoarded and kept secret from others in the pursuit of competitive advantage. Motorola considers the relevant members and beneficiaries of the firm's creative efforts and concern to extend far beyond the firm itself. It is a strong voice for the sharing of knowledge across firms and industries, and pushes strongly for quality-oriented changes in the content, method and assumptions of management education. Motorola's efforts extend to unusual places – a limousine driver, working for Motorola's headquarters, recently explained to one of the authors how his limousine business had become a sole supplier, and what Motorola's six-sigma quality focus had to do with livery service.

20.3.2 Is management the crucial resource and competence?

Two other common strategy perspectives, the *resource-based view* of the firm and *core competence*, highlight the importance of inputs and specialized skills. The resource-based view describes firms as bundles of resources and suggest that the most crucial resources may also be the most difficult to develop, acquire or change (Barney 1986; Dierickx and Cook 1989; Ghemawat 1991; Mahoney and Pandian 1992; Wernerfelt 1984).

Often, however, a firm may recognize a valuable resource only in hindsight, for example after it has gained valuable experience in a particular skill or area. Resources matter, but perhaps the key to business success is not resources per se, but the firm's ability to manage systems. After all, merely identifying resources may give little clue about how to use them. An overemphasis on resources obscures the critical issue of a firm's basic managerial approach and systems. Resources are not much use without a system which makes good use of them. How a firm mobilizes its resources determines what activities it becomes good at. Moreover, the capacity to achieve high quality is difficult to develop, hard to buy and provides a substantial benefit, which sounds much like the definition of a valuable resource. Clearly, a management system which manages for quality is an abstract form of a resource.

Core competence, a variation on the resource theme, suggests that a firm may be particularly good at some fundamental activity which can be leveraged in pursuit of success (Prahalad and Hamel 1990). Again, however, it seems to us that, from a strategic perspective, fundamental competence may lie not in the type of functional activity (such as engineering, marketing or research) but in *how* the activity is carried out. This is the distinction between competence building and competence leveraging. For example, possessing skilled mechanical engineers as does Mercedes-Benz, or chemical expertise as does ICI, does not lead to competence per se. Competence arises from the managerial assumptions and practices which provide the structure for productive activity. Superior assumptions and practices are those which integrate a firm's activities and leverage the firm's value equation.

20.3.3 Does competition hinder systemic improvement?

One controversial thought is the idea that some aspects of competition may be quite destructive. Kohn (1986), for example, argues that logic and evidence do not support the widespread belief that competition between individuals is beneficial. Deming (1986, 1993) believes that such competition conflicts with human psychology and hinders a systemic perspective.

Business competition takes many forms, including the following:

- With suppliers: holding bidding wars, arbitrary price reduction targets, multiple sourcing.

- Internally: competitive resource allocation processes, meritocracies, profit centres.

- With customers: 'shaving' product quality or quantity, price increases to customers with no alternative supply, withholding needed information.

- With other firms and governments: opportunism within consortia and cartels, industrial espionage, tax fraud, shedding of costly consequences of strategic and operating decisions.

A firm can never be fully independent of other parties (including suppliers, customers and direct competitors) in the productive system, but it can choose win-win or win-lose approaches to the interdependencies it must manage (the age-old issue of the individual versus the group). The quality paradigm does not deny the existence of conflicting interests, but suggests that conflict and competition are partly the result of a failure to think on a system level. Indeed, a glaring shortcoming of traditional microeconomic and strategic thought is that they primarily offer theories in which firms are independent competitors attempting to maximize their share of economic wealth. Both microeconomics and strategy have been relatively silent on the issue of interdependent firms co-operating to enlarge the aggregate economic wealth. Figure 20.8 illustrates the interdependence between members of productive chains, and between the chains themselves. As firms strengthen relations in their respective chains, competition is narrowed to some, but not all, facets of the inter-system level.

As a simple example, the 'Big Three' US automakers – General Motors, Ford and Chrysler – once were highly financially vertically integrated, particularly GM. Having de-integrated to some extend (particularly Chrysler and Ford), they now have worked in various ways to strengthen ties with suppliers and customers. The three firms do compete vigorously in the retail markets, but they also share suppliers and produce parts for each other they also share suppliers and produce parts for each other; they are highly interdependent. For example, if GM were to close all of its in-house suppliers tomorrow, automobile production at Ford and Chrysler would be substantially disrupted, at least temporarily. Another perspective on close interaction can be found in the contrast between the tight supply links in the relatively healthy Japanese auto industry (Cusumano and Takeishi 1991) and the more arm's-length links in the fairly troubled British one (Turnbull, Oliver and Wilkinson 1992).

The competition–co-operation issue also sheds light on the question of vertical integration. From a system level, the question of the formal boundaries of a firm appears relatively trivial in comparison to how the broader productive system is managed. In other words, downsizing and outsourcing in integrated firms, and acquisition in the opposite case, are not solutions to the need for a productive way to operationally manage interdependence between steps in the value chain which leads from raw materials to final customers. Whether owned or not, productive activities are interdependent and their links must be managed. Figure 20.8 illustrates linkages and the interdependencies created within and between them.

The standard view is that markets will mesh demand with supply. However, it can be difficult to integrate demand with supply in a competitive environment, since the capacity for co-operation is quite limited. This limited co-operation also hinders the firm's ability to change and learn. Indeed, in some cases fiercely competitive markets create market failures for co-operative learning and system improvement.

For example, Homescape is a regional real estate development company in the US which finances, plans and builds residential subdivisions. In a pattern typical for the industry, the firm has only two employees on direct payroll. They co-ordinate numerous independent contractors including engineers, roadwork firms, realtors, and a builder. The builder then co-ordinates the numerous subcontractors who build a house – masons, carpenters, etc. Homescape explains the tradition of independent contractors as the result of the cyclical nature of housing demand. When demand is strong, construction occurs at a frenzied pace, with multiple developers competing for contractors and subcontractors. Developers and builders have been known to walk on to competitors' job sites and offer contractors cash to leave for another project. Homescape possesses more sophisticated management and much greater capital than most of its competitors.

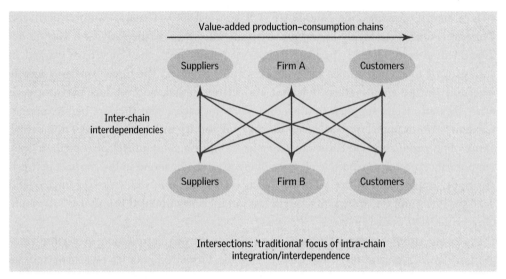

Figure 20.8 Interdependencies

Many developers are not particularly wealthy and, with high debt loads, tend to avoid integrating forward into the activities of their contractor network because they fear high fixed personnel costs and carrying costs for unsold properties which could occur in times of low demand. Although informal relationships certainly continue, low demand typically leads to the laying off of contractors. It is interesting to consider, however, that this response to market cyclicality also makes the cycle *worse*. Rising demand for houses tends to lead to overbuilding, and falling demand often leads to a wave of deferred projects. Given the substantial lead-time in project development, these responses simply widen the market swings. Further, despite the importance of technical skills in construction, developers typically do not invest in training for contractors and subcontractors, since many of the relationships are fairly arm's-length and short term. Contrast this with Motorola, which requires forty hours per year of formal training for each of its employees (Bales 1992).

20.4 **Does organization get in the way?**

Strategy may get in the way of quality and may serve to reduce it. So, too, may organizational factors (*see* Part 4). Wilson (1999, p. 101) observed that many organizational characteristics served to confound or potentially reverse systemic attempts at quality improvement. Some examples are:

- *Sectional interests*: Quality programmes can intensify local rationalities. Those who support the programme will be its (often) fanatical supporters while others may view it with less enthusiasm. The potential systemic effects of quality improvement are thus lost as sectional interests fight among themselves.

- *The sponge effect*: Because quality programmes are systemic in their scope, they can easily become all-embracing processes into which all organizational problems are put. Quite reasonably, the programmes have little hope of solving these problems (such as labour disputes or key decisions such as a reorganization) and so is judged to have failed. Systemic quality programmes are open to soaking up more problems than they can realistically handle.

- *Recreating the rigid organization:* Because programmes are organization-wide, they demand absolute commitment from all parts of the organization. The outcomes of a successful programme can, as a result, simply recreate another level of status quo from which further change becomes difficult. Organization can drive out the intended continuous characteristics of quality change.

- *Distinctions between means and ends become blurred*: Quality programmes can easily slip into becoming ends in themselves rather than means to an end (e.g. creating organizational change to increase levels of customer loyalty or satisfaction). This is particularly true of incremental, step-wise quality programmes where achieving the steps becomes the end in itself rather than the means to systemic organizational change.

Wilson (1999, p. 102) also points out other organizational phenomena which relate to systemic quality programmes. They can, paradoxically, make things worse rather than better. This can occur, for example, where the organization is in a state of decline. Scarce resources mean that allocating key resources to quality could seal the demise of an already declining organization. Finally, much of the evidence from quality programmes is collected from manufacturing organizations with a lesser degree of evidence from service firms. It is unclear to what extent there can be direct translation from manufacturing contexts to service or non-profit organizations and more empirical research is needed before we can answer such questions.

20.4.1 **The complexity of performance**

Financial profit is often stressed as the central goal of firms, but a systemic view of quality suggests a more complex set of purposes, acknowledging customer satisfaction, the interests of employees, the system capacity for continued existence, and benefits to others contributing to the organization (including, certainly, profit for the owners of capital). This is basically the stakeholder argument (e.g. Freeman 1984) with a dynamic emphasis on system improvement. It echoes changes in accounting research and practice, such as activity-based costings (Kaplan 1990) and the balanced scorecard approach to top management reporting practices (Kaplan and Norton 1993).

20.4.2 **The operations basis of strategy**

Despite longstanding calls (Skinner 1969), an understanding of production and systems views is still infrequent in the strategic planning of many firms, particularly those in which finance or marketing have been the traditional path into senior management. Recall the truck equipment maker Trucko. Top management clearly felt driven by marketing and financial concerns, and manufacturing issues literally took the back seat. An underappreciation of the complexities of production also seems to be lacking in some management researchers. For instance, a recent academic seminar discussed a study of changes in workforce management practices due to advanced manufacturing technologies. The audience, consisting mostly of organizational change researchers, seemed fundamentally surprised to learn that many firms in the study fully recognized the importance of changing employees' attitudes and skills to remain in step with new technology. The 'dark Satanic mills' stereotype of manufacturing still has true believers, even among management scholars.

Quality management includes the use of very specific tools developed mostly in the production arena, but this does not limit it to only a narrow functional relevance. For instance, quality and finance both have many tools and methods, but most firms do not keep finance isolated – they train and expect a variety of managers to understand relevant financial concepts (Juran 1981). It seems difficult to develop or study strategy without an elementary understanding of what a firm actually does, and how it does it. This requires basic knowledge of production and operations management issues and concepts.

For example, Porter's (1980) three generic strategies – cost reduction, differentiation and focus – are popular themes for firms. However, in a systems view of quality they are not strategies but mutually reinforcing *elements* of strategy. This suggests that a firm can simultaneously reduce costs by improving processes and relations with suppliers *and* focus on improving service to a well-understood customer set and differentiate itself through both perceived and actual quality. Researchers have demonstrated that these elements can move together (Cho and Lee 1993). The success of a firm such as Toyota suggests the value of using quality as a strategic concept is that it can help integrate specific production (cost-reduction) and marketing (differentiation) skills developed over time.

There is a very substantial body of strategy literature typified by the Porter generic strategies. However, it is worth noting that this literature often seems associated with a particular view of production, one in which long, standardized runs in dedicated, inflexible production systems lead to efficiency and in which high quality is a high-cost craftsman approach. That perspective (*see* Abernathy 1978) is increasingly outmoded by technological changes and new thinking about management.

20.5 Summary

The central theme of this chapter, which stresses an integrative, strategic-level view of quality, is also to raise issues that merit scrutiny. Organizations actually foster problems while trying to solve them:

- A focus on a balance between competition and cooperation creates a market for learning.

- Firms do better to develop strategies that seek improved performance for the value-chain as a whole, rather than pursing success alone.

- A greater appreciation of operations and production improves the way we conceive of and implement the strategy systems process.

It is paradoxical that both strategies and organizational characteristics have the capability to reduce rather than increase quality. Hence the importance of including quality in the strategic portfolio of any organization.

Key terms

Agency theory *758*	Quality matrix *756*
Business operations processes *742*	Six-sigma concept *755*
Customer value *742*	Total quality management (TQM) *742*
Kaizen *753*	Transaction cost theory *758*
Kanban *753*	Value chain *749*
Keiretsu *753*	Vertical integration *752*
Quality control *756*	

Recap questions and assignments

1   Use the Deming philosophy in Figure 20.2 to draw a comparison between Toyota and Ford (or GM).

2   In what sense is 'quality' a strategic rather than an operational issue?

3   Was General Electric under Jack Welch (pp. 754–5) different from Ford and GM in the way in which it used Total Quality Management?

When you have read this chapter, log on to the Online Learning Centre website at www.mcgraw-hill.co.uk/textbooks/mcgee to explore chapter-by-chapter test questions, further reading and more online study tools for strategy.

Case 1 **Wasting disease**

A tale of poor quality and inefficiency

'OUR attempts to deliver today's technologies with today's medical production capabilities are the medical equivalent of manufacturing microprocessors in a vacuum-tube factory. The costs of waste, poor quality and inefficiency are enormous. If the current delivery system is unable to utilise today's technologies effectively, it will be even less able to carry the weight of tomorrow's technologies and an ageing population, raising the spectre of even more variability in quality, more errors, less responsiveness and greater costs associated with waste and poor quality.'

This indictment of America's health-care system comes not from an angry blogger but from the prestigious Institute of Medicine in a landmark report, 'Crossing the Quality Chasm'. The result of years of work by a committee of experts, it is scathing about the poor standards and wastefulness that it found.

One manifest sign of poor quality is the number of people who die because of medical errors. In an earlier report, the institute estimated that such errors in American hospitals were responsible for at least 44,000 deaths a year, and perhaps more than twice that. Medication errors alone, such as incorrect dosages, accounted for 7,000 deaths. According to the institute, health care was 'a decade or more behind other high-risk industries in its attention to ensuring basic safety'.

Not only can medical errors result in human tragedies, they also waste money because of compensation claims and the additional spending needed to try to put things right. Another kind of waste stems from the inappropriate use of medical procedures on patients for whom the risks outweigh potential benefits. This happens on a worryingly large scale; for example, 14% of bypass surgeries in America have been assessed as inappropriate.

The picture in other countries is much the same. Recent studies in Canada and Denmark have documented a high incidence of medical errors in hospitals. Thomas Schioler of the Danish National Board of Health says that in many countries a large number of patients are injured because of medical treatment and not because of their underlying disease. Over-use of medical procedures is also common. In Sweden and Britain, for example, 10% and 16% respectively of bypass surgeries have been found to be inappropriate.

Yet another form of waste is under-use of appropriate medical care. A report from the National Committee for Quality Assurance, an independent watchdog of American health care, estimated in 2003 that over 57,000 American deaths a year could be attributed to a failure to deliver best-practice care. The NCQA calculated that this failure generated an annual bill of $1.6 billion in avoidable hospital costs.

According to a recent survey from the RAND think-tank, American adults receive little more than half the medical care recommended. Reviewing a subsequent comparison of the quality of care in five countries – Australia, Canada, New Zealand, Britain and America –

Elizabeth McGlynn, who led the RAND study, recently wrote in *Health Affairs* that other countries were doing no better than America. Ms McGlynn believes that if the RAND survey were repeated in the other four countries, 'we would find very similar levels of performance to those found in the United States overall.'

Getting it together

Medical systems are inefficient, too. As the Institute of Medicine's report says: 'Surgeons know that operations rarely start on time; doctors and nurses wait 'on hold' as they try to track down vital information, and delays and barriers involved in referrals eat up the time and energy of both referring doctors and consulting specialists.' In Britain's NHS, many operating theatres stand idle unnecessarily, even though there is huge pressure to cut the numbers waiting for operations. Auditors have calculated that operating rooms are used on average 24 hours a week instead of an intended 40.

One of the biggest failings of modern health-care systems is that they so seldom provide integrated medical care. In emergencies, patients head for the local hospital; for minor illnesses they consult their family doctor. But for chronic conditions such as diabetes and cardiovascular diseases, which are becoming increasingly prevalent, they require care and advice both from their primary physician and from the hospital. Effective co-ordination of this care results in better and cheaper treatment, yet too often it does not happen. According to the OECD, 'health-care organizations, hospitals and physicians typically operate as separate "silos", acting without the benefit of complete information about the patient's condition, medical history, services provided in other settings, or medications prescribed by other clinicians.'

Inefficiency also stems from poor allocation of resources across different parts of the health-care system. Too much is done in high-cost hospital

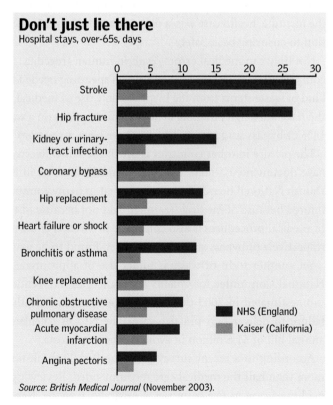

Don't just lie there
Hospital stays, over-65s, days

- Stroke
- Hip fracture
- Kidney or urinary-tract infection
- Coronary bypass
- Hip replacement
- Heart failure or shock
- Bronchitis or asthma
- Knee replacement
- Chronic obstructive pulmonary disease
- Acute myocardial infarction
- Angina pectoris

■ NHS (England)
■ Kaiser (California)

Source: British Medical Journal (November 2003).

settings, and too little in lower-cost primary settings. Traditionally, physicians in primary practice have worked as independents from small offices. Given the demands of patients for round-the-clock access and the increasing complexity of medicine, this structure no longer works well. But it has left a legacy of under-capitalised primary care, even though many treatments are now better carried out away from hospitals.

Germany's medical-delivery system has long been organised in a particularly inefficient way. With only a few exceptions, hospitals have been confined to in-patient care, and hospital specialists have not been able to provide their services in cheaper out-patient clinics. This restriction, which dates back to 1931, has created an opportunity for independent specialists, but half of them work on their own rather than in well-capitalised group clinics. This strict separation of care has prevented effective integration of services between primary-care physicians and hospitals – for example, for cancer patients, says Reinhard Busse of Berlin's Technical University. Not before time, reforms have now been launched to get rid of these restrictive practices.

But Germany is only an extreme example of medical-delivery systems organised to serve the interests of doctors rather than patients. One exception to the rule is Kaiser Permanente, a health-maintenance organization (HMO) that provides care to 8.2m Americans insured with it. Established in 1945, Kaiser has a distinctive model of health care. It owns most of the hospitals and medical facilities that it uses. Its physicians, who are salaried rather than paid on a fee-for-service basis, work together in group practices which they manage themselves. This structure has enabled it to develop a genuinely integrated form of medical care.

Richard Feachem, executive director of the Global Fund to Fight AIDS, Tuberculosis and Malaria, based in Geneva, is impressed: 'There is no perfect system in the world, every one has serious flaws and makes serious mistakes which people suffer from, but Kaiser comes closer to an ideal than any system I know.' Shortly before starting his present job, he led a controversial comparison of Kaiser's operations in California and Britain's NHS, which suggested that Kaiser achieved a better performance overall with roughly the same resources per head as the NHS. But how? Mr Feachem puts it down mainly to better integration. 'Without question Kaiser has achieved a greater degree of integration than the NHS – integration between prevention and cure, out-patient and in-patient services and between primary-care physicians and hospitals,' he says.

This allows Kaiser to treat patients at the most cost-effective level of care, economising in particular on expensive time in hospital. A subsequent comparison of the two systems, led by Chris Ham, director of the strategy unit at the Department of Health in London, dealt with some of the methodological objections to the original study by looking at acute care for those aged 65 and over. Across a range of 11 common clinical conditions, it found that admission rates were mostly higher in the NHS than in Kaiser. Once admitted, NHS patients spent much longer in hospital than

Kaiser patients. The disparity was highest for strokes and hip fractures, where NHS stays were five to six times higher than those in Kaiser hospitals. Kaiser pays a great deal of attention to the patient's journey through hospital, explains Mr Feachem: when a patient enters the hospital, staff are already planning his discharge. This strategy has the 'full backing of physicians, not just managers, because it is good medicine'. A systematic approach to the patient journey is crucial, because 'if you cumulate a small number of delays, you can lose 48 hours'. The patients like it too, he adds, because they feel that staff are on the case.

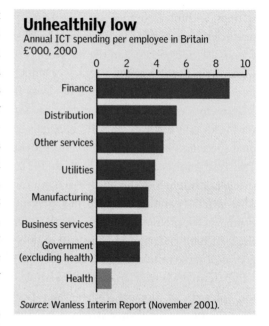

Unhealthily low
Annual ICT spending per employee in Britain
£'000, 2000

Source: Wanless Interim Report (November 2001).

The NHS is taking a leaf out of Kaiser's book. Managers from several hospitals and primary-care organizations have spent time in California observing its methods, and are now trying to implement them in various parts of Britain. It will not be easy. Replicating the Kaiser model has proved tricky even in America.

Deus ex machina

But there is another, more universally applicable way to achieve better, more integrated medical care. Information technology provides a means to avoid many medication errors: computerised systems, including electronic patient cards, would allow checks on the accuracy of doses and improve patient safety by telling doctors about other drugs that patients may be taking. Electronic patient records also make it easier to integrate medical services between physicians in primary care and hospitals in the secondary sector.

Health-care systems are now scrambling to make more use of IT. Germany is investing 1.8 billion to develop electronic patient cards by the start of 2006. In France, Philippe Douste-Blazy, the health minister, has announced a plan to computerise health records, partly to control the excessive use of doctors by the country's notoriously demanding patients.

In America, Medicare will insist on doctors using electronic methods for prescribing drugs to elderly Americans after the government starts bearing part of the cost. 'The question is when, not whether,' says Mark McClellan, administrator of the Centres for Medicare and Medicaid Services (CMS). He also expects IT to play a big role in new chronic-disease management programmes for America's elderly. For example, PacifiCare, a health insurer based in California, uses modem links with patients suffering from congestive heart disease to check daily on whether they are taking their medicine.

The most ambitious project is under way in Britain. At present, notes on patients are often still held on paper; electronic information is fragmented in locally based systems, and there is a great deal of duplication. The aim is to replace this with a comprehensive national electronic system, costing £6 billion ($11 billion), making it the biggest civilian IT project in the world. By 2007, all prescriptions will be created and transferred to pharmacies electronically. By 2010 the system will provide fully integrated access to patient records for appropriate health-care professionals, wherever they work.

These plans hold out much promise, provided they can be implemented without the usual pitfalls of big IT projects. Experience of IT in other service industries suggests that it has plenty of potential to cut waste and raise efficiency in health care. But, even allowing for worries about patient confidentiality, why has it taken so long in health care? In the mid-1990s, a survey of 53 American industries ranked health care 38th in its expenditure on IT per worker. A similar picture emerged from a British survey of IT spending in 2000 (see chart entitled 'unhealthily low'). The banking sector spent nine times as much on IT per employee as the health sector.

This in turn prompts a broader question. The Institute of Medicine report said: 'Because of the high levels of waste in the current system, the committee sees no immediate conflict in the simultaneous pursuit of lower costs through efficiency and better patient experiences through safety, effectiveness, patient-centredness and timeliness.' The international evidence of waste and inefficiency suggests that this conclusion holds not just for America but for most other developed economies. So why have strenuous efforts to control medical costs failed to control all that waste?

Source: 'Wasting disease', *The Economist*, 15 July 2004.
© The Economist Newspaper Limited, London (15 July 2004).

Case Questions

1 Why is this evidence of waste and inefficiency a strategic issue and not simply a matter of operational efficiency?

2 Explain how a Total Quality Management approach should address these problems.

Further reading and references

Abernathy, W (1978) *The Productivity Dilemma: Roadblock to Innovation in the Automobile Industry*, Johns Hopkins University Press, Baltimore, MD.

Aguayo, R (1990) *Dr Deming*, Fireside Books, New York.

Bales, E (1992) 'Making Six Sigma and Quality a Part of the Curriculum', Presentation on Motorola's Quality Efforts at the Academy of Management Annual Meeting, Las Vegas.

Barney, J (1986) 'Strategic Factor Markets: Expectations, Luck, and Business Strategy', *Management Science*, **32**, pp. 1231–41.

Carnegie, A (1920) *Autobiography of Andrew Carnegie*, Houghton Mifflin, New York.

Cho, DS and Lee, DH (1993) 'Dynamic Integration of Cost Leadership and Differentiation', paper presented at the 1993 Strategic Management Society annual conference, Chicago.

Crosby, P (1979) *Quality is Free*, McGraw-Hill, New York.

Cusumano, M and Takeishi, A (1991) 'Supplier Relations and Management: a Survey of Japanese, Japanese-transplant, and US Auto Plants', *Strategic Management Journal*, **12**, **8**, pp. 563–88.

Deming, W (1986) *Out of the Crisis*, MIT Center for Advanced Engineering Study, Cambridge, MA.

Deming, W (1993) *The New Economics*, MIT Center for Advanced Engineering Study, Cambridge, MA.

Dierickx, I and Cook, K (1989) 'Asset Stock Accumulation and Sustainability of Competitive Advantage', *Management Science*, **35**, **1**, pp. 1504–14.

Doyle, P (2000) 'Value-Based Marketing', John Wiley & Sons, Chichester.

Eisenhardt, K (1985) 'Control: Organizational and Economic Approaches', *Management Science*, **31**, pp. 134–49.

Eisenhardt, K (1989) 'Agency Theory: an Assessment and Review', *Academy of Management Review*, **14**, pp. 57–74.

Freeman, RE (1984) *Strategic Management: A Stakeholder Approach*, Pitman, Boston.

Garvin, D (1986) 'Quality Problems, Policies, and Attitudes in the United States and Japan: an Exploratory Study', *Academy of Management Journal*, **29**, pp. 653–73.

Garvin, D (1987) 'Competing on the Eight Dimensions of Quality', *Harvard Business Review*, **65**, 6, pp. 101–9.

Ghemawat, P (1991) *Commitment: The Dynamics of Strategy*, Free Press, New York.

Gitlow, H and Gitlow, S (1987) *The Deming Guide to Quality and Competitive Position*, Prentice-Hall, New York.

Godfrey, AB (1993) 'Ten Areas for Future Research in Total Quality Management', *Quality Management Journal*, **1**, **1**, pp. 47–70.

Hayes, R and Abernathy, W (1980) 'Managing Our Way to Economic Decline', *Harvard Business Review*, **4**, pp. 67–77.

Ishikawa, K (1982) *Guide to Quality Control*, Asian Productivity Organization, Tokyo.

Ishikawa, K (1985) *What is Total Quality Control? The Japanese Way*, Prentice-Hall, Englewood Cliffs, New Jersey.

Juran, JE (1951) *Quality Control Handbook*, 1st edition, McGraw-Hill, New York.

Juran, J (1978) 'Japanese and Western Quality: a Contrast in Methods and Results', *Management Review*, **67** (November), pp. 27–45.

Juran, JE (1951) *Quality Control Handbook*, 1st edition, McGraw-Hill, New York.

Juran, J (1981) 'Product Quality – a Prescription for the West: Part 1: Training and Improvement Programs', *Management Review*, **70**, **6**, pp. 9–14.

Juran, J and Gyma, F (eds) (1988) *Juran's Quality Control Handbook*, 4th edition, McGraw-Hill, New York.

Kaplan, R (ed.) (1990) *Measurers for Manufacturing Excellence*, Harvard Business School Press, Boston.

Kaplan, R and Norton, D (1993) 'Putting the Balanced Scorecard to Work', *Harvard Business Review*, **71**, **5**, pp. 134–42.

Kohn, A (1986) *No Contest: The Case Against Competition*, Houghton Mifflin, Boston.

Leffler, K (1982) 'Ambiguous Changes in Product Quality', *American Economic Review*, **72**, **5**, pp. 956–67.

Mahoney, J and Pandian, J (1992) 'The Resource-based View Within the Conversation of Strategic Management', *Strategic Management Journal*, **13**, pp. 363–80.

Mintzberg, H (1973) *The Nature of Managerial Work*, Harper and Row, New York.

Moen, R, Nolan, T and Provost, L (1991) *Improving Quality Through Planned Experimentation*, McGraw-Hill, New York.

Parasuraman, A, Zeithaml, V and Berry, L (1985) 'A Conceptual Model of Service Quality and its Implications for Future Research', *Journal of Marketing*, **49** (Fall), pp. 41–50.

Pegels, CC (1995*) Total Quality Management*, Boyd and Fraser, Danvers, MA.

Pirsig, R (1974) *Zen and the Art of Motorcycle Maintenance*, Bantam Books, New York.

Porter, M (1980) *Competitive Strategy*, Free Press, New York.

Prahalad, CK and Hamel, G (1990) 'The Core Competence of the Corporation', *Harvard Business Review*, **68**, 3, pp. 79–91.

Shewhart, W (1930) *Economic Control of Quality of Manufactured Products*, Technical publications monograph B-496, Bell Telephone Laboratories, New York.

Skinner, W (1969) 'Manufacturing – Missing Link in Corporate Strategy', *Harvard Business Review*, **47**, May/June, pp. 136–45.

Slack, N and Lewis, M (2002) *Operations Strategy*, FT Prentice-Hall, London.

Susman, G (ed.) (1992) *Integrating Design and Manufacturing for Competitive Advantage*, Oxford University Press, New York.

Taguchi, G (1986) *Introduction to Quality Engineering: Designing Quality into Products and Processes*, Asian Productivity Organization, Tokyo.

Taylor, F (1911) The *Principles of Scientific Management*, Harper and Brothers, New York.

Turnbull, P, Oliver, N and Wilkinson, B (1992) 'Buyer-supplier Relations in the UK Automotive Industry: Strategic Implications of the Japanese Manufacturing Model', *Strategic Management Journal*, **13**, 2, pp. 159–68.

Walker, GE (2003) *Modern Competitive Strategy*, McGraw-Hill, New York.

Wernerfelt, B (1984) 'A Resource-based View of the Firm', *Strategic Management Journal*, **5**, pp. 171–80.

Williamson, O (1985) *The Economic Institutions of Capitalism*, Free Press, New York.

Wilson, DC (1999) *A Strategy of Change*, International Thomson, London.

Womack, JP, Jones, DT and Roos, D (1990) *The Machine that Changed the World*, Newson Associates, New York.

Zeithaml, V, Parasuraman, A and Berry, L (1990) *Delivering Quality*, Free Press, New York.

Chapter 21

Managing business value as a system: value creation from a systems perspective

Introduction

The term 'value' has been contested terrain for a number of years. For example, it has been used to describe **business value** (Parker and Harcourt 1969), **social value** (Carroll 1979) and as a term to replace the much maligned word 'profit' (Glautier and Underdown 2001). As we have seen in previous chapters of this book, over the past two decades, as a result of the globalization of trade and capital markets and the information technology revolution, the strategic attention of many leading companies has focused on the principle of generating and maximizing **shareholder value** for strategy evaluation and performance measurement. From this perspective, the primary task of senior managers is to act as agents for the shareholders and to maximize shareholder value (SVA) in financial terms, typically using an SVA discounted cash flow criterion. This allows share-holders to assess the value of their investment over time, using the rate of interest as the method of assessing the *time value* of money. For example, if the rate of interest is 10 per cent per annum, €1 invested now at 10 per cent will amount to €1.10 in a year. Or, conversely, the *value* of €1.10 a year hence is €1 now. Following Day and Fahey (1990), the SVA model can be depicted as:

- Purpose of strategy   ⟶   Maximize returns to shareholders
- Reference group   ⟶   Shareholders and proxies
- Decision variables   ⟶   Revenues, costs, investments and capital structure
- Level of analysis   ⟶   Company and strategic business unit
- Basis of measurement   ⟶   Share prices, market/book ratios and net present value of cash flows

Doyle (2000) argues that the adoption of SVA has eliminated much of the excess and ineffi-ciency of capitalism in the decades of the 1960s and 1970s. We shall explore this claim later in this chapter.

While economists such as Friedman (1970) and Friedman and Friedman (1980) have stressed that business is in business to make profits and should not be expected and, indeed, is not best suited to do anything other than this, nevertheless, there is increasing recognition in today's environment that businesses cannot exist solely to make a profit. Henry Ford's much earlier statement is important here:

> *Business must be run at a profit, else it will die. But when anyone tries to run a business solely for profit ... then also the business must die, for it no longer has a reason for existence.*

Many writers (e.g. Freeman 1984) have noted that the actions of business affect not only them-selves but also other stakeholders, with sometimes contradictory expectations, such as employees, managers, customers, suppliers, investors, governments and communities. They argue, therefore, that business must recognize its responsibility to those stakeholders and society as a whole. In essence, they suggest that there is a strong mutual interdependence between busi-ness and society. The responsibility of a business to society is to build and improve conditions for wealth creation through such things as commercializing new innovations, investing in new plants and facilities, creating new job opportunities, paying corporate taxes and minimizing negative social or environmental externalities. In turn, business depends on society to create and foster an environment in which business can fulfil its goals of wealth creation (AACSB 2003).

It is clear that the challenges for business, and its corporate strategists, go far beyond simple bottom-line profitability goals. Writers from MIT's Innovation Project (such as Malone *et al.* 1996) also point out some of the critical issues in managing and inventing organizations in the future. They include the need to understand how to tap into the complex sources of competitive advantage in the new economy, in environments where new skills, new sources of continuous innovation and increasing impacts of information technology create new ways of working and constant strategic change.

In consequence, arguably richer conceptions and theories of the firm are now emerging that encompass both the social and economic context of the firm and that seek to balance the 'doing well' and 'doing good' aspects of a firm's performance (Elkington 1997). In the end (*see*, for example, Kay 1995), the success of a company depends on how it meets and balances the often incommensurable and incompatible objectives demanded by its various stakeholders. Kay argues that the purpose of companies is to produce, in their own distinctive fields of capability, goods and services we want as individuals and as a society. The distinctive capabilities (*see* earlier chapters on the resource-based view of the firm) of companies are, in turn, embedded in their relationships with the social and commercial environments in which they operate. The argument is that organizations can succeed only by managing the totality of these relationships.

Kay's views prompt many of the arguments in this chapter. We seek to explore new theories and concepts of the firm from the perspective of the systems viewpoint – the 'web' of relationships, internal and external to the organization, which must be managed in order to create sustainable advantage and long-term wealth creation. Note that the strategy framework used in this book is a systems model and this discussion provides the overarching strategic systems model which links the various elements of the strategic plan together (*see* Figure 1.6). This chapter explores the following:

- The strategic systems framework as a lens for managing value as a system.
- Stakeholder theories of the firm.
- Learning theories of the firm.
- Adaptive theories of the 'living company'.
- Common issues such as trust, accountability and reputation that drive the firm's purpose.
- The role of intangible assets in creating value.
- The concept of managing value from a systems viewpoint.

21.1 **The strategic systems perspective**

> *How do we use the information gleaned about the parts to build up a theory of the whole? The deep difficulty here lies in the fact that the complex whole may exhibit properties that are not readily explained by understanding the parts.*[1] *The complex whole, in a completely non-mystical sense, can often exhibit collective properties, 'emergent' features that are lawful in their own right.* (Kauffman 1995)

---

[1] See, for example, the case study 'Microworld' at the end of Chapter 16.

As we outlined in Chapters 1 and 2, a *system* is a collection of parts that interact to function as a whole. The behaviour of a system depends on its entire structure, the relative strengths of the many connections among its parts at any point in time, and the manner and degree to which these connections change over time. **Systems theory** involves the study of living systems as integrated wholes whose visible properties cannot be reduced to those of smaller sub-units. Viewed from a systems perspective, the world consists of relationships and integration. Instead of concentrating on basic building blocks to learn about the properties of the larger system, the systems approach emphasizes basic principles of organization – how the parts are interrelated and co-ordinated into a unified whole. From that viewpoint, value-creating strategies emerge through learning about the system and can only be understood by analysing the system conditions that give rise to success and strategy innovation. We firmly believe that today's strategist should frame strategic thinking from a 'strategic systems' perspective (Bell *et al.* 1997).

From the systems theorist's perspective, a living system interacts with its environment through **structural coupling** – recurring interactions, each of which triggers structural changes in the system, such as when a cell membrane infuses substances from its environment into its metabolic processes, or when an organism's central nervous system changes its connectivity after receiving information. A structurally coupled system is a learning system. The structure of such a system continually changes in response to its environment. Consequently, adaptation, learning and development are key characteristics of the behaviour of living systems.

At the company level, organizations exhibit emergent behaviour – that is, they behave quite differently from how they would behave if their sub-units were independent of each other. According to Kees van der Heijden, retired executive from Royal Dutch Shell, who headed its Business Environment Division and was in charge of scenario planning:

> *Emergent behaviour is the outside behavioural manifestation of the internal mediating processes. In systems terms, it implies a hierarchical organisation, with the upper level guiding and constraining the actions at the lower. It is the constraints on the lower level members that creates the emergent behaviour at the higher level ... If such constraints did not exist, lower level members would carry on as if they were independent and there would be no emergent behaviour and, therefore, no identity for the larger system.* (Van der Heijden 1996, p. 39)

The level of **complexity** inherent in an organization is a characteristic of the system's structure and is affected by the total number of its individual sub-units, the number of different layers in the structural hierarchy, the number of different business processes that perform business activities and the number and strengths of connections among all of these sub-units and between these sub-units and outside economic agents.

Beer (1981) has studied and written extensively about how to model the dynamics of complex systems such as today's business organizations calling such systems' perspectives 'exceedingly complex' (see Chapter 2 for a summary of Beer's five-level structure).

According to Richardson (1991, p. 187):

> *In Beer's view, every viable system is organised in such a hierarchy of five systems. Furthermore, complex viable systems are composed of viable sub-systems that again have this five-level structure. To be viable, a division of a firm should be organised this way. The entire firm as a set of inter-related divisions should also have the same sort of structure. A viable sector of an economy should have the same structure. Naturally, an entire national economy, to be viable, should be similarly organised. Viewed from the elevated level of the national economy, in the hierarchy an individual firm or sector operates at the level of systems one, two and three. The functions of its own high-level systems four and five are seen as part of the autonomic processes of the more aggregate system.*

To gain the appropriate level of understanding of a firm's business, industry and wider environment for the purpose of conducting a strategic analysis, we argue that strategists should direct their attention to the firm's systems dynamics – its strategic positioning within its environment; its emergent behaviours that impact its attained level of performance; the strength of its connections, or structural couplings, to outside economic agents; the nature and impact of any symbiotic alliances; the specific interrelationships and internal process interactions that dominate its performance; and potential changes in other reaches of the vast economic and social web that might threaten the viability of the client's strategies and niches. These systemic properties determine the strategic competencies and capabilities that enhance the **value** of the organization and that promote *changes in that value* over time.

Figure 21.1 depicts a firm as a complex web of interrelationships embedded within a broader complex economic web.[2] This complex web is what the strategist sees when looking through the strategic-systems lens. The strengths of the many interrelationships comprising this broader economic web reflect the extent of the organization's ability to manage its environment and therefore to **create value** and generate the cash flow needed to sustain growth. A fundamental understanding of the strengths of these connections provides a basis for development of expectations about the quality and creativity of the entity's strategies and its attained level of performance.

An example illustrates how, in an adaptive system, the relevance and strength of the interconnections changes over time (and how, in turn, value can be created or lost). Assume that the organization depicted in Figure 21.1 is a retail bookseller (such as Barnes & Noble or Borders in the USA or WH Smith or Waterstones in the UK) with a heavy capital investment in retail facilities located around the country. Now, assume that a new market niche emerges, involving the use of the World Wide Web in lieu of retail outlets to market and sell books.

---

[2] Figure 1.4 in Chapter 1 provides a simple picture and Chapters 3 and 4 provide a detailed description, of this complex economic web.

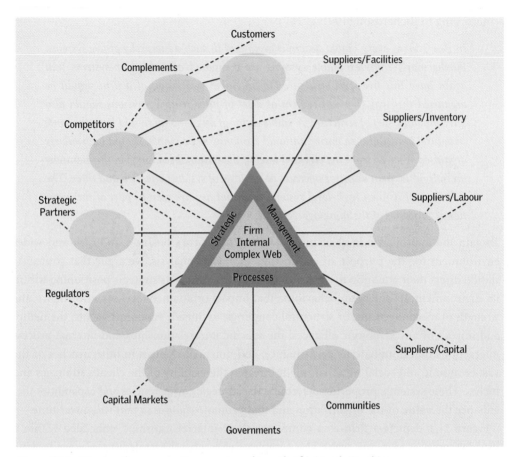

Figure 21.1 Viewing the organization as a complex web of interrelationships

New competitors such as Amazon.com occupying this niche offer access to much larger inventories than any retail outlet can stock, and can price their books at a substantial discount because of lower overhead costs. In addition, consumers can search these massive inventories using search engines provided by the new competitors and can access book reviews by other consumers available through these competitors' websites.

As the number of consumers connected to the World Wide Web grows over time, the connections between customers and competitors occupying this new niche are likely to increase in number. And, in turn, unless it adapts its own operation by moving into this new niche, the strength of connections between the original retailer and most of the other economic agents depicted in Figure 21.1 will diminish. For example, as the original retailer experiences a drop in demand, it will respond by reducing its own demand for facilities, inventory, labour and capital from suppliers.

21.2 The stakeholder management perspective

A particular example of a systems-type model is **Freeman's stakeholder theory**. Many of the stakeholders that have the potential to be most important to organizations are shown in Figure 21.2.

By definition, these stakeholders are individuals or organizations that have an interest in, or some kind of stake in, the firm's ongoing activities. Stakeholder analysis (Freeman 1984) is the process of identifying, understanding and prioritizing the needs of key stakeholders so that the question of which groups of stakeholders deserve management attention is addressed. The knowledge from this analysis is absorbed into the strategic framework, direction and management of the organization.

Clearly, the needs and goals of these stakeholders are sometimes in conflict with each other but stakeholder management is a never-ending task of balancing and integrating multiple relationships and multiple objectives (Freeman and McVea 2001). Some of the alternative stakeholder viewpoints are outlined in the following sections.

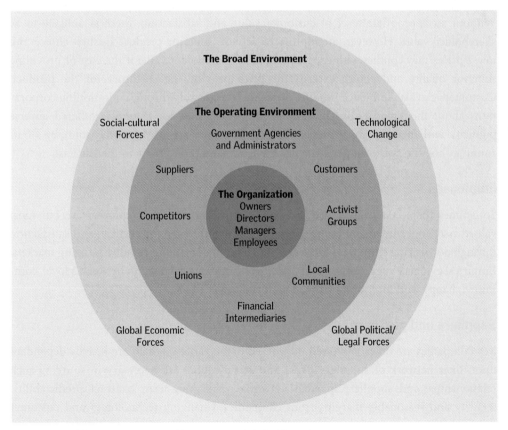

Figure 21.2 The organization and its primary stakeholders
Source: adapted from Harrison and St John, 1998.

Governments and local communities

Emerging conceptual frameworks that reflect changing societal expectations about the role of business in society can be seen in the following areas:

- Socially responsible investment.
- Corporate social responsibility (e.g. negative impacts arising from pollution and environmental damage – e.g. the *Exxon-Valdez* case and the Union Carbide Bhopal crisis).
- Corporate citizenship.
- Corporate governance.
- Sustainability and the 'triple bottom line'.

Local communities, governments and non-governmental organizations try to ensure that organizations act in a socially responsible manner to maintain such things as a 'green' environment, ethical investing and a sustainable level of national resources.

Customers

Without an appropriate level of customer value and satisfaction, there is unlikely to be shareholder value. However, attempting to achieve superior product quality, choice and lower prices may conflict with the attainment of shareholder value if the cost of providing superior quality and choice exceeds the price paid by the customer for the product. Customers can also influence product purchase considerably through questioning corporations about their global sourcing and investments. Nike, for example, suffered adverse publicity and financial consequences from consumers, arising from the sourcing of its running shoes in 'sweat shops' with poor environmental conditions in the Far East.

Employees

Sometimes there is a strategic gap between statements such as 'employees are our most valued asset' and subsequent corporate actions which threaten job security and satisfaction through downsizing employees following shortfalls in demand in rapidly changing markets. Empirical evidence suggests, however, that there is a strong correlation between a loyal, committed, happy workforce and financial performance.

Suppliers and partners

Key companies are nowadays often networked organizations, which are heavily dependent upon their network of suppliers. Trust and social capital are necessary in sourcing such relationships, and suppliers in such networks value long-term contract predictability, security and reasonable margins from companies. Changing technologies and customer needs, however, may from time to time require companies to change suppliers.

These changes will create conflicts in relationships with suppliers that value network stability and corporate commitments but are also in competition with other supplier networks.

Shareholders

Shareholders are often depicted as a somewhat isolated but wealthy group of individuals who act in their own self-interest. However, through the activities of financial institutions and pension funds, most individuals in Western countries own shares in companies and have a very clear interest in ensuring that stock prices and shareholder value continue to rise in order to protect their future pension and social security provision. The rise in shareholder activism (e.g. CALPERS, the California State Pension Fund in the US, and Anthony Bolton of Fidelity in the UK) is probably more due to reaction to financial underperformance by firms than concern about their ethical or corporate responsibility activities, despite such recent corporate failures as Enron, WorldCom and Parmalat.

Freeman (1984) provides a model, a stakeholder grid, shown in Table 21.1, which classifies stakeholders on two dimensions: first, the nature of their stakes in the organization; and, second, the behavioural influence or power they have on the organization.

Businesses (e.g. Nike in shoe manufacture and Toyota in car manufacture) are already moving to organize themselves into networked form (see Chapter 12) and, in doing so, become the hub of a web or nexus of contracts enacted with many of the entities shown in the web of Figure 21. 2 and the stakeholder grid of Table 21.1. Clearly, the effective

Table 21.2 Freeman's stakeholder grid

		Formal or Voting (Contractual or Regulatory)	Economic	Political
	Equity	Internal stakeholders Directors Minority interests	External shareholders	
STAKE	Economic	Outside directors Alliance partners Tax authorities	Customers Employees Suppliers Competitors Creditors	Local communities Local governments Unions Foreign governments
	Social	Regulatory or government agencies	Financial institutions and financial community	National government Activist, lobbying groups Trade associations

POWER OR INFLUENCE ON BEHAVIOUR

Source: adapted from Freeman, 1984, p. 63.

management of the web of stakeholders is critical to wealth and value creation. Research evidence (see, for example, Mohr and Spekman 1994) suggests that effective partnerships are associated with the following:

- Strong quality of communication
- Joint problem solving
- Commitment
- Co-ordination
- Trust

Weak partnerships tend to adversely affect the hub organization's image and reputation in the marketplace.

Writers such as Senge (1998) stress and emphasize the role of processes of learning and adaptability in organizations with regard to understanding the pace of strategic change and in providing new ways of conceptualizing the business environment. Thus, strategists can frame strategic issues in terms of the web of customers, stakeholders, etc. in order to manage the business better (create more value). In the next section we examine the processes of building learning organizations that can create value.

21.3 Learning theories of the firm and value creation

Senge emphasizes the importance of what he calls 'adaptive learning' and 'generative learning' in organizations. Adaptive learning is similar to what Argyris and Schon (1978) call 'single-loop' learning in which individuals, groups and organizations adjust their behaviour according to fixed organizational goals, norms and assumptions. Generative learning, on the other hand, is akin to 'double-loop' learning, in which organizational goals, norms and assumptions as well as behaviour are all open to change. In Senge's terms:

> Increasing adaptiveness is only the first stage in moving towards learning organis-ations. The impulse to learn in children goes deeper than desires to respond and adapt more effectively to environmental change. The impulse to learn, at its heart, is an impulse to be generative, to expand our capability. This is why leading corpo-rations are focusing on generative learning, which is about creating, as well as adaptive learning, which is about coping.

Therefore, Senge is wedded to the idea of the firm both as a system and a social and knowledge web, which is conceptually very close to de Geus's framing of the firm as the 'living company' (1997). This 'living company' survives over the long term through such concrete factors as financial strength and stability, environmental sensitivity and adap-tation to change, and a strong culture, identity and value system which enables it to become a systematic, living organism that continually grows and reinvents itself. Leaders of such organizations are 'systems thinkers' who see the 'big picture' and focus more on understanding the underlying reasons and forces that contribute to change. Important skills for such leaders include:

- The ability to see the interrelationships and processes in systemic change.

- The recognition that problems in change result from poorly designed systems.

- The ability to recognize and understand the dynamic complexity of system problems, i.e. when the cause and effect of strategic problems are distant in time and space, and when the consequences of interventions over time are subtle.

- The ability to focus on areas of high leverage, i.e. systems thinking shows that small, well-focused actions can produce significant enduring improvements if they are in the right place.

- The avoidance of symptomatic solutions, i.e. 'quick fixes' or so-called 'band-aid solutions'. The best solutions rely on the ability to analyse the system and, thus, find enduring solutions. Enduring solutions create value.

21.4 Trust, accountability, reputation and value

From these perspectives, it seems that strategists must make a paradigmatic (or at least ideological) choice. This choice is between whether we should adopt the multiple objective goals of stakeholder and/or learning views of the firm, or adopt the primacy of shareholder value maximization (SVA) for optimizing the value of the firm as a system. The key argument against shareholder value maximization is that it ignores an organization's social responsibilities and fails to balance the different stakeholder interests. Doyle (2000, p. 23) and Sunderam and Inkpen (2004, p. 353) offer spirited arguments for the primacy of shareholder value maximization as the preferred corporate goal or objective. Sunderam and Inkpen summarize their arguments as follows:

- The goal of maximizing shareholder value is pro-stakeholder.

- Maximizing shareholder value creates appropriate incentives for managers to assume entrepreneurial risks.

- Having more than one objective function will make governing difficult, if not impossible.

- It is easier to make shareholders out of stakeholders than vice-versa.

- In the event of contract or trust, stakeholders, compared with shareholders, have protection (or can seek remedies) through contracts and the legal system.

Doyle's fundamental argument (2000, p. 24) mirrors much of the above reasoning. He argues stridently that social responsibilities are not the job of business. He notes that, in a market-based economy, the only social responsibility of business is to create shareholder value legally and with integrity. He believes that there are strong market-based incentives for value-maximizing firms to take into account stakeholder interests. They include:

- The need to attract, retain and motivate key 'knowledge workers' and employees to ensure long-term competitiveness. This means paying competitive salaries to employees and offering safe and attractive workplace conditions.

- The need to satisfy customers through new product development, quality and customer service.

- The need to build trust, reputation and image with customers and society as a whole.

- The requirement to undertake investments to create wealth and value and avoid investments undertaken to 'balance other stakeholder interests' for reasons of prestige and public relations, but not value creation.

- The recognition that shareholders are generally pension funds, financial institutions and other societal institutions that require value-producing investments to meet their fiduciary obligations.

The alternative paradigm emphasizes the social role of organizations in society and argues that value emerges from conducting business in a socially responsible way. Such a perspective has many labels (such as corporate accountability or corporate citizenship) and in this chapter we will use the term **corporate social responsibility** (CSR) to cover the social and ethical roles of business organizations in society. In a basic way, laws already exist for some factors which affect the social good. Organizations are liable in law in many countries for the escape of dangerous substances, failing to provide adequate health and safety cover for employees and for rules about the manner in which accountability of business firms to investors and employees is met. CSR extends beyond this regulatory level. Originating in social and political theories, CSR argues three main points:

- Organizational decisions should be centrally concerned with socially responsible alternatives.

- The implementation of such decisions will help maximize profit (value) since customers will prefer to buy goods and services from ethical and responsible organizations.

- Trust, reputation and image will be enhanced more by ethical and socially responsible strategic decisions than by maximizing shareholder value.

Carroll (1979) argues that organizations should be socially responsive since they are created by and sustained by society. Drucker (1993) argues that organizations should be given rights and duties in society in much the same way as individual citizens are (hence the term corporate citizenship). Increased image and reputation for the organization will help create value. As Rosenfeld and Wilson (1999, p. 353) point out, such value creation from the point of view of ecological responsibility is big business. Since the establishment of an international standard for 'green-ness' (ISO 14001) organizations have quickly recognized the value of being accredited. Shell and Xerox were accredited early and many other firms have publicly announced pro-environmental strategies (e.g. Elf, Union Carbide, Interplan, The Body Shop).

There are some enduring problems with the CSR value-creating perspective. First, it is theoretically very difficult to establish exactly what CSR is and what it is not. There is no agreed (or generally accepted) definition of what CSR is – other than organizations and decision makers should weigh the impact of their actions upon others. Second, the scope of CSR is difficult to determine. Should it apply to every organizational action and operation or to a selection of activities? Third, unless strategists are able to determine a clear view of what are societies' preferences and ethical priorities, then much of what is classed as socially desirable will remain either guesswork or subjective judgement. Arrow's (1963) 'general impossibility theorem' captures this neatly. He argues that if we exclude the possibility of interpersonal comparisons of utility, then the only method of transferring from individual tastes to broad social preferences that will be satisfactory (and defined for a wide set of individual rankings) will either be imposed or dictated by definition.

Nevertheless, the impact of CSR has been substantial and the 'triple bottom line' has reinforced the value-creating aspects of socially responsible performance by organizations. Aware of possible paradigm incommensurability between the SVA and the CSR perspectives, we suggest that, at least in some key aspects (intangible assets), a systems perspective can begin to integrate some aspects of CSR and SVA to create value. We explore this argument in the next section.

21.5 Intangible assets and value creation

Given the theoretical approach we have adopted in this book, we would suggest a marriage to shareholder value maximization and the strategic systems lens offers the strategist the best opportunity for managing the business system from a value-based perspective. Such a marriage will require close attention for the 'embedded firm' to maximize value from the system resources available to it. We regard the following three issues as critical intangible assets to the implementation of a systems model for value maximization – trust, accountability and reputation/image/identity.

Trust

This involves creating a strong sense of mission and values. Collins and Porras (1996) note that core values are enduring, essential tenets for those inside the organization. The core ideology consists of core values and core purpose, where core purpose is the 'raison d'etre' – the reason for being. Core ideology has to be authentic and is the 'glue' that holds the organization together over time. It is a consistent identity that all stakeholders learn to trust over time. For example, Hewlett Packard's core ideology was a code of ethics called the 'HP way'. It includes:

♦ A deep respect for the individual.

♦ A dedication to affordable quality and reliability.

♦ A commitment to community responsibility.

♦ HP exists to make technical contributions for the advancement and welfare of humanity.

A good example of trust in practice is shown in the following case box.

Case box: **Johnson & Johnson and Tylenol**

In 1982, Johnson & Johnson (J&J) found itself facing a corporate nightmare when bottles of its best-selling Tylenol were tampered with, resulting in several deaths. The corporation's immediate response was to pull all Tylenol off the shelves of retail outlets. Thirty-one million capsules were destroyed, even though they were tested and found safe. Although the immediate cost was significant, no other action was possible, given the firm's Credo. Authored almost forty years earlier by president Robert Ward Johnson, Johnson & Johnson's Credo states that permanent success is possible only when modern industry realizes that:

♦ service to its customers comes first;

♦ service to its employees and management comes second;

♦ service to its stockholders, last.

Source: adapted from Senge, 1998.

As Senge notes, such credo statements may look like 'motherhood and apple pie' to those who have not seen how a clear core ideology can affect key business decisions. Johnson & Johnson's crisis management action in this case was based on the credo. It was simple, right and it worked.

Collins and Porras (1996, p. 67) quote Ralph Larsen, a former CEO of Johnson & Johnson, who puts it this way: 'The core values embodied in our credo might be a competitive advantage, but that is not *why* we have them. We have them because they define for us what we stand for, and we would hold them, even if they become a competitive *dis*advantage in certain situations.'

Accountability

A company must have in place 'systems' of accountability to measure performance outcomes for all relevant stakeholders in the system web of its corporate relationships and linkages. SVA on its own measures 'shareholder value', whereas the balanced scorecard approach (Kaplan and Norton 1996, 2001) in Chapter 18 introduces the viewpoint that firms need to develop performance measures along four dimensions – financial, customers, internal processes, and learning and growth – in order to achieve enduringly strong and balanced results along those multiple objectives and manage a strategy-focused organization.

More recently, Kaplan and Norton (2004) have added the notion of a 'strategy map' – a systems view of the organization – which maps the strategy, uncovers problems, monitors progress, identifies critical issues and communicates the strategy both internally to managers and employees and externally to investors, media, local and government communities. Critically, the strategy map incorporates a model to fit intangible assets: human capital readiness (e.g. skills), information capital readiness (e.g. databases) and organizational capital readiness (e.g. teamwork) into the balanced strategy approach. Ultimately, this is a strong attempt to provide a 'systemic' approach to discussing and investigating organizational strategy.

Reputation, image and identity

> 'Reputation, reputation, reputation – the one immortal part of man' (Shakespeare, from Othello).

The modern resource-based theory of the firm (RBV), discussed in Chapter 7, identifies a range of intangible assets including technology, patents, skills, etc. which, when combined with human and organizational resources, define the firm's core dynamic capabilities. A key set of intangible assets are the firm's **reputational assets** and these include the company name, its identity, brands, brand image and customer-based loyalty, the reputation of the firm's products and services, and the integrity of its relationships with the complex web or customers, suppliers, communities and governments. Many of the world's top brands (Coca-Cola, Microsoft, IBM, GE, Intel, Nescafe, etc.) are household names and help to develop a strong relationship of value, trust and goodwill with the customer. As we have recently seen, however, in the accounting industry, with the demise of Arthur Andersen, a hard-won reputation was easily dissipated and lost by the unethical and illegal behaviour of its employees. Therefore, a strong corporate reputation is a key strategic asset in managing value as a system.

21.6 Managing value as a system

What is critical from the strategic systems perspective is the ability to manage the organization strategically to maximize value. This requires:

- Strategy co-ordination – the strategy-focused organization.
- A clear objective of value creation and maximization.
- The ability to balance assets (e.g. trust, reputation, goodwill, etc.).
- The ability to balance financial measures.

- The ability to co-ordinate organization, operations and stakeholders so that the complex web of relationships works effectively.

As we have seen in this chapter, determining who the relevant business stakeholders and constituencies are requires a well-balanced understanding of the business system using, perhaps, Kaplan and Norton's concept of a strategy map. Value for customers results from customer satisfaction associated with product quality, choice and price. For shareholders and investors, SVA measures are appropriate. For employees, value may comprise such things as salaries, on-the-job training, stock options and job satisfaction. For suppliers, value may emanate from long-term corporate relationships and access to new technology and processes, as well as fair prices for their products. For governments and communities, value is measured by good corporate citizenship and social responsibility.

In addressing all these components of value – business strategy, customers, asset portfolios, organization and operations, learning and knowledge growth, supplier relationships, employees, local and government communities – the key skill is to treat them as a system and understand their context through the strategy map. In other words, by examining their interrelationships and treating the components of value concurrently and systematically, strategic decisions are examined relative to their impact on the other value components using SVA and balanced scorecard approaches. The strategy map, or systems diagram, then enables the manager to monitor and adapt strategy, develop organizational learning and growth and provide socially and financially responsible outcomes.

21.7 Summary and other issues in managing value

We continue to argue that the preferred objective for the corporation is the 'maximization of shareholder value', i.e. if an organization maximizes shareholder wealth in the long term, it will maximize firm value and enlarge the pie for all stakeholders. We recognize, however, that, as stated by Sundaram and Inkpen (2004, p. 371), 'All of us seek a path to a promised land in which accountable firms managed by ethical decision-makers create the greatest value for the greatest number of stakeholders'. This may occur using a shareholder value model, as we advocate, or through the development of a well-developed stakeholder theory, which is empirically supported (Freeman *et al.* 2004). In time, we may see such a theory developed but, in the meantime, some or all of the following issues are important in the process of managing the value of the business system:

- Would a company-wide ethical orientation (such as, for example, The Body Shop) or a strong commitment to corporate social responsibility constitute a key strategic resource in terms of the resource-based view of the firm? (*See* Wernerfelt 1984; Barney 1991.) In other words, is an ethical and socially responsible stance a non-imitable, unique source of sustainable long-term competitive advantage for the firm?

- Similarly, would strong organizational trust (Barney and Hansen 1994) create a long-term source of competitive advantage for the firm?

- Would core competencies and capabilities in business–government relations, such as the relationship between an ethical pharmaceutical company and the Federal Drug Administration in the drug-approval process, create a source of sustainable competitive advantage through effective management of the regulatory processes?

- Can a strong organizational identity or core ideology (e.g. Johnson & Johnson's credo) create an identity management competence for long-term sustainable competitive advantage?

- Managing value as a system requires a clear business model or 'Theory of the Business' (Drucker 1994). Drucker identifies four specifications about a valid theory of business:
  - The assumptions about environment, mission and core competencies must fit reality.
  - The assumptions in all three areas have to fit one another.
  - The theory of the business must be known throughout the organization.
  - The theory of the business has to be tested constantly.
  Throughout, Drucker has a systems-oriented view. He states 'when a theory shows the first signs of becoming obsolete, it is time to start thinking again.'

- As Yoffie (1988) points out, companies can strengthen their competitive advantage by forging closer ties with government. A political strategy may offer creative strategic choices in newly opened markets, such as in the dynamics of deregulated markets (e.g. rail, bus and utility companies in the UK).

In conclusion, we offer a couple of quotes and a case example from the challenging and controversial entrepreneur Anita Roddick, drawn from her book *Business as Unusual* (2000). Her stance on business challenges us all to examine the core values that drive business as a system and which create value.

> *One of our greatest frustrations at The Body Shop is that we are still judged by the media and the City by our profits, by the amount of product we sell, whereas we want, and have always wanted, to be judged by our activities in the larger world, by the positive difference we make. The shaping force for us from the start has not been our products but our principles.*

> *In terms of power and influence, you can forget the church, forget politics. There is no more powerful institution in society than business – I believe it is more important than ever before for business to assume a moral leadership. The business of business should not be about money, it should be about responsibility. It should be about public good, not private greed.*

Key terms

Business value *775*

Complexity *778*

Corporate social responsibility *786*

Create value *779*

Freeman's stakeholder theory *781*

Reputational assets *789*

Shareholder value *775*

Social value *775*

Structural coupling *778*

Systems theory *778*

Value *779*

Recap questions and assignments

1 What are the implications of the systems perspective for the work of a board of directors and the top management team? (refer back to the discussion on corporate governance in Chapter 17).

2 Does competition make it more or less difficult to apply a systems perspective? (refer back to the discussion in the previous chapter, pp. 760–2).

Online
***Learning*Centre**

When you have read this chapter, log on to the Online Learning Centre website at www.mcgraw-hill.co.uk/textbooks/mcgee to explore chapter-by-chapter test questions, further reading and more online study tools for strategy.

Case 1 **Oh, the joy of the journey!**

I guess you'd call it one of those defining moments. The year was 1987. The Body Shop was still in its protoplasmic period, but the Confederation of British Industry had chosen us as Company of the Year. Which meant I had to pick up the award.

There, they sat, the captains of industry, the bankers, the analysts, the journalists, just about the entire British financial establishment, all lined up and holding their collective breath as I mounted the podium.

It was irresistible. Every provocative bone in my body was aching to act up. I'd prepared what I hoped would be a mildly inflammatory speech. When I showed it to my husband, Gordon, he advised me to challenge them all. I also showed it to Jilly Forster, a close friend who also happened to be our PR person. She told me I had to say what I'd written. As I started to speak, the tension was such that I could see tears streaming down her face. I could also see our brokers, sitting stoney-faced on either side of her.

What did I say? I stood up for entrepreneurs against the big corporations. I told these business titans they were stuck in the past. (I believe the phrase I used was 'dinosaurs in pin-striped suits'.) What else could I do? 'I've never met a captain of industry who made my blood sing', I declared – at which point I looked up to see Robert Maxwell walking out. For all I know he had another appointment, but still I felt a surge of pride. My blood did sing, thanks, indirectly, to Cap'n Bob.

That speech was a watershed for me. I had the optimistic sensation that The Body Shop way of doing business was the inescapable future.

In the decade or so that followed, the story got a lot more complex – 'richer', but darker too. History did 1800 flips. The Wall came down (so did Robert Maxwell for that matter). The maximalism of the 1980s surrendered to the minimalism of the 1990s. All the while, The Body Shop was growing into one of the most successful retailers in the world. And I found myself on an extraordinary journey, a journey which made me even more passionate about the urgent need for a new model of business. It was also a journey through a minefield, with every explosion a reminder – as if I needed one – of how fragile were the goals we'd set ourselves. That journey is the subject matter of this book.

Looking back from the vantage point of a new century, I can trace how the path I've taken has radicalized me. Whether it was a sally into the forests of Sarawak to photograph illegal logging or up the Amazon to set up the first direct trading link with the Kayapo, it gave me a glimpse of the way in which global corporations threaten to engulf life, not just in our society but also in the communities where businesspeople simply never go. The outrage I felt was no abstract emotion. It grew stronger the more I travelled, the more I met people forced to eke out a bare existence on the margins of the world, denied their fundamental human rights by the fickle voracity of the global business juggernaut.

I'd always known I was in uncharted territory, but sometimes the landscape I found myself in was so alien that the people I thought were friends were actually enemies – and vice versa. Talk about a recipe for paranoia. Life in a minefield isn't easy. There have been many dents in my optimism and challenges to my convictions – our libel action, our mistakes in the American market, that relationship with the Kayapo I mentioned – but this was ultimately a good thing. When you've had some years when everyone – including the stock market – says you can do no wrong, it's good to be reminded that you're running the same race as the rest of the world. What doesn't kill you makes you stronger.

Yet that sentiment is actually too harsh. Be kind, Harvey Keitel writes on Kate Winslet's forehead in the movie Holy Smoke. That's what I wanted to do to the business world – nurture a revolution in kindness. But underlying that ambition has been the recurring theme of my role in the company I founded, now that it has grown into such a huge and complicated organization. So this book actually has another subject as well. It is the story of how I managed to maintain some intimate part of myself – the original core, if you like – in a business gone global. I have had to constantly reinvent the role of the founder entrepreneur. That's tough when your natural tendency is towards a gleeful anarchy. There are no road-maps, no instruction manuals. Passion is your guide. Instinct tells you where to go when a challenge arises.

So this book is more than a chronicle of a decade at The Body Shop, more than a condensed manual for the wannabe business radical. It is also about one individual's attempt to marry the often impersonal wants of a successful business with the very personal needs of a successful businessperson. Despite the enormous constraints of a global company, despite the general intractability of life, I need to find new ways to push the limits of business, to change its language, to make it a force for positive change. **That's what I mean by business as unusual**.

Source: Anita Roddick (2000) *Business as Unusual: The Journey of Anita Roddick and The Body Shop,* Thorsons, London.

Case Questions

1 Discuss Anita Roddick's conception of a responsible business.

2 How do her guiding principles and values allow the business to grow?

3 What is the role of the founder-entrepreneur in the growth of a successful business?

Further reading and references

AACSB (2003) *Ethics Education in Business Schools*, St. Louis, AACSB International.

Argyris, C and Schon, D (1978) *Organisational Learning: A Theory-in-Action Perspective*, Reading, MA, Addison-Wesley.

Arrow, KJ (1963) *Social Choice and Individual Values*, Yale, Yale University Press.

Barney, JB (1991) 'Firm resources and sustained competitive advantage', *Journal of Management*, **17**, pp. 99–120.

Barney, JB and Hansen, MH (1994) 'Trustworthiness as a source of competitive advantage', *Strategic Management Journal*, **15**, pp. 175–90.

Beer, S (1981) *Brain of the Firm: The Managerial Cybernetics of Organisation*, Chichester, John Wiley & Sons.

Bell, T, Marrs, F, Solomon, I and Thomas, H (1997) *Auditing Organisations Through a Strategic-Systems Lens*, Montvale, NJ, KPMG Publications.

Carroll, AB (1979) 'A Three-Dimensional Conceptual Model of Corporate Performance', *Academy of Business Review*, **4**, pp. 497–505.

Collins, JC and Porras, JI (1996) 'Building Your Company's Vision', *Harvard Business Review*, **74**, September/October, pp. 64–77.

Day, GS and Fahey, L (1990) 'Putting Strategy into Shareholder Value Analysis', *Harvard Business Review*, **68**, March/April, pp.156–63.

De Geus, AP (1988) 'Planning as Learning', *Harvard Business Review*, **66**, March/April, pp. 70–5.

Doyle, P (2000) *Value-based Marketing*, Chichester and New York, Wiley.

Drucker, PF (1993) *Post-Capitalist Society*, Oxford, Butterworth-Heinemann.

Drucker, PF (1994) 'The Theory of the Business', *Harvard Business Review*, **72**, Sept/Oct, pp. 95–104.

Elkington, J (1997) *Cannibals with Forks: The Triple Bottom Line of 21st Century Business*, Oxford, Capstone.

Freeman, RE (1984) *Strategic Management: A Stakeholder Perspective*, London, Pitman.

Freeman, RE and McVea, J, (2001) 'A Stakeholder Approach to Strategic Management', in M Hitt, E Freeman and J Harrison (eds) *Handbook of Strategic Management*, Oxford, Blackwell, pp. 189–207.

Friedman, M (1970) 'The Social Responsibility of Business is to Increase its Profits', *New York Time Magazine*, September, pp. 32–3.

Friedman, M and Friedman, R (1980) *Free to Choose: A Personal Statement*, London, Secker & Warburg.

Glautier, MWE and Underdown, B (2001) *Accounting Theory and Practice*, New York, Prentice-Hall.

Grant, RM (1997) *Contemporary Strategy Analysis*, 3rd edition, Oxford, Blackwell.

Harrison, JS and St John, CH (1998) *Strategic Management of Organisations and Stakeholders*, 2nd edition, Cincinnati, Ohio, South Western Publishing.

Kaplan, RS and Norton, DP (2004) 'Measuring the Strategic Readiness of Intangible Assets', *Harvard Business Review*, **82**, **2**, February, pp. 52–64.

Kaplan, RS and Norton, DP (1996) *The Balanced Scorecard*, Cambridge, HBS Press.

Kauffman, S (1995) *At Home in the Universe: The Search for Laws of Self-Organisation and Complexity*, Oxford, Oxford University Press.

Kay, J (1995) *Why Firms Succeed*, Oxford, Oxford University Press.

Magretta, J (2003) *What Management Is*, London, Profile Books.

Malone, TW, Scott-Morton, MS and Halperin, RR (1996) 'Organising for the 21st Century', *Strategy and Leadership*, **24**, July/August, pp. 6–11.

Mintzberg, H (1987) 'Crafting Strategy', *Harvard Business Review*, **65**, July/August, pp. 66–76.

Mohr, J and Spekman, R (1994) 'Characteristics of Partnership Success: Partnership Attributes Communication Behaviour and Conflict Resolution Techniques', *Strategic Management Journal*, **15**, pp. 135–52.

Parker, RH and Harcourt, GC (1969) *Readings in the Concept and Management of Income*, Cambridge, Cambridge University Press.

Richardson, GP (1991) *Feedback Thought in Social Science and Systems Theory*, Philadelphia, University of Philadelphia Press.

Roddick, A (2000) *Business as Unusual*, London, Thorsons.

Rosenfeld, R and Wilson, DC (1999) *Managing Organizations: Text Readings and Cases*, Maidenhead, McGraw-Hill.

Senge, P (1998) 'The leader's new work: Building learning organisations', in S Segal-Horn (ed.) *The Strategy Reader*, Oxford, Blackwell, pp. 296–312.

Sundaram, AK and Inkpen, AC (2004) 'The Corporate Objective Revisited', *Organisation Science*, **15**, **3**, May/June, pp. 350–63.

Van der Heijden, K (1996) *Scenarios: The Art of Strategic Conversation*, Chichester, John Wiley & Sons.

Wernerfelt, B (1984) 'A resource-based view of the firm', *Strategic Management Journal*, **5**, pp. 171–80.

Yoffie, DB (1988) 'How an Industry Builds Political Advantage', *Harvard Business Review*, **66**, May/June, pp. 82–90.

Challenges in strategy: final thoughts and postscript

In this book we have presented a wide-range of analytical and theoretical models to help strategists frame their strategic problems and issues in an effective manner. These models provide concepts, theoretical frameworks and analytical approaches which strategists can use as 'lenses' through which to view their strategic problems and strategy formulation processes.

Indeed, as Ned Bowman (1990) convincingly argues, strategists must learn how to use these models and lenses as frameworks and as tools to promote clear and frank dialogue among members of the strategy team about policy options and strategic decisions. A classic, well-known book on strategic decision-making in the political arena, namely Graham Allison's (1971) *Essence of Decision – Explaining the Cuban Missile Crisis*, illustrates clearly processes of strategic dialogue. It convincingly demonstrates that the decision to block the Russian missile ships approaching Cuba emerged from a combination of rational analyses of the situation and the decision alternatives and of discussion and debate in the top team advising President Kennedy. Bobby Kennedy, the President's brother, acted as a 'devil's advocate' to bring out the alternative views of the military and political establishment that were instrumental in forming the eventual decision.

Similarly we believe that the field of business strategy needs analytical tools such as theories, concepts and frameworks supported by processes of dialogue and debate in the management team. This combination provides the basis for practical insights by managers and prospects for improving the quality of strategic decisions. The role of strategy academics, such as we who have written this book, is to develop the conceptual foundations for the practice of strategy and show how these relate to the realities of decision-making.

For its part, top management must take responsibility in leading organizations to establish a corporate context in which both creativity and foresight are emphasized and which regards strategic thinking as the essential process from which both 'unbounded' or 'blue sky' thinking emerges and also from which sound and sensible business plans are created.

But strategic thinking involves the unknown, the improbable and the unlikely. The track record of organizations, both public and private, is for this reason at least very mixed. Strategic decisions by their nature are highly idiosyncratic and situation-specific. Therefore what works in one context does not necessarily work in another. Thus, there are no convenient blueprints for action. Instead academics, consultants and strategy practitioners repeatedly emphasize the importance of strategic thinking. Strategy in this way is an intellectual discipline and the concepts, frameworks and tools developed by academics, consultants and practitioners are an aid to thought, dialogue and debate. They are not a substitute for them. For these reasons and others to do with the natural distance between academics and practitioners it is evident that strategy theory and practice are not always well connected. Indeed, Bettis (1991) notes that research in strategic management has not yet produced the volume of useful results expected by managers. While the strategy field has clearly advanced over the last twenty years – as evidenced by the rapid growth of both scholarly and practitioner journals in the field (to say nothing of the burgeoning number of books on strategy), research in strategic management has continued to leave gaps between what is known from an academic perspective and what is, or can be, prescribed to managers. The opportunity for all of us in the field, including students of strategy, is to try to bridge this gap between theory and practice. Without such a bridge, managers may start losing interest (and insight) into theoretical developments which do not seem, in their eyes, to either help to explain reality or to facilitate action designed to influence it.

As academics, our research is usually focused on examining data so that we can understand what has happened in the past and why. This is a useful endeavour from which many valuable analytical approaches can be developed. But, in addition, academics, just like managers, have a responsibility to assess future possibilities, examine trends, and debate the turning points and discontinuities of the future. In this postscript, we focus on three elements which we think are important and which can form a platform for research agendas now and in the future.

1 What do leaders do, why are they important, and what difference do they create?

2 How can creativity be achieved through strategy?

3 The development of concepts of 'unbounded' thinking in strategy formulation.

Leadership

Vision without action is a daydream. Action without vision is a nightmare. (Old Japanese Proverb)

In a challenging article, John Kotter (1990) examines what leaders really do. He points out that leadership complements management; it does not replace it. Good management is about coping with, and controlling, complexity. Whereas leadership, by contrast, is about establishing a direction and coping with change. It is clear from the themes developed in this book that the business environment in recent times has become increasingly competitive, complex, turbulent, and subject to rapid change. We have rehearsed many of the reasons for this throughout the book, including new forms of competition, new and occasionally disruptive technologies, the need for new strategic capabilities, and changes in accountability and regulation. All of these are also happening in a rapidly changing demographic, cultural and international context.

Kotter notes that coping with complexity and coping with change are characteristic activities of managers and leaders. Managers and leaders have three tasks in common; namely,

> *deciding what needs to be done, creating networks of people and relationships that can accomplish an agenda and then trying to ensure that these people actually do the job.*

First, in deciding what needs to be done *leaders* set direction and a vision for the future whereas *managers* set plans and associated budgets.

Second, in developing the capacity to achieve the plan, *leaders* communicate the direction and align people to commit to the direction whereas *managers* devise, organize and staff an appropriate organizational structure and system.

Third, in ensuring that the organization's goals and plans are achieved, *leaders* need to motivate and inspire people to follow the strategic direction, whereas *managers* seek to control and monitor the plans in order to reach appropriate targets from a 'balanced score-card' perspective.

In essence, leaders need to develop a leadership culture which promotes values of adaptation to change and in which recruiting quality people to the organization is critical. It is then important to provide them with opportunities to learn by creating new business ideas, opportunities and risks. The simplistic metaphors of the leader as hero or as omnipotent dictatorial power are increasingly inappropriate in today's world. As Porter, Lorsch, and Nohria (2004) point out there are some important and subtle lessons for chief executive officers:

> *First, you must learn to manage organisational context rather than focus on daily operations.*

Second, you must recognise that your position does not infer the right to lead, nor does it guarantee the loyalty of the organisation.

Finally, you must remember that you are subject to a host of limitations, even though others may treat you as omnipotent.

These lessons create dilemmas for leaders, for instance to be coercive or to be democratic, to be authoritative or to be a coach, to be affiliative or to set the pace. These are increasingly important as the structural context in which businesses work becomes more fluid and more unpredictable, and as such, business organizations need to abandon comfortable structures on favour of experimental changes. The effect of leaders and leadership on strategy and strategy-making will become more significant and this will become a major challenge for business and for strategy academics.

Strategy and creativity

A keystone of strategy is innovation. However, a pertinent question to ask here is 'where do new ideas come from'. Typically, the simple answer is from people and human ingenuity. It is people who ultimately design new products, create new software, develop new businesses (e.g. Anita Roddick's Body Shop discussed in Chapter 21) or make existing businesses more efficient through management of the value-chain.

The key to creativity is the availability of high-quality creative individuals in the areas of science, engineering, architecture, education, art and music and more applied knowledge workers in the professional fields of law, business and medicine. From a macro-economic viewpoint (see Chapter 4), this requires an appropriate level of societal investment in both education and research and development in order to create an innovatory entrepreneurial culture. Recently Richard Florida (2004) has pointed out that countries such as Ireland, Canada, Australian, New Zealand and Denmark are spending more on R&D and higher education than either the US or the UK in order to attract and retain creative human capital.

New ideas tend to emerge from entrepreneurs (Drucker 1985) and it is from their highly individualised and personal cognitive maps (Porac and Thomas 2002) that new business ideas are sold to venture capitalists and new business arenas are formed (remember our discussion of entrepreneurs in Chapter 8). Drucker points out that it was through the linkage and integration of previously independent technological developments, i.e. audion tubes, binary theory, Jacquard punchcards and symbolic logic that the concept of the computer was created. Subsequently the modern computer industry with its many entrepreneurs such as Thomas J Watson, Steve Jobs, Tim Berners-Lee, Michael Dell and others, was created.

In all these cases entrepreneurs had to sell their creative visions and product concepts to other stakeholders who were often wedded to existing business models. For example, the business model of Jeff Bezos at Amazon.com needed to be sold to both venture capitalists and consumers. The rapid growth and success of Amazon has forced significant changes to the existing bookseller model favoured by Barnes and Noble in the USA and Waterstones in the UK. Something similar has happened in the internet world in EBay, ably led by the CEO Meg Whitman. This rapidly growing web-based trading network has forced a re-evaluation of auction trading. At a more mundane level the concept of 'Post-it notes' (essentially an adhesive piece of paper which did not adhere very well) at 3M was implemented within 3M's offices and office networks long before it was noticed and considered worthy enough to be launched as a new product by senior 3M managers. In summary, these examples illustrate the point that the strategy literature must more clearly incorporate into its frameworks entrepreneurial values such as the creative, cognitive and emotionally intelligent skills of the entrepreneur. Bill Gates at Microsoft, Herb Kelleher (Southwest Airlines) and Stelios (easyJet) in low cost airlines and Curtis Carlson the inventor of Xerography are all examples of entrepreneurs examined within the pages of this strategy text.

Unbounded thinking

Another characteristic of the entrepreneur is the ability to think 'out of the box'. Richard Branson at Virgin, Phil Knight at Nike, Nicholas Hayek at Swatch, Sochorio at Honda and others all exemplify the ability to think beyond current industry and competitive norms.

How can such 'unbounded' thinking be fostered? Gary Hamel and CK Prahalad's work, well represented in this book, offers concepts such as 'strategic intent', 'strategy as stretch and leverage' and 'strategy as revolution'. These exhort strategists to set 'big, hairy, audacious goals' (Collins and Porras 1996) and think outside current frames of reference in setting the company's vision. Indeed, Gary Hamel argues that it is through the activities of revolutionaries and innovators that sustainable competitive strategies are developed.

Chan Kim and Renée Mauborgne, 2004, advance the concept of *blue ocean strategy* to describe the existence of a previously unknown market space in which demand is created rather than fought over. One of their main examples is Cirque du Soleil – the French circus company. Despite a secular decline in the circus industry, Cirque has profitably increased its revenue over twenty times over the last ten years by reinventing the concept of a circus. This is an example of a company creating a 'blue ocean' by expanding the boundaries of an existing industry. EBay, on the other hand, is an example of a *blue ocean* created in a completely new fashion and defining a new market domain, namely online auctions.

More recently, the work of Johan Roos and his colleagues at the Imagination Lab in Lausanne, Switzerland has married creativity skills with blue ocean thinking. They use Lego blocks and Lego creativity play concepts with top management teams as a vehicle to enable them to think creatively about strategy in a systemic concept. The notion of developing unbounded thinking in organizations is a new and exciting area of study for the future.

As a final note . . .

We have identified a few important and novel themes in this postscript. In our view these are the areas in which strategic thinking and acting can develop both in theory and in practice. The five sections of this book were intended to provide an extensive examination of strategy as analysis and strategy as practice. The three new themes identified here will provide challenges for analysts to extend and develop their models to incorporate more subjective and imponderable characteristics. Similarly, strategy as practice needs also to extend its purview to move from a preoccupation with implementation and change to leadership, creativity and longer term perspectives.

Our other main goal in writing this book was to create for you a sense of enjoyment and fulfilment when you read it. In that respect, we hope that you enjoyed the content, organization, and the range of concepts offered here and are stimulated to think and act strategically as well as critically examine any organization in the future using the strategic systems lens presented in this book.

Further reading and references

Allison, GT (1971) *Essence of Decision: Explaining the Cuban Missile Crisis*, New York, HarperCollins.

Bettis, RA (1991) 'Strategic Management and the Straitjacket: an editorial essay', *Organisational Science*, **2** (3), pp. 315–19.

Bowman, EH (1990) 'Strategic changes; possible worlds and actual minds', in JW Frederickson (ed.), *Perspectives in Strategic Management*. New York, Harper and Row, pp. 9–39.

Collins, JC and Porras, JI (1996) 'Building your company's vision', *Harvard Business Review*, **74**, September–October, pp. 65–77.

Drucker, PF (1985) 'Innovation and Entrepreneurship', New York, Harper and Row.

Florida, Richard (2004) 'America's Looming Creativity Crisis', *Harvard Business Review*, **82**, **10**, pp. 121–39.

Kim, W Chan and Mauborgne, R (2004) 'Blue Ocean Strategy', *Harvard Business Review*, **82**, **10**, pp. 76–86.

Kotter, JP (1990) 'What leaders really do?' *Harvard Business Review*, **90**, **3**, pp. 103–11.

Porac, JF and Thomas, H (2002) 'Managing Cognition and Strategy', in AM Pettigrew, H Thomas and R Whittington (eds) 'Handbook of Strategy and Management', London, Sage, pp. 165–82.

Porter, ME, Lorsch, JW and Nohria, N (2004) 'Seven Surprises for new CEOs', *Harvard Business Review*, **82**, **10**, pp. 62–76.

Case Study Section

A Guide to Using the Case Studies

The main text of our book contains sixty case boxes within the chapters and twenty-one short case studies at the end of the chapters. These have been chosen to exemplify and enlarge upon the concepts and issues raised in each chapter. They are practical examples of how strategy concepts and ideas are manifested in the real world of making strategic decisions. Together with the Recap Questions at the end of each chapter these represent a practical study content that is further developed in the Online Learning Centre that accompanies this book at www.mcgraw-hill.co.uk/textbooks/mcgee.

The case studies that appear in this section take your learning onto a different level. These case studies are written around real, practical problems but in using them you should recognize that they are not intended as illustrations of either effective or ineffective management practice. In reading the previous chapters we hope to have persuaded you that the world of strategy and practice is messy and complicated. It follows usually that it is not easy or indeed sensible to attempt to categorize management practice as good or bad. These case studies are intended to provide a basis for analyzing and discussing a range of different situations in which the decisions to be taken are either not obvious or their implementation carries risks and complexities. These cases are typically quite long and contain considerable detail. Whereas the earlier case boxes and end of chapter cases are designed to be short so as to highlight the learning of concepts, the case studies in this section show the application of strategy theory and concepts in the real world of complex detail that is characteristic of companies and other organizations. The learning objective of analyzing long case studies is to bring together your ability to think conceptually with your ability to collect, select, analyze and interpret considerable amounts of data. Taken together these abilities are the basis for being able to understand and make strategic decisions.

This general and overarching objective can be broken down into specific learning experiences.

1 The first step is to gain practice in identifying key problems. The strategist's usual questions are where are we going? How are we going to get there? How do we expect to be able to succeed? These questions need to be fully articulated so that the context of the case is properly captured in the questions. For example, it is not enough to simply make a distinction between a growth strategy and a share retention strategy. The alternatives have to be expressed in terms of the detail of the situation so that the nature of the required judgments can be understood.

2 The cases are also designed to give practice in specifying what is meant by key concepts such as competitive advantage and core competence in real terms. As intellectual constructs these are powerful ideas but only gain real meaning when placed within the specific context of the individual company.

3 Case studies also allow the analyst to gain practice in how to shape an implementation plan. This should be expressed in terms of the business model, the key functional strategies and tactics, the key decisions to be taken and the risks involved.

4 The complexity of the real worlds of these cases allows you to explore larger issues such as mergers and acquisitions, technical innovation and R&D, performance assessment, corporate governance, and ethics and social responsibility. These represent significant 'strategic issues' that have concepts and content of their own and attract significant debate and controversy.

The summary table that follows displays how the cases relate to the chapters. There is an indication of the main focus of each case and also an indication of the minor focus. Each case may apply to more than one chapter and may cover a variety of concepts. The country location of each case is also shown so that you can choose to focus or diversify your use of cases as you wish.

In using cases you should be aware that before going onto the main theme of the case you will need to carry out a strategy analysis such as that shown in chapters 5, 6 and 7 (where the basic idea of competitive strategy is explained). Thus, a question posed in the case might be: 'Should Unilever buy cosmetics company X?' In order to address this question properly it is first necessary to undertake

Guide to the main focus of cases

Page	Companies/ Industries Featured:	Ch 1 and 2 — Introduction: basic concepts	Ch 3 and 4 — Economics of Strategy	Ch 5 — Industry Analysis & Competitive Strategy	Ch 6 — Competitive Position: competitive advantage	Ch 7 — Strategic Capability: core competence	Ch 8 — Life cycles, turnarounds, entrepreneurs	Ch 9 — Corporate Strategy: parenting advantage	Ch 10 — M&A and Alliances	Ch 11 — Global Strategies	Ch 12 — New Economy	Ch 13 — Strategic Decision Making	Ch 14 — Risk & Uncertainty	Ch 15 — Strategic Change	Ch 16 — Learning	Ch 17 — Corporate Governance	Ch 18 — Performance Assessment: balanced score card	Ch 19 — Knowledge, Information, Innovation	Ch 20 — Total quality, process improvement	Ch 21 — Business value as a system	Country location of case study
C407	Abrakebabra						◆◆										◆				Ireland
C357	British Airways									◆◆				◆◆							UK
C337	Blue Circle							◆◆													UK
C258	BSkyB				◆						◆◆		◆								UK
C106	Canon				◆◆	◆◆						◆									Japan
C195	Cola Wars in China			◆	◆◆		◆			◆			◆								China
C471	Consulting Industry				◆◆																Global
C418	Creyf in the Euro Temping Industry	◆			◆			◆◆	◆◆				◆								Belgium
C437	DSM - Performance Management							◆◆									◆◆			◆	The Netherlands
C079	easyJet			◆	◆◆	◆															UK
C237	Ferrari												◆	◆	◆◆			◆◆			Italy
C059	Finland & Nokia		◆◆								◆◆							◆			Scandinavia
C224	Formula 1 Constructors			◆														◆◆			UK/Europe
C458	Gatetrade: Nordic B2B Marketplace				◆				◆		◆◆		◆								Scandinavia
C324	Grand Metropolitan to Diageo							◆◆	◆							◆					UK

Key: ◆◆ = major focus   ◆ = important subsidiary focus

Page	Companies/ Industries Featured:	Ch 1 and 2 Introduction: basic concepts	Ch 3 and 4 Economics of Strategy	Ch 5 Industry Analysis & Competitive Strategy	Ch 6 Competitive Position: competitive advantage	Ch 7 Strategic Capability: core competence	Ch 8 Life cycles, turnarounds, entrepreneurs	Ch 9 Corporate Strategy: parenting advantage	Ch 10 M&A and Alliances	Ch 11 Global Strategies	Ch 12 New Economy	Ch 13 Strategic Decision Making	Ch 14 Risk & Uncertainty	Ch 15 Strategic Change	Ch 16 Learning	Ch 17 Corporate Governance	Ch 18 Performance Assessment: balanced score card	Ch 19 Knowledge, Information, Innovation	Ch 20 Total quality, process improvement	Ch 21 Business value as a system	Country location of case study
C027	Honda A & B	◆◆	◆◆	◆◆	◆◆								◆								Japan/USA
C376	House of Townend			◆	◆◆						◆◆										UK
C097	Hewlett-Packard				◆◆						◆								◆◆		Global
C143	HSBC							◆		◆◆			◆								China
C245	IKEA				◆	◆				◆		◆									Sweden
C210	Leo Burnett					◆				◆◆		◆									Canada
C310	Low-Cost Airlines Industry		◆	◆◆																	UK
C123	LVMH				◆			◆◆		◆					◆						France
C290	Mobile Telecoms Industry in the UK			◆							◆◆										UK
C005	NEC and GTE				◆	◆◆															Japan
C043	Nike	◆										◆◆		◆							USA
C174	Rank Xerox A,B,C															◆◆	◆◆		◆◆		Europe
C477	Rockware			◆			◆◆														UK
C391	Shell																◆◆				The Netherlands/UK
C152	Virgin						◆◆	◆													UK

Key: ◆◆ = major focus   ◆ = important subsidiary focus

a preliminary strategy analysis in order to understand the major strategic objectives, the nature of the competitive advantage and the degree of success of the implementation of the current strategy. This places the 'buy/not buy' decision in proper context.

The cases are intended to be used as they stand without recourse to more recent information such as financial reports or websites. You may find it helpful to review your recommendations against these data sources but you should bear in mind that the future, as it actually took place, is *not* necessarily the best answer!

亞洲商業案例中心
Centre for Asian Business Cases
School of Business, The University of Hong Kong

Case 1   **Core competence at NEC and GTE**

In 1990, a *Harvard Business Review* article touted NEC Corporation of Japan's 'core competence' and its focus on 'computers and communications'.[1] The same article heavily criticised GTE Corporation of the United States for focusing its attention on 'businesses' rather than 'competencies'. The authors proceeded to predict a bright future for NEC and other 'competence-based' companies, and potential obsolescence for GTE and other 'business-based' companies. The article, 'The Core Competence of the Corporation', which went on to become the best-selling HER reprint in history, ushered in a wave of consulting and academic work that said that 'core competence' was the key to company performance. NEC, with its 'C&C' strategy, became the darling of consultants and business academics around the world and the veritable 'poster child' for strategies

....

Professor Michael J. Enright prepared this case for class discussion. This case is not intended to show effective or ineffective handling of decision or business processes. This case is best used with Prahalad, C.K. & Hamel, G., 'The Core Competence of the Corporation', Harvard Business Review. Vol. 68, No. 3, pp.79–91 (reprints available from Harvard Business School Publishing, reprint no. 90311).

....

[1] Prahalad, C.K. & Hamel, G., (1990), 'The Core Competence of the Corporation', *Harvard Business Review,* Vol. 68, No. 3, pp.79–91.

based on core competencies. By mid-1999, however, NEC was in the midst of unprecedented upheaval. New CEO Koji Nishigaki promised to shake up the company by eliminating unprofitable businesses and by turning the manufacturer of computers, semiconductors, electronic devices, and communications equipment into an Internet-based company. Meanwhile, GTE appeared to be moving from strength to strength and to be well situated in the burgeoning international market for telecommunications.

NEC, GTE, and 'The Core Competence of the Corporation'

In the opening of 'The Core Competence of the Corporation,' authors C. K. Prahalad and Gary Hamel motivated the notion of 'core competence' by comparing NEC and GTE.

> *Consider the last ten years of GTE and NEC. In the early 1980s, GTE was well positioned to become a major player in the evolving information technology industry. It was active in telecommunications. Its operations spanned a variety of businesses including telephones, switching and transmission systems, digital PABX, semiconductors, packet switching, satellites, defense systems, and lighting products. And GTE's Entertainment Products Group, which produced Sylvania color TVs, had a position in related display technologies. In 1980, GTE's sales were $9.98 billion and net cash flow was $1.73 billion. NEC, in contrast, was much smaller, at $3.8 billion in sales. It had a comparable technological base and computer business, but it had no experience as an operating telecommunications company.*
>
> *Yet look at the positions of GTE and NEC in 1988. GTE's 1988 sales were $16.46 billion, and NEC's sales were considerably higher at $21.89 billion. GTE has, in effect, become a telephone operating company with a position in defense and lighting products. GTE's other businesses are small in global terms. GTE has divested Sylvania TV and Telenet, put switching, transmission, and digital PABX into joint ventures, and closed down semiconductors. As a result, the international position of GTE has eroded.*

Non-US revenue as a percent of total revenue dropped from 20% to 15% between 1980 and 1988.

NEC has emerged as the world leader in semiconductors and as a first-tier player in telecommunications products and computers. It has consolidated its position in mainframe computers. It has moved beyond public switching and transmission to include such lifestyle products as mobile telephones, facsimile machines, and laptop computers – bridging the gap between telecommunications and office automation. NEC is the only company in the world to be in the top five in revenue in telecommunications, semiconductors, and mainframes. Why did these two companies, starting with comparable business portfolios, perform so differently? Largely because NEC conceived of itself in terms of 'core competencies', and GTE did not.[2]

NEC to 1990

NEC (Nippon Electric Corporation) was founded in Tokyo on 17 July 1899, by a group of Japanese investors, led by Kunihiko Iwardare, as a joint venture with the US-based Western Electric Company, the manufacturing subsidiary of AT&T. Two years later, the company built its first manufacturing plant and in 1908 established its first foreign sales office in Seoul, Korea. NEC's initial products were telephone lines and equipment made primarily with Western Electric's technology. In 1918, the company successfully completed the installation of its own telephone lines and equipment in Hankow and Wuchang in China. During the rebuilding of Tokyo after the 1923 Kanto earthquake, NEC was chosen to modify automatic telephone exchange equipment from European and US manufacturers. NEC soon began to manufacture its own systems and in 1925 it began to produce vacuum tubes and phototelegraphy equipment, a forerunner of the modern facsimile machine.

---

2 Prahalad, C.K. & Hamel, G., (1990), 'The Core Competence of the Corporation', *Harvard Business Review,* Vol. 68, No. 3, pp.79–80. Reprinted by permission *of Harvard Business Review.* Copyright © 1990 by the Harvard Business School Publishing Corporation; all rights reserved.

The Japanese Government's desire for technological self-sufficiency in the 1930s pushed NEC to develop more and more of its own products. It began manufacturing radio broadcast equipment in 1930 and began research on microwave communications technology in 1935. It extended its business in cables and related technologies, and made history in 1939 by laying one of the world's longest telephone cable lines; 3,000 kilometres from Tokyo, through Korea, and into China. NEC also made efforts to develop technologies related to television relay and broadcasting, aiming at covering the Tokyo Olympic Games scheduled to be held in Tokyo in 1940. However, the Games were cancelled due to Sino-Japanese hostilities, and the research was further interrupted by the outbreak of World War II. By the late 1930s, some 40 per cent of the company's sales were to the Japanese military, a figure that increased to nearly 97 per cent by the end of the war in 1945.

Post World War II product developments

The years after the war heralded a new era in NEC's operations. NEC was able to take advantage of postwar rebuilding in Japan, rapid technological change, and the globalisation of business. In 1949, its shares were listed on the Tokyo and Osaka stock exchanges.

NEC became one of four principal suppliers to Nippon Telegraph and Telephone (NTT), the government-owned company that was formed in 1952 to control Japan's telephone industry. The post-WWII need to repair Japan's telephone systems and the country's continuing economic recovery resulted in strong demand from NTT for NEC's products. In the late 1950s and in the 1960s, NTT business represented over 50 per cent of NEC's sales. NTT provided a firm, protected source of demand for NEC and other Japanese suppliers for decades. NTT, for example, decided to press ahead with microwave communications links for the national telephone system, a decision that provided substantial demand for NEC microwave technology. The 1950 Radio Waves Law, which made radio waves available for use by the private sector, also created a large private-sector demand for radio and television receivers, as well as microwave links. NEC soon became a leading producer of microwave equipment.

The company also began to supply radios, television sets, and other consumer electronics products.

The development of the transistor in 1947 at the Bell Telephone Laboratories in the United States provided the forerunner of modern semiconductor integrated circuits (ICs), which in turn were to form the basis of modern communications and computer technologies. NEC signed a technology licensing agreement with GE from the United States in 1958 (five years after Sony had signed a similar agreement with Western Electric). The company established its Integrated Circuits Division in 1960 and became the first Japanese company to manufacture integrated circuits. The company eventually moved into large-scale integrated circuits (LSIs) in the mid-1960s and very large-scale integrated circuits (VLSIs) in 1967. NEC made its first foray into the computer industry in the 1950s. It demonstrated the world's first working transistorised computer in 1959, made the first Japanese microprocessor in 1974, and developed its first personal computer in 1979. By the end of the 1970s, NEC had established itself as a leader in its three main lines of business: communications equipment, computers, and semiconductors.

International operations

NEC had been cut off from international markets during the Second World War. The company began to expand internationally in the 1950s with the export of communications equipment to Asia. By the late 1950s, NEC was exporting large-scale communications equipment for public telephone networks to the Middle and Near East. It established its first marketing subsidiary for communications equipment in North America in 1963, and later developed a number of local manufacturing subsidiaries there, with product lines ranging from communications systems and computer peripherals to semiconductors. NEC's operations in Latin America began in the 1960s with the sale of microwave communications systems, and it entered the European market in the same period by shipping satellite communications earth stations and microwave communications systems. It continued to expand its European operations and concentrated on building a marketing network throughout Europe.

NEC began operations in Africa in the 1970s,

with an emphasis on building communications networks to promote economic development. NEC introduced its first digital switching system for the overseas market in 1977, although Japanese telephone networks were based on analog technology at the time. In the early 1980s, NEC delivered and installed digital optical communication networks in Argentina using optical fire cables manufactured by Sumitomo and digital switching equipment supplied by NEC. Meanwhile, NEC consumer electronics products were exported throughout the world, with substantial increases in foreign sales in the 1980s.

C & C – computers and communications

In 1964, Koji Kobayshi was appointed NEC president, and in 1976 he became chairman and CEO, a position he held for the next 12 years. In 1977 he articulated his vision of NEC's future as an integrator of computers and communications through semiconductor technology. Kobayashi believed that the integration of computers and communications was inevitable. He refocused the company on equipment to process and transmit information, thus forming the vision of NEC in terms of 'computers and communications', or 'C&C'. The company built on its past experience to focus on developing its capabilities in the technologies that were common to the different products that would emerge from this vision.

At the time, NEC has four separate divisions for its main businesses – communications, computers and industrial electronic systems, electron devices, and consumer electronics. It set up project teams that spanned different divisions. Marketing and sales had a team devoted to the promotion of C&C products, such as office and factory automation equipment and switching technology. Increasingly, however, the company organised itself around its core technologies rather than lines of business.

By the late 1980s, NEC was the largest of Japan's four major telecommunications equipment companies (in many other countries, telecommunications equipment was dominated by a single national champion or monopoly supplier).[3] NTT, which was partially privatised in 1985, still provided

---

[3] The other three companies were Fujitsu, Hitachi and Oki.

an important, though less dominant, market for Japanese companies. NTT accounted for roughly 50 per cent of NEC's sales in 1967, but only 13 per cent in 1985. NEC sold its digital public telephone exchange equipment in 28 countries (but never achieved much success in the United States), and was the world's largest supplier of satellite earth stations and microwave communications equipment. Although numerous competitors, first from Japan and then from Korea, had entered the cyclical and price-sensitive memory chip portion of the semiconductor industry, NEC was the world leader in semiconductor sales (mostly memory chips) and boasted the largest factory for standardised memory chips in the world.

NEC held the third-largest market share for computers within Japan and dominated the Japanese personal computer market, a market it had helped pioneer in the late 1970s and early 1980s. NEC's proprietary operating system helped it to dominate the Japanese PC market and shielded it from the cut-throat competition that broke out among producers in the United States, but also limited its presence in international markets, where systems based on Intel microprocessors and Microsoft operating systems became the norm. In 1987, in an attempt to extend its position in the hotly contested mainframe computer market, where it faced companies such as IBM and Fujitsu among others, NEC formed a partnership with Honeywell (United States) and France's Groupe Bull.

NEC was also a significant player in the home electronics business, an industry that had come to be dominated by several highly competitive Japanese firms, including Matsushita and Sony, and from which many United States and European firms had exited. NEC's home electronics division, which was responsible for about 10 per cent of sales, included televisions, video recorders and hi-fis.

Other firms that tried to carry out 'C&C' strategies, such as AT&T and IBM in the United States and Olivetti and Siemens in Europe, however, had found it impossible to compete in the three areas (or even two out of the three areas) profitably. NEC's foreign sales peaked at 35 per cent of total sales in 1984 and declined to 25 per cent of sales by 1989. As **Exhibit 2** shows, NEC was unique in appearing among the world's top five in its three core technologies: computers, telecommunications, and semiconductor devices. It was this position that Prahalad and Hamel wrote about in 1990.

GTE to 1990

GTE got its start in 1918 when three entrepreneurs, John O'Connell, Sigrid Odegard, and John Pratt, bought the Richland Center Telephone Company. The name was changed to Commonwealth Telephone Company two years later, and by 1935, the company was reorganised as the General Telephone Corporation. The company entered a period of rapid growth in the early post-World War II period, as US demand for telephone services exploded.

General Telephone's initial line of business was the provision of local telephone services. At the time, local telephone service in each area in the United States was provided by a local monopoly supplier. General Telephone created a subsidiary to produce telephone directories in 1926 and acquired a communications equipment-manufacturing company in 1950. In 1955, General Telephone acquired Theodore Gary and Company. Gary's subsidiary Automatic Electric would become General Telephone's main communications equipment-manufacturing operation. Along with the Gary purchase came companies that served 600,000 telephone customers in the United States, the Dominican Republic, and Canada, as well as a minority interest in the Philippines Long Distance Telephone Company. The acquisition of Peninsular Telephone of Florida added another 300,000 customers. By 1957, General Telephone was providing telephone service to 2.8 million customers in the United States, Canada, and the Dominican Republic.

Merger and expansion

In 1959, General Telephone merged with Sylvania Electric Products, and the name of the parent company was changed to General Telephone & Electronics Corporation (GTE). At the time, Sylvania, whose roots went back to 1901, was a major electronics supplier. Its products included light bulbs, fluorescent lamps, flash bulbs for photography, vacuum tubes, speciality chemical products, and metallurgical products for the electronics industry.

The merger with Sylvania, which had 45 plants and sales exceeding US$333 million (making it roughly comparable in size to General Telephone) created a diversified electronics and communications group.

The merger also marked the beginning of a period of tremendous expansion. In the 1960s, GTE expanded its telephone operations by acquiring phone companies in British Columbia, Quebec, Hawaii, and several Western and Midwestern US states, while selling off its Philippine stake. In 1969, GTE installed its ten-millionth telephone. The company expanded its product offerings in other areas in the 1960s and 1970s. It set up a data services subsidiary, acquired a communications company, obtained the name and distribution rights for Philco consumer electronics products in the United States and Canada, and introduced new technologies, such as the world's first fibre-optic communications system to provide a regular telephone service (between Long Beach and Artesia, California, in 1977).

The 1970s also saw GTE consolidating and reorganising its management. Corporate headquarters was relocated to Stamford, Connecticut, from New York City. The GTE Products Group was formed to bring worldwide manufacturing and marketing under a single entity. Foreign manufacturing subsidiaries, which had been under a single international division, were reassigned to their respective global divisions headquartered in the United States. Thomas A. Vanderslice, formerly of GE, was named President and Chief Operating Officer in 1979 with a mandate from Chairman and CEO Theodore F. Brophy to change the company into a leaner and more aggressive operation.

Liberalisation in the US telecommunications industry

The US telecommunications industry experienced dramatic change in the 1980s. In 1984, an anti-trust case resulted in the break-up of AT&T and an end to its virtual monopoly of telephone service in the United States. At the time, telephone service in most countries was provided by a single monopoly supplier. AT&T had been granted a virtual monopoly over telephone service in the United States in 1918, and by 1984 AT&T served the vast majority of the United States with local (80 percent), long-distance

(100 per cent), and international (100 per cent) telephone service, telephone directories, and telephone equipment, including everything from simple handsets to the most complicated central-office switching equipment.

Under the 1984 settlement, AT&T's local telephone companies were formed into seven regional Bell operating companies (RBOCs). Each RBOC was granted a monopoly on local fixed-line services within its region, but was denied the right to manufacture equipment and could not sell inter-regional or international long-distance services. Eventually, the local fixed-line companies were given one of two cellular phone licences granted in each region. AT&T retained its manufacturing, laboratories, and the right to sell interstate and international long-distance call services. The settlement created a totally open market for telecommunications equipment of all types, by separating manufacturing from the provision of local telephone service, as the RBOCs were now free to purchase equipment from any vendor. It left local monopolies in fixed-line local service, but created competition in long-distance and international services by opening these services up to new competitors.

GTE in the 1980s

The AT&T settlement left GTE as the only company in the United States with its own manufacturing arm, local operating companies, long-distance service, and mobile or cellular phone activities. GTE's local telephone companies pre-dated the granting of monopoly status or had been set up in relatively remote areas before AT&T could supply service (sometimes with the latter's blessing). As a result, by 1984, GTE served rural and suburban markets in some 28 states. In its areas, GTE traditionally operated like a mini-AT&T, supplying local telephone service, telephone directories, and telephone equipment, though AT&T provided long-distance and international phone service to GTE customers. By 1984, GTE provided approximately 10 per cent of US local connections, compared to 80 per cent for AT&T and 10 per cent for a host of other small independent companies. GTE's relatively small share meant that there was no effort by the US Government to break up the company. However, the AT&T decision came at an unsettled time for GTE, as President Vanderslice had resigned in December 1983 amid some controversy before he could completely implement his plans for GTE.

GTE decided to realign its business portfolio, announcing in 1984 that it would focus on three 'core' businesses: telecommunications, lighting, and precision materials. The company had already entered new communications businesses. In 1982, GTE Mobilnet® was formed. The following year, GTE acquired a long-distance telephone services company (renamed GTE Sprint), and satellite communications companies (renamed GTE Spacenet), and began offering mobile phone service and developing satellite communications services in 1984. Airphone, a company that provided telephone services from commercial aircraft, was acquired in 1986. By 1989, GTE was the first cellular phone provider to offer service nationally in the United States. The company's research focused on the telecommunications business, by developing advanced ISDN capabilities, beginning the development of advanced network systems (such as video on demand), and creating new military communications systems.

The firm also sold or exited several businesses. Television- and radio-manufacturing operations were sold (many other US and European firms had already exited these businesses), as was the company's cable television equipment, electrical equipment, and structural support (for construction) businesses. In communications equipment, GTE's communications transmission and central-office switch-manufacturing activities were transferred to a joint venture 80 per cent controlled by the German company Siemens in 1986, and its US business systems and PABX businesses were transferred to a joint venture 80 per cent owned by Fujitsu of Japan in 1987. In 1989, its consumer communications products business was divested. GTE also gradually divested its stake in GTE Sprint, which had incurred huge investment costs and substantial operating losses in what had become a fiercely competitive long-distance telephone market.

The end of the decade saw GTE in the midst of restructuring. It announced major job cuts, sold off various businesses, and reorganised the company into six operating groups. Previously the company had had just two units: telephone and communications products/services. Following the

reorganisation, the six operating groups were: Telephone Operations, Electrical Products, Government Systems, Information Services, Mobile Communications, and Spacenet.

The 'Core Competence' take on NEC and GTE

Prahalad and Hamel characterised the evolution of the two companies until 1990 as follows;

NEC versus GTE, again, is instructive and only one of many such comparative cases we analysed to understand the changing basis for global leadership. Early in the 1970s, NEC articulated a strategic intent to exploit the convergence of computing and communications, what it called 'C&C'. Success, top management reckoned, would hinge on acquiring competencies, particularly in semiconductors. Management adopted an appropriate 'strategic architecture', summarized by C&C, and then communicated its intent to the whole organisation and the outside world during the mid-1970s.

NEC constituted a 'C&C Committee' of top managers to oversee the development of core products and core competencies. NEC put in place coordination groups and committees that cut across the interests of individual businesses. Consistent with its strategic architecture, NEC shifted enormous resources to strengthen its position in components and central processors. By using collaborative arrangements to multiply internal resources, NEC was able to accumulate a broad array of core competencies.

NEC carefully identified three interrelated streams of technological and market evolution. Top management determined that computing would evolve from large mainframes to distributed processing, components from simple ICs to VLSI, and communications from mechanical cross-bar exchange to complex digital systems we now call ISDN. As things evolved further, NEC reasoned, the computing, communications, and components businesses would so overlap that it would be very hard to distinguish among them, and that there would be enormous opportunities for any company that had built the competencies needed to serve all three markets.

NEC top management determined that semiconductors would be the company's most important 'core product'. It entered into myriad strategic alliances – over 100 as of 1987 – aimed at building competencies rapidly and at low cost. In mainframe computers, its most noted relationship was with Honeywell and Bull. Almost all the collaborative arrangements in the semiconductor-component field were oriented toward technology access. As they entered collaborative arrangements, NEC's operating managers understood the rationale for these alliances and the goal of internalizing partner skills. NEC's director of research summed up its competence acquisition during the 1970s and 1980s this way: 'From an investment standpoint, it was much quicker and cheaper to use foreign technology. There wasn't a need for us to develop new ideas.'

No such clarity of strategic architecture appeared to exist at GTE. Although senior executives discussed the implications of the evolving information technology industry, no commonly accepted view of which competencies would be required to compete in that industry were communicated widely. While significant staff work was done to identify key technologies, senior line managers continued to act as if they were managing independent business units. Decentralization made it difficult to focus on core competencies. Instead, individual businesses became increasingly dependent on outsiders for critical skills, and collaboration became a route to staged exits. Today, with a new management team in place, GTE has repositioned itself to apply its competencies to emerging markets in telecommunications services.[4]

NEC in the 1990s

NEC, which entered the 1990s as one of the world's most admired corporations, soon faced new challenges. The Japanese economy, which accounted for most of NEC's sales, stalled as asset values collapsed. This in turn exacerbated a banking crisis that had been hidden during the prior decade's growth. Japan's economy slowed for most of the decade and the Nikkei index, which stood at nearly 39,000 at the end of 1989, was just under 19,000 at the end of 1999. The 'Big Bang' reforms in Japan's financial markets in the late 1990s saw a heightened interest in profitability and returns on the part of shareholders. Many Japanese firms found their competitive positions under threat as North American and European firms regained their footing and as production from Newly Industrialised Economies such as Korea, Taiwan, Hong Kong, Singapore, and other Asian economies grew.

NEC lost its status as the world's largest semiconductor maker to Intel (which concentrated on the microprocessors that ran most of the world's personal computers) in the early 1990s. By 1998, market research indicated that NEC had slipped to third place in memory chips behind the Korean companies Samsung Electronics Company and Hyundai Electronics Industries.[5] The memory portion of the semiconductor industry continued to be cyclical, with firms losing as much money in downturns as they made in upturns, if not more, and continued to see governments (in places such as Korea, Malaysia, and Taiwan, among others) supporting new entry into the business.

Competition in the telecommunications equipment industry had changed substantially from the days in which cosy monopolies and oligopolies dominated national markets. The darlings of the industry had become fast-moving specialist companies such as Nokia, Ericsson, and Motorola, rather than slower-moving, broad-line companies such as NEC. Several foreign players made significant inroads into the Japanese market, particularly in newer and more

---

[4] Prahalad, C.K. & Hamel, G., (1990), 'The Core Competence of the Corporation', *Harvard Business Review*, Vol. 68, No. 3, pp.80–81. Reprinted by permission *of Harvard Business Review*. Copyright © 1990 by the Harvard Business School Publishing Corporation; all rights reserved.

[5] MacLellan, A., 'Japan revamps strategies', *Electronic Buyers News*, 5 April, 1999.

advanced applications such as mobile telephony and data transmission and handling equipment.

In October 1992, Compaq Computer Corporation of the United States stunned the Japanese PC market when it introduced its Prolinea series into Japan. The standardisation around the 'Wintel' combination of Microsoft operating systems and Intel microprocessors had made the personal computer industry in the United States a commodity business. NEC's proprietary system based on internal competencies had limited direct price competition in Japan. With the Prolinea, which undercut Japanese rivals by more than 50 per cent in price, Compaq initiated price competition that had not been seen formerly in the Japanese PC market. When NEC's PC operations began to suffer, it responded in 1994 by allowing licensing of PCs based on its operating system for the first time. However, the days of the proprietary NEC system were numbered as even NEC began making 'Wintel' computers in earnest. By June 1995, NEC's share of Japan's personal computer market had fallen to below 50 per cent. It would fall to 27 per cent by 1998.

In the late 1990s, NEC entered into a number of joint ventures and alliances covering its whole range of operations. In 1995, NEC and Packard Bell Electronics, the leader in US retail PC market share, formed Packard Bell-NEC. In 1998, NEC raised its stake in Packard Bell from 20 per cent to 80 per cent. In 1996, in an attempt to improve the yield on the chip production lines of both companies, NEC and Samsung Electronics agreed to jointly research improving production efficiency and to swap sensitive information on manufacturing yields and processing techniques. This was viewed as an attempt to shore up the situation in a commodity business. In the same year, NEC created US subsidiary Holon Net Corp. to make hardware and software for Internet and intranet markets.

In spite of these efforts, by 1998 NEC was in crisis. Tadahiro Sekimoto resigned as chairman in October 1998, taking responsibility for NEC's activities in a defence procurement scandal, in which several NEC officials were indicted on charges of overcharging the Japanese military in procurement contracts. Despite president Hishashi Kaneko's assurances that he would remain in his position, he was forced to resign in February 1999 in the wake of massive losses forecast for the year.

On March 26 1999, Koji Nishigaki was appointed president of NEC. Nishigaki soon announced a plan to eliminate unprofitable business and concentrate on those tied to the Internet. More radical was his intention to create cost-of-capital measurements for individual businesses, set targets for return on that capital, and allocate funds to high-return operations. This move was in stark contrast to traditional Japanese measures of business performance, which were commonly market share and top-line sales growth, regardless of the amount of money invested. It also was in stark contrast to the 'core competence' model of organisation that the company had followed. Mr. Nishigaki was clear that NEC would focus on shareholder value, and even more radically, that each division would have a separate profit and loss account, which would be made public.

We will promote decentralisation by transferring a significant amount of authority to NEC's business groups through the balanced implementation of in-house divisional companies. These in-house companies will develop and execute business plans as well as take responsibility for business results independently of each other.

– Koji Nishigaki.[6]

In September, Nishigaki announced a business plan that put the Internet at the centre of each division's mission statement and positioned NEC as a 'solutions provider' for businesses trying to cash in on e-commerce. The restructuring was to break the company into three separate entities – NEC Solutions, NEC Networks, and NEC Electron Devices. Each company was to be responsible for its own operations, from production to sales, in a business-unit structure. Nishigaki also announced an alliance with Intel, which planned to open 12 worldwide Internet hosting centres, offering systems for service providers, by the end of 2000. Intel planned to establish the first centre in Japan with NEC. Customers of Biglobe (NEC's flagship Internet service provider) were to be able to use Intel's standard e-business application and hosting services once the centre was up and running. Nishigaki also announced a joint venture with Hitachi

6   Nishigaki, K., 'The Path Towards Corporate Excellence', January 2000.

to consolidate their money-losing memory chip oper-ations, the restructuring of Packard Bell-NEC (which laid off 80 per cent of its employees and exited the US retail market), and entered an agreement with Hewlett-Packard to develop a next-generation Internet network for Japan.

GTE in the 1990s

GTE developed substantially in the 1990s. The United States, where GTE had the bulk of its sales, saw substantial economic growth in the decade. Asset prices rose dramatically, with the S&P 500 average going from 353 at the end of 1989 to 1,455 at the end of 1999. The decade also saw dramatic expansion of most communication services in the United States, with data applications and then the emerging Internet driving growing demand.

GTE began the decade with the announcement of what was (at that time) the largest merger in telecommunications history. The merger with Contel Corporation, a major local telephone and cellular service provider, created the fifth-largest domestic telephone company in the United States and, together with the acquisition of additional cellular properties, the nation's second-largest cellular phone service provider. GTE closed the decade with an agreement to merge with one of the RBOCs, Bell Atlantic (1998), the acquisition of cellular phone assets from Ameritech (1999), and the announce-ment of an alliance with Vodaphone Airtouch (1999) to form the largest wireless communications company in the United States.

Throughout the 1990s, GTE's focused its efforts on new and enhanced communications businesses. By 1992, GTE was launching large-scale market trials of two-way personal communications services. It introduced new advanced switching modes, the first wide-area multimedia communications network in the United States, interactive video services, wire-less data and personal communications services, international roaming services for cellular phones, Internet access services, online services, and others. In order to position itself for the Internet revolution and related data communication markets, GTE pur-chased BBN, along with its national IP network, in 1997. GTE also reached agreements with Lycos (online services), Qwest (fibre optic networks),

and Cisco (internetworking capabilities) to enhance its position in Internet-related businesses.

GTE also expanded in foreign markets in the 1990s. In 1991, it announced a joint venture with SOVINTEL to provide instantaneous, high-quality telephone service from the Soviet Union to the West and Asia. In the same year, it led the consortium that acquired a 40 per cent share in the Venezuelan tele-phone company CANTV. GTE also began activities in Argentina (cellular phone services), Belgium (direc-tory services), Mexico (alliance to provide communications services), China (research and development, installation of cellular phone equip-ment on China Southern Boeing 777s, and helping set up a wireless paging network), Japan (cellular phone service), Taiwan (cellular phone service), and Puerto Rico (local telephone services). In several instances, GTE obtained local monopoly or oligopoly positions in its new markets.

Continuing its focus on specific businesses rather than competencies, GTE divested its worldwide lighting, electrical products, space-based communi-cations, and aircraft cellular phone businesses, and its remaining stake in long-distance company Sprint. It also announced that it would sell its Government Systems operation (mostly communications systems for the military). Each of the businesses was described as either under-performing or non-core. The divestitures would free up resources for high-growth initiatives in the company's core businesses.

In the United States, the Telecommunications Act of 1996 had forced the RBOCs to open up their facili-ties so that competitors could connect to them, but also allowed the RBOCs to sell long-distance services once they met a 14-point 'Competitive Checklist' to ensure they had opened their networks to competi-tion. On December 22, 1999, Bell Atlantic became the first RBOC to be granted the right to sell long-distance services. The Act, increased competition, data and voice network convergence, and the emergence of the Internet all contributed to unprecedented growth and transformation in the US telecommunications industry. The barriers that had created separate worlds of wireless, wireline, voice, data, local, and long-distance services were eroding, and a new communications network was being con-structed in its place. Local exchange carriers had gained ground by introducing new services at lower prices using alternative technology, and cable operators who had recognised their capability of transferring voice and data had also entered the market. GTE had positioned itself right in the middle of this communications revolution.

According to GTE management, the company was well positioned in its core businesses, and was confident that these businesses would allow it to compete successfully in the future:

> We understood that, within the first few years of the next century, 80 to 90 per cent of our total traffic would be data, and the kinds of services high-value customers would demand could only be delivered via an IP infrastructure.... To ensure our status as a Tier One company, GTE is establishing itself in three key areas of the data market – transport, access, and value-added services.[7]

The new millennium

For nearly 20 years, NEC had focused on its 'core competencies', while GTE had focused on its 'core businesses'. The two strategies left the firms in very different positions as they faced the start of the new millennium. GTE seemed to remain confident in its business-based approach, whereas NEC had decided that it had to promote decentralisation, a business-unit focus, and individual business group accountability. Senior executives from the two companies adopted very different tones:

> We enter the 21st century with strong core businesses that performed very well in 1999 and provide a solid foundation for future growth.
> – Charles R. Lee, Chairman and CEO of GTE.[8]

> Our short-term target is returning to profitability, our mid-term goal is recreating NEC into a highly valued corporation that sets standards in global excellence.
> – Koji Nishigaki, President, NEC Corporation.[9]

---

7 GTE, 'Investor Information', January 2000.

8 GTE, January 2000.
9 Nishigaki, K., January 2000

APPENDIX 1: What are core competencies?

According to Prahalad and Hamel,

Core competencies are the collective learning in the organization, especially how to coordinate diverse production skills and integrate multiple streams of technologies.[10]

The authors claim that the recognition and development of core competencies rely on communication and co-operation across traditional organisational boundaries, and that this communication and co-operation can make disparate businesses coherent and position a company to take advantage of opportunities for future growth. In addition, they see a core competence as not diminishing with use or deteriorating over time. Instead they conclude the more it is used, the more valuable it becomes.

The authors provide three tests to identify a core competence:

♦ It must have the potential to form the basis for entry into new product markets.

♦ The competence must make a significant contribution to customer perceived value.

♦ It should be difficult for competitors to imitate.

They state that while a company's short-term competitiveness derives from the price and performance of its current products, its long-term competitiveness derives from an ability to build core competencies that generate the products of the future. Therefore, 'the real sources of advantage are to be found in management's ability to consolidate corporate wide technologies and production skills into competencies that empower individual businesses to adapt quickly to changing opportunities.'[11]

Core competencies versus business units

Prahalad and Hamel claim that the 'traditional' corporate focus on business units and industries makes the issue of putting competitive products on today's shelves the most significant one. In their view however, corporations should be seeking to maximise their world manufacturing share of core products, which they define as the link between core competencies and end products, rather than the end products themselves.

According to the authors, there are three dangers in the 'traditional' approach:

♦ If the organisation focuses on business units, no single unit may feel responsible for maintaining a viable position in core products or competencies, and the company may find itself dependent on external sources for critical components.

♦ Competencies developed within a business unit become 'imprisoned' within that unit, denying the corporation the necessary harmonisation and communication across those · boundaries necessary to fully exploit all opportunities.

♦ Opportunities for growth will be missed if the potential for these products crosses SBU (strategic business unit) parameters.

Thus, according to Prahalad and Hamel, in order to prevent the fragmentation of core competencies, which is inevitable for any corporation organised in business units and focused on positioning within 'industries', a corporation needs to establish a corporate-wide strategic architecture for competence-building. They claim that successful organisations of the future will be those that have shifted their focus from that of SBUs to the core competencies of their organisation, as these form the foundations of future growth.

---

[10] Prahalad, C.K. & Hamel, G., (1990), 'The Core Competence of the Corporation', *Harvard Business Review,* Vol. 68, No. 3, p.82. Reprinted by permission *of Harvard Business Review.* Copyright © 1990 by the Harvard Business School Publishing Corporation; all rights reserved.

[11] Prahalad, C.K. & Hamel, G., (1990), 'The Core Competence of the Corporation', *Harvard Business Review,* Vol. 68, No. 3, p.81. Reprinted by permission *of Harvard Business Review.* Copyright © 1990 by the Harvard Business School Publishing Corporation; all rights reserved.

EXHIBIT 1 NEC and GTE, sales, 1980–1990

NEC		GTE	
Fiscal Year Ending	Sales (USD millions)	Fiscal Year Ending	Sales (USD millions)
March 1981	4,711	Dec 1980	9,979
March 1982	4,872	Dec 1981	11,026
March 1983	6,013	Dec 1982	12,066
March 1984	7,830	Dec 1983	12,944
March 1985	8,998	Dec 1984	14,547
March 1986	13,116	Dec 1985	15,732
March 1987	16,779	Dec 1986	15,111
March 1988	21,893	Dec 1987	15,421
March 1989	23,178	Dec 1988	16,460
March 1990	21,798	Dec 1989	17,424

Source: Compustat

EXHIBIT 2 Worldwide electronic supplier ranking

	Computers Sales in US$ billions		Telecommunications Sales in US$ billions		Semiconductors Sales in US$ billions	
1	IBM	49.6	AT&T	17.3	NEC	2.6
2	Unisys	9.4	Alcatel-ITT	7.6	Hitachi	2.3
3	DEC	8.4	Northern Telecom	4.1	Toshiba	2.3
4	Fujitsu	6.6	NEC	3.6	Motorola	2.3
5	NEC	6.3	Siemens	3.2	Texas Instruments	1.8

Source: 'NEC Sets Global Strategy for Medium Term', *PR Newswire*, 19 October 1987.

EXHIBIT 3 NEC Corporation, financial results, 1981–1990 (in USD millions)

Fiscal Year Ending	Sales	Operating Income Before Depreciation	Income Before Tax	Net Income	Total Assets	Shareholders' Equity
March 1981	4,711	579	206	99	5,174	782
March 1982	4,872	590	225	109	5,405	812
March 1983	6,013	794	299	138	6,880	1,194
March 1984	7,830	1,040	417	198	9,243	1,818
March 1985	8,998	1,374	596	267	10,801	1,901
March 1986	13,116	1,732	714	153	14,529	2,798
March 1987	16,779	1,701	420	103	18,944	3,522
March 1988	21,893	2,220	630	205	23,427	4,784
March 1989	23,178	2,682	1,085	485	25,161	5,183
March 1990	21,798	2,737	1,179	539	23,316	5,096

Source: Compustat
Note: Results are reported in accordance with US Generally Accepted Accounting Principles, and are converted at the prevailing exchange rate at the end of the fiscal year.

EXHIBIT 4 GTE Corporation, financial results, 1980–1989 (in USD millions)

Fiscal Year Ending	Sales	Operating Income Before Depreciation	Income Before Tax	Net Income	Total Assets	Shareholders' Equity
Dec 1980	9,979	3,105	1,218	478	19,720	4,851
Dec 1981	11,026	3,518	1,376	722	21,113	5,289
Dec 1982	12,066	3,790	1,469	836	22,294	6,025
Dec 1983	12,944	4,253	1,698	956	24,223	6,785
Dec 1984	14,547	4,708	1,900	1,125	26,364	7,811
Dec 1985	15,732	4,988	(72)	(161)	26,558	7,235
Dec 1986	15,111	5,381	2,182	1,184	27,402	8,017
Dec 1987	15,421	5,489	1,845	1,119	28,745	8,429
Dec 1988	16,460	5,464	1,944	1,225	31,104	8,752
Dec 1989	17,424	5,620	2,193	1,417	31,986	8,518

Source: Compustat

EXHIBIT 5 NEC and GTE, share price, and dividend history, 1979–1989

Year End	NEC Corporation				GTE Corporation		
	Share Price at Year End (USD)	Per Share Div./Year (USD)	Nikkei 225 Average Price Index (Yen)	Nikkei 225 Average Price Index (USD)	Share Price at Year End (USD)	Per Share Div./Year (USD)	S&P Composite Price Index (USD)
1979	7.19		6,569.73		9.42		107.94
1980	11.21	2.763	7,063.13	31.15	9.08	2.72	135.76
1981	15.05	3.153	7,681.84	34.83	10.67	2.75	122.55
1982	17.86	2.712	8,016.67	32.19	13.58	2.86	138.34
1983	28.41	0.624	9,893.82	41.66	14.58	2.94	164.93
1984	24.25	0.690	11,542.60	48.59	13.54	3.02	167.24
1985	32.88	0.850	13,083.18	54.85	15.33	3.10	211.28
1986	63.88	1.168	18,820.64	111.69	19.46	3.18	242.17
1987	73.50	1.414	21,564.00	149.11	17.69*	2.46*	247.08
1988	78.50	1.484	30,159.00	235.34	22.25	2.56	277.72
1989	65.50	0.660	38,915.87	282.08	35.00	2.74	353.40

Source: Datastream, Sequencer, CEIC and Annual Reports.
Note: * In 1987, GTE stock was split three-for-two. The price indicated is the post-split price per share. The dividend is the total annual dividend per post-split share.

EXHIBIT 6 NEC corporation, financial results, 1991–1999 (in USD millions)

Fiscal Year Ending	Sales	Operating Income Before Depreciation	Income Before Tax	Net Income	Total Assets	Shareholders' Equity
March 1991	26,233	3,161	992	386	27,869	6,248
March 1992	28,375	2,685	445	115	30,686	6,604
March 1993	30,565	2,205	(260)	(393)	34,599	7,007
March 1994	35,096	2,852	314	65	39,606	7,667
March 1995	43,326	4,351	995	406	47,716	9,089
March 1996	41,095	4,748	1,473	721	43,767	8,214
March 1997	39,907	3,683	980	739	38,703	8,092
March 1998	36,851	3,581	693	311	37,397	8,051
March 1999	40,334	2,624	(1,958)	(1,339)	42,174	7,230

Source: Compustat
Note: Results are reported in accordance with US Generally Accepted Accounting Principles, and are converted at the prevailing exchange rate at the end of the fiscal year.

EXHIBIT 7   GTE Corporation, financial results, 1990–1998 (in USD millions)

Fiscal Year Ending	Sales	Operating Income Before Depreciation	Income Before Tax	Net Income	Total Assets	Shareholders' Equity
Dec 1990	18,374	6,042	2,365	1,541	33,769	9,210
Dec 1991	19,621	7,194	2,319	1,580	42,437	11,417
Dec 1992	19,984	7,326	2,889	(754)	42,144	10,171
Dec 1993	19,748	7,694	1,692	882	41,575	9,677
Dec 1994	19,944	8,072	4,141	2,441	42,500	10,556
Dec 1995	19,957	8,731	4,253	(2,144)	37,019	6,871
Dec 1996	21,339	9,258	4,668	2,798	38,422	7,336
Dec 1997	23,260	9,497	4,675	2,794	42,142	8,038
Dec 1998	25,473	9,911	4,335	2,172	43,615	8,766

Source: Compustat

EXHIBIT 8   NEC and GTE, share price and dividend history, 1990–1999

Year End	NEC Corporation				GTE Corporation		
	Share Price at Year End (USD)	Per Share Div./Year (USD)	Nikkei 225 Average Price Index (Yen)	Nikkei 225 Average Price Index (USD)	Share Price at Year End (USD)	Per Share Div./Year (USD)	S&P Composite Price Index (USD)
1990	47.50	2.140	23,848.71	164.70	29.13*	1.49*	330.22
1991	48.25	2.290	22,983.77	170.83	34.63	1.61	417.09
1992	26.88	1.705	16,924.95	133.64	34.63	1.73	435.71
1993	38.13	1.955	17,417.24	156.65	34.50	1.83	465.44
1994	57.00	2.123	19,723.06	192.93	30.38	1.88	459.27
1995	61.00	2.298	19,868.15	211.22	43.88	1.88	615.93
1996	60.75	2.187	19,361.35	177.97	45.38	1.88	740.74
1997	53.63	1.919	15,258.74	126.11	52.25	1.88	970.43
1998	45.25	1.807	13,842.17	105.75	65.00	1.88	1,229.23
1999	114.50	1.049	18,934.34	164.75	73.00	1.88	1,455.22

Source: Datastream, Sequencer, CEIC and Annual Reports.
Note: * In 1990, GTE stock was split two-for-one. The price indicated is the post-split price per share. The dividend is the total annual dividend per post-split share.

EXHIBIT 9 NEC, business results, selected years

	1999	1998	1997	1996	1995	1994	1993	1990	1989	1988	1985	1984	1983	1980
Information & Communications Systems														
• Communication Systems & Equipment (% of Total Sales)	31.35	35.03	34.09	27.90	27.25	27.07	27.34	25.41	26.02	27.92	29.22	32.52	36.31	37.59
• Computers & Industrial Electronic Devices (% of Total Sales)	46.02	40.34	42.00	44.19	47.47	49.75	50.90	43.76	43.25	41.62	31.93	30.53	27.72	24.24
• Operating margin (%)	3.18	5.55	5.39											
Electron Devices														
• % of Total Sales	18.39	20.18	19.46	23.49	20.56	18.32	16.87	17.59	18.36	17.05	26.39	24.12	21.76	21.46
• Operating margin (%)	(5.96)	5.36	5.61											
Other														
• % of Total Sales	4.24	4.45	4.45	4.41	4.72	4.83	4.89	13.27	12.36	13.41	12.44	12.83	14.14	16.71
• Operating margin (%)	(1.98)	(0.46)	(1.82)											

Source: Annual Reports.

EXHIBIT 10 GTE, business unit results, 1980–1990

	1990	1989	1988	1987	1986	1985	1984	1983	1982	1981	1980
Telephone Operations											
• % of Total Sales	69.46	71.50	71.00	72.35	71.14	63.44	62.32	64.65	64.74	61.34	59.32
• Operating margin (%)	23.97	22.79	23.26	25.80	27.27	29.34	28.72	27.17	27.66	29.73	28.87
Communication Products & Services											
• % of Total Sales	18.45	16.29	15.78	14.33	16.79						
• Operating margin (%)	4.57	4.51	4.08	2.35	4.97						
Communications Products											
• % of Total Sales						16.66	17.15	19.71	20.34	19.94	20.75
• Operating margin (%)						3.74	0.96	5.64	6.23	5.14	6.28
Communications Services *											
• % of Total Sales						8.54	8.56	4.86	0.89	0.73	0.45
• Operating margin (%)						(18.21)	5.38	14.19	(25.23)	(30.00)	(62.22)
Electrical Products											
• % of Total Sales	12.39	12.53	13.59	13.81	17.72	12.07	12.74	11.43	11.78	14.45	16.83
• Operating margin (%)	10.46	10.16	10.19	10.43	9.36	10.27	11.44	7.16	10.27	12.81	14.40

Note: GTE changed the way it reported results in 1986.
* Communication services consisted mostly of long-distance services
Source: Annual Reports.

EXHIBIT 11 GTE, business unit results, 1991–1998

	1998	1997	1996	1994	1993	1992	1991
Telephone Operations							
• % of Total Sales				79.75	80.15	79.37	79.77
• Operating margin (%)				26.65	17.02	25.43	24.32
Telecommunication Products & Services							
• % of Total Sales				20.25	19.85	20.63	20.23
• Operating margin (%)				15.05	(1.45)	4.42	0.81
National Operations							
Network Services							
• % of Total Sales	59.86	62.44	63.52				
• Operating margin (%)	31.59	32.54	28.69				
Wireless Products & Services							
• % of Total Sales	12.05	12.56	12.34				
• Operating margin (%)	21.07	14.95	18.30				
Data Products & Services							
• % of Total Sales	3.08	1.20					
• Operating margin (%)	(67.09)	(128.31)					
Other National Sales							
• % of Total Sales	12.32	11.38	11.30				
• Operating margin (%)	(13.96)	(1.62)	14.14				
International Operations							
• % of Total Sales	12.69	12.42	12.83				
• Operating margin (%)	22.70	24.65	26.22				

Note: GTE changed the way it reported results in 1995.
Source: Annual Reports.

EXHIBIT 12 NEC selected products, 1999

Computers and Industrial Electronic Systems
Auto electronic
Automated fingerprint
identification systems
CD-ROM drives
Colour plasma display panels
Hard disk drives
Laser equipment
Mainframe computers
Monitors
Optical disc players
Personal computers
Postal automation systems
Printers
Recognition control equipment
Semiconductor manufacturing equipment
Servers
Software
Supercomputers
Test and measurement systems
Video projectors
Workstations

Electronic Devices
Capacitors
Colour display and other tubes
Diodes
Electrical connectors
Gate arrays
Integrated circuits
Memory
Microcontrollers
Microprocessors

Optical semiconductor devices
Relays
Transistors

Communications Systems and Equipment
CATV systems
Cellular phones
Defence electronics systems
Digital switching equipment
Fibre-optic submarine cable systems
Fibre-optic transmission systems
Hubs
ISDN terminal adapters
Microwave communications systems
Mobile communications systems
Modems
Network management systems
Pagers
Radio navigation and radar equipment
Rocket guidance and control equipment
Routers
Satellite communications systems
Satellites
Teleconferencing systems
Television and radio broadcast
equipment
Video and studio equipment

Other
Lighting
Receivers
Televisions

Source: NEC 1999 Annual Report.

EXHIBIT 13 GTE selected products and services, 1999

Home and Family
Additional phone lines
Answering devices
Call waiting
Caller ID devices (displays)
Caller ID displays
Caller ID services
Calling services
Corded phones and accessories
Cordless phones
Digital subscriber lines
GTE calling card services
GTE DSL solutions
GTE easy savings plan
GTE international calling plan
GTE in-touch 800
GTE nationwide saver
GTE total call
GTE unlimited packages
Home and family
Internet services
Integrated services digital network
Long distance
Multi-line corded phones
Multi-line cordless phones
Novelty phones
Phone books
Phone lines
Phones and accessories
Prepaid calling cards
Send a text message
Single phone line
Single-line ISDN
Telephone answering devices
Telephone products for the hearing impaired

Video services/digital cable services
Voice mail
Wireless data
Wireless service

Business
Additional business lines
Business voice messaging
Cable TV advertising opportunities
Caller ID services
Calling services
CentraNet
Custom Networks
Dial-up access
DSL
Frame Relay
Full range of business phones and accessories
ISDN
LAN (ISDN) access
Long distance
Manage my account
Other Internet services
Outsourced e-mail
Platinum value plan
Single business lines
SmartPark services
SuperPages.com
Yellow pages advertising

Wireless
Coverage maps
Store locator
Wireless
Wireless data services
Wireless voice services

Source: GTE 1999 Annual Report

EXHIBIT 14   Worldwide electronic supplier ranking

	Computers* (1996) Sales in US$ billions		Telecommunications Equipment (1998) Sales in US$ billions		Semiconductors (1998) Sales in US$ billions	
1	IBM	36.0	Lucent	26.8	Intel	22.8
2	HP	19.0	Ericsson	23.2	NEC	8.1
3	Fujitsu	18.5	Motorola	20.6	Motorola	7.1
4	NEC	14.1	Alcatel	19.9	Toshiba	5.9
5	Compaq	13.5	Nortel	17.3	Texas Instruments	5.8
6	Toshiba	11.4	Siemens	16.3	Hitachi	4.6
7	Hitachi	11.3	Nokia	13.7	Samsung	4.6
8	Apple	10.2	NEC	11.7	Philips	4.4
9	DEC	6.1	Cisco	8.5	STM	3.8
10	Sun	5.3	IBM	6.1	Fujitsu	3.7

Note: * sales of personal computers, servers, large computers, and computer peripherals
Sources: Datamation, Dataquest, IDATE.

EXHIBIT 15 1997 Results, selected companies

	Sales (USD mil.)	Operating Income Before Dep'n (USD mil.)	Net Income (USD mil.)	Operating Margin Before Dep'n (%)	Pretax Profit Margin (%)	Net Profit Margin (%)	Return on Assets (%)	Return on Equity (%)
NEC	39,907	3,683	739	9.23	2.46	1.85	1.91	9.13
Toshiba	43,979	3,304	541	7.51	2.57	1.23	1.15	5.30
Fujitsu	36,318	4,037	372	11.12	3.26	1.02	0.98	3.91
Hitachi	68,735	6,780	735	9.86	3.09	1.04	0.89	2.69
GTE	23,260	9,497	2,794	40.83	20.10	12.01	6.63	34.76
AT&T	51,319	10,795	4,638	21.04	14.04	8.71	7.63	19.75
Ameritech	15,998	6,181	2,296	38.64	23.03	14.35	9.06	27.64
Bell Atlantic	30,368	12,889	2,455	42.44	13.12	8.08	4.55	19.20
Bellsouth	20,633	9,412	3,261	45.62	26.44	15.85	9.01	21.56
Bellsouth Tel.	15,418	7,592	2,314	49.24	23.97	15.07	10.00	27.24
PAC Bell	9,938	3,926	350	39.50	0.54	0.08	0.05	0.24
US West	11,479	2,776	1,374	24.18	21.16	11.97	7.75	31.46

Note: In addition to GTE and AT&T, the other US companies are RBOCs.
Source: Compustat.

EXHIBIT 16   Country data

Year Ended	USA		JAPAN			
	GDP Current Prices (USD billions)	GDP per capita in Current Prices (USD)	GDP Current Prices (Yen billions)	Average Annual Exchange Rate (Yen to USD)	GDP Current Prices (USD billions)	GDP per capita in Current Prices (USD)
1980	2,795	12,303	240,176	226.74	1,059	7,559
1981	3,131	13,646	257,963	220.54	1,170	8,287
1982	3,259	14,069	270,600	249.08	1,086	7,643
1983	3,535	15,120	281,767	237.51	1,186	8,289
1984	3,933	16,676	300,543	237.52	1,265	8,783
1985	4,213	17,707	320,419	238.54	1,343	9,266
1986	4,453	18,543	335,457	168.51	1,991	13,660
1987	4,742	19,574	349,759	144.62	2,418	16,516
1988	5,108	20,893	373,973	128.152	2,918	19,844
1989	5,489	21,989	399,998	137.96	2,899	19,639
1990	5,803	22,980	430,040	144.80	2,970	20,050
1991	5,986	23,420	458,299	134.54	3,406	22,906
1992	6,319	24,451	471,020	126.65	3,719	24,920
1993	6,642	25,410	475,381	111.18	4,276	28,557
1994	7,054	27,069	479,260	102.23	4,688	31,225
1995	7,400	28,135	483,219	94.06	5,137	34,129
1996	7,813	29,434	500,309	108.79	4,599	30,484
1997	8,301	30,984	507,851	121.00	4,197	27,755
1998	8,760	32,409	495,327	130.90	3,784	24,955
1999	9,222	33,800	499,042	114.93	4,342	28,524

Sources: Datastream, CEIC.

Harvard Business School

Case 2 **Honda A and B**

Honda A

The two decades from 1960 to 1980 witnessed a strategic reversal in the world motorcycle industry. By the end of that period, previously well-financed American competitors with seemingly impregnable market positions were faced with extinction. Although most consumers had an initial preference to purchase from them, these U.S. manufacturers had been dislodged by Japanese competitors and lost position despite technological shifts that could have been emulated as competition intensified.

The Japanese invasion of the world motorcycle market was spearheaded by the Honda Motor Company. Its founder, Sochiro Honda, a visionary inventor and industrialist, had been involved peripherally in the automotive industry prior to World War II. However, Japan's postwar devastation resulted in the downsizing of Honda's ambitions; motorcycles were a more technologically manageable and

Dr. Richard T. Pascale of Stanford Graduate School of Business prepared this case with the collaboration of Professor E. Tatum Christiansen of Harvard Business School as a basis for class discussion rather than to illustrate either effective or ineffective handling of an administrative situation.

Note: This case is based largely on the Harvard Business School's 'Note on the Motorcycle Industry – 1975' (No. 9-587-210) and on a published report of the Boston Consulting Group ('Strategy Alternatives for the British Motorcycle Industry'), 1975.

economically affordable product for the average Japanese. Reflecting Honda's commitment to a technologically based strategy, the Honda Technical Research Institute was established in 1946. This institute, dedicated to improvements in internal combustion engines, represented Honda's opening move in the motorcycle field. In 1947, Honda introduced its first A-type, 2-stroke engine.

As of 1948, Honda's Japanese competition consisted of 247 Japanese participants in a loosely defined motorcycle industry. Most competitors operated in ill-equipped job shops, adapting clip-on engines for bicycles. A few larger manufacturers endeavored to copy European motorcycles but were hampered by inferior technology and materials that resulted in unreliable products.

Honda expanded its presence in the fall of 1949, introducing a lightweight 50cc, 2-stroke, D-type motorcycle. Honda's engine at 3 hp was more reliable than most of its contemporaries' engines and had a superior stamped metal frame. This introduction coincided closely, however, with the introduction of a 4-stroke engine by several larger competitors. These engines were both quieter and more powerful than Honda's. Responding to this threat, Honda followed in 1951 with a superior 4-stroke design that doubled horsepower with no additional weight. Embarking on a bold campaign to exploit this advantage, Honda acquired a plant, and over the next two years it developed enough manufacturing expertise to become a fully integrated producer of engines, frames, chains, sprockets, and other ancillary parts crucial to motorcycle performance.

Motorcycle manufacturers in the Japanese industry tended to minimize risk by investing in one winning design and milking that product until it became technologically obsolescent. Beginning in the 1950s, Honda began to depart from this pattern – seeking simultaneously to (1) offer a multiproduct line, (2) take leadership in product innovation, and (3) exploit opportunities for economies of mass production by gearing designs to production objectives. Most notably, in 1958 Honda's market research identified a large, untapped market segment seeking a small, unintimidating motorcycle that could be used by small-motorcycle businesses for local deliveries. Honda designed a product specifically for this application: a step-through frame, automatic transmission, and one-hand controls that enabled drivers to handle the machine with one hand while carrying a package in the other. The 50cc Honda was an explosive success. Unit sales reached 3,000 per month after six months on the market. Deciding to make this the product of the future, Honda gambled, investing in a highly automated 30,000-unit-per-month manufacturing plant – a capacity 10 times in excess of demand at the time of construction.

Honda's bold moves set the stage for a yet bolder decision – to invade the U.S. market. The following section depicts the sequence of events as taken from a Harvard Business School case on the motorcycle industry.[1]

In 1959 ... Honda Motor Company ... entered the American market. The Japanese motorcycle industry had expanded rapidly since World War II to meet the need for cheap transportation. In 1959, Honda, Suzuki, Yamaha, and Kawasaki together produced some 450,000 motorcycles. With sales of $55 million in that year, Honda was already the world's largest motorcycle producer ...

In contrast to other foreign producers who relied on distributors, Honda established a U.S. subsidiary, American Honda Motor Company, and began its push in the U.S. market by offering very small lightweight motorcycles. The Honda machine had a three-speed transmission, an automatic clutch, five horsepower (compared with two and a half for the lightweight motorcycle then sold by Sears, Roebuck), an electric starter, and a step-through frame for female riders. Generally superior to the Sears lightweight and easier to handle, the Honda machines sold for less than $250 retail, compared with $1,000–$1,500 for the bigger American or British machines.

----

[1] D. Purkayastha and R. Buzzell, 'Note on the Motorcycle Industry – 1975,' HBS No. 9–578–210, pp. 5–7.

Honda followed a policy of developing the market region by region, beginning on the West Coast and moving eastward over a period of four to five years. In 1961 it lined up 125 dealers and spent $150,000 on regional advertising. Honda advertising represented a concerted effort to overcome the unsavory image of motorcyclists that had developed since the 1940s, given special prominence by the 1953 movie *The Wild Ones*, which starred Marlon Brando as the surly, destructive leader of a motorcycle gang. In contrast, Honda addressed its appeal primarily to middle-class consumers and claimed, 'You meet the nicest people on a Honda.' This marketing effort was backed by heavy advertising, and the other Japanese exporters also invested substantial sums: $1.5 million for Yamaha and $0.7 million for Suzuki.

Honda's strategy was phenomenally successful. Its U.S. sales rose from $500,000 in 1960 to $77 million in 1965. By 1966, Honda, Yamaha, and Suzuki together had 85% of the U.S. market. From a negligible position in 1960, lightweight motorcycles had come to dominate the market.

The transformation and expansion of the motorcycle market during the early 1960s benefited British and American producers as well as the Japanese. British exports doubled between 1960 and 1966, while Harley-Davidson's sales increased from $16.6 million in 1959 to $29.6 million in 1965. Two press reports of the mid 1960s illustrate these traditional manufacturers' interpretation of the Japanese success:

'The success of Honda, Suzuki, and Yamaha in the States has been jolly good for us,' Eric Turner, chairman of the board of BSA Ltd., told Advertising Age. 'People here start out by buying one of the low-priced Japanese jobs. They get to enjoy the fun and exhilaration of the open road and frequently end up buying one of our more powerful and expensive machines.' The British insist that they're not really in competition with the Japanese (they're on the lighter end). The Japanese have other ideas. Just two months ago Honda introduced a 444cc model to compete, at a lower price, with the Triumph 500cc. [Advertising Age, December 27, 1965]

'Basically we do not believe in the lightweight

market,' says William H. Davidson, son of one of the founders and currently president of the company (Harley-Davidson). 'We believe that motorcycles are sports vehicles, not transportation vehicles. Even if a man says he bought a motorcycle for transportation, it's generally for leisure time use. The lightweight motorcycle is only supplemental. Back around World War I, a number of companies came out with lightweight bikes. We came out with one ourselves. We came out with another one in 1947 and it just did not go anywhere. We have seen what happens to these small sizes.' [Forbes, *September 15, 1966*]

Meanwhile, the Japanese producers continued to grow in other export markets. In 1965, domestic sales represented only 59% of Honda's total of $316 million, down from 98% in 1959. Over the same period, production volume had increased almost five-fold, from 285,000 to 1.4 million units. In Europe, where the Japanese did not begin their thrust until the late 1960s, they had captured a commanding share of key markets by 1974.

In short, by the mid–1970s the Japanese producers had come to dominate a market shared by European and American producers 20 years earlier...

It was often said that Honda created the market for the recreational uses of motorcycles through its extensive advertising and promotional effort.

The company achieved a significant product advantage through a heavy commitment to R&D and advanced manufacturing techniques. Honda used its productivity-based cost advantage and R&D capability to introduce new models at prices below those of competitive machines. New products could be brought to market very quickly; the interval between conception and production was estimated to be only 18 months. Honda was also reported to have a 'cold storage' of designs that could be introduced if the market developed....

Since 1960, Honda had consistently outspent its competitors in advertising. It had also established the largest dealership network in the U.S. On average, Honda dealers were larger than their competitors. In new markets, Honda had been willing to take short-term losses in order to build up an adequate selling and distribution network.

In 1975, the Boston Consulting Group was retained by the British government to diagnose the British motorcycle industry and the factors contributing to its decline. The remainder of this case, reflecting on Honda's strategy, consists of excerpts from that report:[2]

The market approach of [Honda] has certain common features which, taken together, may be described as a 'marketing philosophy.' The fundamental feature of this philosophy is the emphasis it places on market share and sales volume. Objectives set in these terms are regarded as critical, and defended at all costs.

The whole thrust of the marketing program ... is towards maintaining or improving market share position.... We have seen some ways in which this goal is pursued. It is worth adding, as an example of how pervasive this objective is ... that in an interview with a Honda personnel director, we were told that the first question a prospective Honda dealer is asked is the level of his market share in his local area. 'I don't know why, but this company places an awful lot of emphasis on market share' was the comment.... We shall return to the reasons why market shares are critical for commercial success in the industry.

We were also told by representatives of [Honda] that their primary objectives are set in terms of sales volume rather than short-term profitability. Annual sales targets – based on market share penetration assumptions and market growth prospects – are set, and the main task of the sales company is to achieve these targets. The essence of this strategy is to grow sales volume at least as fast or faster than any of your competitors.

A number of more specific policies follow from this general philosophy, and our descriptions of each of the Japanese competitors provide ample examples of these policies:

1 Products are updated or redesigned whenever a market threat or opportunity is perceived.

2 Prices are set at levels designed to achieve market share targets and will be cut if necessary.

2 Boston Consulting Group, 'Strategy Alternatives for the British Motorcycle Industry,' Her Majesty's Stationery Office, London, 30 July 1975, pp. 16–17, 23, 39–43, 54–55.

3 Effective marketing systems are set up in all markets where serious competition is intended, regardless of short-term cost.

4 Plans and objectives look to long-term payoff.

The results of these policies for the Japanese competitors have, of course, been spectacularly successful. Over the last fifteen years, the rates of growth of the four major Japanese companies have been as shown in [Table A].

Table A Growth of Japanese production

	Production in 1959 (000 units)	Production in 1974 (000 units)	Average Annual Growth Rate (% p.a.)
Honda	285	2,133	14
Yamaha	64	1,165	21
Kawasaki	10	355	27
Suzuki	96	840	16

Source: Japan Automobile Industry Association

Selling and distribution systems. We have so far discussed market share as a function of the product features and prices of particular models. Market share across all cc classes is also influenced by what we shall call the selling and distribution system (s and d system). Within the s and d system we include all the activities of the marketing companies (or importers) in each national market:

◆ Sales representation at the dealer level

◆ Physical distribution of parts and machines

◆ Warranty and service support

◆ Dealer support

◆ Advertising and promotion

◆ Market planning and control.

We also include the effects of the dealer network established by the marketing companies:

◆ Numbers and quality of dealers

◆ Floor space devoted to the manufacturers' products

◆ Sales support by dealers.

The s and d system supports sales of the manufacturer across the whole model range, and its quality affects market shares in each cc class where the manufacturer is represented. **Table B** compares the s and d systems of the four full-line Japanese manufacturers in the USA, and shows that high market shares both overall *and* in each cc class go with high levels of expenditure on s and d and with extensive dealer networks.

The interaction between product-related variables and s- and d-related variables is complex. The better the product range in terms of comprehensiveness, features, and price, and the more sophisticated the s and d system of the sales company, the easier it will be to attract good dealers. This is because good products, which are well supported at the marketing company level, lead to good retail sales. Equally, good dealers themselves improve retail sales, and active competition between dealers can lead to retail discounting which acts as a volume-boosting price cut to the public. The manufacturers' products and s and d system therefore influence sales both directly, at retail, and proximately, through their effect on the dealer network.

In particular cc categories, each manufacturer's position is substantially influenced by its specific product offerings. For example, Kawasaki are strong in the 750cc-and over class due to the Z-1, and Yamaha have been weak due to its poor 750cc model. Outstanding products obtain market shares that are unusually high for a manufacturer, and weak products lead to atypically low market shares. For products of average attraction, however, market shares seem to move towards some equilibrium level. For each manufacturer, this level in the USA appears to be:

Honda	*40–50%*
Yamaha	*15–25%*
Kawasaki	*10–15%*
Suzuki	*9–12%*

As overall market leaders, the Japanese have dominated pricing in the motorcycle industry. It is therefore appropriate to begin this analysis by examining the extent to which the experience curve concept appears to explain the performance of the Japanese. Unfortunately, it is impossible directly to determine   unit   cost   performance   data   for competitors, since the data are not publicly available. Sources can be found, however, for unit price and production volume data. Over the long term, price behavior is a useful guide to movements in the underlying costs, and so an experience curve analysis on prices can be extremely revealing.

Japanese price performance. In **Figure A**, price experience curves are drawn for the Japanese motorcycle industry as a whole, based on aggregate data collected by MITI. These curves show price reduction performance of a consistent nature for each of the size ranges of motorcycle considered, the rate of price reduction being most rapid of all in the largest range, 126–250cc, which is following an experience curve slope of 76%. The other slopes are more shallow, at 81% and 88%, but there is no mistaking the fact that real prices are descending smoothly over time. These experience-based price reductions clearly go a long way towards explaining the historical competitive effectiveness of the Japanese in the marketplace in small and medium motorcycles.

For the purposes of strategy development ... it is

Table B The selling and distribution systems of Japanese companies in the U.S.A.

| | Estimated Total S&D Expenditure by Sales Company 1974 ($m) | Advertising Expenditure 1972 ($m) | Dealers 1974 | | 1974 % Share Total Market (units) | Lowest % Share of any cc Class | Highest % Share of any cc Class |
			Numbers	Units Sold per Dealer			
Honda	90–100	8.1	1,974	220	43	34	61
Yamaha	40–45	4.2	1,515	135	20	4	34
Kawasaki	30–35	2.2	1,018	127	13	9	19
Suzuki	25–30	3.0	1,103	98	11	5	16

Source: R.L.. Rolk, Motorcycle Dealer News, Ziff-Davis Market Research Dept., BCG estimates.

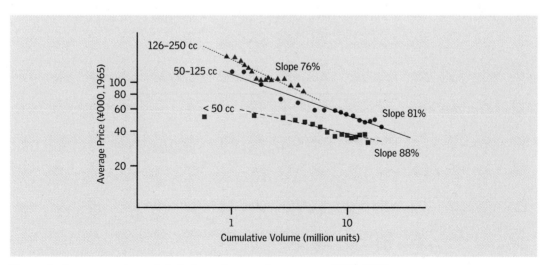

Figure A Japanese motorcycle industry: price experience curves, 1959–1974
Source: MITI

[helpful] to look more closely at price performance in the larger bike models. The Honda CB 750 has been the pacesetter in superbikes in terms of both market penetration and pricing. In **Figure B**, price experience curves are plotted for this product and for two other large Honda bikes. The prices of other Japanese manufacturers have been broadly comparable to Honda's in the equivalent size range (they usually tend if anything to price at a slight premium relative to Honda), so that we may use Honda as a good 'benchmark' for the Japanese competition in big bikes in general.

It is clear from **Figure B** that price performance in the large bikes has been consistent with that in small: real prices have declined along experience curve slopes in the region of 85%–87%. This has

also been true of the price in the United States, when converted into yen terms.

An interesting feature of the curves is that the prices in the United States are so much higher than [those] of the same products in Japan. As shown in **Table C**, the premiums are high across almost the entire range of bikes and are far larger than seems necessary, even allowing for the extra costs incurred for duty, freight, and packing in shipping bikes from Japan to the United States. This certainly suggests that there is no possibility that the Japanese are 'dumping' their products in the U.S. market: quite the reverse. Furthermore, it may well indicate that competitive though the Japanese have been in the United States, based on the downward trends in their real price levels over time, there may well be plenty of

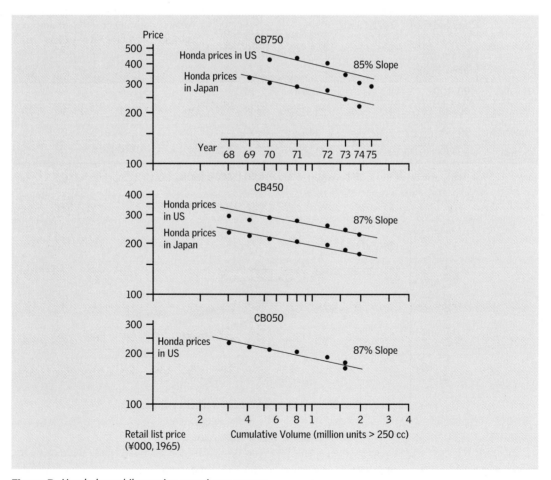

Figure B Honda large bikes: price experience curves

Table C Honda price premium, USA vs Japan

Premium on retail list prices, 1974				
Model	Japan Price		U.S. Price ($)	Premium
	¥000	$ Equiv.		
CB 750	395	1411	2024	43%
CB 550	355	1268	1732	37%
CB 450	303	1082	1471	36%
CB 360	253	904	1150	26%
CB 350	275	982	1363	39%
MT 250	218	779	965	24%
MT 125	158	564	743	32%
CB 125	166	593	640	8%

Premium allowing for freight, duty and packing

CB 750, U.S. retail price 1975 = $2112
 Price to dealer $1584 (75% of 2112)
 Price to distributor $1373 (65%)

 Japan list price   ¥440,000 or
           $1517 (equivalent)
 Price to distributor $ 986 (65%)
 Ocean freight to LA   60
 Duty   63 (3% U.S. Retail Price)
 Packaging costs   40
          $ 163

Thus, indicated price to U.S. distributor for equal manufacturer's margin to that on bikes sold in Japan
      = $ 986 + 163
      $1149

Thus, premium in U.S.A. even after allowing for freight, duty and packing
      = (1373/1149 − 1) × 100
      = 20%

Note: The versions of the smaller bike models shipped to the States may be slightly more expensive than their Japanese equivalents (extra lighting, etc.). The versions of the larger bikes are, however, reported to be identical in both markets.

scope for them to be even more competitive in the future if seriously challenged in that market. They could simply reduce their margins on exports to the United States to levels more in line with those enjoyed in their domestic business.

Japanese cost performance. The implication of the downward trends in real prices for the Japanese is, of course, that there have been underlying experience-based cost reductions: that the decline has not been accounted for simply by a reduction in margins. ... However, the major Japanese manufacturers have been continuously profitable, and this suggests that cost reductions have indeed taken place in parallel with real price reductions. On the other hand, all the Japanese motorcycle manufacturers also make a significant proportion of products other than motorcycles (in 1974 about 35% of Honda's turnover, and about 40% of Suzuki's, was accounted for by cars; of Yamaha Motor's turnover about 40% was in products such as boats and snowmobiles). It is, perhaps, reasonable to question whether these products are sufficiently profitable to 'subsidize' the motorcycle business.

... It seems clear that ... none of [the three major Japanese] manufacturers is subsidizing the motorcycle business from other businesses. Indeed, Honda was actually losing money in its car business in 1974, which suggests that their motorcycle business that year may have shown returns of the order of 20% (BIT) compared with the 12.4% return earned by the company overall. The overall inference from this profit performance must be that each manufacturer has indeed achieved an experience curve effect on costs in parallel with those achieved on price. The existence of this experience curve effect in the motorcycle industry has important strategy implications.

Competitive strategy implications

As we have discussed, failure to achieve a cost position – and hence cost reductions over time–equivalent to your competitors' will result in commercial vulnerability. At some point your competitors will start setting prices which you cannot match profitably, and losses will ensue. The strategic importance of the experience curve is that it explains clearly the two possible long-term causes of uncompetitive costs:

- ◆ Relative growth: failure to grow as rapidly as competitors, thereby progressing more slowly than them along the experience curve.

- ◆ Relative slopes: failure to bring costs down the characteristic experience curve slope achieved by competitors. ...

Summary

From the perspective of the writers of the BCG study, a fundamental cause for the Japanese success was their high productivity. The motorcycle industry was exhibiting the effects that differences in growth rates, volume, and level of capital investment among competitors can have on relative costs. The high rates of growth and levels of production achieved by the Japanese manufacturers resulted in their superior productivity. In terms of value added per employee, Honda outperformed Western competitors by as much as four times. Even the smaller Japanese competitors were able to out perform their Western counterparts by a factor of two or three.

The BCG report also countered the common argument that the relatively inexpensive Japanese labor was the primary source of competitive advantage. The Japanese competitors in fact had higher labor costs than companies in the West. Their relative high growth and scale caused total costs to drop quickly enough to support regular pay increases and price decreases at the same time.

Essentially the argument presented by BCG was that the Japanese emphasis on market share as the primary objective led to high production volume, improved productivity, low costs, and in the long term to higher profitability than their competitors.

Harvard Business School

Honda (B)

Sochiro Honda, an inventive genius with a legendary ego, founded the Honda Motor Co., Ltd., in 1948. His exploits have received wide coverage in the Japanese press. Known for his mercurial temperament and bouts of 'philandering,'[1] he is variously reported to have tossed a geisha out a second-story window,[2] climbed inside a septic tank to retrieve a visiting supplier's false teeth (and subsequently placed the teeth in his own mouth),[3] appeared inebriated and in costume before a formal presentation to Honda's bankers requesting financing vital to the firm's survival (the loan was denied),[4] hit a worker on the head with a wrench,[5] and stripped naked before his engineers to assemble a motorcycle engine.[6]

Dr. Richard T. Pascale of Stanford Graduate School of Business wrote this case with the collaboration of Professor E. Tatum Christiansen of Harvard Business School as the basis for class discussion rather than to illustrate either effective or ineffective handling of an administrative situation. It is based largely on internal Honda sources and interviews with founders of Honda Motor Co., Ltd., and the Japanese management team that founded Honda of America.

[1] Sakiya, Tetsuo. 'The Story of Honda's Founders,' *Asahi Evening News,* June 1–August 29, 1979, Series #2 and #3.
[2] Interviews with Honda executives, Tokyo, Japan, July 1980.
[3] Sakiya, Tetsuo. *Honda Motor: The Men, The Management, The Machines,* Kadonsha International. Tokyo, Japan, 1982, p 69; also Sakiya, 'Honda's Founders,' Series #4.
[4] Sakiya, 'Honda's Founders,' Series #7 and #8.
[5] Sakiya, *Honda Motor,* p. 72.
[6] Sakiya, 'Honda's Founders,' Series #2.

Company background

Postwar Japan was in desperate need of transportation. Motorcycle manufacturers proliferated, producing clip-on engines that converted bicycles into makeshift 'mopeds.' Sochiro Honda was among these, but his prior experience as an automotive repairman provided neither the financial, managerial, nor technical basis for a viable enterprise.

Sochiro Honda viewed 'technology' as the vehicle through which Japanese society could be restored and the world made a better place in which to live. Reflecting the intensity of this commitment, he established the Honda Technical Research Institute in 1946. The term institute was somewhat misleading, since the organization was composed of himself and a few associates and had no practical means of support. Under this organizational umbrella, he began to tinker, and, as a means of livelihood, he purchased 500 war surplus engines and retrofitted them for bicycle use. Lacking marketing know-how, he entered into an exclusive arrangement with a distributor, who packaged a motorcycle conversion kit for bicycles. The Honda Motor Company was formed. Further tinkering led, in turn, to the introduction of the 'A-design' – a 2-stroke, 50cc engine. The engine had numerous defects, and sales did not materialize. Scraping by on occasional orders, the company lost money in 1947 and grossed $55,000 in 1948.

In 1949, Sochiro Honda turned to friends. Raising $3,800, he developed and introduced the 2-stroke, D-type engine. This engine, generating 3 hp, was more reliable than most on the market and enjoyed a brief spurt of popularity. Recruiting a work force of 70 employees, Honda produced engines one at a time and approached an annualized production rate of 100 units per month by the end of 1949.

Success was short-lived, however. Honda's exclusive distributor elected to artificially limit sales to 80 units per month in order to maintain high margins. Sochiro Honda was irate and vowed to avoid such dependencies in the future. In late 1949 he set out to raise additional financing but suffered a second setback when competitors leapfrogged the 2-stroke design and introduced quieter and more powerful 4-stroke engines.

A classic dilemma now faced the struggling enterprise. Honda's engine was obsolete, and his distribution system held him at ransom. Without additional financing he could not correct these deficiencies, and banks and investors did not regard him as a sound management risk.

In late 1949, an intermediary urged him to accept a partner – Takeo Fujisawa. Fujisawa was prepared to invest 2 million yen (about $7,500). More important, Fujisawa brought financial expertise and marketing strengths.

Despite Fujisawa's presence, the firm continued to falter. No further capital could be raised in 1950. Fujisawa pressed his partner to quit tinkering with his noisy 2-stroke engine and join the industry leaders with a 4-stroke design, since it was clear that competition had threatened Honda with extinction. At first too proud to accept this counsel, in 1951 he unexpectedly unveiled a breakthrough design that doubled horsepower over competitive 4-stroke engines. With this innovation, the firm was off and putting, and by 1952 demand was brisk.[7]

Honda's superior 4-stroke engine enabled Fujisawa to raise $88,000 in 1952. With these funds, Fujisawa committed to reduce dependency on suppliers and distributors by becoming a full-scale motorcycle manufacturer. To forestall technological obsolescence, he encouraged Honda to stay abreast of technological developments. He also sought more flexible channels of distribution. Unfortunately, Honda was a relatively late entrant; the best Fujisawa could do was to arrange for several distributors to carry Honda as a secondary line. He compensated for weak product positioning by going directly to the consumer with advertising.

In late 1952 a sewing machine plant was purchased and converted to a crude motorcycle factory. Neither partner had managerial or manufacturing experience, and there was no real plan other than to work as long as necessary each day to keep up with orders. Honda's more powerful engine and superior stamped motorcycle frame created considerable interest, and demand remained strong. Employment leaped from 150 in 1951 to 1,337 by the end of 1952. Honda integrated into the production of chains, sprockets, and motorcycle frames. Altogether, these factors greatly complicated the management task. There were no standardized drawings, procedures, or tools. For several years the plant was, in effect, a collection of semi-independent 'activities' sharing the same roof. Nonetheless, by the beginning of 1959 Honda had become a significant participant in the industry, with 23% market share (see **Exhibit 1**).

Honda's successful 4-stroke engine eased the pressures on Fujisawa by increasing sales and providing easier access to financing. For Sochiro Honda, the higher-horsepower engine opened the possibility of pursuing one of his central ambitions in life: to build and to race a high-performance, special-purpose motorcycle – and win. Winning provided the ultimate confirmation of his design abilities. Racing success in Japan came quickly. As a result, in 1959 he raised his sights to the international arena and committed the firm to winning at Great Britain's Isle of Man – the 'Olympics' of motorcycle racing.[8] Again, Honda's inventive genius was called into play. Shifting most of the firm's resources into this racing effort, he embarked on studies of combustion that resulted in a new configuration of the combustion chamber, which doubled horsepower and halved weight. Honda leapfrogged past European and American competitors – winning in one class, then another, winning the Isle of Man manufacturer's prize in 1959, and sweeping the first five positions by 1961.[9]

Throughout the 1950s, Fujisawa sought to turn his partner's attention from enthusiasm with racing to the more mundane requirements of running an enterprise. By 1956, as the innovations gained from racing had begun to pay off in vastly more efficient engines, Fujisawa pressed Honda to adapt this technology for a commercial motorcycle.[10] He had a particular segment in mind. Most motorcyclists in Japan were male, and the machines were used

[7] Sakiya, *Honda Motor*, pp. 71–72.

[8] Sakiya, 'Honda's Founders,' Series #11.
[9] Ibid.
[10] Ibid., Series #13; also Sakiya, *Honda Motor*, p. 117.

primarily as an alternative form of transportation to trains and buses. However, a vast number of small commercial establishments in Japan still delivered goods and ran errands on bicycles. Trains and buses were inconvenient for these activities. The purse strings of these small enterprises were controlled by the Japanese wife – who resisted buying conventional motorcycles because they were expensive, dangerous, and hard to handle. Fujisawa challenged his partner: Can you use what you've learned from racing to come up with an inexpensive, safe-looking motorcycle that can be driven with one hand (to enable carrying packages)?[11]

The first breakthrough

In 1958 the Honda 50cc Supercub was introduced – with an automatic clutch, 3-speed transmission, automatic starter, and the safe, friendly look of a bicycle (without the stigma of the outmoded mopeds). As a rule of thumb, a 50cc engine is 50% cheaper to make than a 100cc engine. Achieving high horsepower with a small engine thereby reaps automatic cost savings – making the new bike affordable. Innovative design provided a cost advantage without requiring Honda to manufacture more efficiently than its competitors. (This was fortunate since the firm, having expanded into three plants in the 1950s, had still not achieved a well-integrated production process.)

Overnight, Honda was overwhelmed with Supercub orders. Demand was met through makeshift, high-cost, company-owned assembly and farmed-out assembly through subcontractors.[12] By the end of 1959 Honda had skyrocketed into first place among Japanese motorcycle manufacturers. Of its total sales that year of 285,000 units, 168,000 were Supercubs.[13] The time seemed appropriate to build an automated plant with a 30,000-unit-per-month capacity. 'It wasn't a speculative investment,' recalls one executive. 'We had the proprietary technology, we had the market, and the

demand was enormous.'[14] The plant was completed in mid-1960.

Distribution channels

Fujisawa utilized the Supercub to restructure Honda's channels of distribution. For many years, Honda had rankled under the two-tier distribution system that prevailed in the industry. As noted earlier, these problems had been exacerbated by Honda's being carried as a secondary line by distributors whose loyalties lay with older, established manufacturers. Further weakening Honda's leverage, all manufacturer sales were on a consignment basis.

Fujisawa had characterized the Supercub to Honda's distributors as 'something much more like a bicycle than a motorcycle.' The traditional channels, to their later regret, agreed. Under amicable terms, Fujisawa began selling the Supercub directly to retailers – and primarily through bicycle shops. Since these shops were small and numerous (approximately 12,000 in Japan), sales on consignment were unthinkable. A cash-on-delivery system was installed – giving Honda significantly more leverage over its dealerships than the other motorcycle manufacturers enjoyed.[15]

Honda enters U.S. market

Sochiro Honda's racing conquests in the late 1950s had given substance to his convictions about his abilities. Success fueled his appetite for new and different challenges. Explosive sales of the Supercub in Japan provided the financial base for new quests. The stage was now set for the exploration of the U.S. market.

From the Japanese vantage point, the American market was vast, untapped, and affluent. 'We turned toward the United States by a process of deduction,' states one executive. 'Our experiments with local Southeast Asian markets in 1957 and 1958 had little success. With little disposable income and poor roads, total Asian exports had reached a meager 1,000 units in 1958.[16] The European market,

[11] Sakiya, 'Honda's Founders,' Series #11.

[12] Pascale, Richard T., Interviews with Honda executives, Tokyo, Japan, September 10, 1982.

[13] Data provided by Honda Motor Company.

[14] Pascale interviews.

[15] Ibid.

[16] Ibid.

while larger, was heavily dominated by its own name-brand manufacturers, and the popular mopeds dominated the low-price, low-horsepower end.'

Two Honda executives – the designated president of American Honda Motor Company, Kihachiro Kawashima, and his assistant – arrived in the United States in late 1958. Their itinerary: San Francisco, Los Angeles, Dallas, New York, and Columbus. Kihachiro Kawashima recounts his impressions:[17]

> My first reaction after traveling across the United States was 'How could we have been so stupid to start a war with such a vast and wealthy country!' My second reaction was discomfort. I spoke poor English. We dropped in on motorcycle dealers who treated us discourteously and, in addition, gave the general impression of being motorcycle enthusiasts who, secondarily, were in business. There were only 3,000 motorcycle dealers in the United States at the time, and only 1,000 of them were open five days a week. The remainder were open on nights and on weekends. Inventory was poor, manufacturers sold motorcycles to dealers on consignment, the retailers provided consumer financing, and after-sale service was poor. It was discouraging.

> My other impression was that everyone in the United States drove an automobile – making it doubtful that motorcycles could ever do very well in the market. However, with 450,000 motorcycle registrations in the United States and 60,000 motorcycles imported from Europe each year it didn't seem unreasonable to shoot for 10% of the import market. I returned to Japan with that report.

> In truth, we had no strategy other than the idea of seeing if we could sell something in the United States. It was a new frontier, a new challenge, and it fit the 'success against all odds' culture that Mr. Honda had cultivated: I reported my impressions to Fujisawa – including the seat-of-the-pants target of trying, over several years, to attain a 10% share of the U.S. imports. He didn't probe that target quantitatively. We did not discuss profits or deadlines for breakeven. Fujisawa told me if anyone could

succeed, I could, and authorized $1 million for the venture.

> The next hurdle was to obtain a currency allocation from the Ministry of Finance. They were extraordinarily skeptical. Toyota had launched the Toyopet in the United States in 1958 and had failed miserably. 'How could Honda succeed?' they asked. Months went by. We put the project on hold. Suddenly, five months after our application, we were given the go-ahead – but at only a fraction of our expected level of commitment. 'You can invest $250,000 in the U.S. market,' they said, 'but only $110,000 in cash.' The remainder of our assets had to be in parts and motorcycle inventory.

> We moved into frantic activity as the government, hoping we would give up on the idea, continued to hold us to the July 1959 start-up timetable. Our focus, as mentioned earlier, was to compete with the European exports. We knew our products at the time were good, but not far superior. Mr. Honda was especially confident of the 250cc and the 305cc machines. The shape of the handlebar on these larger machines looked like the eyebrow of Buddha, which he felt was a strong selling point. Thus, after some discussion and with no compelling criteria for selection, we configured our start-up inventory with 25% of each of our four products – the 50cc Supercub and the 125cc, 250cc, and 305cc machines. In dollar-value terms, of course, the inventory was heavily weighted toward the larger bikes.

> The stringent monetary controls of the Japanese government together with the unfriendly reception we had received during our 1958 visit caused us to start small. We chose Los Angeles where there was a large second- and third-generation Japanese community, a climate suitable for motorcycle use, and a growing population. We were so strapped for cash that the three of us shared a furnished apartment that rented for $80 per month. Two of us slept on the floor. We obtained a warehouse in a run-down section of the city and waited for the ship to arrive. Not daring to spare our funds for equipment, the three of us stacked the motorcycle crates three-high, by hand; swept the floor; and built and maintained the parts bin.

---

[17] Ibid.

We were entirely in the dark the first year. We were not aware that the motorcycle business in the United States occurs during a seasonable April-to-August window – and that our timing coincided with the closing of the 1959 season. Our hard-learned experiences with distributorship in Japan convinced us to try to go to the retailers direct. We ran ads in the motorcycle trade magazine for dealers. A few responded. By spring 1960, we had 40 dealers and some of our inventory in their stores – mostly larger bikes. A few of the 250cc and 305cc bikes began to sell. Then disaster struck.

By the first week of April 1960, reports were coming in that our machines were leaking oil and encountering clutch failure. This was our lowest moment. Honda's fragile reputation was being destroyed before it could be established. As it turned out, motorcycles in the United States are driven much farther and much faster than in Japan. We dug deeply into our precious cash reserves to air freight our motorcycles to the Honda testing lab in Japan. Throughout the dark month of April, Pan Am was the only enterprise in the United States that was nice to us. Our testing lab worked 24-hour days bench testing the bikes to try to replicate the failure. Within a month, a redesigned head gasket and clutch spring solved the problem. In the meantime, events had taken a surprising turn.

Throughout our first eight months, following Mr. Honda's and our own instincts, we had not attempted to move the 50cc Supercubs. While they were a smash success in Japan (and manufacturing couldn't keep up with demand there), they seemed wholly unsuitable for the U.S. market where everything was bigger and more luxurious. As a clincher, we had our sights on the import market – and the Europeans, like the American manufacturers, emphasized the larger machines.

We used the Honda 50s ourselves to ride around Los Angeles on errands. They attracted a lot of attention. One day we had a call from a Sears buyer. While persisting in our refusal to sell through an intermediary, we took note of Sears's interest. But we still hesitated to push the 50cc bikes out of fear they might harm our

image in a heavily macho market. But when the larger bikes started breaking, we had no choice. We let the 50cc bikes move. And surprisingly, the retailers who wanted to sell them weren't motorcycle dealers; they were sporting goods stores.

The excitement created by Honda Supercub began to gain momentum. Under restrictions from the Japanese government, we were still on a cash basis. Working with our initial cash and inventory, we sold machines, reinvested in inventory, and sunk the profits into additional inventory and advertising. Our advertising tried to straddle the market. While retailers continued to inform us that our Supercub customers were normal everyday Americans, we hesitated to target toward this segment out of fear of alienating the high-margin end of our business – sold through the traditional motorcycle dealers to a more traditional 'black leather jacket' customer.

An advertising twist

As late as 1963, Honda was still working with its original Los Angeles advertising agency, its ad campaigns straddling all customers so as not to antagonize one market in pursuit of another.

In the spring of 1963, while fulfilling a routine class assignment, an undergraduate advertising major at UCLA submitted an ad campaign for Honda. Its theme was 'You Meet the Nicest People On a Honda.' Encouraged by his instructor, the student passed his work on to a friend at Grey Advertising. Grey had been soliciting the Honda account – which, with a $5-million-a-year budget, was becoming an attractive potential client. Grey purchased the student's idea – on a tightly kept nondisclosure basis. Grey attempted to sell the idea to Honda.[18]

Interestingly, the Honda management team, which by 1963 had grown to five Japanese executives, was badly split on this advertising decision. The president and treasurer favored another proposal from another agency. The director of sales, however, felt strongly that the Nicest People campaign was the right one – and his commitment eventually held sway. Thus, in 1963, Honda adopted a strategy that

---

[18] Ibid.

directly identified and targeted that large, untapped segment of the marketplace that was to become inseparable from the Honda legend.[19]

The Nicest People campaign drove Honda's U.S. sales at an even greater rate. By 1964 nearly one out of every two motorcycles sold was a Honda. As a result of the influx of medium-income leisure-class consumers, banks and other consumer credit companies began to finance motorcycles – shifting away from dealer credit, which had been the traditional purchasing mechanism available. Honda, seizing the opportunity of soaring demand for its products, took a courageous and seemingly risky position. Late in 1964 it announced that thereafter, it would cease to ship on a consignment basis but would require cash on delivery. Honda braced itself for a revolt that never materialized. While nearly every dealer questioned, appealed, or complained, none relinquished the Honda franchise. In one fell swoop, Honda shifted the power relationship from the dealer to the manufacturer. Within three years, C.O.D. sales would become the pattern for the industry.[20]

Honda's growth on several dimensions is shown in Exhibit 2. Automobiles were introduced into the product line in 1963, shifting resources and management attention heavily in that direction in the ensuing years.

25 years later

In late 1972, anticipating the company's twenty-fifth anniversary, Fujisawa, 62, raised the issue of retirement. 'We are strong dominating individuals,' he said. 'I must step aside and let the younger men lead our company.' Sochiro Honda, 66, also conceded to retire. In September 1973, the two stepped down. States one source: 'Fujisawa retired early to provide Mr. Honda with an opportunity to retire, also. It is a reflection of Fujisawa's genuine personal friendship with Mr. Honda.'[21]

[19] Ibid.

[20] Ibid.

[21] Sakiya, Tetsuo. 'The Story of Honda's Founders,' *Asahi Evening News,* August 29, 1979.

Exhibit 1 Motorcycle production in Japan by Japanese makers

Calendar Year	Honda	Yamaha	Suzuki	Kawasaki	Other	Total
1950	531	–	–	–	6,960	7,491
1951	2,380	–	–	–	21,773	24,153
1952	9,659	–	–	–	69,586	79,245
1953	29,797	–	–	–	131,632	161,429
1954	30,344	–	–	200	133,929	164,473
1955	42,557	2,272	9,079	–	205,487	259,395
1956	55,031	8,743	18,444	5,083	245,459	332,760
1957	77,509	15,811	29,132	6,793	280,819	410,064
1958	117,375	27,184	66,363	7,018	283,392	501,332
1959	285,218	63,657	95,862	10,104	425,788	880,629
1960	649,243	138,153	155,445	9,261	520,982	1,473,084
1961	935,859	129,079	186,392	22,038	531,003	1,804,371
1962	1,009,787	117,908	173,121	31,718	342,391	1,674,925
1963	1,224,695	167,370	271,438	34,954	229,513	1,927,970
1964	1,353,594	221,655	373,871	33,040	128,175	2,110,335
1965	1,465,762	244,058	341,367	48,745	112,852	2,212,784
1966	1,422,949	389,756	448,128	67,959	118,599	2,447,391
1967	1,276,226	406,579	402,438	79,194	77,410	2,241,847
1968	1,349,896	423,039	365,330	78,124	34,946	2,251,335
1969	1,534,882	519,710	398,784	102,406	21,091	2,576,873
1970	1,795,828	574,100	407,538	149,480	20,726	2,947,672
1971	1,927,186	750,510	491,064	208,904	22,838	3,400,502
1972	1,873,893	853,317	594,922	218,058	25,056	3,565,246
1973	1,835,527	1,012,810	641,779	250,099	22,912	3,763,127
1974	2,132,902	1,164,886	839,741	354,615	17,276	4,509,420
1975	1,782,448	1,030,541	686,666	274,022	28,870	3,802,547
1976	1,928,576	1,169,175	831,941	284,478	20,942	4,235,112
1977	2,378,867	1,824,152	1,031,753	335,112	7,475	5,577,359
1978	2,639,588	1,887,311	1,144,488	326,317	2,225	5,999,929
1979	2,437,057	1,653,891	1,100,778	308,191	79	5,499,996
1980	3,087,471	2,241,959	1,551,127	521,846	–	7,402,403
1981	3,587,957	2,792,817	1,764,120	521,333	–	8,666,227

Source: Japan Automobile Manufacturers Association, Inc.
Note: KD sets and scooters are included.

Exhibit 2 Honda's financial performance and U.S. motorcycle sales

Calendar Year	Gross Sales (million yen)	Honda U.S. Motorcycle Sales (units)	Outside Financing (million yen)	Employees
1948	14.3	–	1	20
1949	34.6	–	2	70
1950	82.8	–	–	90
1951	330.3	–	–	150
1952	2,438	–	15	1,337
1953	7,729	–	60	2,185
1954	5,979	–	–	2,494
1955	5,525	–	120	2,459
1956	7,882	–	–	2,377
1957	9,786	–	360	2,438
1958	14,188	–	720	2,705
1959	26,165	–	1,440	3,355
1960	49,128	1,315	4,320	4,053
1961	57,912	6,052	8,640	5,406
1962	64,552	27,840	9,090	5,798
1963	83,206	65,869	–	6,816
1964	97,936	110,470	–	7,696
1965	123,746	227,308	–	8,481
1966	106,845	272,900	–	9,069
1967	141,179	181,200	–	11,283
1968	193,871	174,706	18,180	13,165
1969	244,895	272,600	–	16,614
1970	316,331	441,200	–	17,511
1971	332,931	656,800	–	18,079
1972	327,702	707,800	–	18,297
1973	366,777	556,300	19,480	18,287
1974	519,897	628,500	24,350	18,455
1975	563,805	343,900	–	18,505
1976	668,677	444,624	25,500	19,069
1977	849,635	439,822	29,600	19,968
1978	922,280	401,114	–	21,316

Note: Above figures are related solely to Honda Motor Co.. Ltd., and are not consolidated with those of its subsidiaries.

Harvard Business School

Case 3 Phil Knight Managing NIKE's Transformation

Woodell as president

After appointing Woodell as president, Knight worked on manufacturing projects in China, and was effectively incommunicado; thereafter he continued to be absent for long periods of time. Typically, Woodell spoke to him about once every two weeks. Woodell tried to run the company as he thought Knight had intended and 'to get done the things that needed to get done.' In his first six months, he focused on NIKE's brand softness, the inventory problem, making sure he had the right people in areas like marketing and sales, and 'dealing with the fact that our founder and our leader was not present. It would have been a real trap to try to copy Phil. Historically, we've had a tendency to go to Knight for decisions. My style is to build the organization so people out there make the decisions.'

Woodell continued to work with the old NIKE management team, and relied extensively on the two other Gang of Four members: Rob Strasser for

marketing and Del Hayes for manufacturing operations. Woodell recalled:

> My approach was to try to identify the issues and get them under control one piece at a time. There may be been other approaches. Knight's approach, quite often, might have been more to 'shake things up.' As founder and CEO, he could do that. A new president and COO couldn't do it that way.

Woodell added that the difficulty of this transition from peer to leader was compounded by the tough business environment, as he, Strasser, and Hayes began to realize that the company's business problems were larger and more deeply rooted than the management team had recognized before Woodell's appointment.

Changing market forces

During fiscal year 1984, growth slowed in the running shoe market, NIKE's core business. As the decade-long running boom diminished, a general fitness boom arose to include other sports. Niche segments like aerobics began to mushroom in 1982. Reebok expanded the market by designing and styling two aerobics shoes specifically for women. Launched in 1982, the 'Energizer' (made of nylon and suede) and the 'Freestyle' (made of garment leather) lifted Reebok's sales from $13 million in 1983 to $66 million in 1984. While the soft garment leather was comfortable and required no break-in period, it also wore out quickly. Still, many consumers preferred comfortable Reeboks – with holes – to durable NIKES.

At Knight's urging, NIKE had produced a prototype aerobics shoe in 1983. The factories in Korea felt, however, that the leather was too thin and would wear out too quickly; it was 'simply unsuitable' for a NIKE product. Furthermore, women employees – who had urged the company to produce an aerobics shoe – thought the prototype profoundly ugly. They did not even want to try it on. And while NIKE shoes were still selling well, even without an aerobics line, Harry Carsh, a senior executive who had joined the company in 1983, suggested another reason behind NIKE's delay – arrogance:

> We could still be purists and talk about shoes that were for runners and athletes. And anybody who didn't make it the way we made it was a fool. We also had the idea that everything we sold, even though we were selling a lot of garbage, was used by an athlete to perform, which was absolute bull.

Reebok's sales exploded as the first-mover into the aerobics segment. By the end of 1983, Nike management realized that Reebok posed a serious threat, but they could not push the company to get a good product to market fast enough to prevent the upstart from reaching a critical mass. Woodell had Hayes visit Exeter to expedite product development. By that time, the Exeter facility had grown into a fairly complex operation. Hayes targeted 10 of the more than 300 shoes that were under development there and introduced 'critical path' procedures for getting select shoes to market quickly.

Inventory problems

The shoe inventory buildup that had first attracted management's attention in late 1982 began to snowball in 1983 and 1984. Just months after receiving its largest Futures order in August 1982 for November 1982 delivery, the market changed. The problem became apparent in March 1983, and by the end of the fiscal year on May 31, 1983, inventories had reached 21 million pairs.

Director of production, Ron Nelson, who coordinated Futures orders with orders to factories, was reluctant to cut factory orders at that time for two reasons. First, he wanted to protect the relationships that NIKE had carefully cultivated with new shoe suppliers so as to reduce its dependence on increasingly expensive Korean sources. He estimated that through the end of calendar year 1982, NIKE ordered about 6 million pairs of shoes for which it had no orders, simply to build up capacity with non-Korean factories. 'We knew we were ordering extras,' said Nelson, 'so we ordered models that we *thought* were safe. Second, Nelson was optimistic

that the product really was still popular, and he anticipated fill-in orders from international operations to take up some of the slack. International orders had grown more than 115% between 1982 and 1983, and seemed a better prospect for growth than domestic orders. Indeed, although international accounted for only 20% of sales, international Futures orders for delivery during the first half of 1983 had grown 1.1 million pairs over the same period in 1982, while domestic Futures orders had grown only 0.6 million pairs. In anticipation of these international orders, NIKE over-built about 2 million pairs per month between January and March 1983 (for delivery three months later).

Woodell saw the growing inventory as 'a cancer that was going to eat us alive,' but was constrained because much of it was tough-to-sell 'athleisure' shoes and apparel. He was also aware that many people within NIKE – including Knight – had strong personal ties to manufacturers in Asia and were reluctant to cut factory orders. Woodell found it frustrating to steer the course between building up even more inventory and 'pissing too many people off:'

> My approach was, let's do what we can and work with what we've got, and that's the best we can do. And that's what we were doing for six months. But every time you told people you had to cut these orders back more, somebody would say, we can't do that because we've worked with these people and Knight's got these personal relationships. My frustration was, we're having trouble doing this crap [cutting factory orders] because everybody has got a reason why we can't do it and the only guy that can do it [Knight] is tough to get a hold of.

Restoring the brand magic

Woodell and his management team decided to focus on restoring some of the 'magic' to NIKE's brand image by asking Rob Strasser to develop and implement a new strategy and implement it. In 1983, Strasser and a small group targeted the 1984 summer Olympics in Los Angeles for a major publicity blitz 'to light the second stage of NIKE's rocket.' Woodell and Strasser believed that a successful advertising campaign would breathe some life into the NIKE brand and give the company some of the time it needed to develop a new product line, requiring about 18 months.

The campaign that began in Los Angeles with a slew of visual advertisements was expanded to include 10 major metropolitan areas. This 'Cities Campaign' featured colorful, oversized, 'outrageous' murals and billboards of well known athletes – some in sweaty contemplation, some performing great athletic feats. John McEnroe, many times the U.S. Open and Wimbledon tennis champion, appeared on the side of New York buildings wearing street clothes and looking like a hometown boy – wearing NIKEs. The murals contained no text, nor did they attempt to sell specific shoes; instead, they simply established a link in the consumer's mind between the athletes and NIKE. The campaign included promotions for Olympic athletes.

In the games themselves, 58 NIKE-supported athletes won 65 medals. One senior marketing manager, who had been working on the Olympics promotions and the Cities Campaign at the time, said:

When you asked who the host of this Olympic Games was, people said NIKE. Converse had paid $5 million for the right to be the official shoe of the Olympics. Well, nobody wore Converse. I don't think we saw one pair of Converse out there [in track and field events].

The campaign received critical acclaim for its creativity, and the marketing department saw it as a great success. The finance department was less impressed, however, seeing no improvement in the inventory situation following the effort. The marketing manager acknowledged, 'We recognized after the '84 Olympics that having the most gold medals was great for our image, but did nothing for our shoe sales, which kept going down. We thought we were missing something.' (See **Exhibit 1** for quarterly financial data.)

'Loading the wagon' with apparel

Woodell, who had been in charge of NIKE's apparel division from 1980 to 1982, thought apparel could potentially keep the company's sales from declining in fiscal year 1984. Sales of the broad product line of athletic performance clothing (including running shorts, warm-ups, soccer jerseys; and tennis outfits)

and comfortable athleisure cloths (shirts, sweaters, jackets, and pants), had grown dramatically from $2 million in 1979 to $107 million in 1983, and sales representatives described demand as 'smoking.'

Woodell believed there were competitive and strategic reasons, too, for continuing emphasis on the apparel business. The shoe company, for example, might 'run out of feet.' Meanwhile, larger competitors, such as Adidas, relied on apparel for as much as 40% of sales. Margins in the apparel business, however, were lower than those in shoes.

In an off-site meeting in December 1983, Woodell and Hayes proposed to Knight, and later the rest of the management team, that NIKE 'aggressively grow apparel' for the Fall 1984 season. By investing an additional $15 to 20 million in inventories, and budgeting another $25 million in sourcing, sales, advertising, promotion and other operating expenses, Woodell thought apparel could boost sales by $100 million over the next fiscal year (ending May 1985), and by $200 million within the next two years. Said Hayes:

We couldn't convince vendors – the mills and people that we would buy from – that we were really in the business. It seemed ridiculous that if you were in the business that you weren't able to buy the apparel [with short lead times] you wanted to sell. So we 'loaded the wagon.' We committed to buy as much apparel [in advance] as our marketing and sales people said we could sell.

With Woodell's backing, NIKE committed to the apparel business with a vengeance. The program quickly established the company's credibility with vendors and retailers.

Organizational developments

One of Woodell's early changes was to reconstitute the old Friday Club's membership and redefine its role to improve decision-making. Woodell thought the old Friday Club meetings had lost much of their focus, and he wanted to run the meetings differently. He told the group: 'Bring up as subject matter only those issues that you think other members of the group *must* be informed about, or important issues where you need their collective counsel.' 'I tried to get answers about a few specific issues in each meeting,' recalled Woodell. 'But I had to get to those answers in a different way than Knight did. I had to use the power of the whole management group.' He explained his view of the new group, which colleagues immediately dubbed 'The Wednesday Club:'

My purpose is to reinforce the NIKE process of debating the issue, collaborating, making decisions, and getting counsel from each other. I don't want to put people out on a limb too quickly, but I'm trying to get people to take more responsibility.

A Policy and Procedures Committee was established to formalize some of the company's key practices that for years had been managed informally. For example, it established subcommittees to consider holidays, sick leave, education reimbursement, leave of absence, termination, and compensation. In July 1983 – his second month as president – Woodell approved PPC recommendations on sick leave, leave of absence, and educational reimbursement policies, and charged the group with addressing NIKE's most difficult personnel problem: how to formalize NIKE's widely divergent compensation practices. Although for years, many managers believed that a more formal salary administration system was needed – any action to develop one had always foundered on the shoal of a deep dislike for 'systems.'

George Porter, who chaired the PPC, said:

Everybody has heard stories illustrating the inconsistencies faced by employees. And most managers can recount the dilemmas they've faced in trying to balance a human responsibility to the company. We shouldn't have to fight this battle each time a situation comes up. There should be a policy that's right for us, that captures what the company is. It can probably deal with about 90% of the cases.

A PPC subcommittee eventually suggested adopting a formal system developed by Hay Associates, a compensation consulting firm. The system rated each job on the basis of three factors required for all jobs: know-how, problem-solving, and accountability. 'Job points' were assigned to each job, and because these were determined by

Hay's objective national standards, NIKE's pay system could be compared to 4,000 other U.S. companies; moreover, NIKE could correlate each person's pay with job points.

Phil Knight returns

'By the Spring of 1984, things were going to hell, and Woodell and I didn't have the communication to stop the bleeding. The more I got into this, I saw I had lost touch and had to step back in,' said Phil Knight, who in September 1984 decided to return full-time as president. Woodell was appointed head of a New Business unit charged with finding new, entrepreneurial business ventures.

Inventory and cost control

Knight's first priority was to reduce swollen inventories and to bring operating costs under control. By March 1984, inventories had reached 22 million pairs of shoes, including unsuccessful experiments in boots and punk-fashion athleisure shoes. On his return, Knight ordered prices slashed, then worked closely with the company's larger national accounts, such as J.C. Penney, to reduce inventory further. He even authorized bartering $12 million worth of surplus inventory for office furniture and airline tickets. By November 1984, the inventory stockpile had fallen to 15 million pairs, and by May 1985, to a manageable 9.8 million pairs.

This experience provoked a change in thinking about inventory within NIKE. Before, the focus on Futures ordering and demand forecasting allowed factories to run at optimal levels, but had masked short-term market changes. Said George Porter:

As a result, we couldn't see the downturn fast enough in our own factories. We wanted to keep them filled. Until that time, the problem had been one of production, not of sales. We could sell everything that we could produce. That attitude eventually catches up with you, and it did at that time.

In 1985, apparel sales were $160 million rather than the $235 million Woodell had projected. Apparel inventory remained high, not only because of the sales shortfall, but also because the company did not have a shippable mix of sizes, tops, and bottoms, and color-coordinated apparel. More inventory-reduction efforts eventually brought results, though at negative gross margins.

Knight planned to adopt stricter controls. He cautioned, however, 'Certainly there's a need to have more formalized procedures, but that doesn't mean a sledgehammer approach. With a 5% increase in sales and a 5% cut in operating expenses, you restore margins and have a very, very healthy performance.' Nevertheless, over the 12 months following his return, Knight discharged 400 people, or about 10% of NIKE's work force. Yielding to financial pressures, he also made the difficult move to close 5 of 30 supplier-owned plants.

Research and development

In December 1984, Phil Knight asked Tom Clarke to relocate the Research and Development Center from Exeter, New Hampshire to Beaverton, Oregon. The decision was controversial within NIKE because it cut about 75 of the Exeter facility's 125 employees. The move was received positively in the business press, which construed it as a cost-cutting measure. Knight's main motivation, however, was to improve communication and eventually collaboration between design and marketing. This was a major reversal of his early philosophy, which held that R&D should be kept away from corporate headquarters to protect designers from pressures that might limit their creativity. However, the old logic was eroding, as Tom Clarke explained:

> The R&D center had been set up in Exeter because of its proximity to some of the East Coast manufacturing. We continued to make our high-tech running shoes there through 1984. Because of that proximity, the R&D center's focus had been on running shoes. As court shoes started to be made in Asia, it became clear that the R&D center was not involved enough in non-running product categories. It was really separated from the decisions being made about the Asian factories. There was a need to unite marketing and design and development.

Organization

As he undertook these early initiatives, Knight stuck with his old management team. At the same time, however, he began to invite a wider circle of people to meetings. By February 1985, Knight was ready to modify the organization. He wanted to fix two major organizational shortcomings: to get NIKE back in touch with the market so it would no longer miss major market trends; and to improve its ability to implement a coordinated response. The reorganization created divisions around the major product categories to supplement the previous function- and geography-based structure. As a consequence, he had 12 vice presidents reporting directly to him.

Knight also used this occasion to shuffle his senior management group again. Among the many changes, Rob Strasser headed up the newly formed New Products Division with a mandate to develop ideas and products and bring them quickly to the marketplace. Knight also made an effort 'to get some I.Q. around here,' and hired several outsiders with MBA degrees and experience in footwear or athletic products. The management style of these new marketing- and production-oriented managers was more formal than NIKE veterans were used to, and some within the company resisted being 'professionalized.' Old-timers did not understand 'how wearing a tie makes us any more professional.'

A proliferation of teams (variously described as 'speed groups,' 'SWAT teams,' and, when organized around product launches, 'launch groups') began to tackle NIKE's problems. Some speed groups were formed as a means of 'getting together the product and marketing concepts.' Others were less product-oriented; for example, the 'Big Fitness' speed group addressed the issue of how to organize and position the shoe company as a fitness enterprise that provided all kinds of fitness products. Generally, speed groups were seen within the company as effective, even if some were overly exuberant (see **Exhibit 2**).

Rob Strasser, a strong advocate of the groups and leader of many of them, saw them as an effective way to implement his management 'principles' (see **Exhibit 3**). Mark Parker, who had worked in marketing, research and development, and design, recalled:

> Strasser wanted to make decisions quickly and keep moving ahead. That's what he really brought to the group. He forced progress. He really forced decisions to be made, and I think

we were able to cut through a lot of bureaucracy that had developed in the company at that time.

Recognizing the power of the team concept and the need to become more responsive to the market, in October 1985, Knight reorganized the New Products group around Launch Teams. Led by product line managers (PLMs), launch teams brought together individuals from all three departments to bring a specific new product to market. It aimed to do so by altering the product development process. Teams were responsible for all stages of developing new products - from the design stage through product development, marketing, production, and sales. After the reorganization, PLMs were designated team leaders of groups including a marketing manager, information manager, and a designer (in most instances). According to Carsh, PLMs formerly had been dedicated to 'getting products built and delivered, not getting products marketed.' Responsibility for new products was divided into three areas, product direction under Strasser, product management under Carsh, and production under Nelson. All three men reported directly to Knight.

Product-market strategy

Knight initiated a strategy review, and concluded that by copying Reebok's strategy, NIKE had let itself stray too far into the athleisure market segment and away from its core business of performance athletic products. Early in 1985, he explained to shareholders his intention to refocus NIKE's strategy: 'NIKE is a sports company,' he contended. 'Our innovation, our technology, and our talents are best suited for providing for the demands of athletes.' Knight pinned NIKE's hopes for restoring high profitability on diversifying into other fitness and sports shoes, especially medium- to high-end products.

As a result of this decision, management decided to review NIKE's 'Air' technology, which incorporated sealed gas bladders in the soles of the shoes to add cushioning and reduce weight. Air technology, patented in 1974, and developed since then, required specialized manufacturing techniques unavailable to NIKE's competitors. Although running enthusiasts recognized that Air technology improved

performance and gave the innovative and successful 1979 Tailwind shoe high marks, the general public did not understand the concept or believed that Air soles enhanced performance. Consequently, NIKE had not exploited the technology more widely in the early 1980s. The management review led to a decision to revive this potential asset.

One of the first products that Rob Strasser drove through the New Products group was the best-selling basketball shoe ever marketed. The shoe was built around Michael Jordan of the Chicago Bulls, the National Basketball Association (NBA) Rookie of the Year, and represented a departure from NIKE's promotion and marketing strategy. First Jordan's agent asked for a million dollars per year to sign a contract with the up-and-coming superstar. This was in contrast to existing practices of promoting 'grass roots athletes' or local stars at maybe one-tenth Jordan's price. To justify paying that price, NIKE 'had to do something special' with Jordan. Second, Jordan's personality and high profile made him a bona fide national star. Signing him gave NIKE the impetus to create a major new product line.

A launch team led by Strasser designed a distinctive red, black, and white shoe for Jordan, gave it its own logo, and called it the 'Air Jordan by NIKE.' They built on the color scheme and the styling to offer a coordinated line of clothing - NIKE's first experiment with collection selling. The coordinated Air Jordan apparel line rekindled the interest of retailers, who had been disappointed by NIKE's previous clothing offerings.

Strasser hired a new advertising agency which created exciting new commercials. After Jordan first appeared in the shoe, the NBA banned it from games, not because of the shoe's structure or technology, but because its red and black color scheme violated NBA dress regulations. NIKE fully exploited the controversy in a follow-up advertisement offering the public the shoe that the NBA banned because of its 'revolutionary design.'

Although Air Jordan was a huge marketing success with fiscal 1986 sales of $88 million – an achievement many credited to Strasser's speed group – the company had problems with logistics. Product quality was questionable, and late supply required expensive air shipment from Korea. When NIKE could not meet demand for the product, the company developed a new distribution strategy, called the 'allocation method.' Basically, those who provided the best distribution got the shoes. That meant targeting the important markets (such as Los Angeles, Chicago, Atlanta, and New York) and the large athletic specialty distributors (such as Foot Locker). A small athletic shoe retailer complained:

NIKE built the company on our backs. We took their product back in 1976 and said this is the best thing out there, and worked real hard to sell it. But when NIKE got hot, it went to the big guys. We little guys weren't treated well. It made us buy six months in advance; it didn't service us well; its sales force was arrogant. The big guys always got the product first. Also, NIKE's product line turned over very fast. We would book our orders six months in advance, and sometimes, before we even got them, they were closing out that line.

Del Hayes explained:

We gave the second tier of accounts some shoes, but we couldn't give them very much. They became very upset with us, but we learned they would come back if you had something that was really hot in the marketplace. Our strategy was to pull all products through the system as opposed to push them. If we convince the consumer with our promotional activities that he has to have that shoe, the hell with the retailer. He doesn't have any choice. This was NIKE's arrogance – using that pyramid theory together with the idea that we'll pull our product right through the marketplace, right through the chain by hitting that consumer. And it was very effective.

Following two years of falling earnings, NIKE rallied in fiscal 1986 to earn a record $59 million, despite $11 million in charges from plant closings and from the sale of its Japanese subsidiary. Unit sales were up 15% over the previous year and the average price per pair rose 12%. The gain reflected strong sales of Air Jordan products. By managing inventory levels and product lines better, and by selling higher-margin shoes, NIKE was able to improve its gross margin from 26.3% in 1985 to 32.4% in 1986. The effects of NIKE's cost-cutting efforts showed up in lower SG&A expenses, which fell from 21.6% to 19.6% of sales, and lower interest expenses, which fell because of reduced interest rates and lower borrowing. Yet, market share declined again as Reebok overtook NIKE. (See **Exhibits 4 and 5** for financial and market share data.)

NIKE's mid-life crisis

By Fall 1986, it was clear that fiscal 1987 was not going to be as profitable as fiscal 1986. Despite initial shortages of the Air Jordan, by the end of the season, NIKE had clogged up its distribution channels with excess inventory. The Air Jordan II was not the profit engine that the first model had been after the product's fadishness cooled, and injuries forced Michael Jordan to withdraw from the Chicago Bulls for the season. In December of 1986, Phil Knight announced a second round of layoffs, displacing 280 of NIKE's 2,150 employees.

Organizational tensions

Over time, speed groups created resentment in the company because of the resources at their disposal and the credit they often received for efforts that represented a larger group's contributions. One manager who worked in some of the speed groups with Strasser, described 1986-1987 as a time of two separate NIKEs, the 'mainstream NIKE' and the 'one running around it.' Often, speed groups duplicated other efforts within the company, and individuals in the mainstream complained of receiving conflicting directions. Moreover, noted Tom Clarke, who also worked in a speed group with Strasser and Parker:

There were people in those groups who were very good, but there was a tendency to jump from project to project, rather than to dive into each one and see the worth of stability, defining roles, defining how the groups would interact with the other divisions.

Harry Carsh, vice president of the Footwear Division, reflected on the difficulties with the organization:

I ran around firing people. It was a nightmare and 1986 was just a horrible, horrible year.

Finally, in early 1987, it came to a head. Brendan Foster, who had been brought over from Europe two years earlier to run marketing, had some really good ideas, but he was an egomaniac, and he took on Phil. He said, 'Hey, Phil, you run a lousy company.' And we were a lousy company. There was nothing wrong with what he was saying, but he was saying it to the wrong person. It wasn't Knight running the company. The rest of us were really doing a horrible job. And basically, Foster blamed it on Knight.

Foster departed, increasing tension between Knight and Strasser, who looked upon Foster as his protege. Meanwhile, Knight was concerned that Strasser was getting too involved in others' activities. Ron Nelson described the tension:

Trying to get Strasser to work on creative things and keep him out of the operations was kind of a balancing act that Knight had for a couple years. In all that time, Strasser didn't truly understand how much you needed the operations. You needed the base in there to make things happen. To go from 2 million to 5 million pairs a month – we could do that because we had all the systems, all of the operations, and the people all set up.

Finally, Strasser decided to take a five-month leave of absence. When he returned, Knight told him that he 'could not micro-manage from the corner office.' Just a few weeks later, Strasser quit. He was the eighth of the founding group of vice presidents to leave in a two-year period. Meanwhile, it became increasingly clear that the outside group of 'professional managers' Knight had hired in 1985 would not be able to fill the gap created. Indeed, all seven of the MBA's recruited 'to get some I.Q. around here' eventually left the company.

Developing people: reorganizing around the matrix

Although Strasser and Foster had been an immensely successful marketing team and had contributed greatly to the success of the Air Jordan and other products, Knight thought their dominance had not allowed others to really perform. He felt that Strasser's strong personal control, combined with

his fleeting zeal for different projects, led to confusion about management direction. Said Parker:

Strasser had difficulty focusing for a very long period of time on any one thing. He zoomed in on something and wanted to play with it for a while, and when something else caught his eye, he'd run over and play with that. What that meant in terms of NIKE was that he'd jump on an idea and stay with it for a little while. He would get everybody moving in that direction, get a little frustrated with it, and eventually shift to another area. The rest of the company was sitting back, trying to figure out what this small cadre of upper management was doing and where they were going.

During Strasser's five-month absence, Knight realized a need to develop other people and decided to reconceptualize the organization to achieve this objective. Harry Carsh recalled the ensuing period of searching as a tense one in which he literally 'got midnight phone calls from Knight asking me who could perform.' There were many people who had been in middle management for a decade or more and who really knew the company. Because many were athletes, they knew the product as well. 'So we started picking these guys out,' he said. 'A lot of them had been on the verge of being fired under the Strasser regime. Some of them had already quit; others were just about to go.'

But many felt that this new generation of internally developed managers could only be effective if NIKE broke out of its old organizational approaches. As he considered what to do, Knight talked to Tom Paine, a board member and consultant who had spent much time doing organizational design within the aerospace industry. Paine felt a matrix organization might fit NIKE's needs, and spent a lot of time educating the management team about the ways in which such organizations worked. Other key managers became persuaded by Paine's arguments. Dick Donahue, another board member with whom Knight communicated closely at the time believed:

You have natural competition for voice [in a company], so you have to try to devise an organization that allows not only competition, but also communication and collaboration. A matrix not only gets people talking; it also reassures them. In other words, if you interrelate with a couple of departments on your decision over sales, design, marketing, or something of that nature, it almost guarantees you're not going to make a colossal mistake. And it does make you consider all the factors.

Key managers such as Mark Parker thought the matrix would coordinate activities without stifling NIKE's entrepreneurial culture:

We were concerned about losing some of the emotional fire within NIKE, some of the risk-taking, some of the spirit of adventure that made NIKE special. The matrix was an attempt to move away from an emotionally driven, dicta-torial situation to one where there's more collaboration on the future of the company.

The matrix helped us look more in depth, not only at the product and marketing aspects of NIKE, but also the operational and business side. It helped us look at the total picture – what it takes to make a business successful – not just the marketing and design aspects. It was also sensitive to the NIKE irreverence, the need to take risks, to punch it out, and to make sure we were not turning into a dry, predictable company.

Rather than developing a classic formal matrix, the managers preferred to create a looser, less formal set of relationships. Yet, despite the need for increased communication and shared responsibility, the management team still wanted Knight very much in charge. So much so that Del Hayes quipped, 'I didn't realize it was a very good matrix organiz-ation. I thought it was more like a wheel with a hub in the middle.'

The essence of the matrix was coordination among four key functional areas, each headed by a divisional vice president reporting directly to Knight. (See **Exhibit 6**, which shows NIKE's organization in late 1987.) Strong personal friendships and the common experience of growing up together as NIKE managers had created a strong bond among these 'matrix heads' and kept communication at the top of the matrix strong. Matrix heads met every week as a group and also communicated informally.

Across these functional divisions, two corporate vice presidents took on what were described as general management roles. One major task was 'to check that the business plans of the divisions were connected.' Contact between the matrix heads and the general managers occurred in staff meetings, which were collaborative, not directional. The two general managers acted as facilitators, who 'made sure decisions were made, but did not actually make the decisions.' The general managers dealt mostly with administrative issues (such as compensation or new company-wide guidelines). Because the people in the matrix reported up to the divisional vice pres-idents, the general managers had less formal power than the divisional vice presidents. However, the div-ision vice presidents clearly valued the general managers' coordinating role, and respected the fact that they, too, reported directly to Knight.

The matrix heads collectively chose the members of cross-functional teams organized to accomplish product launches. Referred to internally as 'P.T. boats,' these intrapreneurial teams were composed of members who were two or three levels below the matrix heads. Typically, teams consisted of a mar-keting manager, a designer, and a development manager. The teams would meet with the matrix heads two or three times per six-month season. The matrix heads, who walked around the departments regularly, were familiar with the goings-on of the P.T. boats.

Changes in style

Within this overall structure, the new generation of managers began to exert a different organizational approach and management style than their prede-cessors. For example, in 1987, Clarke felt that the marketing department had to develop a more disci-plined approach: 'My belief has always been that you have to be organized to be creative. The former mar-keting regime didn't believe in organization. They felt that was stifling creativity.' Under Clarke, the mar-keting department began to write formal marketing plans. At first descriptive in nature, they grew pro-gressively more strategic and market-focused. Also, in 1987, for the first time the marketing department subscribed to independent color services, which tracked the colors and color schemes that were popular in different parts of the country.

Finally, Clarke required employees to focus more on individual projects, rather than bouncing from one to another as they had under Strasser:

> We started to stress that there are these individual teams that have a certain amount of autonomy under a central direction. They're going to spend their whole day working on basketball, or a whole day on running, as opposed to before, when we had people jumping from category to category, kind of wild-catting on various projects. That [old style] just wasn't yielding the best results given the size and scope of the business that we were trying to drive.

With the new organization came more job stability. George Porter recalled the 1984–1986 period, 'I had four jobs in two years. It was impossible in these circumstances to learn the job and to develop relationships.' He believed that organizational stability and job continuity enabled people to really learn their jobs. Clarke concurred:

> It sounds incredibly mundane, but you win in business just by putting some emphasis on the fact that people aren't totally interchangeable, that they have skills, that they need job descriptions.

In 1987, the new managers had confidence in the cohesion of the management team and the clarity of purpose this leant the business. Mark Parker reflected:

> The chemistry among the people in the matrix was really exceptional. People finished each other's sentences and had a sixth-sense of what others were thinking. That chemistry within the group and with the other people around the company appeared in 1987. We had a real shared vision, a sense of what we were and what we needed to do.

New products

One of the new products developed was the cross-training shoe. First introduced in 1986, this was a multiple-use shoe that could be used for running, tennis, basketball, and other sports activities as well. Cross-training shoes were backed by a well-coordinated marketing, advertising, and sales distribution program that was built around multi-sport star athlete, Bo Jackson, and the theme: 'Bo Knows.' In the late 1980s, this cross-training shoe category really took off.

Although NIKE's Air Jordan Shoe had been phenomenally successful, design and marketing people believed that even by 1987, the public did not understand air technology. Management saw the opportunity to change that in a new product line of twelve 'Visible Air' shoes. In 1985, a speed group composed of designers and marketers had started working on this new group of products, the 'Air Pack.' Air Pack shoes contained translucent, gas-filled plastic bladders in their midsoles that were visible through windows in the sides of the shoes. This revolutionary design not only helped the public understand that there really was something structurally different about NIKE's products, but it also enhanced the shoes' performance by increasing the volume of air in the midsole and cutting the shoe's weight.

The 'Air Pack' range of products reflected a more coordinated effort between product design and marketing than had occurred previously. Never had the design of the shoes been pushed so far in order to make that technology marketable. Furthermore, the concept was executed in a range of twelve shoes from running to tennis to basketball. And it was launched in 1987 with a $20 million advertising campaign based on the Beatles' song, 'Revolution.' In 1992, Knight commented[1]:

> Today, when people talk about NIKE, the television ads are practically all they want to talk about. But we became a billion dollar company without television. For years, we just got the shoes out there on the athletes and ran a limited number of print ads in specialized magazines like Runner's World. We didn't complete the advertising spectrum until 1987, when we used television for the first time.
>
> Our first television campaign was for Visible Air shoes. Having gone thorough the painful experience of laying people off and cutting overhead in

---

[1] *Harvard Business Review*, July–August 1992, 'High-Performance Marketing: An Interview with NIKE's Phil Knight.'

the mid-1980s, we wanted the message about our new line of shoes to hit with a punch, and that really dictated television advertising.

The Visible Air launch was a critical moment for a couple of reasons. Until then, we really didn't know if we could be a big company and still have people work closely together. Visible Air was a hugely complex product whose components were made in three different countries, and nobody knew if it would come together. Production, marketing, and sales were all fighting with each other, and we were using television advertising for the first time. There was tension all the way around.

We launched the product with the Revolution campaign, using the Beatles' song. We wanted to communicate not just a radical departure in shoes, but a revolution in the way Americans felt about fitness, exercise, and wellness. The ads were a tremendous hit, and Nike Air became the standard for the industry immediately thereafter.

Back to the future

Fiscal 1987 was NIKE's last year of declining sales, profits and marketshare. Thereafter, sales and profits skyrocketed and NIKE regained market leadership. (See **Exhibit 4**.) In 1989, Knight named 63-year-old Richard Donahue – an 11-year veteran of NIKE's board – as COO. At that time, the matrix heads described the company's organization as a collection of distinct silos rather than a matrix. The vertical chains of command in the functional divisions had remained intact or been strengthened, but the general management roles that sought to promote coordination across functions had atrophied. Cross-functional teams still operated in much the same way as before, but all were now devoted exclusively to one product segment (e.g., basketball) rather than two or three. Communications among the former matrix heads remained strong, and all these divisional vice presidents had been made corporate vice presidents.

In a 1992 interview,[2] Knight commented:

For years, we thought of ourselves as a production-oriented company, meaning we put all our emphasis on designing and manufacturing the product. But now we understand that the most important thing we do is market the product. We've come around to saying that NIKE is a marketing-oriented company, and the product is our most important marketing tool. What I mean is that marketing knits the whole organization together. The design elements and functional characteristics of the product itself are just part of the overall marketing process.

We used to think that everything started in the lab. Now we realize that everything spins off the consumer. And while technology is still important, the consumer has to lead innovation. We have to innovate for a specific reason, and that reason comes from the market. Otherwise, we'll end up making museum pieces.

When the formulas that got NIKE up to $1 billion in sales – being good at innovation and production and being able to sign great athletes – stopped working, we faced a series of problems. For one thing, Reebok came out of nowhere to dominate the aerobics market, which we completely miscalculated. We made an aerobics shoe that was functionally superior to Reeboks', but we missed the styling. Reebok's shoe was sleek and attractive, while ours was sturdy and clunky. We also decided against using garment leather, as Reebok had done, because it wasn't durable. By the time we developed a leather that was both strong and soft, Reebok had established a brand, won a huge chunk of sales, and gained the momentum to go right by us.

We were also having management problems at that time because we really hadn't adjusted to being a big company.

We understood our 'core consumers,' the athletes who were performing at the highest level of the sport. We saw them as being at the top of a pyramid, with weekend jocks in the middle of the pyramid, and everybody else who wore athletic hoses at the bottom. Even though about 60% of our product is bought by people who don't use it for the actual sport, everything we did was aimed at the top. We said, if we get the people

---

[2] Ibid.

at the top, we'll get the others because they'll know that the shoe can perform.

But that was an oversimplification. Sure, it's important to get the top of the pyramid, but you've also got to speak to the people all the way down. Just take something simple like the color of the shoe. We used to say we don't care what the color is. If a top player like Michael Jordan liked some kind of yellow and orange jobbie, that's what we made – even if nobody else really wanted yellow and orange. One of our great racing shoes, the Sock Racer, failed for exactly that reason: we made it bright bumble-bee yellow, and it turned everybody off.

Whether you're talking about the core consumer or the person on the street, the principle is the same: you have to come up with what the consumer wants, and you need a vehicle to understand it. To understand the rest of the pyramid, we do a lot of work at the grass roots level. We go to amateur sports events and spend time at gyms and tennis courts talking to people.

We make sure that the product is the same functionally whether it's for Michael Jordan or Joe American Public. We don't just say Michael Jordan is going to wear it so therefore, Joe American Public is going to wear it. We have people who tell us what colors are going to be in for 1993, for instance, and we incorporate them.

Beyond that, we do some fairly typical kinds of market research, but lots of it – spending time in stores and watching what happens across the counter, getting reports from dealers, doing focus groups, tracking responses to our ads. We just sort of factor all that information into the computer between the ears and come up with conclusions.

We've created lots of new categories under the NIKE brand, everything from cross-training and water sports to outdoors and walking.

But what's interesting is that we've sliced up some of the categories themselves.

We've always believed that to succeed with the consumer, you have to wake him up. He's not going to walk in and buy the same stuff he always has, or listen to the same thing he's always heard. There are 50 different competitors in the athletic shoe business. If you do the same thing you've done before or that somebody else is doing, you won't last more than one or two seasons.

And from the beginning, we've tried to create an emotional tie with the consumer. Why do people get married – or do anything? Because of emotional ties. That's what builds long-term relationships with the consumer, and that's what our campaigns are about. That approach distinguishes us from a lot of other companies, including Reebok. Our advertising tries to link consumers to the NIKE brand through the emotions of sports and fitness. We show competition, determination, achievement, fun, and even the spiritual rewards of participating in those activities. People at NIKE believe in the power of emotion because we feel it ourselves.

In mid-1993, the CEO of one of NIKE's competitors commented:

I believe that NIKE is the class act of the industry. NIKE has a clear point of view on who they are which is incorporated into all of their marketing and product. They sell an attitude and a benefit (performance) which greatly lessens their dependence on a 'hot' shoe or a 'hot' feature.

They have built a high quality, professional organization which is extremely loyal to NIKE. An attitude of investing in their people and business is, in my opinion, widening the gap between NIKE and the rest of the industry.

Exhibit 1 NIKE quarterly statements (fiscal year ending May 31)

		Sales ($million)	Gross Margin	S,G&A	Net Income	RoA	Inventory (Turnover)
II	1983	188.4	32.2%	16.0%	6.4%		
III	1983	199.2	29.3	16.9	4.7	7.3%	2.0
IV	1983	222.9	33.2	15.9	6.7	11.8	2.1
I	1984	270.2	33.4	14.7	8.4	18.6	2.7
II	1984	168.9	28.9	20.7	3.3	4.9	1.9
III	1984	224.0	26.7	19.4	2.9	4.8	2.5
IV	1984	256.7	24.3	17.7	2.3	4.3	2.8
I	1985	284.6	27.5	20.0	2.7	5.4	3.0

Source: Standard & Poors' Compustat.

Exhibit 2 NIKE Inc., cartoon from NIKE's in-house newspaper, 1985
Source: *The Nike Times*, 1985.

Principles

1. Our business is change.

2. We're on offense. All the time.

3. Perfect results count – not a perfect process. Break the rules; fight the law.

4. This is as much about battle as about business.

5. Assume nothing. Make sure people keep their promises. Push yourselves, push others. Stretch the possible.

6. Live off the land.

7. Your job isn't done until *the* job is done.

8. Dangers:

   Bureaucracy
   Personal ambition
   Energy takers versus energy givers
   Knowing our weaknesses
   Getting too many things on the platter

9. It won't be pretty.

10. If we do the right things, we'll make money damn near automatic.

Exhibit 3 NIKE Inc., The principles that Rob Strasser distributed to his marketing team.
Source: Company records.

Exhibit 4 NIKE financial information (fiscal year ending May 31)

	Sales ($million)	% Foreign	Gross Margin	S,G&A	Net Income	RoA	Inventory (Turns)
1983	867.2	10.8%	32.0%	15.3%	6.6%	11.2%	2.4
1984	919.8	17.2	28.4	17.8	4.4	7.3	2.3
1985	946.4	22.9	26.3	21.6	1.1	2.0	3.0
1986	1,069.2	23.6	32.4	19.6	5.5	12.4	3.9
1987	877.4	26.9	32.0	23.3	4.1	7.0	4.0
1988	1,203.4	25.2	33.2	20.5	8.5	14.3	5.0
1989	1,710.8	20.4	37.2	20.7	9.8	20.2	5.1
1990	2,235.2	21.5	38.1	20.3	10.9	22.2	5.2
1991	3,003.6	28.7	38.4	22.1	9.6	16.8	4.1
1992	3,405.2	33.3	38.7	22.4	9.7	17.6	3.9
1993	3,931.0	35.7	39.3	23.5	9.3	16.7	4.5

Source: NIKE Annual Reports, 1983-1992. NIKE's fiscal year ended in May.
Note: Total assets grew from $512 million in 1987 to $2,187 million in 1993. Long term debt decreased from $40 million to $15 million during this period, while shareholders' equity rose from $338 million to $1,646 million (of which retained earnings rose from $254 million to $1,542 million).

Exhibit 5 Athletic footwear market (Branded)

	Market Size ($ million)	NIKE's Share	Reebok's Share
1980	1,700	14.4%	–
1981	1,800	22.2	–
1982	1,900	30.5	–
1983	1,960	34.0	1.1%
1984	1,962	32.6	3.4
1985	2,086	27.2	14.3
1986	2,642	24.6	31.8
1987	3,189	16.0	32.5
1988	3,831	19.8	30.0
1989	4,476	23.5	25.7
1990	5,003	27.3	23.4
1991	5,353	31.3	23.9
1992	5,700	31.7	23.4
1993	6,100	32.0	22.0
1994 (est.)	6,300	33.0	23.0

Source: Company estimates.

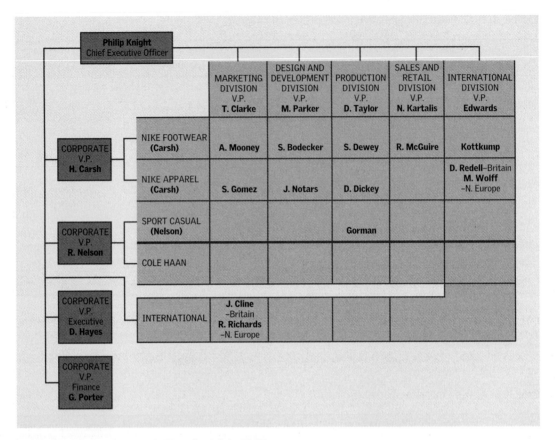

Exhibit 6 NIKE, Inc., organization chart, late 1987

Explanation: Individuals in the matrix (e.g., Mooney, Bodecker, Gomez, etc.) reported up to division vice presidents. Matrix heads (Clarke, Parker, Taylor, Kartalis) established and managed cross-divisional teams. Those on the left side of the matrix were of equal rank to matrix heads and filled a general management role: they provided checks to ensure that cross-divisional coordination was effective, and addressed corporate issues. The company was in the process of acquiring Cole Haan Holdings Inc., which marketed footwear and accessories under the brand name 'Cole Haan'.

Source: Company records.

H A R V A R D | B U S I N E S S | S C H O O L

Case 4 **Finland and Nokia**

Örjan Sölvell
Michael E. Porter

When an inventor in Silicon Valley opens his garage door to show off his latest idea, he has 50% of the world market in front of him. When an inventor in Finland opens his garage door, he faces three feet of snow.
   – J.O. Nieminen, CEO of Nokia Mobira, 1984

Until the 1990s, Finland was considered a remote and sleepy country in the northeastern corner of Europe, lying in the shadow of its large neighbor Russia. Finland had been part of Sweden for six centuries until 1809, when it was ceded to Russia. The Bolshevik revolution in 1917 and the collapse of the Romanov dynasty led Finland to unilaterally declare independence on December 6, 1917 (still the national day). After difficult years during World War II, Finland remained somewhat isolated, and its economy remained highly dependent on the Soviet Union. Following the model of its Nordic neighbors in

Professor Örjan Sölvell and Professor Michael E. Porter, Institute for Strategy and Competitiveness at Harvard Business School, prepared this case from published sources with the assistance of Pekka Yla-Anttila, Laura Paija, and Christian Ketels. HBS cases are developed solely as the basis for class discussion. Cases are not intended to serve as endorsements, sources of primary data, or illustrations of effective or ineffective management.

the post-war years, Finland was characterized by heavy investments in social welfare and public infrastructure. There was a history of reliance on government leadership in many private sector companies. The government had large holdings in many top Finnish companies (see **Exhibit 1**), and through its active involvement in major mergers and acquisitions transactions, influenced the ownership structures of key industries. Finland's prosperity level caught up to the OECD average only slowly. With few exceptions, notably in pulp and paper and specialty shipbuilding, Finnish companies were absent from international business rankings.

By 2001, Finland had become one of the fastest growing and most competitive economies in the world. A member of the European Union, it was known for fiscal stability and was the only Nordic country introducing the Euro in the first wave. In the Competitiveness Rankings of the Global Competitiveness Report, Finland won the top spot from the United States in 2000. One Finnish company, Nokia, had outpaced others to cast a long shadow on the entire economy. Its emergence as the market leader in global mobile telecommunication equipment had made the company the leading influence on Finnish exports, R&D expenditures, and market capitalization.

With the slowdown of the global telecommunication market, however, both Nokia and the Finnish economy were facing challenges, raising questions about the company and the country's recent achievements.

Country background

Finland was a sparsely populated European country, surrounded by the Baltic Sea in the South and the West, a 1,000-mile plus border with Russia in the East, and Sweden and Norway in the Northwest. The country's capital Helsinki was located at the same latitude as southern Alaska and Greenland.

Finland's population of 5.3 million in 2001 was spread thinly across the country's 130,000 square miles. Only the region of the southern cities of Helsinki, Espoo, and Vantaa was more heavily populated accounting for about 20% of the total population.

Finland was one of the world's most homogenous societies with a very low proportion of immigrants. Finns shared one culture, although about 6% of its population belonged to the Swedish minority. Finland had close cultural ties to its Nordic neighbors but had followed a separate path in many other respects. The Finnish language was part of the Finno-Ugrian language group and was related only to Estonian, Hungarian, and to the Inuit language spoken in the far north. Apart from Finnish and Swedish, the two official languages, most of the population also spoke English. With the establishment of the common Nordic labor market in 1954, large numbers of Finnish women moved to Sweden to work in the textile factories, making Finns the largest immigrant group in Sweden. Very few Swedes, however, had moved to Finland.

Beginning in 1919, the Finnish constitution had enshrined a so-called 'semi-presidential' form of government. The president, directly elected by the people for a 6-year term, had significant policy making powers, especially in foreign relations, and the right to dissolve parliament and call elections. He or she (Tarja Halonen was elected the first female Finnish president in February 2000) also nominated government ministers that had to be confirmed by parliament. The 200 members of the one-chamber parliament were elected for four years. Legislative proposals were usually initiated by the government, but could also come from any member of the parliament. On March 1, 2000, Finland adopted a new constitution that integrated four previously separate constitutional acts but did not change the substance of the political system.

The country's vulnerable geopolitical position vis-à-vis the Soviet Union, plus the constitution had allowed President Urho Kekkonen to dominate the country's political agenda during his 26 years of office from 1956 to 1982. The parliament was controlled by coalitions often encompassing the whole spectrum of left- to right-wing parties. Kekkonen had forced these broad coalitions which were accepted out of desire to avoid divergent views on domestic policies that would destabilize Finland's external relations. This logic lived on in the government that had been elected in 1999. Only one party, the rural Center party, was not included in the government coalition.

The Finnish economy prior to 1990

The Finnish economy was historically driven by the wealth of the country's natural resource endowment and its long coastline. The economy was dominated by manufacturing industries and had a service sector smaller than in many comparable European countries. The three largest clusters were pulp and paper, wood products, and engineered metal products. Pulp and paper accounted for 40% of exports, wood products for 16%, and engineered metal (including shipbuilding) for 23% in 1970.

The pulp and paper cluster had grown, based on the large forests and woodland covering 76% of the country's total land area. It achieved a leading role in the world industry, however, despite slower growing forests and higher energy costs than in competing regions of the world. A shipbuilding cluster was focused on specialized ships such as ice-breakers and ferries. Domestic demand, for example by ferry lines connecting Finland to Sweden and to continental Europe, was an important initial market for the cluster.

Finland's post-war economic performance was characterized by slow catch-up to more advanced western economies from an initially low level. In 1950, Finland's GDP per hour worked was at 46% of the U.S. level, in between its Nordic neighbors and war-torn Germany and Austria. GDP per hour had reached 69% of the United States in 1970, closing some of the gap to its neighbors but falling behind Germany and Austria. GDP growth rates stayed between 3 and 5% per year, investment rates were high, and total factor productivity growth outperformed many other European countries from the 1960s through the 1980s. Wage dispersion in the Finnish economy was low. Company profitability in Finland was also historically low compared to other OECD countries.

Finland's trade was dominated by the Soviet Union. Having joined forces with Germany during World War II, Finland was made to pay substantial war indemnities in the form of steel, ships, textiles and machinery to the Soviet Union. This created important business linkages in the east. Some 20% of all Finnish exports were sent east between the 1950s and the 1980s; Finland became an important supplier of manufactured products to the Soviet Union. Payments for these exports were usually made in natural resources, often oil. Other important export markets were in Europe, primarily Sweden and Germany. The United States, accounted for only 3% of Finnish exports in the early 1980s. The country had joined the European Free Trade Association (EFTA) as an associate member in 1961. Finland's economic policy in the 1970s and 80s followed Western European and Nordic patterns. Finland had traditionally been a country with a large public sector and strong welfare aspirations. Taxes were high after an era of active interventionism by government in the 1960s and 1970s. Transfer payments and public spending on services were high. Macroeconomic policy featured a fixed nominal exchange rate, centralized wage bargaining, and an increasing fiscal budget through the 1980s. After World War II, Finland experienced at least one large devaluation every decade; 30.7% in 1949, 28.1% in 1957, 23.8% in 1967, and over 20% in a series of devaluations in the 1970s.

Finland had developed a sophisticated public education and university system. Education between the ages of 7 and 16 was compulsory and most students stayed on for three to four more years in upper secondary or vocational schools. Public spending on education relative to GDP was traditionally above the level in many other European countries, and had increased at a steady growth rate. Quality of education was considered good, and Finnish students generally performed well in international school performance tests. Nearly 60% of the population had completed a secondary education or beyond.

Finland also was home to 20 universities and other institutions of higher education, with a student population of approximately 270,000. A number of universities had a long tradition; the University of Åbo was founded in 1640 but moved to Helsinki in 1828. Nearly 13% of the population had a university degree or the equivalent.

Finland's financial markets were characterized by strong ties between companies and their banks, not unlike the system prevalent in the Germanic countries. Financial regulation was tight, making credit approval restrictive. Finnish competition policy, not unlike other Nordic countries, had a history of lax enforcement. Mergers and acquisitions were decided and negotiated by a small elite group of managers and owners (the so called 'bergsråd'), together with the large banks and government officials.

The Finnish corporate sector had traditionally been dominated by large, often highly diversified groups, such as Valmet, Nokia, and Ahlström, with roots back to the nineteenth century. Valmet was a world leader in sophisticated machinery for the pulp and paper industry with a long history. Nokia had historical traces all the way back to 1865, but was really created in 1967 when Suomen Kaapelitehdas (Finnish Cable Works, founded in 1917 and active in the telecommunications cable and electronics businesses) was merged with Suomen Gummi-tehdas (Finnish Rubber Works) and Nokia, a 100-year-old wood grinding mill. Other parts of the economy, such as the food retail sector, had a strong presence of small companies tied together in co-operatives.

Developments in the 1980s Economic growth in the 1980s was driven by rising government expenditure that led to increasing inflationary pressure. Growing government budgets were financed by public sector deficits and an increasing tax share of GDP. In October 1982 the Bank of Finland devalued the Finnish Markka, first by 3.8% and then by 5.7%.

Throughout the 1980s, a series of policy changes were made in reaction to a growing perception that Finland's economy was losing ground internationally. In science and technology, R&D expenditure as a share of GDP was increased continuously beginning in the early 1980s. Public R&D spending was increased at an annual rate of about 10%, soon making Finland one of the leading OECD countries in public R&D spending relative to GDP.

In 1983 the National Technology Agency (Tekes) was founded, which became the main implementer of technology policy. In March 1987, another research related body, the Science and Technology Policy Council, was founded. Headed by the Prime Minister and including the Ministers of Finance, Trade and Industry, Education, and four other Ministers together with representatives from the main research organizations, the Council was to direct overall research policy and develop strategies in three-year cycles.

In financial market regulation, existing policies came under increasing pressure in the 1980s for making Finland uncompetitive. In the second half of the 1980s the financial markets were liberalized, as they were in Norway and Sweden, making lending much easier for banks. Access to international capital markets was also made easier.

Emergence of the Finnish telecommunications cluster

Unlike in most other European countries, the Finnish telephone network was never monopolized by the state. The deliberately fragmented market structure reflected security concerns dating back to the late nineteenth century when Finland was a Russian Grand Duchy. At the time, the Finnish Senate had granted many licenses for telephone operations in order to complicate any effort by the Tsar to seize the national telephone system.

After independence, a national public telecommunications operator (PTT) Telecom Finland was established to operate the network left behind by Russia. The PTT was not only an operator but also the regulatory body for the industry. There were several attempts over the decades to nationalize poorly performing private operators in the name of harmonizing infrastructure, but these had met with political resistance and never materialized. The threat of nationalizing weak companies, however, stimulated private operators to upgrade their technology. In 1921, the private telephone operators founded the 'Association of Telephone Companies' for administrative cooperation and joint actions vis-à-vis the PTT. The Association became a powerful competitor to the PTT, dominating local telephone operations in major cities while the PTT had a monopoly over long distance and international calls. In the 1930s, there were no less than 815 private local telephone companies in Finland. Finnish operators, who were quite advanced technologically, engaged actively in R&D cooperation with equipment manufacturers.

The seeds of the Finnish radiophone and mobile phone industries were planted in the 1920s in three companies: Salora, established in 1928, was a

regional manufacturer of TV and radio sets. It began the development of radiophones in 1964 after the Finnish Army issued an invitation for tenders; the first in a series of orders by the government which required companies to meet demanding requirements in the development of radio technology. Valtion Sähköpaja (lit. State Electric Works), established in 1925, as the radio laboratory of the Ministry of Defense, was founded to strengthen national development and production of radio technology. Valtion Sähköpaja was merged after the War with the R&D unit of the PTT, renamed Televa. Finally, Suomen Kaapelitehdas (lit. Finnish Cable Works), founded in 1917, was a producer of telecommunications cables, and merged into Nokia in 1967. By the 1970s, Televa and Nokia viewed the Finnish market as too small and its resources too scarce for parallel development of digital exchanges, and combined their R&D and marketing efforts in digital transfer technology in a joint venture, Telefenno. Telefenno introduced the first digital exchange in 1982, only shortly after Ericsson, Alcatel, ITT and Siemens. For years, the product became Nokia's most successful export.

The first two decades of the mobile era In 1969, the 'Nordic Telecom Conference', a body for formal and informal technical cooperation between the Nordic PTTs (in Denmark, Finland, Norway and Sweden), initiated a project on an automatic (analog) Nordic Mobile Telephone (NMT) network. The NMT system, launched in 1981, was unique in several respects. Most importantly, it developed roaming technology (later used in other systems around the world) that made it possible for the system to know where a telephone was located, making it possible to travel across national borders using the same phone. Furthermore, NMT was an open standard. The introduction of the NMT made the Nordic region the world's largest single mobile market at the time.

Expanding at a rapid rate, the market began to attract private operators and manufacturers. In Finland, private license applications were rejected by the PTT in its role as regulator. The Finnish PTT argued that competition would preclude economies of scale and that mobile communications was a natural monopoly. As a countermove, the Association of Telephone Companies formed a joint venture in 1988, Radiolinja, to operate a private network.

The introduction of the NMT marked the start of a fast-expanding new industry. The design of the NMT standard brought the Nordic telecommunications administrators and providers into close cooperation. While active in the development of mobile phones, the Finnish industry had in the past not been able to provide network infrastructure. In 1981, however, pressure from the Finnish PTT led the domestic industry to develop a base station (see Appendix for an overview of the technologies involved). By 1985, the NMT standard had a leading position in a number of foreign markets, and an average annual growth rate of 50%. Several Nordic manufacturers of mobile phones and network infrastructure soon entered the market. In other countries, with closed standards, there was only one operator that also supplied the phones.

By the late 1980s there were some 15 competitors active in the Nordic mobile phone markets. The only other country that had significant competition was the UK, which had a similar number of competitors, while each of the other European markets had about five. In terms of user penetration, the Nordic region was the first to take off. The Nordic region had 523,000 subscribers in June of 1988, The U.K. had 366,000, Germany 70,000, France 69,000, Austria 34,000 and Switzerland 14,000.

With the NMT under way, Nokia and Salora created a 50-50 owned joint venture in 1979 named Mobira (later Nokia-Mobira) to market and develop radio technology, especially new NMT phones. Before 1980 Nokia had sold approximately half of its production in the domestic market. The rest was exported mostly to neighboring countries. During the 1980s, Mobira allied itself with distributors and mobile operators around the world, and the company learned about building a global consumer brand. Nokia began to strengthen its international operations by also acquiring several electronics companies including Luxor (a Swedish manufacturer of TV sets and personal computers) and Standard Elektrik Lorenz's consumer electronics businesses (a German manufacturer of TV sets and other electronics). Nokia also acquired the PC and office electronics business of Ericsson, Ericsson Information Systems. The acquired units operated mostly in the electronics industry and manufactured products such as TV sets, monitors and videos sold directly to consumers. Through these acquisitions Nokia became the largest consumer electronics company in the Nordic region during the 1980s. Nokia's mobile phone unit, Mobira, expanded through global alliances. Together with Tandy Corporation, for example, Nokia established joint ventures in Korea and the United States. Mobile phones were sold under different brand names, including the private label brands of dealers (e.g. Radio Shack in the U.S.) and service operators.

During this period, the Finnish telecommunication equipment industry was further consolidated in Nokia, still a large conglomerate. Through a series of mergers finalized in 1987, Salora, Telefenno, and Televa became parts of Nokia. Salora and units of Suomen Kaapelitehdas ultimately became Nokia Mobile Phones in 1989, and Telefenno and Televa became Nokia Telecommunications (the exchange business) in 1992.

After rapid growth through acquisitions and alliances, however, Nokia ran into a financial crisis. With CEO Kari Kairamo's untimely death in 1988 a new CEO was brought in to try to establish some focus in the company as well as to regain cost control. Company employment decreased by around 15,000 between 1989 and 1992 (see **Exhibit 2**).

Finnish economic policy in the 1990s

The 1990s began with the most severe crisis the Finnish economy had ever experienced. In 1991, real GDP fell by 6.2%. In 1992, it lost another 3.3%. Exports dropped by 13% in dollar terms in 1991. Unemployment rose from 3.5% in 1990 to 17.9% in 1993.

The Berlin wall had come down in 1989 and the Soviet Union was dissolving. Almost overnight, exports to what had been the most important market for Finnish exports dried up. German reunification and the economic integration of Eastern Germany led to an increase in real interest rates throughout Europe. Finland was also experiencing a deteriorating terms-of-trade due to falling world pulp and paper prices, its main export industry. The problems were compounded by domestic economic conditions: In the late 1980s, the Finnish economy had experienced a huge increase in credits from the liberalized banking sector. Property prices increased sharply and inflation rose. The savings rate fell to 12.1% in 1992, less than half of the 24.9% ten years earlier. As a result of the external problems and internal overheating, the Finnish exchange rate came under pressure. In November 1991 the Marka was devaluated by 12%, and in September 1992, Finland was forced to float its currency and fundamentally revisit its economic policy.

Tight macroeconomic policies were quickly adopted. The earlier creeping increase in the tax burden was halted, and tax rates stabilized. With wage growth and profits weak during the crisis, tax revenues on these two items as a share of GDP fell from 19.3% in 1990 to 18.1% in 1995. Government expenditures were cut by nearly 10% of GDP, targeting budget surpluses by the end of the 1990s compared to a deficit of 7.3% of GDP in 1993. Monetary policy was changed to adopt an inflation target of 2% beginning 1995. Interest rates were the main policy instrument, initially reaching levels above 13% on 10-year government bonds in 1992, implying an interest rate differential of up to 500 basis points relative to Germany.

Finland's economy began to rebound in 1993 with real GDP growth reaching 4% and staying between 3.8 and 6.3% throughout the rest of the 1990s. Inflation fell continuously from its peak of almost 7% in 1990 to under 2% from 1993 onwards. Interest rates came down continuously to reach about 6% at the end of 1997, eliminating the differential with Germany. Finland was able to re-establish a stable parity to European Union member currencies in 1996.

During the 1990s, the changes in the science and technology policies initiated in the preceding decade were accelerated. While some parts of the budget were severely cut in the 1992 crisis, the government decided to make additional resources available for research and development (see **Table 1**). Already in 1990, the Science and Technology Policy Council conducted a major review of Finland's economic position that had resulted in two reform initiatives to strengthen the country's national innovative capacity. The Center of Expertise Program, focused on 'strengthening regional competitiveness by increasing innovation, renewing the regional production structure, and creating new jobs in selected expertise areas'. The Cluster Program focused on developing the innovative capacity of industrial clusters by supporting cluster-specific R&D efforts. In parallel, the government set up 15 incubators in proximity to regional clusters throughout Finland to make venture capital available for start-up companies.

Table 1 Finnish research and development expenditure, 1989–1999 (€ millions)

	1989	1991	1993	1995	1997	1998	1999
Enterprises	€924.8	€975.1	€1,048.5	€1,373.4	€1,916.7	€2,252.8	€2,643.9
Public sector[a]	286.1	357.5	379.7	374.4	408.6	443.8	470.1
University sector[b]	290.2	378.0	367.5	424.6	579.5	657.9	764.8
Total	1,501.2	1,710.6	1,795.8	2,172.4	2,904.9	3,354.5	3,878.8
as % of GDP	1.8	2.0	2.2	2.3	2.7	2.9	3.2[c]
Enterprises	61.6%	57.0%	58.4%	63.2%	66.0%	67.2%	68.2%
Public sector[a]	19.1	20.9	21.1	17.2	14.1	13.2	12.1
University sector[b]	19.3	22.1	20.5	19.6	20.0	19.6	19.7
Total	100	100	100	100	100	100	100

Source: *Statistics Finland*, Science and technology statistics.
[a] Including private nonprofit sector.
[b] Including central university hospitals since 1997 and polytechnics since 1999.
[c] Preliminary data

The cluster approach was introduced in Finland through a study coordinated by the Research Institute of the Finnish Economy (ETLA) in the early 1990s. The approach set the design of policy guidelines outlined in 1993 in the White Paper 'A National Industrial Strategy' by the Ministry of Trade and Industry. The central message for policy makers was that all government actions had implications for national competitiveness. Therefore, economic and industrial policies needed to be considered from an extended perspective, beyond sectoral ministries' administrative boundaries. The cluster model stimulated new forums for interaction and coordination between ministries, public and private research units, and companies. The study served to convince policymakers of the relevance of the evolving policy direction first began in the 1980s, clarifying the role of the government as the creator of favorable framework conditions, and emphasizing interorganizational cooperation as well as accumulation and transfer of know-how. Policies concerning technology, education and competition became center stage of the new Finnish industrial policy.

The increasing focus on R&D and technology-intensive activities increased the demand for skilled employees. The government reacted by expanding the capacity of higher education. Between 1993-1998, the total intake of students in universities nearly doubled, and in polytechnics it nearly tripled. Despite growing enrollment, however, Finland ranked 14th—well below the OECD average—in expenditures per student at the tertiary level. In early 1998, the government adopted a program to expand education in the information and communication field between 1998–2001.

The liberalization of the Finnish capital markets that had begun already in the 1980s continued. In 1991, for example, households were allowed to borrow in foreign currency. More rivalry in the domestic banking market and easier access to foreign capital reshaped the traditionally tight relations between companies and their banks. In 1993, restrictions on foreign ownership of Finnish firms were removed. Venture capitalists emerged during the 1990s, stimulated in part by government-sponsored incubators. Successful business plans at the turn of the century attracted increasing amounts of venture capital, which had emerged as the most common source of capital for start-ups. Investors had become more specialized due to the increased number of funds and investment companies. The availability of venture capital had reshaped the role of public funding, traditionally the prime source of capital for risky enterprises. New kinds of investment syndicates were established where the public sector invested alongside venture capitalists.

In 1994, the policy-making powers of the regions were significantly strengthened through the Regional Development Act. Regions were encouraged to develop their own economic development activities and integrate the 'Center's of Excellence' concept developed as part of the new technology policy.

The attitude towards competition shifted in favor of more intense rivalry. However, mark-ups in many Finnish industries still remained above the levels of the United States and other European countries. The centralized wage setting mechanisms between unions and employer organizations remained in place.

Internationally, Finland was redirecting attention from the East to the West: In 1993, Finland joined the European Economic Area (EEA); a decision that eliminated many trade and investment barriers to other Nordic and European countries. Germany, Sweden, and the United Kingdom became Finland's most important export markets. The United States doubled its share of Finnish exports, while the Russian share fell to 4.5%.

In 1995, Finland became a member of the European Union, entering together with its neighbor Sweden. EU membership brought further integration into the European Common Market, and the harmonization of many laws and regulations with the other EU countries. With the opening towards the west, the Finnish economy attracted significant amounts of inward FDI. Large mergers between Swedish and Finnish firms in banking (Nordea), engineering (ABB), electronics (Nokia) and pulp and paper (Stora-Enso, UPM-Kymmene) created larger and more focused Finnish firms with global reach. In 1998, Swedish firms accounted for 50% of FDI in Finland, and 34% of Finnish FDI took place in Sweden. In 1985, the stock of Finnish inward and outward foreign direct investment had been 1.3% and 1.8% of GDP respectively. In 1998, these ratios had increased to 18.3% and 33.8%.

The transformation of Finnish industry could also

be seen in the composition of the economy: In 1999, electronics and telecommunications equipment had become the leading sector, accounting for 21% of value added, followed by pulp and paper (15%), chemicals (10%), and machinery and equipment (9.5%). Within these and other fields the corporate landscape had changed significantly. The pulp and paper cluster, for example, was considered to be a leader in global markets with a broad array of companies including specialized machine manufacturers and service companies.

The three largest sectors also increasingly dominated exports. In 1999, pulp and paper and electronics products each accounted for about 30% of exports. Engineered metal products accounted for another 20%.

In the second half of the 1990s, Finland's average GDP growth rose to about 5%, with Nokia's growth contributing close to 1%. Unemployment rates came down but stayed above the 10%-level throughout the 1990s. In 1999, youth unemployment was above 20%, higher than in other European countries and more than twice as high as ten years earlier.

Finnish telecommunications policy in the 1990s

The Finnish telecommunications sector was subject to standard competition and consumer protection legislation. The telecommunications authorities pursued a policy of minimum interference, acting mainly in cases of insufficient competition, an approach different from most other OECD countries. Some mandatory EU requirements had been enforced in Finland rather reluctantly, as they were considered to go against the liberal functioning of markets.

In 1987, a new Telecommunications Services Act had separated the regulatory and operator functions of the PTT, transferring regulatory authority from the PTT to an independent body under the Ministry of Transport and Communications. The Act also established the right of private companies to offer mobile communication network services. This legislation ended a long dispute over the PTTs monopoly rights that dated back already to the 1960s.[1]

---

[1] The operative Imperial Telephone Decree of 1886 did not provide an unambiguous interpretation of the statutory rights to provide novel network services, such as data transfer, telefax and teletext.

In 1991, privately-owned Radiolinja was the first operator in the world to launch a commercial GSM network. Liberalization meant fundamental organizational changes for the PTT, which was turned into a public company. The PTT began to improve service and worked hard to launch its GSM service soon after Radiolinja, becoming one of the first PTTs in Europe to do so. The government started reducing its ownership in the PTT and indicated further privatization. In 1998, the name of the company was changed to Sonera to reflect a new strategic focus on fixed, mobile and media services.

At the end of the 1990s, the government was mandated by parliament to withdraw from the telecommunications business. These intentions were later frustrated by Sonera's large expenditures on UMTS licenses in Europe which created large borrowings. In 2001, the Government decided to save the company by infusing new equity. This move came despite the government's decision to limit intervention in the sector as much as possible. Finland had, for example, decided not to engage in direct, high-speed network capacity provision, despite the political goal of providing leading infrastructure. This decision, different from neighboring Sweden and more in line with the United Kingdom and other continental European countries, was made to insure technology neutrality and the free functioning of the market. In line with the same liberal policy principles, Finland granted third-generation mobile network licenses without restricting the choice of standards.

The international mobile telecommunications sector

The mobile telecommunications sector grew out of the combination of radiophone technology with wired telephone systems. The basic technology of so-called cellular systems had been developed already in the 1950s in the United States. With the exception of small city systems in some parts of the world, however, cellular or mobile telephony did not develop as a market until the early 1980s.

In 2001, over 500 million mobile phones were sold worldwide. The industry was divided into two parts: mobile communication infrastructure and mobile handsets (often called cellular phones in the

United States. See the **Appendix**). Each part had different competitive characteristics, though the big three, Motorola, Ericsson (including Sony Ericsson) and Nokia were all active in both infrastructure and handsets in 2001.

The use of mobile phones was highest in the Nordic countries, with penetration rates of over 70% in 2000. Italy and Austria also had penetration rates above 70%, whereas most other European countries were around 60%. Japan had a penetration rate of about 50%, the United States 40%, and South East Asia around 10%.

Evolving standards

In 1986, there were mobile networks in 32 countries, most of which were incompatible accross national borders. In 2001, this list had grown to over 150 countries and an emerging global standard had begun to be installed across the most advanced nations. This third generation system, referred to as UMTS, integrated voice and high-speed data communication (see **Table 2**).

First generation systems in the 1980s were analog and incompatible. In Europe alone, there were six systems: NMT, Comvik, TACS, Radiocom 2000, C-450, and RTMS. The leading system was the Nordic NMT system, the only one offering international compatibility (first throughout the Nordic region, and in 1988, in Switzerland and the Benelux region). Comvik was used in Sweden in parallel to the PTT-controlled NMT system. The TACS system from the United States was brought to Ireland and the U.K. in 1985. The Radiocom 2000 system was developed by Matra and used only in France. The C-450 system was developed by Siemens for the German market, and adopted by Portugal. The Italian RTMS system was introduced in Italy in 1985. In the United States, several competing systems and standards evolved, covering limited areas of the nation that were also adopted in Latin America.

Second generation systems involved a shift to digital technology, and were introduced earlier in Europe than in the United States. Digital technology provided major benefits in terms of operating costs, system capacity and enhanced service offerings to customers. The Nordic Conference in 1982 played an active role in initiating the pan-European digital mobile network, or GSM system (an alternative standard proposed by German and French interests was later withdrawn). GSM was launched in 1990 and covered all of Europe, later spreading to Asia and the United States. A GSM group had been

Table 2 Mobile telecommunication standards

	First Generation	**Second Generation**	**Third Generation**
Application	◆ National/local systems ◆ Portable phones ◆ Car phones	◆ Regional systems ◆ Pocket phones ◆ Digital voice services ◆ Digital text: SMS (short message service) ◆ First-generation WAP	◆ Global system ◆ Integrated high-quality audio and data ◆ Music and video ◆ Narrowband and broadband ◆ Multimedia services
Type of System	◆ Analog cellular technology ◆ Macro-cellular systems	◆ Digital cellular technology ◆ Micro-cellular and pico-cellular ◆ Enhanced cordless technology	◆ Digital broadband ◆ Information compression ◆ Higher frequency spectrum ◆ IP packet switching
Standards	◆ AMPS, ETACS, NMT 450, NMT 900, TACS, Radiocom 2000, C-450, RTMS, Comvik	◆ GSM, CDMA, TDMA, PDC, GPRS	◆ WCDMA, CDMA 2000, TDMA 136

formed to secure Europe against Japanese competition and involved cooperation through alliances. For example, Nokia-Mobira developed systems and handsets together with AEG and Alcatel, and had an alliance for processor chip development together with AT&T. Motorola was also active in GSM technology, with a focus on Europe.

In the United States, two digital standards emerged, TDMA and CDMA. In the late 1990s, a number of GSM systems were established offering the ability to use a single phone in Europe and the United States. Qualcomm's Code Division Multiple Access (CDMA) followed a restrictive licensing strategy. Nokia decided not to license the technology and developed its own CDMA phone. In March of 1999, Qualcomm sold its manufacturing operations to Ericsson after a long patent fight. TDMA was championed by AT&T Wireless, Bell South, and Southwestern Bell Mobile. In 2000, GSM had 69% of digital subscribers worldwide, CDMA 13%, TDMA 10% and the Japanese system PDC 8%.

There was fierce competition over third-generation standards. GPRS, sometimes referred to as the 2-1/2 generation system, had been developed in Europe to maintain momentum. The emerging leader in 3G systems was the European WCDMA. Together with Qualcomm's new CDMA 2000 and the leading Japanese companies, WCDMA formed a 'global family' allowing phones to be used all over the world. U.S. proponents of the TDMA system also introduced a third generation system under the name of TDMA 136. The transition to the third generation system was slow and in 2001/2002 investment plans were delayed in most countries. Japan and Korea were the first movers.

Mobile telecommunication systems had initially been separate from the Internet. A first standard allowing access to certain Internet services was the Wireless Application Protocol (WAP), introduced on high-end phones in the late 1990s. With increased bandwidth in third-generation systems, mobile Internet was emerging.

The mobile communications value system

Mobile service was provided by network operators (Figure 1). Once a monopoly in many countries, mobile service providers faced fierce competition in 2001. Three or more mobile operators typically competed in each local market. Verizon Wireless was the largest mobile operator in the United States in 2001 with some 30 million subscribers. Operators had internationalized, and a few global firms or 'families' of firms had emerged.

Operators had begun to segment their services to cater to the differing usage needs of business and residential customers. Handset manufacturers had also begun developing handsets focused on segments.

The growth of fixed-line systems was slowing in advanced countries, and the paging market had recently begun to slow as well. Leading paging manufacturers such as Motorola and Glenayre in the United States were adding more functionality to paging with two-way paging and voice paging. Satellite phones were a long-term threat to mobile phones, but remained expensive in 2001.

Mobile telephone equipment could be divided into infrastructure and handsets; each accounting for about one half of the total manufacturing market. Infrastructure, consisting of base stations and switching equipment, was produced by major telecommunications manufacturers such as Ericsson, Motorola, and Nokia. Handsets, or mobile phones, were manufactured by many new companies, especially as standards became more established.

As the mobile communications industry emerged in the 1980s, two companies became leaders: Motorola from the United States and Nokia-Mobira from Finland (see **Table 3**). Suppliers of first generation analog infrastructure (such as Ericsson, Siemens, Philips, Alcatel, NEC) also developed proprietary phones for their own systems, and some also manufactured phones for open systems such as NMT. Rapid industry growth attracted new handset competitors, many with a background in consumer electronics (such as Samsung, Panasonic, Mitsubishi, Sony). Ericsson and Samsung gained substantial market share in the 1990s, while NEC, Mitsubishi and Toshiba were the losers. In 2002 positions had shifted considerably with Sony-Ericsson (the two companies merged their handset businesses in 2000) far behind Nokia, Motorola, Samsung and Siemens.

Mobile handsets were sold through service operators as well as through independent dealers.

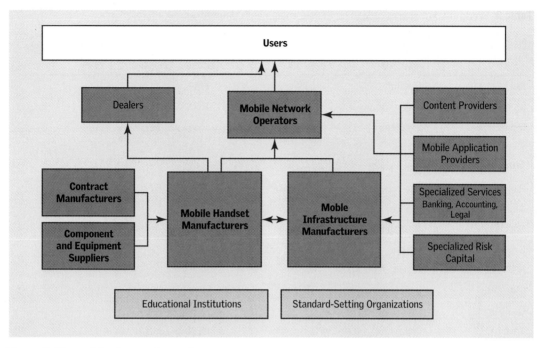

Figure 1 The mobile phone value system
Source: Case writer

Some operators sold phones directly to consumers (sometimes branding the phone themselves or jointly with the OEM), while others concentrated exclusively on subsidized sales of phones through independent dealers, with which they typically had exclusive relationships.

The components for mobile phones included the casing, LCD, circuits, battery, and antenna. Phone manufacturers made some parts themselves but contracted many components from outside suppliers. Some phone manufacturers such as Motorola, Nokia and Samsung had integrated backwards into semiconductors in an attempt to reduce costs and help shorten new product development cycles. In addition, software constituted an increasingly important part of the value of a phone.

Competition

All mobile phone manufacturers were facing intense competition in 2001. Growth rates in major consumer markets were slowing, and incumbents together with new entrants from the consumer electronics industry had capacities that outstripped market demand. Phone companies, were also under financial pressure and less willing to subsidize phones in order to stimulate demand. The three leading competitors in 2001, were Nokia, Motorola, and SonyEricsson.

Motorola Based in the United States, Motorola had long been a leader in two-way radios, paging, mobile phone handsets and mobile infrastructure. Founded by Paul V. Galvin, Motorola successfully commercialized car radios under the brand name 'Motorola' in the 1930s. In the 1960s, the company became a leader in military, space and commercial communications, as well as semiconductors and consumer electronics. It also began expanding into international markets.

After divesting its consumer electronics business, Motorola had, by the end of the 1980s, became the leading worldwide supplier of mobile phones and mobile infrastructure. In the 1990s Motorola invested several hundred million dollars in a new satellite phone system, the Iridium, which did not grow as expected.

Table 3 World market shares of leading mobile equipment competitors

Company	Home Base	Mobile Phones		Infrastructure
		2000	1988	1999
Nokia	Finland	31%	14%	10%
Motorola	United States	15	13	13
Ericsson	Sweden	10	3	30
Samsung	Korea	6	–	–
Siemens	Germany	6	2	6
Panasonic	Japan	5	9	–
Alcatel	France	5	6	3
Philips	Netherlands	3	3	–
Sagem	France	3	–	–
NEC	Japan	3	12	7
Mitsubishi	Japan	2	8	–
Qualcomm	United States	2	–	–
Toshiba	Japan	2	8	–
LG	Korea	1	–	–
Lucent	United States	–	–	11
Nortel	Canada	–	–	9
Fujitsu	Japan	–	–	2
OKI	Japan	–	6	–
Others		6	16	9

Source: 'Nokia-Mobira OY,' Harvard Business School case No. 589-112; Gardner Dataquest.
Note: – = not active or less than 1% share.

Motorola's small and light mobile phones had garnered a strong following. In 1989, the MicroTAC phone was the smallest and lightest phone in the market. In 1996 the 3.1-ounce StarTAC was introduced. The company controlled almost 25% of the world market in the 1990s. However, Motorola was slow to shift from analog to digital phones, and lost its leadership position in the late 1990s. In 2001, Motorola held the number two spot in both mobile networks (13%) and phones (15%). The company was vertically integrated into semiconductors and other components.

Ericsson Founded as a telegraph repair shop in 1876 by Lars Magnus Ericsson, Ericsson copied the newly invented Bell telephone which had not been patented by Bell in Sweden. When Bell entered the Swedish market in 1880, a spirited rivalry began. Ericsson introduced the first half-automatic switch in 1883. Because the Swedish PTT began to manufacture its own telephone equipment, Ericsson turned to international markets in the late 19th century. Ericsson had manufacturing operations in Russia and sales subsidiaries in China and Mexico as early as the 1890s. By 2001, Ericsson served over 130 markets worldwide. Ericsson had entered the radio industry in 1919.

In 1977, when NMT specifications were issued, Ericsson developed a mobile phone and exchange infrastructure. The mobile handset business was seen as peripheral and Ericsson considered selling the division several times. Throughout the 1980s and 1990s, Ericsson became a world leader in network technologies, especially through its digital switches, for both mobile and fixed-line telecommunication systems. Ericsson was known for its strong focus on technology, and invested 16% of revenues in R&D.

In 2000 and 2001, Ericsson sold off or closed a large number of units, concentrating on mobile telecom infrastructure where it was considered the world leader. In handsets, market share fell from 15% in 1998 to less than 10% a few years later. In 2000, Ericsson and Sony decided to join forces, establishing a 50/50-owned company, SonyEricsson, headquartered in London. As 3rd generation mobile systems were implemented beginning in the Japanese market, Ericsson had taken a lead with over 40% of the worldwide infrastructure market.

Exhibit 3 presents comparative data sales, profitability, and employment for the major manufacturers throughout the 1990s.

The Finnish telecommunications cluster in 2001

Finns had been early adopters of mobile phones. As Nokia became an international success story, Finns came to see the mobile phone as a 'national symbol.' Finland was among the world leaders in mobile penetration. In 1998 mobile subscribers outnumbered wired subscribers, and 20% of households had cancelled fixed line service and relied solely on mobile communications.

Finland had also been early to adopt the Internet in the late 1980s, led by students. The world's first graphic-based Internet browser was developed in an IT class at the Helsinki University of Technology in 1992, a year before Mosaic and Netscape. The students were not interested in commercializing the software, but other Finnish students, Tatu Ylönen (SSH encryption program) and Linus Torvalds (Linux operating system) went on to become legends in their own time. Finland ranked number one in the rate of Internet host penetration by 1999. A rapid increase in ISDN subscriptions, due to growing Internet penetration, was driving renewed demand for fixed line services in Finland.

From a modest base in the 1960s and 1970s, the Finnish telecommunications cluster began to emerge in earnest in the 1990s. By 2000, the cluster employed some 83,000 people (just under 4% of national employment) in over 4,000 firms, representing 6.9% of GDP (see **Table 4**). The total value of shipments was EUR 21.4 billion, with manufacturing of equipment and electronic components representing 70% of revenues. The cluster had grown at an average annual rate of 20% (manufacturing 32% and services 12%). See **Table 4**.

Operators In 2001, there were over 100 telecommunications operators in Finland, though most of them utilized leased network capacity. Sonera (formerly Telecom Finland) and the Finnet Group (the renamed Association of Telephone Companies) held 95% of revenue. Sonera had restructured during the 1990s and upgraded employee skill levels. In mobile services, Sonera's main competitor was Radiolinja, owned by the largest private operator Elisa Communications. Swedish Telia had not succeeded in capturing any significant share of the Finnish market since its entry in 1997. The fourth mobile operator, DNA Finland, was launched in early 2001 by a group of private investors. Finland granted licenses for 3rd generation systems (called UMTS) to all four GSM operators, the first country in the world to do so.

Content providers There were over 300 Finnish companies engaged in the provision of digital content, including media, services (e.g., banks and travel agencies) and Internet portals. An expanding number of services were targeted at professional groups (e.g., in health care and education). Nokia offered tools and support for entertainment service providers in an open virtual forum. The National Technology Agency, Tekes, had assumed the role of a facilitator in the emerging digital media industry, and facilitated interaction between firms, venture capitalists, universities, and research institutes.

Equipment manufacturers Nokia was the dominant equipment manufacturer in Finland, producing both handsets and infrastructure. There were also other manufacturers such as Benefon, a company founded by ex-Nokia managers. Much of Nokia's manufacturing was also outsourced to contract manufacturers such as Elcoteq.

Suppliers A large number of specialized suppliers

Table 4 Key economic indicators of the telecommunications cluster (2000)

| | Telecom Manufacturing | | Telecom Services | | | | Cluster Total | |
| | | | Telecom | | Related Software and IT Services | | | |
	EUR Million	Share of Production	EUR Million	Share of Production	EUR Million	Share of Production	EUR Million	Share of Production
Revenues	14,805		3,678		2,947		21,431	
Exports	12,125	82%	118	3%	1,009	34%	13,252	62%
Imports	4,185	28%	151	4%	605	21%	4,941	23%
No. of firms	414		216		3,463		4,093	
No. of employees	38,385		19,294		25,284		82,963	

Source: Adapted from L. Paija (ed), 'Finnish ICT Cluster in the Digital Economy,' Helsinki: ETLA – the Research Institute of the Finnish Economy).
Note: Smaller amounts of non-telecom IT software and services are included in the figures.

and contract manufacturers had emerged in Finland, in part driven by the growth of Nokia. Finnish suppliers tended to produce highly customized inputs (e.g. ASIC, rf filters, customized circuit boards, hybrid circuits), while standard components were imported. Other Finnish companies specialized in process technologies such as surface mounting, robots, and precision moulding equipment for telecom use. Increased outsourcing was coupled with extensive cooperation and long-term commitments between manufacturers and suppliers. Increased technological complexity and shortening product life cycles had pushed firms to closer interaction and risk sharing. Finnish suppliers such as Perlos Ltd, Eimo Ltd and Elcoteq Networks Ltd followed Nokia by establishing or acquiring manufacturing units in such countries as China and the United States.

Equity capital A venture capital market had emerged as a new and important source of funding in the 1990s. In 1999 some EUR 285 million of venture capital was invested in new Finnish companies. A Finnish Venture Capital Association had been formed, which included 36 members in 2001. Some 30% of all venture capital was directed towards telecommunications.

In part due to Nokia, investors and venture capitalists from around the world sought out other leading-edge technology companies in Finland. As a consequence, a number of small Finnish high-tech companies had obtained financing from abroad. The majority of the capital raised in recent private placements in companies such as Solid, Digia, Riot, AVS and LPG came from international venture capitalists. Most of the money went to first or second round investments, rather than seed stage financing. Since the early 1990s, a growing number of foreign portfolio investors had added Nokia to their portfolios. In 1993, Nokia's foreign ownership was 46%, and by July 2001 the share had reached 90%. Nokia's share of the total market capitalization of the Helsinki Stock Exchange (HEX) peaked at 71% in November 2000. Although Nokia was listed in a number of markets, Helsinki had retained its position as the most important place to trade Nokia shares.

Education and research There were 12 colleges and universities in Finland providing education and conducting research in information technology and telecommunications. Finland was recognized as a location for highly skilled IT professionals.

Investment in IT and telecommunications-related R&D had risen substantially, mostly driven by a huge

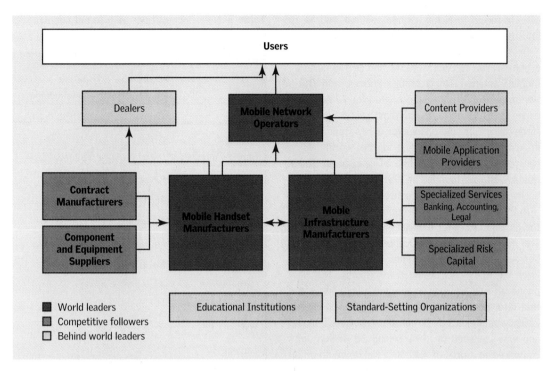

Figure 2 The Finnish mobile telecommunications cluster
Source: Case writer

increase in private sector R&D. University and other public-sector R&D also increased substantially in absolute terms, but not as rapidly as investments by companies. Increased R&D led to an average annual growth rate in patenting of 42%, in these fields between 1992 and 1998. Almost 30% of the United States patents granted to Finnish inventors were in IT and communications. During the 1990s, a number of international companies such as ICL, IBM, Siemens, Hewlett Packard and Ericsson had established R&D activities in Finland. Nokia conducted close to 60% of its research in Finland, and accounted for approximately 45% of all private R&D expenditure in the country.

Nokia in 2001

Nokia's sales were EUR 30.4 billion in 2000, with an operating profit of EUR 5.8 billion, an above average margin. The company employed 60,289 people, 24,000 of whom were located in Finland. The company had production locations in 10 countries, R&D in 15 countries, and sales to over 130 countries.

Nokia had weathered a crisis in the late 1980s as the company tried to cope with growth and diversity. A new CEO cut employment, but Nokia registered large losses in 1992. Jorma Olilla, 41, became CEO in 1992. New capital was raised through a private placement in the United States in 1993, and Nokia was listed on the New York Stock Exchange the following year. In 1994, Olilla got board approved to divest all of Nokia's businesses outside of telecommunications.

Olilla and his team also began to build a new culture. The four fundamental values of Nokia, the 'Nokia Way', were introduced in 1992: customer satisfaction, respect for the individual, achievement, and continuous learning. Nokia's strong culture, shared especially among the Finnish management team, substituted for detailed systems when the company entered new geographies. Nokia was seen as mirroring the Finnish national character: pragmatic, honest, quiet, and serious. The business press often referred to Nokia as 'non-political' and as an informal organization built on trust.

In 2001, Nokia was organized into three business groups: Nokia Networks (GSM and 3rd generation mobile systems), Nokia Mobile Phones, and Nokia Ventures. Mobile phones accounted for 72% of revenues in 2000, and was the most profitable of the three groups. It sold phones for every standard and in just about every market in the world. Nokia Networks accounted for 25% of revenue in 2000. Nokia Ventures, founded in 1998 to search for new business opportunities, accounted for 3%.

In the early 1990s, Nokia controlled about 12% of the global market for handsets, with a goal of 25%. The new sleek Nokia 2100 phone was designed by Los Angeles freelance designer Frank Nuovo (who later became head designer for Nokia). The new phone offered a larger screen and a scrolling menu that later became the industry standard. The Nokia 2100 was Nokia's first consumer-targeted model and was launched in 1994, selling 20 million units compared to a goal of 400,000. Nokia would go on to define a mobile phone as a fashion item and consumer good, instead of a technology product. Nokia's strategy was to serve distinct customer segments with differing needs using technology compatible to whatever standard was utilized in a particular regional market.

In the 1990s Nokia became the world leader in digital phones with a market share of 31% in 2000. The company offered the widest line of phones, covering every segment of the market, and had the broadest geographical coverage. In 1998 Nokia announced that 'mobile Internet' was to be the future guiding star of the company. Foreign sales accounted for 98% of revenue in 2000, up from 70% in 1990. In 2001, Nokia had a total of 19 manufacturing facilities in ten countries. Nokia Networks had five plants in Finland, five plants in China and one in Malaysia. Nokia Mobile Phones had production units in eight countries. See Table 5.

Nokia had R&D units located in 14 different countries, although just over half of total R&D activities were located in Finland. R&D facilities were typically located close to leading universities and research centers. At the end of the 1990s, Nokia spent close to 9% of its revenues on R&D, up from 6% in the first half of the 1990s.

Table 5 Nokia's operations in different countries (2000)

R&D Units	Production Facilities	Listings on Stock Exchanges
Finland	Finland	Finland
Germany	Germany	Germany
United States	United States	United States
Hungary	Hungary	Sweden
China	China	U.K.
Malaysia	Malaysia	France
South Korea	South Korea	
Australia	Brazil	
United Kingdom	Mexico	
Japan		
Italy		
Canada		
Sweden		
Denmark		

In the 1980s, Nokia had used subcontractors mainly as buffers to stabilize its manufacturing capacity. In the 1990s Nokia turned to outsourcing through long-term cooperation agreements. In the latter part of the 1990s, cooperation was gradually expanded from accessories to other components. Nokia also reorganized its supply chain to include contract manufacturers. Furthermore, Nokia began to contract for some software development and R&D. Some of Nokia's partners and subcontractors began international operations, including exports and production abroad not only to Nokia's foreign units but also to other customers. The outsourcing activities of Nokia had created some public concerns, that manufacturing operations would shift to low-cost countries in Eastern Europe and Asia.

One of the main challenges facing Nokia in 2001 was the evolution of standards. New standards in 3rd generation systems were being developed in mobile Internet services as well as software and hardware for phones and infrastructure. Personal digital assistants (PDA), electronic organizers, palmtops, and small-screen handsets were proliferating. A large number of firms and standards were competing, many of which sought enhanced mobility. For example, Microsoft had developed Stinger software and Palm had its own system. Nokia had licensed parts of its phone software and components to other handset manufacturers to encourage the adoption of its standard globally. In November 2001, Nokia announced it would license the source code for its mobile Internet browser and advanced text messaging technology to Samsung in Korea.

Together with Ericsson, Motorola and Phone.com (a small U.S. company), Nokia had established the WAP (Wireless Application Protocol) Forum. By 2000, there were over 200 members. Nokia introduced the first WAP phone in 1999, though the early products encountered some technical problems. In Japan, the i-mode system led by NTT had attracted large demand with millions of users.

Together with Sony, Ericsson (who invented the technology in 1994), Microsoft, IBM, Intel and others, Nokia had also developed Bluetooth, a standard used for short-range (under 30 feet) wireless connectivity. The main competing standard was called WiFi. Bluetooth chips used far less power than WiFi devices and were much cheaper, though WiFi offered a much higher bandwidth.

Research efforts were geared at developing 'smart' mobile phones with multimedia messaging, connections to the Internet, and the possibility of downloading information from Web sites. Here Nokia was pushing the Symbian operating system used by more than 70% of the mobile phone market. Motorola, Sony Ericsson, Psion, (a U.K. based manufacturer of PDAs), and Japan's Matsushita were Nokia's partners in this effort.

Finland in 2001

While Finland had maintained its ranking as a leading competitive nation in 2001, the nation was facing challenges. Overall growth rates were declining, and major export markets appeared weak. The telecommunications cluster especially was experiencing a severe downturn, and Nokia had seen its revenue and profits fall. Given the large role of Nokia and the cluster in Finland's economy, concerns about the level of exposure to one company and one cluster were becoming louder.

Finland was also facing shortages of skilled engineers and scientists. As demand for skilled labor was expected to increase, some universities had started offering programs tailored for foreign students to attract people to Finland. At the same time as IT jobs went begging, however, there was increasing unemployment, especially among the young and the low skilled. The differences in prosperity was creating strains on the traditionally egalitarian Finnish society.

Exhibit 1 Government ownership stakes in the top 25 Finnish companies

Sales Rank	Company	Industry	Government Share (%)
1	Nokia	Electronics	–
2	Stora Enso*	Forestry	15.1
3	Fortum	Energy	70.7
4	UPM-Kymmene	Forestry	–
5	*Metsäliitto*	Forestry	–
6	Kesko	Wholesale trade	–
7	Sampo	Finance	40.2
8	Pohjola	Finance	–
9	Nordea*	Finance	–
10	Metso	Mining / Metals	11.6
11	Varma-Sampo	Finance	–
12	Outokumpu	Mining / Metals	40.0
13	Ilmarinen	Finance	–
14	Tamro	Pharmaceuticals trade	–
15	Huhtamäki	Food	–
16	SOK	Retail	–
17	Rautarruukki	Mining / Metals	40.1
18	Wärtsilä	Machinery / Shipyards	–
19	Kone	Machinery / Shipyards	–
20	Partek	Mining / Metals	30.2
21	Kemira	Chemicals/ Plastics	56.2
22	Elcoteq Network	Electronics	–
23	Merita Henkivakuutus	Finance	–
24	Ahlström	Forestry	–
25	Sonera	Telecommunication	52.8

Source: Talouselämä, Finland's Top500 Companies, 2000.
Note: * indicates companies with broad Nordic Ownership. – = 0% or not applicable.

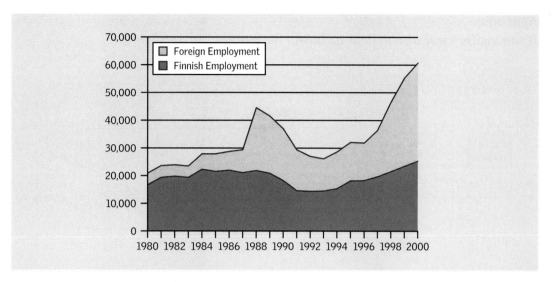

Exhibit 2 Nokia employment, 1980–2001
Source: L. Paija (ed), 'Finnish ICT Cluster in the Digital Economy,' Helsinki: ETLA – the Research Institute of the Finnish Economy and Taloustieto Oy, 2001.

Exhibit 3 Financial overview, major mobile telecommunication manufacturers

	1992	1993	1994	1995	1996	1997	1998	1999	2000
Nokia									
Sales ($ mil)	3,451	4,079	6,368	8,400	8,446	9,702	15,553	19,954	28,608
Net Income ($ mil)	(78)	132	632	509	745	1,154	2,043	2,601	3,709
Employees	26,700	25,800	28,600	31,948	31,723	36,647	44,543	51,777	60,000
Ericsson									
Sales ($ mil)	6,644	7,622	11,342	14,902	18,291	21,219	22,760	25,267	29,026
Net Income ($ mil)	68	340	531	813	1,033	1,511	1,609	1,423	2,230
Employees	66,232	69,597	76,144	84,513	93,949	100,774	103,667	103,290	105,129
Motorola									
Sales ($ mil)	13,303	16,963	22,245	27,037	27,973	29,794	29,398	30,931	37,580
Net Income ($ mil)	453	1,022	1,560	1,781	1,154	1,180	(962)	817	1,318
Employees	107,000	120,000	132,000	142,000	139,000	150,000	133,000	121,000	147,000

Source: Adapted from Hoover's, Inc.
Note: Motorola figures include a number of business units outside the mobile telecommunications sector.

Appendix
A schematic view of a mobile (cellular) network

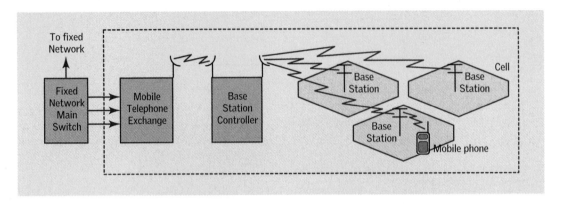

The base station controller coordinates calls among the base stations; it controls and routes calls back to the main switch for routing to other base station controllers or the fixed line system depending on the call. The base station controller is also connected to the base station via fixed line or microwave. The base station covers a certain geographic area, which is called a cell. Base stations are strategically located so as to overlap and connect geographically to surrounding base stations. The combination of these base stations or cells is the overall coverage area of the cellular network. The base station connects to handsets, i.e. mobile phones, via radio signals. These radio signals have traditionally been transmitted using analog coding technology (e.g., AMPS, ETACS, NMT) but are now using digital technology (e.g. GSM, GPRS, TDMA, CDMA and WCDMA) for cost and capacity reasons.

The cellular network broadly consists of base stations (cells), a base station controller, and a mobile telephone exchange (MTX). The cellular concept had been developed by Bell laboratories in the United States already in the 1950s. The MTX is the central coordinator (similar to the CPU in a computer) in the cellular network and gateway to the fixed wire-line system. As the central coordinator, the main switch coordinates/routes calls within the cellular network and externally to the fixed line system. The cellular network customer database and call information reside in the main switch. The MTX connects to the base station controller either via fixed line or microwave. Traditional manufacturers of telephone exchanges for fixed networks, such as Ericsson, had developed the MTX technology based on their expertise in building large-scale switching systems.

INTERNATIONAL

Case 5 easyJet: the web's favorite airline

The safest way to become a millionaire is to start as a billionaire and invest in the airline industry.

Richard Branson,
Founder, the Virgin Group

'If you create the right expectations and you meet or exceed those expectations, then you will have happy customers,' proclaimed Stelios Haji-Ioannou, the 32 year-old founder and CEO of easyJet airlines. Since its launch in November 1995, easyJet had become one of Europe's leading low-cost airlines by adopting an efficiency-driven operational model, creating brand awareness, and maintaining high levels of customer satisfaction.

Stelios, who preferred to be addressed by his first name only, considered himself a serial entrepreneur. Although he gained international fame as a pioneer

Research Associate Brian Rogers prepared this case under the supervision of Professor Nirmalya Kumar as a basis for class discussion rather than to illustrate either effective or ineffective handling of a business situation.

This case was the **Overall Winner** of the *2002 European Case Awards*, granted by ECCH in association with Business Week.

This case also won the *2001 European Case Award*, in the category of **Policy & General Management**, granted by ECCH in association with Business Week.

IMD-3-0873 (EM 873)
V. 11.12.2002

in the airline industry, he first achieved business success at the age of 25 when he created Stelmar, a specialized tanker company. Anxious to replicate his past successes, Stelios aggressively pursued any business opportunity that he believed he could operate profitably.

Despite its early success, easyJet airlines still faced internal challenges that were typical of many startup companies. Growing competition from other small, low-cost carriers, as well as threats from Europe's major carriers, required much of the company's attention and resources. Undeterred, Stelios relished the challenge and moved ahead in his mission 'to offer low-cost airline service to the masses.'

Stelios believed that in order to be successful, it was important to be first to market and to saturate the geographic market. 'You don't need to conquer the world in order to be profitable,' he argued. His strategy for market entry had been successful in the airline industry, but many wondered if he could transfer his low-cost business model to Internet cafés, rental cars, and Internet banking, three ventures he considered in 1999.

Company background

Stelios first became interested in the idea of a European low-cost airline in May 1994, after being asked to invest in a Virgin Atlantic Airlines franchisee. Although he refused, soon thereafter, he flew on Southwest Airlines, a successful low-cost carrier in the US. That experience became the catalyst in his decision to create easyJet. Stelios asked his father, Lukas Haji-Ioannou, a Greek shipping tycoon, to invest in his startup airline. In November 1995, after receiving £5 million from his father, Stelios began operating easyJet with two leased aircraft and a staff primarily comprised of teenagers who served as reservation agents. Although London's Heathrow and Gatwick were major international airports with higher passenger traffic, Stelios chose Luton because it offered lower labor costs and close proximity to downtown London, and charged lower airport fees.

The first easyJet flight, from London to Glasgow, was advertised for a one-way fare of £29. The flight was completely full, in large part because Stelios had launched an extensive public relations and advertising campaign with the slogan, 'Fly to Scotland for the price of a pair of jeans!' Increasing demand soon led to flight service to Edinburgh and Aberdeen. Over the next two years, Stelios raised an additional £50 million in debt and equity to finance the purchase of four additional aircraft and to speed expansion. By early 1998, easyJet owned a fleet of six Boeing 737-300s and flew 12 routes in five countries. However, by November 1999 easyJet owned and/or leased 18 Boeing 737-300s, and flew 27 routes in Europe.

Stelios modeled easyJet after Southwest Airlines. He researched Southwest intensively and even met with the airline's CEO, Herb Kelleher, before launching easyJet. Stelios deeply admired the concept behind Southwest Airlines: one type of aircraft, point-to-point short-haul travel, no in-flight meals, rapid turnaround time and very high aircraft utilization. However, Stelios added his own twist to the Southwest concept: he completely avoided travel agents, issued no tickets, encouraged direct sales over the Internet, and flew brand new Boeing 737s using the maximum seat capacity of 149 seats. Moreover, he decided not to offer free drinks or peanuts; everything would be for sale. Stelios championed the idea of no-frills travel; the only free item on board an easyJet flight was easyRider, the airline's in-flight magazine. He argued, 'When someone is on a bus, he doesn't expect any free lunch. I couldn't see why we cannot educate our customers to expect no frills on board.' (*Refer to Exhibit 1 to view items available from the easyKiosk.*)

The company's headquarters, referred to as 'easyLand,' was located at London's Luton airport. Just like the airline, easyLand was no-frills. Employees were instructed to dress casually, and Stelios sat in the same open-plan office as everyone else. He had no personal secretary, maintained a paperless office, and expected everybody else to do the same.

In 1996/97 easyJet suffered pre-tax losses of £3.3 million.[1] However, in 1998 the company announced annual pre-tax profits of £2.3 million, the first time the airline had posted a profit in its brief history. (*Refer to Exhibit 2 to review easyJet's financial performance.*)

---

[1] £1.0 = US$1.60.

Deregulation of the European Airline Industry

Until the early 1990s the European airline industry had been highly regulated, in large part because individual countries wanted to protect their own national carriers, commonly referred to as 'flag carriers.' However, in December 1992 the European Union passed legislation that deregulated the airline industry. Similar to the deregulation of the US airline industry in the 1980s, the new directive meant that any European carrier could fly to any destination and demand landing slots.

The proliferation of airlines offering highly competitive fares after December 1992 revolutionized European air travel, especially from the United Kingdom. New airlines were created, and travelers could fly from most airports in the UK to almost anywhere in the world for very low prices. This prompted one commentator to reply, 'You can now fly from one end of Europe to the other for the cost of two hardback books.' Richard Wright of the Civil Aviation Authority, which regulated British aviation, postulated that many new carriers set up operations from the UK, rather than other European countries, because the British, along with the Germans, traveled most often.

Deregulation in Europe, however, spawned fewer new competitors than in the US. In 1999, only 3% to 5% of passengers in Europe flew on a low-cost carrier, compared to 24% in the US. On some routes in Europe, high speed rail service competed directly with airlines. Furthermore, industry experts believed that the cost of running an airline in Europe was, on average, 40% higher than in the US.

Understandably, few low-cost carriers enjoyed the same success as easyJet. Of the 80 carriers that had begun operations after 1992, 60 had already gone bankrupt by 1996. Still, analysts predicted that the European low-cost market could grow by as much as 300% by 2004.

Competing on cost

Because easyJet offered low fares, it sought to minimize costs where possible. For example, easyJet saved £14 per passenger by not offering meal service, and estimated that by flying into London's Luton Airport instead of Gatwick, it saved £10 per passenger. The airline also shaved costs by not offering business class seating, thus allowing for more overall seating capacity. (*Refer to **Exhibit 3** to view a comparison of the costs of easyJet and other carriers.*)

Moreover, easyJet encouraged Internet sales. In March 1999, Internet sales accounted for 15% of revenues; however, by October 1999, Internet sales had soared to 60% of revenues. Stelios offered discounted fares to customers who purchased over the Internet because such sales reduced the need to hire additional reservation agents. He avoided computer reservation systems and travel agents because he believed that they added 25% to total operating costs.

Illustration: Saying No To Travel Agents

In 1998, Stelios enraged travel agents in Greece by selling cheap daily flights to Athens and flaunting his commission-free service by advertising to 'forget your travel agent.' Travel agents there took him to court. He won and then immediately thumbed his nose at his foes by plastering 'say no to travel agents' in bright orange letters across the first plane to fly from London to Athens, earning him huge amounts of press.

The airline also turned its airplanes around faster, flying planes 11.5 hours per day, instead of 6 hours, the industry average. Because easyJet flew its planes more hours, Stelios claimed that he could fly just 2 planes, and do the work of 3. Although easyJet had achieved profitability in 1999, margins were quite small; the airline earned £1.50 profit per passenger.

Even though easyJet carefully monitored costs, Stelios emphasized that safety was never compromised. The airline only flew brand new Boeing 737s, and only hired experienced pilots who were paid market rates. Stelios commented:

If you advertise a very cheap price, people expect an old airplane. But when they come on board and see a brand new plane, they are impressed. Likewise, many customers expect an unhappy staff because they believe they are not paid well, but they come on board and see the staff is smiling!

Table 1 Cost of an easyJet flight from London to Geneva

Cost Item	£	%
Airport charges	600	15%
Aircraft ownership	560	14%
Air traffic control	480	12%
Crew	400	10%
Marketing/sales	400	10%
Fuel	400	10%
Maintenance	400	10%
Overhead	400	10%
Ground handling	360	9%
Total Costs	£4,000	100%

Assumptions: The table approximates easyJet's costs for a one-way trip. All costs are fixed.
Source: easyJet

Competing on service

One of the distinguishing characteristics of easyJet was its approach to customer satisfaction. Stelios flew on at least four flights per week, and enjoyed interacting with customers. He had even been known to work the phones selling tickets. Stelios was wary of market research, preferring to cull information directly from passengers. He also read and replied to many of the emails he received from customers. He considered himself a man of the people and worked hard to cultivate this image. (*Refer to **Exhibit 4** to view an example of his communication with customers.*)

To provide our customers with safe, low-cost, good value, point-to-point air services. To offer a consistent and reliable product at fares appealing to leisure and business markets from our bases to a range of domestic and European destinations. To achieve this we will develop our people and establish lasting partnerships with our suppliers.

Figure 1 easyJet mission statement
Source: easyJet

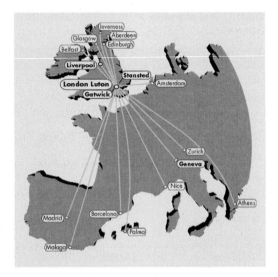

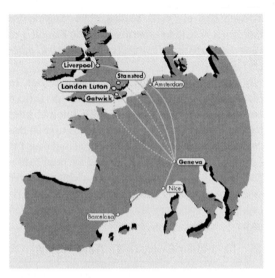

Figure 2 Destinations served from London's Luton Airport
Source: easyJet, November 1999

Figure 3 Destinations served from Geneva
Source: easyJet, November 1999

All of easyJet's fares were one-way fares and had the same restrictions. The cost to change a flight was £10 plus the difference between the two fares. Only 4% of customers failed to show up for their flights, and easyJet offered no reimbursement for missed flights.

To book a flight, customers either purchased their tickets over the Internet or they called a local number and were connected to one of easyJet's reservation agents in easyLand. Because easyJet was a 100% direct-sell operation, the marketing department knew the relative effectiveness of different media and could react quickly. Oftentimes, the company placed different phone numbers on different types of advertisements to measure consumer response precisely.

Customers were required to pay by credit card, after which they received a six-character booking reference number. This reference number was the only information passengers needed to board the plane. Reservation agents were paid on a commission basis, at a rate of £0.80 per seat sold, and could sell 60 to 90 seats during an average eight-hour shift.

The airline did not offer any pre-assigned seating, but instead utilized a priority boarding procedure. Passengers were given a number based on the time they checked in, and those passengers who arrived late for check-in had to sit in whatever seats remained.

Generally speaking, easyJet defined its target customers as 'people who pay for travel from their own pockets.' The target group consisted of travelers visiting relatives, leisure travelers making brief trips, as well as entrepreneurs and managers working for small firms. While easyJet typically ignored the large market of business travelers, on some routes, such as London-Glasgow, London-Edinburgh, and London-Amsterdam, business travelers represented 50% of the passengers. Stelios argued that larger airlines ripped off traveling business customers who usually did not want to stay over a Saturday night or who wanted complete flexibility to change their travel plans.

Using yield management, easyJet tried to fill as many seats as possible. Seats were sold in what could be considered a lottery system; the more people demanded a particular flight, the higher the fare. Put differently, if the load factor (percentage of seats sold) was higher than normal, prices automatically increased. This system worked well for easyJet because it helped avoid selling out popular flights months in advance.

Yield management also served another purpose: it drew potential customers who were in search of

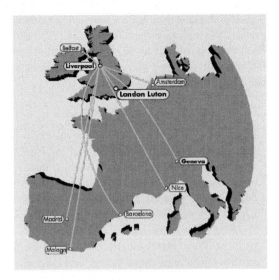

Figure 4 Destinations served from Liverpool
Source: easyJet, November 1999

cheap fares. Once they found there were no more cheap seats, they usually bought a ticket anyway, since the next highest fare was still cheaper than easyJet's competitors. Stelios defended his policy vigorously: 'We decided that people who are willing to give us their money early should get a better price, and those who want the flexibility of booking late should pay a bit more.' (*Refer to Exhibit 5 to view a report on availability of fares.*)

Punctuality at easyJet was important. Because customer satisfaction was linked so closely to punctuality, responding adequately to the needs of customers was very important to Stelios. If a flight arrived more than four hours late, Stelios instructed his staff to write a letter of apology with his signature and to issue a full refund. Because the airline had many repeat customers, Stelios was confident that customer satisfaction was high. (*Refer to Exhibit 6 to view additional data on punctuality.*)

Outsourcing

Initially, Stelios had outsourced many of the airline's operations because it lowered costs and increased efficiency. Typically, the airline provided the planes, pilots, cabin crew, marketing and sales people. Subcontractors handled all other responsibilities, from check-in to the on-site customer information desk.

By early 1998, however, easyJet had acquired its own operating certificate and reached a scale where it would have been possible to bring certain operations in-house. Nevertheless, Stelios still maintained that it made more sense to continue working with subcontractors. The airline's ability to remain ticket-less, meet its goal of a 20-minute turnaround at the gate, and maintain its safety depended on subcontractors.

To improve its relationships with these outside vendors, easyJet often led workshops, role-reversal exercises, and simulations to explain its objectives and expectations. The company evaluated subcontractors not only on quantitative criteria, such as percentage of on-time flights, but also on qualitative criteria, such as understanding of the easyJet concept.

Creating brand awareness

Because Stelios felt that brand awareness was critical to the success of the airline, approximately 10% of easyJet's revenues were spent on newspaper, magazine, and radio advertising. Because of its marketing approach, easyJet's top management believed that easyJet was able to differentiate itself from its competitors. Management was also of the opinion that its efforts had been rewarded through a significant growth in sales and through the company's high level of brand awareness. A 1998 industry poll indicated that the easyJet brand had a recognition rate of 88% in London; in Geneva, brand awareness was 82%.

Stelios also generated publicity for easyJet through highly publicized, and often full-scale attacks on his competitors. According to Philippe Vignon, marketing director, 'Whenever there is an opportunity to make some news, we do it!' (*Refer to Exhibits 7 and 8 to view examples of easyJet's attacking ads.*)

Illustration: The Barcelona Controversy

In early 1999, easyJet advertised for months that the airline was planning to offer service to Barcelona [from Geneva], and had even sold 7,000 seats. However, this new service was contingent upon approval from the Swiss authorities. Swissair, which had a monopoly over the Barcelona-Geneva route, fought against easyJet's entry into the market. The Swiss government ruled in favor of Swissair, stating that easyJet could not fly scheduled flights between the two cities. On the inaugural flight to Barcelona, Stelios appeared and personally issued refunds to passengers, in essence, giving them a free trip to Barcelona. He even emblazoned the words, 'Say no to Swissair monopoly' in bright orange letters across the fuselage of the plane. During the flight, he asked for a donation from passengers in order to 'protect consumers against the Swissair monopoly.' Surprisingly, 50% to 60% of the money he refunded was donated back to easyJet. Undeterred, easyJet found a loophole. The company set up a new company, called easyJet Tours, which offered chartered service to Barcelona as part of a package that included the flight, a bus ticket, and the right to stay in a tent on a campsite near the city. (Staying in the tent was not a requirement.) Stelios believed such acts created affinity. In addition to building brand loyalty, the extra media attention helped easyJet gain widespread support in Switzerland for its willingness to stand its ground against Swissair.

Source: easyJet

Corporate culture

Stelios wanted to build a strong, inclusive employee-culture at easyJet, which led to the creation of the easyJet Culture Committee. The committee, an elected group drawn from company staff, was responsible for establishing company policy on the working environment, communications between management and staff, and social events such as staff parties for the airline's 1,000 employees. Every Friday at Luton, easyJet held a company-sponsored barbecue that the staff used to get to know one another better.

Stelios believed in complete transparency, and all documents had to be scanned and placed on the computer system, so that anyone in the company could access them. This included mail, internal memos, press cuttings, business plans, and sales data (the only confidential information was payroll-related).

Stelios stressed that culture was not something leaders can create overnight. As he put it, 'You build your legend slowly, bit by bit, battle by battle. You talk about it, and then you get together and have fun. I believe that work should be fun.'

Illustration: The Fight with Go

In 1996, Bob Ayling, British Airway's chief, approached Stelios in what appeared to be an offer to buy easyJet. Instead, after a three month courtship, British Airways abandoned the deal, and one year later, launched Go, its own budget airline. Still angry over the incident, Stelios got his revenge by buying several rows of seats on Go's first flight. He commanded his staff to don orange boiler jackets, and they all boarded the flight like a group of merry pranksters, offering free flights on easyJet to Go's passengers. Barbara Cassani, chief executive of Go airlines, was on the inaugural flight to welcome new passengers. When she saw what was occurring, she lapsed into stunned silence. The publicity stunt paid off for easyJet. Go Airlines announced losses of £22 million in 1999. However, Stelios was wounded yet again when British Airways hired away easyJet's lawyer at an estimated annual salary of £500,000.

Source: easyJet

Stelios strongly believed that being the underdog in such a highly competitive industry strengthened his team and brought them closer together. He recalled:

I noticed how much more motivated the staff was when British Airways launched the Go airline and when the whole country was talking about us and we were on television every night. All of these things created a sense of pride for the company. The same thing happened in Switzerland. People at TEA, a Swiss charter airline, were no longer motivated, so we bought the company and turned it around. As soon as we had the run-in with Swissair, morale really picked up. We were the underdogs. Our employees would go home and their neighbors had heard about the company they work for, which gave them the courage to stay and fight.

Because of the airline's high-profile battles, Stelios had become famous and people began to recognize him when he was out in public. When asked about his increasing popularity, he replied:

> It is nice to be considered as sort of a Robin Hood, and have people stop you in the street and say, 'Thank you for flying to London. Now I can go and see my family.' My father was a very successful shipper, but no one ever stopped him in the street and said, 'Thank you for transporting oil to my house.' It is very satisfying to be recognized and to be appreciated.

Competition

Ryanair

Ryanair, based in Ireland, was established in 1985. Initially, Ryanair was a full-service, traditional airline with two classes of seating, but in the early 1990s, the airline changed its focus to become a no-frills carrier. Unlike easyJet, Ryanair used travel agents, issued tickets, and participated in the global distribution system. Utilizing a fleet of 20 Boeing 737s and servicing 26 destinations, the airline had more than 100 scheduled flights per day in late 1999, and planned to expand both its route base and the size of its fleet. (*Refer to Exhibits 9 and 10 for additional information on easyJet's competitors.*)

In 1999, Ryanair experienced its ninth straight year of strong growth. For the six month period ending June 30, 1999, Ryanair had sales of IR£66.2 million[2], and the operating profit margin was 28%.

Go

Go was established by British Airways in May 1998 as a no-frills airline to compete in the low-cost segment of the European market. Financed with £25 million from British Airways, Go was founded in large part to defend British Airway's market share, since easyJet was stealing its passengers. In 1999 the company suffered financial losses, although Go's CEO, Barbara Cassani, expected to achieve profitability by 2001. For the period ending March 31, 1999, Go had sales of £31.6 million, and operating losses of £22 million. Before Go announced that the airline was losing money, Stelios set up a contest offering free easyJet flights to whoever came closest to guessing the amount of Go's losses.

Go's flights were based out of London's Stansted Airport instead of London's Heathrow Airport, where British Airways was headquartered. Stelios considered Go a copycat of easyJet, and believed that Go was heavily influenced by parent company British Airways in the way it structured its fares. Stelios also suspected that British Airways unfairly subsidized Go; therefore, he filed a lawsuit alleging that British Airways violated Article 86 of the Treaty of Rome, which says that dominant players in a market should not operate at below the cost of production.

Virgin Express

Virgin Express Holdings plc, headquartered in Belgium, was set up in 1996 when the Virgin Group acquired a controlling stake in EuroBelgian Airlines. Virgin Express Holdings plc was principally engaged as a low-fare carrier, and provided short to medium-haul jet service to markets principally within continental Europe from the company's base in Brussels. For the fiscal year ending December 31, 1998, Virgin Express had sales of BEF 10.5 billion.[3]

Virgin Express differentiated itself from other low-cost carriers in that it had formed an alliance with Sabena Airlines, the flag carrier in Belgium. This relationship provided Virgin Express with a steady stream of contractual revenue, since Sabena bought seats on Virgin Express in order to offer better connections to destinations throughout Europe.

Buzz

In September 1999 KLM announced that it would enter the low-cost segment of the market with Buzz airlines. From its base at London's Stansted airport, Buzz planned to offer service to Berlin, Dusseldorf, Frankfurt, Milan, Vienna, Paris, and Lyon. KLM already had one brand in place at London Stansted, KLM UK. To avoid confusion, management stated that KLM flights would go to Amsterdam, while Buzz would fly to all other destinations.

---

[2] IR£1.00 = US$1.30.

[3] BEF 40 = US$1.00.

Challenges

Stelios faced several challenges at easyJet. In November 1999, he struggled with the decision of whether to take his privately held company public. On one hand, he believed he could better motivate his staff by offering them shares in the company. On the other hand, however, his team of advisors feared his management style was too entrepreneurial. Regarding the decision to refund passengers who had already paid for the Geneva-Barcelona flight during the battle with Swissair, he remarked, 'Do you think the finance director of a public company would say, "Refund every customer on the Geneva flight" like I did? My finance director was pulling his hair out!' Although plans were underway to float the company on the London Stock Exchange and NASDAQ in early 2000, Stelios frequently asked himself and others around him if the market would trust him to run the company the way he felt was best.

Second, the airline had a history of using subcontractors, but found that at times, the outsourcing of vital functions posed certain problems. For example, at some airports that were not frequently serviced, easyJet hired external ground handlers. Because the handlers were not easyJet employees, they did not attend to customers' needs in a manner that satisfied Stelios. He commented:

Making sure that these subcontractors meet the quality standards we have set is very difficult. The weakest link in the chain is in Mallorca. There, we have people who maybe work on an easyJet flight once a day or once a week, and therefore don't know the company very well. I've been telling my staff, 'If I hear another ground handler refer to easyJet in the third person, I will sack him!' There is nothing worse for a customer to go to a check-in desk and say, 'When is the flight?' and the person responds, 'easyJet is an hour late.' When the customer asks why, the person responds, 'Ask easyJet!'

Third, Stelios believed that easyJet needed to become more corporate in its processes. In his opinion, it took certain skills to start a company from scratch, and people who were good at starting companies were not necessarily good at running big companies. In late 1999, the company was recruiting 3 or 4 senior managers.

A fourth challenge at easyJet was the relative youth and inexperience of some employees. Although it was not unusual to find a 24 year-old handling a monthly budget of £500,000, the airline nonetheless had high rates of absenteeism among phone operators.

Recognizing that easyJet was in a phase where it needed to stabilize itself internally, Stelios decided not to enter any new markets in the short-term. He felt that he needed to consolidate and do more in the countries where they had already set up operations. He asked, 'What's wrong with flying 10 times a day between London and Geneva?' He added, 'One of the biggest mistakes that airlines make is spreading themselves too thin.'

When asked how many low-cost carriers could survive in Europe, Stelios replied:

The market is bigger than most people think, although availability of slots at airports is a problem. London is getting a bit crowded, but then again, London is a big place and just about any city out of London can work as a destination. Start looking around Europe, and there aren't many other low-cost carriers. [...] The big prize in Europe is Paris. There is no low-cost flying in and out of Paris whatsoever. Any city with 3 or 4 million people should be capable of sustaining a low cost airline.

From easyJet to easyEverything

Pleased with his success in the airline industry, Stelios was ready to try his hand at other businesses in 1999. Among his pet projects was the creation of a cybercafé business called easyEverything café. The idea behind easyEverything was 'to offer the Internet to the masses' and 'to be the cheapest way to access the web.' Charging £1 per hour of Web access, Stelios stated that surfing the Internet at easyEverything was less than the cost of a phone call in London. He hoped that customers would come to the café not only to surf the Internet, but also to send emails and do their online shopping. Stelios joked, 'If flying people to Scotland for £29 is crazy, this is crazier!'

The first easyEverything café debuted in London on June 21, 1999 near Victoria Station and was open non-stop 24 hours per day. It was quickly considered one of the hot spots in London, and there was often a queue to get inside, even at 3 AM. Customers could purchase coffee and snacks or rent the services of a tutor, who showed them how to use the Internet to access online bargains.

In June 1999, Stelios signed four more leases for bigger locations in London. The key to success for the café was thought to be size; the first café contained 400 terminals. Another perceived advantage was the use of state-of-the-art hardware, including flat screens and fiber-optic communication lines, which offered much faster connection and downloading than most home systems.

Not content to stop with cybercafés, Stelios also considered entering the rental car business and starting up an Internet-based bank. He wondered if he could successfully apply the concept behind easyJet to these new businesses. Given that Stelios was known to be rather risk-averse, the decision would not be an easy one.[4]

[4] The case was written using interviews and materials provided by the company. Among the materials provided were a case study from the February 1999 issue of the *European Management Journal* written by Don Sull, and an article on easyJet from the November 1999 issue of *Bilan* magazine written by Giuseppe Melillo, which we would like to gratefully acknowledge.

Exhibit 1 Food selections from the easyKiosk
Source: easyJet

Exhibit 2 Financial performance, 1997-1998

easyJet Airline Company Limited PROFIT AND LOSS ACCOUNT	1997 £	1998 £
Turnover	46,034,549	77,000,035
Cost of Sales	(38,963,150)	(61,525,257)
Gross Profit	7,071,399	15,474,778
Distribution and marketing	(6,324,068)	(7,748,225)
Administrative expenses	(4,491,338)	(6,260,124)
Operating profit/(loss)	(3,744,007)	1,466,429
Other interest receivable and similar income	607,392	978,268
Interest payable and similar charges	(135,250)	(125,759)
Profit/(loss) on ordinary activities before taxation	(3,271,865)	2,318,938
Tax on profit on ordinary activities	–	–
Retained profit/(loss) for the year	(3,271,865)	2,318,938
Retained loss brought forward	(5,872,621)	(9,144,486)
Retained loss carried forward	(9,144,486)	(6,825,548)

easyJet Airline Company Limited BALANCE SHEET	1997 £	1998 £
Fixed assets		
Tangible assets	1,529,161	2,601,184
Current assets		
Restricted deposits	343,476	1,416,457
Debtors	3,888,546	10,887,761
Cash at bank and in hand	16,877,623	12,506,665
Creditors	(17,783,292)	(20,237,615)
Net current assets	3,326,353	4,573,268
Net assets	4,855,514	7,174,452
Capital and reserves		
Called up share capital	14,000,000	14,000,000
Profit and loss account	(9,144,486)	(6,825,548)
Equity shareholders' funds	4,855,514	7,174,452

Source: Directors' report and financial statements, September 30, 1998

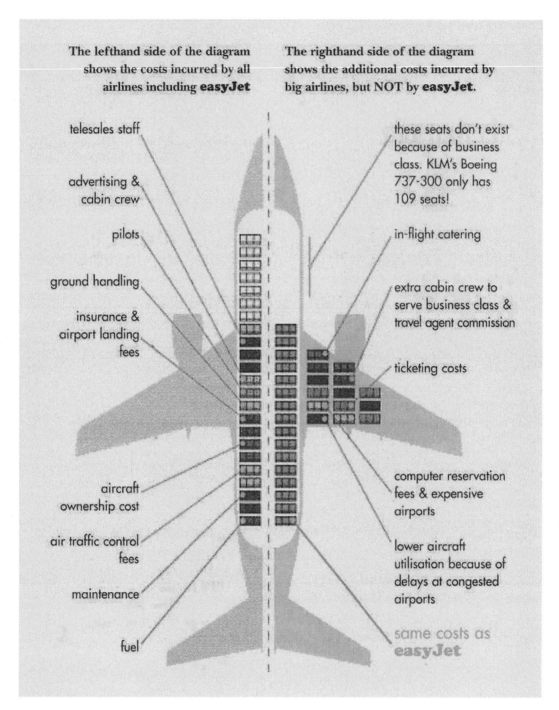

The lefthand side of the diagram shows the costs incurred by all airlines including **easyJet**.

The righthand side of the diagram shows the additional costs incurred by big airlines, but NOT by **easyJet**.

telesales staff

advertising & cabin crew

pilots

ground handling

insurance & airport landing fees

aircraft ownership cost

air traffic control fees

maintenance

fuel

these seats don't exist because of business class. KLM's Boeing 737-300 only has 109 seats!

in-flight catering

extra cabin crew to serve business class & travel agent commission

ticketing costs

computer reservation fees & expensive airports

lower aircraft utilisation because of delays at congested airports

same costs as **easyJet**

Exhibit 3 Cost comparison
Source: easyRider magazine, July 1999

We have arrived! (Well, sort of.) The ultimate magazine for fat cat business travelers did a poll of its readers, and we were voted the best low-cost airline. What pleases me more than anything is that we beat the low-cost clone by British Airways (BA). It's not bad if you think that they lost £22m in the first year alone trying to break into our market.

So we must be doing something right. With our fleet of 18 Boeing 737-300s, one of the youngest in the world, and a far better punctuality record than BA and other so-called flag carriers, we are flying fuller than ever before. We now have 27 routes, and not only will we fly more frequently on our existing routes, but we are also planning new ones later in the year 2000, when the next 15 brand new 737-700s start arriving.

On other fronts, my Internet shops are doing very well and I will expand easyEverything in all the cities that easyJet flies as soon as I can. At the time of publishing this message on the web site, we have signed for five in London with a total of 2300 seats (yes – the biggest has 630 seats!), and have already signed for sites in Edinburgh and Amsterdam.

My easyRentacar.com project is on track for being up and running by April 2000, and you should be able to rent an 'orange car' over the Internet for £9/day.

As you can see, the common theme for all my ventures is the heavy use of the Internet. Take my word for it, all the best deals on the airline will be available on the Net from now on. So, if you don't get online you might lose out. Remember you can always use an easyEverything Internet shop to book your flight or car, coming to a place near you soon!

On another subject, we continue our battle against Swissair. As you may remember, in July we were blocked from operating a scheduled service between Geneva and Barcelona, due to political pressure from Swissair who wanted to preserve their monopoly on this route. So, to get round this, I set up easyJet Tours, a charter operation which offers passengers return flights, transfers, and accommodation (even though this is only a tent!). This service has proved very popular (I mean the flights, not the tents), and we will continue to fly this route throughout the winter. In the meantime, we will carry on lobbying the Swiss government to make changes to the law. I am encouraged by the fact that a large number of Swiss MPs have signed a motion supporting this cause, even before it is debated in Parliament.

Thank you for visiting our web site.

Stelios

Exhibit 4 Message from Stelios
Source: easyJet, November 1999

Four weeks before travel date:

I had to wait 10 minutes before speaking to Richard, a sales assistant. I asked for the cheapest fare to Barcelona, leaving Saturday, September 26 and staying two nights. Richard said that a ticket for the 8:10 PM flight would cost £49 one way (an earlier flight would be much more expensive). The return would cost £99 for the 4:45 PM flight, or £69 for the 6:50 AM flight. So the cheapest fare was £118 including tax. Richard warned me that the 4:45 PM flight was filling up fast and prices would only go up.

Three weeks before travel date:

Prices were the same, but there were then only six seats for the return leg. I felt pressured to book, so I did. There was no charge for using my credit card and no hard sell to take easyJet insurance. I was given a reference number and told I won't be issued a ticket. Confirmation of my flight was faxed through about an hour later; the paperwork arrived in the post a week later, with a discount voucher for train travel.

Two weeks before travel date:

The prices had risen by £10 for the outward flight; the 4:45 PM flight was sold out.

One week before travel date:

My outward flight was £64; there were only two seats left. Interestingly, seven seats were available again on the return flight at £129.

One day before travel date:

The outward flight cost £69, and the return flight cost £139.

Exhibit 5 A Sunday Times reporter investigates availability of easyJet's low fares
Source: 'Fare Play.' *Sunday Times*, October 18, 1998

Exhibit 6 Airline punctuality comparisons for the period ending August 1999: arrivals and departures

		Percentage of Flights Late				
		Early to 15 minutes	16 to 30 minutes	31 to 60 minutes	1 to 3 hours	3 to 6 hours
easyJet	London–Glasgow	90%	8%	2%	0%	0%
	London–Zurich	52%	33%	11%	4%	0%
	London–Mallorca	79%	13%	6%	2%	0%
go	London–Malaga	64%	18%	9%	6%	3%
	London–Mallorca	53%	8%	25%	14%	0%
RYANAIR	London–Dublin	63%	20%	10%	7%	0%
Virgin Express	London–Malaga	70%	0%	10%	20%	0%
	London–Mallorca	78%	11%	11%	0%	0%
swissair	London–Zurich	43%	31%	18%	8%	0%
BRITISH AIRWAYS	London–Glasgow	88%	6%	3%	3%	0%
	London–Zurich	69%	23%	6%	2%	0%

Source: UK Civil Aviation Authority

It's time BA came out of the closet!

On 25 May 1999, British Airways announced their 1998/99 results, but they still refuse to disclose how much of the £25 million they put in their low-cost airline has been lost over that period. Last year **easyJet** convinced a High Court Judge that any cross subsidy between BA and its subsidiary could be illegal. The case is still pending, and BA is doing everything it can to avoid disclosure of the facts.

We are so convinced that BA's low-cost airline has made a substantial loss in their first year that we are having a competition over the Internet to guess the total amount lost in its first year of trading.

The 50 entrants nearest the correct figure will win themselves a pair of **easyJet** flights anywhere on the **easyJet** network! If there are more than 50 correct answers a tie-breaker will apply. The competition will close as soon as the results are released. In due course they will have to file them with Companies House. So if you want the chance to win a prize sooner, why not e-mail Bob Ayling at BA and persuade him to release the results.

COMPETITION
50 pairs of **easyJet** flights up for grabs!

Entries will ONLY be accepted over the Internet at

www.**easyJet**.com
the web's favourite airline

Exhibit 7 Ad attacking British Airways
Source: easyJet

Stelios' pet hates

Air Miles = Air Bribes

Air Miles is a bribery scheme invented by British Airways and designed to induce business travellers to waste their companies' money by travelling business class and then collecting the reward for their personal benefit. (Usually lavish holidays in the Caribbean frequently in the company of their secretaries)!

Those Chief Executives with the best interest of the company and its shareholders at heart must ban the collection of air miles by their staff while travelling on business. It's not going to be a popular decision, which goes to prove the degree of corruption!

In addition, the taxman has done British Airways a huge favour by miraculously not including air miles as a taxable perk, in the same way that company cars are taxed.

Write to your MP about the great Government rip-off!

The last Tory Chancellor increased airport tax (officially called Air Passenger Duty or APD) from £5 to £10. Zurich, outside the EU, has an even higher tax at £20. Contrary to popular belief this money does not contribute to the improvement of airports, but ends up in the pocket of the taxman. This tax is totally unfair to **easyJet** customers as on some occasions the tax has been more than our one-way air fare (Yes, we have sold seats for £8.50). Please write to your MP expressing your dissatisfaction and suggesting that APD should be a percentage of the fare, just like VAT.

www.**easyJet**.com

Exhibit 8 Stelios' pet hates
Source: easyJet

Exhibit 9 Airlines routes of competing low cost carriers

	easyJet	go	RYANAIR THE LOW FARES AIRLINE	Virgin Express
Belgium			Brussels	Brussels*
Czech Republic		Prague		
Denmark		Copenhagen	Århus	Copenhagen
France	Nice	Lyon	Biarritz, Carcassonne, Dinnard, Lyon, Paris, St. Etienne, Toulouse	Nice
Germany		Munich	Frankfurt	
Greece	Athens			
Ireland	Belfast		Cork, Derry, Dublin*, Kerry, Knock	Shannon
Italy		Bologna, Milan, Rome, Venice	Ancona, Genoa, Pisa, Rimini, Turin, Venice	Milan, Rome
The Netherlands	Amsterdam			Rotterdam
Norway			Oslo	
Portugal		Faro, Lisbon		
Scotland	Aberdeen, Edinburgh, Glasgow, Inverness	Edinburgh	Glasgow*	
Spain	Barcelona, Madrid, Malaga, Mallorca	Alicante, Barcelona, Bilbao, Madrid, Malaga, Mallorca		Barcelona, Madrid, Malaga, Mallorca
Sweden			Kristianstad, Malmö, Stockholm	
Switzerland	Geneva*, Zurich	Zurich		
United Kingdom	Liverpool*, London*	London*	Birmingham, Bournemouth, Bristol, Cardiff, Leeds Bradford, Liverpool, London*, Manchester, Teesside	London

* Represents a hub

Sources: <http://www.easyJet.com>; <http://www.Go-Fly.com>; <http://www.Ryanair.com>; <http://www.Virgin-Express.com>.

Exhibit 10 Comparative financial & operational statistics for selected airlines

	easyJet[1]	Go[2]	Ryanair[3]	Virgin Express[4]	Southwest[5]	British Airways[6]	Swissair[7]
	US$ million	US$ million	US$ million	US$ million	US$ million	US$ million	US$ million
Revenue	123	51	303	262	4,164	14,264	7,290
Operating expenses	121	83	233	261	3,480	13,557	6,897
Operating profit/(loss)	2	(32)	70	1	684	806	452
Net profit/(loss)	4	(22)	59	(3)	433	330	233
Market Capitalization	n/a	n/a	1,794	95	8,197	6,504	2,439
Pre-tax Profit Margin	3.0	(63)	25.6	0.5	16.9	2.5	4.9
Return on Assets	32.3	(57)	18.8	(2.8)	9.7	1.6	2.6
Return on Equity	16.6	(177)	31.6	(6.6)	19.7	6.1	13.0
Debt/Equity	1.4	n/a	59.3	140.3	96.7	282.2	385.2
Sales to Assets	10.7	91.1	96.9	292.0	92.9	69.5	82.5
Price-Earnings Ratio	n/a	n/a	21.7	170.8	20.4	21.4	10.0
Capacity ('000) – ASKM[a]	2,801,000	2,052,000	3,000,000[b]	2,657,814	76,069,624	161,291,000	40,560,000
Load Factor	75%	53%	71%	75%	66%	71%	72%
Passengers per year	1,714,761	2,000,000	4,900,000	2,600,000	52,586,400	45,049,000	12,199,000
Number of Aircraft	8	13	20	20	280	278	129
Employees	394	500	1094	639	25,844	63,779	43,696

[1] For the period ending 30.09.98.
[4,5,7] For the period ending 31.12.98.
[2,3,6] For the period ending 31.03.99.
[a] ASKM = Available Seat Kilometers; [b] This figure is an estimate.
Source: Company Annual Reports, Reuters Business Briefing

INTERNATIONAL

Case 6 **Hewlett-Packard: Creating a virtual supply chain (A)**

I want Hewlett-Packard to be able to produce and deliver a tape drive in five days, from supplied parts to customers.

Research Associate Petri Lehtivaara prepared this case under the supervision of Professors Carlos Cordon, Ralf W. Seifert and Thomas E. Vollmann as a basis for class discussion rather than to illustrate either effective or ineffective handling of a business situation.

This case series won the Supply Chain Management Award in the 2003 European Case Writing Competition organized by the European Foundation for Management Development (efmd).

IMD-6-0251
V. 17.12.2003

The words that Derek Gray, supply chain manager in the tape drive unit of Hewlett-Packard, had uttered just hours earlier to a couple of external visitors echoed in his head.

It was early July 2001. Gray sat down in his cubicle in HP's open-plan office in Bristol, United Kingdom. He was preparing for the next day's management meeting at which he had to present his recommendations for moving toward virtual manufacturing.

Gray had been managing a project – started some years ago – to create a virtual supply chain. He had gathered vast experience on the way and wanted to use this knowledge to recommend a good solution. Gray had three alternative routes to choose from:

♦ Path of least resistance: Outsource the final assembly, testing and configuration to one of the suppliers of a major part (Philips).

♦ Create the ultimate supply chain: Develop a lowest total cost supply chain; invest in further redesign and resourcing to maximize long-term efficiency.

♦ Consolidation of the industry: Join forces with a competitor and outsource the final assembly, testing and configuration to it.

HP needed to take manufacturing to the next stage – standing still was not an option.

Hewlett-Packard Company

Hewlett-Packard Company (HP) was a global provider of computing and imaging solutions and services for business and home. In 2000 its sales

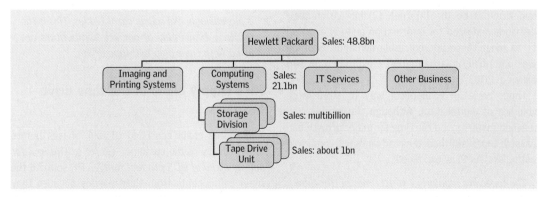

Figure 1 Tape Drive Business Unit
Note: 2000 figures, in $

were US$48.8 billion and it employed 89,000 people. HP's three main segments were imaging and printing systems (41%), computing systems (42%) and IT services (14%); other business accounted for 3%.

CEO Carly Fiorina had reorganized HP to become more customer oriented. The reorganization created a back-end, including product generation units, and a front-end devoted to sales and marketing, delivery channels and the client relationship. In addition, the focus changed from a functional one to a matrix.

Tape drives in HP

The tape drive business unit employed 700 people, 550 of them based in Bristol. The headquarters of the unit was in the United States. (*Refer to Figure 1 for the organizational position of tape drives in HP.*)

Products

HP's tape drive business unit had three main areas: digital data storage (DDS), Ultrium and Storage solutions. In 2000 sales were just under $1 billion, with DDS generating most of this. Ultrium was the product of the future; it was based on an open standard – called linear tape open (LTO) – developed together with IBM and Seagate.

Tape drive business

The tape drive business was part of the storage market. The storage market in general was expanding due to customers' business transformation. Customers were (1) taking advantage of opportunities on the Internet, (2) increasing their demands and need for information and (3) evolving IT to meet these unpredictable demands. Storage was potentially a large market – estimated at $46 billion in 2003.

Tapes were an economical way to store large volumes of digital data. Although the market had reached maturity and the time for major growth had passed, tapes still had their advantages compared with disks. As Gray explained:

The tapes are regularly 7 to 10 times better than disks in cost/gigabyte stored. They will remain around for at least the next seven years.

The type of tape drives most often used had also started to change, and demand was increasingly for higher capacity, more complex equipment.

The performance and quality of the product were qualifying criteria in the business. The key success factors were time-to-market and cost of the product. The cost was especially important in sales to original equipment manufacturers (OEMs).

The life cycle of a product was typically four years. This meant that getting product to market as quickly as possible was critical for the company, to ensure highest possible sales volumes and margins. In the future merely having a good product would not be good enough; it would have to be part of a system.

The business in transition

Tape technology was in a transitional phase. New technology – LTO and super digital linear tape (SDLT) – had been introduced to upgrade from the traditional technologies of DDS and digital linear tape (DLT). Quantum was the major producer of DLT and was the overall market leader in the tape drive business, particularly the high-end segment. HP had kept its lead in the medium segment. DDS technology-based products were still a profitable product line. (*Refer to Figure 2 for characteristics of tape drive products.*)

One emerging trend in the industry was the link between sales of tape drives and media (tape). The media business was a large and growing one. Gray noted:

There is less money in the tape drive business. The money is increasingly in media. The business is increasingly like selling razor blades. This is the strategy that many of our key competitors are using with their high-end tape drives.

HP's supply chain in the tape drive business

The supply chain consisted of four phases before final delivery to the customer. (*Refer to Figure 3 for supply chain of DDS product family.*) HP sourced the main components from third parties because they had special technology and expertise that HP did not have in-house.

Characteristics	Traditional Technology		New Technology
	Medium segment	High-end segment	
Competing products	DDS, AIT	DLT, AIT, Mammoth, 34XX	Super digital linear tape (SDLT), linear tape open (LTO)
Volume (per annum)	1.75 million	400,000	Low
Price comparison	$1,000 (reference price*)	3× to 5×	7× to 10×
Main producers (and market share)	HP (50%–55%), Sony (30%), Seagate	Quantum (80%)	Quantum, IBM, HP, Seagate

Figure 2 Characteristics of tape drive products
* A disguised price that does not reflect actuals.

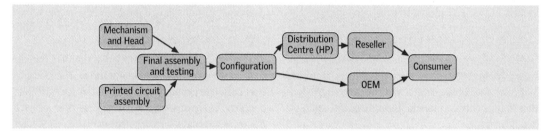

Figure 3 Supply chain for DDS products

Two channels to market

The tape drives were sold to the end consumer either through OEMs or resellers. In volume terms the OEM channel was larger; in sales terms the reseller channel was larger. The reseller channel was pretty profitable for HP, whereas the OEM channel was less so. Danny Berry, OEM supply chain manager, explained:

> OEMs are very demanding. On the other hand, if we deliver it is a good reference. In addition we have a lot of contact with the engineers.

HP delivered the product to its resellers through three regional warehouses – Asia-Pacific, Europe and the US – which had varying degrees of performance. Gray expressed his views on the deliveries:

> [In the reseller channel] we had significant problems with on-time delivery. I am not sure if we

> need distribution centers in our business. I think we should be able to deliver product directly from production to the reseller.

The OEM channel received the products directly from the factory. This worked well and HP had even won awards from Sun Microsystems for being a good supplier.

Outsourcing of DDS products

In 1997 HP decided to start developing the LTO standard together with IBM and Seagate. This meant that the requirement for space and investment in the factory increased, but the manufacturing manager indicated there was no more space or investment for manufacturing. Outsourcing of manufacturing was the only option, even if many people had initially been against it.

Players in the Outsourced Supply Chain with Different Models of DDS					
Model	Start	Mechanism and Head	PCA	FAST	Configuration
DDS1	1990	Sony	CM A	HP Bristol	HP Bristol
DDS2	1997	Mitsumi	CM A	CM A (Scotland)	CM A (Ireland)
DDS3	1998	Mitsumi	CM B	CM A (Scotland)	CM A (Ireland)
DDS4	1999	Mitsumi	CM A	Mitsumi	CM C (Ireland)

Figure 4 Evolution of the partners in the supply chain
Note: CM = Contract manufacturer

Between 1997 and 2000 HP outsourced all its models in the DDS product family, one by one. The organization did not have an overall strategy. The solutions were tailored to each individual situation. *(Refer to Figure 4 for evolution of the partners in the supply chain.)* HP always started the manufacturing in its own facilities in Bristol and transferred production to the contract manufacturer after the ramp-up had been done.

OEM customers had an ambivalent reaction to outsourcing. On the one hand, they did not want to go through a new approval process of a new supplier for the product. On the other hand, their attitude to outsourcing was: 'Just make sure that this is invisible to us in terms of quality, delivery performance and cost.'

Outsourcing assembly and configuration

HP decided to outsource the final assembly and configuration of DDS2. It chose a contract manufacturer in Scotland to keep the risk of outsourcing low: the contract manufacturer was close to HP, the engineering people liked it and the price was competitive, although not the lowest.

Relatively soon after the deal, it became evident that the contract manufacturer could produce drives at a significantly lower cost than HP, largely because of overhead. Both companies put a lot of effort into managing the relationship. HP had three or four people constantly in Scotland and the companies had regular team meetings. The core team consisted of people from materials, finance, engineering and logistics areas in the two companies. There was also a communications matrix by which HP people talked to their counterparts at the manufacturer. Both companies seemed happy with the situation.

HP also outsourced production of the DDS3 model to the same contract manufacturer. The decision was based on capacity and cost. In this case, HP was concerned about the resourcing of the project. Davey Maclachlan, procurement manager, explained:

We wanted the contract manufacturer to have a new product introduction team [for DDS3]. It had one team that needed to manage both DDS2 and DDS3. I think the margins were so small that they had to cut resources. We also noted that they were fire fighting. It felt like their departments were not talking to each other. They fixed one problem and the next came up as a consequence. The vendor management, inbound logistics and throughput suffered.

Divisional finance involvement

In 1998 HP's divisional finance function became involved. It had been investigating opportunities for taking advantage of regional benefits. The tape drive unit assessed whether this would work for them and decided on a location in Ireland. This meant that configuration should move there. Legal issues complicated the matter as HP had to have the management of the operation in Ireland, so communication from Bristol went to the factory via the Irish office.

The regional benefits were so significant that the organization was willing to complicate matters operationally. Calculations showed that the financial advantages would be equal to double the normal returns from supply chain savings and efficiencies.

Worsening relations with the contract manufacturer

The relationship with the contract manufacturer deteriorated. Maclachlan explained:

I went to visit the CM with a colleague in a positive mood. We thought that we would propose some additional business to them. When we met the team we were surprised by their response. Their motivation had clearly diminished and all they could see were problems. We assumed that something had happened to cause their change of heart, potentially in their assessment of the real costs of doing the work. We also felt it necessary to alert them to our needs to consider lower cost geographies (within the same company) and this was not well received.

New outsourcing partner

For the DDS4 model, HP opted to work mainly with Mitsumi and another contract manufacturer. For the new contract manufacturer, which had to configure only one product, this arrangement was not ideal. Also the supply chain had become complex. Gray explained:

We now had three major deals with different generations of DDS products. The relationships with the earlier contract manufacturers were becoming quite difficult due to the limited future. We had hoped to grow the business with the new CM but were having operational problems. The Mitsumi relationship was working very well, however the overhead to manage all of these various relationships was going through the roof. At this stage we also started to have quite heated debates between the functions (accountants, supply chain and engineering) about the relative benefits of each outsourcing decision.

Launch of the new technology: Ultrium

Work on developing Ultrium started in 1997. HP partnered with IBM and Seagate to develop the standard, which was in competition with the Quantum one. Production of Ultrium began in late 2000. The supply chain looked similar to that for DDS products, with three main components: mechanism, PCA and head (*refer to Figure 5*).

After six months' production of Ultrium, Gray decided to collect data to better understand the ramp-up period. He was amazed to see the level of inventory in the supply chain since production began. (*Refer to Exhibit 1 for information on the supply chain.*)

The lead time across the supply chain was theoretically 90 days. Gray's ambition was to be able to deliver a tape drive to the customer in five days. He commented:

It does not take more than a day to manufacture one, and four days are enough for logistics.

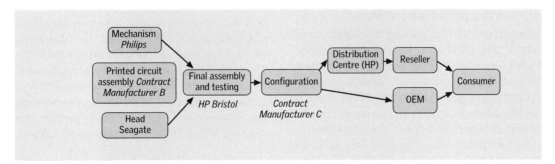

Figure 5 Supply chain for Ultrium

Future alternatives

Gray had come to the conclusion that HP needed to move toward virtual manufacturing and not produce any part of Ultrium. He identified four key issues that should determine the choice of the future alternative:

1   Strategic alignment

2   Total cost of ownership

3   Partner choice

4   Cost of production

The first two were the most important criteria. Strategic alignment included both supply chain and overall strategy of the storage division and meant that HP's investment would be low with quick returns.

Many other companies in the industry had also moved toward outsourcing or virtual manufacturing. Outsourcing had seen the development of a new industry around contract manufacturers, the largest of which had global operations with high-level manufacturing and supply chain management skills. During 1999 and 2000 the deals had become larger, reaching multibillion levels in 2001.

HP had not been convinced of its contract manufacturers' capabilities in tape engineering. HP's experience was that its fixed cost was not reducing as much as expected, as it had to do the engineering itself. In the future HP wanted to move away from its original practice of ramping up the production in-house for six months and moving the production out after that. Now it wanted to change its manufacturing approach radically and get its partner involved from day one. To this end, it had outlined three main alternatives.

Alternative 1: path of least resistance

HP would give the final assembly and testing, configuration and distribution to one of its suppliers, Philips. According to Gray this was an easy-to-do alternative. Philips had superb engineers, who understood the tape business. However, Philips was a bit like HP, with high overhead, and the outsourcing deal did not seem to fit with Philips' overall strategy.

The production would be done in Austria and Hungary with five or six HP people always on site. In this case Gray needed to persuade the accountants of the intangible benefits, since the apparent savings were lower. The key issue was: What would it take for Philips to take on this business and what would be left for HP?

Alternative 2: the ultimate supply chain

This would involve designing the supply chain in the right way, from scratch. HP had talked with Mitsumi, which would ultimately have capabilities to manufacture both the head and mechanism and would also take care of final assembly and testing, configuration and – potentially – distribution. Mitsumi would emerge as a major tape drive manufacturer.

Gray assumed the investment would be high, but that the return would also be high. Ultimately this alternative would provide low cost and flexibility. At the moment Mitsumi did not have enough buying power and capabilities to produce the mechanism. HP would need to assist it with technology development for Ultrium. In the past, HP had had positive experiences working with Mitsumi. However, this time HP would need to assist Mitsumi with technology development and was unsure about the implications of moving in this direction.

Alternative 3: consolidation

The third alternative included collaborating with a competitor. This approach would assume consolidation was necessary in the industry and would concentrate on supply chain efficiency rather than competition. This would be especially true as both companies would be competing against Quantum's standard. The main question would be: Should you help a competitor to survive? The relationship would be complex and troublesome.

Decision looming

Gray also wondered to what extent similar options had come up in other industries. The alternatives were lined up and it was up to him to recommend one. The decision could be a crucial one for the future of the tape drive unit. Gray wanted to achieve efficiency in the supply chain, low cost of products and manageable relationships with HP's future partners. But Gray also acknowledged the fact of the HP culture:

HP is big on consensus. Any one person can kill the proposal.

Exhibit 1 Cumulative volume of parts in the supply chain and sales of ultrium

Month (end)	Supplier to PCA	Head	PCA	Mechanism	FAST	Config.	Sales
Aug 2000	33	9	18	20	4	4	0
Sep 2000	62	26	32	46	13	13	1
Oct 2000	129	34	43	46	21	17	1
Nov 2000	150	70	71	74	42	35	9
Dec 2000	204	100	127	120	73	51	14
Jan 2001	270	136	204	155	96	66	21
Feb 2001	367	185	266	208	130	101	38
Mar 2001	636	237	320	264	174	116	62
Apr 2001	733	294	418	332	220	161	78
May 2001	1,021	343	448	367	265	192	100

Note: The volume information is proportional, with sales in May 2001 being 100 and other volumes proportional to that.
Source: Company information

INTERNATIONAL

Hewlett-Packard: Creating a virtual supply chain (B)

Another 12 months had passed. Derek Gray took a deep breath and sat back and reflected on the developments that had taken place in this time.

> We took a long time to decide, but now we are ready to move forward. A lot of people were involved in the decision and we also lived through some internal organizational changes. The pending merger with Compaq further complicated the process on our side, but frankly there were also a number of surprises on the part of our potential partners.

Gray was relaxed as the roller-coaster experience of reaching the outsourcing decision was behind him and he could look forward to his new challenge of ramping up production at the supplier. It was July 2002. Gray had just moved to Vienna, Austria. This was not the original intention, but Gray explained:

> In autumn 2001 we decided on a variation of the Mitsumi option. We believed that it was worth

Research Associate Petri Lehtivaara prepared this case under the supervision of Professors Carlos Cordon and Ralf W. Seifert as a basis for class discussion rather than to illustrate either effective or ineffective handling of a business situation.

This case series won the Supply Chain Management Award in the *2003 European Case Writing Competition* organized by the European Foundation for Management Development (efmd).

IMD-6-0252
V. 17.12.2003

winning the battle for the tape drive business and thus wanted to create the ultimate supply chain, removing as many nodes as possible to improve efficiency. The idea with the Mitsumi option was to move our mechanism production, including equipment, technology and tools, from Philips to Mitsumi.

> We discussed our decision with the Philips executive and reached agreement on the matter. Somewhat unexpectedly, however, his team resisted the transfer and [through organizational play] effectively made it impossible for us to proceed.

More time passed and Gray needed to take a fresh look at the Philips option. Philips came back with the alternative suggestion of using Flextronics as a contract manufacturer. Flextronics had an assembly plant in Hungary, few hours away from Vienna, where the Philips division was based. Gray noted:

> We got quite excited about this option, as it would provide the lower manufacturing cost but with the engineering expertise of Philips. It felt like Christmas to us, it could be a win-win-win situation. The Philips and Flextronics executives were long-time friends and this helped to establish the relationship. We felt that in the circumstances, this would be a deal worth going for. By then we had finally said no to the Mitsumi option, and our negotiations with Seagate had slowly gone cold. Shortly afterwards, we learned about a management change at Philips. The new executive also subscribed to Philips strategy, but interpreted it slightly differently: It was no longer desirable for Philips to divest the mechanism manufacturing business to Flextronics as was previously proposed. At that point we had gone through all the options and in view of the significant loss of time decided simply to go ahead with Flextronics anyway. The Flextronics option provided ample opportunity for supply chain integration and was geographically close to Philips. It also provided low cost manufacturing capability in its Hungarian facility.

Gray's learning points from the outsourcing decisions

While reflecting on the ups and downs with the outsourcing, Gray was able to identify four dimensions of learning for himself.

- *'People buy from people'* Individuals make a difference and can alter decisions. A change of individuals will have a huge impact on potential deals.

- *'You get the vendor you deserve'* Vendor management and vendor development is extremely important. A partner who is constantly driven on cost is likely to cut resources to the point of poor performance. The vendor's performance often reflects the poorly developed vendor management practices of the customer, and indeed the other customers that the vendor works with.

- *'We need more accountants and lawyers than engineers'* Regional benefits are extremely significant and can distort people's thinking. The supply chain should still be the primary driver of decisions but there is a great deal of opportunity to be taken through these regional benefits.

- *'Like herding cats'* Large companies have difficulty organizing themselves. Bureaucracy and unclear accountability render decision making difficult. This applies to many multinationals and can be frustrating when two multinational companies try to work together.

Gray described the central learning:

Any team halfway capable but focused could make any of the options work, as long as they want to make things happen and have shared values with the supplier. One should not underestimate the value of the right team and the right skills in making almost any option work.

New challenges

Gray and two other people from HP's Bristol plant moved to Vienna to oversee the transition of manufacturing operations to Flextronics. Gray's challenge was to quickly transfer the manufacturing knowledge to the contract manufacturers. This time he wanted to follow a different approach and work toward a true partnership. With this in mind, Gray had to decide on two issues.

- What would be the best approach for knowledge transfer from the HP team to Flextronics?

- How should he define success for himself?

INSEAD

Case 7 Canon: Competing on capabilities

In 1961, following the runaway success of the company's model 914 office copier, Joseph C. Wilson, President of Xerox Corporation, was reported to have said, 'I keep asking myself, when am I going to wake up? Things just aren't this good in life'. Indeed, the following decade turned out to be better than anything Wilson could have dreamed. Between 1960 and 1970, Xerox increased its sales 40 percent per year from $40 million to $1.7 billion and raised its after-tax profits from $2.6 million to $187.7 million. In 1970, with 93 percent market share world-wide and a brand name that was synonymous with copying, Xerox appeared as invincible in its industry as any company ever could.

When Canon, 'the camera company from Japan', jumped into the business in the late 1960s, most observers were sceptical. Less than a tenth the size of Xerox, Canon had no direct sales or service organization to reach the corporate market for copiers, nor did it have a process technology to by-pass the 500 patents that guarded Xerox's Plain Paper Copier (PPC) process. Reacting to the spate of recent entries in the business including Canon, Arthur D. Little predicted in 1969 that no company would be able to challenge Xerox's monopoly in PPCs in the 1970s because its patents presented an insurmountable barrier.

Yet, over the next two decades, Canon rewrote the rule book on how copiers were supposed to be produced and sold as it built up $5 billion in revenues in the business, emerging as the second largest global player in terms of sales and surpassing Xerox in the

....

This case was prepared by Mary Ackenhusen, Research Associate, under the supervision of Sumantra Ghoshal, Associate Professor at INSEAD. It is intended to be used as a basis for class discussion rather than to illustrate either effective or ineffective handling of an administrative situation.

05/92-2253

number of units sold. According to the Canon Handbook, the company's formula for success as displayed initially in the copier business is 'synergistic management of the total technological capabilities of the company, combining the full measure of Canon's know how in fine optics, precision mechanics, electronics and fine chemicals'. Canon continues to grow and diversify using this strategy. Its vision, as described in 1991 by Ryuzaburo Kaku, President of the company, is 'to become a premier global company of the size of IBM combined with Matsushita'.

Industry background

The photocopying machine has often been compared with the typewriter as one of the few triggers that have fundamentally changed the ways of office work. But, while a mechanical Memograph machine for copying had been introduced by the A.B. Dick company of Chicago as far back as 1887, it was only in the second half of this century that the copier market exploded with Xerox's commercialisation of the 'electrophotography' process invented by Chester Carlson.

Xerox

Carlson's invention used an electrostatic process to transfer images from one sheet of paper to another. Licensed to Xerox in 1948, this invention led to two different photocopying technologies. The Coated Paper Copying (CPC) technology transferred the reflection of an image from the original directly to specialized zinc-oxide coated paper, while the Plain Paper Copying (PPC) technology transferred the image indirectly to ordinary paper through a rotating drum coated with charged particles. While either dry or liquid toner could be used to develop the image, the dry toner was generally preferable in both technologies. A large number of companies entered the CPC market in the 1950s and 1960s based on technology licensed from Xerox or RCA (to whom Xerox had earlier licensed this technology). However, PPC remained a Xerox monopoly since the company had refused to license any technology remotely connected to the PPC process and had protected the technology with over 500 patents.

Because of the need for specialized coated paper, the cost per copy was higher for CPC. Also, this process could produce only one copy at a time, and the copies tended to fade when exposed to heat or light. PPC, on the other hand, produced copies at a lower operating cost that were also indistinguishable from the original. The PPC machines were much more expensive, however, and were much larger in size. Therefore, they required a central location in the user's office. The smaller and less expensive CPC machines, in contrast, could be placed on individual desks. Over time, the cost and quality advantages of PPC, together with its ability to make multiple copies at high speed, made it the dominant technology and, with it, Xerox's model of centralized copying, the industry norm.

This business concept of centralized copying required a set of capabilities that Xerox developed and which, in turn, served as its major strengths and as key barriers to entry to the business. Given the advantages of volume and speed, all large companies found centralized copying highly attractive and they became the key customers for photocopying machines. In order to support this corporate customer base, Xerox's product designs and upgrades emphasized economies of higher volume copying. To market the product effectively to these customers, Xerox also built up an extensive direct sales and service organization of over 12,000 sales representatives and 15,000 service people. Forty percent of the sales reps' time was spent 'hand holding' to prevent even minor dissatisfaction. Service reps, dressed in suits and carrying their tools in briefcases, performed preventative maintenance and prided themselves on reducing the average time between breakdown and repair to a few hours.

Further, with the high cost of each machine and the fast rate of model introductions, Xerox developed a strategy of leasing rather than selling machines to customers. Various options were available, but typically the customers paid a monthly charge on the number of copies made. The charge covered not only machine costs but also those of the paper and toner that Xerox supplied and the service visits. This lease strategy, together with the carefully cultivated service image, served as key safeguards from competition, as they tied the customers into Xerox and significantly raised their switching costs.

Unlike some other American corporations, Xerox had an international orientation right from the beginning. Even before it had a successful commercial copier, Xerox built up an international presence through joint ventures which allowed the company to minimize its capital investment abroad. In 1956, it ventured with the Rank Organization Ltd. in the U.K. to form Rank Xerox. In 1962, Rank Xerox became a 50 percent partner with Fuji Photo to form Fuji Xerox which sold copiers in Japan. Through these joint ventures, Xerox built up sales and service capabilities in these key markets similar to those it had in the United States. There were some 5,000 sales people in Europe, 3,000 in Japan and over 7,000 and 3,000 service reps, respectively. Xerox also built limited design capabilities in both the joint ventures for local market customization, which developed into significant research establishments in their own rights in later years.

Simultaneously, Xerox maintained high levels of investment in both technology and manufacturing to support its growing market. It continued to spend over $100 million a year in R&D, exceeding the total revenues from the copier business that any of its competitors were earning in the early 70s, and also invested heavily in large-size plants not only in the U.S., but also in the U.K. and Japan.

Competition in the 1970s

Xerox's PPC patents began to expire in the 1970s, heralding a storm of new entrants. In 1970, IBM offered the first PPC copier not sold by Xerox, which resulted in Xerox suing IBM for patent infringement and violation of trade secrets. Canon marketed a PPC copier the same year through the development of an independent PPC technology which they licensed selectively to others. By 1973, competition had expanded to include players from the office equipment industry (IBM, SCM, Litton, Pitney Bowes), the electronics industry (Toshiba, Sharp), the reprographics industry (Ricoh, Mita, Copyer, 3M, AB Dick, Addressograph/Multigraph), the photographic equipment industry (Canon, Kodak, Minolta, Konishiroku) and the suppliers of copy paper (Nashua, Dennison, Saxon).

By the 1980s many of these new entrants,

including IBM, had lost large amounts of money and exited the business. A few of the newcomers managed to achieve a high level of success, however, and copiers became a major business for them. Specifically, copiers were generating 40 percent of Canon's revenues by 1990.

Canon

Canon was founded in 1933 with the ambition to produce a sophisticated 35mm camera to rival that of Germany's world-class Leica model. In only two years' time, it had emerged as Japan's leading producer of high-class cameras. During the war, Canon utilized its optics expertise to produce an X-ray machine which was adopted by the Japanese military. After the war, Canon was able to successfully market its high-end camera, and by the mid-1950s it was the largest camera manufacturer in Japan. Building off its optics technology, Canon then expanded its product line to include a mid-range camera, an 8mm video camera, television lenses and micrographic equipment. It also began developing markets for its products outside of Japan, mainly in the U.S. and Canada.

Diversification was always very important to Canon in order to further its growth, and a new products R&D section was established in 1962 to explore the fields of copy machines, auto-focusing cameras, strobe-integrated cameras, home VCRs and electronic calculators. A separate, special operating unit was also established to introduce new non-camera products resulting from the diversification effort.

The first product to be targeted was the electronic calculator. This product was challenging because it required Canon engineers to develop new expertise in microelectronics in order to incorporate thousands of transistors and diodes in a compact, desk model machine. Tekeshi Mitarai, President of Canon at that time, was against developing the product because it was seen to be too difficult and risky. Nevertheless, a dedicated group of engineers believed in the challenge and developed the calculator in secrecy. Over a year later, top management gave their support to the project. In 1964, the result of the development effort was introduced as the Canola 130, the world's first 10-key numeric pad calculator. With this

product line, Canon dominated the Japanese electronic calculator market in the 1960s.

Not every diversification effort was a success, however. In 1956, Canon began development of the synchroreader, a device for writing and reading with a sheet of paper coated with magnetic material. When introduced in 1959, the product received high praise for its technology. But, because the design was not patented, another firm introduced a similar product at half the price. There was no market for the high priced and incredibly heavy Canon product. Ultimately, the firm was forced to disassemble the finished inventories and sell off the usable parts in the 'once-used' components market.

Move into copiers

Canon began research into copier technology in 1959, and, in 1962, it formed a research group dedicated to developing a plain paper copier (PPC) technology. The only known PPC process was protected by hundreds of Xerox patents, but Canon felt that only this technology promised sufficient quality, speed, economy and ease of maintenance to successfully capture a large portion of the market. Therefore, corporate management challenged the researchers to develop a new PPC process which would not violate the Xerox patents.

In the meantime, the company entered the copier business by licensing the 'inferior' CPC technology in 1965 from RCA. Canon decided not to put the name of the company on this product and marketed it under the brand name Confax 1000 in Japan only. Three years later, Canon licensed a liquid toner technology from an Australian company and combined this with the RCA technology to introduce the CanAll Series. To sell the copier in Japan, Canon formed a separate company, International Image Industry. The copier was sold as an OEM to Scott Paper in the U.S. who sold it under its own brand name.

Canon's research aiming at developing a PPC technical alternative to xerography paid off with the announcement of the 'New Process' (NP) in 1968. This successful research effort not only produced an alternative process but also taught Canon the importance of patent law: how not to violate patents and how to protect new technology. The NP process was soon protected by close to 500 patents.

The first machine with the NP technology, the NP1100, was introduced in Japan in 1970. It was the first copier sold by Canon to carry the Canon brand name. It produced 10 copies per minute and utilized dry toner. As was the standard in the Japanese market, the copier line was sold outright to customers from the beginning. After two years of experience in the domestic market, Canon entered the overseas market, except North America, with this machine.

The second generation of the NP system was introduced in Japan in 1972 as the NPL7. It was a marked improvement because it eliminated a complex fusing technology, simplified developing and cleaning, and made toner supply easier through a new system developed to use liquid toner. Compared with the Xerox equivalent, it was more economical, more compact, more reliable and still had the same or better quality of copies.

With the NP system, Canon began a sideline which was to become quite profitable: licensing. The first generation NP system was licensed to AM, and Canon also provided it with machines on an OEM basis. The second generation was again licensed to AM as well as to Saxon, Ricoh, and Copyer. Canon accumulated an estimated $32 million in license fees between 1975 and 1982.

Canon continued its product introductions with a stream of state-of-the-art technological innovations throughout the seventies. In 1973 it added colour to the NP system; in 1975, it added laser beam printing technology. Its first entry into high volume copiers took place in 1978 with a model which was targeted at the Xerox 9200. The NP200 was introduced in 1979 and went on to win a gold medal at the Leipzig Fair for being the most economical and productive copier available. By 1982, copiers had surpassed cameras as the company's largest revenue generator (see **Exhibits 1 and 2** for Canon's financials and sales by product line).

The personal copier

In the late 1970s, top management began searching for a new market for the PPC copier. They had recently experienced a huge success with the introduction of the AE-1 camera in 1976 and wanted a similar success in copiers. The AE-1 was a very compact single-lens reflex camera, the first camera that used a microprocessor to control electronically functions of exposure, film rewind and strobe. The product had been developed through a focused, cross-functional project team effort which had resulted in a substantial reduction in the number of components, as well as in automated assembly and the use of unitized parts. Because of these improvements, the AE-1 enjoyed a 20 percent cost advantage over competitive models in the same class.

After studying the distribution of offices in Japan by size (see **Exhibit 3**), Canon decided to focus on a latent segment that Xerox had ignored. This was the segment comprised of small offices (segment E) who could benefit from the functionality offered by photocopiers but did not require the high speed machines available in the market. Canon management believed that a low volume 'value for money' machine could generate a large demand in this segment. From this analysis emerged the business concept of a 'personal side desk' machine which could not only create a new market in small offices, but potentially also induce decentralization of the copy function in large offices. Over time, the machine might even create demand for a personal copier for home use. This would be a copier that up to now no one had thought possible. Canon felt that, to be successful in this market, the product had to cost half the price of a conventional copier (target price $1,000), be maintenance free, and provide ten times more reliability.

Top management took their 'dream' to the engineers, who, after careful consideration, took on the challenge. The machine would build off their previous expertise in microelectronics but would go much further in terms of material, functional component, design and production engineering technologies. The team's slogan was 'Let's make the AE-1 of copiers!', expressing the necessity of know-how transfer between the camera and copier divisions as well as their desire for a similar type of success. The effort was led by the director of the Reprographic Production Development Center. His cross-functional team of 200 was the second largest ever assembled at Canon (the largest had been that of the AE-1 camera).

During the development effort, a major issue arose concerning the paper size that the new copier would accept. Canon Sales (the sales organization for Japan) wanted the machine to use a larger-than-letter-size paper which accounted for 60 percent of the Japanese market. This size was not necessary for sales outside of Japan and would add 20–30 percent to the machine's cost as well as make the copier more difficult to service. After much debate world-wide, the decision was made to forego the ability to utilize the larger paper size in the interest of better serving the global market.

Three years later the concept was a reality. The new PC (personal copier) employed a new-cartridge based technology which allowed the user to replace the photoreceptive drum, charging device, toner assembly and cleaner with a cartridge every 2,000 copies, thus eliminating the need to maintain the copier regularly. This enabled Canon engineers to meet the cost and reliability targets. The revolutionary product was the smallest, lightest copier ever sold, and created a large market which had previously not existed. Large offices adjusted their copying strategies to include decentralized copying, and many small offices and even homes could now afford a personal copier. Again, Canon's patent knowledge was utilized to protect this research, and the cartridge technology was not licensed to other manufacturers. Canon has maintained its leadership in personal copiers into the 1990s.

Building capabilities

Canon is admired for its technical innovations, marketing expertise, and low-cost quality manufacturing. These are the result of a long-term strategy to become a premier company. Canon has frequently acquired outside expertise so that it could better focus internal investments on skills of strategic importance. This approach of extensive outsourcing and focused internal development has required consistent direction from top management and the patience to allow the company to become well grounded in one skill area before tasking the organization with the next objective.

Technology

Canon's many innovative products, which enabled the company to grow quickly in the seventies and eighties are in large part the result of a carefully orchestrated use of technology and the capacity for managing rapid technological change. Attesting to its prolific output of original research is the fact that Canon has been among the leaders in number of patents issued world-wide throughout the eighties. These successes have been achieved in an organization that has firmly pursued a strategy of decentralized R&D. Most of Canon's R&D personnel are employed by the product divisions where 80–90 percent of the company's patentable inventions originate. Each product division has its own development center which is tasked with short- to medium-term product design and improvement of production systems. Most product development is performed by cross-functional teams. The work of the development groups is coordinated by an R&D headquarters group.

The Corporate Technical Planning and Operation centre is responsible for long-term strategic R&D planning. Canon also has a main research centre which supports state-of-the-art research in optics, electronics, new materials and information technology. There are three other corporate research centres which apply this state-of-the-art research to product development.

Canon acknowledges that it has neither the resources nor the time to develop all necessary technologies and has therefore often traded or bought specific technologies from a variety of external partners. Furthermore, it has used joint ventures and technology transfers as a strategic tool for mitigating foreign trade tensions in Europe and the United States. For example, Canon had two purposes in mind when it made an equity participation in CPF Deutsch, an office equipment marketing firm in Germany. Primarily, it believed that this move would help develop the German market for its copiers; but it did not go unnoticed among top management that CPF owned Tetras, a copier maker who at that time was pressing dumping charges against Japanese copier makers. Canon also used Burroughs as an OEM for office automation equipment in order to acquire Burroughs software and know-how and participated in joint development agreements with Eastman Kodak and Texas Instruments. **Exhibit 4** provides a list of the company's major joint ventures. Canon also recognizes that its continued market success depends on its ability to exploit new research into marketable products quickly. It has worked hard to reduce the new product introduction cycle through a cross-functional programme called TS 1/2 whose purpose is to cut development time by 50 percent on a continuous basis. The main thrust of this programme is the classification of development projects by total time required and the critical human resources needed so that these two parameters can be optimized for each product depending on its importance for Canon's corporate strategy. This allows product teams to be formed around several classifications of product development priorities of which 'best sellers' will receive the most emphasis. These are the products aimed at new markets or segments with large potential demands. Other classifications include products necessary to catch up with competitive offerings, product refinements intended to enhance customer satisfaction, and long-run marathon products which will take considerable time to develop. In all development classifications, Canon emphasizes three factors to reduce time to market: the fostering of engineering ability, efficient technical support systems, and careful reviews of product development at all stages.

Canon is also working to divert its traditional product focus into more of a market focus. To this end, Canon R&D personnel participate in international product strategy meetings, carry out consumer research, join in marketing activities, and attend meetings in the field at both domestic and foreign sales subsidiaries.

Marketing

Canon's effective marketing is the result of step-by-step, calculated introduction strategies. Normally, the product is first introduced and perfected in the home market before being sold internationally. Canon has learned how to capture learning from the Japanese market quickly so that the time span between introduction in Japan and abroad is as short as a few months. Furthermore, the company will not simultaneously launch a new product through a new distribution channel – its strategy is to minimize risk by introducing a new product through known channels first. New channels will only be created, if necessary, after the product has proven to be successful.

The launch of the NP copier exemplifies this strategy. Canon initially sold these copiers in Japan by direct sales through its Business Machines Sales organization, which had been set up in 1968 to sell the calculator product line. This sales organization was merged with the camera sales organization in 1971 to form Canon Sales. By 1972, after three years of experience in producing the NP product line, the company entered into a new distribution channel, that of dealers, to supplement direct selling.

The NP copier line was not marketed in the U.S. until 1974, after production and distribution were running smoothly in Japan. The U.S. distribution system was similar to that used in Japan, with seven sales subsidiaries for direct selling and a network of independent dealers.

By the late 1970s, Canon had built up a strong dealer network in the U.S. which supported both sales and service of the copiers. The dealer channel was responsible for rapid growth in copier sales, and, by the early 1980s, Canon copiers were sold almost exclusively through this channel. Canon enthusiastically supported the dealers with attractive sales incentive programmes, management training and social outings. Dealers were certified to sell copiers only after completing a course in service training. The company felt that a close relationship with its dealers was a vital asset that allowed it to understand and react to customers' needs and problems in a timely manner. At the same time, Canon also maintained a direct selling mechanism through wholly owned sales subsidiaries in Japan, the U.S. and Europe in order to target large customers and government accounts.

The introduction of its low-end personal copier in 1983 was similarly planned to minimize risk. Initially, Canon's NP dealers in Japan were not interested in the product due to its low maintenance needs and inability to utilize large paper sizes. Thus, PCs were distributed through the firm's office supply stores who were already selling its personal calculators. After seeing the success of the PC, the NP dealers began to carry the copier.

In the U.S., the PC was initially sold only through existing dealers and direct sales channels due to limited availability of the product. Later, it was sold through competitors' dealers and office supply stores, and, eventually, the distribution channels were extended to include mass merchandisers. Canon already had considerable experience in mass merchandising from its camera business.

Advertising has always been an integral part of Canon's marketing strategy. President Kaku believes that Canon must have a corporate brand name which is outstanding to succeed in its diversification effort. 'Customers must prefer products because they bear the name Canon', he says. As described by the company's finance director, 'If a brand name is unknown, and there is no advertising, you have to sell it cheap. It's not our policy to buy share with a low price. We establish our brand with advertising at a reasonably high price'.

Therefore, when the NP-200 was introduced in 1980, 10 percent of the selling price was spent on advertising; for the launch of the personal copier, advertising expenditure was estimated to be 20 percent of the selling price. Canon has also sponsored various sporting events including World Cup football, the Williams motor racing team, and the ice dancers Torvill and Dean. The company expects its current expansion into the home automation market to be greatly enhanced by the brand image it has built in office equipment (see **Exhibit 1** for Canon's advertising expenditures through 1990).

Manufacturing

Canon's goal in manufacturing is to produce the best quality at the lowest cost with the best delivery. To drive down costs, a key philosophy of the production system is to organize the manufacture of each product so that the minimum amount of time, energy and resources are required. Canon therefore places strong emphasis on tight inventory management through a stable production planning process, careful material planning, close supplier relationships, and adherence to the **kanban** system of inventory movement. Additionally, a formal waste elimination programme saved Canon 177 billion yen between 1976 and 1985. Overall, Canon accomplished a 30 percent increase in productivity per year from 1976 to 1982 and over 10 percent thereafter through automation and innovative process improvements.

The workforce is held in high regard at Canon. A philosophy of 'stop and fix it' empowers any worker to stop the production line if he or she is not able to

perform a task properly or observes a quality problem. Workers are responsible for their own machine maintenance governed by rules which stress prevention. Targets for quality and production and other critical data are presented to the workers with on-line feedback. Most workers also participate in voluntary 'small group activity' for problem solving. The result of these systems is a workforce that feels individually responsible for the success of the products it manufactures.

Canon sponsors a highly regarded suggestion programme for its workers in order to directly involve those most familiar with the work processes in improving the business. The programme was originally initiated in 1952 with only limited success, but in the early 1980s, participation soared with more than seventy suggestions per employee per year. All suggestions are reviewed by a hierarchy of committees with monetary prizes awarded monthly and yearly depending on the importance of the suggestion. The quality and effectiveness of the process are demonstrated by a 90 percent implementation rate of the suggestions offered and corporate savings of $202 million in 1985 (against a total expenditure of $2 million in running the programme, over 90 percent of it in prize money).

Canon chooses to backward integrate only on parts with unique technologies. For other components, the company prefers to develop long-term relationships with its suppliers and it retains two sources for most parts. In 1990, over 80 percent of Canon's copiers were assembled from purchased parts, with only the drums and toner being manufactured in-house. The company also maintains its own in-house capability for doing pilot production of all parts so as to understand better the technology and the vendors' costs.

Another key to Canon's high quality and low cost is the attention given to parts commonality between models. Between some adjacent copier models, the commonality is as high as 60 percent.

Copier manufacture was primarily located in Toride, Japan, in the early years but then spread to Germany, California and Virginia in the U.S., France, Italy and Korea. In order to mitigate trade and investment friction, Canon is working to increase the local content of parts as it expands globally. In Europe it exceeds the EC standard by 5 percent. It is also adding R&D capability to some of its overseas operations. Mr. Kaku emphasizes the importance of friendly trading partners:

Frictions cannot be erased by merely transferring our manufacturing facilities overseas. The earnings after tax must be reinvested in the country; we must transfer our technology to the country. This is the only way our overseas expansion will be welcomed.

Leveraging expertise

Canon places critical importance on continued growth through diversification into new product fields. Mr. Kaku observed,

Whenever Canon introduced a new product, profits surged forward. Whenever innovation lagged, on the other hand, so did the earnings ... In order to survive in the coming era of extreme competition, Canon must possess at least a dozen proprietary state-of-the-art technologies that will enable it to develop unique products.

While an avid supporter of diversification, Mr. Kaku was cautious.

In order to ensure the enduring survival of Canon, we have to continue diversifying in order to adapt to environmental changes. However, we must be wise in choosing ways toward diversification. In other words, we must minimize the risks. Entering a new business which requires either a technology unrelated to Canon's current expertise or a different marketing channel than Canon currently uses incurs a 50 percent risk. If Canon attempts to enter a new business which requires both a new technology and a new marketing channel which are unfamiliar to Canon, the risk entailed in such ventures would be 100 percent. There are two prerequisites that have to be satisfied before launching such new ventures. First, our operation must be debt-free; second, we will have to secure the personnel capable of competently undertaking such ventures. I feel we shall have to wait until the twenty-first century before we are ready.

Combining capabilities

Through its R&D strategy, Canon has worked to build up specialized expertise in several areas and then link them to offer innovative, state-of-the-art products. Through the fifties and sixties, Canon focused on products related to its main business and expertise, cameras. This prompted the introduction of the 8 mm movie camera and the Canon range of mid-market cameras. There was minimal risk because the optics technology was the same and the marketing outlet, camera shops, remained the same.

Entrance into the calculator market pushed Canon into developing expertise in the field of microelectronics, which it later innovatively combined with its optics capability to introduce one of its most successful products, the personal copier. From copiers, Canon utilized the replaceable cartridge system to introduce a successful desktop laser printer.

In the early seventies, Canon entered the business of marketing micro-chip semiconductor production equipment. In 1980, the company entered into the development and manufacture of unique proprietary ICs in order to strengthen further its expertise in electronics technology. This development effort was expanded in the late eighties to focus on opto-electronic ICs. According to Mr. Kaku:

We are now seriously committed to R&D in ICs because our vision for the future foresees the arrival of the opto-electronic era. When the time arrives for the opto-electronic IC to replace the current ultra-LSI, we intend to go into making large-scale computers. Presently we cannot compete with the IBMs and NECs using the ultra-LSIs. When the era of the opto-electronic IC arrives, the technology of designing the computer will be radically transformed; that will be our chance for making entry into the field of the large-scale computer.

Creative destruction

In 1975 Canon produced the first laser printer. Over the next fifteen years, laser printers evolved as a highly successful product line under the Canon brand name. The company also provides the 'engine' as an OEM to Hewlett Packard and other laser printer manufacturers which when added to its own branded sales supports a total of 84 percent of world-wide demand.

The biggest threat to the laser printer industry is substitution by the newly developed bubble jet printer. With a new technology which squirts out thin streams of ink under heat, a high-quality silent printer can be produced at half the price of the laser printer. The technology was invented accidentally in the Canon research labs. It keys on a print head which has up to 400 fine nozzles per inch, each with its own heater to warm the ink until it shoots out tiny ink droplets. This invention utilizes Canon's competencies in fine chemicals for producing the ink and its expertise in semiconductors, materials, and electronics for manufacturing the print heads. Canon is moving full steam forward to develop the bubble jet technology, even though it might destroy a business that the company dominates. The new product is even more closely tied to the company's core capabilities, and management believes that successful development of this business will help broaden further its expertise in semiconductors.

Challenge of the 1990s

Canon sees the office automation business as its key growth opportunity for the nineties. It already has a well-established brand name in home and office automation products through its offerings of copiers, facsimiles, electronic typewriters, laser printers, word processing equipment and personal computers. The next challenge for the company is to link these discrete products into a multifunctional system which will perform the tasks of a copier, facsimile, printer, and scanner and interface with a computer so that all the functions can be performed from one keyboard. In 1988, with this target, Canon introduced a personal computer which incorporated a PC, a fax, a telephone and a word processor. Canon has also introduced a colour laser copier which hooks up to a computer to serve as a colour printer. A series of additional integrated OA offerings are scheduled for introduction in 1992, and the company expects these products to serve as its growth engine in the first half of the 1990s.

Managing the process

Undergirding this impressive history of continuously building new corporate capabilities and of exploiting those capabilities to create a fountain of innovative new products lies a rather unique management process. Canon has institutionalized corporate entrepreneurship through its highly autonomous and market focused business unit structure. A set of powerful functional committees provide the bridge between the entrepreneurial business units and the company's core capabilities in technology, manufacturing and marketing. Finally, an extraordinarily high level of corporate ambition drives this innovation engine, which is fuelled by the creativity of its people and by top management's continuous striving for ever higher levels of performance.

Driving entrepreneurship: the business units

Mr. Kaku had promoted the concept of the entrepreneurial business unit from his earliest days with Canon, but it was not until the company had suffered significant losses in 1975 that his voice was heard. His plan was implemented shortly before he became president of the company.

Mr. Kaku believed that Canon's diversification strategy could only succeed if the business units were empowered to act on their own, free of central controls. Therefore, two independent operating units were formed in 1978, one for cameras and one for office equipment, to be managed as business units. Optical Instruments, the third business unit, had always been separate. Since that time, an additional three business units have been spun off. The original three business units were then given clear profitability targets, as well as highly ambitious growth objectives, and were allowed the freedom to devise their own ways to achieve these goals. One immediate result of this decentralization was the recognition that Canon's past practice of mixing production of different products in the same manufacturing facility would no longer work. Manufacturing was reorganized so that no plant produced more than one type of product.

Mr. Kaku describes the head of each unit as a surrogate of the CEO empowered to make quick decisions. This allows him, as president of Canon, to devote himself exclusively to his main task of creating and implementing the long-term corporate strategy. In explaining the benefits of the system, he said:

Previously, the president was in exclusive charge of all decision making; his subordinates had to form a queue to await their turn in presenting their problems to him. This kind of system hinders the development of the young managers' potential for decision-making.

Furthermore, take the case of the desktop calculator. Whereas, I can devote only about two hours each day on problems concerning the calculator, the CEO of Casio Calculator could devote 24 hours to the calculator ... In the fiercely competitive market, we lost out because our then CEO was slow in coping with the problem.

In contrast to the Western philosophy of stand-alone SBUs encompassing all functions including engineering, sales, marketing and production, Canon has chosen to separate its product divisions from its sales and marketing arm. This separation allows for a clear focus on the challenges that Canon faces in selling products on a global scale. Through a five-year plan initiated in 1977, Seiichi Takigawa, the president of Canon Sales (the sales organization for Japan), stressed the need to 'make sales a science'. After proving the profitability of this approach, Canon Sales took on the responsibility for world-wide marketing, sales and service. In 1981, Canon Sales was listed on the Tokyo stock exchange, reaffirming its independence.

Canon also allows its overseas subsidiaries free rein, though it holds the majority of stock. The philosophy is to create the maximum operational leeway for each subsidiary to act on its own initiative. Kaku describes the philosophy through an analogy:

Canon's system of managing subsidiaries is similar to the policy of the Tokugawa government, which established secure hegemony over the warlords, who were granted autonomy in their territory. I am 'shogun' [head of the Tokugawa regime] and the subsidiaries' presidents are the 'daimyo' [warlords]. The difference between Canon and the Tokugawa government is that the latter was a zero-sum society; its policy was repressive. On the other hand, Canon's objective is to enhance the prosperity of all subsidiaries through efficient mutual collaboration.

Canon has also promoted the growth of intrapreneurial ventures within the company by spinning these ventures off as wholly owned subsidiaries. The first venture to be spun off was Canon Components, which produces electronic components and devices, in 1984.

Building integration: functional committees

As Canon continues to grow and diversify, it becomes increasingly difficult but also ever more important to link its product divisions in order to realize the benefits possible only in a large multi-product corporation. The basis of Canon's integration is a three dimensional management approach in which the first dimension is the independent business unit, the second a network of functional committees, and the third the regional companies focused on geographic markets (see **Exhibit 5**).

Kaku feels there are four basic requirements for the success of a diversified business: 1) a level of competence in research and development; 2) quality, low-cost manufacturing technology; 3) superior marketing strength; and 4) an outstanding corporate identity, culture and brand name. Therefore, he has established separate functional committees to address the first three requirements of development, production and marketing, while the fourth task has been kept as a direct responsibility of corporate management. The three functional committees, in turn, have been made responsible for company-wide administration of three key management systems:

- The Canon Development System (CDS) whose objectives are to foster the research and creation of new products and technologies by studying and continuously improving the development process;

- The Canon Production System (CPS) whose goal is to achieve optimum quality by minimizing waste in all areas of manufacturing;

- The Canon Marketing System (CMS), later renamed the Canon International Marketing System (CIMS), which is tasked to expand and strengthen Canon's independent domestic and overseas sales networks by building a high quality service and sales force.

Separate offices have been created at headquarters for each of these critical committees, and over time their role has broadened to encompass general improvement of the processes used to support their functions. The chairpersons of the committees are members of Canon's management committee, which gives them the ability to ensure consistency and communicate process improvements throughout the multiproduct, multinational corporation.

Using information technology to integrate its world-wide operations, Canon began development of the Global Information System for Harmonious Growth Administration (GINGA) in 1987. The system will consist of a high-speed digital communications network to interconnect all parts of Canon into a global database and allow for the timely flow of information among managers in any location of the company's world-wide organization. GINGA is planned to include separate but integrated systems for computer integrated manufacturing, global marketing and distribution, R&D and product design, financial reporting, and personnel database tracking, as well as some advances in intelligent office automation. As described by Mr. Kaku, the main objective of this system is to supplement Canon's efficient vertical communications structure with a lateral one that will facilitate direct information exchange among managers across businesses, countries, and functions on all operational matters concerning the company. The system is being developed at a total cost of 20 billion yen and it is targeted for completion in 1992.

Managing renewal: challenges and change

Mr. Kaku was very forthright about some of the management weaknesses of Canon prior to 1975:

In short, our skill in management – the software of our enterprise – was weak. Management policy must be guided by a soundly created software on management; if the software is weak, the firm will lack clearly defined ideals and objectives. In the beginning we had a clearly defined objective, to overtake West Germany's Leica. Since then our management policy has been changing like the colours of a chameleon.

In the past our management would order employees to reach the peak of Mount Fuji,

and then before the vanguard of climbers had barely started climbing, they would be ordered to climb Mount Tsukuba far to the north. Then the order would again be suddenly changed to climb Mount Yatsugatake to the west. After experiencing these kind of shifts in policy, the smarter employees would opt to take things easy by taking naps on the bank of the river Tamagawa. As a result, vitality would be sapped from our work force – a situation that should have been forestalled by all means.

Mr. Kaku's first action as President of Canon was to start the firm on the path to global leadership through establishing the first 'premier company plan', a six-year plan designed to make Canon a top company in Japan. The plan outlined a policy for diversification and required consistently recurring profits exceeding 10 percent on sales.

The aim of any Japanese corporation is ensuring its perpetual survival. Unlike the venture businesses and U.S. corporations, our greatest objective is not to maximize short-term profits. Our vital objective is to continually earn profits on a stable basis for ensuring survival. To implement this goal, we must diversify.

By the time the original six-year plan expired in 1981, Canon had become a highly respected company in Japan. The plan was then renewed through 1986 and then again into the 1990s. The challenge was to become a premier global company, defined as having recurring profits exceeding 15 percent of sales. R&D spending was gradually increased from 6 percent of sales in 1980 to 9 percent in 1985 as a prerequisite for global excellence. As described by Mr. Kaku:

By implementing our first plan for becoming a premier company we have succeeded in attaining the allegorical top of Mount Fuji. Our next objective is the Everest. With a firm determination, we could have climbed Fuji wearing sandals. However, sandals are highly inappropriate for climbing Everest; it may cause our death.

According to Mr. Kaku, such ambitions also require a company to build up the ability to absorb temporary reversals without panic; ambition without stability makes the corporate ship lose its way. To illustrate, he described the situation at Canon during the time the yen depreciated from 236 to the dollar in 1985 to 168 to the dollar in 1986. With 74 percent of Canon's Japanese production going to export markets, this sudden change caused earnings to fall to 4.6 billion yen, one tenth of the previous year. Some board members at Canon sought drastic action such as a major restructuring of the company and cutting the R&D budget. Mr. Kaku had successfully argued the opposite:

What I did was calm them down. If a person gets lost in climbing a high mountain, he must avoid excessive use of his energy; otherwise his predicament will deepen ... Our ongoing strategy for becoming the premier company remains the best, even under this crisis; there is no need to panic. Even if we have to forego dividends for two or three times, we shall surely overcome this crisis.

While celebrating the company's past successes, Mr. Kaku also constantly reminds his colleagues that no organizational form or process holds the eternal truth. The need to change with a changing world is inevitable. For example, despite being the creator of the product division-marketing company split, he was considering rejoining these two in the nineties:

In the future, our major efforts in marketing must be concentrated on clearly defining and differentiating the markets of the respective products and creating appropriate marketing systems for them. In order to make this feasible, we may have to recombine our sales subsidiaries with the parent company and restructure their functions to fully meet the market's needs.

While constantly aware of the need to change, Kaku also recognizes the difficulties managers face in changing the very approaches and strategies that have led to past successes:

In order for a company to survive forever, the company must have the courage to be able to deny at one point what it has been doing in the past; the biological concept of 'ecdysis' – casting off the skin to emerge to new form. But it is difficult for human beings to deny and destruct what they have been building up. But if they cannot do that, it is certain that the firm can not survive forever. Speaking about myself, it is difficult to deny what I've done in the past. So when such time comes that I have to deny the past, I inevitably would have to step down.

Exhibit 1 Canon, Inc. – Ten-year financial summary (millions of yen expect par share amounts)

	1990	1989	1988	1987	1986	1985	1984	1983	1982	1981
Net sales:										
Domestic ¥	508,747	413,854	348,462	290,382	274,174	272,966	240,656	198,577	168,178	144,898
Overseas	1,219,201	937,063	757,548	686,329	615,043	682,814	589,732	458,748	412,322	326,364
Total	1,727,948	1,350,917	1,106,010	976,711	889,217	955,780	830,388	657,325	580,500	471,262
Percentage to previous year	127.9%	122.1	113.2	109.8	93.0	115.1	126.3	113.2	123.2	112.5
Net income	61,408	38,293	37,100	13,244	10,728	37,056	35,029	28,420	22,358	16,216
Percentage to sales	3.6%	2.8	3.4	1.4	1.2	3.9	4.2	4.3	3.9	3.4
Advertising expense	72,234	54,394	41,509	38,280	37,362	50,080	51,318	41,902	37,532	23,555
Research and development	86,008	75,566	65,522	57,085	55,330	49,461	38,256	28,526	23,554	14,491
Depreciation	78,351	64,861	57,627	57,153	55,391	47,440	39,995	30,744	27,865	22,732
Capital expenditure	137,298	107,290	83,069	63,497	81,273	91,763	75,894	53,411	46,208	54,532
Long-term debt	262,886	277,556	206,083	222,784	166,722	134,366	99,490	60,636	53,210	39,301
Stockholders' equity	617,566	550,841	416,465	371,198	336,456	333,148	304,310	264,629	235,026	168,735
Total assets	1,827,945	1,636,380	1,299,843	1,133,881	1,009,504	1,001,044	916,651	731,642	606,101	505,169
Per share data:										
Net income:										
Common and common equivalent share	78.29	50.16	51.27	19.65	16.67	53.38	53.63	46.31	41.17	34.04
Assuming full dilution	78.12	49.31	51.26	19.64	16.67	53.25	53.37	45.02	38.89	33.35
Cash dividends declared	12.50	11.93	11.36	9.09	11.36	11.36	9.88	9.43	8.23	7.84
Stock price:										
High	1,940	2,040	1,536	1,282	1,109	1,364	1,336	1,294	934	1,248
Low	1,220	1,236	823	620	791	800	830	755	417	513
Average number of common and common equivalent shares in thousands	788,765	780,546	747,059	747,053	746,108	727,257	675,153	645,473	564,349	515,593
Number of employees	54,381	44,401	40,740	37,521	35,498	34,129	30,302	27,266	25,607	24,300
Average exchange rate ($1 =)	143	129	127	143	167	235	239	238	248	222

Source: Canon 1990 Annual Report.

Exhibit 2 Canon – Sales by product (millions of yen)

Year	Cameras	Copiers	Other Business Machines	Optical & Other Products	Total
1981	201,635	175,389	52,798	40,222	470,044
1982	224,619	242,161	67,815	45,905	580,500
1983	219,443	291,805	97,412	48,665	657,325
1984	226,645	349,986	180,661	73,096	830,388
1985	197,284	410,840	271,190	76,466	955,780
1986	159,106	368,558	290,630	70,923	889,217
1987	177,729	393,581	342,895	62,506	976,711
1988	159,151	436,924	434,634	75,301	1,106,010
1989	177,597	533,115	547,170	93,035	1,350,917
1990	250,494	686,077	676,095	115,282	1,727,948

Source: Canon Annual Report, 1981–1990

Exhibit 3 Office size distribution, Japan 1979

Copier Market Segment	Number of Office Workers	Number of Offices	Working Population
A	300+	200,000	9,300,000
B	100–299	30,000	4,800,000
C	30–99	170,000	8,300,000
D	5–29	1,820,000	15,400,000
E	1–4	4,110,000	8,700,000

Source: Breakthrough: The Development of the Canon Personal Copier, Teruo Yamanouchi, *Long Range Planning*, Vol. 22, October 1989, p. 4.

Exhibit 4 Canon's major international joint ventures

Category	Partner	Description
Office Equipment	Eastman Kodak (U.S.)	Distributes Kodak medical equipment in Japan; exports copiers to Kodak
	CPF Germany	Equity participation in CPF which markets Canon copiers
	Olivetti (Italy) Lotte (Korea)	Joint venture for manufacture of copier
Computers	Hewlett-Packard (U.S.)	Receives OEM mini-computer from HP; supplies laser printer to HP
	Apple Computer (U.S.)	Distributes Apple computers in Japan; supplies laser printer to Apple
	Next, Inc. (U.S.)	Equity participation; Canon has marketing rights for Asia
Semiconductors	National Semiconductor (U.S.)	Joint development of MPU & software for Canon office equipment
	Intel (U.S.)	Joint development of LSI for Canon copier, manufactured by Intel
Telecommunications	Siemens (Germany)	Development of ISDN interface for Canon facsimile; Siemens supplies Canon with digital PBX
	DHL (U.S.)	Equity participation; Canon supplies terminals to DHL
Camera	Kinsei Seimitsu (Korea)	Canon licenses technology on 35 mm Camera
Other	ECD (U.S.)	Equity participation because Canon values its research on amorphous materials

Source: Canon Asia, Nomura Management School.

Exhibit 5 Canon Organization Chart

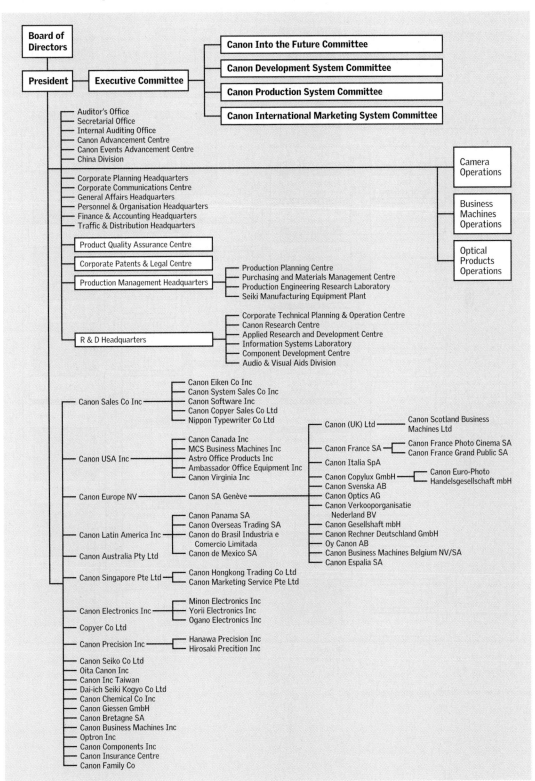

Exhibit 5 continued

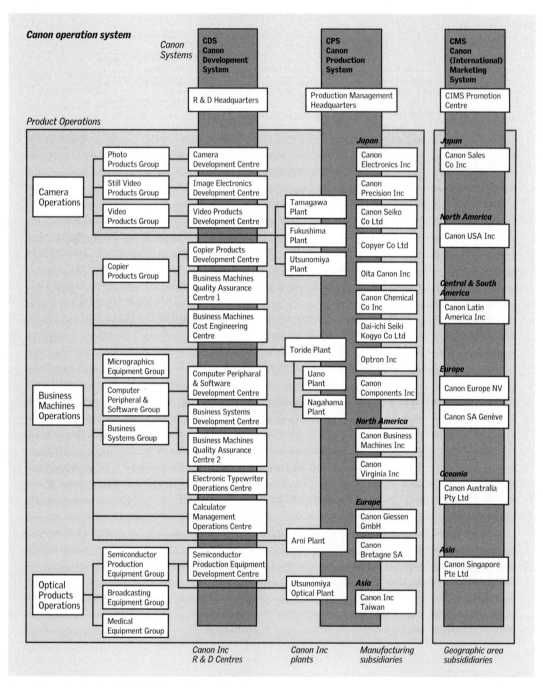

Source: Canon Handbook, published by Canon, Inc.

Case 8 LVMH: Managing the multi-brand conglomerate

LVMH Moët Hennessy Louis Vuitton, based in France, is one of the world's leading luxury goods companies. It operates in wines, spirits, fashion goods, leather goods, perfumes, cosmetics, watches, jewellery and retailing. The company employs approximately 56,000 employees. Its global distribution network grew from 828 stores in 1998 to 1,592 stores in 2004. The majority of sales are derived from the fashion and leather goods division, with Europe (including France) being the biggest regional contributor. The company is the largest and most widely spread luxury goods company, with a strong brand portfolio and distribution skills. LVMH's 'star brands' is a key foundation of the group's strategy. It has built over time one of the strongest brand portfolios in the sector, counting 60 top brands among its five divisions and other operations. At the core of the fashion and leather business is the Louis Vuitton brand itself. This 'star of star brands' is estimated to generate over 80% of earnings in the segment.

....

The case was written by Ashok Som, Assistant Professor of Strategy and Management at ESSEC Business School. It is intended to be used as a basis for class discussion rather than to illustrate either effective or ineffective handling of a business situation. The author gratefully acknowledges Lilly Liu, Deepak Yachamaneni, ESSEC MBA Exchange students, and Boris Gbahoué, ESSEC MBA student, for their research help. The case was compiled from published sources and generalised experience.

© 2004, A. Som, ESSEC Business School, France.

Distributed by The European Case Clearing House, England and USA.

North America: phone: 11 781 239 5884, fax: 11 781 239 5885, e-mail: ECCHBabson@aol.com.

Rest of the World: phone: 144 (0)1234 750903, fax: 144 (0)1234 751125, e-mail: ECCH@cranfield.ac.uk.

All rights reserved. Printed in UK and USA. Website: http://www.ecch.cranfield.ac.uk.

The case discusses the following critical challenges for LVMH:

♦ sustaining its organic growth strategy

♦ competition strategy

♦ managing multi-brand strategy with star brands

♦ managing a decentralized conglomerate

♦ the leadership and charisma of Bernard Arnault in creating, maintaining and managing a global conglomerate

♦ people issues in the luxury industry.

Introduction

The mission of the LVMH group is to represent the most refined qualities of Western 'Art de Vivre' around the world. LVMH must continue to be synonymous with both elegance and creativity. Our products, and the cultural values they embody, blend tradition and innovation, and kindle dream and fantasy. (www.lvmh.com)

On 4 March 2004, 54-year-old Bernard Arnault stood under his Picasso painting at the LVMH headquarters in Paris and pondered the future of his fashion empire. He had just announced a 30% rise in net income for 2003, with improved profits for all sectors of the business except watches and jewellery. Margins for the flagship leather goods brand Louis Vuitton topped 45%, due to the increased publicity spending featuring the actress Jennifer Lopez in its latest global ad campaign.

As the chief shareholder in LVMH Moët Hennessy Louis Vuitton, and his ownership stakes in the high-profile labels of Christian Dior, Givenchy, Louis Vuitton, Christian Lacroix, Kenzo, Céline, Emilio Pucci, Fendi, Loewe, Donna Karan, and a substantial investment in Marc Jacobs, much of the future of world fashion is in his hands. His properties also include Tag Heuer watches, Moët and Chandon champagne, and a chain of duty-free shops that dot many international airports. The fashion conglomerate's leadership in the luxury sector has been sustained by new product launches, store openings and an increased investment in communications. The group has continued its new launches and initiatives in 2004, including the new leather goods Damier Geant line, the Théda bags, an entire new jewellery line at Louis Vuitton, a new perfume for women at Dior, a new fragrance for men at Guerlain, an array of watch and jewellery creations, and the new Ellipse Cognac from Hennessy.

LVMH has continued to develop its worldwide distribution network. The Louis Vuitton brand, which celebrated its 150th anniversary, opened its largest store in the world in New York. Advancements in markets with significant potential for luxury products, such as Asia, have also bolstered the group's performance. Future focus will be likely on new growth markets and regions such as China, a market with considerable potential for cognac, fashion and perfumes; Russia with promise notably for Sephora, which has already shown promise in several Central and Eastern European countries; India, where Louis Vuitton opened its first store in 2003.

However, the €12 billion fashion and liquor conglomerate controlled by Bernard Arnault is not without worries. Wall Street continues to question whether the company's multi-brand strategy can be sustained. He has to consider the increasing importance of succession as he is approaching the legal retirement age; he would soon need to plan about his successor, someone to replace him at the helm of his group.

Company background

History

Established in 1987, LVMH was created by the fusion of two fashion houses: Louis Vuitton, a leather goods specialist founded in 1834, and Moët-Hennessy, a wine and spirits group created in 1971. The luxury group grew through key acquisitions and the development of new products. Under the leadership of Bernard Arnault, the 1990s saw a period of great expansion with the purchase of large stakes in the company's subsidiaries. In recent years, the luxury group has begun to shed some of its portfolio, with the strategy of focusing on its 'star' brands, defined by Arnault as 'timeless, modern, fast-growing and highly profitable' brands (see **Exhibit 1** for a list of the recent acquisitions and divestitures). Observers comment that 'This collection of global brands was the stepping stone for realizing lucrative synergies in the fashion business, which would add to the bottom line.'

With over 56,000 employees and approximately €12 billion in revenues during the fiscal year 2003, the LVMH group operates in five primary sectors: wines and spirits; fashion and leather goods; perfumes and cosmetics; watches and jewellery; and selective retailing. LVMH today controls more than 60 luxury brands across its product lines. The acquisition strategy at LVMH always focused on brands that had strong brand power, resulting in the company reaching leadership positions in almost every segment it served. Each division functions as a strategic business unit (SBU) with its own general manager and a top management team. These divisions also manage overseas sales of their respective lines.

Wines and spirits

The wines and spirits division contributed 18% of sales and 36% of the operating profit in 2003. LVMH, through Hennessy, holds 40% of the cognac market and between 20% and 25% of the overall champagne market. In the premium champagne segment, LVMH has a dominant share of 50% built around exclusive brands such as Moët Chandon and Veuve Clicquot. It has also ventured outside the traditional wine belts in France and Italy to acquire high-end wine producers in California and Australia. Given the rising prominence of both California and Australia in the wine business, these moves allowed the company to market a truly global selection of wines and champagnes. However, considering the total liquor market, LVMH does not figure in the top 10 due to the absence of its drinks in the 'popular segments' such as beers, whisky and vodka. However, this is in line with LVMH's strategy to focus only on high-margin activities. Analysts have suggested spinning off the wines and spirits businesses as a separate unit as they consider it to be non-core to LVMH's fashion image. For example, the sale of Pommery, a profitable champagne brand, in 2001 was a strategic move by LVMH. The brand was bought for the vast lands it owned in the Champagne region; as high-quality land is limited in this region, LVMH wanted more land to produce more grapes for its Moët and Veuve brands of champagne. When Pommery was purchased, its land was also acquired, but when it was sold, the land was retained and only the brand was sold.

Fashion and leather goods

The fashion and leather goods division contributed 35% of sales and 60% of the operating profit in 2003 and had an operating margin of 32%. Much of the sales of this division are concentrated in the Asia-Pacific region, particularly Japan, which accounts for 33% of the sales. Sales in this segment are directly attributable to the Louis Vuitton brand. This label has grown by leaps and bounds under the leadership of its legendary designer, Mr Marc Jacobs. Demand for Louis Vuitton products has often exceeded supply, requiring customers to go on a waiting list that often took several months to clear. The Louis Vuitton label, combined with the strength of the LVMH group, has provided opportunities for expanding into new brands and products. Using this as a launching pad, the company engaged in significant brand expansion efforts to reach a wider audience. These efforts were well supported by fashion buyers.

The company has been able to leverage synergies across its fashion brands. For example, its Kenzo production facility has been transformed into a logistics platform for men's ready-to-wear products serving other brands such as Givenchy and Christian Lacroix. Given the historically lower profit margins in the ready-to-wear market, synergies resulting in cost savings have boosted profitability. As Muriel Zingraff, Harrods' fashion and beauty director, observed:

> What I will say is that we may have more patience with smaller brands if they are owned by a parent company such as LVMH or the Gucci Group.

Perfumes and cosmetics

The perfumes and cosmetics (P&C) division contributed 18% of sales and 8% of the operating profit in 2003. This division has an enviable collection of brands such as Christian Dior, Guerlain, Kenzo, and Givenchy. The company has recently acquired popular US brands such as Bliss, Hard Candy, Urban Decay and Fresh that were geared towards a younger clientele. These acquisitions are an integral part of the drive to internationalize LVMH's perfumes and cosmetics offerings. Europe is the largest market for perfumes, perhaps due to the heritage of the brands that the company offered. The P&C division has been able to leverage R&D synergies across brands; while its R&D expenditure is in line with the industry norms, LVMH has been able to generate twice the average growth rate in the industry. It is believed that these R&D skills would help boost sales of the acquired companies. As part of a larger drive to consolidate margin in this division, the company has been integrating R&D, production, distribution, sourcing and other back-office operations across brands. These moves have been beneficial. For example, integrating the purchasing function across brands has resulted in cost savings in raw materials of 20%. Analysts believe that this division is well positioned to reap the spillover benefits arising from the co-branding strategy under which many of the brands are linked directly to ready-to-wear apparel brands, a unique avenue of differentiation at LVMH.

Watches and jewellery

The latest portfolio addition at LVMH, watches and jewellery, contributed 4% of sales and 2% of the operating profit in 2003. In the watches section, the company owned prestigious brands that included Tag Heuer, Ebel and Zenith, and in the jewellery section, Fred Joallier and Chaumet. The purchase of the Zenith brand was crucial to LVMH's strategy to expand its watches operations. Most watches have an identical manufacturing process and brands reflect minor differences in quality. According to industry sources, there are only three manufacturers in the world from whom all the luxury watchmakers source their products. It is noteworthy that Zenith is the only manufacturer in the world of a certain component used in every watch. LVMH wanted a platform to sell more watches by utilizing its design experience and the production know-how of Zenith. Watches can be one of the most lucrative segments at LVMH with margins as high as 80%.

Unlike its constellation of brands in other divisions, many think that the company does not have quite the same star power in watches and jewellery. Competitors such as Richemont, Hermès and Bulgari seem to have more recognizable brands and more upscale products in this category. However, tangible synergies appear to be a definite possibility because the division could centralize the manufacturing and utilize Tag Heuer's expertise in retail distribution across all brands. The jewellery business is also extremely competitive due to the presence of leading brands such as Cartier and Van Cleef & Arpels. Despite the Place Vendôme heritage of both Chaumet and Fred Joallier, neither of them is currently profitable.

Selective retailing

The selective retailing division contributed 25% of the sales and 5% of the operating profit in 2003. The vertical integration strategy of LVMH came to fruition when the selective retailing arm was established. This division manages LVMH investments in Sephora, DFS Galleria, and Miami Cruiseline Services. While this division contributed 26% of company sales in 2002, it had not made a profit in the previous three years. DFS Galleria, with 150 duty-free and general merchandise stores, is the world's largest travel retailer. Acquired in 1996, this business was a victim of poor timing, since the Asian financial crisis hit soon thereafter. LVMH has since instituted several good management practices, including the execution of a strategy that would reduce DFS's reliance on Asian airports, selective closing of underperforming stores and the creation of DFS Galleria stores in large metropolitan areas. Despite these changes, Japanese travellers are still its most important and loyal customers and any economic development that hurt Japanese travel will invariably find its way to DFS's bottom line.

Miami Cruiseline Services (MCS) was acquired in January 2000. It offers retail services on board cruise ships and includes 76% of the world's major cruise lines (over 100 ships) as its customers. Conceived as an extension of the DFS concept, Miami Cruiseline focuses primarily (90%) on North American passengers, thus counterbalancing the over-reliance on Japanese tourists. It also manages duty-free operations at the Miami International Airport, the gateway to Latin America, opening possibilities of strengthening LVMH's brands in a region of the world where they are still underrepresented.

In addition to these distribution-based assets, LVMH has recently acquired La Samaritaine, the prestigious Paris department store. The company has also entered the retailing end of the made-to-order tailoring business with the acquisition of Thomas Pink, the legendary Mayfair tailoring house

that has a worldwide reputation for excellence in shirts. Thomas Pink has retail outlets in the United States as well. LVMH has also taken a minority stake in the 200-year-old UK fashion retailer Asprey & Garrard, which has global aspirations of its own.

Functioning of the group

LVMH's five product groups are decentralized into production and distribution subsidiaries. Some of the major brands have their own national subsidiaries. Overlaying this, there is a regional structure, with corporate headquarters in Paris, New York, Tokyo and Amsterdam. The wine and spirits operations of Moët Hennessy have their own headquarters, with main offices in France and regional headquarters in Singapore.

Depending on the geographic region, LVMH has different organizational set-ups. In France, the hub of LVMH has individual headquarters for every brand, with an LVMH headquarters handling some centralized activities. In contrast, in New York, the central LVMH office houses the LVMH and Givenchy brands, while Dior and Fendi have their own US-offices. Tokyo centralizes the human resources function, and each brand operates independently on all aspects of business.

The Group's decentralized organizational structure helps the company to foster efficiency, productivity and creativity. LVMH strives to create a highly motivating and dynamic atmosphere for its employees, emphasizing individual initiative and offers real responsibilities – often early on in one's career. LVMH gives each brand almost complete freedom to pursue its creative vision. However, it does realize synergies through almost 20% discount in advertising by negotiating in bulk for all its brands.

The challenge of this structure is that it requires highly entrepreneurial executive teams in each company within the Group. This entrepreneurial spirit requires a healthy dose of common sense from managers, as well as hard work, pragmatism, efficiency and the ability to motivate people in the pursuit of ambitious goals.

Bernard Arnault: 'The Pope of Fashion'

Dubbed the 'Pope of Fashion', Bernard Arnault has spent the past 15 years building LVMH from a small clothing manufacturer to a conglomerate comprising approximately 50 of the world's most powerful brands. Trained as an engineer at the Ecole Polytechnique in France, Arnault joined his family's construction business where he worked for 13 years, before becoming the president of the company in 1978. In 1984, he left his family business to reorganize a French state-owned holding company, Boussac, which owned Christian Dior. In the late 1980s, Bernard Arnault took control of LVMH. With growing success in his business, Bernard Arnault acquired Givenchy (1988) and Kenzo (1993). Today, through a complex web of partnerships, Bernard Arnault owns at least 33% of the company's stock. Bernard Arnault is deeply involved in the creative process, far more than his peers. He believes that in the creative and highly seasonal fashion business, the ability to match effective CEOs with temperamental designers can make the difference between a star and a failure. He believes that *'to have the right DNA in a team is very rare. It's almost like a miracle.'* Deemed the *Billionaire Matchmaker*, in the past 15 years he has formed close creative bonds with designer John Galliano, whose collections for Christian Dior have been hailed by fashion critics. His selection of Hedi Slimane has done wonders for Dior Homme, and his pairing of Marc Jacobs with Luis Vuitton has been a critical and financial success. His vision of the luxury and fashion industry, as he states, is:

> This link to creativity, it's not far from art, and I like it very much. You must like to be with designers and creators. You have to like an image. That's also a key to success. And at the same time, you must be able to organize a business worldwide.

Industry background

> Luxury is not the contrary to poverty, but a contrary to vulgarity. (Gianni Versace)
> We are in the business of selling dreams. The strength of a brand depends on how many dreams it inspires. (Chanel)

The luxury products industry has been estimated to be worth $58 billion, excluding automobiles and

travel. The breakdown by sector is shown in **Exhibit 2**.

Major players in the global luxury goods market include: LVMH Moët Hennessey Louis Vuitton, Richemont, Christian Dior, Gucci, Tiffany, Hermes, Swatch and Bulgari. Traditionally, the luxury sector has been highly fragmented, characterized by a large number of family-owned and medium-sized enterprises. In the past two decades, it has been increasingly dominated by multi-brand luxury conglomerates. Although smaller companies still thrive in this environment by serving niche markets, larger luxury goods companies have acquired or overtaken many of their smaller competitors. (See **Exhibit 3** for luxury market growth, by sector.)

Survival of the multi-brand strategy?

LVMH and France's biggest retail-to-luxury group Pinault-Printemps-Redoute (PPR), which controls Gucci, led the consolidation spree in the luxury industry in the late 1990s. More luxury conglomerates have emerged through acquisitions: many separate brands have united under a holding company structure intended to spread best practice and impose commercial and financial discipline. The goal is to allow firms to grow strongly without overexploiting a particular brand and killing exclusivity. However, Michael Zaoui, Morgan Stanley's head of mergers and acquisitions in Europe, has doubts on the viability of the multi-brand model, citing the slump in luxury M&A activity since 1999. *'It's a hotly debated issue ... but is the multi-brand model holding up?'* asks Zaoui, whose investment bank has been involved in every Gucci acquisition since 1999 as well as the initial public offerings of Bulgari SpA and Burberry PLC.

According to Zaoui, M&A in luxury goods slumped to $800 million in 2002 from $10 billion in 1999, and the rate of return on capital employed in the sector has dropped to 20% in 2001 from 32% in 1997. As companies seek to stretch their brands to target new customers, some 1,400 new luxury goods stores have been opened since 1999 – equivalent to strategic investments of $4.5 billion. Large advertising budgets are required to attract people to these new stores. According to Zaoui, the 10 leading luxury companies spent $1.1 billion on advertising in 2001, equivalent to 8% of sales, compared with 6%

of revenue in 1995. '*This expansion trend increases the inflexibility of the cost base … it can reduce margins if the growth's not there.*'

'Luxury for the masses'

There has been a systemic change in the luxury products market. In the past decade Gucci sunglasses, Prada handbags, and Louis Vuitton suitcases have become must-have items for many thousands of middle-class buyers. According to the Boston Consulting Group's newly released book, *Trading Up: The Transforming Power of New Luxury*, the trend in the market is towards mass elitism. While traditional luxury brands such as Louis Vuitton, Rolls-Royce and Hermes remain items for the elite, luxury has been democratized for all. According to BCG, 'new luxury' could range from a Starbucks frappuccino to a Porsche and can be extended across categories such as personal care, homewares and appliances, oral care, toys, restaurants and wines.

Consumers are in a 'state of heightened emotionalism' and often address feelings of being overworked, isolated, lonely, worried and unhappy by shopping for premium-priced products. 'New' luxury is the idea that middle-class consumers trade up to premium products because of emotional needs, to give them a sense of indulgence and personal fulfilment. They spend a disproportionate amount of their income on such goods, and trade down in other categories that are perceived to be less important. For example, a consumer may visit a Dior boutique to spend several hundred dollars on a Gucci handbag, and then go to a Wal-Mart or Carrefour to buy cotton socks.

This new middle-class market for luxury products creates a wide range of challenges for luxury conglomerates such as Gucci and Louis Vuitton, as they have to understand and cater to a different target consumer.

Market trends

In 2003, the luxury retail market segment was adversely affected by SARS (Severe Acute Respiratory Syndrome) in Asia, the US-led war against Iraq, the strengthening of the euro and a weak 'feel good factor' worldwide. SARS in Asia – which represents 30% of the sales in the luxury retail market segment – led to a general decline in travel and spending. Consumers in the United States also spent less in 2003 due to the war in Iraq and a weak economy. According to a study by Cotton Inc., published by *Women's Wear Daily*, consumers put 39% of their disposable income into savings and 14% to pay down debt in 2003. The strengthening of the euro has also led to a drop in tourism, which translated into lower sales in the luxury retail segment since a significant portion of luxury retail sales is generated by Japanese tourists. A strong euro also means equal sales in foreign currencies now appear as less euro revenues. All of these events contributed to the weak 'feel good factor' in 2003.

The luxury sector is cyclical and partially correlated to economic conditions. The luxury retail market segment appears to be rebounding in 2004 after two years of lacklustre performance. Mr Arnault predicted that the coming years will be '*very good for luxury because the world economy is doing well. The US is booming, interest rates are very low and there is a lot of optimism, Japan recovering, and China and the Far East are growing fast.*' Consumers dug into their pockets during the 2003/2004 holiday season to purchase more of the finer things in life. This turnaround in the luxury retail market segment ends the slump that plagued the market since the 11 September 2001 terrorist attacks.

So, signs of a turnaround in the luxury retail market are surfacing as consumer confidence improves and spending increases. In addition, performance in the luxury retail market segment is expected to improve throughout 2004. According to Mike Niemira, chief economist for the New York-based International Council of Shopping Centers, '*2004 will be a year of transition. Luxury items are strong and I think they are going to continue to be strong.*' Consumer spending in the United States is being propelled by the rebounding stock markets, President Bush's $350 billion tax-cut plan, and improving employment rates. Consumer spending in Asia is also recovering after the SARS epidemic.

In the long term, growth opportunities for the luxury retail market remain positive. The luxury retail market is currently driven by Japan, Europe and the United States. However, this market will include other parts of Asia such as China and

Eastern Europe in the future as these regions become richer.

Competition

Traditionally, the luxury goods sector has been very fragmented and was dominated by small and medium-sized companies that have over the years developed expertise in a particular product. But since the late 1990s – the boom years – the sector has been governed by multi-product and multi-brand conglomerates. Growth by acquisitions has been an important strategy for all the major players in this industry. Conglomerates have been trying to pre-empt each other in acquiring brands that have managed to survive successfully. This race has changed the dynamics of the industry from being 'creativity focused' to more 'financially focused'. The years since 2000 have seriously dampened spirits as sales stagnated and the conglomerates are paying a heavy price for their acquisition spree.

As the luxury goods industry looks to move beyond the three turbulent years, the independent and family-controlled companies that yielded the spotlight to sprawling conglomerates during the boom years are claiming a measure of vindication. The heads of several of the world's leading fashion houses said that their strategy of resisting corporate advances had worked. It gave them better control over production direction at a time when consumers are showing signs of weariness with the glitz and hype of some of fashion's biggest names. *'Never be exploited; don't give up control of design,'* says Giorgio Armani, head of the company he owns.

While keeping it in the family may make sense from a brand-development standpoint, it does have limitations. During the past three years, a weak global economy has tested the financial resources of a number of family-owned luxury goods houses. There is also the question of what happens to companies that become associated with the name, charisma and creativity of a larger-than-life founder. While Armani himself has steadfastly resisted the idea of offering shares to the public, he refused to rule out the option of bringing in a big strategic investor, expressing willingness to partner with LVMH or PPR.

Selling to a bigger holding company does not always mean that a formerly privately controlled designer has to compromise on identity. When Phillips-Van Heusen bought Calvin Klein to help the biggest US shirt-maker compete against department stores, industry insiders were sceptical that Klein would be able to retain complete design control over his empire. Finances at one of the world's most recognizable brands were dismal. The designer had reportedly been losing up to $25 million a year on its couture collection and millions more on retail operations. Rather than clamping down on Klein's creativity, Phillips spun the label into two new mid-range sportswear lines and pledged to cut costs while keeping Klein's 100 designers. Klein continues to play an important role in the image-making of the company. This is an example that shows how designers can funnel their creative energies and coexist with large conglomerates that offer substantial financial support – as both parties have adopted a middle path in the quest for control.

GUCCI–PPR: what after Tom Ford?

Originally a reseller of luggage that was imported from Germany, Gucci took advantage of the economic expansion following the First World War. Since then, the company has displayed an innovative streak, improvising leather alternatives. After the Second World War, Gucci began its global expansion strategy with a store in New York in 1953. The company suffered setbacks in the 1970s and 1980s after scandals and murder plots. There was intense fighting within the Gucci family that resulted in poor strategy and dilution of valuable brand equity. In the late 1980s, Investcorp bought 50% of the company. The revival of Gucci commenced with the appointment of Mr Domenico De Sole as the CEO. The new CEO hired Tom Ford, a highly acclaimed designer who revamped Gucci's product designs. The company took firmer control of the brand, its products, and the distribution. Investcorp sold its holdings through an IPO in 1996, making a fivefold return on its original investment. This was followed by a bitter battle for control of Gucci by LVMH and PPR. Finally, after poison pill measures taken by the Gucci management, which did not deter LVMH, PPR raised its offer and took control of the group. The move was welcomed by the Gucci management comprising Domenico De Sole and Tom Ford, who preferred PPR to LVMH for fear of losing their 'creative license' if LVMH took over Gucci.

Gucci started a multi-brand model later than LVMH. It acquired Yves Saint Laurent's fragrance and ready-to-wear apparel lines and added the renowned shoemaker Sergio Rossi to its umbrella of brands. The multi-brand strategy was expected to deliver important synergies. Unfortunately, the benefits were never realized and YSL pulled down the group's earnings year after year. In the meantime, Gucci continued its aggressive ascent choreographed by De Sole and Ford. The brand is strong in North America today and its strategy of portraying Gucci as a youthful and sensuous brand has appealed immensely to the Americans.

After the PPR group acquired a majority control of Gucci, it started 'infringing' on the independence enjoyed by the creative duo of De Sole and Ford. It is ironic that the very same group that was supposedly chosen to protect the creative freedom was curtailing it. Tensions with the chairman of PPR group, Pinault, led to both De Sole and Ford refusing to renew their three-year contracts after 2004.

According to analysts, 'The decade of revival of Gucci from almost a dead brand to one of the most promising ones today made Mr Tom Ford a bigger name than Gucci and PPR would have immense trouble replacing him.' Adding to PPR's woes, in September 2003 a US court began investigating Pinault for fraud in an unrelated acquisition in the 1990s. These drawbacks have indeed put a question mark on whether Gucci and PPR can continue their growth in the future after Tom Ford exits.

A nagging concern for the PPR group is whether Tom Ford is going to be lapped up by the rival LVMH group. Bernard Arnault has been openly critical of Pinault and De Sole but has refrained from saying anything against Tom Ford since the Gucci episode in 2000. He has recently been quoted as crediting Ford as 'one of the best designers of his time'. These may reflect Arnault's intention to hire Mr Ford after his exit from Gucci. It could significantly affect the dynamics at LVMH if it can lure Tom Ford to its fold. Sources familiar with the situation feel that Tom Ford is more likely to join a smaller company or launch his own label than join LVMH. The reason for his quitting is the constraint over his freedom and,

given the temperament of Mr Arnault, Mr Ford's association with LVMH might not result.

This has created a buzz in the industry as to where Tom Ford is headed and also whom would PPR recruit to replace him. It seems particularly interesting as the new job profile for the position of head of Gucci is to be a person 'out of the Luxury Industry'. It remains to be seen if this proves to be a good option and whether a key figure in this industry can make, break or manage a conglomerate.

Managing a multi-brand conglomerate

Creativity and innovation are synonymous to success in the fashion business. As two analysts recently observed, 'Luxury brands must foster an appreciation and tolerance for creativity that is unconstrained by commercial or production constraints'. In almost all its acquisitions, LVMH had maintained the creative talent as an independent pool without attempting to generate synergies across product lines or brands. Lately though, the sourcing is slowly being centralized to gain synergies and cost savings with a centralized purchasing mechanism.

Bernard Arnault believes that 'If you think and act like a typical manager around creative people – with rules, policies, data on customer preferences, and so forth – you will quickly kill their talent.' The company has been decentralized by design and has a very small cadre of managers.

However, industry insiders cite that all is not well with a financial man like Bernard Arnault at the helm. His management style is described as providing 'constrained freedom'. For example, a manager for Céline could recruit someone himself, independent of the central LVMH human resources department, but he has to send a copy of the CV of the person he hired so that head office is kept aware of the new development. Though Arnault's managers are given autonomy, they know they are being watched and who has the final word in case of any conflict.

Another concern is the ruthless pursuit towards the bottom line. LVMH believes in 'running businesses profitably'. Managers are supported as long as they make money over the stipulated minimum: 'You have the freedom as long as you exceed *your targets. Once you do not ... there is no freedom any more.'* The emphasis is on profit and if any division or company does not deliver, it will promptly be sold off. This approach contrasts with the traditional and creative view of 'Haute Couture', which accepts losses on some collections but waits for the market to accept its designs over a period of time.

Managing 'star brands'

The core pillar of LVMH's current business strategy is 'star brands,' coupled with innovation and quality. More specifically, Bernard Arnault describes the group's stellar financial performance in 2003 as *'a consequence of the priority placed on internal growth and profitability, the development of brands around the dual goals of innovation and quality, and the conquest of new markets.'* (See **Exhibit 5** for key financials.) According to Bernard Arnault, a star brand is one that is:

> *timeless, modern, fast-growing, and highly profitable ... There are fewer than ten star brands in the luxury world, because it is very hard to balance all four characteristics at once – after all, fast growth is often at odds with high profitability – but that is what makes them stars. If you have a star brand, then basically you can be sure you have mastered a paradox.*

According to him, star brands are born only when a company manages to make products that *'speak to the ages'* but the feel is intensely modern. Such products are designed to sell fast, raking in profits for the fashion empire. This is a paradox and he confides that *'mastering the paradox of star brands is very difficult and rare.'*

Bernard Arnault has never specified exactly what those ten 'star brands' were but, using his criteria, the following luxury labels could be considered as star brands: Christian Dior, Louis Vuitton, Hermes, Cartier, Giorgio Armani, Gucci, Chanel and Prada. Of these, LVMH controls just two – Dior and Vuitton, of which he says:

> *if you take Vuitton, which has existed for more than 150 years, I think, today, it is also modern. Dior has been there for 50 years, but also I think it is the most hip fashion brand today.*

Innovation

Bernard Arnault believes that innovation *'is the ultimate driver, of growth and profitability. Our whole business is based on giving our artists and designers complete freedom to invent without limits.'* He has acknowledged past mistakes, including the rapid expansion of the Sephora beauty and fragrance supermarkets, for which he said LVMH had paid too much. After expanding too quickly in the United States, the company had to close stores and reposition the unit. In a business based on giving artists and designers the freedom to create without limits, LVMH allows each brand to run itself, headed by a creative director. Only 250 out of the over 56,000 employees are based in the Paris headquarters; the essence of the business is to identify the right creative people to stimulate new and cutting edge ideas, and trusting their instincts.

Quality

In the luxury products business, quality is essential in production as well as in product development. This is also an essential element in LVMH's success strategy. For example, to exercise the utmost control over the quality of its Louis Vuitton 'star brand,' the company owns manufacturing facilities employing over 4,000 in France, Spain and in the United States, among other countries. While LVMH produces its Louis Vuitton brand in-house, the firm outsources part of the production of its other fashion labels, such as Céline and Fendi. *'For all of our brands we manufacture part of the overall production within our facilities to be sure that there is a consistency between what is done by external subcontractors and what we do,'* explained Jean-Paul Vivier, executive vice president of the LVMH Fashion Group.

Managing people

Human resources and management talent are critical for the luxury conglomerate. When Arnault first began his consolidation, the group was full of problems, and only a few of the companies were profitable. HR Director Concetta Lanciaux confided that his primary concern was to *'have the best managers'*. Lanciaux's challenge was particularly difficult because there was a scarcity of executives in luxury goods at the time. Most firms were small, family-owned companies, without graduates or succession planning. LVMH had to recruit and develop talent from different fields. Regarding the mobilization of LVMH's resources, Bernard Arnault said:

> In a global context the progress of LVMH in 2003 will be based above all on the excellence of the fundamentals and its capacity to mobilize its internal resources. We can rely on our traditional strengths – namely the talent of our managers and employees and their determination to make the difference, the appeal of our major brands, the certain values – more than ever in a difficult period; the creativity and excellence of our products and the power of our distribution networks.
>
> We are continuing to deploy the organic growth strategy ... while still carrying out the sale of non-strategic assets, we will maintain strict management focus, enabling us to reinvest the cost savings achieved in the driving forces of our growth.

LVMH has encouraged and passed on the know-how, skills, the spirit of excellence, and the ethic that conveys, through its creations and products, an exceptional art of living, which is appreciated worldwide. The awakening and education of young people to these values has always constituted an essential part of the Group's goal. LVMH has carried out various original initiatives for young people in France and abroad. It is through these initiatives that primary school children, high school students, art students, young artists and designers, as well as those closer to the Group's new work opportunities such as college and higher education students, can benefit. In 1991, for example, LVMH partnered with Paris-based business school ESSEC to launch the luxury brand marketing LVMH ESSEC chair, funded with FF10 million. Further partnerships have since been launched in Asia as well.

The company had to hire people with experience in other industries, such as consumer goods, and select people with 'good taste'. Lanciaux cited engineering and business schools as specific sources of talent. LVMH also instituted strong company-wide induction and training programmes as well as on-the-job training to introduce the world of luxury to its capable, bright novices. Lanciaux explained:

> With some 40 brands potentially competing against each other in the Group, recruitment and everyday business becomes complex. In the case of our Group, what builds value and profits is the ability to act in an autonomous way and create new products. The business is built on the number of innovative products that come out every year – 20% to 30% of the turnover is based on new products. Therefore, our companies' senior executives have to have a large dose of autonomy and creative capacity. People use these as aspirational products, so we need people who manage and dream – and make others dream.

Despite the group's aggressive growth through acquisition, LVMH has tried to treat such moves sensitively, with a vision of integration. Lanciaux commented:

> First of all, it was about respecting, identifying and then preserving all of the assets of the company – not changing everything at once. One of the mistakes that companies in this situation make is that they want to change everything and bring in their own culture. When we buy these brands, we buy them to develop them. To develop the brand, the first thing you need to know is what makes that brand. Very often it's a number of people who are behind it, often invisible ... You have to find them, make them visible. This means that we have been able to preserve the integrity of these brands. Our style is not to go in there and replace everybody – never.

Jean-Paul Vivier, executive vice president of the LVMH Fashion Group, agrees that the Group seeks to foster creativity not just among its design teams, but also with professionals throughout the business. He compares the process to mixing the perfect cocktail – LVMH tries to build a work environment that promotes creativity and at the same time adheres to strict business disciplines.

Integration, training and top management seminars designed to support business strategies played an essential role in the professional development of the LVMH Group. Since 2001, it steadily increased the number of training days for all personnel categories within the Group and in centres located in Paris, New York, Hong Kong and Tokyo. The total number of training days in 2001 was 103,585 world-wide. Each of the companies is developing a specific training programme that reflects its own vision of excellence and its strategic objectives. At Louis Vuitton, which operates in 44 countries, vendors from all over the world participate in 'brand immersion' seminars organized in Asnières, the company's birthplace and communications centre. They tour the workshops built in 1859 and the Louis Vuitton travel museum. These sites are filled with the spirit of the company, which has remained constant even as it adapts to changing fashions and trends – a spirit embodied in the skills of the craftsmen, the details, and a unique talent for anticipating, analysing and meeting the requirements of the contemporary world. In 1999, Hennessy developed a teaching game called 'Strateco' that takes place over two days. It is designed to make all non-managerial employees more aware of economic influences affecting the companies and their operating realities. Another programme, 'Decompartmentalizing people and their jobs', presents the mission, organization and business of each department in the company's portfolio and brings together participants from the various departments. Finally, the inter-company seminars offered to all the Group's managers focus on topics of mutual interest and are primarily designed to develop or perfect management, communication and leadership skills.

American designer Michael Kors joined LVMH and successfully revived Céline, a dusty brand. However, it didn't seem that anyone at LVMH noticed. During Kors's six-and-a-half-year tenure at Céline, the position of chief executive officer turned five times, from Nan Legeai, to Bernard Divisia, Yves Carcelle, Thierry Andretta and, finally, to Jean-Marc Loubier. At the same time, Bernard Arnault attended only two of Kors's fashion shows for Céline. In total, Kors estimated that he spent a total of three hours in Bernard Arnault's company, including the two shows and two 'hellos' when he ran into Arnault at the Dior store in Paris. Kors said:

Was I mistreated? No. Was I neglected? Yes. I never felt as though there was a strategy at LVMH as far as pitting the designers against each other or the brands against each other.

It's just that I never felt anyone was watching the smaller companies at all, but everybody was spending their time on the two first-born children – Louis Vuitton and Christian Dior. In a way, if you're a nice kid, no one pays attention to you. If you are a bad kid, you get spoiled.

Interesting is the case of Marc Jacobs. In 1997, Marc Jacobs was struggling to keep his namesake brand afloat. Bernard Arnault approached him with an irresistible offer to lend his creative flair to the venerable but stodgy Louis Vuitton label, in return for LVMH underwriting his beleaguered design firm. Jacobs's designs have helped boost sales and buzz around the $3.8 billion Louis Vuitton brand, which accounts for 60% of LVMH's operating profit. His multicoloured Murakami handbag alone drove over $300 million in sales. The 41-year-old designer was also able to develop his own Marc Jacobs label, which soared to about $75 million in sales in 2003, helped by a $50 million investment from LVMH.

However, tensions have arisen between the designer and the company. Mr Jacobs believes his ambitions to develop his own brand are being hindered by LVMH. He complains that the French conglomerate hasn't invested enough in the Marc Jacobs business and has locked him out of critical decisions about the operations at his own line. For example, in May 2003, LVMH, while closing its US fragrance division, sold the Marc Jacobs perfume to Coty Inc. without informing or consulting the designer. None of the proceeds went to Jacobs, instead heading directly to LVMH.

Due to its heavy dependence on creative and modern designs, the departure of key creative personnel would be devastating to Vuitton. Early this year, there was speculation that Jacobs might leave unless LVMH gave more backing to his clothing line. As seen in the example of Tom Ford and Domenico De Sole's departures from luxury rival Gucci, losing its young star designer may spell trouble for the Louis Vuitton brand.

In May 2004 a spokesman in Paris confirmed that Moët Hennessy Louis Vuitton SA has resolved a year-long dispute with the New York designer Marc Jacobs, artistic director of Louis Vuitton, and his business partner Robert Duffy, 49-year-old President of Marc Jacobs, by signing them to new

10-year employment contracts and committing to invest in the partners' Marc Jacobs International fashion house. Under the new agreement, Marc Jacobs and Robert Duffy received salary raises and – for the first time – stock options. According to Robert Duffy, *'Now, Marc and I can achieve our dream of turning Marc Jacobs into a global power-house'.*

Conclusion

Although the Louis Vuitton brand is enormously profitable, none of the other labels rival its level of commercial success. With its current dependence on star designers such as John Galliano and Marc Jacobs, the Group's success is highly correlated to the whim of the creative. Given the current internal politics and recent departure of Michael Kors, will consumers remain loyal to the brand or the designer? The bigger questions are, can LVMH oversee so many luxury brands, make them all profitable and maintain the highest standards of creativity? After Bernard Arnault, how can one manage this 'loose' conglomerate that he has created in the last decade?

Case Questions

1 What does globalization mean in the luxury industry? What is the international strategy of LVMH? How does it differ from its competitors?

2 What are the factors influencing companies to seek growth by acquisitions in this industry? How are they managing and integrating these acquisitions? Is this growth sustainable?

3 Does LVMH's structure support its multi-brand strategy and functioning of the Group?

4 Comment on the nature of the competition in the luxury industry and the multi-brand strategy?

5 How is LVMH managing its creative talents? Does it differ from its competitors? If yes, how? If not, why not?

6 Comment on the leadership of Bernard Arnault and his management style. How is LVMH 'cultivating' leaders for tomorrow?

Exhibit 1 LVMH conglomerate at a glance

Wine & Spirits	Watches & Jewellery	Fashion & Leather	Selective Retailing	Perfumes & Cosmetics
Moët & Chandon*	TAG Heuer*	Louis Vuitton*	DFS*	Parfums Christian Dior*
Dom Pérignon	Ebel*	Loewe*	Miami Cruiseline Services*	Guerlain*
Veuve Clicquot*	Zenith*	Céline*	Sephora*	Parfums Givenchy*
Krug	Christian Dior Watches*	Berluti*	Le Bon Marché*	Kenzo Parfums*
Mercier	Fred*	Kenzo*	La Samaritaine*	Laflachère*
Ruinart	Chaumet*	Givenchy*		Bliss*
Château d'Yquem*	OMAS*	Christian Lacroix*		BeneFit Cosmetics*
Chandon Estates*		Marc Jacobs*		Fresh*
Hennessy*		Fendi*		Make Up For Ever*
Cloudy Bay		StefanoBi		Acqua di Parma*
Cape Mentelle		Emilio Pucci*		Perfumes Loewe*
Newton		Thomas Pink*		
MountAdam		Donna Karan*		

* indicates company status.

Acquisitions

1987	Fashion house Céline
1988	Fashion house Givenchy
1991	Champagne brand Pommery
1993	Fashion house Kenzo
1994	Perfume company Kenzo, cosmetics company Guerlain
1995	Jeweller Fred
1996	Leather goods specialist Loewe
1997	DFS, the luxury goods distribution network
1998	Sephora, the fragrance and cosmetics retail chain
1999	Champagne producer Krug and the watch manufacturer TAG Heuer, a 34% minority stake in the Italian luxury goods maker Gucci
2000	LVMH purchased the US start-up Urban Decay, and Donna Karan apparel line
2001	La Samaritaine department store, Acqua di Parma perfumes, a stake in Fendi
2002	Millennium & Company, prestige wines and alcohol

New business creations

1987   Christian Lacroix

2001   Newton and MountAdam vineyards

       Marketing De Beers diamond jewellery in a 50–50 joint venture

Divestitures

2001   Sale of stake in Gucci to Pinault Printemps Redoute

2002   Pommery champagne brand, Hard Candy and Urban Decay

2003   Canard-Duchene to the Alain Thienot Group

       Final stake of 27.5% in Phillips, de Pury & Luxembourg, an auction house

       Minority stake in Michael Kors, including cosmetics and fragrance licences

       Marc Jacobs and Kenneth Cole fragrance divisions

       Bliss spa line & Ebel watches

Exhibit 2 Breakdown of luxury goods industry

Sector	Percentage share
Tableware	4
Ready-to-wear apparel	26
Leather goods and accessories	17
Wines and spirits	15
Fragrances	12
Cosmetics	12
Watches	9
Jewellery	5

Source: Merrill Lynch Research.

Exhibit 3 Luxury market growth, by sector

Sectors of the luxury products industry	Annual sales growth 1998–2002 (%)
Home fashions	10
Ready-to-wear	10
Accessories	10
Leather goods	10
Watches and jewellery	8
Perfume and cosmetics	6
Crystal and silverware	5
Shoes	4

Source: Eurostat.

Exhibit 4 Representative primary competitors, by business unit

Product Sector	LVMH Businesses	Primary Competitors
Fashion and Leather Goods	Louis Vuitton, Loewe, Céline Berluti, Kenzo, Christian Lacroix, Givenchy, Marc Jacobs, Fendi, StefanoBi, Emilio Pucci, Thomas Pink, Donna Karan	Prada, Versace, Armani, Saint-Laurent, Chanel, Ralph Lauren, MaxMara, Burberry, Ferragamo, Hugo Boss, Gucci, Hermès, Bulgari, Lancel, etc.
Jewellery and Watches	TAG Heuer, Zenith, Dior Watches, FRED, Chaumet, OMAS*	Oméga, Breitling, Vendôme-Cartier, Cartier, Van Cleef & Arpels, Rolex, Ebel*, Baume et Mercier
Perfume and Cosmetics	Parfums Christian Dior, Guerlain, Parfums Givenchy, Kenzo Parfums, Laflachère, BeneFit Cosmetics, Fresh, Make Up For Ever, Acqua di Parma, Perfumes Loewe*	Many brands, including Lancôme, Lanvin et Armani, all brands under L'Oréal, Chanel, Yves Saint-Laurent, Gautier, Calvin Klein, Ralph Lauren, Estée Lauder, Shiseido, Hard Candy*, Bliss*, specialty perfumeries, etc.
Wines and Spirits	Moët & Chandon, Dom Pérignon, Veuve Clicquot, Krug, Mercier, Ruinart, Château d'Yquem, Chandon Estates, Hennessy, Cloudy Bay, Cape Mentelle, Newton, MountAdam	Pommery*, Marne et Champagne, Laurent Perrier, Seagram, Johnny Walker, Smirnoff, Rémy Cointreau, Rémy Martin, Courvoisier, etc.
Distribution	DFS, Le Bon Marché, La Samaritaine, Séphora, sephora.com, Miami Cruiseline Services	Many stores and retailing franchises

* Indicates former LVMH businesses.

Exhibit 5 Consolidated group performance (€million)

	2002	2001	2000	1999	1998	5-Year Growth
Total Current Assets	7,168	8,260	8,280	6,887	5,414	32.40%
Total Current Liabilities	6,890	8,017	9,829	8,615	6,328	8.88%
Total Assets	20,658	22,540	21,124	19,671	16,008	29.05%
Total Liabilities	12,864	15,122	14,947	13,194	9,408	36.73%
Total Common Equity	6,022	5,618	4,696	5,400	5,7365	4.99%
Income Statement	**2002**	**2001**	**2000**	**1999**	**1998**	**5-Year Growth**
Sales	12,693	12,229	11,581	8,547	6,936	83.00%
Cost Of Goods Sold	3,806	3,466	3,821	2,698	2,197	73.25%
Net Income	556	10	705	636	429	29.65%

Source: Thomson Analytics Financial Database.

Exhibit 6a Net sales by business group

Group	2001 (€m)	2001 % total sales	2002 (€m)	2002 % total sales	2003 (€m)	2003 % total sales
Wines & Spirits	2,232	18%	2,266	18%	2,116	18%
Fashion & Leather Goods	3,612	30%	4,207	33%	4,149	35%
Perfumes & Cosmetics	2,231	18%	2,336	18%	2,181	18%
Watches & Jewellery	548	4%	552	4%	503	4%
Selective Retailing	3,493	29%	3,337	26%	3,039	25%
Other businesses and eliminations	113	1%	5	0%	25	0%
Total	12,229		12,693		11,963	

Source: LVMH 2003 Annual Report.

Exhibit 6b Income from operations by business group

Group	2001			2002			2003		
	€m	% total sales	op. margin	€m	% total sales	op. margin	€m	% total sales	op. margin
Wines & Spirits	676	43%	30%	750	37%	33%	796	36%	38%
Fashion & Leather Goods	1,274	82%	35%	1,280	64%	30%	1,311	60%	32%
Perfumes & Cosmetics	149	10%	7%	161	8%	7%	178	8%	8%
Watches & Jewellery	27	2%	5%	13	21%	N/S	48	22%	N/S
Selective Retailing	213	214%	N/S	20	1%	1%	106	5%	3%
Other businesses and eliminations	353	223%	N/S	190	29%	N/S	161	27%	N/S
Total	1,560			2,008			2,182		

Source: LVMH 2003 Annual Report.

Exhibit 7 Net sales by geographic region

2002	
Other markets	6%
United States	27%
France	17%
Rest of Europe	20%
Japan	15%
Rest of Asia	15%
2003	
Other markets	7%
United States	26%
France	17%
Rest of Europe	21%
Japan	16%
Rest of Asia	13%

Source: LVMH 2003 Annual Report.

Exhibit 8 LVMH global reach (number of stores in 2003)

North America	344
Latin America	16
France	277
Europe	401
Africa & Middle East	6
Asia	287
Japan	232
Pacific Region	29

Source: LVMH 2003 Annual Report.

Exhibit 9 Benchmarking Louis Vuitton vs. other luxury brands

Brand	2003 sales ($bn)	Percentage change*	Operating margin (%)
Louis Vuitton	3.80	16.0	45.0
Prada	1.95	0.0	13.0
Gucci**	1.85	21.0	27.0
Hermes	1.57	7.7	25.4
Coach	1.20	134.0	29.9

*   At constant rate of exchange
** Gucci division of Gucci Group
Source: Company reports, *Business Week*.

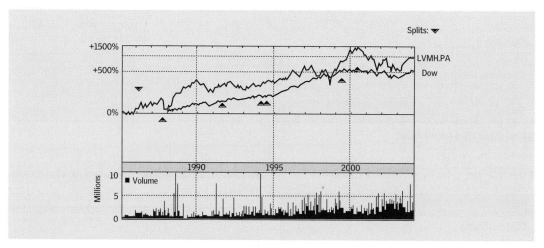

Exhibit 10 LVMH stock performance, 1985 to March 2004
Source: http://uk.finance.yahoo.com. Copyright 2003 Yahoo! Inc.

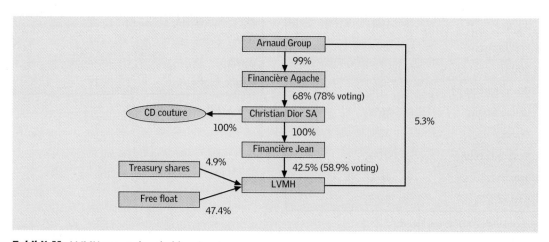

Exhibit 11 LVMH group shareholder structure
Source: Company data, UBS Warburg.

Exhibit 12   The 15 leadership factors
Identified by 450 LVMH Group senior executives during LVMH house sessions (October 2001)

Creativity

Comes up with a lot of new and unique ideas; easily makes connections among previously unrelated notions; tends to be seen as original and value-added in brainstorming sessions.

Strategic Agility

Sees ahead clearly; can anticipate future consequences and trends accurately; has broad knowledge and perspective; is future oriented; can articulately paint credible picture and visions of possibilities and likelihood; can create competitive and breakthrough strategies and plans.

Innovation Management

Is good at bringing the creative ideas of others to market; has good judgement about creative process of others; can facilitate effective brainstorming; can project how potential ideas may play out in the market place.

Managing Vision and Purpose

Communicates a compelling and inspired vision or sense of core purpose; talks beyond today; talks about possibilities; is optimistic; creates mileposts and symbols to rally support behind the vision; makes the vision sharable by everyone; can inspire and motivate entire units or organizations.

Customer Focus

Is dedicated to meeting the expectations and requirements of internal and external customers; gets first-hand customer information and uses it for improvements in products and services; acts with customers in mind; establishes and maintains effective relationships with customers and gains their trust and respect.

Priority Setting

Spends his/her time and the time of others on what's important; quickly zeros in on the critical few and puts the trivial many aside; can quickly sense what will help or hinder accomplishing a goal; eliminates roadblocks; creates focus.

Building Effective Teams

Blends people into teams when needed; creates strong morale and spirit in his/her team; shares wins and successes; fosters open dialogue; lets people finish and be responsible for their work; defines success in terms of the whole team; creates a feeling of belonging in the team.

Action Oriented

Enjoys working hard; is action oriented and full of energy for the things he/she sees as challenging; not fearful of acting with a minimum of planning; seizes more opportunities than others.

Drive for Results

Can be counted on to exceed goals successfully; is constantly and consistently one of the top performers; very bottom-line oriented; steadfastly pushes self and others for results.

Hiring and Staffing

Has a nose for talent; hires the best people available from inside or outside; is not afraid of selecting strong people; assembles talented staffs.

Motivating Others

Creates a climate in which people want to do their best; can motivate many kinds of direct reports and team or project members; can assess each person's hot button and use it to get the best out of him/her; pushes tasks and decisions down; empowers others; invites input from each person and shares ownership and visibility; makes each individual feel his/her work is important; is someone people like working for and with.

Business Acumen

Knows how businesses work; knowledgeable in current and possible future policies, practices, trends, and information affecting his/her business and organization; knows the competition; is aware of how strategies and tactics work in the market place.

Integrity and Trust

Is widely trusted: is seen as a direct, truthful individual; can present the unvarnished truth in an appropriate and helpful manner; keeps confidences; admits mistakes; doesn't misrepresent him/herself for personal gain.

Learning on the Fly

Learns quickly when facing new problems; a relentless and versatile learner; open to change; analyses both successes and failures for clues to improvement; experiments and will try anything to find solutions; enjoys the challenge of unfamiliar tasks; quickly grasps the essence and the underlying structure of anything.

Delegation

Clearly and comfortably delegates both routine and important tasks and decisions; broadly shares both responsibility and accountability; tends to trust people to perform; lets direct reports finish their own work.

INSEAD

Case 9 HSBC: Migrating for value

In September 2000, Raymond Or Ching Fai, General Manager of the Hong Kong and Shanghai Banking Corporation Ltd (HSBC), a subsidiary of HSBC Holdings plc, returned to Hong Kong from a one-week executive workshop at the group's London headquarters. The workshop had been designed to review the progress of each subsidiary in implementing the corporate strategy, 'Managing for Value' (MfV), introduced in 1998. Within HSBC, initial progress had been slow, yet employee grievances and internal conflicts had already emerged. While he agreed with his colleagues in London that it made the best 'commercial sense' for HSBC, Or was not looking forward to his latest task: migrating functions from the company's Network Services Centre (NSC) in Hong Kong to its global processing centre on the Chinese mainland.

HSBC Holdings plc

The HSBC name is derived from the Hongkong and Shanghai Banking Corporation, founded in 1865 in Hong Kong, to provide larger scale and more sophisticated banking facilities to local businesses. Almost immediately after its establishment, the new bank opened an office in Shanghai and began to build a network of offices with an emphasis on China and the rest of the Asia-Pacific region. The group's international acquisition programme did not begin until much later, in 1959, by which time a near monopolistic position in Hong Kong provided a secure foundation from which to finance global expansion.

In 1980, HSBC opened a representative office in Beijing, followed by representative offices in Guangzhou, Shenzen and Xiamen. In 1984, it became the first foreign bank since 1949 to be granted a banking licence, enabling the Shenzen office to be upgraded to a branch. In 1997, HSBC was one of the first banks to be granted permission to conduct renminbi[1] (RMB) business at its Shanghai Pudong Branch. By 1999 it had a network of 19 offices in mainland China, with an expanded renminbi business.

HSBC had also achieved a broad geographical balance of businesses outside Asia. By 2000, it represented one of the largest banking and financial services organizations in the world providing a complete range of personal banking, commercial banking and related financial services through some 5,000 offices in 80 countries and territories worldwide.

Managing for value

In 1998, HSBC responded to global developments in the banking industry by introducing a major group-wide change initiative, *Managing for Value: HSBC into the 21st Century* (MfV). On the banking giant's web site, the introduction to its corporate values emphasised the priorities of this programme:

> As a commercial organisation, our governing objective is to provide a satisfactory return on our shareholders' capital.

The MfV strategy aimed to double shareholder value in the five-year period 1999–2003 and again every five years thereafter. A series of initiatives were introduced across the HSBC group in a bid to align the organisation with this primary objective. These included:

This case was written by Sarah Meegan, Research Fellow, and Steven White, Professor of Asian Business and Comparative Management at INSEAD. It is intended to be used as a basis for class discussion rather than to illustrate either effective or ineffective handling of an administrative situation.

[1] The renminbi (translated literally as 'people's currency') is the official currency of the People's Republic of China. It is sometimes confused with the *yuan*, which is the currency's base unit.

- ◆ Transforming traditional branches to financial service centres.
- ◆ Strengthening the salesforce by recruiting dedicated Financial Services Executives (FSE) and re-deploying back-office staff to frontline operations.
- ◆ Streamlining the business processes and procedures.
- ◆ Migrating back-office operations, currently centralized in the Network Services Center (NSC) in Hong Kong, to the Guangzhou Data Center (GZC) in mainland China.

It was this final initiative which would prove most disruptive to Or's operation in Hong Kong, requiring careful planning and management, and raising myriad issues and concerns across the company.

Back-end jobs to low-cost centres

A guiding principle of the MfV programme was to pursue economies of scale across the various countries and territories covered by the HSBC group. As Keith Whitson, Group Chief Executive, had proclaimed:

> A key initiative is the introduction of global processing. We now have two centers, the first of which was established in Guangzhou, China in 1996, and the second in Hyderabad, India in October 2000. These centers currently employ more than 1,000 people to handle routine workflow from both the UK and the Hong Kong Special Administrative Region (SAR). We plan to double our global processing capacity in 2001.[2]

Previously associated with the manufacturing sector, similar shifts in service industries worldwide had demonstrated an acceleration in the trend of basing low-end jobs in low-cost countries. The acceleration could be attributed, in part, to improvements in infrastructure such as internet connections and falling telecom costs in the host countries. It had also resulted from a corporate desire to concentrate resources on brand-name and customer relations,

leaving the back-office work to contractors. US companies, including General Electric and American Express, had been shifting back-end jobs to lower-cost centres since the mid-1980s, transferring credit card service centres to countries such as India. Other beneficiaries included Malaysia, the Philippines and Australia, as multinationals transferred data entry functions, accounts and call centre work worth millions of dollars.

Network Services Center (NSC) in Hong Kong

The Network Services Center (NSC) in Hong Kong represented HSBC's back-end operations hub, processing all transactions and customer requests on behalf of the branch network. By 2000, the NSC employed more than 1,000 staff divided between five key departments: Account Services (ASV), Payment Services (PSV), Credit Services Personal Banking (CSP), Collections and Recoveries-Secured (CRU-S), and Collections and Recoveries-Unsecured (CRU-U) (Exhibit 1).

Traditional processing and control

Since the NSC had been established, clear segregation of duties and responsibilities had operated across the various departments and between different levels of staff. To iron out a number of grey areas that had arisen over the years, complete sets of operating procedures had been produced and distributed to all employees. For the operations staff in particular, work patterns were extremely routine.

In order to manage the risk exposure and minimize potential errors, the NSC had adopted a 'dual control' approach to most processes: each data-entry input by an operator was subsequently checked by a verifier. In addition to this, a comprehensive set of checks and control measures were enforced, including a maintenance register for transaction processing, multi-level credit approval, and referral to branches/customers for information clarification. Some NSC staff was specifically assigned to perform stringent audit checks on tasks conducted by their colleagues.

Having worked in such a controlled environment for many years, most of the bank's operations staff were focused solely on their own tasks.

---

[2] The Implementation of HSBC's Strategy: a Review by the Group Chief Executive, HSBC Holdings plc, 2000 annual review.

Despite various improvements in the bank's internal systems and a corresponding reduction in risk, over the years the old procedures and practices continued to hold.

NSC review

As part of the bank's major change programme, Or instigated a review of the NSC operation which was carried out between November 2000 and January 2001. The objectives of the study were fourfold:

- To reduce the cost structure of the NSC.
- To identify suitable functions for cross-border processing.
- To identify revenue opportunities in the NSC.
- To optimize customer service levels through re-engineering activities.

Several hundred recommendations on the stream-lining of operational processes, simplification of control procedures, and development of new sources of revenue generation were proposed in the first round of the initiative. One of the most significant suggestions was the migration of functions from the NSC to the Guangzhou Processing Center (GZC), 180km north of Hong Kong, in line with the Chief Executive's directive on global processing. HSBC anticipated creating or facilitating a range of savings from this exercise, including reduction of head-count in the NSC division, reduction in the use of paper, release of premises for business unit expansion, introduction of fee-based services, enhanced process quality, and improved customer service levels.

Function migration to Guangzhou

The processing center at Guangzhou, established in 1996, was designed to house routine clerical tasks which required low-level skills and virtually no decision-making. It was ideally suited to tasks that could be automated and either partially or wholly replaced by computer systems, such as data entry. More complex jobs, which were time-critical, required specialized knowledge or skills, or involved important interactions with other departments such as credit approval or legal matters, would remain at the NSC. As a first step in the migration initiative, the bank conducted a series of re-engineering projects in order to identify process stages already eligible for migration to GZC, and streamline others that could also be transferred. Opportunities for function migration to GZC were greatly increased through the extensive application of computer systems by HSBC.

One of the primary sources of cost reduction achieved through the move to GZC was the pay roll. The average salary of operations staff in GZC was as low as one-fifth of that in the NSC. In addition, a range of fringe benefits enjoyed by staff in Hong Kong, such as low-interest mortgage loans and pension funds, were not offered to their mainland counterparts.

Job losses at NSC

In March 2001, HSBC announced the migration of up to 300 posts (2% of its 14,000 strong workforce) to Guangzhou. Given the variation in duties and responsibilities, relocation of head-count was unevenly distributed across the five departments at NSC: 28% of ASV, 44% of PSV, 26% of CSP, 7% of CRU-S, and 36% of CRU-U would be moved to GZC.

While the NSC would become much smaller, the GZC data center was expanding at an increasing rate. The bank planned to achieve the head-count reduction in the NSC through staff re-deployment, natural attrition, and redundancies. Staff selected for re-deployment would be provided with an intensive one-month training programme to convert them to direct sales positions such as financial services executives. For the new GZC staff, the bank felt that minimal job training was required given the more simple nature of their duties. The bank also considered that each target function could be switched from the NSC to GZC overnight with no requirement for a period of parallel operations or trials.

Employee empowerment

During the NSC Review it had also been concluded that the operating environment was too heavily controlled: excessive checking, unnecessary referrals to branches and customers, and complex and redundant approvals. In order to avoid duplicate efforts, increase the productivity of the center, and better utilize its staff for value-added activities, the decision was taken to relax most of these measures and grant employees greater authority and autonomy in making decisions. For transaction posting and data capture tasks, where error rates had proven negligible, the traditional 100% duplicate checking was replaced by 10% random checking. The widespread use of registers in the NSC was also targeted for elimination.

To compensate for the simplification of the approval structure and decision levels, NSC staff were encouraged to take up additional roles and responsibilities. The existing transaction and credit approval limits, e.g. for invoice signing, loan application, loan restructuring and bad debt write-off, were revised upward for all staff categories and staff at lower grades were authorised to approve transactions below a pre-defined threshold. Employees were also encouraged to take certain decisions without referral to their superiors or further approval from senior management. The clerical staff, for example, could verify customers' signatures by themselves, staff officers (SOs) and section heads (SHs) could post payments to accounts without constant referral to the department manager, and the CRU manager approve a loan reconstruction without counter-approval from a senior manager. At the operations level, the clerical staff and SOs were empowered to amend simple data submission errors at their discretion without referring to the branches or customers. Staff in lower grades were also empowered to sign official documents or letters on behalf of their superiors.

Embarking on the function migration

In mid-March 2001, HSBC management briefed the 1,200 employees in Hong Kong who would be directly affected by the job relocation to GZC. On the same day, copies of a nine-page letter signed by the General Manager explaining the relocation were circulated to all 14,000 employees. In the letter,[3] Or explained:

Whilst we must increase the number of customer interface and sales roles if we are to meet our customers' future needs, back-office processing and support services can more easily be transferred to low-cost offshore locations such as Guangzhou ... The resultant strategy will mean a change in the skills profile and the nature and mix of jobs between Hong Kong and Guangzhou.

The transformation of traditional transaction-based banking into a sales-oriented financial services organization was also confirmed in the letter:

We are now embarking on a major redeployment exercise for those immediately affected ... Equally, we will actually be growing the numbers of employees engaged in positions such as Mandatory Provident Fund[4] processing, customer service and product sales, so the total number employed by the bank in Hong Kong will remain around 14,000 or even increase somewhat over the next three years ... At the maximum, we expect no more than one to two per cent of our total workforce to leave the bank in 2001 as a result of this exercise, and we will be doing all we can to keep this number as low as possible.

However, there was no explicit reference to the exact number of jobs affected or to recent speculation that the bank planned to close many of its branches in Hong Kong. Or's letter remained vague on these points:

Historically, we have been very successful in redeploying those whose jobs have migrated to Guangzhou and elsewhere, and we will make every effort to do so again, through retraining and working with other Group companies in Hong Kong. However, we cannot guarantee that we will be successful in finding redeployment opportunities for everyone.

With the public announcement of the first job move to Guangzhou in March 2001, rumours abounded in the Hong Kong market that HSBC planned to cut as

---

[3] HSBC move may set trend: Group predicts more jobs will switch to 'cheap' mainland as it announces hundreds of transfers, *South China Morning Post*, 14 March 2001.

[4] MFP, the Mandatory Provident Fund was a fully funded, privately managed compulsory retirement scheme implemented by the Hong Kong Government in December 2000. Both the employer and the employee were required to contribute 5% of the employee's monthly cash income.

many as 1,200 jobs. Or responded by dismissing speculation on massive job cuts:

> *The reports are all speculative ... this is an ongoing process. The bank would be committed to retraining and to allow the staff to adapt to a new environment.*

He urged the bank staff, moreover, 'to adopt a positive attitude and try to upgrade themselves'.[5]

Morale, however, was extremely low and staff were left hoping for an early decision on their fate. Some were quite concerned, especially those who had negative-value assets because of the collapse in the secondary housing market.

Employee reactions

An officer in the hotline section of the bank's card center explained that even if he was fortunate enough to be re-deployed to a new frontline sales position, he had little confidence in performing as well as the existing salesforce because he lacked the practical experience and was not personally suited to that type of role. A white-collar staff member in his late forties he preferred the routine provided in his current post, but concluded that he would accept the bank's decision since it was commercially-driven.

Another employee, who had worked in NSC for over 10 years, was worried that she might not fulfil the sales job requirements. However, she needed to retain the low-interest mortgage that came with the job to reduce the burden of her negative-value apartment:

> *The bank has neglected our interests. I work very hard to meet the bank's stringent requirements and plan to stay here until I retire. HSBC has recorded huge profits from Hong Kong virtually every year and we have always had trust in our senior management. The bank should have a moral obligation to provide employment opportunities to us first before offering them to people outside Hong Kong.[6]*

Unlike London and New York, where those released could move to other parts of their respective countries, most employees would find starting a new career in the mainland an unattractive option not least because of its contrasting culture and inferior health-care system. On the other hand, some Hong Kong residents not employed by the bank were considering moving across the border where the price of an apartment was a fraction of the equivalent property in Hong Kong.

A background briefing paper entitled 'Migration of Jobs to Guangzhou—Questions and Answers' distributed to employees with the letter from Raymond Or, had confirmed that labour costs were a significant factor (**Exhibit 2**):

> *The pay packages of Guangzhou employees are structured in accordance with local market conditions. As you will be aware, living costs and salaries in mainland China are, in general, substantially lower than in Hong Kong.[7]*

Reactions from Guangzhou

Contrary to their counterparts in Hong Kong, staff in the GZC processing center welcomed the bank's policy of relocating jobs across the border.[8] In a recent recruitment exercise conducted in Guangzhou, HSBC had hired Derek Cheung, a 28-year-old credit processing officer who had worked previously for the China Construction Bank. When asked why he was interested in working for HSBC, Cheung explained:

> *It is a golden opportunity to work in a company with such a global brand name like HSBC. I will definitely be admired by every one if I succeed. Apart from this, the salary offered is higher, almost double that of similar posts in other banks. There are also opportunities for me to shift to other job positions and learn different operations in a bank.*

Jobs in the banking industry were considered above average if not prestigious. Most employees—usually

---

[5] HSBC confirms moving HK backroom ops to China, *The Business Times Singapore*, 14 March 2001.

[6] Interview with HSBC employee.

[7] HSBC move may set trend: Group predicts more jobs will switch to 'cheap' mainland as it announces hundreds of transfers, *South China Morning Post*, 14 March 2001.

[8] Mainlanders eager for HSBC jobs: Guangzhou staff willing to work for quarter of salaries paid in morale-hit SAR, *South China Morning Post*, 15 March 2001.

university educated—enjoyed housing allowances and received higher wages than the average worker. Vera Wong had already worked in the GZC processing center as a data entry clerk for one year since graduating from Guangzhou University with a Bachelor's Degree in Business Administration. When asked why she chose to stay at HSBC when she had such good qualifications, Miss Wong replied:

> I think it is good to learn and work from the basics. The working experience here will definitely make my resume look better.

Market reaction

In addition to problems within the bank, HSBC faced increasing opposition from the Hong Kong market, and not just from concerned customers. With 220 branches serving 75% of Hong Kong's adult population, the bank found itself at the centre of a controversy over its objectives. Letters and comments from angry residents flooded in to local newspapers:

> I take it that only bottom-line considerations are being taken into account by management to ensure that the bank remains viable amid the increasingly competitive global financial-services market ... Any entity that carries the Hong Kong name but intends to subjugate the job security and welfare of its local staff in order to achieve the practical bottom line should obviously not be allowed to make representations of the SAR in any manner.[9]
>
> Mainlanders used to look up to Hong Kong for everything from the skyscrapers to its vibrant economy. But the sense of envy has eroded since the handover. Guangzhou is getting close to being on a par with it, so Hong Kong should sense the risk it faces in the future.[10]
>
> It may make commercial sense for HSBC to start to transfer its operations to the mainland, but it shows a lamentable disloyalty to the place

that has made the bank one of the richest and most profitable in the world. For generations it has held a privileged position here in Hong Kong, being virtually the central bank of the territory and wielding huge influence over government policy—and never in a way which has been to its own advantage ... It might be thought that all this would promote an allegiance to Hong Kong which goes a little beyond the easy dollars to be made by employing cheap staff in Guangzhou.[11]

The local community was concerned that, as a huge and influential organisation, HSBC was liable to set a trend. HSBC itself had predicted that its relocation to Guangzhou would signal off a trend that other companies would follow. In his nine-page letter to employees, Or explained that:

> While the bank is taking a lead, we believe that more and more Hong Kong companies will undertake similar migration exercises for processing roles.[12]

The company's latest announcement had come on the back of Standard Chartered Bank's attempt to cut staff by 20% by centralising back-office processing and customer support in India and Malaysia. These moves had also sparked alarm among local unions who warned that Hong Kong could see more hollowing out of low-end service sector jobs, as had happened in the 1980s. In a recent protest, several activists from the Confederation of Trade Unions had blindfolded one of the landmark lion sculptures outside HSBC headquarters in Central, symbolising what they perceived as the bank's failure to see the suffering of the people of Hong Kong.

David Hall, HSBC's Head of Public Affairs, was quick to assert that:

> If we are going to make changes, we have to do it in a sensitive way. Will we upset some people? We may. We hope not. We do see the importance of not upsetting the people of Hong Kong

---

[9] Guangzhou & Shanghai Bank a more apt name, Letters to the Editor, *South China Morning Post*, 1 April 2001.

[10] Mainlanders eager for HSBC jobs: Guangzhou staff willing to work for quarter of salaries paid in morale-hit SAR, *South China Morning Post*, 15 March 2001.

[11] Bank's move could start wounding exodus, Letters to the Editor, *South China Morning Post*, 1 April 2001.

[12] HSBC move may set trend: Group predicts more jobs will switch to 'cheap' mainland as it announces hundreds of transfers, *South China Morning Post*, 14 March 2001.

but we live and operate in a commercial and changing environment.[13]

Hall maintained that the group cared deeply about business ethics and supported two international codes of conduct for multinational companies – the United Nations Global Impact and the Global Sullivan Principles.[14]

Hong Kong vs. Mainland China

In addition to the eroding advantages from differences in costs, Hong Kong's position as the gateway to China was also under threat. By mid 2001, the mainland port of Shenzen had boosted the number of containers sixfold since 1996, and with 300,000 Taiwanese working on the mainland and direct shipping and air links across the straits imminent, the comparative erosion was expected to continue. Cities such as Beijing, Shanghai and Shenzen were closing the infrastructure gap as billions of dollars were ploughed into port roads and telecommunications. Moreover, the quality of life in many of China's centres in terms of golf courses, shops, western goods, and high quality housing, meant that Hong Kong was no longer the only—or even preferred—choice for expatriates.

Accordingly, it was not just manufacturing jobs that were moving to the mainland but also service jobs, such as consulting. It was also becoming apparent that large Chinese companies, having established their credibility by listing on the Hong Kong or New York Exchanges, were turning to the higher-rated Shanghai market, giving the underwriting fees to Chinese firms in many cases.

Guangzhou and other Chinese cities near Hong Kong were attractive to employers—even though labour costs were among the highest on the mainland—because the local population spoke Cantonese, the same Chinese dialect used in Hong Kong. The proximity to Hong Kong also meant that documents for processing could be transported by road in a few hours.

---

[13] For Love or Money? *South China Morning Post*, 31 March 2001.

[14] The two codes lay down principles in such areas as protecting human rights, avoiding discrimination, and eliminating forced and child labour.

Cooperation between NSC and GZC

Within a short period of the first tasks being migrated to Guangzhou, it became apparent to Or that the new operations were not running as smoothly as anticipated.

One example of the emerging problems was the processing of customer instructions, such as correspondence address updates, which were received from customers at bank branches and traditionally passed to the NSC. Before the function migration to GZC, the NSC staff were responsible for checking whether the address had been completed or any required fields had been left blank before any information was put into the computer system. After the migration, however, the NSC was only required to consolidate the requests from all branches before forwarding them to GZC for data entry. Within a matter of weeks both branches and the NSC started receiving complaints from customers who had not been sent the standard letters and bills from the bank, or whose account information was incorrect. After checking the customer instructions against the records in the computer systems, it was found that the data was either not entered into the system in the exact format (e.g. wrong order in flat, floor and block) or was simply incorrect (e.g. confusing a 'P' with a 'D' or an 'F' with an 'E').

The NSC staff complained that their GZC colleagues did not understand the format being used and were trying to decipher customers' handwriting themselves rather than checking with NSC first. They also felt that the GZC staff had poor English and a limited knowledge of personal reference fields such as address format and district names, in Hong Kong. They further claimed that the GZC staff were not duly concerned about reading the data carefully as they were not in direct contact with customers and so did not have to answer complaints. Conversely, the GZC staff believed that the NSC was to blame for not checking the data before sending the forms to Guangzhou for data entry and insisted that it was the responsibility of the NSC or the branches to verify data accuracy before forwarding the files to GZC for processing.

A second round

In October 2001, HSBC announced that it would open a second data processing centre in mainland China (Shanghai) in the first quarter of 2002. The group had already moved its China headquarters from Hong Kong to Pudong in Shanghai in 2000.

Pending approval, a wholly-owned subsidiary, HSBC Data Processing (Shanghai), would be established, occupying six floors in Ciro's Plaza in Nanjing Xi Lu, in the Huangpu district of Puxi. The centre was expected to employ 250 people initially, with plans to increase this to 550 by the end of the year, and 1,000 over the next few years. HSBC's Chairman, David Eldon, stressed that although the opening of the new centre represented a transfer of jobs from Hong Kong to the mainland, it did not necessarily mean that staff in Hong Kong would be made redundant.[15] The Shanghai Centre would be engaged in data entry and account maintenance for HSBC operations in the Asia-Pacific in addition to the parent holding company's operations in Canada and Europe. It would be the third such centre serving Asia, alongside the Guangzhou office and a further centre in India. A second centre was also planned for India. Eldon claimed that HSBC would try to avoid involuntary staff cuts but could not guarantee that it would be successful in this endeavour.

Responding to the announcement of a second back-office service centre in China, Or predicted 'obvious' job losses in Hong Kong but countered this with other plans:

> Let's hope we are going to create new jobs by getting into other business areas … I mean this year we went into Mandatory Provident Fund and that helped to create quite a number of jobs to absorb the surplus staff being released due to the migration of jobs to Guangzhou.[16]

In October 2001, HSBC announced that it would be freezing salaries for the bank's 14,000 staff. It was clear that it was still struggling to implement more cost effective work structures and procedures.

---

[15] HSBC arm to freeze staff pay, *Financial Times*, 20 October 2001

[16] HSBC in second mainland centre, *South China Morning Post*, 25 October 2001.

How could the bank learn from its earlier experiences in Guangzhou to facilitate a smoother function migration to Shanghai? What alternative approaches could Or/HSBC have employed in the first round of function migration?

At the same time, HSBC was seeking to significantly expand its business operations in the world's fastest growing market by acquiring stakes in mainland banks. In early 2002, it paid RMB 518 million for an 8% stake in the Bank of Shanghai (BoS). By April 2002, it was in talks with two further mainland banks—Beijing City Commercial Bank (BCCB) and Citic Industrial Bank, owned by mainland giant China International Trust & Investment Corporation (Citic). BCCB and BoS were both local banks, while Citic Industrial Bank was a national concern with 239 branches in 26 leading mainland cities. On 3 April 2002, HSBC became the second Hong Kong bank to obtain a licence to conduct foreign exchange business with mainlanders.

While China represented huge opportunities for new growth and cost-savings, implementing strategies had already proven difficult. HSBC had faced difficult challenges coordinating operations internally as well as harsh criticism from its own employees and customers in Hong Kong. How could the bank achieve a smoother transition and stem the backlash that future changes were likely to elicit?

Functions of NSC

The Account Services (ASV) Department provides account services support to customers. It is responsible for processing automatic payments, performing transactions and maintenance for international deposits, handling pre-processing and post-processing of maintenance requests and supporting all other types of account services such as court order, audit confirmation, Inland Revenue Department enquiries and document microfilming and retrieval.

The Payment Services (PSV) Department handles payments related to transactions and performs all kinds of pre-payment and post-payment processing. These include all types of outward and inward telegraphic transfer, clean cheques, and demand draft.

The Credit Services Personal Banking (CSP) Department conducts the processing of Home Mortgage Loans, Packaged Loans and Personal Financial Services General Banking Facilities.

The handling of Unauthorized Overdrafts and Effects Not Cleared items are also centralized in this department from the branch network.

The Collection & Recoveries Unit—Secured Credit (CRU-S) Department is mainly responsible for the collection and recovery of Home Mortgage Loans, Wayfoon Finance Hire Purchase and General Banking Facilities, arrangement of repossession of distressed properties and legal actions, handling of insurance claims as well as processing of voucher transactions and account maintenance.

The Collections & Recoveries Unit—Unsecured Packaged Product (CRU-U) Department is mainly responsible for the collection and recovery of delinquent or overdue payments on credit cards, and packaged products such as Personal Installment Loan, Personal Overdraft, and SuperEase accounts.

Exhibit 1 Structure of Network Service Centre in Hong Kong

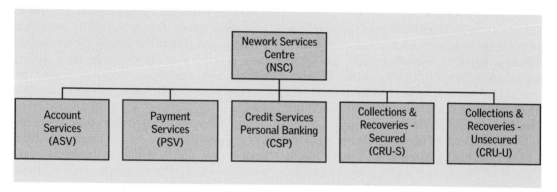

Exhibit 2 A price comparison between Hong Kong and Mainland China

	Hong Kong	Mainland China
Prime Office Space (rent)	US $6.30/sq.ft	US $1.90/sq.ft
Two-bedroom Apartment	$3,500/month	$1,000
Personal Assistant	$3,500/month	$500
International School	$14,500–$16,000/yr.	$17,000–$20,000/yr.
Business Lunch for Two	$51	$24
Taxi to Airport from Downtown	$48	$24
Commercial Broadband	up to $390/month	$180
Office Blessing (by Geomancer)	50 cents/sq.ft	6 cents/sq.ft

Source: A City Under Siege, Business Week International Edition, 23 July 2001.

INSEAD

Case 10 **The house that Branson built: Virgin's entry into the new millennium**

The music stops

Reflecting in 1999 on significant events in the history of the Virgin Group, Richard Branson, its chairman, remained extremely ambivalent about the most momentous decision of his business career – a decision that had been made seven years earlier. It concerned his acceptance of a £510 million cash offer from Thorn EMI, a UK conglomerate with extensive music interests, for his record label Virgin Music. A private company with tangible assets of less than £4 million, Virgin Music was, symbolically, the heart of the Virgin Group, having its roots in the late 1960s, when Branson and his first collaborators founded a record mail-order business in London. Its sale, therefore, meant a great deal more to Branson than simply another business transaction. He would part company with many people he had known since childhood and hand over a business that had been built painstakingly on cash flow using a combination of guile, flair, and luck.

This case was prepared by Robert Dick, Research Associate, under the supervision of Manfred F.R. Kets de Vries, Raoul de Vitry d'Avaucourt Professor of Human Resource Management at INSEAD. It is intended to be used as a basis for class discussion rather than to illustrate either effective or ineffective handling of an administrative situation.

Unless otherwise indicated, all quotes are from interviews conducted by Manfred Kets de Vries and Robert Dick in 1986, 1995, and 1998–2000.

In March 1992, Branson was a reluctant seller, but he was also a realist. He recognized that the cards were heavily stacked against him. The world economy – the airline industry in particular – was in the doldrums in the aftermath of the Gulf War. Virgin Atlantic, the airline he had founded in the mid '80s, had been badly affected by the turmoil in the Middle East. Moreover, it was being targeted in a competitive war by British Airways, which (it would later transpire) was using dubious tactics to gain advantage. Further complicating matters, the media were speculating on Virgin's financial health (prompted, if Branson's allegations are accurate, by misleading stories fed to journalists by British Airways); and behind the scenes, Virgin's bankers were pressing ever more strongly for a sale to reduce debt, reinforcing Branson's disdain for financial organizations that he saw as fair-weather friends.

More personally, Simon Draper, Branson's cousin and the creative force behind Virgin Music, had made it clear that he wanted to cash in his equity and do something different with his life. A vehement opponent of Virgin's move into the airline business from the outset, he envisaged his life's work collapsing with the airline, which was surviving only on the cash flow and guarantees provided by Virgin Music. And Virgin Music provided strong support indeed: only months before, the music label had signed the Rolling Stones, a sign of the position it had attained in the worldwide music business.

Branson realized that the sale of Virgin Music would transform Virgin's financial situation. After settling with the Japanese company Fujisankei, a 25 percent shareholder, and with Simon Draper and Ken Berry (a key collaborator and minority shareholder who had started at Virgin as an accounts clerk and who now runs Thorn EMI's music business), Branson would be left with over £350 million in cash – more than enough to 'fulfill [my] wildest dreams.'[1]

---

[1] Richard Branson, *Losing my Virginity* (London: Virgin Publishing 1998), p. 413.

Growing a business: a strategy for fun

'Putting the world to rights'

Richard Branson's business career started when, at the age of seventeen, he founded *Student* magazine – the 'Voice of Youth' – while still at boarding school. Based on co-operative principles, the magazine employed fellow students as workers and a nearby public pay phone as an office. *Student* was a product of the 1960s, the decade when the post-war 'baby boomers' came of age. Across Western Europe and North America, young people enjoyed educational, employment, and lifestyle opportunities unknown to their parents, all made possible by rapid economic growth. The decade became known for its promotion of a youth culture in which authority was challenged, fashions changed rapidly, and rock stars were the global gurus of a new age.

The initial success of the magazine (Branson optimistically claimed a circulation of 100,000) was not sustained. Seeking new activities to boost his flagging business, he decided to try to tap the potential he saw in the sale of records, still overpriced despite the abolition of retail price maintenance, a UK government policy designed to support certain industries by allowing manufacturers and suppliers to 'recommend' prices to retailers.

Lacking the capital to start a retail outlet, Branson and his associates simply placed an advertisement in the last issue of Student to test the market, listing only records likely to appeal to young people. Prices discounted those offered in stores by as much as 15 percent, and orders (accompanied by cash) came flooding in. Casting around for a name for his new business, he finally accepted a suggestion made jokingly by one of his coterie, who claimed that what they needed was a name that proclaimed their commercial innocence but also had a certain shock value, in keeping with the anti-establishment mood of the times. What better, therefore, than 'Virgin'? The name appealed to Branson and was adopted despite objections from the registration authorities, who deemed it to be in poor taste.

Branson quickly realized that buying and selling records in bulk required proper controls and systems. He turned to a childhood friend, Nik Powell, to help him manage his new business, offering in return a 40 percent stake in the company.

Methodical where Branson was erratic, cautious where Branson would overextend himself, Nik Powell became the ideal counterbalance in the record mail-order company.

In 1971 a national postal strike threatened to push the mail-order company into bankruptcy. Immediately Branson rented retail space, transferred his stock of records, and launched Virgin Retail. True to the emerging Virgin style, the shop's decor was a mix of the outrageous and the shabby, attracting customers more bent on enjoying an experience than spending money. Later that year, Virgin received its first overseas order. Realizing that records intended for export could be purchased by Virgin tax-free, Branson gave in to the temptation to make a quick cash profit by selling 'exported' records through his London store – until the tax authorities pounced.

Shocked and humiliated, Branson spent an uncomfortable night in prison. He was released only after a tearful appeal to his parents to put up £30,000 bail, using their home as security. Eventually, formal charges were dropped in return for an out-of-court financial settlement. Later, Branson would laughingly dismiss his night in a cell, but the pain and embarrassment he caused his parents made him resolve to 'avoid sleepless nights and pay taxes.' Even so, Branson remains an unwilling tax-payer and holds his Virgin shareholding in secret off-shore family trusts, preferring 'to reinvest profits in the business.'

While these setbacks were taking place, Branson had a piece of good fortune. Simon Draper persuaded him to consider backing Mike Oldfield, a nervous, troubled, and talented young musician who arrived at Virgin clutching a handful of recording tapes. Having already been rejected by the major recording studios, the young man was looking for friends and supporters. At Virgin he found them, and his first recording, Tubular Bells, was to launch him and Virgin into the big time.

Tubular Bells and the Sex Pistols

Released in 1973, Tubular Bells was an immediate hit, eventually selling over five million copies worldwide. The massive inflow of funds transformed the company. For Branson, this was the ideal opportunity to launch the Virgin record label and join the ranks of the small independent record producers that were active in the UK market at that time. Within two years, however, financial pressure forced Virgin to reassess its position to avoid becoming a one-hit record label. Its original creative policy, which focused on non-mainstream artists, was not working. Branson needed something fast to re-establish the Virgin name with the record-buying public. He achieved his aim in 1977 with a notorious punk rock band: the Sex Pistols. Debauched and drug-crazed, foul-mouthed and obscene, the Sex Pistols were the subject of intense media coverage and speculation until one of its members, already facing a murder charge, died of a drug overdose and the band disintegrated. But their short existence was a considerable fillip for Virgin.

By the end of the '70s, Virgin comprised a record label, recording studios, music retail outlets, music and book publishing, night-clubs, and cinemas. Virgin had prospered in a buoyant UK market. But as the decade closed, recession and high inflation, combined with changing consumer tastes, severely affected the music business worldwide. Sales contracted and few record companies earned profits. Virgin registered losses of £400,000 in 1980 and £900,000 in 1981. Although well-established, the record company was still a small player living hand-to-mouth in a business dominated by large multinationals.

With financial pressure mounting, Branson was forced to act. Looking to Nik Powell for solutions, he was offered belt-tightening measures that inevitably included laying off personnel, a task Branson has always found daunting and has avoided whenever possible, usually by delegation. The anxiety and ill-feeling that the various measures caused led to talk of union representation.

To some extent Branson himself had inflamed discontent in his company. His personal business philosophy was simple: Why worry about the past? It is over and done. Look to the future to solve difficulties through new opportunities, expansion, and growth. Even as the company was firing staff, closing its US office, and cutting its roster of bands, Branson used scarce financial resources to purchase two night-clubs – Heaven, London's largest venue for homosexuals, and the struggling Roof Garden. He also launched a new London entertainment guide,

Event, founded to challenge the strike-bound market leader, Time Out. The launch was unsuccessful; within a year Event closed at a cost to Virgin of £750,000.

Branson's expansion-oriented actions created tension between him and his senior management, particularly Nik Powell. As Powell's working relationship with Branson soured, he realized that his ambitions were likely to remain unfulfilled while he was number two. Matters came to head over creative policy. Despite limited funds, Simon Draper wanted to invest in new bands and to continue financing existing artists whom he believed would eventually be profitable. Nik Powell, advocating a more cautious, corporate-type approach, pressed for the pruning of loss-making bands. Obligated to make the choice that would settle matters, Branson, with some reluctance and sadness, backed Draper's artistic judgement over the more conventional approach offered by Powell.

His instinct proved right: within a short span of time, Virgin had some of the most profitable bands of the '80s – Phil Collins, Human League, Simple Minds, and the hugely successful Culture Club, led by the transvestite Boy George. Virgin successfully maneuvered itself out of the recession, nearly doubling its turnover from £48 million in 1982 to £94 million in 1983, with profits soaring to over £11 million. But Nik Powell was not around to share the success. Dissatisfied with his position, he had left the company in 1981, selling his shareholding in return for £1 million, Virgin's cinema interests, and a video recording studio. Branson was once again the 100 percent owner of Virgin, with two trusted lieutenants: Simon Draper and Ken Berry. (Both later acquired holdings in the record company after lengthy negotiations.) Branson, depending on Draper for creative decisions and on Berry for contracts and management, kept himself out of the day-to-day administration of the company to concentrate on new ventures.

In France, Germany, and Italy, Virgin companies were established to add local artists to the company roster and to represent UK bands. In the US, the Virgin label was re-established. The huge success of Virgin artists attracted increasing numbers of established and emerging bands to the Virgin stable, creating a portfolio of talent that challenged the industry leaders. In circumstances such as these, conventional business practice would dictate that success should be consolidated and expansion restricted to complementary activities. Such, however, was not to be Branson's way. He wanted to expand his company in a completely new direction. To the astonishment of music industry observers, the horror of Simon Draper, and the ridicule of the music press, Richard Branson was off on a new path: he was going to found an airline.

'Never let the facts get in the way of a good idea'

In early 1984, Branson received a call from Randolph Fields, the 31-year-old California-born lawyer who had founded British Atlantic, a transatlantic airline not yet off the ground that hoped to target business travelers. Fields, one of an increasing number of people arriving at Branson's door with ideas that needed backing, was seeking additional financing to get his airline airborne. Branson was all too aware of the dangers in entering the airline business: his company had no experience in that arena, the business was capital intensive, and revenue was highly seasonal. Furthermore, he recalled the recent experience of a UK cut-price airline, Laker Airlines, which had been pushed into bankruptcy by high debts, currency fluctuations, and ferocious competition from established national airlines. The industry Goliaths had slaughtered the upstart David in a battle whose echoes were still straining UK/US trade diplomacy in the mid '80s.

Yet, despite all these reservations and obstacles, Branson was persuaded by Fields's proposal. Within a week – 'We can decide something in the morning and have it running in the afternoon' is Branson's proud boast – he had formed a partnership with Fields, renaming the airline Virgin Atlantic. It was later dubbed by jokers the airline that Boy George built, a reference to the supposed source of cash injected by Branson into his new project. The launch in June 1984 saw him playing to the cameras dressed as a World War I pilot in leather jacket and goggles, the first in a long line of publicity stunts that were to become Branson's trademark.

One of a number of ex-Laker managers recruited by Branson was David Tait, now President of Virgin Atlantic North America, based in Norwalk, Connecticut. Recalling the launch of the airline he said:

I thought that Virgin was the most stupid name ever for an airline, and I told him that his plan [for business class only] was not a good idea and explained why. But with Richard, you never let the facts get in the way of a good idea! ... Despite what people think, it was never a budget proposition either – more a mix of economy and business class, which in those days only Air Florida had tried with success. Since we went into Newark and not JFK, we could also offer lower fares with less chance of reprisal. But our real secret was to offer value-for-money. Charge the same or slightly less for a much better product: first-class travel at business-class rates.

The creation of his airline took Branson into unfamiliar territory. His business needed skills not previously required in the unregulated, open-market environment of the record industry. The airline business, by contrast, was – and remains – highly political: the awarding of jealously guarded international landing rights to (mostly) nationalized airlines involved protracted inter-governmental negotiations, requiring Branson to lobby the Thatcher government. Informally advised by Freddy Laker, Branson also had an eye to the future; he anticipated predatory pricing from the major airlines that would jeopardize his cost advantage – the Laker scenario all over again.

Randolph Fields, who had brought the airline idea to Branson, did not stay long with Virgin. His management style, Branson concluded, did not fit either the Virgin ethos or the detailed operation of an airline, although Branson recognized Fields's contribution in putting together the initial proposal. Behind the scenes, relations between the two became so acrimonious that Branson felt forced to oust Fields in 1985, buying his shareholding for £1 million. Fields later said that he had fallen in love with Branson on the day they met, but that Branson had fallen in love only with Fields's idea.

'From the rock market to the stock market'

In late 1986 a series of press and TV advertisements appeared in the UK under the slogan 'From the Rock Market to the Stock Market.' The advertisements invited the public to buy shares in the Virgin Group. Richard Branson, for so long a champion of private company status and the independence of entrepreneurs, had succumbed to the blandishments of City investment bankers to sell part of his company during the '80s bull market. He saw the move as an opportunity to raise capital quickly to reduce the company's dependence on short-term bank borrowing – and what Branson saw as demanding and short-sighted bankers – and to further expand without losing control of his company. (When the public company was eventually floated, Branson and his senior collaborators retained control of 63 percent of the voting stock.)

Much of the detail work of the flotation had been handled by Don Cruickshank, appointed Group Managing Director in 1984. A Scottish accountant with an MBA from Manchester Business School, Cruickshank had worked for the consulting firm McKinsey and had been in general management in the media industry. At ease in City circles, he was the kind of executive with whom bankers felt comfortable, an important factor in Branson's decision to recruit him via head-hunters.

Despite the demand for shares, the stock market flotation was not the success that Branson or the investors had expected. Although recording better-than-expected profits, Virgin's share price performed badly post-flotation and later fell precipitously when the London exchange crashed in October 1987. Moreover, relations between Virgin management and City analysts were at best uneasy. Branson was unsuited to cultivating the type of relationship that the chairman of a public company must have with institutional investors. While appreciating the discipline that being a public company had imposed on his company, he nevertheless felt that the City undervalued Virgin and failed to understand the entrepreneurial nature of his business, especially the music division. The analysts in turn were uncomfortable with the vagaries of a business where, it seemed to them, most of the assets – rock musicians and their creative output – were valued against the ephemeral nature of public taste. (More recently there has been evidence to show that established artists can create a steady revenue stream against which investment decisions can be calculated. The sale in 1997 of David Bowie's work via a securitized bond placement is a case in point.)

The analysts' doubts and concerns were reinforced by the unpredictable nature of the Chairman and the demands on his time from his publicity stunts, airline business, and charitable activities. Unwilling to tolerate the constraints placed upon him but determined to help the many small investors who had seen the value of their investment diminish, Branson finally resolved to quit the stock market. In July 1988 he announced his decision to raise privately £200 million to be used to buy out the publicly held shares at the original asking price, in effect compensating the original shareholders, both private and corporate, who at that point faced a considerable paper loss. Richard Branson thus honored a moral debt he felt he owed and was once more master of his own destiny.

'Too old to rock, too young to fly'

The unsuccessful flotation had forced Branson to review Virgin's activities and modus operandi. With a major debt to repay and still in need of a substantial capital injection to finance his ambitions for the company, Branson recognized that he needed external investors. However, his approach in the light of his stock market experience was to be more circumspect.

In the years following privatization, Branson, while still an opportunistic entrepreneur, nevertheless followed a path of growth through joint ventures with established companies. This approach permitted his company to expand, in terms of both product and geography. The most significant deal was the sale in 1989 of 25 percent of Virgin Records to Fujisankei, Japan's largest media company, for £115 million. That same year, another Japanese company – Seibu Saison, the hotel chain – paid £10 million for 10 percent of Virgin Travel, which had recently acquired landing rights in Tokyo through Virgin Atlantic.

In the UK, Virgin's retail interests were consolidated around the Megastore concept in a joint venture with a major retailer. In prestige locations in major cities, Megastores began to sell home-entertainment products – music, videos, and books – on a large scale. They replaced the string of small secondary retail outlets for which Virgin had become known. The success of the Megastore concept was exported to major cities throughout the world, frequently through joint ventures.

Virgin Atlantic had also advanced dramatically from the original operation envisaged by Randolph Fields. Although still a relatively small player, it now competed with the major carriers on the main routes out of London, winning awards for innovation and service as well as plaudits from vital business travelers. Virgin Atlantic had become a serious threat to the major airlines – none more so than British Airways (BA), the UK's national carrier, led by the ebullient and forthright Lord King.

However, the airline had suffered financially as a result of the recession and the Gulf War, perhaps more than Branson was prepared to admit publicly. He was reconciled to finding a major capital investment to ensure the airline's long-term survival, an ambition close to his heart. Internally, such capital could realistically come only from the sale of the record business – the jewel in the Virgin crown and the largest remaining independent record company in the world.

After long discussions with his immediate team, and wrenching soul-searching, Branson, advised by the investment bank Goldman Sachs, entered into negotiations with Bertelsmann of Germany and Thorn EMI, calculating that the time was ripe to conclude a sale on his terms. Thorn's offer of cash or shares (Branson took the cash) to a value of £510 million won the day, allowing Branson to clear his debts and to plan the expansion of his airline in the way he sought. Commercial to the last, Branson and Berry managed to win £9 million on currency speculation by delaying payment to Fujisankei to the last contractual moment.

Virgin Music was combined with EMI records, creating a music business with 18 percent of the world market. City comments that Thorn had overpaid for Virgin were quickly discounted. A rationalization of Virgin staff and bands improved Thorn's profits by more than £80 million in 1993–94. At the time of the sale, some Virgin Music employees felt that they had been let down by Branson. They had assumed they would share in the profits from the sale of the company, although no promises had been made. Many of the long-serving staff attended an emotional farewell party where a tearful Branson and Draper assured them that Ken Berry would be staying with Virgin and that its future independence within the Thorn EMI group was guaranteed. After the sale, Branson said, 'Too many entrepreneurs have gone down because they were not prepared to cash in their chips at the right time.'

The battle between British Airways and Virgin Atlantic, personalized around its two leaders (Lord King dismissing Richard Branson as 'too old to rock and too young to fly'), became increasingly acrimonious. Matters came to a head when a television program alleged that BA had used dirty tricks against Virgin Atlantic, breaking into its computer system to target its customers, spreading misinformation about Virgin's financial state, and diverting its customers at US airports to BA flights. Branson immediately sued BA for damages, claiming £11 million. Lord King's rebuttal was libelous and Branson won substantial damages, humiliating the BA chairman and accelerating his retirement after an otherwise distinguished business career. As a gesture to the airline staff, Branson divided the damages among them.

Coming of age?

The sale of the record company in 1992 saw the departure of many long-serving staff. This, combined with the evolutionary changes in retail, the growth of the airline, and the creation of new companies, moved Virgin away from its roots and previous management structure. From 1992 to 1997, the company was overseen by a triumvirate: Richard Branson, Trevor Abbott (the Group's Finance Director, brought in by Cruickshank), and Robert Devereux (Branson's brother-in-law, who headed the media and entertainment interests). These latter are no longer with Virgin. Robert Devereux, now a wealthy man, has achieved his aim of 'semi-retiring at forty' and spends his time climbing mountains; Trevor Abbott took his own life, motivated, it is believed, by serious personal problems and his diminishing role at Virgin. Their functions are now fulfilled by Simon Burke and Steven Murphy, respectively.

Research on the Virgin brand name in the early 1990s demonstrated the impact over time of quirky advertising and publicity stunts. The brand was recognized by 96 percent of UK consumers, and Richard Branson was correctly identified by 95 percent as the company's founder. The Virgin name was associated by respondents with words such as fun, innovation, success, and trust and identified with a range of businesses, confirming what Branson and others had believed: in principle, there were no product or service boundaries limiting a brand name, provided it was associated with a quality offering.

Encouraged by the research, Virgin began entering new sectors outside of its core activities of travel and retail. Virgin businesses as diverse as radio broadcasting, book publishing, and computer games found a home in the same stable as hotels, railways, personal computers, cola drinks, cinemas, and financial services. To manage this complex empire, Virgin increasingly employed the type of structure and people more usually associated with conventional companies. Branson continued to work at the center, supported by a small business-development group, a press office, and key senior advisors in the areas of strategy and finance. Although the firm is now housed in more elegant surroundings, the early Virgin style of informality and openness remains. There is not the feel of a traditional corporate head office: neckties are rarely worn, denim jeans are common, and everybody is on first-name terms.

Building on that evolutionary process started in the mid '80s, Virgin today is more likely to employ people (particularly at the management level) with direct experience of a relevant business activity, either through a career at Virgin or through training with a competitor. The policy of promotion-from-within that Branson practiced in the early days remains in force, especially in the larger companies, but has become more organized and less driven by short-term exigencies and Branson's whims. In acknowledgement of the fact that promotion cannot always provide the best candidate, the use of headhunters is now an established practice for senior posts. Human resource tools such as assessment centers, personality profiling, and employee development are commonly used. Moreover, many managers have formal business training and qualifications, along with experience with multinationals or management consultancies, a profile that would have been unknown at Virgin in its early days. Despite this, there is still a belief, held by most of the senior management, that there are 'Virgin people' – those who, through their personality, style, or outlook on life, are better suited than others for the organization. (See **Exhibit** 4: Virgin People.)

Having a center did not mean a centralized operation, a notion that Branson resisted – at least until recently. Each operating unit was expected to stand alone, having little interaction with either the head office or other units. Unit managers networked informally (usually at parties and similar events) but were not obliged to follow prescriptive corporate policies; these were 'understood' rather than codified. For example, there was no common human resource policy. Managers knew that employees must be treated 'fairly,' since 'that is what Richard would want,' and they complied in their own way, whether in the UK or overseas. Similarly, there was no group information-technology strategist or central purchasing function, because Branson believed that those roles would constitute interference and discourage managerial creativity. In the same way there was no systematic seeking out of synergy, either at the center or by unit managers. Whenever synergy emerged, it was because the unit managers saw mutual advantage, not because a corporate policy dictated it.

This strategy was Virgin's modus operandi until 1999, when a chance remark from one of his senior executives made Branson rethink his approach. The executive mentioned to Branson that the managing director of a rival organization had commented that if Virgin companies ever decided to collaborate, they would be unstoppable. To test whether this was true, Branson immediately – and for the first time – brought together all his managing directors (some thirty in all) for a retreat at his hotel in Mallorca. The agenda was open, but two themes dominated – e-commerce and a proposed unifying document, the Virgin Charter.

During the discussion at the Mallorca meeting, the participants realized that, more by happenstance than planning, Virgin had found itself in businesses 'that are ideally suited to e-commerce and in which growth is expected to occur – travel, financial services, publishing, music, entertainment.' To exploit this potential, the participants decided to use tomorrow's technology to give all Virgin customers a small mobile device from which they could purchase any Virgin product – from a rail or cinema ticket to a CD or a savings product – and streamline online services with a single Virgin web address: Virgin.com. Virgin Net, another venture, is an Internet service provider created as a joint venture between Virgin and the UK subsidiary of NTL, a US computer technology company. Virgin is responsible for creative content and marketing; NTL provides the backup systems and software. Virgin Net targets the UK consumer market and wants to compete on 'value-for-money, speed, excellent customer service, and compelling content,' according to David Clarke, Managing Director. Much of its content is sourced from specialist suppliers (for example, the Independent newspaper for news). This idea took off in 1999; Virgin Net became a free service, and Virgin.com continued its expansion in e-commerce with a wide range of connections from Megastores online to train booking facilities (total internet revenues 1999 – £150 million).

During the meeting in Mallorca, the group also endorsed Branson's proposed Virgin Charter. Running to some sixty pages, the charter is an agreement between Virgin Management Ltd (in effect, the holding company) and all the subsidiaries. It defines the role of the center vis-à-vis the subsidiaries. The principal benefit the Virgin Charter is expected to bring is to create clearer information and communication flows between the Virgin shareholders, Virgin Management Ltd, and the Virgin companies. It covers topics such as taxation, legal affairs, intellectual property, and real estate, but it also outlines closer links in areas previously left to individual units: IT, people, purchasing. Thus the charter sets out ways for Virgin companies to tackle common activities with a common approach. (**Exhibit 5** shows Richard Branson's introduction to the charter.)

Branson has compared his current operation to a venture capital firm based on the Virgin brand. At the center, ideas (whether sourced internally or externally) are debated and analyzed, deals are struck, and new ventures are created. Potentially good ideas are disseminated outwards – quite often by Branson, who will 'call up [a manager] in his half-apologetic way and ask you to think about

a suggestion.' When deals or joint ventures are finalized, the implementation is delegated out, usually with considerable autonomy. A small example of the process is Virgin Brides. In 1995 Ailsa Petchley joined Virgin Atlantic as a member of its cabin crew. On one of her early flights she met Branson and got talking about weddings and the poor, often disjointed service offered to prospective brides. When she mentioned that she had a business idea offering a comprehensive service, she was given a few months to put together a plan. The net result was the creation of Virgin Brides, with Ailsa in the role of marketing manager, working in collaboration with a bridal-wear specialist from the US. The company is established but has a way to go to be profitable.

Along with the development of Virgin.com, Branson's last bold move at the close of the century was his deal with Singapore Airlines. During 1999 Branson had intimated that he might float part of the airline to raise capital for expansion. As the year was closing, however, he announced a surprise deal with Singapore Airlines that, in terms of fleet and revenues, is about three times the size of Virgin Atlantic. If the deal goes through, in 2000 Singapore will acquire a 49% stake in Virgin Atlantic at a cost of £600 million. The two airlines will work in partnership to maximise cost cutting synergies (eg maintenance, ground facilities, code sharing) but retain their respective identities and develop their own products. Industry observers saw the logic of the deal since in many ways the two airlines are complementary – their routes do not overlap and they both enjoy excellent reputations for service and innovation. There were, however, doubts expressed at the price that Singapore was paying, valuing Virgin Atlantic at more than £1.2 billion, a high figure in many observers' view.

The Virgin Group in 2000 comprised twenty-four individual companies or groups of companies (see Exhibits 2 and 3 for commentary and summary). Nearly all are private and owned entirely by the Virgin Group or by Richard Branson's family trusts. Branson sits on the board of most of the companies and usually, but by no means always, attends board meetings. He relies on others to bring serious problems to his attention: he has little time for reading long operational reports, market research, financial statements, and the like.

Richard Branson: a portrait

Jailbird or millionaire?

Richard Branson was born in July 1950, the first child and the only son of Ted Branson and his wife, Eve, née Huntley-Flint. He was later joined by two sisters, Lindi and Vanessa. The family has remained close, all enjoying what Richard was later to describe as a 'happy and secure' childhood.

Both Ted and Eve came from comfortable Establishment backgrounds. Ted was the son and grandson of eminent lawyers, a fact impressed on young Richard when he visited Tussaud's waxworks museum in London with his father and saw models of murderers sentenced to hang by Sir George Branson, his grandfather. Following family tradition, Ted left his Quaker-run school to study law at Cambridge University. After military service in World War II, he eventually qualified as a lawyer, but (perhaps because of his Quaker education or his naturally kindly disposition) his career in advocacy, where adversarial skills are vital, was slow to get started.

Eve Huntley-Flint came from a family of clerics, farmers, and stockbrokers whose womenfolk were expected to have horizons beyond the home. While still a young girl, she trained as a dancer and appeared in London theatres, both in dance reviews and as an actress, a somewhat risqué career for someone of her background. By the time she met Ted Branson, she had become an air stewardess, travelling to South America when air travel still contained a significant element of adventure and danger. Determined, self-assured and ambitious, at twenty-seven Eve was an attractive, outgoing young woman when she married Ted Branson, the reserved and fair-minded young lawyer.

Eve had decided views on child-rearing. While she was never a martinet, she pushed her children to be self-reliant and responsible, to take control of their own destinies rather than relying on others. One summer afternoon as she and four-year-old Richard were on their way home after visiting his grandparents, Eve told Richard to get out of the car and try to find his own way back. The farmhouse where they were staying was not far, but Richard got lost, ending up at the neighbor's farm to be collected by his alarmed parents. Eve Branson now admits that she may have been overly enthusiastic about encouraging Richard's independence, but she has never regretted it. Clearly, Eve admired strength of character. Furthermore, she was convinced that shyness in children was simply bad manners and a self-indulgence to be discouraged. She believed that her children's ability to overcome challenges would encourage the kind of spirit she wanted to see in them. Accordingly, she used her own considerable energy to organize activities, games, and projects for her children that were not only fun but also served a useful purpose. Holidays, weekends, and other free time were used productively. In line with that goal, the Branson household had no television, since it was 'time-wasting.' If money was short (as it was in the early days, when Ted's father cut off his allowance to protest his precipitate marriage), a solution could always be found in small money-making schemes that Eve thought up. Bemoaning one's lot was never acceptable to Eve, and she lived up to her own standards.

Ted Branson was never a strict and remote father figure. Rather, he acted as a calm and considerate backdrop to Eve's daily management of the children. Sympathetic and supportive by preference, a half-hearted disciplinarian if really necessary, Ted was less directly ambitious for his children than Eve, who expected, for example, that 'Richard [would] one day be Prime Minister.'

Richard grew up to be the archetypal naughty boy, frequently in minor scrapes, scolded for innumerable misdemeanors, and hyperactive in all he did. His parents found him both endearing and fatiguing. According to his father, Branson began his first business venture when he was eleven or twelve years old. He planted a thousand seedlings and then went back to school convinced that he would make a killing selling Christmas trees. Rabbits soon ate the trees, however. About a year later he tried another venture. This time the scheme involved budgerigars, a highly fecund type of small parrot. Another failure.

Richard's parents were particularly concerned about his progress at school, where – thanks to a strong physique and a competitive spirit – his main accomplishments were on the sports field. His schoolboy heroes were sportsmen, particularly cricketers, and adventurers such as Scott of the Antarctic, the famous British explorer and a distant relation by marriage. A serious leg injury, however, forestalled a promising career in athletics, while a period of forced intensive study finally gained his admittance to Stowe School, an exclusive English boys' private school with a liberal reputation. His indifference to schoolwork (not helped by long-undetected poor eyesight and dyslexia) continued, and he achieved only average results, ruling out a legal or other professional career. By contrast, Student magazine excited Branson with its possibilities and offered a timely and convenient exit from the educational treadmill. So, with his parents' reluctant blessing – his father's support was particularly influential – he quit school.

Branson left few friends behind him. While he was not unpopular, his energetic and single-minded pursuit of that which pleased him left little room for others. His indifference to the contemporary social mores and allegiances common in a school like Stowe left him somewhat isolated. His few friends were those he managed to inveigle into his varied and numerous projects. Commenting on the end of his schooldays, Branson said, 'Having left school without going to university, I decided to make money.... I never considered failure.' His headmaster had definite views about his future: 'Richard, you will either go to prison or become a millionaire.'

Working with family and friends

For a long time, Branson's office and home shared quarters in a canal houseboat. One bedroom served as the office of his two secretaries, while Branson operated from a dining table in the small sitting room. On occasion the bathroom served as the boardroom, with Branson conducting meetings from his bath. Eventually, when his two children 'started to answer the phones,' Branson was forced to move to a larger home, but he kept the houseboat as a private office. Nowadays, he runs his business empire from a large, elegant townhouse situated in London's diplomatic quarter. His home is in a similar building nearby.

His (second) wife, a down-to-earth Glaswegian from a working-class background, has no interest or role in his business life. She remains out of the limelight in the interests of their two children, providing an intimate family life to which Branson can retreat. Her stance is something of an anomaly at Virgin.

Contrary to conventional wisdom, Branson has always been a great believer in working with family and friends, convinced that the advantages outweigh the risks. Over time, his cousins, aunts, school and childhood friends, parents, and former girlfriends have all been drawn into his various business activities. His first wife found the situation difficult to accept, but even she is now in a joint venture with Branson, developing hotels in Spain.

The charges of nepotism that such arrangements usually engender were muted at Virgin, because of Branson's promotion-from-within policy. He has given many of his staff opportunities that their gender, lack of experience, or training would have precluded in more conventional companies. Of course, Virgin has been unconventional in other ways, too. Somehow, Branson has created the impression that people work at Virgin for fun rather than simply as a means of earning a living. ('More than any other element, fun is the secret of Virgin's success,'[2] he believes.) Notoriously indifferent to material possessions and unconcerned about everyday financial matters, the young Branson saw no problem in paying modest salaries provided people enjoyed themselves and felt part of an idiosyncratic enterprise that had a heart. If people were down, a party would revive spirits and, incidentally, give Branson the chance to play a practical joke on newcomers, an embarrassing rite of passage at Virgin that is partially maintained to this day. For example, when Branson hands out 'wings' to newly appointed cabin crew, he douses them in champagne. Similarly, the traditional annual company party that Branson used to throw at the recording studios (and now holds at his country home) has grown from a small Sunday event for 200 or so in the '70s to a marathon jamboree to which all Virgin staff and their family and friends can come.

A business philosophy

Much of Virgin's operating style was established not so much by design as by the exigencies of the time when Virgin was getting started. Nonetheless, it has proved to be a successful model that Branson believes he can replicate. His practice is to immerse

---

[2] Ibid. p. 431.

himself in a new venture until he understands the ins and outs of the business, then hand it over to a good managing director and financial controller, the two of whom are usually given a stake and then expected to make the company take off. (Branson can usually be relied on to engage in a publicity stunt of some kind that will give the company some initial awareness, jumpstarting the process. In the case of Virgin Bride, for example, he shaved off his beard and was photographed in a bridal gown).

Branson knows that expansion through the creation of additional discrete legal entities not only protects the Virgin Group but also gives people a sense of involvement with and loyalty to the smaller unit to which they belong, particularly if he trusts the managers of subsidiaries with full authority and offers them minority share options. He is proud of the fact that Virgin has produced a considerable number of millionaires. He has said that he does not want his best people to leave the company to start a venture outside; he prefers to make millionaires within.

His use of joint ventures, an extension of this model, has been reinforced by his dealings with the Japanese. Branson has been impressed by the Japanese approach to business, admiring their commitment to the long term and the way they take time to build a business through organic growth rather than acquisitions. He sees similarities between the Japanese *keiretsu* system (small companies interlocking in a collaborative network) and the structure he has created at Virgin, with numerous small companies around the world operated quasi-independently by the right people. Both systems embody the maxims 'Small is beautiful' and 'People matter.'

Branson explained these and other business maxims that he believes are necessary for success in a speech in London in 1993.[3] 'Staff first, then customers and shareholders' – this should be the chairman's priority if an organization wants better performance, according to Branson. Happy staff who are proud of their company make for happy customers who return. Job satisfaction is hampered when management is remote from all levels of staff,

relying, for example, on trade unions for communication. Branson cites his decision to keep 200 airline staff on the payroll, rather than lay them off during a recession, as a practical manifestation of this staff-first philosophy. Businesses should be 'shaped around the people,' Branson believes, citing his experience of subdividing the record company as it grew. Each new record label was given to up-and-coming managers, creating in-house entrepreneurs who were 'far more motivated to build a business' with which they, and the staff, identified. A natural extension of this is the notion of growing a business organically: 'Build, don't buy.' In accordance with that maxim, Branson has never made a major acquisition (as that term is usually understood).

His rivalry with British Airways illustrates his views on competition: 'Be best not biggest; compete on quality as well as price.' And his habit, since the early days, of recording good ideas in notebooks (dozens of these books have accumulated over time) supports his notion that the innovative business must 'capture every fleeting idea.' In a restless, creative business with an emphasis on experiment and development, 'ideas are lifeblood.' 'Drive for change' is another guiding principle in the Branson business philosophy. Branson is impatient with what he sees as the risk-aversive nature of British industry and commerce, and indeed society at large. 'It is great for tourism ... and airlines ... but has no place in industry.... We [at Virgin] experiment endlessly with new methods, new companies, and new marketing, especially when we can get others to pay for it!'

Formally expounding a business philosophy, however, is not a regular Branson activity. Indeed, in his autobiography he commented, 'Academics analyze ... we just hit the phones and get on with the business.'[4]

'Hero of the World'

In 1990, Richard Branson found himself in northern Japan preparing for take-off in an attempt to make the first-ever trans-Pacific crossing in a hot-air balloon, an event timed to coincide with Virgin Atlantic's inaugural flight to Tokyo. His Japanese hosts had invited a huge crowd to witness the event,

---

[3] Institute of Directors, London, 1993.

[4] Branson, *Losing my Virginity*, p. 12.

and banners had been hung declaring him to be the 'Hero of the World.'

The attempt was just one in a series of exploits undertaken by Branson. They began in 1985 when he attempted to cross the Atlantic in a high-powered speedboat to win the coveted Blue Riband, the prize awarded to the vessel and crew with the fastest time. The vessel sank off Ireland, but a similar attempt the following year was successful. In 1987, he and Per Lindstrand, an experienced balloonist, attempted the fastest trans-Atlantic balloon crossing, an aim achieved – but only after both barely escaped with their lives when the balloon made a forced landing in the Irish Sea. His latest endeavor, a round-the-world balloon flight, has now been abandoned following a rival's successful attempt.

Branson is happy to admit that these exploits were started as an inexpensive way of publicizing his trans-Atlantic airline, but with time they seemed to gain a momentum of their own. Asked how the chairman of a major corporation can justify the risks and expense, he replied, 'People who have to ask the question don't understand.'

Whatever his motives, Branson has come to be seen as a modern buccaneer with an appealing, devil-may-care attitude to physical danger as well as business risks. At the same time, he supports charitable, radical, and humanitarian causes. For example, he still funds a sex counseling clinic that he helped found in his Student days when his girlfriend became pregnant and they had nowhere to turn for advice. He also launched a new brand of condoms, Mates, as a response to the government's laissez-faire attitude towards AIDS and condom use. This is the kind of project that appeals to Branson: there is a benefit for society, money is raised for charity, and he has fun doing it. More controversially, he boycotted a magazine that refused to carry advertisements supporting the legalization of marijuana, although he personally dislikes illegal drugs following an ill-fated experiment with LSD. 'Richard could not stand to be out of control,' according to his girlfriend at the time.

Branson's exploits and causes are diverse, ranging from a health-care foundation supporting AIDS research to financial support for a new political publication. He bought and published a banned video on

security matters, used his aircraft to rescue people trapped by the Gulf War, and led an initiative to help unemployed teenagers (although the initiative soon wound down). He submitted a bid to run the new National Lottery in the UK on a charitable rather than profit-making basis. He lost, later claiming that the winning consortium's representative had tried to bribe him to withdraw from the bidding. The representative sued but lost in court, paying heavy damages to Branson and standing down from his position.

Branson's esteem in UK public opinion at all levels is regularly demonstrated. In the 1980s he was the darling of the former Prime Minister, Margaret Thatcher; in the late 1990s he enjoyed good relations with Tony Blair's Labour government. He has been nominated for awards for enterprise, voted the most popular businessman, and named in polls by Londoners as the preferred choice for the new post of mayor, even though he has never put his name forward. In recognition of his services to entrepreneurship, the Blair government nominated Branson for a knighthood in the new millennium honours list. The soon-to-be Sir Richard Branson expressed his delight at the award, noting that 'neither I nor Virgin have ever made a political donation', underlining his long-held apolitical stance.

In general, Branson is the point of reference whenever comparisons are made between the traditional business leader and emerging entrepreneurs of the '80s and '90s. He is, however, a man of contrasts. The public persona is that of a warm, friendly, idealistic family man. Yet he is also a highly competitive workaholic and an extremely tough negotiator who thrives on bargaining.

The 'real' Richard Branson

Richard Branson has become an international celebrity, the subject of numerous profiles in gossip magazines, the business press, and television programs. Generally, this coverage has been sympathetic – especially in the UK, where he has achieved folk-hero status. Writers focus on his eccentric lifestyle, derring-do exploits, and new business ventures, comparing him favorably to more staid and conventional business leaders. Even the London tabloids, not known for their generosity to celebrities – indeed, often seeking out sensational stories about their private lives – seem willing to give Branson a relatively soft ride. They generally adopt a tone of friendly mockery about his exploits (although the failure to meet expectations in his rail company is starting to encourage negative press). He is frequently cited as a role model by young people wanting a successful business career that does not compromise personal ethics.

His detractors see Branson in different terms: a me-too operator, simply copying other people's ideas; an arch manipulator, fooling staff and consumers with warm words to mask his own grasping ambition; a fool with a death wish, driven by demons from his childhood to undertake ever-more risky exploits – whether commercial or physical – until eventually everything collapses about him.

Whichever point of view is right, in material terms Branson is undoubtedly successful. He became one of the UK's richest people before he turned forty, and recently he ranked as the eleventh-wealthiest person in the UK, with an estimated net worth of £900 million. Asked to explain the strategy that got him to this point, he talks of minimizing risks: 'Protect the downside, always be ready to walk away,' he says. 'But I have never thought of myself as a businessman. In my first venture I saw myself as an editor, only becoming a businessman to make sure my magazine survived.'

Over the years he has made strategic statements that, with hindsight, have not related closely to subsequent events. Most frequently, however, he eschews strategy in favor of fun: he says he simply wants to enjoy himself. But can a strategy for fun really explain the creation of a music company by a founder who, paradoxically, has little interest in or knowledge of music? Equally, it is difficult to explain how a shy man, ill at ease when speaking publicly or in private conversation with strangers, can become a supreme self-publicist. Or how an establishment-born figure with intrinsically conventional views can become the champion of radical and libertarian causes. Or how the man who is almost obsessive about fair play can negotiate ferociously for the last penny in a deal.

A London Sunday Times report on the British Airways affair quoted Lord King as saying, 'If Richard Branson had worn a pair of steel-rimmed glasses, a double-breasted suit and shaved off his beard, I would have taken him seriously. As it was I couldn't.... I underestimated him.' Perhaps Lord King is not alone in being misled by the hippie entrepreneur image that surrounds Branson. But if that image is not the real Richard Branson, then what is?

Virgin in the new millennium

In the year 2000, when Richard Branson celebrates his fiftieth birthday, he will have been leading Virgin for thirty-two years. (See **Exhibit 1** for key dates.) How many more years will he be at the helm? Can a company founded on youth, fun, and anti-establishment sentiments be run by someone with retirement on the horizon? Indeed, will Richard Branson ever *want* to retire? If not, what implications would his continuation have for Virgin and its management? If he does plan to withdraw, either partly or wholly, what impact would his retirement have, given that his persona is so closely associated in the eyes of the public and investors with Virgin and its ethos? Is there anyone else who could act as the public face of Virgin, who could step into Branson's shoes? He has children, but they are still in their teens; the elder, his daughter, has ambitions to become a doctor.

Typically, entrepreneurs do not pass on their heritage successfully. What needs to be done to ensure that Virgin endures? What potential dangers are there, and what preventative steps should be taken? Will it take a commercial or other calamity to force Branson to take a back seat, or will someone (family? friend? business associate?) be able to 'control' his instinctive tendency for expansion, growth, and risk taking, directing his energies towards an orderly transition?

Or is the only real danger the sudden loss of Branson himself? Branson argues that he is not the sole source of the company's success, that each major Virgin company could stand alone, led by an experienced management team. The Virgin brand, he says, is an independent entity that has an existence beyond its association with him. Moreover, the organization has the momentum and strength that would see it through a crisis. Is this assertion correct? If Branson goes, would the company lose the impetus for innovation and the 'can-do' culture that has for so long been its hallmark? Who would maintain the elaborate structure of financial deals, joint ventures, and interlinked companies? Would the abrupt departure of Richard Branson create a crisis of confidence so severe as to endanger the very survival of Virgin?

As time passes, questions about the future of Virgin (often brought to the fore by Branson's dangerous exploits) will increasingly be in the minds of shareholders, bankers, senior managers, potential partners, and myriad other interested parties. Has Virgin come of age to face a robust future, or is it on the cusp, about to enter terminal decline?

Exhibit 1 Key dates

1968	First issue of Student magazine published.
1970/71	Virgin mail-order operation started; first Virgin record shop opened in Oxford Street.
1972/73	First Virgin recording studio opened at The Manor near Oxford; Tubular Bells released; Virgin record label launched; music publishing operation established in the UK.
1977	The Sex Pistols signed by Virgin.
1978/80	First Virgin night-club (The Venue) opened; Human League signed to Virgin; Virgin Records presence in overseas markets expanded.
1981/82	Phil Collins, Boy George, and Culture Club signed to Virgin.
1983/84	Virgin Vision formed: film and video distribution, TV, broadcasting; Virgin Games launched; Virgin Atlantic Airways and Virgin Cargo launched; first luxury hotel launched (in Mallorca); the Music Channel, a 24-hour satellite-delivered music station, launched by Virgin Vision, which also produced the award-winning film 1984, starring Richard Burton and John Hurt.
1985/86	Business Enterprise Award for company of the year won by Virgin; Virgin Holidays formed; £25 million raised via convertible stock; Virgin Group floated on London stock exchange.
1987	Virgin Records America launched; Japanese subsidiary established; Rushes Video, London, acquired; 525, Virgin Communications LA-based post-production facility, launched; Virgin served as founding member of British Satellite Broadcasting Plc; majority holding in Music Channel sold; UK distribution rights for Sega computer games acquired; Virgin balloon company launched; first results from Virgin Group Plc made available – turnover: £279 million; pbt: £28 million.
1988	Olympic Recording Studios opened in London; Virgin Classics established to specialize in high-quality classical music repertoire; first Virgin Megastores opened in Australia, Glasgow, and Paris; smaller UK retail outlets sold to W. H. Smith for £23 million; Virgin Broadcasting formed to further develop Virgin's interests in radio and TV; three major business-class awards won by Virgin Atlantic, designated Britain's second-most-popular long-haul carrier; management buyout announced by Branson following the 1987 October stock market crash.
1989	Doubled pre-tax profits at £10 million announced by Virgin Atlantic, which also established its own engineering operations; 10 percent of Virgin Travel sold to Seibu Saison, Japan; 25 percent of Virgin Music sold to Fujisankei, Japan; long-term European distribution for Sega Video Games signed by Virgin Mastertronics as Sega became the number-one brand for video games in Europe; Virgin Vision sold to Management Company Entertainment Group (MCEG) of Los Angeles for $83 million.

➤

1990   Virgin Music Group launched second US record company based in New York; Megastores opened in Marseilles, Bordeaux, and Belfast; West One Television, a UK post-production company, created by Virgin Communications; joint venture signed with Marui retail group to operate Megastores in Japan.

1991   Ruling by the Civil Aviation Authority (CAA) won by Virgin Atlantic, allowing it to operate extra services to Tokyo by transfer of rights from BA; right won by Virgin Atlantic to operate services out of Heathrow (London) in addition to Gatwick (London), along with UK government approval to fly to South Africa; Virgin Mastertronic, Virgin Communications' European computer games distributor, sold to Sega of Japan for £40 million (though Virgin Communications retained the publishing division and began a rapid expansion of Virgin Games); Virgin Book Publishing formed in joint venture with W. H. Smith and Allison & Busby.

1992   Virgin Music Group sold to Thorn EMI Plc; first video-game software in Europe released by Virgin Games; Westwood Studios Inc., a Las Vegas–based developer of computer software, acquired; Virgin Games SA established in Paris; purchase of DC-3 announced to establish new US carrier Vintage Airtours, to operate a daily service of nostalgic trips from Orlando to the Florida Keys; UK's first national radio rock station launched in joint venture with TV-am Plc; post-production interests consolidated by Virgin TV, which also planned international expansion; Megastores opened in Spain, Netherlands, Australia, USA; joint venture formed by Virgin Retail with Blockbuster of Florida to expand Megastores in Europe, Australia, and North America; Euro-Magnetic, a specialist supplier of PC consumables, acquired by Virgin.

1993   Libel settlement of £610,000 against Lord King and BA won by Virgin Atlantic, which was voted Executive Travel's Airline of the Year for the third year running; Virgin Games K.K established in Tokyo by Virgin Games, which sold minority interests to Hasbro Inc and Blockbuster; the PC market entered by Virgin Euromagnetics, which launched its first range of personal computers; first management contract obtained by Virgin Hotels; daily flight to Hong Kong and San Francisco launched by Virgin Atlantic; joint venture announced with Wheelock Pacific to form Virgin Megastores Hong Kong, aimed at Chinese-speaking Asia market; Our Price chain in UK acquired by Virgin Retail; Saehan Virgin Megastores Korea established in joint venture with Saehan Media.

1994   Virgin Games renamed Virgin Interactive Entertainment (VIE) and Blockbuster raise stake to 75 percent; creative design and brand-development consultancy formed in partnership with Rodney Fitch and Co; Virgin City Jet service launched in January between Dublin and London City Airport; joint venture formed by Virgin Hotels with Shirayama Shokusan to develop London's County Hall; management contracts for four UK hotels awarded to Virgin Hotels; 100 percent ownership of three hotels previously held in joint venture taken by Virgin Hotels, which also acquired 50 percent ownership of the luxury restaurant Le Manoir aux Quat' Saisons; Virgin Hotels Marketing launched to promote owner-managed small hotels operating in Virgin style; Virgin Television Mexico formed; Virgin Trading formed to market FMCG under the Virgin brand name, with first venture in partnership with W. Grant and Sons to market Virgin Vodka; Virgin Radio awarded FM license in London; Virgin Cola Company formed by Virgin Retail and COTT of Canada.

➤

1995   Agreement reached by Virgin Atlantic and Malaysian Airways to operate a twice-daily flight to Kuala Lumpur; agreement between Virgin Atlantic and Delta Airways approved by the US Department of Transportation; Virgin Direct Financial Services launched in a joint venture with Norwich Union Insurance; joint venture formed to acquire MGM Cinemas; Norwich Union bought out by Australian Mutual Provident (AMP); Virgin Atlantic voted airline of the year by Executive Travel magazine; Virgin Cola launched to compete with Coca-Cola and Pepsi; British Airways sued again by Branson, who this time claimed damages in the US.

1996   Flights started by Virgin Atlantic to Orlando and Washington DC; Euro Belgian Airlines acquired by Virgin Travel, which renamed it Virgin Express; Virgin Bride, Europe's largest bridal-wear shop, opened; Virgin Net formed to enter the Internet market; V2 Music launched, signing its first two bands; £3 billion contract to build Channel Tunnel Link and operate Eurostar services to Paris and Brussels awarded to London and Continental Railways, in which Virgin is a minority shareholder; Virgin Rail awarded franchise to operate rail passenger service covering 130 stations in England, Scotland, and Wales; Virgin Atlantic voted best business class and best transatlantic carrier by Executive Travel magazine for the sixth year running.

1997   Virgin Rail awarded InterCity West Coast franchise; three hotels in Wales acquired by Virgin Hotels; 50 percent share in London Broncos rugby team acquired by Branson; Virgin Express quoted on the Brussels and NASDAQ exchanges; Virgin Cinemas and Virgin Megastores World-wide (excluding the UK) merged to form Virgin Entertainment Group; four stores in UK opened by Virgin Vie, a joint venture in cosmetics and beauty care; first banking product – Virgin One Account – launched by Virgin Direct (Financial Services) in joint venture with Royal Bank of Scotland; Virgin Radio sold for £85 million; COTT's share of Virgin Cola bought out by Virgin Trading.

1998   Richard Branson wins G-Tech court case, involving G-Tech the lottery equipment supplier and Guy Snowden its former chairman; 'Diana', the tribute album for Diana, Princess of Wales, released by V2 Records on behalf of the record industry raises over £40m for charity; Virgin Sun, Virgin Holidays' first foray into short-haul holidays is launched; Virgin Express starts flights from Stansted to Continental Europe; Rail Regulator, John Swift, approves Virgin Trains' and Railtrack's massive upgrade of the UK's West Coast Main Line; Stagecoach buys 49% of Virgin Rail Group and Virgin increases its stake from 41% to 51%; Virgin Entertainment Group buys WHSmith's 75% holding in Virgin Our Price retail chain in Great Britain and Ireland.

1999   Virgin Rail Group completes the financing of new high speed tilting trains for both its franchises – West Coast and Cross Country. A total of over £4 billion of private sector investment secured with the introduction of the new trains still on track for 2001-2002. The first new 'Pendolino' destined for the West Coast Mainline rolls off the production line in December 1999; Virgin Atlantic announces further expansion plans on the back of continuing growth and increased profitability. 1999 will see the launch of new routes to Chicago, Shanghai and other destinations. Virgin Sun's first charter flights commence in May 1999. Virgin Atlantic's fleet of wide body jets grows to 28. In December, Singapore Airlines and Virgin announce that the former will buy a 49% stake in Virgin Atlantic for £600m cash. In the same month, Virgin Atlantic also announces a deal with Air India which

➤

will give the airline access to the sub-continent for the first time, with flights due to start in July 2000; Virgin Group announces its intention to enter the telecommunications business; Virgin Net goes free and Virgin continues its expansion in e-commerce with a wide range of connections from Megastores online to train booking facilities (total internet revenues 1999—£150 million); Virgin Mobile, Virgin's first consumer telecommunications venture, announces creation of 500 jobs in Trowbridge, West Wiltshire. The company will establish a management, customer service and call centre from which to market mobile telephony products (joint venture with Deutsche Telekom's One2One unit); Virgin Megastores continue their expansion world-wide with store openings in Miami, Glasgow, Piccadilly Circus, Bluewater, Strasburg, Okayama in Japan, bringing the total of Megastores total up to 381 stores world-wide. As a result of its more focussed retail strategy, Virgin Entertainment Group accepts an offer of £215m from UGC of France to buy Virgin Cinemas, the deal completes in November 1999; Virgin Active launches the first of its expected chain health and lifestyle centres, in Preston, Leeds and Stockley Park; Virgin Express starts a new service from Stansted to Berlin. Virgin also confirms the intention to set up a new independent low cost airline in Australia; Virgin opens its first game park in South Africa. The company also confirms that it has sold some of its smaller UK hotels to a private investor as part of its plan to refocus on exclusive properties around the world.

2000   Virgin Spectrum Limited is formed to participate in SpectrumCo, a new company formed by a number of shareholders to bid for a 3rd Generation Mobile Telephony license in the UK in March 2000. Other partners in the bid include Tesco, EMI, Sonera, Nextel, Marconi and a number of large private equity funds; Virgin Rail Group confirms its intention to bid for the East Coast Mainline; Virgin confirms its intention to launch Virgin.com/cars, a new e-commerce business, selling a wide range of cars direct to the consumer online.

Exhibit 2 Virgin group of companies in 1999: commentary on Major Operations

It is generally acknowledged, both within and outside Virgin, that **Virgin Travel**, especially Virgin Atlantic, is the company closest to Branson's heart. It is the only company in which employees have Branson's direct telephone number and are encouraged to call or write to him with ideas or feedback on customer satisfaction. Branson regularly travels on his planes, helping to serve meals, talking to passengers and cabin crew, and generally listening for suggestions for improvements.

With twenty-nine aircraft and routes from London to about a dozen major cities outside Europe, **Virgin Atlantic** remains a niche player in an industry dominated by global carriers and state airlines. Since its founding, the airline has relied on service, value-for-money, and innovation,

dished up with panache and flair, to differentiate itself in the market. On the first flights, cabin crew in business class were dressed as butlers, serving bought in food from Maxims. Later, in-flight magicians, masseuses, and musicians were used; a limousine service to the airport for upper-class passengers was instituted; and multi-channel music and video systems that can be customized to a passenger's individual needs were installed. More recently, luxurious Virgin Atlantic clubhouses have appeared at London's two airports as well as in Hong Kong, Washington, and San Francisco. Not all of these ideas originated at Virgin, but Branson will happily copy good practice if he sees an advantage. Judging by the numerous awards and citations the airline has won, his approach seems to work.

➤

During 1999 Branson had intimated that he might float part of the airline to raise capital for expansion. As the year was closing, however, he announced a surprise deal with Singapore Airlines that, in terms of fleet and revenues, is about three times the size of Virgin Atlantic. If the deal goes through, in 2000 Singapore will acquire a 49% stake in Virgin Atlantic at a cost of £600 million. The two airlines will work in partnership to maximise cost cutting synergies (eg maintenance, ground facilities, code sharing) but retain their respective identities and develop their own products. Industry observers saw the logic of the deal since in many ways the two airlines are complementary – their routes do not overlap and they both enjoy excellent reputations for service and innovation. There were, however, doubts expressed at the price that Singapore was paying, valuing Virgin Atlantic at more than £1.2 billion, a high figure in many observers' view.

Also included in the deal are the other divisions of Virgin Atlantic—Virgin Holidays, Virgin Sun and Virgin Aviation Services, the group's cargo division. Managing Director Ron Simms describes **Virgin Holidays** as 'the world's largest long-haul tour operator in terms of numbers carried.' The holiday company grew on the back of the airline and has recently moved into the short-haul business. The main destination is Florida, where Virgin is the Disney hotels' biggest customer.

Virgin Entertainment owns **Virgin Cinemas**, a cinema chain formed from the purchase of MGM cinemas. Virgin sold the ninety small sites it acquired, retaining the remainder for conversion to 'Megaplexes.' After substantial refurbishment, Megaplexes offer cafe/bars, shops, and spacious seating; those that offer 'Premier Screen' also have personalized service – coats are taken, drinks are served at the seat, extra legroom is provided. Virgin plans to develop the chain through purpose-built Megaplexes.

Virgin Entertainment is also the Virgin partner in joint ventures that run overseas Megastores. The Megastore concept is exported and refined to adapt to the local culture, but it retains its core values: fun, good design, value-for-money, and choice.

Virgin Retail's core activity is the chain of fifty-plus Megastores in the UK, in partnership with W. H. Smith, a retail chain. It also owns Caroline International, an importer/exporter of music and video media, and has an interest in Sound & Media, a specialist music supplier.

Based in Brussels, **Virgin Express Holdings Plc** is a scheduled airline company serving the main European cities, offering single-class airfares substantially below the norm. It offers its customers a no-frills, simple-to-understand service in which even ticketing has been reduced to a booking confirmation number.

Virgin Direct and **Virgin Direct Personal Finance** were founded to bring Virgin into the personal financial services market, where Branson saw an industry 'ripe for reform': poor service, high charges, disreputable practices, dissatisfied customers. In addition, the market was forecast to grow as people took more responsibility for their own financial security in old age.

Relying for competitive advantage on the Virgin brand's association with trust and value-for-money, **Virgin Direct** was initially a joint venture with Norwich Union Assurance, a large insurance group that supplied the technology and back-office support while Virgin supplied the marketing. Norwich Union withdrew shortly after the launch in favor of Australian Mutual Provident.

Virgin Direct differentiates itself in several ways. First, it does not use a commission-led sales force or agents, relying instead on advertising and telesales, contrary to accepted industry practice. Second, it offers simple saving products, based on tracking financial indices, that the average person can understand. Simplicity of product and lack of commission mean lower costs, which are passed on as lower administration charges. The transparency of its charges are a key selling point in its advertising. In 1999, after four years in operation, Virgin Direct has over 200,000 customers with more than £1 billion under management. Its main products are PEPS (a tax-efficient personal equity plan under a 'tax wrapper'), personal pensions, and life insurance.

▶

Virgin Direct Personal Finance links Virgin Direct with Royal Bank of Scotland to offer the *One* account, a combined, highly flexible mortgage and bank account with a single rate for all lending purposes: car loan, house purchase, overdraft, credit card, etc.

The most recent major investment by Virgin, **Virgin Rail** consists of twenty-year franchises to operate two networks: CrossCountry, a series of routes that traverse the UK, and West Coast, the main route from London to Glasgow and intermediate stations. The franchises were awarded by competitive tendering as part of the long-term denationalization program of the Conservative government. Virgin inherited rolling stock, ticketing offices, and staff, all previously under British Rail ownership and management. The tracks, signaling, and stations are owned and operated by Railtrack.

British Rail was not seen as a customer-friendly and efficient organization. Furthermore, years of under-investment had had an impact on the infrastructure. The result was high prices, unhappy customers, and demotivated (sometimes antagonistic) staff. Industry observers, City analysts, and media commentators all had reservations about the prospects for franchisees given the major turnaround required. In Virgin's case, they forecast considerable damage to the brand. Branson recognized that there was a risk but believed that his project to undertake major investment in modern trains and convert the staff to a customer-service culture would pay off in the long term, particularly with passenger numbers forecast to rise. In the short term, however, Virgin Rail has suffered from poor public relations, with horror stories surfacing frequently about delayed trains, poor food, and dirty trains. Virgin Rail management explains that improvements cannot come overnight.

Virgin Rail was initially a joint venture between Virgin and venture capitalists. In 1998, Branson made plans to float Virgin Rail, intending to offer part of the equity to the public to allow the initial investors to withdraw. There were doubts in the City about whether this would be a success. At the last moment, Brian Souter, chairman of Stagecoach, a private bus company operating mainly in the UK but also overseas, offered to take a 49 percent holding. A Scottish entrepreneur from a modest background, Souter is a born-again Christian with a reputation for running a tight and hard-nosed operation. His company has been accused of predatory actions against competitors, for example. His business was founded in the early '80s and prospered when the Thatcher government privatized many bus companies. With the reputation for being somewhat eccentric (i.e., in the Branson mold), Souter sees synergy between his bus networks and trains.

Obliged by contract to stay out of the music business for three years after the sale of Virgin Music, **V2 Music** is Branson's return to the industry that got him started. It was founded as a global business with a presence in many countries. Still a small, loss-making operator, V2 Music has yet to sign any major artists, but it is investing in creative personnel to seek out new talent.

Virgin Net is an Internet service provider created as a joint venture between Virgin and the UK subsidiary of NTL, a US computer technology company. Virgin is responsible for creative content and marketing; NTL provides the backup systems and software. Virgin Net targets the UK consumer market and wants to compete on 'value-for-money, speed, excellent customer service, and compelling content,' according to David Clarke, Managing Director. Much of its content is sourced from specialist suppliers (for example, the Independent newspaper for news).

Exhibit 3 Virgin group of companies in 1999: summary

Virgin Company	% Virgin interests	Other major shareholders	Turnover 97/98 £m*	Employees	Trading location(s)	Launch date
Virgin Travel Group	100%			4,750	Worldwide	
– Virgin Atlantic Airways	100%		678			1984
– Virgin Holidays	100%		177			1985
– Virgin Aviation Services	90%	Held by management	15			1985
Virgin Entertainment Group	70%	Texas Pacific Group, Colony				
– Cinemas	100%	Capital	100	800	UK	1995
– US Megastores	100%	(formerly MGM Cinemas)	80	400	USA	1992
– Japan Megastores	50%		68	100	Japan	1990
– European Megastores	100%	Marui Co	150	300	Continental Europe	1988
Virgin Retail Group	100%					
– Virgin Retail (Our Price, UK Megastores)	25%	W H Smith	500	4,500	UK	1971
– Caroline International	100%		20	62	UK	1972
– Sound & Media	50%	Held by management (Virgin interest since 1994)	8	68	UK	1994
Virgin Trading Group	100%					
– Virgin Cola, Virgin Vodka	100%		21	45	UK	1994
– Virgin Limobikes	100%		0.3	5	UK	1996
V Entertainment Group	100%					
– Virgin Digital Studios (525, Rushes, W1TV)	100%		27	340	UK, USA	1986
– Virgin Publishing	60%	Robert Devereux	10	42	Worldwide	1991
– John Brown Enterprises	20%	John Brown	12	68	UK	1984
– Rapido TV	50%	Rapido TV Investments	4	12	Mexico	1991
Ginger Media Group	20%	Chris Evans, Apax partners				
– Virgin Radio	100%		18	64	UK	1993
Virgin Express Holdings Plc	50.1%	Guarantee Nominees Ltd, management	150	800	Continental Europe	1996
Virgin Hotels Group	100%					
– Virgin Clubs, La Residencia, Woodhouse Securities, Cribyn	100%		21	587	UK, Spain	1988
– Le Manoir Aux Quat' Saisons	50%	Held by management	7	120	UK	1994
Virgin Direct Ltd	50%	Australian Mutual Provident				
– Virgin Direct Personal Services	100%	(AMP)	608**	450	UK	1995
Virgin Direct Personal Finance	25%	AMP, Royal Bank of Scotland		150	UK	1998
Victory Corporation Plc	49%	Clerical Medical, Foreign & Colonial, GRE				
– Virgin Vie	100%	Morgan Grenfell, Commercial	2.5	150	UK	1997
– Virgin Clothing	100%	Union, McCarthy Corporation		57	UK	1998
Virgin Rail Group	51%	Stagecoach Group	423	3,450	UK	1997
– West Coast Trains	100%					
– CrossCountry Trains	100%					
V2 Music	66%	McCarthy Corporation	10	200	UK	1996
Virgin Net	51%	NTL	10	60	UK	1996
Vanson Developments (property)	100%		30	14	UK	1983
Virgin Bride	100%		0.9	25	UK	1996
Neckar (island resort)	100%		2.5	33	Virgin Islands, WI	1984
Heaven	100%		3	43	London	1982
Virgin Vouchers	100%		0.1	2	UK	1996
London Broncos	50.1%	BAT Trustees (Jersey), King Investments	2	50	London	1997
Virgin Helicopters	100%		0.8	12	UK	1997
The Lightship Group	50%	Lightship America	9	215	UK, USA	1990
Virgin Airships & Balloons	75%	Nerorate	8	47	UK	1987
Storm Model Management	50%	held by management	6	22	Worldwide	1985

* Financial year-ends not concurrent   **Gross Sales   Plc indicates publicly quoted company

Exhibit 4 Virgin people

Is there a 'Virgin person'? From Richard Branson to the most humble employee, those who work for Virgin seem to believe that only a certain type of person will fit into the sprawling Virgin empire, despite its diverse range of businesses. What follows are selected extracts from interviews with Virgin staff, who talked about what it takes to work at Virgin:

Stephen Murphy, Group Financial Director based in Geneva: *We like to hire smart people, people who have had all the schooling and education but who are pissed off with management consultancies, investment banks, and the like. We had one woman who was thrown out of a well-known consultancy because she had a nose earring. We took her on. We don't have those kinds of prejudices.*

Dan Higgott, International Brand Development Manager, Megastores (formerly Manager of the flagship Megastore on London's Oxford Street): *After five years with Virgin, I still find it difficult to describe a Virgin person. You need common sense and need not to be overly concerned with status and formality, but these could apply to any successful business. There are no preconceptions about people at Virgin, and I'm a good example. My training was in fashion, and I fell into retail management by accident. In Virgin Retail we have quite a formal process for developing people, so I've been given opportunities to progress. At twenty-nine I was running a £35 million business. I believe those opportunities genuinely apply to any of the 230 people who worked for me at the Oxford Street store.*

Kenneth Ibbett, Chairman, Virgin Media Group: *I joined Virgin so that I could come to work on a bicycle and not wear a tie – and took a 25 percent pay cut! We don't necessarily pay the best rates, and we're quite open about that. One problem at Virgin is that senior people with creativity and flair move on when they cash in their options. We miss people like that – Robert Devereux is a good example. When recruiting, you have to be open-minded and recognize that you're not looking*

for clones. I've just recruited someone who has nothing in common with me, but she's just right to run our TV business. As to the attributes we look for, it's probably easier to list the negatives to avoid: complacency, fear of failure, lack of integrity, and stupidity are probably the important ones.

Lene Byrne, Flight Supervisor, Virgin Atlantic: *I came from Denmark to college in England and had wanted to fly for a couple of years. That was nine years ago. We've grown a lot since then and are more systemized, less easygoing, but we also have more chance to be transferred or promoted. I like the way we have fun at Virgin; it's more like a family where I know everyone, and that wouldn't be the same at BA, for example. To be employed at Virgin Atlantic you have to have the Virgin Flair – that's the big one – which means thinking young, having a sense of humor, being easygoing but professional at the same time. The longer you're here, the more you get to know Richard. Personally he's a very nice man, very genuine; but when it comes to business, he doesn't do anything without a reason – he's good at it!*

Will Whitehorn, Director of Corporate Affairs, Virgin Group: *Virgin has grown a lot recently and brought in a lot of new people. [To avoid difficulties in a start-up,] a new team will be made up of Virgin people plus new people. The new telecommunications business is a good example of that. We've brought in technical expertise and linked it to our marketing skills. The kind of people we look for are those who want to be the boss sometime and can work in the culture here at Virgin that gives you the confidence to do that. We want people with a clear idea of why they want to be with us, who don't beat around the bush when it comes to expressing a vision they may have. The organization doesn't like 'yes' people or political people; we want people who are happy to enter a discourse and debate things.*

Tim McIntosh, Manager, Union Square Megastore, New York: *In New York the staff do have the feeling that they work for Richard*

➤

Branson and an English company because they've seen him and talked to him when he comes by for [promotional] events. For many of them this is their first job, but they know the history because of the book [Branson's autobiography] and the Virgin record label. We look at resumes [of potential recruits] and on paper they look good but not when you meet them. We're looking for personality – someone you'll notice, friendly and upbeat, people who look like they're going to try. It takes time to find the right people. Once they're here, they have to do a pretty bad thing to get fired –

stealing, racial slurs, drinking, fighting, and that kind of thing. At a senior level, one bad business decision won't get a hatchet thrown at you, but you don't make that decision again.

Whatever the profile of the Virgin Person, the company should not have difficulty in persuading young people to join, at least in the UK. According to a 1999 survey,[5] UK graduates ranked Virgin Group second only to the BBC as the best place to work, ahead of its rival British Airways (ranked sixth) and the accounting and consulting firms.

Exhibit 5 Richard Branson's introduction to the Virgin charter

Virgin is a unique brand, and behind that brand sits an equally unique corporate structure. Over the years Virgin has evolved into something between a branded venture capital organization and a Japanese-style keiretsu (family of businesses).

The consequences of this evolving structure have been twofold. Firstly, each business has become focused and been able to develop in a more autonomous and entrepreneurial environment than their equivalent subsidiaries in large conglomerates. Secondly, the Virgin brand has built up a world-wide reputation out of all proportion to the actual size and market share of any individual Virgin company. Much in the way that other brands have become household names without being associated to any one product, so Virgin is becoming a household name, bound only by the attributes that people want to associate it with – namely, value for money, quality, innovation, challenge and fun.

In a hectic and dynamic business environment, however, autonomy can have its downside – and communication links are usually the first to suffer. This can lead to flaws in the decision-making process and, ultimately, to companies acting on their own and without the common good of the Virgin shareholders in mind. As more responsibility is devolved to a range of individually significant businesses in their own right, links become stretched and frustrated and information stops flowing.

We need to prevent this from happening while respecting and maintaining the spirit of Virgin. Hence the Virgin Charter.

It is intended that the Virgin Charter will evolve into a management system that will allow all Virgin companies to be the best they can possibly be, without the need for obstructive hierarchies which can so easily impede rapid decision-making by those who know their own business.

In the longer term we hope that the Virgin Charter will become a mechanism through which both the individual companies, Virgin Management Ltd. and the Virgin brand can quickly take advantage of the truly exciting opportunities that lie ahead, both in our core businesses and the new frontiers of global electronic commerce. As we move into the twenty-first century there is a real opportunity to turn Virgin into one of the leading global brands, by looking at strategic opportunities for the existing businesses and by forming new ones.

Finally, please don't forget that Virgin's success, both now and in the future, rests with each of us. We are a people brand and a people business in the purest sense of the word.

My greatest hope is that the Virgin Charter will continue to create a culture of praise rather than blame, and family rather than alienation. If that alone can be achieved then all our efforts will have been worthwhile.

5 Universum, Stockholm 1999, graduate survey.

INSEAD

Case 11 Rank Xerox, A, B, C

Rank Xerox (A): Global transfer of best practices

It was early 1995 and Carlos Camarero, the get-things-done, results-oriented leader of Rank Xerox's Team C initiative, was troubled. Over six months into the implementation of Wave II he was perplexed by its negligible impact on Rank Xerox's approach to selling products. The absence of financial benefits from Wave II was particularly worrying compared with the resounding success of Team C's Wave I initiative which had generated US$100 million net benefit in 1994.

The early 1990s had been a time of tremendous change at the European Rank Xerox and its parent company, Xerox Corporation, based in Stamford, Connecticut, US. Faced with changing competitive and technological dynamics in the world copier market, Xerox Corporation CEO Paul Allaire had repositioned the firm as *The Document Company*

This case received the 2003 European Foundation for Management Development Case of the Year Award in the category 'Knowledge Management and Learning in Organisations'

This original version of the case was written by Gary M. Deutsch, Wharton MBA 1997 and Joanna Fueyo, Research Assistant, under the supervision of Gabriel Szulanski, Associate Professor of Strategy at INSEAD. Michael Casaburi, Wharton MBA 1998 and Doctoral Student at Wharton, wrote this revised version. The case is intended to be used as a basis for class discussion rather than to illustrate either effective or ineffective handling of an administrative situation.

06/2004-5138

and transformed its centralized organizational structure into one based on product-centric business divisions. Rank Xerox, however, did not similarly redesign its organizational structure at that time.

In September 1992, Managing Director Bernard Fournier announced the *Rank Xerox 2000* initiative to remedy the company's recent performance ills and restructure its organization using the more customer-responsive business division model of the master corporation. At the core of the 2000 initiative was the concept of best practice transfer – the identification and transfer of best practices across Rank Xerox's individual countries of operation – in response to the realization that valuable information was not being successfully shared between countries.

Fournier had formed a series of expert teams to meet his objectives – Teams A, B and C – and gave them each a specific set of goals and objectives. Team A had been successful in transforming the organizational structure into an information-sharing and customer-focused matrix. Team B had succeeded in slashing costs and eliminating bureaucracy at Rank Xerox's corporate headquarters in Marlow, England. Wave I of Team C's initiative had achieved remarkable revenue improvements by identifying, documenting and transferring best practices associated with discrete sales processes and the marketing of specific products. Next came Wave II, a broader attempt to define overarching sales best practices which was targeted at the core processes of the predominantly sales-focused company. Although Wave II was led by Camarero – as was its predecessor – its results had not been as successful as those of Wave I.

As he prepared to meet with Fournier to discuss Wave II's status, Carlos pondered the intricacies of best practice transfer and analyzed the similarities and differences between Waves I and II.

Rank Xerox

Originally an English motion picture firm, Rank first became involved with Xerox through a joint venture in 1955. Later, Rank became Rank Xerox, the European subsidiary of Xerox Corporation. Rank Xerox was organized into 15 independent national operating companies (OpCos) centered on its European headquarters in Marlow, England. The heads of the largest OpCos reported directly to Fournier. Smaller OpCos were organized into regional clusters whose heads reported to regional general managers who reported to Fournier.

Over the years, Rank Xerox had learned to cope with the difficulties of being a multinational corporation operating across the various countries and cultures of Europe. Some countries were natural rivals (Portugal and Spain, Britain and France, Belgium and Holland) and Rank Xerox managers had come to recognize that certain ideas and initiatives would be better received in some places than others. For instance, calls for technological advancement met with approval more quickly in Holland than in Italy. Likewise, customer demands and needs varied by country.

In 1992 Fournier was concerned about Rank Xerox's recent financial performance, particularly variance across the OpCos. For many years it had been less profitable than Xerox US and its return on assets (ROA) was well below the 20% profit seen in the US. Fournier believed Rank Xerox had the potential to make up the US$200 million cost gap between itself and Xerox US and to improve ROA by 5% or 6% by 1996, but first he felt he needed to align Rank Xerox's organizational structure with that of Xerox US.

Moving toward a solution

Fundamental to Fournier's desired changes was the identification of the strengths of each element of the organisation – features that he wanted to maintain and perhaps use in best practice transfer. Initial examination of the OpCos showed that performance lacked uniformity since Holland, Belgium, Austria, Switzerland, Denmark and Portugal – with ROAs greater than 20% – outperformed other OpCos and Rank Xerox as a whole.

Pressure from Stamford was increasing on Rank Xerox to devise an organizational structure more congruent with its own, and show a dramatic improvement in profits: Stamford set goals of a 40% increase in 1994 and a 38% increase in 1995. In response, Fournier announced the Rank Xerox 2000 initiative in September 1992 with three main objectives. The first was to make the new organization cost effective, flexible, synergistic and pro-active. This meant closing the US$200 million cost gap between Rank Xerox and Xerox US, simplifying processes and increasing productivity, sharing resources and skills at all levels, and getting closer to the customer and thus better able to serve customer needs. The second objective was to position Rank Xerox to move closer to the idea of *The Document Company,* and the third was to restructure the company in line with the organization of the Xerox business divisions.

Team B

Team B was created for the organizational restructuring and streamlining of activities at European headquarters – a focus designed to partially fulfill objectives one and three above. It involved identifying and eliminating activities and layers that did not add direct value to the company or its customers. Team B quickly achieved results and four months into the project had already saved the company US$50 million, mostly by downsizing the corporate workforce.

Team A

Much broader in scope than Team B, Team A was mandated to redesign the Rank Xerox organization. Fournier specifically instructed Team A to propose a structure for the OpCos more congruent with the corporate business divisions model. Team A concluded that a matrix design was best for Rank Xerox. The new organization was centered on the formation of small regional profit centers known as Customer Business Units (CBUs). For the most part, each European country was its own CBU. A CBU had its own sales support, financial analysis, and human resource/quality functions and its general manager held profit/loss responsibility.

CBUs were grouped into territorial 'Entities' that provided governance across the CBUs. France, the UK and Germany were large enough to constitute their own Entities; the other countries were grouped into the Nordic, Central, or Southern Entity. Their role did not involve day-to-day operations (which were now the domain of the CBU); their purpose was to provide resource support to CBUs and help determine national-level policy. To interact adequately with and follow the design of the business division model of Xerox Corporation, Rank Xerox's new structure also included product-line focused Business Division Units (BDUs).

The bottom line impact of Team A's work was dramatic: it was estimated that the reorganization of Rank Xerox led to a US$240 million reduction in the 1993 cost base. However, that was not enough to put Rank Xerox on course to meet the profit improvement goals set by Xerox Corporation for 1994 and 1995 (i.e., projected cost savings would generate 11% profit growth in 1994 and 1995, well below the respective 40% and 38% goals set by Stamford).

Team C

The results for diverse products and services varied dramatically across countries and it was obvious that some CBUs outperformed others. After the success of Teams A and B and their resulting cost savings, Fournier focused on revenues. He created Team C to identify, validate, and document best practices and to mandate their implementation with the overall goal of revenue creation.

Fournier appointed a Spaniard, Carlos Camarero, to lead Team C. In 1993 he had been at Rank Xerox for 22 years, having served as Managing Director in Italy and Portugal as well as in Rank Xerox's Asia-Pacific operations. He had also spent time as Director of Operations in Spain and Region A, which, under the old structure, included all countries in Europe except France, Germany and the UK. Just months before his appointment, Carlos had been transferred from Italy to corporate headquarters in Marlow to assume the position of Corporate Business Division Director. He maintained his responsibilities in that position while committing approximately one-third of his time to the management of Team C. Known for his direct style and get-things-done attitude, he was selected for his operational experience in various OpCos as well as his ability to motivate people and drive projects to fruition. Fournier believed Carlos was vital to the success of Team C since he could negotiate productive agreement between multiple parties.

Since Team C's revenue initiatives would be transferred across the diverse cultures and nationalities of Rank Xerox, Carlos was quick to recognize that its work would have to be simple and easily implementable. He did not want Team C to get lost in the outer realms of 'strategic thinking'. To ensure the accessibility of its work to all the CBUs, Carlos enlisted 'doers' – 25 senior managers (product managers, marketing directors, operations directors and general managers) from CBUs who had ultimate responsibility for confirming that Team C's ideas and plans were realistic and implementable. Both Carlos and Fournier agreed that doers must be the top people in their respective CBUs. To allay possible fears that doers might hurt their careers by spending time away from their CBUs and 'best practicing' themselves out of a job, top management guaranteed their futures in the firm.

It was critical that Team C rapidly identify the origin of revenue growth opportunity best practices and not waste time on the inconsequential. Carlos continually emphasized that they must be broken down into their core drivers, stressing the identification of each best practice by a small number of underlying 'Key Success Factors.' In addition to contributing knowledge and experience, the doers would be instrumental in the prompt implementation of Team C's work. Fournier and Carlos anticipated that the acceptance of Team C initiatives by the top CBU people would inspire their rapid adoption by their CBU peers and subordinates.

Team C's Wave I initiative

Team C's initial project, Wave I, served to identify, document and transfer best practices involved in bringing specific products to market. Beginning in 1994, Team C devoted six months to draw up a list of best practices to be later implemented across different CBUs. Their objective was to find discrete policies within each CBU that could be taught and transferred to others, with the originating CBU serving as model for their specific practice. The original implementation goal was modest – to implement 50% of best practice transfer opportunities in 75% of the CBUs.

Defining the opportunities

Team C laid out the following actions to be taken to successfully identify best practices:

◆ Deep analysis of internal reporting database.

◆ Appointment of 'knowledge' person (Best Practice Champion).

- Promotion of the idea of best practice sharing.
- Creation of the right team to include skills and expertise.
- Recognition that identification effort is not enough.
- Building best practice transfer into annual business planning.
- 100% commitment and support from top managers.
- They also recognized the following potential difficulties in identifying best practices:
- Gaining complete understanding when best practice is complex, cross functional and sequential.
- Establishing sufficient common measurements.
- Thorough documentation of best practices.
- Justification of the opportunity.
- Identification of critical success factors at an early stage.

Since Team C's overall goal was to increase revenue, they began by scanning CBUs for potential easy-to-implement revenue growth opportunities. Opportunities currently being fully implemented by at least one of the CBUs were identified. Carlos described the identification process:

We searched for best performance. Some we found through the database. The others were not so easy. We wrote to every key person (intermediate level) asking them for the best idea from their country. Out of approximately 40 ideas it was very easy to identify the best 10. We then went to each country to observe and understand, and the entire process took six months.

Once the revenue growth opportunities had been identified, Team C benchmarked those CBUs already optimizing such opportunities – essentially making them role models for the company-wide implementation of their specific opportunity. Team C personnel next worked with salespeople and managers at the benchmark CBUs to define the extent of the revenue opportunity as well as to determine a logical scope of implementation. Lastly, a consortium of Team C and CBU personnel laid out a set of Key Success Factors to be implemented simultaneously which served as an action plan for other CBUs.

Carlos believed that although multiple Key Success Factors for each revenue growth opportunity were listed, each opportunity hinged on the identification of one or two core best practices. He illustrated his point with the following story:

In the North of Spain I stumbled across the finest fish restaurant I have ever found. I had to know what the chef was doing to prepare his fish so excellently. Through my persistence, I convinced him to give me his recipe. However, when I tried to duplicate his masterpiece at home I had no luck. The chef later told me with a sly grin that the key to the recipe was not the ingredients per se, rather the precise order in which they are mixed together. For Team C, we knew that we not only had to find the key ingredients of success, but also understand the key drivers which enabled the ingredients to optimally work together.

From their work, Team C developed the following list of nine revenue growth opportunities/best practices that were to be implemented across the CBUs:

- MajestiK: An initiative to increase market share in the European colour copier market.
- Customer Retention: A plan to encourage current customers to repurchase equipment from Rank Xerox by providing special incentives to salespeople for customer retention as well as technological database aids for tracking customer equipment stocks, usage requirements and contract expiration dates.
- DocuTech: An initiative to sell offset printers to commercial and educational users by focusing on overall document solutions rather than on traditional product or price selling.
- New Business Major Accounts: A plan to establish salespeople whose sole responsibility is generating new business.
- DocuPrint: A plan to accelerate sales of the newly launched line of high-speed network printers, particularly to the banking and insurance industries, by emphasizing the product's image printing capabilities and systems integration features.
- CSO Competitive MIF Identification: An initiative for rapid updating of the Rank Xerox

company-wide sales database to track competitive information and provide salespeople with reliable leads.

♦ Analyst Time Billing: A plan to sell the value-adding, problem-solving consulting services of Rank Xerox technical analysts.

♦ XBS: A plan to educate salespeople on how to sell facilities management services effectively through the creation of simple packages and pricing options (i.e., Rank Xerox providing the customer with a packaged service consisting of both equipment and manpower).

♦ Secondhand CEP: An initiative to regain control of the secondhand market for centralized mainframe printers (typically found in data centers) by repurchasing secondhand machines, refurbishing and reselling them to targeted accounts for which price sensitivity is high.

Implementing the opportunities

The first step in the implementation process was convincing Entity and CBU managers that Team C's findings were significant. Carlos and his team had the benefit of Fournier's support but also of hard data which were critical in convincing them of the importance of Wave I. Carlos explained:

We prepared 180 slides full of statistics to convince top management. Even before seeing them the big bosses said, 'Forget it. Everybody here is an expert in marketing and sales. It will never work.' I said, 'Forget it? No! You are going to see the slides. If after that you tell me to forget it, I will forget it. But you are not going to tell me to forget it before you see this.' After only 35 slides we got the go-ahead.

Once Wave I was underway, one of the first challenges facing Team C was logistical coordination and planning. With Team C members scattered throughout Europe holding meeting after meeting and writing up new documentation, it was critical that valuable information did not get lost in the process. Team C enlisted the aid of two secretaries who were immediately immersed in the blood and guts of the project – compiling text, managing schedules and coordinating meetings. The secretaries also became instrumental in the massive

editing project that ensued once the data and ideas for the Wave I implementation books had been gathered.

Team C had essentially created a new corporate language for Rank Xerox. Carlos knew it was critical that the revenue growth opportunities, carefully selected for their simple underlying Key Success Factors, be described in a way that was equally simple and straightforward. Developing such a language proved to be a challenging task requiring several iterations. Several 'laymen' and 'non-experts' in the CBUs were enlisted to read the evolving drafts of the Wave I books. They rejected the first draft due to its complexity and corporate jargon.

Once an easily comprehensible set of Team C books had been completed and distributed, the implementation effort began to gain momentum from the benchmark CBUs. They were more than happy to talk up the best practice for which they had been highlighted. Team C figured that their input, combined with the abundance of data, would help to alleviate many of the problems that typically result when business people in different European countries are asked to agree on a standard. Effectively, Carlos and his team could turn to managers in a given CBU and say, 'You may not think that the French (or Swiss or English or Portuguese, etc.) can do this better than you, but they do, and here are the numbers to prove it.'

Fournier was happy with the way Wave I was proceeding. However, he was still concerned about how the CBU managers would react to change. In an attempt to minimize possible CBU stress, Fournier gave instructions that Entities avoid implementing all nine revenue opportunities at once. Rather, he suggested they pick their four favorites and concentrate on them before proceeding with the other five – a feasible approach as the opportunities were mutually exclusive.

Carlos and Team C believed that as the impact of Wave I would be felt throughout Rank Xerox over a multiple-month roll out, the key to successful implementation would be close monitoring of the process. During implementation, Team C's core group of 10 people dedicated 30% to 40% of their time to traveling to the CBUs for two-day visits to explain the best practices. Carlos was a proponent of a 'champion' system whereby each Entity would dedicate one senior-level person outside Team C to monitor implementation. This would involve monthly progress meetings between the champion, a Team C steering committee, and managers and key people within the CBU. At the meeting, the CBU manager would present a monthly results report detailing the CBU's performance against a set of goals and benchmarks. A major positive side effect of these meetings was that Team C was able to develop a set of 'best practices' for the implementation of the Wave I best practices which could be quickly transmitted across all the other countries.

Success

Wave I proved to be relatively easy to implement despite the fact that some revenue growth opportunities were more challenging than others and that e Entity Champions only gave 50% of their time to the team. Fournier felt that Team C's approach was effective since it entailed each country receiving all information so that the reinvention of the wheel could be minimized. This led to the generation of superb documentation which was followed by the launch of Wave I, the results of which were immediately apparent: it yielded revenue improvements of US$100 million in the first year (1994). All the more impressive was the cost of Team C which was estimated to be about US$1 million.

Fournier was so impressed by Team C's performance that he rewarded team members with significant spot bonuses, dividing participants into three categories of involvement with the project, with the largest bonuses going to the biggest contributors. The two secretaries who dedicated themselves to planning Team C logistics and editing the Wave I books were rewarded at the highest level.

Team C's Wave II initiative

With the success of Wave I, Team C set its sights on a more challenging objective: defining overarching best practices for the company's core sales processes, specifically salesforce productivity and sales process management. Carlos and Team C felt that their efforts could be escalated to a more sophisticated level in Wave II.

Wave II was based upon the concept of best practice transfer and focused predominantly on salesforce productivity. At its core was the notion that a set of best practices – identified by the team from a number of countries – could be combined into a series of modules covering key activities in the Salesforce Management Activities Model. The best practice modules did not exist as a finite, discrete entity. Rather, elements of each existed in several units. Although Wave II would be more difficult to implement than Wave I, Team C felt the bottom line rewards of Wave II could triple those of its predecessor. The highly competitive environment in Europe and the lofty profit growth goals set by Xerox Corporation in Stamford added urgency to their new mission.

Team C knew that replicating the success of Wave I would not be easy. In concrete terms, implementing a comprehensive salesforce management process meant telling salespeople how to do almost every aspect of their job and, in many cases, dramatic changes in a salesperson's assumptions and behavior. For example, it was traditionally believed that the more time a salesperson spent on the road, the more contacts could be made and the more sales closed. By that logic, salespeople should spend as little time as possible in the office and as much time as possible out making contacts. However, the analysis of best practices by Team C showed that salespeople in the best-performing offices spent more time in the office preparing intelligently for their field trips and optimizing the choice of prospects and the timing of visits. Since Rank Xerox was historically a sales-focused company with 5,000 'experts' devoted to the sales process, considerable effort would be needed to change their behavior. Also, in Wave II Team C would be losing one of its strongest proponents from Wave I – the benchmark CBUs.

Generating a new set of opportunities

In practical terms, Wave II differed most from Wave I in that it was a theoretical laboratory model that was a composite of little pieces of information from best practices identified across many countries. Team C sought to develop a model that would optimize salesforce management and all salesforce activities. Specifically, it aimed to identify optimal sales behaviors that were spread randomly (and sometimes deceptively) throughout the CBUs and devise a model that, in essence, would define new action plans for each aspect of the Rank Xerox sales process: territory planning, field salesforce activity management, market engagement programs, lead generation, product training, sales pay and incentive plans. A unique software module would be developed for each of these aspects linked to a market database containing schedules, performance figures, leads, contacts, and other information from all the CBUs. Salespeople would each have a portable computer to access the database at any time. Additionally, managers would be able to track salesperson activity at all times.

Tim Spooner, who was in charge of formulating the Wave II model, describes the generation of the idea as follows:

> We started with data. We sought out the CBUs which were performing best in areas like revenue growth and coverage-to-buy ratios. We then visited those countries and simply sat around for a while, talking with salespeople and watching what they were doing. It was key for us to dig below the sometimes rather slick surface to determine what was really going on. A lot of best practices are hidden, and many of the countries weren't exactly aware of what they are doing right and wrong. The danger we faced was that we would hone in on only the best-performing countries and assume that everything they did was the best thing. It was important that we look at all countries. Actually, the worst-performing countries played an important role in our analysis: we used them to confirm that certain practices were certainly not best. Over time, we did find that most of the 'building blocks' we ended up incorporating into our final model could be found in the best-performing countries, although they were never fully in place.

Implementation

Once Team C had generated its Wave II model and again produced a set of implementation books, it was time to return to the CBUs to put the model into action. But Team C faced several barriers to implementation: a lack of urgency on the part of the CBUs and additional complications. The CBUs' response was very different second time around and there was no urgency for change. Team C knew that getting mass buy-in to a revolutionary plan would be difficult when so many people had the attitude 'We had an excellent 1994 ... outperforming Xerox US, so why make changes? There is no crisis.'

In effect, Team C's ability to convince CBU personnel of the need for further change via Wave II was confounded by the resounding success of Wave I. Additionally, because Wave II was based on a laboratory model, Team C did not have voluminous data to support their cause. In fact, they had no directly applicable data. Neither did they have the help of the benchmark CBUs. For Carlos and Team C, the key to successful implementation for Wave II was somewhere between a rock and a hard place. They also knew that it represented fundamental change for the Rank Xerox environment – a shift from 100% salesforce empowerment to strong process management – and that all players in the implementation would need to be on the same page from day one.

Team C felt that the complexity of implementation highlighted the need for strong leadership and not only from both the Team C doers and top managers: Wave II would require full-time Entity Champions. Unfortunately, just as implementation was gearing up, Team C learned that Fournier and top managers were unwilling to appoint full-time Wave II Entity Champions.

Adding to the complexity of implementation was the timeline aspect of Wave II. Adoption of the various modules had to follow a tight schedule and the software modules had to be installed sequentially. This meant it was much more challenging to implement than Wave I, which had no such constraints since each of its nine revenue opportunities could be implemented separately in any order.

Another complicating factor was the computer hardware and software required for Wave II. First, it injected a group of outside players (computer consultants and technicians) into the process. Second, because it relied more heavily on technology than its predecessor and required greater technological skills from participants, it underscored differences in technical aptitude across the CBUs. Further, a keystone to the Wave II model was the market database software which depended on all databases being at a standard level of quality. Although each CBU had maintained its own database for many years, data quality varied tremendously across countries. Carlos and his team worried about these technology barriers and feared that the less computer adept Southern Europeans would have more difficulty meeting Wave II's strict software/database management demands than the computer savvy Central and Northern Europeans.

The fact that the Wave II initiatives were more process-oriented than the simpler Wave I initiatives highlighted one of the major differences among Rank Xerox CBUs. Although Rank Xerox had a long history as a multinational company successfully operating across the diverse cultures of Europe, Carlos was concerned that while the English, for example, would find comfort in the rigid structure of Wave II's implementation, the Italians and Spanish would hate it. Rank Xerox had long fostered an open and democratic culture in which everyone was encouraged to generate ideas, and he feared a mass rejection since a company-wide program for reinventing everyone's job could evoke some very negative emotions.

Waiting for results

Six months into the implementation of Wave II, no more than 10% of salespeople were using the new software. Team C had run into an empowerment conflict with the CBUs since no one wanted to surrender control of the sales process. Revenue improvements associated with Wave II were negligible in comparison with those of its predecessor. Team C was left wondering what had gone wrong and how it could be successfully re-implemented in the future. Sitting in the lobby of Fournier's office, Carlos compared Waves I and II and contemplated the reasons for the latter's unsuccessful implementation.

Exhibit 1 Team C results

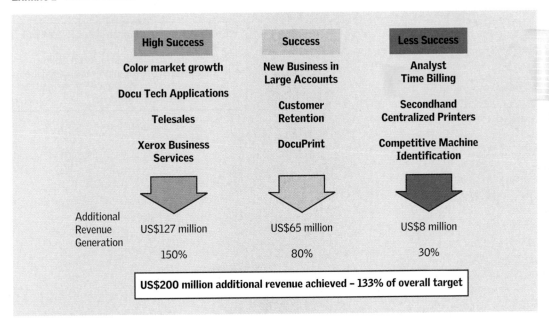

Source: Rank Xerox.

Exhibit 2 Assessments of Team C, Wave I implementation

	UK Jan 95	GERMANY Sept 95	SWITZ Dec 95	AUSTRIA Jun 95	SPAIN Nov 95	NORDIC Sept 95
MajestiK	3	4	4	4	4	4
Customer Retention	3	4	4	4	4	3
Docutech	4	3	4	4	4	4
DocuPrint	3	3	4	4	3	4
New Business Major Accounts	5	-	3	4	5	2
Compet MIF	3	4	2	4	3	3
Analyst Time Billing	3	4	5	3	4	3
Second Hand CEP	4	5	5	1	4	5
XBS	5	5	3	5	4	3

> Validation of Implementation status (1–5 rating)
> 1 = Not implemented
> 2 = Planned implementation in next 3 months
> 3 = Implemented / major improvements required
> 4 = Implemented / minor improvements required
> 5 = Best practice implemented

Source: Rank Xerox Policy Committee 24–26 January 1996.

Exhibit 3 Database-driven marketing and sales processes

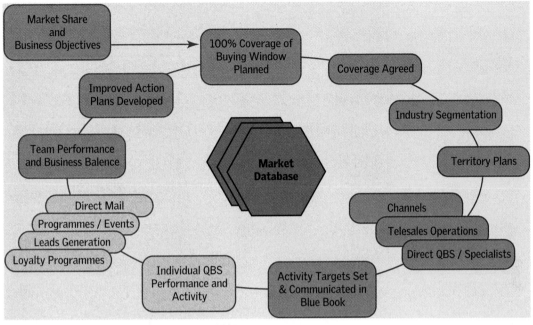

Source: Rank Xerox Policy Committee 24–26 January 1996.

Exhibit 4 Best practice transfer overview

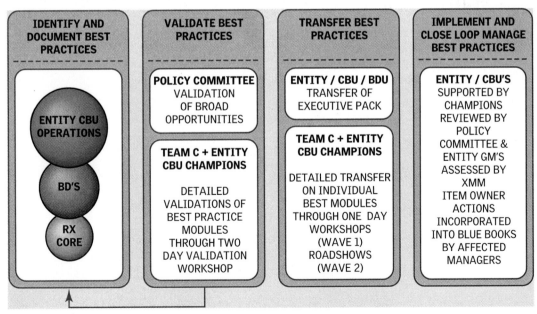

Source: Rank Xerox.

Exhibit 5 Best practice transfer key success factors (sample)

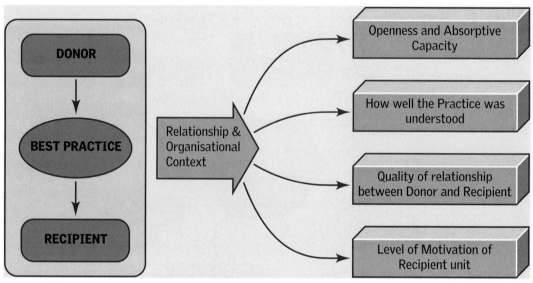

Source: Rank Xerox

INSEAD

Rank Xerox (B): Is 'telemarketing' the answer?

This case received the 2003 European Foundation for Management Development Case of the Year Award in the category 'Knowledge Management and Learning in Organisations'

It was mid-1995 and Carlos Camarero, leader of Rank Xerox's Team C, was not pleased. Having led Wave I to achieve remarkable revenue improvements (over US$100 million in incremental revenue in 1994) by identifying, documenting and disseminating best practices associated with discrete sales processes and the marketing of specific products, his subsequent project, Wave II, was faltering.

Carlos and Team C had set a more challenging objective for Wave II: defining overarching best practices for the company's core sales processes, specifically salesforce productivity and sales process management. But it was producing only lackluster results – for example, sales coverage (the key metric) had remained static.

Carlos asked Bernard Fournier, Rank Xerox's Managing Director, if they could change the approach to implementing Wave II and try again, but the request was rejected: 'Forget it. I'm not going to put my name on something that is never

....

This case was written by Michael Casaburi, Wharton MBA 1998 and Doctoral Student at Wharton under the supervision of Gabriel Szulanski, Associate Professor of Strategy at INSEAD. The case is intended to be used as a basis for class discussion rather than to illustrate either effective or ineffective handling of an administrative situation.

Copyright © 2004 INSEAD, Singapore.

06/2004-5138

going to fly.' Instead, Fournier said that he would like him to investigate something else.

In the early 1990s, in the search for revenue generating opportunities, Fournier had visited various Rank Xerox offices. What struck him was that in Colombia and Dubai (United Arab Emirates) salespeople contacted and interacted with customers primarily by telephone rather than through face-to-face contact. (Dubai called this process 'telemarketing', although the processes involved were very different from those commonly associated with the term.) Contrary to the approach used in Europe, telephone selling was used extensively in these locations because salespeople preferred to be indoors – in Colombia to avoid the risk of being shot while driving, and in Dubai to avoid the heat (typical temperatures exceeded 44°C). During his visits to Colombia and Dubai, local managers made presentations that showed substantially better sales productivity than Fournier had seen in Europe.

Fournier asked Carlos to visit Colombia and Dubai to see first-hand how telemarketing worked and determine whether it was of potential interest for adoption at other Rank Xerox offices. Carlos thought such a trip would be a 'waste of time' – telemarketing intuitively did not make sense, customers needed face-to-face contact before they purchased a copier. Neither Rank Xerox nor its competitors used the telephone in such a way in Europe. Even if Colombia and Dubai had great success with telephone sales, they might simply be special cases because of their small size and unique circumstances.

But given the apparent impending failure of Wave II, Fournier's rejection of his request to re-implement Wave II, and the state of sales operations, Carlos thought he had little to lose by visiting Colombia and Dubai and had his flights booked.

Rank Xerox's sales operations were not performing well. It had less than 30% coverage of buying window decisions; 40% of its customers at risk were not contacted in the six months before the loss of the business to a competitor; and sales costs, which were already high, were rising.

Surprise in Colombia

When Carlos arrived in Colombia, the performance of the operations there appeared, on the face of it, to be astounding: sales were reported by local management to be growing at 40% annually with a 70% profit margin. But he soon learned that all was not as it appeared, as he explained:

> The general manager [in Colombia] made a beautiful presentation, but I couldn't believe it. I developed a huge curiosity to know what it [the truth] was. I couldn't sleep that night. ... In the morning I said to myself, 'If I ask about the details they are not going to tell me.' So what I did was go back and say, 'I would like to talk to someone about commissions and remuneration of the salesforce ...' They looked at me very strangely. Here comes this big guy from Europe to talk to the secretary ... What happened was that I got into the office of that young lady and she started to explain to me what was really going on: the [dollar value of the] revenue and profit [being reported] were correct but they came from different sources [e.g., selling paper to customers] and not from selling Xerox copiers!

What Carlos could see, however, was that Colombia had an excellent operation selling small equipment and other items over the telephone. Salespeople closed deals over the telephone without face-to-face contact with customers. Even with his concern that the products being sold were not what he (or probably anyone else at Xerox outside of Colombia) expected, the telephone operation was intriguing:

> I came back [from Colombia] and said, 'Somehow this looks bloody good.' At the time I was not able to understand the [potential] power of that process. But instinctively you could see that this could be something special.

Carlos's next stop was Dubai.

'Little' Dubai

Compared with the major European countries where Rank Xerox did most of its business, Dubai is very small. A city of approximately 700,000 people, it is the second largest city (after the capital Abu Dhabi) in a country of about two million people with a GDP of US$132 billion (1993). The country's geography is extensive and there are a limited number of geographic concentrations of businesses. Rank Xerox's Dubai location had close to US$5 million in revenue in 1994, compared to approximately US$5 billion for the company overall.

Carlos watched the salesforce in action and interviewed people at all levels of the organization (from clerks to the general manager). He found that Dubai had been using telemarketing since April 1993. Unlike Colombia, he uncovered no surprises as to what was being sold.

Telemarketing originated from the desire of the salesforce to escape the harsh climate. At one point, sales managers in Dubai decided to minimize the frequency of salespeople using the telephone to solicit and transact business because they wanted them to meet customers face-to-face (which they thought was a more effective sales approach). The sales managers set a goal that each salesperson make six face-to-face sales calls per day (given the area's geographic expanse this entailed a lot of traveling). The salesforce protested and as a 'capitulation solution' management agreed to let them stay in the office if they made 40 telephone calls daily with no requirement to make a daily face-to-face sales call.

'Telemarketing' was in some ways a misnomer: while salespeople conducted most of their activities over the telephone (e.g., interviewing potential customers), they still visited customers periodically in-person as required (e.g., to provide demonstrations or to close the transaction). Carlos explained:

> Eventually, there is a big deal [opportunity] available [to bid on] ... [W]hen it is the right time, they go [to the customer or potential customer] for a face-to-face meeting and not before then.

The key objectives of telemarketing were to maximize coverage (i.e., the percentage of buying decisions that Rank Xerox bid on), improve sales productivity and controls, conduct accurate sales analysis, and improve the prospect and customer database.

Increasing coverage was critical because the more buying decisions that Rank Xerox was aware of, the more opportunities it had to bid, and thus the greater the number of contracts it would win. Knowing the timing of the contract bid window in advance was therefore valuable. Using the telephone to call prospects (and existing Rank Xerox customers) to identify such timing was more efficient than setting up face-to-face meetings.

The concept that salespeople would be more productive, however, relied on more than increased coverage. Salespeople also needed better and more information about prospects and existing customers (through an improved database) and to have the hardware and software to fully leverage that data.

A critical part of telemarketing was the central database that was compiled from existing databases and by the salesforce through telephone calls. Using the telephone helped increase the quality of the database much faster than face-to-face visits, as Carlos observed:

The secret of their success was their [database] … because it is so easy and takes five minutes to make a telephone call. Physically you can do six [in person] visits a day, five are to customers. On the telephone you can make 40 calls a day to non-customers.

Sample information in the database included:

◆ Company name, location, telephone number, number of employees, etc.

◆ Identification of decision-making unit (DMU) (i.e., the part of a company that makes the decision as to which copier to purchase).

◆ Market segmentation data.

◆ Impression volume (e.g., of Rank Xerox and competitors).

◆ Contact history (e.g. when salesperson called a prospect and what transpired).

◆ Selling cycle tracking (e.g., date of demonstration, proposal, close, order, and implementation).

The salesforce had clear performance objectives. Sales managers could provide direction and control on a daily (sometimes hourly) basis and had to approve visits by salespeople to prospects or customers. Software measured performance on many of these objectives (e.g., number of calls, call duration, new contacts versus follow-up contacts, prospects, proposals, and orders) and provided managers with tailor-made reports regarding sales statistics, activity levels, and individual/group productivity.

While the technical staff in Dubai was still refining the telemarketing system, Dubai had performed very well on its objectives. For example, from August 1993 to February 1994, the number of companies (decision-making units) in the database had increased over 400% to about 12,000 and Dubai was making several thousand telemarketing phone calls per month.

Moreover, its sales productivity far outpaced that of other countries. In Europe, the average number of contacts-per-day and revenue-per-salesperson were six contacts and US$300,000, whereas in Dubai it was 40 contacts and US$1.2 million respectively (after adjusting revenues for the small size of the Dubai market).

On the return flight, Carlos was elated about the possibilities that telemarketing offered. But would it work outside of Dubai? He knew he had to get the opinion of Ricardo Morias, an expert in relational database management who was well respected within Rank Xerox for his ability to bridge the technical and practical domains. Ricardo had worked with Carlos on a variety of projects (often without additional pay on top of a significant amount of other work) and he trusted Ricardo's judgment regarding practical business issues as much as on technical issues, as he recalled:

[Telemarketing would need to be] translated to our culture, our language, our physical and graphic life, and the only person that could do that was him … I knew that if he [Ricardo] bought [into] the concept, he had the technical capabilities to put that in a package [that would be extremely valuable].

When I came back from Dubai, I said to Ricardo, 'I've found something shocking.' He asked me, 'What have you found?' and I don't remember what I said but Ricardo said, 'You must be joking!' because, at the time, everyone reacted like that. So, I said, 'Go to Dubai and take a look. Take a plane and go there.' … So he went to Dubai, and I thought, 'Oh geez, let's see if Ricardo likes it or doesn't like it, because if he doesn't like it, we'll start again.

Ricardo was thinking in similar terms:

Carlos came to me and told me about Dubai. At that time I was working on a project [for Rank

*Xerox's International Region] looking into poten-
tial software systems we could us ... It matched
perfectly for me to go to Dubai as I wanted to
see what they had and what could be done
with it.*

Dubai revisited

Ricardo's mission was to understand telemarketing
and assess its value for use in other parts of Rank
Xerox. He was concerned that it would not be possible to sell large copiers over the telephone and
wanted to see how Dubai handled such orders.

During the visit, Ricardo was impressed:

*... I was impressed even though their operation
was on a small scale. I saw myself how they sold
through the telephone ... [The] supervisors
showed me information that they had available
by pointing to a [computer] screen and saying
'Look what this guy [salesperson] is doing now
... in the morning he made five contacts ... he is
not doing much now, I am going to have to see
him later.' I was shocked. ... We had spent
US$140 million in the [United] States on soft-
ware development by X [an outside consultant]
and we did not have a clue how to collect information automatically.*

Ricardo found that the telemarketing operations
covered clients of all sizes, from major accounts to
other commercial customers, and included selling
large and smaller copiers.

Telemarketing was a primitive technical system
that Ricardo thought was appropriate for Dubai's
environment. For example, the database had limited
fields for a prospect company's address because
there were no street names in many parts of Dubai.

But he instantly realized that without the
'TeleMagic' software that was the glue holding it
together, there 'would be no telemarketing'. Key
elements regarding database management,
reporting and record keeping were embedded in
TeleMagic, which was the most recent public version
available and was based on the Disk Operating
System (DOS).

To help salespeople fully leverage the power of the
database, TeleMagic put the following productivity
tools at their fingertips:

- Automatic telephone number dialing and tele-
  phone call logging (including call length).
- Electronic diary (controlling appointments and
  meeting scheduling).
- Automatic reminders (e.g., to tell a salesperson
  to call a particular prospect on a given day).
- Mail merge and email.
- Sales quotation and proposal generation models.
- Territory planning.

Each salesperson had a computer and a modem that
was set up in the office and connected to a network.
Salespeople were fully dependent on the workstation, software, database, and telephone/facsimile –
there was no need for 'pen and paper' or secretarial
support.

Ricardo saw a lot of potential in applying telemarketing elsewhere. But he rejected the idea of using
Dubai's version of TeleMagic because as a DOS
program it was outdated. It would need to be available in a Microsoft Windows environment for him to
even attempt to upgrade the software for different
and larger environments (e.g., European operations).

As part of his investigation for Rank Xerox's
International Region, Ricardo had spoken with staff
at the company that sold TeleMagic about potentially purchasing the software. He later found out
that if he were to proceed with upgrading telemarketing, they would provide him with a Windows
version of TeleMagic and all the other things he
needed to customize the software (e.g., Windows
Professional version, hooks, etc.) along with full
information and technical support to assist his
efforts. As he explained:

*Dubai was using something [TeleMagic] that I
knew there was a new version of ... they had
never heard [about]. If I could not get the
Windows version, I would not consider creating
a new package for telemarketing.*

Ricardo came back from Dubai ready to get the ball
rolling on improving telemarketing for use system-
wide in Rank Xerox, as Carlos explained:

*Ricardo came back saying, 'Excellent!' Already in
the plane he was creating out of that [Dubai's]
package a package that was one-hundred*

times better, which was what I knew he was going to do. And, he came like a lion, saying '... I can do it one hundred times better!'

Outside of Dubai

Sales operations in Europe differed from those within Dubai in many ways.

First, no competitor in Europe was using telephone sales to sell copiers. Moreover, while Dubai sold copiers of many sizes via telemarketing, it was unclear whether customers elsewhere would buy copiers, particularly large ones, with such heavy dependence on the telephone by the vendor.

Second, Rank Xerox had a 'marketing buccaneer' culture. The salesforce was used to making decisions independently (e.g., who to approach and how to sell to them) with little management control. The existing approach was to focus on generating revenue by spending as much time on the road (seeing people face-to-face) and as little time in the office as possible. Because salesforce bonuses were based on performance (i.e., revenue generated) and not activity (e.g., prospects contacted), salespeople put greater priority on obtaining signed orders than

on making contact with non-customers to generate leads.

Third, salespeople outside of Dubai had not used computers in the selling process in any substantial way – they were used to pen and paper and secretarial support.

Clearly, considerable effort would be needed to change their behavior, as Carlos noted:

Cultural traditions and history [at Rank Xerox] are as tough as granite ... To change the behavior of salespeople is impossible.

Next move

As he sat in his office, Carlos was still trying to recover from Wave II's waning performance. He was buoyed, however, by the thought of what he had seen in Dubai and how excited Ricardo was about upgrading and implementing telemarketing.

It was now time to decide: should he tell Fournier that he had found a revolutionary tool that would transform Rank Xerox's sales operations, or should he put the whole idea aside and not share the secrets of Dubai?

Exhibit 1 Dubai revenues (1992 to 1994)

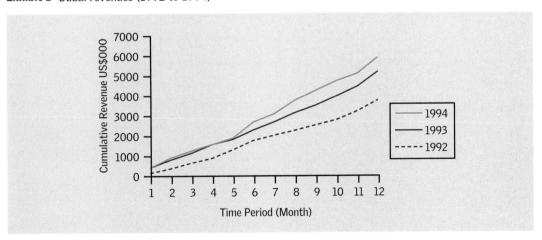

Source: Rank Xerox Order Tracker (Sales).

Exhibit 2 Dubai telemarketing activity (1993 to late 1995)

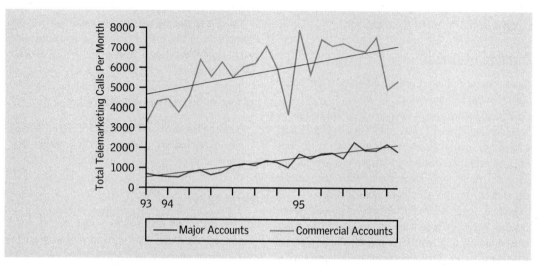

Source: Rank Xerox TeleMagic (Marketing).

INSEAD

Rank Xerox (C): The success of telesales

This case received the 2003 European Foundation for Management Development Case of the Year Award in the category 'Knowledge Management and Learning in Organisations'

It was 1997 and Carlos Camarero was a happy man. His last initiative leading Team C, Telesales, was a resounding success. Within the first six weeks of launch, over 2,000 TeleMagic licenses were sold within Rank Xerox. Within a year, Telesales had been fully implemented in 19 countries (all 15 major Rank Xerox European countries as well as Turkey, Hungary, the Czech Republic, and Morocco) and average sales coverage had increased by 11% over 1995 levels with some units increasing by as much as 30%. The Chairman's Statement in Rank Xerox's 1996 Annual Report noted that Telesales helped improve coverage (i.e., percentage of copier buying decisions that Rank Xerox bid on) and increase market share. Its success was lasting. Over the next two years, direct sales productivity (annual per person revenue) had risen from US$385,000 to US$481,000.

'Telesales' was Carlos's retitled version of 'Telemarketing'. He saw Telemarketing in action first-hand when he visited Rank Xerox's Dubai, United Arab Emirates location. Telemarketing involved increased use of the telephone by sales-people to capture information from prospects and customers to increase coverage and improve sales-force productivity. Carlos described and marketed it as 'Telesales' because it sounded more impressive (which was important when trying to get people at all levels of the organization buy in to the approach). After he had visited Dubai, Carlos obtained approval from senior management to pilot, and ultimately broadly implement Telesales. Telesales was piloted outside of Dubai in 1995 and was launched broadly among Rank Xerox's European offices in 1996.

The Telesales concept was originally a small piece of the Wave I initiative. Hardly anyone, even Carlos, the Team C leader, had noticed at that time or several years later that Telesales was technically part of Wave I. Telesales was presented in 1995 as another module to Wave II, which was struggling at that time. There was such an enormous acceptance of Telesales that Wave II was ultimately declared dead and Team C focused on Telesales.

Carlos, however, was surprised at Telesales' success. He recalled that at a senior committee meeting to gain approval to pilot Telesales, people were asking 'Where is Dubai?' Some executives even scoffed at the idea of attempting to spread a practice from such a small country. When Carlos told Bernard Fournier, Rank Xerox's Managing Director, of the Telesales plan he was impressed but wondered who was going to pay for it. When Carlos told him that Ricardo Morias, a relational database expert within Rank Xerox, was going to do this as a voluntary service (without extra pay) during the night (while working on other responsibilities during the day), Fournier laughed but gave the approval to proceed. Under such circumstances, Carlos wondered how Telesales had become so successful.

Telesales development and pilots

Carlos's objective to implement Telesales in European countries was to restore the momentum lost in Wave II. Following Team C methodology (as used in Wave I and Wave II), Carlos and his team extracted the key elements of the Dubai practice. They then put together a 40 page booklet similar to those used in Wave I detailing the extraordinary performance of Dubai, describing the key factors of the Telesales practice, and explaining how to implement it.

The management in Dubai had embedded the key elements having to do with database management, reporting, and record keeping in a piece of DOS software entitled 'TeleMagic'. Ricardo purchased an upgrade to TeleMagic which operated in a Microsoft Windows environment and then changed the coding in the software so that the language identifying the various fields matched the daily language of Rank Xerox exactly (the company selling TeleMagic gave Rank Xerox the rights to modify the software). Ricardo developed computer screens that were easy to read and easy to use. Ricardo also increased the reporting capabilities of the software and connected it to headquarters' central computers. As Carlos summarized:

> We decided to buy the best package in the market [TeleMagic] and modify and link it to our database. Ricardo Morias did that ... He did a beautiful job. It took him two months. He [worked with] a company in Portugal and for US$50,000, we developed the most amazing piece of sales software ... it basically fills the database and helps salespeople try to get 100% coverage of buying windows by using industry segmentation and territory planning, organizing activity targets, and monitoring of activities (not performance) ...

Telesales was initially implemented in late 1995 in Europe in a series of pilots beginning in Lisbon and later in Birmingham, Lyon, Brussels, and Madrid. To persuade the managers of these units to undertake the initiative, Carlos not only shared with them data proving the superior performance of Dubai but he also flew them to Dubai personally to observe the operations. This approach was effective. As Carlos described:

> It was an opportunistic exercise where theory turned into practice. It allowed potential recipients to see, eat, chew and touch the practice. It was seeing with their eyes that 2+2=4, not just being told.

The Telesales practice is considerably larger and more complex than those transferred in Wave I and implementation was not as smooth as originally anticipated. It took a number of months for the pilots to begin to reproduce the superior results found at Dubai along with a number of iterations back to Dubai to answer questions that were originally unforeseen.

For example, after implementation had been under way in Lisbon for a couple of months they discovered that they didn't know how to operate Telesales for salespeople responsible for Key Accounts, accounts with major corporations. Calling such corporations on the phone to sell copiers did not at first sound like an intelligent idea. However, Carlos went back to Dubai to observe what they did. In Dubai, those responsible for Key Accounts used the telephone as much or more than those responsible for smaller firms because the units of large corporations often buy separately and are headed by people who are too busy for numerous personal visits.

Telesales roll-out

Once the pilot units were operational they were designated as benchmarks for the rest of the corporation. As he had in persuading the pilots, Carlos brought dozens and dozens of managers to the pilot in Lisbon to personally observe the operations in an explicit attempt to increase the motivation to adopt the new practice. The managers who visited Dubai were impressed by the potential opportunity they saw in implementing Telesales in their countries. As Carlos explained:

> It was a cosmic exercise, of almost insulting simplicity. We found out that [in Europe] our salespeople were averaging ten customer visits a day, but only one of them was effective. This way (i.e., using Telesales) they could rapidly complete the effective transaction and had plenty of time left to average 2.5 effective transactions per day, thus doubling their productivity.

In rolling out Telesales, Team C offered a complete package. It was like many franchise operations, according to Ricardo, in that all the necessary elements were pulled together and were easy to follow. Team C integrated the equipment, space, facilities, and network requirements and provided training and support. As Ricardo recalled, 'We even told them how to organize the workspace with the new computers in the office'. Carlos and his team did not publicize the control aspects of the software, which allowed sales managers to closely monitor salepersons' behavior (even by the minute).

Salespeople saw the benefits of using Telesales. As Ricardo explained:

Sales people did not like having to write up their activities (e.g., who they called and when) and the software was viewed as great because the computer was now doing this for them ... The solution is simple. You contact 24 customers instead of 6 customers. People thought, 'I'll buy it' ... it was a magic box.

Salespeople also accepted the introduction of computers (and the attendant requirement to populate the database with data) because the Internet age was emerging and it was seen as being 'high tech'. As Carlos noted:

The computer was fashionable as it was the time of the Internet explosion ... we did not have to explain to them that they would fill in [populate] the database ... we said 'This is state of the art technology and we are helping you' ... it was sexy and fashionable and we did not need to convince them with data [that they should use Telesales].

Looking back

As Carlos reflected on his work with Team C, he tried to piece together what lessons could be learned. Why was Telesales successful? Would Telesales have worked independent of the initial attempt to implement Wave II? Was Telesales Wave II reborn? What were the factors that made Wave I and Telesales successful but Wave II unsuccessful? What could others learn from his experience?

Exhibit 1 Telesales performance

	1995	1996 (Jan – Oct)	1997 (Jan – Oct)	% Difference
Level of Implementation	Pilots in Nine Countries	Jan: 49/59 subunits July: 58/59 subunits	Fully implemented in all countries and all but one of 59 subunits	
Revenue attributable directly to Telesales		US$42 million (US$60 million in all of 1996)	US$47 million	11.9%
Revenue per Teleseller		US$180,000	US$220,140	22.3%
Orders per Teleseller		33	43	29.2%
Boxes per Operator		3.2	4.1	28.5%

Source: Rank Xerox documents.

Exhibit 2 Wave I, Wave II, and telesales metrics

	Pre Wave I (1993)	Post Wave I /Pre Wave II (1994)	Post Wave II /Pre Telesales (1995)	Post Telesales (1996)	Telesales Lagged (1997)
Mean Sales Coverage	Not available	29.14	29.14	32.36	33.11
Mean Direct Sales Revenue/sales person ($US 000)	368	400	385	Not Available	481
Mean Ratio of gross profit to selling expenses	Not available	1.06	1.19	Not Available	2.02

Note: 1995 sales coverage data is available only by geographic region (Northern, Southern, and Central) except for the three largest countries (Germany, France, and the U.K) for a total sample size of seven.
Source: Rank Xerox documents.

Ivey

Richard Ivey School of Business

The University of Western Ontario

Case 12 Cola wars in China: The future is here

On July 7, 2002, Zong Qinghou, the general manager of the Wahaha Group (Wahaha), China's largest soft drink producer, was reviewing market data on Wahaha's Future Cola brand in his office in Hangzhou, Zhejiang Province. Wahaha Future Cola had been launched four years earlier to compete with products from Coca Cola and PepsiCo, the dominant players in the category. At the launch, Zong and his management team had been

tremendously energized by the opportunity to compete with some of the world's best companies. Four years later, despite the failure of several other domestic colas, Wahaha Future Cola and other Future Series carbonated drinks had achieved an impressive 18 per cent of the carbonated drinks market in the first half of 2002. However, as Future Cola's share grew, Zong was preoccupied with how his multinational competitors would respond, how Wahaha should prepare for these responses, and how it should continue to increase its market share. Competition for share in the high-stakes market of the world's most populated country was intensifying.

Wahaha group

Company profile

With 2001 sales revenue of RMB6.23 billion, and profits of RMB914 million,[1] the Wahaha Hangzhou Group Co. Ltd. consisted of more than 40 wholly-owned subsidiaries and majority holding companies in 23 provinces, autonomous regions and cities. With total assets of RMB6 billion and 14,000 employees, the group operated more than 68 advanced automated production lines at various locations. Unlike many other Chinese companies of its size, the group had a solid cash position and no long-term bank debt. Wahaha's 2002 target was to achieve sales revenues of RMB8 billion, and a profit of RMB1.3 billion. In the longer term, the Wahaha Group aimed to become a truly national, and even international, player. Specifically, it was working on establishing subsidiaries in most provinces, maintaining its leading position in water, milk drinks and mixed congee, and on increasing its market share in carbonated beverages, tea and juice drinks.

In 2002, Wahaha competed in six major product categories: milk drinks, packaged water, carbonated drinks, tea and juice drinks, canned food and health-care products. For several years, its milk drink, packaged water and canned mixed congee had been leaders in their respective categories. For the first half of 2002, the total soft drink output for Wahaha was 1.83 million tons (1.66 billion litres), while its

---

[1] *An exchange rate of US$1 = RMB8.27 applied in 2002.*

closest competitors — Coca Cola and PepsiCo — sold 1.61 million tons (1.461 billion litres) and 0.76 million tons (0.689 billion litres), respectively. This was the first time that a domestic company's soft drink output had exceeded that of Coca Cola in China. It was also an unusual situation for Coca Cola that a local competitor had seemingly come out of nowhere to upstage the global giant. In a nation of 1.3 billion people, per capita consumption of Wahaha beverages in China was more than 10 bottles a year.

Wahaha's development

Wahaha was founded in 1987, when it began selling bottled soda water, ice cream and stationery to the children in Hangzhou, Zhejiang Province. Founder Zong Qinghou and two employees discovered in 1988 that although there were 38 companies nationwide producing nutritional drinks, none was specifically targeted toward children. The one-child policy had created a whole generation of 'little emperors' who, due to their parents' and grandparents' indulgences, were fastidious with food, and presented a potentially huge opportunity. By some estimates there were 200 million such children in China. The company developed a nutritious drink called the Wahaha Natrient Beverage for Children and aggressively pursued the children's market. (The brand Wahaha means 'to make children happy.') The product was supported with the slogan 'Drinking Wahaha boosts appetite.' The product was an instant success, propelling corporate revenues to RMB400 million and profits to RMB70 million by 1990.

Management quickly realized that it was not easy to sustain growth with a single product that had low entry barriers and low technical content. Competitors followed close on the heels of Wahaha. Between 1992 and 1994, 3,000 companies entered the market for children's beverages. Zong decided to expand the product range, entering the fruit-flavored milk drinks market. At the time, a couple of companies had already launched fruit-flavored milk drinks, and the product had won market acceptance. Zong felt this was the best time to enter. In what was to become a pattern in several product categories, Wahaha was a fast follower that quickly ramped up production and achieved high retail coverage with its nationwide production facilities, well-known brand,

and well-established distribution network. Its wide range of products made it competitive relative to other domestic producers who tended to have a narrow product line. By the end of 1991, Wahaha launched its fruit-flavored milk drink, followed quickly by Wahaha Milk enriched with vitamins A and D, and calcium. Its catchy advertising jingles rolled off the tongues of tots in many provinces. In 1996, amidst concerns over polluted tap water in several provinces, the company launched Wahaha purified water, which rapidly achieved leading market share, contributing to corporate sales revenues of over RMB1 billion in that year.

Wahaha's brand extensions had aroused much debate among industry observers who held that Wahaha was mainly a children's brand and extending it to categories such as mixed congee and purified water would either not work, or would dilute the brand. Zong, while admitting the advantages of launching different brands for different product categories, held that it would spread the limited financial resources of most Chinese enterprises too thin. Wahaha's logic had been to continue to extend the brand into food and beverage categories in which there was no dominant player. For consumers, the connotation of the Wahaha brand broadened and came to represent health, wholesomeness, happiness, quality and reliability, and not just a brand for children's nutritious drinks. Results from the market rewarded and justified Wahaha's approach. After a series of brand extensions, Wahaha's sales revenue exceeded RMB2 billion in 1997, and the revenue of Wahaha purified water and mixed congee exceeded RMB500 million and 100 million respectively. This was a rare achievement, even in China's rapidly growing food and beverage industry. In 1998, spurred by its success in other beverage categories, Wahaha decided to tackle the prize: the carbonated drinks market. Industry observers were skeptical and predicted that it would last no more than a few months on the market.

Corporate growth was powered not just by the launch of new products, but also through acquisitions, such as loss-making companies that were several times larger, but poorly managed. Acquisitions supported geographic expansion and allowed Wahaha to produce locally in various provincial markets, as well as to increase its market share and brand awareness in other provinces. By 2002, over a third of Wahaha's output was produced outside its home province.

Wahaha's joint ventures with Danone

In 1996, despite Wahaha's excellent performance, management realized that it needed to scale its operations quickly and obtain world-class production technology if it was to survive competition from both local and multinational competitors. After careful consideration, it chose to partner with the giant French food company, Groupe Danone. The two companies established several production-oriented joint ventures. While Danone eventually held a 51 per cent share of the joint ventures, Wahaha retained control of management and marketing. In 2002, among Wahaha Group's 42 companies and RMB3.5 billion registered capital, Danone's investment was 32 per cent. With the injection of capital from Danone, Wahaha launched Wahaha Future Cola and introduced advanced production lines for bottling water, milk and tea. Prior to the joint venture, the annual increase in revenues and profits was about RMB100 million and RMB10 million respectively. Since 1996, both revenue and profit had grown even more rapidly (see Exhibit 1).

Zong Qinghou's management style

Founder and general manager Zong Qinghou was a charismatic leader who liked to 'put his eggs in the baskets he knew best.' Like most of his generation of the Cultural Revolution, he spent 15 years in the countryside after finishing junior school. This experience taught him a lot about rural China. When he came back to his hometown, Hangzhou, he worked in a factory, first as a worker and then in sales. During this period, he traveled extensively throughout China, deepening his knowledge of markets and consumers in various regions. He was 42 when he began his career as sales manager of the two person sales team at the factory. His job included delivering goods to retailers on his cycle.

When asked what made Wahaha so successful, Zong responded that the company understood the Chinese market well:

Market research reports in China are not reliable. You pay the market research firms large amounts of money and you don't know where the money was spent. However, our own marketing people are our market research staff since we are always collecting information about the market, and we make decisions based on their understanding of the market.

Now in his late 50s, Zong worked long hours and still traveled more than 200 days every year 'to keep a finger on the pulse of the market.' He hosted most of the marketing meetings at Wahaha and participated in every product launch and marketing planning activity.

Wahaha's marketing

Marketing, research and development (R&D) and logistics management were centralized at headquarters, while the subsidiaries were engaged in production. Wahaha's marketing was clearly home-grown.

Wahaha's advertising

A typical new product launch followed a pattern established early on in Wahaha's history. In an early launch of Wahaha Natrient Beverage, Zong signed advertising deals worth several hundred thousand RMB with local television stations, exceeding even the company's cash reserves at the time. In its advertisement, Wahaha highlighted data from reports about children's malnutrition and endorsements from experts about Wahaha Natrient Beverage's nutritional benefits for children. On the strength of the advertising, Wahaha would convince the local government-controlled distribution companies to carry the product. If distributors hesitated, Wahaha's marketing staff would call every retailer and smaller distributor in the local yellow pages to inquire if they carried Wahaha Natrient Beverage. This created a buzz that usually resulted in the product being listed with the distribution companies.

In 2001, Wahaha was among the top 10 advertisers in China's US$11.2 billion advertising market, and the only beverage company in the group.[2] Wahaha's total advertising expenditures amounted

---

[2] 'China Market racks up largest ad spending in Asia-Pacific,' www1.chinadaily.com.cn/bw/2002–03–05/60571.html, March 12, 2002.

to more than RMB500 million, with media buys accounting for 80 per cent. Comparatively, Coca Cola's 2001 media expense in China (including cinema, TV, radio, print, and outdoor) was US$19 million. Wahaha's television advertising was mainly intended to build brand awareness and recognition, while print advertising elaborated on product benefits and promotions. Wahaha spent 75 per cent of its marketing budget on television advertising, and half of that was on CCTV Channel 1 (the national news channel). The remainder was spent on print media (five per cent), promotion (10 per cent) and outdoor advertising (10 per cent). Wahaha's advertising targeted the mass market, and not just the wealthier urban consumers. The prices of its products were usually lower than those of comparable products from its multinational competitors.

In addition to Wahaha's advertising, its sponsorship activities had helped build positive associations for its brand. Wahaha established Wahaha elementary school, Wahaha Children's Palace (a recreation center for children), Wahaha Children's Art Troupe and Wahaha Summer Camps to underscore its involvement in child development. In 2001, Wahaha held a campaign to celebrate Children's Day and Beijing's application to host the 2008 Summer Olympic Games.

Wahaha was also the first among Chinese companies to use celebrity product endorsement for its products. In 1996, Jinggangshan, a pop singer, was signed to endorse Wahaha purified water. Celebrity endorsement was also used for Wahaha Future Cola and Wahaha Tea series.

Wahaha's distribution

Key success factors for Wahaha were the unique relationships developed with distributors over the previous 10 years. In a vast country where logistics are notoriously difficult, Wahaha's network was able to quickly deliver its products, reaching even remote corners of China within days. Unlike many multinational and domestic companies which preferred to establish their own distribution networks, Wahaha focused on partnering with local distributors, and its initial promotional efforts on entry into a region included distributors rather than end-consumers alone.

Partnerships with local distributors were not without problems. In particular, accounts receivable and bad debts were a perennial headache and the main reason why multinationals shunned this mode of distribution. In 1994, Wahaha concluded that the problem of accounts receivable was serious enough to jeopardize its growth and success. The company tackled the issue head-on by developing a radical new policy that ensured compliance and on-time payment by introducing incentives for channel members to play for long-term gain: distributors were required to pay an annual security deposit in advance and operate according to Wahaha's payment policy. In return, Wahaha would pay a higher-than-bank interest rate on the security deposit and offered discounts for early payment. At the end of the year, bonuses were awarded to distributors making prompt payments. The policy was replicated down the chain as distributors, in turn, developed secondary wholesalers, some of whom enjoyed preferential policies by paying security deposits to the distributors. It took Wahaha two years to implement the policy. In the process, a number of distributors that had low credibility dropped out of the system. Those that remained were more committed than ever to Wahaha.

Wahaha established offices in more than 30 provinces with sales staff co-ordinating operations with the distributors. Distributors were in charge of carrying inventory, providing funds and delivering to the retailers, and Wahaha's local offices supported them in retail coverage, inventory management, advertising and promotion. Wahaha established coordination teams to monitor prices in different areas to protect the interests of local distributors. Wahaha's staff collected information from the market and provided feedback to headquarters, which enabled the company to adjust its sales strategy and develop new products. Today, Wahaha's 2,000 sales staff work closely with more than 1,000 influential distributors that have the credibility and infrastructure to sell large volumes. Loyalty and stability of the distributors are key, and bad debts have decreased substantially. In 2002, Wahaha began implementing an information system that would enable distributors and Wahaha to exchange information in real time.

The world soft-drink industry

The term 'soft drinks' refers to beverages that do not contain alcohol, and includes packaged water, carbonated drinks, juices and juice drinks, ready-to-drink tea, as well as sports and energy drinks.

In 2000, global soft drink consumption reached 320.2 billion litres. That total was split into 170 billion litres (53 per cent) of carbonated drinks, 77 billion litres (24 per cent) of packaged water, and the 'other' category which included juices, ready-to-drink tea, sports and energy drinks, and miscellaneous drinks accounting for 73.2 billion litres (23 per cent). Worldwide, the growth of carbonated drinks had been slowing in recent years from an average annual rate of four per cent between 1994 and 2000 to a predicted rate of only two per cent in 2003 (see **Exhibit 2**). These numbers masked fast growth in countries such as China and India, which compensated for declines in the more mature markets of North America and Europe. Packaged water was growing worldwide, in some markets due to consumer trends toward a healthier lifestyle, and in others due to the poor quality of tap water. The 'other' category had great growth potential due to increased demand for more healthy, nutritious and tasty drinks. The size of this category had rapidly grown from 52.7 billion litres in 1994 to 73.2 billion litres in 2000. By 2003 volumes were forecast to reach 85.6 billion litres. Within this category, 'ready-to-drink tea' had had the fastest growth since 1994, with an annual increase of over 11 per cent and industry observers believed it still had plenty of untapped potential.

The players in China

The leading soft drink producers in the world included Coca Cola, PepsiCo, Nestlé and Danone, and all four were also present in China. Globally, the first two were dominant in the carbonated category with more than 70 per cent combined market share, while the latter two were strong in the ready-to-drink tea and water categories.

Coca Cola Coca Cola was the world's largest soft-drink company, and the fifth-largest food and beverage company. Its 2001 revenues were US$20.092 billion, with a net income of US$3.969 billion. The firm sold about 300 drink brands, including coffees, juices, sports drinks and teas in 200 nations. Its major brands included Coca Cola Classic, Diet Coke, Sprite, Fanta (carbonated drinks), Minute Maid (juice), POWERade (sports drink) and Dasani (water). It distributed Danone's Evian water in North America and Danone's spring water brands in the United States. Beverage Partner Worldwide, its joint venture with Nestlé, S.A., marketed ready-to-drink coffee and tea. More than 60 per cent of its sales revenues came from outside the United States. Coca Cola's stated aim was to become an all-around beverage company. In 2001, water was the second largest contributor to its growth after carbonated drinks. Coca Cola had recently instituted a 'think local, act local, but leverage global' mandate to empower local decision-makers, in recognition of the need to both respond to local preferences and react to local competitors. In response, its local subsidiaries had launched a wide variety of drinks aimed at local needs.

Coca Cola first opened bottling plants in Shanghai and Tianjin in 1927, which were shut after the communist revolution in 1949. In 1979, when Coca Cola re-entered China, following the re-establishment of relations between China and the United States, it became the first American consumer product to return to China. In 2000, it moved its marketing headquarters for China from Hong Kong to Shanghai. By 2002, Coca Cola had a total of 28 bottling plants in China, with a total investment of US$1.1 billion. In most of these joint ventures, Coca Cola didn't have majority shareholding. Its soft-drink output in China was 16 per cent of the national total in 2001 and its carbonated drink output was about 35 per cent of total carbonated drink output. China was the sixth largest market for the company worldwide. In addition to its global carbonated drink brands such as Coca Cola, Diet Coke, Fanta and Sprite, the company also developed local brands such as Heaven and Earth (non-carbonated fruit juice, tea, water), Jinmeile (tea), Smart (fruit-flavored carbonated drink), Lanfeng (honey green tea) and Qoo (juice drink). In 2001, it launched its water brand 'Sensation' (at the remarkably low wholesale price point of RMB0.50, while the market leader Wahaha water was selling at RMB0.90). In its advertising, the company included Chinese cultural icons such as windmills and dragons. Local film and sports stars were engaged as endorsers, including diver Fu Mingxia, the three-time Olympic gold medalist. It also sponsored the Coca Cola Cup National Youth Soccer Tournament and the China national soccer teams at all levels. Coca Cola also extended its sponsorship contracts with the International Olympic Committee up to 2008, which included US$1 billion in funding for the Beijing Games. In 2001, the total revenue for Coca Cola China was about US$189 million and revenue from carbonated drinks was about US$186 million. However, the annual per capita consumption of Coca Cola products in China was a meager eight servings (about 0.2268 litre per serving). Consumption was still a far cry from the average 415 servings consumed in the United States, 163 in Japan, 98 in Europe and 68 in South Korea.

PepsiCo After the merger with Quaker in 2001, PepsiCo became the fourth-largest food and beverage company in the world. Its 2001 total sales revenue of US$26.935 billion included beverage revenue and profit of US$10.44 billion and US$1.678 billion respectively. Forty-two per cent of its sales were outside the United States. Its powerful soft drink brands included Pepsi-Cola, Diet Pepsi, Mountain Dew, 7Up, Miranda, Gatorade (sports drink), Tropicana (juice), Lipton teas and Aquafina (water).

In 1981, PepsiCo signed a deal with the Chinese government to establish a joint-venture bottling plant in Shenzhen. By 2002, the company had invested a total of US$500 million in China on 14 bottling plants and employed close to 10,000 people. Unlike Coca Cola, PepsiCo sought a majority share in the joint ventures. Its flagship carbonated drink brands in China were Pepsi-Cola, Pepsi Light, Pepsi Twist, 7Up, Miranda and Mountain Dew. It also owned local brands such as Asia, Arctic and Tianfu. Its non-carbonated drink brands in China included Gatorade and Dole (fruit juice). Its non-beverage brands included Lay's potato chips, Doritos and Cheetos. Its soft-drink output in China was about eight per cent of the national total in 2001. According to A.C. Nielsen's market data in Asia, Pepsi-Cola was the most popular soft drink brand for young consumers, a reflection of its positioning for that

demographic market. In its advertising in China, PepsiCo used popular entertainers such as Faye Wang, Guo Fuchen and Chen Huiling as endorsers. Despite its marketing efforts and popularity among China's youth, PepsiCo China had not been profitable during its 20 years in China: high marketing costs and conflicts with joint venture partners were holding the company back.[3]

Nestlé S.A. With revenues of CHF84.698 billion[4] (approximately US$56 billion) and profit of CHF6.681 billion (approx. US$4 billion) in 2001, Nestlé was the world's largest food and beverage company. Its major products included coffee, water, dairy products, breakfast cereals, culinary products, ice cream, frozen food, chocolate and confectionary, and pet care. Its major water brands included Nestlé Pure Life, Nestlé Aquarel, Perrier and Vittel. Other beverage brands included Nestea, Nesquik, Nescau, Milo, Carnation, Libby's and Caro. In 2001, Nestlé was the world leader in bottled water with a market share of 16.3 per cent. Nestlé owned four of the top six water brands in the world.

Nestlé came to China in 1979. By 2002 it had established 14 fully owned enterprises, 19 joint ventures and one R&D center for a total investment of US$72 million. Its 2001 sales in China amounted to US$570 million. Due to the growth of packaged water and its profitability, Nestlé China aimed to be the market leader in this category. It established plants for producing packaged water in Tianjin and Shanghai and was expanding its own sales network to co-operate with distributors.

Groupe Danone The French company ranked sixth in the global food and beverage industry. In 2001, it had revenues of €14.470 billion (approximately US$14 billion), with net income of €132 million (approximately US$127.7 million). It operated in three core businesses: fresh dairy products, beverages and cereal biscuits and snacks. Its major brands included Danone and Dannon for fresh dairy products, Evian, Volvic and Aqua for mineral water, and LU for biscuits. Its leading position worldwide was based on a portfolio of major international brands

---

[3] Yan Shi, 'Pepsi's Business Model Encountering Trust Crisis in China', Economic Observation, *April 24, 2002.*

[4] *1 U.S. dollar (US$) 5 1.35 Swiss Francs (CHF).*

and a solid presence in local markets (about 70 per cent of global sales came from brands that were local market leaders in which Danone had shares). As part of a recent push toward globalization, the company had made about 40 acquisitions in Asia, Latin America, Central Europe, Africa and the Middle East.

Danone's major products in China included biscuits, water, yogurt and milk. Most of these products were sold under the Danone brand. In 1987, the company had begun operations in China by establishing the Guangzhou Danone Yogurt Company. This was followed in 1992 by the Shanghai Danone Biscuit Company. Since then, it had acquired a number of companies: in 1996 it purchased 63.2 per cent of Haomen Beer, 54.2 per cent of Wuhan Donghu Beer and its stake in the five joint ventures with Wahaha. In 1998 it owned 54.2 per cent of Shenzhen Danone Yili Beverages Co. Ltd., and in 2000 it purchased 92 per cent of Robust Group, one of the top 10 Chinese soft-drink producers. In December 2000, it had acquired a five per cent stake in Shanghai Bright Dairy, one of the top milk producers in China. It also purchased 50 per cent of Meilin-Zhengguanghe Water Company and 10 per cent of Zhengguanghe Online Shopping Company.

China's soft-drink industry

With the entry of multinationals into the Chinese market in the 1980s, marketing, advanced production technology and cutting-edge management expertise were injected into China's soft-drink industry, spurring its development. Over the past 20 years, the industry had grown at an annual rate of over 21 per cent, and annual output had increased from 0.288 million tons (261 million litres) in 1980 to 16.69 million tons (15.141 billion litres) in 2001 (see Exhibit 3). Per capita consumption increased from 0.3 litre per annum in 1982 to eight litres per annum in 2001, 27 times that of 1982. Total revenues exceeded RMB40 billion in 2000. In urban areas, soft drinks were no longer seen as an occasional luxury to be consumed only in restaurants and hotels, but a regularly consumed product. Drink package formats diversified to meet new consumption patterns, and now included cans, polyethylene terephtalate (PET) and paper packs.

China's soft-drink industry had sped through three major development stages in a short time: the rise of carbonated drinks in the 1980s, packaged water in the 1990s and tea in the 2000s. In 2001, packaged water accounted for 40.6 per cent of total sales, carbonated drinks for 27 per cent and the 'other' category for 32.4 per cent. The fastest growing product was bottled tea because of its low-calorie, low-fat and low-sugar content, and convenience. It had a share of about 12 per cent and an annual growth of 85 per cent. It was predicted that juice and milk drinks would become the catalyst for growth in the next phase of development. Despite rapid growth, China's national per capita consumption was still only 20 per cent of the world average and 33 per cent of the United States average. Growth potential for all categories remained high. It was predicted that over the next 10 to 15 years, industry output would grow at an annual rate of about 10 per cent, reaching 22.65 million tons (20.548 billion litres) in 2005, and 37 million tons (33.566 billion litres) by 2015. With China's entry into World Trade Organization (WTO) in 2001, China's soft-drink industry was expected to develop even more rapidly and competition was already intensifying as restrictions on foreign investment were lifted.

A number of large companies and brands were present on the national stage, yet the industry remained fragmented in comparison to developed markets. In 2001, the combined output of the top 10 domestic soft-drink producers in China (see Exhibit 4) accounted for 40 per cent of the national total.[5] With Coca Cola China and PepsiCo China, the total output of the top players represented 63 per cent of national output. In the 2000s, several of the top 10 companies were undergoing major changes: Jianlibao, a large domestic player, was in crisis; Danone invested in Wahaha, Robust and Meilin-Zhengguanghe; Xuri Group, the largest tea producer, failed in its competition with two iced-tea brands from Taiwan (named Mr. Kon and President), which now held 75 per cent share, with combined revenues of RMB3.5 billion. Nestlé, despite its leading position in the global tea market, did not do as well in China. Robust, in which Danone had a majority share, had its own problems. Five of its top executives resigned

---

[5] Data from China Soft Drink Industry Association.

due to the company's failure to meet growth targets and because of differences of opinion on the future strategy of the company with Danone. Danone China's CEO took over the management role.

Consumers

According to research conducted in 2001, the target customers for soft drinks were people in the 11 to 40 age group. Income and education level were positively related to soft drink purchase. When purchasing soft drinks, taste was a key criterion. In addition, young consumers were concerned with brand, lifestyle and fashion. Older consumers cared more about health and nutrition. Women and children preferred sweeter drinks, men and young consumers preferred a crisp taste, while older consumers preferred a light taste. Most consumers purchased soft drinks in supermarkets for reasons of price, choice, and the quality assurance the retailer provided. Drinks were also sold through convenience stores, ice cream shops and roadside stalls, especially those near residential areas and schools.

Marketing in the soft drink industry had changed in recent years. Prior to 1997, the emphasis had been on brand-building, and companies had spent heavily on advertising. However, with brand proliferation and several companies adopting similar positioning, distribution had become a key battleground for gaining competitive advantage.

Cola in China

Thanks to Coca Cola and PepsiCo, cola was the most popular soft drink worldwide, with consumption amounting to 70 billion litres, and accounting for 20 per cent of all soft-drink sales. Cola sales were still on the rise, though its role in the overall soft-drinks mix was diminishing.

In the early 1980s, before Coca Cola and PepsiCo entered China, more than 10 domestic cola manufacturers produced cola, but with little marketing, revenues remained small. With the arrival of the two multinational giants, the local producers found it hard to compete, and gradually withdrew from the market or established joint bottling ventures with the two giants.

Coca Cola and PepsiCo's sales volumes rose in line with overall sales of cola until they dominated China's carbonated drink market. The two

companies had replicated their global rivalry in China and were initially determined to seize market share from domestic cola producers, even at the cost of profitability. The headquarters of both companies in China co-ordinated the marketing efforts of the bottling plants. Both used heavy advertising and sponsoring to support their cola brands. By 2000, Coca Cola had an average of 85 per cent distribution penetration in cities, while PepsiCo stood at about 65 per cent but was growing faster (3.7 per cent growth rate versus Coca Coca's 1.3 per cent).[6] Coca Cola expanded its sales nationwide: it first targeted the 150 cities with a population greater than one million by establishing sales channels there. Next, it continued to roll out into cities with populations greater than 0.5 million, and so on. In comparison, PepsiCo focused on key markets and in cities such as Shanghai, Chongqing, Chengdu, Wuhan and Shenzhen, where it had a higher share than its rival.

In 1998 some domestic soft-drink producers, attracted by the rapidly growing market, launched their own cola brands. Among them were Wahaha Future Cola from Wahaha, and Fenhuang Cola from Guangzhou Fenhuang Food Company. Both advertised heavily on CCTV. Wahaha launched its Wahaha Future Cola brand during the soccer World Cup and utilized its well-established distribution channels. Fenhuang Cola signed up the famous martial arts actor Jackie Chan to endorse its brand. Both brands emphasized a 'China's own cola' positioning, and were targeting smaller cities and the rural market where the two big foreign cola producers were comparatively weak. This revitalization of domestic cola brought other competitors into the fray, including Alishan Zhonghua Cola and Yanjing Cola in 2000, as well as Jianlibao's Huating Cola in 2001.

Wahaha Future Cola

By 1998, Wahaha had firmly established its production and distribution system, and its dominant position in non-carbonated drinks was secure. Wahaha could not, for long, neglect the carbonates market which represented almost half of the volume

---

[6] 'An Analysis of the Competition Between Coca Cola and PepsiCo in China,' China Business, October 16, 2001. Market penetration refers to the percentage of consumers of a certain cola brand among total cola consumers.

of the soft-drink industry. Entering the market would provide a much better utilization of its distribution network, and leverage its marketing skills. But it would also mean direct competition with Coca Cola and PepsiCo. In 1997, the total cola output in China was 1.36 million tons (1.234 billion litres) and Coca Cola and PepsiCo held a combined market share of 80 per cent. In 1998, Coca Cola's total beverage output in China was two million tons and PepsiCo 0.8 million tons. Wahaha, despite its number one position among domestic producers, had a total output of 0.93 million tons. Coca Cola and PepsiCo's success against the domestic cola producers in the early stages and their strong brand name and sales network in big cities formed a high entry barrier for new competitors.

Zong firmly believed local companies were capable of competing with the multinational players. He pointed to the computer industry, where domestic companies such as Legend were dominating the local market, and even building global brands. He pointed out that in the food and beverage industry where the technical requirements were relatively low and an understanding of domestic preferences was a distinct advantage, domestic companies had an edge. He concluded that the failure of domestic colas in the early stages was due to their lack of marketing and brand management skills, and that Wahaha had proven that it had these skills. As well, he believed some domestic producers did not want to compete with the multinationals because they lacked the confidence to compete against the giants. Confidence was not lacking at Wahaha.

Zong decided to target the rural market first because he knew and understood this market, and because it was not the focus of Coca Cola and PepsiCo. He reasoned that cola had the potential to be a mass-market product, and the rural areas were where the mass market resided. The 1.1 billion people in the rural market were impossible to ignore. Over the years, China's rural population had become wealthier. In 2000, rural residents' average income was 36 per cent of that of an urban resident (see **Exhibit 5**), but due to their large numbers, they accounted for two-thirds of national spending. A rural resident's spending on food and beverage totaled RMB820.52 a year, 42 per cent that of an urban resident. Meanwhile, the development of mass

communication had made the rural population more accessible, and exposed it to the outside world. Zong believed these trends represented an unparalleled and untapped opportunity.

To develop the product, Wahaha co-operated with R&D institutes and leading domestic flavor producers. To ensure that its cola would be of a high quality, Wahaha sought the advice of global beverage experts and conducted thousands of taste tests worldwide. Its taste was designed to be close to international colas, but a little bit sweeter and stronger to cater to the Chinese consumers' taste. In domestic blind taste tests, consumers preferred Wahaha Future Cola to other colas.

The name Wahaha Future Cola was put forward by Wahaha's employees. The Chinese characters of the brand meant 'unusual,' a reference to the unusual move of launching against entrenched and strong competitive rivals.

Wahaha did not intend to start a price war in the cola category, but it prepared to win such a war if one broke out. At launch, Wahaha offered three pack sizes, the same as Coca Cola and PepsiCo: 355 ml, 500 ml and 1.25 litres. A standard unit case (12 bottles of 500 ml) of Wahaha Future Cola was priced at RMB19 (wholesale), RMB7 lower than Coca Cola and Pepsi-Cola. This translated into a price difference of approximately RMB0.50 per bottle at retail. One reason for the lower price, Wahaha executives explained, was that Future Cola was aimed at the rural market which was more price-sensitive than the urban markets where the international competitors focused. Assessing potential competitive responses, Zong said:

It is possible that Coca Cola might reduce its price. But if it lowers the price per bottle of cola by RMB0.10, it will probably lose profit of about RMB0.5 billion; if it cuts price by RM0.50 it stands to lose RMB2.5 billion. If it is willing to do so, we are willing to follow.

Wahaha reasoned that its revenues from other products could support Future Cola through a price war. As it happened, Wahaha maintained the price difference with Coca Cola and PepsiCo over the years despite the launch of new pack sizes (see **Exhibit 6**).

Wahaha supported the launch with an RMB33.9-million TV campaign, including RMB12.44 million spent on CCTV during the soccer World Cup. Simultaneously, Wahaha greatly increased its brand-building efforts. In 1998, total TV advertising of Wahaha reached RMB368.7 million, of which RMB65.18 million was devoted to Future Cola. CCTV's coverage (national, including rural areas) and credibility (as a domestic national voice) among consumers made it an excellent channel to convey Wahaha Future Cola's brand image. According to a national survey, 61 per cent of rural consumers said TV was their most important source of information and 33.8 per cent said CCTV Channel 1 was the most frequently viewed channel. Favorite programs for rural residents included films, TV series and CCTV news. Prime advertising time was 7 p.m. to 10 p.m. It helped that Wahaha had been advertising on CCTV for 10 years and already had high brand awareness among rural consumers.

Wahaha relied on its nationwide distribution network to get the product to rural consumers. While Coca Cola and PepsiCo had the advantage in large cities where chain stores and supermarkets accounted for half the grocery trade, Wahaha played on its strength in the countryside where the trade was fragmented, and reachable primarily through multi-layered wholesale markets. Distributors who had been working with Wahaha for years and who had benefited from Wahaha's remarkable growth supported the launch of the cola.

The initial success of the cola surprised even Wahaha. The company could not meet demand using its own bottling facilities and even resorted to outsourcing bottling to other bottlers. When Coca Cola bottlers were approached, the answer was a firm 'no.' At the same time, many of Coca Cola's distributors noticed that if they sold Wahaha Future Cola, Coca Cola would stop supplying them and refuse end-of-year bonuses.[7]

On average, advertising expenses of Wahaha Future Cola comprised about 20 to 30 per cent of the company's total advertising expenditure, adjusted for seasonal and promotional focus. Besides advertising on CCTV and other local TV channels, Wahaha used outdoor advertising and point-of-sale advertising. In particular, to tackle the rural market, it used 'wall advertising' — painting walls with advertising slogans — a cost-effective way to promote brand awareness. At busy roads and fairs, Wahaha set up large brand and slogan banners. It also sponsored traveling troupes that performed in rural markets and at fairs. In villages where there was no cinema, Wahaha sponsored traveling film shows. These activities catered to the needs of rural customers and quickly increased Wahaha Future Cola's awareness in the rural market.

In 2000, Yu Chen Qing, a pop singer from Taiwan, was signed on to endorse Wahaha Future Cola, while Coco Li Wen, another pop singer from Taiwan, endorsed the Future Lemon carbonated drink. In 2000 and 2001, Wahaha was the exclusive sponsor for CCTV's spring festival party, a program that attracted a mass audience, building national brand awareness.

In 2001, Wahaha Future Cola launched a new advertising slogan 'Future Cola, the choice for happy occasions.' To support this association, Wahaha provided free cola to wedding parties in some key markets. A co-promotion with liquor producers further reinforced the association.

Before the spring festival in 2002, Zong noticed that Coca Cola changed its original paper case packaging to plastic wrap to save costs. Zong saw this as an opportunity to promote Wahaha Future Cola's paper packaging, which was easier to carry and looked better than plastic wrap. Sales staff promoted the paper case as a gift item for the festival, inserting posters of the image of the god of fortune in each case.

Wahaha Future Cola's focus on rural markets meant that 60 per cent to 70 per cent of total sales came from rural areas. In 2002, Wahaha launched carbonated drinks with fresh apple juice and orange juice. With the wider product range, it increased its sales efforts in supermarkets and big stores, and in larger cities.

During the same period, Coca Cola and PepsiCo began to notice and respond to the domestic upstart, while continuing to compete with each other. In a few markets they offered their cola products at a lower price than Wahaha Future Cola. Meanwhile, they further localized their marketing. For example, Coca Cola adjusted its advertising strategy and

[7] *Wu Xiaobo and Hu Honwei,* Extraordinary Marketing Strategy, *Zhejiang People's Publishing House, 2002, pp. 230–231.*

increased its advertising on CCTV. It also signed on pop singers from Taiwan and Hong Kong, Zhang Huimei and Xie Tingfeng, to endorse its brand. In 2001, to celebrate Beijing's victory in its bid to host the 2008 Olympics Games, Coca Cola announced a new thematic pack design just 22 minutes after the news announcement. The following day the new design (in gold, integrating various architectural and sports themes in Beijing) was launched in key markets. In 2001 during the Spring Festival, Coca Cola packs carried a picture of a traditional Chinese clay doll 'A Fu' (a symbol of luck).

Coca Cola and PepsiCo also began to actively develop the non-carbonated drink market while continuing to promote their carbonate products. Pepsi promoted non-carbonate drinks such as Dole (100 per cent fruit juice) and Gatorade. Coca Cola launched 'Sensation' water in 2001 without any advertising support, and with a wholesale price that was 40 per cent lower than Wahaha purified water in some regions. In 2002, it launched new 600 ml, 1.5 litre and 2.25 litre packages for its cola without increases in price over the 500 ml, 1.25 litre and two litre respectively. Coca Cola also announced its intention to increase the number of bottling plants to 34 from 28 within five years, growing especially in the mainly rural western region.

Both Coca Cola and PepsiCo were also working on their distribution policy, according to a report in *China Business*.[8] Coca Cola and PepsiCo had never been directly involved in the sales of their products. Instead, their bottlers managed sales in their assigned territory, relying on distributors to cover areas their own systems could not serve. The two companies' practice was to set stringent sales targets for bottlers, and in turn bottlers would set targets for distributors. Bonuses were contingent on reaching these goals. Distributors paid upfront for goods and couldn't return unsold merchandise. However, different wholesale prices in different regions and the incentive of the bonus resulted in distributors selling across provinces to achieve their sales targets, even though both companies had strict policies against cross-territory sales. Recognizing

the problems of the current system, the two companies had recently redefined the roles of bottlers and distributors: distributors were in charge of carrying inventory and delivering to the retailer and their profit would come from the volume handled, but they no longer had any discretion over selling prices; bottlers were responsible for order taking, promotion and product display at the retail end, and retained ownership of the product until the retailer bought it. In comparison, Wahaha's sales company bought the products from its wholly-owned bottling subsidiaries and then co-ordinated sales and marketing on a national scale. Its sales company directly dealt with the distributors (see **Exhibit 7**). Coca Cola and PepsiCo both made money from the sales of concentrate, thus limiting the potential profitability (and price flexibility) of third-party bottlers. Wahaha made money from the sales of the final product, as the production of concentrate and the final product was handled by its own subsidiaries. This gave Wahaha greater pricing flexibility in the field.

In 2002, PepsiCo encountered some problems with a local joint-venture partner. PepsiCo was applying to a commercial arbitration court in Stockholm to cancel its contracts with the joint-venture partner in Chengdu, Sichuan Province — a key Pepsi-Cola market. PepsiCo contended that it had been prevented from exercising its rights under the joint-venture contract, and alleged that there were major financial irregularities within the local company, while the latter accused PepsiCo China of bugging its phones. This was unprecedented in PepsiCo's 20 years in China. While PepsiCo was distracted by these internal problems, Coca Cola was launching a campaign to seize market share in Sichuan and Chongqing — other key markets for PepsiCo.

In the meantime, Wahaha steadily increased sales and market share of Future Cola. Between 1998 and 2001, Wahaha Future series' sales volume increased from 73,800 tons (66.95 million litres) to 0.64 million tons (580 million litres), a share of 14 per cent of the carbonated drink market (see **Exhibit 8**). In comparison, 2001 carbonated-drink sales for Coca Cola and PepsiCo were 1.9 million tons (1.724 billion litres) and 1.07 million tons (971 million litres) respectively. In June 2002, Future series market share reached 18 per cent, with sales revenues of RMB930 million.

---

[8] Ma Qiang, 'Comments on Banning the Association of PepsiCo's Bottlers,' *China Business, August 1, 2002.*

In some provinces such as Hunan, Xinjiang, Jiangxi and the three provinces in northern China, Future's market share was higher than that of Coca Cola and Pepsi-Cola. In some provinces, Wahaha Future Cola was the only cola brand carried by retailers. In 2001, the Future brand was extended to tea drinks.

Coca Cola now admitted that it faced competition from domestic companies. According to a *Wall Street Journal* article, Coca Cola had been aggressively ramping up its sales efforts and 'by opening more bottling plants and using recyclable bottles, it has brought the price down to one yuan for a single serving in remote towns.'

During the past three years, Coke and its bottlers have been trying to map every supermarket, restaurant, barbershop or market stall where a can of soda might be consumed throughout much of China. Their army of more than 10,000 sales representatives makes regular visits, often on bicycle or foot, to each outlet to ensure there is enough in stock and to record how much was sold. All the information goes into a central database, updated daily, that gives Coke some of the most accurate consumer profiles available in China. Those data help Coke get closer to its customers, whether they are in large hypermarkets, spartan noodle shops or schools. ... And in a strategy proven in markets such as Africa and India, Coke lets local distributors gradually own their own assets, whether these be tricycles used for deliveries or small refrigeration units.[9]

Wahaha, in the meantime, was planning on expanding its sales and marketing staff from 2,000 to 8,000 in 2002.

As Zong Qinghou reviewed the progress of Wahaha Future Cola, he knew that his strategy had allowed Wahaha to quickly become a player in the soft-drink business in China. As Coca Cola and PepsiCo realized the threat from Chinese domestic cola producers and the vast market potential in the countryside, they would certainly take action to protect their position in the carbonated-drink market and tackle the rural market. Zong wondered what steps he should take next with Wahaha Future Cola and the carbonated-drink market. Meanwhile, changes in the soft-drink industry also posed challenges for all participants. The rapid growth of new drink categories offered both opportunities and risks. As the general manager of China's number one soft-drink producer, he also needed to consider competition in the rapidly growing non-carbonated drink market and the future growth of Wahaha.

Exhibit 1 Wahaha group sales revenue and profit 1996 to 2001 (in RMB million)

	1996	1997	1998	1999	2000	2001
Sales revenue	1,110	2,110	2,870	4,510	5,440	6,230
Profit	155	334	501	875	906	914
Profit margin	14%	16%	17%	19%	17%	15%

Source: Company files.

[9] Gabriel Kahn, 'Coke Works Harder at Being The Real Thing in Hinterland', Wall Street Journal, November 26, 2002.

Exhibit 2 World soft drink average annual growth rate 1994 to 2003

category	1994–2000	2001–2003
Carbonated drinks	4%	2%
Packaged water	8%	6%
Other*	5.70%	5.30%
Juice and nectars	4.10%	4.20%
Non-carbonated drinks	4.90%	6.30%
Iced tea	11.70%	5.80%
Sports and energy drinks	6.40%	5.90%

'Other' category includes juice and nectars, still drinks, iced tea, sports and energy drinks.

Global soft drink category development (billions of litres)

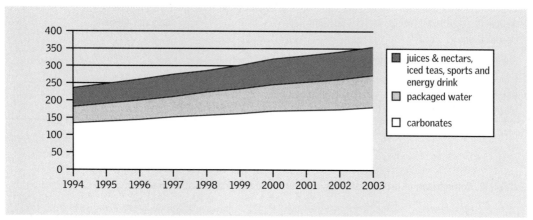

Source: Canadean Ltd.

Exhibit 3 China's soft drink output

Year	Soft Drinks output (in millions of tons)	Carbonated Drinks output (in millions of tons)	Carbonated Drinks as a percentage of total Soft Drinks
1994	6.29	3.14	50%
1995	9.82	5.21	53%
1996	8.84	4.29	49%
1997	10.69	4.92	46%
1998	12.00	5.40	45%
1999	11.86	4.27	36%
2000	14.91	4.62	31%
2001	16.69	4.57	27%

Source: The beverage industry.

Exhibit 4 Top ten domestic soft drink producers in China

Company	Major Soft Drink	Major Brand
Robust (Guangdong) Food & Beverage Co., Ltd.	non-carbonated drink	Robust
Guangdong Jianlibao Beverage Co., Ltd.	sport drink	Jianlibao
Shanghai Maling Aquarius (Group) Corporation	canned food, packaged water	Zhengguanghe
Beijing Huiyuan Juice Group Corporation	juice	Huiyuan
Hebei Xurishen Co. Ltd.	tea	Xurishen
Hebei Lolo Co. Ltd.	almond drink	Lolo
Hangzhou Wahaha Group Corporation	packaged water, carbonated drinks, tea, dairy drink	Wahaha, Future
Hainan Coconut Palm Group Corporation	coconut milk	Coconut Palm
Shenzhen Danone Yili Beverage Co., Ltd.	mineral water	Yili
Cestbon Food & Beverage (shenzhen) Co., Ltd	distilled water	Cestbon

Source: China Soft Drink Industry Association.

Exhibit 5 Comparison of urban residents' and rural residents' disposable income in China

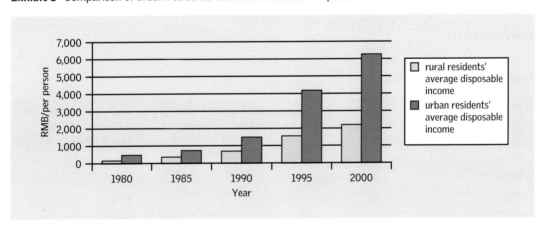

Exhibit 6 Retail price comparison of various pack sizes in 2002 (in RMB)

Size	Coca Cola	Pepsi Cola	Wahaha Future Cola
355 ml	1.8–2.2	1.8–2.2	1.7–2.0
500 ml	2.2–2.5	2.2–2.5	1.9–2.2
600 ml	2.2–2.5	2.2–2.5	none
1.25 l	4.4–4.9	4.4–4.9	3.8
1.5 l	4.4–4.9	4.4–4.9	none
2 l	6.5	6.5	6.0–6.5
2.25 l	6.5	6.5	none

Note: Both Coca Cola and Pepsi Cola offered 600 ml, 1.5 l and 2.25 l at the same price as 500 ml, 1.25 l and 2 l as promotion prices.
Source: Company files.

Exhibit 7 Comparison of product flow and revenue flow

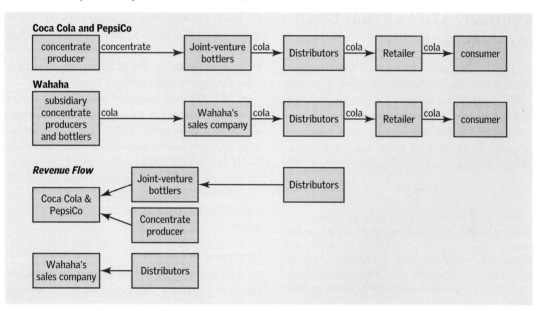

Exhibit 8 Comparison of Coca Cola, PepsiCo. and Wahaha's carbonate sales

	1998		1999		2000		2001	
	Total (in tons)	Market Share	Total	Market Share	Total	Market Share	Total	Market Share
Coca Cola	1,940.0	36%	2,040.0	48%	2,180.0	47%	1,920.0	42%
PepsiCo's	760.0	14%	910.0	21%	1,090.0	24%	1,066.7	23%
Wahaha	73.8	1%	399.0	9%	480.0	10%	640.0	14%
China's total carbonated drink sales	5,400.0	100%	4,273.8	100%	4,620.0	100%	4,571.4	100%

Richard Ivey School of Business
The University of Western Ontario

Case 13 The Leo Burnett Company Ltd.: virtual team management

On July 2, 2001, Janet Carmichael, global account director for The Leo Burnett Company Ltd. (LB), United Kingdom, sat in her office wondering how to structure her global advertising team. The team was responsible for the introduction of a skin care product of one of LB's most important clients, Ontann Beauty Care (OBC). The product had

Elizabeth O'Neil prepared this case under the supervision of Professor Joerg Dietz and Fernando Olivera solely to provide material for class discussion. The authors do not intend to illustrate either effective or ineffective handling of a managerial situation. The authors may have disguised certain names and other identifying information to protect confidentiality.

Version: (A) 2003-11-04

launched in the Canadian and Taiwanese test markets earlier that year. Taiwanese sales and awareness levels for the product had been high but were low for the Canadian market. Typically, at this stage in the launch process, Carmichael would decentralize the communications management in each market, but the poor performance in the Canadian market left her with a difficult decision: should she maintain centralized control over the Canadian side of her team? In three days, she would leave for meetings at LB's Toronto, Canada, office, where the team would expect her decision.

The Leo Burnett Company Ltd. background

LB, which was founded in Chicago in 1935, was one of North America's premier advertising agencies. It had created numerous well-recognized North American brand icons, including The Marlboro Man, Kellogg's Tony the Tiger, and the Pillsbury Dough Boy.

By 1999, LB had expanded around the globe to include 93 offices in 83 markets. The company employed approximately 9,000 people, and worldwide revenues were approximately US$9 billion. In 2000, LB merged with two other global agencies to form b|com³ (the actual company name), one of the largest advertising holding companies in the world, but each LB office retained the Leo Burnett company name.

LB services and products

As a full-service agency, LB offered the complete range of marketing and communications services and products (see Exhibits 1 and 2). The company's marketing philosophy was to build 'brand belief.' The idea driving this philosophy was that true loyalty went beyond mere buying behavior. LB defined 'believers' as customers who demonstrated both a believing attitude and loyal purchase behavior. The company strove to convert buyers into believers by building lasting customer affinity for the brand.

One of the most important measures of an agency's success was the quality of the creative product that was developed to connect brands to their end consumers. Each local office strove to produce outstanding creative advertising to break through the clutter of marketing messages that the general public was subjected to daily and truly reach the consumer in a memorable way. Award shows were held nationally and internationally to recognize this effort, one of the most prestigious being the annual festival in Cannes, France. With each award, individual employees (usually the art director and copy writer who had worked together to develop the ad) were recognized, as was the local agency office where they worked. These creative accolades were instrumental in helping an office win new client business. Even within the global LB network, awards were given to the local offices that produced the most outstanding creative work.

LB internal team structures

A multidisciplinary team serviced each brand. Each team had representatives from all core areas of the agency as well as members from the specialized services as appropriate for the brand. In most cases, team members had two sets of reporting lines.

First and formally, they directly reported to the supervisor of their home department (for example, account management). It was this formal supervisor who was responsible for conducting performance evaluations and assigning and managing an employee's workload.

Informally, the team members reported to a project team leader, the senior account services person, who usually was an account director or a vice-president of client services director. It was this team leader's responsibility to manage the project in question, ensure that the client was satisfied with project progress, and build and manage the overall relationship between the client and the agency. Employees on the project team would be responsible to this person for meeting project deadlines and managing their individual client relationships. This team leader would often provide input to a team member's performance evaluation, along with other agency colleagues (see **Exhibit 3**).

At any given time, an agency employee typically worked on two or three different brand teams, virtually all of them face-to-face teams servicing local clients.

LB typical office environment

Most LB employees were young (in their 20s and 30s) and worked about 60 hours per week. Client needs and project deadlines dictated work priorities, and the volume of work often required late nights at the office. Agency office environments were often open-concept and social. Employees spent many hours each day up and about, discussing projects with colleagues and responding to client requests. The pace was fast and the general spirit was one of camaraderie; it was common for LB employees to socialize together after a late night at the office.

LB Toronto

LB's Toronto office was founded in 1952 to service the Canadian arms of the Chicago-based clients. It was LB's first expansion beyond Chicago. In 2001, it employed a staff of approximately 200 people and billings were approximately $200 million.

LB United Kingdom

LB acquired its London, United Kingdom, office in the mid-1970s as part of an expansion into Europe. By 2001, the office had grown to over 350 employees and billings were approximately $400 million. London was also the regional LB headquarters for all European, Middle Eastern and African offices.

LB's relationship with Ontann Beauty Care

Ontann Beauty Care (OBC)

OBC was a leading global manufacturer of health and beauty care products. In the late 1990s, OBC made a strategic decision to centralize the global marketing of its brands and products, designating a global team to define the global strategy for a given brand and develop the core communication materials as templates for local markets to follow. Local offices were given the responsibility for adapting the global materials and developing local 'below the line' (BTL) materials which would synergize with the global vision and creative templates. Below the line materials included direct marketing, in-store materials, digital marketing, public relations and promotions (that is, everything except strict advertising). In practice, on established brands with well-defined communication templates and strong local knowledge, some local markets (at least key regional markets) were awarded more opportunity to develop their own communication material.

The global team, however, retained veto power to ensure all communications were building a consistent personality and look for the brand.

Each OBC global office had as many teams as it had brands. An OBC brand team usually consisted of the global category director, the brand manager and an assistant brand manager, plus a representative from each of the various departments: marketing technology, consumer, trade/distribution, PR, sales, product development, and production.

Relationship between LB and OBC

OBC, which, like LB, was founded in Chicago, was one of LB's original clients. In 2001, as one of the top three LB clients worldwide, OBC did business with most LB offices. OBC, however, awarded its business to advertising agencies brand-by-brand. As a result, other advertising agencies also had business with OBC. Competition among advertising agencies for OBC business was strong, in particular when they had to work together on joint brand promotions.

OBC had been a client of LB's Toronto office since 1958 and of LB's London office since its acquisition in the mid-1970s. Both the Toronto and London offices initially developed advertising and communications materials for various OBC facial care brands and eventually also worked on OBC's skin care brands.

To better service OBC, LB also centralized its decision marking for this client's brands and appointed expanded and strengthened global teams with the power to make global decisions. For its other clients, LB's global teams were significantly smaller, tending to consist simply of one very senior LB manager who shared learning from across the globe with a given client's senior management.

A new OBC brand: Forever Young

In the fall of 1998, the OBC London office announced a new skin care line called 'Forever Young'. Product formulas were based on a newly patented process that addressed the needs of aging skin. For OBC, this brand presented an opportunity to address a new market segment: the rapidly growing population of people over the age of 50. The product line was more extensive than other OBC skin care brands. It also represented the company's first foray into

premium priced skin care products. Product cost, on average, was double that of most other OBC brands, falling between drug store products and designer products. OBC intended Forever Young to be its next big global launch and awarded the Forever Young advertising and brand communications business to LB.

Global advertising and communications team for Forever Young

Team formation

For LB, a successful launch of this new product would significantly increase revenues and the likelihood of acquiring additional global OBC brands. An unsuccessful launch would risk the relationship with OBC that LB had built over so many years. LB management in Chicago decided that LB London would be the global team headquarters. This decision reflected the experience that the London office had in leading global business teams and the proximity to the OBC global team for Forever Young. It was also likely that the United Kingdom would be the test market for the new product.

In LB's London office, Janet Carmichael was assigned as brand team leader for the Forever Young product line effective January 1, 1999. Carmichael was the global account director for OBC. The 41-year-old Carmichael, a Canadian, had begun her career at LB Toronto as an account executive in 1985, after completing an MBA degree at the University of Toronto. In 1987, Carmichael moved to Europe, where she continued her career with LB. She became an account supervisor in Italy, an account director in Belgium, and finally a regional and global account director in Germany before taking on a global account director role on OBC brands in the United Kingdom in 1996. She was very familiar with OBC's business and had built excellent relationships with the OBC skin care client group.

LB's initial Forever Young brand team had six members who all were employees of the London office: Carmichael as the team leader, an account director, an account executive (she formally supervised these two employees), the agency's creative director, and two 'creatives' (an art director and a copy writer). Carmichael outlined a project timetable (see **Exhibit 4**). The LB team worked with the OBC team on consumer research, market exploration, brand creative concepts (creative), packaging samples and global copy testing throughout North America and Europe. Carmichael viewed marketing a new product to a new consumer segment in a crowded category as challenging; however, after several months of testing, LB's Forever Young brand team developed a unique creative concept that was well received by OBC.

In the fall of 1999, OBC decided that the United Kingdom would be the lead market for another skin care product. Because North America was a priority for the Forever Young brand and Canada was 'clean' (that is, OBC was not testing other products in Canada at that time), Canada became the new primary test market for Forever Young. In addition, Canadians' personal skin care habits and the distribution process for skin care products were more reflective of overall Western practices (i.e., the Western world) than were those in other potential test markets. Taiwan became the secondary test market for Asian consumers. These choices were consistent with OBC's interest in global brand validation.

In keeping with OBC's team structures, LB maintained the global brand team in London and, in January of 2000, formed satellite teams in Toronto, Canada, and Taipei, Taiwan, to manage material execution in their local markets. It was up to the LB Toronto and Taipei offices to determine their members in the Forever Young satellite teams. In Taipei, Cathy Lee, an account director who was particularly interested in the assignment, took the lead on local agency activities. In Toronto, Geoff Davids, an account supervisor from the direct marketing group, was assigned to lead the Toronto team. The global brand team and the two satellite teams now formed the LB side of the global advertising and communications team for Forever Young (see **Exhibit 5**).

Kick-off meeting

In February 2000, a face-to-face kick-off meeting took place in Toronto with the intent to bring all senior members of LB's and OBC's London, Toronto, and Taipei teams onto the same page regarding the new brand and the status of the launch process. One or two senior representatives from OBC London, Toronto, and Taipei participated in the meeting. From LB, the complete London team participated, along with Geoff Davids and a senior agency representative from the Toronto office, and Cathy Lee and a senior agency representative from the Taipei office. Carmichael and her U.K. team members shared their initial brand creative concepts, which had already garnered admiration throughout the LB network, and their knowledge about the product and target audience.

It was decided that Davids and Lee would serve as the main links to LB's London-based global brand team. Specifically, Davids and Lee reported to Annabel Forin, Carmichael's account director in the United Kingdom. Forin then reported to Carmichael and OBC's London team. Besides Forin, Carmichael's primary contacts would be Annabelle Manning, the global creative director at LB United Kingdom and Sarah Jones, OBC's global vice-president of skin care in London. All work produced by LB's satellite teams would require approval from LB's London team.

The creative assignments

The creative assignments for the Canadian and Taiwanese teams were slightly different from each other. Normally, the global team would produce a creative template for a brand (meaning the design of the advertising and communications materials), which would then be passed to the satellite teams to be adapted for the local market.

In the Taiwanese market, this would be the case. The Taiwanese LB team would be responsible for adapting the advertising materials, which would include re-filming the television ad to star an Asian actress, as well as retaking photos for the print ads, again, to demonstrate product benefits on Asian skin. The brand message (meaning the text in print ads and the vocal message in television ads) would be adapted to appeal to the Taiwanese audience.

In Toronto, however, the assignment broke from this traditional format. The LB team in London would produce English television and print advertising, which would be used in the Canadian market. The LB team in Toronto would design and produce the direct marketing and Web site materials because the London office did not have strong in-house capabilities in these areas. While the Toronto office would have control of the design of these communication pieces, the U.K. office would require that certain elements be incorporated into the design (for example, specific photos and colors), in order for the pieces to be visually consistent with the print advertising.

Events leading up to the launch

LB's Taipei office

After returning to Taipei from the kick-off meeting, Lee formed her local team, which consisted of an account executive (Tanya Yang) and a creative team (one art director and one copy writer). In co-operation with OBC's Taipei team, Lee and her team focused first on recreating the television ad. The ad followed the original creative idea developed in the United Kingdom but used a popular Taiwanese actress in the lead. The character differentiation was necessary to demonstrate the product's benefit to Asian skin because the original ad featured a blond, Caucasian actress as the lead. The team moved on to adapt the brand's print advertising and direct marketing pieces and developed a public relations campaign to meet local market needs. These communication elements were visually and strategically consistent with the television ad as they incorporated photos of the same Taiwanese actress.

Throughout this process, the Taipei team regularly updated LB's and OBC's London teams about its progress. Although all work required U.K. approval, the Taiwanese team worked with a significant amount of autonomy because of the cultural differences present in its market. Carmichael and Manning occasionally travelled to Taiwan to meet with the team and approve its creative work, which they generally received well. In addition, the Taipei team communicated with the London offices through videoconference calls and e-mail. The LB Taipei and Toronto teams had contact with each other only during the global team videoconference meetings, held every two months.

LB's Toronto office

After the kick-off meeting, Davids, with the approval of LB's Toronto management, assigned representatives from the direct marketing group and the interactive marketing group to the brand team. This included account management (Tara Powell, account executive for direct; and Liz Nelson, account supervisor; and Alexis Jacobs, project manager for interactive) and creative staff (Shirley Watson, creative director; and one copy writer from each of the direct and interactive groups).

In co-operation with OBC's Toronto team, the LB Toronto team was responsible for developing a full communication plan for its local market. Along with running the television and print ads developed in the United Kingdom, the team would focus on producing the brand's below the line materials (i.e., direct mail, Web site). These communication elements served as the education pieces that supplemented the TV ad. Davids conducted an internal team debrief, outlining the information he had received at the kick-off meeting. From this, the team developed a communications plan that, in Carmichael's opinion, was 'on-brief' (i.e., consistent with the original brand strategic direction) and included some very innovative thinking.

Next, the team began determining a creative look and feel for the direct mail pieces. The look and feel could be different from the television creative but had to be consistent across all of the paper-based (print ads, direct mail pieces and in-store materials) and online communication elements. The creatives in LB's Toronto team developed the direct marketing materials, and simultaneously the creatives in LB's U.K. team developed the print advertising. The two sides' creative work evolved in different directions, but each side hoped that the other would adapt their look and feel. Eventually, however, LB's Toronto team told its London counterpart to 'figure it out,' and they would follow London's lead. Communication between the two sides mostly flowed through Davids and Forin to Carmichael. Carmichael, however, had received a copy of the following e-mail from Watson to Davids:

Geoff, as you know, it's always a challenge to work with someone else's art direction. I don't think the model that London chose is right for this market, and the photography we have to work with doesn't have as contemporary a feel as I would like.

This would be easier if I could connect directly with Annabelle [Manning] but she's on the road so much of the time it's hard to catch her. We weren't asked for our opinion initially and, given the timing constraints at this point, we don't have much choice but to use what they've sent us, but could you please convey to Annabel [Forin] that in the future, if possible, we'd like to have the chance to input on the photography before it's taken? It will help us develop good direct mail creative.

For now, though, I think we'll be able to do something with what they've sent us. Thanks.

There had been other challenges for LB's Toronto team. Davids described an incident that had occurred when his direct marketing team tried to present its creative concept to the team in the United Kingdom during a videoconference meeting:

Our direct mail concept was a three-panel, folded piece. We sent two flat files to the United Kingdom via e-mail, which were to be cut out, pasted back-to-back [to form the front and back of the piece] and then folded into thirds. It took us so long to explain how to do that — somehow we just weren't getting through! Our colleagues in London cut and folded and pasted in different places, and what should have been a simple preliminary procedure took up 45 minutes of our one-hour videoconference meeting! By the time we actually got around to discussing the layout of the piece, everyone on the call was frustrated. That's never a good frame of mind to be in when reviewing and critiquing a new layout. It's too bad our clients were on that call as well.

A greater challenge came in September 2000, when the team was behind schedule in the development of the Web site after encountering difficulties with OBC's technology standards. The budgeting for the Web site development came out of the global budget, not the local budget. This meant that the members of LB's Toronto team who were responsible for the Web site development ('interactive marketing') received directions from OBC's London team. The budgeting for direct marketing, however, came out of the local budget, and the members of LB's Toronto team, who were responsible for the development of the direct marketing materials, dealt with OBC's Toronto team. The instructions from

these two OBC teams were often inconsistent. Compounding matters, the two OBC client teams repeatedly requested changes of the Web and direct marketing materials, which made these materials even more different from each other and forced the LB Toronto team into extremely tight timeframes.

Carmichael learned about this sort of difficulty mostly through the direct supervisors of the team members. She frequently received calls from LB Toronto's Interactive Marketing Group and Direct Marketing Group senior managers. Carmichael repeatedly had to explain the basic project components to these senior managers and wished that the members of LB's Toronto team would just follow the team communications protocol and forward their concerns to Davids, who would then take up matters as necessary with the U.K. team.

Canadian pre-launch test

Despite these challenges, LB's Toronto team produced the materials in time for the Canadian pre-launch test in October of 2000. The pre-launch test was a launch of the complete communications program (TV ad, newspaper inserts, distribution of trial packs, direct mail, and a Web site launch) in a market whose media could be completely isolated. A small town in the interior of British Columbia, Canada's most westerly province, met these conditions. In terms of product trial and product sales as a percentage of market share, the test indexed 120 against its objectives, which had a base index of 100. Subsequently, OBC and LB decided to move immediately into research to test the advertising in the U.S. market. The global OBC and LB teams worked with their Canadian counterparts to conduct this research, the results of which were very poor. As a result, OBC London required that LB's London and Toronto teams revised the advertising materials even before the Canadian launch.

Canadian national launch

The days before the launch were panic-filled, as LB's London and Toronto teams scrambled to revise the advertising. In February 2001, the campaign was launched in Canada with the following elements:

- One 30-second TV ad;
- One direct mail piece;

- The English Web site;

- Product samples available from the Web from direct mail piece, and from an in-store coupon;

- Specially designed in-store displays;

- Trial-sized package bundles (one week's worth);

- A public relations campaign; and

- Five print ads in national magazines.

Research following the national launch showed that the brand did not perform well among Canadian consumers. It indexed 50 against a base index of 100. Because of the success of the Canadian pre-launch test, OBC and LB were surprised. The Forever Young global advertising and communications team attributed the discrepancy between the pre-launch test and national launch, in part, to the fact that the pre-launch test conditions were not replicable on a national scale. The audience penetration in the small B.C. town, the pre-test site, was significantly greater than it was in the national launch. OBC decided that the results of the Canadian launch were below 'action standards,' meaning that OBC would not even consider a rollout into the U.S. market at the current time.

The tension levels on both LB's side and OBC's side of the Forever Young global advertising and communications team were high. LB's future business on the brand was in jeopardy. The OBC side was under tremendous pressure internally to improve brand trial and market share metrics and already planned to decentralize the local teams for the global product rollout. Despite numerous revisions to the advertising, it never tested well enough to convince OBC that a U.S. or European launch would be successful.

A different story in Asia

In Taiwan, the product launch was successful. Test results showed that the brand was indexing 120 per cent against brand objectives. Research also showed that Taiwanese consumers, in contrast to Canadian consumers, did not perceive some of the advertising elements as 'violent.' Moreover, in Taiwan, overall research scores in terms of 'likeability' and 'whether or not the advertising would inspire you to try the product' were higher, leading to higher sales.

By June of 2001, the Taiwanese team was ready to take on more local-market responsibility and move into the post-launch phase of the advertising campaign. This phase would involve creating new ads to build on the initial success and grow sales in the market.

Recovery plan for Canada

By June of 2001, LB needed to take drastic measures to develop a new Forever Young campaign in order to improve the brand's performance in the Canadian marketplace. Whereas, before the launch, there had been a clear division of responsibilities (with the United Kingdom developing the television and print advertising and Canada developing direct marketing, in-store and Web site communications), now the global LB team in London decided that it would be necessary to have all hands on deck. New creative teams from the mass advertising department in the Toronto office, as well as supplementary creative teams from the London office, were briefed to develop new campaign ideas. Each team had only three weeks to develop their new ideas, less than half of the eight weeks they would normally have, and the teams had to work independent of each other. The London and Toronto creative teams had to present their concepts to the entire global OBC and LB team at the same time. Subsequently, the results of market research would determine the winning creative concept. Squabbling between the offices began over which team would present first, which office received what compensation for the development, and whether or not overall remuneration packages were fair. Moreover, the communication between the account services members of LB's London and Toronto teams, which was the primary communication channel between the two agencies, became less frequent, less candid and more formal. The presentations took place on June 25, 2001, in Toronto. Watson, the creative director in Toronto commented:

This process has been exciting, but we're near the ends of our collective ropes now. We have a new mass advertising creative team [who specialized in TV ads] on the business in Toronto, and they're being expected to produce world-class creative results for a brand they've only

*heard about for the past few days. They don't —
and couldn't possibly — have the same passion
for the brand that the direct marketing creative
team members have after working on it for so
long. I'm having a hard time motivating them to
work under these tight timelines.*

*We're even more isolated now in Toronto. Our
connection to the creative teams and the global
creative director in London was distant at best,
and now it's non-existent. And our relationship
with the local OBC client feels very remote, too.
Still, we're moving forward with our work. We're
trying to learn from the Taiwanese experience
and are considering what success we would
have with a nationally recognized actress starring in our television ads.*

Evolution of the Forever Young global advertising and communications team

Personnel changes

Between January and June of 2001, numerous personnel changes in the Forever Young global
advertising and communications team occurred (see
Exhibit 5). In LB's London office, Forin, the U.K.
account director, had been replaced following her
departure for maternity leave. In OBC's London
office, Sarah Jones, the global vice-president for
skin care, took early retirement without putting a
succession plan in place. In LB's Toronto office,
Davids, the Toronto brand team leader, had left the
agency. Tara Powell, who had reported to Davids,
took on his responsibilities, but she had not met
most of the global team members. Liz Nelson, the
account supervisor for interactive, left LB's Toronto
office to return to school. Alexis Jacobs, who had
managed the Web site development, took over her
responsibilities. Powell and Jacobs did not have
close relationships with their international counterparts. At OBC Toronto, Sally Burns, the local brand
manager, who had been LB's main contact in the
local market and had been with the brand since
inception, left OBC. LB's and OBC's Taiwanese
teams remained stable over time. Cathy Lee worked
with a team that was nearly identical to her initial
team.

Communications

Early on (between February and May 2000),
Carmichael had orchestrated frequent face-to-face
meetings to ensure clarity of communication and
sufficient information sharing. In the following
months, the team relied on videoconferences and
phone calls, with visits back and forth between
London and Toronto on occasion. Since early 2001,
the team had relied increasingly on e-mails and telephone calls to communicate. In June 2001,
Carmichael noted that the communication had
become more formal, and she had lost the feeling of
being part of a global team. She wondered if giving
the LB's Toronto team more autonomy to develop
the brand in their market would help the brand
progress. Working together as a smaller team might
improve the Toronto group's team dynamic as well.
Carmichael was concerned that the current discord
between LB's London and Toronto offices would
negatively affect the relationship to OBC.

Budget problems

The extra creative teams assigned to the redevelop-
ment of the brand's television advertising and the
unexpected changes to the Forever Young communication materials had meant that LB's costs to staff
the project had been higher than originally estimated
and higher than the revenues that had been negotiated with OBC. Since OBC did not want to pay
more for its advertising than had been originally
budgeted, LB faced tremendous internal pressure to
finish the project as soon as possible. This situation
created conflict between LB and OBC in the United
Kingdom, who was responsible for negotiating LB's
overall fees. Because all fees were paid to the global
brand office (in this case, LB's London office) and
then transferred to the local satellite teams, this
situation also created conflict between LB's London
and Toronto teams, who had both expended
additional staff time to revise the advertising
materials and wanted 'fair' compensation.

What next?

In three days, Carmichael had to leave for Toronto
to sit in research sessions to test the recently presented new creative concepts. In the meetings that
followed, she would present to the team her

recommendation for how to move forward with the brand. Carmichael reviewed the brand events and team interaction of the past two years (see Exhibit 4) to determine the best global team structure for salvaging the Forever Young brand and maintaining the relationship between OBC and LB.

Carmichael felt torn in her loyalties. On the one hand, she was Canadian and knew LB's Toronto office well — she knew that LB's Toronto brand team worked hard, and she wished them every success. On the other hand, she had now worked in LB's London office for several years, and she had always liked the creative that the U.K. team had initially produced. If she maintained the current form of centralized control of the team, either creative concept might be chosen; however, if she decentralized team control, the Toronto team would almost certainly choose their own creative concept for the television ads. Since the creative direction chosen now would become the brand's advertising in most North American and European markets, it needed to be top calibre. Carmichael thought this posed a risk if the creative development was left to the new Toronto-based mass advertising creative team. It would be a shame to lose the U.K. team's original creative concept.

In making her decision on whether to decentralize the team, Carmichael considered the following:

1   Where was the knowledge necessary to create a competitive advantage for the brand in Canada? Would it be in the Canadian marketplace because they understood the market, or would it be in London because they had more in-depth knowledge of the brand?

2   Where was the client responsibility, and where should it be? Now that the London-based global vice-president of skin care was retiring, the client was considering creating a virtual global team to manage the brand, headquartered in the United States but composed of members of the original United Kingdom OBC team, in preparation for a U.S. launch. If the client team had its headquarters in North America, should LB also structure its team this way?

3   If Carmichael decentralized the brand and gave the Toronto team greater autonomy, who would lead the brand in Toronto now that Davids had left the agency? How would the necessary knowledge be imparted to the new leader?

4   If they remained centralized, would the team make it through before it self-destructed? How much would this risk the client relationship? To what extent would it strain the already tight budget?

Carmichael had to make a decision that was best for the brand, LB and OBC.

Exhibit 1 LB Agency Services

Traditional core agency services included:

Account Management

Account management worked in close partnership with planning, creative, media, production and the client to craft tightly focused advertising strategies, based on a deep understanding of the client's products, goals and competition, as well as insights into contemporary consumer behavior.

Creative Services

In most LB offices, creative was the largest department. Creatives focused its visual art and copywriting talents on turning strategic insights into advertising ideas. This department was a key part of each client's brand team and often interacted with both clients and clients' customers.

Planning

Planners conducted research to gain insights about the consumer and the marketplace. They also provided valuable input to the strategic and creative agency processes in the form of the implications raised by that research, specifically combining that learning with information about a given product, the social context in which it fit and the psychology of the people who used it.

Media

Starcom was the media division for LB's parent holding company. Its role was to identify the most influential and efficient media vehicles to deliver brand communications to the appropriate audience.

Production

Production staff brought creative ideas to life with the highest quality execution in television, cinema, radio, print, outdoor, direct, point of sale, interactive or any other medium.

In addition to these core services, most offices also offered expertise in more specialized services, including:

- B2B Technology Marketing
- Direct and Database Marketing
- Health-care Marketing
- Interactive Marketing
- Multicultural Marketing
- Public Relations
- Sales Promotion and Event Marketing

Exhibit 2 LB agency products

Traditional Advertising Products

<u>Television Broadcast Advertising</u> — Usually 30-second (:30s) or 60-second (:60s) TV ads that ran during local or national television programming. This also included sponsoring specific programs, which usually consisted of a five-second announcement before or after the show, i.e., 'This program is brought to you by ...' accompanied by the visual of the sponsoring company's logo.

Radio Broadcast Advertising — Usually 15-, 20-, or 30-second (:15s, :20s, :30s) radio ads that were placed throughout local or national radio programming. Radio ads could include sponsoring specific programs, which usually consisted of a five-second announcement before or after the show, i.e. 'This program brought to you by ...'

Print Advertising — Included black and white and color print ads in local, national or trade newspapers, journals and magazines. Magazine ads could be single-page ads or double-page spreads (two pages facing each other).

Non-Traditional or 'Below the Line' Advertising Products

Direct Marketing — Normally a series of mail-out items (letters, post cards, product samples, etc.) sent to a specifically targeted population(s) called 'cells', e.g., companies might send promotional mail-outs to current customers, former customers who have not shopped with the company for a period or time, and new prospective customers — each of these groups would be considered a cell.

Digital or Interactive Marketing — Any marketing efforts that were delivered to the consumer online or by wireless networks (e.g., hand-held wireless devices). This could include Web site design and production, banner advertising and promotions on other Web sites, e-mail marketing, and internal corporate marketing tools such as customer relationship marketing or database building tools.

<u>Collateral</u> — Any piece of print material that was not strictly advertising, for instance brochures, annual reports, posters, flyers and in-store materials.

Promotions — Any marketing effort that included a time-limited offer or incentive to either purchase a product or offer personal data. Promotions could involve advertising, direct marketing, interactive marketing, product packaging and/or outdoor marketing.

Exhibit 3 LB agency formal and informal reporting lines

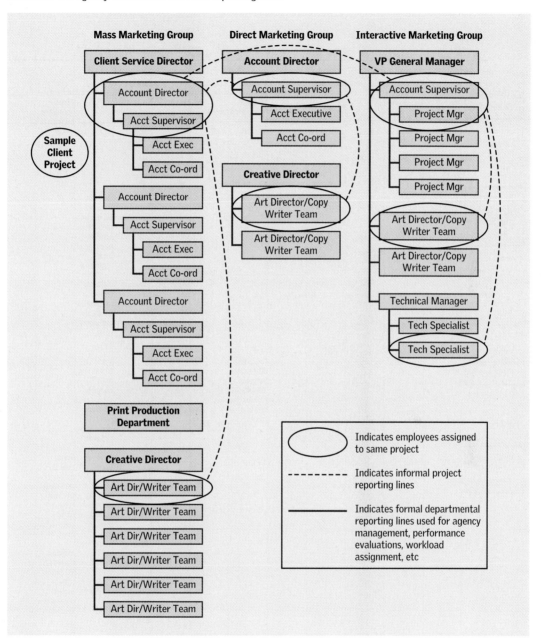

Exhibit 4 Brand development chronology

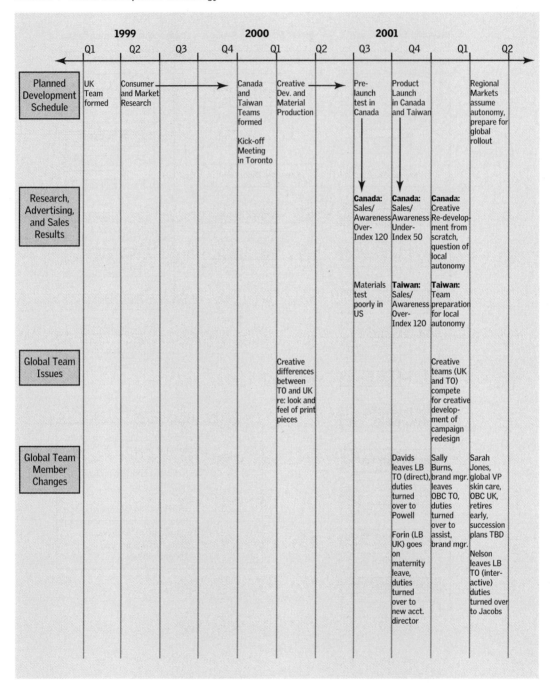

	1999				2000		2001			
	Q1	Q2	Q3	Q4	Q1	Q2	Q3	Q4	Q1	Q2
Planned Development Schedule	UK Team formed	Consumer and Market Research			Canada and Taiwan Teams formed Kick-off Meeting in Toronto	Creative Dev. and Material Production	Pre-launch test in Canada	Product Launch in Canada and Taiwan		Regional Markets assume autonomy, prepare for global rollout
Research, Advertising, and Sales Results							**Canada:** Sales/ Awareness Over-Index 120 Materials test poorly in US	**Canada:** Sales/ Awareness Under-Index 50 **Taiwan:** Sales/ Awareness Over-Index 120	**Canada:** Creative Re-development from scratch, question of local autonomy **Taiwan:** Team preparation for local autonomy	
Global Team Issues					Creative differences between TO and UK re: look and feel of print pieces				Creative teams (UK and TO) compete for creative development of campaign redesign	
Global Team Member Changes							Davids leaves LB TO (direct), duties turned over to Powell Forin (LB UK) goes on maternity leave, duties turned over to new acct. director	Sally Burns, brand mgr. leaves OBC TO, duties turned over to assist, brand mgr.	Sarah Jones, global VP skin care, OBC UK, retires early, succession plans TBD Nelson leaves LB TO (inter-active) duties turned over to Jacobs	

Exhibit 5 The Global Forever Young team

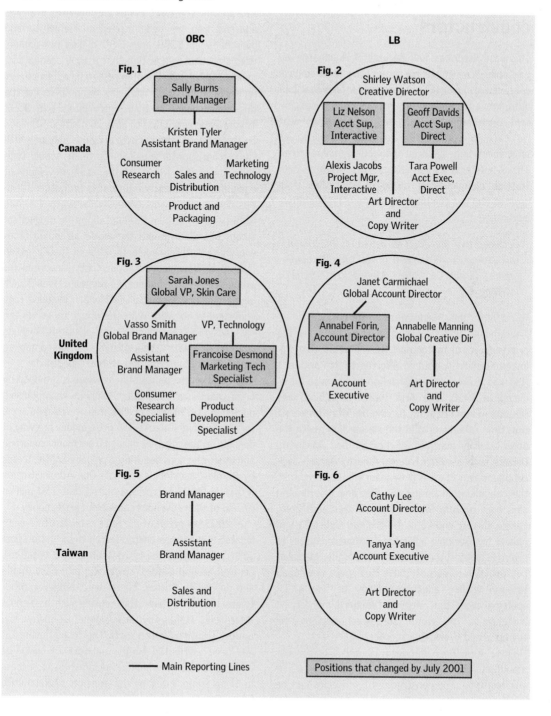

Case 14 **The Formula 1 constructors**

This case describes four periods of dominance by particular firms in a highly competitive technological context. Formula 1 (F1) motorsport is the pinnacle of automotive technology and involves highly special-ized constructors designing and building single-seat racecars to compete for annual championships which bring huge financial and reputational rewards. These four eras explore the stories of three con-trasting companies in terms of how they both created and lost the basis for sustained competitive advantage.

Between two and four on a Sunday afternoon this is a sport. All the rest of the time it's com-merce. (Frank Williams, Managing Director, Williams F1)

In 1945 the Fédération Internationale de l'Automobile (FIA) established Formula A as the premier level of motorsport. In the years that fol-lowed Formula A became referred to as Formula 1 (F1) and a drivers' world championship was intro-duced in 1950. The first world champion was Giuseppe Farina of Italy, driving an Alfa Romeo. At that time Alfa dominated the racing along with the other Italian marques of Ferrari and Maserati. Drivers such as Juan Fangio, Alberto Ascari, Jack Brabham, Jim Clark and Graham Hill were to take the championship during the 50s and 60s driving cars built by Alfa Romeo, Ferrari, Mercedes-Benz, Lancia, Cooper and Lotus. By the mid sixties F1 had moved from being a basis for car manufacturers to promote and test their products to a highly specialist business where purpose built cars were developed through leading edge technology to win a TV sporting event that enjoyed the third highest TV audience in the world, surpassed only by the Olympics and World Cup soccer.

There have been between 10 and 14 race car manufacturers or constructors competing in F1 at any one time. The constructors themselves can be

By Mark Jenkins

© 2004, M. Jenkins, Nottingham University Business School.

grouped into a number of different categories. In 2003 the top three teams were Ferrari, Williams and McLaren, all medium-sized businesses turning over between $250 and $350 million per annum, with estimates suggesting that it took around $50 million capital investment in research facilities to set up the minimum basis for being competitive. For the first three years of their entry into F1 in 2002 Toyota were estimated to have committed $1 billion on capital and running costs of which only one-fifth came from sponsorship. The top teams would typi-cally have their own testing and development equipment, including wind-tunnels and other facili-ties. The larger teams employed between 450 and 800 people in their F1 operations, a quarter of whom travelled around the world attending races every two to three weeks throughout the F1 season (March to November). Labour costs accounted for around 25% of the budget. All the teams would have highly qualified technical staff which included race engineers (who work with the driver to set up the car), designers, aerodynamicists, composite experts (to work with specialized carbon-composite materials) and information systems specialists.

In addition to sponsorship, revenue is provided by prize money generated by winning championship points; in 2003 this was allocated on a sliding scale for the first eight places. The prize money is a way of dividing up the royalties earned from media coverage and other revenues negotiated on behalf of the teams by Bernie Ecclestone's Formula One Administration (FOA). In 2003 Ferrari estimated that $30 million (9.7%) of their revenues came from prize money.

In 2003 seven out of the ten F1 constructors were located in what has been referred to as 'motorsport valley', an area of the UK described by a broad arc centred around Oxford, stretching into East Anglia and down into Surrey. There were, however, other teams located outside this region, such as Ferrari (Maranello, Italy), Toyota (Cologne, Germany) and Sauber (Hinwil, Switzerland). The focus on the UK has been attributed to the network of specialist engineering talent which is fundamental to success in F1, as summarized by the principal of RenaultF1, Flavio Briatore: '*If you like proscuitto you come to Italy. If you like champagne, you come to France. For Formula 1 you come to England. I don't like the English weather, but the best engineering is here.*'

The Formula 1 constructors provide a unique context to consider the competitive advantage of different multi-million-pound organizations over time. The pace of change and the basis of advantage is constantly changing, shown by the fact that since the start of the world championships, only two constructors have won the championship consecutively more than four times (McLaren 1988–91; Ferrari 1999–2003) and only Ferrari (1975–1977) and Williams (1992–1994) have won for three consecutive years. The remainder of the case considers each of these periods of competitive dominance in chronological order.

Ferrari 1975–1979

The period 1975–77 saw a renaissance for the Ferrari team. Their previous F1 World Championship had been won in 1964, one of the few reminders of the glorious 50s and early 60s when the bright red cars of Ferrari dominated motor racing. In the mid 70s they won 15 of the 45 races during 1975, 1976 and 1977.

Ferrari are the oldest of all the Grand Prix teams still racing. Their heritage gives them a special place in the hearts of all motor racing enthusiasts. Founded by Enzo Ferrari, an ex-driver and manager of the Alfa Romeo racing team in 1950, they and other Italian marques of Maserati and Alfa dominated the sport during the 1950s. By the end of 2003 Ferraris had taken part in more than 550 Grand Prix and, despite the variable nature of the team's performance, drivers continue to view a contract with Ferrari as something very special. Perhaps this is why world champions such as Alain Prost, Nigel Mansell and Michael Schumacher have been attracted to the team at times when their cars have been far from the fastest or most reliable.

In an era when the majority of constructors are British specialists who buy in components such as engines and gearboxes, Ferrari had always done everything themselves. Engine, gearbox, suspension, chassis were all made at their Maranello factory, which enjoys the most up-to-date facilities in terms of designing, developing and building all the necessary components of a race-car. While other constructors such as McLaren and Williams would paint their cars whatever colour was required by their flagship sponsor, Ferraris had always been blood red, the national colour of Italy, a throwback from the time when F1 cars were colour coded by country of origin. There was also very little evidence of sponsorship on the Ferrari cars; it has always been the Ferrari emblem – a black prancing horse on a yellow shield – which has the most prominent position. The Italian public see Ferrari as a national icon, as observed by Niki Lauda:

> *The Italians love you when you win and hate you when you lose and whatever you do, win, lose or simply break wind everyone in Italy wants to know about it!*

The influence of Enzo Ferrari, or Il Commendatore as he was frequently known, was pervasive and the myths and stories surrounding him still permeate the team. It was legendary that Ferrari himself hardly ever attended a race and rarely left the Maranello factory where his beloved cars were made. He relied on the media and his advisors for information, which often created a highly political atmosphere in the team. Ferrari's first love was motor racing, this was despite having created a very successful range of road-going cars which he saw primarily as the source of funding for his racing. The merger between Fiat and Ferrari in 1969, when Fiat acquired a 50% stake in the company, provided Ferrari with a huge cash injection. While Fiat would manage the production of the road cars, Enzo, who was then 71, would retain control of the racing operation to concentrate on his first love, motor racing at the highest level: Formula 1.

The resources which Ferrari had at their disposal were the envy of every other team. They had always built their own engines and have a large technical team dedicated to the task of engine design and development. In 1971 they opened their own test track at Fiorano, a few hundred yards from the Maranello factory. At the time it was the most advanced and sophisticated test circuit in the world, enabling the cars to be constantly tested and developed between the track and the factory. This effectively gave Ferrari their own Grand Prix circuit. All their competitors were obliged to hire a circuit such as Silverstone in the UK and transport their cars and equipment for a two- or three-day test. Ferrari himself attended most of the tests and would make sure he was kept informed as to exactly what was being tested and why. Enzo himself had always declared his love for the distinctive sound and power of a Ferrari engine, as indicated by former Ferrari driver Nigel Mansel: *'Enzo Ferrari believed that the engine was the most important part of the race car. Colin [Chapman – head of British constructor Lotus] believed it was the chassis.'*

The early seventies were difficult for Ferrari. The new ownership and influence from Fiat meant increased resources, but also increased pressure for results. At this time F1 was dominated by the Ford DFV engine. Built by Cosworth Engineering near Northampton and funded by the Ford Motor Company, the DFV was purpose built for F1. It was light, powerful and relatively inexpensive. In 1968 the engines were available for £7500 each and were fully capable of winning a Grand Prix. This enabled the British constructors, which specialized in chassis design, to become increasingly competitive. In 1971 and 1973 every Grand Prix was won by a car using a DFV engine.

In 1971 the Ferrari racecars were very fast, but unreliable. It got worse in 1972 and 1973, with cars only finishing every other race and rarely in the points. Enzo himself had been suffering poor health and the team seemed unable to turn around despite having the huge resources of Fiat at its disposal. However, through 1974 things began to change. A few years earlier Ferrari engineers had commissioned a small firm in the UK, TC prototypes to build three chassis for the 1974 car using a monocoque structure, derived from aircraft design and favoured by the English constructors. Mauro Forghieri had also been recalled to Ferrari in 1973 as technical director. Forghieri had been responsible for some of the more successful Ferraris of the 1960s but had fallen from grace and spent the later part of the 1960s working on 'special projects'.

In addition to the arrival of Forghieri, a new team boss was also appointed to try to turn Ferrari fortunes around. At 25 years old and a qualified lawyer with connections to the Agnelli family who owned Fiat, Luca di Montezemolo was an unlikely right-hand man for Il Commendatore. However, he was given a relatively free hand by Ferrari and brought much needed management discipline to the team. While there had always been a huge supply of talent at Ferrari, particularly in the design and development of engines, gearboxes and suspension systems, it had not always reached its collective potential. Enzo's autocratic style of 'divide and rule' had created much confusion and rivalry within the team. Montezemolo defined strict areas of responsibility in order to reduce the amount of interference and internal politics. This created a situation where the various technical teams (chassis and suspension; engine; gearbox) concentrated on, and were fully accountable for, their own area. Montezemolo was also instrumental in the recruitment of driver Niki Lauda. Lauda was of Austrian aristocratic descent, but was totally committed to his racing. He had been very successful in Formula Two but was having a torrid time with the ailing BRM team in F1. In 1973 Enzo Ferrari told Lauda he wanted him to drive for Ferrari, an offer which very few drivers have ever refused.

In 1974 Lauda and the design team had embarked upon an exhaustive testing and development programme at the Fiorano test track. The new car, the 312B, was very fast. However, there were still reliability problems and although Lauda was leading the championship at the British Grand Prix, the lead was lost through technical problems which resulted in Emerson Fittipaldi in a McLaren taking the eventual honours.

In 1975 the fruits of Forghieri's creative ideas and the intensive testing at Fiorano were exemplified in the new 312T, which featured a wide low body with a powerful 'flat-12' 12-cylinder engine and a revolutionary transverse (sideways mounted) gearbox which improved the balance of the car, making it handle extremely well. While the new car was not ready until the season had already started, Lauda, with the support of team-mate Regazzoni, was easily able to secure both the drivers' and constructors' world championships. The Ferraris dominated the 1975 season. With their elegant handling and the power advantage of the engine, they were in a class of their own. Because the majority of the competition all had the same engine gearbox combination (Ford DFV and Hewland gearbox), they were unable to respond to a chassis/gearbox/engine combination which was unique to Ferrari.

The following year, 1976, continued in much the same vein, with Lauda and Regazzoni winning the early races. The intensive testing did not let up and new ideas and innovations, such as a revised rear suspension system, were constantly being tried out. On the management front, Montezemolo had been promoted to head up Fiat's entire motorsport operation, which included the Lancia rally programme as well as Ferrari. Daniele Audetto was moved from managing the rally team to Sporting Director at Ferrari. However, things were not to go as smoothly as in 1975. At the German Grand Prix Lauda lost control of the car in the wet and crashed in flames. He was rescued by four other drivers, but not before suffering severe burns and inhaling toxic fumes. His life was in the balance for some weeks while the Grand Prix series continued with James Hunt (McLaren) reducing Lauda's lead in the championship. Miraculously Lauda recovered from his injuries, and although still badly scarred, he returned to race for Ferrari. He and Hunt went into the last Grand Prix of 1976 (Japan) with Lauda leading by three points. There was heavy rain and Lauda pulled out of the race leaving the drivers' championship to Hunt, although Ferrari still collected the constructors' championship. While, on paper, it was a good year, by rights Ferrari should have dominated 1976 as they had 1975. Audetto, who had been unable to live up to the role created by Montezemolo, returned to the world of rallying. Ferrari went into 1977 in a state of disarray.

In 1977 Ferrari were still the team to beat, although the testing and development lost through Lauda's six-week convalescence had undermined the crushing dominance which the team had earlier demonstrated. The competition were beginning to find ways of catching up. The Brabham team moved away from the Ford DFV and used an Alfa Romeo 'flat-12', similar to the Ferrari engine. Tyrrell launched the revolutionary P34 six-wheeled car which seemed to be the only car able to stay with the Ferrari in 1976. Ferrari themselves were not standing still and launched the 312T2 which was a significant development of the original 312T. Ferrari won the 1977 drivers' and constructors' championship, but this was the end of the partnership with Niki Lauda; the relationship had never been the same since the Nurburgring accident. Lauda left to join Brabham. While Lauda was not perhaps the fastest racer on the track, he was always able to develop a

car and build relationships with the design team which enabled Ferrari to translate the driver's senses into reliable technical solutions.

The unprecedented run of Ferrari success continued in 1978 with the 312T3 car driven by two highly talented drivers: Argentinean Carlos Reutemann was joined by the flamboyant Gilles Villeneuve and, while they were not able to win the constructors' championship, they achieved a very strong second place. In 1979 Reutemann was replaced by South African Jody Scheckter, whose consistency contrasted with Villeneuve's erratic speed. Scheckter won the drivers' championship, with Ferrari taking the constructors' championship. Their greatest moment was when Scheckter and Villeneuve finished first and second in the Italian Grand Prix at Monza.

However, 1979 was the last time that Ferrari were to win a drivers' world championship for 21 years. 1980 was something of a disaster for Ferrari. Scheckter and Villeneuve were totally uncompetitive in the 312T5 car which, while a significant development from the 312T4, was outclassed by the competition. New innovations in aerodynamics brought the 'ground effect' revolution, pioneered by Lotus and quickly adopted by Williams and Brabham. Here the underside of the car featured two 'venturi', or channels, either side of the driver. These were aerodynamically designed to create a low-pressure area under the car which sucked the car to the track, allowing faster cornering. Sliding strips of material or 'skirts' were used to create a seal for the air flowing under the car. While the Ferrari's engine was one of the most powerful, it was a flat-12 meaning that the cylinders were horizontal to the ground, creating a low and wide barrier which gave no opportunity to create the ground effect achieved with the slimmer V8 DFV engines. In 1978 Alfa Romeo had launched a V12 engine to replace their flat-12 for this very reason. No such initiative had been taken at Ferrari which was concentrating on a longer-term project to develop a V6 turbo-charged engine. *Autosport* correspondent Nigel Roebuck commented on this change of fortune: 'Maranello's flat-12, still a magnificent racing engine, is incompatible with modern chassis. Villeneuve and Scheckter were competing in yesterday's cars.' The lowest point came in the Canadian Grand Prix when the reigning world champion, Jody Scheckter, failed to qualify his Ferrari for the race. Once again the full wrath of the Italian press descended on the team.

McLaren Honda 1988–1991

The period from 1988 to 1991 was unusual in the hyper-competitive world of F1, where the pace of change is rarely matched in any other competitive environment. This period was notable because of the dominance of one constructor. In one year the McLaren team won 15 of the 16 races. Such dominance had not been seen before and is unlikely to occur again.

Founded by New Zealander and F1 driver Bruce McLaren in 1966, the McLaren team had their first victory in the Belgian Grand Prix of 1968. Tragically McLaren himself was killed two years later while testing. Lawyer and family friend Teddy Mayer took over as team principal. The team continued to develop and in 1974 secured a long-term sponsorship from Philip Morris to promote the Marlboro brand of cigarettes. This was a partnership that was to last until 1996, probably the most enduring relationship between a constructor and a 'flagship' sponsor. However, in the late seventies McLaren found itself left behind by some of the new aerodynamic advances. In September 1980 Ron Dennis became joint team principal with Mayer, a position which he took over solely in 1982, when Mayer was 'encouraged' by Philip Morris to take a less active role in the management of McLaren. In the previous year McLaren moved from their modest site in Colnbrook to a modern facility at Woking in Surrey, South of London.

Dennis had been a mechanic for the highly successful Cooper team in 1966, but left to set up his own Formula 2 (a smaller, less expensive formula) team in 1971. By the end of the 70s he had built up a reputation for professionalism and immaculate presentation. His Project Four company brought in designer John Barnard, who had some radical ideas about using carbon fibre, rather than metal, as the basis for a race car chassis. These ideas were to provide the basis for the radical MP4 car. Both Dennis and Barnard were perfectionists, with Dennis's obsession with immaculate presentation and attention to detail complemented by Barnard's

uncompromising quest for technical excellence. As John Barnard observed in an interview, the entire nature of the organization shifted: 'We changed from being mechanic-led to a team which was totally controlled by the drawing office. Ron used to tell everyone time and time again, "I don't care if we're the last two cars on the grid, we'll be the smartest and the best presented" and that attitude built into the company once it was launched.'

In 1986 John Barnard left to join the struggling Ferrari team. Barnard was considered by many to be the reason for McLaren's developing dominance. The partnership between Dennis and Barnard had been stormy, but a huge amount had been achieved through the energy of these two individuals. Dennis provided the managerial and commercial acumen and Barnard the highly innovative design skills. To replace Barnard, Brabham designer Gordon Murray was brought into the team, perhaps best known for developing the innovative 'fan car' for Brabham in 1978. Murray, like Barnard, was at the leading edge of F1 car design.

A further factor in McLaren's success had been their relationship with engine suppliers. In the mid eighties turbo-charging became the key technology and in 1983 they used a Porsche turbo engine which was funded by the electronics' company TAG, a sponsor which had previously been with the Williams team. However, the emerging force in engine development was Honda, which had re-entered F1 in 1983 in partnership with Williams. Importantly, the engines were supported by a significant commitment from Honda in both people and resources. Honda used the relationship as an opportunity to develop some of their most talented engineers and to transfer F1 design and development capabilities to their production car programme. In the mid eighties the Williams/Honda partnership was very successful, but following Frank Williams' road accident in 1986, Honda began to have doubts about the future of the Williams team and agreed to supply both McLaren and Lotus for the 1987 season.

Halfway through 1987 McLaren announced that they had recruited two of the top drivers in F1 to their team for the 1988 season: Alain Prost and Ayrton Senna. This was unusual as most teams tended to have a clear hierarchy with a lead driver being supported by a 'number two', who was either regarded as less skilful and/or less experienced than the lead driver. However, McLaren appeared to feel that they would be able to deal with the potential problems which such a structure could cause, as reported in *Motorsport*:

> Ayrton Senna is being moved from Lotus to McLaren to join Prost in one of the most professional and well balanced teams of all time. Prost and Senna have been announced as joint number one drivers, and McLaren International has shown in the past that it is well capable of handling two top drivers, which few other teams have managed.

Ayrton Senna, the young Brazilian, had made a name for himself as being extremely talented and totally committed, but very difficult to manage. In his previous team, Lotus, he is alleged to have blocked the recruitment of second driver Derek Warwick as he regarded him too great a threat and persuaded the team to bring in the less experienced and younger Johnny Dumfries. Prost and Senna were real contrasts: Senna was fast, determined and ruthless. Prost was fast too, but a great tactician and adept at team politics, making sure that the whole team was behind him. It was rumoured that a key reason for Honda moving to McLaren was that they now had Alain Prost. However, it was ultimately Senna who was able to win the psychological battle and change the balance of power within the team.

In 1988 the Honda-powered MP4 car was without question the fastest and most reliable car on the circuit. This meant that effectively the only real competition for Prost and Senna was each other. This competition between two highly committed and talented drivers resulted in one of the most enduring and bitter feuds the sport has ever known. In 1988 Senna swerved at Prost as they raced wheel to wheel at 190 mph. Prost told him, '*If you want the world championship badly enough to die for it, you are welcome*'. In 1990 the acrimony with Senna culminated in Prost moving to Ferrari. Senna now had the team to himself. But the battle between them continued, reaching a dramatic climax at the Japanese Grand Prix when Senna forced Prost's Ferrari off the road, and as a consequence became world champion.

Ron Dennis and his professional management style was synonymous with the success of McLaren, indicating that the era of the 'one-man band' Formula One constructor was past. Eddie Jordan, principal of the Jordan team made the following statement when planning to enter F1 in 1990:

> I know it sounds far fetched, but I want to emulate Ron Dennis. He's won that many Grand Prix, he's won that many championships, he's been on pole that many times and he's got the best drivers. Everyone hates him; but they only hate him because he's the best. I believe I'm as good as he is: I believe I'm in the same league, but only time will tell.

Dennis's negotiating and marketing abilities were legendary throughout Formula One. McLaren also created their own marketing consultancy operation where the smaller teams engaged them to find sponsors. In 1991 *Management Week* had Ron Dennis on the front cover with the question, 'Is Ron Dennis Britain's best manager?' Dennis likens the management of McLaren to that of a game of chess: '... *you've got to get all the elements right, the overall package, the budget, the designer, the engine, the drivers, the organization*.' John Barnard once likened working with Dennis as: '*being in a room with a hand grenade rolling about without its pin, about to go off and make a horrible mess.*' Dennis is renowned for being hyper-competitive and allegedly once chastised a driver who was delighted with finishing second with the comment, '*Remember, you're only the first of the losers*'. Dennis's ambitions went beyond F1 and in 1988 he began a project to build a road-going car, the McLaren F1. In many ways this mirrored the development of Ferrari, which had made the progression from producing dedicated race cars to also develop road-going cars. The McLaren F1 was launched in 1994 and, with a price tag of £634,000 and a top speed of 231 mph, became the most expensive and fastest road-going car in the world.

The McLaren Honda combination had dominated F1 from 1988 through to 1991, and it was difficult to see what more could be achieved. In September 1992, following widespread speculation, Honda confirmed that that they were pulling out of F1 racing. Honda's reasons were simple: they had been hugely successful and achieved all of their objectives; it was now time to stand back from F1 and find some new challenges. While Dennis had been told about Honda's thinking in late 1991, it appeared that he hadn't taken it seriously enough and the team had no realistic alternatives. This meant they lost valuable winter development time as they tried to find a new engine supplier. In 1993 they competed with customer Ford engines available to any team that had the cash to buy them. Senna's skills still gave McLaren five victories, despite having a less than competitive car. However, at the end of 1993 Senna left the McLaren team to move to Williams, which he saw as having the superior car and engine combination. Former world champion and adviser to Ferrari, Niki Lauda saw this as the terminal blow: *'Senna was a leader. He told them exactly what was wrong with the car. Hakkinen* (Senna's replacement) *is not in a position to do that, so the reaction time is much longer. Senna motivated the designers.'* John Hogan, VP of European marketing for Philip Morris and holder of the McLaren purse strings, saw the problem as design leadership and was advocating that Barnard be brought back to McLaren.

The mid nineties was a particularly difficult period for McLaren. Having tried Peugeot engines in 1994, they moved to Mercedes in 1995. However, 1995 was perhaps best remembered for the debacle at the start when neither Nigel Mansell nor Mika Hakinnen could fit into the new £50 million MP4/10 and then Mansell's alleged £4.5 million contract to race for the year fell apart when neither he nor the car came up to expectations. On a more positive note, 1995 was significant in that it heralded a new partnership between McLaren and Mercedes. Mercedes had been considering a major commitment to F1 and in 1995 they concluded a deal which involved their taking equity stakes in McLaren (40%) and also in specialist engine builder Ilmor Engineering, based near Northampton (25%, increased in 2002 to 55%) which was to build the Mercedes engines used in F1. This relationship was wider than just F1 and would lead to the design and manufacture of the new Mercedes SLR sports car using F1 technology and materials.

Williams Renault 1992–1994

If the McLaren MP4 was the dominant car in the late eighties, the Williams F1 FW15 and 16 powered by a Renault V10 was the car to beat in the early 1990s. During the period 1992–94 Williams cars won 27 out of 48 races, they secured the F1 constructors' title for all three years and the world championship for drivers was won in a Williams in 1992 (Nigel Mansell) and 1993 (Alain Prost).

Like most of the founders of the Formula One constructors, Frank Williams began as a driver, perhaps not of the same standing as Bruce McLaren or Jack Brabham, but nonetheless someone who lived, breathed and loved motor racing. His desire to remain in the sport led him to develop a business buying and selling racing cars and spare parts and in 1968 Frank Williams (Racing Cars) Ltd was formed. A series of triumphs, tragedies and near bankruptcies led up to the establishment of Williams Grand Prix Engineering in 1977 when Frank Williams teamed up with technical director Patrick Head. His approach and style owed a lot to the difficult years in the seventies when he survived on his wits and very little else. At one time he was making calls to sponsors from a public telephone box near the workshop as the phones were disconnected because he hadn't been able to pay the bill. His style could be described as autocratic, entrepreneurial and certainly frugal, despite the multi-million-pound funding he managed to extract from the likes of Canon, R.J. Reynolds and Rothmans. Williams saw his role as providing the resources to build the best car; therefore, anything that didn't directly make the car go faster was a waste of money as far as Frank was concerned. His long-standing relationship with Head was pivotal to the team and brought together a blend of entrepreneurial energy and technical excellence needed to succeed in F1.

The first car from this new alliance was the FW06, designed by Patrick Head and with support from Saudi Airlines. The team enjoyed their first real success in 1980/81 by winning the constructors' championship and with Alan Jones winning the drivers' title in 1980. Jones was a forthright Australian who knew what he wanted and was not afraid to voice his opinions; he also simply got on with the job of driving with little fuss or expectations of special treatment. His approach to working with the team was very influential and coloured Frank Williams' view of drivers: *'I took a very masculine attitude towards drivers and assumed that they should behave – or should be treated – like Alan.'*

A further success occurred in 1986/87 with Nelson Piquet winning the drivers' title in 1987 and Williams the constructors' title in both years. This was despite the road accident in 1986, which left Frank Williams tetraplegic and confined to a wheelchair. However, 1988 was Williams' worst season, with Honda having switched to supplying McLaren, they were forced to suddenly switch to 'off the shelf' Judd V10 engines which were available to anyone who wanted one. Williams didn't win a single race, while McLaren won 15 out of the 16 Grand Prix of 1988 and a disillusioned Nigel Mansell left and went to Ferrari. Frank Williams had to search frantically for a new engine deal which he found in 1990 with Renault. At the end of 1985 Renault had withdrawn from Formula One as a constructor, having failed to win a world championship over the previous eight seasons. However, they continued their engine development activities with the aim of building a new F1 engine to meet the new non-turbo standards due to be introduced in 1989. Frank Williams was able to form an agreement for Renault to supply him with the new V10 engine. This relationship became a far reaching and durable one, with Renault putting human and financial resources into the project with Williams. They also sought to develop the relationship further and extended their activities with Renault by running their team of saloon cars for the British Touring Car Championship, and also provided engineering input and the Williams name for a special edition of the Renault Clio.

In 1990 a lack of driver talent meant that the team were only able to win two races. In 1991 Nigel Mansell was persuaded to return from retirement by Frank Williams and narrowly missed taking the 1991 title, but in 1992 the team dominated the circuits, effectively winning the championship by the middle of the season. Nigel Mansell went into the record books by winning the first five consecutive races of the season. However, deterioration in the relationship between Williams and Mansell led to the driver's retirement from F1 at the end of the year.

The Williams approach to design and development of a car was always the highest priority. Patrick Head had always been one of the more conspicuous of the technical directors in Formula One, a role which is often put into the shade by the team principal and driver. In a sport where personnel change teams frequently, the stable relationship between Williams and Head provided enviable continuity compared with the rest of the field. While Head's designs had often been functional rather than innovative, he had always been able to take a good idea and develop it further. These have included ground effect (originally developed by Lotus), carbon-composite monocoque (McLaren), semi-automatic gearbox (Ferrari), and active suspension (Lotus). The car development process was always a top priority at Williams and Head was supported by many junior designers who then went on to be highly influential in Formula One, such as Neil Oatley and Adrian Newey (both with McLaren), Frank Dernie (Ligier, Lotus and Arrows), Geoff Willis (BAR) and Ross Brawn (Benetton and then Ferrari).

This focus on developing the car and engine combination sometimes meant that the driver took second place in the Williams philosophy, despite the fact that a good driver, who could tell the technicians what needed to be done to the car to improve its performance, was essential to the development process. There had been a number of high-profile disputes between drivers and Williams which had, in part, been attributable to Frank Williams' 'masculine' approach to dealing with drivers. Controversy broke out when the relationship between Williams and two top British drivers broke down. In 1992 Nigel Mansell left when he felt his 'number one' driver position was threatened by the recruitment of Alain Prost for 1993 (although Prost himself left the following year for the same reason regarding the hiring of Ayrton Senna). A similar situation arose when the 1996 world champion, Damon Hill was not retained for the 1997 season and was replaced with Heinz-Harald Frentzen. In an interview with the *Sunday Times* Patrick Head set out the reasons for the decision not to hold on to Hill: *'We are an engineering company and that is what we focus on. Ferrari are probably the only team where you can say the driver is of paramount importance and that is because* [Michael] *Schumacher is three-quarters of a second a lap quicker than anyone else.'*

This emphasis on the driver being only part of the equation was not lost on Paul Stewart, who was concentrating on developing the Stewart Grand Prix entry to F1 in 1996:

If you haven't got the money none of it is possible, so money is one key to success – but what makes a difference is how the money is used. It's not down to any one thing like a driver or an engine, but the interaction that matters. If you look at the Williams team, they rely on a solid framework, their organization, their engine, their car design is all amalgamated into something that gives a platform for everyone to work on. They don't believe putting millions into a driver is going to make all the difference.

Williams' emphatic dominance in the 1992 season was due to a number of factors: the development of the powerful and reliable Renault engine was perfectly complemented by the FW15 chassis which incorporated Patrick Head's development of some of the innovations of the early nineties, namely semi-automatic gearboxes, drive-by-wire technology and their own active suspension system. As summarized by a senior manager at Williams F1: '*I think we actually were better able to exploit the technology that was available and led that technology revolution. We were better able to exploit it to the full, before the others caught up ... it wasn't just one thing but a combination of many things, each one giving you another 200/300th of a second, if you add them up you a get a couple of seconds of advantage.*'

However, other teams were also able to use these innovations and in 1993 the Benetton team made a great deal of progress with both the gearbox and suspension innovations largely attributed to the development skills of their new driver, Michael Schumacher. Williams' technical lead coupled with the tactical race skills of Alain Prost, supported by promoted test driver Damon Hill (due to Mansell's sudden exit) secured the 1993 world championship and constructors' championship for Williams F1.

1994 was a disastrous year, but not for reasons of performance as Williams won the constructors' championship for the third successive year (this was always their declared primary objective, with the drivers' championship very much a secondary aim). Frank Williams had, for some time, regarded Brazilian Ayrton Senna as the best driver around and now, with the obvious performance advantage of the FW15 chassis and the Renault V10 engine, Senna was keen to move to Williams. The problem

was that a bitter and prolonged feud between Senna and Prost, originating from their time together at McLaren, meant that if Senna arrived, Prost would leave. This was exactly what happened. Prost decided to retire (though he returned to run his own team) and Ayrton Senna was partnered by Damon Hill for the 1994 season. However, tragedy struck in the San Marino Grand Prix at Imola on 1 May 1994 when Senna was killed in an accident, an event which not only devastated the Williams team but the sport as a whole.

For the remainder of the season Hill found himself as lead driver supported by the new test driver David Coulthard and a couple of 'comebacks' from Nigel Mansell. While Williams lost the drivers' title to the rising star of German driver Michael Schumacher, despite these huge setbacks Williams retained the constructors' title for 1994.

In 1995 the Benetton team was eclipsing the Williams domination. Benetton had developed a car using many of the technological innovations used by Williams (with the help of ex-Williams designer Ross Brawn). In addition, Renault's ambitions to match Honda's previous domination of the sport as an engine supplier from 1986–1991 led them to supply Benetton with their engines as well as Williams, a decision which incensed Head and Williams. 1995 was the year of Benetton and Michael Schumacher, breaking the three-year domination of the Williams team. However, in 1996 Schumacher moved to the then uncompetitive Ferrari team for £27 million, putting him in 3rd place in the Forbes chart of sports top earners. This left the way clear for Williams to dominate the season, with Benetton failing to fill the gap left by Schumacher.

Ferrari: 1999–2003

The 1980s were a difficult period for Ferrari; more and more investment was poured into the Italian facilities but with no effect on performance. A key problem was that new developments in aerodynamics and the use of composite materials had emerged from the UK's motorsport valley. Ferrari had traditionally focused on the engine as their key competitive advantage. This made perfect sense as, unlike most of the competition who outsourced their engines, Ferrari designed and manufactured their

CASE 14 THE FORMULA 1 CONSTRUCTORS C233

own engines. However, it appeared that these new technologies were substituting superior engine power with enhanced grip due to aerodynamic downforce and improved chassis rigidity.

In 1984, in an effort to introduce a greater understanding of aerodynamics in Ferrari, British designer Harvey Postlethwaite became the first non-Italian Technical Director of Ferrari. In 1986 British designer John Barnard was recruited to the top technical role. However, Barnard was not prepared to move to Italy as he felt that his technical team and network of contacts in the UK would be essential to the success of his position. Surprisingly Enzo Ferrari allowed him to establish a design and manufacturing facility near Guildford in Surrey that became known as the Ferrari 'GTO' or Guildford Technical Office. It seemed that rather than being a unique and distinctively Italian F1 team, Ferrari were now prepared to imitate the British constructors who Enzo had once, rather contemptuously, referred to as the 'Garagistes'. The concept of the GTO was that it was concerned with longer-term research and development and would concentrate on the design of the following year's car, whereas in Maranello, under Postlethwaite, they would focus on building and racing the current car. However, the fact that Barnard was defining the technical direction of Ferrari meant that he became increasingly involved in activities at both sites.

Enzo Ferrari's death in 1988 created a vacuum which was filled by executives from the Fiat organization for a number of years. It was written into the contract that on Enzo's death Fiat's original stake would be increased to 90%; this greater investment led to attempts to run Ferrari as a formal subsidiary of the Fiat group. Barnard became frustrated with the interference and politics of the situation and left to join Benetton in 1989. However, at the end of 1991 Fiat brought Luca di Montezemolo back to Ferrari, this time as CEO with a mandate to do whatever was needed to take Ferrari back to the top. Montezemolo had been team manager with Ferrari during the successful period in the mid seventies. After leaving Ferrari he had taken on a range of high-profile management roles including running Italy's hosting of the soccer World Cup in 1990. One of Montezemolo's first actions was to re-appoint John Barnard as technical director and

re-establish GTO. He was quoted in *The Times* as follows: '*In Italy we are cut away from the Silicon Valley of Formula One that has sprung up in England.*' With an Englishman heading up design he followed this up with the appointment of a Frenchman, Jean Todt, to handle the overall management of the team. Both appointments were clear signals to all involved in Ferrari that things were going to change. Todt had no experience in F1 but had been in motorsport management for many years and had recently led a successful rally and sportscar programme at Peugeot.

However, the physical separation between design and development in Guildford and the racing operation in Maranello led to increased problems and eventually Barnard and Ferrari parted company in 1996. This opened the way for Ferrari to recruit a number of the key individuals in the Benetton technical team to join driver Michael Schumacher who had moved from Benetton to start the 1996 season with the Maranello team. Todt and Montezemolo also chose not to make a direct replacement for the role of technical supremo who would both lead the design of the car and the management of the technical activity. They split the role between a chief designer, Rory Byrne, who had overall responsibility for designing the car, and Ross Brawn, who managed the entire technical operation, roles which both had undertaken in working with Schumacher at Benetton. However, the contractual arrangement with John Barnard had been one where the GTO designers were paid through his private company. When he left they all went with him and Byrne and Brawn faced the task of building up from scratch a new design department – around 50 people, based in Italy.

Along with their recruitment of Michael Schumacher in 1996, Ferrari entered into a commercial partnership with tobacco giant Phillip Morris to use their Marlboro brand on the Ferrari cars. In a novel arrangement Phillip Morris, rather than Ferrari, paid Schumacher's salary, and also made a significant contribution to Ferrari's annual operating budget. However, there was one price to pay which troubled many long-term Ferrari officiandos: the blood-red Ferrari of old was now replaced by a vivid red which more closely matched Marlboro 'rocket red' and also, importantly was more effective on television. There was much speculation about the wisdom of these changes, but Montezemolo was clear that these had to be made to move forward:

> For me the company's human resources are critical, the atmosphere is extremely important. I want people, first of all, who love Ferrari and are totally willing to work as a team. You need people able to work together and look forward at the same time. OK, the company has a long history, which holds the lessons for the future, but I don't want people to look at it and stop. The past is the past, important as a point of reference but that's it.

Ferrari also entered into a long-term partnership with Shell to provide both financial and technical support to the team. In these kinds of arrangements Ferrari led a trend away from selling space on cars to long-term commercial arrangements, with coordinated marketing strategies for commercial partners to maximize the benefits of their investments.

This rejuvenated team provided the basis for Michael Schumacher's dominance of F1 in the early part of the 21st century. In 1997 they raced the Barnard-developed Ferrari and finished second in the constructors' championship. Their competitiveness continued to improve and in 1999 they won their first constructors' championship for 12 years – although with an injured Schumacher missing six Grand Prix, the driver's championship went to Mika Hakkinen in a McLaren-Mercedes. However, in 2000 Ferrari secured both championships and it was at this point that they felt they had truly returned to the glory of the mid seventies, it having been 21 years since their last drivers' world championship. In 2002 Schumacher and Ferrari were so dominant that a series of regulation changes were introduced to try to make the racing more competitive. These changes were also prompted by Ferrari's tradition of having a lead driver, which meant that often the second driver was asked to move over in order for the lead driver to maximize his world championship points. This happened at the 2002 Austrian Grand Prix when Ferrari driver Rubens Barrichello moved over just before the finish line to allow Michael Schumacher to win. This produced an angry reaction from fans worldwide and made both the governing body – the FIA – and Ferrari reflect on the wisdom of such a blatant use of team orders.

While Schumacher's talent as a driver and a motivator of the team (he learnt Japanese to converse with an engine technician recruited from Honda) was clearly critical, another key aspect in Ferrari's advantage for 2002 had been their relationship with Bridgestone tyres. Tyres were regarded as a 'black art' in F1, with differing compounds of rubber and different tyre wall construction suiting different cars and different drivers; whereas with changes in aerodynamics teams could make improvements in 100ths of a second, with the right tyre the improvements could result in an advantage in terms of whole seconds rather than tenths or hundredths. In 2000 Bridgestone had been the sole supplier to all F1 teams and therefore tyres were not a source of competitive advantage. However, in 2001 Michelin entered F1 and Ferrari's main rivals – Williams, McLaren and Renault – all switched to Michelin. At the time the regulations stipulated that each manufacturer could create only two specific tyre compounds. For Bridgestone, which now only supplied Ferrari and a number of less competitive teams, the choice was clear: they had to design and develop their compounds specifically for Michael Schumacher and Ferrari. Everyone else would have to make do with this specification. For Michelin the problem was more complex, with many top teams and drivers vying for a compound that specifically suited their car and driving style. Inevitably the Michelin solution was a compromise across many drivers and teams. However, in 2003 the regulations were relaxed and they were able to develop specific compounds for each team/driver. Despite stronger competition from Williams, McLaren and Renault, in 2003 Ferrari were able to secure a record-breaking fifth consecutive constructors title and Michael Schumacher a sixth world championship, breaking Juan Fangio's record which had stood since 1957.

For Montezemolo, all of this was the culmination of a process which had started from the moment of his appointment in 1991:

> At the beginning of the '90s, we reorganized the team and invested a lot in new technology. Now we're getting the benefit of what we did three, four years ago; in Formula 1, you can't change everything in 12 months. We had a strong mechanical knowledge, and it was important to

keep that, but we had to find out about things we didn't know such as aerodynamics, electronics and, perhaps most importantly, team work. It's because of all that change that we have a very strong team today.

Appendix A: summary of world champions			
Year	Driver	Car/Engine	Constructor's Cup
1950	Giuseppe Farina	Alfa Romeo	
1951	Juan Manuel Fangio	Alfa Romeo	
1952	Alberto Ascari	Ferrari	
1953	Alberto Ascari	Ferrari	
1954	Juan Manuel Fangio	Maserati	
1955	Juan Manuel Fangio	Mercedes-Benz	
1956	Juan Manuel Fangio	Lancia-Ferrari	
1957	Juan Manuel Fangio	Maserati	
1958	Mike Hawthorn	Ferrari	Vanwall
1959	Jack Brabham	Cooper/Climax	Cooper/Climax
1960	Jack Brabham	Cooper/Climax	Cooper/Climax
1961	Phil Hill	Ferrari	Ferrari
1962	Graham Hill	BRM	BRM
1963	Jim Clark	Lotus/Climax	Lotus/Climax
1964	John Surtees	Ferrari	Ferrari
1965	Jim Clark	Lotus/Climax	Lotus/Climax
1966	Jack Brabham	Brabham/Repco	Brabham/Repco
1967	Denny Hulme	Brabham/Repco	Brabham/Repco
1968	Graham Hill	Lotus/Ford	Lotus/Ford
1969	Jackie Stewart	Matra/Ford	Matra/Ford
1970	Jochen Rindt	Lotus/Ford	Lotus/Ford
1971	Jackie Stewart	Tyrrell/Ford	Tyrrell/Ford
1972	Emerson Fittipaldi	Lotus/Ford	Lotus/Ford
1973	Jackie Stewart	Tyrrell/Ford	Lotus/Ford
1974	Emerson Fittipaldi	McLaren/Ford	McLaren/Ford
1975	Niki Lauda	Ferrari	Ferrari
1976	James Hunt	McLaren/Ford	Ferrari
1977	Niki Lauda	Ferrari	Ferrari
1978	Mario Andretti	Lotus/Ford	Lotus/Ford
1979	Jody Scheckter	Ferrari	Ferrari
1980	Alan Jones	Williams/Ford	Williams/Ford
1981	Nelson Piquet	Brabham/Ford	Williams/Ford
1982	Keke Rosberg	Williams/Ford	Ferrari
1983	Nelson Piquet	Brabham/BMW	Ferrari
1984	Niki Lauda	McLaren/Porsche	McLaren/Porsche
1985	Alain Prost	McLaren/Porsche	McLaren/Porsche
1986	Alain Prost	McLaren/Porsche	Williams/Honda
1987	Nelson Piquet	Williams/Honda	Williams/Honda
1988	Ayrton Senna	McLaren/Honda	McLaren/Honda
1989	Alain Prost	McLaren/Honda	McLaren/Honda
1990	Ayrton Senna	McLaren/Honda	McLaren/Honda
1991	Ayrton Senna	McLaren/Honda	McLaren/Honda
1992	Nigel Mansell	Williams/Renault	Williams/Renault
1993	Alain Prost	Williams/Renault	Williams/Renault

1994	Michael Schumacher	Benetton/Ford	Williams/Renault
1995	Michael Schumacher	Benetton/Renault	Benetton/Renault
1996	Damon Hill	Williams/Renault	Williams/Renault
1997	Jacques Villeneuve	Williams/Renault	Williams/Renault
1998	Mika Hakkinen	McLaren/Mercedes	McLaren/Mercedes
1999	Mika Hakkinen	McLaren/Mercedes	Ferrari
2000	Michael Schumacher	Ferrari	Ferrari
2001	Michael Schumacher	Ferrari	Ferrari
2002	Michael Schumacher	Ferrari	Ferrari
2003	Michael Schumacher	Ferrari	Ferrari

Note: Constructors' championship is based on the cumulative points gained by a team during the season. Currently each team is limited to entering two cars and drivers per race.

Case 15 **Transforming the prancing horse: Ferrari 1950–2003**

This case describes the transformation of the Ferrari Formula 1 team from 1950 through to the end of 2003. It focuses in particular on the way in which Ferrari reinvented itself during the 1990s into a winning force which has dominated Formula 1 in the early part of the 21st century.

Breaking all the records

In 2003 Ferrari won their fifth successive Formula 1 (F1) constructors' world championship title, the first time this had ever happened since the award began in 1958. Furthermore, driver Michael Schumacher won his fourth successive drivers' world championship, the first time a driver had ever achieved such a concentrated dominance. His previous world championships for the Benetton team in 1994 and 1995 also meant that he had now surpassed Juan Manuel Fangio's record of five world championships with a total of six, making him the most successful world champion since F1 began in 1950. However, this success had not come without controversy: at the Austrian Grand Prix of 2002 Ferrari were accused of unsporting behaviour when their second driver, Rubens Barrichello, having dominated the race, moved over to allow Michael Schumacher to win, thereby maximizing Schumacher's world championship points. While there was a furore in the press, the Ferrari management remained stoical about their approach. After all, this success had been a long time coming, their 1999 constructors' title had been their first for sixteen years, during which the honours had been dominated by the British-based Williams, McLaren and Benetton teams. Moreover Ferrari's focus had always been to secure the drivers' championship and Schumacher's title in 2000 had been Ferrari's first since Jody Scheckter in 1979, a gap of 21 years. The roots of Ferrari's 2000 victory can be traced back to the appointment

By Mark Jenkins

of a new chairman, Luca di Montezemolo, in 1991 and the fact that it took Ferrari almost ten years to reinvent itself into a world championship winner meant that those involved in this journey felt justified in savouring the fruits of victory for as long as possible.

The prancing horse

Born in 1898, Enzo Ferrari achieved his boyhood ambition of becoming a racing driver. Legend has it that on his first victory at the 1923 Circuito del Savio he was presented the prize by Countess Paolina Baracca, the mother of a First World War fighter pilot who had used the image of a prancing horse on the side of his plane. The countess offered Ferrari the horse emblem so that he could use it for his racing cars, an offer he gratefully accepted. However, Ferrari's career as a driver was soon behind him and in November 1929 he created Scuderia Ferrari (SF) based in Modena, between Parma and Bologna in northern Italy. SF focused on the preparation and competition of racecars for enthusiasts, thereby creating one of the first specialist motorsport companies. They exclusively raced Alfa Romeo cars and in 1932 Alfa Romeo outsourced all its motorsport activity to be run by SF; 1932 was also the year that Ferrari used the prancing horse logo, a black horse on a yellow background – the historic colour of Modena – to symbolize Scuderia Ferrari. The partnership with Alfa Romeo proved to be very successful, winning 144 out of 225 races in the period up to 1937. However, during the late thirties the German Mercedes and Auto-Unions began to dominate racing and, following the Second World War, Alfa Romeo split with SF and Enzo Ferrari went on to build his first car.

The Ferrari 125 made its debut in May 1947, having been designed and developed over the previous two years. Most of the design and development had focused on the creation of the Ferrari supercharged 12-cylinder engine, the first in a long line of Ferrari *dodici cilindri* engines. The Ferrari 125 entered the new F1 championship when it began in 1950, but it was not until 1951 that a Ferrari won a Grand Prix and in 1952 driver Alberto Ascari won the drivers' world championship. The early fifties were of unparalleled success for Ferrari and the other Italian teams of Alfa Romeo and Maserati, which were all based in northern Italy. Italy was now the world leader in motorsport engineering with designs that focused on supercharged 4.5 litre engines positioned in front of the driver, their blood red cars a reflection of the earlier days of Grand Prix racing when cars were colour coded by country of origin, with British racing green for the Vanwalls and BRMs, and the silver Mercedes and Auto-Unions from Germany.

The 1950s were also a tragic time for Ferrari; overall safety standards were poor and many drivers died in Ferrari cars. As a consequence Ferrari often had to endure a great deal of criticism from the press; Enzo Ferrari had lost his son Dino in 1956, and for many this loss hardened his attitude to life and to the loss of drivers. The role of the driver was simply to do a job – bring victory to the red cars of Ferrari and if they did not there was always another to take their place. He was also very frugal about drivers' wages, as former world champion Phil Hill remarked: *'The Old Man's line was very much that you drove for Ferrari for the honour of it. And he wasn't kidding.'* Similarly, it was also claimed that Enzo liked to manage the situation so no particular driver was able to gain the credit for success, as former driver Stirling Moss records: *'I never drove for him, but I've no doubts that in my day he would allow different drivers to win by giving them better cars sometimes, thereby giving the impression that the driver didn't count for anything – that it was the car which had won.'*

Ferrai himself had a rather enigmatic approach to running the company. After the death of his son Dino he very rarely left the Modena area, and hardly ever attended races, preferring to spend his time either in the factory or at the Ferrari test facilities. He relied on the Italian media – which had always shown a keen interest in Ferrari – and his closest advisors for information; this often created a highly political atmosphere in the team.

However, Italian supremacy in F1 was soon to end. The British constructor Cooper produced small 2.0 litre cars with the engine positioned behind the driver (mid-engine layout), designed to maximize mechanical grip, as opposed to relying on sheer engine power as preferred by the Italians. Cooper dominated the world championships of 1959 and 1960 using the 'bought in' Coventry Climax engine, which had been originally designed to power water pumps for fire engines. They were followed by Lotus which, like Cooper, produced lightweight agile cars with high levels of mechanical grip.

Ferrari initially resisted this trend and referred to the British constructors as *'assemblatori'* or *'garagistes'*. He defended the engine layout of the Ferrari with the analogy that the 'horse' had always pulled, not pushed, the cart. Although not an engineer himself, the designers who Ferrari employed (Alberto Massimino, Gioachino Colombo, Carlo Chiti and Mauro Forghieri) had learnt their trade as engine designers and so the design of a new car would always start with the engine. Ferrari often referred to *'the song of the twelve,'* underlining the distinctive high-pitched note of the Ferrari engine. However, by 1960 the dominance of the British cars was undeniable and Ferrari built a lighter mid-engine layout car using a highly effective V6 engine. The Dino 156 (1.5 litre, V6) or 'shark nose' dominated 1961 and gave Ferrari a further world title. However, the advances made in chassis construction by other teams had meant that it was increasingly uncompetitive and in 1964 the Ferrari 158 was launched with a similar monocoque-type chassis to the Lotus 25 of 1962. In 1964 Ferrari tried out the 'flat-12' engine developed by Mauro Forghieri, it was this 12-cylinder unit that was seen to be the future for Ferrari.

Ferrari renaissance: the mid seventies

In 1969 SF merged with Italian automotive manufacturer Fiat. This was, in all but name, a benign acquisition, with Fiat acquiring 50% of Ferrari equity. This provided a huge injection of cash to support research and development activities, symbolized by the construction of a purpose-built circuit at Fiorano, close to the SF factory at Maranello, in 1972. The technical team used this facility to engage in a period of intensive development focusing on the 'flat-12' engine.

The new ownership and influence from Fiat meant increased resources, but also increased pressure for results. In the early seventies F1 was dominated by the Ford DFV engine. Built by Cosworth Engineering near Northampton and funded by the Ford

Motor Company, the DFV was purpose-built for F1: it was light, powerful and relatively inexpensive. In 1968 the engines were available for £7500 each and were fully capable of winning a Grand Prix. This enabled the British constructors, which specialized in chassis design, to become increasingly competitive. In 1971 and 1973 every Grand Prix was won by a car using a DFV engine. The DFV engine made the cars both very light and very powerful; at a time when tyre technology was relatively primitive, this left the designers searching for other ways to increase grip. The answer came from aerodynamics with aircraft-type 'wings' being used to create downforce, or aerodynamic grip, allowing the cars to both enter and exit corners at vastly increased speeds.

During this time Enzo, now in his seventies, had been suffering from ill health. He appointed a team manager to help run the day-to-day activities of the F1 team. Luca di Montezemolo was a 25-year-old lawyer who was connected to Fiat's Agnelli dynasty. In addition Mauro Forghieri had been recalled to Ferrari in 1973 as technical director. In 1975 the fruits of Forghieri's creative ideas and the intensive testing at Fiorano were exemplified in the new 312T, which featured a wide low body with a powerful flat-12 cylinder unit and a revolutionary transverse (sideways mounted) gearbox which improved the balance of the car, making it handle extremely well. While the new car was not ready until the season had already started, driver Niki Lauda, with the support of team-mate Clay Regazzoni, was easily able to secure both the drivers' and constructors' world championships. The Ferraris dominated the 1975 season. With their elegant handling and the power advantage of the engine, they were in a class of their own. This unprecedented run of Ferrari success continued through to 1978 and in 1979 when they won both the drivers' and constructors' championships. Their greatest moment came in 1979 when Ferrari's finished first and second at the Italian Grand Prix at Monza, sending the fanatical Italian fans or *tifosi,* and the Italian press into a complete frenzy.

Ferrari: the end of an era, 1980–1990

However, in 1980 the 312T5 car was outclassed by the competition. New innovations in aerodynamics

brought the 'ground effect' revolution, pioneered by Lotus and quickly adopted by Williams and Brabham. Here the underside of the car featured two 'venturi', or channels, either side of the driver. These were aerodynamically designed to create a low-pressure area under the car which sucked it to the track, allowing faster cornering. Sliding strips of material or 'skirts' were used to create a seal for the air flowing under the car. While the Ferrari's engine was one of the most powerful, it was a flat 12, meaning that the cylinders were horizontal to the ground creating a low and wide barrier which gave little opportunity to create the ground effect achieved with the slimmer V8 DFV engines. In 1978 Alfa Romeo had launched a V12 engine to replace its flat-12 for this very reason. No such initiative had been taken at Ferrari, which was concentrating on a longer-term project to develop a V6 turbocharged engine. *Autosport* correspondent Nigel Roebuck commented on this change of fortune: '*Maranello's flat-12, still a magnificent racing engine, is incompatible with modern chassis. Villeneuve and Scheckter were competing in yesterdays cars.*' The lowest point came in the Canadian Grand Prix when the reigning world champion, Jody Scheckter, failed to qualify his Ferrari for the race. This was a disaster equivalent to Italy failing to qualify for the soccer World Cup. Once again the full wrath of the Italian press descended on the team.

In the mid-eighties more and more investment was poured into the Italian facilities but to no effect on performance. A key problem was that new developments in aerodynamics and the use of composite materials had emerged from the UK. This was concentrated in an area to the south and west of London known as motorsport valley, an area which developed from a network of small engineering firms developed from the automotive and aerospace industries.

In 1986 British designer John Barnard was recruited to the top technical role – he was the second senior non-Italian engineer to take up a position with Ferrari, following the recruitment of Dr Harvey Postlethwaite two years earlier. However, unlike Postlethwaite, Barnard was not prepared to move to Italy as he felt that his technical team and network of contacts in the UK would be essential to the success of his position. Surprisingly Enzo accepted his terms and allowed him to establish a design and manufacturing facility near Guildford in Surrey; it subsequently became known as the Ferrari 'GTO' or Guildford Technical Office. The fact that Barnard was defining the technical direction of Ferrari meant that he became increasingly involved in activities at both Guildford and Maranello. However, the geographical separation between the car and engine departments led to development of various 'factions' within Ferrari, making Barnard's job increasingly difficult. In 1987 there was uproar from the workforce when he ordered a ban on the consumption of wine at the midday canteen in Maranello, many seeing this as an insult to their professionalism.

Enzo Ferrari's death in 1988 created a vacuum which was filled by a series of executives from the Fiat organization for a number of years. It was written into the contract that on Enzo's death Fiat's original stake would be increased to 90%, this greater investment led to attempts to run Ferrari as a formal subsidiary of the Fiat group. Barnard became frustrated with the interference and politics of the situation and left to join the Benetton F1 team in 1989. Ferrari had recruited world champion Alain Prost to drive for them in 1990 but, while the car was both competitive and elegant (an example of this Ferrari 641 now resides in New York's Museum of Modern Art), the organization was falling apart and in 1991 Prost was fired by the Ferrari management for criticizing the car and therefore the sacred name of Ferrari. Former driver Patrick Tambay commented on the situation as follows: *'No one's in charge any more. When the Old Man was alive the buck stopped with him. Maybe he took some curious decisions – but at least he took them. I'm not saying that Ferrari will never win again, but the fabric of what the name meant has gone. There are so many layers of management, so many bosses reporting to bosses, until ultimately it gets to Gianni Agnelli (Chairman of Fiat).'*

Transforming the prancing horse: 1990–2003

At the end of 1991, Fiat's chairman Gianni Agnelli appointed Luca di Montezemolo as CEO of Ferrari. His mandate was simple, to do whatever was needed to take them back to the top. After his role as team manager for Ferrari during the successful period in the mid seventies, Montezemolo had taken on a range of high-profile management roles including running Italy's hosting of the soccer World Cup in 1990. Di Montezemolo accepted the role on the basis that Ferrari, and in particular, the racing operation, was independent of Fiat: *'I have not been in the Fiat management stream for ten years. Maranello is another world and has to be treated as such.'* In an article in *Autosport* he described the situation as follows:

After I arrived last December (1991) I spent five months working to understand the situation. To understand the manpower, to understand the potential of the car. Once I had absorbed all this I decided to approach the whole situation in a completely different manner. Ferrari had become an inflexible monolith of a company which was no good for racing. As a result I decided to divide it into three small departments: future developments and special projects in the UK under John Barnard; the engine department in Maranello under Paolo Massai and finally the Scuderia Ferrari under Harvey Postlethwaite which is the place where we build the cars and manage the team.

I also wanted to build up a a strong relationship between our UK facility and Italy in order to take full advantage of the F1 'silicon valley' in England for chassis development and specialist sub-contractors while still harnessing the huge potential of Maranello.

When asked why he was repeating the 'GTO' initiative which Enzo Ferrari had set up with Barnard and which had ultimately ended with Barnard leaving, Montezemolo had a very clear response:

I think that the GTO concept of Enzo Ferrari was a super idea. Unfortunately, at the time Ferrari was very old and the situation was managed in a bad way. But the fundamental idea was very good. For me the approach is slightly different. First of all, I am in charge of the company with full powers, so I can take a decision without anyone else taking a parallel initiative. I take my responsibilities and I want the people in the company to follow my ideas. If they follow, I am very happy. If they don't then there are many other doors, many possibilities available to them outside Ferrari.

My objective is to create a smaller racing department which contains less bureaucracy; of course, there will be a lot of discussion between the engine and chassis departments. In Maranello we have a huge organization geared to building cars, but I want to take advantage of the UK facilities, and for a world-wide company like Ferrari it is certainly not a scandal to have an affiliate in the UK. If you want to make pasta, then you have to be in Parma, I want to make a sophisticated F1 project so I want to be involved in England. Then it is up to me to put everything together.

In August 1992 John Barnard signed a five-year contract with Ferrari to design and develop its new cars. In an effort to avoid a 'them and us' situation between the UK and Italy a number of technical people were swapped over between the UK and Italy.

At the launch of the 1992 car, Montezemolo broke with tradition and introduced a new numbering system based on the year a car would be racing. Prior to this point the numbering of many Ferrari cars had been based on the characteristics of the engine – the 312 of 1971 representing 3.0 litre 12 cylinders, the 126C4 of 1984 representing a 120° 'V' angle with 6 cylinders, and C standing for 'Compression' or turbo-charging:

At Ferrari we have always devoted and will continue to devote, great attention to racing, racing is part of the history, the culture and the traditions of this company. We live in a country which, especially in recent times, people have yelled and complained a bit too much. We hope that the only noise around here will be our engine as it sets new lap records at Fiorano. We are looking for a revival here, and with an eye to the future we have tried to put together a group which combines young engineers, many of them with the highest qualifications, and people whose enthusiasm and abilities will make a notable contribution. We have a lot of work

to do, we have a lot of ground to make up on the opposition. We have code-named the new car F92A to demonstrate that we are turning a new page in our history.

When asked about drivers in 1992 he also gave some indication of his thinking: *'The main priority is the new organization. We are lucky because it is a big challenge to offer a driver the chance to help re-establish Ferrari to a competitive level. I want a driver who is motivated and prepared to work with us. Motivation is everything in a driver, as Niki Lauda reminds us!'*

In addition to the structural changes, Montezemolo had also brought in some familiar faces from Ferrari's successful period in the mid seventies, driver Niki Lauda acted as a consultant to the team and Sante Ghedini took on the role of team manager. With an Englishman heading up design he followed this up with the appointment of a Frenchman, Jean Todt, to handle the overall management of the team. Todt had no experience in F1, but had been in motorsport management for many years and had recently led a successful rally and sportscar programme at Peugeot. Driver Gerhard Berger commented on Todt's team building skills: *'I was able to bring some links in the chain to Ferrari, but it took Todt to join them together. Ferrari is now working as a team for the first time. He has made a huge difference.'* Chief Mechanic Nigel Stepney joined Ferrari in 1993, but his first impressions were not positive. *'When I joined Ferrari at the beginning of 1993, it was like being thrown into the lion's den. I was in a non-position, regarded as John Barnard's spy and not allowed to take any responsibility.'* However, he recalled the arrival of Jean Todt as a turning point in the team: *'It was like Julius Caesar every day. People getting sacked and leaving every five minutes. You never knew who was boss – not until Jean Todt arrived, took control of the situation and instilled organization, stability and loyalty into the team.'*

However, the physical separation between design and development in Guildford and the racing operation in Maranello led to increased problems and eventually Barnard and Ferrari parted company for the second time at the end of 1996. At the start of the year Ferrari had recruited F1 World Champion

Michael Schumacher, formerly with the Benetton team. The departure of Barnard now opened the way for Ferrari to recruit a number of the key individuals from the Benetton technical team which had helped Schumacher to his world titles in 1994 and 1995. The arrival of Schumacher also provided new impetus for the team, as Nigel Stepney recounted: 'Once Schumacher arrived, everyone started putting us under incredible pressure. We weren't quite ready as we still needed key people, but at some point you just have to go for it and get the best driver around. He was the icing on the cake and it sent out signals that we were serious again.'

Todt and Montezemolo also chose not to make a direct replacement for the role of technical supremo who would both lead the design of the car and the management of the technical activity. They split the role between a chief designer, Rory Byrne, who had overall responsibility for designing the car, and Ross Brawn, who managed the entire technical operation; these were roles which both had undertaken in working with Schumacher at Benetton. However, the contractual arrangement with John Barnard had been one where the GTO designers were paid through his private company. When he left they all went with him and Byrne and Brawn faced the task of building up from scratch a new design department – around 50 people, based in Italy. The engine department continued to develop Ferrari's engines but, in line with new technologies and developments, these were now lighter V10s to compete with the Renault and Mercedes engines, rather than the beloved, but now dated, Ferrari *dodici cilindri*.

Along with its recruitment of Michael Schumacher in 1996, Ferrari entered into a commercial partnership with tobacco giant Phillip Morris to use their Marlboro brand on the Ferrari cars. In a novel arrangement Phillip Morris, rather than Ferrari, paid Schumacher's salary, and also made a significant contribution to Ferrari's annual operating budget. However, there was one price to pay which troubled many long-term Ferrari officiandos: the blood-red Ferrari of old was now replaced by a vivid red which more closely matched Marlboro 'rocket red' and also, importantly was more effective on television. There was much speculation about the wisdom of these changes, but Montezemolo was clear that these had to be made to move forward:

For me the company's human resources are critical, the atmosphere is extremely important. I want people, first of all, who love Ferrari and are totally willing to work as a team. You need people able to work together and look forward at the same time. OK, the company has a long history, which holds the lessons for the future, but I don't want people to look at it and stop. The past is the past, important as a point of reference but that's it.

In addition to Marlboro, Ferrari also entered into a long-term partnership with Shell to provide both financial and technical support to the team. In these kinds of arrangements Ferrari led a trend away from selling space on cars to long-term commercial arrangements, with coordinated marketing strategies for commercial partners to maximize the benefits of their investments.

There were also concerns about the way the team now revolved around Schumacher, rather than, as in the past, when the drivers were secondary to the cars of Ferrari. Jean Alesi, a former Ferrari driver observed that '*Schumacher does whatever he wants, and they do whatever he says.*'. This was in marked contrast to Enzo Ferrari who had famously rejected a number of top-class drivers because they wanted too much money, such as Jackie Stewart in 1970 and Ayrton Senna in 1986 whose wage demands Enzo described as '*imaginativo!*'

This rejuvenated team provided the basis for Michael Schumacher's dominance of F1. In 1997 it raced the Barnard-developed Ferrari and finished second in the constructors' championship. Although as this was Ferrari's 50th anniversary and there was high anticipation that this was to be their year – but, as Nigel Stepney recounts: '*1997 was a great disappointment for the team as we so nearly won the championship, we felt we had the right way of working; we just had to keep at it and not panic.*' Their competitiveness continued to improve and in 1999 they won the constructors' championship – although the drivers' championship went to Mika Hakkinen in a McLaren-Mercedes, Stepney again recalls: '*It was a very stressful year, we lost Michael Schumacher after he broke his leg at Silverstone. Then we made mistakes such as the pit-stop at the Nurburgring. But although we paid the price in one respect, we gained from the experiences. We realized that as a team, we had to pace ourselves, to switch off and recharge our batteries sometime.'*

There was clear momentum in the company now to secure the world championships and what followed was a complete domination by Ferrari in the period 2000–2003. For Montezemolo this was the culmination of a process which had started from the moment of his appointment in 1991: *'At the beginning of the '90s, we reorganized the team and*

invested a lot in new technology. Now we're getting the benefit of what we did three, four years ago; in Formula 1, you can't change everything in 12 months. We had a strong mechanical knowledge, and it was important to keep that, but we had to find out about things we didn't know such as aerodynamics, electronics and, perhaps most importantly, team work. It's because of all that change that we have a very strong team today.'

Appendix A: summary of world champions

Year	Driver	Car/Engine	Constructor's Cup
1950	Giuseppe Farina	Alfa Romeo	
1951	Juan Manuel Fangio	Alfa Romeo	
1952	Alberto Ascari	Ferrari	
1953	Alberto Ascari	Ferrari	
1954	Juan Manuel Fangio	Maserati	
1955	Juan Manuel Fangio	Mercedes-Benz	
1956	Juan Manuel Fangio	Lancia-Ferrari	
1957	Juan Manuel Fangio	Maserati	
1958	Mike Hawthorn	Ferrari	Vanwall
1959	Jack Brabham	Cooper/Climax	Cooper/Climax
1960	Jack Brabham	Cooper/Climax	Cooper/Climax
1961	Phil Hill	Ferrari	Ferrari
1962	Graham Hill	BRM	BRM
1963	Jim Clark	Lotus/Climax	Lotus/Climax
1964	John Surtees	Ferrari	Ferrari
1965	Jim Clark	Lotus/Climax	Lotus/Climax
1966	Jack Brabham	Brabham/Repco	Brabham/Repco
1967	Denny Hulme	Brabham/Repco	Brabham/Repco
1968	Graham Hill	Lotus/Ford	Lotus/Ford
1969	Jackie Stewart	Matra/Ford	Matra/Ford
1970	Jochen Rindt	Lotus/Ford	Lotus/Ford
1971	Jackie Stewart	Tyrrell/Ford	Tyrrell/Ford
1972	Emerson Fittipaldi	Lotus/Ford	Lotus/Ford
1973	Jackie Stewart	Tyrrell/Ford	Lotus/Ford
1974	Emerson Fittipaldi	McLaren/Ford	McLaren/Ford
1975	Niki Lauda	Ferrari	Ferrari
1976	James Hunt	McLaren/Ford	Ferrari
1977	Niki Lauda	Ferrari	Ferrari
1978	Mario Andretti	Lotus/Ford	Lotus/Ford
1979	Jody Scheckter	Ferrari	Ferrari
1980	Alan Jones	Williams/Ford	Williams/Ford
1981	Nelson Piquet	Brabham/Ford	Williams/Ford
1982	Keke Rosberg	Williams/Ford	Ferrari
1983	Nelson Piquet	Brabham/BMW	Ferrari
1984	Niki Lauda	McLaren/Porsche	McLaren/Porsche
1985	Alain Prost	McLaren/Porsche	McLaren/Porsche

1986	Alain Prost	McLaren/Porsche	Williams/Honda
1987	Nelson Piquet	Williams/Honda	Williams/Honda
1988	Ayrton Senna	McLaren/Honda	McLaren/Honda
1989	Alain Prost	McLaren/Honda	McLaren/Honda
1990	Ayrton Senna	McLaren/Honda	McLaren/Honda
1991	Ayrton Senna	McLaren/Honda	McLaren/Honda
1992	Nigel Mansell	Williams/Renault	Williams/Renault
1993	Alain Prost	Williams/Renault	Williams/Renault
1994	Michael Schumacher	Benetton/Ford	Williams/Renault
1995	Michael Schumacher	Benetton/Renault	Benetton/Renault
1996	Damon Hill	Williams/Renault	Williams/Renault
1997	Jacques Villeneuve	Williams/Renault	Williams/Renault
1998	Mika Hakkinen	McLaren/Mercedes	McLaren/Mercedes
1999	Mika Hakkinen	McLaren/Mercedes	Ferrari
2000	Michael Schumacher	Ferrari	Ferrari
2001	Michael Schumacher	Ferrari	Ferrari
2002	Michael Schumacher	Ferrari	Ferrari
2003	Michael Schumacher	Ferrari	Ferrari

Note: Constructors' championship is based on the cumulative points gained by a team during the season. Currently each team is limited to entering two cars and drivers per race.

This case study is drawn from material contained in Performance at the Limit: Business Lessons from Formula 1 Motor Racing (2005) Jenkins, M. Pasternak, K. and West, R., Cambridge University Press, Cambridge, UK.

CHAMBRE DE COMMERCE ET D'INDUSTRIE DE PARIS
CENTRE DE PERFECTIONNEMENT AUX AFFAIRES

Case 16 IKEA culture as competitive advantage

I IKEA the worldwide standard setter

After firmly attaining leadership within Sweden, where it holds more than 20% of the overall market, IKEA has succeeded over the last twenty five years to do what no furniture distributor has ever attempted: to become a global player in an industry considered by nature to be local.

Today IKEA delivers low priced quality furniture to key markets throughout the world. It is the only distributor in its field to have successfully established itself in all parts of Europe, including Southern and Eastern Europe, and more notably in North America, including the USA. It has stores today in the Middle East, Singapore and Hong Kong and is preparing to enter the Chinese market sometime in the early part of the next century. Recently Ingvar Kamprad has secured his position in Europe with the acquisition of British based Habitat, IKEA's chief rival in the UK and France.

To provide some idea of its worldwide presence, IKEA receives annually over 120 million visitors in its 125 stores, and distributes 35 million catalogues. Its sales revenues increased steadily over the last 10 years by an average of 12% annually, in spite of the flattening out of its business in Western Europe which still represents nearly 80% of its annual volume. (See **Exhibit 1.**)

Founder Ingvar Kamprad's stubborn insistence that people will buy more furniture if the price is

low enough, the furniture of decent quality and no delays in delivery has gradually revolutionized the conservative national furniture markets in Europe and beyond. Kamprad intuitively anticipated the rise of consumerism in the 1950's and 60's, and virtually invented the practices of cash and carry, self-service, and volume buying in Europe.

IKEA was to invent many other concepts and new ways of dealing with logistics, sourcing, and retailing, many of these innovations have become industry standards: knock-down furniture that can be stored and shipped in flat boxes; involving customers in the value adding process by handling the transportation and doing easy home-assembly themselves; and turning shopping into a family event by creating attractive open store environments that contain IKEA trademarks like the children's areas with brightly colored plastic balls, and the buffet style restaurants where you can eat Swedish meatballs.

IKEA has affected the way furniture is sold and distributed in every country where it is doing business, inspiring imitation and drawing respect, sometimes begrudgingly, from traditional furniture dealers.

One aspect of IKEA's success has been the development of unique product design capabilities, based on an almost religious dedication to the simple, yet graceful design of contemporary Swedish furniture. In so doing it has introduced millions of households around the world to the Swedish style that it more than others have come to typify. (See **Exhibit 2.**)

IKEA's strength today comes from their mastery of three key aspects of the value chain: **unique design capabilities, unique sourcing, and tightly controlled logistics**. This means that they are able to produce products that are distinctive enough to provide market recognition, secure sourcing for long runs at profitable levels, and reduce inventory costs through regional warehouses which work very closely with stores. In this way they have been able to buck industry trends and steadily increase their share of slow growing, sometimes shrinking markets.

IKEA has become a household reference as much in Warsaw, as in Los Angeles, attracting customers who just want to come to a store, look around and have some fun. Something universally irresistible about IKEA makes it very difficult for people to come away from one of its stores without making a purchase and instills unprecedented loyalty among its customers and employees.

IKEA'S successful development, particular organizational capabilities, and the bold and inspired leadership of its entrepreneur-founder have all been largely written up and commented on. Its organization, communication, marketing, product range, and store layouts all tell the same story – the story of the 'IKEA-Way'. A way strongly rooted in the personality of found Ingvar Kamprad and the Swedish (regional) culture that he grew up in.

II THE 'IKEA-way': doing things differently

What is it that makes IKEA so different? Is it just 'low priced quality goods at affordable prices'? Or is there a deeper explanation? When asked these questions, IKEA managers and personnel become mystical and somewhat vague. 'It is really a winning combination of price and a merry feeling, a feeling of delight' a Dutch marketing manager answers. This feeling and a conscious awareness that, in addition to the competitive advantage there is something strong and intangible at IKEA that drives and motivates its success, is shared by IKEAns throughout the organization. Could it be that the IKEA-Way's combination of vision, charismatic leadership, sound business principles is subtly reinforced by the influence of Swedish culture? Could it be that Swedish, or Scandinavian culture contains elements that facilitates international expansion?

Can a company's national culture in this case be a competitive advantage? Throughout our investigation of IKEA we have kept these questions in the back of our minds, and we invite you to consider them as we explore the IKEA-Way more closely.

How it all started

IKEA'S name is derived from the initials of the company's founder, architect, and driving force

Ingvar Kamprad, those of the farm where he was raised, Elmtaryd, and those of his native village Agunnaryd, located in Smaland a poor farming region in the south-east of Sweden. Coming from a modest background, Kamprad began as a trader in everything from matches to Christmas cards, he almost accidentally got into the furniture business after buying out a failed furniture plant in the early 1950's. He demonstrated from the very beginning a combination of strong salesmanship, practical business acumen, thrift, an identity with ordinary people, and an unconventional perseverance in the face of adversity. Always modest he was none the less a true entrepreneur, and more significantly a nonconformist who was not the least bit restrained by the conventions and traditions of the Swedish furniture trade of his day.

His habit of staying close to his customers and his reluctance to own manufacturing furniture plants gave him freedom to focus and innovate on all the facets of distribution. With nearly furniture producers he co-designed furniture to meet very specific requirements for quality products that average customers could afford, and then printed them up in catalogues, which he had discovered as an economical and effective way of marketing to a growing customer base in his early days as a trader.

In 1953 he opened his first showroom at the furniture plant he had bought earlier in Almhult which has become the heart of his furniture empire. The only transportation link to the factory was by road at a time when more and more working class Swedes were purchasing their first automobiles, so what was originally a problem would become a solution.

Kamprad was obsessed with low prices, and the only way to offer them was to keep costs as low as possible: this conviction became a driving force of his business development. He would constantly seek new ways to lower prices. For example he bought fabrics for his furniture directly from textile mills, placing large orders and then supplying the material himself to his network of small furniture manufacturers. In this way at the same time he was able to cut costs a bit more, and ensure that his customers would have a wider selection of upholstery to choose from in the catalogue. Unwittingly he had introduced the notion of vertical integration, which provided

IKEA even then with a strong competitive advantage compared to traditional distributors who only displayed and sold furniture.

Such practices enabled him to have close contact with his suppliers, and eventually to learn intimately the parameters of furniture production. His relationship between him and his suppliers were so good that to obtain their commitment he needed only to draw rough sketches of the furniture he wanted and discuss with them how to adapt production to their capabilities. In so doing, he established over the years another cornerstone of his business philosophy: marrying the customers' need for low prices with the suppliers' need for profit through efficiency and long production runs. This was a strong departure from the kind of relationship that distributors traditionally maintained with their suppliers, buying furniture as it was ordered piece by piece at high prices with long waiting periods for delivery.

Balancing customers' requirements and producers' needs, which enabled him to sell furniture at prices 30 to 50% below traditional distributors, is now the foundation of the IKEA-Way. This notion is so basic and even imperative that a store manager in Germany told me, when walking through the accessories department where some Chinese gadgets were displayed, that this balancing of optimal product design with the supplier with the needs of the customer is the 'Yin and Yang' of the IKEA strategy. It was already present in the way Ingvar Kamprad developed his business through the fifties when his innovative ways provoked stubborn counter attacks from his more established Swedish competitors.

A legendary showdown took place at the Sankt Erik's Fair in Stockholm where, for the first time, IKEA introduced its products. Feeling threatened by Kamprad's unexpected success and many new customers, the Swedish furniture cartel tried to block IKEA's entry at the fair. They failed, but soon thereafter managed a successful boycott of IKEA by Swedish furniture manufacturers accusing Kamprad of unfair practices. Undaunted by this seemingly insurmountable obstacle, Kamprad looked for and found new suppliers in Poland at the height of the Cold War.

Although Polish manufacturers were willing to sell at prices well below their counterparts in Sweden, the cost of transportation offset this advantage. This new obstacle was at the origin of yet another IKEA invention, as Kamprad discovered that by 'knocking down' furniture into disassembled parts it could be packed and shipped in flat cardboard reducing by more than 80% the cost of transporation. To further save on costs, the furniture could be sold directly to customers in these same flat boxes. To help customers participate in the distribution cycle IKEA offered to rent roof racks and invented the simple assembly tool which had become another of its trademarks.

To reach the largest possible market and benefit fully from volume sales, in 1964 IKEA opened Europe's first large 'warehouse scale' store in Stockholm. Unexpectedly large crowds of people attended the grand opening causing yet another problem. Seemingly endless queues formed at the check-out stands as employees scurried to the storage areas to fetch the purchased furniture. Instead of hiring more employees, Kamprad simply opened the storage area to customers and invited them to fetch the furniture themselves. Such practices were unheard of then, but understanding that this would lead to lower prices, customers willingly complied. In just a few years IKEA had invented the concept of 'prosumers' whereby customers actively participate in the distribution cycle.

Suddenly the whole system was in place: customers were able to purchase attractive quality furniture at low prices; furniture suppliers benefited from long production runs, and IKEA, through volume sales, was able to make a considerable profit from small margins.

IKEA'S business strategy did not evolve from 'strategic planning' which is still scorned today in the company as 'too sophisticated'. It evolved from creative responses to difficult problems, turning them into solutions pragmatically and often with considerable risk. Not going by the book, or adopting conventional solutions. Learning by doing appears to be a distinguishing trait of Ingvar Kamprad's and IKEA'S intuitive way of doing business.

The IKEA mission

As IKEA grew Ingvar Kamprad found ways to explain his unique way of doing business always using simple language and metaphors. He has consistently maintained that IKEA's mission is **to offer 'a wide range of home furnishing items of good design and function, at prices so low that the majority of people can afford to buy them'**. This statement is at the heart of the IKEA's philosophy and has shaped all of the phases of its business, particularly product range. The concept is protected through numerous guidelines and special legal entities. Changes in the criteria for product range can only be made by joint decisions of INGKA Holding BV and Inter IKEA Systems BV both of which are outside the sphere of management.

The essential guidelines appear in a 1976 publication 'Testament of a Furniture Dealer' in which Kamprad emphasizes the company's ambition to cover furnishing and decorative needs of the total home area with a distinctive style that reflect 'our thoughts and be as simple and straightforward as ourselves'. The guidelines also express such modern ideals as furniture that is durable and easy to live with, reflects a natural and free life style, and appeals to youthfulness with color and joy. Most of IKEA's products are designed by Swedes in Almhult who consciously reproduce the designs that reflect these values which are very consistent with Swedish culture. At the same time there is something universally appealing in that specific design in markets throughout the world.

Business principles

IKEA has developed unique competencies and ability to deliver products which are distinctly Swedish, attractively presented in warm value adding environments, and at consistently lower prices than competition.

What has made IKEA so different from other distributors is the balanced focus it has maintained on product range, sourcing, vertical integration, mass marketing, cost leadership, and a distinctive image. As such they are not market driven, and tend to react rather slowly to new consumer trends, studying them to see how they can fit into their operating systems and what value IKEA can add

within their proven framework, before adopting them into their range. The issue of range is vital for them as, when they introduce new products they must insure that the volumes they produce are leveraged from within sourcing-logistics-store layouts.

The Yin/Yang metaphor mentioned earlier illustrates the imperative balance of strategic sourcing and marketing mix.

The balance and complementariness of:

Strategic Sourcing   and   the Marketing Mix

In the area of **strategic sourcing**, IKEA has established a long-standing competitive advantage. The durable partnerships that it has developed with furniture producers and other suppliers is based on the producers capacity to provide long runs of parts, and their willingness to comply with IKEA's quality standards and IKEA's guaranteed purchase of all parts produced. IKEA considers their producers as key stakeholders and provide them with technical assistance to increase their productivity sometimes underwriting investments of new technology. Together they actively contribute to both cost reduction and quality enhancement, that optimise the marketing mix.

Through such partnerships IKEA has virtually integrated production into its value-added chain without the heavy investments of actually owning and running its own furniture plants.

Management style and practices

IKEA management style is described by non-Swedish members as informal, open, and caring. Hierarchy is not emphasized and in a typical store there are only three levels of responsibility between the store manager and co-workers (which is what employees are called). A pragmatic approach to problem solving and consensus-based decision-making are also strongly embedded in IKEA management practice.

Co-workers at all levels are encouraged to take initiatives, and making mistakes is considered a necessary part of 'learning by doing'. Managers are expected not only to share information with co-workers but also their knowledge and skills. IKEA wants their co-workers to feel important, they can express their ideas, and should feel responsible for improving the way things are done.

An entrepreneurial zeal for getting the job done in the most direct way and a distaste for bureaucratic procedure are basic managerial attitudes that have long been promoted within IKEA. Managers are expected to be close to their co-workers with few if any status barriers, and not to take themselves seriously. This egalitarian approach to management has also made it easy for motivated employees to work their way up the organization with little formal training. It is significant that Swedish managers' titles do not appear on their business cards, and that company cars are the same economy models for all of those who need them for work or business regardless of their position.

Rather than establish extensive training programs and detailed rules on procedures to propagate its unique culture, IKEA prefers a softer approach through discussion and explanation. The IKEA-Way has been spelled out through wide distribution of Kamprad's 'Testament', which has been translated into a dozen languages. Kamprad himself explains that IKEA has 'a strong and living culture' based on doing things differently. 'It has grown step by step', and together with its business principles is the 'cornerstone of our operations. … Which helps us retain the spirit and vitality of the early years … and create a feeling of belonging in a large international organization. Our corporate culture binds us together.' To ensure that the IKEA-Way is understood, the organization relies heavily on managers to act as 'missionaries' carrying all that it embodies through their example and willingness to explain to new and older employees why things are done the way they are. This, as much as anything else, provides the reason for the extensive presence of Swedish managers in IKEA's international units, as their knowledge stems from their direct exposure to Ingvar Kamprad and IKEA's subtle way of doing business and managing people. For those managers who do not have that exposure, week-long IKEA-Way seminars are organized periodically in Almhult, the IKEA equivalent of Mecca and the heart of its culture.

III IKEA's strategy of international expansion: flexibility within established parameters

Patterns of international expansion

IKEA's international expansion has taken place progressively over the last twenty-five years with an eye towards markets in countries with growth potential. Expansion outside of Scandinavia was driven by Ingvar Kamprad's intuitive quest for new opportunities, and his previous successful search for suppliers outside of Sweden more than by any formal development strategy. Some insights are provided by one of IKEA's Swedish executives, an early companion of Ingvar Kamprad. 'When we opened our first store outside Scandinavia in Switzerland, people asked why there? It was a difficult market. Ingvar said that if we could succeed there, we should succeed anywhere. He had intuitions, he spoke to people on the streets to learn what they were looking for.' Such an empirical experiential approach goes against the orthodox rules of international retailing which are preaching extensive market studies before entering a new market, catering to local tastes, and gaining expertise through acquisitions and joint ventures.

When IKEA expanded into Germany, competition was strong and German distributors didn't take them seriously. 'They called us those crazy Swedes, but we didn't mind, we even used this label in our advertising. It took them five years to really react, but by then we had eight stores and were setting the standards.'

Charting its own course, IKEA has developed internationally, finding cheap land for stores, availability of sourcing, proximity to central warehouses, or lowering marketing costs. When in the late 70's they decided to go into Belgium because it was cost effective to service the country from their central warehouse in Germany they ran into problems with building permits and so decided to develop in France instead. The preference has been for leveraging market costs by concentrating several stores in the same area. This explains why they opened four stores in the Philadelphia/Washington DC/New Jersey area sometimes in locations that were rather isolated. They also preferred concentrating four stores in the Paris area even if this could dilute store sales and creates potential competition between stores.

Typically development has been done on a store by store basis. IKEA opens a beachhead in a given country with a group of trusted and experienced Swedish 'Missionaries'. Together they form a right-knit group who can solve problems and make decisions quickly. They supervise the building, lead operational teams who open the store, and run the store until local management has learned how the system works. After a short while store management is turned over to local managers, while most of the key national positions remain in the hands of Swedes until the operation and market has reached maturity.

Adapting to national markets

Adapting to new markets in Western Europe throughout the 70's and early 80's was fairly simple. Catalogue offerings were virtually the same. However concessions had to be made, particularly in bedroom furnishings since bedding could be substantially different from country to country.

'When we entered a new country we did things our way. The idea was to be IKEA everywhere, after all, our furniture is a cultural statement. But as the years went by we learned to be more flexible, particularly when demand in Sweden declined and we became more dependent on our non-Scandinavian markets.'

Adapting to the US market was a real learning experience for IKEA, since many standards were different. Few product managers from IKEA of Sweden had traveled to North America since the price of air travel was prohibitive to IKEA's cost-conscience policies. They expected their European range to sell just as easily in the US, which did not turn out to be the case. As a former US country manager explains: 'IKEA ran into problems in the US so we had to ask ourselves what can we offer to Americans. Should we become an American company, or merely adapt our merchandising to American customers? We finally decided on a solution: Merchandising to the American customer by speaking English with a Swedish accent. Capitalizing on our strengths as an outsider.'

Development of the range is now closely monitored by IKEA of Sweden (IOS) and the Board of Directors of INGKA Holding. The issue of range is vital for them as, when they introduce new products they must ensure that the volumes they produce are balanced from within (sourcing-logistics-store layouts). It took IKEA of Sweden several years to introduce 'futons' in Europe, and American store managers had to work hard to convince them that a 'Home Entertainment' line was feasible in North America.

As a former French country manager described, obtaining concessions from product managers to take into account specific national preferences was a consensual process that required many negotiation skills. 'Some room is allowed for national considerations in our catalogue range. But since changes mean that it will be more expensive for the country manager, only a limited number is requested. Still 90% of our range is the same all over, only 5 to 10% is country specific. The product manager has the final word, but he usually listens to the country manager. There is a healthy tension between the two and this enables us to adapt but not to over-adapt and weaken our cost effectiveness.'

Although IKEA's stated mission is to provide home furnishing for the 'greatest number' and its business is conducted on a volume basis, outside of Scandinavia it is in reality a niche player, appealing to the educated population with mid to upper level incomes. This segment is looking for non-traditional lines of furniture, and finds the Swedish style of IKEA suitable to its modern taste.

'In spite of our image as the "common man's store" the majority of our customers have a university degree' admits a French store manager. This may appear paradoxical considering IKEA's avowed mission statement, but the paradox has proven successful as it keeps IKEA at the same time close to its roots and still makes it highly distinctive in foreign market places. It also plays neatly into its strengths of sourcing, volume, long runs, and cost-efficient distribution.

Human resource management

Management of international operations has largely followed the IKEA-Way and its strong Swedish flavor. The belief in IKEA is that their way of managing people has universal appeal. 'People like to participate in making decisions. They like to feel respected, and that they can take responsibility', one Swedish expatriate states.

For recruitment, IKEA looks for people who have good communication skills, open minds, positive work attitudes and have good potential without necessarily having diplomas. It attracts people with its pleasant working environment, job security, and the **care that shows** towards the individual. IKEA employees regardless of nationality are more than likely to have strong preferences for cooperative informal relations, being independent and have a tolerant approach to others. 'We look for people who know how to listen, and who are able to transmit their knowledge to others. They should not feel they are better than others and be curious about what is going on around them.'

Being an IKEA manager overseas isn't just running the stores and distribution systems smoothly. They must be able to explain to employees and managers why things are done that way, and win people's hearts and minds to the 'IKEA-Way'. They are expected to be ambassadors and must educate their non-Swedish co-workers through patience, common understanding, and example. It is not always easy to transmit IKEA's egalitarian management style. While it goes down easily in the Netherlands, it is less easy for Germany or for France. But for different reasons. In the United States long term employees generally feel more comfortable with Scandinavian managers than with Americans, younger American managers don't seem to know how to show 'equalness'.

The challenge IKEA may be facing is that, with its extended international network, it is becoming more difficult to find enough Swedish IKEA managers who are willing to work overseas for long periods. IKEA had to hire Swedes from outside the company. In the past the company has not systematically searched out and developed its international 'high potentials' early enough, although it does send its most loyal and successful foreign managers to week-long seminars in Sweden and encourages its co-workers to learn something about the culture.

It is still very difficult for non-Scandinavians to work their way up the corporate ladder. To do so they need to learn all of IKEA's key trades: retailing, logistics, product design, and purchasing. Non Swedes can work their way up in retailing through

the national organizations and sometimes in the logistical organizations which are run regionally, but very few have gone into product management because this function is part of IKEA of Sweden in Almhult, where IKEA's product managers and furniture school are located. It is a very remote area and only Swedish is spoken. So, speaking the language as well and knowing the culture becomes a prerequisite that very few managers from the foreign branch have been able to fill.

There are no formal career paths for advancement as a long term Swedish expatriate executive admits. 'To get ahead in IKEA you first have to know the range intimately, then you have to know and use the informal internal network, and then you have to understand the subtleties of the IKEA-Way, its cultural roots. It is really difficult for an outsider to know his way around. In reality it is a difficult company to understand. Humbleness is not a sign of weakness. It comes from Ingvar. People are expected to learn from their experience, and this takes time and patience, you can't be in a hurry to move up the ladder.'

Dealing with the Europeans – Germany

Germany is the largest national organization of the IKEA group accounting for ±30% of the total group sales with more than 20 stores, including the nearly opened stores in former East Germany.

Although IKEA has been established in Germany for more than two decades, (its first store was opened in Munich in 1974), Swedish management is still perceived by German IKEA members as peculiar. As described by Thomas Larson, the store manager of Cologne: 'Some older co-workers still have problems addressing me by my first name or use the German "Du" (the informal equivalent for you, "tu" in French).' 'Dutzen', using the informal you, is often felt as undermining the respect and prestige of the boss. As Heike Oestreich, the personnel manager said: 'There are two different "Du's", the IKEA Du and the Du which is used between friends.'

The Germans are very disciplined and precise. They do exactly what the boss asks them to do and what is agreed is put down in writing. A problem is that the Swedish notion and cornerstone of our work policy 'to take your own responsibility' is not perceived in the same way by the Germans. There is a tendency to adhere very closely to precisely defined rules and instructions. When IKEA translated the corporate brochure 'the IKEA-Way' into German, a need was felt to sharpen and make more explicit the original Swedish text, which presented key IKEA concepts in sometimes vague terms in order to give freedom to people to adapt them and take personal responsibility for carrying them out. Once Anders Moberg, I. Kamprad's successor, suggested in a letter that certain merchandising displays could be used in a variety of places. In Germany department managers interpreted this as an order, and systematically set up the displays in every part of their stores.

In general German employees feel that the Swedes are more result oriented and treat every problem as a challenge that should be met. However they believe that Swedish management does not sufficiently assess risks before taking action. According to Heike Oestreich, Human Resource Manager in Cologne: 'The Swedes', to reduce bureaucracy, 'would like to dump all our office desks in the back yard'. The lack of formality is also dismaying to Germans. To implement a decision 'notes on the back of a cigarette package are often sufficient' for the Swedes. In contrast, Germans are more comfortable adhering to formal procedures; 'We need procedures and forms. Germans love administration because it provides them with security.'

Dealing with the Europeans – France

Development in France, which has fewer than half the number of stores in Germany, was always considered problematic because of multiple administrative regulations on the retail trade and a hostile attitude towards discounters that prevailed in the late 70's and early 80's. By carefully avoiding too much public attention and with only a limited number of store openings it managed to secure a safe place for itself on the market and develop an 8% share of market.

The main challenge for IKEA management in France is the French tendency to judge informality as a sign of weakness, or indecision. People here are accustomed to formal rules and strong hierarchy. In the words of a former Swedish country manager when IKEA first started in France: 'Some French managers felt that with Swedish informality they could do whatever they wanted. When we told them that they should inform their subordinates they did not take us seriously.' Some aspects of the informality can be irritating to the French at such as the lack of formal job descriptions and written procedures. Whereas Swedish managers will justify this by saying that they don't like to limit responsibility, and that they get more out of people with an informal approach, the French tend to be suspicious of informality for the same reasons.

In the view of IKEA's French Human Resource manager: 'Working here isn't for everyone. It is very difficult for someone over 35, because this place is different from all of the others in France. When you join IKEA, you enter another world: we do not behave like a normal French company. Status is not recognized which can cause an identity problem: everyone is put on the same level – no one stands out, and you can get lost in the crowd. It is hard to explain what IKEA is, everyone will give a different answer, one shouldn't freeze the system, it is flexible, it should stay that way.'

Two of the main reasons given for IKEA's appeal to French candidates are:

- The esthetics of our stores – they look nice and are pleasant to work in.
- Also the intelligent way in which we work – it makes sense!

However, to make things clearer to employees, a formal communication platform has been developed in France to spell out in facts and figures which compare IKEA's benefits to those of competitors. Also more formal training programs are being developed because in France 'learning by doing' is not perceived as credible way of developing competency. You typically would not trust your boss to develop your skills in France, and more faith is placed in 'off-site programs'. In France tolerance has its limits and when IKEA hired 'too many' people of non-French origins, they received complaints from their customers, so now they make a point of keeping 'non-French' workers to a minimum.

Four years ago relations with unions were hostile. There was a nasty strike and widespread discontent. French labor unions did not trust or understand IKEA's Swedish management style with its tendency to seek consensus. More recently IKEA's management has taken a more affirmative attitude, and relations have improved notably. They may continue to improve now that IKEA France is run by a Frenchman, Jean Louis Baillot whose wife is Swedish and who has worked in Almhult.

Doing things differently in the United States

Expanding into the US market in the 80's was certainly the boldest developmental decision that IKEA had made up to that time. From an historical perspective the venture seemed unlikely to succeed. First the culturally specific requirements for home furnishing in the United States are considerably different than the European markets, particularly concerning the size and functions of furniture. Secondly the American market had come to be known as the 'graveyard' of European retailers with a long list of unfortunate ventures by such successful firms as Casino, Carrefour, and Marks & Spencer. But somehow IKEA seemed confident that going about it in their own way would prove an exception to the laws of failure that seemed to doom European entrants to the US market.

Initially development in the US was quite consistent with IKEA's pattern in Europe: Identifying prime markets with volume potential; purchasing cheap land in the periphery of big cities; relying on mass advertising and a unique message emphasizing its Swedishness; focusing on range and price through the catalogue, establishing a beachhead from which to launch and develop its organization. Also its approach was empirical and pragmatic, and it did not set out to take the US by storm, but merely to test its tried and true formula and learn through experience how they could succeed. In fact from the mid seventies to the early 80's IKEA opened a series of franchised stores in Canada, developing during this time its logistic capabilities and demonstrating that its European range could sell in America's back yard, before it finally entered the US market in 1985.

Its first stage of development in the US began on the East Coast with the opening of Plymouth Meeting in Philadelphia's northwest suburbs, followed by a cluster of four other stores. 'Development was initially based on the potato field approach. Find someplace where there is cheap land, build and the people will follow.' This approach ignored the rule of American retailing based on fine tuned segmentation and targeting. Their choice of locations, driven by cost-consciousness, led them to establish their stores in shopping centers that had no upscale 'anchors stores' to draw the high income customers that IKEA appeals to. This should have been a relative disadvantage, since competitors like Home Depot locate their stores in centers with 'anchors' like Nordstrom's and Macy's. But by maintaining the profile of a 'different kind of store', very Swedish, with a wide range of products, it apparently has overcome this obstacle. Here the catalogue has served them well, as people can plan their purchases before they come and thus optimize their time investment.

Up until the early 90's IKEA enjoyed a honeymoon of sorts. The American public was attracted by the novelty of Scandinavian style, and IKEA's unique merchandising, which resembles a European village market place. Its advertising was a success. People drove six to eight hours to come to the stores and they initially came in large numbers. Riding on a high dollar, IKEA had appeared to have gotten off to a fast start as they had in Germany and other European markets. The honeymoon ended abruptly in the late eighties when the dollar went down, revealing multiple weaknesses.

First and foremost even if Americans were initially attracted by IKEA's advertising and novelty, their range of furniture was unsuited to American standards and sold poorly. One often told anecdote illustrates just how far from those standards they really were. Customers would purchase flower vases thinking they were American size drinking glasses. Americans furnish their master bedrooms with king-size beds, whereas IKEA's largest beds were 5 inches narrower. Also Americans are harder on sitting room furniture, and IKEA's soft and armchair offerings proved too lightly dimensioned. Additionally IKEA did not offer furniture suitable to the 'Home Entertainment Centers' that blossomed through the 80's and into the 90's in American households with proliferation of widescreen television, VCR, and hi-fi equipment. With declining sales revenue and shrinking profits, by 1989 the 'graveyard effect' seemed to have caught up with IKEA.

A courageous decision was then made by Anders Moberg and a new management team was brought in to head the US organization. Faced with the alternatives of: holding on and waiting for better times, withdrawing humbly, or fighting back, the latter course was chosen. In 1990 the American retail management group, under the leadership of Göran Carstedt, recently hired from Volvo, convinced the product managers at IKEA of Sweden that the IKEA European range has to be adapted and American based sourcing stepped up while reassuring them that IKEA would not lose its soul. In the words of Carstedt: 'The IKEA strategy in North America will still be blue and yellow, but we will put more stars and stripes and more maple leaves in it.'

It was not easy but they succeeded in changing the design of many household products. To make the point one US manager brought a plastic American-sized turkey with him to Almhult and before a surprised group of product managers placed it on one of the best selling dining tables in the European range. Given the size of the bird there was only room for two table settings instead of the normal six. He had made his point.

However there was a condition attached to adapting the range, and that condition was volume. Lines of furniture specifically designed for the American market would have to be produced in long enough lines to meet IKEA's commitment to suppliers and be priced at the lowest levels possible.

A combination of luck and bold counter attacking led to an unexpected expansion on the West Coast that was to ease pressure on its pricing and provide needed growth to its retail business. An imitator 'Stor' inspired by IKEA's success had illicitly acquired knowledge of IKEA's floor plan and merchandising schemes and successfully opened four stores primarily around Los Angeles, far from IKEA's base on the East Coast. Responding as much to the threat to their image as to the opportunity to capitalize on Stor's advertising of Swedish style furniture, IKEA decided to counter attack. It opened a store in Los Angeles and eventually, through its price and sourcing advantage, drove Stor to the brink of bankruptcy. It then bought out its imitator at a bargain price and established a solid base in a prime market on the West Coast. If IKEA's low profile stance stressed its humble origins and culture, it definitely did not mean that the company was a weakling. IKEA showed that it could be tough and decisive in that

toughest of tough markets. The current US country manager Jan Kjellman is comparing the US market to his previous European experience used the following words: 'The biggest difference is competition. Competitors are everywhere, and they are strong. The market is crowded, but still there always seem to be new competitors. Even with a million and a half customers, we are small. It is a total struggle for us, and it is tough to survive.' Could IKEA adapt to such competition and still remain faithful to the 'IKEA-Way'?

Swedish managers are impressed with the professionalism of American salesmanship. 'Over here retailing is a profession. Sales persons are subjected to a lot of pressure for short term results because large retailers are publicly owned and shareholders measure quarterly results. So they are very time-efficient and masters of the hard sell,' relates Kjellman. IKEA has always maintained a soft approach believing that people know what they want, so that sales personnel are there to help them find it. Moreover the strategy is that most of the selling is done by the catalogue so that people arrive with specific purchases in mind. Impulse buying takes place for smaller items like candleholders, or accessories that are sought for as bargains. On this point IKEA has stood firm, and sales personnel from competitors such as Macy's or Bloomingdale have to unlearn the hard sell approach.

Americans are always looking for convenience, which means more space, more information, anything that reduces effort and saves time. To respond to these demands IKEA had to redesign its store layouts providing more directions and short cuts for people who don't want to just wander through the store. 'Customers were screaming: let us out, before we remodelled our layout' reports a store manager, 'They couldn't find their way out of our maze of displays, there were no windows or signs they felt lost and panicky.' While making these adjustments in store layout, which have been criticized by IKEA International headquarters, IKEA has maintained its policy of minimal service. Customers who want home delivery or someone to assemble their furniture must pay the full add-on cost. In fact IKEA stores carefully outsource these services to local providers and they never promote such services in their advertising, they rather encourage their customers to do it the IKEA-Way, which means renting a roof rack and assembling it yourself.

Adapting IKEA's floor plans and furniture to American dimensions paid off, and sales has increased 25 to 30% compared to the late 80's. By 1994 IKEA had turned around the situation in the USA. Through its acquisition of Stor and by adapting its range to US requirements sales have increased steadily by about 10% annually providing them with the volume base necessary to sustain long production lines and keep prices low. Whereas only 15% of the furniture in American stores was produced locally, the figure is now at about 50%.

In the view of several IKEA senior US managers, the key to this successful turn around was the granting of more autonomy to the American country management than their European counterparts had enjoyed. 'You can't steer America from Europe', admitted Anders Moberg in 1994. 'When we went in we hadn't planned a clear strategy of how to supply the American market at a low cost'. Learning how to succeed in the United States through its own painful expense took more than five years. Although its US operation has shown a profit over the last three years it still has not received its initial investment. With flat growth in Europe, heavy investment in longer term expansion into Eastern Europe and China putting pressure on IKEA's capital reserves, focus in the US is now on developing sales and profit from its existing stores before expanding into new regions. Following its bold actions in the early 90's, IKEA has entered into a more conservative phase of consolidation, perhaps it has also learned that the price of being different means that you also have to be more careful about where you invest.

Unresolved issues: management and human resource development

From an American perspective Swedish managers don't show emotion in the work place, 'praise is given for looking calm in all situations. They do not feel comfortable in conflictual situations. Also they tend not to set themselves apart, and self-promotion is frowned upon. They don't like drum beating, or cheer leading in a culture where both are common ways of motivating workers.'

'The biggest conflicts stem from the Americans who need to know who's in charge. People expect their managers to tell them what to do here.' However, at IKEA the manager's role is more subtle and they tend to have a long-term approach to management. 'It takes longer but we want to train people to know how to do things the IKEA-Way.' Since there are few written procedures, the golden rule for managers is helping people understand why things are done in a particular way. This can be taken for indecision by American employees new to IKEA who are more used to rules and procedures spelled out clearly and managers who take responsibility for quick decision making.

American employees perceive IKEA as being more employee oriented than average American employers. IKEA attracts and selects people who value security, job enrichment, and benefits, which are more generous than American typical employers (like five weeks of paid holiday) more than career advancement. However, with full employment in the US it is becoming more difficult to find candidates, particularly for management positions, who have the necessary job qualifications and whose values match IKEA's.

Although IKEA has recently initiated an American style performance review procedure, which requires documenting employee's individual performance strengths and weaknesses, Swedish managers feel uncomfortable with the formality of the system and the need to provide negative feedback. Since they hold the more senior positions their ambivalence has resulted in little real discrimination in pay increases which are directly linked to the reviews. Although turnover at IKEA is lower than the industry average, and co-workers generally appreciate IKEA's caring environment, there is some latent discontent with the way pay increases are distributed even among long term employees who feel that their individual achievements are not always rewarded.

In the opinion of one American manager 'A lot of people have left IKEA because they can't move up fast enough here. Some left the store to go to the Service Center (IKEA's national headquarters) then left because it was too hard for them to adjust, there was not clear frame of reference – policies, procedures. We have lost some key American managers because they didn't have a clear idea of their role or future in the organization.'

Acknowledging that there are not enough American managers in senior positions, IKEA is trying to attract management trainees through presentations at Business Schools. However its low keyed image and lack of structured career pathing is not easy to sell to 'high potentials' more attuned to the packages offered by retailers such as Home Depot which forcefully promote rapid promotion and individualized pay incentives. There is a general consensus that IKEA needs to develop young American managers who can play a bigger role in the organization than at present. However there is no agreement yet on how critical the need is, nor on how to solve the problem.

Two differing views that could be overheard in a fictitious debate between two long term Ikeans illustrate the unresolved issues facing IKEA USA at the end of 1996:

The view of a young American manager: *There is a glass ceiling here. I am at a level at which my growth will stop because I'm not Swedish. IKEA should be made less complicated for Americans, easier for us to adapt to, and develop in. Our management needs to be much more professional in managing human resources. We need to bring new people into the organization and reward individual accountability for results. This would lead to a better balance between the IKEA-Way and American management. Becoming a successful manager at IKEA requires a lot of time and effort to understand how everything fits together. Yet not everyone can go to Sweden or learn Swedish and today too many talented Americans choose to go to the competition. Competition is catching up on us in terms of benefits, and with full employment we should be much more competitive than we are on the American job market.*

The Swedish view: *Being the underdog, not doing things the traditional way over here is vital to IKEA's success in the United States. We must keep a unique image and work better at getting our message across to employees and customers so that they understand why we are successful. Pride in being a part of IKEA must be built locally and since our system is unique this takes time. The real danger is assimilation. We are becoming too American. Giving people bonuses and pay incentives doesn't make them more intelligent; people are motivated by learning and improving in an organization that provides them room to grow. Rewards should be more on a give and take basis, when the company makes more it can give more, but we must remain flexible. Although we must seek balance between adapting and sticking to our proven ways we must protect our unique concepts and way of doing. This means that we will always need a strong Swedish presence in the US, they are our 'on site missionaries' who can develop loyalty to and understanding of our uniqueness.*

IV Clouds on the horizon

By the mid 90's, in spite of its undisputed international success and expansion over the past 25 years, signs appeared that the pattern of growth and steady profit were slowing down. Costs were rising, complaints on quality were more frequent, and unaccustomed delays appeared in product delivery. External factors had changed from the early times in Europe. Economic growth slowed as baby boomers moved into middle age with new tastes and demands, and fewer new homes being sold. Competition had also learned from IKEA's pioneering distribution and were offering better furniture at lower prices, seeking low cost furniture suppliers in eastern Europe which put pressure on IKEA's unique sourcing.

IKEA had become a rather large international organization and in an effort to adapt to the requirements of its many domestic markets its product range had grown from 10.000 to 14.000 items thus weakening returns from long product runs and overburdening logistic supply lines. Increasingly greater attention had to be given to bringing costs down, often through productivity gains which put unprecedented pressure on retail staffs to improve sales to staff ratios. During the years of rapid growth many recruits were bought in from outside the company, who were not steeped in IKEA culture. The company's extended network made it difficult to provide employees and mid-level managers with a clear perception of how their local business impacted on the corporation as a whole. Local initiatives were taken without regard to their impact on the whole system.

Was this the price of diversity or was IKEA in many ways suffering from too much decentralization.

In 1993 to cope with this situation, Anders Moberg and IKEA's senior management launched a company wide operation 'Nytt Läge' (New Situation) with task forces and project teams to suggest ways of improving communication and eliminating snags in distribution. Many suggestions were implemented, including creation of new regional divisions in Europe for closer coordination of country operations, and the hiring of more professionals at headquarters to provide guidelines and more efficient corporate control systems. Although the 'Nytt Läge' program met with a lot of enthusiasm and did achieve improvement in some areas, it soon became clear to Ingvar Kamprad that a more radical change in the organization was needed.

In early 1996 a major organizational change was introduced to 'shorten the value chain' between customers and suppliers. Regional organizations were eliminated to bring stores in more direct contact with IKEA of Sweden. New emphasis was given to the importance of a living corporate culture based on the IKEA values of simplicity and self-discipline, rather than relying on formal policies and procedures. At the same time IKEA's expansion plans in Europe and the United States were delayed. The fear at corporate headquarters was that the IKEA had drifted too far from the basic principles that were behind its legendary success.

Back to the roots

In May Ingvar Kamprad gathered IKEA's 250 worldwide store managers and senior managers at an important meeting in Poland to explain IKEA's need to re-focus and re-direct its efforts. He actually used the word 'rejuvenate'.

'Our product range and purchasing people often have an unequal battle with retailers and their far too many interests. Many of our suppliers got stuck in the middle. Our IKEA idea as one of the world's few production oriented companies is under threat.

Perhaps we were blinded by the boom years of the 80's, which increased geographical spread of our operations to new markets, both on retail and the trading side. Internal communication also became difficult, our administration expanded and our overheads became increasingly heavy. Our costs rose, and our customers and suppliers felt lost, many of them got in touch with me directly.

Decision-making took longer and longer, and endless discussions took place. It became more difficult to see the company as a whole. Far too much of our product development had too little to do with the tastes and wallets of the majority of people. Our product range expanded in every direction and could not be handled in a reasonable way on our sales floors. Our price advantage compared to competitors began to shrink. Even IKEA's soul, our fine corporate culture was in danger. Have we forgotten to explain to our new workers about the IKEA-Way? Have our desks removed us too far from reality? Have we lost our way?'

The managers who attended that meeting felt galvanized by their founder's strong message, and their confidence and belief in the IKEA-Way had been doubtlessly reinforced. In an increasingly complex world environment, simplicity indeed appeared to be a true virtue that had guided the company in the past. Several wondered as they left how Kamprad's intuitive ability to see through the complexity of a worldwide organization and re-ignite the dynamics of IKEA's success could be transmitted throughout the organization? Others wondered if they would have as much autonomy as they had previously enjoyed in adapting to very different markets? Some wondered if the company could regain its developmental thrust through the late 90's.

Case 17 BSkyB: Embracing the digital revolution

Introduction

At the end of 1998 BSkyB faced multiple challenges to its immensely profitable position as the dominant player in UK pay-TV. The imminent launch of digital television meant the end of channel scarcity and created opportunities for new entrants to grab a share of the growing pay-TV market. ONdigital, backed by the UK's two main commercial terrestrial broadcasters and offering consumers digital television via their existing TV aerials, was gearing up for a mass-market launch in November. Another challenge came from the three largest cable companies. Cable and Wireless, Telewest, and NTL were all planning to offer low-cost 'triple-play' packages that included digital television, telephony, and internet access from early 1999. With so many competitors moving into digital television it seemed only a matter of time before BSkyB's margins and market-share were eroded and its dominant position in pay-TV came to an end.

By the end of 2002, however, the picture was very different. BSkyB had doubled its annual revenues to £2.8 billion, almost doubled its subscriber base to 6.6 million, and increased its market-share to 70% of the pay-TV market. By contrast most of its competitors were either down or out. ONdigital, renamed ITV Digital in 2001, had shut down in May 2002 with losses of £1.25 billion (although Freeview – a free-to-access service backed by the BBC – rose from the ashes six months later). The two remaining cable companies, NTL and Telewest, were more focused on restructuring their combined £15 billion debt and simply surviving than on leading the digital revolution.

This case study was researched and written by Ian Maude under the supervision of John McGee, Warwick Business School. Special thanks to Claire Enders and Toby Syfret for their help with proof-reading. Also thanks to Jon Beaumont, Tom Betts, David Chance, David Elstein, Chris Goodall, Mathew Horsman, Marija Radaković, David Raybould, Paul Simmonds, Joe Smithies, Ray Snoddy, David Thatcher, and several others that cannot be named for their assistance.

How did BSkyB manage to see off the competition and extend its domination of pay-TV into the digital era? Why did its competitors fail so spectacularly? What were BSkyB's strategic advantages and how did they change over time? By 2002 BSkyB had fully converted its customer franchise to digital but was the decision to launch Sky Digital in 1998 the right one? What other options did BSkyB have? Finally what threats, challenges, and opportunities lie ahead for the satellite television company?

The analogue era

UK pay-TV up to 1998

By 1998 pay-TV had grown significantly in the UK since its launch in the 1980s. At the end of the year 6.3 million UK households – 25% of TV households – received cable or satellite television.[1] The majority subscribed to Sky's satellite service although an increasing number was signing up to cable services such as those run by Cable & Wireless and Telewest.

Until the mid-1980s the UK had only four terrestrial free-to-air television channels: BBC1 and BBC2, advertising-free channels owned by the public service BBC and funded by a compulsory television licence, ITV, a commercial channel formed by a number of independent regional franchises, and Channel 4, a public service commercial channel. In 1986 the television regulator invited bids to broadcast television channels into UK homes via a government-controlled satellite. At the time Rupert Murdoch's Sky was a small satellite television company broadcasting a single advertising-supported channel across Europe. Sky bid for the new UK satellite licence but lost out to British Satellite Broadcasting (BSB), a consortium including Granada and Anglia, two of the ITV regional franchises, and Richard Branson's Virgin Group. BSB's plan was to launch a high-quality subscription-based service in late 1989. Unwilling to give up, Murdoch decided to launch a competing, advertising-supported free-to-access service before BSB went

---

[1] *UK: TV Market Overview*, Screen Digest, London, November 2003.

on air. Sky bought content rights, leased transponder capacity on the Luxembourg-based Astra satellite, and set up alliances with consumer electronics companies to develop set-top boxes and satellite dishes. Cash was tight and much of the necessary equipment had to be leased rather than bought. Hollywood studios refused to license their movies to Sky until Murdoch restricted access to paying customers. Movies were 'must-have' content so Murdoch was forced to switch from his original advertising-based business model to a subscription-based model. To control access to Sky's channels he invested in encryption technology and subscriber management systems.[2]

The revamped Sky went on air on 5 February 1989 with four channels: Sky News, the UK's first 24-hour news channel, Sky TV, an entertainment channel, Sky Movies, and Eurosport. Retailers were initially reluctant to stock the set-top boxes required to access the new service so Murdoch hired hundreds of salesmen to sell Sky door-to-door. News Corporation, Sky's parent company, promoted the service heavily in its UK media assets which included *The Sun* and *The Times* newspapers. When BSB finally launched in April 1990 Sky had around 750,000 subscribers. Sky's earlier launch and aggressive marketing enabled it to attract far more subscribers but the competition between the rival services drove up costs and increased uncertainty amongst consumers, resulting in both companies haemorrhaging cash. By the end of 1990 the competitors were forced to merge to stave off bankruptcy. Rumour had it Murdoch himself approached the Prime Minister, Margaret Thatcher, who nodded the deal through. Although touted as a merger, Murdoch's News Corporation had a controlling share and Murdoch wasted no time in exercising it. Almost all BSB's staff were sacked. Brutal cost-cutting by Sam Chisholm, the pugnacious Australian television boss picked by Murdoch to run the merged company, helped British Sky Broadcasting (BSkyB)

to achieve its first operating profit in 1992.[3] But massive debt meant the company was still losing money.

The new Premier League presented an opportunity and Chisholm grabbed it. The Premier League (also known as the Premiership) was formed in 1992 by the top 22 football clubs in the UK Football League breaking away to have more control over their own destiny and specifically over television rights. Sport in the UK is dominated by the top football clubs and Chisholm saw the potential of the new league to drive subscriptions. BSkyB bid £191.5 million for exclusive broadcast rights to live Premier League football for five years from 1992/93. With the addition of the BBC's bid for exclusive recorded highlights, the combined BSkyB/BBC offer was £214 million – significantly more than was bid by ITV for live rights and recorded highlights. It was alleged Chisholm resubmitted his bid after being told the value of ITV's offer but for a company with a turnover of £93 million and which lost £759 million in 1991 it was still a very big bet. It paid off immediately. After it was announced Sky had exclusive live Premier League football Chisholm said subscriptions rolled in as if it was 'Christmas every day'.[4] Within two years Sky doubled in size to more than 2.5 million satellite (also known as direct-to-home or DTH) subscribers. In 1994 BSkyB achieved its first pre-tax profit of £93 million on revenues of £550 million. Murdoch immediately capitalised on Sky's success and floated 17.5% of BSkyB's stock on the London and New York Stock Exchanges, valuing the company at £4.4 billion.

Over the next few years BSkyB took advantage of additional satellite capacity to add more channels. It negotiated exclusive carriage deals with popular US cable channels and moved into new areas such as pay-per-view (PPV). In 1996 660,000 subscribers each paid up to £15 to watch Mike Tyson's heavyweight boxing match with Frank Bruno. That same year BSkyB negotiated a new contract with the Premier League, paying £670 million for exclusive live rights for another four years. Its negotiating position was aided by a clause in the 1992 contract

---

[2] Murdoch realised secure encryption was key to charging for content over networks. In 1988 he invested $3.6 million in News Datacom Research Ltd which had licensed Israeli academic Adi Shamir's encryption algorithms, the basis for the VideoCrypt conditional access system later used by Sky.

---

[3] The pay-TV service continued to operate under the Sky brand name.

[4] 'Everything to play for at BSkyB', John Cassy, *The Guardian*, Manchester, 23 April 2003, p.19.

that allowed it to match any other bid. BSkyB also tied up rights for the Football League, the three professional football divisions below the Premier League, for five years for £125 million. By now Sky offered 33 basic and seven premium channels. In 1997 BSkyB had 3.5 million DTH subscribers and generated profits of £374 million on turnover of £1.25 billion. The broadcaster was the dominant player in UK pay-TV but subscriptions had stagnated. BSkyB had become highly profitable on the back of exclusive live Premiership football but it looked as if the football dividend had been used up. Sky also had a downmarket image in part due to the large satellite dishes required to receive the weak Astra signal. Analysts began to question BSkyB's prospects and by the end of 1997 its market value had fallen 30% from a peak of £12.7 billion.

Cable television launched in the UK in 1984 with licences based on geographic areas. Unlike the US, networks had to be installed underground and the high cost meant there was little money for original programming. By 1990 there were 26 cable operators but only 270,000 subscribers. In 1991, to kick-start the market, the Government granted cable companies the right to provide telephony. Offering cheap telephone calls gave them a competitive edge over Sky but it was this that drove much of their growth. This was compounded by a lack of compelling, attractively-priced programming. US cable companies built their franchises on the back of premium content but in the UK BSkyB had exclusive rights to 90% of first-run Hollywood movies and, from 1992, live Premiership football. UK cable operators felt obliged to go to BSkyB for content. It didn't refuse access but it did require them to take a range of channels and set strict rules about packaging through the use of Minimum Carriage Requirements (MCRs) and buy-through conditions.[5] These forced cable operators to sell Sky channels on the same basis of tiering and buy-through as did Sky.

This meant including Sky's basic channels in their basic tiers and its premium channels in a premium tier with subscribers having to buy through a basic tier to subscribe to premium channels. Sky's wholesale prices were based on 59% of its retail prices with discounts and penalties according to several factors that included the Pay-to-Basic Ratio (PBR), the ratio of premium Sky channel subscribers (weighted for the number of premium Sky channels to which they subscribed) to basic subscribers. Some cable companies argued such policies made pay-TV more expensive by making it more premium-oriented and preventing price competition and meant it was impossible to resell Sky channels profitably. In late 1995 BSkyB's position in the wholesale pay-TV market became the subject of an Office of Fair Trading (OFT) investigation. In its defence BSkyB argued it did not dominate the supply of premium or other content, pricing policies such as tiering and buy-through were commonplace in pay-TV markets, and an efficient company would eventually make a profit reselling its channels. After a year-long inquiry the OFT announced there was no evidence BSkyB was abusing its position although it asked the company to make certain voluntary undertakings, to which it agreed.[6] These included publishing its wholesale pricing and discount policy and agreeing to submit any future changes to the OFT for approval. Other undertakings included reducing the upper limit on MCRs from 100% to 80% of a cable operator's base and publicly reaffirming other broadcasters had non-discriminatory access to its conditional access system (which had become the de facto UK standard). The OFT also referred the Premier League and its broadcast agreements with BSkyB and the BBC to the Restrictive Practices Court on the basis the League was acting as a cartel by brokering exclusive deals which reduced consumer choice and increased the cost of watching games on television.

The huge costs of installing underground networks and resulting losses led to rapid consolidation in the cable industry and by 1998 there were only five major operators. But despite its problems cable had

---

[5] Minimum Carriage Requirements required channels to be made available to a certain proportion of a cable operator's subscriber base. An MCR of 100% meant a channel had to be included in an operator's most widely available tier. Buy-through conditions applied to premium channels. They required pay-TV subscribers to buy through a basic tier before they could subscribe to a premium channel.

---

[6] *The Director General's Review of BSkyB's position in the Wholesale TV Market*, OFT, London, December 1996.

started to grow rapidly. By 1997 there were 2.3 million cable television subscribers compared to Sky's 3.5 million and in 1998 cable subscriptions increased by 20% compared with virtually no growth in satellite.[7] Some analysts predicted it would not be long before cable overtook satellite as the dominant pay-TV platform in the UK, as it was elsewhere in Europe and in the US.

The game's afoot

Government Acts

Digital technology converts sound and pictures into a digital format – a series of 1s and 0s – which is compressed before transmission. Six or more digital television channels can be supported by the same 'bandwidth' (broadcast spectrum or frequency) required for a single analogue channel. This allows broadcasters to deliver more channels as well as other services and makes transmission costs per channel far cheaper. Transmitting digital signals also reduces data loss enabling higher quality sound and pictures to be delivered.

In 1996 Parliament passed the Broadcasting Act which set out the legislative framework for the development of digital terrestrial television (DTT) in the UK.[8] This came into force in October 1996 when the Independent Television Commission (ITC), the commercial television regulator, invited bids for four digital terrestrial multiplexes (equivalent to analogue channel licences). Two additional multiplexes were reserved, one for the BBC and one for ITV/Channel 4. Channel 5, a terrestrial channel launched in 1997, and S4C, a Welsh-language channel, were guaranteed carriage on a non-specified multiplex. Value was added to the multiplexes by the fact the Government planned to switch off analogue television by 2006–2010 so the spectrum could be sold off for other purposes.

In June 1997 three multiplexes were awarded to British Digital Broadcasting (BDB), a three-way venture owned by Carlton and Granada, the two largest regional ITV broadcasters, and BSkyB.

[7] *UK: TV Market Overview*, Screen Digest, London, November 2003.
[8] *Broadcasting Act 1996*, HMSO, London, July 1996.

Under pressure from EU competition authorities, however, the ITC forced BSkyB to pull out of the consortium because of concern its position as both programme buyer and seller could allow it to control prices. In May 1998 the fourth multiplex was awarded to SDN Ltd, owned by NTL, S4C, and United News & Media, the latter being a major shareholder in Channel 5.

The arrival of DTT meant digital television could now be broadcast via three different platforms:

◆ DTT: signals are received via a conventional aerial but require a digital adaptor (set-top box) or integrated digital television (including a digital adaptor) to decode them back into analogue form.

◆ Cable: digitally encoded signals are piped into the home via cable and decoded via a set-top box.

◆ Satellite: received via a satellite dish the digital signals are decoded via a digital adaptor or integrated digital television.

Since cable and satellite broadcasters controlled their own networks they could transmit as many channels as they wanted, limited only by the capacity of the technology they used, and switch to digital whenever they wished.

Digital ambition

The key groups planning to launch digital television services in the UK were the BBC, ITV/Channel 4, BDB, BSkyB, and the cable companies.

The licence fee funded BBC planned to make its two existing channels plus three new channels available on all three digital platforms. It also planned to launch four more channels as part of a commercial venture with Flextech, the programme supplier. The first digital channel, BBC News 24, was scheduled to launch in November 1997, to be followed by BBC Choice and BBC Parliament in 1998. To help to fund its digital expansion the BBC sold its transmitter network to Crown Transmission Services Ltd for £244 million.

ITV and Channel 4 set up a joint venture, Digital 3&4 Ltd, to manage their multiplex and planned to launch existing and new channels on all digital platforms by the end of 1998. New channels included ITV2, a free-to-access entertainment and sports channel, and FilmFour, a subscription-based movie channel. Free-to-access channels would be available to anyone with an integrated digital television or set-top box but subscription channels would only be accessible via pay-TV services.

BDB, holder of three digital multiplexes, planned to launch in late 1998. After BSkyB's forced withdrawal Granada and Carlton became sole owners with Carlton's Chairman, Michael Green, becoming Chairman of BDB. Green recruited Stephen Grabiner, Managing Director at Express Newspapers, to be BDB's CEO. With the 12-year DTT licences won and the analogue switch-off scheduled for 2006–2010, confidence at BDB was high. Grabiner and his team spent 1998 putting together the new service. They set up a transmission agreement, awarded the contract for the encryption system to Canal+ subsidiary SECA, appointed BT to handle subscriber management, and placed orders for set-top boxes with six consumer electronics companies. In July BDB changed its name to ONdigital and announced it would launch with 15 channels. These included 12 basic channels from Granada, Carlton, and BBC/Flextech, and three premium channels from Sky. Free-to-air channels would also be available. The big selling point was consumers wishing to access these channels had only to plug the ONdigital set-top box into their existing aerial and television – they didn't need a new aerial, cable, or satellite dish. The DTT broadcaster was targeting what Green called 'Middle England' or the three quarters of the UK population that didn't subscribe to multi-channel television and it had ambitious targets, aiming to double the size of the UK pay-TV market by signing up around six million subscribers.[9] Grabiner told analysts ONdigital would achieve breakeven with two million subscribers and make annual profits of £165 million once it reached three million.[10] In late September the company confirmed it would launch its service on 15 November with set-top boxes costing £199 and a range of subscription packages starting from £7.99 a month. With a marketing budget of £90 million, plus promotion on the ITV network, it would be one of the largest ever launches of a consumer product in the UK.

At BSkyB Chisholm was not sold on digital television, believing it would reduce profitability. However Murdoch saw 'digital' as the future and thought it was essential to switch before the competition, so Chisholm pushed on. Despite his reservations Chisholm was determined not to let anything loosen BSkyB's highly lucrative grip on UK pay-TV. As well as planning a satellite-based service, dubbed Sky Digital, he entered into a joint venture with Carlton to bid for the DTT licences. Chisholm believed the best approach was to be platform agnostic, telling analysts 'Sky is in everything ... it's a horizontally integrated business, that's why it's in digital terrestrial, cable, satellite, smoke signals, whatever the platforms are, we're a programme deliverer'.[11] He also set up British Interactive Broadcasting (BIB), a consortium of BSkyB, BT, HSBC, and Matsushita, which would offer a range of interactive services such as home banking and shopping via a set-top box. Initially the partners were to invest £265 million in BIB, which was projected to breakeven after five years. Sky Digital and other services would be accessed via set-top boxes developed by BIB. These would feature an Electronic Programme Guide (EPG), an on-screen display controlled by a dedicated remote control which would enable viewers to search and select channels and services. Return-path information for interactive services would be via a telephone connection. Conditional access technology would be supplied by NDS (formerly News Datacom Research Ltd), a News Corporation subsidiary, and subscriber management would be handled by BSkyB's state-of-the-art customer service centre.

Murdoch and Chisholm had considered launching Sky Digital as early as May 1996 but delayed several times. Ostensibly this was for technical reasons but Chisholm's concern about the impact on profitability and the lack of pressure from the competition were also factors. The delays did have one upside in that Sky's digital set-top box and EPG technology was, in the words of one executive, 'road-tested to death'.[12] On 17 June 1997 it was announced Chisholm was to step down as BSkyB's CEO because of ill-health.

[9] *Sky High: The Inside Story of BSkyB*, Mathew Horsman, Orion, London, 1998, p.247.

[10] 'UK's BDB stays on track for Q4 digital TV launch', *Reuters Newswire*, London, 8 May 1998.

[11] Horsman, op. cit., p.198.

[12] Case study interview, June 2004.

A few days later news leaked out BSkyB would have to pull out of BDB and David Chance, Chisholm's highly regarded deputy, would leave later in the year. That same week the *Financial Times* ran a story that the Premier League was considering setting up its own pay-TV venture.[13] In the space of a few days the shares fell 24%, reducing the company's value by £2.6 billion. Before he left, one of Chisholm's last significant acts was to negotiate a settlement with Granada and Carlton in which they agreed to pay £75 million for BSkyB's stake in BDB. As part of the deal BSkyB contracted to supply certain of its premium channels to BDB for five years, although the DTT broadcaster had to consent to a high Pay-to-Basic Ratio.

Two weeks before Chisholm's departure was announced Murdoch appointed Mark Booth, COO at JSkyB – News Corporation's Japanese pay-TV operation, as his successor. There were plenty of issues for the new CEO to deal with. From February 1998 BSkyB was in dispute with Carlton and Granada, claiming it was owed £60 million for the programming it was due to supply to BDB. Granada had agreed to pay but Carlton's Green held out on the basis BSkyB hadn't delivered the promised content. It had emerged BSkyB's deals for Premiership football and Hollywood movies didn't include digital terrestrial rights and Green refused to pay the full amount after slow progress made him believe BSkyB hadn't tried hard enough to resolve the issue. In April BDB's decision to use SECA's MediaGuard conditional access system rather than VideoCrypt from NDS led Booth to issue a writ against BDB, arguing this breached a commitment to make its set-top boxes interoperable. BSkyB also had to deal with an ITC investigation into its policy of requiring cable companies to purchase two Sky movie channels if they wished to carry the Disney Channel (the company dropped the requirement prior to the outcome of the inquiry).[14] All this time BSkyB's share price was falling.

Despite these issues BSkyB's digital plans moved ahead. The company negotiated exclusive or preferential carriage deals with key channel providers such as Disney, Turner Broadcasting, and Viacom, and set up PPV deals with the major film studios. It also leased transponder capacity on digital satellites from SES-Astra and ordered set-top boxes from Pace and other manufacturers. In May, after BSkyB and BT had made concessions, the EU commission gave BIB, now renamed Open, the go ahead.[15] The following month the row with ONdigital over its conditional access system was settled after Booth accepted viewers only needed a plug-in adaptor to switch to Sky Digital. In July BSkyB signed agreements with the BBC, Flextech, Discovery, and Channel 4 to add their channels to its digital service. Not everything went BSkyB's way. Following an investigation into channel bundling and in an attempt to make access to pay-TV cheaper, the ITC announced MCRs were to be prohibited. Even so BSkyB saw it could turn the situation to its advantage by creating a low-cost entry level package for Sky Digital with only a few channels included (in effect ditching channels it didn't own from the basic package) while leaving prices for top tier packages unchanged.

Available to a limited number of analogue subscribers from June, Sky Digital's official launch was scheduled for 1 October. Initially it would offer 140 channels. Many of these were extensions of channels on Sky's analogue service, multiplexed PPV movie channels showing the same movies at short intervals (known as Near Video On Demand or NVOD), and audio-only music channels. Booth's business strategy remained the same as Chisholm's but a new marketing strategy focused on attracting premium subscribers to Sky Digital by emphasising its extensive movie and sports content whilst continuing to market the basic analogue service to value-conscious consumers. A smaller, redesigned satellite dish aided Sky Digital's more upscale positioning.

The three leading cable companies – Cable & Wireless, Telewest, and NTL – planned to launch

---

[13] 'Top football clubs consider pay-TV launch: Premier League told it could fare better without BSkyB', Patrick Harverson, *Financial Times*, London, 24 June 1997, p.1.

[14] BSkyB had exclusive UK distribution rights for the Disney Channel.

[15] The concessions included guaranteeing third parties access to the set-top box and removing the requirement for users to sign up for BSkyB's pay-TV service. BT also had to agree to divest its UK cable television interests.

cable-based digital television services from late 1998/early 1999.

At the end of 1997 the UK's largest cable operator, Cable & Wireless Communications (CWC), a subsidiary of telecoms giant Cable & Wireless plc, had 5.9 million passed homes and nearly 600,000 cable television subscribers. In early 1998 CWC committed £100 million to developing its digital television service, started consumer trials, and made plans to roll the service out to all the homes covered by its network the following year. In October 1998 the company ordered 100,000 digital set-top boxes in anticipation of launching the service in spring 1999.

Telewest Communications plc was set up in 1992 as a joint venture between US West, one of the Baby Bell telcos, and TCI, the US cable operator. By 1998 it had a cable network covering 20% of the UK and 600,000 television subscribers. At £281 per annum Telewest had the highest average revenue per user (ARPU) of all cable television companies although it also had the highest churn, losing 34% of its customers a year. In March it bid £666 million for General Cable and announced it would buy Comcast's cable franchises in Birmingham and London, to be financed by share issues and debt. After these acquisitions Telewest had more than 720,000 cable television subscribers and debts of £2.3 billion. At the end of the year the company announced plans to launch a digital service by the end of 1999.

National Transcommunications Ltd (NTL) began life as the UK's transmission network for commercial television. In 1996 it was bought by CableTel, a fibre optic network company which owned cable licences for several UK cities. In 1997 NASDAQ-listed CableTel renamed itself NTL and set about buying more cable licences. That same year it led an unsuccessful bid for the DTT multiplexes. In April 1998 CEO Barclay Knapp announced plans to launch a 'triple-play' of digital services later in the year saying, 'We just want to pump everything we can down the wires'.[16] Telephony and internet access would be available from September with digital television to follow. As was the case with all

cable companies, NTL's services could only be accessed in areas covered by its network. After acquiring Diamond Cable and the majority of Comcast's UK cable operations, NTL reached 5.2 million homes and had 690,000 cable television subscribers. Knapp and his team spent the year raising money, planning acquisitions, and managing the company's debt. They even bought a stake in Newcastle United football club.[17] By the end of 1998 debt had risen to $5 billion but delays in agreeing technical specifications meant there was still no firm launch date for NTL's digital services.

Digital TV arrives

DSAT and DTT launch

Sky Digital went on air on 1 October 1998. It offered a range of pricing options starting from £6.99 per month for a six channel package up to all 140 channels including all Sky Sports and Sky Movies channels for £29.99 a month.[18] To access Sky Digital viewers had to purchase a new set-top box, the Sky Digibox, and satellite dish for £200 (£160 for existing subscribers) and pay an installation fee of £30 (£25).[19] BSkyB promoted the new service aggressively with TV spots on Sky's analogue service and the terrestrial television channels. *The Times* and *The Sun* ran daily promotions. At the end of the month Booth announced Sky Digital had 100,000 subscribers.

ONdigital went live six weeks after Sky Digital. Although available in less than 70% of households and despite problems with delivery of set-top boxes, hopes were high with Grabiner proclaiming, 'Digital television made simple, through an aerial, is here' (BSkyB's Booth responded by saying ONdigital was

---

[16] 'Hot wires', *The Economist*, London, 20 June 1998, p.98.

[17] This aped an earlier bid by BSkyB for Manchester United football club. NTL planned to make a full bid for Newcastle United but drew back after the OFT disallowed BSkyB's bid for Manchester United in April 1999.

[18] The entry level package for Sky's analogue service cost £11.99 a month – all 40 analogue channels cost £29.99 a month.

[19] Subscribers who didn't renew their subscriptions could still access free-to-air digital satellite channels via their set-top box.

more 'plug and pray' than 'plug and play').[20] ONdigital's set-top boxes cost £200 and there was a £20 connection fee. The basic subscription package cost £7.99 a month. This included six out of a possible 15 subscription channels, plus the free-to-air channels from the BBC, ITV, Channel 4, and Channel 5. Five premium channels were also available – the most expensive being Sky Sports 1, featuring live Premiership football, which cost an extra £11 per month. All 31 channels were available for £29.99 a month.

Analysts were quick to predict rapid growth in consumer take-up of digital television. Almost all saw digital television as a non-zero-sum game since there were more than enough households not yet subscribing to multi-channel television to support Sky Digital, ONdigital, and, eventually, the cable companies. Henderson Crosthwaite forecast by 2005 Sky Digital would have 3.8 million subscribers with 2.7 million on ONdigital and 4.7 million for digital cable.[21]

At BSkyB Booth was determined to ensure Sky Digital offered the widest possible choice and was incensed when ITV made its channels available via cable but not on satellite. He complained to the OFT and the ITC, claiming ITV's decision was anti-competitive. He complained again to the ITC when Carlton and Granada refused to carry commercials for Premiership football on Sky Digital. At the end of 1998 Sky Digital had 225,000 subscribers, mostly existing customers switching to digital. ONdigital's decision not to release year-end figures was somewhat undermined by a statement in mid-January by Philips, the only supplier to have distributed set-top boxes for the new service, which said, 'By the end of January, we hope to have sold 100,000 ONdigital boxes'.[22]

The battle between BSkyB and ONdigital was also fought out over content rights, mostly for sporting events. In February 1999 ITV and ONdigital successfully bid £265 million for exclusive broadcast rights to UEFA Champions League football for four years.[23] Matches would be shown exclusively on ITV and ITV2 which were not available on Sky Digital. In retaliation BSkyB switched events, such as Ryder Cup golf, from Sky Sports 1, which was available on ONdigital, to Sky Sports 2, which was not. Grabiner complained to the ITC that BSkyB was abusing its position by refusing to supply Sky Sports 2 to ONdigital. BSkyB countered by arguing doing so might put it in breach of the Broadcasting Act's limits on the supply of services by one supplier. In March the ITC found against Carlton and Granada over their refusal to carry ads promoting Premiership football on Sky Digital but decided ITV should not be forced to supply ITV or ITV2 for satellite distribution (the OFT later came to the same conclusion). Even without the ITV channels Sky Digital grew faster than ONdigital and by the end of March had 350,000 subscribers compared to 110,000 on the DTT service.

Cable consolidation and free set-top boxes

In January 1999 Microsoft agreed to buy 5.25% of NTL's convertible preferred stock for $500 million. In return NTL undertook to use Microsoft servers and software in its digital services. Whilst undoubtedly a high profile strategic partnership, the deal meant further delays before NTL could confirm the technical specifications for its digital cable service. At Telewest (where Microsoft also took a non-controlling stake) the management team spent the first part of the year organising credit facilities for acquisitions. To a degree the cable companies' focus on deal-making was understandable. Analogue cable subscriptions continued to grow and the stock markets were charging ahead, particularly in the US where the Dow Jones and NASDAQ Composite both rose 20% in the first half of the year. Media stocks were being valued on a per subscriber basis and investors were rewarding scale and ambition. Further consolidation seemed inevitable. In fact the first move was made by CWC which, having decided

[20] 'First shots in Digital TV war', *BBC News web site*, 15 November 1998, <URL:http://news.bbc.co.uk/1/hi/business/the_company_file/214809.stm>, Accessed 1 June 2004.

[21] 'First shots in Digital TV war', op. cit.

[22] 'The First 100k ... we hope!', *Digital TV Group web site*, 16 January 1998, <URL: http://www.dtg.org.uk/news/archive/sum_9801.htm>, Accessed 4 June 2004.

[23] UEFA Champions League football is an annual cup competition between the top 32 European football clubs.

to focus on business and data services, started talks about selling its cable division to Telewest. The cable operators finally made their first digital moves in May when CWC started trials of its digital cable service, offering a package of 14 television channels and a telephone line for £10 a month. The following month NTL announced it would launch its digital service in September. Knapp confidently predicted NTL would have 250,000 digital subscribers by mid-2000 with customers attracted by the company's low cost packages.

Although Sky Digital was growing, Sky's overall DTH subscriber numbers had been static at 3.5 million since 1997. With cable about to enter the race it was clear something dramatic was needed to boost growth. Free trials were not feasible but Martin Stewart, BSkyB's CFO, suggested giving away the set-top box to new digital subscribers in return for a 12 month commitment.[24] It was estimated the subsidy would cost £187 million in 1999. Booth approved the strategy but, as with all key decisions, the critical approval was that of Murdoch. To help finance the promotion the company made a provision of £450 million in its accounts. Booth also raised Sky Digital's retail prices by £2 a month, increased the installation fee to £40, and cancelled dividend payments until further notice. The offer started on 5 May and encouraged mass-market retailers like Dixons, Comet, and Argos, to offer Sky on a national basis for the first time – although their commission per sale went down BSkyB was able to persuade the retailers higher volumes would more than compensate. Again the bet paid off. BSkyB had to hire an extra 2,000 installation engineers and 600 call centre staff to cope with demand.

Grabiner knew ONdigital had to match Sky's free set-top box offer. It did so two weeks later, even offering free connection as an additional inducement, but the £220 per subscriber subsidy wasn't factored into the business plan, forcing Carlton and Granada to allow it to draw down

more cash.[25] However, the move did encourage analysts to increase their forecasts for the DTT service. Merrill Lynch raised its forecast to 480,000 subscribers by the end of 1999 and 1.66 million by 2002.[26]

Back in April Booth had announced he was leaving BSkyB in June to head up e-partners – a venture capital fund set up by News Corporation. Murdoch quickly appointed Tony Ball, President of News Corporation's Fox Sports network in the US, as the new CEO. Soon after, ONdigital also lost its CEO when Grabiner resigned after a series of disagreements with Green. During the summer ONdigital lost a number of other key staff and Carlton and Granada were forced to restructure the management team. Grabiner was replaced by Stuart Prebble, previously Director of Channels at Granada and regarded as having strong management and programming skills.

By the end of June Telewest still hadn't agreed terms with Cable & Wireless. NTL's Knapp decided to contact CWC with an offer and within a few weeks the deal was agreed. NTL would buy CWC's cable business for £8.2 billion. NTL was backed by France Telecom which agreed to pay $5.5 billion for 25% of the merged company. When the deal closed NTL would be the UK's biggest cable operator with a network covering half the country and 2.8 million residential customers. According to Knapp, NTL/CWC would have the scale to compete with BT in telephony and with BSkyB in pay-TV. But with management focused on completing the buyout, which was referred to the competition authorities after BSkyB objected, the launch of NTL's digital service was delayed once more.

Declaring 'I don't just want Sky in every home – I want it watched in every home', BSkyB's Ball set his team the goal of changing Sky from a sports-led broadcaster to an all-round entertainment service.[27]

---

[24] Chisholm and Chance had used the same razor-and-blades strategy in the analogue era. Free trials were not considered viable or desirable, mainly due to the cost of dish installation. Under the terms of the free set-top box offer subscribers had to connect the set-top box to their telephone line.

[25] Unlike Sky, ONdigital required the free set-top box to be returned when the subscription came to an end or was cancelled.

[26] 'Cheap integrated sets and free boxes push button for high-street blast-off', Hugo Davenport, *New Media Markets*, 27 May 1999, p.1.

[27] 'Tony Ball: Murdoch's solid enforcer', Ian Youngs, *BBC News web site*, 23 September 2003, <URL: http://news.bbc.co.uk/1/hi/entertainment/tv_and_radio/313020 6.stm>, Accessed 29 May 2004.

More family-oriented channels were signed up but it was the free set-top box offer that drove take-up. By July Sky Digital had 1.2 million subscribers although BSkyB's results revealed the high cost – the previous year's profit had become a loss of £388 million. Ball publicly announced targets of 5 million DTH subscribers and ARPU of £300 per annum (including £50 from interactive) by the end of 2000 and suggested Sky's analogue service could be switched off by the end of 2001. The company also moved into interactive services. In July it added internet access and discounted telephone calls to Sky Digital's offering. The following month saw the launch of Sky Sports Extra – an on-screen interactive icon which provided the ability to change camera angles and call up replays during football matches. Also in August, Open, the interactive banking and shopping service backed by BIB, finally launched. There was good news on another front when the Restrictive Practices Court rejected the OFT's case against the Premier League's practice of collective bargaining of broadcast rights.[28] The markets welcomed the company's subscriber land-grab and interactive strategy and by the end of September BSkyB was valued at over £20 billion.

At ONdigital Prebble and his team faced a number of challenges:

♦ Lower than expected signal strength for DTT transmissions meant less than 70% of the UK population could receive ONdigital rather than 90% as per the business plan.

♦ Although its marketing focused heavily on the plug and play nature of ONdigital some viewers experienced poor reception and picture quality unless they upgraded their TV aerials.

♦ Significant numbers of customers were cancelling their subscriptions with many switching to other providers of multi-channel television.

♦ ONdigital's encryption technology had been hacked making piracy commonplace.[29]

In spite of its problems ONdigital had 411,000 subscribers by September, ahead of expectations and on track to its target of two million by May 2002. Whilst Sky Digital had more subscribers many of these were existing customers switching to digital whereas, as Prebble regularly pointed out, 90% of ONdigital's subscribers were new to multi-channel television. Many commentators felt ONdigital's simple offering and ease of installation would attract customers that had so far resisted the lure of pay-TV. The company was certainly making progress, adding channels such as MTV, Nickelodeon and, after a long battle with BSkyB, Sky Sports 2 to its line-up. New marketing programmes had been launched such as 'pre-paid' set-top boxes which included a year's subscription to ONdigital for £119. These could be bought in stores, taken home, and plugged in for instant digital television – a significant advantage over Sky where customers had to wait up to seven weeks for the dish to be installed. Low-cost integrated digital televisions (idTV) with built-in ONdigital decoders were also coming onto the market. Analysts believed idTVs would soon represent a big slice of the 4 million televisions sold in the UK every year and become the main driver of ONdigital's growth. In the meantime the free set-top box offer was severely affecting the company's cash flow. Merrill Lynch estimated the subsidy accounted for over 90% of revenues in 1999.[30] Nevertheless the company received a boost when the Government restated its goal of switching off analogue television by 2010.

Increasing consumer choice

Digital cable finally arrived in October 1999 when Telewest launched Active Digital. This offered 150 television and radio channels, including 50 PPV

---

[28] 1996 No.1 (E&W) in the Restrictive Practices Court (in England and Wales), The Court Service, London, 28 July 1999. Although the Court agreed the agreements were restrictive it found they were in the public interest as they helped to fund ground improvements and the money was shared equitably by the clubs.

[29] By 2002 ONdigital estimated there were over 100,000 hacked smart cards in circulation. In March 2002 Canal+, makers of the MediaGuard conditional access system used by ONdigital and other pay-TV broadcasters, filed a lawsuit against NDS alleging it had leaked the encryption code. No link was proven and the case was settled out of court.

[30] 'ONdigital terrestrial TV forecasts', New Media Markets, op. cit., p.3.

movie channels, and low-cost telephony with the promise of broadband internet access to come. The basic package, including 18 television channels and a telephone line, was priced at £13 per month. Additional channels, costing between £2 and £12 a month, could be picked from an 'à la carte' menu which allowed subscribers to select and pay for only those they wanted. Subscribers had to pay a connection fee of £30 but the set-top box came free.[31] To attract new customers Telewest even offered a free one-month trial. The company planned to rollout the new service to the 4.2 million homes covered by its network by the middle of 2000. Telewest also moved into interactive services. In December it announced a flat-rate internet access service, SurfUnlimited, for £10 a month – the first company in the UK to do so. It also announced plans to offer home banking, home shopping, email, and internet access via its high speed cable network from early 2000.

Most analysts assumed it would not be long before the acquisitive Knapp made a play for Telewest. Instead Telewest sprang its own surprise when it announced the takeover of Flextech, the programme supplier which owned or had a stake in 13 television channels.[32] Telewest's shareholders would own 80% of the merged company, worth £10.5 billion, with 20% owned by Flextech's shareholders. Adam Singer, CEO of the smaller Flextech, would be CEO. Singer's strategy was to build mass and increase ARPU by using the company's low-cost bundled packages to attract customers and then persuading them to trade up to higher margin services such as high speed internet access. Singer pushed the idea that Telewest/Flextech's branded content, high speed network, and focus on new interactive services would create the UK's first 'Broadbandcaster'.[33] Investor reaction was positive and by the end of the year the share price had risen over 40% in

two months, valuing the pre-merger Telewest at over £10 billion.

In May 2000 NTL at last launched its digital cable service. NTL Digital Plus featured the much-vaunted 'triple-play' of digital television, telephony, and internet access, although the latter would only be available from July. Channel packs and premium channels could be bolted onto the basic package which cost £13 per month and included a telephone line, 14 television channels, and access to multi-plexed PPV movies. Whilst the set-top box came free subscribers had to pay a £40 connection fee.[34] Like Telewest, NTL planned a phased rollout. NTL also put heavy emphasis on interactivity, promising full web-browsing via both TV and PC. Knapp believed NTL's interactive services would distinguish it from its competitors and set a target of 500,000 digital subscribers by the end of 2000. Later that month the last regulatory obstacle to NTL's buyout of CWC's cable business was cleared when France Telecom received approval for its investment in NTL/CWC.

The view from 30,000 feet

By June Continental Research estimated there were 4.65 million digital television subscribers in the UK, equivalent to 19% of TV households.[35] In many areas, consumers could now choose between three different services: Sky Digital, ONdigital, and either Telewest or NTL. Heavyweight marketing campaigns from the key players throughout the year increased consumer demand. In a survey by Gallup, 44% of adults said they intended to get digital television within three years with greater choice of viewing and better quality sound and pictures the main attractions.[36]

The UK was the first country to launch digital terrestrial television but digital cable- and satellite-based services had launched in the US, France, Germany, and elsewhere from 1994 onwards.

---

[31] In fact the set-top box was rented and had to be returned if the subscriber cancelled their subscription.

[32] The deal was partly driven by fears that OFTEL, the telecoms regulator, would open up cable networks to competition.

[33] *1st Quarter Results 2000*, Telewest, London, 18 May 2000, p.2.

[34] As with Telewest the set-top box was rented and had to be returned if the subscription was cancelled.

[35] *Digital Satellite and Cable Monitor No. 135*, Continental Research, June 2000.

[36] 'Digital TV Hitting Home', *Pace Micro Technology web site*, 30 November 2000, <URL: http://www.pace.co.uk/news room/index.asp>, Accessed 10 June 2004

By 2000 a number of governments had set firm dates for analogue switch-off. National regulatory regimes as well as language and cultural differences had conspired against the creation of global or even regional television companies but the development of digital technology and the resulting convergence of television, telecommunications and the internet were creating new opportunities.

Murdoch was keen to establish satellite operations in Europe and the US but, with much of the world's television industry still highly regulated, genuine opportunities were hard to find. At the end of 1999 he decided to take a minority share in Premiere World, a fledgling German digital satellite pay-TV service, via a 24% stake in KirchPayTV Gmbh, with a view to securing a position in Europe's largest television market. The £962 million investment was made through BSkyB, funded by cash and shares.[37] NTL's Knapp also had ambitions beyond the UK, spending over $5 billion on his corporate credit card to acquire or take stakes in a number of cable companies across Europe.

Football matters

In the latter half of 1999 and early part of 2000 the stock markets were rising fast, largely driven by increasing internet frenzy. BSkyB's Ball invested in a number of dotcom ventures including spending £287 million to acquire Sports Internet Group, a sports web site and online betting service. The satellite broadcaster also continued to buy sports rights, adding more cricket and rugby union to its roster. However the biggest prize was top flight football. BSkyB had maximised its return from the Premiership over the previous eight years but the television rights were up for negotiation once more and this time Sky's competitors had a better understanding of their potential value. In May 2000 the League invited sealed bids for four broadcast packages each lasting three years. Rumours of a massive bid from NTL led to a 40% drop in BSkyB's share price, wiping £13.8 billion off its market value in less than three weeks.[38] On 9 June Richard Scudamore,

Managing Director of the Premier League, announced there would be a second round with only three packages on offer. Any one bidder could win only one package and winning bids had to be 10% higher than the next offer or a new round would be held. The deadline for bids was 2pm on Wednesday 14 June.

The three Premier League broadcast packages were:

◆ The Main Deal: the most valuable package, comprising 66 live games each season.

◆ The Pay-Per-View Deal: consisting of 40 PPV games per season in which all 20 teams had to be featured at least once.

◆ The Terrestrial Deal: open only to free-to-air terrestrial broadcasters: the BBC; ITV companies; Channel 4; and Channel 5; this only included recorded highlights.

BSkyB's bid team was led by Tony Ball supported by the company's in-house strategic planning team. The only package they were really interested in was the Main Deal. Stories that Bill Gates was bankrolling NTL and Barclay Knapp would bid £1.7 billion were all over the press and BSkyB's share price bounced up and down as the markets considered the implications. Ball and his team agonised over how much to offer. Finally they decided NTL wouldn't bid more than £1 billion for the live rights. Ball added 10% and another £10 million for good measure. BSkyB's bid was £1.11 billion.[39] If NTL bid less than £1.01 billion BSkyB would win. If NTL bid more than £1.01 billion but less than £1.22 billion BSkyB would have another chance. But if Knapp bid more than £1.22 billion NTL would walk away with the prize and BSkyB would lose its 'battering ram'.[40]

If Ball was at all uncertain, analysts seemed to have a clear sense of how much he should bid. Mathew Horsman, Research Director at Investec, told the BBC, 'If they [BSkyB] pay less than £1.2 billon and win it, we will be buying the shares. If they pay substantially more, we will be back sharpening

---

[37] Murdoch also invested in several other pay-TV companies around the world via News Corporation.

[38] BSkyB's share price had peaked at £22.64 on 7 March 2000, valuing the company at more than £43 billion.

[39] *Virtual Murdoch: Reality Wars on the Information Superhighway*, N Chenoweth, Vintage, London, 2000, p.335.

[40] Murdoch's famous description of how sports could be used to drive pay-TV subscriptions.

our pencils, but if they lose them altogether we will watch the shares dive.'[41]

An hour after the deadline on 14 June, Scudamore telephoned BSkyB to tell them they had won the live broadcast package outright. NTL won the PPV deal for £328 million and ITV outbid the BBC for the recorded highlights with a bid of £183 million. In total the auction generated over £1.6 billion. The general view of most analysts was BSkyB had won the live rights with a high but justifiable bid but NTL had overbid for the PPV package.[42]

Prebble was determined to find a 'killer-app' to drive ONdigital subscriptions. An opportunity came in the form of the Football League, consisting of the 72 clubs below the Premier League, whose broadcast rights were up for sale at the same time. Although the Premiership grabbed the headlines, more fans attended Football League matches every week. ONdigital quickly won exclusive rights with a bid of £315 million for a three year deal starting in 2001/02. The deal gave ONdigital the right to show 88 live matches plus a number of PPV matches every season. The contract was signed by the Football League and ONdigital on 15 June. With exclusive live UEFA Champions League and Football League matches as well as Premiership football via Sky Sports, ONdigital could now legitimately claim it offered more comprehensive coverage of the national sport than any other broadcaster. Soon afterwards ONdigital also announced its interactive service – ONnet, offering internet access and email via TV for £5 a month, would launch in September.

Sky high

Regardless of the competition Sky Digital maintained its rapid, if costly, growth. In July 2000 Ball announced it had more than 3.6 million subscribers

and set a new target of seven million by the end of 2003. With digital churn a mere 3.5%, customer satisfaction was rising, as was ARPU, up to £287 per annum. Sky Digital's growth pushed revenues in 1999/2000 up to £1.85 billion but the set-top box subsidy continued to hit the bottom line with pre-tax losses exceeding £260 million. Investor reaction to the results was downbeat with analysts expressing concern about the costs of going digital, although the fading love affair with technology, media, and telecoms stocks was also a factor. In July BSkyB was forced to buy out HSBC and Matsushita from Open, its underperforming interactive shopping service, for £525 million in an all-share deal – that same month Murdoch told all his senior managers there was to be no more spending on internet businesses. By September Sky Digital had over 4.5 million subscribers, well on track to the year-end target of five million DTH subscribers, but BSkyB's share price had halved from its peak of six months earlier.

BSkyB's competitors faced their own problems. In August Carlton and Granada had announced plans to float ONdigital in the autumn with a capitalisation of between £1.5 and £2 billion, partly to raise funds to support the DTT broadcaster through to 2003 when it was expected to move into profit. However, the initial public offering (IPO) was postponed after several analysts downgraded their valuations to under £1 billion. As many predicted, NTL couldn't make the numbers add up for its PPV deal with the Premier League. Knapp had planned to offer free games to attract new subscribers and to bundle games with other programming but the Premier League objected. The row still wasn't resolved by the start of the 2000/01 football season and in October NTL pulled out of the deal.[43] At Telewest problems with the supply of set-top boxes, sourced exclusively from Pace, and service reliability forced it to relaunch Active Digital and reduce its targets for digital subscribers.

In November BSkyB raised its retail prices for Sky Digital – the second set of increases since launch – triggering rises of up £4 a month in Sky's

[41] 'TV giants gamble on sport', *BBC News web site*, 14 June 2000, <URL: http://news.bbc.co.uk/1/hi/business/791321.stm>, Accessed 10 June 2004.

[42] The logic for believing NTL had overbid was as follows. Each game would cost NTL £2.7 million. If NTL charged £5 per match, after factoring in costs of say £1, it needed to attract over 680,000 viewers per game – more than the UK record for a PPV event. Since many matches would be between less popular teams and NTL had only 1.26 million cable TV subscribers such a target seemed unattainable.

[43] Eventually the Premier League made the PPV rights available on a non-exclusive basis. This raised £181 million.

wholesale prices. Prebble complained BSkyB was behaving as a monopoly leading the OFT to announce it was reopening its investigation into Sky's wholesale pricing. ONdigital's priority however was to hit its target of one million subscribers by the end of the year. With Granada and Carlton planning an IPO for the DTT broadcaster and profits unlikely in the near future the subscriber target was critical. As the year-end approached there were reports of subscribers threatening to cancel being offered packages worth £37 a month for as little as £1 a month. Whatever the tactics ONdigital hit its target. By the end of the year the Digital TV Group estimated the number of digital television homes had risen to nearly 7 million, including satellite, DTT and cable services.[44] A fourth platform was also opening up. After regulations preventing the delivery of broadcast television via telephone lines were lifted, BT confirmed it was considering launching a digital television service in 2001 using high-speed ADSL (Asymmetric Digital Subscriber Line) technology.

Decreasing investor patience

After the longest bull market in history the Dow Jones, NASDAQ Composite, and FTSE-100 had all fallen in 2000. By 2001 slowing economic growth in the US and Europe was having a significant impact on global equity markets. Business confidence and capital investment were declining for the first time in nearly a decade. For businesses still in the investment phase and with little experience of managing in a bear market the situation was problematic to say the least.

By spring 2001 the stock market bubble had burst and Telewest and NTL faced mounting pressure from shareholders. NTL's shares had fallen to less than a quarter of their peak value of $110. Despite losses of more than $3 billion in 2000 and debts in excess of $15 billion Knapp was as confident as ever,

predicting NTL would achieve breakeven by 2004 and cable would soon overtake BSkyB to become the dominant DTV platform in the UK. Not everyone agreed – with interest payments of more than $1 billion a year some questioned how NTL could survive. At the end of March, although churn was still 25%, Telewest's digital television service had reached 500,000 subscribers. But by now its share price had fallen from a high of 569 pence to around 115 pence. In spite of this Singer was able to restructure £2.25 billion of Telewest/Flextech's debt and free up £300 million for expansion.

The deteriorating economy and dotcom crash also had a negative impact on the advertising market. As advertising was their sole source of revenue this was especially hard on Granada and Carlton whose shares fell throughout the latter half of 2000 and early 2001. At ONdigital Prebble told journalists the company's target of achieving two million subscribers and breakeven by 2002 'is not a hope, it is entirely realisable' but net subscriber growth in the first quarter of 2001 was rumoured to be less than 40,000.[45] This was partly due to high churn caused by pre-paid customers returning set-top boxes at the end of the 12-month subscription. Sales of ONdigital-enabled idTVs had also been very disappointing. Granada and Carlton decided a new approach was needed for their main businesses and ONdigital. In April Charles Allen, Granada's Chairman, and Carlton's Green announced plans to reorganise their assets under the ITV banner and to rebrand ONdigital as ITV Digital. Prebble was appointed CEO with responsibility for ITV's terrestrial network, ITV Digital, and ITV.com. ITC rules had restricted the level of promotion ITV could offer ONdigital but the new structure would allow it to promote ITV Digital more heavily. At a press conference to publicise the new structure Prebble announced new goals for the DTT broadcaster. ITV Digital's targets for the end of 2002 included:

- Reaching 1.6 million subscribers.

- Increasing ARPU from £225 to £300 (including VAT).

[44] 'Another digital milestone!' *Digital TV Group web site*, 20 December 2000, <URL: http://www.dtg.org.uk/news/archive/sum_0012.htm>, Accessed 17 June 2004. As well as nearly five million Sky Digital and one million ONdigital subscribers, this included 500,000 NTL and 300,000 Telewest digital cable subscribers. In addition it was estimated 100,000 digital television sets, allowing access to free-to-air channels, had been sold.

[45] 'Ondigital fights for growth', *BBC News web site*, 17 January 2001, <URL: http://news.bbc.co.uk/1/hi/business/1121929.stm> Accessed 18 June 2004.

- Reducing churn from 25% to 18%.

- Cutting acquisition costs from £200 to £120 per subscriber.

- Achieving a gross margin of 44% on programming.[46]

Prebble planned to use sport to grow ITV Digital the same way Sam Chisholm had done at Sky in the early 1990s. As part of this strategy the different ITV units were to pool their sports rights to create a new subscription-based channel, ITV Sport, which would launch on ITV Digital the following August. For £6.99 subscribers would be able to watch live UEFA Champions League and Football League matches as well as various other sports. A new marketing campaign would promote ITV Digital and the new ITV Sport channel. Prebble planned to boost ARPU through a mixture of price rises and increasing the Pay-to-Basic Ratio by selling more premium channels such as ITV Sport.[47] Falling set-top box prices would cut acquisition costs and programming costs would be reduced by renegotiating contracts with suppliers – a clear reference to BSkyB. If all the targets were achieved ITV Digital would breakeven by 2003/04. Reaction to the strategy was mixed with some analysts seeing it as long overdue and others seeing it as the last throw of the dice.

Since advertising represented a small proportion of its revenues BSkyB was less vulnerable to falling advertising spend than Carlton and Granada. The free set-top box offer continued to drive growth and by June 2001 Sky Digital had more than 5.5 million digital subscribers, allowing Ball to bring forward the analogue switch-off to September. More digital than analogue subscribers took the top tier package,

helping to push ARPU up to £313 per annum (including £11 in interactive ARPU). BSkyB continued to innovate by launching Sky+, a Sky-branded Personal Video Recorder (PVR) enabling programmes to be recorded onto a hard drive. It wasn't all good news. Losses had doubled over the previous year to £515 million and net debt had risen to £1.55 billion. BSkyB had been forced to buy out BT from Open and many of the company's investments had gone sour. Despite owning the rights to Bundesliga football (the German Premier League) and other high profile sports, Premiere World had struggled in the traditionally free-to-air German television market. By 2001 KirchPayTV was staggering under the weight of debt taken on to buy broadcast rights at what turned out to be the top of the market. Ball's new media investments fared no better. BSkyB had invested over £800 million in interactive services but the only interactive bet that paid off (and even this was debatable) was TV betting which generated £78 million in 2000/01 out of total interactive revenues of £93 million, the rest coming from Open. In July the EU Commission announced it would investigate an agreement between BSkyB and Disney which prevented the latter from offering its channels to ITV Digital. In spite of the challenges Ball and Stewart forged ahead, promising to increase ARPU to £400 per annum by 2005 and to deliver positive cash flow by the end of the year and profits by 2002–2004.

Cash is king

By the end of 2001 falling stock markets and declining ad spend meant cash was king. Telewest continued to grow its digital television service, up to 644,000 subscribers by October, but debt was now £4.7 billion. In November, with its share price down to 25 pence and under pressure from bondholders, Singer announced plans to convert Telewest's debts into equity. At NTL, in spite of reaching 1.25 million digital subscribers, Knapp announced the company would have to shed 8,000 staff and increase prices to meet its cash flow targets. He also put many of NTL's assets up for sale, although most were worth a fraction of their purchase price – leading to write-downs of $11.5 billion. With TV advertising revenues down an estimated 25% year-on-year in the last quarter, cash flow was also becoming a problem for

---

[46] *ITV Digital – Between a Rock and a Hard Place?*, Claire Enders, Enders Analysis, Dundee, July 2001, p.2.

[47] The high PBR that had been agreed with BSkyB back in 1997 as part of the deal for Sky programming meant that, in the words of a senior manager at one of ITV Digital's shareholders, "When we sell one pay channel to a subscriber, we lose money. When we sell two, we break even. When we sell three, we make between 0 and 5%. When we sell four, we make between 5 and 10%". Quote from *The Gross Margin from Retailing Premium Pay-TV Channels*, Chris Goodall, Enders Analysis, Dundee, July 2001, p.5.

Granada and Carlton. They had pumped £800 million into ITV Digital and analysts were now openly calling for them to pull the plug. While admitting to considering their options they continued to support their DTT offspring. In part this was because of signs of improvement at ITV Digital but it was also in the belief the Government would soon set a firm date for analogue shutdown. However in November they succumbed to pressure from advertisers and signed a deal with BSkyB for carriage of ITV1 (previously ITV) and ITV2 on Sky Digital.[48] Despite losing one of ITV Digital's key selling points versus Sky, with subscriptions up to 1.2 million Prebble was still upbeat. But the underlying situation was worsening. ITV Sport was not attracting significant numbers of subscribers to ITV Digital, forcing the DTT broadcaster to seek additional distribution for the new channel. A carriage fee was agreed with NTL but Telewest and BSkyB refused to take ITV Sport on the terms offered.[49] The Football League deal bombed. Some matches had such poor viewing figures Prebble was compelled to try to renegotiate the cost but the League refused. As the year ended BSkyB's competitors were at last able to claim a victory. In December the OFT announced it proposed to find the satellite broadcaster guilty of infringing UK competition law by unfairly squeezing the margins of its premium channel distributors and using its wholesale pricing policies to prevent rival premium channel providers from entering the market.[50] Possible sanctions included a fine of 10% of turnover for up to three years. Unusually BSkyB's shares rose on the news, reflecting the markets' confidence it would beat the rap.

At the end of the year the fierce competition between the different service providers had driven penetration of digital television up to 37% of all TV households.[51] However a poll in November found switching to digital was still not on the radar for 30% of the population.[52]

Winners and losers

ITV and the cable companies

Poor sales in the last quarter of 2001 and early 2002 and continuing losses of £1 million a day led Granada and Carlton to announce ITV Digital needed a 'fundamental restructuring ... as a matter of urgency'.[53] In February they called in Deloitte & Touche. The accountants laid off 500 staff and attempted to cut ITV Digital's costs although not everyone was sympathetic. One source quoted Adam Singer, Telewest's CEO, as saying 'If ITV Digital come to us and say we have to lower our prices or they die, then as a competing platform owner the death bit sounds good to me. Bring it on.'[54] Attention focused on the deal with the Football League. Deloitte & Touche tried to persuade the League to accept less than the £178.5 million it was still owed but the League rejected all offers, believing it could force Carlton and Granada to honour the original agreement. After failing to restructure the business or find a buyer Deloitte & Touche finally shut ITV Digital down on 1 May 2002 with the loss of 1,300 jobs and debts of £1.25 billion. The pioneering digital

---

[48] As well as increasing their audience reach the agreement increased the rebate Granada and Carlton received from the Government against the levy they paid for their analogue licences. Analysts estimated adding BSkyB's subscribers to ITV's digital audience would generate an annual windfall of £50 million for the network owners. ITV also received undisclosed carriage fees from BSkyB for ITV2, which became part of Sky's pay-TV packages. Against this the network had to pay BSkyB's conditional access charges of £17 million.

[49] NTL was rumoured to have agreed to pay a guaranteed carriage fee of around £40 million per annum. The offers rejected by BSkyB and Telewest were reputed to be £80 million and £20 million per annum respectively. There were also discussions with BSkyB based on the idea of marketing ITV Sport directly to satellite TV viewers using Sky's conditional access system but ITV didn't pursue the idea.

[50] *OFT proposes to find BSkyB in breach of law PN 51/01,* OFT, London, 17 December 2001.

[51] *2001 Report: Commercial Television in the UK: an overview,* ITC, London, April 2002.

[52] 'Digital Switch Fails to Spark Public Imagination', *Pace Micro Technology web site,* 16 November 2001, op. cit.

[53] 'ITV Digital in crisis, owners say', *BBC News web site,* 27 February 2002, <URL: http://news.bbc.co.uk/1/hi/business/1843673.stm>, Accessed 17 June 2004.

[54] 'ITV Digital's flickering future', Nick Higham, *BBC News web site,* 5 March 2002, <URL: http://news.bbc.co.uk/1/hi/entertainment/tv_and_radio/1853678.stm>, Accessed 15 June 2004.

terrestrial pay-TV service had been unable to compete with BSkyB. In total Carlton and Granada had pumped £1.2 billion into the venture.

In the glory days the cable companies had pushed their 'convergence' model but by 2002 they were just trying to stay alive. In the last months of 2001 NTL sold assets to cut debt and made thousands of staff redundant to cut costs. It even shut down its marketing department as it couldn't afford to take on new customers. It was all too late and the shares continued to fall until being suspended at the end of March 2002, trading at 20 cents. NTL finally sought the refuge of Chapter 11 bankruptcy protection in May, emerging the following January after bond-holders forgave $10.9 billion of debt in return for control of the company. Telewest fared little better. In February 2002 it announced it had lost £1.9 billion in 2001 – mostly a write-down against Flextech. Having lost the confidence of his fellow directors, Singer resigned in July to be replaced by Charles Burdick, the Finance Director. Telewest narrowly avoided administration with a financial restructuring which gave bondholders 98.5% of the company. The cable companies had stopped building out their networks in 2000. By the end of 2002 they faced scaling back their ambitions even further and the number of cable television subscribers was in decline.

The BBC

Although the Government rejected a BBC plea for a digital levy in 2000, above-inflation rises in the licence fee and internal cost cutting enabled it to expand its digital television services to eight channels by 2002. When bids were invited for the defunct ITV Digital's DTT multiplexes the BBC approached BSkyB and Crown Castle (formerly Crown Transmission Services) with the idea of launching a low cost free-to-air service. After winning the licence, subject to the condition BSkyB wasn't involved in running the new service, the BBC-led consortium moved quickly. Freeview launched in October 2002 with 30 channels, including free-to-air channels from the BBC, ITV, Channel 4, Five (previously Channel 5), and BSkyB. Consumers wishing to access the new service only required a set-top box costing £99 or an integrated digital television, no subscription was needed. Ex-ITV Digital subscribers could also access it via their set-top boxes. Freeview got off to a flying start and by the end of 2002 over 330,000 people had bought set-top boxes for the new service. The BBC had taken control of a key digital distribution channel and made a significant and politically astute contribution towards the Government's goal of switching off analogue television by 2010.

BSkyB

In the year to June 2002 BSkyB made an operating profit of £115 million on turnover of £2.76 billion. The former became a loss of £1.28 billion after goodwill and exceptional charges (principally a write-down of the investment in KirchPayTV) but Ball and Stewart delivered on their promise of generating positive cash flow (albeit only £18 million). They also continued to improve the Sky Digital offering, increasing the number of channels to 380. The demise of ITV Digital helped Sky grow to 6.6 million DTH subscribers by the end of 2002. With net growth of over 200,000 per quarter and ARPU of £350 per annum the company was well on track to its targets of 7 million subscribers and ARPU of £400 with the prospect of significant free cash flow. Throughout 2002 the OFT's provisional decision to find BSkyB in breach of the 1998 Competition Act had hung over the company but in December, following further submissions by the satellite broadcaster, the regulator announced there was insufficient evidence it had abused its position.[55] With the threat of action by the UK competition authorities removed BSkyB was able to face the future with confidence. Despite the enormous risks and challenges it had managed the transition to digital and reinforced its position as the dominant UK pay-TV platform. Furthermore, through its partnership with the BBC and Crown Castle, it had secured distribution for several of its channels on the new free-to-air DTT service.

At the end of 2002 BSkyB's position seemed unassailable, although the emergence of Freeview and increasing interest of EU regulators presented potential future threats. How would BSkyB deal

---

[55] *Decision of the Director General of Fair Trading No CA98/20/2002*, OFT, London, 17 December 2002.

with these and other challenges? Could it ever again produce the 30% margins it achieved in 1997? With over 40% of the UK population already signed up for digital television and another 30% seemingly uninterested, where would long-term growth come from?

Exhibit 1 Glossary

ADSL (Asymmetric Digital Subscriber Line)	Digital technology allowing high speed data transfer over copper wire.
Analogue	Traditional method of transmitting information in continuous wave form.
ARPU (Average Revenue Per User)	The average revenue generated by a user in a specific period, usually per month or per annum.
Buy-through	The practice of forcing pay-TV subscribers to buy through basic channel packages before they are allowed to subscribe to premium channels.
Churn	The ratio of subscribers cancelling their subscriptions to total subscribers within a specific period, usually per annum.
Conditional access system	A system for encrypting content to control access. Users require a decoder in the form of a set-top box or integrated digital television.
Digital	Digital technology converts information into binary digits which can be compressed, allowing more efficient transmission with less data loss.
DTV (Digital television)	Television signals are converted into digital format, transmitted and decoded back into sound and pictures.
DTT (Digital Terrestrial Television)	Digital television received via an aerial.
DTH (Direct-to-Home)	Satellite signals received via a dish receiver. Also known as satellite TV.
EPG (Electronic Programming Guide)	An application enabling users to search and select channels and services via an on-screen display, usually controlled by a dedicated remote control.
FTA (Free-to-air or free-to-access)	Free channels or services.
idTV (integrated digital television)	A television with an integrated digital decoder.
MCRs (Minimum Carriage Requirements)	Agreements requiring channels to be carried to a pre-set percentage, usually 80%, of a platform's subscribers. Banned, with some exceptions, by the UK's commercial television regulator in 1998.
Mux (Multiplex)	A stream of digital data able to carry several channels or services.
Passed homes	The number of homes covered by a cable network.
Pay-TV	Encrypted television services only accessible by paying subscribers.
PBR (Pay-to-Basic Ratio)	Ratio of premium channel subscribers (weighted for the number of premium channels to which they subscribe) to total subscribers.
PPV (Pay-Per-View)	Service allowing specific programmes such as movies or sports events to be ordered in return for a one-off payment.
PVR (Personal Video Recorder)	An enhanced set-top box which enables television programmes to be recorded onto an internal hard-drive.
Subscriber acquisition cost	The average cost of acquiring a new customer or subscriber.
STB (Set-top box)	Device enabling television signals to be decoded and accessed.
Tiering	The practice of creating separate basic and premium pay-TV channel packages (see buy-through).
VOD (Video On Demand)	Service allowing customers to order and see a specific programme at a time of their choosing.

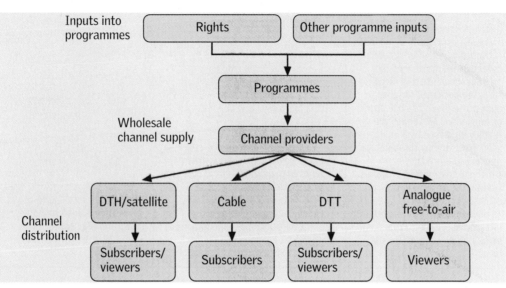

Exhibit 2 The TV supply chain
Source: *Decision of the Director General of Fair Trading No CA98/20/2002*, OFT, London, 17 December 2002, p.6.

Exhibit 3 The history of multichannel TV in the UK

1989	Sky Television launches UK satellite TV with a four channel service.
1990	British Satellite Broadcasting (BSB) launches. Sky and BSB merge to form British Sky Broadcasting (BSkyB).
1992	BSkyB buys exclusive rights to live FA Premier League football coverage.
1993	Sky launches multichannel pay TV package.
1997	Independent Television Commission licenses digital terrestrial TV multiplexes to Digital 3&4 and British Digital Broadcasting. The BBC is also allocated one multiplex.
1998	BSkyB launches UK's first digital TV service and attracts 100,000 customers in its first month. Digital terrestrial TV broadcasts start. British Digital Broadcasting launches its pay TV service under the ONdigital brand name.
1999	Sky and ONdigital begin to offer free set-top boxes. NTL and Telewest launch digital cable TV services. Sky introduces interactive services. Secretary of State announces ambition to complete digital switchover and defines switchover targets.
2000	NTL acquires the consumer operations of Cable and Wireless Communications (CWC) to become largest cable operator. Telewest merges with Flextech.
2001	BSkyB reaches five million digital subscribers and switches off its analogue service. ONdigital relaunched as ITV Digital. NTL and Telewest launch broadband Internet services. Government launches Digital TV Action Plan.
2002	ITV Digital closes down. Freeview launched. New BBC digital TV and radio services begin broadcasting. NTL applies for Chapter 11 protection in the US; it later secures recapitalisation. Half of all UK viewers have multichannel TV.

Source: *Driving digital switchover: a report to the Secretary of State*, OFCOM, London, April 2004, p.29.

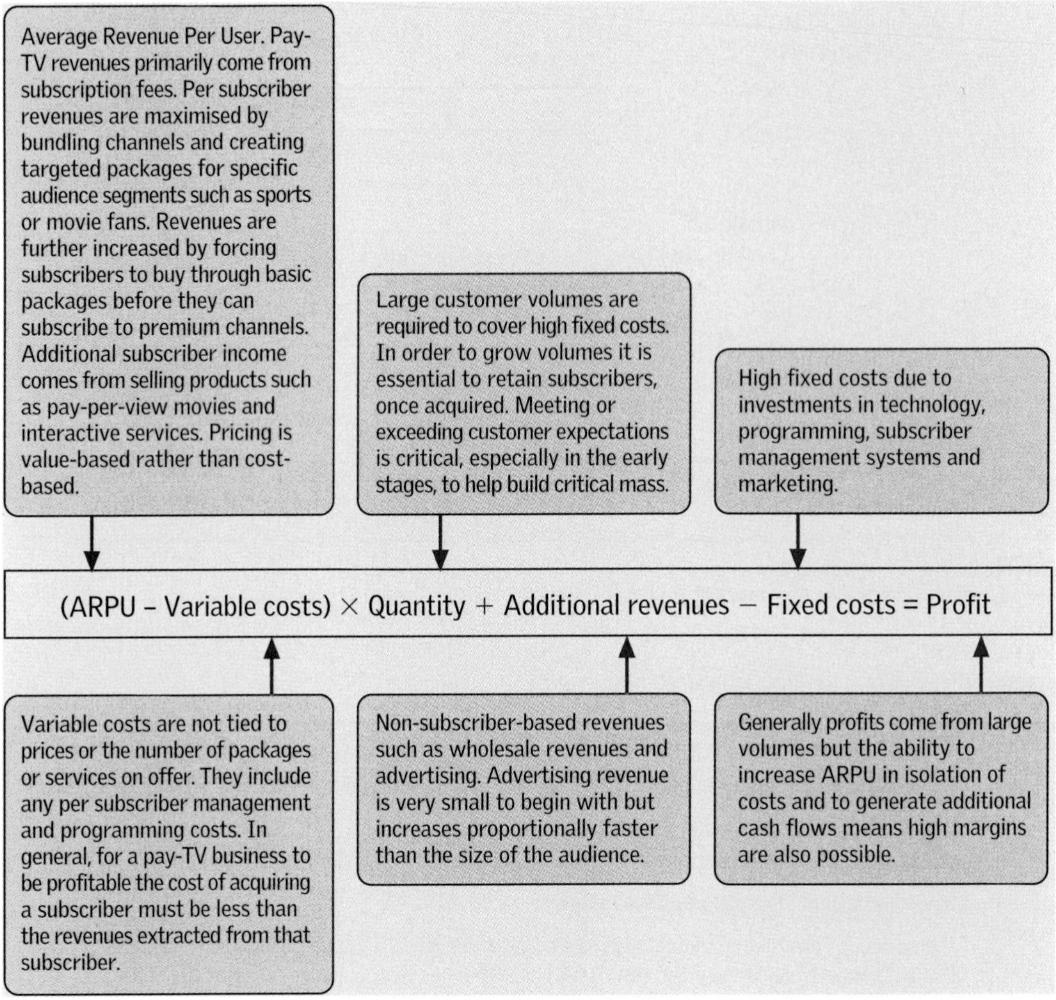

Average Revenue Per User. Pay-TV revenues primarily come from subscription fees. Per subscriber revenues are maximised by bundling channels and creating targeted packages for specific audience segments such as sports or movie fans. Revenues are further increased by forcing subscribers to buy through basic packages before they can subscribe to premium channels. Additional subscriber income comes from selling products such as pay-per-view movies and interactive services. Pricing is value-based rather than cost-based.

Large customer volumes are required to cover high fixed costs. In order to grow volumes it is essential to retain subscribers, once acquired. Meeting or exceeding customer expectations is critical, especially in the early stages, to help build critical mass.

High fixed costs due to investments in technology, programming, subscriber management systems and marketing.

$$(\text{ARPU} - \text{Variable costs}) \times \text{Quantity} + \text{Additional revenues} - \text{Fixed costs} = \text{Profit}$$

Variable costs are not tied to prices or the number of packages or services on offer. They include any per subscriber management and programming costs. In general, for a pay-TV business to be profitable the cost of acquiring a subscriber must be less than the revenues extracted from that subscriber.

Non-subscriber-based revenues such as wholesale revenues and advertising. Advertising revenue is very small to begin with but increases proportionally faster than the size of the audience.

Generally profits come from large volumes but the ability to increase ARPU in isolation of costs and to generate additional cash flows means high margins are also possible.

Exhibit 4 Pay-TV business model

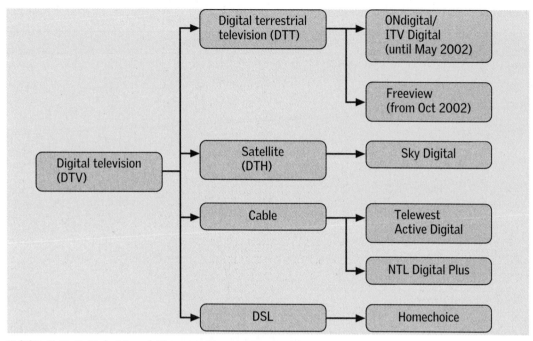

Exhibit 5 Digital television platforms and key service providers

Source: Adapted from *Digital television for all: A report on usability and accessible design*, DTI, London, September 2003, p.9. Freeview can be accessed by anyone with an idTV or digital set-top box and doesn't require a subscription. Other companies providing free-to-air digital channels accessible via an idTV or digital set-top box include the BBC, Digital 3&4 Ltd, and SDN Ltd. Other digital cable service providers include Kingston Interactive Television and Isle of Wight Cable. By the end of 2002 DSL-based digital television services delivered via a telephone connection, such as Homechoice, had a user base of a few thousand homes.

Exhibit 6 Digital terrestrial multiplexes

Multiplex	Operator	Free to air	Subscription	Coverage
1	BBC	BBC1 BBC2 BBC Choice BBC News 24 BBC Knowledge BBC Text BBC Parliament (audio only)		91%
2	Digital 3 & 4	ITV ITV2 Channel 4 Teletext digital	Film Four*	91%
A	SDN	Channel 5 S4C		90%
B	Ondigital		Carlton Cinema Cartoon Network Sky One British Eurosport Sky Sports 1* and 3 Sky Premier*	88%
C	Ondigital		Granada Plus Shop!** UK Gold MTV ON Sport** Sky MovieMax*	77%
D	Ondigital		UK Style UK Horizons (BBC) UK Play _____ Discovery Kids AM Carlton Food Network Granada Breeze _____ Discovery Wings PM Adult Channel Granada Men & Motors	69%

* Premium channel ** Free bonus channels
Note that this listing is subject to change quite dynamically.
Source: *Development of Digital TV in Europe: 2000 report: United Kingdom*, iDate, Montpellier, Decemeber 2000, p.9–10.

Exhibit 7 Sky Digital channel line-up

Sky One	Sky Sports Extra	Discovery Animal Planet	VH1
UK Gold	MUTV	Cartoon Network	VH1 Classic
UK Gold 2	Skysports.comTV	Nickelodeon	The Box
Living	British Eurosport	CNBC	UK Play
Granada Plus	Sky Premier	Discovery	44 Music Choice channels
Challenge TV	Sky Premier 2	Discovery Travel & Adv.	QVC
Bravo	Sky Premier 3	Discovery Civilisation	BBC1
Paramount Comedy Channel	Sky Premier 4	Discovery Sci-Trek	BBC2
Sci-Fi	Sky Premier Widescreen	Adventure One	Channel 4
Discovery Home & Leisure	Sky MovieMax	The History Channel	Channel 5
Granada Breeze	Sky MovieMax 2	UK Horizons	BBC Choice
Granada Men & Motors	Sky MovieMax 3	[.tv]	S4C
Sky Travel	Sky MovieMax 4	Nick Jr.	BBC News 24
UK Style	Sky MovieMax 5	Trouble	BBC Parliament
UK Drama	Sky Cinema	Fox Kids	CNN International
TARA Television	Sky Cinema 2	Disney Channel	BBC Knowledge
Hallmark Entertainment	FilmFour	MTV	Money Channel
Sky Sports 1	Sky Box Office	MTV Extra	22 digital radio channels
Sky Sports 2	Sky News	MTV Base	
Sky Sports 3	Bloomberg	MTV2	

Source: *2000 Annual Report*, BSkyB, Isleworth, June 2000, p.38–39.

Exhibit 8 ONdigital channel line-up

BBC1	Carlton Cinema	Granada Men & Motors	Sky Sports 1
BBC2	Carlton Food Network	Granada Plus	Sky Sports 2
ITV	Carlton Kids	ITV2	Sky Sports 3
Channel 4	Carlton Select	MTV	UK Gold
Channel 5	Carlton World	Nickelodeon	UK Horizons
BBC Choice	Cartoon Network	S4C	UK Play
BBC Knowledge	Eurosport	Sky MovieMax	
BBC News 24	FilmFour	Sky One	
BBC Parliament	Granada Breeze	Sky Premier	

Source: *D2K: Just Zeros and Ones? A Report into Viewing Behaviour in Digital Homes*, Television Research Partnership, Taunton, December 1999, p.12.

Exhibit 9 Telewest Active Digital channel line-up

Sky One	Challenge TV	Channel One Liverpool	Zee TV
UK Gold	Granada Men & Motors	Turner Classic Movies	B4U
Granada Plus	UK Style	FilmFour	QVC
Paramount Comedy	Travel Channel	Front Row Guide	Shop!
Sci-Fi Channel	Discovery Home & Leis.	Television X	TV Travel Shop
Bravo	Discovery Travel & Adv.	Playboy	Travel Deals Direct
Scene One	Granada Breeze	Sky Sports 1	Screenshop
E4	Carlton Food Network	Sky Sports 2	BBC1
UK Drama	MTV	British Eurosport	BBC2
Play UK	MTV2	Racing Channel	BBC News 24
Tara	MTV Base	Sky News	BBC Choice
Carlton Cinema	MTV Extra	CNN	BBC Parliament
Discovery	VH1	Bloomberg	BBC Knowledge
Discovery Animal Planet	VH1 Classic	Cartoon Network	ITV
Discovery Civilisations	Performance Channel	Nickelodeon	ITV2
Sci-Trek	Sky Premier	Nick Jr.	ITN News 24
UK Horizons	Sky MovieMax	Disney Channel	regional ITV
National Geographic	Sky Cinema	Trouble	Channel 4
The History Channel	CNBC	Asianet	Channel 5
Living	The Money Channel	Sony Entertainment TV	S2

Source: Zap (Telewest Digital magazine), January 2001

Exhibit 10 NTL Digital Plus channel line-up

BBC1	Sky News	UK Play	Sky Sports 2
BBC	The Box	BET Jazz International	Sky Sports 3
ITV	UK Drama	MTV	Sky Premier
Channel 4	Tara TV	VH1	Sky Moviemax
Channel 5	Challenge TV	Cartoon Network	Sky Cinema
BBC News 24	Carlton Cinema	Rapture	Disney Channel
BBC Choice	Granada Plus	Trouble	Playboy TV
BBC Knowledge	Carlton Food Network	Nickelodeon	Adult Channel
BBC Parliament	UK Gold	Discovery	Television X
CBBC Digital	Performance Channel	UK Horizons	The Fantasy Channel
BBC Cbeebies	Discovery Home & Leis.	Discovery Civilisation	FilmFour
TV Travelshop	Granada Breeze	Discovery Travel & Adv.	Racing Channel
Bloomberg	UK Style	Discovery Sci-Trek	Sony Entertainment TV
MTV2	Sci-Fi	Discovery Animal Planet	Christian Channel
British Eurosport	TCM	History Channel	Zee TV
QVC	Granada Men & Motors	CNN	Front Row PPV movies
ITN News	Bravo	National Geographic	PPV Events
E4	Living	Travel Channel	8 Music Choice channels
Sky One	Paramount Comedy Ch.	Sky Sports 1	

Source: Adapted from NTL Home Digital Pricing NI, *Irish Cable & Digital Guide web site*, c. 2002, <URL: http://myhome.iolfree.ie/~icdg/tuning_ntl_nidigital.htm>, Accessed 22 August 2004. Excludes channels only available in Northern Ireland.

Exhibit 11 Cost of digital television

All figs £	Connection Fee	Basic Package	Basic with Movies	Basic with Sport	Basic with Both	Full Range
NTL	40	120	324	360	396	468
ONdigital	Free	84	264	264	324	396
Sky Digital	40	84	324	324	384	384
Telewest	20	108	288	288	348	504

Source: 'Annual Cost of Digital Television', *Which?* magazine, December 2000.

Exhibit 12 Sky Digital retail prices

All figs £	1998	1999	2000	2001	2002
Entry level package	7	7	7	10	10
Entry level plus Movies	25	27	27	28	30
Entry level plus Sports	25	27	27	30	30
All channels	30	32	32	34	37

Source: Enders Analysis. All prices per month.

Exhibit 13 Estimated BSkyB wholesale pricing

All figs £	Wholesale price from BSkyB	Approximate market retail price (ex-VAT)
1 Premium channel	10.50–11.00	10.00–13.00
2 Premium channels	13.50–14.10	13.50–17.00
3 Premium channels	15.20–15.90	16.50–17.50
4 Premium channels	16.45–17.25	18.00–20.00

Source: *The Gross Margin from Retailing Premium Pay-TV Channels*, Chris Goodall, Enders Analysis, Dundee, July 2001, p.5. All prices per subscriber per month. UK VAT is 17.5%.

Exhibit 14 UK digital TV households

All figs 000s	1998	1999	2000	2001	2002
Sky Digital	225	2,075	4,669	5,716	6,562
ONdigital/ITV Digital	c.100	552	1,012	1,263	–
NTL/CWC	–	c.100	531	1,253	1,229
Telewest	–	23	339	724	857
Free-to-air/Freeview	–	–	c.100	c.275	c.1,550
Total	c.325	c.2,750	c.6,651	c.9,231	c.10,198

Sources: Company reports, ITC. All figures to end December. Free-to-air/Freeview figure for 2002 includes integrated digital televisions, legacy ITV Digital set-top boxes and 25% of Sky Digital's former subscribers as well as Freeview set-top boxes.

Exhibit 15   Integrated digital TV sales forecasts

All figs 000s	1999	2000	2001	2002	2003	2004	2005
ABN Amro	21	114	185	338	613	1,060	1,710
BREMA	27	93	195	375	375	1,500	3,000

Source: *Future Reflections: Data and Context*, ITC, London, November 2001, p.4. According to the report 'BREMA's forecast of 195,000 idTV sales in 2001 is already looking doubtful; in reality, sales could be as low as 130,000 this year and 200,000 in 2002'.

Exhibit 16   UK: TV market overview

		1997	1998	1999	2000	2001	2002
UK population	000s	59,090	59,357	59,623	59,863	60,120	60,148
UK households	000s	25,089	25,429	25,597	25,820	26,048	26,197
TV households	000s	24,239	24,489	24,639	24,972	25,267	25,411
Cable penetration	%	9.79	11.54	13.17	14.26	14.32	13.21
DTH penetration (pay)	%	14.78	14.12	16.1	20.23	22.62	25.82
DTH penetration (free)	%	2.98	4.54	3.51	0.99	3.46	2.2
DTH penetration (total)	%	17.76	18.66	19.61	21.21	26.08	28.02
DTT penetration (pay)	%	–	0.11	2.24	4.05	5	–
DTT penetration (free)	%	–	–	–	–	–	5.23
DTT penetration (total)	%	–	0.11	2.24	4.05	5	5.23
Analogue terrestrial penetration	%	–	–	–	–	–	–
Analogue pay TV penetration	%	24.57	24.74	20.54	12.31	6.49	4.97
Digital pay TV penetration	%	–	1.03	10.97	26.23	35.45	34.06
Pay TV penetration	%	24.57	25.77	31.51	38.54	41.94	39.03
Digital TV penetration (pay & free)	%	–	1.03	10.97	26.23	35.45	39.29

Source: 'UK: TV Market Overview', *Screen Digest*, London, November 2003.

Exhibit 17   UK digital TV forecasts

All figs millions	2002	2003	2004	2005	2006
Digital satellite TV households	6.30	6.75	7.10	7.25	7.40
Digital cable TV households	2.09	2.25	2.40	2.55	2.65
Digital terrestrial TV households	0.70	0.95	1.15	1.30	1.50
Digital TV dual platform households	0.22	0.25	0.27	0.29	0.30
All digital TV households	8.87	9.70	10.38	10.81	11.25
Analogue cable TV households	1.30	1.10	0.90	0.80	0.70
Free-to-air satellite	0.30	0.35	0.40	0.45	0.50
Multi-channel TV households	10.47	11.15	11.68	12.06	12.45

Source: *UK Digital TV Forecasts: 2002–2006*, Enders Analysis, Dundee, November 2002, p.6.

Exhibit 18 BSkyB results

	2002 £m	2001 £m	2000 £m	1999 £m	1998 £m	1997 £m
DTH subscriber revenues	1,929	1,537	1,189	979	968	861
Cable and DTT subscriber revenues	279	299	303	253	228	191
Advertising revenues	251	271	242	217	195	150
Interactive revenues	186	93	5	–	–	–
Other revenues	131	106	108	96	43	48
Turnover	2,776	2,306	1,847	1,545	1,434	1,249
Programming	−1,439	−1,134	−946	−787	−688	−569
Transmission and related functions	−147	−129	−105	−91	−70	−47
Marketing	−417	−378	−381	−216	−168	−102
Subscriber management	−291	−243	−200	−154	−92	−92
Administration	−203	−187	−130	−112	−76	−65
Gaming	−88	−75	–	–	–	–
Operating expenses, net	−2,585	−2,146	−1,762	−1,360	−1,094	−875
Goodwill amortisation and exceptional items	−137	−67	−105	−456	–	–
Operating profit	54	93	−20	−271	341	374
Share of operating results of joint ventures	−76	−256	−122	−58	−17	−10
Joint ventures' goodwill amortisation	−1,070	−101	−14	–	–	–
Profit on sales of fixed assets	2	−70	−15	–	–	–
Amounts written off fixed assets investments	−60	−39	–	–	–	–
Release of provision for loss on disposals	10	−10	–	–	–	–
Net interest payable	−137	−132	−92	−60	−53	−50
Profit on ordinary activities before tax	−1,277	−515	−263	−389	271	314
Tax on profit on ordinary activities	−107	−24	65	103	−22	−26
Profit on ordinary activities after tax	−1,384	−539	−198	−286	249	288
Capital expenditure	101	133	58	76	82	42
Fixed assets	1,129	2,411	1,886	343	219	148
Working capital	−17	15	32	2	90	150
Provisions, tax and dividend	115	182	−127	−305	−92	−92
Net debt	−1,528	−1,547	−1,145	−665	−518	−628
Net assets	−301	1,061	646	−625	−301	−422
Direct-to-home (DTH) subscribers (000s)	6,101	5,453	4,513	3,460	3,547	3,532
Sky Digital subscribers (000s)	6,101	5,308	3,583	753	–	–
Cable subscribers (000s)	4,091	3,486	3,735	3,778	3,352	2,327
DTT subscribers (000s)	0	1,105	740	204	–	–
Total subscribers (000s)	10,192	10,044	8,988	7,442	6,899	5,859
DTH subscriber acquisition cost (£)	234	250	n/a	n/a	n/a	n/a
DTH annual churn (%)	10.5	10	10.5	13.4	15.1	12.2
DTH ARPU (£ per annum)	347	313	287	281	272	252
DTH pay-to-basic ratio (%)	267	272	284	291	302	253

Sources: Company reports (UK GAAP), company presentations, Merrill Lynch. Annual results to end June. ARPU includes revenues from television and interactive services and is net of VAT.

Exhibit 19 NTL results

	2002 $m	2001 $m	2000 $m	1999 $m	1998 $m
Consumer revenues	2,074	2,515	1,820	834	355
Business revenues	880	841	720	453	249
Broadcast and other revenues	311	344	319	297	140
Total revenues	3,265	3,699	2,841	1,584	747
Operating expenses	−1,503	−1,809	−1,388	−799	−372
Selling, general and admin.	−770	−1,182	−1,109	−575	−300
EBITDA	993	708	344	211	75
Asset impairment	−445	−11,124	–	–	–
Other charges and expenses	−408	−409	−140	−62	−38
Depreciation and Amortisation	−1,542	−3,181	−2,123	−791	−266
Operating profit	−1,402	14,006	−1,919	−643	−229
Net interest	−750	−1,390	−1,035	−631	−283
Profits from investments	−98	−399	−121	506	4
Recapitalisation	−152	–	–	–	–
Profit before tax	−2,402	15,795	−3,075	−768	−507
Income tax	26	−63	111	35	3
Profit from early extinguishment of debt	–	–	–	−3	−31
Net profit	−2,376	15,858	−2,964	−736	−535
Preferred stock dividends	–	−326	−194	−74	−19
Net profit to common shareholders	2.376	−16,184	−3,158	−809	−553
Working capital	−554	18.151	−849	2,261	601
Fixed assets, net	7,894	12,573	12,693	5,598	3,854
Total assets	11,248	16,834	28,384	12,212	6.194
Long term debt	6,540	102	15,044	8,798	5,044
Redeemable preferred stock	–	2,774	2,083	142	124
Shareholders' equity	2,928	−6,542	8,367	2,137	355
Homes passed (000s)	8,404	8,404	8,800	4,291	n/a
Telephony subscribers (000s)	2,412	2,589	2,537	n/a	n/a
Cable TV subscribers (000s)	2,055	2,262	2,301	n/a	n/a
Digital Plus subscribers (000s)	1,229	1,253	531	c.100	–
Internet subscribers (000s)	987	845	859	625	200
Total subscribers (000s)	2,686	2,840	2,842	1,846	1,172
Annual churn (%)	15.9	21.3	20.4	12.7	n/a
ARPU (£ per annum)	492	488	428	420	n/a
Pay-to-basic ratio (%)	n/a	n/a	n/a	91	n/a

Source: Company reports (UK GAAP). Annual results to end December. Assets and liabilities for 2002 are pro-forma. Digital Plus subscribers includes all NTL/CWC digital TV subscribers. ARPU is annualised Q4 ARPU, includes revenues from telephony, cable TV and internet services, and is net of VAT.

Exhibit 20 Telewest results

	2002 £m	2001 £m	2000 £m	1999 £m	1998 £m
Residential cable TV	336	329	279	258	202
Residential telephony	495	488	445	343	233
Internet and other	79	40	16	17	21
Business telephony & services	267	274	271	174	84
Content division (inc UKTV backout)	42	66	82	–	–
Total	1,283	1,260	1,093	793	539
Programming costs	−128	−142	−132	132	−103
Telephony costs	−218	−238	−235	158	−82
Content division costs	−70	−83	−46	–	–
Selling, general and admin. costs	−499	−491	−445	281	−208
Total costs of revenue	−915	−954	−846	571	−393
EBITDA	368	306	247	222	146
Depreciation and amortisation	−609	−626	−541	−403	−238
Operating profit	−241	−320	−294	−181	−92
Total interest payable and similar charges	−274	−477	−407	−349	−234
Profit before income taxes	−506	−797	−701	−530	−314
Income tax	−1	−5	−5	–	–
Extraordinary items	−1,712	−1,134	–	–	–
Net profit	−2,219	−1,936	−706	−530	−312
Fixed assets	3,911	5,789	6,891	4,086	3,405
Current assets	640	340	235	236	353
Net current assets	−3,770	−330	−270	−270	23
Creditors: amounts due after > 1 year	−1,932	−5,031	−3,580	−3,061	−2,570
Net assets	−1,790	427	2,355	754	858
Equity shareholders' funds	−1,790	427	2,355	754	858
Homes passed (000s)	4,896	4,914	4,922	4,918	4,183
Cable TV subscribers (000s)	1,293	1,342	1,250	1,192	999
Active Digital subscribers (000s)	857	724	339	23	–
Residential telephony subscribers (000s)	1,614	1,616	1,538	1,476	1,261
Internet subscribers (000s)	540	388	287	70	–
Total subscribers (000s)	1,759	1,766	1,691	1,649	1,370
Cable TV annual churn (%)	21.5	18.7	26.0	26.7	29.7
Cable TV ARPU (£ per annum)	250	249	234	253	270
Pay-to-basic ratio (%)	80	72	n/a	n/a	n/a

Source: Company reports (UK GAAP). Annual results to end December. ARPU is net of VAT. Pay-to-basic ratio is for Q4.

Exhibit 21   ONdigital operating results

	2001 £m	2000 £m	1999 £m	1998 £m
Revenues	176	107	n/a	n/a
Cost of sales	−104	−69	n/a	n/a
Gross profit	72	37	n/a	n/a
Subscriber management	−71	−54	n/a	n/a
Fixed costs	−69	−61	n/a	n/a
Customer acquisition costs	−134	−106	n/a	n/a
Direct costs	−47	−58	n/a	n/a
ITVSelect/ITVActive/Sport	−92	−47	n/a	n/a
Rebranding	−10	–	–	–
Profit before interest and tax	−351	−289	−153	−31
Fixed assets	104	104	n/a	n/a
Current assets	206	228	n/a	n/a
Gross liabilities	−1,034	−560	n/a	n/a
Subscribers (000s)	1,263	896	411	–
Subscriber acquisition cost (£)	200	n/a	n/a	n/a
Annual churn (%)	25	n/a	n/a	n/a
ARPU (£ per annum)	225	n/a	n/a	n/a

Sources: Carlton, Enders Analysis. Annual results to end September. Figures for 2000 and 2001 include ITV Digital and ITV Sport channel. SAC, ARPU and churn for 2001 taken from *ITV Digital – Between a Rock and a Hard Place?*, Claire Enders, Enders Analysis, Dundee, July 2001, p.2. ARPU includes VAT at 17.5%.

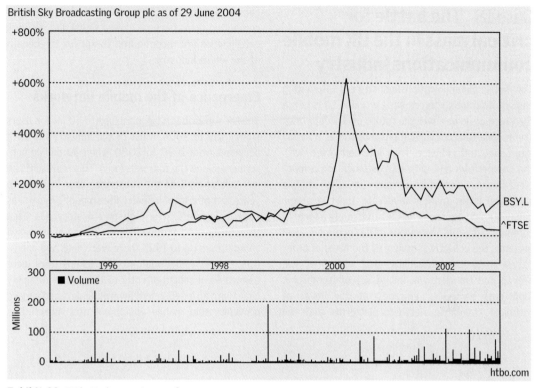

British Sky Broadcasting Group plc as of 29 June 2004

Exhibit 22 BSkyB share price performance
Source: *Yahoo! UK & Ireland Finance web site*, 28 June 2004, URL:http://uk.finance.yahoo.com/q?s=bsy.l&d=c>, Accessed 29 June 2004.

Case 18 **The battle for critical mass in the UK mobile communications industry**

The mobile communications industry is a fascinating case of interacting forces each working to retain a threshold of power over the future of the networks. The mobile telecommunications industry is a highly interconnected industry. It is interconnected with the competitors and with its customers on a long-term basis. Industry players in the mobile communications market moderate their strategic behaviour and opt for strategies that imply a form of complex adaptive behaviour. The common goal becomes the collective survival of the firms in order to eliminate the probability that one firm will prevail and the rest will fail. A set of isomorphic (copy-cat) strategies emerges at the level of technical standards, network platforms and the

consumer platform. As a result market shares of competing firms become almost equal and network externalities are reconfigured to act for the benefit of the whole industry.

Emergence of the mobile networks

The UK subscriber base increased to 50 million users from 1985 to 2004. Most of the industry's growth occurred from 1999 to 2000 when 30 million subscribers joined the four networks. This represents an increase of 66% of the subscriber base in just two years, out of a total industry life span of 17 years, as seen in Figure 1. The industry's history has been through a period of duopoly and a period of increased competition. Up to 1993 there were only two operators, Cellnet[i] and Vodafone. The competitors were banned from selling directly to the public. A supply chain with an independent level of dealers and service providers sold mobile equipment and subscription

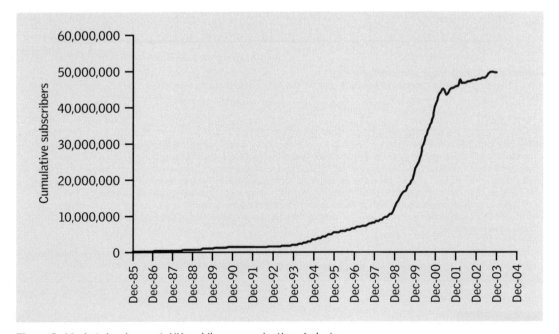

Figure 1 Market development: UK mobile communications industry

By Tanya Sammut-Bonnici

The material in this case is taken from original research conducted by the author at Warwick Business School under the supervision of John McGee.

© Tanya Sammut-Bonnici, 2004

[i] Cellnet later became O2 in November 2001.
[ii] One2One became T-Mobile in April 2002.

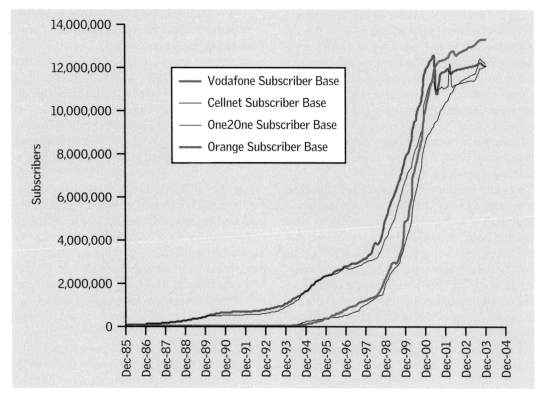

Figure 2 Industry network performance

airtime to consumers. One2One[ii] and Orange entered the market in 1993 and 1994 respectively.

The UK Government granted licences to Vodafone and Cellnet for the operation of mobile communications networks in 1983. Vodafone was initially owned by Racal Electronics and was later floated on the stock exchange as a separate company. Cellnet was 60% owned by British Telecom, and 40% by Securicor. The two companies launched their networks concurrently in 1985. Further licences were granted to One2One and Orange in 1993 and 1994 respectively. One2One, was originally owned by Mercury Personal Communications. Orange was created by the Microtel consortium led by British Aerospace, which was subsequently purchased by Hutchison Telecommunications. The industry started with analogue networks in 1985 and moved on to digital network in the 1990s. Vodafone and Cellnet switched on digital networks in 1992 and 1994. One2One and Orange entered the market with digital networks from their launch date.

Industry leadership

Figure 2 summarises the network size of the four MNOs from 1985 to date. Three out of the four MNOs held the position of the largest networks at different periods. Only One2One failed to attain the largest subscriber base at any point in its history. Cellnet, Vodafone, and Orange became industry leaders in 1985, 1986 and 2001 respectively.

Cellnet was the industry leader up to the third quarter of 1985. The company never regained the lead position but came close to having the same market share as Vodafone in 1996 and in 2001. The Cellnet story defeats the idea of 'first mover advantage', and the concept of a seed value[iii] from the innovations diffusion literature.

Cellnet started to relinquish market share to

[iii] The seed value, which is the initial size of a network, is thought to provide enough impetus for a network to grow at an increasing rate, outstripping competitors.

Racal-Vodafone[iv] in mid 1986. At that point, it had 32,000 subscribers, representing 54% of the UK mobile market. In just nine months, Cellnet made three price changes in fixed and variable rates. Its pricing structure was cheaper in the London areas, but more expensive in what were called the provincial areas. Growth in connections and traffic in the provincial areas was increasing in significance. Cellnet suffered because of real and perceived price differentials, and its miscalculation of growth potential of non-London territories.

In an effort to protect margins, Cellnet attempted to increase its connection and standing charges in April 1986. It withdrew them only four days after they had been introduced. The move followed the decision by the rival operator, Racal-Vodafone, to hold its prices steady and to increase the usage charge. Racal-Vodafone's increase was confined to the London area. Cellnet increased all its call charges at the beginning of this month. Racal, which had 27,000 customers at the time, said that its move was not designed to put pressure on Cellnet. Its mix of charges was intended to meet its target of another 35,000 customers over the next year, and that it decided to hold down connection and standing charges. These types of charges were viewed as the 'most emotive issues' for customers. Vodafone intended to act according to the psychological response of the consumer.

The fact that Cellnet cancelled its plans to increase prices meant that it would not meet its planned target to reach break-even point by 1987. The company, which was 60% owned by British Telecom, thought that the proposed increases would be reasonable, and that they would have been acceptable to the market. The results showed otherwise, and new customers drifted slowly towards Racal-Vodafone. In spite of the freeze in prices, Cellnet continued to lose market share. It claimed that the average customer would pay 6% less than under Racal, but it believed that customers perceived the Vodafone offering to be better. As a result, Cellnet was losing out in provincial areas where Racal's charges were cheaper. At that point in the industry's timeline, Vodafone was getting about 60% of its traffic from outside London, while Cellnet got 40–50%.

By January 1987, the pressure from customers increased and Cellnet was forced to introduce a new price structure. The move marked an attempt by Cellnet to win back market share from Racal, which had gained 53% of the UK's 114,000 subscribers. Cellnet announced a decrease in price of its basic cell phone by £450 to £899. However, the company lost its opportunity to gain a price differential in the eyes of its customers because Racal-Vodac followed suit the next day. Cellnet had started another price war. When sales were slow in August 1986, Cellnet brought the price of its cheapest unit below £1,000 for the first time. This move was the subject of a complaint to Oftel, but it did not lead to an investigation since Cellnet put its prices up again after six weeks. In May 1987, Cellnet instigated another price war against Vodafone with the announcement that new subscribers to its network would only pay half the subscription price for the first six months.

The competition battles were played through pricing strategies as well as advertising strategies. In May 1987, Cellnet unveiled a £5 million promotional drive, including a £1 million TV campaign through its agency Doyle Dane Bernbach. The campaign featured celebrities such as Joan Collins and Ian Botham. Vodafone rapidly took up battle in its fight with Cellnet for dominance in the UK mobile telephone market. It launched a £2 million TV campaign through Saatchi and Saatchi just two weeks after Cellnet's release. Interestingly Vodafone used its new campaign to push the other services it offered, besides the mobile telephone network. The move may have enhanced the image of Racal-Vodafone in terms of its size, reliability, experience in communications and its overall capability to build and sustain a mobile network. This drive to promote Racal-Vodafone's overall product offering was set to balance Cellnet's strong corporate image as a subsidiary of British Telecom.

Once Vodafone gained the position of the largest network in 1986 (Figure 3), Cellnet slipped into second place and remained there for the next twelve years. Orange challenged both Cellnet and Vodafone's positions in the year 2001 when it rapidly gained market share and became the largest mobile communications network. In July 2001 Vodafone's market share was seen to trail that of Cellnet and Orange. Vodafone slipped behind the two companies to become Britain's third largest mobile phone operator.

[iv] Racal and Vodafone demerged in September 1991.

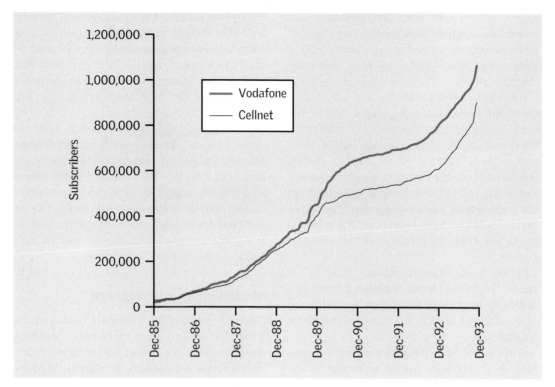

Figure 3 Cellnet and Vodafone network performance

Orange was the last operator to enter the industry yet it grew rapidly to become the largest network to date. Orange's story defies all notions of first mover advantage as it challenged One2One, Cellnet, and finally Vodafone in its race for the largest portion of market share. Orange overtook One2One in 1996. Its strategy to overtake competitors started prior to the date it switched on its network. Its main strategies were: to set off with a network which had a larger coverage than its closest competitor; to offer better handsets; to offer simplified pricing structures.

When Mercury launched One2One in September 1993, Hutchison was close to launching Orange. However, research had showed 50% coverage of the UK population to be the minimum level acceptable to customers. While Mercury had a strong proposition, with new phones and cheaper calls, its 30% coverage of the UK market was not enough to challenge large operators. After the launch of One2One both Vodafone and Cellnet initially resisted calls to cut

their prices. One2One felt the pressure to reduce its tariffs because it did not offer national coverage like its competitors. In view of the price cuts, Orange's launch was delayed further.

Hutchison felt that it was important to have a minimum of 50% coverage on entry into the UK market and to rapidly achieve over 90% coverage. An investment of £450 million was allocated for 1994 when the service was to reach 70% of the population. This commitment required considerable capital outlay by Hutchison, the owner of Orange. Commitment of capital outlay on this scale made the challenge of Orange to Vodafone and Cellnet of a different order to that of Mercury. It allowed Orange to take the process of change in the mobile telephone market forward, benefiting from the effect One2One had as an earlier catalyst of change.

The Orange network was attractive to consumers from the outset. Since it covered the main UK metropolitan areas and the connection motorways at launch, it immediately had a significant advantage over its closest rival One2One. From its launch period, Orange offered more benefits than One2One. Its Nokia handsets doubled as radio pagers, and had screens that could display voicemail and caller identification.

The target market for Orange was described by the head of product marketing Graeme Oxby as: 'Not those right at the top of the corporate market, but the remaining 90% of the populace.' Business customers were initially the principal target, predominantly middle managers and small business owners. The new target was largely ABC1 customers and predominantly younger age groups attracted by the possibilities of digital technology. Orange was to benefit from the larger population of the new target segment.

In July 2001, Orange's network grew to 3.4 million subscribers, which challenged Vodafone's position as industry leader. Orange was attracting more customers on both the subscription and the pre-paid tariffs.

At the beginning of 2002, Orange and Vodafone were in dispute over market leadership claims. Orange claimed a lead over Vodafone, while calling for the industry to use the same definitions for 'active' customers. Orange did not include 'inactive' users in its calculations and was pressing for a common, industry-wide definition of active customers. It said that if it used the industry's current definition of an active customer it could add another 656,000 users to its 12.4 million UK customer base. Graham Howe, Orange's deputy chief executive and finance director, said: 'I thought about using the industry definition but it just didn't make sense because you add in customers you know are inactive. I'm not saying the Orange definition is the perfect one but I think we need to get a group together to figure out what the industry definition should be.'

The debate saw the rise in popularity of a most important acronym in the mobile industry: average revenue per user ARPU. Operators in developed mobile markets were struggling to push up ARPU, even at the expense of growth in terms of subscriber numbers. Vodafone said it was still the UK's biggest mobile phone operator in terms of both revenue and profits and noted that the industry was now more focused on ARPU. Vodafone, which had

99.9 million customers worldwide in 2002, reported an ARPU of £274 in 2001. Orange, on the other hand, was reporting revenues alongside customer data. The company reported 2001 revenue up 25% at £8.3 billion. It added 8.8 million customers in that year, to take the total to 39.3 million, a 29% increase.

In the period under analysis there is no overall industry leader in the mobile communications industry. Vodafone is seen to have held the longest lead, from 1986 to 2001, yet Orange's meteoric rise is equally significant. The industry shows evidence of shifting patterns of leadership. This implies that the growth of MNOs is not a result of positive feedback from previous subscribers, but a result of other factors such as network externalities.

Market share convergence

Figure 4 provides an interesting picture of the trends in market share of Cellnet, Vodafone, One2One and Orange. Cellnet started out with a high market share, relinquishing it to Vodafone over a period of 2 years. Vodafone and Cellnet held their positions at a stable level, until the entry of One2One and Orange in 1993 and 1994. At that point the market share of the older companies diminished as the new companies rapidly increased their hold on the market.

Cellnet held the highest market share from the start of the industry up to August 1985. Vodafone held the longest lead, from 1985 to 2001. Orange's dramatic growth moved it to the top position in 2001. The change in industry leadership clearly shows that winner-takes-all strategies were not, or could not be, exploited in this industry.

At the time when Orange overtook Vodafone, Cellnet's subscriber base dropped for the first time ever. Cellnet's subscriber base fell by 268,000 in accounting terms over the quarter to settle at 10.9 million in July 2001. The operator also saw a decline of 20,000 in its post-paid base. This decline was due to a move towards a three-month accounting standard similar to Vodafone. At this point Cellnet started to count only those customers who had used the phone at any point in the last three months. The new accounting measure reduced the bias on over-inflation of subscriber figures.

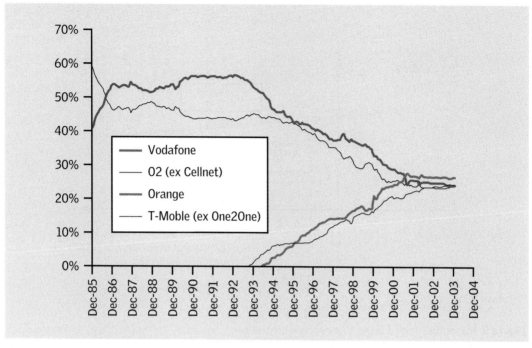

Figure 4 Market shares in the UK Mobile communications industry

Orange had the fastest growth rate in the industry. Orange saw its contract base increase by 222,000 net new customers to 3.4 million in the three months to the end of June, compared with 89,000 in the first quarter and with Vodafone's overall growth of 269,000. Orange, which allowed for 1 million inactive prepaid customers in its accounting, was outperforming Vodafone, even in the battle for more valuable post-paid customers.

Brand consistency

Figure 5 shows the number of times the companies changed ownership and brand names. It can be assumed that change in ownership does not have a direct effect on network growth. Orange underwent three ownership changes and it grew into the largest network. Vodafone had one change in ownership, when it separated from Racal and floated its stocks in 1991. Cellnet and One2One changed ownership twice. Orange was originally owned by Hutchison Whompoa and BAE, which shed its ownership

in 1998. Mannesmann bought Orange in 1999. Orange was bought out again by France Telecom in 2000, when Vodafone took over Mannesmann. Vodafone was the only network operator that was not bought out by third parties. Cellnet was originally owned by British Telecom and Securicor. It became wholly owned by British Telecom in 1999. Cellnet was demerged from British Telecom in the same year and floated on the stock exchange in 2001. One2One was originally owned by Cable and Wireless and US West Media Group. It was partly floated in 1997, and bought out by Deutsche Telekom in 1999.

From the four companies there is some indication that consistent branding can be linked to performance. Brand name consistency is the common characteristic of Orange and Vodafone, which have the highest brand equity in our research sample. They kept their brand name unchanged for the duration of their life span in mobile communications. Orange and Vodafone are almost equally successful. On the other hand, One2One was rebranded twice from Mercury One2One to One2One to T-Mobile.

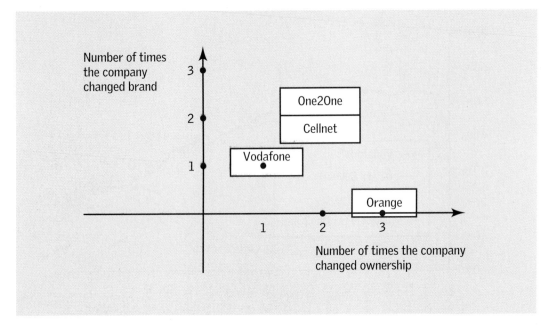

Figure 5 Perceptual map of ownership vs brand consistency

Cellnet was rebranded from BT Cellnet to Cellnet to O2.

Critical mass and market growth

In the early days of the mobile communications industry, the achievement of a critical mass was a clearly stated goal. Vodafone and Cellnet, the pioneers in the industry, invested substantially to set the 'watershed' of subscribers in motion. The industry was striving to gain enough subscribers to move into an area of the demand function where it would be easier to attain more subscribers. In its objectives, the industry was verbalising the characteristics of a positive feedback system to reach a hyperactive state of development. Figure 6 illustrates important turning points in the mobile industry's market development.

Critical mass may be evaluated in terms of inflection points on the demand function of mobile telephone subscribers. An inflection point occurs when the rate of change, or the gradient of the curve, changes in magnitude and direction. A typical diffusion of innovation curve has an S-shape with a first-order inflection and two second-order inflection points.[1]

♦ The first-order inflection point (Point B) occurs when the increase in the adoption rate is the fastest for the entire diffusion. By and large, the first-order inflection point occurs when 50% of the population has adopted the innovation.

♦ The two other second-order inflection points occur when the rate of adoption switches from a slow rate to a faster one, and vice versa. The standard deviation of subscribers, gives the values of the second-order inflection points before and after the first-order inflection point.

Inflection Point A (co-ordinates: 9.8 million subscribers, mid 1998) represents the most important turning point for the industry. The coefficient of determination for network externalities at that point was around 65%.[v] At the same time, important changes were taking place in pricing and

---

[v] The correlation between number of new customers and network size was R = 0.8. The coefficient of determination $R^2 = 0.65$ is a rough indication that 65% of the new subscriber data is attributed to network size. The value is a relative rule of thumb measure for the strength of network externalities.

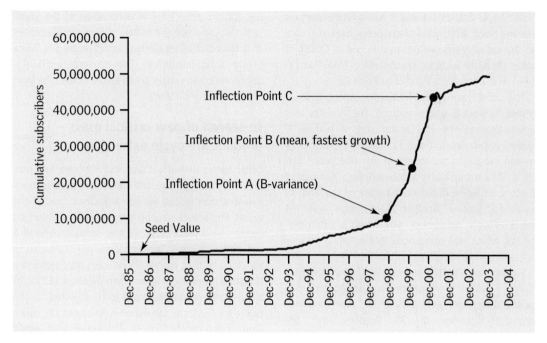

Figure 6 Inflection points

distribution policies, which were to transform the industry's landscape. The mobile phone networks started to sell handsets in supermarkets nationwide. Furthermore, pre-paid phone cards were introduced which addressed potential users' apprehension of the subscription system.

Critical mass acts on the adoption of the MNO plat-forms in a similar manner for all companies. The deviations in the occurrences of critical mass are limited to a maximum of eighteen months, notwith-standing that the second set of MNOs entered the market a decade after the first set. The individual MNO network size has a small effect on the date of attain-ment of critical mass. The dates registered for Point A, the lower second-order inflection point, are in the order of the network size: Vodafone being the largest followed by Cellnet, Orange and One2One. The lag in the dates, however, has no relationship to the date of entry. The lag in attainment of inflection points dimin-ishes through Point B and Point C, as the networks grow similar in size and market shares converge.

The exponential rise in demand was combined with a rapid reduction in cost of sales effort per subscriber. At Point A, the demand exceeds supply[vi] by a wide margin and the marketing strat-egies changed from a 'push' strategy to one of distribution efficiency. Prior to the critical mass point, the companies had aggressive direct sales forces which sold mobile telephones on a door-to-door basis. In 1999, both Vodafone and Cellnet changed their sales strategy significantly. Post critical mass, the sales forces were transformed to support high street and supermarket distributors, where most of the sales were occurring on a cash and carry basis.

Marketing practitioners can readily identify when inflection Point A has been reached, but mathemat-ical models and statistical techniques are required to forecast the other two inflection points.

Inflection Point B (co-ordinates: 23.5 million subscribers, end 1999) was less apparent to marketers when it occurred. It showed a very small decline in the rate of increase of demand.

[vi] The demand exceeds supply only temporarily, because supply was increased as a response to demand.

However, in statistical terms it was a very important turning point, which could have predicted the arrival of the industry's downturn by the end of 2000. It takes the same increase in subscribers from Point A to B, as it takes from Point B to Point C.[2]

The occurrence of the first-order inflection point (Point B) went largely unnoticed. The industry was going through the spectacular rise of text messaging, which rose from 11 million to over 100 million messages per month in just one year.[3] The UK's SMS explosion is attributed to a number of factors, including the service's ease of use and its value for money. Another main factor was the breakthrough agreement on network interoperability, which was announced by the country's four operators at the beginning of April 1999.[4]

Furthermore, by the end of 1999, when the first signs of decline were noticeable, the industry was anticipating major upheaval with the impending government auctions of 3G licences and the announcement of Vodafone Airtouch's takeover of Mannesmann. The 3G auctions were to determine the future survival or lack thereof of Cellnet, Vodafone, One2One and Orange. The takeover was to affect two out of these network operators, as Mannesmann owned Orange at the time.

There was no reference to the small decrease in growth in a sample of 400 articles from industry publications and the general business media from November 1999 to October 2000. Even up to October 2000, just a few months prior to the slow down, the industry was still reporting signs of a growing market and record sales.

Inflection Point C (co-ordinates: 37.1 million subscribers, end 2000) marked the start of the decline in growth of the UK mobile communications industry. The demise was not apparent for over two years, when clear signs of saturation started to emerge. The decline in sales growth was picked up by the stock market. In May 2002, Vodafone shares closed below 100p, the lowest since February 1988. The weakness in mobile stocks spread across the sector. Analysts said investors were concerned about the short-term outlook for revenue growth, and the delays in bringing out commercial products and services related to GPRS and 3G.[5]

Another factor that affected the decline in the industry's growth was the population threshold at the current price level. A percentage of the population would never use mobile phones, which implies that the point of saturation occurs below the figure of the total population. The demand function is asymmetric and settles down faster at the later part of the industry's history.

In search of new critical mass – product life cycle extension

Other forces that affect demand will come into play in the future of the UK mobile communications industry, and indeed similar industries around the world. The actual demand function will be dislodged further from an S-shape, as the characteristic of a subscriber changes. These changes are attributed to two factors: first, mobile phone users may own more than one telephone. The mathematical calculation of the S-curve would thus have to be adjusted, as the figure for the total population is no longer the upper limit of the demand curve. The upper limit would shift above the population threshold. Second, the mobile phone industry will expand its product life cycle by promoting subscriptions on automated equipment, which will relay consumption information through a mobile connection. The industry would thus push out the population threshold even further, and extend its full potential to encompass individuals as well as machinery.

As the statistical total population for the industry is pushed beyond the national population, the total potential population becomes less finite and more extendable. For example, a household with two adults has the potential to provide the mobile industry with a minimum of two subscriptions. The same household could also provide a number of additional mobile subscriptions for energy and water meters, feedback channels for satellite television channels, and remote operation of domestic appliances. M-commerce, which is commerce conducted via mobile telephony, has the potential to boost the sales figures even further. Wireless shopping, travel information, ticketing, mapping, banking and trading are some of the applications that will see m-commerce revenues rise.

Copycat strategies

Isomorphism is a form of mimetic behaviour or strategic herding that is in vogue in some of the most dynamic industries of the new information economy. The copycat strategies between among Cellnet, Vodafone, One2One and Orange are a good example. Strategic isomorphism has strong appeal because of its risk reduction properties, which ensures the survival of more firms in the industry. However, there are some serious caveats. Industry profit margins are likely to decline, as shown in a study of the German mobile market.[6]

Deutsche Telekom's D1 and Mannesmann's D2 joined the incumbent C-Tel in 1992. Herding effectively removed divergence among the MNOs' services, tariffs and customer niches. When another MNO, E-Plus, emerged in 1994, it differentiated itself with pricing packages for low-volume private users, including students, families and senior citizens. Within a few months, the other networks copied E-Plus's strategy, destroying its brave effort to increase differentiation in the industry. Nattermann's (1999) analysis of the impact of such crowding shows that a 10% decline in the wireless industry's SDI[vii] resulted in an 11.2% decline in profit margins. Between 1992 and 1998 the SDI fell by 83%, taking margins down 50% from their maximum point. The reduction in strategic differentiation created by the incumbent operators was responsible for the lost earnings, which amounted to more than £495 million in 1998 alone. As strategic differentiation and margins decline, companies anxiously endeavour to reintroduce differentiation from competitors, typically by expensive brand enhancement campaigns and higher marketing spending.

A study by the Federal Reserve Bank in 2000 shows that the US personal-computer industry is another field which suffered a lowering in margins due to isomorphism.[viii] From 1976 to 1988 the PC industry's SDI went down by over 37% as companies copied the now dominant IBM-clone model. As a result of the decline, margins fell by 56%, representing £1.8 billion in destroyed margins by 1988. The increased herding effect in product design diminished 'brand' effects, which would have been developed over time from the firms' distinguishing characteristics. Brand effects, including

vii Strategic Differentiation Index. See Nattermann (1999).[7]

viii The findings are summarised by Nattermann in *McKinsey Quarterly* (2000) Number 2, pp. 22–31.

such intangibles as reputation and image, are the drivers of price differentiation, which creates premium pricing margins. If isomorphism erodes distinctive brand characteristic, it will also erode the opportunity to charge for intangible factors.

Industry landscape and structure

The mobile communications industry can be divided into five interacting levels. Each of the levels in our framework has its own economic dynamics and each contributes to the overall network, with technology and regulation in the background (Figure 7).

Regulatory background

In the UK, mobile communications companies fall under the UK Wireless Telegraphy Acts 1948–1967 and the UK Telecommunications Act 1984. The Radio Communications Agency has the authority to grant licences under the Wireless Telegraphy Act. The Department of Trade and Industry is responsible for the sector under the Telecommunications Act. The Office of Communications (Ofcom) is responsible for the enforcement of the licences' issues.

The regulatory institutions' main concern was to encourage and preserve competition. In order to stimulate the growth of a new supply chain, Cellnet and Vodafone were not allowed to market their services directly to the consumer from 1985 to the mid 1990s. The direct sales restriction was lifted when the third and fourth licences came into operation. Orange and One2One were not subject to such restrictions as they were viewed to be at a disadvantage compared to earlier entrants.

The regulation of the UK MNOs has a balancing effect on how the mobile networks develop and on competition. Regulation is starting to match the demands of complex dynamic markets. Regulation is creating new forms of control that fall under the definition of self-organising systems. In this case the regulatory objective is to create self-correcting mechanisms that preserve competition. Although the original objective is maintained, the way of doing it is novel as the outcomes are not entirely predictable.

A classic example would be the 3G spectrum auctions in the UK and across the globe (see Figure 8).

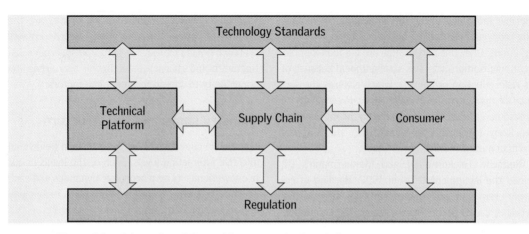

Figure 7 The multilevel dynamics of the mobile communications industry
Source: Sammut-Bonnici and McGee, 2002.[8]

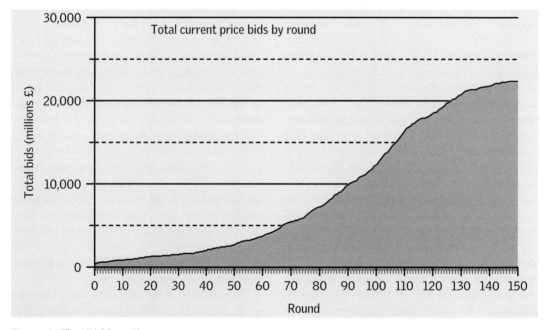

Figure 8 The UK 3G auctions
Source: DTI.

The auctions were designed to match the industry's predicted profitability of the introduction of a new generation of technology. The idea was that firms would bid to the maximum of the technology's feasibility. Thus governments found a way of introducing a licensing system that generated a self-correcting form of revenue, which gauged future profitability.

However, as with all complex systems, the outcome was unpredictable and other factors took hold of the system. The auctions were essentially a taxation procedure on an infant industry, and a key factor to allow MNOs to continue operating. Prospective MNOs faced the situation of having to bid for their future existence, or give up their operation once and for all. Thus the bidding did not stop at the profitability limits, but moved into the limits of what the companies could borrow from their banks. The mobile spectrum in Europe generated £200 billion, with Britain and Germany raising £22.5 and £60 billion respectively. The result was the depletion of cash flow, a delay in third-generation launches and uncertainty in the stock markets.

Another form of self-correcting regulation is the concept of 'market influence' inbuilt into the licence agreements of the MNOs. The definition set in the Telecommunications Act licences implies that MNOs should not exploit price inelasticity that may arise for the demand-side of the market. Market influence behaves as a self-regulatory measure whereby MNOs keep their market strength in check, in order to preserve their licence agreements. As competition in the industry grew, the need for market influence mechanisms diminished and this form of regulatory control was reduced substantially throughout Europe.

Technology standards

Mobile communications technology has evolved along a logical path, from the simple first-generation analogue products designed for business use to second-generation digital wireless telecommunications systems being used in B2B, B2C and C2C markets.

TACS (Total Access Communication System) and ETACS (the extended version) formed the first generation of mobile systems in Europe. The GSM (Global System for Mobile) standard is the second generation of mobile communication systems in Europe, supporting digital voice telephony, SMS text messaging and, more recently WAP and GPRS. Throughout the 1990s, every country in Europe implemented cellular networks based on the GSM specification.

Third-generation (3G) technologies are coming in two versions: CDMA2000 and WCDMA. The technology promises the introduction of video over and above what is already provided by second-generation technologies: images, Internet, voice and data services. Japan was the first to launch 3G in October 2001. The UK followed in 2003. Europe and the US are following slowly. The launch of 3G has been delayed by major regulatory, technical and commercial barriers. This uncertainty about 3G occurred at a time when GSM penetration was approaching saturation in many European countries and when regulators were increasing pressure on operators to reduce excessive profits.

The licence for CDMA technology worldwide is owned by Qualcom. The company is facing an exceptional situation. Every operator in the word that uses 3G technology will have to pay licence fees to Qualcom. (As the names of the standards imply, both CDMA2000 in the US and WCDMA in Europe and Asia use CDMA technology.)

The telecommunications standards we have today are a product of protracted market strife. Mobile technology has become widespread and practical only after going through a period of struggle between competing standards. The process is reminiscent of VHS vs Betamax, and Microsoft vs everyone else. As the wireless industry moves into 3G, it is going through the same arduous process.

The mobile telecommunications industry has also experienced hybrid standard setting. This type of standardisation emerges as private firms adopt strategies to undercut collaborative decisions taken in negotiated standardisation. They introduce new products which not only initiate unprecedented developments, but also create incompatibilities, lock-in effects and pockets of market power. Mobile Internet is a typical example, where companies, standards organisations and governments create a hybrid standard setting environment.[9]

Standards organisations are playing an increasingly important role in the strategy for versioning standards. The GSM Association is guiding the evolution of the mobile industry through a family of wireless technology standards from today's standard through to GPRS (General Packet Radio Service), EDGE (Enhanced Data Rated of GSM Evolution) and 3GSM. Each subsequent standard offers a higher level of service. GPRS provides open Internet. EDGE facilitates faster data streaming, and 3GSM will provide video streaming.

Switching costs are minimised when standards are designed to evolve from one another. The introduction of revolutionary standards would be costly. The pay-off is superior performance against the high cost of switching standards. The example is the price paid by mobile telephone operators to switch to third-generation licences. Mobile spectrum auctions earned European governments £200 billion. The mobile operators had to bid. To renounce third-generation spectrum was to sign their own death warrant. The outcome of these auctions left mobile operators no option but to increase debt to survive. The result was the depletion of cash flow, a delay in third-generation launches and uncertainty in the stock markets.

Physical platforms

Physical platforms in mobile communications are the technical networks connecting mobile phones, base stations, mobile exchanges and landline exchanges. The system extends from a national to an international level. Telecommunications platforms have had to cope with the complexity of interoperability among different systems, and to master the agility required to shift rapidly to newer standards.

Interoperability As in the supply chain case discussed earlier, companies divided their platform structure into separate modules, each with some degree of autonomy.[10] Each module is designed with the flexibility for rapid change, such as the shift from ETACS to GSM. The complexity feature is retained because each module is interoperable with other modules to form a weblike complex system. The modules are therefore interdependent through the nodes, or joints between the modules. Interoperability between modules creates value for the user, as we observe in the ability to call overseas on a mobile telephone. Roaming of mobile telephones from country to country is another example.

Interoperability exists between platforms of different MNOs[ix] in the same country, or different platforms in different countries. Physical platforms have evolved from the simple structures, such as the older regional railway system, to a complex structure of interconnected sub-platforms.

For this reason, the joints between the sub-networks become the strength of the whole structure, or conversely it could be its Achilles heel. It is therefore vital to define standards for joints. The

standards that govern how a system and its modules interact are called the network's architecture (Morris and Ferguson, 1993).[11] Henderson and Clark (1990)[12] review two kinds of dynamic processes in modular systems: modular innovation and architectural innovation.

The former type retains the architecture of the network including its joints, but modifies the modules. By preserving the basic architecture of a system, MNOs offer users enough compatibility to shift from one product generation to the next. The changes occur in the innovations and improvements of the modular components. They are fitted into the system when required, and will be removed when obsolete. The result is a hybrid dynamic of change that preserved the platform's architecture, while creating innovations within the module structure. A series of minor incremental modular changes can lead to an overall network platform that is radically new.

Capacity

A further aspect of network platforms concerns communication capacity and its expansion over time. Valletti and Cave (1998, p. 112)[13] make some observations on how this is addressed in the UK industry:

> On the one hand, there is the obvious investment decision of firms. As more cells are added, more subscribers can be supported by a network. Such a decision can be made by a firm on the ground of the optimal choice of coverage and capacity of its network. However, the choice is constrained by the regulatory requirement of 90% of the population being served by a certain date, assuming that there are no regulatory flaws. On the other hand, capacity has also increased over time, for technological reasons. Continuous improvements have allowed for a more efficient use of the existing spectrum so that more people can be handled by the same number of base stations. Finally, and equally importantly, the Government can decide to release significant amounts of additional radio spectrum for the mobile communications sectors.

Telecommunications networks fall under an 'integrative class' of complex networks, because of their tendency to integrate information from a large

---

[ix] Vodafone, Cellnet, Orange and One2One are mobile network operators (MNOs).

number of sources. Other networks that form part of this class are air traffic control and management systems, military command and control systems and electricity network sharing. The integrative class is characterised by: a large number of diverse information sources; the need to interoperate and integrate both equipment and information; the need to detect events in a complex network of connections; the need to operate across techno-socio barriers; and the need to operate as an open system which includes interoperability, portability, scalability; and the need to evolve.

The interconnectivity in mobile communications hinges on two important factors: the interconnections in the networks and the sharing of call revenue. The original objective of operating an open platform determined the survival of all the competing mobile platforms, which could evolve from one generation of transmission standards to the next in a concerted effort. Call revenue sharing ensured that the interconnectivity was kept at a high level of reliability across all the networks, in order to preserve revenue streams.

Interconnectivity in the information economy leads to the concept of 'co-evolution'. Evolving to meet the needs of other members in the value chain is becoming a more effective strategy than satisfying the company's own needs. Adapting to meet other companies' need leads to more business. Riding the new wave of co-evolution, companies are avoiding costly races against each other, in favour of a strategy to joining forces to gain more customers. We are observing this effect in NEC and Siemens, which have joined forces to supply the networks for Hutchison 3G, which will be a key network provider for third-generation telecommunications in Europe.

Co-evolution and collaboration are even more relevant in industries where network externalities are a vital part of corporate success. The more customers join a network, such as a telecommunications service, the higher is the incentive for other customers to join. This effect is causing companies to collaborate on issues of compatibility. With 3G mobile phones on the horizon for Europe and the US, the standards war for a mobile Internet operating system has begun. Microsoft, Linux, Symbian and Openwave are in the race to establish a widely accepted standard. This is an example of old-style competition, but it has caused a wave of co-evolution in another layer of competitors.

The issue of standards has motivated Nokia and Siemens, Europe's largest manufacturers of mobile phones, to collaborate. They have teamed up to accelerate the introduction of third-generation mobile services. The collaboration of the companies will guarantee that Nokia and Siemens handsets can communicate with each other seamlessly. In this way the two companies, which have a combined global market share of 45%, will benefit from network externalities and the positive feedback generated from a larger compatible technology platform. Nokia and Siemens anticipate that other equipment vendors will link up with them to minimise industry fragmentation.[14]

Image phones gave the Japanese market a boost similar to when DoCoMo introduced I-Mode wireless web service. DoCoMo, which had planned to concentrate on the introduction of 3G system with video capabilities, still bolstered its line of second-generation phones with a camera phone called the I-shot. DoCoMo President Keiji Tachikawa said: 'we recognise there is strong demand for cellular phones with cameras, so we will increase the number of current-generation camera models.' Companies saw their revenue from basic voice phone services decline, while sales of those equipped with cameras and related services were bringing in more money. The new models were reinvigorating a market that was becoming sluggish.

In Figure 12 the x and y-axes are normalised to reflect the penetration of the population by the UK and the Japanese mobile networks. The S-shape pattern of diffusion remains largely similar. This time UK's superior population diffusion rates are seen to be much higher than Japan's, although the comparison is not entirely on the same level as larger populations would have different economic demographics.

Japan was one of the first countries in the world to introduce the 3G standard, almost two years before it appeared in Europe. DoCoMo led the world in starting 3G services in October 2001, followed by KDDI in April 2002, and J-Phone in December 2002, so all three have a 3G presence. The European market gradually saw 3G services coming online in 2003 and 2004.

Supply chain

The mobile communications industry occupies an important position in the information economy. The structure is built on layers of communication network companies, hardware and software manufacturers, Internet service providers, e-commerce transaction companies, media and content companies, and myriad service companies (Figure 9).

The network infrastructure suppliers are companies such as Alcatel, Nortel Networks, Motorola and Ericsson that provide communications networking equipment. Intel and 3Com form a subset of companies in this category, which supply interfacing hardware and software.

The network operators provide the basis of the exchange of information between companies and

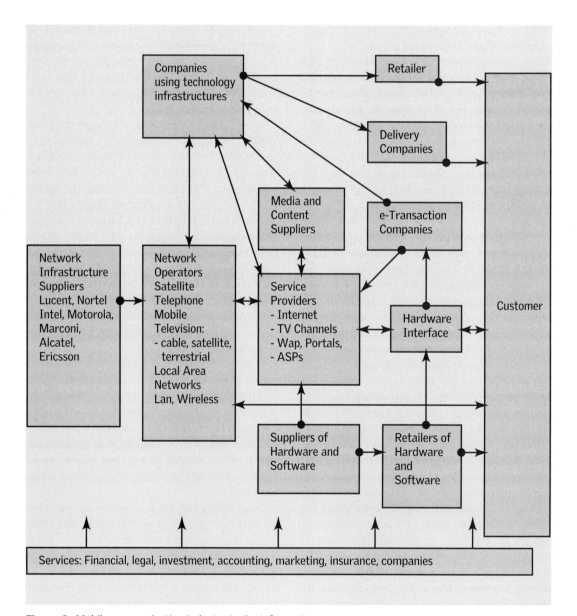

Figure 9 Mobile communication industry in the information economy

their customers. The medium they operate could be based on satellite, telephone, mobile, television or area networks. British Telecom, AT&T, Vodafone and T-Mobile offer landline and mobile telecommunications networks. The operation of these companies is interconnected with other companies. For example, Vodafone uses BT's network. Credit card companies use Vodafone's mobile network for offsite credit verification. Vodafone has sold fixed-line telephone services from Energis and Racal Telecom networks. The interoperability of different telecom networks has become a complex business operation.

The 3G telephone, which will become the new customer interface, would dictate a change in Internet transmission management and the nature of media content, all the way down the supply chain. The supply chain in the information economy shown in Figure 9 takes the form of a weblike network where each member may have to collaborate with all the other members. Inter-collaboration is necessary partly because of software and hardware compatibility. An example of this weblike structure is the relationship between e-transaction companies, ISPs, media content providers, and the companies that own the web pages.

The nature of the supply chain of the UK mobile communications industry changed dramatically as the network operators became more powerful.

When the UK mobile licences were granted, Cellnet and Vodafone were not allowed to sell direct to the customer. The regulators posed this restriction to create two tiers of firms in the industry that would balance each other's power. The first tier was the network operators (Cellnet and Vodafone) that were to have an engineering orientation and would focus on the technical platform. The second tier of firms consisted of distributors and service providers, which would market the product to the public. In spite of the regulators' intention to equalise power in the supply chain, the network operators grew more and more powerful. They progressed to the top of a hierarchical distribution pyramid in just a few years, through a deliberate strategy of controlling the supply chain population. This was achieved through the three stages described below.

1   Buyouts and mergers of distributors and service providers: By reducing or freezing prices,

Vodafone and Cellnet eroded the margins of hardware retailers. Survival of distributors and service providers became a direct function of market share. The larger companies were able to stay in business while the smaller ones were forced to merge or to sell-out. In the late 1980s we see the takeovers of National Radiophone, Advanced Car Telephone, and the sale of 40% in Air Call. Takeovers continued through the 1990s. The service provider arm of Robert Bosch, Hi-Time, MCP, and Excell were the next companies to be bought out of the supply chain, by competitors in their own tier.

2   Acquisition of suppliers by Vodafone and Cellnet: In the mid 1990s, acquisitions changed in nature. This time the MNOs started to buy into the supplier tier, further strengthening their power in the supply chain. Vodafone bought Hawthorn Leslie and Peoples Phones. It acquired shares in Astec Communications, Martin Dawes, and Talkland. By the end of 1996, Vodafone had direct control of 70% of the customers connected to its network. Cellnet joined the acquisitions game in the late 1990s. In 1997, it bought shares in The Link and acquired Martin Dawes, and DX Communications in 1999. It bought the Mobile Phone Store in 2000.

3   Supply chain control strategies: In the history of mobile communications, we see repeated evidence of the mobile operators determining the prices of phones and tariffs, even though the regulator intended that service providers would have some market power.

In 1992, the Federation of Communications Services (FCS), the mobile communications industry criticised Vodafone for quoting prices in its advertising. At the time, Vodafone was not allowed to sell its service direct to the customer. Oftel issued a report on unfair practices by Vodafone and Cellnet against independent providers. The companies were cross-subsidised by BT Mobile Communications, Securicor Cellular Services and Vodac, which were daughter companies. The regulator concluded that cross-subsidies were in contravention of the Cellnet and Vodafone licences.

Over the years, in spite of Oftel's efforts to moderate market power, the market share of the

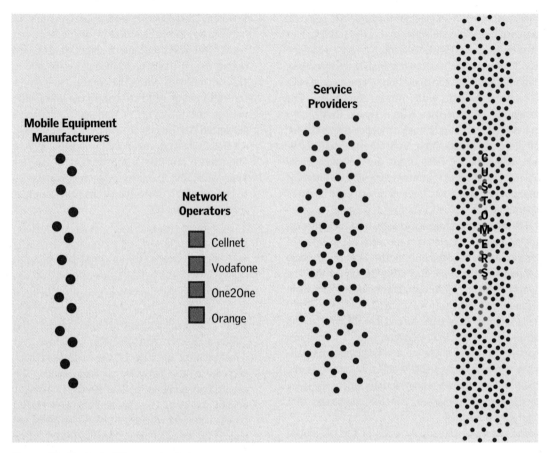

Figure 10 Control of the supply chain

independent cellular service suppliers continued to diminish. By 1996, the network operators owned 10 service providers that captured 77.5% of the market.

A determining factor of the power of the network operators was that they controlled the bottleneck of the supply chain (Figure 10). The number of network operators that could enter the market was determined by government licences and limited to four firms. On the other hand, the suppliers to the left and the right of the network operators in the figure operate in a competitive market with no controls on entry and exit.

Consumer networks

The consumer network is the final level of inter-acting dynamics in the mobile communications industry. The behaviour of consumers is affected by regulation (choice and pricing), technology standards (service offering), physical platforms (reliability) and the supply chain (retail access). Nonetheless, the consumer network exhibits strong characteristics of its own, such as network externalities.[x] Consumers affect each other's buying behaviour in a positive feedback loop, resulting in critical mass effects and exponential growth.

Network externalities are a powerful force in the

---

[x] Network externalities are observed in products where the possession of a product by one consumer affects the value of product for some other consumer. Telecommunications is a classic example where the value of the telephone for any individual depends on the number of colleagues, friends and relatives in possession of a telephone.

UK mobile communications industry. The correlation between number of new customers and network size was R = 0.8. The coefficient of determination $R^2 = 0.65$ is a rough indication that 65% of the new subscriber data is attributed to network size. The value is a relative rule of thumb measure for the strength of network externalities.

Network externalities affect the individual firms from the industry's total installed base and not the individual network platforms. This is the main difference between competing platforms that are independent (VHS and Betamax) and communications platforms that are typically interconnected (telecommunications). This effect shows us how and why market shares converge in the presence of strong network externalities and how market shares become similar for the four companies over the long run.

The increase in subscribers is interdependent with the utility of the whole network as well as with the utility of competing networks. The utility of other networks has a similar stronger effect on new subscribers to a company's own utility. Thus we can start to understand why market shares converge even in the presence of strong network externalities.

Comparison of UK and Japanese market development

The model of development for the UK mobile market is replicable in other environments. The UK's demand curve exhibits the characteristics of an S curve with a mixed influence model of diffusion. The diffusion of the product is determined by external and internal influences. The external influences are derived from the demand side characterised by network externalities and critical mass. Internal influences in the UK market are marketing effects determined by product, price, distribution and promotion policies.

The internal and external influences are present in mobile industries around the world. Network interconnectivity, technology and regulation are experienced to varying degrees in all countries. As a consequence marketing strategies are similar to the UK scenario, and internal influences on consumer demand are also similar. External influences, largely driven by network externalities, are a mathematical function of network adoption and operate irrespective of geographical location.

Japan's population is 122 million, just over double that of the UK. The market for mobile phones in its current state is nearly saturated, as in the UK industry. There are still possibilities for growth in automated mobile commerce, and in the new 3G technology that will allow video transmission. With 60% of the Japanese population (around 73 million subscribers) using mobile phones by 2003, companies can no longer expect rapid growth of the overall market. Towards the end of our data collection period, competition had started to show signs of recovery with the introduction of 3G.

The main difference between the UK and the Japanese diffusion processes is that Japan's industry started in 1980, five years earlier, and that 3G was introduced in 2001 two years earlier than the UK. We shall discuss the implications of these differences and whether they affect the similarity in the diffusion processes of the two countries. Figure 11 illustrates the UK and Japan adoption curves, normalised by the number of years of operation of the industry.

In the figure we see the UK and Japanese diffusion functions following an S curve shape, typical of mixed influence models of diffusion. Interestingly critical mass is reached at the same period within thirteen years from the date of introduction of the mobile industry. Although this means that Japan approached critical mass in 1993, five years before the UK, it is striking that the market dynamics retained the same time frame to move into exponential growth.

While the two countries' diffusion models are similar in their general trend and nature, earlier technological adoption on the part of the Japanese introduces interesting differences. While Europe and the US were experiencing a downturn in sales in 2000, Japan's market was undergoing an upturn. The growth in e-mail photo services started with J-Phone's launch in November 2000 of its Sha-mail model. KDDI followed in April 2001, followed by NTT DoCoMo in June 2001. Image telephones were so fashionable during the year that demand exceeded supply. The demand for the phones even outstripped the production of digital cameras. The industry sold 15 million camera phones by the end of 2002. Figure 12 illustrates the UK and Japan adoption curves, normalised by the number of years in operation and penetration.

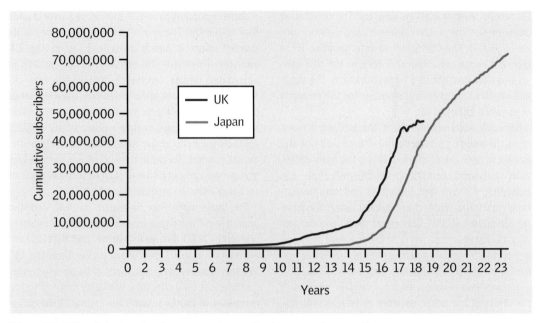

Figure 11 UK and Japan adoption curves – normalised by years in operation

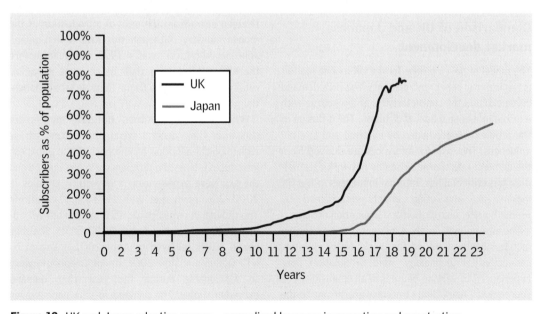

Figure 12 UK and Japan adoption curves – normalised by years in operation and penetration

The future of the mobile communications industry

The future of mobile telephony lies beyond picture and video transmission promised by third-generation technology. It will depend on the development of technical capability that generates a personal transaction environment that supports identity and payment.

Digital money transacted through electronic cash payments and billing will have a revolutionary impact on the industry. The industry is moving towards multi-application SIM cards integrated with network services. The technology opens up opportunities for non-telecom applications whereby a mobile phone would act as a bank payment card. New technologies will sustain electronic identity through public key infrastructure (PKI) and biometrics. Identification of users will be integral to ordering and paying through a mobile phone. Data transmission of wireless will increase dramatically and information exchange protocols such as XML are expected to evolve accordingly.

Voice recognition and synthesis technologies are expected to create the next wave of usage in mobile communications. The lack of space for a keyboard on a mobile handset has limited its range of use. Voice recognition would open up new possibilities for the mobile industry as the capability of a mobile phone moves closer to that of a personal computer. The impact of voice technologies is expected to increase mobile usage dramatically, as it opens the channels for people to speak directly to machines, without a keyboard interface.

Mobile network operators, such as Vodafone, T-Mobile, O2 and Orange, will need to adapt as they move from a model based on the economics of utilities to a model that is rooted in the wireless economy.

Strategic challenges

The challenge for future mobile phone products and services lies in the significance of interdependence between consumers and networks. Network externalities need to be addressed directly rather than tacitly as the evolution from one technological generation to another will follow in rapid success. New products face the challenge of having to replace older platforms. Each new product faces the gradual climb towards critical mass, a period of exponential growth and the limitation of market size. The strategies to be adopted are wide and varied. Should the strategy of open platforms be retained? When is the best time for a network operator to introduce a new service? What is the role of innovation and process efficiency in the quest for new subscribers? Would the current copycat strategies lead to a reduction in innovation, or would the equipment providers balance out this factor?

References

1   Valente, T (1995) *Network Models of the Diffusion of Innovations*, Hampton, VA: Hampton Press Communication Series.
2   Valente, ibid p. 9.
3   *Mobile Communications*, Nov 11, 1999.
4   *Mobile Communications*, 261/3.
5   *Financial Times*, May 4, 2002
6   Nattermann, PM (2000) 'The German Cellular Market: A Case of Involuntary Competition?' *McKinsey Quarterly*, 2, pp. 22–31.
7   Nattermann, PM (1999) 'The German Cellular Market: A Case of Involuntary Competition?' *McKinsey Quarterly*, 1(4) August.
8   Sammut-Bonnici T. and McGee I (2002) 'Emerging Strategies for New Industry Structures', *European Business Journal*, December pp. 174–185.
9   Vercoulen, F and Wegberg, M (1998) 'Standard Selection Modes in Dynamic, Complex Industries: Creating Hybrids Between Market Selection and Negotiated Selection of Standards', Maastricht: Nibor Working Paper, Nib98006.
10 Langlois, RN and Robertson, PL (1992) 'Networks and Innovation in A Modular System: Lessons from the Microcomputer and Stereo Component Industries', *Research Policy*, 21(4), pp. 297–313.
11 Morris, CR and Ferguson, CH (1993) 'How Architecture Wins Technology Wars', *Harvard Business Review*, 71(2), pp. 86–96.
12 Henderson, RM and Clark (KB) (1990) 'Architectural Innovation: The Reconfiguration of Existing Product Technologies and the Failure of Established Firms', *Administrative Science Quarterly*, 35, pp. 9–30.
13 Valetti, TM and Cave M (1998) 'Competition in UK Mobile Communications', *Telecommunications Policy*, 22, pp. 109–131.
14 Sammut-Bonnici, T and Wensley, R (2002) 'Darwinism, Probability and Complexity – Transformation and Change Explained through the Theories of Evolution,' *International Journal of Management Reviews*, 4, pp. 291–315.

WARWICK
BUSINESS SCHOOL

Case 19 **The low-cost airline industry in Europe**

After 31 years and several economic downturns, Southwest continues to validate its founding philosophy: maintaining permanent low-costs as a basis for permanently low fares is the only way to run a permanently profitable airline. Air Transport World, 22nd July 2002

History

The European low-cost airlines copied the format from Southwest Airlines, based in Texas. After 31 years of operations, Southwest has proved that the business model is sustainable. In 2003 Southwest's pre-tax profits of $483 million were more than all the other US airlines combined. In the same year American Airlines (the worlds largest carrier) posted a loss of $1.2 billion, while another of the US major carriers – Delta – lost $773 million Furthermore, in May of the same year Southwest boarded 6.54 million domestic passengers, which was more than Delta (6.34 million) and American Airlines (6.22 million). For the first time in aviation history a low-cost airline was the market leader.

Southwest offers a low-fare, high-frequency, point-to-point no-frills service that is in marked contrast to the established market offering from the US major carriers that provide a hub-based network (meaning that customers will often fly via an intermediate point in order to reach their destination), which incurs greater costs and results in higher fares for passengers. The relative success can be seen through Southwest's financial results (see Appendix 1 for a full details), the year-end results for 2003 marked Southwest's 31st consecutive year of profitability. During the same year, United Airlines lost $47 on every passenger that boarded one of its aircraft. In the USA the low-cost airlines now account for 32% of all domestic passenger traffic, and JP

Morgan's market forecasts show this could reach 40% by 2006.[1]

Considering the financial success of Southwest, it comes as little surprise that the majors are fighting back with a low-cost formula of their own. Early in 2004 both United Airlines and Delta Airlines started to operate with a low-cost subsidiary airline. Delta's discount airline is branded separately as 'Song', United's as 'Ted'. The perennial problem for the majors operating offshoot airlines is the ability to reduce their cost base to competitive levels. Often the subsidiary will be penalized by legacy contracts in place at the parent company (for example with the unions or suppliers). Moreover, segmenting the market between the full service and low-frills service offerings is complex. This makes the sustainability of dual operations extremely difficult to achieve in the long term.

The market is also attracting a new breed of airline that has many characteristics of the low-cost model, including point-to-point services and single aircraft type but with superior in-flight service. JetBlue, which started operations in 2000, is the leader of this group, having worked hard to reduce their operating costs to 7 cents per mile, which is 0.5 cents less than Southwest.[2] To date, however, JetBlue has studiously avoided head-to-head competition with Southwest and consequently downward pressure on yields for both airlines has not occurred. Notwithstanding, JetBlue harbours ambitious expansion plans (intending to spend $7 billion to take the fleet size to 290 by 2011), so ultimately direct competition in an overcrowded market is likely to occur.

The key attributes of Southwest's success

Southwest was the first airline to consider going back-to-basics with air travel. It determined that a basic product offering could strip away unnecessary operating expenses. First to be discarded was the assignment of seats and the provision of in-flight meals. Not only did this save on catering and cleaning costs, but it also allowed for an alternative cabin configuration that eliminated the on-board galley, thus freeing up space for more seats to generate more revenue.

Stephen Hodge prepared this case under the supervision of John McGee as a basis for class discussion rather than to illustrate either effective or ineffective handling of a business situation.

---

[1] 'Trouble in low fare land', *Wall Street Journal*, 13 February 2004.

[2] *Smart Money*, June 2002, pp. 102–106.

Operational efficiency is achieved via the utilization of a single aircraft type (Southwest started with three B737s in 1971; at the end of 2003 it operated 398). This simplifies scheduling and flight operations, reduces maintenance cost by decreasing spare parts inventory and rationalizes training of both engineers and crew. Another critical benefit of operating a single aircraft type is the potential to negotiate favourable terms with the aircraft manufacturers; Southwest was the launch customer for three versions of the B737 – the 300, 500 and 700 series. Moreover, Southwest quickly realized that aircraft make no money when they are sitting on the ground, so it pioneered the concept of a quick turnaround. The average amount of time spent at the gate is 20 minutes. For an industry characterized by high fixed cost high asset utilization is the key to success; by reducing the time aircraft spend on the ground Southwest are able to offer more services with fewer aircraft – Southwest's fleet of B737s are in the air 11.09 hours per day, more than any other major airline.[3]

Further efficiency is achieved through employee productivity. The US airline industry has a long history of having poor labour relations. However, Southwest's employees, which are non-unionized, are considered an integral part of their success; the pilots fly 80 hours per month in comparison to 50 hours at United Airlines, while flight attendants work 150 hours per month compared to 80 hours at many rival airlines. Herb Kelleher, Southwest's charismatic founder, is quoted as saying, 'We are not a company of planes; we are company of people'.[4] By placing staff at the centre of the business Southwest is able to find employees willing to complete multiple tasks, for example flight attendants assist with the aircraft cabin cleaning, enabling the quick turnaround. Although the Southwest employees work longer and smarter they are still employed by one of the top 10 businesses to work for in the US, as recognized by *Fortune* magazine.[5]

Employee productivity has been achieved without sacrificing service to customers; in 2002, the *Wall Street Journal* ranked Southwest first among airlines for customer satisfaction, according to a survey by the American Customer Satisfaction Index. The unique culture instilled by Herb Kelleher has had a large part to play in the employee and customer relations. 'If the employees are happy, satisfied, dedicated, and energetic, they'll take good care of the customers. When the customers are happy, they come back. And that makes the shareholders happy.'[6] From the beginning, the employees of Southwest Airlines created a family atmosphere that fostered creativity, independence and friendliness between employees. As Southwest grew larger it interviewed the top employees in each job function; this enabled them to identify their common strengths and create 'job profiles'. These profiles were then used for training and development of existing employees. Furthermore, consistency in new recruits was maintained by the instigation of peer interviews – pilots hired pilots, and gate agents hired gate agents

Another key facet of Southwest's business model is to operate from secondary airports. Not only are these less congested, thus preserving the quick aircraft turnaround time, but they also offer convenience to passengers with locations closer to city centres than principal hub airports (e.g. Houston Hobby, Chicago Midway). By avoiding the major hub airports Southwest are able to select markets which are underserved in terms of frequency and have high fares. The strategy of choosing to compete in these markets means that Southwest avoids head-to-head competition with other low-fare airlines, instead choosing to attack the domain of the major carriers. Consequently it is common for fares to drop by much as 70% once Southwest enters the market. This strategy has proved to be so successful that Southwest has a 69% market share on their top 100 city-pair markets.[7]

Deregulation of the European airline industry

One of the catalysts for Southwest's growth was the deregulation of the US domestic market for air travel in 1978. Within Europe complete liberalization of the air transport industry was not completed until 1993. Until this time the industry was highly regulated, mostly because of the protectionism offered by countries whose objective was to promote their

---

[3] Southwest Annual Report, 2003.

[4] Southwest Annual Report, 2003.

[5] Southwest Annual Report, 2003.

[6] Jon Magratta, *What Management is: How it works and why it's everyone's business*, The Free Press, 2002, p. 199.

[7] Southwest Annual Report, 2002.

own national carriers. The industry was characterized by government interference, over capacity, poor management, large-scale losses and state aid. The effect of liberalization was to reduce the barriers to entry for new airlines and open up routes for competition. Prior to liberalization, most routes within Europe were operated solely by the (mostly state-owned) national flag carriers. As a result, competition was limited and consumers had little choice except to pay high fares. However, in spite of there being a highly regulated market most nationalized airlines contrived to mount up large losses, often requiring national government subsidies in order to maintain the prestige associated with airline operations. Paradoxically the liberalization of European air transport services initially increased the level of state aid for European airlines as they undertook massive restructuring programmes in order to become more competitive in the future. SAS – the Scandinavian-based airline – reported that European airlines were granted $12.5 billion during the period 1991–1997.[8] See Appendix 2 for a full breakdown.

In theory, liberalization allowed EU-based airlines to operate on routes between member states but, in practice, this proved difficult to execute; in order to fly between two points an airline needs take-off and landing permission (known as a slot) from the relevant airport authorities. For historical reasons the national flag carriers control a large percentage of the slots at the principal hub airports of London Heathrow, Paris Charles De Gaulle and Frankfurt, thus creating a barrier to entry. Increasingly, the flag carriers are realizing the value of these slots and a grey market in slot trading has now opened up – in 2003 BA paid SN Brussels (the airline created from the bankruptcy of Sabena) £30 million for eight daily slot pairs.[9]

The low-cost airlines have been attracted by new market opportunities away from these principal airports. However, most ventures have proved to be short-lived. Of the 80 carriers that began operations after 1992, 60 were bankrupt by 1996.[10] Of the starts-ups born in the 1990s two airlines have successfully exploited market opportunities: Ryanair and easyJet. Although deregulation reduced the barriers to entry, a review of low-cost airline industry over the past few years indicates that a good deal more than access to financial capital and a couple of leased B737s is required in order to set up a profitable airline. Excluding Ryanair and easyJet, the European low-cost segment accumulated losses of almost $300 million between 1996 and 2001.[11] Casualties of these losses included Debonair, AB Airlines and ColorAir. easyJet and Ryanair have also seen off potential competitors through acquisition (easyJet purchased GO in 2002, while Ryanair acquired Buzz), and between them they account for 88%[12] of the scheduled low-cost market in Europe. Considering that Southwest Airlines has a market share of 50% of the US low-cost market, the advantage of entering the market early, building brand recognition and establishing a route network is clear. Later entrants have difficulty in matching the cost base, providing sufficiently low fares and building up traffic. Although the low-cost airlines now account for 7% of intra-European air travel as measured by the number of passengers flown, many forecasts predict that penetration rates have the potential to reach 25%.[13] The winners in capturing this growth will be, as per Southwest's model, those with the greatest cost advantage.

Ryanair

We want to be the Wal-Mart of the Airline business. No one will beat us on price. Ever. (Michael O'Leary, Ryanair CEO, Ryanair Annual Report 2002)

Ryanair began operating in 1985 with small fifteen-seater aircraft on point-to-point routes between England and Ireland. By 1990 Ryanair was serving

---

[8] 'Air France aid attacked', *Air Transport World*, August 1998, Vol. 35 Issue 8, p. 9.

[9] 'Swiss Slots', *Financial Times*, London, 24 September 2003, p. 20.

[10] Thomas Lawton, *Cleared for takeoff: Structure and strategy in the low fare airline business*, Ashgate Publishing.

[11] Ibid.

[12] Bingelli and Pompeo, *The McKinsey Quarterly*, 'Hyped hopes for Europe's low-cost airlines', 2002, No. 4.

[13] Ibid.

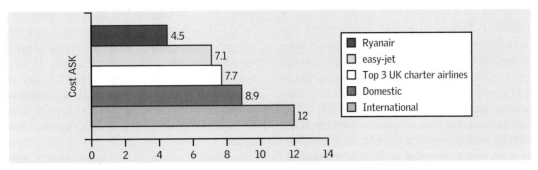

Figure 1 Cost comparison: Ryanair versus other airlines (costs are quoted per available seat kilometre (ASK) 2001 in cents)
Source: Bingelli and Pompeo, *The McKinsey Quarterly*, 'Hyped hopes for Europe's low-cost airlines', 2002, No. 4.

26 city pairs and carrying 700,000 passengers but it was in financial difficulties.[14] The reincarnation of Ryanair began when Michael O'Leary was sent to Texas to examine Southwest's operations. Consequently the Ryanair business model is a clone of Southwest's and O'Leary is now the CEO of Ryanair. O'Leary has many traits in common with Southwest's Herb Kelleher. O'Leary is a fiercely competitive character who relishes a fight and has spurred Ryanair on to become Europe's most successful, most profitable and highly valued airline. By 2002 Ryanair had a market capitalization of €4.9 billion, some 45% larger than British Airways.

Ryanair's growth has been based on defining the market for low-cost travel. New routes have provided a low-cost alternative to the flag carriers with the average price of a one-way ticket on an international intra-European route of €50–€85,

Table 1 Breakdown of Ryanair cost advantage versus top 3 major international flag carriers (all costs are per ASK and quoted in cents)

Cost item	Cost advantage	Ryanair's advantage per ASK
Overhead	Lower general, administration cost	0.5
Distribution	Internet sales account for 94% of bookings. No travel agents' commission paid	1.7
Passenger services	No catering costs	0.8
Crew costs	Higher crew productivity, pilots paid according to hours worked. Commonality due to single aircraft type	0.6
Airport charges, ground handling	Lower charges due to use of secondary airports. Negotiated better ground handling charges	2.6
Seat density	15% more seats per aircraft	1.3
Total		7.5

Source: adapted from Bingelli and Pompeo, *The McKinsey Quarterly*, 'Hyped hopes for Europe's low-cost airlines' 2002, No. 4.

[14] Thomas Lawton, *Cleared for takeoff: Structure and strategy in the low fare airline business*, Ashgate Publishing, p. 91.

compared to €180–€200 on British Airways or Lufthansa. Moreover, Ryanair has provided consumers with an alternative transport means – some of their routes compete directly with rail or possible car journeys e.g. Stansted–Newquay. By making air travel affordable Ryanair has fuelled their own growth, as passenger numbers increase it is able to benefit from operating efficiencies, thus creating a multiplier effect of ever decreasing costs and fares. However, at the same time, profits have continued to rise from 2000 to 2003 profits grew by 44%, 44% and 59%, with the highest operating margins in the industry. Appendix 3 contains more detailed information on Ryanair's financial performance.

The basis for Ryanair's success has been the cloning of Southwest Airlines efficient operations with low fares made possible by lower operating costs. Figure 1 and Table 1 provide a cost comparison between Ryanair and other European airlines.

As Table 1 indicates, a part of Ryanair's cost advantage comes from the way that O'Leary has also cleverly exploited his suppliers. Away from the congested hub airports there is a vast amount overcapacity in secondary airports across Europe. O'Leary took advantage of this by exploiting local regeneration efforts – in Charleroi, Belgium, Ryanair received €15 million as a sweetener from the regional government. However, in February 2004 the European Commission ruled that this amounted to state aid (the regional government provided the funds as a spur for economic regeneration) and Ryanair were forced to pay back €4 million of the subsidy. The implication of this ruling for Ryanair is that future route development will become more difficult. Subsidies from regional governments enabled them to slowly build the critical mass of passengers required for profitable operations. Without the subsidy it is likely that some of Ryanair's thin routes will be cancelled. Furthermore, it also sends a signal to airports competing for Ryanair's business that the balance of power may shift back in their favour.

With an operating model of ruthless cost control, quick aircraft turn time (Ryanair match Southwest's 20-minute average) and servicing secondary airports, Ryanair is able to stimulate the demand for air travel by providing a cost-effective alternative to other transport modes. All of these factors are a mirror image of Southwest's operations. However, one area that Ryanair has conspicuously chosen not to copy Southwest is in customer care. O'Leary's mantra is low fares, not customer service. In contrast to Herb Kelleher, O'Leary views the two as being mutually exclusive. Customer service is seen as an additional expense and a barrier to keeping fares low. One of O'Leary's politer quotes regarding customers is 'What part of no refund don't they understand?'[15] His mission is to re-educate customers that flying should be akin 'to taking a bus' and that low fares can only be achieved through cutting of costs across the board. Unlike easyJet there is no compensation for delayed flights and customer complaints are given only cursory attention.

easyJet

If you create the right expectations and you meet or exceed those expectations, then you will have happy customers. (Stelios Haji-Ioannou, easyJet's founder, IMD Case Study easyJet 'The Web's Favorite Airline')

Around the same time that Ryanair were copying the Southwest model, Stelios Haji-Ioannou (who likes to be known as just Stelios) was developing his own version of a low-cost airline, based out of London's Luton airport. Stelios is the son of a Greek shipping magnate and persuaded his father to invest £5 million in his start-up airline. Stelios started operations at the end of 1995 with two leased B737s and, in order to keep costs down, acted as a virtual airline by contracting-in everything required from pilots to check-in staff.

easyJet's inaugural flights were from Luton to Edinburgh and Glasgow, which were promoted via innovative advertising on the side of the aircraft 'Fly to Scotland for the price of a pair of Jeans'. In the early days easyJet used aggressive marketing techniques in order to build up brand recognition and attack the competitors. easyJet has probably been the most successful low-cost airline at attacking the market space traditionally occupied by the full service airlines, especially British Airways and BMI

---

[15] 'Ryanair talks of disaster, but the low-cost revolution flies on', *Financial Times*, 7 February 2004.

in the UK and Swiss in Switzerland. Until now, as in the US, direct competition between the low-cost airlines is rare.

Stelios became famous for high-profile media battles with competitors, for example when British Airways launched it's own low-cost subsidiary GO, which ironically was later purchased by easyJet; with suppliers, when Luton airport wanted to raise landing charges associated with easyJet's operations; or with government as Stelios successfully lobbied for fairness on air passenger duty (airport tax). All of these stunts were orchestrated in order to educate the general public on the true costs of air travel and to promote the benefits of a low-cost alternative. The spin-off was that customers saw that there was a real benefit to flying on a low-cost carrier, while companies with large travel budgets also recognized that low-cost provided a real alternative to full service airlines. In October 1999, readers of *Business Traveller* magazine voted 'Best Low-cost Airline' easyJet.

easyJet increased profits during the 5-year period 1999–2003 from £21.1 million to £138.6 million, however, the pre-tax profit margin remained unchanged at 15% (see Appendix 4). A part of easyJet's success is attributed to the unique working culture that Stelios instilled in the airline. In common with Southwest Airlines, the objective was to build a strong, inclusive employee-led culture at easyLand – the airline's headquarters. The culture was determined to a large extent by the easyJet Culture Committee, an elected group drawn from company staff, whose remit was to establish company policy on the working environment and management communications, as well as organize the social calendar. Stelios's belief was that 'work should be fun' and even went as far as to make the position of 'party animal' an official one. The objective was to instil a sense of pride in the staff, which would enable superior customer service.

The confidence that Stelios had in his staff was portrayed in January 1999 when he allowed ITV to provide a fly-on-the-wall documentary of life for both the passengers and staff at easyJet. By the end of the year the programme had become ITV's most successful docu-soap with 9 million viewers. For easyJet it provided priceless publicity. However, without a strong culture of customer service this

venture may well have proved to be a spectacular own goal. In contrast to O'Leary, Stelios took customer satisfaction extremely seriously, often taking easyJet flights in order to interact with the passengers. Stelios believed that this was the best form of market research possible. easyJet's approach to customer service was acknowledged in March 2001 when it was the only low-cost airline to be ranked in the first division of a customer satisfaction table in a *Holiday Which?* survey. All of easyJet's core values are summarized in their mission statement.

easyJet's mission statement

To provide our customers with safe, low-cost, good-value, point-to-point air services. To offer a consistent and reliable product at fares appealing to leisure and business markets from our bases to a range of domestic and European destinations. To achieve this we will develop our people and establish long lasting partnerships with our suppliers.

Source: www.easyjet.com.

easyJet's business model is based on direct sale to the end customer. Unlike Southwest Airlines it does not pay travel agents for even a small proportion of their business and it estimates this saves them 25% on distribution costs. Since April 1998 easyJet has been encouraging customers to book online and within 18 months had achieved one million sales via the Internet. In order to encourage online sales easyJet were the first to provide a discount for seats booked via the web. Furthermore, it amended their online booking policy so that seats purchased more than two months in advance could only be booked online. Moreover, web bookings provided customers with complete control over their itinerary; they could quickly compare the costs of alternative travel dates and times, which was aided by the one-way fares on offer. The flexibility over fares offered was extended to cover changes to existing bookings – for £10 plus the difference between the two fares, easyJet provided full flexibility on time of travel. This was in marked contrast to the traditional full service airlines which placed a large number of restrictions on their 'economy' tickets. Because easyJet had transparent and flexible pricing it quickly started to attract business travellers eager to find cost-effective travel solutions. On some routes business travellers soon accounted for 50% of the passengers.

In contrast to Ryanair, easyJet's expansion has been based around operations from Europe's principal cities – easyJet now have bases in Geneva, Amsterdam, London Gatwick, Paris and Berlin to support Luton. In this context easyJet has drifted away from the original low-cost model of operations to secondary airports in order to preserve the quick aircraft turnaround times and efficient asset utilization required for low-cost airline operations. However, the focus is still very much on filling as many seats as possible. The objective is to maximize the revenue per passenger. This is achieved through a yield management system – as demand for a flight increased then so does the fare. The system is designed to ensure the optimal balance between available capacity, the number of seats sold and the revenue each passenger contributes. Appendix 4 contains detailed load factor data from 1999–2003.

Another golden rule of low-cost airline operations has also been breached by easyJet. After a yearlong head-to-head battle between the two principal aircraft manufacturers easyJet announced in October 2002 its intention to appoint Airbus as its preferred aircraft supplier. As part of the deal easyJet placed a firm order for 120 Airbus A319 aircraft for delivery over 5 years from September 2003, with an option to purchase a further 120 with protected prices. By turning to Airbus, easyJet has lost the efficiencies in training, maintenance and the lower operating costs that are associated with single fleet operations. Despite the additional complexities of operating another type of aircraft easyJet maintain that the financial benefits of the deal far outweigh the integration costs. Sir Colin Chandler, easyJet's Chairman, stated that the Airbus deal was 'significantly better value than the offer made by Boeing'.[16] Moreover, easyJet expects that the Airbus will offer a cost decrease of 10% against their current B737 fleet. However, it should be noted that Ryanair has chosen the B737-800 as the basis for their fleet, which provides 28 more seats than the A319.

Appendix 9 contains data on the number of seats by aircraft type.

easyJet's strategy of serving Europe's primary airports, targeting the business traveller and mixing the fleet, creates an impression of a conventional airline business model, when compared with Ryanair. This would provide an explanation of, as per Figure 1, easyJet's cost disadvantage of 2.6 cents per ASK versus Ryanair. In the long run this may prove to be a critical source of competitive advantage for Ryanair.

Competition

The response from British Airways

The effect of the low-cost airlines targeting passengers from the traditional full service airlines has been catastrophic on the profitability of British Airways (BA) (see Appendix 5), the response to which was to announce the 'future size and shape' programme in February 2002. BA's CEO Rod Eddington described the programme as being 'based on three simple tenets: to reduce cost, restructure the short-haul operations, and remove complexity from the business'. The target is to deliver £650 million in annualized saving by March 2004,[17] the majority of which comes from manpower savings. In essence BA are playing catch-up with the low-cost carriers; it is applying elements of the low-cost business model to a full service airline. These include increasing the number of Internet bookings, price flexibility and rationalizing operations.

After flirting with their own low-cost airline operation (GO) BA was one of the first to realize that the market for short-haul traffic was undergoing a structural change as a result of low-cost airlines rather than a cyclical change. BA sold GO in June 2001 to a venture capital backed management buyout led by Barbara Cassani. At the time of the sale Eddington was quoted as saying that the £110 million. BA received for GO represented a good return on the initial investment of £25 million made three years earlier.[18] The sale of GO was one of

---

[16] easyJet letter to shareholders, 24 February 2003. Available on www.easyjet.com.

[17] 'BA keeps taking the medicine', *Financial Times*, 10 Feb. 2004.

[18] BA press release, 14 June 2001, available on www. britishairways.com.

Eddington's first acts when he took the helm at BA, the rationale being that operating a no-frills service alongside a full service strategy was not sustainable in the long term. More specifically BA were finding it difficult to justify a substantial price premium for the full service offering, effectively it was eating into its own profits. Subsequently, in August 2002, easyJet acquired GO for £374 million, creating Europe's largest low-cost airline.

Although BA is not yet breaking even on short-haul operations, previous losses have been greatly reduced. As a result of adjusting their business model full service airlines are now able to offer an alternative to low-cost travel. Having finally realized that in the post deregulation age supply of capacity is not tightly controlled and price-sensitive customers' demand can be manipulated, the full service airlines are now able to sell the benefits of additional product features. For customers that value convenience, i.e. being flown directly to their destination, as opposed to a satellite airport up to 100km away, and the level of service associated with a traditional airline including assigned seating and onboard meal service, the established airlines have started to provide an affordable alternative to the low-cost carriers. Indeed, much of BA's current advertising is explicit in promoting the benefits of travel with a full service airline. However, as Willie Walsh of Aer Lingus points out, the size of the premium charged for additional service features has shrunk forever.

BMI

As the UK's second largest airline after BA, BMI has proved vulnerable to the growth of low-cost carriers. BMI's main base is at London Heathrow, where it holds 14% of the available landing slots. BMI operates around 2000 flights per week with a fleet of 53 aircraft. Although the primary focus has been on domestic and short-haul travel, BMI, as a member of the Star Alliance, is attempting to break into the more lucrative intercontinental market. As a medium-sized carrier with a relatively high fixed operating cost base BMI has lost market share to easyJet and Ryanair. See Appendix 7 for summary financial data on BMI.

BMI's response to the threat posed by the low-cost airlines has been to open its own low-cost subsidiary – bmibaby, which now has three operational bases at East Midlands, Cardiff and London Gatwick, effectively making it the third-largest low-cost operator in the UK. However, the rationale behind operations appear to be stuck somewhere in the middle between the true low-cost model and the full service airline. Some of BMI's old habits such as express check-in for business travellers, allocated seats and in-flight service have proved hard to give up. Moreover, it would appear that BMI has not heeded the warnings apparent when BA gave up trying to run a full service and a low-cost airline in tandem. In particular there is evidence that bmibaby is cannibalizing some of BMI's business by operating head-to-head on certain routes. From summer 2004 both airlines will serve Prague: BMI from London Heathrow and bmibaby from London Gatwick.

The global perspective

The low-cost revolution is now becoming a global phenomenon. In Australia, Virgin Blue, founded by Sir Richard Branson, started operations and has precipitated a vicious price war in the Australian domestic market. From mid 2004 Quantas will be fighting back with a low-cost format of their own, flying under the brand Jetstar. A similar success story can be found in Malaysia. Air Asia, formed in December 2001, now operates 15 B737-300s on point-to-point routes between Indonesia, Malaysia, Thailand and Singapore. With some one-way fares as low as $13, stimulating demand from the 500 million people who live within three hours of Air Asia's bases in Kuala Lumpur, Bangkok and Singapore is not proving to be problematic.[19] The success of these low-cost airlines is creating political pressure for further liberalization of air transport services within Asia, and at the end of 2003 Singapore Airlines (SIA), one of the world's most profitable airlines and second in terms of market capitalization, announced a joint venture in a low-cost subsidiary Tiger Airways. In some respects this a defensive move against the plans of former SIA executives to open a third low-cost carrier in Singapore during 2004, ValuAir.[20]

---

[19] 'Having fun and flying high', *The Economist*, 13 March 2004, Vol. 370, Issue 8366, p. 63.

[20] 'SIA to release Tiger in Asia low-cost airlines', *Financial Times*, p. 32, 10 December 2003.

Sustainability

As the UK market for low-cost travel becomes more saturated fewer new routes are becoming viable. As a consequence the low-cost airlines have turned their attention towards Europe in order to provide growth. easyJet and Ryanair have opened new bases in markets that are poorly served by the national airlines; seven out of the ten routes operated by Ryanair from Frankfurt Hahn were not served by Lufthansa, while easyJet's success in Geneva coincided with the decline of the Swiss national carrier Swissair. In May 2003 easyJet revealed that it was the number one carrier at Geneva airport with 26% of passengers, ahead of Swiss, Air France and BA.[21] easyJet's success in Switzerland has been a major factor in the reborn national carrier Swiss, which emerged from the high-profile bankruptcy of Swiss Air, continuing to mount losses. As witnessed in the US, in selected markets the low-cost airlines are now starting to replace the traditional flag carriers.

The advantage of this expansion strategy is that in the medium term direct competition between the low-cost carriers is avoided. However, new entrants are continuously being encouraged to fight the low-cost market. In Germany, Air Berlin has remodelled itself from being a charter carrier into a flight-only seller with operations from eight German airports to London, Milan, Vienna, Barcelona and Zurich as well as operating domestic flights within Spain from its Malaga hub. Air Berlin, with 9.6 million passengers in 2003 is now Germany's second-largest airline after Lufthansa[22] and Europe's third-largest low-cost carrier. Appendix 8 provides a comparison between Air Berlin, Ryanair and easyJet.

Outside Germany and the UK, however, the low-cost carriers may experience difficulties stimulating enough demand. Other transport modes provide greater competition, for example the high-speed rail network in France, and the propensity to travel great distances for holiday and leisure activities is much reduced. In the long run it's likely that low-cost airlines will need to compete more on a head-to-head basis, something that has largely been avoided until now. Another market segment that could come under attack from the low-cost carriers is Europe's €45 billion package-tour market. Presently the charter airline industry accounts for 21% of intra-European travel – some 45% of flights for German holidays are purchased as part of a package, a figure that has remained constant for the past five years.[23] However, as demand for package tours stagnate the vertically integrated tour companies are looking to spin off their airline operations and compete in the low-cost segment. Thompson holidays are now following My Travel's lead in starting up its own low-cost airline operation.

Any fool can grow in the airline industry whilst losing money and we are surrounded by many fine examples of this in Europe at present. The difference with Ryanair is that we achieve consistent growth, but deliver equally consistent profit growth at high margins despite offering the lowest air fares in Europe. The challenge facing us over the coming years will be to maintain our growth, whilst improving customer service, upgrading the fleet with the new Boeing B737 aircraft, but continuing to lower our unit costs and maintaining industry leading margins.
(Michael O'Leary – Ryanair Annual Report 2003)

The low-cost airlines are also susceptible to cost pressure from their suppliers. The deal for landing and passenger charges at Ryanair's biggest base – London Stansted – expires in 2006, when the airport operator BAA is commencing work on a £2 billion second runway. As the expansion must be paid for by the airlines using the airport this will force higher charges for the incumbents. At the same time, existing airport deals between secondary airports and the low-cost airlines are coming under close scrutiny from the European Commission, which is eager to stamp out any cross-subsidization. Moreover, as the industry matures the opportunities for manufacturing large cost savings become scarcer, for example switching sales on to the Internet lowered costs sharply; however,

---

[21] Source: www.easyjet.com

[22] 'An old hand at low fares', *Air Transport World*, January 2003.

[23] 'Bingelli and Pompeo, *The McKinsey Quarterly*, 'Hyped hopes for Europe's low-cost airlines', 2002, No. 4.

with easyJet and Ryanair selling about 95% of sales via the web the scope for further cost-cutting becomes limited.

As the competition increases and the established airlines start to realize operating efficiencies that allow them to compete on price with low-cost airlines, the low-cost airlines have started to experience growing pains. There is likely to be some turbulence ahead if Ryanair are to achieve their forecast of carrying 50 million passengers per year by 2009 with a fleet of 149 aircraft; recent experience has shown that as capacity has increased the yield per passenger has declined. Much of the recent growth in passenger numbers has been achieved by special promotions and giveaways to passengers with the flexibility to fly at off-peak times. In February 2004 Ryanair announced a profit warning for the first time, the root cause for which was an average year on year decline in fares of 30%. This was matched by a corresponding fall in the load factor from 81% to 77%.[24]

As the industry matures, easyJet's culture has also been evolving. In 2003 Stelios stepped down as chairman of easyJet – a sure sign that the entrepreneurial spirit required to set up the airline was less relevant in the running of a maturing business. Sir Colin Chandler, who has a long list of directorships to his name, replaced Stelios. Nonetheless, easyJet has been subjected to the same pressures on yield as Ryanair; in the six-month trading period to the end of March 2004 easyJet lost £18.5 million, which created nervousness for investors as the share price dropped by 25%.[25] The result of these financial pressures on easyJet and Ryanair is a decline in their price earnings ratios. (The price earnings (PE) ratio is generally accepted as an indicator of future profitability.) Although easyJet is presently trading at a PE ratio of 35, Ryanair's is down to 15, as compared with 35 four years ago.[26] The suggestion from analysts is that the declining revenue per passenger could be symptomatic of ambitious expansion plans (see Appendix 10 for share price data). On a more positive note, however, there is still a substantial difference between the pre-tax profit margins for the established carriers and the low-cost carriers, despite both easyJet and Southwest experiencing diminishing returns in the past couple of years.

One of the consequences of this evolution is that Ryanair entered negotiations with Boeing to reschedule the new aircraft delivery. For the next few years Ryanair are looking to maintain capacity growth at no more than 20–25%. Considering that easyJet and Ryanair have between them placed orders for 245 new aircraft there is likely to be a shakeout across the industry, particularly once head-to-head competition commences.

---

[24] 'Source: www.ryanair.com.

[25] 'easyJet takes brunt of airline sector woes', *Financial Times*, London, 6 May 2004.

[26] Data from http://finance.yahoo.com.

Appendix 1 Southwest Airlines load factor and financial data

	1999	2000	2001	2002	2003
Turnover $bn	4.735	5.649	5.555	5.521	5.937
Pre-tax profit $m	474	625	631	417	483
Pre-tax profit margin	10%	11.1%	11.4%	7.6%	8.1%
Passengers m	57.5	63.7	64.4	63	65.5
Load factor	69%	70.5%	68.1%	65.9%	6.8%
Fleet size (B737)	312	344	355	375	398

Source: company reports.

Appendix 2 State aid to European airlines 1991–1997

Air France	1991	$570
Sabena	1991	$970
Iberia	1992	$1300
Aer Lingus	1994	$250
Air France	1994	$3700
Olympic	1994	$2300
TAP	1994	$1100
Iberia	1996	$710
Alitalia	1997	$1600

Source: SAS as reported in 'Air France aid attacked', *Air Transport World*, August 1998, Vol. 35, Issue 8, p. 9.

Appendix 3 Ryanair load factor and financial data

	1999	2000	2001	2002	2003
Turnover €m	295.8	370.1	487.4	624.1	842
Pre-tax profit €m	57.5	72.5	104.5	150.1	239.4
Pre-tax profit margin	19.4%	19.5%	21.4%	24%	28.4%
Passengers m	5.3	6.1	8.1	11.1	15.7
Load factor	71%	n/a	n/a	82%	81%

Source: company reports.

Appendix 4 easyJet load factor and financial data

	1999	2000	2001	2002	2003
Turnover £m	139.8	258.9	354.9	551.8	931.8
Pre-tax profit £m	21.1	47.0	63.0	156.8	138.6
Pre-tax profit margin	15.1%	18.2%	17.8%	28.4%	14.8%
Passengers m	3.1	5.6	7.1	11.4	20.3
Load factor	75.9%	80.8%	83.0%	84.8%	84.1%

Source: company reports.
Note: Ryanair's financial data are published in €, easyJet in £.

Appendix 5 British Airways load factor and financial data

	1999	2000	2001	2002	2003
Turnover £m	8915	8940	9278	8340	7688
Pre-tax profit (loss) £m	225	5	150	(200)	135
Pre-tax profit (loss) margin	2.5%	0.5%	1.6%	(2.4%)	1.7%
Passengers m	45.0	46.6	44.4	40.0	38.0
Load factor	70.7%	69.8%	71.7%	70.4%	71.9%

Source: company reports.

Appendix 6 American Airlines load factor and financial data

	1999	2000	2001	2002	2003
Turnover $m	17730	19703	18969	17420	17440
Pre-tax profit (loss) $m	985	813	(1762)	(3511)	(1228)
Pre-tax profit (loss) margin	5.5%	4.1%	(9.2%)	(20%)	(7%)
Passengers m	n/a	n/a	n/a	94.1	88.8
Load factor	69.5%	72.4%	69.0%	70.7%	72.8%

Source: company reports.

Appendix 7 BMI selected statistics

	2000	2001	2002	2003
Turnover £m	739.2	756.9	723.8	772
Pre-tax profit (loss) £m	8.2	12.4	(19.6)	(9.8)
Pre-tax profit margin	1.1%	1.6%	(2.7%)	(1.3%)
Passengers m	7.1	6.7	7.5	9.4

Source: www.flybmi.com.

Appendix 8 Summary Table 2003 data

	easyJet	Ryanair	Air Berlin	British Airways
Profit	€76.4 m.[1]	€239.4 m.	€30 m.[2]	€198[3]
Turnover	€1370 m.	€842 m.	€880 m.	€11301
Passengers	20.3 m.	22.4 m.	9.6 m.	38.0 m.
Load factor	84.1%	81%	79.3%	71.9%
Routes	151	127	N/a	170
Aircraft				
B737	67	68	42	19
A319	5			21
BAE146		6		5
Other			3	171
Total	72	74	45	216[4]
Confirmed aircraft orders	120 (A319)	125 (B737)	n/a	20[4]

[1] The easyJet results have been converted from £ to € at the exchange rate £1 = €1.47 (http://uk.finance.yahoo.com, 4 May 2004).
[2] The Air Berlin figures are an estimate from *Air Transport World*. The company publishes no financial data.
[3] The British Airways results have also been converted from £ to € at the exchange rate £1 = €1.47.
[4] As at 31 December 2002. Source: www.bashares.com.

Appendix 9 Aircraft type and seat numbers

Aircraft	Maximum no. seats
A319	156
B737-700	149
B737-400	167
B737-800	189
BAE 146	110

Notes: easyJet is the launch customer for the A319 in a single-class cabin configuration. The maximum number of seats available on the aircraft is 156.
Ryanair inherited the BAE146 following the acquisition of Buzz in 2003. This aircraft type will be phased out and replaced by the B737-800.
Both Ryanair and Air Berlin operate the B737-800; however, Ryanair squeeze an additional 5 seats into their version (189 vs 184).
Source: Company websites.

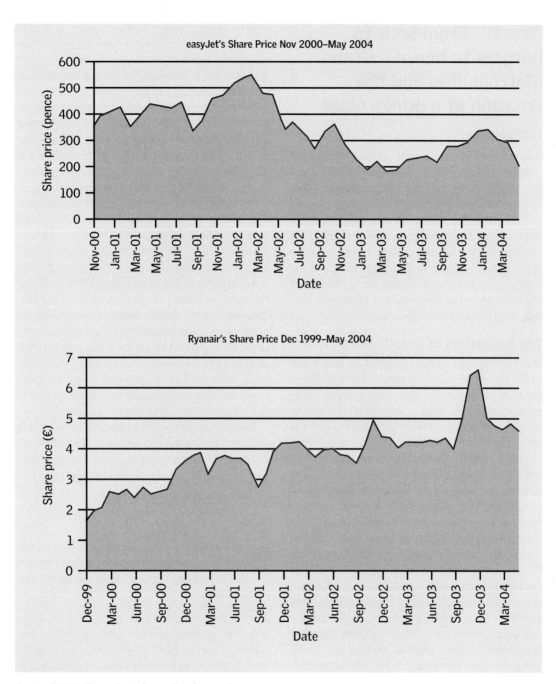

Appendix 10 Ryanair and easyJet share prices
Source: adapted from data published on http://uk.finance.yahoo.com.

This case study was prepared for this textbook by faculty members at Warwick Business School, University of Warwick, UK. This case study may not be reproduced in any form without prior permission. For more information, visit www.wbs.ac.uk.

Case 20 From beds to burgers to booze – Grand Metropolitan and the creation of a drinks giant

Introduction

Diageo is the world's largest alcoholic beverages company and was formed in December 1997 from the merger of its two predecessor firms, Grand Metropolitan and Guinness. This case examines the transformation of Grand Metropolitan from its origins as a hotel company in post Second World War London, through the various changes of direction it experienced prior to the merger with Guinness in 1997 and follows the story through to the present day to analyse the problems and challenges that have and continue to face Diageo.

The foundation of Grand Metropolitan

The foundation of Grand Metropolitan in the late 1940s was down to the entrepreneurial activities of one man – Max Joseph. Joseph was a career entrepreneur, who had been a successful real estate investor and estate agent prior to the start of the Second World War. He began purchasing a serious of hotels from 1947 onwards. These hotels were originally focused on London but gradually expanded to cover various overseas locations including Paris, Amsterdam, Monte Carlo and New York.

During this initial period of Grand Metropolitan's development and expansion, the culture of the organisation remained relaxed and non-bureaucratic. For example, the purchase of hotels was undertaken quickly, based on Joseph's innate business judgement and without the aid of detailed business analysis. The growth of the business, however, gradually forced a change and introduced a demand for more advanced management control systems and resulted in the hiring of Stanley Grinstead, a future CEO of the business, as its Chief Accountant in 1960. This move was quickly followed by the firm's IPO in 1961.

Robert Salter prepared this case under the supervision of John McGee as a basis for class discussion rather than to illustrate either effective or ineffective handling of a business situation.

© Robert Salter, Warwick Business School, 2004.

Although Grand Metropolitan started to acquire various non-hotel businesses from the mid 1960s, during this period of the company's history, Joseph was still keen to follow the same basic business concepts and ideas that had worked with his acquisitions in the hotel trade. Throughout this period, the core principle was that the business acquired 'trading property assets', with the idea being that the cash flow from the business needed to be sufficient to cover the costs of servicing any debts that had been built up to acquire the properties concerned.

While Joseph focused on only acquiring those assets which he believed would innately rise in value (e.g. because of the increasing demand for hotels), his management style didn't specifically focus on the subsequent ongoing control and management of the acquired business. The focus of Grand Metropolitan at this time was based on 'making deals' rather than specifically looking to add shareholder value from the acquired entities. It was therefore standard practice for Grand Metropolitan to leave the existing management of an acquired organisation in place following an acquisition, while the CEO or Chairman of any significant businesses that were acquired was typically invited on to the Grand Metropolitan board of directors.[1]

Though the acquisitions of the mid to late 1960s extended the company's original management and business philosophy into new areas, Jospeh insisted that all acquisitions satisfied the following criteria:

1 the companies acquired needed to be in businesses that were in some generic sense related to the hotel trade; and

2 the businesses were required to be property intensive – this was an extension of the 'trading property assets' concept that has been mentioned above.

Among the businesses that were acquired during this period were several catering firms, pub-restaurants and a chain of off-licences. However, by the late 1960s, the firm's requirements regarding its future acquisitions were gradually relaxing and the early 1970s saw a move into less related industries and segments. This period saw the acquisition of

---

[1] The practice of inviting the Chairman/CEO of acquired businesses on to the Grand Metropolitan board resulted in the company's board growing to 18 at one stage.

Express Dairies in 1969,[2] and Mecca, a dance hall, bingo hall and casino group, in 1970.

Most acquisitions until this stage had been undertaken on a friendly basis (Express Dairies was the one notable exception). However, this focus on friendly acquisitions changed with the takeover of the brewer Truman, Hanbury and Buxton (THB) in 1972 after an acquisition process that lasted 9 months. The eventual price paid (£48 million) was the most paid by Grand Metropolitan for any acquisition up to that date and was approximately 50% more than the price for Express Dairies only 3 years earlier.

The acquisition of THB subsequently led to the the acquisition of British brewer, Watney Mann, later in 1972. Watney Mann was a significantly bigger brewer than THB and also included its own distillery subsidiary, IDV. As with the THB acquisition, the takeover process was drawn out and Grand Metropolitan was required to make three separate offers for the company before a bid of £435 million was eventually agreed upon. This price was the most ever paid for an acquisition in Britain up to that date and left Grand Metropolitan with significant debt levels, just as economic conditions in Britain began to deteriorate significantly.

The years of struggle

From 1973, Britain was racked with a serious of economic problems, caused by the effects of international oil price rises and intensive industrial action by Britain's coal miners, which resulted in a 3-day working week being introduced by the British government due to serious energy shortages. At the same time, Grand Metropolitan was being seriously squeezed because of its high debt levels and these problems were being compounded by the following circumstances:

1   Its failure to successfully divest the spirits division (IDV) of Watney Mann, as had originally

been planned when the acquisition was undertaken.

2   A significant fall in UK property values, which threatened to undermine the strength of Grand Metropolitan's balance sheet.

The pressures faced by the company during this period resulted in it having to announce its first fall in trading profits in 1974, and resulted in the firm focusing on trying to improve the trading performance of its various divisions to avoid a genuine threat of bankruptcy. As part of the focus on improving the group's trading performance, Allen Sheppard was recruited by Joseph to specifically head up the brewing division of Grand Metropolitan. At the same time, the group's spirits division, IDV, was separated from the brewing division and placed under the leadership of Anthony Tennant.

Sheppard and Tennant both set about improving the performance of their respective divisions aggressively, but did this in very different styles. While Sheppard successfully revitalised and strengthened the sales of Watney Mann's regional beers, his core focus during this period was on reducing head count within the division and on cutting costs. In contrast, the focus at IDV was very much on improving the marketing and promotion of IDV's brands and there was no significant focus during this period on product or cost rationalisation.

Despite the very different business philosophies that had been followed by Sheppard and Tennant, both approaches proved highly successful. By the late 1970s, Grand Metropolitan's profits and cash flows had significantly improved and the firm was once again in a strong financial position – this was the result of both the improvement in the firm's trading income and the revitalised UK property market which helped increase the value of the assets shown on the company's balance sheet.

US diversification

Joseph and Grinstead were aware that Grand Metropolitan had been on the edge of bankruptcy during the mid 1970s and took from this experience a determination that the firm should never again be as dependant purely on the UK economy as it had been at that stage. Therefore, as the company's

---

[2] Although the Express Dairies business did include hotel and restaurant subsidiaries, the door-to-door milk delivery business was at the core of its operations. At this time, the firm controlled approximately 25% of all door-to-door milk deliveries in the UK.

financial position improved in the late 1970s, they became increasingly receptive to the idea of international expansion.

The first serious opportunity for international expansion resulted in the acquisition of the US-based Liggett Group in 1981. While the Liggett Group included the distributor of IDV's products in the US, the firm was involved in a wide range of other products (e.g. pet food, cigarettes and fitness equipment), and had only a limited focus on property. Although Joseph was unconvinced about the merits of this acquisition, it was pushed through by Grinstead who had by this stage replaced Joseph as Chairman of Grand Metropolitan, despite the fact that it brought the company into areas of business in which they had little or no experience.

Following the acquisition of the Liggett Group, Grand Metropolitan acquired Intercontinental Hotels from Pan-Am Airlines. As with many of the acquisitions of the 1950s and 1960s, the Intercontinental Hotels acquisition was completed quickly (within one week). However, while the Intercontinental deal offered Grant Metropolitan the 'comfort' of being in a business which it new well, this acquisition did at the same time represent a step away from the focus on acquiring 'trading property assets'. In reality, few of the Intercontinental hotels were actually directly owned – rather, they were typically operated by the group under management contract and franchise arrangements.

Following Joseph's death in the early 1980s, Grinstead continued to focus on acquiring further companies in the US. During this period, Grinstead's principles when considering potential purchases and acquisitions were based around the following:

1 Acquiring service companies in general, on the basis that he believed the service sector in general would expand more quickly over the coming years than manufacturing.

2 Looking to continue diversifying away the risks associated with only doing most of Grand Metropolitan's business purely in the UK.

During the period up until the mid 1980s, the span of acquisitions undertaken by Grand Metropolitan under Grinstead's chairmanship was wide ranging and diverse. The companies acquired provided services ranging from childcare, home-based healthcare and optical retailing.

While Grinstead was focused on the US acquisitions policy during the early to mid 1980s, the company also became increasingly focused on trying to increase the operational performance of its business units, in contrast to the very 'hands-off' management style that had traditionally been a feature of Grand Metropolitan's philosophy. The process of focusing on operational improvement was, in many respects, led by Sheppard, and his team pursued an aggressive policy of rationalising the business units for which they were responsible. The 'Sheppard approach' to operational improvement focused on the divestment of underperforming or peripheral facilities or business units, but also tried to combine this rationalisation focus with improved marketing performance and a decentralised management policy that provided operational managers with real autonomy.

The Sheppard approach worked very effectively in the areas under his responsibility (basically the UK brewing and food businesses). However, Tennant at IDV continued to pursue a very different policy and was in some respects even more successful. IDV gradually became Grand Metropolitan's largest profit source, based on a strategy that focused heavily on trying to control the distribution channels, so that IDV could get as close as possible to the end-customers of its products, and an ongoing heavy investment in product marketing and branding. During this period under Tennant, IDV also successfully focused on the development of a range of new alcoholic beverages.[3] Under Tennant, throughout this period there continued to be no specific focus at IDV on cost control and product rationalisation.

However, despite the successes of Tennant and Sheppard, by 1986, the investors in the City of London had begun to lose confidence in Grinstead's emphasis on expansion. Grand Metropolitan's earnings per share growth had ceased by 1986 (although the company remained profitable), and around this

---

[3] Among the products that were developed by IDV during this period was Bailey's Irish Cream, which became the best selling product in its market segment worldwide. During the 1980s, IDV introduced 32% of all the new products of the world's 7 biggest alcoholic beverages companies.

time, the Grand Metropolitan's shares were being downgraded by the City. By the time that Grinstead stepped down in 1987, to be replaced by Sheppard as CEO and Chairman, there were strong rumours and suggestions in the City that a corporate raider might try to take over Grand Metropolitan with the aim of selling off the individual divisions of the firm.

The Sheppard years

Despite the City's dissatisfaction with the acquisitions policy that had been pursued by Grand Metropolitan during the early to mid 1980s, acquisitions continued under Sheppard's leadership. The two key acquisitions during the Sheppard years were Heublein from RJR Nabisco in 1987 (a move which doubled the size of IDV's spirits business) and Pillsbury in 1989. The acquisition of Pillsbury enabled Grand Metropolitan to expand its food business on an international scale,[4] while also providing it with significant rationalisation opportunities in accordance with Sheppard's tried and tested approach to business.

The Grand Metropolitan team that moved into Pillsbury's operations after its acquisition was led by Ian Martin, one of Sheppard's key disciples. This team removed about one-third of Pillsbury's existing management within 12 months of the acquisition as part of its stated policy of cutting the division's operating costs, improving the impact of the well-known Pillsbury brands and developing new products and/or markets.

While Sheppard oversaw the acquisition of these two businesses, there was a simultaneous focus on divesting unwanted or unnecessary Grand Metropolitan businesses in a move that became known as 'Operation De-cluster'. The strategic focus under Sheppard was for Grand Metropolitan to increasingly focus on food, drinks and retailing, with all businesses that remained in the group needing to show that they could satisfy the following three criteria:

1 a good brand image;

2 good market shares; and

3 an international scope.

The decision to focus on only the food, drinks and retail businesses was based on the idea that it was better to be a leader in a few areas than a real 'jack-of-all-trades' with no specific strengths. As part of this policy of greater specialisation, Grand Metropolitan did consider the possibility of focusing on purely one market area, but at the end of the day, the company was not at this stage willing to 'put all of its eggs in one basket'. This was despite the fact that Sheppard was aware that the highly focused approach would provide Grand Metropolitan with the opportunity to benefit from the maximum amount of specialist knowledge and focus.

In addition to the big acquisitions and the wide ranging series of corporate disposals, the Sheppard years were characterised by a significant focus on trying to change the overall management philosophy and corporate culture within Grand Metropolitan. Many of Sheppard's key management team from his time in charge of the UK food and brewing businesses replaced the existing central Grand Metropolitan management teams in areas such as personnel and finance. At IDV, where George Bull had replaced Anthony Tennant,[5] the influence of Sheppard and his management policies was slightly more muted than elsewhere within Grand Metropolitan, because of IDV's long history of closely guarded independence and overall level of profitability relative to other areas of the business. However, even so, IDV saw a greater emphasis on cost reduction and rationalisation during these years than had previously been the case.

At the same time, under Sheppard, Grand Metropolitan placed a great deal of emphasis on the training of managers – e.g. via an organised policy of internal transfers throughout the group, in an attempt to spread best practices as widely as possible. Per Sheppard, the role of the corporate centre during this period encompassed the following factors:

1 It was responsible for providing a 'tough and challenging culture' for top management that

---

[4] Among the businesses owned by Pillsbury were Burger King, Pillsbury Doughboy, Haagen Dazs Ice Cream and Green Giant.

[5] Tennant left IDV in 1990 to become CEO of Guinness.

was focused on demanding superior operational performance and cost leadership.

2   It focused on spotting and nurturing management talent within the various Grand Metropolitan business units.

3   It should focus simultaneously on improving operational performance with the business units and improving the branding and promotion of Grand Metropolitan's products.

The post-Sheppard years

Sheppard retired as Chairman and CEO of Grand Metropolitan in 1993. Although he had originally proposed that he should be replaced by Ian Martin, who had been responsible for overseeing the rationalisation and turnaround of the Pillsbury acquisition, Sheppard's recommendation in this respect was ignored by Grand Metropolitan's board of directors. They argued that George Bull's experience in successful brand building at IDV was more appropriate for the CEO role of a consumer products company in the 1990s than Martin's traditional focus on cost cutting and rationalisation. Therefore, Bull replaced Sheppard as CEO in 1993, while Martin subsequently left the company to pursue other interests.

Under Bull's leadership, the period from 1993 to 1996 was characterised by a continuous focus on the divestment of Grand Metropolitan's non-branded businesses, combined with ongoing attempts to acquire strong brands and to widen the international scope of the business. While the focus on cost control and restructuring remained from Sheppard's era, under Bull the group was also keen on maximising its international strengths, opportunities and alliances as he believed that Grand Metropolitan's growth potential depended on its ability to successfully access the high growth potential offered by the alcoholic drinks market in the world's emerging economies. However, while it remained a profitable company under Bull, it was also recognised by commentators and analysts that Grand Metropolitan struggled to effectively manage the demands of trying to build up an international business with far-flung operations.[6]

Furthermore, the group's share price continued to 'underperform' on the London Stock Exchange.[7] This continued underperformance, combined with the desire to strengthen Grand Metropolitan's international access, provided the background for the decision to merge Grand Metropolitan and Guinness in 1997. The new group was originally led by Bull and Tony Greener of Guinness, until Bull's retirement in 1998, when Greener took over sole responsibility. At the time of the merger, Diageo (as the merged group was called), consisted of the following core businesses:

1   Guinness Brewing; this included a wide range of brewing businesses around the world, including Spain's biggest brewer (Cruz Campo) and Desnoes & Geddes in the West Indies.

2   Pillsbury.

3   United Distillers and Vintners (this was the merged name for the combination of Guinness's United Distillers subsidiary and Grand Metropolitan's IDV division).

4   Burger King.

Diageo: the early years

The merger of Grand Metropolitan and Guinness created the world's sixth largest food and drinks business and was initially well regarded by City analysts, who saw genuine opportunities for the new business. At the time of the merger, it was claimed that the merged entity would be able to 'cut costs and exploit marketing synergies, while building global economies of scale.'[8] The perceived attractiveness of the merged company can be found by comparing the pre- and post-merger share prices. Immediately prior to the merger announcement, Grand Metropolitan and Guinness stock had been trading at 516 and 515 pence respectively; after the formal merger went through in December, the market price of the combined group was 590 pence per share.

At the time of the merger, the idea had been for the combined entity to continue operating and growing in all of the two predecessor firms' existing

6   Ernest Beck, Wall *Street Journal*, 19–01–98.

7   Ernest Beck, *Wall Street Journal*, 19–01–98.

8   Article in the *Wall Street Journal*, 20–05–00.

business units. In both the brewing and food divisions, it had famous and popular brands, while in the spirits area it had, through the merger, become the world's biggest spirits company. Nine of the world's top 25 global spirits brands, including such famous names as Smirnoff, Johnnie Walker and Bailey's, were owned by the group.

At the time of the merger announcement, there was, despite the general City approval of the alleged benefits that would arise from the fusion, some criticism of the proposal for the merged entity to continue operating in both the food and alcoholic beverages markets. Perhaps the strongest critic of the proposed strategy was Bernaud Arnaut, a non-executive director of Guinness at the time and Chairman of the French drinks company LVMH Moet Hennessy, which was a major shareholder in Guinness at this time. Arnaut strongly argued for the benefits that would arise from his alternative proposal to merge the alcoholic drinks divisions of LVMH, Guinness and Grand Metropolitan while selling off Grand Metropolitan's Pillsbury and Burger King divisions. Despite Arnaut's proposals to the contrary, the merger of Grand Metropolitan and Guinness went through as originally proposed in December 1997, after a delay of approximately seven months.

The early months of Diageo appeared to be well regarded by the City and in July 1998, the Diageo share price reached a high of over 700 pence per share – a rise of over 18% in the seven months since the merger of Grand Metropolitan and Guinness was finalised and the shares started trading on the London Stock Exchange. At this time, Diageo was already able to announce that the anticipated annual savings of £195 million that were due to arise as a result of the merger would be reached and analysts were suggesting that annual savings from the merger would actually be approximately £50 million greater than originally estimated.[9]

However, despite the fact that Diageo shares were still well regarded by the City in 1998, the merged entity was experiencing a range of problems at this stage. In 1998, John McGrath, the CEO of Diageo, admitted that the group's performance was actually destroying shareholder value – while its weighted average cost of capital was 10.5%, its actual return on total invested capital was during this period, only 9.5%.[10] While Diageo was one of the few British companies in this period to publicly focus on shareholder value creation as a core aim of the business, the fact that the business was, at least initially, undermining real shareholder value creation shows that there was plenty of work to do in improving the performance of the business as a whole.

Throughout 1998 and 1999, despite relatively moderate overall financial results, Diageo continued to argue that there was nothing wrong with the Diageo business model. Paul Walsh, who led Diageo's Pillsbury division at the time of the merger and who would go on to replace McGrath as CEO on the latter's retirement in 2000, publicly stated in 1998 that 'Pillsbury will be a principal contributor in achieving Diageo's aims of doubling total shareholder returns every four years.'[11]

In an attempt to improve Diageo's performance and support the combined food and drinks business model, McGrath announced plans for the formal sharing of best practice throughout the Diageo group. These plans focused on having the executives of the various Diageo divisions take responsibility for 'looking at each other's patches to transfer best practice across the group'.[12] In addition, in January 1999, Diageo set up a cross-divisional marketing excellence team with members from Burger King, Guinness, UDV and Pillsbury in order to try to achieve marketing and promotional synergies and best practice across its various business divisions. However, while Diageo was able to develop and exploit minor marketing synergies (e.g. Burger King was able to utilise Pillsbury products in some of its restaurant promotions), by 2000 Diageo was admitting that the marketing synergies and benefits of the merger were negligible and journalists and commentators were pointing out that Diageo's shares had under-performed the market by 31% between January 1999 and September 2000.[13]

[9] *Financial Times*, 07–07–98.

[10] Report of interview with John McGrath, *Financial Times*, 18–03–98.

[11] Paul Walsh reported in the *Financial Times* by Maggie Urry, 21–10–02.

[12] John McGrath quoted in the *Financial Times*, 18–03–98.

[13] John Thornhill, *Financial Times*, 08–09–00.

At the same time that Diageo had been struggling to make the merger a clear success in its core business areas, the policy of sell-off and disposal continued as it had at Grand Metropolitan throughout much of the 1980s and the first half of the 1990s. While the disposal of many of the group's minor spirit brands was often because of the need to satisfy the various regulatory bodies around the world, other disposals (e.g. the disposal of the Spanish brewer Cruz Campo in 1999) were undertaken because of the perceived need to dispose of underperforming units and could be compared to the disposals that had been undertaken by Grand Metropolitan under Sheppard and Bull's leadership.

Diageo: the Paul Walsh era

At the time of McGrath's retirement as CEO of Diageo in 2000 and his replacement by Paul Walsh, a long-time Grand Metropolitan employee who had been partially responsible for the turnaround at Pillsbury, the company still faced a difficult post-merger future. The promised marketing synergies had largely failed to materialise while the performance of Burger King and Pillsbury was perceived by analysts to be undermining the success of the group's drinks divisions. In addition, franchisee holders at Burger King had become increasingly restless at what they perceived to be the failure of Diageo to manage the fast-food restaurant business effectively,[14] and had begun to publicly call for the Burger King business to be spun off as a separate entity.

The problems facing the company during this period resulted in Diageo agreeing to merge its Pillsbury division with General Mills, Inc., in 2000 (as part of the agreement, Diageo took a substantial minority stake in the expanded General Mills, Inc.). This development followed the announcement of Diageo's plans to put up 20% of Burger King for sale via an Initial Public Offering. Although Diageo under Walsh was clearly keen to dispose of Burger King in its entirety, US capital gains tax rules worked against the idea of initially offering more than 20% of Burger King for sale.

While the disposal of Pillsbury to General Mills went through without any significant problems, the planned partial disposal of Burger King was a much more drawn out and convoluted process. The initial plan to offer 20% of Burger King to the public via an IPO was eventually dropped because of stock market problems in 2000 and 2001 and Diageo didn't manage to dispose of Burger King until 2002, when it agreed to sell the business to a private equity consortium. Even then, Diageo had to accept getting only $1.5 billion for the business (when the original IPO plan had been launched, the business had been valued at $2.5–3.0 billion), while also having to provide the buying consortium with a wide range of financial assistance and guarantees.[15]

At the same time that Diageo was disposing (or trying to dispose) of Burger King and Pillsbury, it focused on trying to acquire some of the brands held by the spirits division of the Canadian drinks company Seagram, in an association with the French company Pernod Ricard. Diageo entered into a consortium with Pernod to acquire them, because it was keen to stop major rivals from acquiring them and it was not in a position to acquire the Seagram spirits brands in their totality, because of regulatory constraints in various countries. Although the acquisition process was long-drawn-out and convoluted, Diageo eventually agreed to pay $5.3 billion to obtain famous Seagram brands such as Crown Royal and Captain Morgan Rum. However, while Walsh called the deal a success, some commentators argued that Diageo's partner did better from the Seagram deal. In addition, despite having entered into the alliance with Pernod to specifically avoid getting into problems with the competition regulators around the world, this move was only partially successful, as US regulators insisted that Diageo needed to sell off either its newly acquired Captain Morgan Rum brand or its existing Malibu brand.[16]

---

[14] For example, during the 1990s under Grand Metropolitan and Diageo, Burger King was led by four separate Chief Executives.

[15] According to Newspaper reports (e.g. *Financial Times*, 20–02–04), Diageo's financial guarantees in respect of the Burger King sale amounted to $1.05 billion.

[16] Diageo eventually disposed of Malibu to Allied Domecq in 2002.

Diageo: what does the future hold?

Following the generally successful integration of Seagram's spirit brands and the disposals of Pillsbury and Burger King, the divisions that had been holding back Diageo's growth since the merger, one would perhaps imagine that the company's future is assured. However, while Diageo's stated goal for the future is now based clearly 'on delivering high quality growth in premium drinks',[17] there are still significant problems and issues which the company needs to address if it is going to enjoy significant growth over the coming years.

The volume growth in the alcoholic beverages market is limited (typically 1–2% per annum),[18] and this means that the innate future growth prospects for Diageo are also limited. In addition, while being the largest alcoholic beverages company in the world may be an attractive position to be in, it does also bring potential disadvantages in Diageo's case, as it would appear that the pure size of the company and the dominant position that it enjoys in many areas of the drinks markets may limit its ability to undertake any further significant acquisitions. Furthermore, Diageo in general (and Guinness in particular) is struggling in the core UK and Irish markets, as drinkers increasingly move away from going to pubs and prefer to buy their drinks in supermarket to enjoy at home. This development could result in Diageo facing thinner profit margins on its products, as they become increasingly squeezed by the powerful supermarkets.

Given the above problems and issues, future profit increases may therefore have to be achieved by one (or more) of the following methods:

1 Focusing on continually cutting the company's costs.

2 Stealing market share away from other firms and types of alcoholic beverage (e.g. from wine).

3 Continuing to successfully develop new alcoholic products that can help attract new drinkers.

4 Improving marketing and getting closer to the customer than any of the competition.

While Diageo (and previously Grand Metropolitan) have shown that they have been able to successfully develop new alcoholic beverages over an extended period of time, some commentators have questioned the long-term viability and/or stability of such a tactic. In this regard, one should note that some of Diageo's more recent innovations have only met with limited market success, while serious concerns have also been raised about the long-term market sustainability of some of Diageo's more successful, recent introductions such as Captain Morgan Spiced Rum in the US which, although produced like a beer (to benefit from lower US tax duties), is specifically designed to taste like a spirit (these types of drink are called malternatives). Overall, critics argue that too many of Diageo's new products are akin to brand extensions rather than the introduction of genuinely new products that help steal market shares from rivals.

Some commentators have also pointed out that the aggressive way in which Diageo has tried to change the 'rules of the game' in respect to the boundaries that apply to the alcoholic drinks industry has not always been successful. For example, Diageo has tried to persuade the major US TV broadcasters to remove their voluntary ban on the advertising of spirits without long-term success.[19] Additionally, the aggressive way that Diageo exploited the brewing rules in the US when developing the 'malternative' drinks concept resulted in heavy government lobbying from the influential US brewing industry. This lobbying has provisionally succeeded in that the US government agreed to change the rules so that 'malternative'-style drinks can only qualify for the reduced beer tax rates if they actually 'taste more like beer'. As one journalist has said, it has often appeared 'one step forward and two steps back for Diageo'.[20]

In addition, some commentators have raised question marks about the long-term future of Guinness within the Diageo empire. Although Diageo publicly remained committed to the Guinness brand, sales of

---

[17] Chief Executive's Review, Diageo Annual Report, 2003.
[18] *Business Week*, May 2003.

[19] Although Diageo was initially successful in persuading NBC to drop its advertising ban on spirits, NBC backed down under pressure and never screened the advertisements.
[20] Gerry Khermouth and Kerry Capell, *Business Week*, 19–05–03.

the stout are falling in both the UK and Ireland and Diageo have recently announced plans to close the Guinness brewery and Park Royal in London and centralise all European and North American Guinness production in Dublin. One also needs to ask whether the values associated with a traditional beer or stout are actually closely linked with the various spirits brands with which Diageo is most closely associated and whether there are genuine and significant marketing and distribution synergies between spirits and beers for the company.

However, despite the above concerns, it is clear that under Walsh's leadership Diageo will aggressively challenge the status quo in its markets and is keen to try new products and to challenge old market assumptions. Walsh remains publicly committed to ensuring that Diageo grows by more than the 1–2% market average growth rates, and it is clear that Diageo is willing to copy the successful practices of potential rivals to help achieve this growth. In this respect, Diageo in the US has started to use it power in the spirits sector to follow the example of Anheuser-Busch in the US beer market by increasingly centralising its US distribution network (with one distributor now taking responsibility for one whole state). As part of this pattern of increased centralisation, Diageo have started to simultaneously demand that each distributor appoints a specialist team to look after the whole of the Diageo account in their region as one of the requirements for being awarded the account.

Despite possible concerns about the company's long-term growth prospects, during the first part of the 21st century Diageo shares have outperformed the overall London Stock Exchange and its shares are continuing to trade at a premium compared to some of its major rivals such as Allied Domecq, while it remains well regarded by City analysts. The company has also shown that it has a strong cash flow stream over a period of several years and has shown itself over the past few years to be happy to return excess cash to shareholders. Perhaps the real question is, however, whether Diageo can continue to satisfy and exceed stock market expectations in the longer term with its present format and focus, or whether it will need to reinvent and redefine its strategic direction to maintain this favoured position with investors.

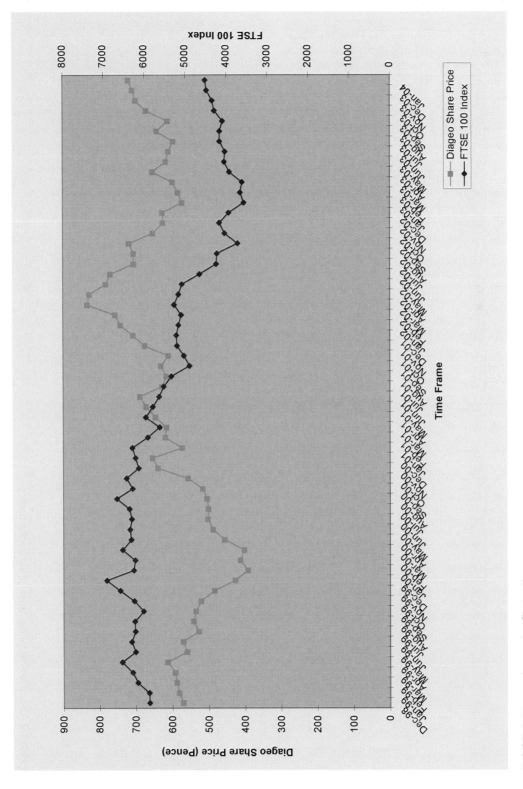

Exhibit 1 Diageo share price fluctuations

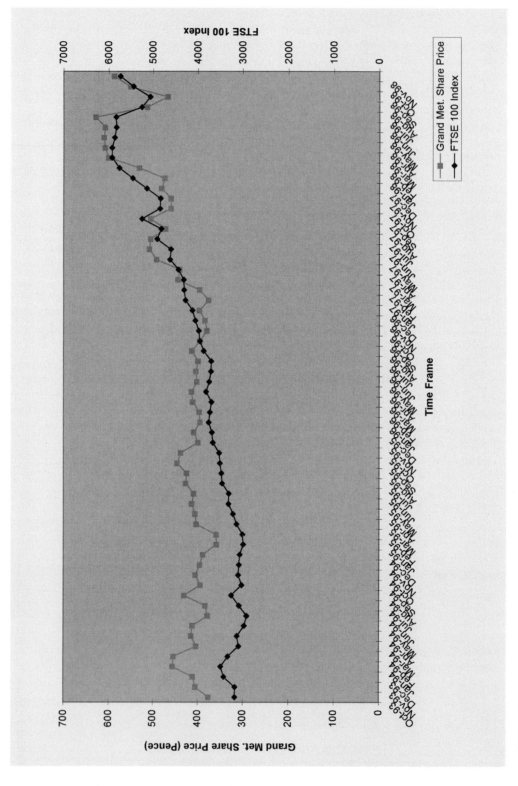

Exhibit 2 Grand Metropolitan share price fluctuations

Appendix 1 Diageo profit figures

	30 Dec 1996	30 June 1998	30 June 1999	30 June 2000	30 June 2001	30 June 2002	30 June 2003
Turnover – continuing activities	12,753	17,596	11,795	11,870	8,622	9,254	8,961
Turnover – disposals	687	106			4,199	1,455	479
Turnover – acquisition						573	
Group turnover	13,440	17,698	11,795	11,870	12,821	11,282	9,440
Profit on ordinary activities before tax	1,332	2,368	1,467	1,451	1,722	2,336	654

Notes:
1 The accounting period ended 30 June 1998 covers a period of 18 months. All other accounting periods cover a period of 12 months.
2 The accounts for the period ended 30 June 2003 include a special provision of £1.5 billion in respect of the disposal of Burger King.
3 Accounts have not been adjusted to reflect any changes to UK Generally Accepted Accounting Principles (GAAP) during the above periods.

Appendix 2 The core Diageo brands as at July 2003

Smirnoff – The world's best selling premium vodka.
Johnnie Walker – The world's best selling Scotch whisky.
Captain Morgan – The world's number two selling rum.
Bailey's – The world's number one cream liqueur.
J&B – The number two selling Scotch whisky in the world.
Cuervo – The number one selling tequila in the world.
Tanqueray – The number one selling premium gin in the US market.
Guinness – The world's best selling (and best known) stout.

Appendix 3 A summary of major acquisitions and disposals within Grand Metropolitan and Diageo between 1988 and 2002

2002 calendar year
– Sale of Burger King to a private equity consortium is finalised.
– Sale of the Malibu brand to Allied Domecq is finalised.

2001 calendar year
– Acquisition of Seagram spirit and wine business (in association with Pernod Ricard) is finalised.
– Disposal of Pillsbury via a combination with General Mills, Inc., is finalised.

2000 calendar year
– Diageo initially decides on the partial flotation of Burger King (subsequently not executed).

1999 calendar year
– Sale of Cruz Campo (Spain's largest brewer) to Heineken.
– Disposal of a range of 'minor' spirit brands including Cinzano Vermouth (to Campari).

1998 calendar year
– Acquisition by Pillsbury of the bakery products business of Heinz.
– Disposal of Dewar's whisky and Bombey gin to Bacardi.

1996 calendar year
– Sale of Pearle Vision Optical Retailers to the Cole National Corporation.

1995 calendar year
– Purchase by Pillsbury of Old El Paso Mexican-style food products.

1993 calendar year
– Disposal of Chef & Brewer pub-restaurant chain to Scottish & Newcastle brewers.

1992 calendar year
– Sale of Express Dairy and Eden Vale businesses to Northern Foods.
– Purchase of Cinzano Vermouth.
– Sale of Burger King's distribution services arm.

1991 calendar year
– Disposal of Grand Metropolitan's brewing interests.
– Sale of Wienerwald (a German/central European restaurant chain).

1990 calendar year
– Disposal of Wimpy table service restaurants.
– Disposal of Berni pub-restaurants.

1989 calendar year
– Grand Metropolitan acquires the Pillsbury food chain (including its Burger King subsidiary).
– Purchase of UB chain of fast-food restaurants.
– Purchase of Eyelab optical retailers in the US.
– Sale of UK casino interests.

1988 calendar year
– Sale of Intercontinental hotel chain.
– Purchase of various US optical retail firms including Vision Express and Eye & Tech.
– Disposal of Grand Metropolitan's soft drink bottling facilities.

Case 21 **The hostile bid for Blue Circle**

Introduction

Early summer 1999, Rick Haythornthwaite, the CEO of Blue Circle PLC, became aware that one of its largest rivals, Lafarge, under its Chairman and CEO Bertrand Collomb, was considering a takeover bid. In fact, Lafarge had started planning for the acquisition in June 1997, some two years earlier. Both companies were leading global players in the world cement industry: Blue Circle, a FTSE 250 PLC, was capitalised at £2.752 billion,[1] while Lafarge, a French giant, was capitalised at FFR76.591 billion. The takeover, launched on 31 January 2000 was an all-cash hostile bid, which valued Blue Circle at £3.4 billion. If the takeover bid succeeded, Lafarge would become the largest cement company in the world.

Blue Circle and its advisers started work on updating its defence plan, which consisted of valuations on several bases together with expected lines of attack and potential responses to these issues.

Industry background

World demand for cement is approximately 1.5 billion tonnes per annum, and between 1990 and

....

This case is intended as a basis for class discussion rather than to illustrate either effective or ineffective handling of a business situation.

© Duncan Angwin, Philip Stern, Sarah Bradley, Warwick Business School, 2004.

....

[1] 1999 estimate.

1997 demand grew at a compound rate of 5.5% compared with population growth of 1.5% over the same period. Production and consumption data are shown in Appendix 1. Regional differences can be significant and consumption is increasing in the developing world much more than in the developed world. Since 1990 per capita consumption grew by 7.1% in Asia whereas in Europe it fell by 1.4%, although this latter figure partly reflects the fall in consumption in former Eastern Bloc countries. Regional cement trends are shown in Appendix 2.

Per capita cement consumption varies between regions, with the North American and European markets consuming approximately four times as much cement per person as Africa. Regional consumption per capita is shown in Appendix 3. Regional averages can, however, mask country differences, and within Europe Portugal consumes nearly 1000kg per person while the UK only uses 210kg, largely because of different construction methods for residential and infrastructure work.

Industry consolidation

The main players in the cement industry can be divided into four strategic categories, as shown in Figure 1.

International producers have a strong home base, which has supported limited investment overseas. The businesses remain largely independent and there is limited sharing of skills and expertise. Multinational producers are larger groups that have been investing internationally for some years. Production decisions remain largely domestic although some trading of cement takes place.

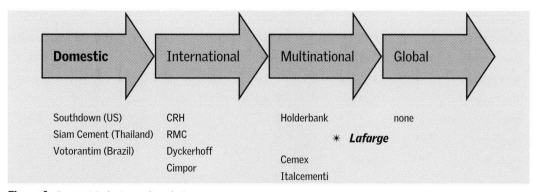

Figure 1 Cement industry value chain
Source: *European Cement Review*, January 2000, HSBC.

Trading and operational synergies increase as the groups expand and returns are therefore generally higher than those for international producers. Global producers are currently a theoretical category where production and capacity decisions are taken on a global basis. The advantage would be the erosion of price discrepancies and the rising of average prices as a result of less competition (*European Cement Review*, January 2000, HSBC).

The last few years have seen large-scale consolidation of the cement industry with nearly 80 million tonnes capacity acquired by the leading producers in the four years to the end of 1999 (see Appendix 4). This represents over 8% of global cement capacity, excluding China. The top six multinational producers have 30% of global capacity at the end of 1999 compared with 11% in 1988.

Appendix 5 shows major deals entered into in the last three years, and Table 1 gives the capacities of the largest companies.

Key expansion opportunities lie in the regions where national players still dominate. The percentage of regional markets controlled by international and domestic producers are shown in Table 2.

Blue Circle

In 1999, Blue Circle was the sixth largest cement producer in the world with a total kiln capacity of 40.6 million tonnes. Blue Circle was the parent company of an international group of companies whose core businesses were cement, aggregates and ready-mix concrete. Cement contributed the majority of group sales and operating profit. It was quoted on the London stock exchange and its market capitalisation at 31 December 1999 was €4.7 billion.

Blue Circle had market leader positions in the UK, Malaysia, Greece, Nigeria, Denmark and Kenya and was number five in the US. The Group's market share and major competitors by country are shown in Appendix 8. Although some way behind Holderbank and Lafarge in size, Blue Circle doubled its cement capacity between 1997 and 1999 with acquisitions in Asia and Greece. In addition, during 1999, the non-core heating and bathrooms divisions were disposed of. (Selected financial information is shown in Appendix 6.)

Lafarge

In 1999, Lafarge, the French heavy building materials group, was the second largest cement pro-

Table 1 Cement kiln capacity by largest companies and by region

	Total kiln capacity (millions tonnes)							
	Western Europe	Eastern Europe	Africa	Asia	Oceania	North America	C & S America	Total
Holderbank	16.4	6.6	5.7	17.4	1.2	15.3	21.3	83.9
Lafarge	24.7	12.0	12.0	6.0		13.2	8.2	76.1
Cemex	10.4		4.0	10.2		1.1	41.1	66.8
Italcementi	30.2	2.6	3.6	3.9		5.4	0.7	46.3
Heidelberger	33.8	12.5	1.2	3.0		10.5		61.0
Blue Circle	16.7		4.1	12.3		6.7	0.9	40.6
CRH	5.8							5.8
RMC	8.9	6.5			3.1	1.0		19.5
Dyckerhoff	10.7	2.6				4.7		18.1
Cimpor	7.1		2.4				2.8	12.3

Source: *European Cement Review*, January 2000, HSBC.

Table 2 Regional markets controlled by international and domestic producers

Region	National players market share (%)	International majors market share (%)
Asia (excluding China)	90	10
Middle East	84	16
Eastern Europe	73	27
Africa	71	29
Latin America	70	30
Western Europe	37	63
North America	37	63
Total (excluding China)	70	30

Source: *European Cement Review*, January 2000, HSBC.

ducer in the world, with total kiln capacity of 76.1 million tonnes (see Table 1), behind Holderbank of Switzerland. Lafarge was also the world's largest producer of roof tiles and the third largest ready-mix concrete producer. Lafarge was quoted in Paris and London and its market capitalisation at 31 December 1999 was €12.1 billion. Lafarge's other building materials activities include aggregates, plasterboard and speciality materials.

Lafarge has market leader positions in France, Poland, Morocco and Canada, is number two in Venezuela and Turkey, and is number three in the US, Brazil and Spain. Lafarge's market share and major competitors by country are shown in Appendix 9. Cement contributes approximately one-third of sales but more than half of operating profit. (Selected financial information is shown in Appendix 10.)

Haythornthwaite: Blue Circle's new CEO

Rick Haythornthwaite, CEO of Blue Circle at the time of the hostile takeover, had previously held a number of positions at BP and had been a director of Premier Oil plc. He joined Blue Circle in October 1997 and had initial responsibility for Heavy Building Materials in Asia where he was the architect of Blue Circle's strategy for investing in Malaysia. He later took responsibility for Europe. He became Chief Executive designate in December 1998 and finally CEO in July

1999 on a salary of £390,000; a discount of 20% of the median level to reflect his lack of experience in such a role.

The first rumours that Blue Circle might be a potential bid target occurred in October 1999, after the Group issued a profits warning. This came only six weeks after the announcement of the half-year results and severely undermined the credibility of the new Chief Executive. The following month it was reported that Lafarge had engaged an investment bank to assist them in preparing a bid. Little further was heard until 30 January 2000 when the *Sunday Telegraph* reported that a bid was imminent.

Bertrand Collomb, the Chairman and Chief Executive of Lafarge, telephoned Rick Haythornthwaite that weekend to discuss a possible takeover. The price of £4.30 per share was mentioned, but this was dismissed by Haythornthwaite.

The hostile bid

On 1 February 2000 Lafarge announced a pre-conditional offer for Blue Circle of £4.20 per share. The offer represented a premium of only 1.4% over Blue Circle's closing middle market price of £4.14 on 31 January, although it was a premium of 33.6% over the closing middle market price of £3.1425 on Thursday 27 January, the day before there was significant speculation in the market concerning a possible bid for Blue Circle. It was acknowledged by analysts that the two groups were strategically a good fit, but the consensus was that the price would have to be close to £5.00 per share for the bid to succeed.

Lafarge attacked Blue Circle primarily for mistakes made in the past, including the diversification strategy of the 1980s and early 1990s. By diversifying, Blue Circle had fallen behind its international competitors and it was now heavily dependent on 'too few countries'. Lafarge asserted that *this "over-dependence" on a small number of operating territories means that Blue Circle's profitability is inherently volatile'*.

Defence plan

Blue Circle's financial advisers at the time of the bid were the merchant bank Lazards. They had been heavily involved in producing the defence plan in 1999. They now steered the conduct of the defence itself. The first critical issue was what value to put on Blue Circle? The valuations prepared by City analysts (see Table 3) were all based on information in the public domain and on the analysts' expectations of future growth in the various markets.

The analysts' valuations were generally around 500 pence, with some exceptions, namely Oddo Equities[2] (25 January 2000) and Credit Suisse First

Table 3 Analysts' valuations of Blue Circle

Date	Source	Nature of valuation	Pence per share
March 1999	Lazard Brothers for BCI	DCF	433
September 1999	Warburg Dillon Read	Target price	500
January 2000	HSBC	Target price	430
13 January 2000	Lazard Brothers for BCI	DCF mid-point	486
25 January 2000	Oddo Equities	Stand alone value Discounted free cash flow	390
31 January 2000	Warburg Dillon Read	Target price	500
22 February 2000	Goldman Sachs	Target price	471
	HSBC	Target price	500
	Warburg Dillon Read	Target price	500
24 February 2000	Credit Suisse First Boston	Stand alone value Discounted free cash flow	390
24 February 2000	Teather & Greenwood	Exit price	500
3 March 2000	Commerzbank	Break up value, before premium for control	446
7 March 2000	Robert Fleming & Co	Target price	500
12 April 2000	Oddo Equities	Take out price	519
20 April 2000	Robert Fleming & Co	Target price (post Asia and OIP announcements)	550
1 December 2000	Schroder Salomon Smith Barney	Take out price	490–495

Note: BCI is Blue Circle Industries.

2 Oddo Equities later increased their valuation to in excess of 500 pence towards the end on the bid process and after the release of the OIP and Asia documents.

Table 4 Blue Circle forecasts against actual results

Date prepared	Source	Operating profits 2001 forecast £m
November 1999	2000–2002 Business Plan	560
November 2000	2001–2003 Business Plan	519
June 2001	Full year forecast	491
September 2001	Full year forecast *	385

Note: *£33 million of the reduction between the June and September 2001 forecasts is due to the sale of Blue Circle's Canadian cement business.

Boston (24 February 2000). Lazards had access to Blue Circle financial information including management accounts, forecasts and budgets. Their valuation presented to the board in January 2000 was prepared based on the 2000–2002 business plan. This valuation seemed a reasonable estimate provided the profit forecasts in the Business Plan were considered achievable. Blue Circle, however, tended to achieve actual results lower than plan, and profit projections were sometimes wildly optimistic (see Table 4).

Lazards were instructed to reduce the profit forecasts in the 2000–2002 plan to bring them down to more achievable levels. Their discounted cash flow analysis prepared for the board of Blue Circle valued the business at 486 pence, which was seen as relatively conservative. This valuation provided support for the claims of management that the Lafarge bid of 430 pence undervalued the group.

Blue Circle's response

The initial response of Blue Circle to the Lafarge approach was to dismiss the bid as significantly undervaluing the company. There was then a delay until Lafarge issued its offer document on 10 February 2000. Blue Circle's response to this document was to reiterate the earlier assertion that the offer undervalued the company, but also to claim that the Lafarge bid was a 'quest for our Asian assets' and that this 'validates the investment strategy' of the group.

The first significant document issued by Blue Circle was the early release of the group's 1999 results on 21 February 2000. The publication date was brought forward by five weeks, partly because the original date would have been after day 39, the latest date on which Blue Circle could issue new information, and partly to provide a solid base from which to launch the defence in which management attempted to justify their current strategy. The document stated that:

Lafarge's chairman has congratulated our management for 'doing all the right things'. He is right to.

- ♦ *We have a business that is fundamentally changed, refocused on our strengths in cement, aggregates and concrete.*
- ♦ *We have invested carefully, building leading positions in our chosen markets.*
- ♦ *We have exciting growth prospects.*
- ♦ *We will deliver substantial performance improvement and cost savings in the near term.*

The document also showed that the final dividend for 1999 would be 10.95 pence per share, which was an increase compared with internal plans (see Table 5).

On 23 March 2000 Blue Circle issued a document setting out the open market value and development value of the group's land holdings in Kent and elsewhere. The open market value was estimated at £227 million and the development value at £546 million.

On 28 March 2000 Blue Circle issued a profit forecast for its Asian businesses where it had been investing heavily. Indeed, this heavy investment had been at a time when profits in Asia were falling and these difficult trading conditions had been

Table 5 Dividends declared and paid for the years 1994 to 1999

	Interim dividend (pence per share)	Final dividend (pence per share)
1994	3.75	8.0
1995	4.0	8.5
1996	4.25	9.0
1997	4.65	9.85
1998	4.85	10.35
1999	5.05	10.95

responsible for the profits warning. Under the rules of the Takeover Code, the group would not normally have been permitted to issue such a forecast, but because Lafarge had itself issued forecasts for the prospects in Asia, Blue Circle was permitted to respond.

The document set out forecasts for profits for Asia for 2000–2002 to convince shareholders that the investments in Asia would pay off in the short term. In defending management's strategy the document stated that *'Blue Circle has followed a deliberate strategy of increasing investment in Asia in anticipation of what is now a strong and sustainable recovery.'*

On 6 April, Blue Circle announced its operational improvements programme (OIP). The document announced details of the projected benefits arising from such cost savings and included forecasts of the benefits to be achieved to be of the order of £116 million per annum by 2002. The document also reiterated that the Lafarge bid undervalued the company.

The final salvo in Blue Circle's defence was launched on 11 April 2000. Blue Circle was so confident it would deliver on the promises in the property, Asia and OIP documents that it would return £800 million to shareholders in advance. The first tranche of £400 million was to take place by way of a tender offer for Blue Circle's shares, although the form of the second tranche was left open.

The return of capital was in effect a down payment to shareholders, demonstrating the confidence of management in delivering the promises they had made. It had the consequence of increasing Blue Circle's gearing significantly from 17.2% (end of

1999) to 107.7% (end of 2000), and of dramatically reducing the free cash flow available for future projects.

The return of capital document issued on 11 April summarised the main defence themes of property, performance improvement, Asia, and strong market positions, under the headline *'Blue Circle is a business with renewed momentum'*.

Other options

At the same time as these actions were being taken, Blue Circle considered a number of other options.

Management buy-out

An MBO team was put together, headed up by Operations Director David Lovett and staffed by the Finance Director and other managers from Blue Circle's North American operations. The MBO would have been the eighth largest ever and work needed to start early if it was to have any chance of success. The then Head of Mergers and Acquisitions at Blue Circle stated in interview that he believed that Lazards had effectively sabotaged any chance of success with an MBO as they had advised Haythornthwaite that the financing could be arranged in a short period of time. This opinion was not voiced by the Strategy Director, although he agreed that work on the MBO started too late in the defence process to have any chance of success.

The Blue Circle Strategy Director stated that he believed that the process of preparing the MBO case was very divisive within the organisation and that it distracted attention from the main fight. Within the organisation the MBO was unpopular as it would have been a North America takeover of the group and would have required significant disposals of operations to be feasible. Externally the Strategy Director believed that it did create noise in the markets and therefore may have unsettled Lafarge. The MBO option was examined but not pursued.

Acquisitions by target

Prior to Lafarge's bid, Blue Circle had started talks with Southdown, a US cement manufacturer, in 1999 with a view to agreeing a takeover. The two parties were close to agreeing a deal in early 2000 when the bid by Lafarge was launched, and indeed the bid may have been precipitated by leaks of the talks. If Blue Circle had acquired Southdown, the combined group would have been too large for Lafarge to afford.

Blue Circle remained in contact with Southdown during the defence process, although Southdown were not prepared to contemplate a deal until such time as Blue Circle had defeated Lafarge.

White squire defence

In this instance Votorantim would invest in new equity to enable Blue Circle to acquire Southdown. Some discussions were held with Votorantim but this option was not pursued further.

White knights

Management examined the possibility of a merger with a number of parties including Italcementi, Cemex, Holderbank, Hanson, RMC and Aggregate Industries. White knight deals failed on several fronts. Haythornthwaite commented that the potential white knight deals failed to provide the cash that the shareholders seemed to want and the potential white knights were also reluctant to become involved. The Strategy Director stated that Collomb had spoken to the other majors and effectively warned them against becoming involved in the bid.

Dawn raid

On 19 April, day 46 under the City Takeover Code, Lafarge launched a dawn raid and picked up 19.9% of Blue Circle directly and a further 9.6% through its bankers. Lafarge then increased its offer to £4.50 per share. Lafarge was confident of victory.

There were very few legal or regulatory defences available to Blue Circle at this point. Competition clearance from the European Commission was a formality, and the only areas where there were competition issues were the United States and Canada, so the scope for action by Blue Circle was limited.

Blue Circle appealed to the Canadian regulatory authorities following Lafarge's dawn raid. Under Canadian law, Lafarge was only permitted to acquire up to 20% of Blue Circle before receiving clearance, but the stake held by Lafarge's bankers meant that Lafarge effectively controlled nearly 30% of Blue Circle. Lafarge claimed it had agreed to make divestitures as required by the relevant authorities and that it had received prior approval from the Canadians. However, the Canadian authorities denied this. Even so, the authorities declined to take action against Lafarge.

The hostile bid fails

Early on in the defence process shareholders did not want to talk to Blue Circle. Investors were not prepared to sit down and talk to management until the final offer had been made by Lafarge and no further information could be released. During the last ten days of the offer period Haythornthwaite and James Loudon, Blue Circle's Finance Director, held a number of meetings with institutional investors in an attempt to persuade them to back management and reject the bid.

As day 60 approached, the lobbying of shareholders paid off when Schroeder's publicly backed the incumbent management on 26 April. This was followed by other shareholders and the bid was rejected. On 3 May Lafarge announced that it had received acceptances that, together with its holdings amounted to 44.5% of Blue Circle. The bid therefore lapsed. This was the first all-cash bid for a FTSE 100 company to fail for fifteen years.

Lafarge's reaction

Collomb and Lafarge had been severely shaken when the 2000 bid failed, particularly as they already controlled nearly 30% of Blue Circle following the dawn raid in April 2000. Collomb was very heavily involved with the hostile bid and the defeat was seen by many as a personal failure, particularly as it was rumoured that Lafarge's advisers recommended a revised offer in the range 460–470 pence in April 2000, and Collomb had ignored this advice by only increasing the bid to 450 pence. It is highly unlikely that Collomb would have launched another hostile bid for Blue Circle in 2001 as he would not have been prepared to risk failure again.

Blue Circle's reaction

Immediately following the successful defence in 2000 the remuneration committee of the board met and agreed that Haythornthwaite's package should be reviewed. His base to salary was increased to £490,000 per annum, being the median for a Chief Executive in the industrial sector. In addition, Haythornthwaite was granted a large number of executive share options and stock appreciation rights to take his entitlement up to the maximum four times salary that was permitted. It would normally have taken four years to build up to the full holding. It should be noted that Haythornthwaite's options were granted outside the normal timetable for such options, and that other directors were not granted additional options at this time.

At the time of the first bid in 2000 Haythornthwaite held options and SARs over a total of 431,166 shares. This would have realised a profit of approximately £340,000 at the original offer price of £4.20 and £469,000 at the revised price of £4.50. The recommended bid in 2001 gave rise to a potential profit on Haythornthwaite's share options and SARs of approximately £1.1 million.

The stated motivation of the remuneration committee was retention. The committee was aware of Haythornthwaite's increased profile in the market following the successful defence of Blue Circle, and felt that it was important for the group that he continued in office to ensure delivery of the defence promises. The additional salary and options were designed to prevent Haythornthwaite from leaving Blue Circle.

Post-deal options for Blue Circle

Blue Circle was left with a major competitor effectively owning 29.5% of its shares, and this increased to 32.2% after the first tranche of the return

of capital, by way of tender offer, was completed. To be able to remain independent Blue Circle needed to undertake a major acquisition or merger, but potential partners were unwilling to participate while Lafarge owned more than 30% of the Group.

Late in June 2000 a two-day board meeting was held to review strategy. It was acknowledged that Lafarge had few strategic growth options as attractive to it as Blue Circle, and it was considered that a price of £5.00 to £5.50 could be justified. Delivery on the defence promises was vital, but the directors also considered that step-change acquisitions should also be pursued.

At the time of the announcement of the group's interim 2000 results in September, Haythornthwaite wrote to Collomb, offering to brief him, in his capacity of major shareholder, on the results. The two Chief Executives met and agreed that they would not allow pride to get in the way of achieving the best deal for the shareholders of both groups. Haythornthwaite said that he was not ready to sell yet, but that if a deal were to be done the price would have to be 'a long way north' of what was previously offered. This was followed by a meeting in a London hotel where Haythornthwaite and Collomb discussed a possible link-up.

At the October board meeting Haythornthwaite explained to the board the difficulties facing the group in the current operating environment and also reported that the first draft of the 2001–2003 business plan was forecasting operating profits for 2001 of £511 million, significantly below brokers' consensus of £539 million. Haythornthwaite presented three strategy options to the board, which dealt with the relative short-term strength but medium-term weakness of the group. These included achieving an early deal with Lafarge; an acquisition to move out of Lafarge's reach; and a merger with another party. Considerable time and resources had been devoted to evaluating acquisitions of or mergers with various parties following the strategy meeting in June. The board decided that negotiations should begin with Lafarge, but that the other options should remain open to avoid undermining the current position of strength.

Haythornthwaite's approach to Lafarge was timed to maximise his negotiating position. The OIP was expected to achieve results in 2000 in excess of those promised during the defence. Total operating profits for 2000 were forecast to meet market consensus, although the quality of earnings was relatively poor, with higher than consensus profits from property disposals and a number of one-off accounting adjustments. Profits for Asia were forecast marginally below market consensus but in line with defence promises. However, the forecasts for 2001 and 2002 showed operating profit below market consensus, and it was considered that these forecasts were challenging, with more potential for downside than upside.

At Lafarge, Collomb's confidence was dented and he may not have been prepared to risk failure again. Even so, under takeover regulations he would not have been able to bid again until May 2001. Haythornthwaite took advantage of this by initiating negotiations well before that time.

Haythornthwaite met Collomb again to start the negotiations. By early December 2000 it was clear that a deal could be done with Lafarge or else a dignified exit. It was in the interests of both groups to resolve the position and it was known that Collomb was unwilling to risk another hostile takeover. Both sides were extremely anxious that there should be no leaks, and had there been any Haythornthwaite would have walked away.

Lafarge started at £4.70 with no dividend but Haythornthwaite had been adamant that he needed to be able to present the deal as being worth over £5.00 per share in order to recommend it to shareholders. However, the Blue Circle board agreed privately that they would accept an offer price less than the discounted cash flow valuation of £5.00 per share as management credibility would be lost if they rejected a 'reasonable value'. The reasonable value they agreed upon was £4.70 to £4.75 per share. The advisers to both sides worked in the period up to and over Christmas, finally agreeing a deal at £4.95 per share plus a final dividend.

A board meeting was held on Sunday 7 January 2001 to decide whether to recommend the Lafarge offer to shareholders. A revised discounted cash flow valuation had been prepared by Lazards based on the 2001–2003 business plan forecasts, and by coincidence this gave a value for the group of £4.95 per share. The directors therefore had no hesitation in recommending the offer to shareholders.

The vast majority of Blue Circle's shareholders were institutions and they readily agreed to the bid. However, many individual shareholders, who were mainly ex-employees with an emotional attachment, voted against the takeover, as they saw Blue Circle as a 'British Institution'.

The agreed takeover at £4.95 per share was described in February 2001 as 'a sensibly priced deal' by analysts at HSBC. Lafarge's shares responded favourably, rising sharply immediately after announcement and remained relatively stable at this higher level.

After the completion of the takeover

Haythornthwaite left Blue Circle on 11 July 2001 following completion. On 24 July 2001, it was announced that he would be appointed CEO of Invensys with effect from 1 October.

Case Questions

1 Why was Blue Circle bid for?

2 Was it in the interests of Blue Circle's shareholders for the hostile bid to fail?

3 Were the defence strategies adopted by Blue Circle consistent with reducing the chance of takeover but not prejudicial towards its shareholders?

4 Did Hawthornthwaite act in his own best interests or his shareholders'?

Appendices; Financial Information

Appendix 1 Global cement market (including China)

	1990	1991	1992	1993	1994	1995	1996	1997	1998e	1999e	Av. growth rate 1990–99e	Av. growth rate 1990–97
Production (millions tonnes)	1008	1042	1130	1206	1308	1388	1440	1473	1449	1494	4.5%	5.6%
% change		3.4%	8.4%	6.6%	8.5%	6.1%	3.7%	2.3%	−1.7%	3.1%		
Imports (millions tonnes)	71	72	76	78	90	100	102	102	101	102	4.1%	5.3%
% change		0.8%	6.6%	2.7%	15.5%	10.8%	1.9%	−0.4%	−0.6%	0.5%		
Exports (millions tonnes)	70	72	75	81	93	101	105	105	105	110	5.1%	6.0%
% change		2.0%	4.9%	7.2%	15.0%	9.3%	3.9%	0.2%	−0.1%	4.1%		
Consumption (millions tonnes)	1006	1037	1127	1197	1296	1376	1427	1458	1440	1483	4.4%	5.5%
% change		3.1%	8.7%	6.2%	8.3%	6.2%	3.7%	2.1%	−1.2%	3.0%		
Population (millions)	4972	5075	5179	5226	5276	5360	5443	5518	5589	5663	1.5%	1.5%
Kg per capital	202	204	218	229	246	257	262	264	258	262	2.9%	3.9%
% change		1.0%	6.5%	5.2%	7.3%	4.5%	2.1%	0.8%	−2.5%	1.6%		

Source: *European Cement Review*, January 2000, HSBC

Appendix 2 Regional cement trends

1990–97 growth	Consumption	Production	Population growth	Per capita growth
Europe	−0.9%	−0.4%	0.5%	−1.4%
N. America	2.1%	2.7%	1.1%	1.0%
Asia	8.9%	8.9%	1.6%	7.1%
S & C America	3.3%	3.2%	0.3%	3.0%
Africa	2.6%	2.6%	2.6%	–
Oceania	2.9%	2.1%	2.0%	0.9%
Total	5.5%	5.6%	1.5%	3.9%

Source: *European Cement Review*, January 2000, HSBC

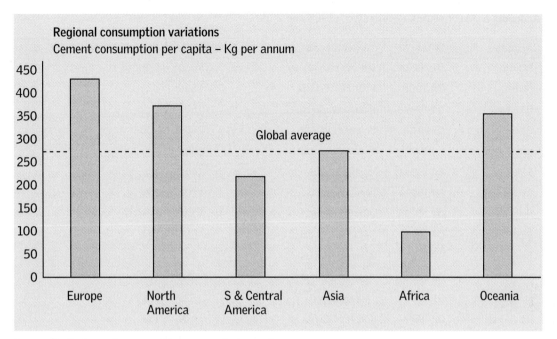

Appendix 3 Cement consumption per capita by region

Appendix 4 Acquisitions by large cement producers 1996–1999

Area	Tonnage (m)
Eastern Europe	22.3
Asia (excluding China)	20.3
Western Europe	11.5
Latin and South America	8.8
Africa	7.1
North America	6.6
Middle East	3.1
Total	79.7

Source: *European Cement Review*, January 2000, HSBC

Appendix 5 Major cement deals between 1998 and 2000

Acquirer	Date	Target/Country	Price $m	Price per tonne
Lafarge	Q1 2001	Blue Circle/various	7050	179
Cemex	Q4 2000	Southdown/USA	2850	225
Hanson	Q4 1999	Pioneer/various	2600	na
Heidelberger	Q2 1999	Scancem/various	2400	200
Anglo American	Q4 1999	Tarmac/UK, USA	2000	na
RMC	Q4 1999	Rugby/various	1400	176
Dyckerhoff	Q4 1999	Lonestar/USA	1200	294
Heidelberger	Q4 1999	CBR minorities/various	1100	175
Blue Circle	Q4 1999	Heracles & Halkis/Greece	680	124
Cimpor	Q3 1999	Brennand/Brazil	594	212
Cimpor	Q2 2000	Ameriyah/Egypt	550	187
Suez Cement	Q1 2000	Tourah/Egypt	523	108
Blue Circle	Q2 1999	Kedah/Malaysia	499	130
CRH	Q2 1999	Finnsementti/Finland	440	210
Blue Circle	Q4 1998	APMC/Malaysia	421	125
CRH	Q3 1999	Thompson McCulley/USA	420	na
Cemex	Q1 1999	Apo/Philippines	400	166
Italcementi	Q1 1998	24% Ciments Français/various	400	125
Cemex	Q4 1999	Assiut/Egypt	373	104
CRH	Q1 2000	Shelly/USA	362	na
Lafarge	Q1 1999	Beni Suef/Egypt	358	265
Valderrivas	Q4 1999	Giant/USA	343	202
RMC	Q2 1998	Wulfrather/Germany	280	90
CRH	Q4 2000	Jura/Switzerland	265	na
Valderrivas	Q4 1998	Atlantico/Spain	260	190
Semapa	Q1 2000	Gabes/Tunisia	250	220
Lafarge	Q3 1998	BC South Africa/South Africa	248	92
Cimpor	Q4 1998	Ciments de jebl Oust/Tunisia	243	200
Holderbank	Q4 1999	Siam City Cement/Thailand	228	100
Holderbank	Q3 1998	Phinma/Philippines	287	105
Blue Circle	Q4 1999	Alexandria/Egypt	200	130
Uniland	Q4 1998	Cements d'enfidha/Tunisia	168	159
Holderbank	Q3 1998	Siam City Cement/Thailand	153	100
Total			$29.5bn	

Source: *European Cement Review*, February 2001, HSBC

Appendix 6 Selected financial information on Blue Circle

Blue Circle Industries PLC	Selected financial data *£millions*				
	1995	1996	1997	1998	1999E
Group turnover	1,775	1,815	1,939	2,021	2,301
Operating profit (before exceptional items)	290	309	360	349	330
Operating margin	16.3%	17.0%	18.6%	17.3%	14.3%
Profit before tax (before exceptional items)	273	298	342	318	267
Earnings per share (before exceptional items) (pence)	21.4p	23.5p	29.0p	28.0p	23.5p
Net dividend (pence)	12.5p	13.25p	14.5p	15.2p	16.0p
Net assets	1,235	1,275	1,293	1,457	1,520
Net debt	36	1	245	565	596
Gearing (%)	2.9%	0.1%	18.9%	38.8%	39.2%
Market capitalisation at 31 December	2,510	2,625	2,586	2,414	2,752

Source: 1995–1998 actuals – Blue Circle Industries PLC 1995–1998 annual accounts
        1999 estimates – *European Cement Review*, January 2000, HSBC

Appendix 7 Blue Circle's share price performance

Appendix 8   Blue Circle's market share and competitors by country

Country	Market share	Competitors
UK	47%	Heidelberger (24%), RMC (20%)
USA	6%	Holderbank (12%), Southdown (10%), Heidelberger (7%), Lafarge (9%), Ash Grove (6%), Dyckerhoff (5%), Ciments Français (5%)
Malaysia	47%	CIMA (9%), Perak Hanjoong (6%), Pahang (6%), CMS (8%), Tasek (7%), Holderbank (5%)
Chile	40%	Holderbank (34%), Cemex (22%)
Philippines	20%	Holderbank (34%), Cemex (20%), Lafarge (15%), Northern (5%)
Denmark	90%	Imports
Greece	53%	Titan (40%), Ciments Français (6%)
Canada	13%	Lafarge (42%), Holderbank (17%), Heidelberger (18%), Ciments Français (7%)
Singapore	24%	Jurong (14%), National (14%), Ssangyong (13%), Sin Heng Chang (11%), Singapore Cement (8%), Asia Cement (6%)
Egypt	c2%	Holderbank (7%), Lafarge/Titan (5%), Cemex (12%), other domestics (10% each)
Nigeria	c30%	3 state owned companies
Kenya	c90%	1 domestic company

Source: *European Cement Review*, January 2000, HSBC

Appendix 9 Lafarge's market share and competitors by country

Country	Market share	Competitors
France	33%	Ciments Français (30%), Holderbank (14%), Vicat (Heidelberger) (14%)
Germany	7%	RMC (16%), Dyckerhoff (23%), Schwenk (15%), Heidelberger (14%), Holderbank (7%)
Italy	3%	Italcementi (32%), Unicem (20%), Cementir (10%), Holderbank (7%)
Poland	20%	Heidelberger (20%), CRH (20%), RMC (15%), Dyckerhoff (8%)
Czech Republic	15%	Heidelberger (47%), Dyckerhoff (19%), Holderbank (19%)
Turkey	12%	Heidelberger (15%), Ciments Français (7%), locals (66%)
Morocco	30%	Ciments Français (30%), Cimpor (9%)
Philippines	15%	Holderbank (34%), Cemex (20%), Blue Circle (20%), Northern (5%)
Indonesia	4%	Cemex (35%)
Egypt	4%	Suez (12%), Tourah (12%), Cemex (12%), Helwan (11%), National (11%), Amreyah (8%), Holderbank (7%), Blue Circle (2%)
Canada	33%	Holderbank (18%), Heidelberger (12%), Blue Circle (16%), Ciments Français (7%)
Spain	14%	Cemex (23%), Valderrivas (17%), Ciments Français (6%), Holderbank (8%), Cimpor (5%),
Venezuela	30%	Cemex (50%), Holderbank (20%)
Brazil	10%	Votorantim (40%), Jao Santos (11%), Holderbank (9%), Cimpor (9%)
USA	9%	Holderbank (12%), Southdown (10%), Heidelberger (7%), Blue Circle (6%), Ash Grove (6%), Dyckerhoff (5%), Ciments Français (5%)

Source: *European Cement Review*, January 2000, HSBC

Appendix 10 Selected financial information on Lafarge

	FF millions 1995	1996	1997	1998	1999E
Group turnover	33,218	35,262	42,066	64,294	68,500
Operating profit	4,110	3,755	5,178	8,238	9,725
Operating margin	12.4%	10.6%	12.3%	12.8%	14.2%
Profit before tax	3,720	3,333	4,647	6,714	8,075
Earnings per share (FF)	26.6	20.4	27.2	31.3	37.2
Net dividend (FF)	10.0	10.0	11.0	12.0	13.0
Net assets	23,204	24,160	26,121	29,521	31,776
Net debt	4,446	10,912	33,884	36,553	40,284
Gearing (%)	12.9%	37.0%	97.1%	93.3%	93.4%
Market capitalisation	30,332	29,226	35,512	51,528	76,591

Source: 1999 estimates – *European Cement Review*, January 2000, HSBC

Figures and tables

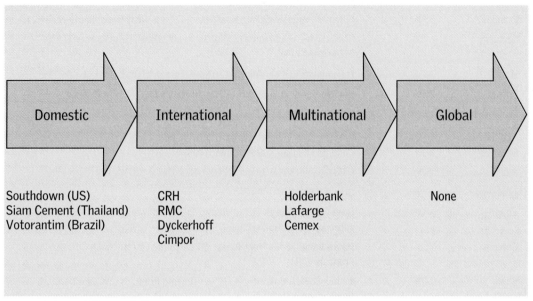

Figure 1 Cement firm evolution
Source: *European Cement Review*, January 2000, HSBC

Table 1 Cement kiln capacity by largest companies and by region

Total kiln capacity (millions tonnes)								
	Western Europe	Eastern Europe	Africa	Asia	Oceania	North America	C & S America	Total
Holderbank	16.4	6.6	5.7	17.4	1.2	15.3	21.3	83.9
Lafarge	24.7	12.0	12.0	6.0		13.2	8.2	76.1
Cemex	10.4			4.0	10.2	1.1	41.1	66.8
Heidelberger	33.8	12.5	1.2	3.0		10.5		61.0
Italcementi	30.2	2.6	3.6	3.9		5.4	0.7	46.3
Blue Circle	16.7		4.1	12.3		6.7	0.9	40.6
RMC	8.9	6.5			3.1	1.0		19.5
Dyckerhoff	10.7	2.6				4.7		18.1
Cimpor	7.1		2.4				2.8	12.3
CRH	5.8							5.8

Source: *European Cement Review*, January 2000, HSBC

Table 2 Regional markets controlled by international and domestic producers

Region	National players market share (%)	International majors market share (%)
Asia – (excluding China)	90	10
Middle East	84	16
Eastern Europe	73	27
Africa	71	29
Latin America	70	30
Western Europe	37	63
North America	37	63
Total (excluding China)	70	30

Source: *European Cement Review*, January 2000, HSBC

Table 3 Blue Circle's acquisition history 1979–2000

Company acquired	Acquisition year	Comments
Cemento Melon	1979	Chilean cement manufacturer
Armitage Shanks	1980	UK sanitaryware manufacturer Sold at a profit 1999
Tulsa cement works	1984	Oklahoma, USA
Ravena limestone quarry	1988	New York, USA
Birmid Qualcast	1988	Included Potterton heating boilers, Qualcast, Atzo and Webb lawnmowers, New World cookers, foundries, Qualitas bathroom products, Wrighton and Elizabeth Ann kitchen furniture, • Foundries and kitchen furniture businesses sold 1990 • Garden products sold at a loss in 1992 • New World cookers sold at a loss in 1994
Blue Circle Aggregates	1989	US aggregates operations
Ockley Brick Company	1990	UK based brick manufacturer Sold at a loss in 1997
Myson	1989	Radiators, heating pumps
Georgia Marble	1989	US aggregates company
Ceramica Dolomite, Italy	1990	Italian sanitaryware manufacturer Sold at a profit 1999
Aalborg	1990	50% share in Danish cement producer Sold at a loss in 2000
Harleyville cement works	1991	South Carolina, USA
Basic Energy	1991	Small clinical incineration business Sold at a loss 1998
Thermopanel	1991	Swedish heating group – radiators, valves, towel warmers
Celsius, France	1992	Heating equipment manufacturer and suppliers in France and Germany Sold at a loss in 1999
Total losses on acquisitions for period		Estimated at £235m
	1992	Keith Orrell-Jones takes over as Chief Executive Autumn 1992
St Marys Canada	1997	Canadian cement company
Needler Group Ltd	1998	Canadian aggregates and concrete block manufacturer
Philippines	1998–9	Various cement manufacturers in Philippines
APMC	1998	50% of Malaysian cement group
Kedah Cement	1999	Malaysian cement manufacturer
	1999	Rick Haythornthwaite takes over as Chief Executive July 1999
Alexandria Portland Cement	2000	Egyptian cement manufacturer
Heracles Cement Company	2000	Greek cement manufacturer
West African Portland Cement Company and Ashaka Cement	2000	Controlling interests in Nigerian cement manufacturers

Table 4 Analysts valuations of Blue Circle

Date	Source	Nature of valuation	Pence per share
March 1999	Lazard Brothers for BCI	DCF	433
September 1999	Warburg Dillon Read	Target price	500
January 2000	HSBC	Target price	430
13 January 2000	Lazard Brothers for BCI	DCF mid-point	486
25 January 2000	Oddo Equities	Stand alone value Discounted free cash flow	390
31 January 2000	Warburg Dillon Read	Target price	500
22 February 2000	Goldman Sachs HSBC Warburg Dillon Read	Target price Target price Target price	471 500 500
24 February 2000	Credit Suisse First Boston	Stand alone value Discounted free cash flow	390
24 February 2000	Teather & Greenwood	Exit price	500
3 March 2000	Commerzbank	Break up value, before premium for control	446
7 March 2000	Robert Fleming & Co	Target price	500
12 April 2000	Oddo Equities	Take out price	519
20 April 2000	Robert Fleming & Co	Target price (post Asia and OIP announcements)	550
1 December 2000	Schroder Salomon Smith Barney	Take out price	490–495

Note: BCI is Blue Circle Industries

Table 5 Blue Circle forecasts against actual results

Date prepared	Source	Operating profits 2001 forecast £m
November 1999	2000–2002 Business Plan	560
November 2000	2001–2003 Business Plan	519
June 2001	Full year forecast	491
September 2001	Full year forecast *	385

*£33 million of the reduction between the June and September 2001 forecasts is due to the sale of Blue Circle's Canadian cement business

Table 6 Dividends declared and paid for the years 1994 to 1999

	Interim dividend (pence per share)	Final dividend (pence per share)
1994	3.75	8.0
1995	4.0	8.5
1996	4.25	9.0
1997	4.65	9.85
1998	4.85	10.35
1999	5.05	10.95

This case study was prepared for this textbook by faculty members at Warwick Business School, University of Warwick, UK. This case study may not be reproduced in any form without prior permission. For more information, visit www.wbs.ac.uk.

Case 22 **BA profits in flight**

To be the undisputed leader in world travel (BA Mission, 1997)

The Chairman of BA was sitting at his desk in 'The Hub', located on the top floor of Waterside, the new British Airways HQ, observing BA planes taking off from Heathrow. He was trying to take stock and detemine how successful (or otherwise) the implementation of the global strategy had been at both a domestic and international level. He was reflecting upon whether this had been an appropriate strategy at this time and if it had been effective in fortifying the airline in an increasingly competitive context.

Company background

We have the skills, style, spirit and financial strength that are the envy of our competitors. (Lord King, Chairman 1992)

The airline sector is still a highly regulated industry, constrained by national and international operating laws and conventions; however, this has not prevented many international airlines from promoting themselves as 'global airlines'. In the UK airline sector, historically there have been only a few major players, including British Airways, the original national carrier, which was privatised and inherited prime locations at all major UK airports, including Heathrow, and is still perceived by many as the national carrier.

British Airways plc (BA), is a public company listed on the London Stock Exchange and based near London's Heathrow Airport. BA's history can be traced back to the early days of the aviation industry from 1919 to the birth of the package holiday mass market and the expansion of international travel which began in the late 1960s and 1970s. BA formed as the result of a merger in 1972 between British Overseas Airline Corporation (BOAC) and British

European Airways (BEA). In 1987, BA was privatised from being a state-owned national carrier.

BA has undergone significant structural and cultural changes since being privatised. To cope with increasing competition both domestically and internationally, management at BA has had to adjust the culture and structure of the airline in an effort to make it more competitive and customer focused. This posed several key challenges for senior managers. A brief summary of the airline's recent history follows.

Preparing to privatise (1980–1987)

Lord King was appointed Chairman, charged with restoring the Group to profitability and preparing for privatisation. With an overall deficit of £544m declared for 1981/82 including special provisions to pay for an extensive 'survival plan', which included staff cuts, suspension of unprofitable routes and disposal of surplus assets, the task of re-establishing the company as the world's leading airline began in April 1983. In 1982 a new CEO, Sir Colin Marshall, was appointed. This heralded a period of change of image, change of culture and a focus on increasing profitability, including repositioning of the carrier as the *World's Favourite Airline*, introducing a new corporate identity for the airline called 'Manhattan' and, in 1983, a corporate training programme called 'Putting People First' when 40,000 employees attended a two-day training programme.

During this phase, attempts were made to reposition the organisation within the changing environment, with the goal of making BA more competitive in the new 'global' marketplace and for the company to embrace the concept of the 'customer is king'. However, the culture at the time remained operationally focused:

> *At this time British Airways was a classical transport bureaucracy, somewhat analogous to the railways, whose primary agenda was to keep the aircraft flying safely. This operational orientation had been inherited after the War from the RAF. It was a viable approach in the highly regulated and stable market of the 60s and 70s. The systems were rule bound designed to operate on the assumption that people could not be really trusted.* (Management Communications Report 1988)

In the early 1980s, the airline was facing large financial losses and the public opinion of the airline was in decline. Market research found that the

---

By Dr Bridgette Sullivan-Taylor, Warwick Business School.

The material in this case is taken from original research conducted by the author and from a selection of working papers.

service provided by BA was seen as 'cool, aloof, professional and impersonal' and that passengers were dissatisfied if their basic needs were not being met. The results suggested that: 'Passengers wanted to be treated as individuals whose problems, cares and anxieties were responded to in a personal and caring way rather than a piece of cargo to be shipped from A to B' (Management Report 1988).

Management realised that if BA wanted to become a people-oriented organisation, responsive to the needs of its customers, both management behaviours and the wider corporate culture had to change. In response, BA attempted to rebrand itself as the 'World's Favourite Airline' and adopted a new corporate identity known as 'Manhattan':

> *Changing the culture was much more difficult than revamping the image. Staff were focused on our customers. But research revealed significant gaps between customers' expectations of what 'good service' was and those of our staff. Our staff concentrated on getting the routines right, the operational aspects of the job and the mechanics of service. Customers took that for granted; they were more interested in human aspects of service-spontaneity, warmth, concern, friendliness and attention to individual needs.*
> (Gurassa, Head of World Sales, 1997)

Internally, a number of new programmes were initiated in an attempt to change the organisation's values and belief systems. These programmes used a variety of innovative people-management practices. One such programme was known as 'Putting People First', when 40,000 employees attended a two-day workshop, aimed at instilling a heightened focus on both the internal and external customer.

Privatisation (1987–1995)

King and Marshall began to turn the airline into 'one of the world's most successful' (Harper, 2000:42). During this period, significant changes occurred within the organisation in the early to mid 1980s. These included a rationalisation of almost 24,000 jobs down to 36,000; the significant reduction in the number of routes serviced and the introduction of a new corporate mission with the objective of the company becoming the best airline in its class: *'to be the best and most successful company in the airline industry'.*

Once privatisation was completed, the airline faced a different business climate within the industry. Changes in legislation enabled BA to develop alliances with a variety of other carriers. BA also differentiated its service offering through the launch of new products and services, which culminated in a new corporate identity. At the same time, the airline underwent a period of rationalisation and restructuring with non-core activities being outsourced, leading to redundancies and labour disputes.

However, the characteristics of a state-owned organisation continued to permeate BA's culture. The company had been a government institution and a civil service culture, characteristically bureaucratic, hierarchical and status oriented, was endemic. These characteristics were reflected in the norms, behaviours and attitudes of employees (Bruce, BA Management Report, 1998:7).

As the UK's national airline, BA had operated within a monopolistic context and had become operationally focused. For example, it had a propensity to invest in state of the art engineering development and maintenance programmes. The Concorde project required a level of R&D investment that was far above that which any private sector airline could afford.

The merger with British Caledonian in 1987 resulted in an industrial dispute between the airline and the stewards and stewardesses association (BASSA). After the dispute was resolved, a period of significant investment occurred which led to the development of new brands and new cabin services features as detailed in Table 1.

In 1991, the Gulf War began. This resulted in a decrease in traffic which had a significant impact on the airline's profitability. BA reduced its network activity in response to a decrease in demand for flights by consumers, who felt unsure about travelling at this time. During this retrenchment phase 4,600 employees were offered redundancy packages and early retirement and another 2,000 employees were asked to work half-time until demand had returned to normal levels. Simultaneously, in an attempt to boost demand, the airline began an innovative marketing campaign called the 'World's Biggest Offer' in an effort to increase consumer confidence and recover from the downturn in traffic.

Table 1 1987–1991 (*BA Fact Book*, 1997)

		The 1987–1991 Period
Dec 1987	Brands	BA and United Airlines announced a worldwide marketing partnership.
1988	Profit	$300 million [profitable for the first time].
Jan 1988	Brands	New Club World and Club Europe Brands introduced. Investment of over $100 million on upgrading and improving business class products.
March 1989	Brands	New First Class service introduced.
May 1990	Network	At BA's initiative, the world's airlines set up an Infrastructure Action Group based in Geneva and operating under IATA, to work for the elimination of restraints which threatened to stifle the growth of the aviation industry. BA carried 25 million people.
Jan 1991	Brands	World Traveller and Euro Traveller brands were introduced.

The 1990s were also significant due to the change of leadership and a refocusing of the organisational philosophy, as Sir Colin Marshall succeeded Lord King as Chairman. This period is summarised in Table 2. At this time, the organisation's initials, BA, were still often taken to stand for *'Bloody Awful'* due to the inconsistent standard of service being delivered. Marshall stated that in the 1990s, however, *'customer service had joined "motherhood" as one of the unassailable virtues of our time, and consequently there is growing pressure to improve the responsiveness of organisations to those whose interests they exist to serve'* (Bruce, 1998:2). Marshall was pivotal in introducing a customer-focused vision for the organisation and supported the 'Managing Winners' programme, aimed at renewing the airline's commitment to delivering internal and external quality customer service. The challenges, which followed, are summarised by the Head of World Sales:

Our first challenge for the rest of the 1990s is growth. The second challenge is cost. The third challenge is management style. The outdated style of managing by control, setting standards and targets, dictating work designs and schedules and operating through bureaucracies and structure has to be replaced. The demand from employees today is for more participation and involvement in decision making, less bureaucracy and paternalistic care, and more respect and value as individuals. If this is what drives employee satisfaction in the 1990s, this is what we intend to provide.' (Head of BA World Sales, *BA Fact Book*, 1997:10)

During the remainder of the early 1990s, the airline enjoyed stable growth, achieved through an expansion of the route network and through the introduction of innovative products and services. This is summarised in Table 3.

The 'Ayling' era: Ayling as CEO (1995–2000)

In 1995 there was a key change in leadership in 1995, when Robert Ayling was promoted from Managing Director to the position of CEO. This marked the beginning of the 'Ayling' era. At this time BA was regarded as one of Britain's blue-ribbon companies, as both a prestige private company and a privatised national organisation. BA's performance results was also strong during this period:

- 1995 The airline announced record Group pre-tax profits of £430m for the six months that ended 30 Sept 1995, up 23.2% on the previous year. The interim dividend is up by 10% to 3.85 pence a share.

- 1996 BA announced pre-tax profits of £104m for the three months ended 31 Dec 1995, up 30% compared with the previous year.

- 1996 BA announced record pre-tax profits of £585m, up 29.4% on the £452m (before the US Air provision) achieved in the previous year. Basic earnings per share increased (before US

Table 2 1992–1993 (*BA Fact Book* 1997)

		The 1992–1993 Period
April 1992	Corporate Culture Programme	A renewed commitment to keep BA ahead in quality passenger service was pledged by the airline with the launch of 'Managing Winners', the new management programme and 'Winners', the new corporate event.
July 1992	Leadership change	Lord King announced he was to step down as Chairman in July 1993 after 12 years. Sir Colin Marshall, later Lord Marshall, takes over full executive management responsibility for the airline with immediate effect.
Sept 1992	Market	BA was assigned one of the highest credit ratings in the world.
Oct 1992	Global strategy	The airline unveiled its first fully integrated global advertising campaign called 'Feeling Good'.
Dec 1992	Network: Partnership Investment	US and UK governments did not approve of BA's attempt to invest in US Air due to a bilateral air services agreement.
Jan 1993	Alliance Investment	BA and US Air alliance, e.g. code-sharing opportunities.
Jan 1993	Legal case	BA paid £610,000 in settlement of a libel action brought by Richard Branson and Virgin Atlantic Airways.
Feb 1993	Leadership change	Lord King retired as chairman. The board of BA appointed Sir Colin Marshall as Chairman and Robert Ayling as Group Managing Director. Sir Michael Angus continued as non-executive Deputy Chairman. BA also intended to increase the non-executive representation on the Board. Lord King is invited by the Board to become the first President of British Airways.

Table 3 1993–1995 (*BA Factbook* 1997)

		The 1993–1995 Period
1993	Industrial dispute	Strike between management and BASSA.
March 1993–94	Network Devpt	Extension of global network.
1994	Industrial dispute	Strike between management and BASSA.
August 1995	Profits	BA announced pre-tax profits of £135m for the three months ended 30 June 1995 an increase of 57% in comparison to the same period last year. The result set a new first quarter record for the airline, ignoring asset disposals.
Sept 1995	Campaign	BA announced a £500m 3-year plan that intended to revolutionise air travel. The programme was called 'Insight' and began with the relaunch of Club World and Executive Club frequent flyer programmes. A completely new First Class service was launched in the winter and the other cabins were relaunched later.

Air provision) by 25.7% with dividends per share up by 10.1%.

As part of this key leadership change the global strategy was adopted including a handful of decisions including introducing the BEP programme (which involved restructuring, outsourcing and downsizing), as well as introducing a new corporate identity and developing the global network through joining an alliance.

BA had implemented international strategies in the past. These had been either operational, through ongoing extensions to the network into new market destinations, through mergers (BOAC and BEA in 1972–1974), through product extensions such as providing charter airlines when mass package holidays became the vogue in the 1970s, as well as through new innovations such as developing Concorde with Air France in 1976. Then, in the 1980s, during the privatisation process the airline was repositioned as the 'World's Favourite Airline' and the new mission introduced in 1987 was for BA 'To be the Best and Most Successful Company in the Airline Industry'. Through most of the late 1980s and 1990s BA continued to extend its products and services offering to its broad range of customers in order to grow its market share.

Then in 1995 BA introduced the 'Insight' programme intended to 'revolutionise air travel' and began to relaunch its brands. As part of this overhaul, in 1996 the Business Efficiency Programme (BEP) was introduced, aimed to save the airline £1 billion in costs by 2000. The programme involved both the reallocation of current investment into new initiatives and the restructuring and centralisation of activities.

Ayling recognised that one of BA's strengths was its identity as an upmarket international airline, but he also recognised the need to balance the aspiration to globalise and compete internationally with the desire to achieve greater efficiency through cost cutting:

Our job is to find ways of reducing expenditure while increasing the value for money that our customers get. If the customers value something and you want to keep their business, you don't take it away and say, 'Will you please pay the same fare', or worse still, 'Will you please pay more'. They will go somewhere else. (Ayling, 1999:66)

The manifestations of the BEP are illustrated in Table 4.

Although BA had implemented a variety of international initiatives to create a more outward focused airline, it was not until 1997 that it decided to adopt a strategy of becoming a global airline, when the new mission was introduced 'To be the undisputed leader in world travel' which included an integrated approach to globalising the airline's service and product offering under the new corporate mission – to become 'truly global' – and a new identity, 'Utopia,' was introduced as part of BA's new 'global' focus.

The corporate strategy was intended to globalise the airline through achieving scale and scope efficiencies. However, implementing many of these decisions involved managing the fine balance between investing in the launch of new products to improve customer service, developing a global network and simultaneously reducing overall operating costs, within the context of a highly competitive industry and a highly unionised workforce, each providing specific challenges for management and for the execution of a global strategy.

However, at the same time that this new corporate strategic intent was launched, Ayling had also decided that in order for the airline to maintain its position in such a competitive context, £1 billion in costs needed to be removed from across the airline by 2000. This created an internal tension which resulted in conflict. During the summer of 1997, in response to the introduction of the aggressive cost-cutting programme (called BEP), a major industrial dispute occurred. This dispute was a critical event in the airline's history and affected future management-worker relations.[1] This dispute was a reaction by the cabin crew community who had perceived that the

----

[1] BA has a long history of industrial disputes. In the recent past there had been several major strikes with various unions including in 1972 during the merger between BEA and BOAC; 1987 with BASSA over the merger with British Caledonian; 1993–1994 with BASSA; in 1996 a potential strike by BALPA was averted.

Table 4 1996–1997 (*BA Fact Book*, 1999)

		The 1996–1997 Period
	Network development	BA continued to code-share with American and Canadian carriers.
July 1996	Labour dispute	A threatened strike by members of the pilots union, BALPA, was averted.
	Alliance	The proposed alliance between BA and AA received approval from the House of Commons Transport Select Committee.
August 1996	Profit	BA announced a record pre-tax profit of £150m for the 3 months to 30 June 1996, up 11.1% on the £135m achieved in the same period last year.
Sept 1996	Restructuring	BA unveiled plans for a transformation of the group for the year 2000. The plans aimed to meet new market and customer needs, and included the restructuring of the workforce to ensure the company had the right skills in place to achieve £1B of efficiencies. To ensure it had the right people with the right skills in the right jobs for the new millennium, the airline carried out an extensive programme of redeployment and retraining. Severance and early retirement was offered to 5,000 volunteers and around the same number of new staff, skilled in customer services and languages, were recruited.
November 1996	Restructuring	The airline announced a restructuring of its Passenger Revenue Accounting Dept, which resulted in a reduction of around 600 UK jobs. Half of these jobs became obsolete through automation, while another third were contracted to World Network Services, a new development based in India.
February 1997	Restructuring	BA announced a £250m investment in a new World Cargo Centre at Heathrow. The significant increase in automation led to a reduction of almost 400 jobs from the current workforce.
February 1997	Restructuring	BA announced that it was combining its general accounting activities at a new Global Accounting Centre in London. The result was a reduction of around 290 posts over three years.
March 1997	Restructuring	BA announced an agreement with 2,800 ground services staff in its Aircraft Services department at Heathrow. The agreement included a two-year pay freeze, best practice throughout the department and lower starter rates for new recruits.
March 1997	Restructuring	Outsourced: BA transferred its Ground Fleet Services business, which provided vehicle management and maintenance services at Heathrow and Gatwick for 5 years.
March 1997	Investment in route	BA announced it was investing US$100 million to improve facilities for passengers travelling to and from New York. The project included the expansion of the airline's own terminal at John F. Kennedy International Airport, major new road access to the building, and new premium passenger facilities at Newark International Airport.
April 1997	Restructuring	The airline announced a streamlining of its Engineering department including outsourcing arrangements.
May 1997	Mission	New Mission 'To be the undisputed leader in world travel'.
May 1997	Restructuring	Staff at the BA World Cargo Centre voted for a proposal that included a two-year pay freeze, changes to working practices and simplified grading structure.

Table 5 May 1997–Sept 1997 (*BA Fact Book*, 1999)

		The May 1997–September 1997 Period
May 1997	Restructuring	BA members of Cabin Crew 89 union voted overwhelmingly in favour of proposals, which included pay restructuring and lower starter rates.
June 1997	Brand	Utopia. BA unveiled its new corporate identity designed to help establish the company as the undisputed leader in world travel. Changes included the new tailfin designs.
July 1997	CEO	First calls were made for Ayling to be sacked at AGM.
August 1997	Restructuring	BA Engineering announced a strengthened focus on maintaining and servicing BA's own aircraft. It continued to sell services to other operators, but on a more selective basis. This policy enabled the department to streamline its organisation and resulted in a reduction of 450 managerial and support jobs.
July 1997	Labour Dispute	Some of the cabin crew workforce at the airline held a three-day strike. Talks progressed between BA, the Transport and General Workers Union and the BA Stewards and Stewardesses Association (BASSA) and aimed to resolve the industrial dispute.
Sept 1997	Labour Dispute	Settlement of the issues central to the cabin crew dispute. The agreement, which came into immediate effect, secured the £42 million annual savings targeted from cabin crew as part of the Business Efficiency Programme. It also paved the way for a new relationship between airlines and the unions that represented cabin crew.

BEP programme would have a detrimental impact upon their working practices. Although the strike lasted for only three days, it was estimated to have cost the airline £125 million. The dispute led to a loss of morale by employees and a loss of confidence in the CEO by shareholders, who called for his dismissal at the AGM.[2] This period is summarised in Table 5.

In the continued pursuit of the BEP cost savings target, management continued to downsize and outsource large departments within the airline, such as catering, landing gear business and other non-core functions, despite ongoing resistance from internal stakeholders affected by these changes. This period is summarised in Table 6.

Table 6 Sept 1997–August 1998 (*BA Fact Book*, 1999)

		The September 1997–August 1998 Period
Sept 1997	Downsize	BA announced the sales of its Landing Gear business.
Dec 1997	Outsource	BA completed the sale of its Heathrow catering production units to Gate Gourmet. The 1200 staff transferred to Gate Gourmet.
May 1998	Profits	BA announced its preliminary results for the full year 1997/98. Driven by the BEP which delivered £250 million of cost efficiencies, pre-tax profits for the year were down just 9.4% to £580 million compared to the previous year's record levels. The result was achieved despite the industrial dispute, which cost £125m and the strength of sterling, which at the pre-tax level cost the group £180 million.
Aug 1998	Route	BA announced that it will suspend services to Osaka as a result of worsening passenger demand and the continued fall in the value of the Japanese Yen.

[2] However, it was not until January 2000 that the board requested that Ayling relinquish acting as CEO.

The Asian economic crises occurred in 1997–98, affecting capacity on major passenger routes in the Asian region. In 1999, the BA Chief Economist wrote a report entitled 'Globalisation: expanding our horizons' that discussed the implications of these global trends for the airline:

This year, we have been provided with a painful reminder of the increasing interdependence of the global economy. The shock waves from the economic and financial crisis in East Asia have spread far and wide. Financial instability has spread to Russia and South America. Banks have lost money and multinational companies are reporting reduced profits – hitting stock markets. Jobs are being lost in the financial sector and in the manufacturing industry. Globalisation is no longer a gleam in the eye of business school theorists. It is an established part of business life. And the fact that a downturn in Asia is now causing job losses in the Northeast of England and Scotland provides us with stark and graphic illustration of the new realities of the global marketplace ... The service sector also needs to brace itself for a period of restructuring, particularly as information technology opens up new markets and revolutionises traditional ways of delivering existing activities. We see this happening in our own industry as video-conferencing and other forms of business communication offer alternatives to business travel. (Sentence, BA Economics Department Report, BA Intranet, 1999)

Many airlines, including BA, had realised that due to sheer cost considerations and the highly regulated air transport environment, they were unable to provide a global network which covered every possible destination. To overcome these factors, BA began to forge alliances with other airlines in a move to provide a '*single global network*':

I think people who stop and think certainly understand that this industry has to participate in the global situation that is taking place in all industries. Unfortunately we are so hamstrung with regulations that we have to operate under bilateral agreements, formed in 1944 before the industry really existed, so we can't do it like other industries and so we can't go in, take over countries, able to operate their licences out of their countries at least outside of the EU. The only way we can participate in globalisation as an organisation is by striking these alliances or relationships with other carriers. Yes there are some problems felt over the franchise programme that we are operating essentially in this country, where there is a degree of overlap and a degree of concern that is created, but our first partnership we entered into in 1987 – I think it was with United Airlines – this sort of thing has been around for quite some time. (Lord Marshall, Chairman)

In September 1998, the oneworld™[3] alliance was launched. This was an attempt by a variety of airlines to 'globalise' their service offering, within the industry constraints, through marketing alliances with other carriers, who operated within specific disparate regions. Details of the oneworld™ alliance are in Table 7.

Throughout 1998 and 1999, considerable investment continued into a variety of brand relaunches to align the airline's strategic focus with the business travel market. This narrowing of strategic focus altered the way BA serviced its main premium markets, operated its flight schedules,

Table 7 September 1998 (*BA Factbook*)

		The September 1998 Period
Sept 1998	Alliance	oneworld – American Airlines, British Airways, Canadian Airlines, Cathay Pacific Airways and Qantas Airways announced the new oneworld global alliance. Combined total of 220,000 employees in 138 countries. 600 destinations are served and access to over 200 lounges was provided.

[3] A profile of the oneworld alliance can be seen on page 374.

Table 8 1998–1999 (*BA Factbook*, 2001)

		The 1998–1999 Period
Nov 1998	Brands	BA launched a range of new services and benefits for 'World Traveller' passengers.
April 1999	Strategy	BA took delivery of its last Boeing 747-400 aircraft in keeping with the airline's new global strategy geared towards focusing on the most profitable segments of business and thereby improving returns.
May 1999	Brands	BA announced that it would be developing radical new products, which would redefine long-haul business travel and set new benchmarks in comfort and design. The plans included improvements to Club World featuring completely flat beds, a new state of the art entertainment system with bigger screens, in-seat power for lap top computers, email, phones and fax.
	Products	BA launched BA Global Financial Services and products.
	New Centre	New World Cargo Centre opened.
	Profits	BA reported pre-tax profits of £225 million for the year ended 31 March 1999, including Business Efficiency Programme benefits of £610 million.
June 1999	Downsizing	In line with its strategy of reducing the rate of its capacity growth, the airline announced that it will terminate the lease on one Boeing 767-300, as permitted under the lease agreement. BA sells its shares to Galileo International Inc (a travel agency reservation company) releasing a profit before tax of £149 million. BA sells its in-flight catering facility at Gatwick for £14 million.
August 1999	Restructuring	BA announces its intention to accelerate its reduction in capacity. The airline plans to reduce its mainline scheduled capacity by 12% over the next 3–4 years. BA announces its intention to save a further £225 million (excluding one-off severance costs) in the current financial year to support profitability in a challenging trading environment. The main focus of the actions will be on improving efficiency in support areas of the company. Plans include the deferral of some non-fleet capital expenditure, an acceleration of other cost saving plans and reduction of 300 managers (a 10% cut) is targeted. Staff reductions are expected to be managed by voluntary means, the cost of which is expected to be in the region of £40 million. The airline will continue to invest in its new strategy and in innovative products. More code-sharing plans announced and upgrade of Concorde.

and configured its fleet and the associated manpower planning. The various initiatives are detailed in Table 8.

One of the results of the new strategic focus on the premium market was the increased investment in new innovations for the business club brands and the purchase of smaller aircraft with a larger number of business class seats which were scheduled to operate more frequently on the core business routes. These developments are detailed in Table 9.

Despite the investment in new products and services, such as the launch of new premium cabin related brand features and the aggressive cost cutting of the BEP, profits continued to decline over this period and BA became known in the press as *'the ailing airline'*. The board of BA dismissed Robert Ayling in March of 2000. Lord Marshall stood in as acting CEO and was succeeded by the new CEO, Rod Eddington, in May 2000.

The next section details the content of the global strategic intent.

Table 9 1999–2000 (*BA Factbook*, 2001)

		The 1999–2000 Period
Sept 1999	Brands	The airline announced a £50 million programme of improvements to Club Europe.
Oct 1999	Fleet	BA ordered 12 new 100-seat Airbus 318s with options to purchase 12 more aircraft. The move to the new, smaller A318 was a further step in the airline's fleet strategy, which aimed to modernise the fleet, increase average yields and reduce capacity.
Nov 1999	Global alliance	BA and AA file an application with the US Department of Transportation to code-share on flights serving 75 destinations in the UK, USA, Europe and Africa, as part of their plans to develop a global marketing alliance.
Dec 1999	Brands	London Eye opened by Prime Minister – Ayling on Board of BA-sponsored London Eye. Millennium Dome opened New Year's Eve – Ayling on Board of Millennium Dome.
Jan 2000	Chain relationships	BA announced plans for fundamental change to the way the airline works with UK travel agents.
Jan 2000	Brands	BA presented its new products and announced the introduction of a new cabin class. 'Lounge in the Sky' concept set for rollout in both Club World and World Traveller Plus.
Jan 2000	Strategy	BA took delivery of its first two Boeing 777 Extended Range aircraft. This signalled the next stage of the strategy implementation that focused on smaller, more profitable aircraft.
Jan 2000	E-commerce	World's first commercial interactive TV travel section on a UK cable company. Will be developed for on-line bookings.

The global strategic intent – why 'go global'?

Global network, global outlook: recognised everywhere for superior value in world travel. (BA Global Goal, BA Factbook, 1997:13)

In the late 1990s management had decided to reposition the airline as *'the world's favourite airline'* focusing on being both 'global and caring'. This change in focus had been driven by an awareness during the mid-1990s that British Airways was facing increasing competition from both domestic and international carriers. In order to increase market share, management felt that BA needed to differentiate the offering to appeal to the diverse needs of the 60% of its passengers whose journey originated from outside the UK. Prior to this the focus had been mainly on meeting the needs of the 40% of domestic customers, who also travelled internationally.

This view was further supported by market research undertaken during the early 1990s which indicated that BA was considered by passengers from overseas markets as providing service which

Table 10 2000 (*BA Fact Book*, 2001)

		The 2000 Period
March 2000	Change in Leadership	Robert Ayling resigned and Lord Marshall acted as CEO and as Chairman of BA until a new CEO could be found.
May 2000	Change in Leadership	Rod Eddington appointed as CEO

was 'too cool and aloof' and therefore too British oriented. In late 1995, senior management then commissioned a large market research study across several of its key target markets. BA customers were carefully selected to represent a cross-section of travellers in terms of: age, gender, reasons for travel and frequency of travel. The research indicated that the traditional BA corporate identity, known as the 'Landor' image, was seen by the public as *distinctly British, masculine, catering more for business travellers, arrogant, traditional and old-fashioned.*

The research also found that the notion of being 'British' was perceived by these customers to have changed. Results from this research are found in Table 11.

On the basis of these results regarding the change in 'Britishness', management commissioned further market research to determine whether the airline should also change its corporate identity to align with the new corporate mission, vision and values. Table 12 provides an overview of the market research findings in regard to the shift in perception of 'Britishness' and the perceived positive and negative associations.

The market research also indicated that in the worldwide context, societal values had significantly changed from the 1980s to the 1990s. The changes are detailed in Table 13. It was found that across all major markets researched, a backlash against the customer values of the 1980s had occurred.

The research suggested that the BA brand should be repositioned to reflect the changing values of the 'new' world. It should be seen as bringing people together, a world 'glue', a network, a web making the connection at both the macro and micro levels.[4] The new identity would embrace the notions of a global and caring world, fragmentation, a shift in gender balance, tolerance, individuality and corporate responsibility and would be executed through initiatives that were tangible and grounded in reality. In the light of the research, BA was seen to need to reposition itself in the global marketplace, with a new corporate mission, vision and values, and to take the '*opportunity to take a moral stance, which was visible, tangible and experienced at ground level*' (Research International Report, 1995).

Thus, by adopting a globally focused strategy the Chairman considered that the CEO was appropriately responding to changes in the competitive airline industry:

> *Over the last few years we have changed our strategy quite a lot because the market has fundamentally changed. The pound has become much stronger and our competitors in Europe have got much better too, and we used to have the market to ourselves.* (Chairman)

In order to implement a '*Think Global, Act Local*' strategy, however, a significant number of operational decisions needed to be made regarding the

Table 11 Changing notions of 'Britishness'

The traditional Britain	The modern Britain
Britain as a theme park; with the monarch, heritage, mother of parliaments, leader of democracy, a nation of integrity	A multiracial society living in harmony. International 'mecca' (esp. London). Fun, quirky, eccentric. Leaders in style, fashion, music. Youth influencing other parts of the world. Centre of world communication, manufacturing excellence

Source: adapted from Curtis, 1997:19, BA market research report, 1997.

[4] The new youth generation also brought new views and perspectives relating to gender, greater tolerance, post-materialism, individuality/autonomy, freedom institutions and hierarchy. The implications of these societal changes meant that British Airways needed a new identity to reflect the changing values.

Table 12 Views of 'Britishness'

Negative Associations		Positive Associations		Areas in which Britain excels
Tradition	Proud	Creativity	Independent	Scientific research
Conservativeness	Stubborn	Ingenuity	Self-confident	Fashion
Insularity	Rigid, formal	Individualism	Traditional	Software
Exclusivity	Inflexible, dogmatic	Invention	Integrity	Design
Stiff	Not open-minded	Classy	Tolerant	Media
Distant	Insular	Gentlemanly	Harmonious	
Square	Exuberant and	Polite, courteous	Humorous	
Arrogant	Eccentric	Reliable	Sociable	

Source: adapted from Curtis, 1997:19, BA market research report, 1997.

extent to which the organisation needed to appeal directly to the vast number of different customer groups and regarding what competencies needed to be developed in order for the customer service delivery platform to deploy the global strategy. Decisions needed to be made as to how to implement this strategy in practice and how far the organisation should go in localising such a service offering on a global scale in order differentiate BA further from its global competitors.

Components of the global strategy

This section describes the nature of the corporate mission, vision and values of the airline at the time the global strategic intent was formulated, as well

as how the strategic intent was translated into product and service propositions, which were then interpreted into service specifications for the strategy to be operationalised.

The emergence of the global strategy arose from these market research activities and management perceptions. BA responded by adopting themes and values from this new world, with goals such as becoming a 'global and caring' airline. One of the four goals, therefore, was to become 'Truly Global', which was also defined by these research activities.

The 'Truly Global' goal reflected the changing competitive structure in our industry. It recognises the new ways customers can be served

Table 13 Changes in wider society

1980s	1990s
– 'yuppie' consumerism	– a focus on individual; time for self, rather than work
– curbing of excesses	– respect for individuals rather than companies/organisations
– greater restraint	– time for community and family; looking after each other, 'traditional values (individualism also can be seen as a threat)
– a move back to 'traditional values'	
– a greater self-awareness of 'others', especially the 'have-nots'	– safety and security (risk aversion)
	– moving from material to spiritual values; quality of life, rather than success, soul searching, moral and ethical questioning (e.g. nuclear testing)
	– environmental consciousness

Source adapted from Curtis, 1997:19, BA market research report, 1997.

Table 14 Global goals

FACTORS	ACTIVITIES
Global Passenger Benefit	Consistency of customer satisfaction across markets and partners
Global Travel Network	Relative quality of connections offered between the projected top 40 international business cities
Brand Recognition	Spontaneous recognition of BA as international airline compared with other carriers in key markets
Multicultural	Fit between customer contact staff/management nationalities and those of BA's customer base

by effective international alliances. The major airlines and, more importantly, their most frequent customers, are beginning to see the attractions in such alliances.

For British Airways to succeed as these changes take effect we need to concentrate on how customers can be better served by a global alliance network, based on seamlessness and consistent standards. We also need to be a company with a positive global outlook, through developing the competitive strength of our alliance network and the global impact of our brands; we will also be seeking profitable new ways of meeting customer needs for travel-related products worldwide.

We must commit to our value of being 'global and caring', recognising the culturally diverse nature of our customers and aiming to serve them with a high level of awareness and sensitivity. This will be measured by asking customers of different cultures about how well their needs are met when they travel with us. Overall we must aim to be truly global, with a truly global network and a truly global outlook. (BA Goals, BA Intranet 1999)

The goals of becoming a 'Global network, global outlook: recognised everywhere for superior value in world travel' and of having a 'Share of worldwide air passengers who provide income to BA or its alliances' was broken down further into sub-goals, as described in Table 14. The goals of developing a global network and outlook and to be known for superior value were underpinned by four key factors, namely providing global customer benefits, a global travel network, brand recognition and being multicultural.

The strategic intent of the airline was to become 'the undisputed leader in world travel'. The corporate 'Strategy Plan' further detailed the specific nature of this new focus:

British Airways has adopted a focused strategy for the 21st Century. It encompasses four main elements: offering our customers the industry's leading premium brands, with world beating customer service delivered by inspired people, while building an airline, with alliances, that can truly serve the world, all contributing to a renewed drive towards greater profitability and shareholder value. Focused on the world, focused on our customers, focused on our people and, focused on profitability. As the world industry faces fundamental change, British Airways is undergoing its fourth strategic evolution since privatisation. In this year's annual report, while reviewing the past 12 months, we also focus on our vision for the future. We outline the steps we are taking to ensure we fly into the new millennium firmly on track to become the undisputed leader in world travel. (BA Annual Report 1998–99:2)

The corporate strategic plan was then further translated into several strategic elements. These four strategic elements show where the global strategic intent was to fit in to the strategic agenda of the organisation. The 'official' description of each of the four strategic elements and the associated specific functional initiatives used to deploy the corporate strategy are detailed in Table 15.

The mission, vision and goals

At the time of privatisation, the mission, values and goals of the airline were redesigned to align the

Table 15 The four strategic elements

Strategic Element	Overall Focus	Initiatives	Directors' Comment
1. Focused on profitability	Our new fleet and network refinement strategies are building on our business efficiency programmes, enabling us to concentrate on strong profitability into the future.	New fleet and network strategies New World Cargo Centre (May 99) Business Efficiency Programme Premium Focus	*'Our fleet and network refinement programmes will enable us to deliver real benefits to the business – and to our customers.' Director of Strategy.*
2. Focused on customers	Customers remain at the heart of everything we do and exceeding our customers' expectations is of paramount importance to our future.	World Traveller (economy) relaunch New Club World business in the wings Smoother service on the ground	*'We are completely committed to customer service and innovation. We will continue to invest in providing our customers with ground-breaking products and services into the future, whenever and wherever it makes good commercial sense.' Director of Marketing.*
3. Focused on the world	We are using our worldwide network and our new alliance relationships to offer customers the best choice and flexibility and to enable us to concentrate on the most profitable markets.	oneworld™ takes off A growing world network Alliance partnerships strengthened More franchises and partners	*'With oneworld™ British Airways is at the centre of a world-leading alliance that more than matches any competitor.' Director of Alliances.*
4. Focused on our people	Our people are the key to our success. We are investing in providing the best possible working environments to inspire our people all over the world.	State of the art workplaces – Waterside, World Cargo Centre, 'hot desking', cyber surfing. Putting People First Again Share ownership Good people management and In Touch programmes Changes to union agreements (pilots)	*'People who feel good about their working world deliver the best results. That is the philosophy that lies behind British Airways' approach to its employees.' Director of Human Resources.*

Source: BA Annual Report 1998-1999:30.

organisation more closely with the expectations of the airline's customers:

In 1986, Sir Colin Marshall, then its Chief Executive, set out the Mission for British Airways – 'To be The Best and Most Successful Company in the Airline Industry'. Then it seemed an impossible dream for a BA dubbed 'Bloody Awful' by customers. But by improving customer service and by redefining its marketing, sales and managerial approach ready for life in the private sector, the company transformed its reputation and its finances. Customers were impressed by a new-found focus on service.

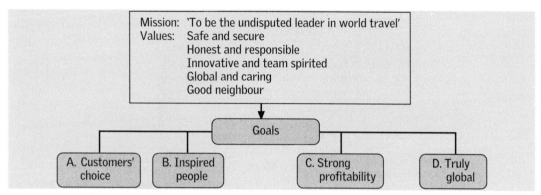

Figure 1 Mission, values and goals
Source: *BA Fact Book*, 1997:13.

Investors, including most employees, also bene-fited from the growth in the value of its shares. (*BA Fact Book*, 1997:13)

The TMT redefined the mission, values and goals, towards better customer services, achievement of financial and operational targets and improved ways of working between employees and management. The new mission, values and goals are detailed in Figure 2. Four areas that needed to be addressed were identified: the global economic climate, the challenge of competition, what customers were asking for and what employees wanted.

The new mission statement became '*to be the undisputed leader in world travel*'. The new values included being *safe and secure, honest and respon-sible, innovative and team-spirited, global and caring, a good neighbour*. The new goals became cus-tomers' choice (airline of first choice in key markets), *strong profitability* (meeting investors' expectations and securing the future), truly global (global network, global outlook recognised everywhere for superior value in world travel), *inspired people* (building on success and delighting customers), as detailed in Figures 3 to 5 (*BA Fact Book*, 1997:13).

These diagrams indicate the linkages between the mission, vision, values and associated goals and detail the objectives of each of the goals. This overview illustrates where the 'Truly Global' goal was positioned within the overall corporate vision.

The global strategic implementation initiatives

Many different organisation-wide change initiatives were introduced to execute the 'truly global'

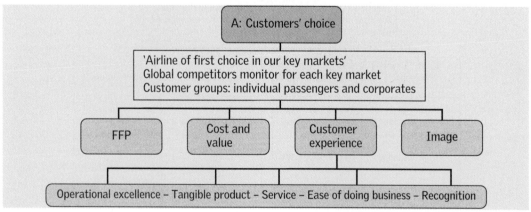

Figure 2 Goal A
Source: *BA Fact Book*, 1997:13)

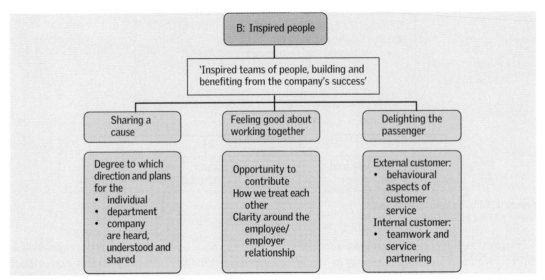

Figure 3 Goal B
Source: *BA Fact Book*, 1997:13)

strategic intent. The following section provides an overview of the nature and extent of these initiatives specifically designed to deploy the new global strategy into practice. These included a highly visible corporate identity change, the launch of a global alliance, a new flagship HQ and a new corporate communication programme. These organisation-wide initiatives are listed in Table 16.

Utopia

In 1997, Ayling declared that the new corporate image on the aircraft was *'the physical manifestation of a fundamental review of our mission. No longer will the airline be just a UK carrier but a global airline based in Britain'*. The changes to the image of the airline required the repainting of over 300 aircraft at an estimated cost of £60 million (*BA News*, 2000:10).

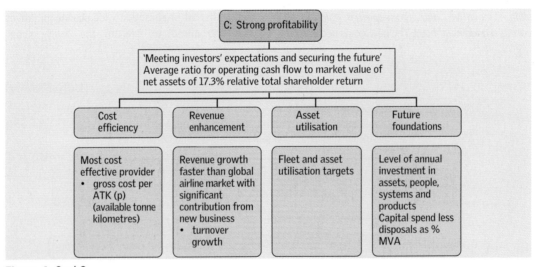

Figure 4 Goal C
Source: *BA Fact Book*, 1997:13)

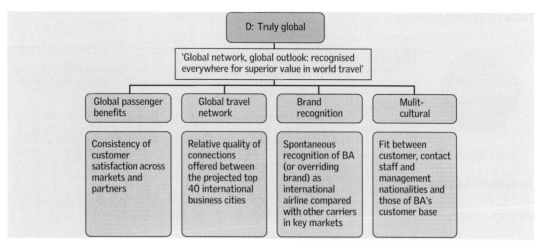

Figure 5 Goal D.
Source: *BA Fact Book*, 1997:13)

The most visual symbol of the change in strategic emphasis was the attempt to change the airline's corporate identity. It was believed that such a change would help to communicate the new mission, vision and values:

One of the issues faced was the question of how to interpret and deliver the positioning identified in the Masterbrand Research – 'Global and Caring'. Reflected in the metaphor 'nothing is too big and nothing is too small'. The positioning was expressed as: 'an airline of its world and for that world, born and based in Britain – citizen of the world' (global); 'a passionate commitment of the British Airways community to serving the communities of the world' (caring). The change in identity is to reflect that British Airways is building from British to global; from premium/business to all people who place value on the travel experience; from long-haul, to both short and long-haul; from masculine and upright to warmth and humanity. (The Research Business International Report: 1995)

BA developed a new marketing campaign, called Utopia, based around the use of global images. The market research indicated that this new identity would help convey BA's aspirations for the future, by appealing to travellers worldwide and indicating that the airline was a 'British' airline. BA wanted to be both a British airline and also a 'global' airline. Using images from five different continents BA hoped to convey values of cultural sympathy and diversity.[5] In June 1997, the new BA corporate identity was launched. Another marketing campaign attempting to create the perception that the organisation was a global operator was the oneworld™ alliance. The logo that represented the alliance was then added to any visual representations of the airline, as part of the corporate identity.

Table 16 Corporate level initiatives

Year	Initiative
1997	Utopia, the new corporate identity
1997	The Waterside building and its particular design features
1999	oneworld™
1999	Putting People First Again, corporate communications event

[5] Market Research Department Reports 1997 and 1998.

Table 17 Benefits to oneworld Members

oneworld Features

Aer Lingus

AmericanAirlines®

BRITISH AIRWAYS

CATHAY PACIFIC

FINNAIR

IBERIA

LAN

QANTAS

More people to support you
- Together we employ over 260,000 people in over 130 countries. Our employees will be there to help you, on the ground and in the air, wherever your journey takes you in the oneworld network of over 550 destinations around the globe.

Greater rewards for frequent flyers
- If you are a member of the American Airlines Advantage, British Airways Executive Club, Cathay Pacific Marco Polo Club, Finnair Plus, Iberia Plus, Qantas Frequent Flyer, LanChile LanPass or Aer Lingus TAB you will find that the rewards and privileges of membership have been greatly enhanced. You will earn miles in your particular program whenever you travel on eligible flights and fares of the oneworld alliance airways. Qualifying flights will also count towards the maintenance or advancement of your tier status. 2 And, when you are ready to redeem your miles, you can do so to over 550 destinations worldwide.

  Because our eight frequent flyer programs have different names for their various membership tiers, we have created a set of oneworld symbols: oneworld Emerald, Sapphire and Ruby.

Smoother transfers
- We place great emphasis on the service we provide, in flight and on the ground, especially to passengers with onward connections. We hope to make your transfers between oneworld member airlines as smooth as possible.

More value
- oneworld Global Products bring a new simplicity to planning both regional and around-the-world itineraries to your choice of over 550 destinations.

Access to airline lounges
- The oneworld alliance airlines provide over 400 lounges across the globe. If you are a top-tier member of one of our frequent flyer programs, you will have access to our lounges prior to departure.

  At peak periods, access to certain lounges may be restricted due to capacity constraints. Access is available on the day of departure when your next onward flight is with a oneworld member airline. Access may not apply at a limited number of third-party-operated lounges.

Source: www.BA.com

Waterside

Another attempt by management to change the culture of the airline was to move the functional managers into one custom-built, open-plan environment known as 'Waterside'. This transition into the new 21st-century working mode (which included 'hot desking') was another of Ayling's high-profile changes.

The move to Waterside was a further attempt to create culture change by bringing together many departments in one location and to reinforce the 'global and caring' strategic intent.

The design was such that each wing of the building was named after a region of the world and each workspace, meeting and training room was named after particular cities within that region. The idea was to provide a global perspective to daily work.

oneworld™

The oneworld alliance was launched in 1998 and embraced 220,000 employees in over 138 countries,

serving 600 destinations and providing access to over 200 lounges. Table 17 lists features of oneworld including the various airline partners involved in the oneworld alliance and the benefits offered to oneworld members.

Putting People First Again (PPFA)

To give effect to this strategic intent, the external image and customer perception of the airline needed to be aligned with the internal image, culture and behaviours of the employees. At the corporate level, initiatives such as corporate training programmes were introduced in an attempt to change the internal culture. One of these programmes, 'Putting People First Again' (PPFA), attempted to broaden attitudes, to promote a more outward-looking perspective and to increase the focus on customer service. PPFA emphasised the importance of meeting individuals' needs through an increased understanding of different cultural needs. Employees from all levels across the network were flown to the

UK HQ to attend this one-day training event. This programme followed on from the previous PPF programme that had been introduced by Sir Colin Marshall in 1983 when the organisation had first been privatised and which was designed to reinforce a more customer-driven organisational culture. The PPFA communication programme revolved around a common charter that was communicated to all those who attended the training programme. The charter is described in Figure 6 below.

Putting People First Again
Charter
'So, what's it all about?'
'Honest, direct communication'
You told us in the Employee Opinion Survey that you wanted more. This is your chance to get it!
'Our Customers'
They are critical to our profitability. We'll be discussing what they want and how we deliver those needs.
'Today's business'
An honest picture of what's going on in the company at the moment.
'Tomorrow's World'
A glimpse of what the future holds for our business and what we need to do to secure that future.
'So, what do we want from you?'
'Involvement'
Your expertise, your knowledge.
'An open mind'
Listen and respect the contributions of colleagues.

Figure 6 BA PPFA Charter 1999

Case 23 House of Townend Limited

Wine Online: new competition in the UK wine trade

Introduction

Throughout the late 1990s unprecedented growth in e-commerce had a profound effect on many industries, yet the fine wine trade was surprisingly slow to react to the changes brought about by this new technology. Towards the close of the decade a handful of traditional wine merchants cautiously entered the market, faced with new competition from dedicated Internet operators. Although wine would seem to be a product perfectly suited to selling online, many long-established wine businesses have found that they did not have the skills or resources to compete effectively in this new medium. This case examines the position at the end of 2000 for a company approaching its 100th anniversary: Yorkshire-based *House of Townend*.

House of Townend Limited

The company is a wholly owned subsidiary of J. Townend & Sons (Hull) Limited, a holding company controlled by J.E. Townend and his immediate family. House of Townend Limited ('*Townend*') is an importer, wholesaler and retailer of high-quality wine. These three trading activities generate three discrete revenue streams through various trading divisions.

Overseas agency agreements, foreign market purchases and imports are managed by the agency division *Cachet Wine*. This relates purely to quality wines sourced directly with the producers, for which a sole supply agency is in place. Foreign currency transactions are carried out through the main

Townend operation, which remains responsible for all wholesale activity.

The wholesale division is the core business, supplying quality hotels and restaurants and a limited number of resellers. A team of 10 experienced salespeople is supported by a permanent telesales operation and own-fleet distribution. A cash-and-carry operation has recently been launched, at the main site in Hull, serving regional pubs and off-licences.

The retail arm operates 11 shops under separately branded *House of Townend* wine shops and *Booz Brothers* off-licences. Only one is a fine wine shop, attached to the *Willerby Manor Hotel*, a related Townend Group undertaking. Three further shops are wine-led, although positioned further downmarket. The seven Booz Brothers shops are downmarket off-licences selling a range of beers, spirits and CTN lines, with wine taking a secondary role.

Case background

In preliminary interviews, the Managing Director suggested that the firm was under-utilising its assets. He was keen to investigate the possibility of launching an online operation.

Within the retail division a small mail-order business had been operating on a low-key basis since 1995. It used essentially the same wine list as the wholesale supply list, with different pricing and VAT presentation, and contributed approximately £200k in revenues. This operation was recently used as the vehicle to test a pilot e-commerce project. A Website was constructed, which was effectively little more than a price list published on the Web. This operated under the domain name www.houseoftownend.co.uk.

The commercial effect of the pilot project was negligible and the site was aborted to allow a refocusing of the strategy. The domain names remain active and new site formats are being considered for a relaunch in 2001.

The UK wine market

The UK wine trade is almost exclusively an import business, with exports (mainly consisting of re-exports) amounting to less than 1% of total revenues. The wine sector is only one element of the booming alcoholic beverages market, in which the

This case was prepared by Andrew Bramley, Warwick Business School.

The material in this case is taken from the original research conducted by the author. This case is intended as a basis for class discussion and is not intended to illustrate either ineffective or effective handling of a business situation.

© Andrew Bramley 2004.

UK is one of the most important European consumers with a total market value of £32 billion.

Britain has traditionally played an important role in shaping the European and global wine market. British wine merchants are greatly respected, exerting considerable influence over prices and the ratings of wines in each new vintage. It is significant that France's biggest market is the UK, accounting for 18% of French wine exported. The UK is also the most important market for Germany, Australia and New Zealand.

The supply side of the global wine market is dominated by geographically fixed factors of production. The locus of primary production cannot shift, since wine nomenclature is strictly controlled and linked to geography, vineyard site and grape variety, along with a host of contingent factors such as the age and provenance of vines, mandatory vinification techniques and the quantifiable chemical composition of the wine itself.

Although larger operators from both Europe and the New World are continually seeking new foreign vineyard sites to establish a physical position and production base in their respective export markets, the market remains highly fragmented in terms of both supply and distribution. Of particular relevance to wine merchants contemplating e-commerce supported by outsourced logistics and distribution is the particular deficiency the UK market has in its physical distribution channels. The haulage and freight service infrastructure is poor, especially in provincial areas. This remains a problem for traditional wine merchants dependent on carriers for deliveries.

The world's best classic wines are scarce and demand far exceeds supply. Many of the better producers and well-established estates strictly limit the quantities sold to any one merchant, and allocation levels tend to be set in direct proportion to the length of the trading relationship and perceived prestige of the intended destination or sale point. Many top French winemakers, for example, like to see their wines sold in internationally renowned restaurants and perceive that an association with a celebrated chef enhances the credibility of their wine.

For this reason a key factor in the supply-side economics is the need to maintain sources of rare wines, establish new ones, or seek out the rising stars of the future and secure consistent supply through working closely with growers in product development. It is in this area that New World producers have the greatest impact on the changing market.

For example, although Australian wine only accounts for 2.3% of world production, Australia generates around 25% of the world's leading scientific papers on oenology and viticulture. Californian vinification expertise is similarly sought after, and 'flying winemakers' from Australia, New Zealand and the Americas are advising vineyards and winemakers in all areas of the world, even in the classic French heartlands of Bordeaux and Burgundy.

In the late 1980s circa 85% of all the wine exported in the world came from just four Western European countries (France, Italy, Portugal and Spain). By 1997 this had fallen to 72%. The current figure is 69%, yet New World exports have grown at an astonishing rate over the past decade. To take just two examples, Australia has grown by 350% and Chile by 400%.

Excessive fragmentation and over-regulation are undermining the fine wine producers of the Old World. *The Economist* has called this a global market-wide battle, fought between 'Terroir' and 'Technology'. The desire to protect regional identity and the integrity of famous vineyards has produced a plethora of legislation, such as the French *Appellation Contrôlée* (AC). The strictness of AC confines core production methods and means the French vignerons are less able to react to changing consumer tastes or adapt to new technology. The new breed of winemaker is less constrained by such legislation and this is driving greater innovation in vinification.

Further down the value chain at the wholesale level, which primarily concerns Townend, the market is characterised by high asset specificity, coupled with potential labour mobility. In this context, human capital specificity arises because skills are uniquely specific to the area of expert knowledge surrounding fine wine, to precise knowledge of certain rare wines from growers in their portfolio, and to knowledge of the regional peculiarities of the hotel and restaurant business.

Buyers in that industry view their wine suppliers as valued and trusted advisers. Having invested time and learning in the relationship, and time in understanding the range of wines and their growers, they are likely to consider that sales relationships on a personal level are of equal importance to the corporate trading history. This is a market of considerable and growing importance for the specialist merchant. Between 1995 and 1999 the UK hotel trade grew 25% in value terms, followed by the restaurant sector at 20%.

Hence, specificity also extends into complementary markets and, unfortunately for merchants such as Townend, the people acquiring special skills, contacts and knowledge may easily move from one organisation to another without any significant retraining.

Sales of all alcoholic drinks are sensitive to price and, therefore, to changes in tax and duties. The anticipated introduction of the euro is expected to bring greater pan-European fiscal alignment although, to date, there has been limited harmonisation in duties since the formation of the Single European Market in 1993. At a retail level there has been a significant growth in cross-border shopping to take advantage of EU tax differentials.

This has also affected the hotel and restaurant trade. For those restaurateurs or hotel groups willing to outlay larger sums, parallel imports are an increasingly attractive option, especially in premium product sectors, in which UK agencies typically set significantly higher prices relative to those in the country of origin. The clearest example of this was in the sales of champagne during the build-up to the millennium celebrations. Many hotel operators went directly to the producers, anticipating both scarcity and high prices in the UK. In reality, however, the expected boom did not arrive, leaving high stocks within the hospitality industry and causing a further slowing down of champagne sales through legitimate agency channels.

In recent years domestic demand for local wines in producing countries has declined, while wine consumption in traditionally strong beer-drinking countries is on the increase. Major wine producers have been forced to pay attention to their export markets to compensate for falling domestic sales of even their generic wines. The rise in wine consumption in the UK has been especially strong, making this an increasingly important market (see Figure 1).

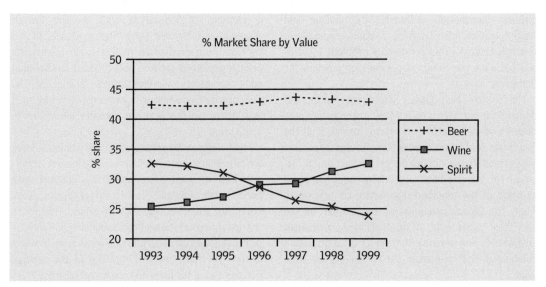

Figure 1 Shift in UK market shares of alcoholic drinks, 1993 to 1999
Source: Mintel/ACNielsen.

The major retailers and supermarket chains have been instrumental in developing the profile of the wine market and lately have done much to assist the specialist merchant. By bringing good quality wine to the shelves, they encourage its purchase as a regular weekly item, and a high information content in their marketing strips away the traditional mystique and cultural barriers that may have previously inhibited buyers.

Now high-street multiples are engaging in sophisticated micro-segmentation and strategic marketing to better understand the UK wine drinker, and most have their own expert tasters, buyers and consultants – previously the domain of the specialist wine merchant. This has been one of the main factors underpinning the increase in popularity of New World wines and in the sheer range and global representation of wines on the shelves of major supermarkets and off-licences.

The changing UK market shares of the key wine-producing countries are shown in Figure 2.

Bringing better wine into mainstream domestic consumption has had a spin-off effect in increased media exposure, which plays a key role in educating consumers. An example of this is the wider appreciation of different grape varieties today, in contrast to 10 years ago, when consumers who might buy wine on the basis of region or AC had no idea which grapes were used in its make-up. High-profile media coverage promotes the idea that wine is fashionable and knowledge of wine is a desirable social skill; an image also perpetuated by positive television exposure. At a higher level of consumer knowledge, media such as *The Wine Advocate*, *The Wine Spectator*, *Decanter* and various independent Web-based commentators such as www.wine-pages.com do much to increase consumer awareness.

Research by Mintel into UK wine buyers' changing preferences, carried out by survey between 1994 and 1998, showed definite trends suggesting increasing acceptance of higher-quality wine:

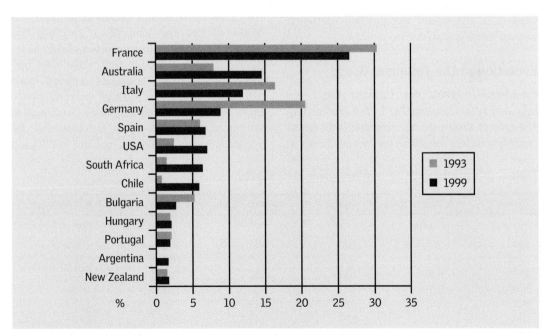

Figure 2 Patterns in UK wine consumption, % share by country of origin[a]
[a]Aggregate % changes by volume.
Source: *The Economist* Intelligence Unit.

- A willingness to experiment with higher-priced wines from new areas
- Greater awareness of differing wine 'styles' based on grape variety
- Greater reliance placed on advice and information at point of sale
- Increasing purchases of different wines to match food

The value of the overall market has increased faster than volume as customers have traded-up in quality to more costly wines. Between 1993 and 1999 the UK market's value increased by 67%, or 43% in real terms (see Table 1).

The slight decline in 1995 was due in part to falling production after poor harvests in Australia, California, Italy and Spain. The resultant pressure on supply and pricing, allied to shortfalls in the production intended for domestic use in these markets, meant that UK retailers found difficulty in sourcing wines at lower price points, which are vital for bringing new consumers into the market.

The upper levels of the trade, however, were not greatly affected and overall values continued to rise, suggesting that this is a surprisingly resilient segment of the market incorporating consumers who are increasingly less price-sensitive.

Evolution of the Townend Group

Established in 1906, the Townend Group has remained in family ownership to the present day. The present Chairman, J.E. Townend, was fundamentally a retailer and during his previous tenure as MD the scale of the business grew to 35 retail outlets. Gradually the emphasis has shifted in favour of wholesale activity with a commensurate reduction in the number of shops throughout the past 20 years.

Under the leadership of the current MD, John Charles Townend, the profile of the business has been substantially changed. At the time of his joining the company in 1988, the portfolio of retail shops numbered 14, with wholesale turnover relatively static and in the region of £0.5m annually. The majority of that revenue consisted of low margin fast-moving lines, sold into supermarkets and grocery multiples. A significant boost to wholesale turnover came in 1992 when Townend won the national supply contract to the TUCO university purchasing group, worth £0.5m per year for 3 years.

From this point onwards the focus of the business development was almost exclusively on wholesale supply, mainly to hotels and restaurants, and between 1997 and 2000 the retail portfolio has diminished at the rate of one shop per year.

The direction of this expansion was aided by the judicious recruitment of specialists in the field of wholesale supply to the on-trade, and in the acquisition of smaller businesses already in this field. The demise of two key competitors, *Yorkshire Fine Wines* and *Chennell & Armstrong*, provided scope for the recruitment of several high-calibre sales personnel. Both these businesses enjoyed good reputations in the region and their sales teams were highly respected. The current Sales Director, Alan Whitehead, was employed in the same role for Yorkshire Fine Wines. He was recruited in 1994 and

Table 1 UK market for still wine of fresh grape 1993 to 1999[a]

	Volume Sales	Index	Value Sales	Index	Inflation adj.
	M litres		£m		£m
1993	617	100	3,500	100	3,500
1994	651	106	3,800	109	3,714
1995	645	105	4,000	114	3,787
1996	678	110	4,400	126	4,074
1997	740	120	4,930	141	4,437
1998	794	129	5,410	155	4,724
1999	839	136	5,850	167	5,038

[a]excludes champagne, sparkling wine and fortified wine.
Source: Mintel/ONS/HM Customs & Excise.

several members of his old team have since joined Townend, most notably Mike Luke, a specialist in wholesale on-trade accounts.

Acquisitions and divestments

This changing profile has been underpinned by a series of divestments and acquisitions.

A major divestment took place in 1986, when 18 retail shops were sold to Blayneys. The proceeds of this sale were invested into the Willerby Manor Hotel, now a wholly owned subsidiary of the holding company J. Townend and Sons (Hull) Ltd. The hotel currently turns over circa £2.3m p.a. and sources its wet purchases, worth around £200k, through Townend.

The continued expansion of the wine division has reflected the relative significance in the industry of human capital and intangible assets. The refined skills and expertise of the people selling the wine, allied to their personal contacts and network of loyal customers are of equal importance to factor inputs, tangibles and capital assets. John Charles Townend set about recruiting several key people through acquisition of their businesses and assets.

The purchase of *Cachet Wine* in 1995 is a case in point. This was a small business run by Graham Coverdale in York, turning over circa £500k p.a. Essentially the trading assets and stock were bought along with the intangible assets and network of contacts associated with Mr. Coverdale. A similar deal took place in 1999 with the absorption of *Phil Parrish Wines*, a local business with revenues of circa £200k.

The attractive aspect of these deals was in the acquisition of new customer accounts and revenues in the hotel and restaurant on-trade, and both these people are now important members of the sales team. Immediately following its purchase, Cachet Wine was used as the platform to develop Townend's agency wines division, which effectively came on stream in and around 1997.

Group restructuring

Significant group restructuring took place between 1995 and 1999. At the start of this period, the majority of the principal wine and spirits trading activity, at circa £4.5m, remained in the holding company. Various smaller operating companies

came within this umbrella and the group structure was characterised by close divisional interrelationships, with several reciprocal participating-interest holdings and extensive cross-billing between divisions. There are also unlimited multilateral guarantees and cross-guarantees within the group, between group undertakings, and between companies in which the holding parent has participating interests. The controlling family has historically viewed the group as one complete entity, inseparable by divisions. In addition to the sales made between Townend and the hotel, substantial management charges are levied between divisions.

In 1998 there was a reported change of trade in J. Townend and Sons, from wine merchants to a holding company with property letting interests. There were a number of transactions between divisions, including transfers of assets, write-back on taxable-event disposals, and revaluation of investments to reflect the underlying net assets of wholly owned subsidiaries. At the height of this reorganisation there were nine separate entities within the group activities.

The reorganisation was phased in to bring alignment and coherency to the group trading activities, since all the wine revenues and trading assets at wholesale and retail levels have gradually been subsumed within House of Townend Ltd. In the 1998–1999 period freehold and leasehold land and buildings with net book values of £2,072,680 and £300,620 were transferred to the holding company from Willerby Manor and House of Townend respectively. The above restructuring has culminated in a streamlining of the group into three key areas as at the end of 1999:

- **J. Townend and Sons (Hull) Ltd:** Holding company controlling all group property
- **House of Townend Ltd:** All wine and spirit importing, wholesaling and retailing
- **Willerby Manor Hotels Ltd:** All hotel and catering activities

Consolidated wholesale and retail wine trading figures for 1995 to 1999 are shown in the 5-year financial performance analysis (see Figure 3).

In calculating the aggregate sector performance the accounts of 117 companies engaged in the same area of the wine trade were analysed and a control group of 66 extracted from the total sample. This control group was chosen on the basis of similar size, operating parameters and customer profile to Townend.

Systems and processes

I spend as much time placating irate customers and sorting out incorrect deliveries as I do selling wine ... either the customer has got someone else's wine, or the vintages are wrong, or they only get half the stock they ordered because the warehouse couldn't find everything. The problem is this Dickensian warehouse system and the fact that nobody talks to anyone else in the different departments. (Mike Luke, Sales Executive)

The company has grown up within a range of Victorian canal-side warehouses, each with its own warren of offices and interconnecting staircases. Mike Luke felt that this in itself contributed to poor communication throughout the company and reduced the accountability of individuals for errors by limiting regular face-to-face contact.

As an importer, Townend has a Customs-bonded warehouse registered with HM Customs & Excise, with a strictly licensed record system for import stock based on an old UNIX platform. The company's main information system is similarly built on UNIX, which has been gradually upgraded and expanded over the past 15 years. There is no interface between the two systems.

The bonded warehouse stock is scrupulously monitored at the time of delivery, due to mandatory Customs compliance and audit procedures. Any incorrect deliveries are notified and records amended before the wines go into storage. However, through regular observation in the warehouse it became clear that there are no formal locations in the bonded section and no layout or plan of the wines in long-term and short-term storage. The process is entirely dependent on the memory of the bondsman, one of the company's longest-serving employees.

In the main warehouse serving the daily deliveries, staff turnover is high and errors are frequent. The orders office generates a manual picking list, which is taken around the warehouse by staff compiling the orders. Each boxed order is given a dispatch note in duplicate, the carbon copy of which is eventually used for compiling the customer invoice. It takes between 7 and 10 days to generate the invoice, which is then mailed to the customer.

All the retail shops are equipped with proprietary DOS-based EPOS systems. The hardware in each shop is basically a till with bar code scanner. Each unit relies on remote dial-up to interface with the management system at head office, which is by text file exchange. This system frequently leads to stock errors. The calibre of shop staff was acknowledged as a weak link in the process. Wine product knowledge is scarce and very little training is carried out, or requested by staff. Notably, the viability of some of the remote shop sites, as stand-alone units, was questioned by the Sales Director and most were not viewed as complementary to the core wholesale fine wine business.

Sales and marketing

Alan Whitehead believes his team of salespeople to be unrivalled in terms of their maturity and the respect they command in the trade. Most have been in the wine business all their lives, and since many have run their own businesses they are extremely profit-aware and have a good range of personal contacts at all levels in the supply chain.

The relatively recent telesales operation is primarily an order-collecting function, since the salesforce is responsible for the selling-in of new lines. All the relationship building is done at the client premises face-to-face, and it is here that long-standing trust is built between client and sales force. The convivial nature of both hospitality business and wine trade means that this may often take place in a semi-social context.

John Townend has developed notable wine tasting and buying skills over the years, and works closely with Alan Whitehead on the development of the trade list and the range of suppliers in the portfolio. The trade list represents a unique range of products, since the 94-year history of Townend has influenced the willingness of better vignerons to supply limited allocation wines in realistic quantities. Hence, the classic regions such as Burgundy and Bordeaux are well represented by top producers. The addition of

Consolidated wholesale and retail trading activities 1995 to 1999

Year Ending	1995	1996	1997	1998	1999	key changes
						1995–1999%
Turnover	6,613,288	6,875,942	7,278,226	7,855,466	8,529,966	28.97
Gross profit	1,186,008	1,217,030	1,482,777	1,645,102	1,896,166	59.87
PBIT	36,193	3,497	72,256	108,111	142,146	292.74
Interest	27,999	11,146	26,349	41,833	42,264	
Taxation	4,655	807	3,775	4,979	6,635	
PAIT	3,539	−37,458	42,132	61,299	133,182	
Dividend	-	-	-	-	-	
Retained Earnings	3,311	−37,458	42,132	61,299	133,182	3922.41
Fixed Assets	966,367	846,790	854,158	933,349	1,268,249	31.23
Current Assets	2,747,292	3,392,840	3,320,667	3,765,864	3,240,077	17.94
Stocks	1,223,491	1,196,934	1,402,944	1,635,626	1,880,860	
Trade Debtors	674,090	716,678	870,792	953,267	1,018,882	
Cash	3,665	2,859	2,857	3,200	2,721	
Total Assets	3,713,659	4,239,630	4,174,825	4,699,213	4,508,326	21.39
Current Liabilities	2,233,873	2,791,154	2,681,271	3,205,727	3,092,196	38.42
Trade Creditors+accruals	751,597	1,003,555	1,030,789	1,202,219	1,435,751	91.02
STL [Bank Overdraft]	705,215	1,115,956	1,080,291	1,200,753	1,312,810	86.16
Capital Employed	1,479,786	1,448,476	1,493,554	1,493,486	1,416,130	−4.3
LTL {debt > 1 yr]	-	6,148	9,094	2,878	240,836	
ShareHolders' Funds	1,479,786	1,442,328	1,484,460	1,490,608	1,175,294	−20.57

Ratio Analysis	note	1995	1996	1997	1998	1999	sector avg
							1999
Performance							
ROCE [PBIT / CE]	a	2.45%	0.24%	4.84%	7.24%	10.04%	22.21%
ROI [PBIT / TA]	b	0.97%	0.08%	1.73%	2.30%	3.15%	6.61%
Gross margin		17.93%	17.70%	20.37%	20.94%	22.23%	22.15%
[~ Movement yr-on-yr]		datum	−1.30%	15.10%	2.79%	6.15%	0.82%
Net margin	aⁱ bⁱ	0.55%	0.05%	0.99%	1.38%	1.67%	2.60%
[~ Movement yr-on-yr]		datum	−90.71%	1852.02%	38.63%	21.08%	0.12%
EVA	c	−£123,433	−£150,425	−£88,270	−£78,118	£24,310	
Efficiency							
Sales: Capital Employed	aⁱⁱ	4.47	4.75	4.87	5.26	6.02	8.54
Asset Turnover	bⁱⁱ	1.78	1.62	1.74	1.67	1.89	2.54
(Debtors*365) / Sales		37.20	38.04	43.67	44.29	43.60	49.37
(Creditors*365) / Sales		41.48	53.27	51.69	55.86	61.44	61.72
Sales : Stocks		5.41	5.74	5.19	4.80	4.54	7.29
Liquidity							
Current Ratio		1.23	1.22	1.24	1.17	1.05	1.20
Acid Test		0.68	0.79	0.72	0.66	0.44	0.91
Stability							
Gearing [on total debt]		47.66%	77.47%	72.94%	80.59%	109.71%	84.52%
Interest Cover		1.29	0.31	2.74	2.58	3.36	5.98
Growth							
Sales growth yr-on-yr		datum	3.97%	5.85%	7.93%	8.59%	8.94%
[~ Inflation-adjusted]		datum	3.88%	5.67%	7.67%	8.44%	8.79%
PBIT Growth yr-on-yr		datum	−90.34%	1966.23%	49.62%	31.48%	1.25%
[~ Inflation-adjusted]		datum	−88.22%	1907.11%	47.99%	30.96%	1.23%

Economic Indicators		1995	1996	1997	1998	1999	1995–1999%
RPI % change yr-on-yr	d	3.54	2.43	3.12	3.42	1.67	11.11
GDP % change yr-on-yr	e	2.83	2.63	3.52	2.21	2.14	10.86
Interest rates %	f	6.57	5.79	6.73	7.34	5.69	−13.39

ab Component elements of ROCE and ROI may not agree due to rounding
c   An EVA cost-of-capital substitute rate was estimated from LIBOR +2%
d   RPI from aggregate quarterly RPIX underlying rate. Index: 1995=100
e   GDP seasonally adjusted, at constant market prices. Index 1995=100
f   Annualised rate calculated from LIBOR expressed as weighted daily averages. Source: Bank of England

Figure 3 Townend Group: 5-Year Financial Performance Analysis

specialist wines from some of the foremost growers in the New World through agency agreements with Cachet Wine means it is feasible for Townend to supply all the needs of quality hotels and restaurants.

Sales meetings are held in a 4–6 week cycle and while these are performance-based and target-led there is very little exchange of information or training relating to the actual products and the portfolio of specialist producers. More importantly, the unique knowledge that has been built up within the team is not disseminated, exploited or added to.

> *Strategy? I think if you ask all ten of us you'll get ten different answers … we are not really told anything about marketing, or the planned Website, or any new things coming up. It would be helpful if we could have a bit more information passed around – sometimes our sales meetings seem more like a collection of strangers who occasionally sit in the same room together. We don't really talk about promotion, marketing, new brands or suchlike.* (Graham Coverdale, Sales Executive)

The issue of brand proposition in this specialised sector is complex. Wine trade marketing tends to be concerned with, for example, 'The Wines of Australia' or 'Fine Wines of Chablis' as general concepts, and the exposure of specific wines, and certainly of their agents or wholesalers, is limited. Due to a fragmented supply market there are no major world-class brands to speak of and, with the exception of the top champagne houses, the concept of mainstream 'branded wine' is anathema to the high-quality specialist merchant.

Branding in the upper reaches of the market is subtle, and may best be described as a nested hierarchy, ranging down from country level, to regional Appellation, to the grower or négociant-éleveur and then, on a micro level, to the estate or vineyard site. The difficulty for wholesalers like Townend is that they get little exposure in this branding hierarchy.

New competition in e-commerce

In the 12 months to the end of 2000, competition in wine e-commerce intensified. The evolution of this relatively new sector has followed similar trends seen in the US market during its own growth period some two years earlier. In the USA, the more advanced state of development may be attributed to the generally earlier public acceptance of Internet technology and the fact that the majority of USA consumer demand is for domestic wines.

In the UK, several key players have emerged, with a small number of highly resourced Internet-focused operators establishing a first-mover advantage in the upper reaches of the market. These same trends in changing structure were apparent in the US market, when just a few significant players such as *Virtual Vineyards* established an early lead.

However, there is evidence from both sides of the Atlantic that e-commerce may not yet destroy the established business model of the traditional wine merchant, since both US and UK markets are afflicted with similar problems of physical distribution. While in the US this is due to restrictive distribution laws still remaining from the Prohibition era, the net result is the same: wine e-tailers are experiencing a boom in sales, yet these are not necessarily at the expense of revenues in existing channels.

Important UK merchants with a mix of both wholesale and retail revenues are reporting differing customer reactions to e-commerce. *Bibendum* and its close rival, 300-year-old *Berry Brothers & Rudd*, were two of the first London merchants to launch Websites in 1998.

Bibendum completely closed down its retail shops in favour of an Internet operation in 1999. In-company research showed that 60% of existing Bibendum customers had Internet access and the majority generally supported the company's e-commerce initiative. However, while the core of its £20m operation is in wholesale revenues, its retail operation is positioned quite differently to Townend, being based purely on minimum 1-case order quantities for home delivery within the M25 boundary. Despite widespread use by the company's retail customers, the online operation generated little increase in total retail sales.

Berry Brothers took a different approach, offering to deliver any quantity to any UK address. It did not have a major retail presence at this time, with no dedicated retail shops. The majority of existing retail mail-order customers did not use the new Website.

The Berry Brothers site still only accounts for 5% of total sales, although recent e-commerce compound growth is significant, with 60% of purchases each month from first-time visitors.

The most significant entrant this year is *Virgin Wines*, a pure online operation headed by Virgin Direct founder Rowan Gormley. Although it has no history in the wine trade, as a highly capitalised business prepared to withstand losses for three years, with the backing of the Virgin group, at face value it poses a serious threat. Many new start-ups have underestimated the time and capital needed to build an Internet-compatible brand and a core of loyal customers. Virgin Wines has a marketing director with a background in pure e-commerce rather than the wine trade, and a loyal captive audience of over 1 million online Virgin customers. It has quickly gained market share from other online operations, even those of long-established merchants such as Bibendum and Berry Brothers.

A new breed of virtual intermediary is emerging, following the model of info-mediary 'navigator': in the US a first-mover was winesearcher.com, essentially an intermediary/search facility representing the list content of wine sellers. Although represented as a source of advice, price comparison and impartial recommendation, its revenues clearly came from commission paid by the merchants. Once more, UK market development is emulating that of its American counterpart, although since it is now two years further on in technological terms, the solutions are more creative.

One such example is uvine.com, the first 'stock exchange' for fine wine. Headed by Christopher Burr, former head of wine at Christie's, uvine.com is an Internet-only business offering investment advice and managed transactions between trade and private wine buyers and sellers. They are able to emulate the advice and expertise element in the package offered by a wine merchant, broker or auctioneer, yet their reach and audience is far wider. This effectively disintermediates traditional businesses through competing on information content, quality of advice, speed and timeliness of response, yet allied to commission rates of only 3.5% as against 10–15% with the major auction players, or the typical wholesale trade gross margins of between 20 and 25%.

A way of fighting this type of disintermediation is through inimitability of product and Internet-enabled introduction and dynamic visual promotion of channel-specific products. The US market again provides the best and earliest examples of this strategy, exemplified by the specific labelling and visual product differentiation adopted by the Mondavi Corporation for some of its premium Californian wines offered over the Web. Berry Brothers are already evaluating a number of specific wines for this treatment, for example a small range of specialised late-harvested Gewürztraminer and Tokay wines from a little-known grower in Alsace, in unusual bottle sizes and with avant-garde one-off painted label designs.

Interactive survey: WWWine Focus Group

The current state of the competition and the relative Internet presence of competitors' Websites was assessed through an interactive focus group of private and professional wine buyers and food and wine writers in Britain and the USA. Entitled the *WWWine Focus Group*, the two-stage survey was based on an interactive online survey instrument disseminated by e-mail to 41 participants.[†]

The group first provided an assessment of the desirable qualities of wine Websites, and generated a list of the keywords, search engines and portals most likely to be used in any speculative Web-search. From the list of key words suggested by participants, a detailed Web-search was made using 10 different search engines, 5 food and wine-related portals and links from leading sites serving the food and wine industry. In total, 114 search or link permutations were executed. The results from part 1 of the survey are summarised in Table 2.

In phase 2, sites with the greatest exposure in the Web-search were then graded by the focus group. Participants provided a critique of those sites on various levels, which generated a ranking of each operator according to the perceptions of more discerning consumers.

In the survey section providing contextual comments, most criticism was levelled at the juvenile

[†] The survey was conducted by the author during research at Harvard Business School. The guidance offered during this project by Professor Stephen Greyser of Harvard is gratefully acknowledged.

Table 2 Focus group ratings of Website attributes and content

Critical Dimensions of Websites	Other Web Services Requested	
Rated 1–6 in order of importance	Rated as Essential	Rated as Desirable
1 Information Content	Declared stock levels	Wine recommendations
2 Fast Download Time	Tasting notes	Discussion forum
3 Ease of Navigation	Rating of vintages	Technical information
4 Range/Quantity Offered	Search facility	Tailored Q&A service
5 Price of Wines	Private access by PIN	Market reports
6 Presentation and Graphics	Secure transactions	Profiles of producers

nature of much of the general material and advertising throughout the Internet. It was considered extremely important to be able to avoid this type of material, get to the target site quickly, navigate it efficiently and place an order as simply as possible. In addition to the major evaluation criteria set out in Table 2, the following points were consistently raised:

♦ It is not desirable to have specialised and detailed oenological information or scarce, unusual or limited-allocation wines listed for the general public to see.

♦ Buyers are likely to spend more on unique or sole-supply wines if *genuine* expert comment and technical information are available.

♦ The simplistic language used on the Internet, the basic level of advertising and the technologically led 'jargon' are detrimental to serious wine buying.[‡]

Table 3 shows the results of part 2 of the survey. Essentially this suggests the likely competitors to Townend's future online operation.

Websites of competitors

The site drawing the most favourable comments was Berry Brothers'. Extracts from the site Webpages are shown at Exhibits 1 and 2.

Exhibit 1 shows a buying window, with a profile of *Jean-Paul Droin*, a small grower in Chablis, along with a description of his wines. Exhibit 2 demonstrates the

Table 3 Focus group results: ratings of top 10 UK wine Websites

Rank	Company	Profile of Main Business [a]	URL
1	Berry Bros. & Rudd	Traditional London merchant	http://www.bbr.com
2	Bibendum	Modern wholesaler	http://www.bibendum-wine.co.uk
3	Oddbins	High-street off-licences	http://www.oddbins.co.uk
4	Chateau Online	Internet operation	http://www.chateauonline.co.uk
5	Wine Planet	Internet operation	http://www.wineplanet.co.uk
6	Majestic Online	Wine cash & carry warehouse	http://www.majestic.co.uk
7	Virgin Wines	Part of diversified brand group	http://www.virginwines.com
8	Uvine	Fine wine 'stock exchange'	http://www.uvine.com
9	Bordeaux Direct	Mail order/wine club model	http://www.bordeauxdirect.co.uk
10	Lindbury Wines	Ex mail order – now all www	http://www.itswine.com

[a] Where different – note certain operators are Internet-only and, in the case of uvine.com, while this is not strictly speaking a merchant, it is nonetheless taking revenues from the traditional merchants' market.

[‡] Particular criticism was reserved for terms such as 'shopping trolley', cartoon images of supermarket baskets and splash screen 'stings' or animated banners on click buttons such as 'Buy It Now' or 'Add To Shopping Basket'.

considerable time and expense involved in updating and maintaining the site content. The underlying technology of the page construction is exploited with the 'recommended wine' window, which changes at random, suggesting different wines to the visitor as the click-stream increases. The site's search facility was the most highly rated of all, and it was noted that the buying section of the site also allows the customer to screen searches on the basis of style of wines, advice content, producer profile or growing regions. It also incorporates a 'bypass' mode to go straight to the ordering facility.

Surprisingly, the site most criticised was Virgin. Over 70% of the group commented that, while there were some good wines listed, finding them was too difficult. Virgin scored lowest on 'ease of navigation' and 'information content'. Criticisms centred on illogical layout, with too many questions put before wine could be bought, and the site's reliance on adolescent humour and oversimplification of the subject matter. As well as causing annoyance it was felt this prevented the search facility from working adequately, and resulted in the 'wine wizard' recommendations falling short of expectations. By way of example, if Australian Shiraz was not noted as a preference in a 'wine wizard' search, the list of recommended wines excluded all Rhône such as Hermitage or Côte Rôtie, classic Italian reds such as Barolo or Amarone, and all Spanish red wines apart from Rioja. The site structure is clearly conceived by technical designers and e-commerce mass retailers rather than wine specialists. Since the search facility works on case-based reasoning it is apparent that the wines have been inappropriately classified from the outset, based on an oversimplified model and limited understanding of the wine consumer.

Exhibit 3 provides an example from uvine.com. The e-mail shown was actuated by a contemporaneous transaction on the site. Although it is automatically activated, it imparts elements of 'news' and 'information', allied to tailored recommendations based on past buying patterns. This proactive approach has effectively 'hijacked' recent information from static media (such as the *Wine Spectator* ratings) and reprocessed it, although the mode of delivery gives it a feeling of timeliness and spontaneity. This system combines proactive and reactive customer contact, with some overlap between personal telephone contact, Internet-enabled CRM and automated transaction processing offered in multiple foreign currencies. The focus group commented widely that the sort of tailored personal recommendations made show a deep understanding of the product, matching the type of advice normally expected from a high-quality wine merchant.

Summary

This case has shown that protected supply chains and inimitable products are important success factors in establishing a sustainable and resilient e-commerce model. New online operators deploying new types of resources threaten the established skills of traditional wine merchants in maintaining and protecting their unique product knowledge.

A key element in Townend's future strategy, therefore, must be to concentrate on high information content and differentiated or preferably unique and non-comparable wines. John Charles Townend has already declared that further expansion into the area of sole agency wines is his preferred route. Such a move would also protect key elements of a difficult supply market plagued by scarcity and vagaries of price, weather and economic uncertainty.

While there is an ever-present threat of disintermediation without exclusive supply contracts in place, important personal relationships with trade customers must also be strengthened and protected. Retail consumers have negligible switching costs and hence their loyalty is transient. However, in the wholesale on-trade sector, merchants have the opportunity to create more permanent associations.

This is an industry driven by people. Townend's future success depends on its relationships with leading producers, a deep knowledge of their unique wines, and the cumulative experience of its salespeople. There is an underlying caveat to this case: the successful integration of a wholly effective online operation requires skills, resources and specialised knowledge that may, at present, be unattainable for Townend without significant investment.

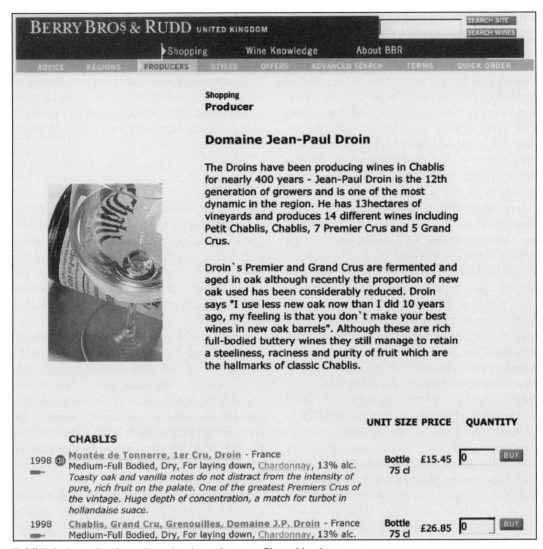

Exhibit 1 Berry Brothers site extract: producer profile and buying screen
Source: http://www.bbr.com.

Exhibit 2 Berry Brothers site extract: interactive news board in wine knowledge section
Source: http://www.bbr.com.

```
From:      enquiries@uvine.com
To:        a.bramley@Bradford.ac.uk
Subject:   uvine - good offers on the uvine exchange
Date:      8 Sept 2000 12:56:59 +0100
```

Reply	Reply All	Forward	Previous	Next	Close

Dear Mr Bramley

uvine.com has now changed the way that wine is bought and sold - with the world's first fully functional exchange for quality wines.

In a further ground-breaking step, uvine now gives you the opportunity to:

- Open an account in any one of a wide range of currencies
- Trade wines in a variety of locations around the world

This will enable online wine trading within and between different areas of the world while settling balances in the currency of your choice.

The service is open to everyone, free to join and the quality and provenance of all the wine is guaranteed. All this with the lowest commission rates in the world* - just 3.5% on either side.

Find out more about the new service, at http://www.uvine.com

As you know, we offer the latest in wine information, investment advice and wine trading strategies for your own p ortfolio. Up-to-the-minute market reports and expert appraisals are available for network members. Here are some more recommendations and hot tips selected from the wines on the exchange today, based on the sort of trades and investments you have been making lately.........................

Ch. Duhart-Milon-Rothschild 1995
Best offer GBP 190

Ch. Pavie 1999 (En Primeur)
Best offer GBP 640

Charles Heidsieck Brut Millésime Champagne 1990
Best offer GBP 145 per 6x75cl bottles: rated 97 by Wine Spectator magazine

Barolo, E Pira 1990
Best offer GBP 375

Tirecul Lagravière Cuvée Madame 1996
Best offer GBP 520 per case of 12x50cl bottles

Offers are per case of 12x75cl bottles in b ond unless otherwise stated and are correct at time of writing.

If you have any questions about the wines in these offers, the trading process or about uvine, please do not hesitate to contact us. We would be happy to recommend further wines if these do not match you current requirements. You can reach us by e-mail at enquiries@uvine.com or by telephone on 0800 328 8448, or, if calling from outside the UK, +44 20 7518 1555.

Yours sincerely,

uvine.com

If you do not wish to be contacted with details of further good offers on the uvine exchange, please send an email to unsubscribe@uvine.com

*As at September 2000

Exhibit 3 uvine.com automated message: low cost services and personalised offers

WARWICK
BUSINESS SCHOOL

This case study was prepared for this textbook by faculty members at Warwick Business School, University of Warwick, UK. This case study may not be reproduced in any form without prior permission. For more information, visit www.wbs.ac.uk.

Case 24 Shell shock: why do good companies do bad things?

Introduction

On 9 January 2004 the Royal Dutch/Shell Group became involved in Britain's biggest business scandal since the Guinness Affair of 1986, after it emerged that the company had overstated its proven reserves of oil and gas. This concerns 'a reduction of 4.47 billion barrels (23%) from the previously reported end–2002 figures of 19.5 billion barrels' (Malcolm Brinded, Managing Director of Shell Transport).[1]

'Proved reserves'

Royal Dutch/Shell define proved reserves as follows:

> Proved reserves are the estimated quantities of oil and gas which geological and engineering data demonstrate with reasonable certainty to be recoverable in future years from known reservoirs under existing economic and operating conditions … Oil and gas reserves cannot be measured exactly since estimation of reserves involves subjective judgment and arbitrary determinations. All estimates are subject to revision.[2]

During January 2004, relative to the FTSE World Oil & Gas Index, shares in Shell Transport & Trading fell by 17% and shares in Royal Dutch Petroleum fell by 10%.[3]

Britain's most admired company

Shell 2001: Britain's most admired company

Shell is one of Britain's most admired companies. Each year *Management Today* asks the chief executives of Britain's ten largest companies in 24 sectors to rate each company in their sector on a scale of one to ten against nine criteria. In December 2001 these 240 chief executives rated Shell Transport & Trading Britain's 'most admired' company with a score of 73.72 out of 100. The citation said: 'Chairman Philip Watts exemplifies the good sense that made Shell this year's winning company.' One of the academic researchers, Dr Michael Brown of Nottingham Business School, explained the choice as a reaction to 11 September and the economic recession: 'When it's raining and the landscape is flooding, people cluster around the strongest mountains – they go where they feel safest' (*Management Today*, December 2001).

> Pragmatic Shell headed by the anonymous Philip Watts since Sir Mark Moody Stuart retired in the summer, was seen as a secure haven. Shell's marketing success is often overlooked. It is one of the few companies in the world (Mercedes and Nike are others) and possibly the only one in the UK that can advertise its products merely by showing its logo minus a name. In uncertain times, such reassurance, built up over the years with campaigns like 'You can be sure of Shell' supplies a warm comfort blanket.
>
> Shell's drive to the summit may have been helped by the sector's advanced knowledge of a smart deal in the offing. Soon after the deadline for voting passed, Shell disclosed that it had become the largest US petrol retailer after concluding a deal worth £2.5bn with a Saudi partner to take over Texaco service stations. That left Shell with 22,000 retail sites in the US. Even so, if analysts and fund managers had

---

This case was written by Professor Bernard Taylor, Executive Director, Centre for Board Effectiveness, Henley Management College. It is intended to be used as the basis for class discussion rather than to illustrate either effective or ineffective handling of a business situation. The case was compiled from published sources.

© 2004 Professor Bernard Taylor, Henley Management College, UK, 24 August 2004.

---

[1] The Shell Transport & Trading Company plc Annual Report and Accounts 2003, p.3.

[2] *Meeting the Energy Challenge: The Shell Report 2002*, 5 March 2003, p.26.

[3] Source: Thomson Datastream, quoted in 'Shell Accounts Get Signed off at Last', *Financial Times*, Tuesday 25 May 2004, p.21.

been voting, Shell would not have topped the rankings.[4]

In the summer Shell took a pasting, with analysts accusing it of offering the market inconsistencies, vagueness and contradictions. The outcry was sparked by a presentation to analysts by the company's exploration and production division, in which Shell admitted it was downgrading its annual growth target from 5% to 3%.

In the *Fortune* Global Hundred published in July 2001, Royal Dutch/Shell Group was ranked sixth among 'the world's largest corporations' and second to DaimlerChrysler in 'Europe's Top 25'. As the editors pointed out, 'higher crude-oil prices meant that oil producers were able to turn black gold into black ink' and 'on average petroleum refiners' revenues grew 39% and their profits increased 124%, an earnings jump bigger than in any other industry.'[5] According to *Fortune* in the fiscal year 2000/2001 Shell reported revenues of $149bn, up 42% on 1999/2000, and profits were $13bn, an increase of 48% over the previous year. At this time Shell had 90,000 employees.

Corporate social responsibility

In the Shell Annual Report for 2001 Philip Watts wrote a personal message as Chairman of the Committee of Managing Directors:

In a troubled and unsettled world, we delivered our second best ever earnings in 2001. Our returns were among the best in the industry and we have met the challenging promises we made to our shareholders three years ago. We continue to focus on delivering robust profitability, while leveraging our competitive edge to grow value.

At the same time we are striving to fulfil our commitments to society based on our strong Business Principles. This included using the principles of sustainable development in all our operations – taking account of their social and

environmental consequences as well as the economic dimension. We believe long-term competitive success depends on being trusted to meet society's expectations.[6]

The Shell Report 2001 provided a comprehensive analysis of Shell's economic, social and environmental performance, and many of the results were independently verified.

Alois Flatz, Head of Research at Sustainable Asset Management, an independent consultant to companies on social and environmental reporting, was favourably impressed by the Report:

Shell's commitment to sustainability has increasingly gained credibility as key strategic decisions have been made to back up their high profile communication on this subject. Moreover, the clear links between business principles and performance indicators establishes Shell's reporting on sustainability as being best in the class.[7]

'Our business principles'

Shell's business principles are communicated to management, employees and all stakeholders. They can also be found in Shell's Annual Report to Shareholders. They recognise the company's responsibilities to its shareholders, customers, business partners and the societies in which they operate. Shell wishes to make a contribution to social and economic development, to safeguard the environment and to mitigate the risks to their investments.

They also stress the need for Shell's people 'to compete fairly and ethically', to maintain safe and healthy operations and 'to provide full relevant information about their activities to legitimately interested parties subject to any overriding consideration of business confidentiality and costs'.

Business integrity is a core value: 'Shell companies insist on honesty, integrity and fairness in all aspects of their business and expect the same in their relationships with all those with whom they do business.' Also, 'all business transactions on behalf of a Shell company must be reflected accurately and fairly in the accounts of the company in accordance

[4] Chris Blackhurst, '2001: Britain's Most Admired Companies', *Management Today*, December 2001.
[5] Jeremy Kahn, 'The World's Largest Corporations', *Fortune*, 23 July 2001, p. 96.

[6] Philip Watts, 'Message from the Chairman', *People, Planet and Profits: The Shell Report 2001*, p.1.
[7] Quoted in *The Shell Report 2001*, p.9.

with established procedures and be subject to audit'.[8]

Implementing business principles

The Shell Report had a special feature on 'Doing Business with Integrity', which was in two parts: bribery and whistleblowing.

Bribery On the subject of bribery the company reported that:

> Shell companies seek to compete fairly and ethically – no bribes, no political payments and fair competition. In 2001, 13 cases were reported in which bribes were offered to Shell staff or they were detected soliciting and/or accepting bribes directly or indirectly. In nine of these cases, employees refused the bribes and the cases were reported. In three cases employees were dismissed. The remaining case is under investigation. We report only the number of proven cases, but investigate many more suspected incidents; even when not proven thorough investigations make it clear that we mean what we say with 'no bribes'.[9]

The Report includes a table indicating the number of bribes offered and the dollar values involved for the years 1998 to 2001.

Whistleblowing The Report also included a whistleblowing case study:

> Increasingly Shell companies are providing means for employees to raise concerns in confidence and without risk of reprisal, using mechanisms such as hotline numbers or whistleblowing schemes.
>
> In the USA a 24-hour, seven-days-a-week Ethics and Compliance Helpline is open to Shell people who have a query on legal and ethical conduct or who want to report concerns or violations ... The US helpline is part of a programme to ensure that all employees are aware of the Group's Business Principles and Code of Conduct in the USA which includes key

policies unique to the USA. A Corporate Ethics and Compliance Officer supports this effort.[10]

In 2000, Shell companies in Nigeria also introduced a policy encouraging staff to report unethical behaviour (anonymously if necessary) and as a result of this policy nine employees were dismissed and eight contractors were removed from Shell's suppliers' list.

The present oil crisis

The oil crisis

On Friday 30 July 2004 oil prices surged to a 21-year high, reaching $43.80 a barrel on the New York Mercantile Exchange. In London Brent crude climbed to $41.74, a 15-year high.[11] On the other hand, despite high oil prices the largest oil companies have in recent years replaced only three-quarters of their production. The result of growing demand and companies' unwillingness to plough more resources into finding oil is a tight supply situation. Add to this the continuous threat to oil supplies in Iraq and Saudi Arabia and the likelihood of government restrictions on oil supplies in Russia.

So what is the future prospect? Experts are forecasting that the demand will rise by more that 50% in the next 20 years. Yet there is little prospect of a significant increase in supplies. According to the International Energy Agency, demand will grow at 'a breakneck pace' but investment is unlikely to follow suit. This means higher prices for the foreseeable future.[12]

The high prices are having a magical effect on the profits of the international oil companies. In the last week of July 2004 Exxon Mobil reported that the company had earned almost $6bn in the second quarter of the year, an all-time record for any US company in a three-month period.

> But the major oil companies are not responding to higher prices and earnings by increasing their

---

8 *The Shell Report 2001*, p.25.
9 *The Shell Report 2001*, p.9.

10 *The Shell Report 2001*, p.8.
11 'Oil prices keep gushing upwards', *The Sunday Times*, 1 August 2004.
12 Irwin Stelzer, Director of Economic Policy Studies, Hudson Institute, 'Soaring oil price lubricates the advance of Kerry', *The Sunday Times*, 1 August 2004.

search for oil. Exclude Russia and BP's output is declining. So are Shell's and Chevron Texaco's. Production at Exxon Mobil is more or less flat. Only Total with its commitment to Africa and Asia seems to be stepping up production.[13]

The new chairman/chief executive

Philip Watts was appointed Chairman and Managing Director of Shell Transport and Trading plc in August 2001 at the age of 56. He had had an outstanding career with Shell spanning 30 years, which had taken him to South East Asia, Africa, the Middle East and Continental Europe. He had worked on virtually every job in Exploration and Production – from seismologist and geophysicist to Exploration Manager before being appointed Chief Executive of Exploration and Production in 1997.

During the 1990s he moved into general management, first as Managing Director, Nigeria, next as Coordinator of Regulatory Affairs, Europe; and then as Director for Planning, the Environment and External Affairs in London. His abilities were also recognised outside Shell. He was elected to the Executive Committee of the World Business Council for Sustainable Development and at around the same time he became Chairman of the UK's governing body of the International Chamber of Commerce (ICC).

The overbooking of reserves

Philip Watts was no doubt chosen to be Chairman and Chief Executive of Shell because of his successful track record in Exploration and Production.

From 1991 to 1994 he was Managing Director of the Shell Petroleum Development Corporation in Nigeria. Shell has extracted an estimated $30bn worth of oil from Nigeria but at a huge environmental cost, particularly in the region of Ogoni. When Ken Saro-Wiwa started a popular protest movement that threatened to disrupt oil production, the Nigerian government, which receives a substantial income from oil revenues, reacted quickly by sending troops into the protesters' villages.

Eventually Ken Saro-Wawa was arrested and hanged. Shell formed a crisis group to rebuild its reputation with environmentalists and the task force was led by Philip Watts. Another factor that clinched his promotion was his unflinching determination to deliver results for the company. Unfortunately the record shows that he may have been too optimistic in forecasting the performance which might be achieved from the Nigerian and other fields that he knew well.

An independent report by Davis Polk, a US law firm, states that by early 2000 it was clear to Shell's exploration and production unit, of which Philip Watts was then Group Managing Director, that the Nigerian reserves 'could not be produced as originally projected or within its current licence periods'.[14]

Leaked company memos also show that production from the Yibal field in Oman began to decline in 1997, but Watts believed that a new technology called 'horizontal drilling' might enable the company to 'extract more from such mature fields' and that year the proven oil reserves figures for Oman were mistakenly increased as a result.

In Australia too, Shell had celebrated the discovery of half a billion barrels of oil, equivalent in the Gorgon gas field. But it was going to be very hard to exploit these reserves. Although Shell had a small exploration base there, the company would need to build a large gas liquification plant on Barrow Island, which was a Class A protected nature reserve. So the gas plant would be subject to environmental impact studies and the Australian government would be under intense pressure to protect the unique wildlife. Shell's partners in the Gorgan project, Exxon Mobil and Chevron, have not included the Gorgon field in their lists of proven reserves.[15]

On the other hand, in 2003 Sir Philip Watts and Walter van de Vijver, working together, scored a major success. By a spate of shuttle diplomacy involving many flights to Russia, they convinced President Putin to allow Shell to have access to 'the world's next big oil province'.[16]

[13] Irwin Stelzer, *The Sunday Times*, 1 August 2004 (op cit).

[14] Paul Durman and Lucinda Kemeny, 'Another brutal week for Shell as report makes Watts the fall guy', *The Sunday Times*, 25 April 2004. pp. 3.8 and 3.9.

[15] Rajan Datar, *Shell Shock*, BBC2 programme, 21.50–22.30, Thursday 15 July 2004.

[16] Lucinda Kemeny "Ready to Blow", *The Sunday Times*, 18 April 2004, p.5.

Enron, WorldCom and Sarbanes-Oxley

Enron

Philip Watts became Chairman and Chief Executive of Shell Transport and Trading in the summer of 2001 and in the autumn of the same year the world business community was rocked by the Enron Affair, the first of a series of high-profile corporate scandals and failures that led to a radical reform of company law and regulation in the USA.

In mid October 2001, Enron, the Houston oil and gas company, reported a third-quarter loss of $638m and disclosed a $1.2bn reduction in shareholder equity, partly related to off-balance-sheet partnerships which had falsified the company's results. This was the largest corporate bankruptcy in American history and the consequences were appalling. Their auditors, Arthur Andersen, one of the world's leading accountancy firms, was convicted of obstruction, fined $500,000 and the Andersen partnership was dissolved. Chairman/CEO Kenneth Lay and the Chief Financial Officer (CFO) Andrew Fastow resigned and they were prosecuted for fraud. Investors lost billions of dollars on their shares and Enron's employees also lost their pensions and thousands of them lost their jobs.[17]

WorldCom

After the Enron debacle, President Bush was asked to tighten up the regulation of corporations and auditors. He refused saying that he did not want to punish the majority of company executives who were acting properly because of what seemed to be the bad behaviour of 'a few bad apples'. Then came the WorldCom scandal. On 25 June 2002 the board of WorldCom, America's second largest mobile phone operator, revealed that their top executives had inflated the company's profits by $3.8bn. (This number has since grown to $9bn.) During 2002 alone, WorldCom's shareholders lost $3bn; many thousands of employees lost their jobs and the company was put up for sale. WorldCom's auditor was Arthur Andersen and, as at Enron, it had turned a blind eye to the fraud in which the company's accountants had categorised billions of dollars of annual operating costs as capital expenditures, so that the expenses could be stretched out over a number of years. In the financial year 2001 this allowed the company to turn an annual operating loss of $662m into a $2.4bn profit.[18]

After this revelation the FBI and the Securities and Exchange Commission (SEC) indicted WorldCom's top executives and CalPERS, the US's largest state pension fund launched a suit to regain some of the $580m which the fund had lost on its WorldCom shares.

Other restatements

In the summer of 2002 Xerox Corporation also revealed that their accounts for 2001 had overstated their operating earning by $1.4bn. In fact, during 2002, 240 companies notified the SEC that they wished to re-state their accounts. This was four times the number of restatements that was recorded only 5 years earlier in 1997.[19]

The Sarbanes-Oxley Act

After Enron, WorldCom, Xerox and a spate of other accounting scandals, the US Congress and business leaders urged the President to take action to reassure investors, to restore confidence in the integrity of US corporations and financial markets and to discourage fraudulent corporate behaviour.[20]

On 30 July 2002 President Bush signed the Sarbanes-Oxley Act, which established a new, much tougher regime of regulations to control the actions of boards of directors, corporate executives, accountants and auditors. The Act included the following arrangements:

♦ *Tougher penalties for corporate fraud* The legislation creates penalties for corporate fraud of up to 20 years for destroying or altering documents sought in federal investigations.

---

[17] Richard Lacay and Amanda Ripley, 'Persons of the Year: The Whistleblowers', *Time*, 30 December 2002, pp. 18–43.

[18] Richard Lacay and Amanda Ripley, op. cit.
[19] John A Byrne, 'Let's really clean up those numbers – Now', *Business Week*, 15 July 2002, p.73.
[20] Doug Cameron, Andrew Hill and Tally Goldstein, 'New Set of Controls on Corporate America', *Financial Times*, 12 August 2002. Also Louis Lavelle and Mike McNamee, 'Will Overseas Boards Play by American Rules', *Business Week*, 16 December 2002, p.38.

Also chief executives who certify false financial reports will face prison terms of 10–20 years and fines of $1m to $5m.

- *An Independent Accounting Oversight Board* The new law creates a new (independent) five-member private sector board to oversee the accounting industry – with subpoena authority and disciplinary powers.

- *Restrictions on auditors' consulting* The law would restrict consulting and other non-auditing services that accounting firms could provide to clients.

- *Curbs on financial analysts* The SEC is empowered to impose new rules on financial analysts to prevent conflicts of interest.

- *Facilitation of investors' lawsuits* The Act also extends the period of time in which defrauded investors might bring lawsuits against companies.

- *Form 6K filing* The requirements on Form 6k filing came into force on 29 August 2002 – a more detailed and onerous reporting system.

- *Empowering the audit committee* The audit committee of the board, consisting of independent directors should have the authority to propose external auditors to the shareholders.

- *Loans to top executives* The Act placed a ban on subsidised personal loans to top executives and required prompt disclosure of share dealings to repay company loans.

- *Vouching for financial statements* Separately, 700 companies with annual revenues of more that $1.2bn must meet an SEC deadline to confirm that their Chief Executives and Chief Financial Officers will vouch for the veracity of their companies' accounts.

- *Dual listings* Shortly afterwards the SEC made it clear that European and Asian companies with US listings would be covered by the Sarbanes-Oxley Act but the application of certain provisions would be negotiable.

In the summer of 2002 the impact of the Sarbanes-Oxley Act was reinforced by the new listing requirements issued by the New York Stock Exchange and NASDAQ which require firms

- to get shareholder approval for all stock-option plans;

- to have a majority of independent directors on their boards;

- to have only independent directors on the audit committee and the committees that select chief executives and deal with executive compensation.[21]

Corporate governance in the UK

The corporate scandals in the USA and the Sarbanes-Oxley Act prompted a review of regulation across the European Union and particularly in the UK. In Britain there was a traditional bias in favour of self-regulation – for Codes of Practice rather than new laws, and reliance on professions to set standards and discipline their own members.

Ever since the bankruptcy of Enron, British accountants had been quietly congratulating themselves that 'it couldn't happen here'. But, particularly after the Sarbanes-Oxley Act the regulation of British auditors and accountants seemed inadequate. In the last five years the US SEC has required 1,200 companies to correct their audited accounts. By comparison Britain's Financial Reporting Review Panel – with only one full-time accountant – acted as a kind of ombudsman. The Panel only investigated if there was a complaint. In 12 years the Panel had made only 67 inquiries and had requested 15 restatements, and in most cases the companies had been let off with a caution.[22]

However, behind the scenes the British government was planning to establish an independent regulator along the lines of the US Accounting Oversight Board and early in 2004 they announced the establishment of the Financial Reporting Council, which incorporates the Financial Reporting Review Panel and is also responsible for regulating the accounting profession and the inspection of audits.[23]

[21] 'Reforming Corporate Governance: In search of honesty', *The Economist*, 17 August 2002.

[22] 'Accounting: Holier than Thou', *The Economist*, 8 February 2003, p.85.

[23] Lucinda Kemeny, 'Watchdog with real bite for number crunchers', *Sunday Times*, 28 March 2004.

After the publication of the Cadbury Report in 1992, Britain became a pioneer in corporate governance and the Cadbury Code became a model for the self-regulation of quoted company boards in other countries. The past decade saw over a dozen inquiries advocating:

◆ an expanded role for non-executive directors;

◆ tighter control of executive remuneration;

◆ fuller disclosure and transparent financial reporting;

◆ the active engagement of institutional shareholders; and

◆ independent regulation of accountants and auditors.

These recommendations were brought together in a New Combined Code, which took effect in July 2003 and was intended to make boards more independent and more effective in controlling chief executives and their management teams.

At the same time, the Netherlands and other Continental countries were reviewing their company laws and developing their own corporate governance codes. Particularly relevant to Shell was the Tabaksblat Committee Code, which was also published in 2003. So Philip Watts's watch from July 2001 to March 2004 coincided with a period of intense activity that led to the reform of laws, regulations and codes of practice aimed at imposing tighter controls on executive teams, their accountants and auditors.

Corporate governance at Shell

Shell was founded in 1907 through a merger between a Dutch oil company, which was partly owned by the Dutch royal family, and Shell, which was an international trading company. However, instead of forming one company with one set of shareholders they established the Royal Dutch/Shell Group as a joint venture between two companies and two groups of shareholders. The Royal Dutch Petroleum Company, which is based in The Hague and listed on the Dutch stock exchange, has a 60% interest in the Group. Shell Transport and Trading plc has its headquarters in London, is listed on the London stock exchange and owns a 40% interest in the Group. For this reason, Shell has two boards of directors. Under Dutch law, Royal Dutch has a two-tier structure with a supervisory board and a management board and Shell Transport operates under the British system with a unitary board.

These two 'parent company' boards are responsible for appointing the directors to the two 'holding companies': Shell Petroleum NV and the Shell Petroleum Company Ltd. The Group Managing Directors of these companies form the Committee of Managing Directors – the top management team which runs the Royal Dutch Shell Group which consists of Service Companies, Operating Companies and Regions (see Figure 1). One or two of these Group Managing Directors also sit on the parent company boards, i.e. on the management board in the Netherlands and on the unitary board in Britain.

In practice the Royal Dutch supervisory board and the Shell Transport board do a great deal of work together. For example, their three main committees – Group Audit, Social Responsibility and Remuneration and Succession – have members from both boards but Shell Transport has a separate Nomination Committee (see Figure 2).

From 2001 to 2003 Sir Philip Watts was both Chairman of the Board and Managing Director of Shell Transport. He was also Chairman of the Committee of Managing Directors (CMD) and the other members of the CMD were the other Group Managing Directors Jeroen van den Veer, Chief Executive of Chemicals, and Walter van de Vijver, Chief Executive of Exploration and Production.

Under Sir Philip Watts's chairmanship, the board of Shell Transport included a number of eminent and experienced non-executive directors:

◆ Sir Mark Moody-Stuart KCMG (UK), Managing Director and Chairman of Shell Transport from 1997 to 2001.

◆ Lord Oxburgh KBE, FRS (UK), former Chief Scientific Advisor to the Ministry of Defence.

◆ Nina Henderson (US), previously Corporate Vice President of Bestfoods, a major US foods company.

◆ Luis Giusti (Venezuela), fomerly Chairman/CEO of Petroleos de Venezuela.

◆ Sir Peter Job KBE (UK), previously Chief Executive of Reuters.

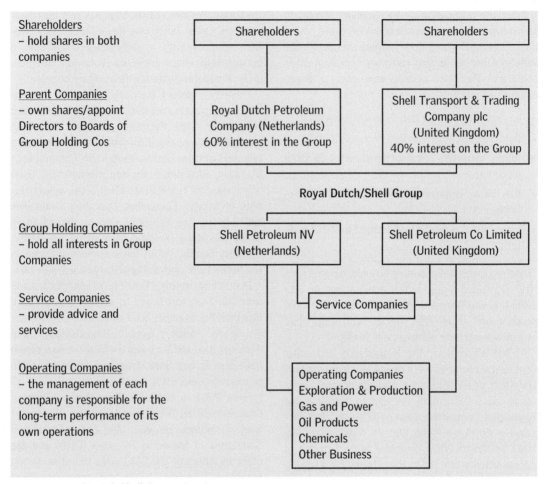

Figure 1 Royal Dutch Shell Group structure
Source: The Shell Transport & Trading Company plc, Annual Report & Accounts 2003, p.6.

- Sir John Kerr GCMG (UK), previously Head of the Diplomatic Service and Principal Private Secretary to the Chancellor of the Exchequer.
- Teymour Alireza (Saudi Arabia), Chairman of the National Pipe Company, Saudi Arabia.
- Sir Peter Burt FRSE (UK), Executive Deputy Chairman of HBOS plc and former Governor of the Bank of Scotland.
- Dr Eileen Buttle (UK), former government scientist. Trustee of environmental non-governmental organisations.

During 2003 there were a total of 17 board meetings and they were well attended. Judith Boynton, the Group Chief Financial Officer was appointed a Group Managing Director and Executive Director of Shell Transport in July 2003 and she regularly attended the board meetings until she resigned on 18 April 2004.

The Group Audit Committee

The Royal Dutch Petroleum Company also had an impressive supervisory board and some of the directors were members of the Group Audit Committee (GAC).

- Aad Jacobs (Netherlands), Chairman of the Committee, a former Chairman of the Board of Management of ING Group, a major Dutch financial services company.

	Royal Dutch	Shell Transport
Group Audit	Aad Jacobs Lawrence Ricciardi Henny de Ruiter	Sir Peter Burt Luis Giusti Nina Henderson
Social Responsibility	Jonkeer Aarout Loudon Maarten van den Bergh Wim Kolc	Lord Oxburgh Teymour Alireza Dr Eileen Buttle
Remuneration and Succession	Jonkeer Aarout Loudon Lawrence Ricciardi Henny de Ruiter Prof. Hubert Markl	Sir Peter Job Nina Henderson Sir John Kerr
Shell Transport Nomination	Lord Oxburgh Sir Peter Burt Sir Peter Job Sir John Kerr	

Figure 2 Royal Dutch Shell Group board committees
Source: The Shell Transport & Trading Company plc Annual Report & Accounts 2003, p.9

- Lawrence Ricciardi (USA), previously President of RJR Nabisco Inc.
- Henry de Ruiter, Managing Director of Royal Dutch 1983–1994.

The other committee members were: Sir Stephen Burt, Luis Giusti and Nina Henderson – all directors on the Shell Transport Board.

During 2003 there were a total of six meeting of the GAC and the members attended virtually all the meetings.

In the 2003 Annual Report and Accounts the Shell Transport & Trading Company plc reviewed its corporate governance arrangements against the requirements of the New Combined Code. The key points from this review are listed below:-

- *Independent directors* Of the nine non-executive directors on the Shell Transport Board, seven are wholly independent of any personal business connection with the companies of the Royal Dutch/Shell Group. Accordingly, the structure of the board during the year observed the New Combined Code provision that it should have a majority of 'independent non-executive directors'.
- *The Chairman* Sir Philip Watts was Chairman of the Board and Group Managing Director of Shell Transport throughout 2003.
- *The Chairman's other commitments* Sir Philip Watts's other commitments during the year included mambership of the World Business Council for Sustainable Development and Chairman of the International Chamber of Commerce's UK governing body.[24]
- *Performance evaluation* During 2003 the Shell Transport board carried out a series of evaluations of
  - the board as a whole;
  - individual members;
  - the Chairman, and;
  - board committees.

The Chairman evaluated the directors individually. For the collective appraisal they used a questionnaire. The Chairman was evaluated by the Senior Independent Director, Lord Oxburgh, and the non-executive directors.[25]

- *Dialogue with shareholders* The dialogue with institutional shareholders was maintained through an investor relations programme agreed by the board. In 2002 the board nominated Lord

[24] Shell Transport & Trading Company plc Annual Report & Accounts 2003, p.121.
[25] 2003 Annual Report, p.121.

Oxburgh as Senior Independent Director and arranged for him and other directors to attend quarterly institutional investors' presentations when appropriate.

♦ *Auditor's remuneration*   Audit fees for Shell Transport amounted to £129,000 in 2003 – up from £31,000 in 2002. The fees payable to PriceWaterhouseCoopers LLP for non-audit servcies in the UK were £31,600 in 2003.

'Unbooking' the reserves

♦ *9 January 2004* a Shell public relations executive told journalists and investors that the company had carried out a review of its 'proved' oil and gas reserves. As a consequence the figures would be reduced by 20%. This revision would cut the value of the reserves by 3.9bn barrels of oil equivalent (boe) from 19.5bn to 15.6bn.

Shell shareholders were shocked by this surprise announcement and in a few days they saw the price of their shares fall by over 10%. The institutional investors also complained about the way they had been treated – that this important announcement had been made by a middle manager – and not by Sir Philip Watts himself.

♦ *5 February*   Sir Philip Watts apologised on television for his absence from the presentation of the revised figures. However, he was being overtaken by events.

♦ *19 February*   The US SEC launched an investigation into the downgrading of the reserves.

♦ *3 March*   Sir Philip Watts, the Chairman/Chief Executive, and Walter van de Vijver, the Chief Executive of Exploration were forced to resign.

♦ *17 March*   The US Department of Justice opened a criminal investigation into Shell's unbooking of reserves.

♦ *18 March*   The company reduced its estimate of reserves for a second time by a further 250m barrels and postponed the publication of the Annual Report and Accounts, and the Annual Meeting with the shareholders.

♦ *22 March*   There was a meeting between Shell's directors and their institutional shareholders.

♦ *19 April*   The company announced a third cut in oil reserves and Judy Boynton the Chief Financial Officer, resigned.

♦ *24 May*   Shell's proved oil reserves were reduced for a fourth time to 14.35bn barrels of oil equivalent. This represented a reduction of 23% on the initial figure. Shell's Annual Report was finally published and the two Annual General Meetings were scheduled for 28 June.[26]

Estimating reserves

These revelations about the company's reserves have left many former executives puzzled. Shell's internal processes for checking the state of its reserves were thought to be as safe as Fort Knox. Each year in The Hague around 30 of the company's most senior staff, including Philip Watts, would hear evidence from the exploration and production people in the field. The annual 'programme discussions' could take three hours – starting with technicalities and moving on to detailed explanations by staff about their estimates of reserves.[27]

The process started in the field. Teams of technical staff would regularly review the data coming in from the wells. If they found any indications that underground reserves were greater or lower than expected, the new information had to be reported immediately to the head office of Shell's Dutch business in The Hague. If the adjustment was significant – more than 5% – a team would arrive from head office. But at some stage in the past three years something had started to go wrong. As early as 2002 Shell's management realised that the company was not finding enough oil to replace production – a key measure of an oil company's future profitability. Years of opportunistic investments had left Shell with a legacy of small fields which did not match the company's production requirements. To remedy this, it would require a major new initiative – an acquisition or an entry into a new field.

It is alleged that a decision was made to relax the rules by which the company accounted for proven reserves – a measure used by the SEC to determine

26 Clay Harris, 'Shell accounts get signed off at last', *Financial Times*, 25 May 2004.

27 Lucinda Kemeny, 'Ready to Blow', *Sunday Tines*, 18 April 1004, pp.3–5.

whether oil and gas can be produced with 'reasonable certainty' using current technology. Shell's decentralised management – which is often cited as a strength – became, in this case, a weakness. Some units were run as small kingdoms with different practices adopted in different subsidiaries and divisions.

The dam broke in January 2004 when Shell admitted the 20% overstatement of reserves. The reclassification was blamed largely on the overbooking of developments in Nigeria and at Ormen Lange, a gasfield off the Norwegian coast.

The issue now is, 'who knew what and when?' Company documents from late in 2003 which were leaked to the *New York Times*, said that Shell's top management had concluded that 1.5bn barrels, 60% of its Nigerian reserves, did not meet the SEC's accounting standards for proven reserves. However, the management were reluctant to change the figures for fear of damaging the relationship with the Nigerian government.

Philip Watts and Walter van de Vijver may have been forced to take the blame for the overbooking of the reserves. But it seemed unlikely that they, and Judy Boynton, Shell's CFO, were the only senior executives who knew about the 'cover-up'. In early April, Walter van de Vijver issued a public statement making this clear:

From the inception of my tenure as head of Exploration and Production I worked diligently to diagnose and improve the health of the business. I regularly communicated to the Committee of Managing Directors the nature and quantity of the potentially non-compliant reserves and our efforts to assess the magnitude of the problem, prevent recurrence and implement off-setting measures.

Analysts and investors hoped that the company would not merely blame the three senior managers but would offer some broader proposals to improve corporate governance and internal control in the Shell Group. Eric Knight, who represents CalPERS, the largest US public sector pension fund, said: 'The question is who is running the group and who is responsible when there is a problem. The truth of the matter is that it is everybody and nobody.'[28]

What went wrong?

Press reports show that Shell was not the only oil company that had to recalculate and restate its estimates of proved reserves. On 29 June 2004, Norsk Hydro had cut its global reserves figure by 6.6%. Also, differing interpretations of the SEC rules have led to different companies booking different estimates for the same field. For example, for the Ormen Lange gas field in the North Sea the companies booked the following proved reserves: BP: 80%; Norsk Hydro: 49%; Exxon Mobil: 35%; Statoil: 25%; Shell: 20%.

On 29 June 2004 BP also restated its proved reserves to bring them in line with the SEC's definition. BP raised its proved reserves by 23m barrels to 18.36bn. This was because, in deciding whether a project is a sound investment, BP uses its own planning price of $20 per barrel to determine its reserve levels and the SEC used the end-of-year price, which was $30.10. As BP explained, 'An investment is made for 20–25 years, therefore we wouldn't make an investment decision based on one day's price'.[29]

How Shell's management came to overestimate their reserves of oil and gas is unclear. A number of possibilities have been advanced:

1 *Over-optimistic forecasting* In their forward planning, senior executives of oil and gas companies must rely on the estimates which they receive from geophysicists and exploration managers. The estimation of reserves is not an exact science. Both technologists and executives need to make assumptions about the volume and quality of the reserves, their accessibility and the rate at which they can be extracted etc. Shell's managers might well have believed that there were more reserves in the ground or that a higher proportion of the oil could be extracted using modern technologies.

2 *Decentralisation* Shell's organisation is highly decentralised. National organisations were semi-autonomous and their executives might have overestimated their production e.g. in Australia and Nigeria.

[28] Lucinda Kemeny, 'Ready to Blow', *The Sunday Times*, 18 April 2004, p.5.

[29] James Boxall, 'BP surprises with upward adjustment' and Nicholas George, 'Norsk Hydro restates reserves', *Financial Times*, 30 June 2004, p.29.

3 *The executive bonus*   In the late 1990s Shell's management had been encouraged to aim for 'stretch targets' and these numbers were linked to an incentive bonus. This too could have motivated them to inflate their estimates of reserves.

4 *Philip Watts's drive for success*   Philip Watts was highly motivated and willing to take risks. He had worked his way up the levels of the organisation, finding and producing oil in Indonesia, Sierra Leone, Malaysia and Brunei. In Nigeria he had continued to produce the oil despite the opposition of local protesters and international pressure groups. Clearly, he thought he could do it again.

5 *The Securities and Exchange Commission (SEC)*   It is conceivable that the regulators in London and The Hague would not have investigated Shell's estimates of their oil and gas reserves. In the event it was the US SEC that queried the figures; the British and Dutch authorities took action only after the SEC had started their formal investigation.

The internal investigation

In early February 2004 the Group Audit Committee (GAC) commissioned an internal investigation into how the overbooking had occurred. The investigation was carried out by the US law firm Davis, Polk & Wordwell and they were given access to the internal memos and the minutes of the Committee of Managing Directors (CMD). When their report was published on Monday 19 April, Lord Oxburgh, the non-executive director who took over Sir Philip Watts's role as Chairman said the company sought to limit the blame for what went wrong at Shell to 'the human failings' of a few individuals.

Jeroen Van der Veer, the new Chief Executive of Shell and Chairman of the CMD, promised 'behavioural and cultural change' at the company to ensure its reserving policy was accurate and to create a clear line of command at the top of the company. He stated: 'We want to foster a culture where bad news can be passed up the line without fear of reprisal'. Malcolm Brinded, who had taken over as head of Exploration and Production at Shell, attempted to reassure the financial markets that there would be no more bad news. He said the company had carried out a 'painstaking and thorough' review that would 'draw a line' under Shell's difficulties.[30]

The Davis Polk Report published the in-company emails which passed between Walter van de Vijver and Sir Philip Watts from the time when Mr van de Vijver had taken over from Sir Philip Watts in August 2001. From the start Mr van de Vijver felt they were 'caught in a box' 'due to aggressive booking of reserves in 1997–2000'.[31]

As early as 11 February 2002, van de Vijver told the CMD that the company might have overstated its reserves by 2.3bn barrels because they were ignoring SEC guidelines.[32] He wrote, 'Recently the SEC issued clarifications that make it apparent that the Group guidelines for booking reserves are no longer fully aligned with the SEC Rules' – because of 'potential environmental and commercial showstoppers'.[33]

Under the SEC definition reserves are called 'proven' if thay can be extracted economically and sold for profit. If reserves are not 'proven' in this way oil companies are required to admit that and say that the reserves are only 'probable'.[34] In van de Vijver's opinion the 'showstoppers', i.e. factors that were preventing Shell from getting these reserves to market, were being ignored. He pointed to overbookings in Australia, Norway, the Middle East and, most of all, Nigeria, where there was political unrest and environmental damage.

On 28 May 2002, Philip Watts wrote to van de Vijver, emphasising that it was vital not to unbook the unproven reserves until new reserves had been found to replace them. He should consider 'the whole spectrum of possibilities ... leaving no stone unturned'.

----

[30] Katherine Griffiths, 'Shell looks to draw a line under reserves fiasco with shake-up of board structure', *The Independent*, 25 April 2004, p.19.

[31] Paul Durman and Lucinda Kemeny, 'Another brutal week for Shell as report makes Watts the fall guy', *The Sunday Times*, 25 April 2004, pp. 9–10.

[32] Jeremy Warner, 'Shell's convoluted whodunit script is worthy of fiction', *The Independent*, 20 April 2004.

[33] Rajan Datar, 'Shell Shock', *The Money Programme*, BBC2, 15 July 2004, 21.50 to 22.30.

[34] Rajan Datar, op. cit.

On 2 September 2002, Van de Vijver sent a note to the CMD with a copy to Judith Boynton, Shell's finance director, emphasising the difficulty Shell would have in achieving 100% reserves replacement ratio (RRR) for 2002 – the target which had been set. 'Unfortunately we are struggling on all key criteria ... RRR remains below 100% due to aggressive overbooking in 1997–2000.'[35] (Shell is replacing only between 50% and 60% of the oil it produces. BP and other big rivals manage 100% to 150%.)

The whistleblower

Eventually it was through Walter van de Vijver that the issue was made public. In the autumn of 2003 he asked Frank Coopman, the Chief Financial Officer of the Exploration and Production unit to make an assessment of Shell's proved reserves. Coopman made his analysis and reported that the figures for 'proved reserves in Shell's 2002 financial statement were materially wrong'.[36] He wrote that to hide this fact would 'constitute a violation of US Securities law and the multiple listing requirements'.

Walter van de Vijver replied in no uncertain terms: 'This is absolute dynamite, not at all what I expected and needs to be destroyed'. Walter van de Vijver said he wanted a report with some positive suggestions that he could present to the CMD. However, Frank Coopman, like some other whistleblowers, lost his job and has since left the company. Judith Boynton, Shell's Chief Financial Officer, complained that she had not been consulted about the report on the reserves position that had been prepared by Frank Coopman. She had somehow been cut out of the loop and she also resigned from her position in April 2004.

In the autumn of 2003 van de Vijver could see the writing on the wall. On 9 November he wrote to Sir Philip Watts in some desperation: 'I am becoming sick and tired about lying about the extent of our reserves and the downward revisions which need to be done because of far too aggressive/optimistic bookings.' Then in December he wrote to a colleague: 'We are heading towards a watershed reputational disaster ... The problem was created in the 90s and foremost in 1997–00. I will not accept cover-up

stories that it was OK then but not OK with the better understanding of SEC rules now, and it took us two and a half years to come to the right answer.'[37]

On 8 December van de Vijver submitted a 42-page report to the CMD. A comprehensive audit of reserves had just been completed and this showed the reserves had been overstated by 3.6bn barrels. With the SEC investigation in progress the CMD had no alternative but to inform shareholders and the public about the real situation and the announcement was planned for 9 January. Shortly afterwards a Dutch acquaintance of van de Vijver told a journalist, 'It's because he respected the company so much that he didn't want to blow the whistle but instead ordered an investigation and tried to remedy the problem through the company. He is a man who has invested his whole life in Shell and believed its ethos of looking after its employees fairly and for life. He was the archetypal company man who was on course to take over the company.'[38]

The fines and the court cases

On 15 July 2004 the BBC *Money Programme* interviewed investors, regulators and lawyers to discover what their reactions had been to the 'Shell Affair'. US oil analyst Fadel Gheit said, 'Most investors and analysts had almost blind faith in the company and its management. Unfortunately all this came to a screeching halt after this disclosure.' Peter Montagnon of the Association of British Insurers said, 'Most people will have a stake in this, if they have a pension; Shell is such a large company that, if you have a pension pot, some of it is in Shell. So when you have an announcement like this, the value of your pension pot is reduced accordingly.'

Within a few days of the Shell announcement, the price of Shell Transport shares fell by 8% and the market value of the company fell by 8%. The video reporter concluded, 'Millions and millions of people had investments either directly in Shell or through their pension plans. They may not have known they

[35] Damian Reece, 'Revealed: bitter power battle that put Shell in the firing line', *The Independent,* 20 April 2004, p.4.
[36] 'Blowing the Whistle', *CFO Europe,* May 2004, p.46.
[37] Damian Reece, op. cit.
[38] Paul Durman and Lucinda Kemeny, *The Sunday Times,* op. cit.

were investors in Shell, but now they know that Shell lied to them and cost them money.'

Stanley Bernstein, a New York lawyer also contributed to the programme. He is leading a class action against Shell on behalf of a group of shareholders, based on the false declaration that Shell's CMD signed and submitted to the SEC in March 2003. This booked 19.3bn barrels of oil reserves, whereas the corrected figure agreed on 24 May 2004 was only 14.35bn barrels. He said, 'Shell had lied intentionally and had deceived the public about how much oil it had in the ground and how certain it was that the oil could be brought to market. Once the truth came out the stock price dropped precipitously to reflect the fact that the company was not as valuable as its competitors were.' He also spoke of the reactions of the regulators: 'When you have a fraud perpetrated over a long period of time. When you have a fraud perpetrated by the very heads of the company with specific responsibility for this core issue, the regulators are going to get their teeth into this and make sure there is appropriate punishment for the individuals involved.'

Executive payoffs and bonuses

Shareholders were concerned that the executives who were responsible for exaggerating the estimates of Shell's proved reserves were given large grants of salaries and pensions. For example, Sir Philip Watts received a final payoff of £1m and an annual pension of over £580,000.[39] Newspaper reports suggested that both Walter van de Vijver and Judith Boynton also received payoffs of around £1m each.[40]

Shareholders also suggested that the executive bonus system might have encouraged managers to overbook the reserves. However, a Shell spokesperson replied that this measure of operational peformance accounted for only 6% of annual bonus payments.[41]

The fines

On Friday 30 July 2004 Shell paid £83m ($151m) in fines to draw a line under its disputes with the US SEC and UK's Financial Services Authority (FSA). The SEC had accused the company of having breached fraud, internal control and reporting requirements. The FSA said the Group had committed 'market abuse'.[42] Press reports stated that there was still a strong chance that Shell will face a criminal prosecution before the US Department of Justice. There was also a possibility that individuals might face civil and criminal cases.

How did Shell respond?

Jeroen van der Veer, who as Chairman of the Committee of Managing Directors (CMD) replaced Sir Philip Watts when he resigned in March 2004, is working with the new non-executive Chairman of Shell Transport & Trading, Lord Oxburgh, to clarify Shell's complex governance structure and to install a stronger and more independent system of financial reporting and control. All the time, Shell management is under intense scrutiny from shareholders and the media. Jeroen van der Veer said, 'It is by far the most difficult part of my career. There is huge pressure all the time and you are living absolutely in a glass house with magnifying glasses on top wherever you go.'[43]

In the Annual Report & Accounts for 2003 Shell described the measures which had been taken to strengthen their corporate governance and financial control systems:

1 *An independent Chairman*   After the departure of Sir Philip Watts, who was both Chairman and Chief Executive of Shell Transport the two roles have been separated and Lord Oxburgh, a non-executive director has been appointed to the job of non-executive Chairman.

2 *The internal inquiry* The Group Audit Committee (GAC) commissioned an independent review by US lawyers Davis Polk of the the overbooking of the reserves. They also sanctioned the publication of a summary of the report and accepted its recommendations.

[39] Rajan Datar op. cit.

[40] Katherine Griffiths, *The Independent,* 25 April 2004, op. cit.

[41] Michael Harrison, *The Independent,* 16 July 2004.

[42] Carola Hoyos *et al,* 'Shell pays $15m in fines to Watchdogs', *The Financial Times,* 30 July 2004.

[43] Deborah Hargreaves, 'Shell fighter begins the big clean-up', *Financial Times,* 30 July 2004.

3 *Booking of reserves* In future, the CMD and the GAC will take a formal role in reviewing the booking of reserves and there will be a 'systematic use of external reserves' expertise to provide challenge and assurance at critical points in the reserves booking and reporting process'.[44]

4 *Corporate governance codes* The Annual Report & Accounts and the board's processes had been adapted to ensure that they conformed to the UK Combined Code, the Sarbanes-Oxley Act and the rules of the New York Stock Exchange. In the Netherlands the company would take account of the Tabaksblat Committee's Code.

5 *The overbooking of reserves and compliance with regulations* The investigation and report to the GAC by Davis Polk & Wordwell listed the deficiencies which had led to the overbooking of reserves:

- the Group's guidelines for booking proved reserves were inadequate;
- the Group's CMD and the Parent Company Boards were not provided with appropriate information to form disclosure judgements;
- the Chief Financial Officers of the businesses did not have direct reporting responsibility to the Group Chief Financial Officer;
- there was a lack of understanding of the meaning and importance of the SEC rules; and
- there was a control environment that did not emphasise the paramount importance of the compliance element of proved reserves decisions.[45]

All these issues had been addressed to strengthen and clarify reporting procedures. Also to emphasise the importance of compliance with the requirements of regulators, in future the company's lawyers would be involved at every stage and the Group Legal Director would attend meetings of the CMD and the parent company boards.[46]

6 *Unifying the two boards and a possible merger?* In response to further pressure from institutional investors, Shell formed a steering committee of Shell board members to look at alternatives to the present dual board structure and commissioned Citigroup and NM Rothchild to act as financial advisers to the steering committee on corporate restructuring. On 11 August 2004 the company announced that it had reached a 'preliminary agreement' to unify its two boards and had asked its financial advisers to assess the feasibility of merging its Dutch and British holding companies.

What further action is required?

So what went wrong and what should be done to prevent it happening again?

1 'A few individuals'?

The Davis Polk Report and Lord Oxburgh, the Chairman of Shell, suggested that the overbooking was the fault of 'a few individuals'. Hopefully, these individuals could be asked to resign, the control systems would be improved and it would be possible to draw a line under the whole sequence of events. But Walter van de Vijver made it clear, in his opinion, that he had told everybody who counted at Shell, certainly the CMD and the board of directors, about his concerns over the state of the company's reserves.[47]

2 A simpler organisation structure?

Some of Shell's institutional investors thought the problems could be much broader. Eric Knight who represents CalPERS, said 'the question is who is running the group and who is responsible when there is a problem. The truth of the matter is that it is everybody and nobody.'[48]

The company is a joint venture between two companies that are subject to different laws and

[44] Malcolm Brinded, Managing Director of Shell Transport, *Shell Transport & Trading Company Annual Report: 2003*, 23 May 2004, p.3.

[45] *The Shell Transport & Trading plc Annual Report 2003*, pp.40 and 41.

[46] *The Shell Transport & Trading plc Annual Report 2003*, pp.41 and 42.

[47] Lucinda Kemeny, 'Ready to Blow', op. cit.

[48] Lucinda Kemeny, op. cit.

different governance codes. There are two sets of boards and a 'Conference', where the Dutch supervisory board and the British unitary board meet to discuss strategy. At the executive level the Group is coordinated by three Group Managing Directors meeting in a Committee of Managing Directors. It is not surprising that some investors called the present structure Byzantine.

3 Big-hitting non-executive directors?

Other investors are asking for 'the injection of some senior big-hitting independent directors who will take an unjaundiced view of Shell's predicament'.

4 Tighter controls?

Certainly the SEC will demand a reorganisation of Shell's internal processes for checking the state of its reserves and its accounts generally – including the internal audit and the relationship with the external auditors – where were the external auditors?

5 Finding new reserves

A gulf still separates Shell from BP and Exxon Mobil. Last year Shell replaced its oil and gas at 63% of the production rate. So at the current rate of production Shell has 10.2 years of oil left in the ground. BP and Exxon have between 13.5 and 14 years, so Shell is starting from a base 30% lower than its rivals.

As Sir Philip Watts insisted, the first objective must be to raise the replacement rate from 63% to 100% – so that the reserves in the ground will be maintained. This will involve routine development work to rebook the downgraded barrels by bringing them up to SEC criteria. According to Clay Smith of Commerzbank, Shell expects that of the 4.7bn downgraded reserves, 85% will be reclassified as 'proven reserves' over the next ten years.[49]

6 Increased investment or acquisitions

To get access to new fields, for example in Iraq, Iran, Libya or China, Shell will probably have to spend more money and take more risks. Shell is planning to increase its capital expenditure from an average of $13bn a year to $14.5bn for future years – the majority of which will be spent on exploration and development.

BP has spent $14bn a year over the past two years – including some fairly risky deals in Russia In addition BP has acquired reserves through acquisitions and mergers with Amoco, Atlantic Richfield and Burmah Castrol. To quote one analyst, 'You have to ask whether Shell can do it by itself, or whether it is going to do it like BP – by acquisition.'[50] This also raises the question whether Shell could manage a merger or acquisition with a corporate structure in two countries.

7 Loss of trust

Finally, Shell's leadership faces a deeper problem. Shell, once regarded by many as a paragon of honesty and fair dealing has had its reputation spoiled by the actions of its top management team. Thousands of Shell's employees around the world will feel that they too have lost something valuable – the pride of working for a company that has an unblemished reputation for integrity and ethical behaviour.

It took Shell many decades to build this reputation. How can this reputation be rebuilt? And how is it possible to prevent Shell executives, at the top level, from risking the company's reputation in the future?

---

[49] Oliver Morgan, 'Shell's Ground Zero', *The Observer,* 30 May 2004, p.5.
[50] Oliver Morgan, op. cit.

Case 25 **Abrakebabra: surviving the franchisee revolt**

A brief history of Abrakebabra

In 1982 two brothers, Wyn and Graeme Beere, founded what in 20 years' time would become Ireland's largest Irish-owned fast food franchise. In the early 1980s Graeme was selling fast food at the front of an off-licence (Deveney's) in the Rathmines area of central Dublin. Wyn was working as a chartered surveyor in a prestigious international property firm. Dublin lacked the restaurant culture of other European cities. Instead Dublin's social life centred on its vibrant pub culture, with bars focusing on drink sales, rather than offering a variety of food to customers. All pubs closed simultaneously at 11pm nightly. Graeme noticed an important gap in the market – where do people go for food after a night out?

The entrepreneurial solution was to create a fast food restaurant that specifically catered for this market. The offering would be new for Dublin: a product mix of kebabs, burgers and chips, popular in London at the time, and late opening until 4am. Searching for a name for this venture, Graeme chose a play on words: a mix of the name of a Steve Miller number one record in 1982 'Abracadabra' and the kebab as the central product. In 1982 the newly named 'Abrakebabra' opened, a 'licence to print money', as one of the founders put it.

The two brothers went from one owner-operated, small fast food restaurant in 1982 to a peak of 59 franchised outlets in the late 1990s. Through entrepreneurial leadership they survived two recessions and a franchisee revolt. This partnership was unbroken until 2001 when one of the brothers, Wyn, decided to retire from the business. His 50% stake was bought out by Gaiety Investments Ltd, the venture capital vehicle of leading Irish entrepreneur Denis Desmond. The exit of Wyn and the entry of Gaiety Investments Ltd present both a challenge and an opportunity to the company. The challenge is how to move from an entrepreneurial mode of control to a more formal managerial control system. The opportunity is that a fresh equity injection by Denis Desmond can help fuel the expansionary strategy of Abrakebabra.

The franchisee revolt

> They [the franchisees] forgot the help that they got. They forgot about the brand and they started thinking that they could do it themselves. We had a little bit of a revolution there in the last couple of years, but all the guys went out of business.[1] (Managing Director of Abrakebabra)

By 1997 Abrakebabra ran 11 company-owned restaurants. These restaurants had delivered powerful advantages to the brothers in the past. They had been an important source of cash flow during the development of the business-franchising model. Company owned restaurants were also an important learning mechanism. By 1997, however, these company-owned units were consuming the majority of the brothers' management time.

This case was written by **Rosalind Beere**, Trinity College Dublin, and **Peter McNamara**, University College Dublin, UCD Business Schools, Department of Business Administration, Belfield, Dublin 4, Ireland. Financial support of a grant from **Davy Stockbrokers** to undertake a series of teaching case studies is gratefully acknowledged. This case study is a reprint which was originally published by the European Case Clearing House. Copyright remains the property of UCD Business Schools.

We wish to also acknowledge the help of Abrakebabra Limited who have co-operated in this research by giving access to management, staff, franchisees and company documents. In particular we wish to thank the 13 interviewees for their time and insights into the company.

Disclaimer: This case is intended to be used as a basis for class discussion rather than to illustrate either effective or ineffective handling of an administrative situation.

[1] Interview with Graeme Beere, founder and Managing Director.

Resources spent on these restaurants meant less managerial attention could be given to the running of their franchising system, which at that time represented over 80% of the company's restaurants.

A decision needed to be made about the long-term strategy of the firm as to whether it could continue to function effectively with such a split focus, between being a franchiser and a restaurateur. In response to the strategy crisis the decision was made to franchise out all company-owned restaurants. Graeme Beere recently summarized the strategic logic of moving to a franchise-only management system as follows:

> The success of Abrakebabra is all about location, location, location. It is a hands-on cash business and we don't want investors, we want owner-occupiers. . . . We found the key was to franchise out the outlets and concentrate on the brand. The wake-up came when our accountant told us that 80 per cent of our income came from franchising, but that 80 per cent of our time was spent on the 11 stores. We put franchisees into all of our stores and turnover increased immediately. All our head office time is now spent looking after the brand and franchisees who need help.[2]

However, trouble was on the horizon in the form of a group of franchisees who expressed concerns over the management of the Abrakebabra franchising network. Some of them claimed they were unhappy with the lack of management focus. It became apparent that a number of franchisees were arranging secret meetings to which the Abrakebabra management team were not invited. The brothers decided to confront this possible revolt head on. They called individual meetings with the franchisees. During these meetings the benefits of being an Abrakebabra franchisee were clearly communicated. Any franchisee that was not clearly committed to the Abrakebabra ethos was then released from their contract.

The experience of the franchisee revolt highlighted issues faced by the partners and their control mechanisms. The Abrakebabra management team created a new identity centred on an exclusively franchise driven business growth model. This case explores the extent of goal alignment between the franchisees and the franchiser and the management control systems that the brothers installed to maximize value creation for both parties.

Performance of Abrakebabra

By 2003 Abrakebabra's new managerial control system had yielded considerable dividends. Abrakebabra had maintained its position as the largest Irish-owned franchise network in its business domain – with 55 franchises. Only McDonald's, with 66 franchise outlets was larger (see Table 1 for size of main competitors). This success had also facilitated the exit of one of the founding brothers, Wyn and a fresh injection of capital with the entry of by Gaiety Investments as a major shareholder. Gaiety Investment's 50% stake cost a reported €3.8 million, valuing Abrakebabra at €7.6 million by the end of 2002.[3]

In 2003 Abrakebabra had sales of €33 million, with the typical franchisee restaurant generating individual sales of €300,000 to €380,000. Franchisees pay a fee of 6% on gross sales, after Value Added Tax, with a further 1% advertising levy. The set-up costs for a franchisee are estimated to be €50,000 (all financial figures from www.Abrakebabra.net). These charges grant franchisees use of the Abrakebabra brand name, purchasing systems and franchisee supports, as outlined below. Profit margins for franchisees are estimated to be as high as 20%.[4] The *Sunday Business Post* indicated that expected profits for the year ended December 2002 were €1.1 million[5] for the Abrakebabra group, while actual profits were later reported to be over €900,000, up 350% on 2001 profits.[6]

---

[2] McMahon, S. (2003) 'Franchising for the Future', *Sunday Business Post*, 25 May 2003.

[3] 'Desmond Invest €3.8 million in AbraKebabra,' *Business and Finance*, 11 April 2002.

[4] O'Halloran, B. (2002) Abrakebabra to Take a Bigger Bite of Fast Food Market', *Business and Finance*, 11 April 2002.

[5] McMahon, S. (2003) 'Franchising for the Future', *Sunday Business Post*, 25 May 2003.

[6] Business News (2004) 'Abrakebabra works its magic', *Sunday Business Post*, 22 February 2004.

Table 1 Main franchise restaurant outlets operating Ireland in 2003[7]

Name	Seating availability	Number of restaurants	Ownership
Abrakebabra	**Seating**	**55**	**Irish**
Supermacs	Seating	45	Irish
McDonald's	Seating	66	US
Burger King	Seating	22	UK
Four Star Pizza	No Seating	26	US
Domino's Pizza	No Seating	17	US

The exact profitability of both the franchising network and individual franchisees are difficult for external third parties to independently confirm. This is because the size of Abrakebabra means that full profit and loss accounts do not need to be made publicly available by the Irish Companies Registration Office (CRO). An analysis of the abridged accounts (primarily balance sheet information) that are publicly available from the CRO is complicated by changes in the structure of the organization. Over the last ten years Abrakebabra operations have encompassed a number of companies including Abrakebabra Holdings, Abrakebabra Limited, Abrakebabra Franchising, and Abrakebabra Meats, among others. An analysis of the abridged accounts of these firms does not offer significant insights into the underlying profitability of the franchiser.[8] These firms are not required to publish sales figures through the CRO, thus external parties cannot observe the amount of levies raised from franchisees.

What lies behind the valuation of Abrakebabra itself, and the profits generated by individual franchisees, is the franchise lead growth strategy and managerial control systems installed in the wake of the 1997 franchisee revolt. It is to these that we now turn our attention.

Goal alignment and value added from the franchising model

We went through a phase where the franchisees were controlling the business ... we reversed the whole process and are now far stronger ... I'd know exactly how to deal with them [the franchisees]. I've learnt![9] (Managing Director of Abrakebabra)

From 1997, emphasis was to be placed on running Abrakebabra as a core franchising support system. With no company-owned restaurants to manage, the two brothers were able to formulate a new strategy that focused exclusively on a franchising business model. A number of unsuitable franchisees did not adhere to the Abrakebabra ethos and exited the franchising system. The process of franchising out company-owned restaurants, the experience of the franchisee revolt, and exit of unsuitable franchisees led management to a realization that the quality of their franchisees was just as important as the total number of franchisees in the network. Thus, management looked at the franchising system with a new perspective.

The franchiser

The single most important thing in a franchise chain is the franchisee.[10] (Abrakebabra Financial Accountant)

The Abrakebabra management team, having franchised out the remaining company-owned

---

[7] All competitor information was obtained by contact with each company's head office.

[8] As part of this case study the authors undertook an analysis of the abridged accounts of Abrakebabra Holdings and Abrakebabra Limited using the published accounts from the CRO (www.cro.ie) in February 2004. Abrakebabra Franchising and Abrakebabra Meats were not in operation in 2004.

[9] Interview with Graeme Beere, Founder and Managing Director.

[10] Interview with Dominic Kelly, Company Financial Accountant.

restaurants, to began seriously reassess their role as a franchiser. In the aftermath of the franchisee revolt the management sought clarification of the value Abrakebabra Ltd created for its franchisees, both in its role as the strategic centre and as operational services provider. At this time, Abrakebabra decided to reconsider their key objectives as a franchiser. The financial accountant, Dominic Kelly, noted that:

> Your average Managing Director's role in life is to increase his shareholders wealth. Ultimately that means [getting] rich. Shareholder value is [created] in two ways ... You either create profits which generate dividends or you create a business that is worth money even if it's not necessarily paying dividends.[11]

The firm sought to maximize long-term shareholder value through a twin focus on profit maximization and sustainable growth of its franchising network. These goals were achieved by delivering and capturing value for the franchisees. Abrakebabra now saw their core competencies as being divided into four domains. The first domain was brand identity. Second, new product development. Third, centralized purchasing to attain economies of scale. Fourth, training, mentoring and franchisee management. Additionally the franchiser would provide support services to the franchisees such as legal services, capital acquisition, and property management advice. Do franchisees believe that these benefits accrue from membership of the Abrakebabra franchisee network? Seven franchisees' perspectives on why they are members of Abrakebabra are provided in Appendix 1. This evidence indicates that in general franchisees concur with management on the benefits of being a franchisee.

The management team could see the obvious benefits of franchising as a system of growth and they redefined and reasserted the advantages of such a structure. The company had achieved rapid expansion and market penetration with relatively low capital investment. Abrakebabra had been able to expand the number of outlets, increase market coverage, market share and brand equity with limited financial exposure. In addition, individual restaurant operational duties were delegated to franchisees, and profits increased through the enhanced motivation of these individual operators; attributed to the fact that individual franchisees have made significant financial investments in their business and are thus more likely to be motivated to maximize sales and minimize costs, when compared with hired managers in the same position. Furthermore, Abrakebabra also benefits from a positive cash flow and risk is transferred away from the company because the franchisees accept all financial, human resource and business risk themselves, limiting the financial liability of Abrakebabra should an individual franchise fail.

However, after identifying the positives, to achieve their new focus the Abrakebabra team set about looking at the disadvantages of franchising and the potential problem areas needing to be addressed. Key problems were the control and monitoring of the franchisees' performance in terms of financial performance and restaurant standards. The management team acknowledged the difficulty in exercising tight controls over the franchisees, due to the nature of the relationship as stipulated in the franchise agreement. Indeed, a crucial problem faced by the management team is to ensure that franchisees declare their true level of business activity. Another challenge is to verify that franchisees are achieving and maintaining the highest standards in their restaurants. The Abrakebabra management team knew that they needed to readdress these key areas. In doing this they also needed to define their franchisees' objectives and try to further align both parties' goals and priorities.

The franchisee

> Why did you want to become an Abrakebabra franchisee? I thought it was going to make loads of money. (Abrakebabra Franchisee)

An important goal of a franchisee is the maximization of wealth. How can Abrakebabra help maximize wealth? What benefits should the franchisees be receiving from Abrakebabra?

The Abrakebabra website points to three benefits of becoming a franchise, namely, that it is easier to

---

[11] Interview with Dominic Kelly, Company Financial Accountant.

raise finance, the risk of failure is lower, and franchisees can use a product of proven appeal (www.abrakebabra.net). The management team recognized that Abrakebabra's proven track record and success with earlier franchisees had provided new franchisees with a tried and tested business formula. Dominic Kelly points out:

The franchisee will pay his money to join the chain, we say here's your store opening manual, here's your shop fitting manual, here's your sandwich or kebab making manual, so that literally they can sit down and read it and from day one and have a 95 per cent chance of making money ... because that's why he is paying his money.[12]

He also links the financial goals of the franchisee with the success of the franchiser:

When a franchise chain succeed, you get at least 95% of your franchisees making money, profitable and happy and once that happens then they are quite happy to pay the franchise fee.

Other benefits experienced by the franchisee are as follows. First, access to Abrakebabra's investment in new product development and large marketing programmes. Second, the opportunity to be their own boss, while having access to the Abrakebabra experience through supervision and consultation. Third, economies of scale in purchasing, advertising, and staff training and reducing operating costs. These advantages lie beyond the reach of a sole trader, but are available to a franchisee.

However, possible shortcomings of Abrakebabra as a franchiser needed to be considered by the management team. Franchisees may find the restrictions of the non-negotiable franchise agreement unattractive. Abrakebabra may not live up to a franchisee's expectations. Brand mismanagement by Abrakebabra might harm the whole system. The franchisee may not be able to avail themself of new supply opportunities because they are locked into buying from a designated supplier of Abrakebabra. So the management team needed to ensure that such problem issues were avoided.

The contract: The franchise agreement

A comprehensive document it deals with everything ... right down to termination.[13]

In looking at the relationship between Abrakebabra and its franchisees, the management team needed to assess the most critical document governing this relationship: the franchise agreement. This defines each party's legally binding obligations, duties and rights. Abrakebabra writes the contract; the terms are non-negotiable because the company is the owner of the brand and its associated trademarks. The agreement grants the franchisee exclusive rights to operate an Abrakebabra restaurant at an approved location and to use Abrakebabra's trademarks and other rights of the company in conjunction with the operation of the restaurant. The rights and responsibilities associated with an Abrakebabra franchise agreement require that all franchisees pay an initial fee for a single restaurant, a 6% franchise royalty fee and 1% for group advertising. In order to calculate this figure franchisees are required to submit to the company weekly sales reports for their respective restaurant.

In return for the initial fee and royalty payments, Abrakebabra helps to set up a franchisee's restaurant, with provision of training and general assistance in central services such as: brand awareness, bulk buying, health and safety training and standards maintenance. The Abrakebabra management also lend their expertise in property selection and the fitting out of a new restaurant. In addition franchisees receive continuous supervisory support from head office and have an assigned area supervisor who carries out regular visits. A quarterly newsletter is also produced at head office and distributed to all franchisees, describing operational changes, current food prices, management advice and assistance and so on. If a franchisee has any issues, they contact head office or their area supervisor via telephone and assistance is immediate.

After assessment the management team considered that the contract was not the central issue which needed to be addressed. In their view the key

---

[12] Interview with Dominic Kelly, Company Financial Account.

[13] Interview with Wyn Beere, founder and retired Director and Company Secretary.

problems were ones that could arise after the contract is signed, such as ongoing monitoring of operational and financial performance of a franchisee. Careful selection of franchisees could assist in minimizing both performance problems and the risk of a future franchisee revolt.

Franchisee selection

If the franchisee isn't making money, he can't pay you. So if you have a franchise that doesn't work you are not going to get your franchise fee . . . and the thing collapses . . . so your number one priority is to pick the right franchisee.[14]

Abrakebabra realized that the success of their franchising system was highly dependent upon the quality of their franchisees and so an important issue facing them was how to ascertain a potential franchisee's level of quality. The problems that Abrakebabra faced in selecting a new franchisee was that potential candidates could appear to be suitable at first glance but over time be deemed unsuitable.

Originally, first franchisees had been chosen on the basis that they had the financial resources and background necessary to run a successful franchise restaurant. Abrakebabra's management quickly made themselves acquainted with the background of franchising laws and issues. As a result of the success experienced by the company during 1982–1990, Abrakebabra was inundated with interested candidates. Consequently Abrakebabra was able to be more selective in choosing its franchisees. However, the recruitment process had remained relatively informal. Dominic Kelly states:

The stronger your brand gets the easier that [franchisee selection] gets because if you have a good brand then people [franchisees] get attracted to it.[15]

However, after the franchisee revolt the management team decided to make the process more formal. They set about formulating a selection system to help identify suitable franchisees. The process is as follows: first of all potential franchisees have to fill out a formal application form, providing basic personal details and capital available for investment. If chosen, they are interviewed in a first round of interviews by David Zebedee, the Franchise Director. He evaluates each franchisee's ambitions, intentions and personal characteristics. The initial steps of franchisee selection are described by David as follows:

Firstly they would read our brochure, they would fill out the application form and sign a confidentiality form and then we would move to the preliminary interview phase . . .[16]

Abrakebabra looks for commitment to the company, because each new franchisee signs a ten-year contract. They do not want investors who only give monetary investments and fail to run the restaurant properly.

Educational and business background

Abrakebabra wants people with experience in management and entrepreneurship. They want people with ambition and passion to run a restaurant full time, serving customers to the best of their ability. People with ideas and drive and with a strong sense of responsibility to the franchiser, their customers and community. Previous education is not as important as previous experience in business, especially in the food business, or any business dealing with customers and staff. Franchisees vary from those who have completed primary education through to university graduates. The best combination is experience and education.

Training of a franchisee

Before the shop opens we'll send them [franchisees] off to a local shop [Abrakebabra restaurant] to be trained . . . we'll pick out a shop which is near enough to them, and Karen [an Abrakebabra trainer] will oversee how they are trained.[17]

When a franchisee is selected and deemed suitable to run and operate an Abrakebabra franchise,

[14] Interview with Graeme Beere, Founder and Managing Director.
[15] Interview with Dominic Kelly, Company Financial Accountant.
[16] Interview with David Zebedee, Franchise Director.
[17] Interview with Sinead Reid, Operations Manager.

official training begins. The company has found that over the years the best possible form of training is on the job with another franchisee. A new recruit is assigned to an established franchisee and works up through the ranks in a restaurant until they are capable of operating and managing it. This form of training can take from two weeks to three months.

The trainee must have a thorough knowledge of the restaurant and all its internal procedures and activities. At this point, if both Abrakebabra and the new recruit are still committed they both sign the franchise contract. Dominic Kelly describes the extensive training process for new franchisees as follows:

> *The training programme is set up for them [franchisees], Sinead who is here will go and work with them building the store ... Then Karen will come on board. Karen will help them recruit their staff and look after operational procedures in the store ... Then Natalia who is here [in Abrakebabra headquarters], she stays on for a period of 4–5 weeks with that franchisee giving them full back-up. She works in the store for 4–5 weeks so it is quite intensive. At the end of the actual training ... they should know the A–Z of Abra.*[18]

The franchisee must be competent in all tasks needed to run a successful Abrakebabra franchise restaurant such as: cooking techniques, till operation, financial management and reporting, supplier management, stock control, health and safety requirements, human resource management and customer management, among other skills and competencies. Once selected and trained as a franchisee, they enter a long-term ten-year contract with Abrakebabra. The ongoing management of this relationship is described below.

Managing the relationship between franchisee and franchiser

Wyn Beere described the affiliation Abrakebabra had with its franchisees as being of a maternal nature:

> *I look upon a franchisee as someone ... when they are with us for the first year ... they are like a baby ... they need everything ... you're like the mother ... they take everything from you ... Then after about five years they learn to read and write, and they start to do their own thing. Then they become a teenager and they think they know everything ... more than you. When they get ... say to about ten years with us they actually want to do their own thing. That's what we found ... If you keep them for ten years you are doing very well ...*[19]

Abrakebabra the franchiser makes its profits from each individual franchisee's entry fee (lump sum) and an ongoing 6% levy on all franchisees' gross revenues (excluding the 1% advertising levy). For this fee Abrakebabra needs to ensure that all franchisees deliver consistent product and service quality levels to the end customer. In return Abrakebabra provides good support infrastructure for their franchisees.

> *I think the main thing is support, that there is someone at the end of the phone ... who can help them deal in any aspects ... [from] suppliers, staffing ... to the business end of things – [preparing and selling] the food. ... Support is our main end of things – guidance and leading them.*[20]

Franchisees make their profit by efficient management of operations and attraction of customers into their restaurant in preference to rival operations. Dominic Kelly states:

> *So if you consider that your food is costing you say 35% for an average week ... your wages are costing you 25%; that's 60% of your turnover gone. Now out of that you've got 40% left to pay all the rest of your overheads, including financing costs, so really you can see where all of a sudden that 5% of your gross profit becomes critical because the difference between having 40% or 45% left, that might be the difference between*

---

[18] Interview with Dominic Kelly, Company Financial Accountant.

[19] Interview with Wyn Beere, founder and retired Director and Company Secretary.

[20] Interview with Sinead Reid, Operations Manager.

make or break. With the franchising system, profits are maximized.[21]

Franchisees pay the franchiser for their expertise in operational issues, access to economies of scale, supply chain management, bulk buying, marketing and branding. All of these benefits make the franchisee more cost efficient than if they acted as a sole trader. One example of the benefits that access to bulk purchasing is the supply deal with C&C for soft drinks. In return for exclusive supply of soft drinks C&C (distributors of Pepsi and Club orange) contributes about half of the total marketing budget of Abrakebabra.[22] This enables the network to keep the advertising levy at 1% of franchisee sales. Abrakebabra management have suggested that 'bulk buying offers Abrakebabra operators an extra 10 per cent profit margin over and above the industry norm of 60 per cent'.[23]

Broadly speaking the franchisees appear to concur with Abrakebabra's perspective on the royalty fee. As one franchisee put it:

The franchiser effectively makes income from the franchisees, so it's very hard to have a paternal attitude towards someone you're trying to make money from. Theoretically it works very well and in actual fact I've a very good relationship with the franchiser in this respect because of the way we evolved together ... So long as the individual unit is successful and it falls into that category that there is a division of a third or two thirds ... in terms of the actual net profit ... and they're helping. If your net profit drops ... they come in and say you know we'll help you ... to develop, to fight for your profit ... On a bad day you know we'll split the difference.[24]

However, Abrakebabra needs to ensure that franchisees maximize their gross revenue and maintain high levels of product and service quality. Maximization of revenues means increased profit for

Abrakebabra through the franchisee royalty fee levied on each franchisee's operation. Maintenance of high levels of product and service quality ensures that Abrakebabra will be successful as a franchising system in both end-consumer markets and in the attraction of future franchisees. Thus, Abrakebabra needs to ensure that franchisees are consistent in the following: use of the brand, restaurant design and maintenance, health and safety, product quality, and customer service. Franchisees face a difficulty in that maintenance of these standards may suppress their profits. The central question is how can Abrakebabra ensure that on the one hand these standards (costs) are maintained equally by all franchisees and on the other hand that franchisees accurately report weekly gross revenues to head office (thus attracting a total 7% levy; 6% for royalty fee and 1% for advertising budget)? Over the years Abrakebabra have installed and modernized a series of monitoring and control systems to manage these two key issues.

Monitoring: operational controls

The challenge faced by Abrakebabra is the large cost involved in monitoring these standards, all of which must be absorbed from the revenues that it derives from the 6% levy on franchisee's revenues (excluding the 1% advertising levy). In relation to franchising, the quality of service at individual outlets needs to be consistent and must meet a pre-ordained minimum standard. The franchisee's quality of effort and meeting of contractual requirements needs to be continuously monitored.

The Abrakebabra management team looked at a number of contractual clauses in the franchise agreement, which stipulated how the franchisees should operate their outlets. The clauses specify and regulate how the business should be run on a daily basis and shape its long-term development. These control systems fall into two categories: monitoring of operational tasks and attainment of strategic goals.

The first category is designed to regulate day-to-day business. Detailed in the operations manual, it includes hours of operation, prices, product quality, accounting systems, layout, décor and Abrakebabra's right to inspect the premises and make changes unilaterally. These contractual clauses allow the company to control their franchisees' daily

[21] Interview with Dominic Kelly, Company Financial Accountant.

[22] O'Halloran, B. (2002) 'Abrakebabra to Take Bigger Bite of Fast Food Market', *Business and Finance*, 11 April 2002.

[23] McMahon, S. (2003) 'Franchising for the Future', *Sunday Business Post*, 25 May 2003.

[24] Interview with an Abrakebabra franchisee.

operations and ensure that the franchisees uniformly follow the 'ideal' business format model.

The second category involves more strategic controls that shape the longer-term business trajectory. This group of controls include sales targets and objectives, expansion triggers, contract duration, contract renewal and a contract termination option. Abrakebabra creates operational controls to establish, maintain and increase the business's turnover (upon which it received percentage fees), whereas franchisees are more interested in maximizing profit.

The Abrakebabra management team then turned to how they physically monitored franchisees. The first of these methods is via financial monitoring. Every Monday, franchisees must call in their previous week's sales figures to head office. These figures are then checked off the previous year's, with profit and loss assessments being checked and maintained over time. To improve both the accuracy and efficiency of monitoring revenues the franchiser's management team have begun to put modems in every Abrakebabra franchisee till. This means that all sales information from a till is immediately relayed to head office, ensuring that Abrakebabra maintains direct contact with a franchisee's sales status. The modems not only allow the management to monitor sales figures but in addition give vital information on the success of their product mix, and whether certain products are increasing in popularity. If on the other hand certain products are underperforming, promotional campaigns can be targeted at these products. In addition, the sales information helps the company monitor year-on-year sales progress. This use of technology is an important monitoring asset for the management team. As the Franchise Director states:

> Now we are introducing modem systems whereby we can read their [franchisees] tills from head office; we have four shops currently online and the plan for the rest of this year is to get the whole group. The till-monitoring system would give us the exact turnover of what the shop did ... What we had in the past – we were taking the franchisees' word on his turnover, so now its automatic.[25]

The benefits of this new system would at first appear to be weighted in favour of the franchiser. However, the weekly chore that every franchisee faces on a Friday and a Monday of calculating their weekly turnover and relaying this information to head office will be eliminated, thus benefiting them in saving time and effort.

The second and equally important method of monitoring for the Abrakebabra management team is the use of standards checking. Abrakebabra has a team who are divided into four areas in Ireland: north, south, east and west. Regional team supervisors visit their respective franchisees on a systematic and regular basis. As Franchise Director David Zebedee states:

> It's ongoing monitoring. Each franchisee will be visited at least twice a month by somebody from head office ... [who] check standards ... [A] hygiene audit is done at least every six weeks in every store ... [as well as] ongoing monitoring ... In addition to this, Abrakebabra has a health and safety officer who also must check and maintain records of each restaurant's standard. All of the above monitoring checks are recorded in report form and delivered to head office. Any problems are dealt with immediately.[26]

Ian Beere, Health and Safety Officer confirms:

> There are four of us, geographically, north, south, east and west. We have our own fourteen or so [shops]; we are in there every month, that gives us another continuous contact with the franchisees.[27]

Customers are also a great source of monitoring. Customer comment cards are available in all restaurants. Customers can (and do) phone Abrakebabra headquarters directly if they wish to make a complaint about service provision in an individual franchise restaurant. The information received from this form of direct consumer response monitoring is essential for the management team. Ian Beere states:

> ... we are watching their turnovers ... we get customer complaints, [which] are good indicators of what is going wrong ... If you get a

---

[25] Interview with David Zebedee, Franchise Director.

[26] Interview with David Zebedee, Franchise Director.
[27] Interview with Ian Beere, Health & Safety Officer.

number of complaints you know there is some-thing going wrong. [There is] one good monitor and that's the customer ... .[28]

Finally, mystery shoppers are also employed by the Abrakebabra management. The feedback received from this method of monitoring is a great way of surveying franchisee standards and competence levels.

The mystery shopper idea was to find out how the food was going ... and we paid the mystery shoppers so they wouldn't go in with a voucher and say we are from head office ... Ian organ-ised that. It works ... and is monitored closely.[29]

Conclusion

From a franchisee's perspective it is clear that the changes in strategy, post 1997, have delivered increased value for them. As one franchisee put it:

I'd say that the brand has really improved in the last couple of years ... I think they have taken a far more professional approach – to the business ... You know, when I was setting up they did everything they could for me.[30]

From the perspective of the franchiser, the changes post 1997 have also been successful. From a difficult position in 1997, with franchisees in open revolt, the management have turned the firm around. Franchisees now see the value that the franchiser creates. New franchisees are being attracted to the venture and opportunities to attract fresh capital have arisen.

The question for the management team at Abrakebabra now is how far and how long can the growth model be sustained?

---

[28] Interview with Ian Beere, Health & Safety Officer.
[29] Interview with Wyn Beere, founder and retired Director and Company Secretary.

[30] Interview with an Abrakebabra franchisee.

Appendix 1 **The franchisee's perspective of Abrakebabra membership.**

Franchisee 1: 'Why Abra? Well at the time I looked at others. McDonald's, Supermacs, Abrakebabra, the whole package, you know. I'd met every one of them and I'd just found them [Abrakebabra] to be the most attractive package out of the whole lot.' We [franchisees] are part of a big, bigger picture [in terms of] marketing and branding ... more than independent outlets. And also from a financial point of view we are better off because we are purchasing at least 12–13% cheaper than the small independent body would be doing.'

Franchisee 2: 'Why did I decide to franchise? I saw a strong name, with a strong product in a strong location and I went for it. Why did I decide to go Abra? Very strong and powerful product range, innovative [and] different.'

Franchisee 3: 'I was already in the business ... and I knew that somebody would open up in [my area] if I didn't ... so I got in there first! Why Abra? Because it was ... how would you say ... size basically. They had a presence ... and [their design specifications] fitted the site ... It wasn't big enough for McDonald's.'

Franchisee 4: 'We owned our own restaurant and McDonald's came to town. It [Abrakebabra] was something to do battle with McDonald's because it affected our business up to about a third of our trade dropped ... because of that ... I looked around at other franchises ... I remember that I ate in Abrakebabra before and loved the food and so I made inquiries [about becoming a franchisee] and as a consequence we went for it.'

'Yes, advertising and bulk buying would be the two main benefits ... their back-up services are pretty good as well.'

Franchisee 5: 'I had looked around and McDonald's and Burger King had come to [my area] and I had seen Abra [also]. I thought it would be good. I had gone along to a show in O'Reilly Hall in UCD and there was an Abra stand, a Pizza Hut stand ... I went away and I didn't really know what to do. Then a while later I saw an ad in the paper and made the call to Abra and went from there.'

'Advertising, and bulk buying, yes ... they would be the biggest benefit ... and of course they [Abrakebabra] help to solve problems with suppliers if a delivery hasn't been made or other stuff. Oh and the name is the biggest benefit of course.'

Franchisee 6: 'Advertising and bulk buying ...'

Franchisee 7: 'Advertising, bulk buying, and legal [expertise] ... Wyn has a huge amount of experience in relation to landlords, dealing with neighbours, rights of way, all this sort of thing. So that's always been a big, big help; they have a huge expertise which they accumulate ...'

INSEAD

Case 26 Creyf's (Solvus Resource Group): David against Goliath in the European temping industry

This case received the 2003 European Foundation for Management Development Case of the Year Award in the category 'International Business'

Prologue

The board meeting scheduled for Wednesday, 28 March 2001 was looking set to be one of the most challenging for Creyf's CEO Michel Van Hemele in his attempt to gain support for acquiring the IT consulting group, Bureau Van Dijk Computer Services (BvD).[1]

Creyf's, a Belgian company that provided a wide range of staffing services and solutions at local, national and European level, was present in nine dif-

This case was written by Eline Van Poeck, Research Assistant, Katholieke Universiteit Leuven, with Paul Verdin, Affiliate Professor at INSEAD and Professor at Solvay Business School (ULB) and Katholieke Universiteit Leuven. Constructive comments by Nick Van Heck of Executive Learning Partnership, and Steve Nysten, Research Assistant at Solvay Business School (ULB), are gratefully acknowledged. It is intended to be used as a basis for class discussion rather than to illustrate either effective or ineffective handling of an administrative situation.

[1] Although only the computer division of Bureau Van Dijk ('Computer Services') was for sale, we will nevertheless simply refer to this acquisition as 'Bureau Van Dijk' and abbreviate it to 'BvD'.

ferent countries and consisted of four main business units: general temping, specialized temping, secondment and projects, and other HR services and consulting. On a European scale the company was ranked fifth after Adecco, Manpower, Vedior and Randstad.

Since 1988, Bureau Van Dijk CS had helped customers to build high-value solutions in information technology. The company designed the solutions, implemented them and assumed responsibility for the continuous management and execution of the process. It offered a wide range of competencies but mainly focused on four core domains: enterprise resource planning solutions (mostly SAP), e-consulting, infrastructure management and information and communication technology. (Exhibit 9 shows more detailed information on BvD).

Van Hemele felt that this acquisition would fit perfectly into his most recent strategic plan to expand Creyf's specialized divisions and reduce the focus on general temping as it was both very expensive and nearly impossible to remain profitable in all the different domains in which the company was involved.

However, others in the company felt that the existing dual strategy, which was both profitable and in line with customers' needs, should not yet be abandoned. Moreover, BvD, capitalizing on the expected growth potential in its sector, was asking an astronomical price. Several members of the board feared that the acquisition might be 'a bridge too far' for a company that had hitherto been successful in rather small-scale acquisitions. In addition, the financial markets were sceptical about the potential investment and the risk that management was prepared to take for something that was not even Creyf's core business.

Nonetheless, Van Hemele was convinced that the takeover was the logical, necessary step in developing a clearer, more profitable strategy in the future. He entered the meeting room ready to take up the challenge, confident that he could prove his many opponents wrong. The board was prepared for a lively debate.

Temporary labour services: in the grip of globalisation

The early 1990s had changed the temporary work services industry ('temping' for short)[2] dramatically. The diminishing role of national legislation in the unified labor market, the liberalization in some European countries of temporary work contracts, and the growing trend in cross-border contracts between European multinationals with temporary work businesses (TWBs) were all factors that explained the industry's evolution.

Consequently, a group of European (some global) TWBs had formed competing on a more international level. In 1994 the most successful players in terms of market share were: Manpower (10%), Ecco (8.8%), Randstad (6.9%), Bis (4.3%), Adia (4.3%) and Vedior (3%).

Given the clear trend towards internationalization, the temping industry was dominated by European rather than local business at the beginning of the 90s. Ironically, it was then that Creyf's decided to reverse its internationalization strategy and refocus on the traditional Belgian market.

Restructuring at Creyf's in the early 90s: 'back to local'

When, in April 1992, Michel Van Hemele traded in his career at the Generale Bank, (Belgium's largest bank at that time) for the position of CEO at Creyf's Interim, he found a company in serious trouble. Latterly, the small temporary staffing company established by Herman Creyf in 1963 had got 'carried away' creating a European dimension. This had become particularly pressing in view of the advent of the Single Market which was expected to significantly change the landscape as a result of the ambitious Internal Market Program (IMP) or 'Europe 1992' as it was called, launched by the

European authorities. According to Herman Creyf, 'You need to establish Europe 1992 yourself. It's eat or be eaten.'[3]

It was an ambitious dream, but one which ended up in a nightmare of loss-making and even fraudulent agencies, acquired across Great Britain, France, Spain and Portugal (see Exhibit 3).

Creyf had left his company after an IPO on the Brussels stock exchange a year earlier and had sold most of his shares to the Antwerp holding Ackermans & Van Haaren (AvH). Van Hemele was invited by this new 'reference shareholder' (which owned 40.57% of the shares) to help the recently hired CFO, Bart Gonnissen, put the company back on its feet.

Van Hemele and Gonnissen would soon become an inseparable and largely effective team, complementing each other in many ways. While Van Hemele turned out to be the more charismatic and prominent leader of the two, Gonnissen was the wizard at figures who, often behind the scenes, took care of all the financial and fiscal aspects of the CEO's decisions. Their critical analysis of the company's situation very soon led to the conclusion that 'The end is near. The foreign adventure of Creyf's is over. The group will concentrate again on the familiar Belgian market.'

In no time the company was drastically reorganized leading to the liquidation of the French agencies, closure of the Spanish activities and a management buy-out in Portugal. The disastrous British agencies had been sold to Herman Creyf a couple of years before. Indeed, it had been one of the major conditions of AvH when agreeing to purchase Creyf's shares.

At the same time, Creyf's had managed to hold an honorable third position in its home market, trailing two Dutch temporary services companies: Gregg Interim (the number two) and Interlabor (the number one). From then on, Creyf's would focus purely on growth in the Belgian market. After all 'Interim work is rather local. You can only create limited added value across borders.'[4]

---

[2] We will concentrate on the notion of temporary work in the sense of *travail intérimaire*. It involves a tripartite relation between a temporary work business (TWB), a temporary worker and a user-firm (client). More details on the temporary service industry can be found in the Industry Note: '*The European Temporary Work Services in 1994*', Nick Van Heck and Paul Verdin, INSEAD/K.U.Leuven, 1999.

[3] Herman Creyf, FET 27/04/1990 (Financieel Economische Tijd, a leading local newspaper).

[4] The two previous quotes of Michel Van Hemele can be found in FET 31/10/2002 and FET 29/12/1992.

Two important decisions were taken. Firstly, the main goal was to eliminate Creyf's disadvantage with regard to coverage of the home market (c.f. its main competitors). The number of agencies was expanded and some important blind spots on the Belgian map got filled up. By 1995, the Belgian network consisted of 60 offices.

Secondly, cost management and profitability became the core of Van Hemele's strategy. In 1993 this led to the disposal of the Acmé Group, a small, unprofitable temporary services group from Liège acquired by Creyf's in 1990 (see Exhibit 3).

Henceforth, Creyf's reverted to being a profitable local company. However, many analysts started wondering whether it would continue to buck the trend in the temping industry or get on board the internationalization train that was passing through the European landscape. This question became increasingly pressing when things started to get rough in the Belgian temping market.

Renewed growth in the mid-90s

In very little time the Belgian general temping sector fell victim to the keen price competition between Gregg and Interlabor, resulting in a significant reduction of profit margins. Van Hemele realised that, despite Creyf's present comfortable situation on the Belgian market, its narrow focus on general temping in one small European market made the company too vulnerable in the future: 'Big international companies start to purchase on a European scale. Besides, Creyf's has become the ideal prey for foreign groups wanting to buy market share in Belgium.'[5]

His concerns resulted in a 'dual strategy' from the mid-90s which acknowledged that it was important to be present in more than one market (regionalization), while offering more than one product (diversification). Van Hemele had clearly heard the whistle of the passing internationalization train.

Diversification in services

Herman Creyf had resisted a diversification strategy for his company and concentrated purely on

general temping. This refers to the temporary recruitment and dispatching of workers in all kinds of industries, with emphasis on quality and flexibility. While generally high volumes can be generated in this segment of the market, profit margins tend to be rather low. His successors were convinced that only by diversification could the company be successful. Specialized temping was the first new activity to be developed. It also refers to the temporary recruitment and dispatching of workers, yet in very specific industries where higher profit margins can still be found.

By 1994 the company thus consisted of four specialized divisions,[6] with Express Medical Interim, acquired in April 1994, being the most important and most profitable.

In 1997 the company acquired ADV Consult (see Exhibit 5), resulting in the development of a third activity for Creyf's, dubbed other HR services, which refers to complete recruitment services – plus selection programs, training programs, career advice, job search training and mobility programs.

Regionalization strategy

The first move towards regionalization was made in the business of general temping. In November 1994 the company acquired Lux Conseil International, the third largest temporary services company in Luxembourg. Over the period 1996–1997 the company rode this trend and acquired Pro Consultant and SFI in France, Van Den Boom in The Netherlands and BGT Personalservice in Germany (see Exhibit 5). All were markets with considerably higher profit margins in general temping than Belgium.

We have no intention of becoming a European group, but our economic territory does not end at the country's borders. In the long term we would like to be active, where our clients are.[7]

In 1998 the acquisition of Draft Engineering in the Netherlands marked the beginning of its regional expansion with regard to a fourth new segment, secondment and projects. This refers to the provision

[5] Michel Van Hemele, Trends 03/10/1996.

[6] Creyf's Data, Creyf's Engineering, Creyf's Maritime, Creyf's Express Medical Interim.
[7] Michel Van Hemele, FET 02/11/1994.

and outsourcing of engineering and IT managers to fulfill certain projects in other companies. It was regarded as a profitable activity.

In less than a year the company had expanded in this segment in the Dutch market by buying Promates, Beaver Software and the Done Group (see Exhibit 5).

The take-over of the large Dutch group, Content, in 1999, could be seen as the perfect illustration of the dual strategy followed by the company since the mid-90s. On the one hand, the acquisition signified an important expansion of its segmentation strategy. The group's specialised temping services were enlarged with Content, StarJob and Carrière (all elements of the Content Group) and its other services segment could benefit from the integration of Schroevers, SBO and Info Opleiders (see Exhibit 5). On the other, it also strengthened the group's international presence: from then on 75% of the group's turnover was realized outside Belgium (nearly half of it in the Netherlands).

By the end of 1999 Creyf's was clearly an international company once more, despite the memories of its hapless foreign adventures in the early years. Commenting on the U-turn, Hamele said, 'From a strategic perspective, Herman's [Creyf] choice to internationalise was definitely the right one. However, one can question the way it was done.'[8]

An acquisition-based strategy

Van Hemele's internationalization strategy was clearly based on some key characteristics as most acquisitions followed a similar pattern with regard to the selection of new markets and targets, the financing of the operations, and the integration of the acquired units.

The selection of new markets and targets

It was on the basis of the 'pigeon' strategy, the 'oil slick' strategy[9] or the 'euroregio' strategy that the international market penetration of the group took shape. As staffing was in essence a local business, Creyf's focused mainly on markets with similar culture, language or legislation. This meant that the company sought potential targets within a limited perimeter around the head office in Antwerp. Thus it first tried to build up a dominant position in Northern France, the Benelux, and West Germany. (Exhibit 6 shows the geographically expansion of the group from 1993 until 1998.)

Moreover, the proximity of the acquired units made it possible for the CEO/CFO management duo, Michel Van Hemele and Bart Gonnissen, to regularly visit their local businesses to make sure that everybody remained on the same wavelength at all times. After all, it was the personal fit with the local company's management that had determined the deal in the first place:

> Before we buy a company, we pay them a couple of visits to check if they are on the same wavelength. It has happened that we decided not to buy an excellent company only because it didn't match. Conversely, we have already bought companies with poor results simply because we believed in its management.[10]

Suitable local managers were typically open-minded entrepreneurs, ready to take initiative and to improve business. They believed in the group's mission and were keen to pursue the company's interest at all times. As one local manager put it: 'You always try to do what's best for the company because you know that, in the end, it will be the best for you too.'[11]

Financing the operations

A second characteristic of Creyf's internationalization strategy had to do with the financing of the acquisitions. Local management was never paid in shares. All transactions were effected in cash to avoid dilution of Creyf's stock. Consequently, Creyf's had to seek a couple of capital increases to raise its own funds and to make possible the financing of the internationalization strategy (see Exhibit 7). AvH, the reference shareholder, contributed to those capital increases in accordance with its participation.

Moreover, Creyf's would rarely buy an entire company at once, preferring to acquire only a part of

---

[8] Michel Van Hemele, FET 24/11/1999.

[9] 'Pigeon' refers to the limited distance a pigeon can fly. 'Oil slick' refers to the way an oil slick expands over the water surface.

[10] Bart Gonnissen, FET 10/11/2001.

[11] Gé Geurts, General Manager, Creyf's Netherlands.

it at first. According to the operational results of the company after the acquisition, local management would receive either more or less for the remaining shares:

> The local managers are of course super motivated because of this earn-out construction. We have already carried out different deals in which the management received more for the last 30% of the shares than for the first 70%.[12]

Integration of the acquired units

> You need to buy the right target at an acceptable price and integrate it afterwards in a correct way. The real work always started after the deal was done.[13]

A high level of decentralization characterized the organizational structure of Creyf's. The acquired businesses would be managed as a network of autonomous business units in which maximum flexibility around a strategic design was guaranteed. In the belief that temping was in essence a local business, the acquired companies were allowed to keep their autonomy after the deal was done.

Thereafter, coordination within the Creyf's group mainly consisted of the financial reports, the IT system and regular visits by the management team. The holding staff in Antwerp consisted of only 15 people, a number that was still too high according to Van Hemele.

The company's flat structure and its short decision lines made it possible to take quick decisions and to act promptly. Creyf's also benefited in that this unique operational structure meant that it could regularly buy a company at a lower price than its competitors. As Gé Geurts, general manager of Creyf's Netherlands, put it at the moment of the acquisition: 'A take-over by a larger Dutch agency had no added value for us. We wanted to maintain our autonomy.'

Entering the new millennium

Continuing acquisitions

From the end of the 90s, Creyf's dual strategy speeded up. In the year 2000, it started to take over

[12] Bart Gonnissen, De Standaard 10/11/2001
[13] Michel Van Hemele, FET 24/11/1999.

companies at an average speed of one company per month, resulting in the tremendous expansion of its product and geographical scope (see Exhibit 4a/b).

The end of the 90s brought the long overdue legalization of the Spanish and Italian temporary staffing industry (see Exhibit 2). Creyf's immediately focused on further expansion of its general temping segment in those markets to capitalize on all possible growth potential. In Italy, Interiman was bought (July 2000). In Spain, Verticce Business (October 2000) was taken over. The general temping segment also expanded into France with the acquisition of SPIA (October 1999) and IPS (November 1999). The Dutch general temping business would benefit from the purchase of VDN Group (August 2000). Creyf's also penetrated two new general temping markets. Firstly, in June 2000, it acquired Alpha Personal Service in Austria. Secondly, in October 2000, a start-up of Creyf's Interim was launched in Switzerland.

The secondment and projects segment expanded into Luxembourg with the acquisition of World Fiduce (June 1999), into the Netherlands by acquiring Applicon Group (January 2000), and into Belgium with the takeover of Wevecos (December 2000). Specialized staffing was further developed in Belgium with the acquisition of Orange Consult (July 2000), and in Spain with the acquisition of Verticce Business Consulting (October 2000).

Creyf's and its European market position

Over six years Creyf's had developed from a virtually unknown Belgian general staffing agency into a major European provider of HR services. The key to this unique track record had been its decentralized structure in combination with a strong entrepreneurial spirit. The current management had carried out complementary and mostly small-scale acquisitions, building Creyf's into one of the most important players in Belgium, the Netherlands and France (see Exhibit 4b). The company had over 30 brands, offered four different services, and was present in nine different countries (see Exhibit 4a)

In the year 2000 Creyf's consolidated turnover was €1.27 billion. Its consolidated operating profit was €66 million. (Exhibit 4c shows in detail how Creyf's turnover and operational result was divided over its international network, and its different services.)

On a European scale, Creyf's was ranked number five after Adecco, Manpower, Vedior and Randstad. Adecco, the outcome of the mega merger between Adia and Ecco in 1996, had clearly become the world's leading Goliath: it was No. 1 or 2 in 12 of the top 13 staffing markets and its market position conferred important unit cost advantages, resulting in higher EBITDA margins than its peers despite similar capital intensity. (More information on these key players can be found in Exhibit 1.)

As a huge gap existed between the industry Goliaths (with a European market share of about 10-15%) and Creyf's (with a European market share of only a few percent), one might wonder whether David could ever win this battle.

The fear of 'getting stuck in the middle'

Although the company had clearly done well with its dual strategy, Van Hemele and Gonnissen started to fear that the same approach could no longer be maintained in the new millennium.

In the six year period, the company had developed a fragmented portfolio on the basis of national and international small-scale acquisitions. They felt that its scope of activities had become too large to guarantee maximum productivity. After all, nobody could be good at everything.

Moreover, as the international network of Creyf's had grown tremendously, Michel Van Hemele was no longer able to visit all subsidiaries on a regular basis. This raised some concern as his 'management by travelling' had always been a key factor in the coordination and supervision of the group's activities.

Therefore, Creyf's management duo believed that time had come to narrow down the company's strategy and focus on a specific activity as the basis for further expansion. As general temping was differently positioned than the three other segments of the group, the feeling was that in the future the emphasis should either be more on general temping, or on the rest.

General temping had increasingly become a commodity market, weighed down by keen price competition and low profit margins (see Exhibit 4c). Only an overall cost-leader could still make money in this segment. From the start, Adecco had clearly focused on this business. The company's relatively high-market share and its heavy up-front investments and aggressive pricing had resulted in a low-cost position and an above-average return in general temping. For Creyf's it was too late to follow this strategic line. It would require huge capital investments without any realistic hope of ever catching up on Adecco's international coverage.

Of our four activities, only one is concentrated on general temping. This activity is very cyclical and generates low profit margins: although it contributes 70% to our turnover, it only generates 49% of our operational results. I'm not convinced we should go for a volume increase in general temping.[14]

It was clear therefore that a debate – if not a fight – was shaping up between the successful small players like Creyf's and the big four industry Goliaths.

David against Goliath

Van Hemele felt that the David vs. Goliath battle could not be won by 'doing what the competition does' – a 'me too' strategy would not bring prosperity. Hence, the strategic aim was to focus attention and investments on the other three activities of the company, i.e., specialized temping, detachment and projects, and other HR services. The idea was to realize a unique, high-quality service. For the detachment and projects segment, this implied a development from simple 'manpower provision' into 'total solutions provision', i.e., instead of merely offering flexible employment to a client, Creyf's wanted to provide total solutions with regard to IT and engineering. The subsidiaries Draft and Cluster were already solution providers for engineering, while Beaver Software was mainly a capacity provider for IT.

So when in March 2001 the IT consulting group, Bureau Van Dijk Computer Services (BvD), was put up for sale, Michel Van Hemele was more than interested to buy in order to establish the solution approach in the IT segment. But not all stakeholders of Creyf's seemed to be supportive of the CEO/CFO duo's intended strategic shift.

---

[14] Michel Van Hemele, De Standaard 08/05/2001.

First of all, several members of the board were not convinced that the current strategy had to be abandoned, particularly as the company's financial results (see Exhibit 4e) and its share price (see Exhibit 4d) had showed a positive evolution over the last few years. They wondered why Creyf's would change a strategy which was clearly rated positively by its key clients and shareholders.

Some of Creyf's key clients (Bosch, Nike, Daikin) were all large users of Creyf's general temping services but made only sporadic use of its other services. The main added value of working with Creyf's was founded in the stability of the relationship and the pro-activity and the willingness of the company to invest in their general temping services. One could wonder how far the company would be able to continue pampering its key clients if the strategy was merely focused on specialized services. Moreover, if future investments in general temping were at risk, would then a key client like Nike, who had a purchasing contract with Adecco on a European basis but did work with Creyf's in Belgium, maintain this exclusive partnership?

Thus board members feared that the CEO/CFO duo had overlooked the opportunity cost of the potential acquisition of BvD, which would definitely seal the intended strategic shift. Furthermore, convinced of the growth potential in its segment, BvD was asking more than €69 million – a huge amount of money for Creyf's, whose profits from ordinary business operations stood at €66 million at that time.

Clearly such an investment in specialized services would lock out similar investments in general temping in the future. Although low profit margins were common in the Belgian general temping industry, higher margins were still to be found in some European countries. By focusing purely on specialized services Creyf's would miss out on these opportunities. Italy, for example, which had only legalized its temporary staffing industry in 1999, still carried considerable growth potential. However, Adecco was clearly taking advantage of the Italian market's liberalization and had opened more than 150 offices in the last year. If Creyf's wanted to become a dominant player in this high-growth market, they would be forced to quickly expand their Italian network. However, to do so they needed money – money which now risked being spent on a non-core segment.

Secondly, the financial world was also sceptical about Creyf's intention to acquire BvD. Although it had always been successful in small-scale acquisitions (with lower P/E), Creyf's was now planning to take over a company with a higher P/E ratio (see Exhibit 8). Many analysts wondered why the company would be willing to pay such a high premium for the expected future earnings of BvD. Was it indeed realistic to expect continuous growth for the IT company? Hadn't the latest financial results of BvD shown signs of the negative pattern which had affected so many technology shares? What if this expected growth failed to materialize? They also questioned the way the company intended to finance the operation, i.e., by issuing converted Creyf's bonds in exchange for BVD shares. Would this not increase Creyf's debt ratio and threaten the financial balance of the company?

For Michel Van Hemele, however, further growth in the IT sector could be anticipated. BvD's high price incorporated a large amount of goodwill. As the founder and director of BvD, Jean-Paul De Nys, explained, further growth potential in his segment was only to be expected: 'IT people are like undertakers. They will always be necessary.' De Nys was particularly attracted by Creyf's established international network on which he hoped to be able to further BvD's international expansion.

Thirdly, for Ackermans & Van Haaren, Creyf's reference shareholder, temping was clearly a local business. For them the key to success would be *being better than the competition in every single location/business you are in'. So* the real question was not which segment Creyf's had to focus on, but how to create critical mass in every segment they were active in.

The proposed acquisition: a unique opportunity or a bridge too far?

The board meeting was scheduled on the night of Wednesday 28 March to decide on this highly contentious takeover of BvD. Michel Van Hemele was ready to convince the other board members of the strategic importance of the acquisition. He feared that without an urgent strategic focus, the company risked getting stuck in the middle – not able to continue the positive results of the past nor keep up with the Goliaths in the future. But would the board be supportive of his arguments?

Would they regard it as reasonable to significantly change the approach and put at risk what had been built up carefully over the years? Would they feel time had come to get rid of the dual focus and start concentrating on where the money was? Would they consider BvD as the best catch the company could go for? Did they believe in its growth potential, which Michel Van Hemele clearly saw? Or would they listen to the needs of the key clients and the concerns of the financial world and continue the safe path that had turned the company into a successful European player? Which future strategy would guarantee David winning the coming battles against the Goliaths of the temping industry? Could the acquisition of BvD be the crucial 'stone in the sling' leading to victory?

Exhibit 1 Competitive analyses
a. Ranking of European Staffing Companies
Market Shares in Continental Europe (2000)

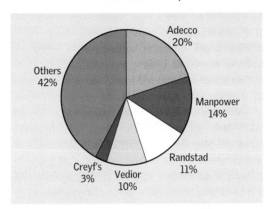

Source: ING Barings.

b. Financial Overview of Top Five European Staffing Companies

In EUR billion	Group Revenue		Group EBITDA		Group EBITDA/Revenue	
	1999	2000	1999	2000	1999	2000
1. Adecco SA	11,515	17,506	580	929	5%	5,30%
2. Manpower Inc	9,702	11,55	292	402	3%	3,50%
3. Vedior NV	4,057	6,584	185	344	4,60%	5,20%
4. Randstad Holding NV	5,565	6,168	350	305	6,30%	4,90%
5. Creyf's	929	1,273	67	93	7,20%	7,30%

Source: Sector Analysis 'The Dutch Staffing Sector', NIB Capital Bank.

c. The Key Players
Adecco SA (Headquarter: Chéserex, Switzerland)
Adecco was formed in August 1996 from the mega merger of Adia and Ecco. Since 1996 the business had grown to become the industry Goliath. In 2000 it generated nearly €18 billion, making it 75% larger than its nearest competitor, Manpower. Adecco had over 6,000 branches in 58 countries and had 700,000 temporary staff working for 250,000 clients per day. Adecco had

a global market share of 12% and a very strong global market position – it was No.1 or 2 in 12 of the top 13 staffing markets, which collectively accounted for 90% of the total market. The only market where Adecco was below No.2 was the Netherlands. France and the US were Adecco's most important markets.

Therefore, Adecco positioned itself as being the global leader. According to some analysts, however, prudence was in order. Adecco consisted of three different divisions.

➤

Adecco Staffing was its mainstream staffing division which offered light industrial and clerical temporary staffing on a global scale and generated the bulk (74%) of the group EBITDA. Ajilon was its specialist division. It was mainly US focused and operated in the IT and telecom markets (70% of sales) but also had a small finance business. Ajilon generated 15% of EBITDA. The third division was Career Services, which mainly covered its outplacement business, Lee Hecht Harrison, and contributed 11% of EBITDA.

Adecco's market position conferred important unit cost advantages, given the economies of scale in staffing, and partly explained why Adecco had higher EBITDA margins than its peers despite similar capital intensity.

Manpower Inc (Headquarter: Milwaukee, USA)

In 1955 Manpower was established in Canada. The first European offices opened in 1956 in the United Kingdom. Manpower France was established in 1957. In 2000 it was the second largest employment service organization with group revenue of nearly €12 billion. It was engaged in delivering high-value staffing and workforce management solutions worldwide. The company consisted of a network of 3,900 offices in 63 countries. Its largest operations, based on revenues, were located in the United States, France and the United Kingdom. Manpower was organized and managed primarily on a geographic basis. The company's operating countries were United States, France and EMEA (Europe, Middle East and Africa, excluding France). The firm provided employment to more than 2.7 million people worldwide and was the industry leader in employee assessment and training. Manpower also provided a range of staffing solutions, engagement and consulting services worldwide under the subsidiary brands of Brook Street, Elan, The Empower Group and Jefferson Wells.

Vedior NV (Headquarter: Amsterdam, The Netherlands)[15]

After the acquisition of Bis in 1997 and Select in 1999, Vedior became the world's third-largest temporary staffing company after Adecco and Manpower. In 2000, the company had over 2,000 branches in 29 countries and 10,500 temporary staff working for one million clients. It generated revenues of €6.58 billion and had a global market share of 4%. Vedior had greater exposure to specialist staffing than Adecco and Manpower. Specialist staffing accounted for 58% of EBITDA in 2001, compared to 15% at Adecco and 10% at Manpower. Vedior consisted of three divisions: Select, VediorBis and Vedior Europe. Select was its global specialist staffing business and its largest division. Select earned the highest EBITDA margins in the group. Select's revenues were evenly split between the US, UK and Europe, with some minor exposure to both Asia-Pacific and Latin American markets. VediorBis was the third-largest French general staffing business. Vedior's smallest division was Vedior Europe which operated across Europe (with the exception of France) but whose operations were mainly focused in the Netherlands, where it was No.3, and Belgium, where it was No.2.

Randstad Holding NV (Headquarter: Diemen, The Netherlands)

Randstad was the fourth largest in the world after Adecco, Manpower and Vedior, having group revenues of over €6 billion. It was only one third of the size of Adecco and half the size of Manpower. It had only minimal permanent placement exposure and only 5% of its revenues were generated from specialist staffing. 77% of Randstad's revenue, and all of its EBITDA were generated in Europe. Randstad focused on the SME[16] segment, major accounts represented only 5-10% of Randstad's revenue.

....

[15] More background information on Vedior can be found in the following case: 'Vedior International's European Strategy: The French Revolution', Nick Van Heck and Paul Verdin, INSEAD/K.U.Leuven, 1999.

[16] Small and Medium Enterprises.

Its business was split evenly between clerical and industrial staffing. Benelux (48% of gross profit), the US (21% of gross profit) and Germany (10% gross profit) were Randstad's three largest markets. Randstad had the leading market position in the Netherlands with a 35% market share, and to an extent in Germany, where it was the No.1 but with only 7% market share. It also had strong market positions in two of the minor European markets: Spain (16% share) and Denmark (13% share). However, Randstad had a weak position in the US, with less than 2% market share. It also had weak market positions in France, the UK and Italy and Switzerland. Randstad had five divisions. Its three general temping divisions (Randstad Europe, Randstad North-America and Tempo Team), a small specialist division, Yacht, and a low cost bulk staffing division, Capac.

Exhibit 2 Changes in regulation (1989–1997)

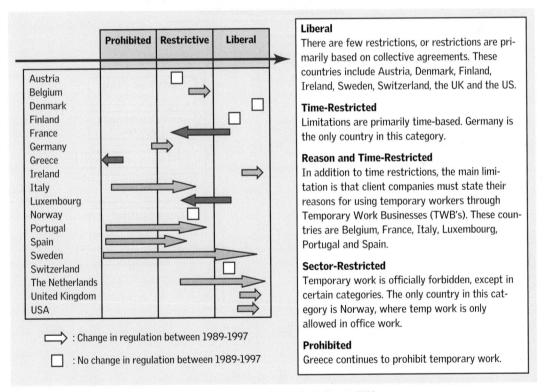

	Prohibited	Restrictive	Liberal
Austria			
Belgium			
Denmark			
Finland			
France			
Germany			
Greece			
Ireland			
Italy			
Luxembourg			
Norway			
Portugal			
Spain			
Sweden			
Switzerland			
The Netherlands			
United Kingdom			
USA			

⇨ : Change in regulation between 1989-1997

□ : No change in regulation between 1989-1997

Liberal
There are few restrictions, or restrictions are primarily based on collective agreements. These countries include Austria, Denmark, Finland, Ireland, Sweden, Switzerland, the UK and the US.

Time-Restricted
Limitations are primarily time-based. Germany is the only country in this category.

Reason and Time-Restricted
In addition to time restrictions, the main limitation is that client companies must state their reasons for using temporary workers through Temporary Work Businesses (TWB's). These countries are Belgium, France, Italy, Luxembourg, Portugal and Spain.

Sector-Restricted
Temporary work is officially forbidden, except in certain categories. The only country in this category is Norway, where temp work is only allowed in office work.

Prohibited
Greece continues to prohibit temporary work.

Source: 'European Temporary Work Business Gaining Ground', Staffing Industry Report, 1999.

Exhibit 3 The results and organigram of Creyf's International BV (31/12/1990, €)[17]

	Great Britain	France	Spain	Portugal	Crey's International BV
Turnover	547,200	17,848,433	1,377,346	95,860	19,868,840
Operating Profit	−428,236	65,320	51,339	−83,664	−393,928
Profit to be distributed	−524,171	−51,934	41,844	−13,386	−595,713

Source: Annual Report 1991 Creyf's Interim.

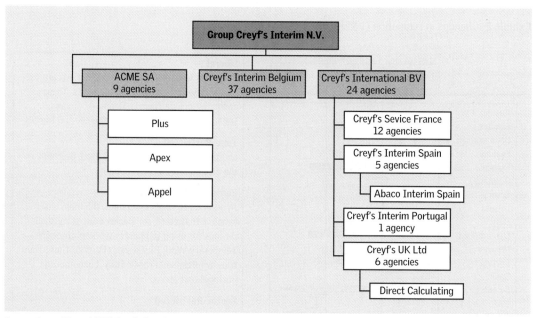

Source: Annual Report 1991 Creyf's Interim.

....

[17] Local currencies have been converted into Euro in order to enhance comparison.

Exhibit 4 The Creyf's Group (2000)
Leading Brands

		Belgium	Netherlands	Luxembourg	France	Spain	Italy	Germany	Austria	Switzerland
General Temporary Employment	Creyf's Interim	●	●	●	●	●	●			●
	BGT							●	●	
	VDN		●							
	BBB		●							
	Intersales		●							
	ASA		●							
	APS								●	
	Nord West Personal							●		
Specialized Temporary Employment	Content	●	●							
	Carrière		●							
	StarJob		●							
	ASA		●							
	Alter Ego				●					
	Express Medical	●								
	Prolink	●								
	Technitemps	●								
Secondment and Projects	Beaver	●	●	●						
	Orange	●								
	Wevecos	●								
	Draft		●							
	Done	●	●					●		
	Promates		●							
	Cluster		●							
Other HRM Services	SBO		●							
	Schoevers		●							
	Creyf's Select	●	●				●			
	BGT Select								●	
	ADV	●								
	Info Opleiders		●							
	BCR		●							
	Qualibre		●							
	BGT Outsourcing							●		

Source: Annual Report Creyf's 2000.

International Network

Country	Number of Agencies	Market Position
The Netherlands	220 agencies	4
France	160 agencies	6
Belgium	92 agencies	3
Germany	22 agencies	15
Luxembourg	6 agencies	1
Austria	4 agencies	/
Spain	5 agencies	/

Source: Presentation Michel Van Hemele: 'Value Creation through growth Commitment', 21/06/2000.

Turnover and Operational Results

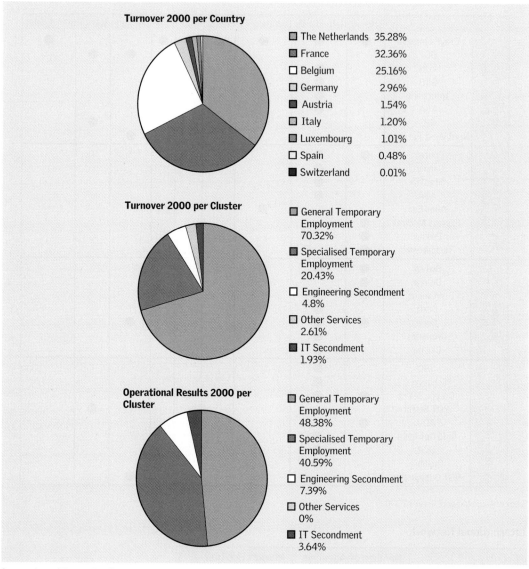

Turnover 2000 per Country

The Netherlands	35.28%
France	32.36%
Belgium	25.16%
Germany	2.96%
Austria	1.54%
Italy	1.20%
Luxembourg	1.01%
Spain	0.48%
Switzerland	0.01%

Turnover 2000 per Cluster

- General Temporary Employment 70.32%
- Specialised Temporary Employment 20.43%
- Engineering Secondment 4.8%
- Other Services 2.61%
- IT Secondment 1.93%

Operational Results 2000 per Cluster

- General Temporary Employment 48.38%
- Specialised Temporary Employment 40.59%
- Engineering Secondment 7.39%
- Other Services 0%
- IT Secondment 3.64%

Source: Annual Report Creyf's 2000.

Historical Share Price Information Creyf's Group

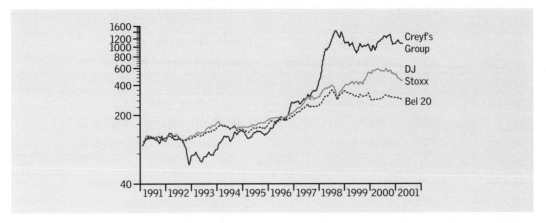

Financial Results Creyf's Group (1999–2000)

X €1000	2000	1999	Δ
Turnover	1,221,971	1,037,515	+17.78%
Operating Result	78,303	58,822	+33.12%
Profit on Ordinary Activities	70,133	54,380	+28.79%
Net Result	41,248	28,492	+44.77%

Source: Annual Report Creyf's 2000.

Exhibit 5 List of major acquisitions 1994–2001

1994			
April	100%	Express Medical	Belgium (Specialized Temping)
November	60%	Lux Conseil International	Luxembourg (General Temping)
1996			
January	80%	Pro Consultant	France (General Temping)
May	100%	SFI/SFB	France/Belgium (General Temping)
October	90%	Van Den Boom	The Netherlands (General Temping)
1997			
April	100%	ADV	Belgium (Other Services/Consulting)
September	80%	BGT Personalservice	Germany (General Temping)
1998			
March	100%	Draft	The Netherlands (Second/Projects)
April	100%	Alter Ego	Luxembourg (Specialized Temping)
April	N/A	Partner/Iso	France (General Temping)
November	100%	Innotiv	The Netherlands (Second/Projects)
December	100%	Beaver Software	The Netherlands (Second/Projects)
1999			
January	100%	Done Group	The Netherlands (Second/Projects)
September	100%	Content Beheer*	The Netherlands
October	100%	SPIA	France (General Temping)
June	100%	World Fiduce	Luxembourg (Second/Projects)
November	75%	IPS	France (General Temping)
2000			
January	100%	Applicon Group	The Netherlands (Second/Projects)
June	100%	Alpha Personal Service	Austria (General Temping)
July	100%	Orange Consul	Belgium (Specialized Temping)
July	60%	Interiman	Italy (General Temping)
August	100%	VDN Group	The Netherlands (General Temping)
October	100%	Verticce	Spain (General Temping)
October		Start-up Creyf's Switzerland	Switzerland (General Temping)
December	100%	Wevecos	Belgium (Specialized Temping)
December	100%	Cluster	The Netherlands (Specialized Temp)
2001			
January	100%	Technitemps	Belgium (Other Services)
February	100%	BBB Uitzendorganisatie	The Netherlands (General Temping)
February	90%	Nord West Personal AG	Switzerland (General Temping)
March	100%	Lestor Group	Spain (General Temping)
March	100%	Mentor Group	Spain (General Temping)

*Content, StarJob, Carrière (Specialized Temping); ASA Studenren Uitzendbureau, InterSales (General Temping); Schroevers, SBO, Info Opleiders (Other Services)

Exhibit 6 Geographical expansion on the basis of the 'Oil Slick'-Strategy

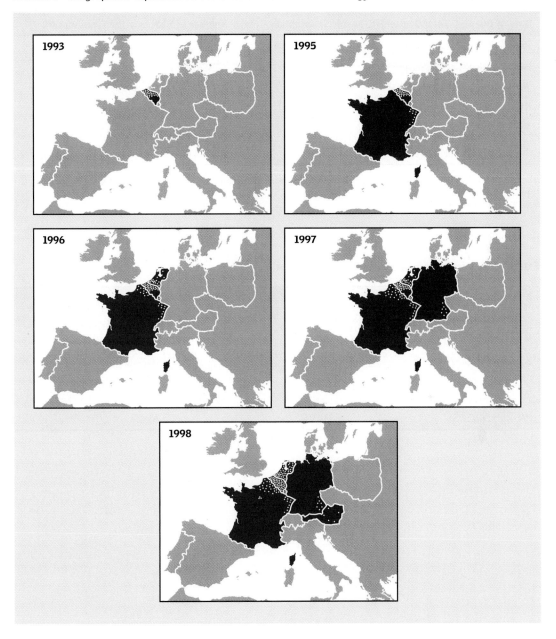

Exhibit 7 Capital increases of Creyf's

Date of Deed	Total Capital ([E]) after Transaction	Number of Shares after Transaction*
16/12/1998	16,991,950	1,408,292
24/12/1998	17,198,455	1,425,407
29/06/1999	67,968,817	21,727,033
03/08/1999	69,683,679	22,275,209
22/06/01	172,149,643	24,735,894
04/07/01	174,576,769	25,084,644

*For comparison purposes, the number of shares was calculated taking into account the stock-split of '99, i.e. 1 share was split into 10 shares.
Source: Annual Report Creyf's 2001.

Exhibit 8 Key financial data on acquisition and target

X €1000	Creyf's	BvD
Number of Shares	25,084,644	2,660,719
Net Profit	43,927,000	2,022,146
Earnings Per Share (EPS)	1.75	0.76
Share Price (P) (End of March '01)	25.5	18.6
P/E Ratio (P/EPS)	14.75	24.47

Exhibit 9 Financial information on Bureau Van Dijk

Evolution of Turnover (1997–2000)

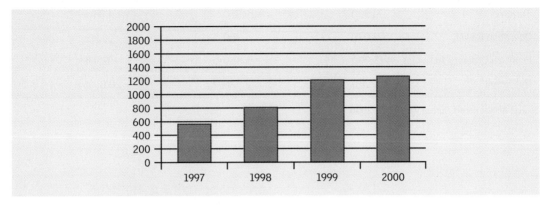

Breakdown of Turnover by Activity (1997–2000)

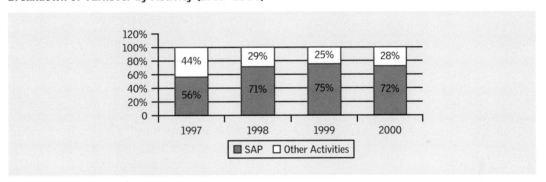

Breakdown of Turnover by Country (1997–2000)

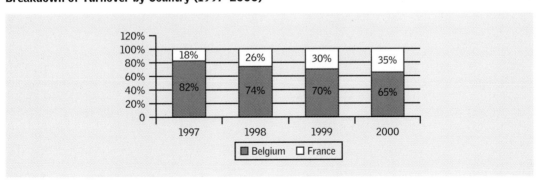

Financial Results (1999–2000)

X €1000	2000	1999	Δ
Turnover	31,320	29,870	+4.85%
Operating Result	4,070	5,980	−31.9%
Profit on Ordinary Activities	3,990	5,860	−31.9%
Net Result	2,310	2,920	−20.89%

Source: Annual Report Bureau Van Dijk CS 2000.

INSEAD

Case 27 **Strategy and performance management at DSM**

It was April 2003, and Hans Dijkman, Business Group Director of DSM Melamine, had just attended a Business Strategy Dialogue (BSD) meeting. DSM Melamine was the global leader in the manufacture and marketing of melamine, a chemical compound used to make highly resistant surfaces, supplying almost one third of world demand. However, Dijkman and his team faced significant challenges in terms of cost competitiveness, aggressive competition, market maturity in Europe and the US, and emerging growth, particularly in China.

Business Strategy Dialogues had been introduced at DSM in the mid-90s to help structure the firm's strategy development process. The BSD process consisted of five distinct phases resulting in a thorough review of the industry, market trends, customer needs, competition and the position of the relevant business group. In 2001, as part of its new

This case was written by Marjolein Bloemhof, Research Associate at INSEAD, under the supervision of Philippe Haspeslagh, Professor of Strategy and Management, and Regine Slagmulder, Associate Professor of Accounting and Control, both at INSEAD. It is intended to be used as a basis for class discussion rather than to illustrate either effective or ineffective handling of an administrative situation. Support from DSM in assembling the information presented in the case is gratefully acknowledged. Some case facts have been disguised for confidentiality reasons.

The authors gratefully acknowledge the financial support provided by the ABN AMRO Research Initiative in Managing for Value.

01/2004-5165

Value Based Business Steering (VBBS) system, DSM had also started to align its strategic planning and financial management processes by introducing Strategic Value Contracts. These contracts contained both performance indicators to monitor the implementation of strategy, and value drivers to measure economic value-creation.

BSDs were initiated whenever either the business or corporate felt the need, on average every three years. DSM Melamine was currently performing its fourth BSD at the request of Dijkman who felt that the current 'actively maintain' strategy would soon fail to achieve the financial performance targeted in his Strategic Value Contract.

Management of DSM Melamine had been discussing the possibility of pursuing a 'grow and build' strategy. They felt that they had reached the limits of cost reduction and that the only way to grow for DSM Melamine was by investing in new melamine plants. Dijkman, however, doubted whether corporate management would agree with this change. Would they emphasize the corporate strategy of becoming a specialties company and thus be reluctant to invest heavily in a commodity such as melamine, or would they let VBBS principles prevail and let themselves be swayed by Melamine's financial track record?

From state mines to specialty company

DSM origins go back to 1902 when the Dutch government founded Dutch State Mines (DSM) as a state-owned coal-mining company. In the 100 years of its existence DSM reinvented itself several times from what was originally a coal mining company, first, as a petrochemicals business, then a commodity chemicals business, and more recently a specialties company.

DSM became a public company in 1989. In 1993, Simon de Bree was appointed CEO and under his leadership DSM continued working on a portfolio shift towards advanced chemical and biotechnical products for the life sciences industry and performance materials. These activities were characterized by good earnings, quality, and strong growth. When de Bree stepped down in July 1999 he was hailed for having reduced the company's exposure to cyclicality and improved its structure by shifting towards a larger share of value-added products. He left the company in good shape both financially and portfolio-wise. Peter Elverding, the board member in charge of integrating Gist Brocades at that time, succeeded de Bree as CEO. Under his guidance, DSM was able to complete its strategic transformation into a specialty chemical company.

By 2003, the company had more than 20,000 employees spread across 200 offices and production sites in 40 countries. It was the leading producer of life science products, performance materials and industrial chemicals, and had a turnover of €6 billion in 2002 (see Exhibit 1 for key figures). Its headquarters were located in Heerlen, in the south of the Netherlands, close to the site of the former coalmines. In 2002, on the 100th anniversary of its foundation, DSM was given royal status and renamed Royal DSM.

Vision 2005: 'Focus and Value strategy'

One year after his appointment, Elverding announced the outcome of the Corporate Strategy Dialogue conducted in 2000 and labeled 'Vision 2005: Focus and Value'. With the implementation of Vision 2005, DSM would complete its strategic transformation into a specialty chemicals company. Elverding announced that DSM was planning to spin off its petrochemical business. This decision was not without emotion as the petrochemicals business was regarded by many as the 'roots' of the chemical company.

In addition, Elverding announced ambitious targets of increasing annual sales by approximately 60% to €10 billion by 2005, despite the planned withdrawal from the petrochemicals business, which provided one-third of the company's turnover in 2000. At least 80% of sales would have to be generated by specialty products; the rest would come from industrial chemicals, such as melamine and caprolactam, where DSM was already the global leader. Acquisitions would account for half of the sales increase and the remainder would be achieved through organic growth, roughly 6% per year.

Besides focusing on a global leadership position in the specialties business, Vision 2005 also

addressed DSM's desire to increase its market capitalization as management felt that the company's stock was undervalued. There were several reasons for this underperformance, including concerns about DSM's portfolio breadth relative to the size of the company, but management believed that the main reason was the market's perception that DSM still was a cyclical stock with predominantly a commodity profile. Management hoped that the implementation of Vision 2005 would turn DSM into a real specialties company, leading to a re-rating and appreciation of its market capitalization. A major part of the Vision 2005 strategy was accomplished when DSM successfully sold its petrochemicals business to Saudi Arabian Basic Industry Corp (SABIC) in June 2002. With a total net consideration of €2.25 billion, this transaction was the largest single deal in DSM's history. In a separate transaction, DSM sold its entitlement to an annual portion of the net profits of EBN[1] to the Dutch government in December 2001. These transactions created a solid cash cushion of over €3 billion to fund the expansion of the specialty portfolio targeted in Vision 2005. To protect its cash trove from unwanted parties, and to keep the funds and transformation process transparent, DSM took the unusual step of placing the revenues from the disposals of EBN and the petrochemicals business into a new subsidiary, DSM Vision 2005 BV. The use of these resources required approval by the governing board of the foundation, which consisted of three members of DSM's managing board and three members of the supervisory board. After the divestment of petrochemicals, DSM had become a substantially smaller company, but with a portfolio that matched the desired profile. Specialties now represented well over two-thirds of total sales, justifying a reclassification from 'bulk commodity player' to 'specialty player'.

In February 2003, Elverding was able to announce the next step in implementing Vision 2005 as DSM

---

[1] EBN: Energie Beheer Nederland, the entity controlling the state participations in the exploration, production and marketing of natural gas in the Netherlands, the management of which was entrusted by the State to DSM.

signed a contract to acquire Hoffman-La Roche's vitamins, carotenoids and fine chemicals business for €1.75 billion, the largest acquisition it had ever made.[2] The acquisition would help restore its total sales, which had been reduced to less than €6 billion as a result of the divestment of petrochemicals, to over €8 billion. More importantly, it would boost the specialty part of DSM's portfolio and help achieve the goal of 80% of sales in specialties two years ahead of the scheduled date (2005). Various analysts were skeptical about the acquisition, however, because of the price pressure and the low growth prospects of the business.

The DSM organization

DSM had a decentralized organizational structure built around 15 business groups (consisting of various business units) that were empowered to execute all business functions. The business groups were grouped into three strategic clusters, mainly for reporting purposes (see Exhibit 2). DSM believed that this structure ensured a flexible, efficient and fast response to market changes. The business group directors reported directly to the managing board of directors. Staff departments at corporate level supported the managing board and the business groups. The business groups contracted the services of a number of shared service departments, DSM Research, and intergroup product supplies at market prices.

The managing board of directors was a collegial board with five members. It was responsible for making decisions about the company's strategy, its portfolio policy, and the deployment of resources. Most board members were 'board delegates' for various business groups. The top management team consisted of the 15 business group directors and the corporate vice-presidents reporting to the board. The third layer of management consisted of 300 senior executives. The top 300 were considered 'corporate property'; they were on one central payroll

and Corporate had the authority to relocate these executives within DSM if they felt the need to do so.

DSM's corporate culture was traditionally informal and consensus-oriented, as is the case in many Dutch companies. Long-standing careers at DSM were encouraged. However, because DSM had been a cyclical company where 90% of the business results were the outcome of external circumstances that could not be influenced, DSM historically did not have a strong accountability culture.

The strategic planning process at DSM

Until the early 1990s, DSM had operated a traditional strategic planning process with planning and budget cycles taking place throughout the year However, DSM management was no longer satisfied with this process. They felt that Corporate Planning owned the strategic planning process and that it served too many different purposes (corporate, divisional, business and functional strategy, internal and external). The process had become routine over time and had degenerated into a 'numbers exercise'. The link between strategy and performance was not clear, but more importantly, top management felt that the quality of strategy development was poor. Most of the strategies focused mainly on cost reduction. The primary beneficiary of such strategies was not the company but its customers, since most of the cost savings were typically passed on to them through price reductions. To enhance the quality of the strategy development process, a new approach called the Business Strategy Dialogue (BSD) was introduced in 1992. These BSDs led to Corporate Strategy Dialogues (CSDs) which were intended to improve the corporate strategy development process.

Corporate strategy dialogue

DSM's strategy development process started with an extensive study of the current situation and the outlook for the company for the next few years. The Corporate Strategy Dialogue was held every three years with a team of 40-50 company-wide executives. It was aimed at developing a long-term corporate strategy, with evaluations and choices being made about portfolio composition,

---

[2] The deal was closed in September 2003, after the final approval of the anti-trust authorities was obtained. Roche's Vitamins & Fine Chemicals business was renamed DSM Nutritional Products (DNP).

investment priorities and geographical spread. The whole process took six to nine months and was wide-ranging, involving intensive discussions in DSM Corporate top meetings, with the supervisory board and the Central Works Council. The end product was a shortlist of corporate top priorities.

The first CSD was performed in 1994, followed by another in 1997 and a third in 2000. Besides new themes that were defined in each CSD, a number of common themes had consistently been part of the CSD, such as profitable growth, leadership position, coherent portfolio, reduction of cyclicality, growth markets, reduction of dollar-sensitivity, geographical spread, and being an attractive employer.

Once the priorities were set, the corporate strategic plan was to be implemented over the next two to three years. Focusing all energy on realizing its corporate priorities had allowed DSM to achieve most of them before their target dates.

Business strategy dialogue

The businesses were responsible for developing and implementing their (approved) Business Strategy Dialogues (BSDs). The purpose of a BSD was to provide a consistent method and terminology to help structure the strategy development process and improve its quality. BSDs were mostly initiated by the business groups themselves, but were sometimes requested by corporate. They occurred at regular intervals of three years on average.

The BSD process consisted of five phases with several steps within each phase. The five phases were: Characterizing the Business Situation; Analyzing the Business System at Macro Level; Analyzing the Business System at Micro Level; Options and Strategic Choice and Action Planning and Performance Measurement (see Exhibit 3). But before a BSD could be started, some preparatory work had to be done.

Starting up One of the first things to be done was to identify a facilitator and a challenger. To facilitate the implementation of the BSDs, Corporate had trained around 30 'facilitators' to support the business teams in its creative thinking process. They were selected from the top 350 executives and asked by the Chairman of DSM to become a facilitator. The task of a facilitator was to prepare the

strategy development process with the business group director by defining the scope of the exercise, discussing the composition of the core team, examining the time schedule, drafting a list of important strategic issues, and appointing a project manager who was responsible for the operational part of the strategy development process. The most important role of the facilitator, however, was to make sure that the BSD led to real strategic options and a real choice, as expressed by Marthijn Jansen, facilitator:

> *The role of the facilitator is to make sure that the BSD focuses on the right issues, that in the 'options phase' the conversation diverges, and that in the defining of the KPIs phase, everything converges to a clear path and a clear view of the implications of the choices made.*

In addition to a facilitator, a 'challenger' was selected. The challenger had an important role as he/she had to question the BSD team about the assumptions, analyses and conclusions it made. Challengers were chosen from the top 100 managers within DSM. In addition to the internal challenger, a business group could also ask 'outsiders' to challenge them on specific issues. These outsiders – often (technology) specialists – also shared their knowledge.

The core team in the BSD typically consisted of the complete business management team supported by specialists from further down the organization. They were advised not to have more than 10 to 12 people as management felt that larger groups did not allow for effective discussion and hampered the creativity of the process. In large or complicated businesses sub-groups were formed to address specific questions. The BSD process consisted of workshops and discussion sessions led by the facilitator. Input and participation by all concerned was considered very important.

Characterizing the business situation The objective of this phase was to collect and structure the necessary information to be used as input to the BSD. The Group provided the businesses with a strategic data checklist of the information that might be useful for the BSD such as environmental and market analysis, competitor assessments and analysis of manufacturing, R&D, HRM, finance and processes. Data were supplied by functional discipline. In addition to data gathering, the checklist offered a useful format for summarizing and presenting the information. The data set was structured in accordance with questions such as:

◆ What business are you competing in?

◆ Which other businesses and products are you competing with?

◆ How attractive is the industry in terms of growth and profitability?

◆ What is your competitive position (benchmarks)?

◆ What are the dynamics? What trends can be expected in your business system?

Practice showed that this phase could take two to four months. Corporate management emphasized that the businesses should not view this information-gathering phase as a checklist exercise but rather approach it from an 'issue-driven' angle.

Analyzing the business system at macro level In this phase, which took approximately two days, the industry in which the business unit competed was analyzed from the outside in, based on Porter's Five Forces model. The discussion focused on the examination of the value added in the business chain, the customers, the competitors, the business dynamics and the drivers of the industry. An important step was the analysis of the different generic strategies followed by key competitors. Understanding generic strategies forced the businesses to categorize the different ways in which a business could compete in the industry. A strategic group was defined as a cluster of companies following the same generic strategy. The outcome of this phase included a basic understanding of the 'rules of the game', i.e. the strategic groups in which the business might compete and a preliminary view of the key success factors (KSFs) that must be met in order to compete successfully within a certain strategic group.

Analyzing the business system at micro level In this phase the organization was analyzed from the inside out, by looking at the internal process. Important tools for the analysis of the internal value chain were market segmentation, activity-based costing, internal or (preferably) external benchmarking of functions, and assessment of the technological position. The conclusions of the micro-discussion included an analysis of the business unit's capabilities – both strengths and weaknesses – to compete in its strategic group. This phase took on average two days.

Options and strategic choice After having assessed the competitive environment and the business unit's capabilities to compete successfully in its environment, the outcome of both steps were compared, i.e. internal capabilities were compared with the list of KSFs (see Exhibit 4 for an example of DSM Melamine). This allowed the business to make a choice as to the strategic group in which it wanted to compete. Furthermore, it allowed the business to verify whether it really could serve the selected market segments and determine what steps were necessary to achieve or sustain leadership within the strategic group.

Action planning and performance measurement Once the strategic choice had been made, the strategy had to be translated into an action plan and linked to performance measurement. Based on the strategic mission and objectives of the business unit a limited number of performance indicators that were important to the corresponding KSFs were selected. Performance indicators monitored the implementation of the strategy and were the measurable part of the KSFs, allowing comparisons with competitors and performance monitoring over time. Examples of performance indicators included market share, pipeline of products, quality, customer satisfaction, and cost per unit. The objective of performance measurement was to provide periodic information on the progress made toward the defined targets for each performance indicator. Furthermore, it helped management set objectives and target levels for the next period.

Annual strategic review (ASR) The Annual Strategic Review (ASR) was performed by each business group, and comprised a progress report on the implementation of the BSD, an update or reassessment of major business risks, an updated sensitivity analysis and updated financial projections. The ASRs of the business groups constituted the building blocks of the corporate ASR whose purpose was to monitor the execution of the Corporate Strategy Dialogue. An important element in the review was the confirmation that the chosen strategy in the BSD was still valid and that the implementation was on track. Therefore, the validity of the main assumptions on which the strategy was based had to be checked and the consequences of changes in the business environment for the strategy evaluated.

Benefits and challenges of the BSD system

Benefits In 2000, six years after its implementation, the BSD had become an accepted system for developing business strategy. DSM management was pleased with the improved quality of strategy formulation and the team-building aspects. One business group director coming from outside DSM commented:

The strategic planning process is very good at DSM. It is a robust and effective process. And it is a living system, contrary to many other companies where people just 'feed' the system.

Many people valued the 'challenger' part of the BSD, where someone from outside the business group challenged the assumptions and outcomes of the BSD. One business group director recalled:

Corporate said to us: 'The BSD is nice but not rigorous enough. Come back when you have really looked at the intrinsic value of each market segment. Not at macro level, but at market segment level.' This was very good because it forced us to get a real grounding in segments.

People agreed that the BSD process greatly enhanced the insights and understanding of the business. In addition, it forced alignment, both across functions in the business unit and with respect to the strategy. Furthermore, people felt that the BSD gave legitimacy to initiate changes later on when the business got to the implementation phase. Another big advantage of the process was that strategy development became a three-yearly process with just an annual update. One top executive of corporate planning commented:

Performing a BSD is a lot of work. But once you are done, you are done for two to three years.

Challenges The final phase of the BSD – translating strategy into performance measurement – remained a challenge. Hein Schreuder, Corporate Vice President Strategy & Development, expressed his concern:

DSM invests heavily in a good strategic diagnosis, but the ultimate focus should be on delivery.

Although DSM had improved the quality of strategic thinking in the planning process, the question remained indeed how to link it with execution.

Value based business steering

In 2000, Henk van Dalen, Director of the DSM Polyethylenes business group, was appointed to the managing board. He believed that the necessary step to implement Vision 2005 and its promise for performance was a more intense focus on value-creation in the businesses. According to the newly introduced Value-Based-Business Steering (VBBS) concept, the overall target for DSM was to create value for all of its stakeholders, i.e. shareholders, employees, customers, and society.

DSM approached VBBS from three different angles. The first was accountability as the basis for financial control. The second was alignment of DSM's strategic business planning processes to materialize its promise for performance. The third was the introduction of new financial operating metrics that translated Vision 2005 and BSDs into economic value terms. DSM decided to start with the third angle because it had the biggest impact on the organization and was a first step in aligning strategy with performance measurement. As a result, VBBS was strongly driven by the finance department – at least initially.

New financial business steering metrics

A new set of performance metrics was developed for internally measuring and managing financial performance in terms of value-creation (see Appendix 1). Cash Flow Return on Investment (CFROI) became DSM's new yardstick for measuring the performance of its businesses. Contrary to other value-based management companies, DSM decided to use CFROI only for internal reporting and financial performance measurement, while ROI remained the performance measure for external reporting. A reason for this decision was that DSM felt that the complex CFROI calculations were difficult to explain to investors. Furthermore, DSM first wanted to see if the new metrics would work.

Total Shareholder Return was an important external performance indicator related to value-creation for DSM as a whole, but could not be directly linked to the performance of individual business groups. DSM chose to introduce Cash Value Added (CVA) to translate value-creation from a capital market point of view into an objective internal DSM measure. CVA represented the cash surplus generated ('value realized') by a business once all capital providers had been compensated. To determine the 'value created' by a business, DSM measured the increase in value (delta CVA) from year to year. Because DSM was a decentralized company, the group did not impose delta CVA targets; instead, target setting was done in a bottom-up fashion. To achieve a positive delta CVA and thus create value, a business could work on two key value drivers: by improving CFROI or by investing in profitable projects.

Investments were evaluated against the Internal Rate of Return (IRR) hurdle, i.e. the before-tax weighted average cost of capital (WACC). If an investment met the WACC hurdle, it created value. However, DSM imposed an additional performance standard by plotting the current business position and the historical performance of a business group on a so-called 'C-curve' (see Exhibit 5).

The C-curve provided a clear indication of the pre-ferred route to value-creation for a business depending on its current return. Three basic scenarios could be distinguished. For businesses that generated returns below the WACC, restructuring and improving the return was priority number one. Businesses that had returns around the WACC needed to improve their performance and were encouraged to explore methods to increase CFROI. Finally, businesses that had returns well above the WACC found themselves in a position that was profitable; the way to create value for this kind of businesses was to grow while improving or maintaining CFROI.

Operationalizing VBBS Value-creation for DSM as a whole was translated into the internal value-creation measure delta CVA. This measure could be applied at the business group level, but also at lower levels such as business units or product/market combinations. The next step in the VBBS process was to translate the abstract concept of value-creation into operational actions using the concept of value drivers. DSM defined a value driver as an 'operational variable which can be influenced by acts of management and which has a direct link with value-creation.' Examples of value drivers included: working capital as a percentage of sales, raw material costs per ton, production costs per ton, and sales price per ton.

At this stage, the difference between value drivers and performance indicators became clear. Performance indicators were developed during the BSD and monitored the implementation of the strategy. Value drivers were developed during the VBBS analyses and monitored how the implemented strategy resulted in economic value-creation. Performance indicators applied to the strategic and tactical level and provided early warning signs ('leading indicators'). In contrast, value drivers applied to the operational level of the organization and were financial and often results-based and therefore 'lagging indicators'.

Value drivers and performance indicators did not necessarily have a one-to-one relationship. One per-formance indicator (e.g. market share) could influence multiple value drivers (e.g., volume, margin, cost), and vice versa, one value driver could be affected by several performance indicators. For the commodity businesses, value drivers and perform-ance indicators often covered the same variables. For example, a value driver could be cost per ton, while the corresponding performance indicator would be a relative measure – costs compared to competitors. However, the link was much less clear for the specialty activities where factors such as the management of the innovation pipeline would be decisive for success. There could be a significant time lag between the filling of the pipeline with new products and the value-creation caused by higher sales volume resulting from these new products.

Once the metrics were defined and the concept of VBBS was clear, DSM started with the strategic assessment of its various businesses. These assess-ments yielded valuable new insights into the positioning of specific businesses. For example, some businesses that accounting wise (i.e., based on ROI) looked like diamonds in the portfolio, turned out to be value-destroying businesses from a CFROI perspective. Loek Radix, Director of Corporate Finance, explained:

> I was almost physically attacked when I delivered that message. But the strategic assessments were a huge eye-opener about how we should manage a certain type of business. Before, there was an atmosphere of complacency in successful businesses. There was no mindset at all about delta value. However, it is not important what today's value is; it is important what the evolution in value is.

Although people got excited about the results from the VBBS assessments, implementing the new metrics and coming up with value drivers turned out to be a technically difficult and time consuming process. Although the consultants were able to explain the concept of CFROI and CVA, translating this into specific measures was extremely complex. According to Radix:

> The sweaty part starts when you really have to develop the metrics in detail. Questions like: 'What do I do with foreign investment?' or 'What is the percentage of economic depreciation?' were difficult to answer. We had to re-define items during the process. That was not really helping us in the introduction of VBBS and we got pushback from the operating managers.

In early 2002, the general knowledge of the VBBS system in the DSM organization was still limited. Although top management understood the big picture, a survey testing more detailed knowledge showed that even at the executive level a lot still had to be learned. One corporate manager estimated that it would take three to five years for people to really understand and work with the new system. However, at corporate level, VBBS thinking had already significantly changed the strategic approach vis-à-vis the businesses. Whereas previously corporate finance used to strive for consensus, the department was now more able to challenge the businesses, helped by the C-curve. According to Radix:

> Before we had a culture of managing conflict in our department. Now we are able to say, 'No, we don't agree, we oppose this investment.' We now challenge businesses whose CFROI is above the WACC to grow, and we refuse to give additional investment money to businesses whose CFROI is below WACC. We now say 'If you don't have 8% CFROI, then your first task is to get that CFROI before you get money for investments.' As a business unit manager you can no longer say: 'I will grow out of the misery.' VBBS and the C-curve really helped to challenge in a different way.

More than new metrics: creating strategic alignment through strategic value contracts

Although VBBS within DSM was still very much metrics oriented, right from the early days DSM was aware that it was much more than just adopting new metrics: DSM management felt that it gave them the tools and insights to align the business strategies to performance measurement. The connection between strategy and performance measurement was made by elaborating the BSD into Strategic Value Contracts (SVCs).

From 2001 on, each new BSD had to result in a SVC. A SVC was a summary of the main conclusions of a BSD translated into measurable targets for the next three years. It contained two main sections which had to be explicitly approved by the managing board: 1) bottom line results focusing on CFROI and CVA and the breakdown thereof in controllable value drivers, and 2) strategic goals laid down in the strategic mission and the implementation specified in terms of key success factors, performance indicators and strategic milestones. Thus, both performance indicators for monitoring strategy implementation, and value-based measures for monitoring value-creation were incorporated into the contract. Future performance of the business would be monitored against the agreed-upon SVC.

DSM felt that the SVC was a strong communication tool and helped the implementation of strategy and VBBS at the business group levels. It explained the steps of how businesses were planning to execute their strategy. This led to more transparency and helped the management board ask the right questions and challenge the business groups. One management board member explained:

What always had frustrated me about the BSD was that a strategy was developed, but monitoring the implementation of this strategy was difficult. I am very pleased with the Strategic Value Contract because people are now forced to implement the strategy. Now, people really have to finish the BSD. That is much clearer.

The SVC was signed by the business group director and the business group referee in the managing board, who signed on behalf of the entire managing board. A successor taking over responsibility for someone's business also had to take over the existing SVC. Proposals for substantial modifications to the contract could only result from major changes in the business environment and had to be approved by the managing board. In early 2002, two business groups had their SVC and five other contracts were in progress. By 2003, nearly all business groups had their SVC.

Compensation

In the past, not meeting targets was widely tolerated at DSM, largely as a result of the fact that DSM had been a cyclical company where 90% of the businesses results were beyond the firm's control. DSM management felt that it had to change this 'culture of excuse' and high level of 'cyclicality tolerance' as DSM transformed into a specialties company. The implementation of SVCs supported this change in culture.

DSM felt that the next step in the implementation of VBBS was to link it with the managers' performance evaluation system. In 2002, it rolled out a new performance appraisal system for its executives which evaluated managers based on their ability to develop sustainable strategies and get them approved (BSD), the achievement of targets set in the SVC, and a number of enabling factors, such as having the right processes and workforce in place. The management board evaluated the top 30 executives, who in turn appraised the managers below them. This appraisal was used to determine managers' salary evolution.

The second element of the compensation system was a short-term incentive program which ranged from 20% to 30% on top of the base salary. This incentive scheme was linked to VBBS by replacing ROI with delta CVA and calculating bonuses based on the current year's delta CVA. Thus, executive compensation was linked both to personal targets and to financial performance measures, such as CFROI, delta CVA and CVA. Lower management was held responsible for the relevant value drivers. Finally, DSM introduced a personnel share option scheme alongside the existing management option scheme in 2001.

When SVCs and the new performance appraisal system were first introduced, managers felt uncomfortable as the pressure on them gradually mounted. On the other hand, the contracts made it clear what was expected of them and improved communication both between the business groups and Corporate and within the business group itself. SVCs also led to a demand from the business group directors with respect to key individuals in their organization. Previously, corporate HR had the authority to move people around and managers typically changed jobs every 18 months to two years. Under the new system, however, some business group directors claimed that they were unable to achieve their SVC targets if they could not keep their key managers. DSM management therefore decided that employees would not move around for a period of three years, but also stated that business group directors had 'corporate' responsibilities in terms of training and follow up of people.

In 2002, DSM was unable to meet its ambitious profitability targets due to unfavorable economic developments. However, a number of corporate improvement targets relating to safety, health and the environment, and a number of targets linked to the Group's strategy were realized. The overall realization was 20%. Moreover, the Supervisory Board had used its discretionary powers to grant an additional bonus to the members of the Managing Board amounting to 10% of their fixed annual salary, in recognition of their extraordinary efforts in strategically repositioning the company.[3]

The BSD and VBBS process at work at DSM Melamine

The DSM Melamine business group was part of the 'Industrial Chemicals' cluster. It was the global

---

[3] Source: DSM Annual Report 2002, page 43.

leader in the manufacturing and marketing of melamine, supplying almost one third of global demand. Melamine is a heat- and scratch-resistant plastic mainly used in impregnating resins and adhesive resins for laminated flooring and panels in the wood-processing industry. It is also used in car paints, durable plastic tableware, euro bank notes, and flame-retardants. The gas-phase production technology that DSM Melamine used to produce melamine was a proprietary technology developed in 1967 and was a highly sophisticated process technology. The raw materials for the production of melamine were natural gas, ammonia, carbon dioxide, and urea. Since ammonia and carbon dioxide were by-products of melamine production, melamine plants had to be built close to a urea plant.

In 2001, world consumption of melamine was nearly 700,000 metric tons, valued at approximately $700 million. DSM Melamine was well established with advanced production plants on three continents and a sophisticated technical support system in place for its customers. In 2002, DSM Melamine's image was one of a global reliable supplier of 'hassle-free' product in Europe, Americas, and Asia Pacific. It earned more than half of its sales from long-term contracts with large customers who considered melamine a strategic purchase item and valued security of supply.

The melamine market was subject to high volatility. Demand for most downstream markets for melamine was greatly influenced by general economic conditions. Consequently, demand followed the fortunes of the leading world economies. Furthermore, demand and capacity had not always been in balance, leading to significant price fluctuations. In 1998, for example, the melamine market was characterized by supply shortages caused by technical problems at several melamine producers worldwide. High imports from overseas by melamine consumers via traders raised spot prices to levels of €3,500/ton. In 1999, however, prices collapsed to €800–900/ton. One of the major challenges for melamine producers was therefore to balance supply and demand.

Forecasting demand was not sufficient, however. An accurate estimate of global melamine supply was also needed to avoid major under- or over-supply. This was hard to predict because of the many unplanned maintenance shutdowns at several melamine producers worldwide. The management of DSM Melamine had worked hard to improve its estimates of capacity utilization vis-à-vis global nameplate capacity.

The early BSDs

DSM Melamine started in 1992 with its first BSD, followed by others in 1995 and 1999. The BSD process proved to be very helpful in addressing the problems and challenges the business group was facing and dramatically changed its performance (see Exhibit 6 for the C-curve for DSM Melamine for the period 1992–1997).

BSD 1992 The main outcome of the 1992 BSD was the final approval of a US$80 million project to dismantle a relatively new melamine plant at Geleen in the Netherlands, and reconstruct it in Indonesia. DSM Melamine had made the decision to build the plant in Geleen in 1989 when it predicted a 5% annual growth in melamine in Europe. However, since then melamine sales and prices in Western Europe had declined as demand in key markets in the former Soviet Union stagnated and exports to Eastern Europe slumped. The management team of DSM Melamine had to decide whether to close, sell, or relocate the plant that had been built only in 1992. Management decided to rebuild it in Indonesia where its Jakarta-based business Joint Venture, DSM Kaltim Melamine, in which it had a 60% stake, would own and operate the plant. DSM had wanted to build a Southeast Asian melamine plant for some time as the Asia/Pacific region was a fairly new market that was developing at a fast pace, especially in countries with major wood-processing industries. The Geleen plant was dismantled in 1994 and rebuilt in Indonesia in 1997, thereby reducing the company's worldwide melamine capacity for three to four years. The plant was the largest melamine plant in the Far East and the first to be built in Southeast Asia.

BSD 1995 In 1995, the second BSD led to a major strategic breakthrough in the eyes of management. The strategy was to 'actively maintain' its global leadership position in terms of market share, technology, cost and customer image. Competition was based on 'price over volume' and DSM Melamine wanted to grow at the prevailing market rate. A breakthrough in the BSD process occurred when DSM Melamine woke up to the fact that it did not have the right technology to grow with the market. Instead of continuing to build large plants with gas-phase production technology – which would cover the growth of the market for the next four to five years – management decided to acquire Shortened Liquid Phase (SLP) technology in 1997. This technology, which required fewer production steps to produce high-quality melamine, would enable DSM Melamine to build smaller plants while still being cost competitive with the traditional gas-phase plants. However, to achieve the same quality level as the melamine obtained in DSM's gas-phase process, the SLP technology had to be upgraded.

BSD 1999 In 1999, a third BSD was performed. The project motivated by the new review was to build a fourth Melamine plant in Geleen based on the new liquid phase technology, which required an investment of €90 million. A portion of that investment would be used to expand urea production at the site. The melamine plant was expected to come on-stream by end 2003.

> The strategy that followed the 1999 BSD was to continue the 'actively maintain' strategy. Management of DSM Melamine expected worldwide consumption of melamine to grow by 5–6% per annum. This growth was concentrated in Europe and to a lesser extent Asia (China) and the Americas. Accordingly, DSM Melamine planned to expand its global capacity by 30kt every two to three years in addition to de-bottlenecking the existing plants.

Key success factors for the actively maintain strategy were 'lowest cost delivered' by de-bottlenecking existing gas-phase plants and new low cost technology, and 'security of sales'. The latter could be achieved by negotiating long-term contracts with global key customers, meeting the requirements for strategic customer alliances, and differentiating service levels.

The strategic value contract

In 2001, the first SVC was drafted for DSM Melamine. Since it was DSM's first experience with these contracts, it was primarily viewed as a learning experience. The subsequent 2003 contract, signed in September 2002, was considered the first 'real' contract. It was based on the 1999 BSD and would be revised at the end of 2003, once the 2003 BSD was finished. (Exhibit 7 shows an extract of the SVC for the period 1999–2003.)

The 2003 BSD process

The 2003 BSD was initiated by the management of DSM Melamine (DMM), as the Annual Strategic Review of 2002 had shown that its current strategy would not enable the business group to achieve the ambitious targets set forth in the SVC. Projections by DMM showed that the group would have a zero or negative delta CVA from 2004 onwards and reach a major negative delta CVA in 2007. These calculations were based on assumptions from the corporate planning group which had predicted a major economic slowdown for 2007.

In addition, the environment had changed considerably. After experiencing strong demand in 1998 and most of 2000, melamine markets declined or remained stagnant in most regions in 2001. High natural gas costs, lower margins, depressed demand, and significant capacity additions during 1998–2001 forced many melamine producers to curtail production in 2001. Producers such as Melamine Chemicals and Namhae Chemical exited the market. However, industry experts expected the demand for melamine in the US and Western Europe to recover and grow at nearly 3% per year from 2001 to 2006. Demand in Southeast Asia, particularly in China, was expected to experience much higher growth rates because of increasing production of laminates for both domestic use and exports. In the 1999 BSD, DMM had not actively looked into China, as the main investment opportunities were seen to be in Europe (see Exhibit 8 for regional growth forecasts and realization). However, because of the impressive annual growth rate (15%) of the Chinese melamine market, the management of DMM wanted to investigate the impact of China on its current strategy.

Kick-off The BSD 2003 of DMM started with a kick-off meeting in September 2002 with the BSD global management team, including the management team from Sittard, the general manager of America, the general manager of Indonesia, and the facilitator. Although the facilitator typically came from outside the business group, DMM decided to ask its own Director of Planning and Projects, Marthijn Jansen, to act as facilitator. In his former function at corporate planning, Mr. Jansen had been facilitator for various business groups and was therefore perceived as very experienced in this role. He was expected to spend half of his time on the BSD process for a period of six months. The challenger, Jos Goessens, Business Group Director of Plastic and Engineering, was asked to join the BSD team in January 2003.

One of the criticisms of previous BSDs was that people felt that they were used to 'sell' a project to top management. The BSD team wanted to prevent this from happening again in 2003 and therefore stressed the importance of challenging each other during the whole process and making a serious effort at identifying alternatives.

As DMM wanted to perform an 'issue-driven' BSD, the BSD team started with identifying the subjects on which they thought decisions were needed. A total of 35 issues were identified ranging from subjects such as marketing & sales, operations, R&D, personnel & organization, and finance, to regional issues related to DMM Indonesia, America, Europe, and China. The next step was to decide which information was needed on these issues to make decisions and who should provide it.

Value teams The BSD team decided to create so-called 'value teams' for each issue, who were responsible for gathering information (i.e. phase I of the BSD – characterizing the business situation) and performing phase II (i.e., analyzing the business system at macro level). By implementing value teams DMM wanted to involve as many people as possible in the BSD process, thereby creating a large platform for the BSD. The value teams presented the results of phase I and II to the BSD team in December 2002. The micro analysis was finalized in February 2003. The next phase was options and strategic choice (phase IV).

Options and strategic choice A main point of discussion in the BSD 2003 was DSM Melamine's position in the US, Indonesia and China. Its 50-50 joint venture with Cytec was the largest player in

the US with the highest prices. However, the business was not profitable because of high raw material costs. DSM Melamine had the best plant in the world located in Indonesia, but profits there were unsatisfactory due to unstable raw material supply and the negative impact on demand of the Asian crisis. Consequently, it was unable to realize the low cost production necessary. Furthermore, DSM Melamine did not yet have a position in China, which the marketing managers viewed as the fastest growing market.

Management felt that the existing 'actively maintain' strategy may no longer be the best, especially since VBBS required businesses to deliver a positive delta CVA every year. According to one of the managers at DMM:

> VBBS has its limits. It is nice for a start-up business but for a mature business it is very difficult to produce a positive delta CVA year after year. It is not easy to create value within a three-year contract in a business like melamine where it takes two to four years for a plant to be operational. So VBBS can lead to short-termism. You have the choice to either increase CFROI on the existing asset base by cutting costs or raising prices, or you can increase the asset base. However, the latter takes more time and involves greater risk.
>
> If DSM did not have VBBS, we would probably continue with our current 'actively maintain' strategy.

In February, after the macro and micro session, management felt that it should present Corporate with the basic choice to either grow the business – as Dijkman and his team felt that they had reached the limits of cost reduction – or otherwise divest.

Growing the business

In the ASR 2002, it was concluded that DSM Melamine could grow faster than was currently the case but that it lacked the capacity to do so. Management wondered if it should be more aggressive and investigated growth opportunities in, for example, Trinidad, a Caribbean island with natural gas production, the Middle East, Europe, and China (see Exhibit 10 for the choice on growth ambitions, ranging from 'give up market share' to 'aggressive growth'). In Europe, DMM's main competitors, such as Agrolinz, were following 'grow/build' scenarios in response to growing worldwide demand. Leon Halders, Vice-President Marketing & Sales DSM Melamine, noted:

> Our two main competitors in Europe are growing heavily, one is tripling and the other is doubling. They are not part of a large company like DSM, but part of a company where melamine is the most attractive business. Melamine is profitable, but because we are part of DSM with a certain strategic mission, we are not the spearhead of DSM strategy.

Although DMM had looked into several growth options, China still seemed the most natural and promising market because of its high growth rates. However, questions remained. First of all there was the question of how DMM, which positioned itself as a main supplier, should enter the Chinese market which was currently a spot market. Another issue was the fact that DMM's existing customers had no significant production base yet in China, which meant that it would have to build a customer base. Finally, a wave of capacity expansion in 2004–2006 was expected to result in oversupply. According to industry analysts, approximately 210 thousand metric tons of melamine was added between 1998–2001, with China accounting for nearly half of new capacity. If all announced capacity expansions were completed, global capacity utilization was expected to fall to approximately 80% in 2006 from 86% in 1998. Some anticipated melamine projects were likely to be postponed or cancelled as a result. But, despite the above challenges, the BSD team still believed in major growth opportunities in China.

As DSM Melamine's financial performance exceeded the WACC, requests for investment to build new melamine plants were justifiable from a VBBS point of view. Dijkman, however, wondered if corporate management would agree with this new strategy, as it was not in line with DSM's corporate strategy of becoming a specialties company. Furthermore, investments in melamine plants always involved large amounts of money (between 50 and 100 million euro), which in the first few years would significantly lower DMM's CFROI.

The corporate perspective on DSM Melamine

At corporate level, DSM management faced a dilemma. From a financial perspective and in line with VBBS principles, investments in DSM Melamine would make perfect sense. On the other hand, following the corporate strategy of becoming a specialty company, one could question how much more to invest in the remaining commodities business such as melamine. It was also important to think through how investors and analysts would react if DSM were to invest further in its melamine business. Earlier in 2003, the management board had already committed to a €50 million proposal of Caprolactam, its other remaining commodity business.

Another issue confronting the management board was the permanent challenge of balancing short-term requirements and long-term value. Big investments would significantly lower DMM's CFROI and only increase CVA in the long-term.

While debating the dilemma on the growth opportunities for DSM Melamine, however, Corporate was also challenging the business on the cost side. It agreed that DSM Melamine had a good low cost position, but as one corporate executive explained:

> We push DSM Melamine. The business has excellent low costs but we are not interested in costs per ton. We would like DSM Melamine to benchmark itself against competitors in its BSD 2003 so that they can see their relative cost position.

The broader issues In addition to the strategic issues facing DSM Melamine, Corporate also had to tackle the remaining challenges of the BSD and VBBS processes. First, VBBS implementation was heavily centralized in the sense that the corporate center, as opposed to the business groups, was driving the change. Although the corporate center had trained facilitators and provided tools to support the implementation, the process was complex and somewhat slow, with significant differences in progress on implementation between the various business groups. The question was how DSM could speed up the process. Top management hoped that the new appraisal system would help the implementation move forward.

Another concern related to how BSDs and SVCs could be effectively translated into specific actions and program management. Thus far, it had been entirely up to the business groups whether and how to operationalize the chosen strategy in terms of value drivers, or how to integrate the SVC with the performance measurement system such as the balanced scorecard. Business groups chose their own way to resolve these issues, with the outcome often being dependent on the consultant that had been hired.

The real test for the future was 'consequence management'. What should DSM do if a business group did not meet its contract, given DSM's historical culture of tolerance for mediocre performance?

Finally, there were some more fundamental questions. Implementing the new financial metrics had led to greater emphasis on short-term performance. DSM felt that this short-term focus could be hazardous for a specialty company that heavily depended on innovation and R&D. For example, in 2000 one of DSM's most successful and profitable products was Stanyl, a product which had been 10 years in development, with negative EPs throughout all those years. How would these kinds of investment projects be handled under the new approach?

Exhibit 1 Key figures on DSM

Balance Sheet (€million)	2002	2001
Fixed assets	3,639	4,442
Current assets	5,357	4,133
Total assets	8,996	8,575
Capital employed	4,570	5,763
Group equity	5,186	4,298
Provisions	682	809
Net debt	−1,038	867
Total group equity and liabilities	8,996	8,575

Income Statement (€million)	2002	2001
Ongoing Activities		
Net sales Life Science Products	2,168	2,237
Net sales Performance Materials	1,767	1,855
Net sales Polymers & Industrial Chemicals	1,268	1,302
Net sales Other Activities	433	357
Total, ongoing activities	5,636	5,751
Operating profit plus depreciation and amortization (EBITDA)	767	741
Operating profit (EBIT)	383	336
Capital expenditure (including acquisitions)	496	561
Discontinued activities		
Net sales	1,029	2,219
Operating profit plus depreciation and amortization (EBITDA)	125	301
Operating profit (EBIT)	67	185
Total		
Net sales	6,665	7,790
Operating profit plus depreciation and amortization (EBITDA)	892	1,042
Operating profit (EBIT)	450	521
Capital expenditure (including acquisitions)	536	652
Profit on ordinary activities after taxation	349	369
Net profit	1,188	1,415
Dividend	199	199
Depreciation and amortization	442	521
Cash flow	1,630	1,936
Workforce at 31 December	18,375	21,504

Exhibit 2 Organizational structure, as of March 2003

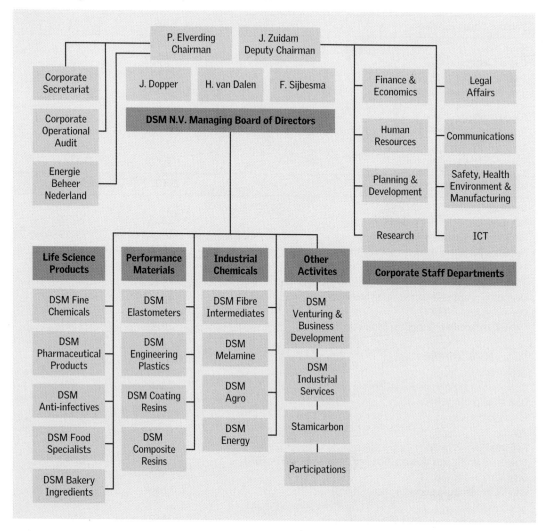

Exhibit 3 The strategy development process

Phase	I Business Situation	II Macro Business System	III MicroBusiness System	IV Options/ Strategic Choice	V Actions & Performance Measurement
Tools	Strategic data checklist	Facilitators	Facilitators	Facilitators	Management reporting format
Duration	2–4 months	2 days	2 days	1–2 days	Continuous
Objective	Gather basic information for BSD	Analyze business dynamics, drivers and strategic groups	Understand own capabilities, analyze strength/ weaknesses	Understand options, select performance indicators and targets	Continuously measure progress
Tasks	◆ Environmental and market analysis ◆ Competitor assessment ◆ Analysis of manufacturing, R&D, technology, HRM, finance, processes	◆ Discuss business chain ◆ Analyze dynamics ◆ Determine industry drivers ◆ Characterize strategic groups	◆ Formulation and evaluation of options ◆ Detailed KSF analysis ◆ Qualifiers ◆ Differentiators ◆ Formulation of indicators ◆ Targets from competitive benchmarking		◆ Progress control ◆ Action plan ◆ Target setting ◆ Continuous improvement program
Output	◆ Document with required information ◆ Strategy support database	◆ Strategic groups ◆ Industry drivers	◆ Capabilities ◆ Organizational/ HR assessment	◆ Strategic plan outline ◆ Strategic mission ◆ KSFs ◆ Indicators ◆ Targets	◆ Strategic contract versus targets

Exhibit 4 DSM Melamine: strategic groups, BSD 1999

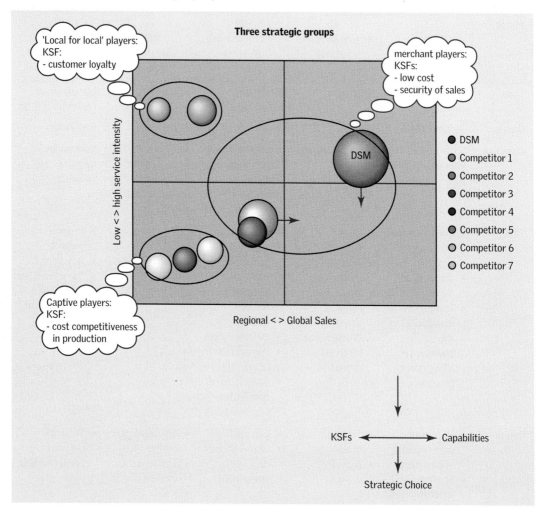

Exhibit 5 C-curve

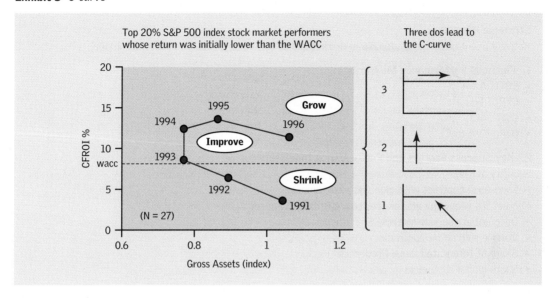

Exhibit 6 C-curve for DSM Melamine 1992–1997

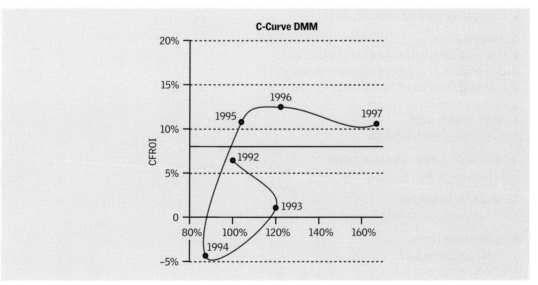

Exhibit 7 Extract of the strategic value contract for DSM Melamine 1999–2003

Strategic mission.
Actively maintain global leadership in market share, technology, cost, and customer image.

1. Financial Performance Measures:
- EBITDA (m€)
- CFROI (%)
- CVA (m€)
- Delta CVA (m€)

2. Key Success Factors and Performance Indicators
Security of sales
- Long-term contract with global key-customers
- Meet the requirements for strategic customer alliances
- Differentiate service levels
- Volume sold under contract
- Share of Integrated Panel Producers
- Share global customers

Lower cost
- De-bottlenecking existing gas-phase plants
- New low cost technology
- Capability to Produce (CTP)
- Controllable fixed out of pocket cost/m ton

3. Value Drivers:
- Unit production cost DSM Kaltim Melamine
- Unit production cost DSM Melamine Americas
- Unit production cost DSM Melamine Europe
- Production volume
- Average sales price
- Sales volume existing plants

4. Strategic Actions and Milestones
- Defined per project

5. Required Resources
- Pre-approval for the next 3 years

6. Sensitivity Items
- Global utilization rate
- USD/EUR currency rate

Exhibit 8 BSD 1999 regional growth rates: forecasts versus realization

	1999 Forecast	**1998–2002 Realization**
Europe	4.0%	4.5%
Americas	5.4%	0.0%
Asia Pacific (APAC)	5.9%	2.9%
China	7.7%	33%

Exhibit 9 DSM Melamine choice on growth ambitions

Market Share Target			
20%	**25%**		**30%**
Give up market share	Organic growth	Active growth	Aggressive growth

• Price over volume
• 'Europe only'
• Lose market leadership
• Max short term cash
• Irreversible:
  – give up China
  – lose scale economies
  – technology standstill
  – competitors build
	• Organic growth with existing customer base
	• China as opportunity market only
	• No new production capacity
	• Accept gradual loss of market share
		• Gain market share
		• Access to new Integrated Panel Producers customers
		• Significant market share in China
		• Build lowest cost plant, leave high cost plant
		• Signal commitment to leadership
			• 'volume over price' policy for plant load
			• Secure lowest cost position worldwide
			• Acquisition may bring growth without price erosion

Appendix 1 **Definition of Metrics**

CFROI: The Cash Flow Return on Investment is a return measure that is the ratio of the Sustainable Cash Flow divided by the Gross Assets.

CVA: Cash Value Added is the Sustainable Cash Flow remaining after a reservation has been made for the capital charge. Formula: (CFROI − WACC) * Gross Assets.

EBITDA: Earnings Before Interest & Tax, Depreciation & Amortization. EBITDA equals the Revenue minus the Cost of Sales.

Gross Assets: The sum of all historical costs of the assets that are being used by a business plus Working Capital and Economic Goodwill paid for any acquired company.

IRR: Internal Rate of Return. Discounting of future cash flows to the year in which the planned investment is made.

ROI: Return on Investment. This is a return measure expressed as the ratio of the Operating Profit of a business and the Capital Employed.

Sustainable Cash Flow (SCF): EBITDA − Tax − Economic Depreciation + Other SCF from non-consolidated companies.

Total Shareholder Return (TSR): Dividend + stock value increase.

WACC: Weighted Average Cost of Capital is the average return on invested capital (debt and/or equity) that capital providers demand from a business. In the case of DSM, the WACC equals 8%.

INSEAD

Case 28 Opening the gate on gatetrade.net: The making of the first Nordic B2B Marketplace (A)

To be or not to be in the marketplace: September 2000

Gerda Norstrand, the number three executive at Post Danmark (PDK) the Danish postal service, looked back on the brief trimester that had passed since Carsten Lind, director of IT services, had come to her with a major piece of news. Three companies representing a significant share of the national economy – Danske Bank, TDC and Maersk Data – were en route to establishing the first online B2B marketplace in Denmark. Could and would PDK join their alliance?

From the start, Norstrand and her CEO, Helge Israelsen, were convinced that the online marketplace did fit with PDK's core business of logistics – a term which, for them, covered more than the traditional letters and parcels. It could also be an important strategic development for PDK in a new domain. PDK's board of directors and executive board agreed to proceed and Norstrand took PDK into the alliance that was forming.

This case was prepared by Dr. Mark Hunter, Senior Research Fellow at INSEAD, under the supervision of Dr. Yves L. Doz, The Timken Chaired Professor of Global Technology and Innovation and Professor of Business Policy. It is intended to be used as a basis for class discussion rather than to illustrate either effective or ineffective handling of an administrative situation.

Staying in the alliance, however, required the final approval of the board of directors. The timing of board meetings meant that by September 2000, PDK was the only alliance member that had not yet signed its shareholder agreement. As the crucial meeting approached when Norstrand and Israelsen would have to carry the board with them, victory seemed far from guaranteed. How could she and her boss persuade the board that this venture offered new markets for PDK's core businesses? And what other benefits could they point to?

Delta, Tango, and Coffee: Spring 2000

In the first months of 2000, Den Danske Bank's new senior vice-president for e-finance, John Andersen, wondered how his company could expand in the New Economy. The trick was to turn 'a threat into an opportunity,' he said.[1] Danske Bank needed more online products for its corporate clients, and its competitors were developing them too. Although it was the biggest bank in Denmark and the second-largest in the 'Nordic-plus' countries (Denmark, Sweden, Norway and Finland),[2] it needed to grow beyond that base – virtually, if not physically.

There was top-level commitment behind Andersen's search. In 1999, Danske Bank announced that 'internet distribution [would] compete with and partly replace' its traditional outlets, such as retail branches.[3] By the end of 2000, one quarter of all securities transactions through the bank would be done via the Internet.[4] A major part of the bank's future was online – yet for the moment it was overwhelmingly a bricks-and-mortar company. The Danske Securities division, its online leader, had a

---

[1] Mr. Andersen was interviewed by David Midgley, Professor of Marketing at INSEAD, in May 2001. We gratefully acknowledge his permission to use his notes.

[2] By year-end 2000, following a merger with RealDanmark, Danske Bank disposed of 626 branches in Denmark, 67 in Norway, 42 in Sweden, plus branches in the U.K., U.S., and Germany, and subsidiary banks in Luxembourg and Poland. Ibid., p. 6.

[3] Den Danske Bank Annual Report 1999, p. 9.

[4] Danske Bank Annual Report 2000, pp. 6, 24.

turnover of just 242 million Danish kroner (Dkr)[5] in 2000 – a sliver compared to the 3.5 billion Dkr of the traditional retail banking sector and overall income of 18 billion Dkr.[6]

Andersen knew that some of Danske Bank's competencies – in areas like electronic transaction systems, databases, and call centers – would be valuable assets in any online project, but those core skills would not suffice for some of the opportunities Andersen had begun studying during a visit to the United States. On his return, he began meeting regularly with executives from two other Danish blue-chip companies, looking for an idea they could develop together.

They called themselves the 'Delta Tango' group, but because they were still working on an informal basis one member dubbed them 'the coffee group'. Danske Bank was already a partner with one player – Maersk Data, the information technology (IT) subsidiary of the A.P. Moller group, the most powerful industrial and shipping conglomerate in Denmark.[7]

Maersk Data, a group in itself, owned all or part of eleven New Economy firms, including the data warehousing company DMdata, a 50-50 joint venture with Danske Bank. The bank was also DMdata's biggest customer. Though Maersk Data was still relatively small, with net revenues of 125 million Dkr on turnover of 1.68 billion Dkr in 1999, CEO Steen H. Knudsen aimed at nothing less than making his company 'world-class' by providing clients with 'any IT service they require.'[8]

The group was completed by Frank Olesen, senior vice-president for corporate strategy at Tele Danmark (soon to be renamed TDC)[9], the recently privatized Danish national telecoms company for which Andersen had previously worked. A giant in the Danish economy, TDC's market capitalization of 119 billion Dkr – twice the value of its shares only two years earlier – represented over one-fifth of all the capital on the Danish KFX stock exchange. But Olesen felt the company had to exploit the Internet more or risk seeing its annual growth rate of nearly 16% fall.

For him, Internet technologies were a 'game changer' that would soon transform entire industries and value chains. Communications, transactions and content would become a single industry, based on data moving via Internet protocols. There were powerful signs in his own company that the shift was underway. TDC's core businesses in mobile and fixed telephones and networks were reaching maturity. In stark contrast, Internet services and traffic had increased by 79% in 1999, along with a 114% burst in revenues from high-speed ISDN lines.[10] And while voice traffic on TDC's network grew only 3% annually, data traffic was exploding at the rate of 5-10% *per month*.[11] In Internet lingo, TDC needed 'more like this.'

Olesen thought TDC's best chance in the New Economy lay in 'alliances focussed on strategic assets that each partner can bring, and how these assets fertilize each other.'[12] The other options – like intensifying product development in-house, or outsourcing it – didn't seem as promising to him. The problem wasn't just developing new products but getting them to market, he said: 'The list of products that the market can hold is larger than what we can do alone.' But in fact, TDC had barely any experience with alliances. It was time, thought Olesen, 'to learn to operate in an environment where partnerships and alliances are part of daily life.'

The members of Delta Tango were part of a homogenous culture whose corporate elite is a small club. In that circle, violations of the 'Jante Law,' a national tradition that bans boasting or American-style shows of affluence, are frowned upon; so are attempts to build independent networks outside

[5] The exchange rate for the kroner versus the U.S. dollar on May 22, 2001 was 8.61 Dkr = 1 $US.

[6] Op. cit., Danske Bank Annual Report 2000, pp. 7, 21.

[7] The A.P. Moller Group's 1999 revenues were over 49 billion Dkr. Source: Preliminary accounts 2000, A/S Dampskibsselskabet Svendbord, Dampskisselskabet AF 1912 A/S.

[8] 'About the Maersk Data Group – business principles.' Via www.maerskdata.com/mdw/en/business.nsf/nval/$First.

[9] On April 26, 2001, Tele Danmark A/S officially changed its name to TDC A/S.

[10] Ibid., p. 29.

[11] Private communication, May 2001.

[12] Interviewed May 1, 2001. All quotes from interview, unless otherwise specified.

the club. Steeped in those values, the group quickly found common ground, said Olesen:

> In terms of corporate culture and values, the three companies do have some similarities – a relatively conservative approach, a thorough approach ... not the habit of undertaking very risky projects. Not a high degree of risk aversion but prudence as to what we go into. ... [So] we sit together, discuss opportunities, and find we think similarly and have the same picture of the future. But where should we start?

The first list: February–March 2000

By February, the Delta Tango group had narrowed its focus to four areas: Wireless (WAP) applications for portable telephones (such as an Internet portal, plus consumer and business services), e-commerce, systems integration services, and standardized workstations.

The latter two offered big markets that already existed: systems integration services alone were already worth over 10 billion Dkr annually in Scandinavia and the market was expected to double within three years. But there was tough competition from established providers. Likewise, computer and electronics industry heavyweights were fighting over the hardware side of the workstation market, while pushing their own software solutions. Though Delta Tango were confident that they could develop attractive services in both markets, they reckoned that earnings would be low.

WAP applications and e-commerce offered new and far larger fields. Of the two, WAP seemed more interesting. International Data Corporation, a respected New Economy research company, estimated that WAP applications would generate 40 billion Dkr in turnover across Scandinavia within eight years. Delta Tango thought they could capture one quarter of that revenue. Only another alliance could provide all the assets and skills that were required to get in the game – and none had yet appeared. Delta Tango's large existing customer base might be enticed onto a WAP portal. And the first-mover advantage would be worth 15% of the market.

But the risks included development costs that were hard to predict – a problem that applied

equally to e-commerce. The major cost for WAP was developing 'content' – information, services and a portal. That would absorb half of revenues for at least three years, while Delta Tango's members confronted a steep learning curve. Notwithstanding, the group favoured higher risks and higher returns, and recommended going for WAP applications. E-commerce was consigned to fourth place on the list.

Listening to the Oracle: Spring 2000

Back in January 2000, product manager Stig Brandt of Oracle Denmark – a subsidiary of the California-based Oracle Corporation, the world's leading supplier of information management software[13] – had noticed that Danske Bank was expanding online. He made a cold call on the bank to pitch Oracle's solutions for financial services. In the next meeting, he recalled:

> We talked about how Danske Bank could achieve higher customer retention by establishing a B2B marketplace – a list of things like order services and financial services, hosting, trade validation online, escrow services on the Internet. These were the services we could offer through our platform.[14]

B2B marketplaces – Internet-based exchanges of goods and services among companies – were the hottest topic in the New Economy. They represented 'simply the next generation of productivity growth for the United States economy,' said a participant in a landmark Federal Trade Commission conference in June 2000.[15]

The reasoning behind that claim looked rock-solid: In the U.S. alone, B2B transactions accounted for 85% of the $20 trillion in annual exchanges of goods and services, according to the Federal Department

---

[13] Oracle's revenues in 2000 were $US10.1 billion. See www.oracle.com/corporate/overview/.

[14] Interviewed May 1, 2001. All quotations from interview, unless otherwise specified.

[15] Staff of the Federal Trade Commission, 'Entering the 21st Century: Competition Policy in the World of B2B Electronic Marketplaces.' Washington, Oct. 2000, p. 7. Despite a tone of unrelenting optimism among participants, this report can be considered essential reading for anyone interested in this subject.

of Commerce. Moving those deals online promised to shave up to 90% off transaction costs by streamlining or eliminating paperwork, handling and other processes.

And the shift seemed to be underway. In 1999, Forrester Research estimated that $109 billion worth of B2B deals were done through the Internet and predicted that the figure would grow to $1.3 trillion by 2003. The IT advisory firm Gartner Group was even more optimistic: it said the turnover would be no less than $7.2 trillion and that 7,500 B2B marketplaces would be competing for that action.[16] At the time, there were only 300 B2B marketplaces worldwide. If the pundits were right, this was a gigantic opportunity for new players.

But Andersen felt that the idea made sense only if there were partners. He brought it to the Delta Tango group, which had considered e-commerce before choosing WAP applications. Danske Bank changed the situation, said Olesen: 'E-commerce and B2B became number one of the priorities.' A meeting was set to begin drawing up detailed plans in June.

The Post gets the message: June 2000

At Post Danmark, IT director Carsten Lind was implementing an unrelated project with Oracle. He heard about the meeting and got himself invited. As it happened, he said, 'I was doing the identical business case for a hypothetical B2B marketplace with the Post as a major player, or the only player.'[17] He concluded that the Post couldn't do it alone – nor, he said, could any of the eventual gatetrade.net owners: 'What is a B2B exchange? A financial flow, a physical flow, and an information flow. None of these companies on their own can supply that skill set.'

Unlike the others in the group, PDK is a public service company – in legal terms, an 'independent public company' whose sole shareholder is the Danish Ministry of Transportation. But it had already declared its intention to become a limited liability company with its capital open to the private sector.[18] Since 1995, PDK it had been operating like

a private company in some ways, publicly reporting net profit of 285 million Dkr on turnover of 10.8 billion in 1999.[19] Yet in the public mind it remained a government bureaucracy. 'I say we're like a private company, but who knows it?' commented Gerda Norstrand, Lind's boss.

Like other state-owned companies in the European Union, market liberalisation exposed PDK to new threats, including a price war with delivery companies like Federal Express,[20] not to mention the Deutsche Post and Royal Mail. PDK responded by diversifying into internet, warehousing, international and remail operations but with mixed success: by 1999 it owned between 25% and 100% of six subsidiaries with combined losses of 29 million Dkr.[21] Nonetheless, sales dropped in parcel delivery, PDK's second most important revenue stream.[22] An inside position in a B2B marketplace could change that trend, thought Norstrand: 'Being part of the marketplace, we would see what kind of new services are needed, so we're better able to meet demands in our core business.'

Norstrand believed that the Internet would change PDK's core business in any case: 'We think in two years all our parcels will be IT parcels – registered electronically in one way or another.' PDK had just introduced its WebPack service, offering electronic track-and-trace of parcels to small businesses. It wanted to turn its offline PFS service (the Danish acronym for 'the Post's dispatch system') into an

---

[16] Op. cit., 'B2B Marketplaces in the New Economy', p. 2.

[17] Currently CEO of Transynergy. Interviewed May 2, 2001.

[18] Post Danmark, 'Annual Report and Accounts 2000', p. 12.

[19] Post Danmark, 'Annual Report and Accounts 1999', p. 12.

[20] 'All Post Danmark's important competitors in Denmark are now attached to international networks which have sufficient strength to create a large competitive power and consequently cause a price war in the Danish market.' Op. cit., 'Annual Report and Accounts 2000', p. 15.

[21] These ventures included the remail companies Belgian Mailhouse BV, Scandinavian Distribution and Postal Service A/S, and Nordic Mail AB; the courrier company Budstikken Transport A/S; Pan Nordic Logistics AB, a parcel distribution service; Weblogistics A/S, a distribution and warehousing service for e-commerce companies; and Billetnet A/S, an online ticket service. PDK owned between 33 and 100% of each. See Post Danmark, 'Annual Report and Accounts 2000', p. 38.

[22] While PDK's turnover in parcels increased by 1.9% in 1999, sales fell 3.4%, partly because of an increase in the weight limit for letters to 2kg. Ibid., p. 13.

online product for major corporations, too. Joining the new marketplace in the 'fine company' of Denmark's biggest companies could speed up that move, said Lind: 'You'd be branded with those people and their customers.'

Behind their thoughts was the fact that there wasn't room for many B2B marketplaces in Denmark. If only one could succeed, Norstrand wanted PDK's logistics infrastructure to be part of it. At the June meeting, Lind argued that without a ready-to-go logistics wing, a marketplace would never fly:

> My card was, with all the problems dot-coms had with fulfilment [of online orders], I said, 'Why not build an exchange that differs in that we have end-to-end control for the users? They can get all logistics services from one point integrated into the engine.'

Lind came back with a first victory: PDK was admitted into a project team that would make the business case for a B2B marketplace. Said Lind, 'We wrote a memo of understanding so no partners would get married to someone else. We had it a month but nobody signed it. But there was trust that nobody would exit.'

Backing out would carry invisible but high costs for whoever tried it. In Denmark, a small country that has historically faced expansionist threats from its neighbors Germany and Sweden, keeping one's word and sticking together are ingrained survival traits. They are also crucial to business reputations. 'We have a saying: "A man is a man and a word is a word,"' noted Andersen. 'A lot of deals have been closed on that phrase.' And with four of the biggest companies in Denmark at the table, no one wanted to break his word to the others.

The key word in everyone's mind was 'speed.' Said Brandt, 'It was very important to close down other initiatives, so that nobody came in from outside [Denmark]. That was my argument: "Close the market, be the first mover, and expand."'

A matter of goals: June 2000

The Delta Tango group became a project team of 15, with members from all four companies, plus Oracle. Said Lind, 'In that period of constructing, TDC,

PDK and Danske Bank were putting in lots of hours. Danske Bank was the strongest player because they're financially very strong. Maersk Data was not as present.'

Some of the others sensed that Maersk Data might not need them as much as they needed Maersk Data. Its in-house expertise covered logistics, retail and other IT systems, as well as Web development. And Maersk Data belonged to a group that owned massive logistics capabilities, plus immense financial resources. In short, it could assemble most of the necessary assets for a marketplace itself. Moreover, only Maersk Data already had the hot New Economy image that the others – all known as conservative, traditional companies – wanted for themselves.

When conflict emerged, however, it was on other grounds. Some members didn't understand that Oracle was providing a standard platform and thought they would have to underwrite a major development project. Once Oracle had walked the group through the technical solutions, another difference appeared. Said Brandt:

> It depends on what kind of people you put in. Danske Bank put in business people – they did not focus on functions, they focussed on business value. PDK put in IT people. If you talk to IT people, they look at problems. The business people look at opportunities. . . . If you're four different players from different areas, they don't have a common knowledge of the main goal.

Unlike PDK or TDC, the alliance was 'not strategic to us as such,' said Kenn Herskind Jorgensen, president of Maersk Data's subsidiary Venture IT, who represented his group on the project committee. 'It's not part of our core business,' he explained. 'One of the challenges in that alliance is we're a venture company. We make money on dividends or exits. And we don't want to get trapped by not being able to exit.'

As Herskind – and to some extent, Danske Bank – saw it, the point was to profit from the marketplace, even if that meant giving it up someday:

> A likely scenario is that, if successful, we would be approached by one or more internationals – other online marketplaces – to make an alliance

or an acquisition. What's going to happen is a smaller number of online marketplaces, international consolidation. If we're buying paper, why not link to other marketplaces to source internationally? The technology supports that. It won't happen overnight but we'll see consolidation. And I would go for having it acquired.

Maersk Data also had a major interest in the IT that would be developed and implemented here. Much of its revenue came from consulting, and a win here would enhance its reputation in a hot sector of the Web. Oracle, too, wanted that prize, said Brandt: 'Marketplace operations are very new, and they're secretive about their experiences. Maybe because their experiences are not so good – or because their knowledge is valuable. If you have a success, the elements will be very valuable to sell.'

Olesen, too, was looking far down the road: 'At the time of decision-making, I don't think TDC considered the amount of profit.' One of his concerns was keeping an eye on Maersk Data, whom Olesen considered 'a potential competitor'. Someday soon, he thought, Maersk Data might move from IT services to telecoms infrastructures, which was TDC's core business:

One of the more forward elements of the value chain is applications. Our competitors are moving to these elements and using them to gain customer relationships. When they have customer relationships in the forward parts of the value chain, they use that to work back to the infrastructure. I see that constantly with our competitors: very often it's IT companies, with systems integration and applications expertise. In that sense, Maersk Data is a competitor of TDC. I think it was an underlying understanding of both parties.

Olesen hoped the marketplace could lead to future collaborations with Maersk Data – a vision he considered 'quite compelling.' Herskind saw it, too: 'TDC and us could have done this alone, strategy- and tech-wise.' But TDC was aware that an alliance with Maersk Data could be even more risky than outright competition. The close relations between Maersk and Danske Bank might put TDC at a permanent disadvantage.

Danske Bank saw the venture as a way to extend its leadership in cash management solutions throughout the Nordic countries. Cash management involves sophisticated methods of routing cash, netting balances and computing interest, plus some IT integration between a bank and its clients. The integration increases customer retention because access to the cash flows of large companies opens doors to additional banking business. Likewise, a B2B marketplace could begin with online procurement, then push for IT systems integration between its customers and Danske Bank's financial services. The bank would grow closer to its major clients.

Moreover, the marketplace would provide 'a new product in the basket' when Danske Bank called on potential customers, said Andersen. He was thinking of new value-added services like digital certificates, payment guarantees, online credit evaluation, credit scoring and invoice handling. Finally, as Brandt suggested, it might offer the bank an opportunity to do more business with the public sector, which was looking for ways to cut its procurement costs – exactly the benefits a B2B marketplace could provide.

Making the business model: June–July 2000

Oracle now took the lead in writing the business case, with Lind and Maersk Data closely involved. Olesen recalled: 'A key strategic decision – the founding decision – was that the marketplace is a process improvement company.' Unlike many online marketplaces, this one would not only function as an auction platform whose main benefit is to knock a few points off prices, Olesen explained:

Our vision was improving processes for buyers and sellers. Auctions [alone] won't facilitate that. It is trading, where the integration of the ERP [enterprise resource planning] systems of the buyer and seller are key – into the warehousing, distribution, and financial systems of buyer and seller. You improve the processes throughout the full value chain, removing costs for both buyer and seller. We are not in the price game.... The price will be lower, but that's a secondary effect. The real benefit is in the processes.

That idea appealed to PDK's purchasing director, Holger B. Nielsen, who wanted to see 'hard benefits' from the marketplace. Nielsen had already used online procurement to reduce the Post's grocery supply transaction costs by 90%. He estimated that an overall online procurement system at the Post would pay for itself in a year 'if people use it for every transaction. Even at 50% [of all transactions], it's a winning proposition.'

A second crucial decision was led by Danske Bank, recalled Brandt. This would be a 'horizontal' marketplace offering goods from different sectors, not a 'vertical' exchange serving one industry. A vertical marketplace carried the risk that a minority of suppliers would quickly establish dominance, thus scaring away new vendors. And it would be far harder to scale up into new industries or new territories.

However, a horizontal marketplace requires a catalogue structure – the only means by which buyers can compare multiple sources and specifications for similar products on a computer screen. The decision of whether they should create their own catalogues, or simply 'aggregate' suppliers' existing catalogues, remained open.

The catalogue issue raised a concern for Post Danmark, which as a public entity is subject to European Union government procurement rules. These rules dictate that purchases over a minimum level be made through tenders.[23] They were written before online marketplaces existed and made no provision for the supply chain integration processes that were at the heart of the exchange's future development. Thus PDK might find it legally impossible to fully profit from the marketplace, a fact that was acknowledged in the business case but not resolved.

The business case called on the owners to build liquidity quickly by channeling a maximum of their non-strategic procurement (goods that are not essential to production) through the marketplace. Ultimately, the goal was for each owner to put all their non-strategic purchasing on the marketplace, but they formally committed to putting in a 20–25% share of these purchases.

It wasn't an equal load for each partner, noted Olesen: 'There is a clear indication of who will be doing the most purchasing on the marketplace – us, because we have the most non-strategic buying.' A rough calculation[24] shows that TDC could put a maximum of about 1.5 billion Dkr of purchases on the marketplace, followed by the Post, at about 1 billion. Maersk Data, in contrast, could not approach those figures. 'We weren't expected to compensate,' said Herskind. 'At the time we were the drivers – that's a significant contribution, to get the thing off the ground.'

The allies' best guess was that value-added services (VAS) could generate between one quarter and half the venture's revenues after a year. The business plan mentioned logistics and financial services such as payment, billing and collection, or credit rating and approval. Supply-chain management through integration between the marketplace and its customers' back-end systems was also evoked. But it could not be predicted which VAS would be feasible, technically or commercially. Marketplaces around the world were still trying to discover the answer to that question.

Left unsaid was that each partner could provide services that could also be provided by another partner, or by the marketplace itself. For example, TDC offered electronic signature certification. PDK had created a similar service, then dropped it. The marketplace might be a chance for PDK to try again. However, there was a real possibility that the value-added services would be captured primarily by Maersk Data.

What *was* spelled out was that any deals between the marketplace and its owners had to be conducted on an 'arm's length' basis, according to 'sound commercial principles'. No owner could be compelled to purchase anything in gatetrade.net (as the marketplace would be called) that it could buy cheaper elsewhere, and no owner could force services upon the marketplace.

But, Herskind wondered, what if one of the owners had the choice between passing a deal to gatetrade.net and getting 25% of the revenue, or keeping it in-house?

---

[23] The limit is 1.6 million Dkr, or about $US200,000.

[24] Approximately one-third of all business purchases are non-strategic goods, and in 2000, TDC reported 4.6 billion Dkr in purchases of goods and services.

If a Norwegian marketplace comes to us to host it, and gatetrade.net could do it, do we put it in there or do it ourselves? A similar case came up – two, in fact – one for us, the other at TDC. Small cases. They came up during the formation period, before the launch. That was a danger. Our CEO saw that and said, 'I'll give that up, put it in gatetrade.net. But I expect if that happens for you guys, you'll do the same.' TDC did the same. [But] if this were a $1 billion order, what would you do? Keep it, or share it with your partners?

Oracle in question: August 2000

As the business case neared completion, Oracle was threatened by a counter-proposal from IBM, which the founders seriously considered for several weeks. Despite its driving role from the start, Oracle was perceived by some as 'a partner without financial commitment,' in Holger Nielsen's phrase. Its risks were limited to the licensing fees it would lose if the project failed. And Maersk Data believed that the price Oracle charged for its software license and consulting was too high.

Brandt countered that Oracle was making a strategic commitment: under no circumstances would it work with another marketplace in Scandinavia. Moreover, he pointed out that under Oracle's deal with gatetrade.net, 'The more liquidity and trade on the marketplace, the more license fees we get. So we will do whatever we have to do to make gatetrade.net successful.'

Oracle's supporters within the alliance raised the following points, summarized by Herskind, who led the re-negotiations with Oracle:

We not only needed the solution – we needed an international brand. Everything associated with this platform had to be associated with quality and professionalism. People are very dubious about going online. Some of the suppliers are really small – 100, 200 people. We had to be sure that everything they saw was something they recognized. That was part of the marketing strategy. And the business case still works.

But the debate remained unresolved as the allies drew up a shareholder agreement. Oracle or not, they were going ahead.

The core of the business: September 2000

Gerda Norstrand considered the shareholder agreement's terms. Each of the four founders put in 25 million Dkr for a 25% share of the capital. Any one of the founders could exit, but the others retained a right of first refusal on the shares and a right of approval of new investors. PDK had joined exclusive company as an equal.

But to move forward, the change represented by gatetrade.net must now be accepted by both the board and employees. The investment was minimal for a company of PDK's size and Norstrand had no doubt it would pay off in the short and long term. She believed gatetrade.net would be profitable and that it would reinforce PDK's existing investments in online procurement. It would also complement PDK's portfolio of ventures in parcel distribution and warehousing. The experience gained, in terms of making alliances work and exploring a new industry, would be very valuable. And if the core letter and parcel businesses were indeed going online, like everything else, PDK had to be there or watch its business migrate elsewhere.

Was she right? Was the business case strong enough to prove her point? And were these the allies PDK needed to take her company into new markets and synergies?

Exhibit 1 Gatetrade co-founder portraits

Maersk Data: The Importance of Being Somebody

In Denmark, the name 'Maersk' denotes the heart of the A.P. Moller Group, the country's most powerful industrial and shipping conglomerate. Maersk Sealand, Maersk Air, Maersk Olie og Gas and Maersk Data contributed some 30 billion Dkr to A.P. Moller's total 84 billion Dkr (about 10.5 billion $US) of revenue in 2000.

The Maersk corporate culture takes careful groundwork and execution as a given, and disdains publicity. In the latter regard Maersk Data is an exception within the group. It was originally created in 1970 to service the information technology (IT) needs of A.P. Moller. By the end of the 1980s, Maersk Data graduated from an internal division to a separate corporation with subsidiaries in the US and Japan. A decade later, it owned all or part of 28 companies in seven different countries, including 11 New Economy ventures spanning a range from B2C e-commerce to data warehousing and web design. And it began to seek wider recognition, arguing that if it weren't known to other venture capital players, it wouldn't get invited to the table when major deals went down.

In keeping with Maersk style, however, the shift was anything but impulsive. With the approval of its parent, Maersk Data was running a real-world experiment in the benefits of getting attention from the media – a strategy that included gatetrade.net. The New Economy was growing within A.P. Moller in more ways than one.

Den Danske Bank: Straining at the Seams of Denmark

How big can you get in Denmark? In 2000, following a merger with its competitor RealDenmark, Danske Bank had 626 branches on Danish soil, about four-fifths of its worldwide presence. Its 3 million retail customers were equivalent to about 60% of the Danish population. If Dansk bank wanted to grow, it had to move further and faster abroad and into new business sectors.

It was moving from a solid, profitable base. At the end of 2000, the bank held assets of over 1.3 trillion Dkr. Its activities were divided into six core sectors – mortgages, retail banking, wholesale banking, insurance and pensions, investment banking, and investment management. In 2000, every one of those sectors showed significant earnings growth – in the case of retail banking, 86%. Income was 26 billion Dkr (up from 22 billion Dkr the previous year), and net profit was over 6 billion Dkr. For shareholders, Danske Bank had provided an annual 27% return on capital (including dividends) since 1995.

Could Danske Bank keep it up? Pressure was growing from competitors like Nordea, the largest financial conglomerate in Scandinavia, with 10 million retail customers. By no coincidence, Nordea announced, as gatetrade.net got underway, that it was keeping a close watch on the venture. Danske Bank had to move fast and well.

TDC: How Far Can You Spread on Your Own?

Following its privatization in 1995, the former Tele Danmark placed foreign acquisitions at the core of its strategy. By the end of 2000, nearly half of its 47 billion Dkr in annual revenues – twice its revenues in 1996 – came from TDC's subsidiaries abroad. And between 1997 and 2000 the company's customer base nearly doubled to 11.5 million accounts by adding mobile and landline subscribers in Switzerland, Poland, Lithuania, the Czech Republic, Hungary, Austria, Belgium, the Netherlands and Germany.

However, TDC's domestic revenues were nearly flat in 2000, growing slightly from 21 to 22 billion Dkr, as its traditional core telephony business reached maturity. Competition abroad was fierce, notably in Switzerland, where the newly-renamed TDC captured 13% of the mobile telephone market, and 26% of the landline business from the established operator, Swisscom, by the end of 2000.

TDC Switzerland was one of seven business divisions around which the company reorganized in 2000. The others included a broadband and communications solutions provider, a mobile operator, an Internet division, a directories publisher, a cable-TV operator, and TDC Services, which mainly supported the other divisions. While they shared common expertise in network technologies, each division had a different geographic focus: the Internet branch concentrated mainly on Denmark and Switzerland, the directories branch aimed at the Nordic region, and the mobile operator bought third-generation UMTS licenses from the Netherlands to Poland.

TDC was fighting on numerous industrial, service and territorial fronts. Could it secure its gains without allies?

Post Danmark: Beyond Letters and Parcels

In 2000, Post Danmark (PDK) faced changes in its business and culture that could fairly be called revolutionary. The European Union's goal of 'liberalizing' public service monopolies forced PDK to confront the likelihood that, in the near future, its exclusive rights to carry letters and parcels would apply only to the smallest and least profitable. Meanwhile, as PDK's annual report predicted, 'Competition will intensify from other countries' postal operators', not to mention the likes of Federal Express.

The Post's executives argued that PDK would ultimately have to 'be converted into a limited liability company' with capital open to the private sector. But consensus on this goal, let alone how to achieve it, was limited. Public service employees, who represented some 40% of PDK's workforce of 30,000, were reluctant to change their status and privileges. Nor was it clear that PDK would be a great success as a listed corporation: Only once in the years 1996-2000 did either its growth or its operating profit margin exceed 5%.

In this context, PDK's strategy of investing in acquisitions or start-ups on the edges of its core logistics business – including an online ticket service, software for electronic parcel services, and e-commerce warehousing – revealed not only its ambitions, but the human and financial constraints on them. PDK, too, had to move toward the future, but not too far or fast at once.

Exhibit 2 The promise and trials of B2B marketplaces

Online B2B marketplaces can be simply defined as Internet-driven exchanges, in which buyers and sellers are brought together through auction or catalogue sales.

The added value of the concept resides in cost reductions. By exchanging information electronically, both buyers and sellers can streamline paperwork and handling of orders. Comparing multiple vendor offerings online makes it possible for buyers to negotiate better prices. Conversely, sellers can find new customers through an exchange at less expense than through tradeshow exhibits or in-person calls.

There are currently about 1,000 e-marketplaces in operation. 'Vertical' operations service a single industry, while 'horizontal' marketplaces span several sectors. Within those broad categories, marketplaces are mainly distinguished by their business models. 'Buyer-driven' marketplaces are exemplified by Covisint, founded by General Motors, Ford, and DaimlerChrysler in 2000 to rationalize supply processes and prices across the automobile industry.[25] 'Seller-driven' marketplaces like PlasticsNet.com, which deliver qualified leads to buyers, often represent a defensive response to the power of buyers. There are

[25] See www.covisint.com for the exchange's own view of its operations and ambitions.

specialists in B2B auctions, like the used equipment marketplace Tradeout.com. 'Reverse auctioneers' such as Freemarkets.com are used by buyers to post offers, with sellers bidding down the price until a deal is made. Catalogue aggregators offer comparisons of different list prices (which may then be nego-tiated) and specifications across product categories.[26]

Whatever the type, marketplaces generally derive revenues from membership fees, transaction fees, or services (such as logistics and industry information). Their greatest current appeal is that they help drive down prices, by putting suppliers in competition. Ford says that it saved $US70 million over one year in process costs and price reductions through Covisint, and that these savings 'easily' covered its investment in the exchange (which Ford did not disclose).[27]

The future benefits of e-marketplaces, it is promised, will be far greater – maybe even 'the next gener-ation of productivity growth for [the] economy.'[28] Once users' enterprise resource planning (ERP) systems are linked to an exchange, control of manufacturing, inventory, logistics and warehousing can be stream-lined. Managers can clamp down on 'maverick' buying – purchases made outside company procurement guidelines, which have been estimated to account for between 30% and 50% of corporate procurement.[29] Ultimately, buyers and sellers might jointly develop products and services, using data from the exchange to model future needs.

There is a precedent for these claims in the decade-old creation of electronic data interchange (EDI) systems, private networks designed to foster supply chain integration between a large company and its suppliers. The retail giant Wal-Mart, a pioneer in this domain, reportedly used EDI to lower costs by up to 95% and to stay in close touch with consumer demand. But as equities analyst Todd C. Weller noted, 'EDI has never achieved critical mass due to its proprietary nature, lack of flexibility, and significant investment requirements.'[30]

E-marketplaces promise many of the benefits of such private systems at a far lower cost – plus a stupe-fying business opportunity. The U.S. Department of Commerce estimates that B2B transactions account for 85% of the $20 trillion in annual exchanges of goods and services in that country. For some observers, the question is when – not if – a giant share of those B2B transactions will migrate online.

In a now-famous prediction, the IT advisory company Gartner Group said that by 2003 the turnover on B2B exchanges would be no less than $7.2 trillion, and that 7,500 marketplaces would be competing for the action.[31] Software application providers like Ariba predicted a dire fate for those who resisted the trend: 'Ultimately, all businesses will buy on a marketplace, sell on a marketplace, host a marketplace, or be marginalized by a marketplace.'[32]

---

[26] These categories are partially adapted from a glossary published by NetMarkets.com at http://www.nmm.com/nm101-b2basics/index.asp, which has the merit of categorizing e-marketplaces or 'net exchanges' by their functions. A stan-dard nomenclature for this industry, like the industry itself, is still under development.

[27] See Carlos Grande, 'Ford recoups investment in Covisint web exchange.' *Financial Times*, July 1, 2001 (via www.ft.com).

[28] Staff of the Federal Trade Commission, 'Entering the 21st Century: Competition Policy in the World of B2B Electronic Marketplaces.' Washington, Oct. 2000, p. 7. The document summarizes a landmark FTC-sponsored conference. Though the quote reflects the often uncritical optimism among participants, this report can be considered essential reading on the subject.

[29] The lower figure is drawn from 'Entering the 21st Century', p. 25. Consultants such as Carsten Sennov, a vice president of Cap Gemini Denmark, consider 50 percent a more likely figure for maverick buying, noting that 'the larger and more dispersed the organization, the more maverick buying there is.'

[30] Todd C. Weller, 'B to B Commerce: The Rise of Marketplaces', Legg Mason Equity Research, Spring 2000, p. 4.

[31] Ariba, 'B2B Marketplaces in the New Economy', Mountain View, CA, March 7, 2000, p. 2.

[32] Ibid.

Perhaps – but meanwhile software providers have discovered that creating stable and highly functional marketplace platforms is a daunting task.[33] 'Suppliers remain leery of the pressure [exchanges] will put on prices,' notes the *Washington Post*.[34] And after the energy marketplace Pepmarket.com shut down in March 2001 with losses of $1.4 million, president Jay Demarest commented that buyers and sellers alike were 'just not ready to adopt that technology in daily business processes yet.'[35]

As the U.S. Federal Trade Commission noted, 'The most important requisite for the survival of a B2B marketplace is to have sufficient transaction volume.'[36] The same could be said for the industry as a whole. Once e-marketplaces become a standard way of doing business, and can deliver on their promises, the sector will surely explode. At the same time, it will very likely see intense consolidation (as is already happening in the online logistics market). But as with dot-coms, it is taking longer and proving more difficult than the New Economy prophets foresaw.

Exhibit 3 The pricing of Gatetrade.net

Devising the pricing model for gatetrade.net was 'one of the key issues – and coming up with it was a difficult exercise,' said Kenn Herskind Jorgensen, president of Maersk Data subsidiary Venture IT and a gatetrade.net board member. In fact, it is still ongoing, especially where value-added services are concerned, as we'll see shortly.

1. Buying and Selling: the Basic Fee Structure
The guiding principles behind gatetrade.net's fee structure were two-fold: encourage customers to enter by reducing up-front costs, and discourage them from exiting by increasing their investment in the marketplace over time. But the founders realized that there was no ideal, ready-made way to set the fees, said Herskind:

> *Oracle did a lot of numbers, we looked at the market prices, then we did the groundwork in groups. The fine-tuning was done [later on] by the management. We didn't go out and do models, scenarios, downside protection analysis. We threw the numbers on the table, had discussions and said, 'This is it.' We could've done it a million ways. We thought, focus on kroner, like the customers. Look at what any purchasing person is looking for: 'If I buy 100 kroner's worth on gatetrade.net, what does it cost me to buy?'*

The first cost to the customer is a one-time registration fee of 10,000 Dkr, plus an annual subscription fee of 1,000 Dkr per user. (In other words, a corporation with 10 purchasing agents using gatetrade.net pays 10,000 Dkr annually, in addition to the registration fee.)

Placing a tender offer or auction on gatetrade.net costs 2,500 Dkr. The marketplace also takes a commission fee of up to 100,000 Dkr on each completed auction from the seller, based on a sliding rate of 0.5%–2% (the bigger the deal, the less the percentage). For example, a 'lot' of computers auctioned through gatetrade.net for 10 million Dkr will cost the seller 2,500 Dkr to place the auction, and 20,000 Dkr in commissions – a total of 22,500 Dkr (assuming that the seller has already registered with the marketplace).

Catalogue users pay no commissions on their purchases through gatetrade.net; instead, they pay 6 Dkr for each 'document', or catalogue search. Suppliers, however, pay a commission of between 1% and 0.2%

---

[33] For example, in May 2001, a promotional event sponsored by Ariba at Las Vegas became the occasion for public criticism of the company. See Mark Jones, 'Ariba Strives to Prove it's Still in the Game', www.infoworld.com, May 4, 2001.

[34] 'Business-to-business e-commerce arena faces shakeout', Washington Post, May 7, 2001 (via Internet).

[35] Erich Luening and Margaret Kane, 'Why B2B went bust', CNET News.com , May 7, 2001 (via Internet).

[36] Op. cit., 'Entering the 21st Century', p. 20.

based on their average number and volume of transactions annually: the greater the size of both, the less the commission.

Thus a supplier who does 25 million Dkr of business on gatetrade.net, but with an average transaction value under 1000 Dkr, will pay 200,000 Dkr in commissions – a rate of 0.8%. A supplier with the same overall volume, but whose average transaction value is 50,000 Dkr, pays 137,500 Dkr in commissions, or 0.55%. This raises a customer relations issue: if you were the first supplier, would you try to negotiate a better rate?

Suppliers also absorb catalogue costs, starting with 5 Dkr per 'stock keeping unit' (SKU), or separate item hosted. Use of the Requisite Corporation's 'e-merge' catalogue creation tool costs between 3 and 5 Dkr per item, depending on volume (and may be negotiated). Gatetrade.net will create catalogues for the customer at approximately 16 Dkr per item – its own cost for making this content. In other words, catalogue costs – the most significant upfront expense by far – are kept to a minimum, though gatetrade.net passes them on to the customer.

2. What Price for Value-added Services (VAS)?

Recall that gatetrade.net's business case foresaw that value-added services would generate between 25% and 50% of revenues within a year. The founders also realized that VAS create an exit barrier for customers because each service deepens the customer's dependence on the marketplace. But which services should a marketplace provide, and what can it charge for them?

The first VAS for gatetrade.net were planned to be online by the end of 2001 – financial services such as certification, payment guarantees, online credit evaluation, credit scoring and invoice handling, plus supply chain management and logistics. Billing and revenue collection would follow. (Gatetrade.net hoped to capture interest revenue, based on the time elapsed between collecting payments from buyers and disbursing the monies to sellers.)

Eventually, gatetrade.net could also look at ways of packaging and selling data from transactions as 'marketplace intelligence' (in other words, 'whom buys what from whom'). However, respecting clients' confidentiality would impose certain limits. For example, gatetrade.net could not reveal the transactions of specific customers, only movements within industry segments.

In an address to the Oracle Postal Forum at Brussels on 11 December 2000, Gerda Norstrand of Post Danmark noted that a major VAS domain would involve integration between gatetrade.net and customers' back-end systems. 'This entails a range of solutions,' she said, 'spanning from very individualized ones to big businesses, to almost 'plug-in' solutions to smaller businesses.' Creating those solutions would lead to implementation and other IT services, as well as what Norstrand called 'an educational process to make such companies understand the real rationale' behind the marketplace. That process, too, would be a billable service.

But it remains unknown what price gatetrade.net or its partners will charge for such services; in September 2001, no standard fees for VAS appeared on its site. This discretion – or in some cases, secrecy – is typical of e-marketplaces in general. Quite simply, there are no benchmark prices for VAS in the industry. This reflects the ferocious competition among exchanges to capture and keep customers, which entails that fees for services be quietly negotiated rather than published. It also reflects the fact that until more marketplaces get past the start-up phase and begin to deliver measurable benefits, no one can specify the real worth to their customers of specific services.

What this means is that gatetrade.net, like other e-marketplaces, will have to rely partly on trial-and-error to learn what its VAS are worth to clients. And it will have to do so quickly because, as its management is aware, over time value-added services are increasingly regarded by customers as basic services whose delivery should be included in the registration fee.

Case 29 **The consulting industry in the new world of information**

Does the internet change everything? The impact of the internet on consulting has been widely reported (Brown, Colvin, Moran, Stepanek). The main thrust of these reports is that the old guard just doesn't get it, leading to the influx of a new breed of firms with a different consulting model for an e-services market estimated to grow from $12.9 billion in 1999 to $80 billion in 2003 (Stepanek). There are a number of important differences from the traditional approach and assumptions in the consulting industry.

First, e-business demands consulting at much faster speed. First-mover advantage and high levels of uncertainty make it more important for companies to iterate, learn and reiterate:

> There is no time for separate advice, the situation demands an approach of do, learn and adjust. (Financial Times, July 2000)

This has led to a typical engagement of 90–180 days, compared to the many months or even years spent on enterprise resource planning (ERP), the mainstay of consulting revenues in the 1990s (Stepanek). Fees are more likely to be on a fixed project basis than the time-plus-costs model, which encourages overruns. The greater number of projects carried out in a year also accelerates learning.

Second, technology and strategy are now completely intertwined. Added to the need for speed, this demands an integrated approach that combines business strategy, creative design and technological implementation within the same cross-functional team. Teams tend to be smaller, comprising 12–18 consultants rather than the small armies of ERP projects (Sammer).

Third, the consultant-client relationship is changing; e-business firms are often much more intimately involved with the organisations they advise.

This case study is extracted from an MBA Project al by Simon Kitchen 'Connections in the Wireless World', Warwick Business School September 2000.

© John McGee & Simon Kitchen, 2000, Warwick Business School.

Equity in exchange for consulting is a common practice and e-firms can take on the entire operational requirements or incubation of a dot.com start-up. This kind of *total immersion* is much closer to the behaviour of venture capitalists and represents a significant departure from the detached independence of the traditionalists (Colvin).

Fourth, given that talent is a key resource, e-firms have succeeded in attracting the brightest and the best from business schools (Hamel). This can be explained by differences in ownership structure and culture. Most e-firms are publicly quoted and offer stock options to all staff. This is in sharp contrast to structures in which up-or-out rules apply and only the partners at the apex of the organisation can hope to share in the greatest rewards (Milgrom and Roberts offer an explanation based on agency theory for this apparent disincentive). The culture of e-firms is much more relaxed, with no strict dress code, less travel and 'sexy' working environments (Sweeney 2000). They also have a compelling sense of vision, with Sapient, for example, claiming it is 'changing the way *the world* works' (Sapient). The combined effect of all these can be seen in staff attrition, with Scient claiming a rate of 11% versus an industry average of 25% (Scient). The skills shortage that exists in e-business is even more marked in the wireless arena where very few people have any experience of the complex blend of skills required.

How successful has been this new breed of e-firms? They have enjoyed triple-digit growth (Stepanek), with approximately 80% of their business coming from Fortune 1000 companies, the hunting ground of traditional consultants. According to a Forrester survey, 76% of companies do not look to their usual suppliers for advice on e-business, although the size of projects is typically much smaller at $1–3 million (Sweeney). E-firms may also be guilty of claiming more than they actually deliver: even the top performers in a survey of FTSE 500 clients earn unimpressive scores. No single provider offers an end-to-end service and there is a perceived need for firms to help structure complementary offerings (Forrester Research).

Response of the incumbents

Almost every firm has either repositioned itself as internet-savvy or set up a discrete e-business practice.

Andersen Consulting claims that 30–40% of its projects now have e-commerce content (Brown 1999), and IBM's e-business services were worth $3 billion last year (IBM 2000b). Andersen has created its own venture capital unit and McKinsey is taking a stake in some of its own clients for the first time. McKinsey are also adopting 'parallel processing', with strategic framing and implementation happening concurrently, and less data-driven analysis (Sweeney). Andersen, McKinsey and PricewaterhouseCoopers (PwC) are exploring the use of internal talent exchanges in an attempt to retain staff by giving them greater control over their own careers. Many firms are adopting new compensation models with greater risk-based elements, such as PwC's share unit plan (Sammer). Andersen has almost doubled its number of partners (Kennedy Information Research Group). All of this suggests that the incumbents recognise the need to remould themselves, if they are to provide picks and shovels for the internet Gold Rush. However, to replicate the capabilities of the upstarts, they need to realign themselves on many dimensions, not just one or two. Of course, that is much harder with a large organisation, with its embedded values and structure, than it is when starting from scratch.

Enter the vendors

The threat to consulting incumbents is not confined to the e-firms. Many hardware and software vendors are attempting to move up the food chain and emulate the success of IBM Global Services:

All equipment vendors are moving towards a solution-selling focus that helps customers harness value from products more quickly. (Arnold et al.)

In the wireless space, almost every vendor claims to offer consulting as part of its end-to-end service. Some, like Ericsson Business Consulting created in January 1999 (Baladi), are quite explicit about their objectives:

Ericsson is undergoing a fundamental shift from being a technology supplier to also becoming a leading consultancy. (www.ericsson.com August 2000)

There are several motivations for these moves. In the new economy, information is the most valuable element and consulting offers higher margins than selling boxes. Vendors also recognise that consultants wield considerable influence over the purchasing decision for hardware and software. By moving into that space, they can gain significant pull-through revenues. For example, IBM operates on the basis that for every $ in consulting fees, $3 will be generated for other services and products (IBM 2000a).

Scale and scope, mergers and acquisitions

Although the emergence of new competition is reshaping the consulting industry, its effects are only beginning to be felt on the incumbent oligopoly shown in Table 1. Taking O'Shea and Madigan's estimate of the total value of the global consulting market as $62 billion, the 10-firm concentration ratio is 78% and the five-firm ratio is 51%. As Segal-Horn predicted, economies of scale and scope mean that the largest multi-national firms enjoy a huge concentration of market power. Despite their rapid organic growth, the e-firms are still minnows by comparison – Sapient, one of the largest, has 2,800 employees and revenues of only $319 million.

Consolidation seems set to continue with a recent spate of mergers, acquisitions, alliances and joint ventures. Cap Gemini has acquired Ernst & Young for $5 billion (echoing the purchase of AT Kearney by EDS in 1995). Andersen and Microsoft have combined to form Avenade, which plans to have 5,000 consultants helping to sell Microsoft-based internet services (Colvin). From the vendor side, Hewlett-Packard has announced plans to buy PwC for £14 billion (*Sunday Times*, September 2000). Cisco has invested $835 million for a 5% stake in a joint venture with Cap Gemini, and taken a 20% stake in KPMG. This is indicative of its strategy to partner with services firms in ecosystems, rather than build up an internal consulting practice (*Consulting Magazine*, March 2000).

A separate driver at work is regulatory pressure by the SEC in the United States for accounting firms to divest their consulting arms, because of the potential for conflict of interest. This lies behind KPMG Consulting's planned partial flotation at $2.5 billion (*Consulting Magazine*, September 2000).

Table 1 Consulting firms by revenue

FIRM	REVENUE $m	CONSULTANTS	$REV per CONS
IBM (est)	8,043	65,000	123,738
ANDERSEN	7,514	53,248	141,113
PwC	7,170	40,560	176,775
DELOITTE	5,050	28,625	176,419
ERNST & YOUNG	4,050	17,348	233,456
CSC	3,640	22,000	165,455
KPMG	3,500	17,000	205,882
CAP GEMINI	3,161	25,337	124,758
McKINSEY	2,900	5,670	511,464
MERCER	1,950	14,100	138,298
ARTHUR ANDERSEN	1,400	9,810	142,712

Source: Colvin.

The telco view

The attitude of telcos to vendors may be critical for the relationship between consulting and the wireless world. As we have already noted, vendors favour deep relationships across global markets with one or two other key vendors, with perhaps occasional strategic input from a specialist. Other suppliers are regarded as point solution providers, to whom the primary vendor may decide to subcontract some elements (IBM 2000a). If telcos, rather than brands, portals or enterprises, are the key players in this space, these conservative attitudes will make it very difficult for consulting firms to gain a foothold without the aid of the telco equipment vendors.

Sense and respond?

To enjoy economies of scale and scope, consulting firms leverage their knowledge and offer services with minimum customisation to their clients. This underpins their business model, with large numbers of young inexperienced consultants charged at high hourly rates feeding the high income of a few senior consultants. At worst, this can result in projects where little more than the name is changed from one client to the next (O'Shea and Madigan). This model may prove inadequate in an environment characterised by high levels of instability. The challenge will be to develop a more dynamic approach that enables clients to feel they are getting a service tailored to their individual needs.

Strategic groups

One could group consulting firms based on any number of factors such as size, ownership structure, market segmentation and so on. Figure 1 shows a grouping along two dimensions: product/service focus and speed of response. Focus means the degree of specialisation in a particular area versus the offering of an integrated, end-to-end service to a wide variety of clients from different industries. Responsiveness means both how quickly a firm can move from analysis to execution (this could be quantified by average project length), and how swiftly it has adapted to environmental change. Clearly, it would take a variety of metrics to assess each dimension and one would then have to weight each one. Therefore, the assessment in Figure 1 is based on qualitative observations and subjective judgement. Naturally, the groups described below do not encompass all consulting firms and undoubtedly there are some hybrids, which have the characteristics of more than one group.

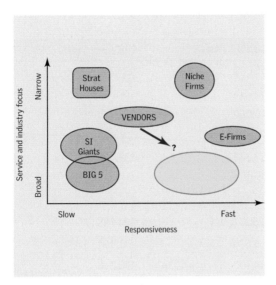

Figure 1 Strategic groups in the consulting industry

Big 5

This refers to the consulting arms of the large accounting firms of Ernst & Young, Pricewaterhouse Coopers, KPMG, Arthur Andersen, and Deloitte Touche. Their strengths lie in large-scale projects, long-term relationships and deep knowledge of vertical industries. Their entry point to consulting came with the introduction of information technology to accounting departments. While this bias remains today, they offer a wide range of services including business strategy, enterprise resource planning, IT consulting and outsourcing, and change and knowledge management. Their natural inclination is to extend assignments to as many layers over as long a time frame as possible. Combined with their size, this results in slow responsiveness.

SI giants

Systems integration is dominated by a few huge organisations: IBM, Andersen Consulting, CSC, EDS and Cap Gemini. Between them, they control most of the world's important databases. While they often compete with the Big 5, they are typically selected for their expertise in complex, large-scale IT assignments rather than business strategy. Their industry experience is broad, though perhaps not as deep as

that of the Big 5. Recently, Andersen and IBM have added services to create an integrated e-business offering. Size and history slow their response speeds.

Vendors

As we have already seen, hardware and software vendors are entering the consulting market. In the wireless world, key players include Nokia, Ericsson, Hewlett-Packard, Oracle, Cisco, Nortel, Lucent, Siemens and Unisys. In many ways, they are attempting to emulate IBM's successful reinvention of itself as a services provider. Their strengths are their technological understanding and monopoly on market access. Their weaknesses are the lack of independent consulting experience in many industries and across service lines. They are not a homogeneous group in terms of speed of response: while most are regarded as slow. Cisco is seen as one of the most dynamic companies in the fast-moving internet space.

Strat houses

These include McKinsey, Bain, Boston Consulting Group, Booze Allen Hamilton, Mercer, Monitor and numerous others. Typically organised as partnerships, they command fees of up to $500,000 per consultant per annum (four times that for the outsourcing of computer services). Weak on implementation, they provide an intellectual approach rooted in the design, planning and positioning schools of strategy. Their greatest asset is probably their access to clients at the CEO level via the old-boy network. While covering all industries, they focus exclusively on strategy and do not offer end-to-end integration. The pursuit of analytical rigour is often at the expense of speed: months of work can result in little more than a thick report.

Niche firms

These firms are even more tightly focused than the strat houses. There are a number that specialise in strategy and research in the digital arena, including Analysys, Decipher, Informed Sources, Ovum and Spectrum. They offer deep knowledge of the telco, media and internet industries, often advising regulators and government on strategic or business modelling issues. Their small size, independence and narrow focus make them nimble and able to punch beyond their weight in terms of influence.

E-firms

This group is highly fragmented, with many players including Viant, Scient, Sapient Proxicom, Razorfish, Agency.com, Organic, IXL, marchFIRST, Digitas and Cambridge Technology Partners. Although coming from diverse backgrounds (web design, advertising, systems integration, direct marketing and pure-plays), all have moved to offer an end-to-end integrated service focused on the internet. The enthusiasm of investors and favourable demand conditions has enabled these publicly traded companies to build global scale quickly, often through multiple acquisitions. With strong cultures and a sophisticated understanding of knowledge management, fast response seems embedded in e-firms. However, as well as coping with their own rapid growth, they now face a number of other challenges. The bursting of the e-bubble has resulted in plummeting stock prices (Viant's market capitalisa-tion has fallen from $2 billion to $236 million during six months in 2000, for instance), which will restrict further expansion. A slowing in demand growth has made it imperative that they begin to differentiate from one another. The maturing of e-business means there is a growing need for vertical industry knowl-edge.

White spaces and other opportunities

Figure 1 throws an interesting light on current industry moves. Cap Gemini's acquisition of Ernst & Young appears to be designed to broaden the focus of the vendors and improve channel access. The partnership between IBM and the strategy house Mercer increases the ability of both parties to claim an end-to-end service. IBM's merger of its consulting and systems integration businesses into Business Innovation Services formalises the breadth of its offering. All of these moves ignore the dimension of speed of response.

One of the benefits of strategic group analysis is that it can highlight white spaces – areas not cur-rently occupied by any group – that represent opportunities to extract future rents (McGee and Thomas). Thus, we can see a large space in the bottom right, 'broad and fast' quadrant. While this would represent the optimum strategy for the wire-less world, it requires competencies that in some ways are juxtaposed – these constitute mobility barriers. What kind of organisation could offer com-plete breadth at the same time as being agile enough to respond quickly to environmental changes?

The strat houses and niche firms are pursuing narrow differentiation strategies and seem unlikely to want to compete in this space. Niche firms may be targets for those who want to buy some speed, although it is doubtful whether the qualities that make them suc-cessful can be preserved through the acquisition process. We believe that all but the most prestigious strat houses may find their position increasingly diffi-cult unless they can provide a faster response. One solution could be to break firms into 'virtual niche firms', harnessing their reputational assets without the dead weight of organisational inertia.

Although the e-firms are currently best positioned to move into this space, to do so would require major investments in new capabilities. This will be hard to finance given current market conditions in 2000. Nevertheless, one might expect a few players such as Sapient and Scient to attempt this. The rest appear vulnerable to consolidation.

The Big 5 and SI Giants will have to struggle against legacy structures and thinking in order to reposition themselves. Some members of the Big 5 seem to lack any clear sense of direction.

The vendors are a mixed bunch but their lack of tenure as consultants may be an advantage: learning new skills can be easier than unlearning old ones. Cisco has proved itself adept at strategic acquisition and choreographing its entire business web in deliv-ering value. Although its origins are in network equipment, Cisco describes its value proposition as 'advice and the intellectual property around it' (Tapscott et al.). This could be the firm most capable of success in this space.

References

Arnold *et al.* 'Wireless, not Profitless', *McKinsey Quarterly*, 2, 1998.

Baladi, P 'Knowledge and Competence Management: Ericsson Business Consulting', *Business Strategy Review*, Winter, 1999.

Brown, E 'The E-Consultants', *Fortune*, 12 April 1999.

Colvin, G 'Old Consultants Never Die: They Just Go E', *Fortune*, 12 June 2000.

Forrester Research, 'Scoring Europe's E-business Help', February 2000.

Hamel, G 'Waking up IBM', *Harvard Business Review*, Sept/Oct 1999.

IBM (2000a) 'Cheryl Altany Wireless Consulting Unit BIS North'.

IBM (2000b) 'IBM.com Annual Report 1999'.

Kennedy Information Research Group, 'E-services Report', April 2000.

McGee, J and Thomas, H (1992) 'Strategic Groups and Intra-Industry Competition', *International Review of Strategic Management*, 3.

Milgrom, P and Roberts, J (1992) *Economics, Organization and Management*, Prentice Hall.

Oran, N (2000) 'Impact on Consultancies', *Financial Times*, 5 July.

O'Shea, J and Madigan, C (1997) *Dangerous Company*, Nicholas Brealey Publishing.

Sammer, J (2000) 'Paying for Performance', *Consulting Magazine*, May.

Sapeint (2000) 'Architects for the New Economy', www.sapient.com, August.

Scient (2000) 'Annual Report'.

Segal-Horn, S (1993) 'The Internationalisation of Service Firms', in *Advances in Strategic Management*, 9, pp. 31–55.

Stepanek, M (2000) 'Clash of E-Consultants', *Business Week*, 19 June.

Sweeney, J (2000) 'McKinsey at the Crossroads', *Consulting Magazine*, January.

Tapscott, D, Ticoll, D and Lowy, A (2000) *Digital Capital: Harnessing the Power of Business Webs*, McGraw-Hill.

Case 30 **Rockware plc**

In September 1983 Sir Peter Parker returned from a seven-year spell running the state-owned British Rail to resume his former role as Chairman of Rockware, a manufacturer of glass bottles and jars. With him he brought a newcomer to the glass container industry, Frank Davies, who had been head of the aluminium extrusion division at Alcan, and had now been appointed Managing Director of Rockware.

When Sir Peter had left Rockware, as plain Peter Parker, in 1976, things looked pretty good. Demand for glass containers was booming. Rockware's shares were growing by around 15% a year in real terms, while operating profit had doubled in the past two years. By September 1983, however, the picture was very different. Having peaked in 1979, demand for glass containers had declined each year since then. Despite high levels of inflation, prices had remained static in money terms and had even started to fall slightly. Rockware, in common with other manufacturers, had been forced to close furnaces and make workers redundant, and by 1983 the workforce had dropped to just 4500 from a 1979 peak of 7600. The redundancy and rationalisation costs of £19 million had virtually wiped out the modest operating profits of the years 1980–82, and for the first six months of 1983 the firms had declared a loss of about £8.5 million. The full year figures would show an operating loss of over £6 million with further interest costs and exceptional losses over £6.5 million.

A successful placing of £10 million worth of convertible preference shares by the firm's merchant bankers in the summer of 1983 had given some breathing space.

But although these shares had been placed without difficulty (Pilkingtons, the large British float and safety glass manufacturer, which owned 20% of Rockware's ordinary shares, took up a large tranche of the preference shares, and this helped

This case was prepared by John Hendry as the basis for class discussion rather than to illustrate either effective or ineffective handling of an administrative situation.

© 1988, 1990 by John Hendry

City confidence), the ordinary share price had collapsed to around 20–30p from 80p in the spring of 1982; before the year ended it would drop further to just 16p. Looking to the future, the prospects for glass containers were not encouraging. Capacity cuts across the industry were beginning to restore the balance between supply and demand with the prospect of a stabilisation of real prices. But there seemed little prospect of any growth in the market, and every prospect of a continuing shrinkage as glass containers lost market share to plastics, and in particular to polyethylene terephthalate (PET). Launched commercially in 1979, PET was still not an adequate substitute for glass in many applications, but technological development, funded by the large multinational petro-chemical companies, was proceeding rapidly. PET bottles were already beginning to eat away at the glass bottle market, and this process looked likely to continue and accelerate. Rockware itself had had an interest in plastic containers for many years, and in 1980, after a series of acquisitions, these accounted for about 30% of its turnover. But a combination of management problems with overseas plants, continuous price squeezing in an intensely competitive market, and the need to raise extra cash to support the glass manufacturing rationalisation had since led to a series of disposals, so that by the end of 1983 plastics accounted for just 12% of turnover.

Glass container technology and materials

Modern glass container manufacture differs little in essence from traditional glass-blowing. The main raw materials are silica sand (about 70%), soda ash (12%), and lime (12%); these are heated with other additives in furnaces to about 720–750° C to make molten glass. After refining to remove impurities, the molten glass is machine blown in blobs into hollow moulds and then cooled under controlled conditions. Each furnace feeds several bottle-making machines, each of which produces 10 or 12 bottles at a time. The furnaces are fuelled by natural gas. In Britain this is supplied by a monopoly supplier, British Gas, and accounts for about 60% of total production costs. Silica sand is supplied by BIS, with about 70% of the market, and soda ash by ICI, with about 80% of the market. Both these companies have strong control over the available sources of supply.

The main feature of the manufacturing technology is its lack of flexibility. A glass container plant cannot be used for the manufacture of any other form of glass product (such as flat glass, or optical glasses). Nor does the technology allow transfer of operations between different types of colours of bottle glass. Thus a brown glass bottle plant is effectively dedicated to brown glass bottle manufacture, and similarly for green, clear or opal glasses. Because of the energy costs of keeping a furnace going, the costs of running a plant at under full capacity (i.e. with one or more of the bottle-making machines idle) are severe, as are the costs of switching from one product to another: to change the moulds is a significant and time-consuming operation, during which the furnace has to be kept going.

The glass container industry

The British glass container industry has traditionally been very fragmented, but by the mid-1970s it had become concentrated into six major companies of which Rockware, with a market share of about 25%, was the largest. The others were Redfearn (about 14%), Beatson Clark (9%), and three subsidiaries of major bottle users who had integrated backwards: United Glass (owned jointly by Distillers and Owens, Illinois, 25%), Canning Town (Arthur Bell 9%) and the glass division of the Co-operative (9%). Of these Beatson Clark specialised in brown glass pharmaceutical containers, and Rockware in opal glass. But both Rockware and Redfearn supplied a wide range of bottles and jars in clear, brown, and green glass, and with United Glass they dominated the open market for glass food and drink containers.

Elsewhere in Europe, and in the US, the industry structure tended to be rather different, with each national market being dominated by one or two glass manufacturers, each diversified across a range of different glass process technologies and products. Although diversified, most of these companies were much larger glass container producers than Rockware. Thus the glass container business of Saint Gobain in France, for example, was one-and-a half times the size of the entire British glass container industry.

The bottling business of BSN, a French brewing, mineral water and soft drinks company which, like Distillers and Guinness, had integrated backwards, was even bigger. Part of the difference of scale was due to a much larger demand for glass bottles in Europe, primarily for the packaging of wine, mineral water and bottled beers, than existed in Britain.

In the late 1970s there had still been very little overlap between national glass container markets, and given the high transport costs of empty glass containers this situation had been expected to continue. From a base of about 4%, however, imports to Britain had grown to 11 % in 1982, and were still rising as customers, uncertain of the future of the precariously placed British industry, placed orders with the diversified European manufacturers as a precaution against the possible bankruptcy and close-down of the British firms. Meanwhile, imports of ready-bottled products were also increasing, at the expense of bulk shipments for local UK bottling and, though difficult to measure, this was clearly having a significant impact on the British bottle market.

The container market: glass, cardboard, PVC and PET

As a container material, glass has many distinct advantages. Rigid as a material it is flexible as a design medium. It is strong, attractive, chemically inert, and almost totally impervious. It is also recyclable. Against this, it is breakable and, above all, heavy, and in the early 1980s it was losing ground to three substitutes: cardboard, PVC and PET.

The use of cardboard was restricted largely to the packaging of milk and fruit juices, but nevertheless posed a serious threat to the bottle manufacturing industry, especially in the case of milk. In Britain milk has traditionally been delivered by the dairies in glass bottles, which are then returned and recycled. Although a glass bottle costs about twice as much as a cardboard container to manufacture, the fact that it can be used 20 or more times makes the delivery system extremely cost effective. Glass is much less suitable, however, for packaging milk for sale in supermarkets and other retail outlets. Although the weight of a pint milk bottle has been halved in the last 50 years, it still adds almost half as much again to the overall weight of the milk, and this is a nuisance to both shoppers and stock-handlers. Glass bottles are less easily packed in bulk than square cardboard containers, and the supermarkets do not find it cost effective to accept empty returns, which both destroys the cost advantage of glass and creates an extra nuisance for the customer who has to dispose of the bottle. During Sir Peter's absence from Rockware, the supermarkets' share of milk sales doubled to about 15%, and a move towards the European and American situation, where all milk is sold in retail stores with no deliveries, was a distinct possibility. On the other hand, some of the supermarket chains had no wish to carry large stocks of milk. The dairies had an interest in maintaining the delivery system, as foreign experience showed that its demise was accompanied by a drop in milk consumption, and consumer research indicated that customers believed milk tasted better from bottles and kept fresher in them.

Of wider significance was the increasing use of plastics, in particular PVC and PET, both of which were cheaper, lighter and less breakable than glass. As yet this use had been limited by the technical properties of these materials, which did not share glass's imperviousness. In the early stages of their development, they could not be used for fizzy drinks, wines, beers, or sauces subject to oxidisation because of the migration of gases through the containers. The technology was improving all the time, however, especially in respect of multi-layer PET bottles. By 1983 these had been developed sufficiently to allow for their use as large soft drinks bottles, where the high volume-to-surface ratio minimised the problem of gas containment, and there was every reason to expect that they would in due course provide potential substitutes for the great majority of glass container applications. Work was even progressing on a recyclable PET. When PET products did become available they would certainly be cheaper than glass (because of much lower energy costs – about half those of glass), lighter, and easier to handle: significant advantages to retailers and consumers alike.

The situation at Rockware: glass

The Rockware group had been built up in the 1960s and early 1970s through the acquisition of three long-established independent glass manufacturers, Garston, Forster and Jackson, and glass manufacturing had remained a decentralised activity. The four sites (five plants), scattered right across Britain, retained their individual characters and loyalties and, although group marketing was centralised in the wake of the acquisitions, they had continued to operate in most respects as independent companies. During the boom years of the mid-1970s this had resulted in a healthy spirit of competition, but with the industry recession the limited degree of centralisation had been abandoned and, with closures threatening, competition between the sites had become more pointed and less friendly, with accusations being made of factories stealing each other's customers. As with other long-established craft-based industries, there was still a strong craft tradition, with long periods of training and with firm and industry loyalties built up over lifetimes and generations. This personal, emotional investment made the recession both harder to accept and harder to bear.

Throughout the industry there remained a deep-seated conviction that things must get better and that the current downturn could only be a temporary phenomenon. As the recession bit, workers had to be made redundant and furnaces closed, but this process lagged well behind the fall in demand and overcapacity continued. The situation was not helped by the economics of bottle manufacture, discussed above, which encouraged firms to run their furnaces at full capacity even if the demand was not there to meet it. Price cutting had inevitably followed, and although Rockware had tried to hold out against this they had lost market share as a result and had ended up having to follow the market. They had, however, led the move to rationalisation. By September 1983 Rockware had spent £19 million on rationalisation, closing furnaces, making workers redundant and eventually closing down the original Rockware factory at St Helens. United Glass and Redfearn were also on the point of closing down factories, and the overcapacity problem looked to be coming to an end. But Rockware were will manufacturing on negative margins, the glass container market was still declining and imports were still rising.

The situation at Rockware: plastics and engineering

Besides its dominant glass container business, Rockware also manufactured in two other areas. The engineering businesses, Burwell Reed and Kinghorn, and the Birstall Foundry served primarily to provide moulds and other equipment for use in Rockware's own container manufacture, though they also traded outside the group. Plastic container manufacturing had begun under Sir Peter's earlier tenure as Chairman and had grown to form a major part of the group's overall business before being cut back again during the downturn in the glass business.

The main growth in Rockware's plastics business had come in the late 1970s. In late 1978 they had taken over Alida, a producer of flexible plastic film packaging, for £4.7 million. The following year they had bought the overseas plastic bottle-making concerns of Dart Industries Inc. of America, with a book value of £6.4 million, for £2.94 million, and paid £0.75 million for two small plastics companies. This gave them a total of 12 plastics factories in Britain, Spain, Holland, Belgium and Australia. The move into plastics had appeared to make sound strategic sense, but in a highly competitive industry all the Rockware plastics operations experienced a chronic squeeze on prices and margins. Some of the businesses also experienced technical and managerial problems, and far from boosting group profits, plastics proved a severe drain on resources at just the time the core glass manufacturing business was running into serious problems. In 1981 the overseas Dart operations were all disposed of, and in late 1982 negotiations began with the Alida management on a management buy-out of that company. This was agreed upon in 1983 and the sale finally took place at the end of that year. The agreed price of £2.9 million was in real terms under half what Rockware had paid for the company but, with glass manufacturing losses, the money was badly needed.

With the sale of Alida, Rockware was left with three plastics divisions specialising in clean air injection blow moulding and extrusion blow moulding, and supplying PVC bottles primarily for the pharmaceuticals and cosmetic markets. Two of these, at Norwich and Kingston, were expanding, profitable businesses, but the other two, at Golborne and Reading, were encountering serious problems at both the technical and managerial levels, and their losses more or less cancelled out the others' profits.

Back from the brink

Despite the capacity cuts being made by all the leading British glass container manufacturers in 1983, the industry had not yet come fully to terms with a declining market. Many people still treated the recent problems as a temporary aberration, and thought in terms of 'reserves of capacity to meet an upturn of business', rather than of overcapacity in a declining business. Right across Europe, the overwhelming response was still to cut prices rather than capacity, while at the same time planning on the basis that they would soon rise again.

To Frank Davies, this was ludicrous. Coming into the industry as an outsider, he saw a 27% decline in the UK glass container market in the previous four years and a level of prices at which no one in the industry could make a profit. As PET development continued, the best that could be hoped for was a stabilisation of the glass container market, while a continued decline looked more realistic. In any price-cutting war, the continental manufacturers, with their diversified product ranges and much greater corporate resources, would inevitably be the victors. Rockware could only be a heavy loser.

Faced with this view of the situation, Frank Davies and Sir Peter Parker determined on a package of short-term measures to save the company. The £10 million issue of convertible preference shares, arranged by Sir Peter in anticipation of his return to the company, provided them with necessary resources and breathing space, but with losses running at £1 million a month they had to move very fast (see Exhibit 1 for a ten-year financial summary).

The first step, taken by Davies on his first day, was to raise prices by 7.5%. Nobody followed, and the company lost volume in the short term. But the move was necessary if losses were to be stemmed, and it was well-timed to coincide with plant closures at both Redfearn and United Glass. A strike at United Glass also helped. Within a month or two it was becoming clear that Rockware's customers would stick with the company and, shortly afterwards, their competitors also began raising prices.

Exhibit 1 Rockware 10 year summary (£000)

	1975	1976	1977	1978	1979	1980	1981	1982	1983	1984
Sales										
Glass	52,630	67,697	80,794	96,684	106,178	116,178	112,971	103,980	101,310	107,410
Plastics	3,165	4,146	7,134	9,825	33,812	48,919	46,221	33,163	26,914	15,240
Engineering	668	711	1,295	1,910	3,261	4,668	2,388	4,610	3,246	1,521
Total	56,463	72,554	89,223	108,419	143,251	169,765	161,580	141,853	131,470	12,4721
Operating Profit(loss)										
Glass								4,504	(8,344)	5,700
Plastics								935	537	0
Engineering								(384)	(84)	300
Total	5,748	7,155	8,014	7,970	7,893	5,773	5,558	5,215	(6,216)	5,909
Interest and exceptional losses	(442)	(1,230)	(603)	(951)	(2,709)	(5,301)	(4,659)	(4,610)	(6,611)	(2,741)
Profit before taxation	4,306	5,925	7,411	7,019	5,184	472	899	605	(12,827)	3,168
Capital expenditure	6,863	5,234	9,549	10,778	13,901	10,829	5,369	9,593	6,569	7,053
Average number of employees	6,321	6,238	6,955	7,048	7,643	7,595	6,593	5,174	4,541	3,669
Share capital and reserves	17,839	32,317	40,517	43,905	58,698	56,559	49,420	49,412	30,437	33,050
Preference shares										10,700
Loans etc	22,060	6,353	10,505	16,001	31,650	39,256	42,447	41,524	29,107	20,786
Fixed assets plus net current assets	39,899	38,670	51,022	59,906	90,348	95,815	91,867	90,936	70,244	64,536
Inflation rate (RPI: 1.1.1974 = 1002)	134.8	157.1	182.0	197.1	223.5	263.7	295.0	320.4	335.1	351.8

Six months later, in May 1984, Davies raised prices again, this time by 8%, and this time the industry followed.

The second measure taken was to make a further 1000 Rockware staff redundant and, at the same time, negotiate a six-month wage freeze (in the face of wage increases elsewhere in the industry of about 6%) with the remaining employees. This step was made possible by very generous redundancy packages (helped by the £10 million of new finance), and by the personal skills of Parker and Davies. Sir Peter Parker is a warm, approachable, and extremely articulate man with a strong sense of public justice. When, on leaving British Rail, he chose to return 'fully committed' to the relatively small Rockware company rather than take up one of the more lucrative and prestigious appointments that would have been his for the taking, the Rockware workforce responded by returning his loyalty. He believes in being open and straightforward with his firm's employees, treating them as 'citizens', and his powers of communication were such that no one in the company could be in any doubt as to the seriousness of the position they were in. Frank Davies is also a friendly and approachable figure, who shares Parker's commitment to honest and plain speaking, and though an outsider to both firm and industry, he was quickly accepted on the basis of these qualities, reinforced by Parker's own recommendation.

Alongside these two very drastic measures, Davies also set about pulling the company together, improving its cohesion and tightening controls. The separate companies in the group (including the three glass bottle companies) continued to be run at local level, with a large degree of operating autonomy. But a new Marketing Director, Don Fairly, was recruited from Britain's largest packaging company, Metal Box, to build up a central marketing organisation and co-ordinate between the different factories, and between the glass and plastic groups, which were previously quite isolated: 'don't think glass, think customer' was the new message. Group financial controls were also strengthened, and the practice of running over orders so as to improve capacity utilisation was stopped: a directive was made to the glass factories to manufacture to orders only, and stocks were cut dramatically as a result, freeing up further capital. To increase productivity and cut down on energy costs, the existing programme of furnace modernisation was accelerated. An improved ordering and order call-off system was introduced. A strategic group, comprising heads of business units and of staff functions, was set up.

These measures between them enabled Rockware to turn in a profit of £3.2 million in 1984, as against a loss of £12.8 million the previous year (see Exhibit 1), but with the basic problem of industry-wide overcapacity unresolved, they could afford only a temporary respite. Rockware needed a strategy.

Exhibit 2 Proportion of glass bottles recycled (selected European countries mid 1980s)

Holland	53%	Italy	24%
Belgium	36%	Denmark	20%
West Germany	31%	Great Britain	9%
France	25%		

Exhibit 3 Estimated non-glass packaging turnovers of selected UK companies, 1984 (£million)

Metal Box	850	DRG	200
Reed	300	Rockware	15
Lin Pac	280		

Case Questions

1 What were the problems facing Rockware when Peter Parker returned? How appropriate were the measures taken so far and what were the alternatives?

2 How were the senior management able to implement the tough measures as smoothly as they did?

3 Analyse the structures of the principal industries in which Rockware is competing. How attractive are these industries? How can Rockware position itself to compete in them in the future?

4 Should Rockware consider diversification, and if so what type of diversification would be appropriate?

Exhibit 4 UK glass container industry

	1980	1981	1982	1983	1984
Million units	6800	6500	6100	5925	5976
£ million	384	381	386	366	376
Imports (%)	6%	7%	11%	12%	14%
By end use (million units)					
Drink					3180
Food					1920
Chemicals and pharmaceuticals					515
Toiletry and perfume					361

Note: these figures do not allow for indirect imports, e.g. wines, waters and beers bottled in country of origin.

Exhibit 5 Forecast UK PET container market

	1985/86	1986/87	
Million units			
Carbonated soft drinks			
1 litre bottles	139	166	
1.5 litre bottles	147	164	
>1.5 litre bottles	314	395	
Other	93	117	
Total	693	842	
Turnover (approximate)	£85 million	£105 million	
Market shares			
In-plant operations *	46%	Metal Box	10%
Fibrenyl	23%	LinPac	10%
Redfearn	11%		

*Aggregate of ten firms manufacturing and bottling products who have backwards integrated to make their own bottles.

Index

Case Study Section Index